EXCLUSIVE FREE OFFER TO BOOK PURCHASERS

Register on-line **now** and become a founder member of Best Loved's

Red Rosette Club

Thank you for purchasing the 2001 Edition of **Best Loved Hotels – UK/Ireland**. Each copy of the 2001 edition has a unique serial number which can be seen above. This gives us the chance to make sure this book works even harder to fulfill your travel needs.

How? Well if you have access to the Internet simply go on-line and type the URL:

http://www.bestlovedhotels.com/register

Why registering your book is a must:

- Experience **bestlovedhotels.com**, the state of the art tool for all your travel planning needs
- Create your very own **myBestLoved** Profile which will save you time when you want to find that special hotel

Plus, as a Red Rosette Club member you will receive special benefits including:

- Receive a £5 discount on your next 8 visits (£40.00 value) to a Best Loved Hotel (participating hotels only)
- Automatic entry in our monthly Best Loved's Hotels **'Night Away Sweepstakes'** (2 winners each month)
- Exclusive weekly Best Loved's Hotels special offers (email recipients only; monthly for non-email registrants)
- Specially designed discounts and offers, promotions from our complementary sponsors

For a full list of benefits see overleaf 

BLD01 BB

Don't have Internet access but you still want to join? Simply answer the questions below, tear off and post us your registration and you to can become a member!

Title ________ First Name ____________________
Last Name ____________________
Company *(if applicable)* ____________________
Address ____________________
____
____
____________________ City ____________________
St/Prov ____________________ Zip/Postcode ____________________
Country ____________________
Tel *(country code)* ________ *(local code)* ________ *(number)* ____________
Fax *(country code)* ________ *(local code)* ________ *(number)* ____________
Email ____________________

Date of purchase ____________________
Place of purchase ____________________

I plan to use **Best Loved Hotels** primarily for: *(please tick)*
Pleasure ❑ Business ❑ or Both ❑

BB0240880408

By registering by post you agree to allow us to contact you by telephone in order to create your **MyBestLoved** Profile. Your registration will not be complete and your benefits will not be sent without this short interview.

Do you prefer to be contacted in the:
morning ❑ afternoon ❑ or evening ❑ *(please tick)*

At a specific time

What days of the week would you prefer?
____
____

From time to time we publish special offers, news and hotel updates as well as share your data with other reputable third parties. If you do not wish to receive anything from third parties simply tick here ❑.

BLD01 BB

Special benefits for the Red Rosette Club member

- Receive a £5 discount on your next 8 visits (£40.00 value) to a **Best Loved Hotels** (participating hotels only)
- Receive a 25% discount on the next edition and/or additional gift copies
- 10% discount on your first purchase from the **Initial Ideas** (**http://www.initialideas.com**) electronic gift and travel catalogue (also available in print)
- Automatic entry in our monthly Best Loved's Hotels **'Night Away Sweepstakes'** (2 winners each month)
- Receive a specially selected travel gift. Guaranteed to be useful!
- Exclusive weekly **Best Loved Hotels** special offers (email recipients only; monthly for non-email registrants)
- Invitations to attend Best Loved Regional Events
- Specially designed discounts, offers, and promotions from our complementary sponsors

If you haven't registered your copy please see overleaf for details 

No stamp needed UK only

Clientbase Fulfilment Ltd,
FREEPOST (SWB40527)
IVYBRIDGE PL21 OZZ

ENGLAND ◆ SCOTLAND ◆ WALES
IRELAND ◆ CHANNEL ISLANDS

BEST LOVED HOTELS OF THE WORLD
Suite 11, The Linen House, 253 Kilburn Lane,
London W10 4BQ, United Kingdom

Telephone: +44 (0)20 8962 9555 ◆ Fax: +44 (0)20 8962 9550

North America:
c/o DDS, 20770 Westwood Drive, Strongsville, OH 44136, USA
Telephone: 440-572-7263 ◆ Fax: (toll free) 800-572-8131

E-mail: mail@bestlovedhotels.com ◆ Website: www.bestlovedhotels.com

A World Media Publishing Limited Publication

Cover story:

Rowing, Henley Regatta (oil on canvas)
by Frank Wootton (1911 - 1998)

Private Collection/Wingfield Sporting Gallery, London

The Battle of Britain Memorial Trust

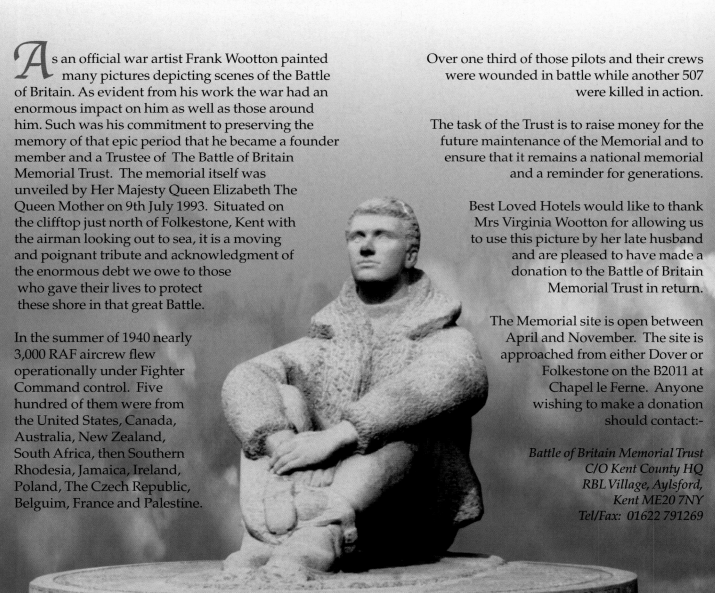

As an official war artist Frank Wootton painted many pictures depicting scenes of the Battle of Britain. As evident from his work the war had an enormous impact on him as well as those around him. Such was his commitment to preserving the memory of that epic period that he became a founder member and a Trustee of The Battle of Britain Memorial Trust. The memorial itself was unveiled by Her Majesty Queen Elizabeth The Queen Mother on 9th July 1993. Situated on the clifftop just north of Folkestone, Kent with the airman looking out to sea, it is a moving and poignant tribute and acknowledgment of the enormous debt we owe to those who gave their lives to protect these shore in that great Battle.

In the summer of 1940 nearly 3,000 RAF aircrew flew operationally under Fighter Command control. Five hundred of them were from the United States, Canada, Australia, New Zealand, South Africa, then Southern Rhodesia, Jamaica, Ireland, Poland, The Czech Republic, Belguim, France and Palestine.

Over one third of those pilots and their crews were wounded in battle while another 507 were killed in action.

The task of the Trust is to raise money for the future maintenance of the Memorial and to ensure that it remains a national memorial and a reminder for generations.

Best Loved Hotels would like to thank Mrs Virginia Wootton for allowing us to use this picture by her late husband and are pleased to have made a donation to the Battle of Britain Memorial Trust in return.

The Memorial site is open between April and November. The site is approached from either Dover or Folkestone on the B2011 at Chapel le Ferne. Anyone wishing to make a donation should contact:-

Battle of Britain Memorial Trust
C/O Kent County HQ
RBL Village, Aylsford,
Kent ME20 7NY
Tel/Fax: 01622 791269

Peter Jarvis
(Communications Director)

Jeffrey Epstein
(Publisher/Founder)

Joanna Whysall
(Marketing Executive).

Joining Up

This edition brings together two very quintessentially British, Scottish, Welsh and Irish themes; the passion for creating and visiting beautiful gardens, and both viewing and taking part in sports activities. This book tries to extol both our love for our physical environment, as well as, showing the numerous ways to enjoy it. Combine these themes with a compilation of characterful and interesting places to stay and we are sure that you, the reader, will be more than satisfied.

With this eighth edition of **Best Loved Hotels - United Kingdom & Ireland** we can truly say that we have bridged the worlds of traditional print with the new age of electronic media through the Internet. We are pleased to use this book as a bridge to this new medium by providing you, the reader, to take the opportunity to log on and review the first ever edition of bestlovedhotels.com. Although not new to the Internet, we launched the Virtual Tour of Britain and Ireland way back in 1996, bestlovedhotels.com has been developed totally with you in mind. By registering your copy of Best Loved you will be among an elite, those members of either the consumer's 'Red Rosette Club' or the travel industry's 'Five Hearts Club'.

The entire Best Loved Hotels team and many people outside our company have gone to great lengths to bring out this volume. But the greatest thanks goes to the hotels that appear on these pages. All have been invited to participate in this book because they have created a unique product that we feel deserves to have a wider audience and we appreciate their confidence in allowing us to present them. Secondly, we wish to thank American Express for their past and continued support.

On behalf of everyone at Best Loved we hope you enjoy using this book to fulfill your dreams.

Jeffrey M Epstein

The traditional coaching inn
Example: The Lifeboat Inn, Thornham, Norfolk

A restaurant with rooms
Example: The Three Chimneys, Isle of Skye

Stately homes & country house hotels
Example: Hunstrete House, near Bath

Representing the best of their kind

A farmhouse
Example: Biggin Hall, Buxton, Derbyshire

This book offers a huge selection of hotels in Great Britain and Ireland from the stately palace to the welcoming inn, each the best of its kind within its locality and price range.

Here, we show a sample of that variety. There are hundreds of places where you might choose to stay. They all have character and are an integral part of the delights and attractions of their region.

And each, in its own special way, is best-loved by someone who's been there.

A resort hotel
Example: Sheen Falls Lodge, Co Kerry, Ireland

A city centre hotel
Example: Flemings Mayfair, London

Castles
Example: Inverlochy Castle, Fort William

A bed & breakfast
Example: The Groes Inn, North Wales

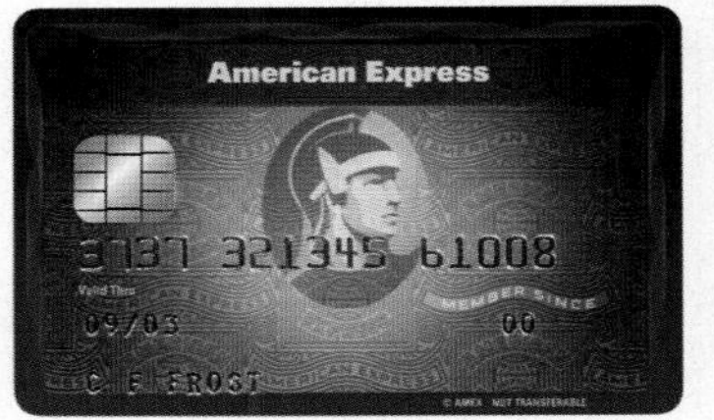
American Express
321345 61008
MEMBER SINCE
09/03
00
C F FROST

Contents

Contacts

Published by
World Media Publishing Limited
Suite 11, The Linen House,
253 Kilburn Lane, London, W10 4BQ
Tel: +44 (0)20 8962 9555
Fax: +44 (0)20 8962 9550
E-mail: mail@bestlovedhotels.com

Book sales: See insert at back of book or go to www.bestlovedhotels.com

United Kingdom
Clientbase Fulfilment Ltd
FREEPOST (SWB40527),
IVYBRIDGE PL21 0ZZ
Tel: +44 (0)870 5862010
Fax: +44 (0)1548 831074

United States
c/o DDS, 20770 Westwood Drive,
Strongsville, OH 44136
Administration Tel: 440-572-7263
Book Sales (Toll Free): 800-808-7682
Fax (Toll Free): 800-572-8131

Publisher
Jeffrey M Epstein

Communications Director
Peter C H Jarvis

Marketing Executive
Joanna Whysall

Designer
Joe Newall

Administration
Ashok Patel

Production Assistant
James Jarvis

Design Consultancy by
The Broadbent Consultancy Ltd, London

Reprographics by
Graphic Ideas, London

Printed by
Jarrold Printing, Norwich, England

Acknowledgments

We are grateful to the following for their help with supplying photographs:

Action-Plus Photographic/ *Steve Bardens*
Bord Failte Photo Library/ *Brian Lynch*
The Bridgeman Art Library
British Horseracing Association
British Tourist Authority
Chelsea Physic Garden
Cornwall Tourist Board
East of England Tourist Board
Edinburgh & Lothian Tourist Board
English Heritage Photo Library:- *Kim Williams/Peter Anderson/ Nigel Corrie/Anne Hyde/Andrew Tryner*
The Highlands of Scotland Tourist Board
Kew Gardens
London Tourist Board
MCC/*James Finlay*
Museum of Garden History

Continued column opposite ☛

SCOTLAND

Highlands & Islands
The braes, burns and lochs
The Whisky Trails
Castles and Palaces

THE NORTH

The Yorkshire Moors and Dales
The Forest of Bowland
The Lake District
Hadrian's Wall

WALES

Snowdonia
The Brecon Beacons
The valleys of song
Land of castles

MIDSHIRES

The Norfolk Broads
The Derbyshire peaks and dales
The Cotswolds
Shakespeare country

INDEX

WEST COUNTRY

Roman & Regency Bath
Dartmoor and Exmoor
Beaches and the coastal path
Maritime heritage

THE SOUTH

The New Forest & Dorset
Londoner's playground
Palaces and stately homes
The Thames Valley

LONDON

Heathlands and The Royal Parks
The entertainment capital
Focal point of British culture
The Royal palaces

IRELAND

The wild west of Connemara and Donegal
The romance of the lakes and mountains
Sacred myths and legends
Stones that tell tales

ACKNOWLEDGMENTS *(continued)*

The National Trust Photo Library:-
Jonathan Bailey/Andrew Butler/ Brian Gallagher/Brian Granger/ Jerry Harpur/Nick Meers/Stephen Robson/ M Trelawny/Rupert Truman
The National Trust for Scotland
John Peters
Scottish Highland Photo Library
Shannon Development
Skyscan Balloon Photography
South East Tourist Board
South West Lakes Trust
Sutton Motorsport Images
United Artists (Courtesy Kobal)
Wales Tourist Board Photo Library
The Wimbledon Lawn Tennis Museum
Wisley Garden Photographic Collection:-
MC Sleigh
Yorkshire County Cricket Club

How to use this book

This book is about places to stay in the United Kingdom and Ireland: castles, stately homes, country house hotels, city centre hotels, town houses, leisure resorts, health spa's and welcoming inns. Each has its own page with comprehensive details including a recommendation in the form of a "Best Loved" quotation from someone who has been there. When you plan a holiday, a friend's advice is usually helpful; our aim is to provide that kind of information. The structure and design of this book is aimed to make the business of making a choice as simple as possible and, given that there are 403 places to choose from, we feel sure you will appreciate some help.

General Structure

The book is divided into eight regions starting with Scotland and moving south; the London region (starting page 368) is the last on the mainland and Ireland is the last in the book. The geographical areas are shown in the map above.

The hotels are listed in alphabetical order by name within their region.

Each region has a four-page introduction that picks out some of the highlights in the region and is designed to spark off some ideas.

At the end of the book are 32 pages of indexes to help you find the hotel of your choice.

Within the indexes are detailed regional maps to help you plan an itinerary.

The Hotel Pages

Whilst every hotel page has a relaxed look (see right), it is packed with information which is broadly itemised as follows:

Good quality **pictures** to give you some idea of the look of the place.

Descriptive editorial intended to give you a feel for the character of the hotel and the people who run it.

A **"Fact column"** (with the yellow

Best Loved Hotels of the World

"Charingworth Manor stands for unadulterated pleasure and I am not ashamed to enjoy it"

Patrick Marlagan, Berkshire

14th century manor

CHARINGWORTH MANOR

The perfect retreat from the twentieth century

The ancient manor of Charingworth lies amidst the gently rolling Cotswold countryside, three miles from Chipping Campden, described as having "the most beautiful High Street in the whole of England". The 14th century manor house is set in its own gardens and grounds of fifty acres and offers peace, tranquillity and breathtaking views.

Inside Charingworth is an historic patchwork of intimate public rooms with log fires burning during the colder months. The atmosphere is warm and relaxed, the service friendly and attentive. There are 26 bedrooms, all furnished with antiques and fine fabrics. Outstanding cuisine creates imaginative dishes where great emphasis is placed on the finest produce available. Recognition has come in the form of two rosettes from the A.A.

To enhance your stay there is an elegant romanesque leisure spa, entirely in keeping with the relaxed comfort found throughout Charingworth. It offers an indoor heated pool, sauna, steam room, solarium and billiards room, there is also a tennis court in the grounds.

The lovely Cotswold villages, Warwick Castle and famous gardens of Hidcote and Kiftsgate are very close by. Also easily reached are the historic Stratford-upon-Avon and Oxford.

LOCATION

Charingworth is situated on the B4035 between Chipping Campden and Shipston-on-Stour. 2 1/2 miles from the A429.

Nr Chipping Campden, Gloucestershire GL55 6NS

Telephone 01386 593555

Fax 01386 593353

GENERAL MANAGER

ROOM RATES

CHARGE/CREDIT CARD

RATINGS & AWARDS

FACILITIES

RESTRICTIONS

ATTRACTIONS

AFFILIATIONS

NEAREST

RESERVATIONS

ACCESS CODES

For things to see and do, visit our Website at www.bestlovedhotels.com

background) which brings together all the information you need about the hotel, how to make contact, its facilities and location. The illustration opposite shows the breadth of scope and how useful this panel can be.

Directions. A green shaded panel supplies information on how to find the hotel. Some, like those in London, are easy to find by the address alone but others may be tucked away in the country where directions are essential.

The Route Planner Maps

The regional route planning maps (see pages 494 to 509) are designed to give you instant help in two main ways:

- To find the nearest Best Loved Hotel to where you want, or have, to be.
- To find a Best Loved Hotel within a price band to suit your pocket or celebrate a special occasion.

All the Best Loved Hotels are denoted by colour coded rosettes as shown below:

Each colour represents a price band of the hotels room rates including applicable

taxes estimating the average of the lowest to the highest tariff throughout the year. For hotels which include meals, an

How to use this book

adjustment has been used to arrive at the average rate.

When these rosettes appear on the maps they also include the hotel's page number. At this stage, you may not know which hotel it is but you can easily find out by either going to the page number quoted OR by turning to the regional index of hotels on page 485.

Regional Index

This index lists all the hotels in the book and gives you an 'at-a-glance' guide to hotels by price and region. The same rosette colour coding is used as well as the page, the county and the map reference so you can find all the information quickly.

Children-Friendly Hotels

Hotels that can accommodate children can be found in the A - Z index, page 506. Details also appear on the hotel page.

Pet-Friendly Hotels

Hotels that can accommodate pets are listed on page 481.

Meetings Facilities

If an hotel has facilities for meetings (for 8 or more people), you will find details on the hotel page in the fact column and in the index on page 476.

General Facilities

Although every hotel page itemises its facilities, you may prefer to look at the index of facilities where we list hotels with swimming pools, health and beauty and tennis as well as those offering riding and tennis. The index starts on page 472.

Golf

Hotels with their own courses or with courses nearby are listed on page 478.

Out of season reservations

If a hotel closes for the season, you can still call to make a booking or get information.

*Address, phone number and fax so you can make your booking or get more information. Or, look for a reservation number below. Always quote **Best Loved**.*

E-mail will also help you find out more or make a booking. NOTE: This service is closely monitored and all commercial solicitations will be discarded.

Room rates that are only a guide giving the lowest seasonal rate to the highest. Most rates are "per room for two people sharing, per night". There are a few exceptions where the rate is "per person per night".

Credit/charge cards accepted by the hotel. Nearly all the hotels in this book accept American Express and these display the company logotype.

Other abbreviations are as follows:

DC = Diners Club
MC = Mastercard and Access
VI = Visa
JCB = Japan Credit Card

Ratings & Awards are taken from the most recent published information from tourist boards, the Royal Automobile Club (RAC) and the Automobile Association (AA). The ratings systems are described on page 11. Awards from other industry recognised organisations are included where relevant and if permitted.

Affiliations. Some hotels belong to consortia or marketing groups and this is given as another source of information or for making a reservation. Details of affiliations are given on page 14.

Reservations are provided to make the booking process easier especially if you are trying to make contact outside Britain or Ireland. Always quote Best Loved.

The Access Codes have relevance only to travel agents.

Holbeck Lane, Windermere, Cumbria LA23 1LU

Telephone 01539 432375
Fax 01539 434743

E-mail: holbeck@bestloved.com

OWNERS
David and Patricia Nicholson

ROOM RATES
18 Doubles/Twins £130 - £200
2 Four-posters/Suites £175 - £200
Includes full English breakfast and VAT
Enquire for 5-course dinner inclusive rates

CHARGE/CREDIT CARDS

• DC • JCB • MC • VI

RATINGS & AWARDS
E.T.C. ★★★ Gold Award
R.A.C. Blue Ribbon ★★★ & Dining Award
A.A. ★★★ ❀❀❀
Cumbria Tourist Board Hotel of the Year 1998

FACILITIES
On site: Health spa, croquet, putting green, gardens, woodland walks, cycling, tennis court, licensed for weddings
2 meeting rooms/max 60 people
Nearby: Golf, riding, fishing

RESTRICTIONS
No children under 8 years in restaurant
No facilities for disabled guests
No dogs in public rooms

ATTRACTIONS
Wordsworth's Dove Cottage, Beatrix Potter's home, lake cruises

AFFILIATIONS
Small Luxury Hotels
Fine Individual Hotels

NEAREST
MAJOR CITY:
Manchester - 90 miles/1½ hrs
MAJOR AIRPORT:
Manchester - 90 miles/1½ hrs
RAILWAY STATION:
Windermere - 3 miles/5 mins

RESERVATIONS
Toll free in US/Canada: 800-525-4800
or 800-544-9993
Quote **Best Loved**

ACCESS CODES
SABRE/ABACUS LX 31195
AMADEUS LX VEMHGC
APOLLO LX 21650
WORLDSPAN LX BWFHG

Sport Museums Guide 2001

To put sport and sporting achievements into their proper contexts, we could not publish this edition without giving recognition to their great historical pasts and the evolutionary changes that have taken place, both in terms of the sports themselves and the fitness levels of the athletes; from footballers to racing drivers. These Museums represent a fascinating log of how British sport has evolved.

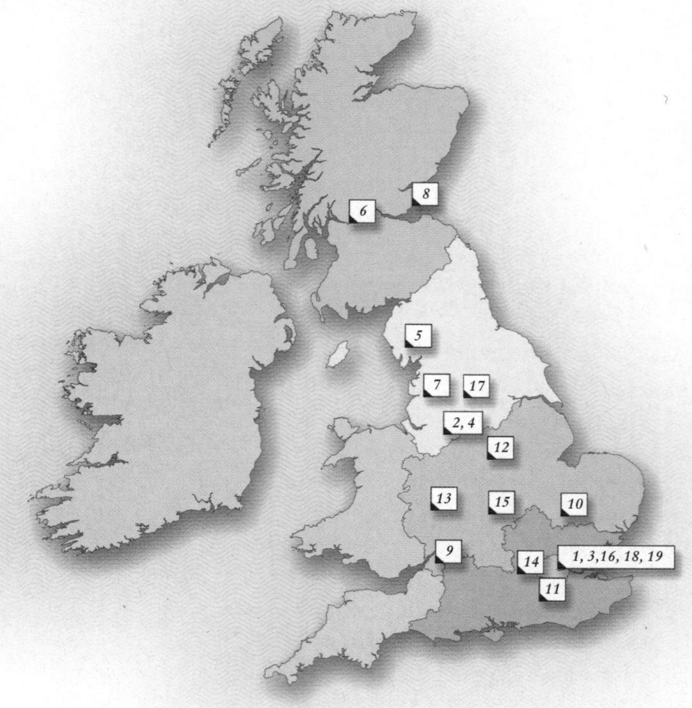

1. **MCC Museum**
   Lord's Cricket Ground, London.
   For further information call 020 7289 1611.

2. **Lancashire County Cricket Club Museum**
   Lancashire County Cricket Club, Old Trafford, Manchester.
   For further information call 0161 282 4000.

3. **The Arsenal Museum (Football)**
   Highbury, London.
   For further information call 020 7704 4000.

4. **Manchester United Museum**
   Old Trafford, Manchester.
   For further information call 0161 868 8631.

5. **The Home of Football Museum**
   Ambleside, Cumbria.
   For further information call 015394 34440.

6. **Scottish Football Association Museum**
   Hampden Park, Glasgow.
   For further information call 0141 946 6190.

7. **National Football Museum**
   North End Football Club, Sir Tom Finney Way, Deepdale, Preston.
   For further information call 01772 902020.

8. **The British Golf Museum**
   Bruce Embankment, St Andrews, Fife.
   For further information call 01334 478880.

9. **Cheltenham Racecourse Hall of Fame**
   Cheltenham Racecourse, Cheltenham, Gloucestershire.
   For further information call 01242 513014.

10. **The National Horseracing Museum**
    99 High Street, Newmarket, Suffolk.
    For further information call 01638 667333.

11. **Brooklands Museum (Motor Racing)**
    Brooklands Road, Weybridge, Surrey.
    For further information call 01932 857381.

12. **The Donington Grand Prix Collection**
    Donington Park, Castle Donington, Derbyshire.
    For further information call 01332 811027.

13. **Much Wenlock Olympian Society Collection**
    Much Wenlock Museum, Much Wenlock, Shropshire.
    For further information call 01952 727773.

14. **River and Rowing Museum**
    Mill Meadows, Henley on Thames, Oxfordshire.
    For further information call 01491 415600.

15. **The James Gilbert Museum (Rugby)**
    5 St Matthews Street, Rugby, Warwickshire.
    For further information call 01788 333888.

16. **The Museum of Rugby**
    RFU, Rugby Road, Twickenham, Middlesex.
    For further information call 020 8892 2000.

17. **The Rugby League Hall of Fame**
    George Hotel, St Georges Square, Huddersfield.
    For further information call 01484 515444.

18. **Royal Tennis Court**
    Hampton Court Palace, London.
    For further information call 020 8977 3015

19. **Wimbledon Lawn Tennis Museum**
    The All England Club, Church Road, Wimbledon, London.
    For further information call 020 8946 6131.

HOTEL RATINGS & AWARDS

A Guide to Ratings

For a quick assessment of an hotel's qualities, we have used rating systems from the tourist boards, the Royal Automobile Club (RAC) and Automobile Association (AA). In addition, we have included the Consumer Association's The Good Food Guide 2001 and WHICH? Hotel Guides 2001. All ratings and awards are supplied to us by the hotels and verified by us where possible. If you need more specific information, we suggest you approach the relevant organisation direct; the addresses are given on page 484.

But symbols are not everything!

A lack of stars, diamonds and rosettes does not necessarily convey the whole picture: some hotels are so new, they have not been rated at all as yet, while others are so non-conformist that they cannot satisfy the standard criteria but who are, nevertheless, interesting and comfortable places to stay. All the hotels in this have been visited by at least one member of the Best Loved team and we can confirm the personal quotations at the top of every page in this book make them best-loved by someone – and for a very good reason!

Scottish
TOURIST BOARD

★★★★★

The system awards stars as follows:

★ - ***Fair and acceptable***
★★ - ***Good***
★★★ - ***Very Good***
★★★★ - ***Excellent***
★★★★★ - ***Exceptional***

Establishments are rated by category: small hotel, hotel, guest house, inn, restaurant with rooms and serviced apartments. They should only be compared with those within their own category.

BWRDD CROESO CYMRU
WALES TOURIST BOARD

★★★★★

The system awards stars as follows:

★ - ***Fair***
★★ - ***Good***
★★★ - ***Very Good***
★★★★ - ***Excellent***
★★★★★ - ***Exceptional***

Establishments are rated by category: hotel, country hotel, country house, guest house, lodge, b&b, farmhouse, inn and restaurant with rooms. They should only be compared with those within their own category.

Irish Tourist Board

★★★★★

Star ratings, ranging upwards from one to five Stars are used to classify hotels throughout Ireland.

Royal Automobile Association (R.A.C.)

★★★★★ ◆◆◆◆◆

Star ratings, from one to five, relate to hotel size and facilities; diamonds relate to guest accommodation.

Gold Ribbon & Blue Ribbon Awards

The Gold Ribbon is the highest accolade awarded by the RAC, followed by the Blue Ribbon. Due to the timings of the presentation of these awards in some cases we have published ratings from 2000.

There are other awards for Guest accommodation:

Little Gem - for all round quality
Sparkling diamonds - for hygine
Warm Welcome - for hospitality

There are also five levels of Dining Awards for both hotels and guest houses indicating quality of *all* meals.

ISBN 1-898889-35-X

The Automobile Association (A.A.)

★★★★★ 76%

Star ratings, from one to five Stars are related to hotel size as well as its facilities. Percentage ratings indicate the level of quality within the category. These are constantly updated.

★★★

Red Stars are given annually to a very few hotels considered to be the best in their star category.

Rosettes range from one up to five, denoting the quality of food.

◆◆◆◆◆

Diamond ratings cover private smaller hotels, guest houses, farmhouses and inns. They are similar to star ratings for hotels and range from one to five, the more there are, the higher the quality.

When you see the stars or diamonds you can be sure the establishment has been inspected and meets the council's standards for facilities and service under the English Tourism Council's quality assurance scheme. The more stars or diamonds, the better the facilities on a scale from one to five. Stars are awarded to hotels and diamonds for guest accommodation.

★★★★★ ◆◆◆◆◆

In addition to stars and diamonds, establishments of all kinds may receive an additional gold or silver award in recognition of the highest levels of quality in areas that guests regard as of the greatest importance.

BEST LOVED HOTELS SPORTING HIGHLIGHTS 2001

January

47th London International Boat Show

Earls Court Exhibition Centre,
Warwick Road,
London

Further Information:
Tel: 0121 767 4600
Fax: 0121 767 3849

February

Six Nations Rugby Football Championship kicks off with England v. Italy at Twickenham (through April)

Rugby Football Union Ground,
Rugby Road, Twickenham,
London

Further Information:
Tel: 020 8892 2000
Fax: 020 8892 9816
Website: www.rfu.com

Motorsport Day, Brooklands Museum

Brooklands Museum rust Ltd,
Brooklands Road,
Weybridge KT13 0QN

Further Information:
Tel: 01932 857381
Fax: 01932 855465

March

Oxford v. Cambridge Boat Race, London (TBC poss. April)

Ketchum, Tower House,
8-14 Southampton Street, Covent Garden,
London WC2E 7HA

Further Information:
Tel: 020 7465 7036
Fax: 020 7240 7729

Flat Racing season opens (Mar-Nov)

United Racecourses Ltd,
Sandown Park, Portsmouth Road, Esher,
Surrey KT10 9AJ

Further Information:
Tel: 01372 470047
Fax: 01372 470427

Cheltenham Gold Cup National Hunt

Cheltenham Racecourse,
Prestbury Park, Cheltenham,
Gloucestershire GL50 4SH

Further Information:
Tel: 01242 513014
Fax: 01242 224227

April

Martell Grand National Festival, Liverpool

Aintree Racecourse Co Ltd,
Aintree Racecourse, Ormskiark Road, Aintree,
Liverpool L9 5AS

Further Information:
Tel: 0151 523 2600
Fax: 0151 522 2920

County Cricket Season opens (Apr-Sept)

MCC, Lords Cricket Ground,
St Johns Wood Road, London NW8

Further Information:
Tel: 020 7289 1611
Fax: 020 7432 1061

May

Badminton Horse Trials

Badminton, Gloucestershire

Further Information:
Tel: 01454 218 272

FA Cup Final (soccer) – Venue TBC

The Football Association, 16 Lancaster Gate,
London W2 3LW

Further Information:
Tel: 020 7402 7151
Fax: 020 7402 2721

International Test Match Cricket England v. Pakistan

MCC, Lords Cricket Ground,
St Johns Wood Road, London NW8

Further Information:
Tel: 020 7289 1611
Fax: 020 7432 1061

Royal Windsor Horse Show

Royal Windsor Horse Show Club,
The Royal Mews, Windsor Castle,
Windsor SL4 1NG

Further Information:
Tel: 01753 860633
Fax: 01753 831074

June

Goodwood Festival of Speed, West Sussex

Goodwood House, Goodwood,
West Sussex PO18 0PX

Further Information:
Tel: 01243 755000
Fax: 01243 755005

The Derby

Epsom Racecourse,
Epsom, Surrey

Further Information:
Tel: 01372 470047
Fax: 01372 470427

Stella Artois Tennis Championships, Queen's Club, London

Queens Tennis Club, Pallister Road,
Barons Courts, London W14 9EQ

Further Information:
Tel: 020 7385 3421
Fax: 020 7386 8295

Royal Ascot

Ascot Racecourse, Ascot SL5 7JN

Further Information:
Tel: 01344 876876
Fax: 01344 628299

Curragh Derby Festival

Further Information:
Tel: +353 (0)1 676 5871 (Bord Failte)

Wimbledon Lawn Tennis Championships (Jun-Jul)

All England Lawn Tennis & Croquet Club,
P O Box 98,
Church Road, Wimbledon,
London SW19 5AE

Further Information:
Tel: 020 8946 2244
Fax: 020 8947 8752

July

British Grand Prix

Silverstone Circuit, Towcester,
Northamptonshie NN12 8TN

Further Information:
Tel: 01327 850100
Fax: 01327 320300

Henley Royal Regatta

Henley Reach, Regatta Headquarters,
Henley-on-Thames RG9 2LY

Further Information:
Tel: 01491 572153
Fax: 01491 575509
Website: www.hrr.co.uk

Golf: The Open Championship 2001, Royal Lytham St. Anne's

Royal Lytham St Anne's Golf Course, Links Gate,
Lytham St Anne's FY8 3LQ

Further Information:
Tel: 01253 724206
Fax: 01253 780946

Murphy's Irish Open

Fota Island, Cork, Republic of Ireland

Further Information:
Tel: +353 (0)1 269411

International Test Match Cricket England v. Australia (The Ashes)

MCC, Lords Cricket Ground,
St Johns Wood Road NW8

Further Information:
Tel: 020 7289 1611
Fax: 020 7432 1061

August

Cowes Week, Isle of Wight

18 Bath Road, Cowes,
Isle of Wight PO31 7QN

Further Information:
Tel: 01983 295328
Fax: 01983 295329

Highland Games at Skye, Perth and Crieff

Highland Games Ltd, 24 Florence Place,
Perth PH1 5BH

Further Information:
Tel: 01738 627782
Fax: 01738 639622

Football (soccer) season begins (Aug-May)

The Football Association,
16 Lancaster Gate,
London W2 3LW

Further Information:
Tel: 020 7402 7151
Fax: 020 7402 2721

Glorious Twelfth marks start of grouse shooting season (to mid-Dec)

Countryside Alliance,
The Old Town Hall, 367 Kennington Road,
London SE11 4EJ

Further Information:
Tel: 020 7840 9220

Grasmere Lakeland Sports and Show (wrestling, hound trails, mountain bike races), Lake District

Sports Filed, Stock Lane,
Grasmere, Cumbria

Further Information:
Tel: 015394 32127
Fax: 015394 32127

International Canoe Federation Marathon Racing World Championships, Stockton-on-Tees

British Canoe Union,
Adbolton Lane, West Bridgford,
Nottingham NG2 5AS

Further Information:
Tel: 0115 982 1100
Fax: 0115 982 1797
Website: www.bcu.org.uk

Manx Grand Prix Motorcycle Fortnight, Isle of Man

Department of Tourism and Leisure,
Sea Terminal, Douglas,
Isle of Man IM1 2RG

Further Information:
Tel: 01624 686801
Fax: 01624 686800

September

Blenheim Horse Trials Three Day Event, Oxfordshire

Blenheim Palace, Woodstock, Oxon OX20 1PS

Further Information:
Tel: 01993 813335
Bookings: 01993 813225

Ryder Cup Golf Tournament

The Belfry, Warickshire

Further Information:
Tel: 01675 470 333

Goodwood Revival Meeting, West Sussex

Goodwood House, Goodwood, West Sussex PO18 0PX

Further Information:
Tel: 01243 755000
Fax: 01243 755005

Horse of the Year Show, Wembley

Wembley Arena, Empire Way, Wembley HA9 0DW

Further Information:
Tel: 020 8902 0902

October

Motor Show - Earls Court, London

SMMT Ltd,
Forbes House, Halkin Street, London SW1X 7DS

Further Information:
Tel: 020 7235 7000
Bookings: 0870 464 2000

British Superbike Championships, Donington

Donnington Park Circuit,
Castle Donnington, Derby DE74 2RP

Further Information:
Tel: 01332 810048
Fax: 01332 850422

World Conker Championships, Peterborough

The Village Green, Ashton, Peterborough PE8

Further Information:
Tel: 01832 272735
Fax: 01832 272735

November

RAC Veteran Car Run, London to Brighton

Madeira Drive, Brighton, Brighton and Hove

Further Information:
Tel: 01273 290000

Network Q Rally of Great Britain/FIA World Rally Championships, Cardiff

Motor Sports Association,
Riverside Park,
Colnbrook SL3 0HG

Further Information:
Tel: 01753 681736
Bookings: 01327 850291

December

Olympia International Show Jumping Championships, London

Olympia Exhibition Centre,
Hammersmith Road,
London W14

Further Information:
Tel: 020 7370 8206
Fax: 020 7370 8347

Oxford v. Cambridge Varsity Match (rugby), Twickenham

Rugby Football Union Ground,
Rugby Road, Twickenham
London TW1 1DZ

Further Information:
Tel: 020 8892 2000
Fax: 020 8892 9816
Website: www.rfu.com

FLOWER SHOW CALENDAR

May

Spalding Flower Festival

Springfields
Camelgate, Spalding PE12 6ET

Further Information:
Tel: 01775 724843
Fax: 01775 711209

Carlisle and Borders Spring Flower Show

Carlisle City Council Community Support Unit,
5th Floor, Civic Centre,
Carlisle CA3 8QG

Further Information:
Tel: 01228 817359
Fax: 01228 817048

Chelsea Flower Show

Royal Horticultural Society,
80 Vincent Square,
London SW1P 2PE

Further Information:
Tel: 020 7649 1885
Bookings: 0870 9063781

June

Covent Garden Flower Festival

Covent Garden Plaza,
London WC2

Further Information:
Tel: 020 7735 1518
Fax: 020 7735 9163

Corpus Christi Carpet of Flowers and Floral Festival

Cathedral of Our Lady and St Philip Howard, Cathedral
West Sussex BN18 9AY

Further Information:
Tel: 01903 882297
Fax: 01903 885335

Wisbech Rose Fair

Saint Peters Patish Church, Church Terrace,
Wisbech, Cambridgeshire

Further Information:
Fax: 019045 584884

July

British Rose Fair

Hampton Court Palace,
Hampton Court,
London

Further Information:
Tel: 01727 850461
Fax: 01727 850360

RHS Hampton Court Palace Flower Show

Hampton Court Palace,
Hampton Court,
London

Further Information:
Tel: 020 7649 1885
Bookings: 0870 9063791
Website: www.rhs.org.uk

August

Ambleside Summer Flower Show and Craft Fair

Ambleside Horticultural and Craft Society,
Lattrigg, Lake Road,
Ambleside LA22 0DF

Further Information:
Tel: 015394 32904
Fax: 015394 32252

Shrewsbury Flower Show

Quarry Park, Shrewsbury,
Shropshire SY1 1RN

Further Information:
Tel: 01743 364051
Fax: 01743 233555

AFFILIATIONS

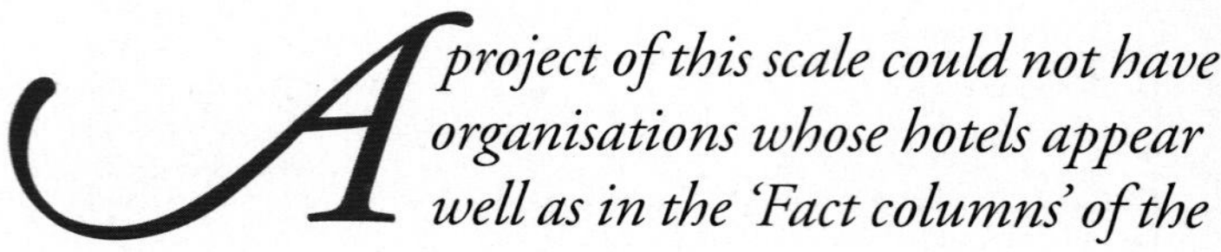

A project of this scale could not have organisations whose hotels appear well as in the 'Fact columns' of the

Langshott Manor, page 335

The Celebrated Hotels Collection/Preston's Global Hotels

Historic deluxe country house and city town house hotels each display in their own individual way, traditional elegance and personal service reminiscent of a bygone age, and provide for the needs of the modern sophisticated traveller.

US: 3816 Briar Oak Drive, Birmingham, AL 35243
US Toll Free (CHC): 800-322-2403
US Toll Free (PGH): 800-544-9993
Tel: 205-967-7054: *Fax:* 205-967-5192

UK: Suite 11, The Linen House,
253 Kilburn Lane, London W10 4BQ
Tel: 020 8962 9555
Fax: 020 8962 9550

Lovelady Shield, page 116

Fine Individual Hotels

Havens of luxury for those who enjoy life with a certain style. The charming, personally-managed hotels offer delightful accommodation, menus ranging from classical to contemporary, a connoisseur's wine list and courteous attention.

All reservations and enquiries should be made direct with each individual hotel.

St Clerans, page 462

Ireland's Blue Book

High standards of accommodation, traditional hospitality and good food in the rural beauty of Ireland. Members of ICHRA offer an opportunity to enjoy quality that is fast disappearing. Guests are welcomed with 'cead mille failte' at every door.

Ardbraccan Glebe, Navan, County Meath, Ireland
Tel: +353 (0)46 23416 • *Fax:* +353 (0)46 23292
US Toll Free: 800-323-5463

Bailiffscourt, page 316

Josephine Barr's Selected British Hotels

Josephine Barr has chosen hotels that offer charm, character and superb food, with easy access to beautiful gardens, stately homes and places of historical importance. Josephine and her team look forward to helping you plan your individual itinerary.

519 Park Drive, Kenilworth, IL 60043
US Toll Free: 800-323-5463 *Tel:* 847-251-4110 • *Fax:* 847-251-6845

Dundrum House, page 429

Manor House Hotels of Ireland

Manor House Hotels, are a superb collection of Irish Country Houses and Castles in the most picturesque of locations. They consist of three and four star properties that are as unique as you are.

1 Sandyford Office Park, Foxrock, Dublin 18, Ireland
Tel: +353(0)1 2958900 • *Fax:* +353(0)1 2958940

come together without the support of many in this book. We acknowledge them below as pages dedicated to their hotels.

Pride of Britain

This collection of privately owned and owner run country house properties offers a glimpse of style and tradition that is uniquely British. Each strives to produce extra special hospitality for their guests.

PO Box 1535, Andover, Hampshire SP10 1XZ
US Toll Free: 800-98-PRIDE *Tel:* 01264 324400 • *Fax:* 01264 324024

Bindon Country House, page 259

Relais & Chateaux

Abbeys, manor houses, mills, fine country houses and chateaux have become very comfortable hotels and elegant restaurants. They are run with an enthusiasm expressed in the famous 5 Cs: Character, Courtesy, Calm, Charm and Cuisine.

UK: Grosvenor Garden House, 35-37 Grosvenor Gardens, London SW1W 0BS
Tel: 020 7630 7667 • *Fax:* 020 7828 9476

US: 11 East 44th Street, New York, NY 10017. *Tel:* 212-856-0115 • *Fax:* 212-856-0193

Sheen Falls Lodge, page 465

Scotland's Hotels of Distinction

Quality hotels and inns, all individually owned and managed. World-renowned hospitality, with highest standards of ambience and quality of food and service. A warm welcome, the finest Scottish cuisine, and excellent value for money.

UK: PO Box 14724, St Andrews, Fife KY16 8WA. *UK Toll Free:* 0800 975 5975
Tel: 01333 360888 • *Fax:* 01333 360809

US: McFarland Ltd, 365 Gaines School Road, Athens, GA 30605
US Toll Free: 800-437-2687 • *Fax:* 706-549-1515

Enmore Hotel, page 51

Small Luxury Hotels

The SLH stamp guarantees an unequalled level of privacy, luxury and exclusivity. These fine quality hotels embrace the sophistication of city centres, the glamour and charm of resorts, historic chateaux and country houses throughout the world.

James House, Bridge Street, Leatherhead Surrey KT22 7EP
Tel: 01372 361873 • *Fax:* 01372 361874

US Toll Free: 800-525-4800

The Grand Hotel, page 329

Welsh Rarebits

They are all in interesting houses, in good locations, with superb food, imaginative decor and indefinable atmosphere. Wales's top country house hotels and traditional farmhouses, seaside hotels and historic inns are all included, and each in its own way is exceptional.

Princes Square, Montgomery Powys SY15 6PZ
Tel: 01686 668030 • *Fax:* 01686 668029

Fairyhill, page 153

Tee time: With 600-plus golf courses from coastal links to peaceful parkland settings, Scotland boasts more golfing options per head than anywhere else on earth. From the swing to the serene, the gardens at Crathes Castle (inset) are arranged in intimate 'rooms' by centuries-old hedges.

scotland

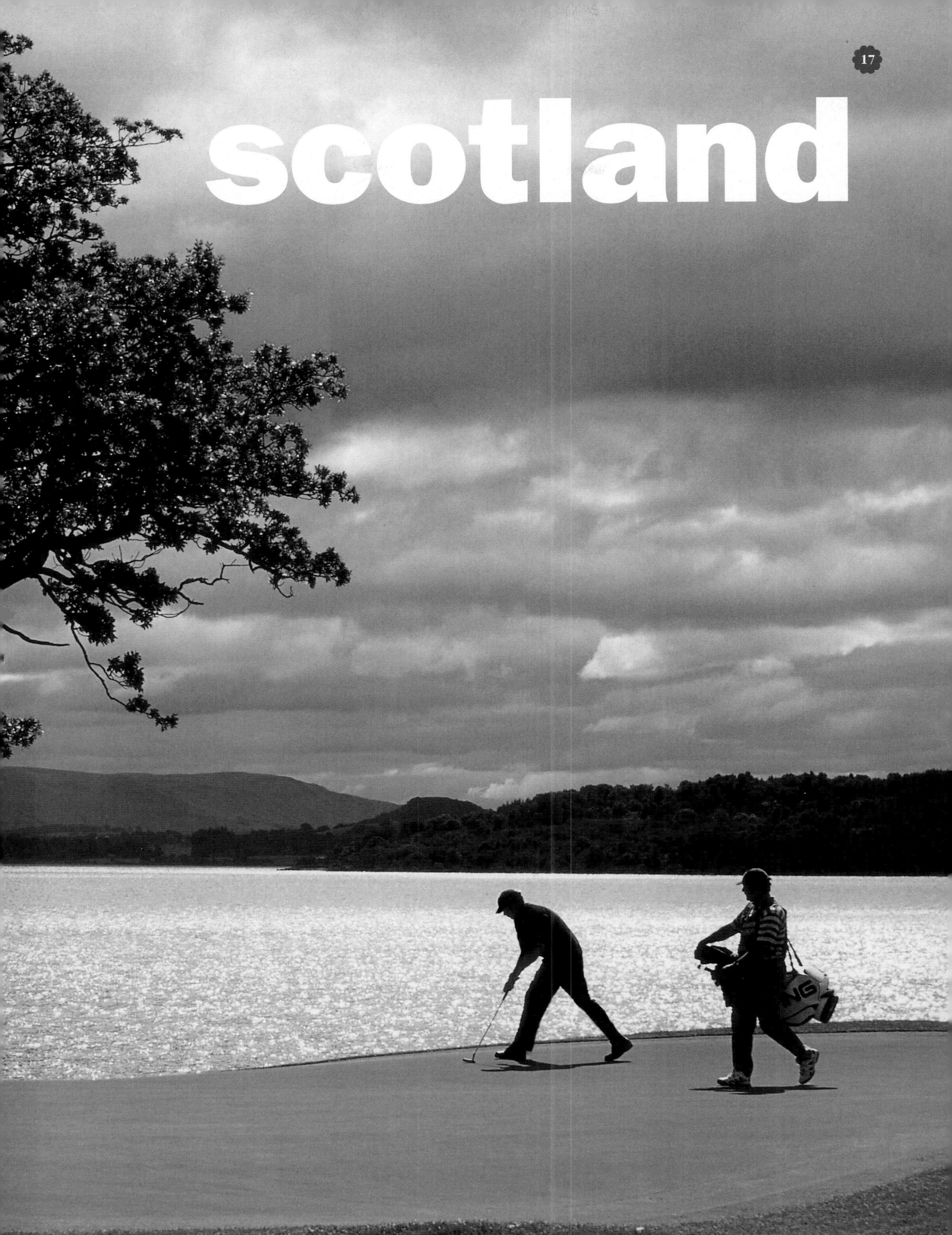

scotland

Scotland is one of Europe's great areas of outstanding natural beauty. The Highlands are majestic with rugged mountains, purple moors, shimmering lochs and tumbling rivers teeming with salmon and trout.

The Border country has gentle hills and rich farmlands that give way to the tranquil rolling countryside and forests of Dumfries and Galloway as you travel west. Then north, the magic coastline winds up to Ayrshire and to the Firth of Clyde, Oban and Argyll.

Offshore is the lure of the Orkneys, the Shetlands, the Inner and Outer Hebrides where Mendelssohn discovered his Fingel's Cave and, just off the mainland, Bonnie Prince Charlie's romantic Isle of Skye.

The country has over 600 castles, many clustered around the great cities of Edinburgh, Glasgow and Aberdeen. More recent building accomplishments include the Forth Railway Bridge and the Caledonian Canal engineered by Thomas Telford.

No visit to Scotland would be complete without a taste of the 'wee dram' and that's a pleasure to be found on many a Whisky trail.

Map Symbols

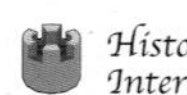

Horse sense

Pony-trekking originated in Scotland using sturdy Highland ponies to ferry visitors to local beauty spots. Now there are stables all over the country offering horse-back excursions far away from the madding crowds into the hills or along sandy strands of deserted beach.

Head for heights

Climbers and walkers with a head for heights are spoilt for choice in Scotland. There are 279 mountains over 3000ft, known as Munros after Hugh T. Munro, who first classified them in 1891. Experienced climbers will head for the Highlands and the spectacular scenery of Glen Coe, Glen Nevis or maybe the ski resort of Aviemore which makes a great base for winter mountaineering in the Cairngorms. On the Isle of Skye, the jagged peaks of the Cuillins lure the bravehearted.

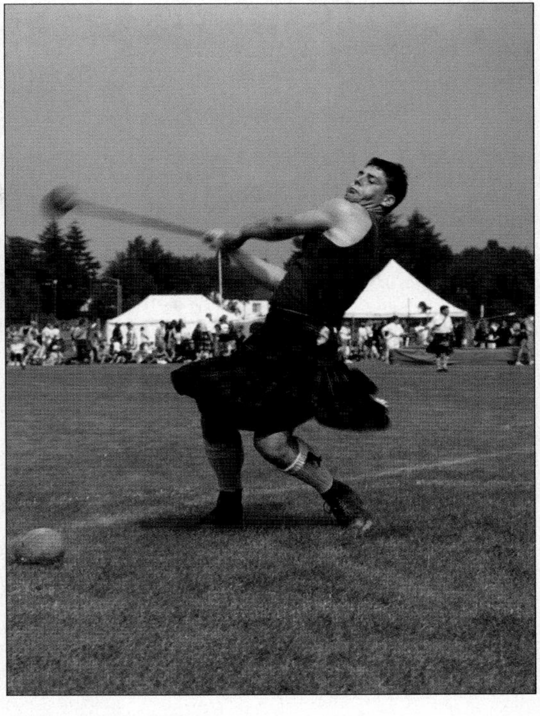

Highland fling

Putting the stone, throwing the hammer and tossing the caber are three of the 'heavies' or trails of strength in Highland Games that chiefs once used to select their warriors.

Micro-miracle

The famous Inverewe Gardens on Scotland's west coast rejoice in the same chilly latitude as distant Labrador. Yet the passage of the Gulf Stream just offshore creates a temperate micro-climate that allowed Osgood Mackenzie to transform a corner of the Highlands into a remarkable garden in a labour of love that lasted over half-a-century between 1862 and 1922.

Ayrie faerie

Ayrshire's top attraction, Culzean (pronounced Kul-ain) Castle looks as though it has leapt straight out of a medieval fairytale and into 3-D reality. In fact it dates from 1777, and is a showcase for the work of celebrated architect and designer Robert Adam. The surrounding country park features extensive formal gardens, a deer park and woodland walks as well as cliff top views to the Isle of Arran.

Arduaine Garden
Arduaine, by Oban, Argyll PA34 4XQ
Tel: 01852 200366
Located on the west coast of Scotland with a notable collection of Azaleas and Rhododendrons

Crarae Gardens
Minard, Argyll
Tel: 01546 8866 14
A unique Himalayan experience in a Scottish Highland glen

Castle Kennedy Gardens
Stair Estates, Rephadm Stranraer, Dumfries & Galloway Tel: 01653 648444
The home of the Earl & Countess of Stair, the gardens are open from Apr - Sep

Drummond Castle Gardens
Mthill, Crieff, Perthshire
Tel: 01764 681257
Scotland's most important formal gardens dating back to the 17th century

Find out more. There are many more attractions listed on the Best Loved Website: **www.bestlovedhotels.com**
Further information about Scotland can be found by contacting: **The Scottish Tourist Board.** 23 Ravelston Terrace, Edinburgh, EH4 3EU. Tel: +44 (0)131 332 2433

• Map p.494 ref: D9

"A little paradise in the middle of Scotland"

Ros & Peter Logan, Croydon, Surrey

ARDANAISEIG

19th century country house

Kilchrenan by Taynuilt, Argyll PA35 1HE

Telephone 01866 833333
Fax 01866 833222

E-mail: *ardanaiseig@bestloved.com*

OWNER
Bennie Gray

MANAGER
Robert Francis

ROOM RATES

Single occupancy	*£87 - £150*
13 Doubles/Twins	*£114 - £240*
3 Four-posters	*£208 - £240*

Includes full breakfast and VAT

CHARGE/CREDIT CARDS

• *DC* • *MC* • *VI*

RATINGS & AWARDS
S.T.B. ★★★★ *Hotel*

FACILITIES
On site: *Gardens, croquet, tennis, heli-pad, 1 meeting room/max 30 people*
Nearby: *Boating, fishing, snooker, walking*

RESTRICTIONS
No pets in public rooms
No smoking in restaurant or drawing room
No facilities for disabled guests

ATTRACTIONS
Oban and the Hebrides, Mull and Iona, Inveraray Castle, skiing and biking at Glencoe and Ben Nevis

AFFILIATIONS
Independent

NEAREST
MAJOR CITY:
Glasgow - 90 miles/2 hrs

MAJOR AIRPORT:
Glasgow - 80 miles/1½ hrs

RAILWAY STATION:
Taynuilt - 10 miles/15 mins

RESERVATIONS
Direct with hotel
Quote with ***Best Loved***

ACCESS CODES
Not applicable

The perfect place to discover the highlands and islands of Scotland

In a remote place of quiet tranquillity and almost surreal natural beauty, where the slopes of Ben Cruachan fall into the clear waters of Loch Awe, there is a small and wildly romantic old country house hotel. Ardanaiseig sits alone overlooking the mysterious islands and crannogs of the Loch, in deeply wooded gardens teeming with wildlife.

Built in 1834, overlooking its own island, Ardanaiseig, with its log fires, freshly picked flowers, antique furniture and fine works of art, has a special stately and timeless atmosphere. It is ideally situated for visits to Argyll's many castles and sites of historic interest.

The 100 acres of wild woodland gardens of Ardanaiseig were laid out in the 1820s. Since then thousands of exotic shrubs and trees including the famous rhododendrons have been imported from many parts of the world - including the Himalayas.

The restaurant is noted for its imaginative use of fresh produce, particularly seafood. Herbs from the walled garden enhance the subtle flavours created by the young award-winning chef.

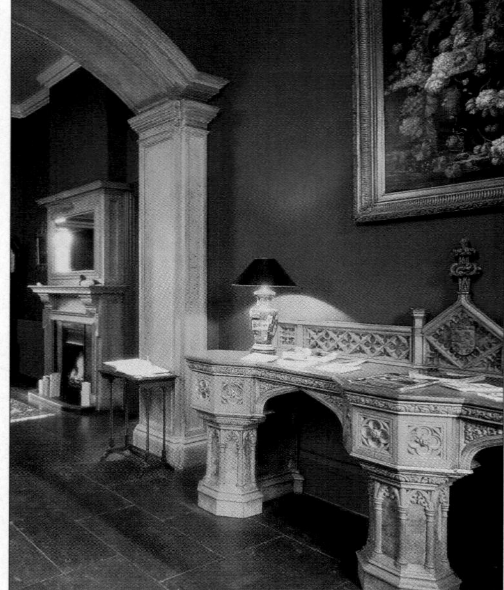

LOCATION

On the Scottish west coast, Loch Awe side, 85 miles from Stirling and 90 miles from Glasgow. From A85 to Oban turn off at Taynuilt on B845 to Kilchrenan and on to Ardanaiseig.

“ Memorable and wonderful to find such accomplished hosts, delicious food and courteous attention ”

Lord Wilson of Tillyorn

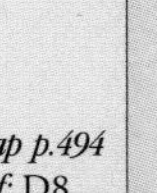

• Map p.494 ref: D8

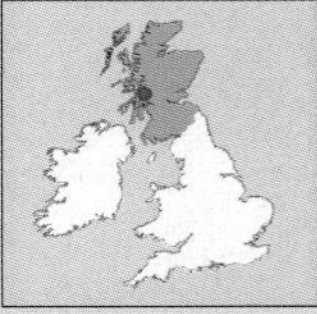

Highland family home and estate

ARDSHEAL HOUSE

Well-cooked food and a welcome on an historic Highland estate

The first Ardsheal House was destroyed by fire as a result of the 1745 uprising. It was rebuilt in about 1760 by Duncan Stewart of Ardsheal from the Stewart of Appin Clan. Constructed of granite and other stone, it stands on a natural promontory of pink marble. It is set in its own 800-acre estate, with one of Scotland's oldest woodlands and marvellous views over Loch Linnhe and the mountains of Morvern.

The family of Neil and Philippa Sutherland originally bought the estate in 1906. The gardens contain a Victorian rockery and are being restored to their former glory. The six comfortable bedrooms are furnished with family antiques and pictures. The oak-panelled hall with its unique barrel window has a crackling log fire on most days. The food, wine and malt whiskies are wonderful. Vegetables, herbs and fruit are from Ardsheal's own garden. Salmon, prawns, oysters and trout are abundant locally. Prime meats and game in season come from the local butcher. Jellies, jams and preserves are homemade; the bread rolls are home-baked.

Ardsheal is a superb base for trips to the Highlands, islands, castles, lochs, mountains and glens. To the north is Ben Nevis; north-west lies the fabled Isle of Skye; south are the seaports of Oban and the Isle of Mull.

LOCATION

Ardsheal is reached from the A828 5 miles south of the Ballachulish Bridge between Glencoe and Appin. 20 miles south of Fort William and 30 miles north of Oban.

Kentallen of Appin, Argyll PA38 4BX

Telephone 01631 740227
Fax 01631 740342

E-mail: *ardsheal@bestloved.com*

OWNERS

Neil and Philippa Sutherland

ROOM RATES

1 Single	£45
4 Doubles/Twins	£90
1 Four-poster	£90

Includes full breakfast and VAT

CHARGE/CREDIT CARDS

• MC • VI

RATINGS & AWARDS

S.T.B. ★★★★ Small Hotel
A.A. ◆◆◆◆◆

FACILITIES

On site: *Garden, snooker*
Nearby: *Water sports, skiing, riding*

RESTRICTIONS

No facilities for disabled guests

ATTRACTIONS

Glencoe, Nevis Range and Gondolas, Glenfinnan, Mull and Iona, Loch Ness

AFFILIATIONS

Independent

NEAREST

MAJOR CITY:
Glasgow - 100 miles/3 hrs

MAJOR AIRPORT:
Glasgow - 100 miles/3 hrs

RAILWAY STATION:
Fort William - 20 miles/40 mins

RESERVATIONS

Direct with hotel
*Quote **Best Loved***

ACCESS CODES

Not applicable

Ferries can make the crossing between Scotland and Ireland in 45 minutes

“We wish we could have stayed longer to enjoy the beautiful gardens and scenery. However, the food, our rooms and everything was delightful”

Ronald Reagan, Former President of the United States of America

AUCHTERARDER HOUSE

19th century baronial hall

Auchterarder,
Near Gleneagles,
Perthshire PH3 1DZ

Telephone 01764 663646
Fax 01764 662939

E-mail: *auchterarder@bestloved.com*

GENERAL MANAGER
Ian Fleming

ROOM RATES

Single occupancy	£125 - £275
6 Turret Wing doubles	£160
3 Junior suites	£195
6 Main Wing doubles	£295

Includes full breakfast and VAT

CHARGE/CREDIT CARDS

• DC • MC • VI

RATINGS & AWARDS
S.T.B. ★★★★ Hotel
A.A. ★★★ ❀❀ 77%

FACILITIES
On site: *Gardens, croquet, putting green, fishing, heli-pad*
2 meeting rooms/max 60 people
Nearby: *Golf, riding, shooting*

RESTRICTIONS
No facilities for disabled guests
No children under 10 years

ATTRACTIONS
Doune, Glamis and Huntingtower Castles, Scone Palace, Drummond Castle Gardens, Branklyn Gardens, Perth, Gleneagles

AFFILIATIONS
The Celebrated Hotels Collection
The Wren's Hotel Group
Grand Heritage Hotels

NEAREST
MAJOR CITY:
Edinburgh/Glasgow - 60 miles/1 hr

MAJOR AIRPORT:
Glasgow - 60 miles/1 hr
Edinburgh - 60 miles/1 hr

RAILWAY STATION:
Gleneagles - 4 miles/10 mins

RESERVATIONS
Toll free in US: 800-322-2403
Quote ***Best Loved***

ACCESS CODES
Not applicable

A magnificent family home a putt or two away from Gleneagles

Auchterarder lies amongst the rolling hills and glens of Perthshire on the royal route between Scone Palace and Stirling Castle. The area is world famous as the home of golf but those dedicated to field sports will know this is the finest hunting, shooting and fishing area in all Britain.

Built as a family home in 1832 and one of the finest Jacobean style country houses in Scotland, Auchterarder is proud of its reputation as a ‘special place’. It is run with the informality of a home but to a standard of service expected of a top flight hotel - the sort of place where chance acquaintances slip easily into lasting friendships.

Dining at Auchterarder House is an occasion to be savoured. Scottish food is presented with the finesse of French cuisine and the world-renowned qualities of Scottish fare. The wine list is extensive and informative; the cellars have obviously been stocked by someone who not only knows his subject but has a passion for it.

Special arrangements can be made for golf (now including Gleneagles), fishing and shooting locally and, if you are out for the day, an Auchterarder picnic lunch will remind you what an exceptional place this is.

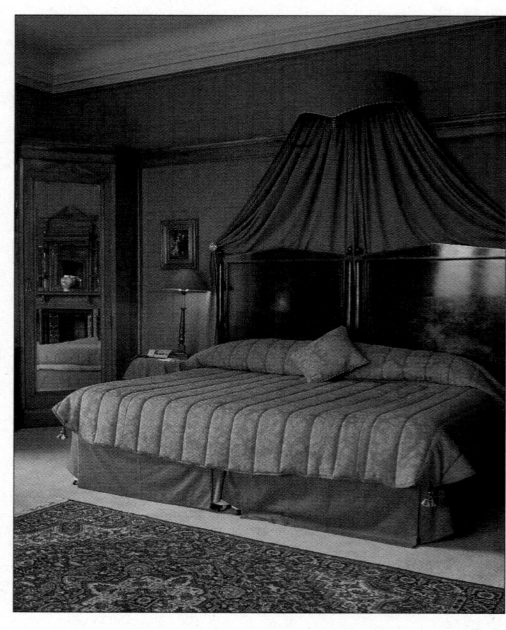

LOCATION

1½ miles north west of Auchterarder.

"We look forward to our next opportunity to visit – Next to excellence is the appreciation of it"

Beryl Barnett

• Map p.494 ref: G9

Georgian mansion BALBIRNIE HOUSE HOTEL

A beautiful country house between Edinburgh and St Andrews

Balbirnie House is a quite unique multi-award winning country house hotel which combines understated luxury with superb service and value. The building is a Grade 'A' listed Georgian country mansion and is set in a beautiful 400-acre estate in the heart of the Kingdom of Fife. Following a caring restoration a few years ago Balbirnie is now a delightful small luxury hotel, privately owned and managed.

A natural inheritance of gracious public rooms and period reflections create a quite individual ambience, skillfully combined with attentive service for the needs of today's house guests.

Views from the house extend over well-manicured lawns, picturesque flowering borders and ancient yew hedges to Balbirnie Park golf course, an undulating and scenic par 71 challenge.

With its unrivalled geographical location it is possible to visit the local quaint fishing villages or explore the countryside and heritage of Fife. Visit Edinburgh and the mecca of golf, St Andrews. Balbirnie is 30 minutes equidistant between both. Varied leisure pursuits can be arranged.

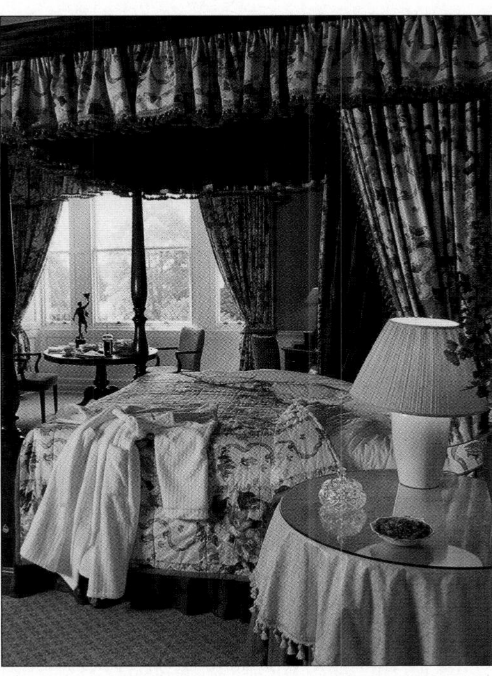

LOCATION

Half an hour equidistant from Edinburgh and St Andrews on the A92. Branch off on to the B9130 to Markinch Village.

Balbirnie Park, Markinch, Glenrothes, Fife KY7 6NE

Telephone 01592 610066
Fax 01592 610529

E-mail: *balbirnie@bestloved.com*

OWNERS

The Russell Family

ROOM RATES

2 Singles	£125 - £160
25 Doubles/Twins	£185 - £245
1 Four-poster	£245
2 Suites	£245

Includes full breakfast and VAT

CHARGE/CREDIT CARDS

• DC • MC • VI

RATINGS & AWARDS

S.T.B. ★★★★

R.A.C. Blue Ribbon ★★★★ Dining Award 3

A.A. ★★★★ ❀❀

Taste of Scotland 'Hotel of the Year'

FACILITIES

On site: *Golf, croquet, snooker, garden, heli-pad*

5 meeting rooms/max 300 people

Nearby: *Riding, fishing, shooting, luxury guided tours*

RESTRICTIONS

Pets by arrangement

ATTRACTIONS

Falkland Palace, Scone Palace, Glamis Castle, Stirling Castle, Edinburgh Castle, The Royal Yacht Britannia

AFFILIATIONS

Pride of Britain

Small Luxury Hotels

NEAREST

MAJOR CITY:
Edinburgh - 28 miles/35 mins

MAJOR AIRPORT:
Edinburgh - 25 miles/30 mins

RAILWAY STATION:
Markinch - 1 mile/5 mins

RESERVATIONS

Toll free in US: 800-98-PRIDE or 800-525-4800

Toll free in UK: 0800 964470

Quote ***Best Loved***

ACCESS CODES

AMADEUS LX EDIBHH
APOLLO/GALILEO LX 20905
SABRE/ABACUS LX 23430
WORLDSPAN LX EDIBH

• Map p.494 ref: G10

"The most charming and stylish stay ever"

Nicola Conyers, Scotland

THE BONHAM

Victorian town house

35 Drumsheugh Gardens,
Edinburgh EH3 7RN

Telephone 0131 623 6060
Fax 0131 226 6080

E-mail: *bonham@bestloved.com*

OWNER
Peter Taylor

GENERAL MANAGER
Fiona Vernon

ROOM RATES

10 Singles	£135 - £155
36 Doubles/Twins	£165 - £235
2 Suites	£295

Includes continental breakfast and VAT

CHARGE/CREDIT CARDS

• DC • MC • VI

RATINGS & AWARDS
S.T.B. ★★★★ Hotel
A.A. ★★★★ ❀ Town House
WHICH? Hotel of the Year 2000

FACILITIES
On site: *1 room with disabled facilities*
1 meeting room/max 80 people
Nearby: *Golf, fitness centre*

RESTRICTIONS
No pets, guide dogs only

ATTRACTIONS
Edinburgh Castle, Royal Mile, West End, Princes Street, Holyrood Palace, Waters of Leith, Dynamic Earth, Royal Yacht Britannia

AFFILIATIONS
Preston's Global Hotels
Selected British Hotels

NEAREST
MAJOR CITY:
Edinburgh
MAJOR AIRPORT:
Edinburgh - 6 miles/25 mins
RAILWAY STATION:
Waverley - 1 mile/10 mins
Haymarket - ½ mile/5 mins

RESERVATIONS
Toll free in US: 800-323-5463 or 800-544-9993
Quote **Best Loved**

ACCESS CODES
AMADEUS HK EDIDRU
APOLLO/GALILEO HT 88207
SABRE/ABACUS HK 1451
WORLDSPAN HK DRUMS

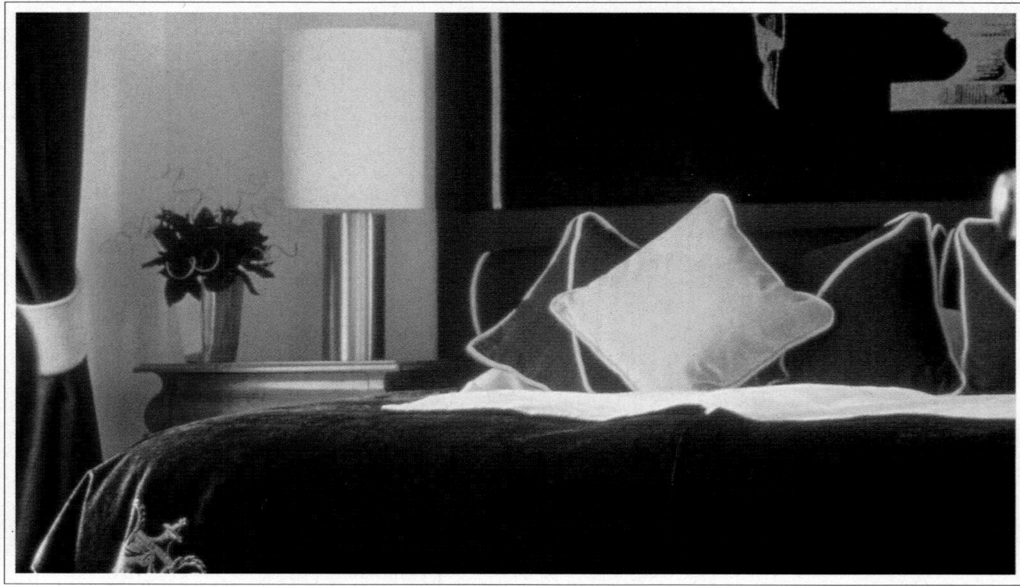

Setting new standards in Edinburgh and beyond

Close to Edinburgh's West End and its famous sites, are three beautifully converted town houses; they are The Bonham, a relaxing boutique-style hotel that could be anywhere but a city centre.

It has been designed for tomorrow; luxurious without being fussy, theatrical with every facility for today's business and leisure traveller. The spacious guest rooms and suites have an avant garde elegance and opulent simplicity made the more dramatic by contemporary furniture and Scottish paintings in rich, bold colours. Crisp lines are broken by luscious fabrics and the windows keep you in touch with the older beauty of Edinburgh, the Village of Dean and the Firth of Forth.

The Bonham is one of the first hotels to offer cutting-edge technology - every guest room is a virtual office and entertainment centre. eTV, as it is known, provides a range of on-line facilities via the television and infra red keyboard including e-mail, The Internet and Microsoft Office. DVD video, audio CD and video games are also on hand.

The Restaurant at The Bonham focuses on unpretentious fresh Scottish produce, with modern Californian influences, in a relaxed and informal 'café bistro' atmosphere.

The Bonham, with its impeccable standards and individuality, belongs firmly in the new millennium.

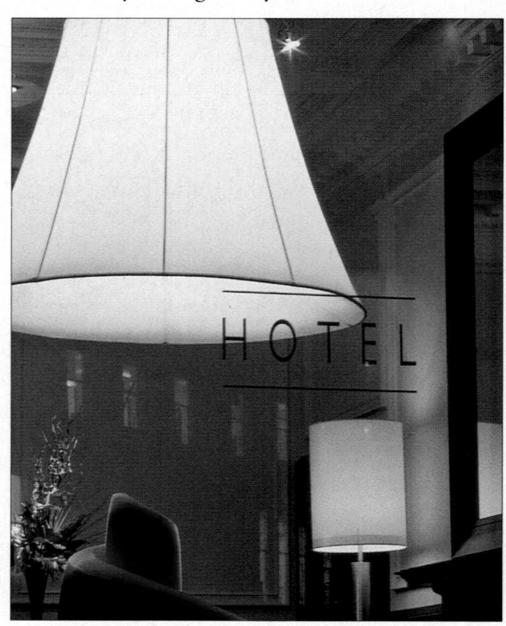

LOCATION

5 minutes walk from Edinburgh's West End/City Centre.

A keen Angler? Refer to page 472 for our Fishing Index

"Relaxation personified"

Ken & Caroline Venters, Aberdeen

Map p.494 ref: E6

Baronial mansion

BUNCHREW HOUSE HOTEL

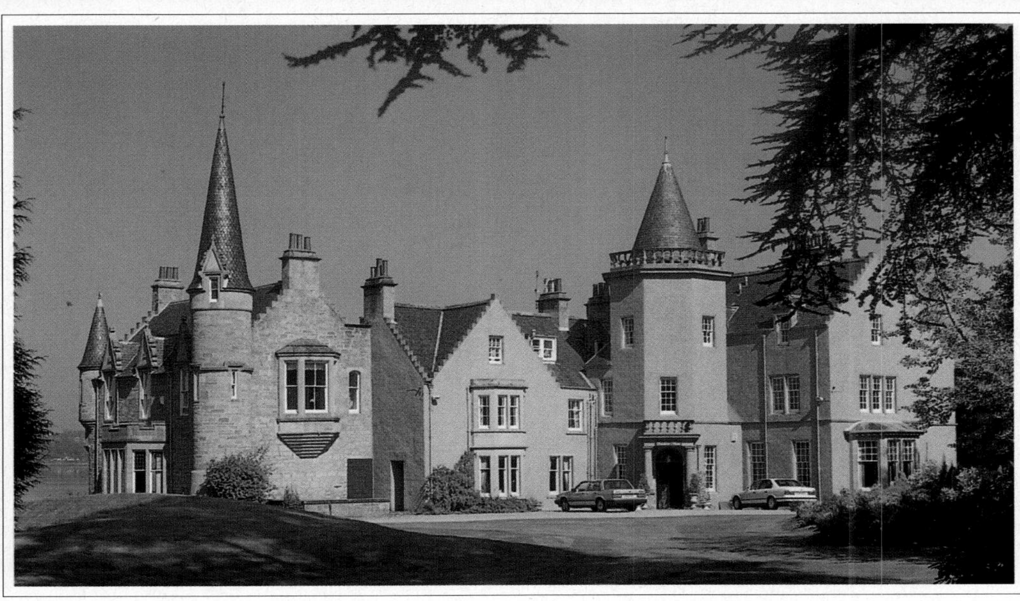

Timelessness and tranquillity by the banks of the Beauly Firth

Steeped in history and tradition, this beautiful 17th century Scottish mansion stands in 20 acres of landscaped gardens whose wall is lapped by the sea in the Beauly Firth. It was built by Simon Fraser, the eighth Lord Lovat, whose marriage to Jean Stewart in 1621 is commemorated by a stone marriage lintel above the fireplace in the drawing room.

Magnificent views from the hotel include the Black Isle and Ben Wyvis. While the dining room – filled with contemporary paintings of the Frasers – overlooks the sea. Traditional cuisine includes prime Scottish beef, fresh lobster and langoustines, local game and venison, and fresh vegetables cooked with herbs from the hotel's own herb garden. These superb dishes are complemented by a comprehensive wine list.

Eleven comfortable guest rooms include two with luxurious four-posters and one with a sumptuous half-tester; all are furnished to an extremely high standard and all benefit from 24-hour room service.

This is an area offering a number of outdoor sporting activities and a diversity of castles, glens, gardens, and, of course, the intriguing legend of the Loch Ness Monster.

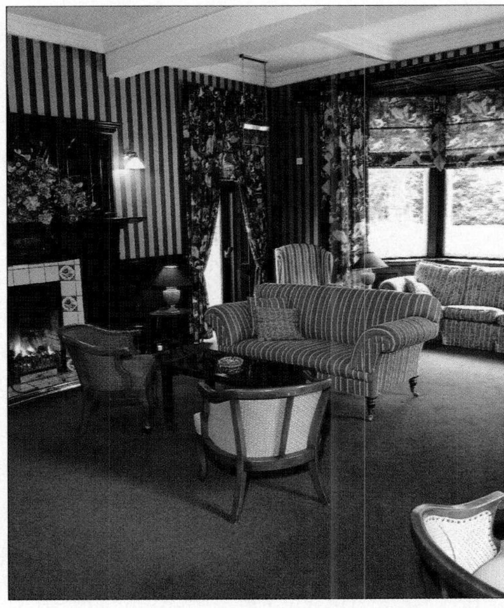

LOCATION

A short distance from both Inverness Airport and railway station, off the A862 between Inverness and Beauly.

By Inverness, Inverness-shire IV3 8TA

Telephone 01463 234917
Fax 01463 710620

***E-mail:** bunchrew@bestloved.com*

SCOTLAND

OWNERS

Graham and Janet Cross

ROOM RATES

Single occupancy	*£70 - £120*
8 Doubles/Twins	*£90 - £160*
3 Four-posters/Half tester	*£120 - £190*

Includes full breakfast and VAT

CHARGE/CREDIT CARDS

• *JCB* • *MC* • *VI*

RATINGS & AWARDS

S.T.B. ★★★★ Small Hotel
A.A. ★★★ ❀ 72%
Morrison Bowmore Scottish Field Restaurant of the Year Award
Taste of Scotland - Scotch Beef Club

FACILITIES

***On site:** Garden, fishing, heli-pad*
3 meeting rooms/max 100 people
***Nearby:** Golf, riding, fishing, shooting, skiing, walking*

RESTRICTIONS

No facilities for disabled guests
No pets in public rooms

ATTRACTIONS

Loch Ness, Culloden Battlefield, Glens of Affric, Cawdor Castle, Strathfarrar and Strathglass, Cannich

AFFILIATIONS

Preston's Global Hotels

NEAREST

MAJOR CITY:
Inverness - 3 miles/10 mins
Edinburgh - 150 miles/ 2½ hrs

MAJOR AIRPORT:
Inverness - 9 miles/20 mins
Edinburgh - 150 miles/2½ hrs

RAILWAY STATION:
Inverness - 3 miles/10 mins

RESERVATIONS

Toll free US: 800-544-9993
*Quote **Best Loved***

ACCESS CODES

Not applicable

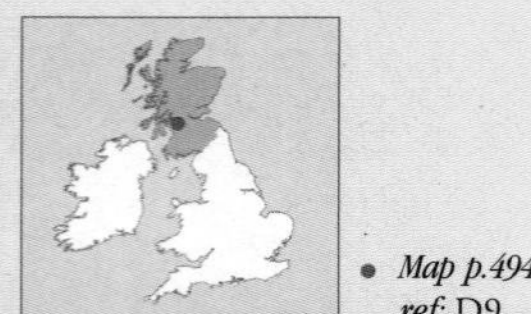

• Map p.494 ref: D9

"So relaxed, our kind of place"

Jean and Ken Hooper, USA

CAIRNBAAN HOTEL

Traditional coaching inn

SCOTLAND

By the Crinan Canal
Near Lochgilphead
Argyll PA31 8SJ

Telephone 01546 603668
Fax 01546 606045

E-mail: *cairnbaan@bestloved.com*

OWNERS
Darren and Christine Dobson

MANAGER
Colin Bell

ROOM RATES

Single occupancy	*£55 - £65*
10 Doubles/Twins	*£90 - £110*

Includes full breakfast and VAT

CHARGE/CREDIT CARDS
MC • VI • JCB

RATINGS & AWARDS
S.T.B. ★★★★ Hotel
A.A. ★★★ ❀ 68%
Taste of Scotland

FACILITIES
On site: *Garden*
2 meeting rooms/max 150 people
Nearby: *Golf, fishing, water skiing, yachting, tennis, fitness, hunting/shooting, riding, forest walks, mountain biking*

RESTRICTIONS
No smoking in bedrooms
No facilities for disabled guests

ATTRACTIONS
Inveraray Castle, Ancient Cairns & Standing Stones, The Crinan Canal, Islands of Islay and Jura, Dunadd Fort, Sea Life Centre, Kilmartin House

AFFILIATIONS
Scotland's Heritage Hotels

NEAREST
MAJOR CITY:
Glasgow - 80 miles/2 hrs

MAJOR AIRPORT:
Glasgow - 80 miles/2 hrs

RAILWAY STATION:
Glasgow - 80 miles/2 hrs

RESERVATIONS
Direct with hotel
Quote ***Best Loved***

ACCESS CODES
Not applicable

The perfect place to watch the world slip by

Cairnbaan Hotel was built in the late 18th century as a coaching inn to serve fishermen and puffers trading on the Crinan Canal. Now refurbished, it offers you the warm welcome typical of the West Coast. Traditional and special dishes are served at dinner in the restaurant. Lunches, snacks and a variety of home-baking can be enjoyed in the 'Bar Lock 5' or The Conservatory.

It is an ideal base from which to tour Argyll and the Islands of Islay and Jura. Local places of interest include Inveraray Castle, where some of Scotland's finest treasures are on show, Dunadd Fort where the ancient Kings of Scotland were crowned, and ancient cairns and standing stones.

Inveraray Jail is an unusual holiday attraction: guides dressed in the uniforms of prisoners and warders re-enact its 19th century past. At newly opened Kilmartin House Argyll's ancient past comes alive. The Highland Wildlife Park at Kincraig features herds of red deer, Highland cattle and many species now extinct to the wild: bison, ancient breeds of sheep and Przewalski's horses, one of the world's rarest mammals.

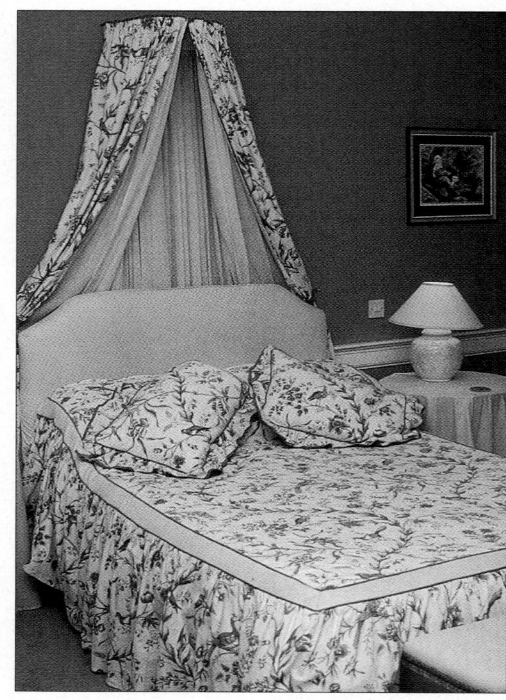

LOCATION

2 hours from Glasgow Airport via A82 and A83 to Lochgilphead. Take A816 to Cairnbaan.

"For me, its luxurious and peaceful setting is the ideal spot to get away from it all, and simply relax"

Lorraine Mollison, Havant, Hampshire

• Map p.494 ref: E9

Baronial mansion

CAMERON HOUSE

The complete leisure destination made exceptional by the food and the location

Since 1400, there has been a famous house on the strip of land that juts into Loch Lomond. Today, only the cellar of the first house remains but in its place, stands Cameron House, a magnificent mansion lovingly restored and provided with a magnificent leisure complex.

Set within 100 acres of gardens and woodlands sweeping down to the shores of the famous loch, its hard to conceive the beauty of the setting or the immense scope of activities available. The facilities for fitness, sport and exploring are so numerous, we can only list them in the yellow column on the left. But the golf course needs a special mention: for a nine-hole course it has a devilish reputation. The other feature that deserves a word or two is the resort's 225-berth marina from which watersports are launched and Celtic Warrior, the resort's own luxury cruiser, will take you on a voyage around the islands.

In sharp contrast to the wealth of technology that has gone into the leisure facilities are the good, old-fashioned virtues of deep-cushioned comfort and impeccable service. Heritage is overlaid by the finest traditional fabrics; antique fixtures and furniture contrast with up-to-the-minute amenities. The international cuisine in the elegant Georgian Room thrives off local produce from the sea, the loch and the highlands. Cameron House is the complete destination.

LOCATION

After crossing the Erskine Bridge take the A82 towards Crianlarich. After about 14 miles take the exit from the roundabout towards Luss. The hotel entrance is 1 mile further on.

Loch Lomond, Dunbartonshire G83 8QZ

Telephone 01389 755565
Fax 01389 759522

E-mail: cameron@bestloved.com

GENERAL MANAGER

Roddy Whiteford

ROOM RATES

Single occupancy	£160 - £170
80 Doubles/Twins	£225 - £235
9 Family rooms	£225 - £235
7 Suites	£350 - £450

Includes full Scottish breakfast, newspaper, residential use of leisure club and VAT

CHARGE/CREDIT CARDS

 • DC • MC • VI

RATINGS & AWARDS

S.T.B. ★★★★★ Hotel

A.A. ★★★★★ ❀❀❀ 72%

FACILITIES

On site: Croquet, tennis, indoor pools, squash, gym, health & beauty, 9 hole golf, fishing, heli-pad, creche, children's club and pool, sailing, windsurfing, archery, off-road driving

5 meeting rooms/max 300 people

Nearby: Golf, fishing, water skiing, hunting/shooting, clay pigeon shooting, riding

RESTRICTIONS

No smoking in bedrooms and restaurant

No pets

ATTRACTIONS

Loch Lomond, Glasgow's museums and galleries, The Trossachs, Dumbarton Castle, Rennie Mackintosh's Hill House

AFFILIATIONS

De Vere Hotels

NEAREST

MAJOR CITY:
Glasgow - 26 miles/30 mins

MAJOR AIRPORT:
Glasgow - 24 miles/25 mins

RAILWAY STATION:
Balloch - 1½ miles/5 mins

RESERVATIONS

Toll free in US: 800-276-7517

Quote **Best Loved**

ACCESS CODES

AMADEUS FT GLACHH
APOLLO/GALILEO FT 76133
SABRE/ABACUS FT 23310
WORLDSPAN FT GLACH

• Map p.494
ref: G8

"You clearly have a terrific facility which we look forward to returning to at an appropriate point in the future"

P D Fleet, Ford Motor Company

CARNOUSTIE GOLF RESORT & SPA

Resort

The Links,
Carnoustie,
Angus DD7 7JE

Telephone 01241 411999
Fax 01241 411998

E-mail: *carnoustie@bestloved.com*

GENERAL MANAGER

Mike McCartan

ROOM RATES

Single occupancy	*£115 - £148*
75 Doubles/Twins	*£125 - £160*
10 Suites	*£300 - £700*

Includes full breakfast and VAT

CHARGE/CREDIT CARDS

• *DC* • *MC* • *VI*

RATINGS & AWARDS

S.T.B. ★★★★ *Hotel*
R.A.C. ★★★★
A.A. ★★★★ *66%*
Taste of Scotland

FACILITIES

On site: *Golf, indoor pool, gym, sauna, heli-pad, health & beauty, jacuzzi, steam room*
6 meeting rooms/max 400 people
Nearby: *Fishing, tennis, clay pigeon shooting, off-road driving, yachting*

RESTRICTIONS

Pets at manager's discretion

ATTRACTIONS

Barry Mill, Glamis Castle, St Andrews, Dundee, Blair Castle, numerous golf courses

AFFILIATIONS

The Celebrated Hotels Collection

NEAREST

MAJOR CITY:
Dundee - 15 miles/20 mins

MAJOR AIRPORT:
Edinburgh - 65 miles/1½ hrs;
Dundee - 15 miles/20 mins

RAILWAY STATION:
Carnoustie - 1 mile/5 mins

RESERVATIONS

Toll free in US: 800-322-2403
Quote ***Best Loved***

ACCESS CODES

AMADEUS HK DNDCAR
APOLLO/GALILEO HT 07092
SABRE/ABACUS HK 46401
WORLDSPAN HK CARNO

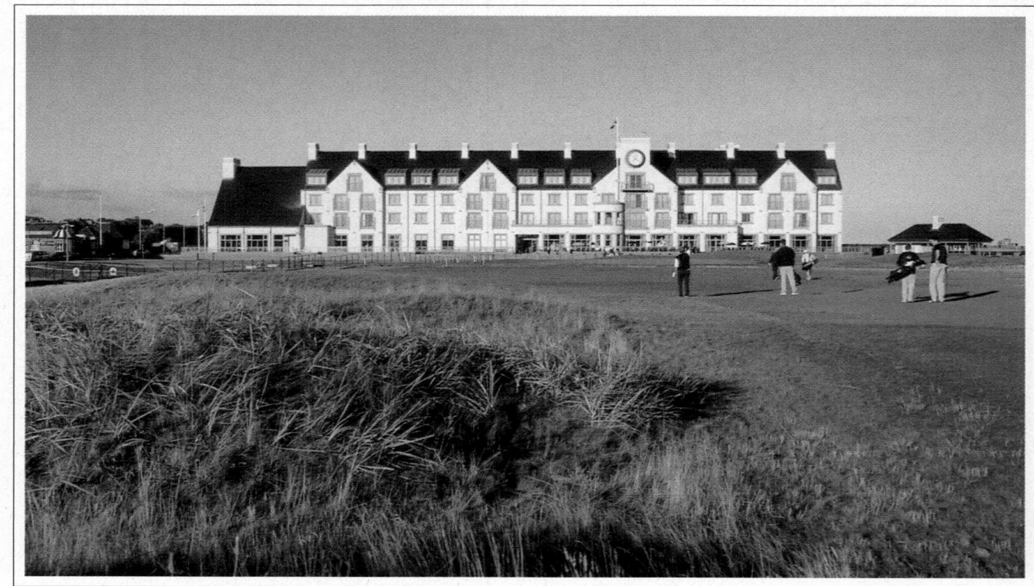

Pampered luxury, overlooking the world's toughest links golf course

As any golfer will tell you, golf is a seriously competitive game: you are not just playing against the opposition but yourself, your handicap, the course and the elements. No surprise then that when The Carnoustie Golf Course Hotel & Resort was being planned, it set out to be better than anything else of its kind in the world. Certainly, the Championship Course (home of the 1999 Open) is arguably the toughest in the land and the other two, the Burnside and The Budden Links, throw down their own particular gauntlets. Whichever one you are playing, take your eye off the ball and do look at the scenery; now that is hard to beat!

There's a competitive edge to the restaurant, too. Floor to ceiling panoramic windows look out over the first tee and the eighteenth green; the decor is luxurious with tables spaced well apart; and there's no argument about the food. Premier Scottish produce like local seafood and salmon, venison from the glens and Aberdeen Angus beef form the basis of French haute cuisine at its best.

The bedrooms try to be grander and more opulent than anywhere else. How well they succeed is for you to decide but it won't be easy, they are a triumph of colour, comfort and design.

One more thing: as a guest, you have guaranteed tee times on any of the three courses and that, without fear of contradiction, is unique.

LOCATION

From Edinburgh take the M90 then the A90 then the A92 to Carnoustie. From there follow the signs to the hotel and golf courses.

"You have achieved a simple perfection. Thank you. P.S. Great staff"

Kenneth H Millstein

• *Map p.494 ref:* G10

Edwardian town house

CHANNINGS

A discreet, boutique-style, country house in town

Walk through the quiet cobbled streets of Edinburgh city centre, just a small distance from the Castle, and you will find a row of five beautifully maintained Edwardian town houses. Together, they make up Channings, a boutique-style hotel with a cosy, traditional club-like atmosphere. The style of Channings has a feeling of classic care, from the peaceful, fire-lit lounges to any of the 46 luxurious guest rooms; several of which offer wonderful panoramic views over the Firth of Forth to the hills of Fife.

The traditional, richly coloured Restaurant with Edwardian features, complements the Conservatory, which is simple and uncluttered with its pale wooden floors and subtle directional downlights offering a light and airy feel. The Restaurant prides itself on honest food and excellent, personable service. After dinner, the Wine Bar provides a relaxed environment and welcomes you with an interesting range of malt whiskies. In the warmer months, take your lunch into the sun-lit terraced garden.

The quiet, classical feel of the hotel makes it the ideal venue for private or corporate dinners or small meetings. Any such gathering can be held in the oak-panelled Library, the Kingsleigh Suite or, indeed, the Conservatory.

LOCATION

Channings is only ½ mile from the city centre (10 minutes walk) and only 20 minutes from the airport by taxi.

12-16 South Learmonth Gardens, Edinburgh EH4 1EZ

Telephone 0131 332 3232
Fax 0131 332 9631

E-mail: *channings@bestloved.com*

OWNER
Peter Taylor

GENERAL MANAGER
Marco Truffelli

ROOM RATES

5 Singles	*£125 - £155*
37 Doubles/Twins	*£155 - £195*
1 Four-poster	*£185 - £205*
3 Suites	*£235 - £240*

Includes full breakfast and VAT

CHARGE/CREDIT CARDS

 • *DC • MC • VI*

RATINGS & AWARDS
S.T.B. ★★★★ *Hotel*
A.A. ★★★★ ❀❀ *75% Town House*

FACILITIES
On site: *Garden, patio, conservatory, Channings Restaurant & Wine Bar*
3 meeting rooms/max 100 people
Nearby: *Golf, fitness centre*

RESTRICTIONS
No facilities for disabled guests
No pets, guide dogs only

ATTRACTIONS
Dynamic Earth, Royal Yacht Britannia, Botanical Gardens, Edinburgh Castle, Holyrood House, Royal Mile, National Art Gallery of Scotland

AFFILIATIONS
Scotland's Hotels of Distinction
Selected British Hotels
The Small Hotel Company

NEAREST
MAJOR CITY:
Edinburgh
MAJOR AIRPORT:
Edinburgh - 6 miles/20 mins
RAILWAY STATION:
Waverley or Haymarket - 1½ miles/5 mins

RESERVATIONS
Toll free in US: 800-323-5463
or 800-544-9993
Quote ***Best Loved***

ACCESS CODES
AMADEUS UI EDICHA
APOLLO/GALILEO UI 22312
SABRE/ABACUS UI 22560
WORLDSPAN U114126

• Map p.494 ref: E6

"Very much the country house with a relaxed and welcoming atmosphere, and refreshingly unpretentious"

D J Robertson, A.A. Inspector

COUL HOUSE HOTEL

Highland mansion

SCOTLAND

Contin, by Strathpeffer, Ross-shire IV14 9EY

Telephone 01997 421487
Fax 01997 421945

E-mail: coulhouse@bestloved.com

OWNERS

Martyn and Ann Hill

ROOM RATES

3 Singles	£53 - £70
6 Doubles/Twins	£76 - £110
6 Superior Doubles/Twins	£88 - £122
1 Four-poster	£100 - £134
1 Suite	£112 - £158
3 Triple/Family rooms	£76 - £165

Includes full breakfast and VAT

CHARGE/CREDIT CARDS

• DC • JCB • MC • VI

RATINGS & AWARDS

S.T.B. ★★★★ Hotel
A.A. ★★★ ❀ 74%
Taste of Scotland

FACILITIES

On site: Garden, 9-hole golf course
2 meeting rooms/max 50 people
Nearby: Golf, fishing

RESTRICTIONS

None

ATTRACTIONS

Strathpeffer Spa Victorian village, Loch Ness, Strathconon, Cromarty Firth, Loch Achonachie salmon lift, Rogie Falls and Torrachilty Forest Trail, Beauly Priory, Castle Leod

AFFILIATIONS

Scotland's Hotels of Distinction
Best Western

NEAREST

MAJOR CITY:
Inverness - 20 miles/30 mins
MAJOR AIRPORT:
Inverness - 25 miles/35 mins
Glasgow - 180 miles/4 hrs
RAILWAY STATION:
Inverness - 20 miles/30 mins

RESERVATIONS

Toll free in US: 800-437-2687
Quote **Best Loved**

ACCESS CODES

SABRE/ABACUS UI 30594
APOLLO/GALILEO UI 83655
AMADEUS UI INVCOU
WORLDSPAN UI 26195

So much to see and enjoy in such a perfect Highland setting

The ancient Mackenzies of Coul picked the supreme situation for this secluded country mansion, with magnificent, uninterrupted views over forest and mountain. For 23 years, it has been the home of Martyn and Ann Hill, who offer high standards, friendly service and a warm Highland welcome.

The candlelit Restaurant and new Tartan Bistro are appointed for 'Taste of Scotland' cooking, which is personally supervised by head chef, Karl Taylor, who has been at Coul for many years. Smoked seafoods, fresh salmon and succulent roasts are on the menu. The wine list is equally superb, and the Mackenzie's Bar has a fine selection of single malts. The three elegant lounges all have log fires. The bedrooms are individually designed and decorated, and thoroughly well equipped.

The hotel is a favourite with anglers and golfers. It has salmon and trout fishing nearby, and offers a 5-course golf package that includes Royal Dornoch. Using the hotel as a base you can easily cruise Loch Ness, visit Macbeth's Cawdor Castle, or sail to the Summer Isles. You can also pony-trek and go on guided 'Insight' rambling, or follow the Highland Heritage Trail.

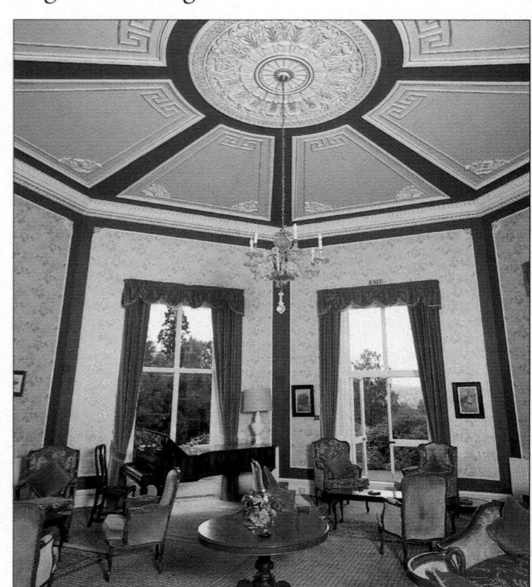

LOCATION

From south, by-passing Inverness, continue on A9 over Moray Firth Bridge. After 5 miles, follow A835 to Contin. Hotel is ½ mile up private drive to the right.

"Deep-cushioned comfort amongst the historic castles of Scotland"

Mr & Mrs Miller, Vancouver, Canada

Map p.494 ref: G6

Victorian hotel

CRAIGELLACHIE HOTEL

Boundless Highland hospitality on the banks of the River Spey

The Craigellachie Hotel occupies a pre-eminent position crowning a low rise above lawns that lead down to the banks of the River Spey. The fast-flowing Spey is one of Scotland's top salmon fishing rivers and a magnet for keen anglers, while the surrounding countryside proves equally appealing to guests who just want to enjoy some of the Highlands' finest scenery. At the very heart of the Malt Whisky Trail, the award winning Quaich Bar serves over 350 single malts and is a celebration to the hotel's many world famous neighbours.

Generously proportioned rooms give a welcome sense of space and provide many quiet corners where guests can steal themselves away either to read a good book by the fire, have a game of snooker or sit and chat over tomorrow's touring plans. Recent refurbishments have garnered considerable praise for the elegant yet unfussy décor which blends cleverly with the period of the building and extends to the charming bedrooms decorated with subtle combinations of colours and fabrics.

Modern Scottish cuisine with an international twist is the order of the day in the ambient Ben Aigan restaurant and after dinner, what better way to spend the rest of the evening than sampling a dram, or two!

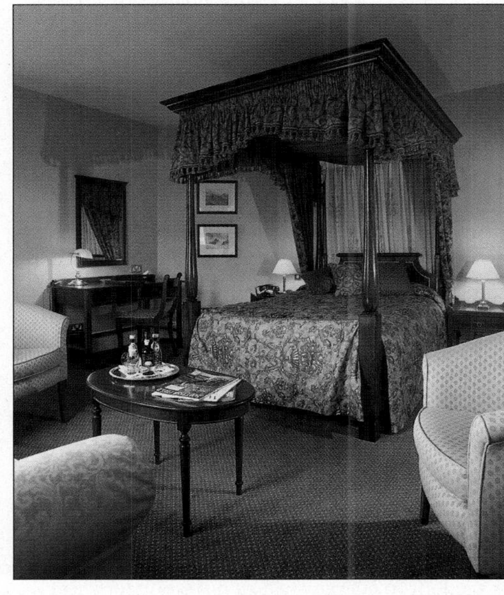

LOCATION

In Craigellachie on the A941 Elgin road. The hotel is on the right hand side.

SCOTLAND

Craigellachie, Speyside, Banffshire AB38 9SR

Telephone 01340 881204
Fax 01340 881253

***E-mail:** craigellachie@bestloved.com*

GENERAL MANAGER

Duncan Elphick

ROOM RATES

15 Doubles/Twins	*£95 - £115*
6 Superior Doubles/Twins	*£110 - £130*
4 Deluxe Doubles/Twins	*£125 - £145*

Includes full breakfast and VAT

CHARGE/CREDIT CARDS

• DC • JCB • MC • VI

RATINGS & AWARDS

S.T.B. ★★★★ Small Hotel
A.A. ★★★ ❀❀ 76%
Glenmorangie Hotel Bar of the Year 1999

FACILITIES

***On site:** Garden, tennis*
3 meeting rooms/max 50 people
***Nearby:** Golf, fishing, hunting, riding, cycling, off road driving*

RESTRICTIONS

No facilities for disabled guests
Pets by arrangement

ATTRACTIONS

Loch Ness, the Highlands, Balmoral Castle, Malt Whisky Trail, Culloden Battlefield, Cairngorms

AFFILIATIONS

The Celebrated Hotels Collection
Grand Heritage Hotels

NEAREST

MAJOR CITY:
Inverness - 50 miles/1 hr

MAJOR AIRPORT:
Aberdeen - 55 miles/1 hr

RAILWAY STATION:
Elgin - 12 miles/20 mins

RESERVATIONS

Toll free in US: 800-322-2403 or 888-93-GRAND
*Quote **Best Loved***

ACCESS CODES

Not applicable

• Map p.494 ref: G10

"You've either got, or you haven't got style. Cringletie House has got more than its fair share of the stuff"

Bill Clapperton, Edinburgh Evening News

CRINGLETIE HOUSE HOTEL

Country mansion

SCOTLAND

Peebles, Borders EH45 8PL

Telephone 01721 730233
Fax 01721 730244

E-mail: cringletie@bestloved.com

MANAGER
Kellie Bradford

ROOM RATES

1 Single	£75 - £95
13 Doubles/Twins	£150 - £180

Includes full breakfast and VAT

CHARGE/CREDIT CARDS

• MC • VI

RATINGS & AWARDS
S.T.B. ★★★★ Hotel
A.A. ★★★ ❀ 79%
S.T.B. Award 2000 for Consistant Excellence
R.A.C. Housekeeping Award

FACILITIES
On site: Gardens, croquet, tennis, fishing, heli-pad, open air theatre
4 meeting rooms/max 100 people
Nearby: Golf, riding, fishing

RESTRICTIONS
No facilities for disabled guests

ATTRACTIONS
Edinburgh, Traquair, Abbotsford, Melrose Abbey, Jedburgh Abbey

AFFILIATIONS
The Wren's Hotel Group
Preston's Global Hotels

NEAREST
MAJOR CITY:
Edinburgh - 20 miles/35 mins

MAJOR AIRPORT:
Edinburgh - 25 miles/40 mins

RAILWAY STATION:
Edinburgh - 20 miles/30 mins

RESERVATIONS
Toll free in US: 800-544-9993
Quote **Best Loved**

ACCESS CODES
AMADEUS UI EDICHH
APOLLO/GALILEO UI 16821
SABRE/ABACUS UI 12038
WORLDSPAN UI 40791

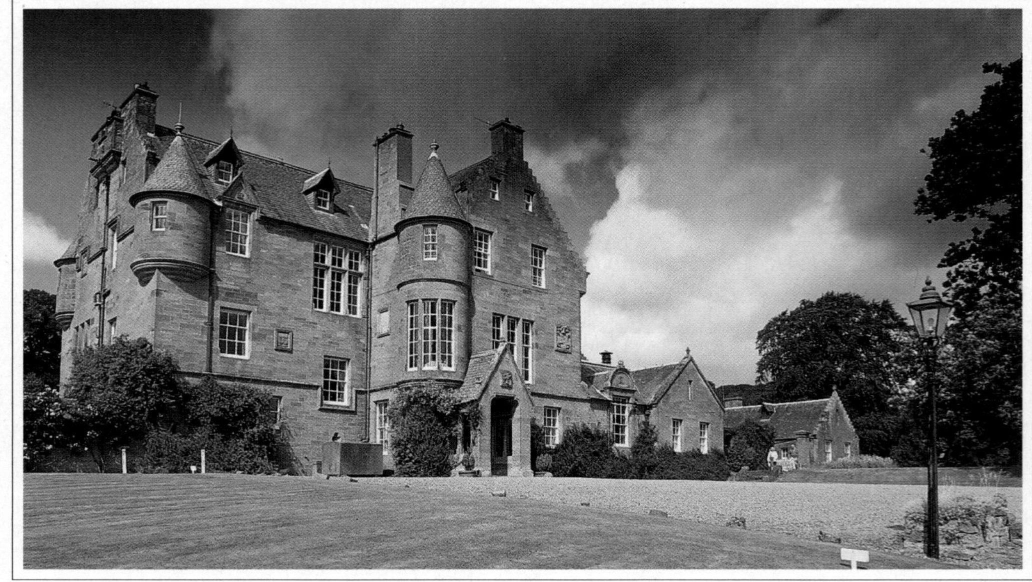

Splendidly romantic – and the food comes highly recommended

Cringletie House Hotel is a romantically splendid mansion house, set in 28 acres of gardens and woodland, twenty miles south of Edinburgh, and two miles north of Peebles. Its location, just half an hour's drive from Edinburgh, makes it a convenient overnight stop from which to visit the city, and return to peaceful rural surroundings.

Cringletie retains the atmosphere of a private country house. The bedrooms are all tastefully decorated and furnished to a high standard of comfort. There are magnificent views, an all weather tennis court, putting green, croquet lawn as well as their very own open air theatre seating 250 people.

Recommended for good food since 1971, the kitchen team provide imaginative dishes. Fresh local produce is used, including fruit and vegetables from the two acre walled kitchen garden.

Quotes from independent guidebooks include: 'Excellent in every way. Friendly, efficient service and outstanding food. Probably the best country house hotel we have visited during the past five years.' 'A very peaceful place; the only noise is the sheep and the birds.

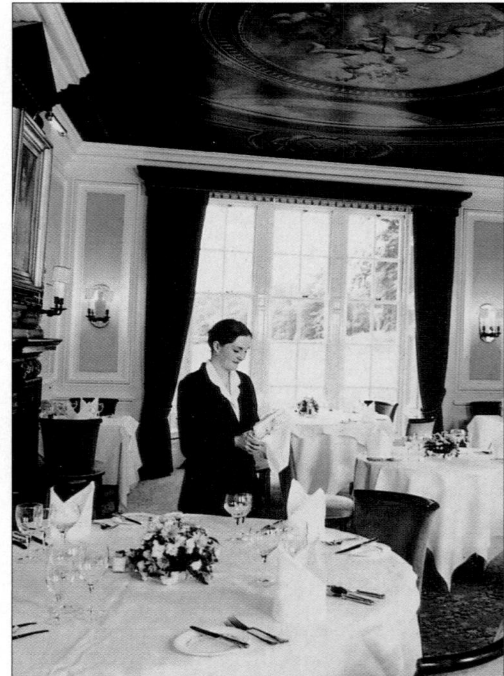

LOCATION

20 miles from Edinburgh, 2 miles north of Peebles on A703.

" A magical experience! By far our best ever in many years of quality travel. A must on any quality itinerary. Authentic excellence "

Sally Miller, California

Map p.494 ref: F9

Baronial mansion and estate

CROMLIX HOUSE

An absolute treasure close to Edinburgh and Glasgow

Built in 1874 as a family residence in a 2000 acre estate, Cromlix retains its original character and features, including a charming chapel perfect for weddings. The imposing exterior belies a 'comfortable' and 'homely' interior. The feeling is that of a much loved home which invites relaxation. In the true traditions of country house hospitality, nothing is 'too precious' or pretentious; everything about Cromlix is genuine, including the sense of history.

As you would expect, Cromlix is furnished throughout with antiques, fine furniture and paintings. The six bedrooms and eight very spacious suites with private sitting rooms, offer comfort and luxury. Two of the five public rooms are typical of a Victorian shooting lodge.

Dining at Cromlix is an experience to be savoured. The award winning staff prepare a fresh menu daily. Vegetarian, special and lighter diets are readily catered for.

Country pursuits include fishing, shooting or simply enjoying the wildlife. By advance arrangement: trout and salmon fishing; sporting, clay shooting. Nearby : 10 golf courses.

LOCATION

5 minutes off the A9 north of Dunblane through Kinbuck Village on the B8033.

Kinbuck By Dunblane, Near Stirling, Perthshire FK15 9JT

Telephone 01786 822125
Fax 01786 825450

E-mail: *cromlix@bestloved.com*

OWNERS

David and Ailsa Assenti

ROOM RATES

Single occupancy	*£110 - £150*
6 Doubles/Twins	*£195 - £235*
8 Suites	*£235 - £325*

Includes full breakfast and VAT

CHARGE/CREDIT CARDS

• *DC* • *MC* • *VI*

RATINGS & AWARDS

S.T.B. ★★★★★ Hotel
A.A. ★★★ ❀❀
Taste of Scotland
Andrew Harper Hideaway of the Year 99/2000

FACILITIES

On site: *Garden, croquet, tennis, riding, fishing, heli-pad*
3 meeting rooms/max 50 people
Nearby: *Golf, riding, salmon & trout fishing*

RESTRICTIONS

No facilities for disabled guests
No pets in public rooms

ATTRACTIONS

Stirling Castle, Scone Palace, Glenturret Distillery, The Trossachs

AFFILIATIONS

Pride of Britain

NEAREST

MAJOR CITY:
Glasgow - 30 miles/35 mins
Edinburgh - 38 miles/45 mins

MAJOR AIRPORT:
Edinburgh - 35 miles/40 mins
Glasgow - 40 miles/55 mins

RAILWAY STATION:
Dunblane - 4 miles/10 mins

RESERVATIONS

Toll free in US: 800-98-PRIDE
*Quote **Best Loved***

ACCESS CODES

Not applicable

• Map p.494 ref: F6

"Excellent food, superb rooms and good hospitality. Simply the best - we shall return"

The Gill family, Yorkshire

CULDEARN HOUSE

Country house

SCOTLAND

Woodlands Terrace, Grantown-on-Spey, Moray PH26 3JU

Telephone 01479 872106
Fax 01479 873641

E-mail: *culdearn@bestloved.com*

OWNERS
Isobel and Alasdair Little

RATES PER PERSON
1 Single £75
8 Doubles/Twins/Kings £75
Includes full breakfast, dinner and VAT

CHARGE/CREDIT CARDS

• *DC* • *JCB* • *MC* • *VI*

RATINGS & AWARDS
S.T.B. ★★★★ Hotel
R.A.C. ★★ Dining Award 3
A.A. ★★ ❀ 77%
Taste of Scotland
Scotch Beef Club
Green Tourism Business - Gold Award

FACILITIES
On site: *Garden*
Nearby: *Golf, fishing, riding, birdwatching*

RESTRICTIONS
No children under 10 years
No pets

ATTRACTIONS
Ballindalloch, Cawdor and Brodie Castles, Culloden Battlefield, Malt Whisky distilleries

AFFILIATIONS
The Circle Group

NEAREST
MAJOR CITY:
Inverness - 30 miles/35 mins

MAJOR AIRPORT:
Edinburgh - 140 miles/2½ hrs

Inverness - 35 miles/40 mins

RAILWAY STATION:
Aviemore - 15 miles/20 mins

RESERVATIONS
Direct with Hotel
Quote ***Best Loved***

ACCESS CODES
Not applicable

True Scottish warmth, hospitality and a kilted laird

Voted 'Scotland's Best Small Hotel' by the RAC, this beautifully furnished hotel makes an ideal place to sample Scottish country life.

Culdearn House is situated in the lush surroundings of picturesque Grantown-on-Spey. Each of the nine immaculate guest rooms is individually styled and named after the famous and romantic castles of Scotland. All inclusive in the price of your room are breakfast and dinner so the generosity of the hospitality is quickly apparent.

The elegant lounge provides a relaxing place to mingle with the other guests before dinner. Whilst enjoying a locally produced whisky, perhaps (for which the area is renowned), one can anticipate the pleasures suggested by the menu.

Alasdair Little, 'the kilted laird' himself, a perfect host, with his wife, Isobel, the award-winning chef, will ensure your complete satisfaction. With her staff, she will prepare your meal using fresh produce from nearby estates and the Moray coast. To complement the food, the laird will suggest a wine or two from his personal selection while kilted girls will attend you with smiling, efficient service.

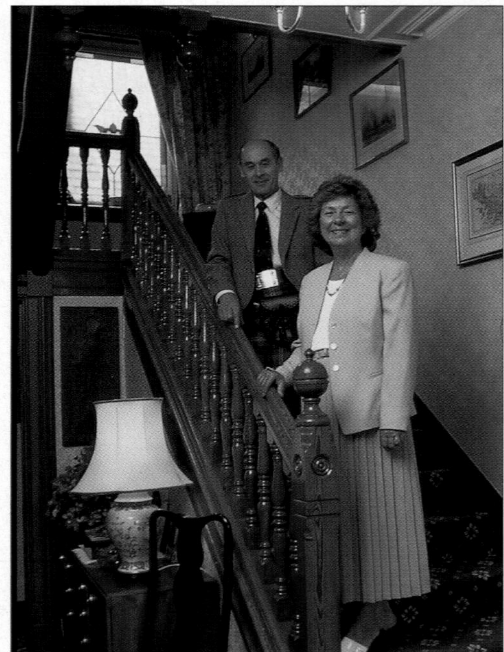

LOCATION

Approaching Grantown from the south west on A95 turn left at the 30 mph sign. Culdearn faces you.

Planning a wedding reception? Turn to 'Meeting Facilities' on page 476

“ Princes past and present have enjoyed the ambience and hospitality of this elegant Palladian mansion ”

Captain Edmund Burt, Letters from a Gentleman in the North of Scotland, c 1730

• Map p.494 ref: F6

18th century country house

CULLODEN HOUSE

Princely Palladian hospitality in a very special Highland setting

Culloden House is a gracious Georgian mansion, refurbished in 1788 incorporating a fortified mid-16th century castle, set in 40 acres of stately parkland. As early as 1730, the Forbes family established a tradition of fine hospitality. On arrival guests could refresh themselves with a pint of fine claret, and stay the night if they chose to. They always chose to.

The house's history features spies, sieges, proud Highland chieftains and romance. Bonnie Prince Charlie buckled his sword as he dashed from the house to fight his last battle. The recent guest list includes politicians, film stars and royalty. The house is decorated and furnished in Palladian style. The main rooms feature ornate Adam plasterwork and fireplaces. Here you can listen to Scottish folk music played on pedal harp, bagpipes and clarsach. Bedrooms are appointed to a very high standard, many having four-poster beds or tester. Dinners are a delight, featuring fresh and smoked Scottish game, meat, fowl and produce cooked and presented imaginatively.

Close by are Culloden Battlefield, the Highland glens, Cawdor Castle, Clava Cairns, the Caledonian Canal and 35 golf courses. Dolphins wait near Inverness harbour, and so may something else in Loch Ness.

LOCATION

1 mile down the A96 from Inverness, turn right at sign for Culloden. 1 mile further, turn left at Culloden House sign.

Culloden, Inverness, Inverness-shire IV2 7BZ

Telephone 01463 790461
Fax 01463 792181

E-mail: *cullodenhse@bestloved.com*

GENERAL MANAGER

Stephen Davies

ROOM RATES

3 Singles	*£135 - £145*
17 Doubles/Twins	*£175 - £230*
8 Suites	*£235 - £270*

Includes full breakfast, newspaper and VAT

CHARGE/CREDIT CARDS

• DC • JCB • MC • VI

RATINGS & AWARDS

S.T.B. ★★★★ Hotel

A.A. ★★★★ ❀❀ 76%

FACILITIES

On site: *Garden, croquet, boules, tennis, sauna, heli-pad*
3 meeting rooms/max 60 people
Nearby: *35 golf courses, fishing, riding, fitness centre, tennis, yachting*

RESTRICTIONS

No facilities for disabled guests
Pets by arrangement

ATTRACTIONS

Cawdor Castle, Clava Cairns, Loch Ness, Caladonian Canal, Fort George, Aviemore, 21 Distilleries

AFFILIATIONS

The Celebrated Hotels Collection
Grand Heritage Hotels

NEAREST

MAJOR CITY:
Inverness - 3 miles/10 mins
MAJOR AIRPORT:
Inverness - 3 miles/10 mins
RAILWAY STATION:
Inverness - 3 miles/10 mins

RESERVATIONS

Toll free in US: 800-322-2403
Toll free tel/fax in US: 800-373-7987
Toll free in UK: 0800-980-4561
Quote ***Best Loved***

ACCESS CODES

AMADEUS UI INVCHH
APOLLO/GALILEO UI 24800
SABRE/ABACUS UI 49776
WORLDSPAN UI 41006

• Map p.494 ref: G10

“ To all, to each, a fair good-night, and pleasing dreams, and slumbers light! ”

Sir Walter Scott whilst staying at Dalhousie in 1808

DALHOUSIE CASTLE & SPA

Historic castle

Bonnyrigg, Edinburgh EH19 3JB

Telephone 01875 820153
Fax 01875 821936

E-mail: *dalhousie@bestloved.com*

MANAGING DIRECTOR

Neville S Petts

ROOM RATES

Single occupancy	*£90 - £130*
29 Doubles/Twins	*£105 - £260*
3 Triples/Quads	*£165 - £220*
1 Themed suite	*£230 - £260*

Includes full breakfast and VAT

CHARGE/CREDIT CARDS

• DC • JCB • MC • VI

RATINGS & AWARDS

S.T.B. ★★★★ Hotel
A.A. ★★★ 71%
Taste of Scotland

FACILITIES

On site: *Garden, health & beauty, spa, falconry, archery, mini-highland games, heli-pad, Private Chapel*
5 meeting rooms/max 120 people
Nearby: *Clay pigeon shooting, golf, riding, fitness, tennis, off-road driving, fishing, hunting*

RESTRICTIONS

No pets in public rooms
No smoking in bedrooms

ATTRACTIONS

Edinburgh City and Castle, Glenkinchie Distillery, Edinburgh Crystal, Glasgow City, Holyrood Palace

AFFILIATIONS

Preston's Global Hotels
Grand Heritage Hotels

NEAREST

MAJOR CITY:
Edinburgh - 7 miles/20 mins
MAJOR AIRPORT:
Edinburgh - 14 miles/30 mins
RAILWAY STATION:
Waverley - 7 miles/20 mins

RESERVATIONS

Toll free in US: 800-544-9993 or 888-93-GRAND
Quote ***Best Loved***

ACCESS CODES

AMADEUS UI EDIDCH
APOLLO/GALILEO UI 78139
SABRE/ABACUS UI 30846
WORLDSPAN UI 40637

A 13th-century castle with a state-of-the-art spa

The Ramsays of Dalhousie laid the foundations of their family seat over 700 years ago and its ancient stones have witnessed a fascinating procession of historical events and famous guests from Edward I and Oliver Cromwell to Queen Victoria and Sir Walter Scott. However, the new millennium has probably heralded the most revolutionary development in the castle's long and distinguished history with the arrival of the Aqueous Spa.

A short drive south of Edinburgh, the castle is set in its own estate of forest and parkland. Ten of its 29 sumptuously furnished and thoughtfully-equipped bedrooms are historically themed, for example the James VI Room, and there are a further five rooms in the century-old Lodge, two-minutes walk away overlooking the South Esk River. The hydrotherapy spa is the first of its kind in Scotland offering invigorating and rejuvenating hydro facilities combined with relaxing treatments to reduce stress levels and promote a healthy body and mind. Spa packages or individual treatments are available. Adjacent to the spa, the Orangery offers a Scottish-Mediterranean menu of light and healthy options as a counter-balance to the traditional Scottish-French cuisine served in the more formal vaulted Dungeon Restaurant.

LOCATION

From Edinburgh take A7 south through Newtongrange. Right at junction onto B704. The hotel entrance is ½ mile along on right.

"Loved it!"

Neil Sedaka

• Map p.494 ref: E10

Victorian town house

THE DEVONSHIRE HOTEL

An establishment of distinction and stylish splendour

The Devonshire Hotel is set in the West End of Glasgow, minutes from many famous attractions; The Burrell Collection, Glasgow University, Kelvingrove Art Gallery & Museum to name a few.

A majestic central staircase, painstakingly restored to the carved glory of a bygone era, sweeps to the upper floors past a charming conservatory on the half-landing highlighted by original stained glass windows. Against this splendid backdrop, guests are assured individual, traditional grand country-style hospitality. Subdued lighting and countless original paintings put this hotel amongst the best in the city. There is an intimate dining room for residents only which has superb standards and quality of food.

Loch Lomond is just 30 minutes drive from the hotel. Edinburgh is forty five minutes by train, which runs twice-hourly.

The hotel is the ideal place to enjoy some of a vast collection of malt whiskies. Famous past guests include Michael Jackson, Whitney Houston, Bryan Adams to name a few.

LOCATION

Exit 17 off M8. Turn right onto A82. After Grosvenor Hotel turn left at 2nd traffic lights into Hyndland Road. Take first right and right at roundabout. Hotel is at end of road on right.

5 Devonshire Gardens, Glasgow G12 0UX

Telephone 0141 339 7878
Fax 0141 339 3980

E-mail: *devonshire@bestloved.com*

SCOTLAND

OWNER

Robert C Hyndman

GENERAL MANAGER

Jeanette Montgomery

ROOM RATES

Single occupancy	*£120 - £160*
10 Doubles	*£140 - £200*
2 Four-posters	*£160 - £210*
2 Suites	*£160 - £240*

Includes VAT

CHARGE/CREDIT CARDS

• *DC* • *MC* • *VI*

RATINGS & AWARDS

S.T.B. ★★★★ *Hotel*
A.A. ★★★ ❀ *77%*
A.A. Romantic Hotel

FACILITIES

On site: *Private dining room*
2 meeting rooms/max 60 people
Nearby: *Golf, riding*

RESTRICTIONS

No facilities for disabled guests
Pets at manager's discretion

ATTRACTIONS

Burrell Collection, Mackintosh House, Dumbarton and Bothwell Castles, Glasgow University

AFFILIATIONS

Scotland's Hotels of Distinction
The Celebrated Hotels Collection

NEAREST

MAJOR CITY:
Glasgow - 1½ miles/10 mins

MAJOR AIRPORT:
Glasgow - 12 miles/20 mins

RAILWAY STATION:
Glasgow - 1½ miles/10 mins

RESERVATIONS

Toll free in US: 800-322-2403
Quote ***Best Loved***

ACCESS CODES

AMADEUS HK GLADEV
APOLLO/GALILEO HT 25902
SABRE/ABACUS HK 31789
WORLDSPAN HK DEVOS

• Map p.494 ref: F11

"Let us hope that the Sturman's achieve in Scotland what they achieved south of the border"

A.A. Inspector

DRYFESDALE COUNTRY HOUSE HOTEL

18th century vicarage

SCOTLAND

Lockerbie, Dumfries & Galloway DG11 2SF

Telephone 01576 202427
Fax 01576 204187

E-mail: *dryfesdale@bestloved.com*

OWNERS
Clive and Heather Sturman

ROOM RATES

3 Singles	*£55 - £85*
12 Doubles/Twins	*£95 - £140*

Includes full breakfast and VAT

CHARGE/CREDIT CARDS

• DC • JCB • MC • VI

RATINGS & AWARDS
S.T.B. ★★★ Hotel
R.A.C. ★★★ Dining Award 2
A.A. ★★★ ❀ 69%
Taste of Scotland

FACILITIES
On site: *Garden, croquet, fishing, putting green, heli-pad*
3 meeting rooms/max 150 people
Nearby: *Fishing, shooting, riding*

RESTRICTIONS
Pets by arrangement

ATTRACTIONS
Edinburgh, Solway Coast, Gretna Green, Caerlaverlock Castle, Lockerbie Garden of Remembrance, Burn's House & Museum

AFFILIATIONS
Independent

NEAREST
MAJOR CITY:
Dumfries - 10 miles/15 mins

MAJOR AIRPORT:
Glasgow - 73 miles/1 hr

RAILWAY STATION:
Lockerbie - 3 miles/10 mins

FERRY PORT:
Stranraer - 70 miles/1½ hrs

RESERVATIONS
Direct with hotel
Quote ***Best Loved***

ACCESS CODES
Not applicable

A convenient and comfortable break just across the Border

In rolling countryside, just minutes off the main A74(M) Carlisle to Glasgow road, The Dryfesdale makes an ideal overnight break on the road north, or extend your stay for a few days to explore the Solway Coast and Dumfries, a notable stop on the Robert Burns Trail.

The Dryfesdale's elevated parkland setting affords panoramic views across the Borders landscape a short distance outside the market town of Lockerbie. It is an unassuming spot in a former manse, or vicarage, dating from 1762. There is a cosy bar and sun lounge offering informal meals and a rich choice of some 160 single malt whiskies, or guests can dine in the more formal restaurant, which specialises in local Scottish cuisine.

With time to spare, there is plenty to see and do in the area. The 'Queen of the South', bustling Dumfries is the gateway to southwest Scotland and home to the Robert Burns Centre. Scotland's most famous poet spent his twilight years here and was buried in St. Michael's Church. South of Dumfries, triangular Caerlaverock Castle is an unusual and fascinating construction founded in the 13th century. Nearby, the Wildfowl and Wetlands Centre on the marshy Solway shore is a real birdwatcher's haven.

LOCATION

½ mile from Junction 17 of the M74. The hotel is well signposted from the motorway roundabout.

Thinking of pampering yourself? See the 'Health & Beauty' index on page 472

"** We travel around a great deal. No other hotel in the British Isles has so invariably combined caring service and beautiful cooking all in a completely relaxed atmosphere **"

Sonia & Patrick Stevenson

• *Map p.494 ref: E6*

Georgian shooting lodge

DUNAIN PARK HOTEL

A seasoned traveller's delight. Something to write home about

Dunain Park Hotel was originally a shooting lodge, built in Georgian times by the Duke of Gordon, and extended in Victorian times. Edward and Ann Nicoll have owned and run Dunain Park as an hotel for twelve years, which they have upgraded and refurbished to the highest standard. In the original part of the house there are five bedrooms all with private facilities. The Nicolls then added on six de-luxe king-bedded suites. The two garden cottages are fully serviced and furnished to the same high standard of the main building and overlook the walled garden. The hotel has full central heating and there are open fires in both main lounges.

Mrs Nicoll is in charge of the kitchen and is a Master Chef of Great Britain. The à la carte menu changes daily and uses the best local produce such as salmon, venison and highland beef. Accompanied by soft fruits, lettuce, vegetables and herbs from the kitchen garden, as well as home-made jams, jellies and chutneys, the meals prove to be innovative and irresistible.

Dunain Park is set in six acres of gardens and woodlands. It is just a short trip from Inverness crossing over the Caledonian Canal. The hotel is only three miles from Loch Ness.

LOCATION

Heading west from Inverness on the A82, 1 mile from the town boundary on the left hand side.

Inverness, Inverness-shire IV3 8JN

Telephone 01463 230512
Fax 01463 224532

***E-mail:** dunain@bestloved.com*

OWNERS

Ann and Edward Nicoll

ROOM RATES

3 Doubles/Twins	*£138 - £158*
2 Superior Doubles	*£198*
6 Suites	*£198*
2 Cottages	*£158*

Includes full breakfast and VAT

CHARGE/CREDIT CARDS

• DC • MC • VI

RATINGS & AWARDS

S.T.B. ★★★★ Hotel
Taste of Scotland

FACILITIES

***On site:** Garden, croquet, indoor pool, sauna*
***Nearby:** Golf, fishing*

RESTRICTIONS

None

ATTRACTIONS

Loch Ness, Cawdor Castle, Culloden Battlefield, Whisky Trail, Eden Court Theatre

AFFILIATIONS

Independent

NEAREST

MAJOR CITY:
Inverness - 2 miles/5 mins

MAJOR AIRPORT:
Inverness - 8 miles/30 mins
Glasgow - 188 miles/3¾ hrs

RAILWAY STATION:
Inverness - 3 miles/10 mins

RESERVATIONS

Direct with hotel
*Quote **Best Loved***

ACCESS CODES

Not applicable

• Map p.494 ref: C7

"Still a great pleasure to stay at the best hotel in Skye, lovely welcome, gorgeous food and homely atmosphere"

Lady Christian Innes, Ross-shire

HOTEL EILEAN IARMAIN

Victorian house

Isle Ornsay, Sleat,
Isle of Skye IV43 8QR

Telephone 01471 833332
Fax 01471 833275

E-mail: *eilean@bestloved.com*

OWNERS

Sir Iain and Lady Noble

GENERAL MANAGER

Morag MacDonald

ROOM RATES

Single occupancy	*£90*
9 Doubles/Twins	*£120*
1 Four-poster	*£150*
2 Triples	*£160*
4 Suites	*£180 - £250*

Includes full breakfast and VAT

CHARGE/CREDIT CARDS

• *DC* • *MC* • *VI*

RATINGS & AWARDS

S.T.B. ★★★ *Hotel*

R.A.C. ★★ *Dining Award 3*

A.A. ★★ ❀❀

A.A. Romantic Hotel

FACILITIES

On site: *Garden, shooting, stalking, fishing, heli-pad*

2 meeting rooms/max 100 people

Nearby: *Golf, riding, pool*

RESTRICTIONS

No pets in public rooms

ATTRACTIONS

Armadale Castle & Gardens, Dunvegan Castle, Aros Heritage Centre, Talisker Distillery, Hotel Eilean Iarmain Art Gallery, 'Bella Jane' Boat trips, Serpentarian Reptile Centre

AFFILIATIONS

Independent

NEAREST

MAJOR CITY:

Glasgow - 148 miles/4 hrs

MAJOR AIRPORT:

Inverness - 93 miles/2 hrs

RAILWAY STATION:

Kyle of Lochalsh - 14 miles/30 mins

FERRY PORT:

Mallaig/Armadale - 8 miles/15 mins

RESERVATIONS

Direct with hotel

Quote ***Best Loved***

ACCESS CODES

Not applicable

An enchanted atmosphere reflecting the legends and romance of Skye

Built in 1888, this small, privately owned hotel has retained its Victorian charm and old-world character. Hotel Eilean Iarmain is situated on the small rocky bay of Isle Ornsay in the south of Skye, with expansive views over the Sound of Sleat to the Knoydart hills. Eilean Iarmain has welcomed visitors from all over the world for over 100 years and has won many awards for its' hospitality and cuisine.

The 16 bedrooms are decorated and furnished in traditional style and include four new suites, housed in the restored stables, one of which is specially suitable for disabled guests. Each bedroom has its own charm: 'The Tower Room', panelled in old pine, and 'The Leabaidh Mhor', with a canopied bed from nearby Armadale Castle, to name two of them. There are log fires in the reception rooms, and a panelled dining room where candlelit dinners can be enjoyed overlooking the bay.

The dinner menu, of 5 courses, combines imaginative cooking with the variety of fresh local produce, including fish and shellfish landed at the old stone pier, oysters and game from the estate, home baked bread and oatcakes. The extensive wine list has been selected by the proprietors with the aim of offering some unusual wines with fascinating historical provenances, as well as a very good range of more famous wines. Hotel Eilean Iarmain is open year round.

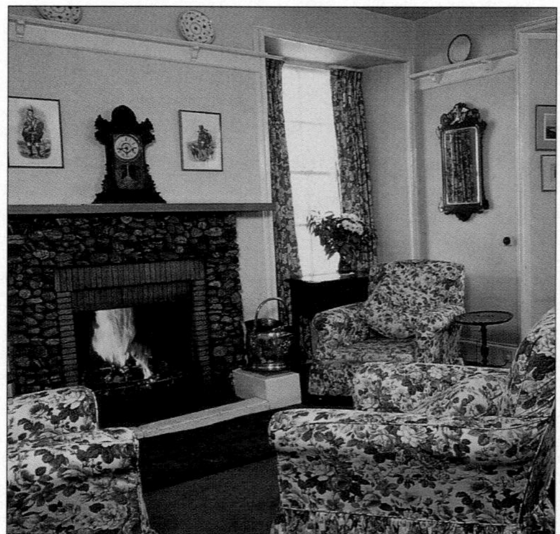

LOCATION

Approximately 20 minutes from Skye Bridge; 20 minutes from Kyle of Lochalsh Rail Station; 30 minutes from Kylerea ferry.

Looking for an hotel with a golf course on site? See our 'Golf Guide' on page 478

“At the Enmore Hotel everything doth gel”

Anne & John Mancino, Plymouth

• Map p.494 ref: D10

Gentleman's retreat

ENMORE HOTEL

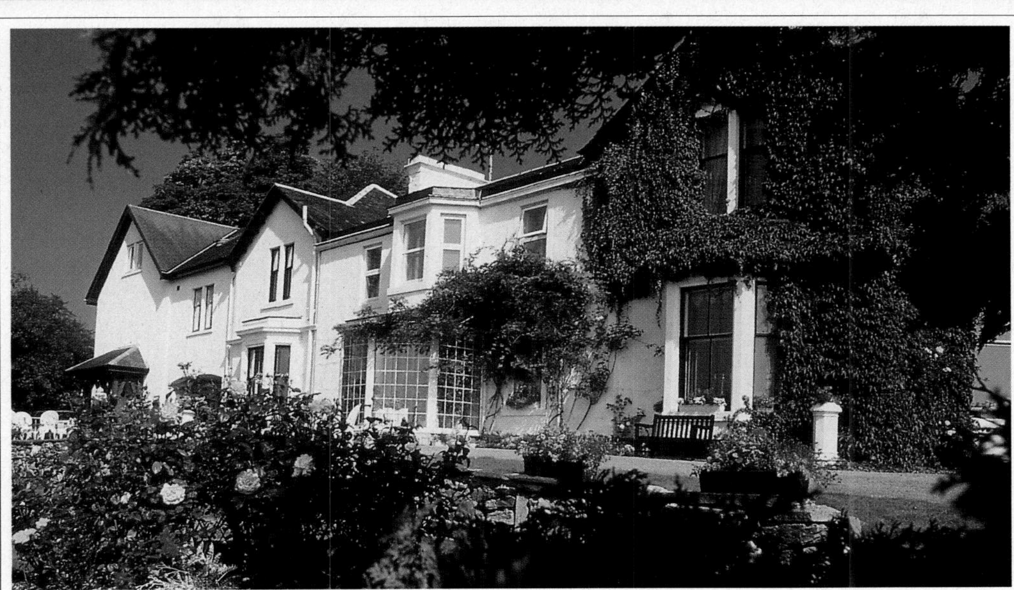

A lot of love has been lavished on this luxury home by Holy Loch

Originally built in 1785 as a gentleman's retreat for a wealthy Glasgow businessman (named Wilson but absolutely no connections with the present Wilsons), the Enmore Hotel has been enlarged over the years to now present the very best in accommodation with no less than four honeymoon/luxury suites, some with jacuzzi. The warmth and hospitality of this small but luxurious hotel is very evident – a family run hotel of the best kind.

Angela and David Wilson came to the Enmore in 1979 to find a 'way of life' running their own hotel with their two children. They have spent the intervening years lovingly restoring this very pretty house into one of the best-loved hotels and restaurants in the area.

For many years until 1992, the principal US naval base was just a few miles away at the beautiful Holy Loch, so the hotel is well used to American ways with even French toast and cinnamon on the breakfast menu. David Wilson is the chef/patron who puts the same care into the menu as Angela does in creating a very special place for the traveller.

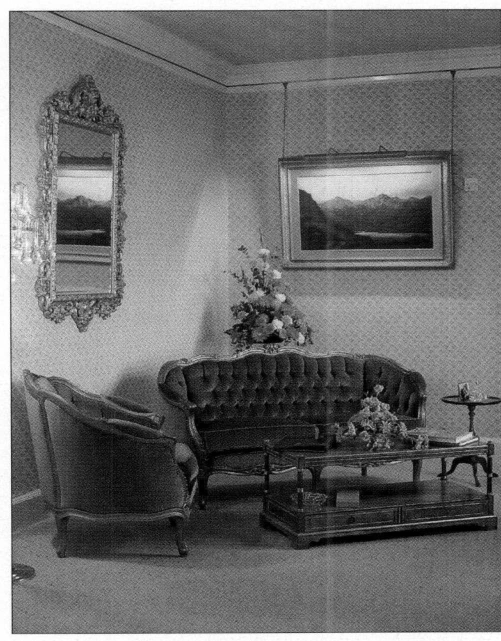

LOCATION

Travel from Glasgow either on the M8/A8 through Greenock and Gourock and over on one of the two ferries or via Loch Lomond and the A815 to Dunoon.

Marine Parade, Dunoon, Argyll PA23 8HH

Telephone 01369 702230
Fax 01369 702148

E-mail: enmore@bestloved.com

OWNERS

Angela and David Wilson

ROOM RATES

1 Single	£45 - £89
4 Doubles/Twins	£90 - £110
4 Four-posters	£120 - £150

Includes full breakfast and VAT

CHARGE/CREDIT CARDS

• MC • VI

RATINGS & AWARDS

S.T.B. ★★★★ Hotel
A.A. ★★ ❀ 76%
A.A. Courtesy & Care Award
Taste of Scotland

FACILITIES

On site: *Garden, squash, private shingle beach*
2 meeting rooms/max 40 people
Nearby: *Golf, riding, fishing*

RESTRICTIONS

No facilities for disabled guests
Closed 25 - 26 Dec

ATTRACTIONS

Dunoon Golf Course, Inverary, Loch Lomond, Stirling, Dumbarton Castle, Rothesay Castle, Mount Stuart

AFFILIATIONS

Scotland's Hotels of Distinction

NEAREST

MAJOR CITY:
Glasgow - 70 miles/1 hr

MAJOR AIRPORT:
Glasgow - 50 miles/1 hr

RAILWAY STATION:
Glasgow - 40 miles/40 mins

FERRY PORT:
Gourock - 20 mins by ferry

RESERVATIONS

Toll free in US: 800-437-2687
Quote **Best Loved**

ACCESS CODES

Not applicable

• Map p.494 ref: F8

"It was really the highlight of our honeymoon tour in Scotland. One cannot express in words the excellence of the dinners we took and the service was as perfect"

Mr & Mrs H Seidersstricker, Germany

FARLEYER HOUSE

16th century dower house

Aberfeldy,
Perthshire PH15 2JE

Telephone 01887 820332
Fax 01887 829430

E-mail: *farleyer@bestloved.com*

OWNER
Janice Reid

GENERAL MANAGER
Andy Cole

RATES PER PERSON

4 Ghillies Cottage Rooms	£60 - £75
1 Family (2 bedrooms)	£60 - £95
5 Superior Doubles/Twins	£60 - £95
4 Keepers Cottage Doubles	£65 - £105
5 Deluxe Doubles/Twins	£65 - £105

Includes full breakfast, dinner and VAT

CHARGE/CREDIT CARDS

• DC • JCB • MC • VI

RATINGS & AWARDS
S.T.B. ★★★★ Hotel

FACILITIES
***On site:** Garden, croquet, golf, fishing, heli-pad*
2 meeting rooms/max 60 people
***Nearby:** Golf, riding, pool, hunting, fishing*

RESTRICTIONS
No pets

ATTRACTIONS
Pitlochry, Loch Ness, The Locus Trails, Blair and Menzies Castles, Dewar's World of Whisky

AFFILIATIONS
Scotland's Hotels of Distinction

NEAREST
MAJOR CITY:
Glasgow/Edinburgh - 75 miles/1½ hrs

MAJOR AIRPORT:
Glasgow/Edinburgh - 70 miles/1½ hrs

RAILWAY STATION:
Pitlochry - 15 miles/30 mins

RESERVATIONS
Toll free in US: 800-437-2687
*Quote **Best Loved***

ACCESS CODES
Not applicable

An ancient croft situated in the heart of the old Castle Menzies Estate

Following the 1745 rebellion, when Charles Stuart was given refuge in the Castle, the croft was enlarged to become the bailiff's residence. Later, when Lady Stair married Sir Neil Menzies, Farleyer, by then the dower house, was again enlarged to its present size to be the main residence for the head of the Clan Menzies.

Farleyer became known far and wide for its own particular style of exceptional hospitality, tranquillity and warmth. A flavour of that hospitality awaits you at Farleyer today, greatly enhanced by some of the most imaginative and exciting cuisine to be found in Britain.

Farleyer stands in some of the most beautiful scenery in Scotland. A leisurely stroll in the grounds, or a quick fun round of golf on the novel, yet challenging, six-hole course, will produce the most wonderful feeling of peace. It provides a perfect base from which to visit numerous attractions and beauty spots.

Although discreetly hidden away in the beautiful Tay Valley, Farleyer is surprisingly easy to reach.

LOCATION

A9 to Ballinghuig, A827 to Aberfeldy, then the B846 out of Aberfeldy 1 mile past Menzies Castle. (The hotel is the Dower House).

"It is worth beating a path to Flodigarry which enjoys one of the finest situations of any country house in Scotland"

Neil MacLean, Sunday Times

• *Map p.494 ref:* C5

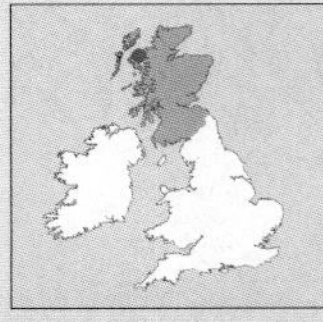

19th century country house FLODIGARRY COUNTRY HOUSE HOTEL

A romantic castle with dreamy views, good food, fine wine and Gaelic charm

The quintessential escapists dream, Flodigarry Country House Hotel is set amidst one of the most stunningly beautiful and dramatic landscapes in the British Isles. Nestling beneath the towering pinnacles of the Quiraing Mountain in the remote north east of Skye, the hotel overlooks the magnificent broad sweep of Staffin Bay, one of the most beautiful on Skye.

Unspoilt by progress, the area is steeped in history from the Vikings to the more recent Jacobite rising of 1745. The family home of Highland heroine, Flora MacDonald stands in the hotel grounds (see right).

The comfortable public rooms and cosy bedrooms all enjoy superb views over the mountains and sea. In addition, there are seven luxury bedrooms in Flora's cottage now lovingly restored and refurbished.

Winning awards for both its fine cuisine and accommodation, Flodigarry prides itself on the warmth of its old-fashioned Highland hospitality where there's a sense of Victorian ease without stuffiness. Named the Macallan Country House Hotel of the Year and recommended by The Sunday Times, Flodigarry is a breath of fresh air.

Bide a while, soak up the wonderfully timeless atmosphere, the superb panoramic views and Gaelic charm of this island gem.

LOCATION

From Portree, A855 north 20 miles to Staffin. Hotel is a further 4 miles north on right.

Staffin, Isle of Skye IV51 9HZ

Telephone 01470 552203
Fax 01470 552301

E-mail: *flodigarry@bestloved.com*

OWNERS

Andrew and Pam Butler

ROOM RATES

Single occupancy	*£29 - £99*
13 Doubles/Twins	*£58 - £120*
4 Family rooms	*£78 - £120*
2 Four-posters	*£108 - £160*

Includes full breakfast and VAT

CHARGE/CREDIT CARDS

• *MC* • *VI*

RATINGS & AWARDS

S.T.B. ★★★★ Hotel
Taste of Scotland
Macallan Country House Hotel of the Year
Talisker Awards for Best Service & Best Accommodation

FACILITIES

On site: *Garden, croquet, fishing, heli-pad*
1 meeting room/max 40 people
Nearby: *Yachting, fishing, watersports, riding*

RESTRICTIONS

No pets in public rooms
No smoking in bedrooms or dining room

ATTRACTIONS

Dunvegan Castle, Quiraing, Talisker Distillery, Old Man of Storr, Trotternish ridge walk, Skye Museum of Island Life

AFFILIATIONS

Independent

NEAREST

MAJOR CITY:
Inverness - 120 miles/3 hrs
MAJOR AIRPORT:
Glasgow - 250 miles/5 hrs
Inverness - 120 miles/3 hrs
RAILWAY STATION:
Kyle of Lochalsh - 50 miles/1 hr
FERRY PORT:
Uig - 8 miles/20 mins

RESERVATIONS

Direct with hotel
*Quote **Best Loved***

ACCESS CODES

Not applicable

• Map p.494 ref: E9

"In addition the food was excellent - very relaxed and friendly service. Why can't all hotels be like this?"

Mr and Mrs M Ennis, Derbyshire

THE FOUR SEASONS HOTEL

Lochside hotel

St Fillans,
Perthshire PH6 2NF

Telephone 01764 685333
Fax 01764 685444

E-mail: *fourseasons@bestloved.com*

OWNER
Andrew Low

ASSISTANT MANAGER
Mary McDiarmid

ROOM RATES

Single occupancy	*£56 - £64*
12 Doubles/Twins	*£72 - £88*
6 Chalets	*£64 - £128*

Includes full breakfast and VAT

CHARGE/CREDIT CARDS

• *MC* • *VI*

RATINGS & AWARDS
S.T.B. ★★★ *Small Hotel*
R.A.C. ★★★ *Dining Award 3*
A.A. ★★★ ❀❀ *67%*

FACILITIES
On site: *Garden, fishing*
3 meeting rooms/max 120 people
Nearby: *Golf, fishing, riding, shooting, mountain biking, watersports*

RESTRICTIONS
No facilities for disabled guests
Closed mid Jan - mid Mar

ATTRACTIONS
Edinburgh, Scone Palace, Deil's Cauldron, Rob Roy's Grave, Mull & Iona, Loch Tay Crannog

AFFILIATIONS
Independent

NEAREST
MAJOR CITY:
Perth/Stirling - 30 miles/45 mins

MAJOR AIRPORT:
Edinburgh - 60 miles/1¼ hrs

RAILWAY STATION:
Perth/Stirling - 30 miles/45 mins

RESERVATIONS
Direct with hotel
Quote ***Best Loved***

ACCESS CODES
Not applicable

A breathtaking loch side setting where nature provides the entertainment

Set against a steep, forested backdrop on the shores of Loch Earn, the Four Seasons occupies one of the most enviably picturesque locations in the whole of Scotland. The main house was built in the early 1800's for the manager of the local limekilns. Later it served a term as a schoolmaster's house before being gradually extended into a small and comfortable hotel.

Here you will find spacious bedrooms, many with views over the loch, and for the privacy minded, six secluded chalets on the wooded hillside behind the hotel, which are perfect for families.

The view from the Four Seasons stretches southwest down the loch and can honestly be described as magnificent. Spectacular sunsets, mist-wreathed mornings and the snow-covered Bens exercise a mesmeric fascination.

Perhaps one of the best places to watch the ever-changing scenery is from one of the hotel's two restaurants. Both restaurants offer all the things you dream about; Orkney scallops, Loch Fyne mussels, Tweed Valley partridge, East Coast halibut and Border lamb, appearing on the menu.

Nearby, there are all sorts of day trips to choose from such as the steam train to Mallaig on the West Coast, a visit to Scotland's smallest whisky distillery, fishing and sailing, or hill walkers can conquer a Munro or two.

LOCATION

On the north east edge of Loch Earn on the A85, Comrie to Lochearnhead road.

"Glenapp Castle is now the standard by which we shall judge all other hotels"

Mr & Mrs Kenneth Ley, Renfrewshire

• *Map p.494* *ref:* D12

Scottish baronial castle

GLENAPP CASTLE

A unique experience in a fairytale Scottish Castle

High above the village of Ballantrae, looking out over the Irish Sea towards Ailsa Craig and the Mull of Kintyre, Glenapp Castle is indeed a magical sight. The ancestral seat of the Earls of Inchcape is now the home of the Cowan family and opened as a luxury hotel in April 2000.

In order to preserve the peaceful ambience of a traditional country house, Glenapp Castle is only open to guests who have made an advanced reservation. On arrival, you will find that everything you could possibly wish for, including the splendid meals prepared by head chef Laurent Gueguen and his team, and specially selected house wines and spirits from the comprehensive cellar lists are included in your daily rate.

The interior of this spectacular Scottish Baronial castle has been totally preserved including the magnificent Austrian Oak-panelled entrance hall and staircase. The bedrooms and suites are spacious, elegant and furnished with antiques and original oil paintings to provide an ambience of traditional luxury.

The thirty acres of delightful gardens and woodland that surround the castle abound with specimen rhododendrons and many rare and unusual shrubs and trees. The showpiece walled-garden boasts a 150-foot Victorian glasshouse.

The Cowans' intention is to create something unique at Glenapp: they are well on the way!

LOCATION

Approximately 15 miles north of Stranraer and 35 miles south of Ayr and Prestwick Airport on the A77 near village of Ballantrae.

Ballantrae, Ayrshire KA26 0NZ

Telephone 01465 831212
Fax 01465 831000

E-mail: *glenapp@bestloved.com*

OWNERS

Graham and Fay Cowan

ROOM RATES

13 Doubles/Twins	*£410*
2 Luxury suites	*£450*
2 Master rooms	*£500*

Includes meals, house wines & spirits and VAT

CHARGE/CREDIT CARDS

• *MC* • *VI*

RATINGS & AWARDS

Independent

FACILITIES

On site: *Garden, croquet, tennis, heli-pad*
3 meeting rooms/max 34 people
Nearby: *Hunting, shooting, fishing, curling, walking, boat trips*

RESTRICTIONS

No children under 5 years in dining room after 6 pm
Closed Nov - Mar

ATTRACTIONS

Culzean Castle & Country Park, Logan Botanical Gardens, Galloway Forest Park, Ayrshire - Robert Burns country, Castle Kennedy Gardens, Mull of Galloway

AFFILIATIONS

Independent

NEAREST

MAJOR CITY:
Glasgow - 70 miles/1½ hrs

MAJOR AIRPORT:
Glasgow Prestwick - 35 miles/50 mins

RAILWAY STATION:
Stranraer - 17 miles/20 mins

RESERVATIONS

Direct with hotel
Quote ***Best Loved***

ACCESS CODES

Not applicable

• Map p.494 ref: F5

"Thank you for looking after me so very well during my stay. The ambience, hospitality and cooking were such that it will take little persuasion to come back"

Derek Reid, Former Chairman, Scottish Tourist Board

Glenmorangie House

16th century country estate

SCOTLAND

Cadboll, Fearn, By Tain, Ross-shire IV20 1XP

Telephone 01862 871671
Fax 01862 871625

E-mail: glenmorangie@bestloved.com

HOUSE MANAGER
Michael Andrews

ROOM RATES
9 Doubles/Twins £150 - £400
Includes full breakfast, dinner and wine, service and VAT

CHARGE/CREDIT CARDS

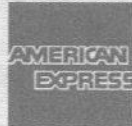

• MC • VI

RATINGS & AWARDS
S.T.B. ★★★★★ Small Hotel
A.A. ★★ ❀ 79%
Taste of Scotland

FACILITIES
On site: Garden, croquet, heli-pad
1 meeting room/max 50 people
Nearby: Golf, fishing, tennis, fitness centre, hunting/shooting, riding

RESTRICTIONS
Pets by arrangement
No smoking in bedrooms
Limited facilities for disabled guests

ATTRACTIONS
Glenmorangie and Glen Moray Distilleries, Urquhart and Dunrobin Castles, Loch Ness, Dolphin watching, beaches and coastal walks, Tain and Dornoch Golf Courses

AFFILIATIONS
Independent

NEAREST
MAJOR CITY:
Inverness - 36 miles/40 mins

MAJOR AIRPORT:
Inverness - 36 miles/40 mins
Edinburgh - 180 miles/3½ hrs

RAILWAY STATION:
Tain - 6 miles/10 mins

RESERVATIONS
Direct with hotel
Quote **Best Loved**

ACCESS CODES
Not applicable

Let a famed distillery's 'Home in the Highlands' be your home!

If Scotland is famous for anything, it has to be whisky. And, for connoisseurs, the single malt varieties. Situated in Easter Ross, amongst the driest regions in all the UK, is the famed Glenmorangie Distillery. Of the many hundreds of whisky producers, Glenmorangie has been one of the industry's leaders for many years and is currently Scotland's top-selling brand.

Twelve years ago, Glenmorangie made a corporate decision to convert a nearby 14th century estate into a 'Home in the Highlands' for their best corporate clients and customers. The result was Glenmorangie House. In 1998, the policy of accepting guests was extended to the public.

What can you expect? Gorgeous panoramic views of the sea, log fires in the Morning Room and cosy 'Buffalo Room', profusion of fresh flowers and memorabilia throughout. Sleeping arrangements are exceedingly comfortable without pretentiousness whether in the main house or one of several cottages. Topping off your visit is the food. The Glenmorangie House kitchen makes best use of the freshest salmon, home grown vegetables and herbs and local lamb and beef, creating classically influenced modern cuisine that is both homely and delicious. So stay here and toast your good fortune with a 'wee dram' at Glenmorangie House.

LOCATION

The hotel is 33 miles from Inverness. From there, take the A9 then B9175 towards Nigg. After 2 miles turn left towards Hilton. The hotel is 5 miles on the right and signposted.

"Thank you for a wonderful stay, please pass our thanks on to your super team, we were made very welcome by every one of them"

J and I Posnett, Lancashire

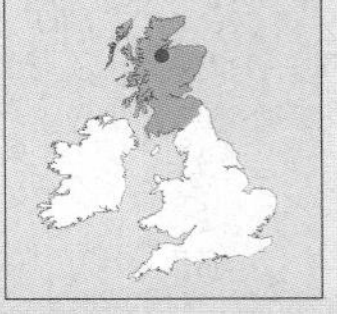

• *Map p.494 ref: E7*

18th century coaching inn **GLENMORISTON ARMS HOTEL**

Character, comfort and creative cuisine just a short stroll from Loch Ness

Glenmoriston Arms Hotel is situated close to Loch Ness at the foot of one of the most beautiful Highland glens. For more than 200 years it has warmly welcomed travellers and drovers.

Owners Neil and Carol Scott make sure that guests enjoy a unique blend of warmth, elegance and informality. There are just eight high quality bedrooms, so each guest is welcomed as an individual. The atmosphere carries over to the hotel's restaurant which was deemed recently by one guest as 'one of the most superb culinary experiences in Scotland'. The Glenmoriston Arms is in the very heart of Highland history. Day trips include touring the enchanting Isle of Skye where you can visit Dunvegan Castle and the Clan Donald Centre. You can follow the route of Bonnie Prince Charlie by visiting the Battlefield at Culloden, where, after his defeat, he escaped to Skye passing through Glenmoriston en route. Loch Ness and loch fishing are on the doorstep. A short drive away is Fort Augustus golf course, nine testing holes on heather-clad moorland.

Given the warm, sociable atmosphere and great position, it is easy to see why so many guests return to 'The Arms' year on year.

LOCATION

From south follow A82 from Fort William; continue 6 miles north of Fort Augustus. From north follow A82 from Inverness; continue 12 miles south of Drumnadrochit.

Invermoriston,
Near Loch Ness,
Inverness-shire IV63 7YA

Telephone 01320 351206
Fax 01320 351308

E-mail: *glenmoriston@bestloved.com*

OWNERS

Neil and Carol Scott

ROOM RATES

Single occupancy	*£55 - £65*
7 Doubles/Twins	*£70 - £100*
1 Four-poster	*£90 - £115*

Includes full breakfast and VAT

CHARGE/CREDIT CARDS

• JCB • MC • VI

RATINGS & AWARDS

S.T.B. ★★★★ Hotel
A.A. ★★ ❀ 76%

FACILITIES

On site: *Garden, jacuzzi, fishing*
1 meeting room/max 24 people
Nearby: *Fishing, stalking, riding, golf, boat trips*

RESTRICTIONS

No pets
No facilities for disabled guests

ATTRACTIONS

Loch Ness, Skye, Ben Nevis, Inner and Outer Hebrides, Aonach Mor Ski Centre, Culloden Moor Battlefield, Urquhart and Eilean Donan Castles, Great Glen Cycle Route

AFFILIATIONS

Preston's Global Hotels

NEAREST

MAJOR CITY:
Inverness - 26 miles/35 mins

MAJOR AIRPORT:
Inverness - 26 miles/35 mins

RAILWAY STATION:
Inverness - 26 miles/35 mins

RESERVATIONS

Toll free in US: 800-544-9993
Quote ***Best Loved***

ACCESS CODES

Not applicable

• Map p.494 ref: G9

"Many guests mentioned to us that it was the best wedding they had ever been to. I believe that this is due to all the efforts and welcoming they received from the Green Craigs"

Sarah and Keith Thomson, Edinburgh

GREEN CRAIGS

Seaside country house

SCOTLAND

Aberlady,
East Lothian EH32 0PY

Telephone 01875 870301/870306
Fax 01875 870440

E-mail: *greencraigs@bestloved.com*

OWNERS
Ray and Olly Craig

MANAGER
Lucy Wood

ROOM RATES

Single occupancy	*£65 - £85*
2 Doubles/Twins	*£110*
1 Suite	*£140*
3 Family rooms	*£110*

Includes full breakfast and VAT

CHARGE/CREDIT CARDS

• DC • JCB • MC • VI

RATINGS & AWARDS
Independent

FACILITIES
On site: *Garden, croquet, heli-pad*
1 meeting room/max 40 people
Nearby: *Golf, tennis, fitness centre, riding, water skiing, hunting/shooting*

RESTRICTIONS
Limited facilities for disabled guests
Pets by arrangement

ATTRACTIONS
Edinburgh, Edinburgh Castle, Glenkinchie Distillery, Deep Sea World, Museum of Flight, Tantallon & Hailes Castles, numerous golf courses

AFFILIATIONS
Independent

NEAREST
MAJOR CITY:
Edinburgh - 18 miles/25 mins

MAJOR AIRPORT:
Edinburgh - 25 miles/30 mins

RAILWAY STATION:
Longniddry - 3 miles/5 mins

RESERVATIONS
Direct with hotel
Quote ***Best Loved***

ACCESS CODES
Not applicable

At the 'white house on The Point' your complete satisfaction is a pleasure

Dramatically situated by the sea, Green Craigs enjoys spectacular views across Gosford Bay to Edinburgh and over the shoreline of Fife. It is an exceptional country house, a small hotel of quality, and the family home of Ray and Olly Craig. Built in 1924, the high ceilings, cornices, nooks and crannies are decorated in sympathy with the original style. 'As a family,' says Olly Craig, 'we have loved each minute of bringing out the individuality of each room, and making it sparkle with warmth and delight.'

The dining room glows with the colours of the setting sun across the bay. The food is fantastic. Exceedingly pleasant menus are devised by chef Duncan McInnes. The modestly priced bar meals are also something special.

Green Craigs is next to the eighth green of Kilspindie golf course. Muirfield and 17 other courses are nearby. So are Edinburgh Castle, and the Glenkinchie Distillery. Green Craigs itself is part of the holiday environment. The Craigs look on it as 'their little piece of heaven'. They are happy when guests share their enjoyment of the house and garden.

LOCATION

One mile west of Aberlady on the A198.

"Long live Greywalls, so dear in our hearts"

Edouard Van Vyve, Antwerp

• *Map p.494 ref: G9*

Country retreat

GREYWALLS

Follow in the footsteps of Nicklaus, Faldo, Edward VII and King Hussein

Sir Edwin Lutyens, architect of the British Embassy in Washington and the Cenotaph in Whitehall, designed Greywalls in 1901. King Edward VII stayed here: you can write your postcards in the panelled library he loved. King Hussein of Jordan was a more recent visitor.

Greywalls is next to Muirfield golf course. Past guests including Arnold Palmer, Jack Nicklaus, Lee Trevino, Greg Norman and Nick Faldo are all part of the Greywalls story.

Greywalls still feels like a family home. The warmth of hospitality from Giles and Ros Weaver today makes guests feel like honoured family friends. There are 23 comfortable, cosy bedrooms each with its own bathroom; many are furnished with antiques. There is a Steinway grand piano, a sunny Edwardian tea room and a small bar with a fine stock of whiskies. The very best of local produce is used to create outstanding meals from hearty breakfasts to fulsome dinners!

Outside are the gardens that Lutyens himself helped to plan. Within eight miles are 10 golf courses, long sandy beaches, nature reserves renowned for bird life, and ancient ruined castles.

LOCATION

Link from M8, M9 or M90 Motorways to A198 via Edinburgh City Bypass A720.

Muirfield, Gullane,
East Lothian EH31 2EG

Telephone 01620 842144
Fax 01620 842241

E-mail: *greywalls@bestloved.com*

OWNERS
Giles and Ros Weaver

MANAGER
Sue Prime

ROOM RATES

4 Singles	*£110 - £188*
19 Doubles/Twins	*£185 - £215*

Includes full breakfast and VAT

CHARGE/CREDIT CARDS

• *DC* • *MC* • *VI*

RATINGS & AWARDS
S.T.B. ★★★★ *Hotel*
A.A. ★★★ ❀❀

FACILITIES
On site: *Garden, croquet, tennis*
1 meeting room/max 30 people
Nearby: *Golf, shooting, fishing, walking, beaches*

RESTRICTIONS
No facilities for disabled guests
Pets by arrangement

ATTRACTIONS
Tantallon Castle, Dirleton Castle, Edinburgh and Edinburgh Castle, Holyrood House

AFFILIATIONS
Independent

NEAREST
MAJOR CITY:
Edinburgh - 18 miles/35 mins

MAJOR AIRPORT:
Edinburgh - 25 miles/40 mins

RAILWAY STATION:
Drem - 2 miles/5 mins

RESERVATIONS
Direct with Hotel
Quote ***Best Loved***

ACCESS CODES
Not applicable

• Map p.494 ref: G10

"Absolutely fantastic in every way – many, many thanks"

Lady Clare Macdonald, Skye

THE HOWARD

Georgian town house

34 Great King Street, Edinburgh EH3 6QH

Telephone 0131 315 2220
Fax 0131 557 6515

***E-mail:** howard@bestloved.com*

OWNER

Peter Taylor

MANAGER

Shaune Ayers

ROOM RATES

2 Singles	£140 - £175
11 Doubles/Twins	£250 - £280
2 Suites	£325

Includes full breakfast and VAT

CHARGE/CREDIT CARDS

• DC • MC • VI

RATINGS & AWARDS

S.T.B. ★★★★★ Small Hotel

A.A. ★★★★ ❀❀ Town House

FACILITIES

***On site:** '36' Restaurant*

3 meeting rooms/max 50 people

***Nearby:** Golf, swimming pool, cycling & jogging route*

RESTRICTIONS

No facilities for disabled guests

No pets, guide dogs only

ATTRACTIONS

Edinburgh Castle, Holyrood House, National Gallery, Edinburgh Festival & Military Tatoo, 'Old Town' and 'New Town', Dynamic Earth, Royal Yacht Britannia

AFFILIATIONS

The Celebrated Hotels Collection

The Small Hotel Company

NEAREST

MAJOR CITY:
Edinburgh

MAJOR AIRPORT:
Edinburgh - 8 miles/25 mins

RAILWAY STATION:
Waverley - 1 mile/5 mins

RESERVATIONS

Toll free in US: 800-323-5463 or 800-322-2403 or 800-98-PRIDE

*Quote **Best Loved***

ACCESS CODES

AMADEUS HK EDIHWO
APOLLO/GALILEO HT 96963
SABRE/ABACUS HK 08591
WORLDSPAN HK HOWAE

Select, intimate and beautifully furnished

Edinburgh's New Town is a neo-classical masterpiece commissioned in the 1820's and preserved today as Britain's largest classified monument. It is in this area of Georgian elegance that you will find The Howard looking much as it did when it was first built.

The Howard is a gem among small hotels. Beautifully decorated with paintings and antique furniture, each of the rooms in this elegant Georgian terrace is an oasis of gracious calm. The panelled breakfast room, deep roll-top baths and original Bakelite telephones evoke a quality of service and comfort that is redolent of a bygone age.

Following a day spent exploring Edinburgh's architectural treasures, shops and galleries, guests are greeted with tea and home-made shortbread, reinforcing the feeling that you are a private rather than a paying guest.

'36', one of the city's smartest eateries - where booking is recommended - just happens to be adjacent to the hotel, going to dinner then 'home' is simply part of The Howard vernacular.

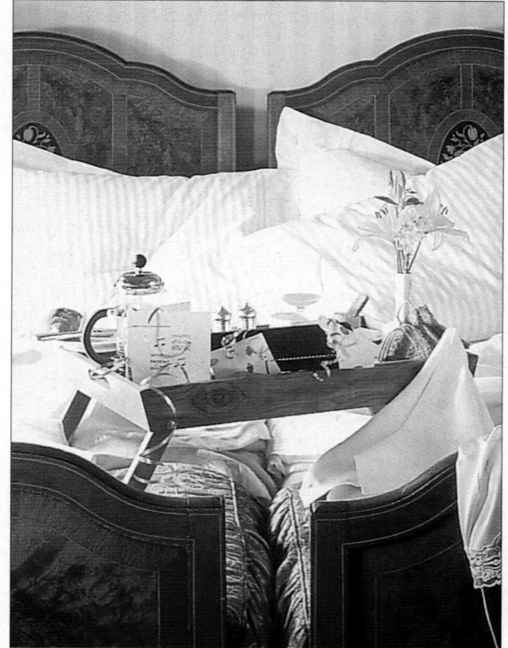

LOCATION

Travelling west along Queen Street, turn right into Queen Street Gardens East. Great King Street is the 3rd on the right.

A keen Angler? Refer to page 472 for our Fishing Index

“ Very friendly staff. Everything runs very efficiently. Delicious food ”

J Trumper

• *Map p.494 ref:* F8

Edwardian hotel

HUNTINGTOWER HOTEL

King James VI was very sorry to leave the Huntingtower!

The Huntingtower is an elegant Edwardian house set in its own four acres of glorious landscaped gardens, three miles west of Perth. Owned by the Brown Family, they have completely and lovingly restored and refurbished the hotel to its original splendour. For dining their are two superb options: The award-winning oak-panelled Restaurant offers a daily changing table d'hôte menu focusing on the best of Scottish produce or the more informal Conservatory for lighter meals. All of the bedrooms have been equipped to offer up-to-the-minute facilities.

The area provides many leisure opportunities including salmon and trout fishing on the river Tay, hillwalking and horse riding in the Highlands, shooting, cycling, or simply relaxing in the peaceful and tranquil surroundings. There are also interesting historic connections. In 1582, at Huntingtower Castle, James VI of Scotland was kidnapped by discontented Protestant nobles. Other examples worth visiting are Blair Castle and the Black Watch Museum at Balhousie Castle. In Curfew Row, Perth you can see the Fair Maid of Perth's House where Sir Walter Scott observed the beauty of the neighbourhood.

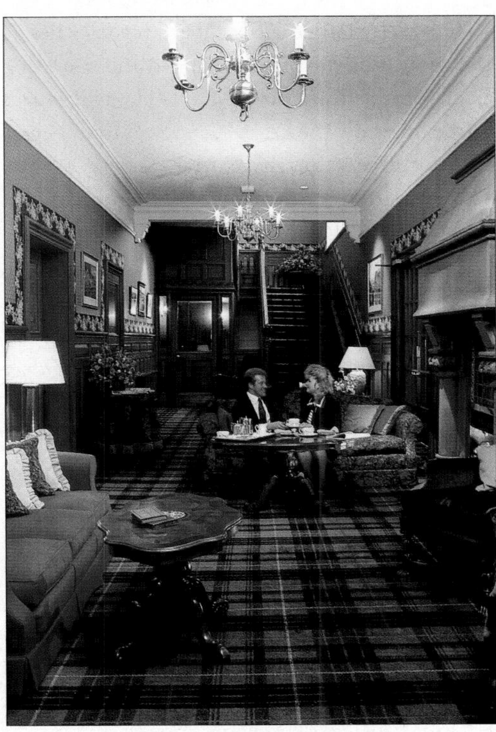

LOCATION

The hotel is 3 miles west of Perth on the A85.

Crieff Road, Perth, Perthshire PH1 3JT

Telephone 01738 583771
Fax 01738 583777

E-mail: *huntingtower@bestloved.com*

OPERATIONS DIRECTOR

Michael Lee

ROOM RATES

3 Singles	*£55 - £90*
12 Doubles/Twins	*£85 - £110*
3 Suites	*£110 - £140*
16 Executive suites	*£110 - £140*

Includes full breakfast and VAT

CHARGE/CREDIT CARDS

• *DC* • *MC* • *VI*

RATINGS & AWARDS

S.T.B. ★★★★ Hotel
A.A. ★★★ ❀ 75%
Taste of Scotland
Sunday Times Golden Pillow Award

FACILITIES

On site: *Garden, pitch & putt, heli-pad*
6 meeting rooms/max 200 people
Nearby: *Golf, tennis, fitness, fishing, water skiing, hunting/shooting, riding*

RESTRICTIONS

Pets by arrangement

ATTRACTIONS

Scone Palace, Ochil Hills, Pitlochry Salmon Ladder, Crieff, Glenshee Ski Centre, Blair Castle

AFFILIATIONS

Scotland's Hotels of Distinction

NEAREST

MAJOR CITY:
Perth - 3 miles/10 mins

MAJOR AIRPORT:
Edinburgh - 30 miles/40 mins
Perth Scone - 5 miles/15 mins

RAILWAY STATION:
Perth - 3 miles/10 mins

RESERVATIONS

Toll free in US: 800-437-2687
Quote ***Best Loved***

ACCESS CODES

Not applicable

"What a wonderful place. Dinner was excellent and the room enchanting. Will come back when we return to Scotland"

Mr Cary, Dallas

THE INN AT ARDGOUR

Highland inn

Ardgour, Fort William,
Highlands PH33 7AA

Telephone 01855 841225
Fax 01855 841214

E-mail: ardgour@bestloved.com

OWNER
Graham Marshall

ROOM RATES

Single occupancy	*£35 - £55*
6 Doubles/Twins	*£55 - £120*
1 Triple	*£70 - £150*
2 Family rooms	*£70 - £150*
1 Family suite	*£80 - £165*

Includes full breakfast and VAT

CHARGE/CREDIT CARDS
MC • VI

RATINGS & AWARDS
S.T.B. ★★★★ Inn
Best Inn in Britain 1999
The Good Beer Guide
Glenmorangie Maltmaster

FACILITIES
On site: *Drying room*
Nearby: *Golf, fishing, water skiing, climbing, sailing*

RESTRICTIONS
No smoking in bedrooms

ATTRACTIONS
Ben Nevis, Glencoe, Sea Life Centre, Glenfinnan, Castle Tioram, Isle of Skye

AFFILIATIONS
Preston's Global Hotels

NEAREST
MAJOR CITY:
Glasgow - 95 miles/2½ hrs

MAJOR AIRPORT:
Glasgow - 80 miles/2 hrs

RAILWAY STATION:
Fort William - 8 miles/15 mins

RESERVATIONS
Toll free in US: 800-544-9993
Quote ***Best Loved***

ACCESS CODES
Not applicable

The highest rated Highland inn - bursting with personality

This welcoming old Highland hostelry lies at the mouth of the Great Glen on the shores of Loch Linnhe near Fort William. The oldest part of the inn, now the But 'n Ben restaurant, began life as cottages for the Corran ferrymen after Hanovarian troopers burned their homes to the ground after the 1746 rebellion.

Every one of the cosy bedrooms is at the front of the inn to catch the spectacular mountain-framed view of the loch. In the foreground the ferry plies back and forth across the loch as it has done for many hundred's of years, because this is the original 'Road to the Isles'. This is also the beginning of the Caledonian Canal, so many visiting yachts and fishing boats, and even Scotland's last working paddle steamer, Waverley, can be spied.

When you can finally bear to tear yourself away from this captivating view, the Western Highlands offer outdoor diversions: from hiking and wildlife watching, otters, seals, golden eagle, red deer and wild goats; to day trips to the Hebridean islands of Mull, Iona and Skye. For duller days the inn has a great selection of books in the library bar, where the craich (chat) is good and the whiskies plentiful. The Innkeeper is a Glenmorangie Maltmaster and there are tutored whisky tastings in the summer.

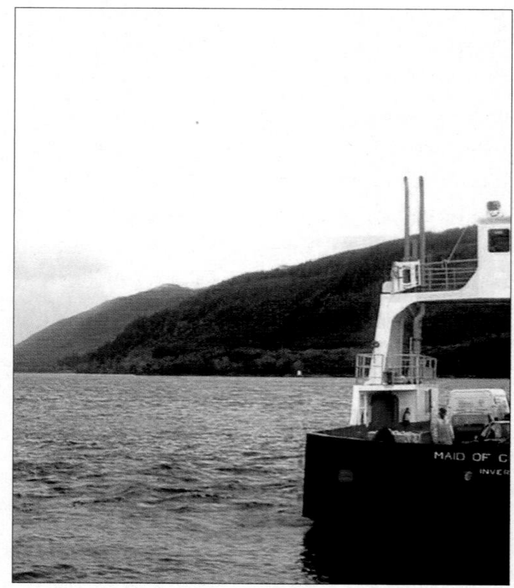

LOCATION

From A82 Onich to Fort William take the ferry (4 mins) across to Ardgour from Corran.

"Personal service, a family atmosphere with food comparable to Gleneagles and Turnberry"

John Huncharek, Houston, Texas

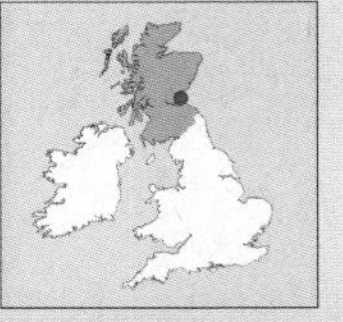

• *Map p.494 ref: G9*

16th century coaching inn

INN AT LATHONES

By Largoward, St Andrews, Fife KY9 1JE

Telephone 01334 840494
Fax 01334 840694

E-mail: *lathones@bestloved.com*

SCOTLAND

Discover the food and hospitality that attracted the 'Wee Mad MacGregor'

A local legend has it that, in this part of Fife, lived a disfigured midget highwayman known as 'Wee Mad MacGregor.' After a successful 'outing,' he liked to enjoy himself at a small inn in the village of Lathones. True or not, visit the Inn at Lathones today and you will meet another colourful and interesting character in the form of owner Nick White.

The Whites came to Lathones in June 1997 and, recognising the beauty of this neglected Inn, bought and renovated it.Their aim was to create a friendly hostelry and a great place to go for good food and wine. For, like the outlaw MacGregor, Nick knows a thing or two about the finer things of life. At the heart of the Inn is the restaurant whose creative menus are derived from excellent Scottish seafood, lamb and local game.

The Inn's white-washed buildings are in perfect harmony with the lush green landscape of rolling hills beyond. The comfortable bedrooms are simple yet tastefully furnished and, best of all, very accommodating on the pocket! The Inn is the perfect touring base for visiting St Andrews and its famous golf courses and the fishing villages along the Forth coast.

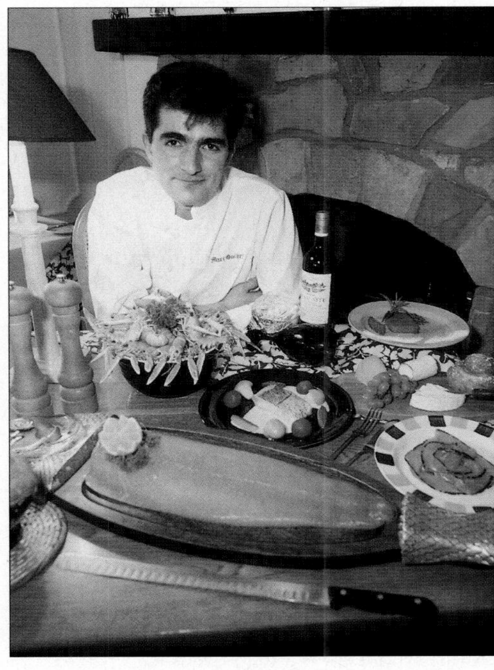

LOCATION

Situated 5 miles south from St Andrews on the A915, which is the main road between St Andrews and Leven.

OWNERS

Nick and Jocelyn White

ROOM RATES

2 Singles	*£55 - £85*
10 Doubles/Twins	*£99 - £110*
2 Master rooms	*£100*

Includes full breakfast and VAT

CHARGE/CREDIT CARDS

• DC • MC • VI

RATINGS & AWARDS

S.T.B. ★★★★ *Inn*
A.A. ★★ ❀❀ *72%*
Investors in People
Taste of Scotland
Scottish Beef Club

FACILITIES

On site: *Patio, children's play rooms, outdoor play area*
1 meeting room/max 60 people
Nearby: *Golf, fishing, water skiing, yachting, tennis, fitness centre, hunting/shooting, riding, clay pigeon shooting*

RESTRICTIONS

Limited facilities for disabled guests
Small dogs welcome only

ATTRACTIONS

Kellie Castle, Isle of May Bird Reserve, St Andrews Cathedral, 18 hole golf courses, Sea-Life Centre, Secret Bunker, Royal and Ancient Golf Museum

AFFILIATIONS

Minotel
Preston's Global Hotels
Grand Heritage Hotels

NEAREST

MAJOR CITY:
St Andrews - 5 miles/10 mins
MAJOR AIRPORT:
Edinburgh - 50 miles/1½ hrs
Dundee - 10 miles/20 mins
RAILWAY STATION:
Leuchars - 7 miles/15 mins

RESERVATIONS

Toll free in US: 800-544-9993
Quote ***Best Loved***

ACCESS CODES

AMADEUS UI ADXINN
APOLLO/GALILEO UI 27836
SABRE/ABACUS UI 52266
WORLDSPAN UI 41354

• Map p.494 ref: E10

" Keen attention to detail and decor. Every member of staff provided a personalised touch, it was the highlight of our stay "

Mr & Mrs Butler, London

THE INN ON THE GREEN

Hotel & restaurant

SCOTLAND

25 Greenhead Street, Glasgow G40 1ES

Telephone 0141 554 0165
Fax 0141 556 4678

***E-mail:** onthegreen@bestloved.com*

GENERAL MANAGER
Philip Raskin

ROOM RATES

Singles	*£55*
Doubles/Twins	*£75 - £90*

Includes continental breakfast and VAT

CHARGE/CREDIT CARDS

• *MC* • *VI*

RATINGS & AWARDS
S.T.B. ★★★ Hotel
Taste of Scotland

FACILITIES
***On site:** Bar & Restaurant*
***Nearby:** Golf, tennis, fitness centre*

RESTRICTIONS
Limited facilities for disabled guests
No pets

ATTRACTIONS
Glasgow Cathedral, Kelvingrove Art Gallery, The Burrell Collection, Rennie MacIntosh's Hill House, Loch Lomond, The Trossachs

AFFILIATIONS
Preston's Global Hotels

NEAREST
MAJOR CITY:
Glasgow

MAJOR AIRPORT:
Glasgow - 9 miles/15 mins

RAILWAY STATION:
Glasgow - 4 miles/10 mins

RESERVATIONS
Toll free in US: 800-544-9993
*Quote **Best Loved***

ACCESS CODES
AMADEUS LM GLA864
APOLLO/GALILEO LM 26168
SABRE/ABACUS LM 51722
WORLDSPAN LM 05864

Innovative design marks out a winner in the 'dear green place'

The Inn on the Green restaurant has been a local institution since the 1980's. Across the street from Glasgow Green and the People's Palace, this cosy basement bistro combines its role as a favourite watering hole renowned for great live piano jazz with that of a gallery showcasing contemporary art.

The hotel is a recent development and also displays considerable creative flair in its innovative styling. Each individual room at the Inn is custom-designed from the textured hessian, silk, grass and bamboo wallcoverings to the chunky wooden beds and Burberry bed linen. Individually-forged wrought iron curtain rails and picnic hampers chockfull of tea, coffee, hot chocolate and biscuits add another distinctive note, and the bathrooms are graced with sculpted Italian tiles. Even the mirrors are special - steam one over if you can, they are designed to remain reflective however hot your shower!

Glasgow was nominated the UK's City of Architecture & Design in 1999, and offers a wealth of museums, galleries and architectural highlights such as Charles Rennie Mackintosh's Art Nouveau Glasgow School of Art. Reinvented as both fashionable and dynamic in the 1990's, it is the third most popular British destination for foreign visitors after London and Edinburgh.

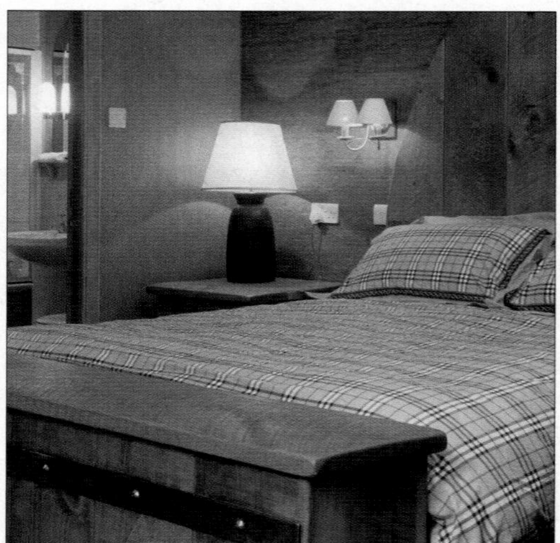

LOCATION

From M74 follow London Road to Bridgton. Pass Bridgton Station and at next major lights take the slip road on left into Arcadia Street. Follow road round left hand bend and take 1st left and left again into Greenhead Street. Hotel is on right.

For information about hotel affiliations see page 14

"I never saw a lovelier or more romantic spot"

Queen Victoria, 1873

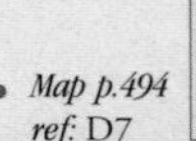

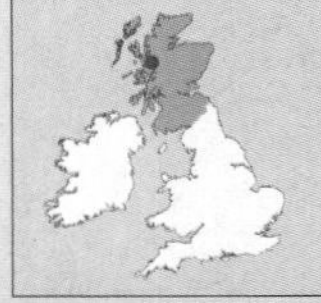

• Map p.494 ref: D7

Highland castle

INVERLOCHY CASTLE

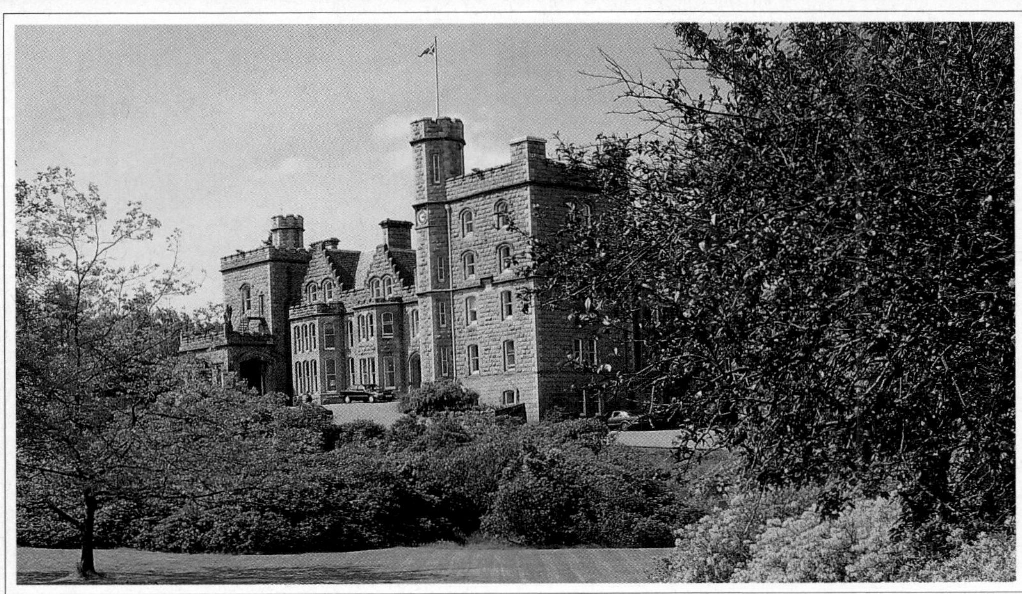

A passionate commitment to your needs in the grandeur of the Highlands

Inverlochy was built by the first Lord Abinger in 1863, near the site of the original 13th century fortress. It is set against some of the most magnificent scenery in the Western Highlands, and stands amongst the foothills of Ben Nevis in its own 500-acre estate. The castle is surrounded by landscaped gardens and rhododendrons.

The baronial Great Hall has beautiful frescoed ceilings, with crystal chandeliers and a handsome staircase. Fine decorations throughout befit the Victorian proportions of the rooms which have been recently refurbished to provide an even higher standard of comfort and luxury. There are 17 individual suites and bedrooms with private bathroom and all modern facilities.

Centrepiece of the dining room is an elaborate carved breakfont sideboard, presented as a gift to Inverlochy by the King of Norway. The menu features international cuisine with emphasis on fresh Scottish produce which changes on a daily and seasonal basis.

Tennis, loch fishing and many beautiful walking paths are within the grounds. Highland scenic attractions, and sports and leisure activities are situated within a short drive. Such is the reputation of Inverlochy that it is advisable to book well in advance!

LOCATION

From Fort William, take A82 north. After 4 miles pass Fort William Golf Club and take next left to Inverlochy – the hotel is clearly signposted.

Torlundy, Fort William, Inverness-shire PH33 6SN

Telephone 01397 702177
Fax 01397 702953

E-mail: *inverlochy@bestloved.com*

GENERAL MANAGER
Michael Leonard

ROOM RATES

14 Doubles/Twins	*£250 - £450*
3 Suites	*£390 - £450*

Includes VAT

CHARGE/CREDIT CARDS

• MC • VI

RATINGS & AWARDS
S.T.B. ★★★★★ Hotel
R.A.C. ★★★★ Gold Ribbon Dining Award 4
A.A. ★★★★ ❀❀❀
Courvoisier's Book of the Best

FACILITIES
On site: *Garden, croquet, tennis, snooker, fishing, heli-pad*
1 meeting room/max 22 people
Nearby: *Golf, fishing, skiing, riding, stalking, guided hill walking, yachting, hunting/shooting*

RESTRICTIONS
No pets
No facilities for disabled guests

ATTRACTIONS
Glencoe, Glenfinnan, Culloden, Isle of Skye, Blair Castle

AFFILIATIONS
Connoisseurs Scotland
Relais & Châteaux

NEAREST
MAJOR CITY:
Glasgow - 100 miles/2½ hrs
MAJOR AIRPORT:
Glasgow - 100 miles/2½ hrs
Inverness - 70 miles/1¾ hrs
RAILWAY STATION:
Fort William - 4 miles/15 mins

RESERVATIONS
Toll free in US: 888-424-0106
Quote ***Best Loved***

ACCESS CODES
Not applicable

"Excellence reigns and not a detail out of place"

The Good Hotel Guide

ISLE OF ERISKA

Victorian baronial mansion

Ledaig, Oban,
Argyll PA37 1SD

Telephone 01631 720371
Fax 01631 720531

E-mail: eriska@bestloved.com

OWNERS
The Buchanan-Smith Family

ROOM RATES
Single occupancy £175
17 Doubles/Twins £220 - £270
Includes full breakfast, complimentary newspaper and VAT

CHARGE/CREDIT CARDS

• MC • VI

RATINGS & AWARDS
S.T.B. ★★★★★ Hotel
A.A. ★★★★ ❀❀❀
The Good Food Guide – Restaurant of the Year 1999
WHICH? Secluded Charm Award 2001

FACILITIES
On site: *Garden, croquet, outdoor tennis, indoor pool, gym, sauna, health & beauty, sea fishing, heli-pad, 6 hole golf course, 3 meeting rooms/max 32 people*
Nearby: *Golf, riding, river and lake fishing*

RESTRICTIONS
No pets in public rooms
Closed Jan

ATTRACTIONS
Sea-Life Centre, Glencoe, distilleries, Isle of Mull, Dunstaffnage Castle, Loch Linnhe

AFFILIATIONS
The Celebrated Hotels Collection
Pride of Britain

NEAREST
MAJOR CITY:
Glasgow - 90 miles/2½ hrs

MAJOR AIRPORT:
Glasgow - 90 miles/2½ hrs

RAILWAY STATION:
Oban - 12 miles/20 mins

RESERVATIONS
Toll free in US: 800-322-2403
or 800-98-PRIDE
Quote **Best Loved**

ACCESS CODES
Not applicable

Accessed by private bridge, Eriska is all about fulfilling dreams

Eriska is a small, secluded island less than 100 miles from Glasgow and Edinburgh. It is the only island in Britain solely devoted to the care and wellbeing of guests. The Big House was built in 1884 at the height of Scottish baronial style. Blazing log fires in the burr oak panelled Hall make for a very Scottish holiday. So does a glass of malt whisky in the library. Since 1973 Eriska has been owned by the Buchanan-Smith family. They set high priority on peace and tranquillity, and these qualities attract people back to the island again and again.

Eriska lives up to the Scottish country house requirement for 'A good table' throughout the day from the delicious breakfasts to the acclaimed formal candlelit dinners.

Sporting facilities include 6-hole golf course, 17-metre swimming pool, steamroom, sauna, gymnasium, all weather tennis court, croquet, golf putting and clay pigeon shooting. The island is virtually a nature reserve with designated nature trails. Seals, otters, badgers and roe deer are all around. Eriska has its own road bridge to link with the mainland. It is only 30 minutes to the seaport of Oban, whence steamers ply to Iona and Staffa. Mainland attractions include Glencoe and Inverary Castle, seat of the Clan Campbell.

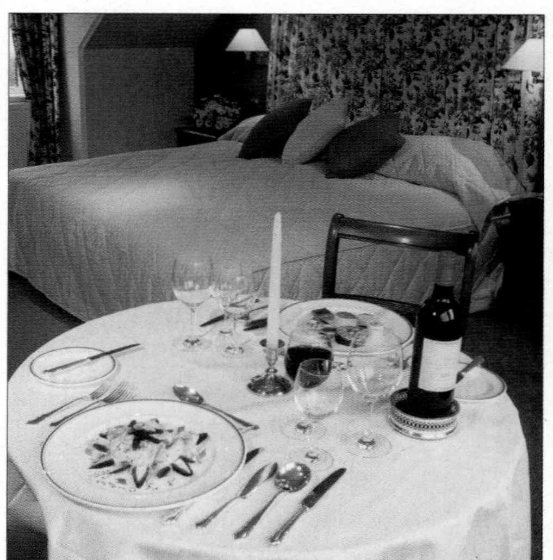

LOCATION

From Edinburgh and Glasgow, drive to Tyndrum, then follow the A85 towards Oban. At Connel proceed by bridge on the A828 for 4 miles to north of Benderloch. Then follow the signs to the hotel.

Planning a wedding reception? Turn to 'Meeting Facilities' on page 476

“ Warm hospitality and delectable food, beautiful rooms, perfect! ”

Robert & Sue Armstrong, Herefordshire

• *Map p.494 ref:* C8

Former estate lodge KILLIECHRONAN HOUSE

Sheer inspiration set within 5000 acres

Beautifully situated at the head of Loch na Keal in the centre of the Isle of Mull, Killiechronan, together with its estate of over 5,000 acres, offers hospitality in its original Highland Lodge, built in 1846. Killiechronan is the family home of the Leroy family who have another fine hotel at Oban. It contains a magnificent collection of antiques and pictures.

All six bedrooms are now transformed so that each one has its own bathroom, radio, direct dial telephone and all the little extras that make guests feel at home. Chef Graham Horne had already established a fine reputation for his cuisine at the Manor House, Oban. He prepares mouthwatering dinners, complemented by a fine wine list. Donna Ingram manages the rest of Killiechronan's facilities. You can rely on the expert attention of Donna and her staff to make sure you enjoy your stay.

Mull and the neighbouring mainland are renowned for their outstanding scenic beauty. Like Mendelssohn, you can visit Fingal's Cave. For less musical inspiration, you can see the white beach at Calgary, Duart Castle, Moy Castle on Loch Buie and its water-filled dungeon.

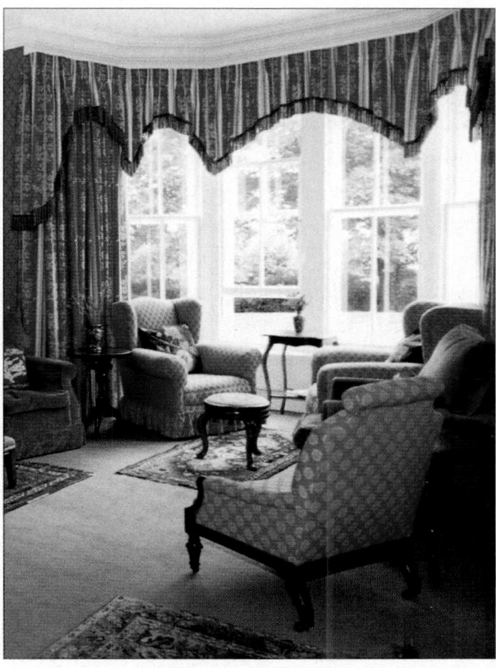

LOCATION

Mull is reached by ferry from Oban or Lochalin. Take A849 to Salen. Left onto B8035. Turn right after 2 miles.

Killiechronan, Isle of Mull PA72 6JU

Telephone 01680 300403
Fax 01680 300463

E-mail: *killiechronan@bestloved.com*

MANAGER
Donna Ingram

RATES PER PERSON

1 Single	*£77 - £85*
5 Doubles/Twins	*£60 - £80*

Includes dinner, full breakfast and VAT

CHARGE/CREDIT CARDS

• *MC* • *VI*

RATINGS & AWARDS
S.T.B. ★★★★ Small Hotel
A.A. ★★ ❀
Taste of Scotland

FACILITIES
On site: *Garden, croquet, fishing, riding, sailing*
Nearby: *Golf*

RESTRICTIONS
No children under 12 years
No facilities for disabled guests
No pets in public rooms
No smoking in bedrooms or dining room
Closed 31 Oct - 1 Mar

ATTRACTIONS
Tobermory, Torosay, Duart Castle, Calgary Sands, Iona, Staffa and Ulva Islands

AFFILIATIONS
Independent

NEAREST
MAJOR CITY:
Glasgow - 107 miles/3 hrs

MAJOR AIRPORT:
Glasgow - 107 miles/3 hrs

RAILWAY STATION:
Oban - 14 miles/1 hr

FERRY PORT:
Craignuir - 14 miles/30 mins

RESERVATIONS
Direct with Hotel
Quote ***Best Loved***

ACCESS CODES
Not applicable

“ Simply the best ”

Duncan Glass, Fife

KINFAUNS CASTLE

Highland hotel

SCOTLAND

**Near Perth,
Perthshire PH2 7JZ**

**Telephone 01738 620777
Fax 01738 620778**

E-mail: *kinfauns@bestloved.com*

OWNERS
James and Julia Smith

GENERAL MANAGER
Nigel W Liston

ROOM RATES
Single occupancy £120 - £180
16 Doubles/Twins £180 - £300
Includes full breakfast, newspaper and VAT

CHARGE/CREDIT CARDS

• DC • JCB • MC • VI

RATINGS & AWARDS
S.T.B. ★★★★ Hotel
A.A. ★★★ ❀❀ 80%
Scottish Chef of the Year 1999

FACILITIES
On site: *Garden, parkland, croquet, heli-pad, health & beauty treatments available by arrangement*
3 meeting rooms/max 60 people
Nearby: *Golf, fishing, tennis, fitness, riding*

RESTRICTIONS
Restrictions apply to children under 12
No facilities for disabled guests
No pets in public rooms

ATTRACTIONS
Pitlochry, Edinburgh, St Andrews, Carnoustie, Glamis Castle, Scone Palace, Loch Tay

AFFILIATIONS
The Celebrated Hotels Collection

NEAREST
MAJOR CITY:
Perth - 2 miles/5 mins

MAJOR AIRPORT:
Edinburgh - 50 miles/1 hr

RAILWAY STATION:
Perth - 2 miles/5 mins

RESERVATIONS
Toll free in US: 800-322-2403
*Quote **Best Loved***

ACCESS CODES
Not applicable

Family history and wonderful food in the fair land of Gowrie

Kinfauns Castle stands in 26 acres of parkland whose history dates back to the 12th century. Built in the Gothic style, there are many features that express an impressive provenance: the handsome carriage way whose steps lead to the Hall of Entrance in which the tartans of previous families are displayed, the ribbed and panelled gold leaf ceiling of The Gallery, the stained glass bay windows and the richly carved chimney piece bearing armorial insignia. The wallpaper is by William Morris and seven magnificent marble fireplaces grace the public rooms.

The oak staircase ornamented by two foot high heraldic wood carvings, one of the most outstanding features, grandly leads to the suites and bedrooms, some with four-poster beds. It is a continuing theme; the bathrooms feature Verona Rosa marble and every convenience is on hand to make your stay both comfortable and memorable.

Kinfauns Castle has quickly achieved a culinary reputation. Continental overtones have a definite Scottish touch which is no surprise - this part of Scotland has an astonishing larder from both land and sea. The wine list is well-chosen and includes a wide range of wines from Europe and the New World - all properly priced.

LOCATION

2 miles east of Perth on the main A90 Dundee Road. Follow signs for Kinfauns Castle.

" One of the very best country house hotels in the region - everything surpassed my expectations "

Geoffrey Hedge, Oxford & County Newspapers

• Map p.494 ref: E6

Private hotel

KINKELL HOUSE

A private house in a beguiling setting and Marsha - the genius in the kitchen

All is not quite as it seems on The Black Isle, the peninsula that separates the Firths of Moray and Cromarty. It is not an island for a start, and it's not black in the chromatic sense, anyway. The guide books will tell you it gets its name because the snow won't settle but the locals will tell you of paganism, witches and trees garlanded with rags - and that's how it got its name, they insist!

And the intrigue does not end there; take Kinkell House, for instance. Don't be deceived: pretty as it looks, most beautifully set in its own garden, it has very much more to offer than the dramatic view that shanghai's the eye across Cromarty Firth to the brooding heights of Ben Wyvis (3,433ft). It's an award-winning restaurant!

A private house, too, owned by Steve and Marsha Fraser. Marsha brings top class culinary experience to the kitchen. "The menu depends on what my regular suppliers have brought in fresh on the day", she says. With such wonderful produce all around, it does not take a genius to put on a feast. But, then, Marsha is a genius! And Steve has a nose for good wine. Best of all, it does not cost an arm and a leg for the privilege.

Everything is done to make you welcome. The bedrooms are furnished all cosy and comfortable. Home-from-home and ever so friendly.

When you escape Kinkell's Elysian fields, you'll find the eastern highlands just as beguiling.

LOCATION

Ten miles north of Inverness, on the B9169 about a mile from the A9 and the A835.

Easter Kinkell, by Dingwall, Ross-shire IV7 8HY

Telephone 01349 861270
Fax 01349 865902

E-mail: *kinkell@bestloved.com*

OWNERS

Steve and Marsha Fraser

ROOM RATES

7 Doubles/Twins	*£65 - £90*
2 Family Rooms	*£95 - £130*

Includes full breakfast and VAT

CHARGE/CREDIT CARDS

• MC • VI

RATINGS & AWARDS

S.T.B. ★★★★ Small Hotel
A.A. ★★ ❀ 76%

FACILITIES

On site: *Garden, croquet*
2 meeting rooms/max 50 people
Nearby: *Golf, riding, fishing, stalking*

RESTRICTIONS

No smoking in bedrooms or restaurant

ATTRACTIONS

Royal Dornoch Golf Club, Loch Ness, Dolphin watching, Glenmorangie Distillery, Culloden Battlefield, Cawdor and Urquhart Castles

AFFILIATIONS

Scotland's Hotels of Distinction

NEAREST

MAJOR CITY:
Inverness - 10 miles/15 mins

MAJOR AIRPORT:
Edinburgh - 170 miles/2½ hrs
Inverness - 15 miles/30 mins

RAILWAY STATION:
Inverness - 10 miles/15 mins

RESERVATIONS

Toll free in US: 800-437-2687
UK: 0800 975 5975
*Quote **Best Loved***

ACCESS CODES

Not applicable

• Map p.494 ref: F8

"This excellence really precludes us from wanting to go elsewhere. Your Head Chef's imaginative cuisine continues to give us great pleasure"

Brian McKibbin, Ludlow, Shropshire

KINLOCH HOUSE HOTEL

Victorian manor house

SCOTLAND

By Blairgowrie, Perthshire PH10 6SG

Telephone 01250 884237
Fax 01250 884333

E-mail: kinlochhse@bestloved.com

OWNERS

The Shentall Family

RATES PER PERSON

4 Singles	£77 - £101
9 Doubles/Twins	£50 - £106
5 Four-posters	£50 - £106
2 Suites	£80 - £130

Includes continental or full breakfast, complimentary newspaper, dinner, service and VAT

CHARGE/CREDIT CARDS

 • DC • JCB • MC • VI

RATINGS & AWARDS

S.T.B. ★★★★★ Hotel

A.A. ★★★ ❀❀❀

FACILITIES

On site: *Garden, croquet, indoor pool, gym, sauna, health & beauty, jacuzzi, fishing, heli-pad*

1 meeting room/max 18 people

Nearby: *Golf, fishing, tennis, hunting/shooting, hill walking*

RESTRICTIONS

No children under 7 years in dining room

Closed 19 - 29 Dec

ATTRACTIONS

Scone Palace, Glenshee Ski Centre, Blair Castle, Black Watch Museum, Glamis Castle and Cluny Gardens

AFFILIATIONS

The Celebrated Hotels Collection

Small Luxury Hotels

NEAREST

MAJOR CITY:

Perth - 18 miles/30 mins

MAJOR AIRPORT:

Edinburgh - 70 miles/1¼ hrs

RAILWAY STATION:

Dunkeld - 8 miles/15 mins

RESERVATIONS

Toll free in US/Canada: 800-525-4800 or 800-322-2403

Toll free in UK: 0800 964 470

Quote ***Best Loved***

ACCESS CODES

AMADEUS LX PSLKLH

APOLLO/GALILEO LX 57720

SABRE/ABACUS LX 31056

WORLDSPAN LX EDIKH

The art of good living in the very heart of Scotland

Some hotels seem to spring up, others, like a good wine, mature and mellow with age. Kinloch House is an example of the latter. It starts off propitiously with its location; put your finger on the centre of Scotland and you're spot on.

It was built in 1840, extended in 1911 becoming an hotel in 1981. But the transition is seamless; it still has the look and feel of a private house. It stands in 25 acres of parkland grazed by highland cattle, with views over the Marlee Loch to the Sidlaw Hills beyond. The walled garden is a recent resurrection which serves two purposes: as a place to relax in scented seclusion and as a kitchen garden much of whose goodness ends up on your plate. The gifted Bill McNicoll, head chef for 17 years, is to be envied, supplied as he is from coast to coast; Aberdeen Angus Beef, lobsters from Kyle of Lochalsh, game from the highlands. His efforts are blessed by a wide-ranging wine list. 'Dinner is regarded as the signature to an enjoyable day', says the brochure. True, but a single malt from a choice of 160 adds a certain flourish before bedtime!

Working up an appetite is easy. There are 30 golf courses within an hour's drive, a 16ft dinghy on the loch and fishing can be arranged. The state-of-the-art health, beauty, fitness and therapy facilities are beautifully tucked away so that the character of this great house is not compromised.

LOCATION

Located 3 miles west of Blairgowrie on the A923 to Dunkeld.

"The welcome is wonderfully warm, service is immaculate and discreet, comfort is considerable, and the food is famously good. Balm for body and soul"

Philippa Davenport, Financial Times Weekend

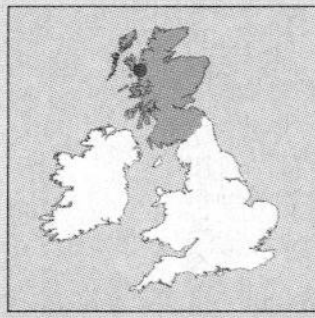

• Map p.494 ref: D7

61

Lochside island hotel

KINLOCH LODGE

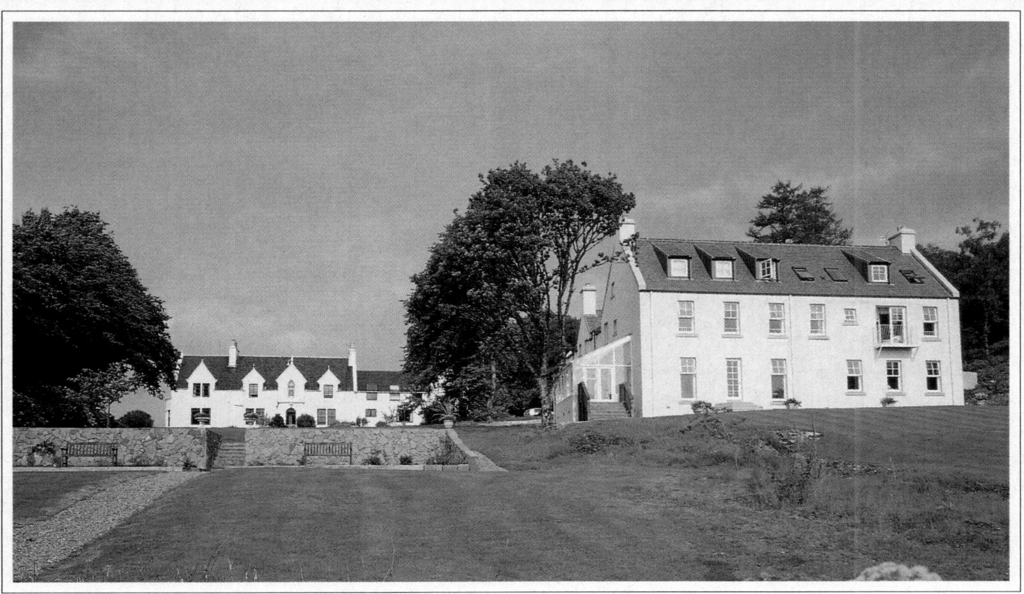

At home with Lord and Lady Macdonald

Kinloch Lodge is an elegant country house dating from the early 1600s, whose gardens slope down to meet the sea loch, Na Dal, on the Isle of Skye in the Highlands of Scotland. It is the ancestral home of Lord Macdonald of Macdonald, High Chief of Clan Donald, who runs it as a small, very personal hotel with his wife, the world-renowned cookery writer Claire Macdonald. In 1998 the Macdonalds built a new house adjacent to the Lodge and in similar style, known as Kinloch, providing 15 bedrooms in all.

The setting is romantic, beautiful and incomparably peaceful. Secluded between a wooded hillside and the sea loch on two sides, the surrounding area is fascinating for those who love and appreciate nature, with notable flowers and plants, five golden eagles on the hill behind the house, seals galore and a colony of otters. The bird life is varied and plentiful.

Here, in view of Skye and the spectacular Cuillin Hills, the Macdonalds dispense the warmest hospitality from their family home. The atmosphere is very relaxed, with comfortable rooms decorated in traditional country house style, log fires and a five-course dinner that features the freshest of ingredients that are naturally available in season.

LOCATION

1 mile off A851. 6 miles south of Broadford and 10 miles north of Armadale.

SCOTLAND

Sleat, Isle of Skye, Highland IV43 8QY

Telephone 01471 833214
Fax 01471 833277

E-mail: *kinlochlodge@bestloved.com*

OWNERS

Lord and Lady Macdonald

ROOM RATES

15 Doubles/Twins £100 - £200
Includes full breakfast and VAT

CHARGE/CREDIT CARDS

• *MC* • *VI*

RATINGS & AWARDS

S.T.B. ★★★★ *Hotel*
A.A. ★★ ❀❀ *75%*
Courvoisier's Book of the Best

FACILITIES

On site: *Gardens, heli-pad, fishing, stalking*
Nearby: *Riding*

RESTRICTIONS

No facilities for disabled guests
Pets by arrangement
No smoking in bedrooms or dining rooms
Closed Christmas week

ATTRACTIONS

Isle of Skye, Clan Donald Centre, Inverewe Gardens, Dunvegan Castle

AFFILIATIONS

The Celebrated Hotels Collection
Scotland's Hotels of Distinction

NEAREST

MAJOR CITY:
Inverness - 100 miles/3½ hrs

MAJOR AIRPORT:
Inverness - 100 miles/3½ hrs

RAILWAY STATION:
Kyle of Lochalsh - 12 miles/45 mins

FERRY PORT:
Kyle of Lochalsh - 12 miles/45 mins

RESERVATIONS

Toll free in US: 800-322-2403
or 800-437-2687
Quote ***Best Loved***

ACCESS CODES

Not applicable

"A lovely haven with superb food"

Joan and Brian Rigley, Warrington

• Map p.494 ref: E10

18/19th century farmstead

KIRKTON HOUSE

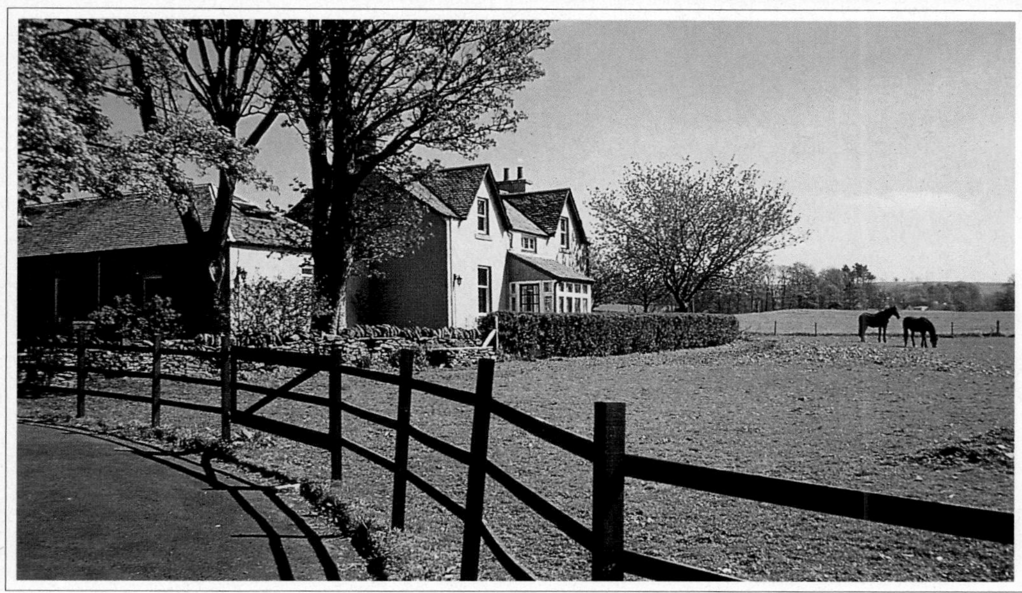

A great little country place in easy reach of Glasgow Airport

Commanding panoramic views of the River Clyde and the Argyll Hills, Kirkton House is handy for Glasgow Airport, Loch Lomond, the West Highlands and Glasgow City. There are excellent local walks and golf courses.

Kirkton House is a conversion of a traditional 18/19th century Scottish farmhouse and barns around a courtyard. The lounge and dining areas have exposed stone walls and rustic fireplaces (including the original 'swee' for hanging the pots). Guests can enjoy a drink in the guest lounge (beside a roaring open fire on chilly evenings), and savour the 'homey', informal and unpretentious ambience. Your well-travelled proprietors have a natural gift for hospitality.

All the well-appointed bedrooms (two on the ground floor) have a bath and/or shower and toilet, direct dial telephones, television, writing table, hairdryer, iron and ironing board, and hospitality tray. Wholesome home cooked dinners are served at individual tables per party: orders are taken at about 7 pm from the extensive menu. Tables should be pre-booked for this house party experience.

'A luxurious and delightful experience' JF, Mass, USA. 'How does one improve on perfection?' HH, Pinner, UK. - just two of many compliments from the guest book.

LOCATION

Turn north off A814 at west end of Cardross village, up Darleith Road. Proceed ½ mile out of housing line and Kirkton House drive is on right after 3 cottages.

Darleith Road, Cardross, Argyll and Bute G82 5EZ

Telephone 01389 841951
Fax 01389 841868

E-mail: *kirkton@bestloved.com*

OWNERS

Stewart and Gillian Macdonald

ROOM RATES

Single occupancy	*£41 - £45*
2 Doubles/Twins	*£61 - £70*
4 Family rooms	*£71 - £86*

Includes full breakfast and VAT

CHARGE/CREDIT CARDS

• *DC* • *JCB* • *MC* • *VI*

RATINGS & AWARDS

S.T.B. ★★★★ Guest House
R.A.C. ◆◆◆◆◆ Sparkling Diamond
Warm Welcome Awards
A.A. ◆◆◆◆◆
Taste of Scotland

FACILITIES

On site: *Garden*
Nearby: *Golf, riding, fishing*

RESTRICTIONS

Limited facilities for disabled guests

ATTRACTIONS

Loch Lomond, The Trossachs, Hill House, Glasgow, Burrell Collection, Loch Lomond International Golf Club, Scottish Exhibition Centre, West Highlands, golf courses

AFFILIATIONS

The Circle Group

NEAREST

MAJOR CITY:
Glasgow - 18 miles/35 mins

MAJOR AIRPORT:
Glasgow - 15 miles/25 mins

RAILWAY STATION:
Cardross - 1 mile/2 mins

RESERVATIONS

Direct with hotel
Quote ***Best Loved***

ACCESS CODES

Not applicable

• Map p.494 ref: E12

“ A delightful experience ”

Professor and Mrs Ian Richardson, Auchterarder

KIRROUGHTREE HOUSE

18th century mansion

Newton Stewart, Wigtownshire, South West Scotland DG8 6AN

Telephone 01671 402141
Fax 01671 402425

E-mail: *kirrough@bestloved.com*

OWNER
Douglas McMillan

GENERAL MANAGER
Jim Stirling

ROOM RATES

2 Singles	£75 - £135
11 Doubles/Twins	£130 - £150
1 Four-poster	£150
3 Suites	£150 - £170

Includes full breakfast and VAT

CHARGE/CREDIT CARDS

• MC • VI

RATINGS & AWARDS
S.T.B. ★★★★ Hotel
R.A.C. Blue Ribbon ★★★
Dining Award 3
A.A. ★★★ ❀❀❀
Winner Taste of Scotland Prestige Award

FACILITIES
On site: Garden, croquet, tennis
1 meeting room/max 20 people
Nearby: Golf, riding, fitness, hunting/shooting, fishing, curling

RESTRICTIONS
No facilities for disabled guests
No smoking in dining rooms

ATTRACTIONS
Gem Rock Museum, Culzean Castle, Whithorn Dig, Drumlanrig Castle, Logan Botanical Gardens, Mill on the Fleet

AFFILIATIONS
Scotland's Hotels of Distinction

NEAREST
MAJOR CITY:
Glasgow - 90 miles/2 hrs
MAJOR AIRPORT:
Glasgow - 90 miles/2 hrs
RAILWAY STATION:
Barhill - 18 miles/30 mins

RESERVATIONS
Toll free in US: 800-437-2687
Quote **Best Loved**

ACCESS CODES
WORLDSPAN RX KIRNE

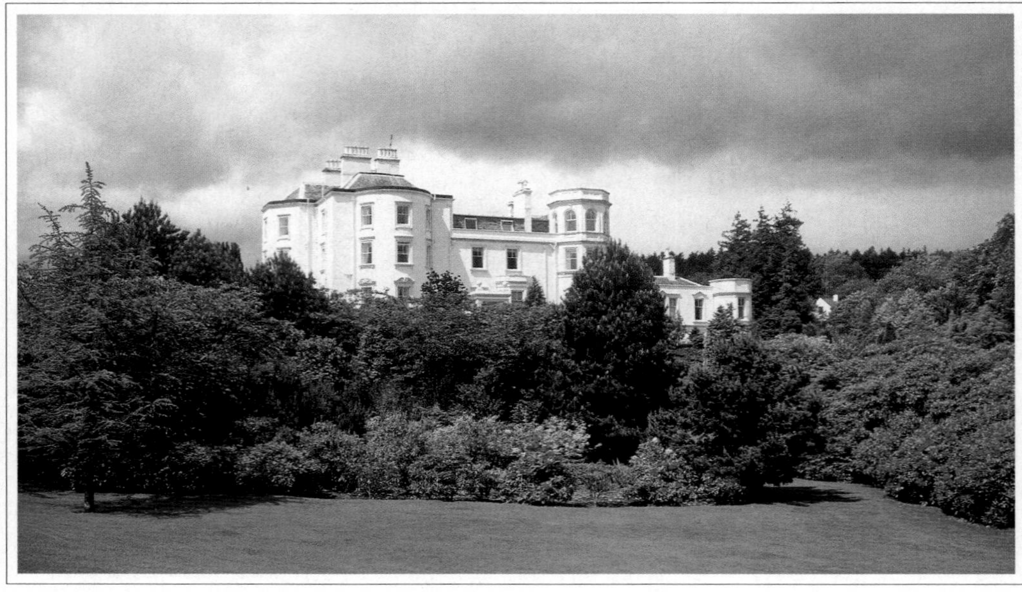

An award winning hotel that inspired Robert Burns

Kirroughtree House is an inspiringly beautiful mansion built by the Heron family in 1719. The Rococo furnishings of its oak-panelled lounge reflect the style and grace of the period. From the lounge rises the original staircase where Robert Burns recited his poems to the Heron family and their guests. He composed four of his ballads, and a song to Elizabeth Heron's music, in this house.

Kirroughtree House is owned and managed by the McMillan family. Individual attention is given to guests by the friendly management and staff. The elegant restaurant has a fine reputation for excellent food. The very best of local produce is used in creating meals of great originality and finesse. Kirroughtree's past awards include Scotland's Hotel of the Year, a standard that it has maintained with its three rosettes for cuisine.

The hotel stands in eight acres of landscaped gardens on the edge of Galloway Forest Park in the foothills of the Cairnsmore of Fleet. You can relax on the terrace and enjoy the spectacular views or play tennis, pitch and putt or croquet. Special golf packages on the exclusive Cally course, salmon and trout fishing, rough shooting and deer stalking can all be arranged.

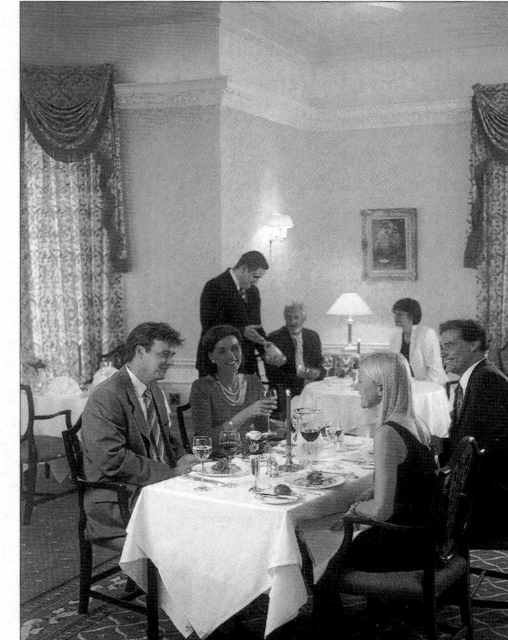

LOCATION

Travelling west on the A75, take the A712 towards New Galloway. The hotel driveway is 300 yards on the left.

"My wife was adorned by a heavily plastered arm. At the quiet, comfortable and efficient Knipoch, the attentive staff looked after us with their usual expertise"

Mr S A H Haddow, Glasgow

• *Map p.494 ref:* D9

Country hotel

KNIPOCH HOUSE HOTEL

A house with its own history and it smokes its own salmon

Knipoch is a historic family home, at one time owned by members of the Campbell Clan. In 1592 Campbell, Thane of Cawdor, was murdered at the 'House of Knipoch in Lorne.' In 1981 the Craig family opened Knipoch as a high quality hotel. Today every bedroom has full modern facilities, with either a view of the loch or the magnificent surrounding countryside.

Knipoch prides itself on its good food. The restaurant has won awards for cuisine and is famed for its own smoked salmon. The cellar has more than 350 wines, and some very fine old malt whiskies. An ancient spring on the side of the hill provides crystal water as the perfect accompaniment.

In this ancient land, history gives way to myth and legend. Nearby is much to see and do. Inverary Castle was the home of the Campbell Clan. Inverary Jail is a living 19th century prison. Oban has highland games and a fine distillery. Close by are Ben Nevis (Britain's highest mountain) and Aonach Mor (Scotland's only mountain gondola system) and the islands of Iona, Staff and Mull. It is a land of great charm and tranquil beauty that belies the savagery of the past. You will never forget it.

LOCATION

Six miles south of Oban on the A816, halfway along Loch Feochan. The hotel is well signposted.

By Oban, Argyll PA34 4QT

Telephone 01852 316251
Fax 01852 316249

E-mail: *knipoch@bestloved.com*

OWNERS

The Craig Family

ROOM RATES

Singles	*£37 - £97*
13 Doubles/Twins	*£77 - £154*
2 Family rooms	*£77 - £154*
1 Suite	*£100 - £200*

Includes full breakfast and VAT

CHARGE/CREDIT CARDS

• DC • MC • VI

RATINGS & AWARDS

S.T.B. ★★★★ Hotel
Taste of Scotland

FACILITIES

On site: *Garden, boating, heli-pad*
2 meeting rooms/max 25 people
Nearby: *Golf, hunting/shooting, game and sea fishing, fitness, riding, diving*

RESTRICTIONS

No pets in public rooms
Closed mid Dec - mid Feb

ATTRACTIONS

Mull & Iona, Nevis Range, Glencoe, Whisky Distilleries, Dunstaffnage Castle and Chapel, Arduaine Gardens

AFFILIATIONS

Scotland's Hotels of Distinction

NEAREST

MAJOR CITY:
Glasgow - 96 miles/2 hrs

MAJOR AIRPORT:
Glasgow - 96 miles/2 hrs

RAILWAY STATION:
Oban - 6 miles/15 mins

RESERVATIONS

Toll free in US: 800-437-2687
or 800-223-6510
Quote ***Best Loved***

ACCESS CODES

Not applicable

• Map p.494
ref: D12

"The epitome of what a fine country house hotel should be – warm, inviting and totally enjoyable"

Helen Worth & Michael Angelis, TV personalities

KNOCKINAAM LODGE

19th century hunting lodge

Portpatrick, Near Stranraer, Dumfries & Galloway DG9 9AD

Telephone 01776 810471
Fax 01776 810435

E-mail: *knockinaam@bestloved.com*

OWNERS

Michael Bricker and Pauline Ashworth

RATES PER PERSON

1 Single	£100 - £140
5 Doubles/Twins	£85 - £120
4 Master rooms	£110 - £165

Includes full breakfast, dinner and VAT

CHARGE/CREDIT CARDS

• DC • MC • VI

RATINGS & AWARDS

S.T.B. ★★★★★ Small Hotel

A.A. ★★ ❀❀❀

Macallan Country House Hotel of the Year 1999

FACILITIES

On site: *Garden, croquet, fishing, heli-pad*
1 meeting room/max 40 people
Nearby: *Fishing, shooting, golf, walking*

RESTRICTIONS

No children under 12 years in dining room for dinner
No facilities for disabled guests
No pets in public rooms

ATTRACTIONS

Logan, Ardwell and Glenwhan gardens, Castle Kennedy, Culzean Castle, Galloway Forest

AFFILIATIONS

The Celebrated Hotels Collection
Pride of Britain

NEAREST

MAJOR CITY:
Stranraer - 8 miles/15 mins
MAJOR AIRPORT:
Glasgow - 98 miles/2 hrs
RAILWAY STATION:
Stranraer - 8 miles/15 mins
FERRY PORT
Stranraer - 8 miles/15 mins

RESERVATIONS

Toll free in US: 800-322-2403
or 800-98-PRIDE
*Quote **Best Loved***

ACCESS CODES

Not applicable

One of Churchill's and Eisenhower's best kept secrets

In its beautiful 30-acre setting beside the Irish Sea, Knockinaam enjoys one of Scotland's most romantic settings. Built in 1869 as a hunting lodge by Lady Hunter-Blair and extended to its present size in 1901, it has marvellous sea views and sunsets, gardens, public rooms with open log fires and 10 comfortable en suite bedrooms. It is the ideal place for a relaxing getaway. Sir Winston Churchill chose Knockinaam as his secret meeting place with General Dwight D. Eisenhower during the Second World War.

The AA 3-rosette restaurant serves the most delicious and innovative cuisine, using only the freshest ingredients. The menu features Scottish beef and lamb, as well as local seafood. To complement the food, the wine list has over 500 varieties. The hotel is noted for its display of over 124 malt whiskies, a pleasure for the connoisseur and an education for the novice!

Knockinaam has an international reputation for service, hospitality and attention to details, provided by proprietors Pauline Ashworth, Michael Bricker and their wonderful staff.

There is superb fishing and shooting close by, and the nearby golf clubs include Turnberry, Royal Troon, Prestwick, Brunston Castle, Southerness, Stranraer and Portpatrick.

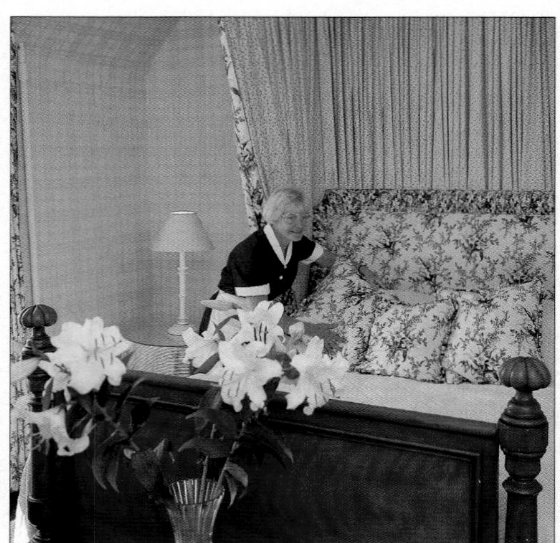

LOCATION

From A75 or A77, follow signs to Portpatrick. 2 miles west of Lochans, turn left at sign to Knockinaam Lodge, pass Colfin Smokehouse and follow signs for 3 miles to the Lodge.

Ferries can make the crossing between Scotland and Ireland in 45 minutes

"We came wondering. We went in wonderment"

George & Florence Wilson, Musselburgh

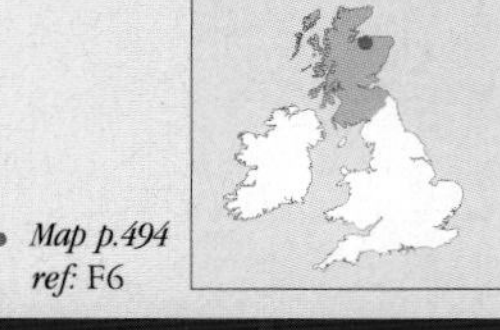

• Map p.494 ref: F6

19th century house

KNOCKOMIE HOTEL

Pampered comfort surrounded by a wealth of sights and sports

Overlooking the Royal Burgh of Forres, Knockomie is ideally situated to visit castles, distilleries and golf courses, while salmon and deer await the keen sportsman. The front hall is panelled in Scots Pine, while all 15 bedrooms are individually decorated with soft furnishings and period furniture. Some have four-poster or half-tester beds; others, with patios, are on the ground floor, including one for the disabled.

Knockomie House was built in 1821, added to in the Arts and Crafts style in 1914 and extended in 1993. The restaurant uses the best of Scottish produce to specialise in the Taste of Scotland. This is complemented by an extensive wine list and a large collection of malt whiskies.

An ideal location to visit the many castles, including Cawdor, Brodie and Ballindalloch or the unique Whisky Trail in the Spey Valley. Loch Ness is less than an hour away waiting to reveal its secret. Other opportunities include stalking and shooting in the glens, or fishing in the lochs and rivers. Local golf courses include Lossiemouth, Hopeman, Forres, Nairn (championship) and Dornoch (championship).

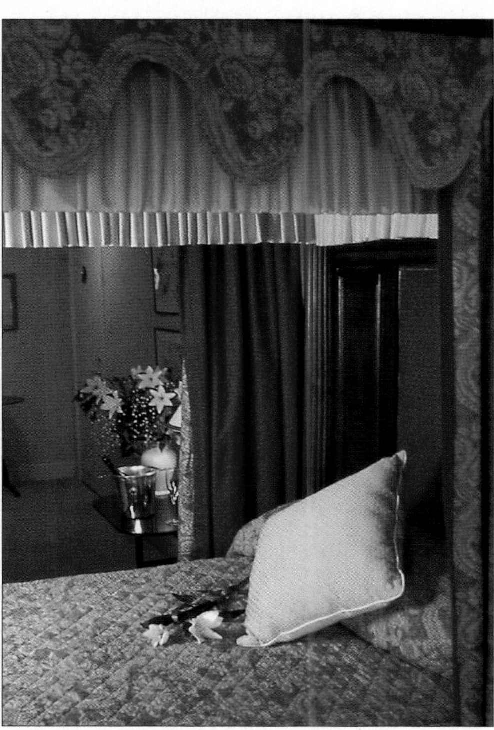

LOCATION

1 mile south of Forres on A940.

Grantown Road, Forres, Moray IV36 2SG

Telephone 01309 673146
Fax 01309 673290

E-mail: *knockomie@bestloved.com*

DIRECTOR

Gavin Ellis

ROOM RATES

1 Single	*£74*
11 Doubles	*£90 - £115*
1 Family room	*£127*
1 Four-poster	*£150*
1 Suite	*£179*

Includes full breakfast and VAT

CHARGE/CREDIT CARDS

• *DC* • *JCB* • *MC* • *VI*

RATINGS & AWARDS

S.T.B. ★★★★ *Hotel*
A.A. ★★★ ❀❀ *74%*
Taste of Scotland

FACILITIES

On site: *Garden, croquet, heli-pad*
2 meeting rooms/max 40 people
Nearby: *Golf, fishing, shooting, stalking*

RESTRICTIONS

None

ATTRACTIONS

Brodie Castle, Cawdor Castle, Ballindalloch Castle, Benromach and Glen Grant Distilleries, Johnston's of Elgin

AFFILIATIONS

Preston's Global Hotels
Grand Heritage Hotels

NEAREST

MAJOR CITY:
Inverness - 27 miles/30 mins
MAJOR AIRPORT:
Inverness - 25 miles/30 mins
Aberdeen - 75 miles/1½ hrs
RAILWAY STATION:
Forres - 1 mile/5 mins

RESERVATIONS

Toll free in US: 800-544-9993 or 888-93-GRAND
Quote ***Best Loved***

ACCESS CODES

AMADEUS UI FSSKNO
APOLLO/GALILEO UI 73447
SABRE/ABACUS UI 32407
WORLDSPAN UI 40671

• Map p.494 ref: E11

" Ladyburn exemplifies life as it used to be lived and ought to be lived "

Jack Macmillan MBE, Edinburgh

LADYBURN

Country house

SCOTLAND

by Maybole, Ayrshire KA19 7SG

Telephone 01655 740585
Fax 01655 740580

E-mail: ladyburn@bestloved.com

OWNERS
David and Jane Hepburn

ROOM RATES

Single occupancy	£100 - £115
5 Doubles/Twins	£145 - £175

Includes full breakfast and VAT

CHARGE/CREDIT CARDS

• MC • VI

RATINGS & AWARDS
R.A.C. Blue Ribbon ★★ Dining Award 3
A.A. ★★ ❀

FACILITIES
On site: Garden, croquet, heli-pad
1 meeting room/max 100 people
Nearby: Golf, fishing, stalking, clay pigeon shooting

RESTRICTIONS
No children under 16 years
Smoking permitted in the Library only
No pets, guide dogs only

ATTRACTIONS
Burns' Centre, Tam O'Shanter Experience, Culzean Castle, Glentrool, Crossraguel Abbey

AFFILIATIONS
Independent

NEAREST
MAJOR CITY:
Glasgow - 45 miles/1 hr

MAJOR AIRPORT:
Glasgow - 50 miles/1¼ hrs
Prestwick - 12 miles/30 mins

RAILWAY STATION:
Ayr - 12 miles/20 mins

RESERVATIONS
Direct with Hotel
Quote **Best Loved**

ACCESS CODES
Not applicable

Character, comfort and good food tied with a Blue Ribbon of excellence

Ladyburn and Jane Hepburn are, as they say, an item! Indivisible. Praise one and you praise the other. It's not obvious from the picture above but there is a clue in the yellow column on the left: you will not find another Blue Ribbon (the second highest accolade the RAC can give) sitting next to only two stars (representing size and facilities).

Ladyburn is about as original as you can get! It most certainly is not an hotel; but the service and comfort could shame the best five stars in the world. And it's not really a restaurant, but you would be hard put to find better food - anywhere!

So what is it? Ladyburn is a combination of irrepressible enthusiasm, total understanding of what people want when away from home and an instinctive genius for cooking. Jane Hepburn is to hospitality what Einstein was to science!

There are only five rooms in the house but what rooms! What comfort! Real coffee on the side and, at bedtime, not just chocolates but a hot water bottle, too!

You will not find a menu in sight; Jane will ask you what you would like and make a suggestion or two if you need a prompt, then go out and buy whatever is necessary.

And by the way, there is plenty nearby to see and do: golf at Turnberry and Royal Troon, fishing for trout and salmon, racing at Ayr …

Ladyburn - there is nothing to match it!

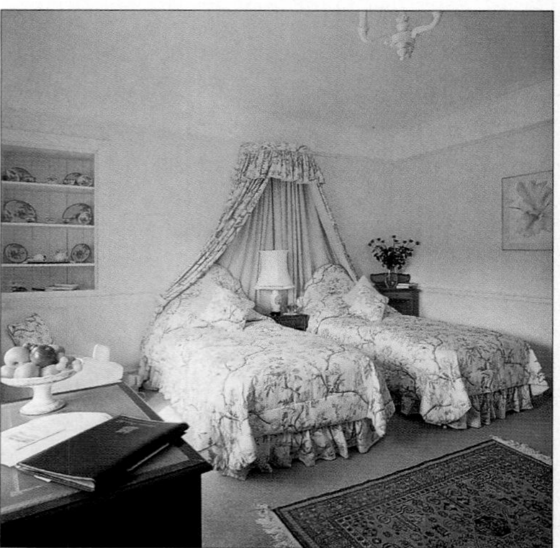

LOCATION

Take the A77 to Maybole. Turn onto B7023 to Crosshill and right at War Memorial. 2 miles further along, turn left. Ladyburn is ¾ mile on right.

Thinking of pampering yourself? See the 'Health & Beauty' index on page 472

"This is a magical place"

Dr & Mrs A Mitchell, Bray -on-Thames

• Map p.494 ref: E9

Lakeside hotel

THE LAKE OF MENTEITH HOTEL

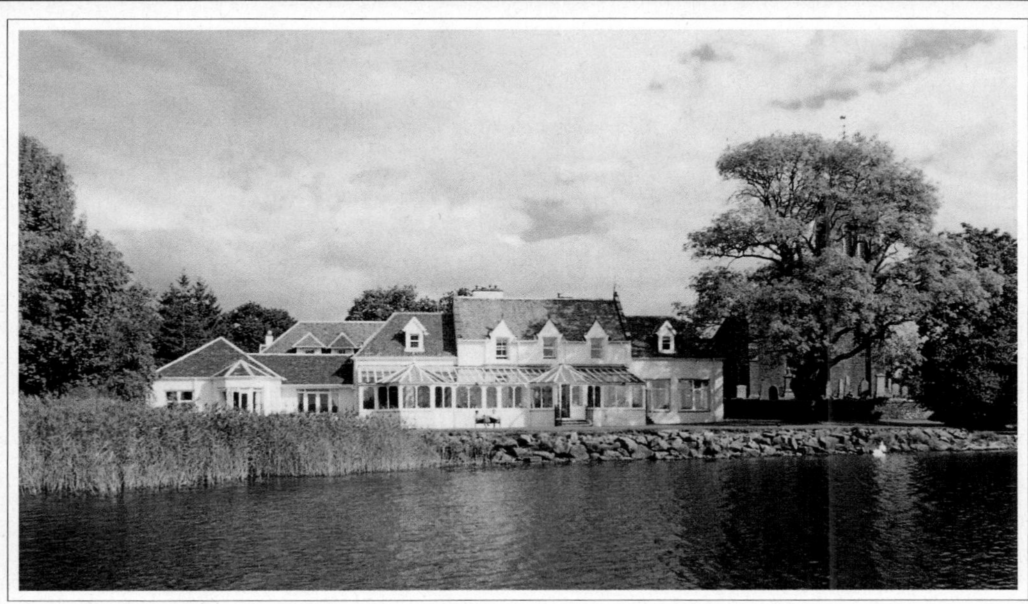

Choice foods, and a grandstand vista of lake and mountains

The Lake of Menteith Hotel is set in a splendid sheltered position on the banks of Lake Menteith in the Trossachs. Its lawn runs down to the edge of the lake. As a guest, you are assured of all the amenities of an STB 3 Star hotel. All bedrooms have en-suite facilities, with all the little details that will make your stay much more comfortable.

The à la carte and table d'hôte menus offer a varied choice of imaginatively prepared dishes. The table d'hôte menus are particularly good value: start with pheasant terrine topped with slivers of smoked venison, followed by a sorbet, then, after a main course of halibut cooked in fennel and cream sauce, enjoy a light Drambuie parfait before your coffee and home-made petits fours. Special rates are available for mini-breaks of two nights or more.

In winter the lake often freezes over, and it is not unusual for locals to bring out their skates for a skim over the ice. Throughout the year the hotel is within easy reach of mountains, wildlife and other leisure activities, including golf. Nearby are Stirling Castle and Loch Lomond.

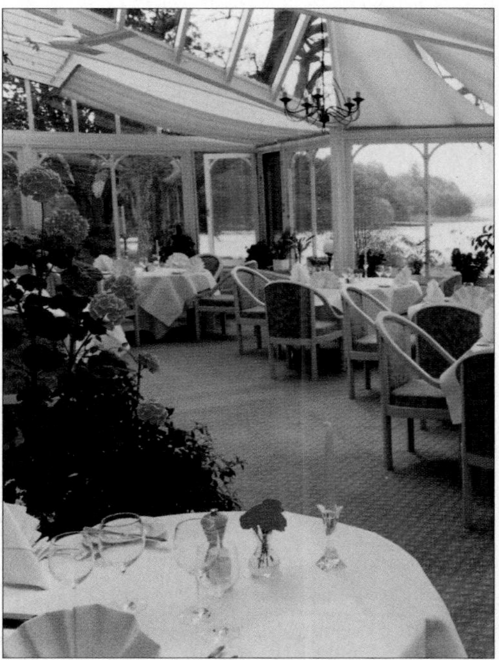

LOCATION

M9 Exit 10. Take the A84/A873/A81 to Port of Menteith. The hotel is on the left next to the church.

Port of Menteith, Perthshire FK8 3RA

Telephone 01877 385258
Fax 01877 385671

E-mail: lakehtl@bestloved.com

MANAGERS
Graeme and Ros McConnachie

RATES PER PERSON
Single occupancy £45 - £96
16 Doubles/Twins £41 - £90
Includes dinner, full breakfast and VAT

CHARGE/CREDIT CARDS

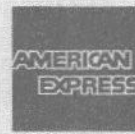

• MC • VI

RATINGS & AWARDS
S.T.B. ★★★ Hotel
A.A. ★★ 74%

FACILITIES
On site: Garden, fishing
2 meeting rooms/max 20 people
Nearby: Golf, riding

RESTRICTIONS
No children under 8 years
No pets in public rooms
Closed Sun evenings - Tues dinner Nov - Mar

ATTRACTIONS
Inchmahome Priory, The Trossachs, Stirling Castle, Rob Roy Centre, Loch Katrine

AFFILIATIONS
Independent

NEAREST
MAJOR CITY:
Glasgow - 33 miles/50 mins

MAJOR AIRPORT:
Glasgow - 35 miles/50 mins

RAILWAY STATION:
Stirling - 17 miles/25 mins

RESERVATIONS
Direct with hotel
Quote **Best Loved**

ACCESS CODES
Not applicable

For a portrait of this region see page 16

• Map p.494 ref: G8

"We have enjoyed our break tremendously. The staff have been refreshingly friendly and helpful. Food excellent"

Mr & Mrs Candlish

LETHAM GRANGE HOTEL & GOLF COURSE

Golf resort

Colliston, Near Carnoustie, Arbroath, Angus DD11 4RL

Telephone 01241 890373
Fax 01241 890725

E-mail: letham@bestloved.com

OWNER
D G Liu

HOST
Allan Robertson

ROOM RATES

Single occupancy	£100
38 Doubles/Twins	£145
1 Four-poster	£180
2 Mini suites	£180
1 Suite	£210

Includes full breakfast and VAT

CHARGE/CREDIT CARDS

• DC • MC • VI

RATINGS & AWARDS
S.T.B. ★★★★ Hotel
R.A.C. ★★★★ Dining Award 2
A.A. ★★★★ 64%
Taste of Scotland

FACILITIES
On site: Garden, croquet, 18 hole golf course, tennis, curling, archery, shooting, quad biking
5 meeting rooms/max 500 people
Nearby: Fitness centre & spa, gliding, watersports, fishing, riding, skiiing

RESTRICTIONS
Limited facilities for disabled guests

ATTRACTIONS
Arbroath Abbey, Glamis Castle, Angus Glens, Kirriemuir, hill walking, numerous golf courses

AFFILIATIONS
Scotland's Hotels of Distinction

NEAREST
MAJOR CITY:
Dundee - 17 miles/30 mins

MAJOR AIRPORT:
Edinburgh - 75 miles/1½ hrs

RAILWAY STATION:
Dundee - 17 miles/30 mins

RESERVATIONS
Toll free in US: 800-437-2687

ACCESS CODES
Not applicable

Tee up for the 'Augusta of Scotland' or just take a leisurely break

First things first, you do not have to be a golfer to enjoy Letham Grange's country house comforts and the peace and quiet of the Angus countryside. If the idea of a relaxing (non-sporting) break appeals, there is fine dining to enjoy, sampling malt whiskeys in the Oak Bar, and side trips to the traditional fishing port of Arbroath, the rugged Angus Glens, and Glamis Castle, legendary setting for Macbeth, and childhood home of Queen Elizabeth, the Queen Mother.

Letham Grange offers a choice of accommodation either in the splendidly renovated Victorian mansion or the Golf Estate. The mansion rooms are individually themed - particularly outstanding is the Rapunzel Tower on three levels linked by a spiral staircase. The Golf Estate buildings are close by and feature refreshingly modern amenities.

Within the grounds there is not just one but two golf courses: the more challenging 72-par Old Course (or 'Augusta of Scotland'), and the 68-par New Course. Golfing breaks are offered throughout the year. The resort also has its very own curling rink, lawn tennis, croquet and excellent conference facilities which can include group activities such as off-roading, shooting and quad-biking.

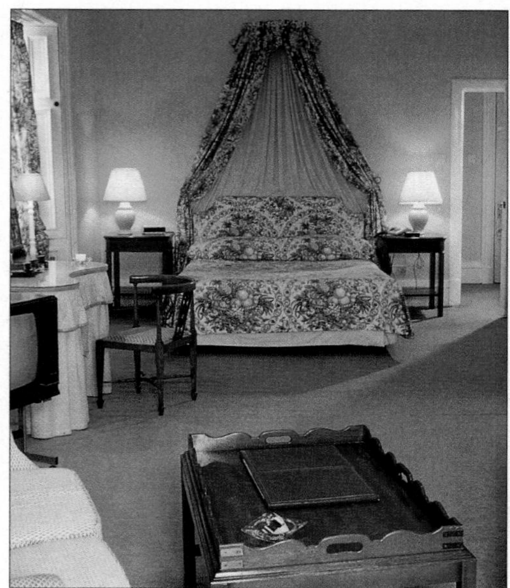

LOCATION

From Dundee take the A92 to Arbroath and then the A933 towards Brechin. After Colliston take the first right for hotel.

Planning a wedding reception? Turn to 'Meeting Facilities' on page 476

"It is the kind of view you could watch all day and it accompanies everything you do in the hotel like silent music – the food matches the setting"

Iain Crawford, freelance journalist

• Map p.494 ref: D9

Hotel and Restaurant — LOCH MELFORT

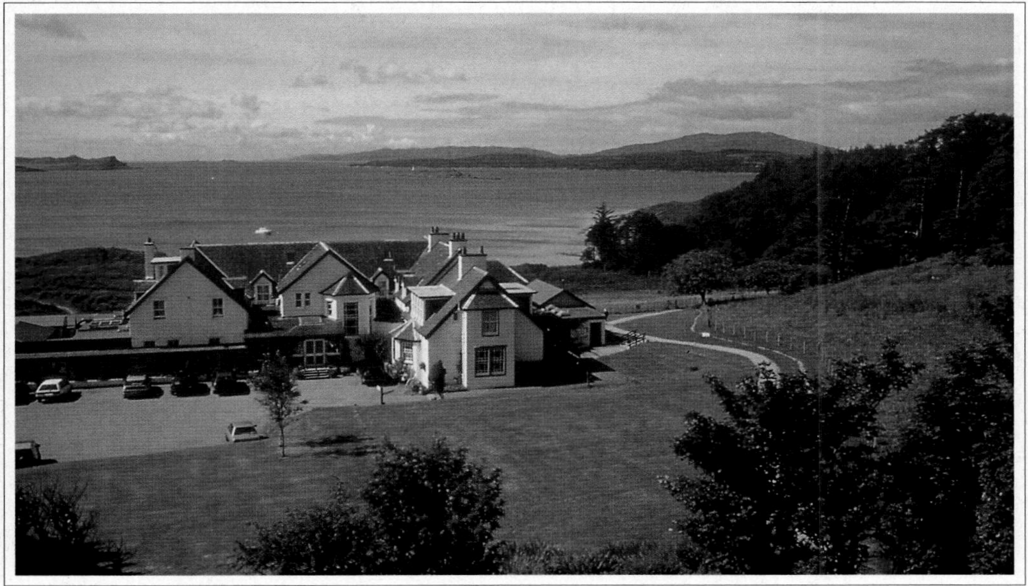

Spectacular location on the west coast with uninterrupted views

The finest location on the west coast of Scotland awaits visitors to this award-winning hotel and restaurant, the perfect place for a relaxing holiday or short break at any time of the year. Personally run by Nigel and Kyle Schofield, they and their friendly and attentive staff are always on hand to make sure your stay is an enjoyable one.

The comfortable bedrooms all have private bathrooms, TV, radio and direct dial telephones. Most have stunning views across Asknish Bay to the islands of Jura, Shuna and Scarba.

The restaurant, with its two AA rosettes for cuisine, offers superb dining comprising only the best of fresh local produce particularly locally-caught fish and shellfish, meats and cheeses. Mouth-watering home-made puddings and ice-creams provide the perfect finale to the menu which changes daily. A carefully chosen and comprehensive wine list offers an excellent choice. Lunches, suppers and afternoon teas are served in the hotel's Skerry Bistro.

The hotel lies next to the National Trust of Scotland's famous Arduaine Gardens, one of 20 National Trust properties within easy reach, all revelling in the mountain grandeur of Argyll.

LOCATION

Midway between Oban and Lochgilphead on A816.

Arduaine, by Oban, Argyll PA34 4XG

Telephone 01852 200233
Fax 01852 200214

E-mail: lochmelfort@bestloved.com

SCOTLAND

OWNERS

Nigel and Kyle Schofield

ROOM RATES

Single occupancy	£55 - £75
24 Doubles/Twins	£80 - £115
2 Superior Doubles	£110 - £155

Includes breakfast and VAT

CHARGE/CREDIT CARDS

• MC • VI

RATINGS & AWARDS

S.T.B. ★★★★ *Hotel*
A.A. ★★★ ❀❀ *76%*

FACILITIES

On site: *Garden*
1 meeting room/max 40 people
Nearby: *Fishing, riding, sailing, windsurfing, walking, mountain biking*

RESTRICTIONS

Limited facilities for disabled guests

ATTRACTIONS

Arduaine Gardens, Mull, Iona, Kerra, Gigha and Arran Islands, Inveraray, Glencoe, Dunstaffnage Castle and Chapel

AFFILIATIONS

Scotland's Hotels of Distinction

NEAREST

MAJOR CITY:
Glasgow - 110 miles/2 hrs

MAJOR AIRPORT:
Glasgow - 100 miles/2 hrs

RAILWAY STATION:
Oban - 19 miles/30 mins

RESERVATIONS

Toll free in US/Canada: 800-223-6510 or 800-437-2687
Quote ***Best Loved***

ACCESS CODES

SABRE/ABACUS UI 21454
APOLLO/GALILEO UI 83670
WORLDSPAN UI LOCHA
AMADEUS UI GLALOC

For information about hotel affiliations see page 14

• *Map p.494*
ref: D8

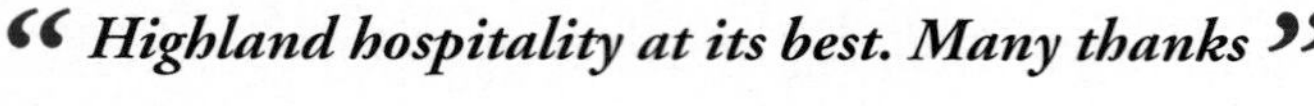
“ Highland hospitality at its best. Many thanks ”

Mr & Mrs McAlpine, Kent

THE MANOR HOUSE

18th century duke's residence

SCOTLAND

Gallanach Road, Oban,
Argyll PA34 4LS

Telephone 01631 562087
Fax 01631 563053

E-mail: *manoroban@bestloved.com*

MANAGER
Gabriella Wijker

RATES PER PERSON
Single occupancy £70 - £110
11 Doubles/Twins £50 - £80
Includes full breakfast, dinner and VAT

CHARGE/CREDIT CARDS

AMERICAN
EXPRESS
• *MC* • *VI*

RATINGS & AWARDS
S.T.B. ★★★★ *Hotel*
A.A. ★★ ❀ *76%*
Taste of Scotland

FACILITIES
On site: *Garden*
Nearby: *Golf, fishing, riding*

RESTRICTIONS
No children under 12 years
No facilities for disabled guests
Pets by arrangement
Closed Sun evening thru Tues mid Nov - Feb

ATTRACTIONS
Ferries to the Western Isles,
Distilleries, Glencoe,
Rare Breeds Park,
Salmon Centre,
Mull of Kintyre

AFFILIATIONS
Independent

NEAREST
MAJOR CITY:
Glasgow - 95 miles/2¼ hrs

MAJOR AIRPORT:
Glasgow - 90 miles/2 hrs

RAILWAY STATION:
Oban - ¼ mile/2 mins

RESERVATIONS
Direct with hotel
Quote ***Best Loved***

ACCESS CODES
Not applicable

The elegance of bygone days and gateway to the Western Isles

Late Georgian style, The Manor House was built in 1780 as the principal residence of the Duke of Argyll's Oban estate. Today it is an hotel which preserves the elegance of bygone days. The Manor House Hotel occupies a prime position overlooking Oban Bay, the adjacent islands and the mountains of Movern and Mull.

The elegant dining room offers guests a fine blend of Scottish and French cooking, with an emphasis on local seafood and game in season. The hotel has a fine cellar of wines and a wide selection of malt whiskies.

All bedrooms are twin or double bedded, and all have en suite bathrooms, TV and tea-making facilities.

The hotel is quietly located, yet within easy walking distance of the town. Oban is Scotland's main port for trips to the Western Isles. Towering above Oban is McCaig's Folly, an unfinished replica of the Roman Colosseum, built by a local banker in the 19th century. On the mainland, nearby Glencoe is one of Scotland's wildest and most celebrated glens. Special mini-breaks are available for stays of two nights or more.

LOCATION

Follow signs to MacBrayne Ferries. Continue past ferry entrance for 300 metres. Manor House is on the right hand side.

"Your staff were courteous and greatly contributed to my new found love of Scotland"

Kyle Gibson, USA

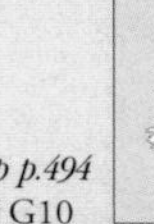

• Map p.494 ref: G10

Edinburgh town house

MELVIN HOUSE HOTEL

Stop Press! A new comer to Edinburgh's fashionable West End

In 1766, 22-year-old James Craig won a public competition to design a New Town for Edinburgh which would expand the city beyond the confines of the rocky outcrop dominated by Edinburgh Castle. Craig's neo-Classical plan extended north of Princes Street, and by the late-19th century the final piece of the New Town development, the West End, neared completion.

It was here, in 1883, that John Ritchie-Findlay, legendary owner of Scotland's national newspaper, 'The Scotsman', built himself a handsome terraced house, which has now been transformed into a first class hotel. Renowned architect, Sidney Mitchell, was instructed to 'cut no corners' in the construction of his elegant and spacious home. Extensively restored, Melvin House remains full of grand Victorian character, intricate mouldings, dark wood panelling and imposing marble fireplaces in the public rooms. The generously sized bedrooms, which can provide exceptional value-for-money family accommodation, boast views over the city to the castle or the ancient kingdom of Fife. A short walk from the Princes Street shops and major attractions such as the National Gallery of Scotland, Melvin House's location is hard to beat and business travellers are well-placed for the city's financial and business communities as well as the hotel's own stately conference rooms.

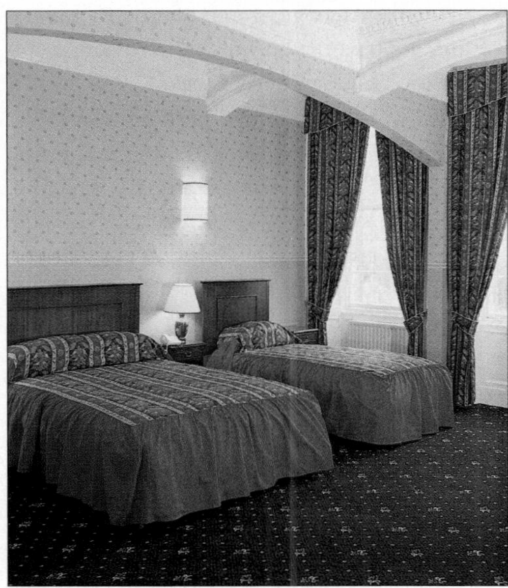

LOCATION

5 mins from the west end of Princes Street.

3 Rothesay Terrace, Edinburgh EH3 7RY

Telephone 0131 225 5084
Fax 0131 226 5085

E-mail: *melvinhouse@bestloved.com*

OWNER

Ian Mackenzie

MANAGERS

Colin and Graeme MacKenzie

ROOM RATES

Single occupancy	*£75 - £115*
10 Doubles/Twins	*£120*
6 Executive Doubles/Twins	*£140 - £160*
6 Family rooms	*£140 - £180*

Includes full breakfast and VAT

CHARGE/CREDIT CARDS

• DC • MC • VI

RATINGS & AWARDS

S.T.B. ★★★ Hotel

FACILITIES

On site: *4 meeting rooms/max 80 people*
Nearby: *Golf, swimming*

RESTRICTIONS

No facilities for disabled guests
Pets by arrangement

ATTRACTIONS

Edinburgh Castle, Holyrood House, Royal Mile, National Art Gallery of Scotland, Dynamic Earth, Royal Yacht Britannia

AFFILIATIONS

Preston's Global Hotels

NEAREST

MAJOR CITY:
Edinburgh

MAJOR AIRPORT:
Edinburgh - 8 miles/25 mins

RAILWAY STATION:
Haymarket - ¼ mile/10 mins

RESERVATIONS

Toll free in US: 800-544-9993
Quote ***Best Loved***

ACCESS CODES

Not applicable

• Map p.494 ref: E6

“ If, like me, you want the very best of both worlds - a remote location with a high level of comfort and hospitality - Mullardoch House provides that very rare blend of both ”

Harry Eastman, Winchester

MULLARDOCH HOUSE HOTEL *Edwardian hunting lodge*

SCOTLAND

Glen Cannich, by Beauly, Inverness-shire IV4 7LX

Telephone 01456 415460
Fax 01456 415460

E-mail: *mullardoch@bestloved.com*

OWNER

Andy Johnston

ROOM RATES

Single occupancy	*£59 - £65*
6 Doubles/Twins	*£94 - £106*
1 Suite	*£94 - £134*

Includes full breakfast and VAT

CHARGE/CREDIT CARDS

• *MC* • *VI*

RATINGS & AWARDS

S.T.B. ★★★★ *Hotel*

FACILITIES

On site: *Garden, stalking, mountain biking, fishing, boating*
1 meeting room/max 30 people
Nearby: *Golf, riding*

RESTRICTIONS

No facilities for disabled guests
No pets in public rooms

ATTRACTIONS

Culloden Battlefield, Loch Ness, Isle of Skye, Urquhart Castle, Eilean Donan Castle, Inverewe Gardens, Cawdor Castle, Whisky Trail

AFFILIATIONS

Independent

NEAREST

MAJOR CITY:
Inverness - 37 miles/1 hr

MAJOR AIRPORT:
Edinburgh - 185 miles/4 hrs
Inverness - 47 miles/1¼ hrs

RAILWAY STATION:
Inverness - 37 miles/1 hr

RESERVATIONS

Direct with hotel
Quote ***Best Loved***

ACCESS CODES

Not applicable

A remote oasis of refinement in the majestic wilderness of the highlands

There is little hope of losing your way along the eight mile single track road as it winds its way along the River Cannich to Mullardoch House; it leads nowhere else! But within this highland wilderness of lochs, glens and munros (mountains of over 3000 feet), you will feel as remote as it is possible to be in the British Isles.

Mullardoch House was built in 1912 as a hunting lodge. Today, it stands dwarfed amongst the giants of Glen Cannich, an oasis of refinement and luxury - and most reasonably priced. The rooms are big and comfortable, silently in awe of the vast landscapes beyond the picture windows. The decor, too, soft and traditional, complements the splendour all around. Indeed, on fine days as you sit in the garden, you will think twice before contradicting the tranquillity with conversation. The food is exactly as it should be: lots of local game - venison and salmon - and seasonal vegetables contrasting with delicious, freshly-caught west coast seafood. Typically in these parts, the excellent wine list includes a choice of over 40 malt whiskies.

Being so central in the highlands, there is no shortage of things to see and do; sightseeing the great fortresses, castles and stone circles; riding or walking amongst the woodlands and munros; stalking, shooting and fishing; or sniffing out your favourites on a whisky trail. Sheer heaven!

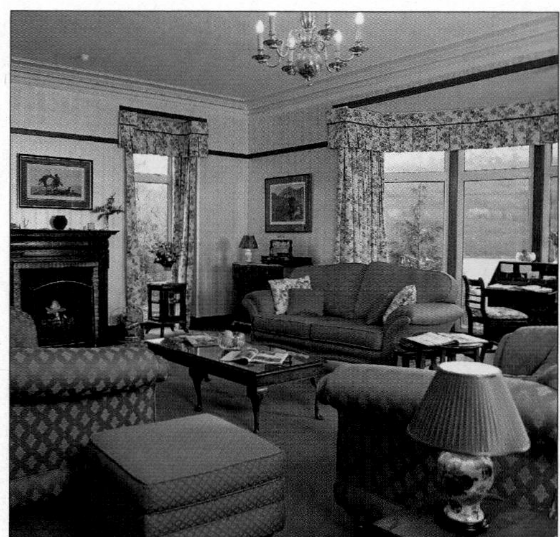

LOCATION

West from Inverness on the A862, then onto the A831 at Beauly. At Cannich, take the Glen Cannich road signposted to the hotel. Courtesy transport from Inverness available on request.

" There is a distinctive difference at your hotel, it shines with warmth, kindness and understanding for the traveller "

Anne M Wenninger, Hartford, WI USA

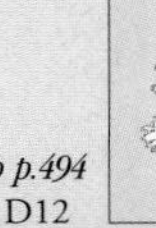

• Map p.494 ref: D12

Regency town house

NORTH WEST CASTLE HOTEL

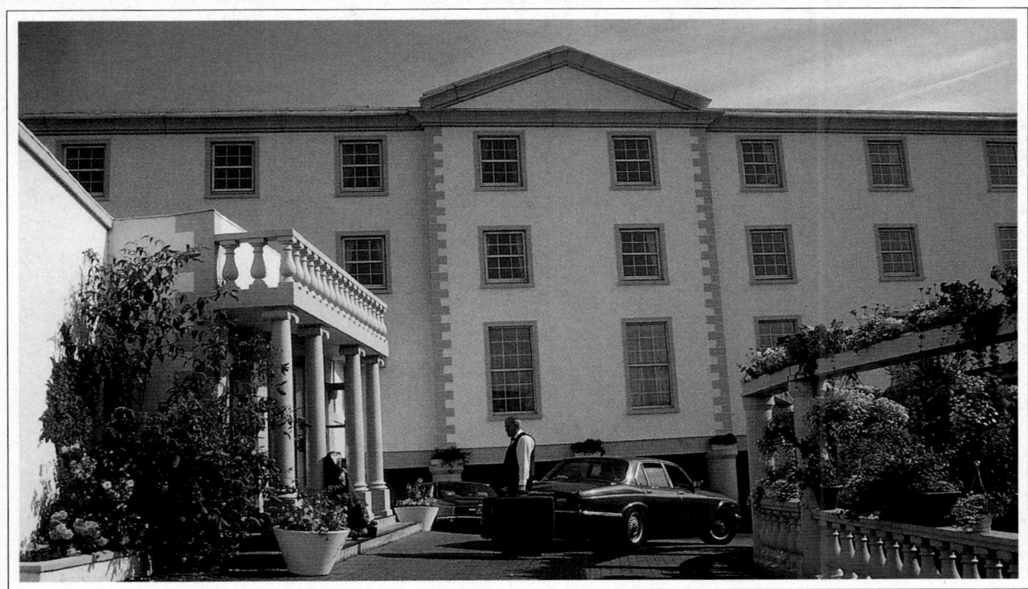

The warmest of welcomes in a polar explorer's historic home

The hotel is in the south-west corner of Scotland, but there is good reason for its name. It was built in 1820 by polar explorer Sir John Ross, famed for his efforts to find the North West Passage above the American continent. Ross put his love of seafaring into the house. He made it face north west. Its front windows command the whole length of Loch Ryan. In 1833 he added a cabin room, facsimile of his cabin aboard his steamship 'Victory'.

North West Castle retains its Regency elegance. Its Royal Suite was once occupied by His Royal Highness the Duke of Edinburgh. All 73 bedrooms are graciously furnished with comfortable extras. The Regency Dining Room is widely acclaimed for its fine cuisine. A local pianist plays each evening during dinner.

North West Castle was the first hotel in the world to have its own indoor curling rink. Other facilities include a heated swimming pool with spa bath, saunas, sunbeds, multi-gym, short carpet bowling, snooker, pool and table tennis. For the golfer, the hotel has all inclusive packages at three local courses. Other nearby options include riding, tennis, sailing and free squash at the local club.

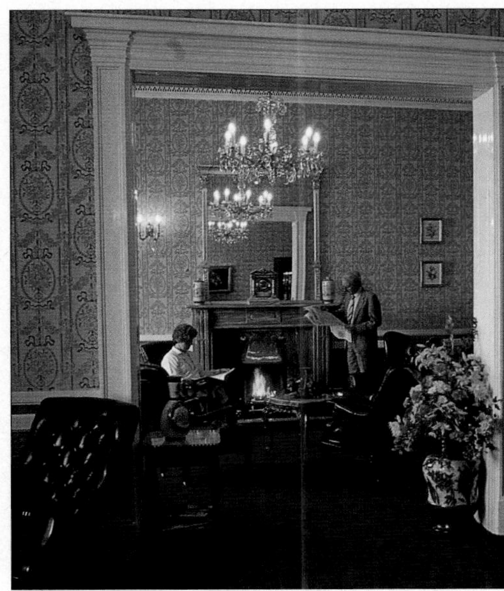

LOCATION

When approaching Stranraer on A75 or A77, follow signs for the ferries. Turn sharp left opposite the Stena ferry terminal.

Stranraer, Dumfries & Galloway DG9 8EH

Telephone 01776 704413
Fax 01776 702646

E-mail: *nwcastle@bestloved.com*

SCOTLAND

OWNERS

The McMillan family

GENERAL MANAGER

Hamilton McMillan Jr

ROOM RATES

3 Singles	*£55 - £80*
64 Doubles/Twins	*£77 - £110*
1 Four-poster	*£97*
5 Suites	*£97 - £107*

Includes full breakfast and VAT

CHARGE/CREDIT CARDS

• MC • VI

RATINGS & AWARDS

S.T.B. ★★★★ *Hotel*
R.A.C. ★★★★ *Dining Award 1*
A.A. ★★★★ ❀ *68%*

FACILITIES

On site: *Garden, indoor pool, sauna, jacuzzi, gym, snooker, carpet bowls, table tennis, pool, curling (in season)*
2 meeting rooms/max 200 people
Nearby: *Golf, riding, fitness, tennis, fishing, hunting/shooting, yachting, squash*

RESTRICTIONS

None

ATTRACTIONS

Logan Botanical Gardens, Gem Rock Museum, Castle Kennedy Gardens, Culzean Castle, Whithorn Dig, Glenluce Abbey

AFFILIATIONS

Independent

NEAREST

MAJOR CITY:
Glasgow - 85 miles/2 hrs

MAJOR AIRPORT:
Glasgow - 85 miles/2 hrs

FERRY PORT/RAILWAY STATION:
Stranraer - 1 mile/5 mins

RESERVATIONS

Direct with hotel
Quote ***Best Loved***

ACCESS CODES

Not applicable

• Map p.494 ref: G9

"Henry and I (Tessa the Scottie) choose the Old Manor for the nice friendly atmosphere and good walks - it's like staying with friends"

Tessa, with Henry & Elspeth Borthwick, Oxton

OLD MANOR HOTEL

Country house hotel

Lundin Links, Near St Andrews, Fife KY8 6AJ

Telephone 01333 320368
Fax 01333 320911

E-mail: oldmanor@bestloved.com

OWNERS

The Clark Family

ROOM RATES

1 Single	£80
8 Doubles/Twins	£135
14 Superior Doubles/Twins	£180

Includes full breakfast and VAT

CHARGE/CREDIT CARDS

• DC • JCB • MC • VI

RATINGS & AWARDS

S.T.B. ★★★★ Hotel
A.A. ★★★ ❀❀ 74%
Taste of Scotland

FACILITIES

On site: Garden
3 meeting rooms/max 180 people
Nearby: Golf, fishing, riding, tennis, squash, bowls, beaches

RESTRICTIONS

No pets in public rooms
Limited facilities for disabled guests

ATTRACTIONS

Deep Sea World, Crail, Anstruther, St Andrews Cathedral, St Andrews Golf Course, Falkland Palace

AFFILIATIONS

Scotland's Hotels of Distinction

NEAREST

MAJOR CITY:
St Andrews - 12 miles/20 mins
Edinburgh - 35 miles/40 mins

MAJOR AIRPORT:
Edinburgh - 30 miles/45 mins

RAILWAY STATION:
Markinch - 6 miles/10 mins

RESERVATIONS

Toll free in US: 800-437-2687
Toll free in UK: 0800 980 2420
Quote **Best Loved**

ACCESS CODES

AMADEUS HK EDIOLD
APOLLO/GALILEO HT 28503
SABRE/ABACUS HK 53935
WORLDSPAN HK OLDMS

A choice of two restaurants, excellent service and golf galore

This pleasant hotel is only 20 minutes from St Andrews itself, looking out on to the Lundin Links and Leven Open qualifying golf courses. The Old Manor is a fine old country house, situated in its own grounds with impressive views over Largo Bay. All of the public rooms are comfortably furnished to provide an easy place to relax. Many of the comfortable bedrooms have delightful sea views; all are en suite.

Chef Alan Brunt and his team have won two AA rosettes and credits in top guides for their imaginative use of local produce and seafood. The old Coachman's Grill in the grounds offers fine chargrilled steaks and seafood in a less formal atmosphere with its real ale and over 100 malt whiskies.

Golf enthusiasts will enjoy the hotel's 'golf à la carte' programme, where you can choose convenient tee times at over 30 courses within an hour's drive. There is also a great deal for non-golfers. St Andrews has beautiful beaches and Scotland's oldest university. The surrounding area has plenty of leisure parks, museums, castles, stately homes and gardens.

A wonderful venue for a wedding reception or a honeymoon.

LOCATION

Exit 2a from M90 on to A92 to St Andrews. At roundabout take third exit - A915 to St Andrews. Lundin Links is 1 mile past Leven. The Old Manor is on right as you enter village.

"A perfect oasis"

Gail and Diane Nelles, USA

• *Map p.494 ref: G8*

SCOTLAND

13th century castle

OLD MANSION HOUSE

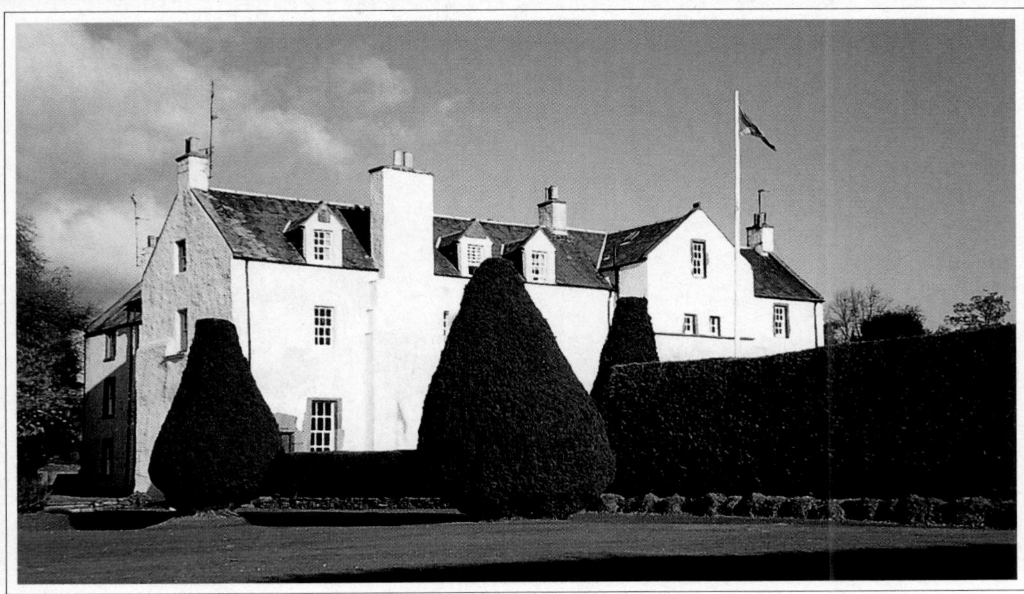

Braveheart remembered in this haunt of bon vivants

Cross the threshold of the Old Mansion House and you walk into centuries of Scots history. In the 13th century, it was an important castle in Sir William (Braveheart) Wallace's crusade to rid Scotland of the English. A monument to his soul stands in the estate. The castle was converted in the 17th century to a country mansion by The Earl of Strathmore who built the famous French style Glamis Castle, the birthplace of the Queen Mother, which lies just over the Sidlaw Hills.

The Old Mansion House is now a small luxury hotel to be remembered as much for splendid rooms as for the talents of its award-winning chef. Six comfortable bedrooms (all named like the Earl of Strathmore Suite on the right) and a Lodge House are luxuriously appointed and brimming with character. As is the Library from whose comprehensive collection of malt whiskies from all over Scotland there is much to learn!

Dining is something of a ritual and dedicated to bon vivants! Chateaubriand is carved at the table with a variety of flambéed dishes to follow. The Angus beef is reared on its home ground, the Scottish Tay Salmon is fresh from its native river and the wine list does everything required of it to complement the excellence of the cuisine.

The Old Mansion House is ideal for walking, shooting and lovers of Scottish heritage. For golfers, it's a seventh heaven with such courses as Carnoustie, Gleneagles, St Andrews and many more within about a 20 minute drive.

LOCATION

Take the A923 Coupar Angus slip road off the Dundee Kingsway, through Birkhill/Muirhead village, to the B954. Follow the tourist signs and the hotel is 2½ miles on the left.

Auchterhouse, By Dundee, Angus DD3 0QN

Telephone 01382 320366
Fax 01382 320400

E-mail: *oldmansion@bestloved.com*

OWNERS

Jannick and Maxine Bertschy

ROOM RATES

Single occupancy	*£85*
5 Doubles/Twins	*£110*
1 Honeymoon Suite	*£150*
1 Family suite	*£145*
2 Bedroomed Lodge House	*£170*

Children under 12 years free when sharing with parents

CHARGE/CREDIT CARDS

• *DC* • *MC* • *VI*

RATINGS & AWARDS

S.T.B. ★★★★ Hotel

A.A. ★★★ ❀❀ 77%

Taste of Scotland

Booker Prize for Excellence 2000 for 'Best Hotel in the UK'

FACILITIES

On site: *Woodland and gardens, croquet, squash, tennis, outdoor heated pool, heli-pad*

2 meeting rooms/max 50 people

Nearby: *Golf, shooting, riding, walking, skiing*

RESTRICTIONS

No pets

No smoking in bedrooms

ATTRACTIONS

The Discovery, Glamis Castle, The Glens, Affleck Castle, Blair Castle, Arbroath Castle, Claypotts Castle, Glenshee, St. Andrew's, Carnoustie and Gleneagles golf courses

AFFILIATIONS

Independent

NEAREST

MAJOR CITY:

Dundee - 7 miles/10 mins

MAJOR AIRPORT:

Edinburgh - 60 miles/1 hr

Dundee - 7 miles/10 mins

RAILWAY STATION:

Dundee - 7 miles/10 mins

RESERVATIONS

Toll free in US: 800-437-2687

Quote ***Best Loved***

ACCESS CODES

Not applicable

• Map p.494 ref: G9

“One of the most honest and enterprising restaurants in Britain”

R W Apple Jnr, The New York Times

THE PEAT INN

Restaurant with rooms

Peat Inn, by Cupar, Fife KY15 5LH

Telephone 01334 840206
Fax 01334 840530

E-mail: peat@bestloved.com

OWNERS
David and Patricia Wilson

ROOM RATES
8 Suites £135 - £145
Includes continental breakfast and VAT

CHARGE/CREDIT CARDS

• MC • VI

RATINGS & AWARDS
S.T.B. ★★★★★ Restaurant with Rooms
A.A. ★★ ❀❀❀
A.A. Romantic Hotel
Andrew Harper Award - Hideaway Report
Taste of Scotland

FACILITIES
On site: Garden
1 meeting room/max 12 people
Nearby: Riding

RESTRICTIONS
None

ATTRACTIONS
St Andrews, East Neuk fishing villages, Falkland Palace, Inchcolm Abbey, Kellie Castle

AFFILIATIONS
Independent

NEAREST
MAJOR CITY:
Edinburgh - 40 miles/1 hr

MAJOR AIRPORT:
Edinburgh - 40 miles/1 hr

RAILWAY STATION:
Cupar - 6 miles/10 mins

RESERVATIONS
Direct with hotel
Quote **Best Loved**

ACCESS CODES
Not applicable

Inspirational Scottish cuisine in a class of its own

The Peat Inn is one of Scotland's most celebrated restaurants and attracts food lovers from around the world to the tiny rural village which takes its name. David Wilson has been cooking here for some 28 years, promoting the very best of Scottish produce and the virtues of simple but innovative cooking skills, passionate beliefs that have inspired a whole generation of Scottish chefs to follow in his footsteps. The restaurant is a delight with open fires to welcome you in the seating areas, glorious arrangements of fresh flowers and tapestries adorning the walls. David's enthusiasm is as strong today as ever and both he and his dedicated team strive to provide exemplary service and great cooking accompanied by remarkable wines from a wine cellar notable for its breadth, interest and value-for-money price list.

The inn offers eight wonderfully comfortable and peaceful suites in the garden residence behind the restaurant. Sympathetically designed by Patricia Wilson, seven of the suites are split level, while one is single level, and each and every one features a marble bathroom, a pretty sitting room and welcome extras such as a selection of homemade cakes and fresh fruit.

LOCATION

Situated in the village of Peat Inn at the junction of the B940/B941, 6 miles south west of St Andrews.

"This is by far the friendliest and best hotel, with delicious food that is beautifully presented. I love all the little extras"

Angela Taylor, Ashton-under-Lyne, Lancashire

• Map p.494 ref: E10

Whisky family home

PIERSLAND HOUSE HOTEL

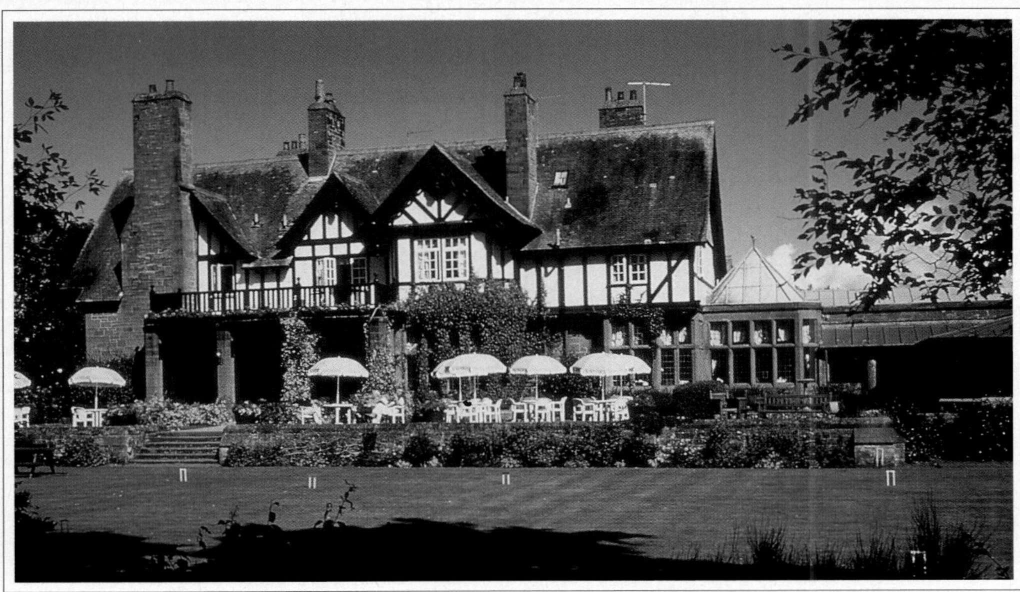

Enjoy Royal Troon - in the world's finest setting for a single malt

Piersland was built at the end of the 19th century by Alexander Walker, grandson of Johnnie Walker who founded the firm and gave his name to the whisky. A most attractive building, Piersland has two extra reasons to be chosen for a Scottish holiday. Royal Troon Golf Club, scene of the 1997 Open Championship, is just across the road. Alexander's own Walker Lounge, luxuriously panelled in oak and with its original wood carvings and fireplaces today offers the choice of 60 fine single malts. There is no better place in the world to enjoy Scotland's most famous product.

Piersland is set in landscaped grounds that include an oriental garden. You enter through the elegant Minstrel Hall. Sumptuous meals are served in two restaurants and the verandah is the perfect place to enjoy a traditional afternoon tea. Within ten miles is the birthplace of Robert Burns and Culzean Castle, home of the Kennedy clan. Turnberry, Old Prestwick and eight other top golf courses are within 30 minute's drive. Glasgow, Edinburgh, Stirling, Loch Lomond and the Trossachs are within easy reach.

LOCATION

5 miles north of Ayr.

SCOTLAND

Craigend Road, Troon, Ayrshire KA10 6HD

Telephone 01292 314747
Fax 01292 315613

E-mail: piersland@bestloved.com

GENERAL MANAGER
Karel Kuhler

ROOM RATES

1 Single	£63 - £83
13 Doubles/Twins	£110 - £119
13 Suites	£115 - £135
1 Four-poster	£115 - £165

Includes full breakfast and VAT

CHARGE/CREDIT CARDS

• DC • MC • VI

RATINGS & AWARDS
S.T.B. ★★★★ Hotel
A.A. ★★★ ❀❀ 74%

FACILITIES
On site: Garden
3 meeting rooms/max 150 people
Nearby: Golf, riding, fitness, yachting, tennis, hunting/shooting

RESTRICTIONS
Pets by arrangement

ATTRACTIONS
Turnberry, Culzean Castle, Burns Cottage, Isle of Arran, Brodick Castle

AFFILIATIONS
Independent

NEAREST
MAJOR CITY:
Glasgow - 25 miles/30 mins

MAJOR AIRPORT:
Prestwick/Glasgow - 3 miles/10 mins

RAILWAY STATION:
Troon - ½ mile/5 mins

RESERVATIONS
Direct with hotel
Quote **Best Loved**

ACCESS CODES
Not applicable

"Cosy, very Scottish and a lovely atmosphere"

Sonia & William Macleod, Auckland, New Zealand

PRESTONFIELD HOUSE

17th century Scottish mansion

**Priestfield Road,
Edinburgh EH16 5UT**

**Telephone 0131 668 3346
Fax 0131 668 3976**

E-mail: *prestonfield@bestloved.com*

OWNERS
The Stevenson family

GENERAL MANAGER
Richard Scott

ROOM RATES

Single occupancy	£145 - £245
29 Doubles/Twins	£145 - £245
2 Suites	£290 - £490

Includes full breakfast, complimentary newspaper and VAT

CHARGE/CREDIT CARDS

• DC • MC • VI

RATINGS & AWARDS
S.T.B. ★★★★ Hotel

FACILITIES
On site: *Garden, golf, heli-pad*
6 meeting rooms/max 600 people
Nearby: *Riding*

RESTRICTIONS
None

ATTRACTIONS
Edinburgh Castle, National Art Gallery, Royal Mile, Botanical Gardens, Holyrood House, Princes Street

AFFILIATIONS
Selected British Hotels

NEAREST
MAJOR CITY:
Edinburgh

MAJOR AIRPORT:
Edinburgh - 10 miles/25 mins

RAILWAY STATION:
Waverley - 2 miles/7 mins

RESERVATIONS
Toll free in US: 800-323-5463
Quote **Best Loved**

ACCESS CODES
SABRE/ABACUS HK 25739
AMADEUS HK EDIPRE
WORLDSPAN HK PREST
APOLLO/GALILEO HK 92198

The elegant country mansion in the heart of Edinburgh

Prestonfield House is one of Scotland's finest historic mansions. Its location, five minutes from Princes Street, makes it ideal for visiting Edinburgh. The house and the unique early 19th century Round Stables are surrounded by a golf course and set in 13 acres of parkland and gardens which are designated as a landscape of outstanding historical and scenic beauty.

Prestonfield was built in 1687 for Sir James Dick, Lord Provost of Edinburgh. The Tapestry, Leather and Italian Rooms contain their distinctive late 17th and early 18th century decorative schemes and much of the family collection of paintings and furniture remain in their original settings. Great care has been taken to ensure that the introduction of modern facilities does not conflict with the historic fabric nor the character of this important building.

Continuing the tradition of 'kindness on kindness, cheerful meals and balmy rest' that Benjamin Franklin found in 1759, Prestonfield has a high quality à la carte restaurant in the Old Dining Room. Few hotels in any capital city anywhere in the world match Prestonfield for its comfort as a country house hotel, combined with its nearness to the city centre. There is ample parking within the grounds, and shops, amenities and historic sites of Edinburgh are nearby.

LOCATION

Turn off the A7 Dalkeith Road into Priestfield Road, a little to the north of Cameron Toll roundabout. Prestonfield House is signposted.

"If there's anywhere better than here then it must have pearly gates"

Lyn Foggo & Walter Butler, Edinburgh

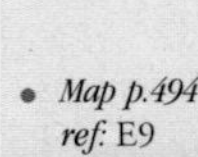

17th century hunting lodge — ROMAN CAMP COUNTRY HOUSE

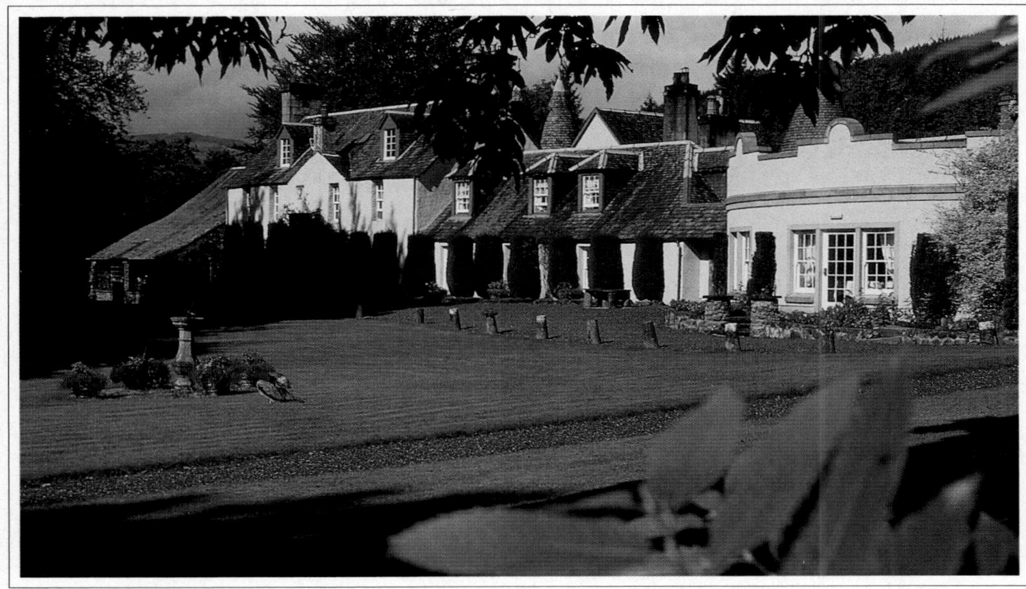

Historic house centrally situated for Callander and the Trossachs

The house takes its name from earthworks to the east of its walled gardens, believed to be the site of a Roman fort. It was built originally as a hunting lodge in 1625 for the Dukes of Perth. It passed into the ownership of Viscount Esher in 1897. The turrets that give the building its unique character were added at that time. The house became an hotel in 1939.

Each of the 14 bedrooms has its own distinctive style and character. Some have coombed walls and furniture dating back 200 years. All are equipped with the little thoughtful extras that make your stay comfortable and enjoyable.

The library, panelled in 16th century oak, has a log fire, lit even in summer. The oval-shaped restaurant features tapestries of English cathedrals woven by Elizabeth Esher in the 1930s. Menus are prepared from local ingredients in season. There are tasty à la carte and vegetarian menus.

Beyond the 20 acres of tranquil parkland and gardens with views of the River Teith are the Trossachs and the Highlands. This is a land of mountain and glen, rolling pasture and heather moor. It is a marvellous base for your Scottish holiday.

LOCATION

From M9 Exit 10, head north on the A84 through the village of Callander, then turn left down a 300-yard drive at the east end of Callander main street.

SCOTLAND

Off Main Street, Callander, Perthshire FK17 8BG

Telephone 01877 330003
Fax 01877 331533

E-mail: roman@bestloved.com

OWNERS

Eric and Marion Brown

ROOM RATES

Single occupancy	£80 - £140
4 Doubles/Twins	£100 - £120
7 Superior Doubles	£160
3 Suites	£180

Includes full breakfast and VAT

CHARGE/CREDIT CARDS

• DC • MC • VI

RATINGS & AWARDS

S.T.B. ★★★★ Hotel
R.A.C. Blue Ribbon ★★★ Dining Award 4
A.A. ★★★ ❀❀❀ 74%
Taste of Scotland

FACILITIES

On site: Garden, fishing, heli-pad
2 meeting rooms/max 100 people
Nearby: Golf, fishing, shooting

RESTRICTIONS

Pets by arrangement

ATTRACTIONS

Rob Roy country, Castle Campbell, Inchmahome Priory, Stirling Castle, Loch Lomond

AFFILIATIONS

Selected British Hotels

NEAREST

MAJOR CITY:
Edinburgh - 52 miles/1 hr

MAJOR AIRPORT:
Edinburgh - 46 miles/50 mins

RAILWAY STATION:
Stirling - 17 miles/30 mins

RESERVATIONS

Toll free in US: 800-323-5463
Quote **Best Loved**

ACCESS CODES

Not applicable

• Map p.494 ref: H11

"Drinks mysteriously appeared on silver trays and waiters attended to our every need. Had I coughed or sneezed, one of them would surely have proffered a perfumed handkerchief"

Giles Milton, The Mail on Sunday

THE ROXBURGHE HOTEL & GOLF COURSE *18th century retreat*

**Heiton, Kelso,
Roxburghshire TD5 8JZ**

**Telephone 01573 450331
Fax 01573 450611**

E-mail: *roxburgh@bestloved.com*

OWNERS
The Duke and Duchess of Roxburghe

GENERAL MANAGER
Stephen Browning

ROOM RATES

2 Singles	£120
13 Doubles/Twins	£120 - £165
5 Four-posters	£205
2 Suites	£255

Includes full breakfast and VAT

CHARGE/CREDIT CARDS

• DC • MC • VI

RATINGS & AWARDS
S.T.B. ★★★★ Hotel
R.A.C. ★★★
A.A. ★★★ ❀❀ 74%
Taste of Scotland

FACILITIES
On site: *Croquet, tennis, gardens, health & beauty, trout loch, clay pigeon shooting school, heli-pad, 18-hole championship golf course*
3 meeting rooms/max 150 people
Nearby: *Fishing*

RESTRICTIONS
£8 surcharge per night for dogs

ATTRACTIONS
Floors Castle, Kelso Abbey, Jedburgh Abbey, Edinburgh

AFFILIATIONS
The Celebrated Hotels Collection
Selected British Hotels

NEAREST
MAJOR CITY:
Edinburgh - 58 miles/1 hr
Newcastle - 60 miles/1 hr
MAJOR AIRPORT:
Edinburgh - 58 miles/1 hr
RAILWAY STATION:
Berwick-upon-Tweed - 20 miles/35 mins

RESERVATIONS
Toll free in US: 800-322-2403
Quote **Best Loved**

ACCESS CODES
Not applicable

In 200 acres, an old country house with its own championship golf course

Roxburghe is a beautiful country house hotel situated in the heart of the Scottish Borders owned by the Duke and Duchess of Roxburghe. You are invited to experience the unique character of this fine old gentleman's retreat.

Crackling log fires in spacious rooms, high levels of comfort and attentive, friendly attention are redolent of an earlier age. Only a small, intimate country hotel like Roxburghe can put you so entirely at ease. 22 bedrooms, fully equipped to care for today's discerning guest are luxuriously appointed. Some have four-poster beds with open log fires whilst others are romantically located in the delightful stables courtyard.

The 18-hole championship Roxburghe Golf Course was offically opened in July 1997 by HRH The Duke of York who was joined by Gavin Hastings, Nick Faldo and Colin Montgomerie competing in the first Roxburghe Challenge Charity Match. The course was designed by Dave Thomas to take advantatage of the stunning setting and the natural contours and character of the estate. His hallmark of deep challenging bunkers and generous rolling greens make this a truly competitive course.

A week or a weekend heaven sent for golfers!

LOCATION

From the A68 Edinburgh-Newcastle route, take A698 Jedburgh-Kelso road. The hotel is 3 miles south of Kelso on the outskirts of Heiton village.

"What a joy it is for world weary travellers to find an oasis of such calm and caring attention"

Sarah Lord, Calvin Klein Inc

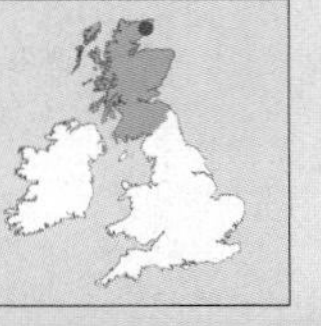

• *Map p.494 ref: F5*

83

Edwardian country house

ROYAL MARINE HOTEL

A place of comfort and calm in a wild and beautiful environment

The renowned Scottish architect, Sir Robert Lorimer, originally designed this as a private country house in the 1900s. A recent extensive restoration has taken place providing the modern amenities expected of a quality hotel. Features include a number of carved wooden fireplaces and an elegant stairway and reception foyer, all complemented by the chef's cuisine in the traditionally styled dining room.

The hotel is especially attractive to sportsmen. Nearby are local championship links golf courses including Brora, Golspie, Royal Dornoch and Tain.

It has its own boat on Loch Brora for fly fishing, its newly built leisure centre has a host of activities and facilities available to all residents.

Situated midway between Inverness and John O'Groats, Brora is ideal as a centre for touring the Northern Highlands and the Orkney Islands. The sparsely populated region abounds with birds and wild life. The rock formations are of particular interest to geologists and provide excellent hill walking.

LOCATION

One hour north of Inverness, just off A9 adjacent to James Braid's 18 hole links golf course.

SCOTLAND

Golf Road, Brora, Sutherland KW9 6QS

Telephone 01408 621252
Fax 01408 621181

E-mail: *royalmarine@bestloved.com*

GENERAL MANAGER

Robert Powell

ROOM RATES

Single occupancy	*£65*
18 Doubles/Twins	*£90 - £120*
2 Suites	*£120 - £150*
1 Family room	*£120*

Includes full breakfast and VAT

CHARGE/CREDIT CARDS

• *DC* • *MC* • *VI*

RATINGS & AWARDS

S.T.B. ★★★★ Hotel
A.A. ★★★ ❀ 72%
The Taste of Scotland

FACILITIES

On site: *Garden, indoor pool, sauna, steam rooms, spa bath, gym, solarium, curling, snooker, disabled bedroom*
2 meeting rooms/max 100 people
Nearby: *Golf, fishing, tennis*

RESTRICTIONS

Pets by arrangement

ATTRACTIONS

Dunrobin Castle, Orkney Islands, Clynelish Malt Whisky Distillery, Hunters of Brora Woollen Mills, Falls of Shin

AFFILIATIONS

Scotland's Hotels of Distinction

NEAREST

MAJOR CITY:
Inverness - 60 miles/1 hr

MAJOR AIRPORT:
Inverness - 70 miles/1¼ hrs

RAILWAY STATION:
Brora - ¼ mile/2 mins

RESERVATIONS

Toll free in US: 800-437-2687
Quote ***Best Loved***

ACCESS CODES

Not applicable

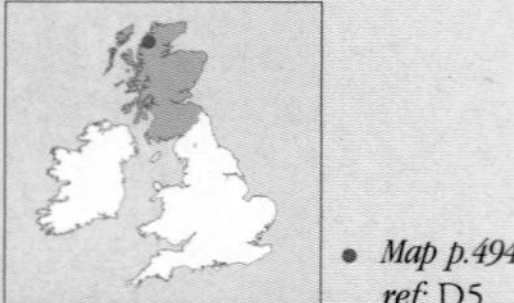

• Map p.494 ref: D5

" The views over the Summer Isles are still stunning and the food remains a major attraction "

Derek Cooper, Scotland on Sunday

SUMMER ISLES

19th century fishing inn

Achiltibuie, Ross-shire IV26 2YG

Telephone 01854 622282
Fax 01854 622251

E-mail: summer@bestloved.com

SCOTLAND

OWNERS
Mark and Geraldine Irvine

ROOM RATES

Single occupancy	£65 - £100
9 Doubles/Twins	£98 - £120
4 Suites	£170 - £200

Includes full breakfast and VAT

CHARGE/CREDIT CARDS
MC • VI

RATINGS & AWARDS
S.T.B. ★★★★ Hotel
The Good Food Guide - Restaurant of the Year 2000
Taste of Scotland

FACILITIES
Nearby: *Birdwatching, walking, fishing, scuba diving, sailing*

RESTRICTIONS
No facilities for disabled guests
No children under 6 years

ATTRACTIONS
Inverewe Gardens, Inverpolly Nature Reserve, Sutherland coast, Western Isles, Highlands

AFFILIATIONS
Independent

NEAREST
MAJOR CITY:
Inverness - 85 miles/2 hrs

MAJOR AIRPORT:
Edinburgh - 220 miles/5 hrs

RAILWAY STATION:
Garve - 60 miles/1½ hrs

RESERVATIONS
Direct with hotel
*Quote **Best Loved***

ACCESS CODES
Not applicable

An oasis of civilisation in wild, untouched landscape

Mark and Geraldine Irvine run this individual but sophisticated hotel which has belonged to the family since the late 1960s. It has established itself as an oasis of civilisation hidden away in a stunningly beautiful, but still wild and untouched landscape.

Nearly everything you eat there is home produced or locally caught. Scallops, lobsters, langoustines, crabs, halibut, turbot, salmon, venison, big brown eggs, wholesome brown bread fresh from the oven – the list of real food is endless. With such fresh ingredients, chef Chris Firth-Bernard provides delicious, healthy fare. Two new additions to the family of very finely appointed bedrooms are the Boathouse and William's Cottage, the latter sleeping four. Both are exquisite with stunning views.

After breakfast, Mark and Geraldine are happy to talk to you about fishing, walking or bird-watching. A local boat, the Hectoria, sails round the islands to show off seals and rare birds. You can also explore the scenery sub-aqua with the local diving school. Inverewe Gardens, Inverpolly Nature Reserve and the Sutherland coast are all within easy reach. This place has a huge amount to offer.

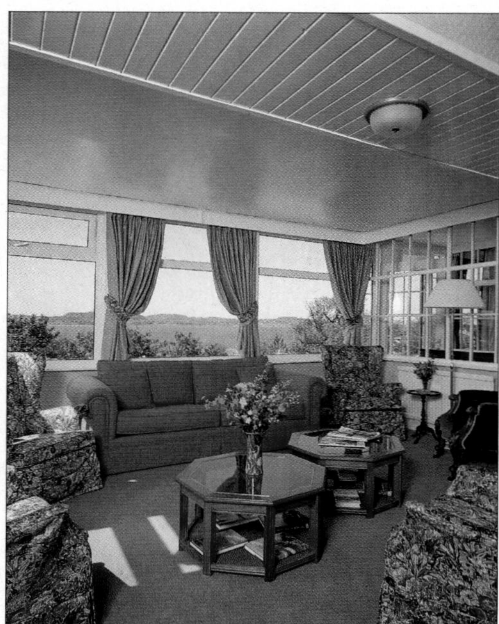

LOCATION

10 miles north of Ullapool, turn left on to a single track road. After 15 miles you reach the village of Achiltibuie. The hotel is just past the post office.

"An amazing hotel - every detail had been thought of - the food was fantastic and the staff made us feel special"

J Money, London

• *Map p.494 ref: D9*

Drover's inn

TAYCHREGGAN

Mountain grandeur, fascinating wildlife and lochside beauty

Surrounded by the grandeur of mountains, Taychreggan Hotel has nestled on the shores of magnificent Loch Awe for the past 300 years. Originally a cattle drover's inn, the old stone house and its cobbled courtyard form the centrepiece of the hotel where the aim is to woo visitors into feeling like house guests. Most of the beautiful en suite bedrooms overlook the loch; all offer high standards of quality, style and comfort.

Owner Annie Paul and her friendly and experienced staff have received great trade and consumer recognition and have scooped many prestigious awards. The magnificent view from the dining room is matched by superb Scottish cuisine, a comprehensive list of French wines and fine single malt whiskies.

You can visit historic places such as Inveraray or Kilchurn Castle, or choose from many outdoor activities. For hill walkers there are 13 peaks over 3,000 feet within an hour's drive. The hotel has its own fishing rights, boats and ghillie. Birds of prey and rare species can be seen in these breathtaking surroundings. Horse riding, deer stalking, water sports, loch cruises, golf and rough shooting can all be arranged.

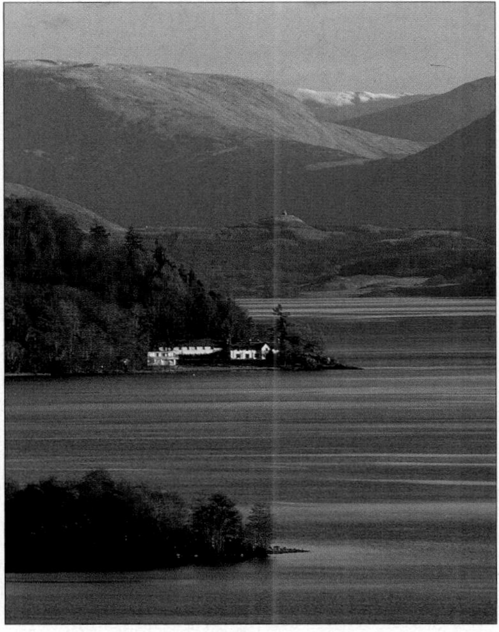

LOCATION

From Edinburgh: exit 10/M9 to Stirling, A84 to Callander, A85 to Crianlarich/Oban & left on to B845 to Kilchrenan/Taychreggan. Hotel is 7 miles on, at end of this single track road.

Kilchrenan, By Taynuilt, Argyll PA35 1HQ

Telephone 01866 833211
Fax 01866 833244

E-mail: *taychreggan@bestloved.com*

GENERAL MANAGER
Alastair Stevenson

ROOM RATES
19 Doubles/Twins £115 - £215
Includes full breakfast and VAT

CHARGE/CREDIT CARDS

 • *MC* • *VI*

RATINGS & AWARDS
S.T.B. ★★★★ *Hotel*
A.A. ★★★ ❀❀ *77%*
Taste of Scotland
Scotland The Brand
Investors in People

FACILITIES
On site: *Garden, fishing*
2 meeting rooms/max 14 people
Nearby: *Walking, gliding*

RESTRICTIONS
Not recommended for children under 14 years
No facilities for disabled guests
Pets by arrangement

ATTRACTIONS
Kilchurn Castle, Inveraray, loch cruises, forest walks, the gardens of Argyll

AFFILIATIONS
Preston's Global Hotels
Grand Heritage Hotels
Scotland's Hotels of Distinction

NEAREST
MAJOR CITY:
Glasgow - 90 miles/2 hrs
MAJOR AIRPORT:
Glasgow - 90 miles/2 hrs
RAILWAY STATION:
Taynuilt - 7 miles/15 mins

RESERVATIONS
Toll free in US: 800-544-9993 or 800-437-2687
Toll free in UK: 0800 975 5975
Quote ***Best Loved***

ACCESS CODES
Not applicable

For route planning map of Scotland see page 494

• Map p.494 ref: B6

"Absolutely fantastic. I definitely want to come back with more time"

Rick Stein, Seafood Restaurant, Cornwall

THE THREE CHIMNEYS

Restaurant with rooms

Colbost, Dunvegan, Isle of Skye IV55 8ZT

Telephone 01470 511258
Fax 01470 511358

E-mail: *3chimneys@bestloved.com*

OWNERS

Eddie and Shirley Spear

ROOM RATES

Single occupancy	*£130*
5 Suites	*£160*
1 Family room	*£250*

Includes buffet breakfast and VAT

CHARGE/CREDIT CARDS

• *MC* • *VI*

RATINGS & AWARDS

S.T.B. ★★★★★ *Restaurant with Rooms*

A.A. ★★ ❀❀❀ *82%*

WHICH? Hotel of the Year 2000

Scottish Chef's Special Award 1999 for outstanding contribution to the industry

FACILITIES

On site: *Garden, heli-pad*

1 meeting room/max 85 people

Nearby: *Canoeing, yachting, fishing, riding, mountain biking, walking*

RESTRICTIONS

No pets

No smoking in bedrooms or dining rooms

ATTRACTIONS

Dunvegan Castle, Bella Jane Boat Trips, Clan Donald Centre, Skye Silver, Outer Isles, Talisker Distillery, Neist Point Lighthouse, local art and crafts, local walks

AFFILIATIONS

Independent

NEAREST

MAJOR CITY:

Inverness - 130 miles/3 hrs

MAJOR AIRPORT:

Inverness - 130 miles/3 hrs

Edinburgh/Glasgow - 280 miles/5½ hrs

RAILWAY STATION:

Kyle of Lochalsh - 50 miles/1 hr

RESERVATIONS

Direct with hotel

Quote ***Best Loved***

ACCESS CODES

Not applicable

A cottage on the Isle of Skye with an international reputation for good food

The Isle of Skye is a wild place with a romance that is born of heroic lost causes and an island folk of indomitable spirit. You could argue that the idea of creating a gastronomic restaurant at the far north-west of the island was a folly as grand as Bonnie Prince Charlie's cause. That the venture is a resounding success with the world, it seems, beating a path to its door, says more about Shirley and Eddie Spear than words ever could.

Shirley is at the top of her profession, admired by her fellow chefs, with a string of awards to her name. In May last year, The Scottish Chefs Association presented her with a 'Special Award' elevating her to the elite of her kind. She was also one of 50 top chefs to prepare the banquet at the inaugural opening of the Scottish Parliament.

Eddie knows his wine. The list covers the New World and the traditional regions of France - but without the cliché; He sniffs out interesting wines from small, dedicated growers thereby paying his own personal compliment to his wife's brilliance.

A word about the restaurant: The copy reads, 'sympathetically reburbished in keeping with a crofter's cottage'; in fact, it is a very chic interpretation by artist and designer friends. The same goes for the sensational bedrooms across the courtyard in The House Over-By. No half measures here: five-star facilities with floor-to-ceiling windows admitting the vast panorama.

A wild and wonderful dream you can share!

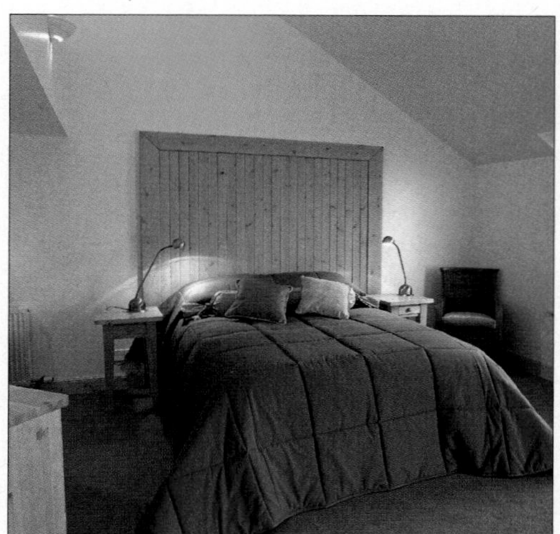

LOCATION

From Dunvegan village, take B884 to Glendale. Colbost is 4 miles from main road turn off. Follow Glendale signposts.

A keen Angler? Refer to page 472 for our Fishing Index

" A warm welcome, the freshest local food; and a great night's rest ... a charming hotel set in the most spectacular scenery "

Sir Chris Bonington

• Map p.494 ref: D6

Seaside hotel

TIGH AN EILEAN

A highland inn surrounded by dramatic sea and landscapes

Tigh-an-Eilean (House of the island) stands in a 200-year old fishing village on the seafront within a short stroll from the old jetty where the fishing boats unload their catch.This quiet unspoilt village, set in the Torridon Mountains, faces the Scottish National Trust's Isle of Pines, and has glorious views over Loch Shieldaig to Loch Torridon and the open sea beyond.

Cathryn and Christopher Field greet you with a warm welcome. There are two lounges and a cosy residents' honesty bar. The dining room, looking across the sea towards the sunset, offers menus that place emphasis on the finest local and regional produce from sea, river and hill. Specialities include seafood delivered direct from boat to the kitchen door that day. The reasonably priced wine list is short but thoughtfully chosen.

All bedrooms are en suite, most with a sea view. The furnishings, prints and paintings give each of them a character and charm all of their own.

This is the great outdoors where the aromatherapy of heather, Caledonian Pines and the sea is free; where the hill walker, the angler and the golfer will find their own paradise and sightseers by car can take in the spectacular scenery - try the the Beinn Eighe Nature Reserve or the 2000 ft Benlach na Bo pass to Applecross with its views across the sea to Skye. Astronomers will find a soul-mate in Christopher whose telescope is set up in the garden. The lure of Tigh an Eilean is ever present; one visit is never enough.

LOCATION

Take the A832 from Inverness to Kinlochewe. Turn left on to the A896 to Shieldaig.

Shieldaig, by Strathcarron, Ross-shire IV54 8XN

Telephone 01520 755251
Fax 01520 755321

E-mail: *tighan@bestloved.com*

SCOTLAND

OWNERS

Christopher and Cathryn Field

ROOM RATES

3 Singles £49.50
8 Doubles/Twins £110
Includes full breakfast and VAT

CHARGE/CREDIT CARDS

• MC • VI

RATINGS & AWARDS

S.T.B. ★★★★ Hotel
R.A.C. ★ Dining Award 3
A.A. ★ ❀ 74%

FACILITIES

On site: *Boat hire, fishing*
Nearby: *Hill walking, mountain climbing*

RESTRICTIONS

No facilities for disabled guests
No dogs in public rooms

ATTRACTIONS

Applecross Peninsula, Inverewe Gardens, Torridon loch and mountains, Beinn Eighe Nature Reserve, Isle of Skye

AFFILIATIONS

Independent

NEAREST

MAJOR CITY:
Inverness - 68 miles/1¾ hrs

MAJOR AIRPORT:
Glasgow - 223 miles/4¼ hrs
Dalcross - 78 miles/2 hrs

RAILWAY STATION:
Strathcarrow - 12 miles/30 mins

RESERVATIONS

Direct with hotel
*Quote **Best Loved***

ACCESS CODES

Not applicable

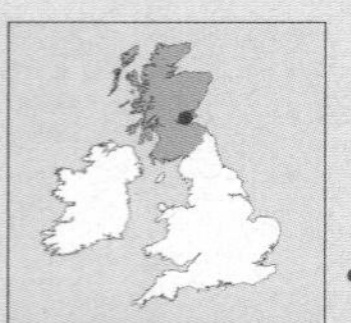

• Map p.494 ref: G9

" A truly remarkable find "

Gordon Walker, Inverness, Scotland

THE WOODSIDE HOTEL

Victorian hotel

Aberdour, Fife KY3 0SW

Telephone 01383 860328
Fax 01383 860920

E-mail: *woodside@bestloved.com*

OWNER
Stuart Dykes

GENERAL MANAGER
Avril Crichton

ROOM RATES

2 Singles	£45 - £80
14 Doubles/Twins	£50 - £80
1 Four-poster	£55 - £80
2 Family rooms	£55 - £75
1 Suite	£100 - £120

Includes full breakfast, newspaper and VAT

CHARGE/CREDIT CARDS

 • JCB • MC • VI

RATINGS & AWARDS
S.T.B. ★★★ Hotel
R.A.C. ★★★ Dining Award 1
A.A. ★★ 68%

FACILITIES
On site: *2 meeting rooms/max 80 people*
Nearby: *Golf, tennis, fitness, yachting, fishing, riding, hunting/shooting*

RESTRICTIONS
No facilities for disabled guests

ATTRACTIONS
St Andrews town & golf course, Edinburgh City & Castle, Blair Castle, Bells Whisky Distillery, Glasgow, Stirling Castle

AFFILIATIONS
Independent

NEAREST
MAJOR CITY:
Edinburgh - 15 miles/25 mins

MAJOR AIRPORT:
Edinburgh - 13 miles/20 mins

RAILWAY STATION:
Aberdour - ¼ mile/10 mins

RESERVATIONS
Direct with hotel
Quote ***Best Loved***

ACCESS CODES
Not applicable

Modern comforts, good food and a warm welcome in an historic mansion

The influence of the sea can be felt throughout this warm and friendly hotel. The original owner's great grandfather founded the Russian Navy, but it is the elaborate mahogany and glass ceiling in the smoking lounge which grabs the most attention. It was brought to the hotel in 1926 from the steamship 'Orontes' which sailed between Australia and the UK.

The hotel was completely refurbished in 1995 and is located in the centre of the picturesque town of Aberdour. Each of the hotel's bedrooms is decorated and furnished in a very individual style and is named after a Scottish clan. The Rennie Room, for example, is an apartment with four-poster bed and private sitting room, while the Thomson Room is a luxury family room with views across the Firth of Forth to Edinburgh.

Fresh fish are taken directly to the hotel's excellent restaurant from the local harbour quayside. In fact, the hotel's consistently good food and imaginative menus have earned the owner, Stewart Dykes, a deserved reputation. A bar bistro offers lighter variations of the fare you can enjoy in the fine dining room.

Aberdour has the distinction of being the only Scottish Beach to have been awarded a blue flag; just one of many attractions besides Edinburgh that makes Woodside an ideal touring base.

LOCATION

From Forth Road Bridge take exit 1/M90. Turn right under M90, to Kirkcaldy. Pass over five roundabouts and enter Aberdour; hotel is on left after a garage.

Looking for an hotel with a golf course on site? See our 'Golf Guide' on page 478

The National Trust for Scotland

We care for Scotland's heritage

When visiting Scotland, you are never far from one of our awesome attractions. With over 100 properties in our care, including castles, gardens and battle sites, you are spoilt for choice!

For a free brochure, *Visit the National Trust for Scotland*, please contact:
Public Affairs Department (BLH)
The National Trust for Scotland,
Wemyss House, 28 Charlotte Square,
Edinburgh EH2 4ET
Phone: (0131) 243 9387
Fax: (0131) 243 9589
E-mail: information@nts.org.uk
Website: www.nts.org.uk

north

The beautiful game: Soccer supremos Manchester United celebrate another triumph in the game that has inspired a rash of recent British creativity including Sir Andrew Lloyd-Webber's latest musical. Another set-piece success is the magical topiary garden at Levens Hall (inset) in Cumbria.

north

The people of the North of England are proud of their heritage - and there's a lot to be proud about. You will see it in the way they support sporting heros and in their art and music. They are resilient and determined, characteristics exemplified by the Angel of the North.

You can walk the Lake District where Wordsworth found his inspiration, where Beatrix Potter created Peter Rabbit. Amongst the Moors and Dales of Yorkshire, home of the Bronte Sisters and James Herriot. You will hear echoes of great music in Leeds, Huddersfield, Manchester and Buxton. And the mellow strains of brass bands playing in gritty mining villages. You will see Bradford through the eyes of David Hockney, and Salford immortalised by L S Lowry.

Cricket, Rugby League and Football, divisive during the game, unite players and spectators alike in the bar afterwards. At Aintree near Liverpool, The Grand National thrills punters worldwide.

The area is famous for its stately homes and gardens, like Castle Howard, Harewood House and Chatsworth, as well as, the romantic ruins that wear the scars of ancient wars or pay tribute to the mission of Cistercian monks.

Holy Island
Carter Bar
Belsay Hall
Northumberland National Park
Newcastle -upon-Tyne
Hadrian's Wall
Carlisle
Elizabeth
Castlerigg Stone Circle
Hamsterley Forest
The North Yorkshire Moors
The Lake District
Sutton Bank
Rievaulx Abbey
Little Voice
The Pennine Way
Holker Hall
The Yorkshire Dales
Castle Howard
Scarborough
York
Fountains Abbey
Forest of Bowland
Leeds
Hull
Manchester
The Peak District
Liverpool
Tatton Park
Chester

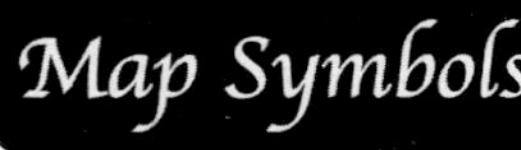

Great Trails

Famous Film Locations

Scenic Views

Historical Interest

Cities & Major towns

Gardens

Sports mad

Whether it be the exploits of the Yorkshire County Cricket Team (pictured) or Newcastle United, mountain biking or climbing, greyhound racing, steeplechasing or the gentle art of pigeon fancying, all forms of sport raise real passions in the north of England.

Take to the water in Lakeland

World-renowned for Wordsworth's golden daffodils and its scenic majesty, the Lake District is also a major watersports centre. There are 16 major lakes and a variety of ways to explore them from dinghy sailing and windsurfing to rowboats and cruises.

A life of [quiet] contemplation

Autumn mists and colours cast a mellow light in the grounds of historic Mount Grace Priory on the North York Moors. Among the ruins of the 14th-century priory buildings, the foundations of the two-storey cells where Carthusian monks once lived out their solitary existence separated by high walls can still be seen. There is also a herb garden and nature trail.

Romantic Rievaulx

The most evocative approach to the supremely graceful ruins of Rievaulx Abbey is on foot, hiking up the Cleveland Way from the Yorkshire market town of Helmsley to the tranquil wooded valley where the mother church of the Cistercian order was founded in 1132. Another wonderful view point is from Rievaulx Terrace and Temples, a charming 18th-century landscaped vista.

Border glory

The spectacular gardens at Newby Hall, near Ripon, are famous for the massed colours of their double herbaceous borders set against trimmed yew hedges. The 17th-century Hall is adorned with rich Gobelins tapestries and classical statuary collected by an ancestor of the owners on his Grand Tour of Europe.

Garden Guide

Belsay Hall
Belsay, Nr Ponteland, Northumbria NE20 0DX
Tel: 01661 881636
30 acres of magnificent landscaped gardens set amidst the Northumberland countryside

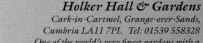

Castle Howard
York, North Yorkshire, YO60 7DA
Tel: 01653 648444
One of England's most dramatic stately homes and landscape gardens with impressive fountains

Holker Hall & Gardens
Cark-in-Cartmel, Grange-over-Sands, Cumbria LA11 7PL Tel: 01539 558328
One of the world's very finest gardens with a lime-stone cascade and beautiful rose garden

Tatton Park
Knutsford, Cheshire WA16 6QN
Tel: 01502 730224
One of England's most important gardens with a wonderful orangery and tree fernery

Find out more. There are many more attractions listed on the Best Loved Website: **www.bestlovedhotels.com**
Further information about the North can be found by contacting: **North West Tourist Board.** Tel: +44 (0)1942 821222. **Yorkshire Tourist Board.** Tel: +44 (0)1904 707961.

• Map p.496
ref: B5

" A house of perfect and irresistible atmosphere "

Hugh Walpole

ARMATHWAITE HALL HOTEL

17th century hall

Bassenthwaite Lake, Keswick, Cumbria CA12 4RE

Telephone 017687 76551
Fax 017687 76220

E-mail: *armathwaite@bestloved.com*

OWNERS

The Graves Family

ROOM RATES

2 Singles	£65
36 Doubles/Twins	£124 - £210
1 Four-poster	£220 - £240
3 Studio suites	£220 - £240

Includes full breakfast and VAT

CHARGE/CREDIT CARDS

• DC • MC • VI

RATINGS & AWARDS

A.A. ★★★★ ❀❀ 70%

FACILITIES

On site: *Indoor pool, croquet, tennis, gym, sauna/spa, beauty therapy, snooker, riding, fishing, rare breeds farm, heli-pad, archery/clay shooting/quad bike safaris by prior arrangement*
Licensed for weddings
4 meeting rooms/max 100 people
Nearby: *Golf*

RESTRICTIONS

No pets in public rooms

ATTRACTIONS

Beatrix Potter Museum & House, William Wordsworth's homes, Rheged Discovery Centre, Hadrian's Wall, Roman wall and forts

AFFILIATIONS

Independent

NEAREST

MAJOR CITY:
Carlisle - 20 miles/40 mins
Newcastle - 70 miles/1½ hrs

MAJOR AIRPORT:
Manchester - 120 miles/2½ hrs

RAILWAY STATION:
Carlisle - 20 miles/40 mins

RESERVATIONS

Direct with hotel
Quote ***Best Loved***

ACCESS CODES

Not applicable

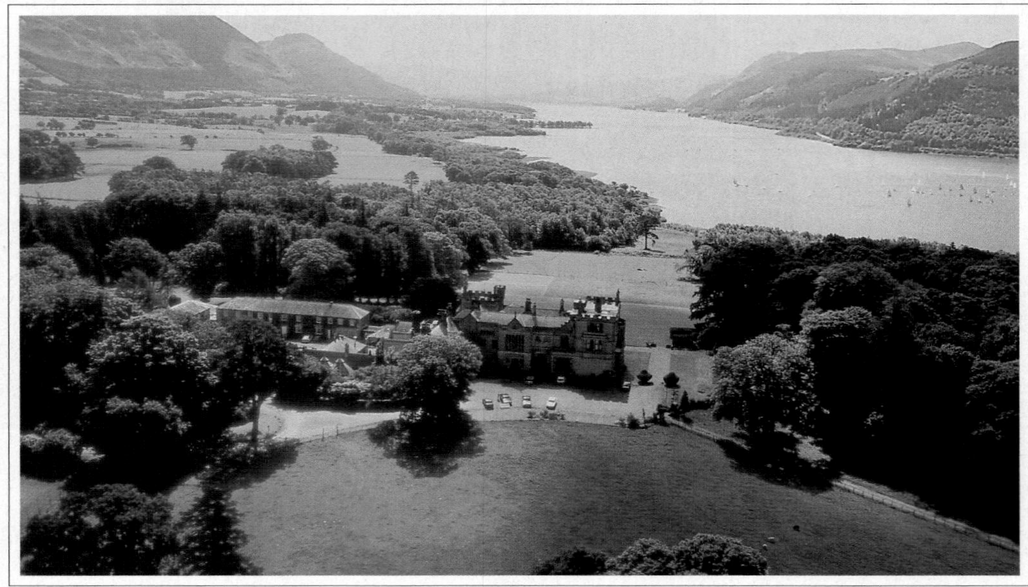

A stately home that will appeal to sportsman and connoisseur alike

Armathwaite Hall is set in a magnificent private estate encompassing park and woodlands and lake frontage. The present hall, part of which dates from 1650, stands on the site of an ancient manor owned by Sir Adam de Bassenthwaite in the reign of Edward II.

The Hall is run personally by the owners who pursue the continuing development of their hotel, its leisure and conference facilities with painstaking regard for the warm, elegant nature of this genuine English stately home.

Connoisseurs of fine cuisine will find much to appreciate at Armathwaite Hall. Master Chef Kevin Dowling takes full advantage of a wealth of local seasonal produce and Cumbrian specialities to create a variety of gastronomic delights.

Management training, personnel motivation courses and corporate hospitality days are popular with delegates and guests making full use of the extensive sports and leisure facilities available on the estate.

An interesting feature is a safari on Quad bikes in an area famed for its spectacular views. This is the perfect centre for either business or pleasure to explore the Lake District.

LOCATION

Turn off the M6 at Exit 40 and follow the A66 to the Keswick roundabout. Then take the A591 to Carlisle for 8 miles and turn left at Castle Inn. The hotel is 300 yards ahead.

"Our most favourite place – the perfect balance between peacefulness, efficient service, friendly staff and outstanding food"

T A Knowlton, Chairman, The Kellogg Company of Great Britain

• Map p.496
ref: B5

Victorian house BORROWDALE GATES COUNTRY HOUSE HOTEL

A rich stroke of fortune amongst the majestic Lakeland mountains

Baddeley's Guide to the English Lakes says: "... there can be no doubt that Borrowdale holds the first position amongst its (the Lake District's) valleys". In the north of the valley is Derwentwater, 'The Queen of the Lakes' and all around are the majestic Lakeland mountains, changing colour with the weather and the seasons. Within this idyllic picture is Borrowdale Gates secluded in its own two acres of wooded gardens.

The house was built in 1860 as a private residence and its air of comfortable informality continues; this is a wonderful place to shed one's cares and release the tensions. The furniture and fabrics contribute to the feeling of mellow good living. Antiques and fresh flowers add a personal touch that can only come from the owners Christine and Terry Parkinson. The bedrooms (ten on the ground floor) make the most of the breathtaking views, as do the lounges and restaurant with their picture windows.

The restaurant, which has won critical acclaim from numerous food guides, serves award-winning food from a daily-changing menu which is inspired by the use of the finest local produce.

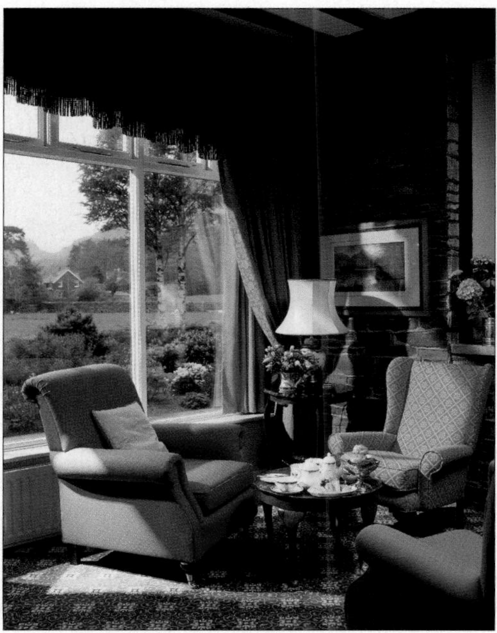

LOCATION

Exit 40 off M6, A66 to Keswick. From there take B5289 and after 4 miles, turn right at the double humpback bridge into Grange. The hotel is about a quarter of a mile past the village on the right.

Grange-in-Borrowdale, Keswick, Cumbria CA12 5UQ

Telephone 01768 777204
Fax 01768 777254

E-mail: *borrowdale@bestloved.com*

OWNERS

Terry and Christine Parkinson

ROOM RATES

3 Singles £65 - £87
26 Doubles/Twins £115 - £170
Includes dinner, full breakfast and VAT

CHARGE/CREDIT CARDS

• MC • VI

RATINGS & AWARDS

E.T.C. ★★★ Silver Award
R.A.C. ★★★ Dining Award 2
A.A. ★★★ ❀❀ 77%

FACILITIES

On site: *Garden*
Nearby: *Fishing, riding, golf, boating, cycling/hiking/climbing in Borrowdale fells*

RESTRICTIONS

No pets
Limited facilities for disabled guests
No children in restaurant under 7 years

ATTRACTIONS

Borrowdale Valley, Cockermouth, Grasmere, Wordsworth's birthplace and Dove Cottage, Carlisle Castle, Muncaster Castle, Hadrian's Wall

AFFILIATIONS

Independent

NEAREST

MAJOR CITY:
Carlisle - 30 miles/45 mins

MAJOR AIRPORT:
Manchester - 120 miles/2 hrs

RAILWAY STATION:
Penrith - 22 miles/30 mins

RESERVATIONS

Direct with hotel
Quote ***Best Loved***

ACCESS CODES

Not applicable

NORTH

• Map p.496 ref: B9

“ One year on and still idyllic ”

Sue & Bill Black, Berwyn, Pennsylvania

BROXTON HALL

17th century Tudor house

**Whitchurch Road,
Broxton, Chester,
Cheshire CH3 9JS**

**Telephone 01829 782321
Fax 01829 782330**

E-mail: broxton@bestloved.com

OWNERS

George and Rosemary Hadley

ROOM RATES

1 Single	£70
7 Doubles/Twins	£85
1 Four-poster	£110
1 Junior suite	£120

Includes full breakfast and VAT

CHARGE/CREDIT CARDS

• DC • MC • VI

RATINGS & AWARDS

R.A.C. ★★★ Dining Award 1
A.A. ★★★ 64%

FACILITIES

On site: Garden
1 meeting room/max 20 people
Nearby: Golf, riding, fishing

RESTRICTIONS

No children under 12 years
No facilities for disabled guests
No pets in public rooms

ATTRACTIONS

Peckforton and Beeston Castles, Snowdonia National Park, Chester, Erdigg Hall, Staveley Water Gardens, Chester & Bangor-on-Dee Racecourses

AFFILIATIONS

Independent

NEAREST

MAJOR CITY:
Chester - 10 miles/15 mins

MAJOR AIRPORT:
Manchester - 30 miles/40 mins
Liverpool - 25 miles/35 mins

RAILWAY STATION:
Chester - 10 miles/15 mins
Crewe - 12 miles/15 mins

RESERVATIONS

Direct with hotel
Quote **Best Loved**

ACCESS CODES

Not applicable

An historic house of character a league or so from Roman Chester

Built in 1671, Broxton Hall is a black-and-white half-timbered Tudor house set in five acres of grounds and extensive gardens. The historical walled city of Chester, famed for its Roman and medieval remains and buildings, is eight miles away.

The hotel provides modern comfort yet retains the ambience of a bygone age. The reception area reflects its character in the furnishings, oak panelled walls, carved oak staircase and a massive Jacobean fireplace, where a welcoming log fire burns most evenings.

All ten bedrooms are beautifully furnished with antiques and offer every facility for your comfort. All have full central heating.

Overlooking the gardens, the restaurant receives consistent praise from regular diners. French and English cuisine is served, using local game in season and freshly caught fish. You can breakfast in the sunny conservatory beside the lawns.

Broxton Hall is ideally placed for visiting the delightful North Wales seaside and the dramatic scenery of Snowdonia. There are excellent golf courses locally and for the racing enthusiast, Chester and Bangor-on-Dee races are nearby.

LOCATION

From Chester, take the A41, signposted to Whitchurch. After 9 miles, you cross the A534. Broxton Hall is shortly after the A534 junction, on the left.

"Nothing is ever too much trouble"

Dawn Tickle, Cabot Carbon, Ellesmere Port

• *Map p.496 ref: B8*

Tudor manor house **THE CHESTER CRABWALL MANOR**

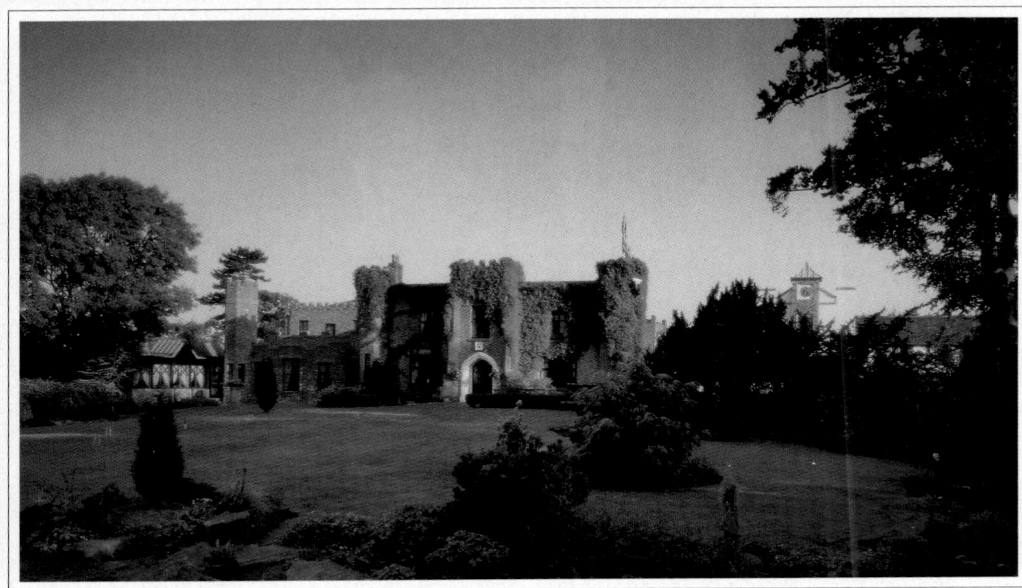

A well-established hotel and restaurant with a state-of-the-art fitness centre added

The origins of Crabwall Manor began long before the Norman Conquest of 1066 but the very recent addition of one of the country's most comprehensive spa facilities puts it firmly into the new century. An hotel that spans three millennia!

Whilst the spa was being built, the hotel itself underwent a radical refurbishment programme under the direction of Laura Ashley designers. The paradox of ancient and modern has no better expression than here at Crabwall. The grand old building lends itself wonderfully to indulgence.

The bedrooms seem to soothe your tensions away; one look is enough. Spacious, sumptuous and softly furnished, each one has its own way of drawing you into a private world of luxury.

Crabwall is highly praised for its cuisine: new ideas and superb renditions of the classics are supported by a formidable wine list. However, the Sommelier's Selection helpfully narrows the field.

Residents have free use of the Spa at Crabwall although the huge range of treatments and therapies are extra. The facilities, supervised by professionals, are exceptional and include a 17 metre pool, air conditioned gym, aerobics room, beauty treatment room, juice bar … you name it!

Inviting as all this may seem, it counts for nothing without people. In this respect, Crabwall has few rivals; you couldn't meet a happier band who really enjoy looking after you. Top marks!

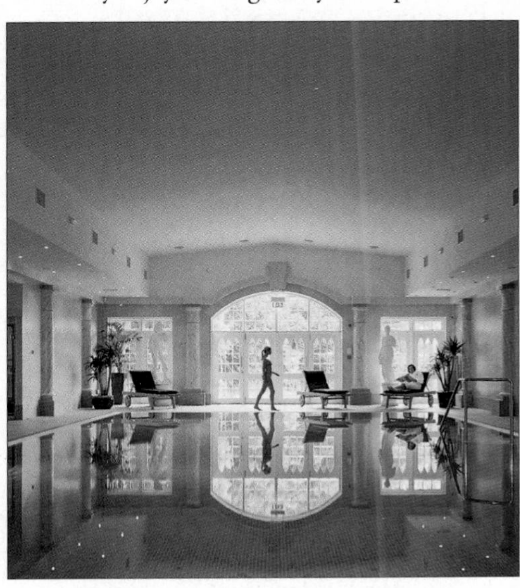

LOCATION

2½ miles from Chester on the A540 Hoylake road. The hotel is set back from the main road.

Parkgate Road, Mollington, Chester, Cheshire CH1 6NE

Telephone 01244 851666
Fax 01244 851400

E-mail: *crabwall@bestloved.com*

GENERAL MANAGER

James Harding

ROOM RATES

Single occupancy	*£129*
42 Doubles/Twins	*£157*
5 Suites	*£197*
1 Four-poster	*£257*

Includes VAT

CHARGE/CREDIT CARDS

• DC • JCB • MC • VI

RATINGS & AWARDS

E.T.C. ★★★★ Silver Award
R.A.C. Blue Ribbon ★★★★
Dining Award 4
A.A. ★★★★ ❀❀ 77%

FACILITIES

On site: *Garden, croquet, snooker, indoor pool, gym, aerobics, beauty treatments, heli-pad, Licensed for weddings*
5 meeting rooms/max 100 people
Nearby: *Golf, tennis, water skiing, yachting, fishing, riding, shooting*

RESTRICTIONS

No pets, guide dogs only

ATTRACTIONS

Roman Ampitheatre, Chester Zoo, Cheshire Oaks Shopping Centre, Blue Plant Aquarium, North Wales, Liverpool

AFFILIATIONS

Marston Hotels

NEAREST

MAJOR CITY:
Chester - 1½ miles/3 mins

MAJOR AIRPORT:
Manchester - 34 miles/30 mins

RAILWAY STATION:
Chester - 3 miles/5 mins

RESERVATIONS

Direct with hotel
Quote ***Best Loved***

ACCESS CODES

Not applicable

For a portrait of this region see page 90

• Map p.496 ref: C9

"To say I was stunned by the place would be an understatement ... everything was perfect, we couldn't fault the arrangements in any way ..."

Jayne Ferguson, Leicester

CREWE HALL

Jacobean mansion

Weston Road, Crewe, Cheshire CW1 6UZ

Telephone 01270 253333
Fax 01270 253322

E-mail: *crewehall@bestloved.com*

DIRECTORS

Philip Humphreys and Glyn Newman

ROOM RATES

Single occupancy	*£125 - £310*
7 Doubles/Twins	*£150 - £250*
6 Superior Doubles/Twins	*£175 - £350*
7 Four-posters	*£195*
5 Suites	*£195 - £290*

Includes full breakfast and VAT

CHARGE/CREDIT CARDS

• *DC* • *MC* • *VI*

RATINGS & AWARDS

A.A. ★★★★ ❀❀

Cheshire Life 'Hotel of the Year'

FACILITIES

On site: *Garden, football pitch, tennis, croquet*
16 meeting rooms/max 350 people
Near by: *Golf*

RESTRICTIONS

None

ATTRACTIONS

Arley Hall & Gardens, Beeston Castle, Biddulph Grange, Chester, The Potteries, Tatton Park, Bridgemere Garden World

AFFILIATIONS

Grand Heritage Hotels

NEAREST

MAJOR CITY:
Chester - 20 miles/40 mins

MAJOR AIRPORT:
Manchester - 35 miles/30 mins

RAILWAY STATION:
Crewe - 2 miles/5 mins

RESERVATIONS

Toll free in US: 888-93-GRAND
Toll free in UK: 0800 0560457
Quote **Best Loved**

ACCESS CODES

AMADEUS UI XVCCWE
APOLLO/GALILEO UI 24840
SABRE/ABACUS UI 49965
WORLDSPAN UI 41056

NORTH

A stately home setting a standard by which all other country houses will be judged

This quiet corner of England has historically been an affluent one and this affluence is made evident by the great collection of grand houses and stately homes. Names like Arley Hall, Dunham Massey and Lyme Park are familiar far and wide with Tatton Park being one of the most famous of them all. Another Cheshire monument to this era of opulent living is the Jacobean mansion house of Crewe Hall.

Dating back to 1615, the Hall was originally built by the Earls of Crewe to impress and entertain on the most lavish of scales and in its' hey-day was served by 20 gardeners and over 100 household servants.

The exterior is majestic and stunningly impressive, the interior ornately decorated with elaborate mouldings, fine paneling, imposing marble fireplaces and magnificently painted ceilings. The bedrooms, some with very high, antique four-poster beds, are elegantly and extravagantly furnished with richly coloured wall coverings and fabrics. It's from the bedrooms, perhaps, that you get the best view of the beautifully maintained and manicured gardens.

The seven splendid State rooms provide a wonderful setting for a meeting, conference or banquet with the Long Gallery, seating as many as 220 people. It's surprisingly accessible, located just 7 minutes from the motorway and is convenient for both Manchester and Birmingham airports.

Driving up to Crewe Hall, is like driving back to these grander times but unlike Tatton Park, this is a place that invites you to experience, enjoy and re-live them.

LOCATION

Leave the M6 at Junction 16. Follow A500 towards Crewe. First roundabout take 2nd exit. At next roundabout take the 1st exit. Crewe Hall is a few hundred yards on the right.

“ What a treasure ”

Colin McKenzie, The Great British Experience

• *Map p.496 ref:* B4

99

Georgian house

CROSBY LODGE

The splendours of good living in the neighbourhood of the Scottish border

This romantic and splendid Georgian house, is the home of the Sedgwick family. The lodge stands high above the village of Low Crosby, with a marvellous view of the River Eden and surrounded by wooded areas and parkland. The house, built in 1802 and altered some years later to the castellated appearance of today, is beautifully furnished with family antiques, complemented by stunning flower arrangements.

Perfectionist and Chef Patron James Sedgwick and his young team serve up deliciously exciting menus featuring authentic continental cuisine and the very best of traditional British fare. The Crosby Lodge sweet trolley, along with their home-made bread and preserves, are renowned far and wide.

Patricia looks after front of house and will greet you personally. The wine list, written and supplied by daughter Philippa, is exceptional.

The house has eleven bedrooms tastefully designed by Patricia. The friendly, efficient staff make this the ideal venue for a peaceful holiday, short break, shooting party or golfing holiday.

LOCATION

Situated just off the A689, 5 miles east of Carlisle. 3½ miles from Exit 44 on M6, on the right, just through Low Crosby.

High Crosby, Crosby-on-Eden, Carlisle, Cumbria CA6 4QZ

Telephone 01228 573618
Fax 01228 573428

E-mail: *crosby@bestloved.com*

OWNERS

Patricia and Michael Sedgwick

ROOM RATES

1 Single	*£82*
5 Doubles/Twins	*£110*
2 Four-posters	*£120 - £150*
3 Family rooms	*£145*

Includes full breakfast and VAT

CHARGE/CREDIT CARDS

• *JCB* • *MC* • *VI*

RATINGS & AWARDS

E.T.C. ★★★ *Silver Award*
A.A. ★★★ ❀ *77%*

FACILITIES

On site: *Garden*
2 meeting rooms/max 20 people
Nearby: *Golf*

RESTRICTIONS

Limited facilities for disabled guests
Pets by arrangement

ATTRACTIONS

Hadrian's Wall, Wetheral Woods, Carlisle Castle and Cathedral, Gardens, Lake District, Lanercost Priory, Brougham Castle, Penrith Castle

AFFILIATIONS

Independent

NEAREST

MAJOR CITY:
Carlisle - 5 miles/8 mins

MAJOR AIRPORT:
Newcastle - 58 miles/1 hr
Glasgow - 100 miles/1½ hrs

RAILWAY STATION:
Carlisle - 5 miles/15 mins

RESERVATIONS

Direct with hotel
Quote ***Best Loved***

ACCESS CODES

Not applicable

NORTH

For information about hotel affiliations see page 14

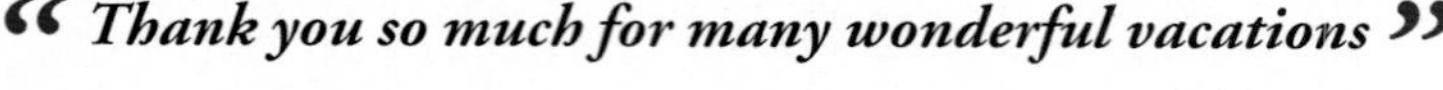

"Thank you so much for many wonderful vacations"

Laura Clark, New York

DALE HEAD HALL

Elizabethan manor house

Lake Thirlmere, Keswick, Cumbria CA12 4TN

Telephone 017687 72478
Fax 017687 71070

***E-mail:** dalehead@bestloved.com*

OWNERS
Alan and Shirley Lowe

MANAGER
Hans Bonkenburg

ROOM RATES

Single occupancy	*£93 - £95*
5 Doubles/Twins	*£100 - £150*
4 Superior Doubles/Twins	*£105 - £170*
3 Four-posters	*£110 - £180*
2 Suites	*£130 - £200*

Includes dinner, full breakfast and VAT

CHARGE/CREDIT CARDS

• MC • VI

RATINGS & AWARDS
E.T.C. ★★★ Silver Award
R.A.C. ★★★ Dining Award 1
A.A. ★★★ ❀❀ 72%

FACILITIES
***On site:** Gardens, croquet, fishing*
***Nearby:** Golf, sailing, canoeing, riding*

RESTRICTIONS
No facilities for disabled guests
No children in restaurant under 10 years
Smoking permitted in bar only
No pets

ATTRACTIONS
Wordsworth's Dove Cottage, Beatrix Potter's museum and house, Brantwood, Cumbrian fells

AFFILIATIONS
Independent

NEAREST
MAJOR CITY:
Carlisle - 40 miles/45 mins

MAJOR AIRPORT:
Manchester - 100 miles/2 hrs

RAILWAY STATION:
Penrith - 10 miles/20 mins

RESERVATIONS
Direct with hotel
*Quote **Best Loved***

ACCESS CODES
Not applicable

NORTH

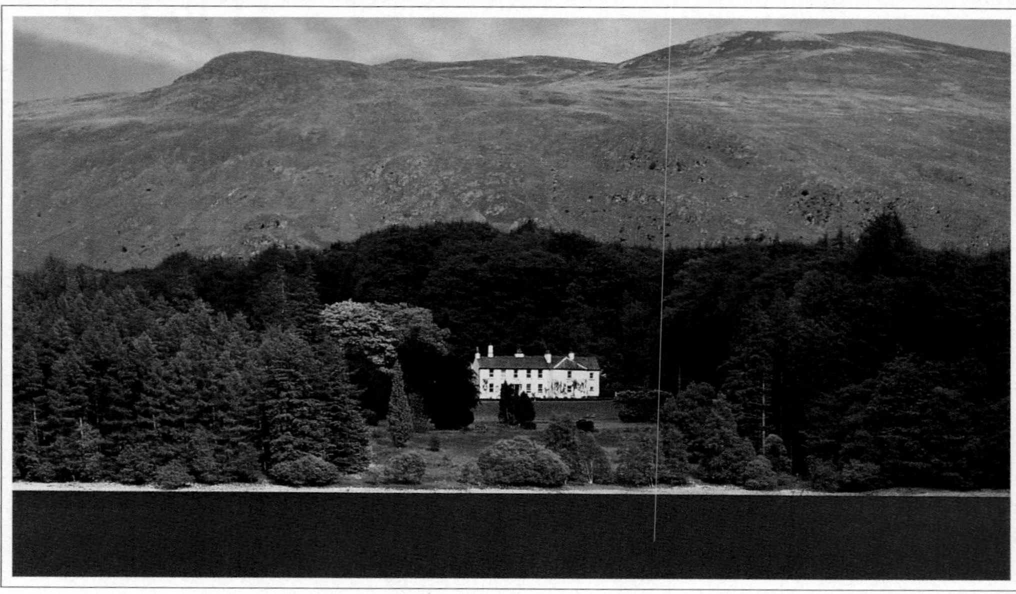

Blissful solitude on the shores of Lake Thirlmere

Beside Lake Thirlmere, surrounded by lush woodland, stands this glorious 16th century house. Rich green lawns sweep towards the water. The tranquillity of the location cannot be surpassed, since the house stands alone on the shores of the 3¹/₄ mile lake.

The Leathes family came to Dale Head Hall in 1577; in 1877 lake and hall were purchased by Manchester to provide the city with clean drinking water and successive Lord Mayors with an idyllic summer retreat.

Today Alan and Shirley Lowe and their family offer exceptional accommodation and service. In restoring the hall, they set high priority on recreating its 16th century authenticity. The bar and lounge are delightful.

The 5-course table d'hôte dinner is served in the oak-beamed Elizabethan dining room, which has an inglenook fireplace. The food is fresh and imaginatively prepared. It is complemented with a good choice of fine wines.

All the splendours of the Lake District are adjacent. Helvellyn is on the doorstep and Borrowdale is close by. Fishing, sailing and canoeing can all be enjoyed; please be sure to take your own equipment as this cannot be supplied by the hotel.

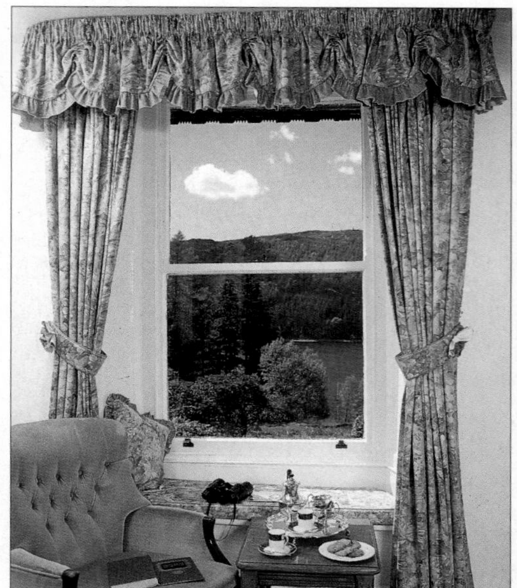

LOCATION

On A591, halfway between Keswick and Grasmere. Hotel is situated along ¼ mile of private driveway overlooking Lake Thirlmere.

"Thank you for being so special"

Christopher Timothy (TV's James Herriot)

• Map p.496 ref: D7

18th century country house

THE DEVONSHIRE ARMS

Bolton Abbey, Near Skipton,
North Yorkshire BD23 6AJ

Telephone 01756 710441
Fax 01756 710564

E-mail: devonskip@bestloved.com

OWNERS
Duke and Duchess of Devonshire
MANAGING DIRECTOR
Jeremy Rata
ROOM RATES

Single occupancy	*£125 - £350*
30 Doubles/Twins	*£175 - £350*
8 Four-posters	*£215*
3 Suites	*£350*

Includes full breakfast and VAT

CHARGE/CREDIT CARDS

• *DC* • *MC* • *VI*

RATINGS & AWARDS
R.A.C. Blue Ribbon ★★★★
Dining Award 3
A.A. ★★★ ❀❀
FACILITIES
On site: *Garden, croquet, indoor pool, tennis, sauna, solarium, spa, gym, beauty therapy, steam room, fishing, heli-pad Licensed for weddings*
4 meeting rooms/max 150 people
Nearby: *Golf*
RESTRICTIONS
No facilities for disabled guests
ATTRACTIONS
Bronte Parsonage, Bolton Priory, Skipton Castle, Castle Howard
AFFILIATIONS
The Celebrated Hotels Collection
Small Luxury Hotels
NEAREST
MAJOR CITY:
Leeds - 17 miles/30 mins
MAJOR AIRPORT:
Manchester - 60 miles/1¼ hrs
Leeds/Bradford - 12 miles/20 mins
RAILWAY STATION:
Ilkley - 5 miles/10 mins
RESERVATIONS
Toll free in US/Canada: 800-322-2403
or 800-525-4800
*Quote **Best Loved***
ACCESS CODES
AMADEUS LX MANDCH
APOLLO/GALILEO LX 44518
SABRE/ABACUS LX 11172
WORLDSPAN LX MANDC

NORTH

Fabulous facilities in the breathtaking Yorkshire Dales

The word 'dale' is derived from the Viking dalr or valley, and the picturesque village of Bolton Abbey lies in a typical fold of the landscape surrounded by scenery of unparalled beauty. Set in 12 acres of gardens and grounds, The Devonshire Arms has been owned by the Devonshires since 1753, forming part of the family's North Yorkshire estates.

Behind the traditional Dale's coaching Inn exterior, the hotel reveals a wonderfully warm and welcoming interior furnished with numerous antiques from the Devonshire's family seat at Chatsworth. The Duchess personally supervised the decoration of the comfortable lounges and the exquisitely appointed bedrooms which include eight romantic four-poster rooms.

The Burlington Restaurant has a fine reputation for the outstanding quality of its cuisine, impeccable service and wine list, while The Brasserie provides a lively and less formal alternative. A sympathetically converted 17th-century barn houses the exceptional leisure facilities of The Devonshire Club. Here, guests can use the gym, pool, steam room and sauna, and enjoy beauty and relaxation treatments. There is also an all-weather tennis court and walking opportunities abound in the Dales landscape which so inspired the Brontë sisters, J.M.W. Turner and, more recently, James Herriot.

LOCATION

On the B6160 to Bolton Abbey, 250 yards north from its roundabout junction with the A59 Skipton to Harrogate Road.

• Map p.496 ref: C6

“ You'll talk about it. Most important you'll enjoy it ”

Yorkshire Life

NORTH

THE DEVONSHIRE FELL

Victorian country house

Burnsall, Skipton, North Yorkshire BD23 6BT

Telephone 01756 718155/718111
Fax 01756 729009

E-mail: *devonfell@bestloved.com*

OWNERS
Duke and Duchess of Devonshire

MANAGING DIRECTOR
Jeremy Rata

ROOM RATES

Single occupancy	*£70 - £90*
10 Doubles/Twins	*£110 - £120*
2 Suites	*£140*

Includes full breakfast and VAT

CHARGE/CREDIT CARDS

• DC • MC • VI

RATINGS & AWARDS
Independent

FACILITIES
On site: *Garden, fishing*
Licensed for weddings
1 meeting room/max 70 people
Nearby: *Golf, tennis, fitness, fishing*

RESTRICTIONS
No facilities for disabled guests

ATTRACTIONS
Bolton Abbey, Skipton Castle, Fountains Abbey, Harewood House, Castle Howard, Bronte Parsonage

AFFILIATIONS
Preston's Global Hotels

NEAREST
MAJOR CITY:
Leeds - 26 miles/1 hr

MAJOR AIRPORT:
Leeds/Bradford - 20 miles/30 mins

RAILWAY STATION:
Skipton - 8 miles/10 mins

RESERVATIONS
Toll free in US: 800-544-9993
Quote ***Best Loved***

ACCESS CODES
Not applicable

Fishy tales in the Dales...

The Devonshire Fell is blessed with a truly glorious position poised on a hillside overlooking the River Wharfe to the rolling uplands of the Yorkshire Dales beyond. Built around 1885, the hotel has recently undergone a complete transformation under the direction of Lady Hartington, daughter-in-law to the owner, the Duke of Devonshire.

The new-look Fell is every bit as eye-catching as its setting, but there are a few surprises in store for traditionalists. Stuffy Victoriana has been ousted in favour of chic, vibrant colour schemes and natural materials from local stone and wood to giant wicker arm chairs. There are open fires (traditional) and live goldfish swimming in the cisterns of the ladies' loos (downright exotic for North Yorkshire), and the hotel has been nominated for both Best Newcomer and Hotel of the Year for Yorkshire by Yorkshire Life magazine.

The glassed-in Bistro and Conservatory make the best of the views while collecting numerous accolades for good food. Specialities include local game and a Fish Board, which might feature lobster, scallops and sea bass. Another big plus is the Fell's young and enthusiastic staff who add a real buzz to the friendly and informal atmosphere.

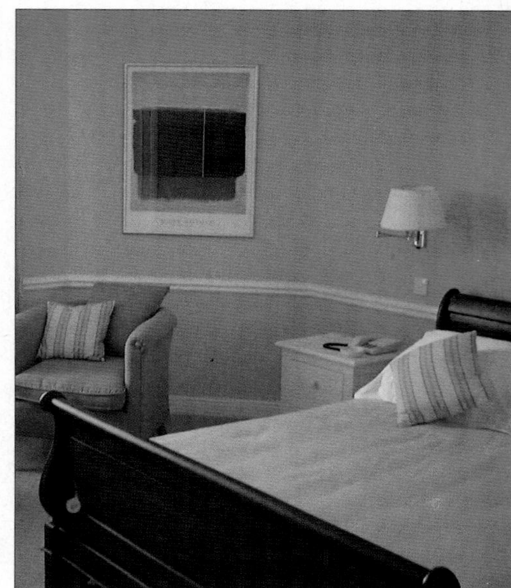

LOCATION

Take B6160 past Bolton Abbey from junction with A59 (Skipton to Harrogate road). Follow for 6 miles, hotel is on left.

" On arrival, I thought 11 was the street number. On leaving, I realise it is your rating out of 10. Many thanks for many things "

Greg Mauchline

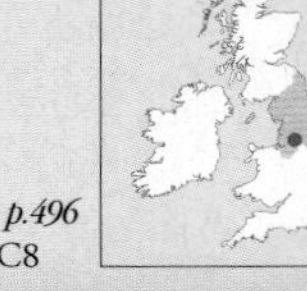

• *Map p.496* *ref:* C8

Victorian residence

ELEVEN DIDSBURY PARK

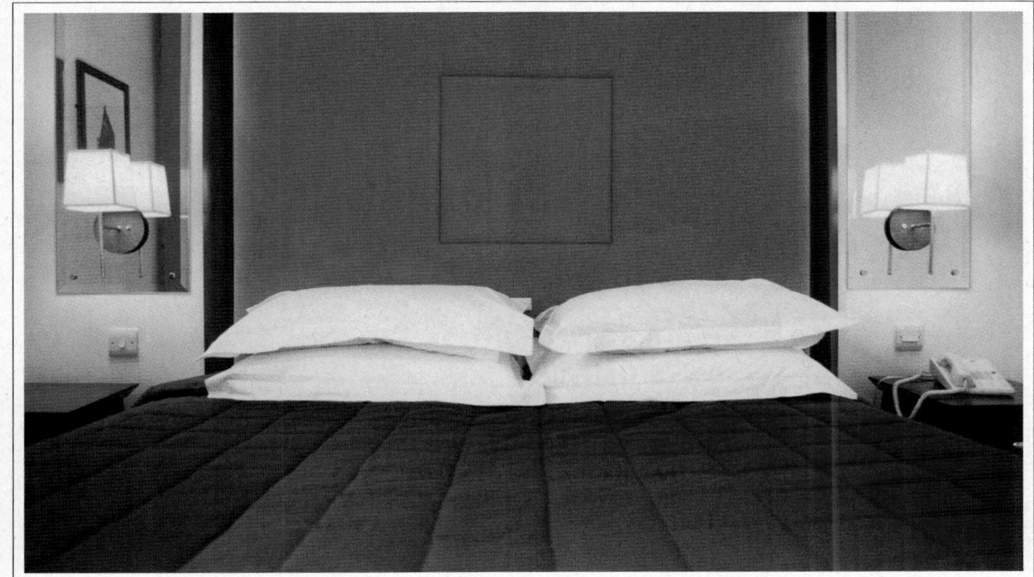

A stylish urban retreat reflecting Manchester's new-found dynamism

Prosperous mill owners and industrialists founded the exclusive south Manchester suburb of Didsbury in the 1850's. Just 15 minutes from the city centre, this leafy neighbourhood of imposing Victorian homes has metamorphosed into a cosmopolitan enclave brimming with hip restaurants and bars, and now a brand new boutique hotel in the form of Eleven Didsbury Park.

Eammon and Sally O'Loughlin have transformed a series of outbuildings arranged around a Victorian walled garden into a model small hotel. There is not a shred of chintz or an over-stuffed armchair in sight, but instead a vision of artful contemporary chic and the odd quirky feature such as the Indian sideboard which serves as a bar. Sally's work as a TV make-up artist may account for her creative flair with colours, fabrics and the striking flower arrangements (admire the herbaceous borders, too). Eammon's innate sense of Irish hospitality is echoed by the boy Fergal the tabby cat - just so long as you don't sit on His chair.

The O'Loughlins offer a scrumptious breakfast and there are plenty of restaurants nearby for dining out (and a courtesy four wheel drive to take you there). A decked roof area with hot tub, plus a small gym are planned for early 2001. Easy access to the city centre makes Eleven Didsbury a good base for business visitors disenchanted with soulless chain hotels, it is also on the right side of the city for the airport and Old Trafford.

LOCATION

From M60 take A34, signposted Manchester City Centre. Turn left onto A5145 and continue down Wilmslow Road. Turn right into Didsbury Park opposite entrance to Towers Business Park. Hotel is half way down on left.

11 Didsbury Park,
Didsbury Village,
Manchester M20 5LH

Telephone 0161 448 7711
Fax 0161 448 8282

E-mail: *11didsbury@bestloved.com*

OWNER

Eamonn O'Loughlin

ROOM RATES

Single occupancy	*£70 - £110*
13 Doubles/Twins	*£70 - £110*
1 Junior suite	*£125 - £155*

Includes service and VAT

CHARGE/CREDIT CARDS

 • *DC* • *JCB* • *MC* • *VI*

RATINGS & AWARDS

Sunday Times Top Five Hotel Town Houses

FACILITIES

On site: *Garden, croquet*
1 meeting room/max 25 people
Nearby: *Tennis*

RESTRICTIONS

No facilities for disabled guests
No smoking in public rooms
No pets

ATTRACTIONS

Lowry Centre, Old Trafford, Manchester United Museum, Bridgewater Hall, The Opera House, Lyme Park

AFFILIATIONS

Design and Planet Hotels

NEAREST

MAJOR CITY:
Manchester - 3½ miles/10 mins

MAJOR AIRPORT:
Manchester - 4 miles/10 mins

RAILWAY STATION:
Stockport - 3 miles/10 mins

RESERVATIONS

Direct with hotel
Quote ***Best Loved***

ACCESS CODES

Not applicable

NORTH

• Map p.496 ref: B6

"Redefining the standards others love to match"

John Gordon, BBC Southampton

FAYRER GARDEN HOUSE HOTEL

Edwardian country house

Lyth Valley Road, Bowness-on-Windermere, Cumbria LA23 3JP

Telephone 015394 88195
Fax 015394 45986

E-mail: fayrer@bestloved.com

NORTH

OWNERS
Iain and Jackie Garside

RATES PER PERSON

2 Singles	£48 - £85
10 Doubles/Twins	£49 - £75
6 Four-posters	£69 - £105

Includes full breakfast, dinner and VAT

CHARGE/CREDIT CARDS

• MC • VI

RATINGS & AWARDS
E.T.C. ★★★ Silver Award
A.A. ★★★ ❀❀ 70%

FACILITIES
On site: Garden, fishing, heli-pad
1 meeting room/max 50 people
Nearby: Golf, tennis, squash, sauna, pool, fishing, riding, watersports, ballooning, cycling

RESTRICTIONS
No pets in public rooms
No children under 5 years in restaurant
Closed 7 - 19 Jan

ATTRACTIONS
Ambleside, Dove Cottage, Holehird Gardens, Beatrix Potter's House, National Park Centre, steamer cruisers

AFFILIATIONS
Independent

NEAREST
MAJOR CITY:
Manchester - 90 miles/1½ hrs

MAJOR AIRPORT:
Manchester - 100 miles/1½ hrs

RAILWAY STATION:
Windermere - 2 miles/5 mins

RESERVATIONS
Direct with hotel
Quote **Best Loved**

ACCESS CODES
Not applicable

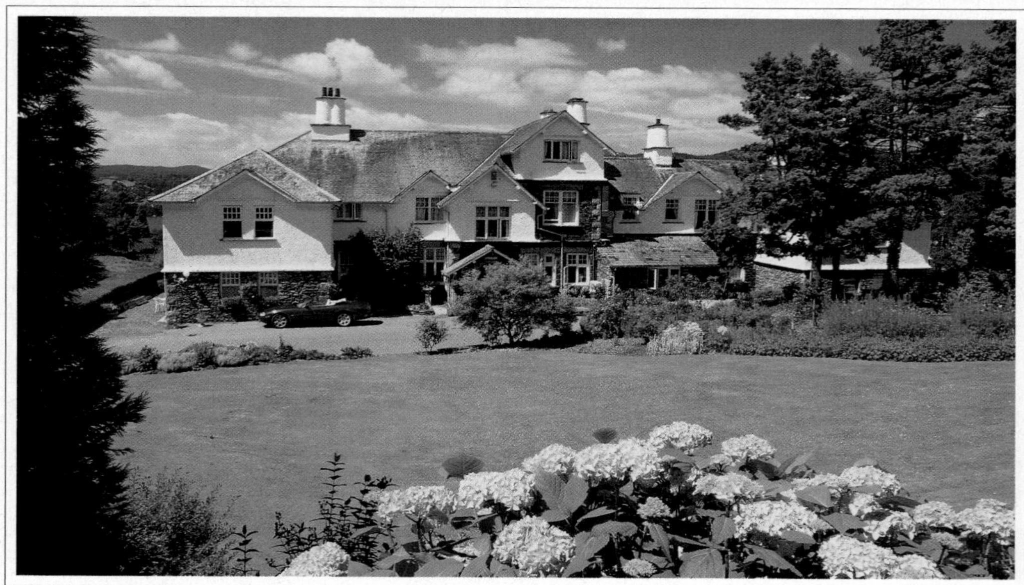

A house, garden and restaurant that are the life and soul of the owners

If there was such a thing as the gastronomic Olympics, the Lake District would be a good place to hold them. Many of the hotels in the area possess a fine track record and compete (mostly in Olympian fellowship) for your custom. It follows you are unlikely to be disappointed but, at Fayrer Garden House, the feast is ambrosial!

It is not just the comfort nor the good food, nor even the stunning location that makes this place exceptional. It owes all to the owners, Iain and Jackie Garside, who bought the house in 1991 and made it their home, their life and their pleasure. Since then it has been completely renovated and furnished into the luxury home it now is and one they choose to share with friends.

Notice the word Garden in the title; the house and its garden were planned together back in 1904 and it is no accident that it blooms all year round. Now, as you survey the scene from the house, the terrace or the lawn, the panorama of lake and mountains is fringed with colour as pretty as any postcard.

The love that Iain and Jackie have for Fayrer turns to a passion in the dining room where Edward Wilkinson and his team excel themselves aided and abetted by wines supplied by a local paragon among wine merchants. As you dine on these Olympian heights, don't miss the view.

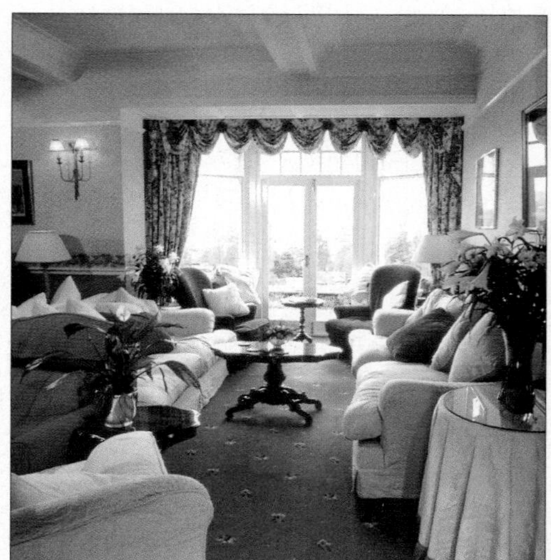

LOCATION

Exit 36/M6 onto A591. After 8 miles take left onto B5284 at roundabout (signed Crook) and turn left at end stop sign (7.5 miles) onto Lyth Valley Rd. Hotel is 400 yds on right.

“ Heaven ”

Audrey Johnson, North Carolina

• Map p.496
ref: B6

Edwardian country house

GILPIN LODGE HOTEL

Crook Road, Near Windermere, Cumbria LA23 3NE

Telephone 015394 88818
Fax 015394 88058

E-mail: *gilpin@bestloved.com*

OWNERS
John and Christine Cunliffe

MANAGER
Richard Marriott

RATES PER PERSON

Single occupancy	£100 - £125
9 Doubles/Twins	£60 - £125
5 Four-posters	£90 - £125

Includes full breakfast, dinner and VAT

CHARGE/CREDIT CARDS

• DC • JCB • MC • VI

RATINGS & AWARDS
E.T.C. ★★★ *Gold Award*
R.A.C. ★★★ *Blue Ribbon Dining Award 3*
A.A. ★★★ ❀❀❀

FACILITIES
On site: *Gardens, croquet*
Nearby: *Golf, riding, tennis, fishing*

RESTRICTIONS
No children under 7 years
No pets
No facilities for disabled guests

ATTRACTIONS
Wordsworth's Dove Cottage, World of Beatrix Potter, Lake Windermere, Holker Hall, Levens Hall

AFFILIATIONS
Selected British Hotels
Pride of Britain

NEAREST
MAJOR CITY:
Manchester - 80 miles/1¼ hrs

MAJOR AIRPORT:
Manchester - 90 miles/1¾ hrs

RAILWAY STATION:
Windermere - 2 miles/10 mins

RESERVATIONS
Toll free in US/Canada: 800-98-PRIDE or 800-323-5463
Quote ***Best Loved***

ACCESS CODES
Not applicable

NORTH

Idyllic scenery, tranquillity and a highly acclaimed restaurant

Gilpin Lodge is an elegant, friendly, relaxing country house set in 20 acres of woodlands, moors and country gardens two miles from Lake Windermere. The original Edwardian building dates from 1901 and, since then, has been converted to incorporate all the comforts and conveniences of a luxury hotel. Indeed, it has been recognised for its excellence by The Good Hotel Guide with a César Award for 2000.

Flowers in profusion, picture-lined walls, antique furniture and log fires in colder weather are all part of John and Christine Cunliffe's perception of hospitality. The bedrooms all have en suite bathrooms and many have four-poster beds, whirlpool baths, French windows and private patios.

The food earns three AA Rosettes and the award-winning wine list suits all tastes and pockets. The service is attentive and, happily, unpretentious.

The beautiful gardens are the perfect place in which to savour the stunning lakeland scenery. Windermere golf course is a half mile away and almost every kind of outdoor activity can be pursued in the vicinity. This is Wordsworth and Beatrix Potter country and nearby there are many stately homes, gardens and castles.

LOCATION

Gilpin Lodge is 12 miles from the M6. Leave motorway at Exit 36 and take the A590/591 to roundabout north of Kendal. Then take the B5284 for 5 miles.

• Map p.496
ref: E7

"A charming place, I hope you didn't mind me bringing my own wine, your food complements it perfectly"

Baron Eric de Rothschild, Château Lafite

THE GRANGE HOTEL

Regency town house

1 Clifton, York, North Yorkshire YO30 6AA

Telephone 01904 644744
Fax 01904 612453

E-mail: *grange@bestloved.com*

OWNER
Jeremy Cassel

GENERAL MANAGER
Shara Ross

ROOM RATES

3 Singles	*£99 - £160*
24 Doubles/Twins	*£120 - £170*
2 Four-posters	*£185*
1 Suite	*£215*

Includes full breakfast and VAT

CHARGE/CREDIT CARDS

• *DC* • *MC* • *VI*

RATINGS & AWARDS
E.T.C. ★★★ Silver Award
R.A.C. Blue Ribbon ★★★ Dining Award 3
A.A. ★★★ ❀❀

FACILITIES
On site: *Licensed for weddings*
2 meeting rooms/max 60 people
Nearby: *Golf, fitness*

RESTRICTIONS
Pets by arrangement

ATTRACTIONS
York Minster, The Shambles, National Railway Museum, Castle Howard, York Racecourse, Yorkshire Moors & Dales

AFFILIATIONS
Selected British Hotels

NEAREST
MAJOR CITY:
York

MAJOR AIRPORT:
Leeds/Bradford - 30 miles/50 mins

RAILWAY STATION:
York - 1 mile/15 mins

RESERVATIONS
Toll free in US: 800-323-5463
Quote ***Best Loved***

ACCESS CODES
Not applicable

NORTH

Luxury, fine cuisine and all the splendours of York and The Dales

Given its history of conquerors, (Roman, Saxon, Viking and Norman), it is not surprising that York boasts of being one of Britain's most interesting cities - and you would be hard pressed to find anywhere more convenient or comfortable for its exploration than The Grange. Within walking distance are the Minster (dating from 1100) and its remarkable stained glass, the City Walls, the Jorvik Viking Centre, the National Railway Museum and the medieval Shambles. Within easy driving distance are stately homes, The Yorkshire Dales and the renowned York Racecourse.

The Grange itself is a Regency townhouse, built in 1834 and carefully restored to create a luxurious 30 bedroom hotel. Light streams down the original vine leaf cast iron staircase which leads from finely decorated bedrooms. English chintz and fine antiques pervade and all rooms offer satellite television.

Not only is the hotel ideally situated for the explorer, the gourmet has a choice of three restaurants. From the elegance of the award-winning Ivy Restaurant - mixing classic French and modern British cuisine, or the Seafood Bar with the freshest of fish and seafood (recommended with a glass or two of chilled champagne), to the relaxed Brasserie converted from the old brick-vaulted cellars. Eat, drink, relax, explore - The Grange Hotel conquers all.

LOCATION

About 500 yards outside York's city walls on the A19, York-Thirsk road. The hotel is on the left going out of York.

At the time of printing the exchange rate for £1.00 was US$1.55

"The best of Yorkshire and a great deal besides"

Gina Lazenby

• Map p.496 ref: D7

Victorian town house

GRANTS HOTEL

Elegant and individual hospitality in the heart of historic England

Harrogate is a beautiful spa and floral town in the heart of an area rich in English history. James Herriot, the world's most celebrated vet, was a regular weekly visitor for many years, finding a convivial refuge from the nearby Yorkshire Dales, scene of his adventures.

Within a short distance is the Roman city of York with its Jorvik Viking Centre or, alternatively, Fountains Abbey, England's largest Cistercian Monastery, disestablished by Henry VIII now preserved as a World Heritage Site.

You can explore Middleham Castle, home of Richard III, immortalised by William Shakespeare, visit Bolton Castle where Mary Queen of Scots was imprisoned or Haworth, home of the Brontë Family.

Grants is a family-run hotel with a reputation for quality service, combining modern efficiency with old fashioned hospitality. Each of the tastefully decorated bedrooms offers a full range of facilities and a lift serves all floors. Chimney Pots Bistro provides an imaginative menu in an elegant air-conditioned atmosphere and is a firm favourite with local gourmets.

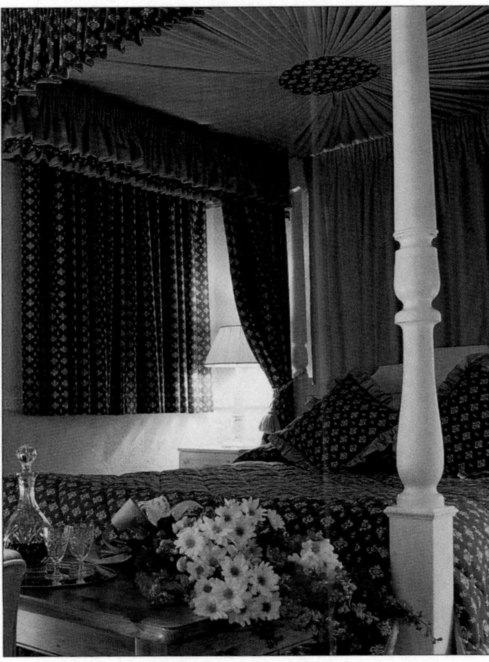

LOCATION

From M1 or M62 at Leeds, take A61 to Harrogate, then 2nd left after The Royal Hall traffic lights into Swan Road.

Swan Road, Harrogate, North Yorkshire HG1 2SS

Telephone 01423 560666
Fax 01423 502550

E-mail: grants@bestloved.com

GENERAL MANAGER
Pam Grant

ROOM RATES

13 Singles	£75 - £110
26 Doubles/Twins	£85 - £142
1 Four-poster	£105 - £155
2 Suites	£100 - £165

Includes full breakfast and VAT

CHARGE/CREDIT CARDS

• DC • JCB • MC • VI

RATINGS & AWARDS
E.T.C. ★★★
R.A.C. ★★★ Dining Award 1
A.A. ★★★ 72%

FACILITIES
On site: Patio gardens, disabled facilities
5 meeting rooms/max 100 people
Nearby: Golf, health & leisure club, riding, fishing

RESTRICTIONS
Pets at management's discretion

ATTRACTIONS
Fountains Abbey, Middleham and Bolton Castles, Herriot Country, Yorkshire Dales, York, Harrogate

AFFILIATIONS
Independent

NEAREST
MAJOR CITY:
Leeds - 15 miles/25 mins

MAJOR AIRPORT:
Leeds/Bradford - 12 miles/20 mins

RAILWAY STATION:
Harrogate - ½ mile/5 mins

RESERVATIONS
Toll free in UK: 0800 371343
Quote **Best Loved**

ACCESS CODES
APOLLO/GALILEO RM 48485
SABRE/ABACUS RN 04297

NORTH

• Map p.496 ref: B6

" I'm fussy but I can't fault it. For the money it's superb value, right down to the Imperial Leather "

J A O'Brien, Berkshire

GRAYTHWAITE MANOR HOTEL *Victorian country house*

Fernhill Road,
Grange-over-Sands,
Cumbria LA11 7JE

Telephone 015395 32001
Fax 015395 35549

***E-mail:** graythwaite@bestloved.com*

GENERAL MANAGERS
Iain and Christine Blakemore

ROOM RATES

5 Singles	*£50 - £75*
15 Doubles/Twins	*£90 - £136*
1 Family suite	*£90 - £136*

Includes full breakfast, dinner and VAT

CHARGE/CREDIT CARDS

 *• JCB • MC • VI*

RATINGS & AWARDS
E.T.C. ★★★
R.A.C. ★★★ *Dining Award 1*
A.A. ★★★ *64%*

FACILITIES
***On site:** Tennis, gardens, putting, snooker*
2 meeting rooms/max 50 people
***Nearby:** Golf, riding, fishing*

RESTRICTIONS
Children at management's discretion
Limited facilities for disabled guests
No pets

ATTRACTIONS
Hill Top - Beatrix Potter's House,
Holker Hall, Cartmel Priory and Village,
Wordsworth's Dove Cottage

AFFILIATIONS
Independent

NEAREST
MAJOR CITY:
Manchester - 80 miles/1½ hrs

MAJOR AIRPORT:
Manchester - 90 miles/1½ hrs

RAILWAY STATION:
Grange-over-Sands - 1 mile/5 mins

RESERVATIONS
Direct with hotel
*Quote **Best Loved***

ACCESS CODES
Not applicable

A beautiful country manor noted for its cuisine

Graythwaite Manor is one of many excellent reasons for choosing Grange-over-Sands as your weekend or holiday venue. Started by the Blakemore family in 1937, the hotel is now under the supervision of the third generation of the same family. A warm welcome and personal care and attention remains their constant aim.

This beautifully furnished country house provides an exclusive, comfortable and tranquil setting in which to relax. It is set in eight acres of landscaped gardens and woodland, on the hillside looking out over Morecambe Bay.

Elegant, spacious lounges with fresh flowers and antiques are part of the atmosphere. Each bedroom is tastefully furnished, and has private bathroom, colour television, telephone and tea/coffee-making facilities. Many provide superb views across the gardens and bay to the Pennines beyond.

The hotel is noted for its superb cuisine, the head chef working closely with the proprietors to ensure the highest standards. You can look forward to a six-course dinner, a choice of carefully prepared dishes and good wine from their extensive cellar. They use fresh local produce as much as possible. A traditional English roast is a regular feature on the menu.

LOCATION

Turn left at top of main street, then 4th road on the right (almost opposite Fire Station).

“ Why anyone would choose to stay in any of the modern boxes in the city when they could stay here is beyond me ”

R Rennison

• *Map p.496 ref: D7*

19th century town house HALEY'S HOTEL & RESTAURANT

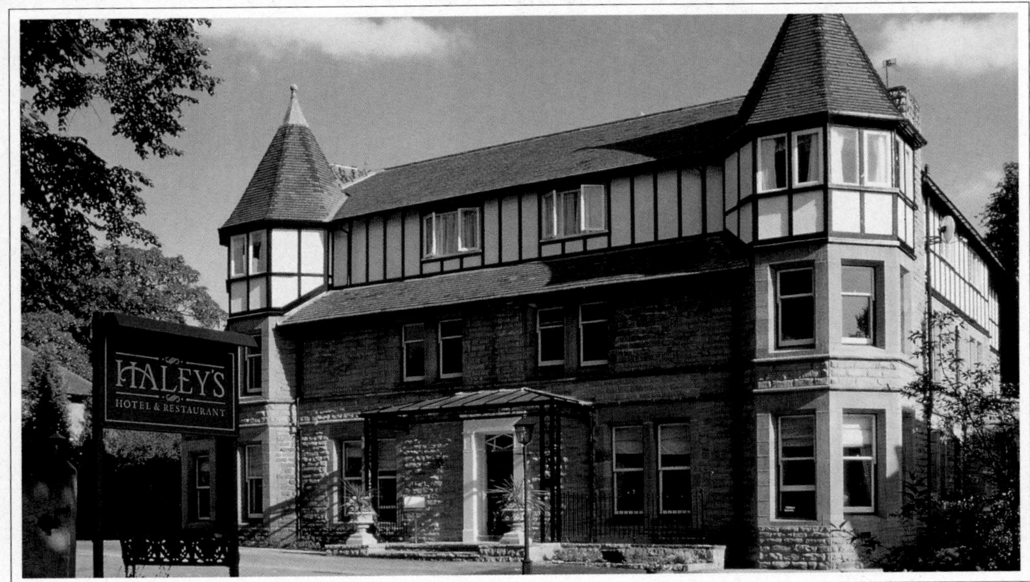

The perfect base for the famous Yorkshire Dales and the 'Cultural Capital of the North

Haley's Hotel and Restaurant is firmly established as one of the finest hotels in Leeds and has a string of prestigious awards to its name particularly for its cuisine. With two AA Rosettes and the title of 'County Hotel of the Year' under its belt, cricketers and bon viveurs amongst you should add this to your list of places to visit.

Located in Headingley just two miles out of the city, Haley's still retains the cosy semblance of being the home of some well-to-do Victorian gentleman - which indeed it once was. Antiques and rich furnishings abound and considerate touches like Harrogate toffee and late suppers give Haley's a very homely feel. Good taste and style come naturally to this highly individual hotel and the restaurant's track record in earning the worthiest of cooking awards speaks for itself.

Leeds itself is now one of Britain's most cosmopolitan and exciting cities and regarded as so 'in' that Harvey Nichols chose the city for its very first store outside London. Together with the fabulous Victorian shopping arcades, lively theatre and opera, famous Corn Exchange and Royal Armouries Museum, Leeds is a city that thoroughly deserves to be rediscovered. Be sure to take time, however, to venture beyond the city boundaries where the sights and scenery of the Yorkshire Dales and 'Herriott Country' are just a short drive away.

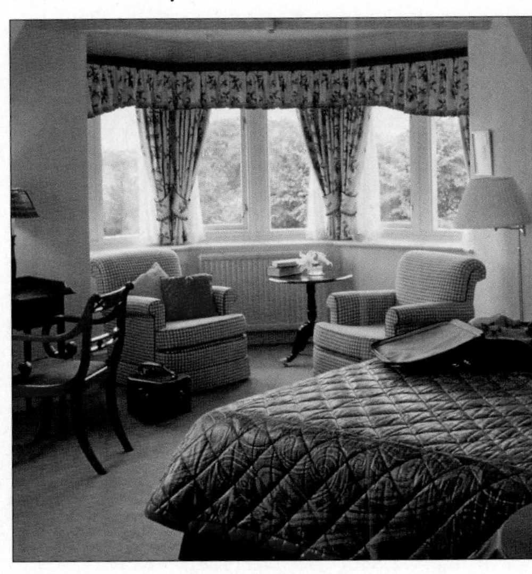

LOCATION

2 miles north of Leeds city centre off A660 (Otley Road). Turn off A660 between HSBC and Yorkshire Banks in Headingley Village.

Shire Oak Road, Headingley, Leeds, West Yorkshire LS6 2DE

Telephone 0113 278 4446
Fax 0113 275 3342

***E-mail:** haleys@bestloved.com*

OWNER
John Appleyard

GENERAL MANAGER
Tim Howard

ROOM RATES

Single occupancy	*£85 - £140*
9 Singles	*£60 - £110*
19 Doubles/Twins	*£85 - £175*
1 Four-poster	*£95 - £175*

Includes full breakfast and VAT

CHARGE/CREDIT CARDS

• DC • JCB • MC • VI

RATINGS & AWARDS
A.A. ★★★ ❀❀ 80%
Charmin Most Comfortable Loo of the Year 2000 Award

FACILITIES
***On site:** Licensed for weddings*
3 meeting rooms/max 100 people
***Nearby:** Golf, tennis, fitness, riding*

RESTRICTIONS
No facilities for disabled guests
No pets, guide dogs only
Closed 26 - 30 Dec

ATTRACTIONS
Royal Armouries, City Art Gallery, Opera House, Thackray Medical Museum, York, Harewood House, Yorkshire Dales

AFFILIATIONS
Preston's Global Hotels

NEAREST
MAJOR CITY:
Leeds - 2 miles/10 mins
MAJOR AIRPORT:
Manchester - 40 miles/1 hr
Leeds/Bradford - 8 miles/15 mins
RAILWAY STATION:
Leeds - 2 miles/10 mins

RESERVATIONS
Toll Free in US: 800-544-9993
*Quote **Best Loved***

ACCESS CODES
AMADEUS UI LBAHAL
APOLLO/GALILEO UI 27508
SABRE/ABACUS UI 52185
WORLDSPAN UI 241333

NORTH

• Map p.496 ref: B6

"Not only was the view unbelievable, it was quite easily the best and friendliest service we have ever experienced"

Will Carling, former England Rugby Captain

HOLBECK GHYLL HOTEL & SPA — *19th century hunting lodge*

NORTH

Holbeck Lane, Windermere, Cumbria LA23 1LU

Telephone 015394 32375
Fax 015394 34743

E-mail: *holbeck@bestloved.com*

OWNERS

David and Patricia Nicholson

ROOM RATES

18 Doubles/Twins £130 - £240
2 Four-posters/Suites £160 - £250
Includes full breakfast and VAT.
Enquire for 5-course dinner inclusive rates

CHARGE/CREDIT CARDS

• *DC* • *JCB* • *MC* • *VI*

RATINGS & AWARDS

E.T.C. ★★★ Gold Award
R.A.C. ★★★ Blue Ribbon Dining Award 3
A.A. ★★★ ❀❀❀
Cumbria Tourist Board
Hotel of the Year 2000 – 2001

FACILITIES

On site: *Health spa, croquet, putting green, gardens, woodland walks, cycling, tennis court, Licensed for weddings*
2 meeting rooms/max 60 people
Nearby: *Golf, riding, fishing*

RESTRICTIONS

No children under 8 years in restaurant
Limited facilities for disabled guests
No pets in public rooms

ATTRACTIONS

Wordsworth's Dove Cottage,
Beatrix Potter's home, lake cruises

AFFILIATIONS

Small Luxury Hotels
Pride of Britain

NEAREST

MAJOR CITY:
Manchester - 90 miles/1½ hrs
MAJOR AIRPORT:
Manchester - 90 miles/1½ hrs
RAILWAY STATION:
Windermere - 3 miles/5 mins

RESERVATIONS

Toll free in US/Canada: 800-525-4800 or 800-544-9993 or 800-98-PRIDE
Quote ***Best Loved***

ACCESS CODES

SABRE/ABACUS LX 31195
AMADEUS LX VEMHGC
APOLLO LX 21650
WORLDSPAN LX BWFHG

A connoisseur's hotel with sensational views of Lake Windermere

Back in 1888, Lord Lonsdale (of boxing's Lonsdale Belt fame) was so taken by the views across Lake Windermere and the Langdale Fells that he bought Holbeck Ghyll for use as his Hunting Lodge. His idea of the perfect country residence has made a lasting impression on its style and appearance. Over 100 years on, the view has hardly altered at all but the house is now an hotel of outstanding character, chosen by the Cumbria Tourist Board as Hotel of the Year 2000. Our congratulations go to David and Patricia Nicholson whose quest for excellence has made this charming hotel such a pleasure to visit.

The interiors are styled in the manner of Charles Rennie Mackintosh with a wealth of oak panelling and stained glass. Into this magnificence are interwoven the luxuries of a first class hotel and a connoisseur's clutter of a home; antiques, original paintings, flowers, really comfortable furniture .... Success is evident in the recent addition of six luxury, lake view rooms in The Lodge, only 45 metres from the old house itself.

Part of the Holbeck experience is the five-course dinner which features dishes classically prepared and artistically presented, much in the English style with a hint of France. Exciting and unusual vegetarian items are included in every course. Gourmets should go for the inclusive rate that includes dinner; they won't be disappointed.

LOCATION

M6 Exit 36. To Windermere, pass Brockhole Visitors' Centre, then after ½ mile turn right into Holbeck Lane (signed Troutbeck). Hotel is ½ mile on left.

Planning a wedding reception? Turn to 'Meeting Facilities' on page 476

" An overall outstanding stay. We will be back! "

Steve & Sue Becker

• Map p.496 ref: D5

Victorian hall

JUDGES AT KIRKLEVINGTON HALL

The verdict is unanimous approval for this former judges' lodging

Kirklevington Hall was built on the edge of the North Yorkshire Moors in 1881, as a family residence for the Richardsons of Hartlepool, prosperous and successful engineering entrepreneurs. Decimated by the First World War, the family hung on until the last Richardson died in 1940, and in the 1970's it was transformed into a country lodging for circuit court judges - hence the name.

Kirklevington has been a hotel since 1994, and the carefully restored house, replete with glossy Victorian woodwork, has a comfortably clubby and relaxing atmosphere which is known to play havoc with guests' short stay plans as they find it difficult to tear themselves away. Part of the charm is the lovely garden with its sunny terraces, Victorian walled garden where fruit and vegetables are grown for the kitchens, and extensive woodlands criss-crossed by shady paths. This is also a terrific base for exploring the moors, visiting the ancient abbeys of Rosedale and Rievaulx or Mount Grace Priory, and heading to the coast for Whitby, where Bram Stoker wrote Dracula, fossil-hunting is a must, and Captain Cook is celebrated with his own museum and monument.

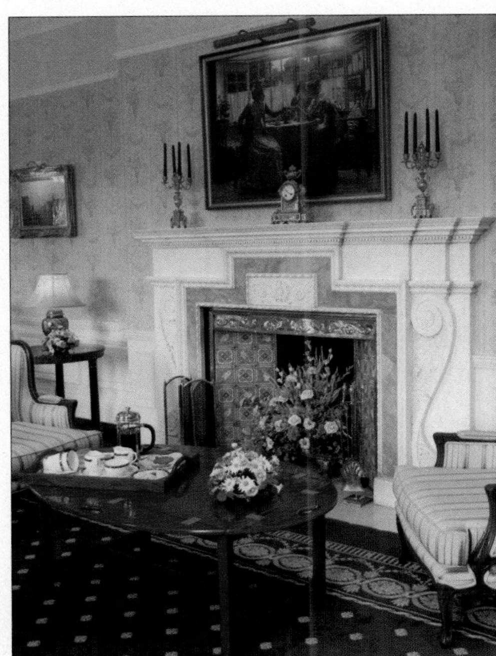

LOCATION

From A19, take A67 towards Yarm. The hotel is on left hand side just after Kirklevington village.

Kirklevington, Yarm, North Yorkshire TS15 9LW

Telephone 01642 789000
Fax 01642 782878

E-mail: *judges@bestloved.com*

OWNERS

Michael and Shirley Downs

ROOM RATES

2 Singles	*£132*
18 Doubles/Twins	*£167*
1 Four-poster	*£167*

Includes full breakfast and VAT

CHARGE/CREDIT CARDS

• *DC* • *MC* • *VI*

RATINGS & AWARDS

A.A. ★★★ ❀❀ *75%*

FACILITIES

On site: *Garden, croquet, heli-pad*
Licensed for weddings
3 meeting rooms/max 200 people
Nearby: *Golf, tennis, riding, fishing, swimming, health & beauty*

RESTRICTIONS

Limited facilities for disabled guests
No pets

ATTRACTIONS

Whitby Abbey, Yorkshire Moors, Rievaulx Abbey, High Force Falls, Pickering Castle, H. M. Bark Endeavour

AFFILIATIONS

Independent

NEAREST

MAJOR CITY:
Middlesbrough - 8 miles/20 mins

MAJOR AIRPORT:
Teeside - 10 miles/30 mins

RAILWAY STATION:
Yarm - 1 mile/5 mins

RESERVATIONS

Direct with hotel
Quote ***Best Loved***

ACCESS CODES

Not applicable

NORTH

Looking for an hotel with a golf course on site? See our 'Golf Guide' on page 478

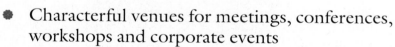

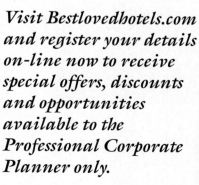

" Once again you have exceeded all our expectations "

Stephen Beresford & Lesley Haynes, Toshiba, Surrey

• *Map p.496 ref: B6*

17th century coaching inn

LAKESIDE HOTEL

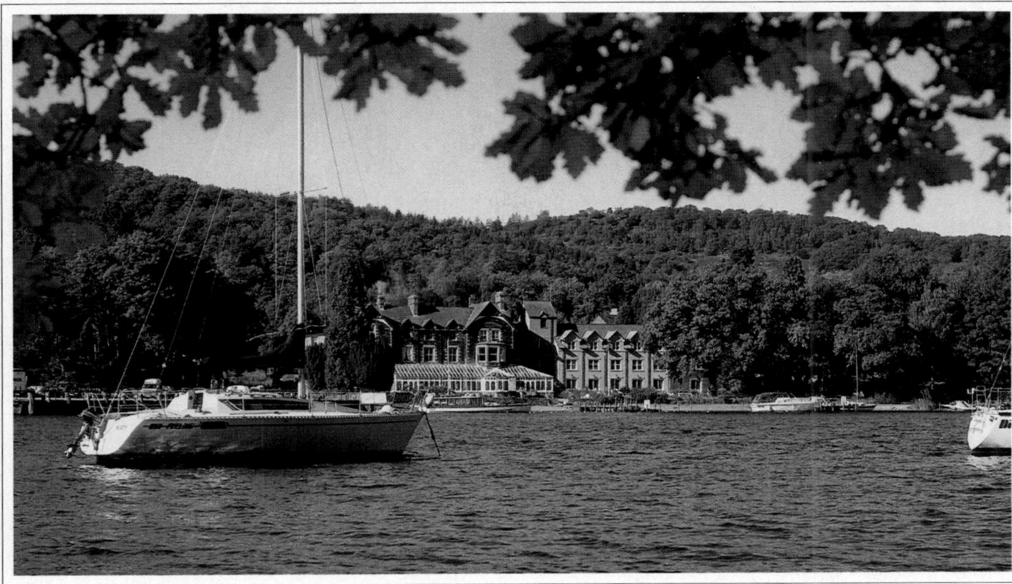

They overlook nothing but the lake

Enviably positioned right on the shores of Lake Windermere, the Lakeside is a classic personally owned and managed Lakeland hotel, and a long-time favourite with regular visitors to the area. The secluded setting provides a wonderful escape from everyday distractions and allows guests to really relax and enjoy the view. The scope for watersports, climbing and walking is boundless and lake cruises depart from the waterfront outside the hotel.

The Lakeside has a long tradition of hospitality dating back to its origins as a 17th-century coaching inn. The spacious and comfortable lounges and cosy bars retain original antique oak panelling and beams, and many of the bedrooms offer breathtaking views of the lake. There is fine dining in the Lakeview Restaurant, while John Ruskin's Brasserie serves a more contemporary menu in less formal surroundings, and The Lakeside Conservatory serves drinks and light meals throughout the day.

Guests can also enjoy the brand new facilities at the on-site Leisure Club, which include a 17 metre indoor pool, gymnasium, sauna, steam room, and a range of health and beauty treatments. Outdoor activities, such as fishing, horse-riding, golf, clay pigeon shooting and hot air ballooning can be arranged within easy reach of the hotel.

LOCATION

From Exit 36 of M6, join A590 to Barrow and follow signs to Newby Bridge. Turn right over the bridge and the hotel is 1 mile on the right.

Lake Windermere, Newby Bridge, Cumbria LA12 8AT

Telephone 015395 31207
Fax 015395 31699

E-mail: *lakeside@bestloved.com*

OWNER
Neville Talbot

GENERAL MANAGER
Clive Wilson

ROOM RATES

4 Singles	*£95 - £145*
72 Doubles/Twins	*£140 - £205*
4 Suites	*£250*

Includes full breakfast and VAT
Self Catering Lodge - Price on application

CHARGE/CREDIT CARDS

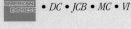

• DC • JCB • MC • VI

RATINGS & AWARDS
E.T.C. ★★★★ Silver Award
R.A.C. ★★★★ Dining Award 1
A.A. ★★★★ ❀❀ 75%

FACILITIES
On site: *Garden, croquet, fishing, indoor pool, gym, sauna, steam room, health & beauty*
Licensed for weddings
7 meeting rooms/max 140 people
Nearby: *Riding, complimentary use of leisure club*

RESTRICTIONS
None

ATTRACTIONS
Lake District National Park, Lake cruises, Lakeside Steam Railway, Beatrix Potter's home, Wordsworth's cottage, John Ruskin's home

AFFILIATIONS
Fine Individual Hotels
The European Connection

NEAREST
MAJOR CITY:
Manchester - 80 miles/1½ hrs
MAJOR AIRPORT:
Manchester - 90 miles/1½ hrs
RAILWAY STATION:
Oxenholme - 12 miles/15 mins

RESERVATIONS
Toll free in US: 800-544-9993
Quote ***Best Loved***

ACCESS CODES
Not applicable

• Map p.496 ref: B5

"A totally enjoyable experience"

B E Crockford, Suffolk

LEEMING HOUSE

Country house

Watermillock, Penrith, Cumbria CA11 0JJ

Telephone 01768 486622
Fax 01768 486443

E-mail: leeminghouse@bestloved.com

GENERAL MANAGER

Christopher Curry

ROOM RATES

Single occupancy	£79 - £99
39 Doubles/Twins	£118 - £178
1 Mini suite	£148 - £188

Includes full breakfast and VAT

CHARGE/CREDIT CARDS

• DC • JCB • MC • VI

RATINGS & AWARDS

R.A.C. Blue Ribbon ★★★★
A.A. ★★★ ❀ 73%
Lake District Restaurant of the Year 1999

FACILITIES

On site: Gardens, croquet, fishing, heli-pad
Licensed for weddings
2 meeting rooms/max 20 people
Nearby: Golf, riding, sailing, quad biking

RESTRICTIONS

Limited facilities for disabled guests
No pets in public rooms

ATTRACTIONS

Tree Trail, Bird of Prey Centre, Aira Force Waterfall, Dalemain House, Ullswater boat trips, hill walking

AFFILIATIONS

Heritage Hotels

NEAREST

MAJOR CITY:
Carlisle - 30 miles/40 mins

MAJOR AIRPORT:
Manchester - 130 miles/2 hrs

RAILWAY STATION:
Penrith - 8 miles/15 mins

RESERVATIONS

Toll free in US: 800-225-5843
Quote **Best Loved**

ACCESS CODES

AMADEUS FE MAN228
APOLLO/GALILEO FE 5757
SABRE/ABACUS FE 10831
WORLDSPAN FE 0228

Splendid seclusion in a stunning setting

Leeming House lies on the western shores of Ullswater, the second longest lake in Cumbria, and the one which William Wordsworth reckoned enjoyed "the happiest combination of beauty and grandeur, which any of the Lakes affords". It would seem little has changed at Leeming, which was built in the early 1800s during the poet's era, and remains seductively cocooned from the outside world by 20 acres of gardens and woodland.

A country house hotel for over 30 years, this is not only a lovely spot from which to explore the Lake District, but a well-established property where guests can truly relax in the elegant yet charmingly informal surroundings. Of particular note is the Regency Restaurant (selected 1999 Lake District Restaurant of the Year), and 14 of the pretty and luxurious bedrooms boast private balconies with views across the gardens towards the lake. Within the grounds is a croquet lawn and the renowned Tree Trail, a half-mile woodland walk planted with an intriguing variety of mature trees from around the world. Popular local diversions include a lake cruise on the Ullswater Steamer, the Aira Force waterfall, hiking and sailing. Fishing can be arranged through the hotel.

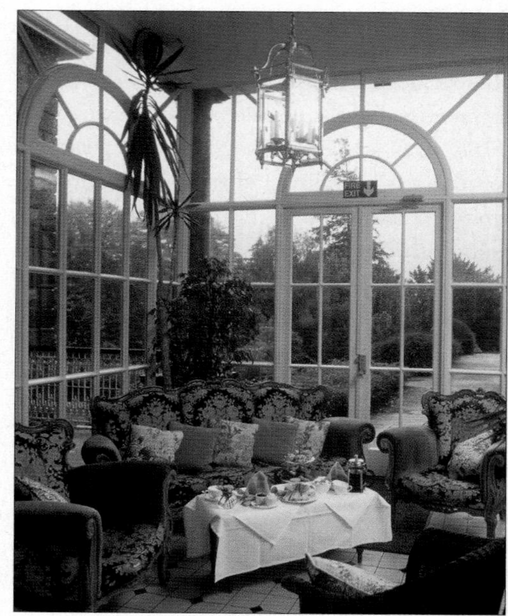

LOCATION

10 minutes from the M6 at Junction 40, on the western shore of Lake Ullswater on the A592.

“ The welcoming atmosphere, good food and magnificent views will mean you'll readily return to Linthwaite . . . ”

Los Angeles Times

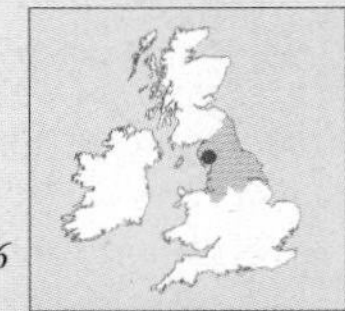

• Map p.496 ref: B6

Victorian country house

LINTHWAITE HOUSE

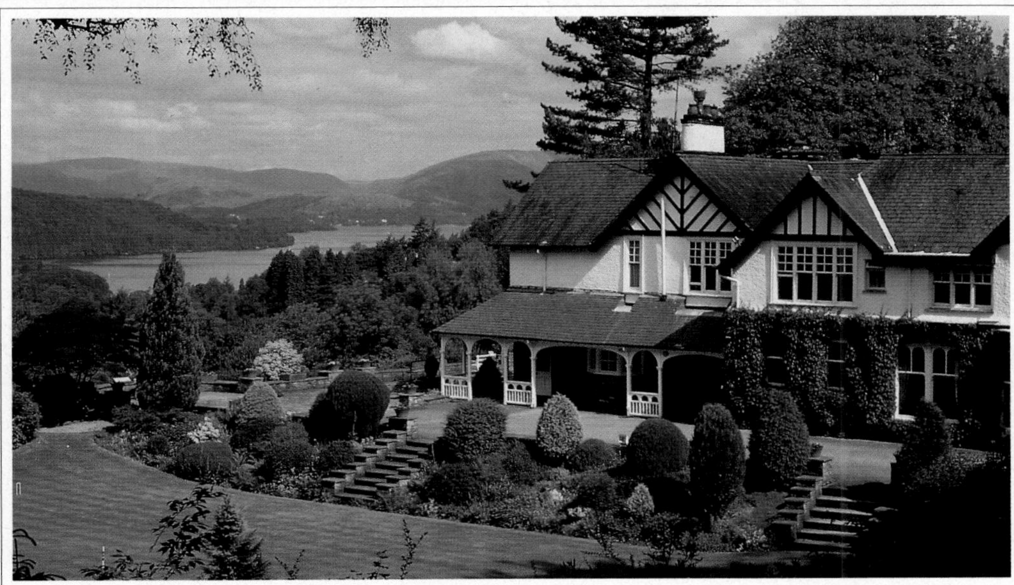

A relaxing break among the hills and valleys of the Lake District

Situated in 14 acres of glorious hilltop gardens overlooking Lake Windermere and 'Coniston Old Man', Linthwaite House is a haven for those with distinctive tastes who appreciate the finer things in life. Breathtaking sunsets, superb scenery and a multitude of places of special interest within easy reach, including the home of William Wordsworth, Beatrix Potter's home, museum and gallery, historic houses, theatre and cinema. Sweeping fells and Lakeland villages have been the source of inspiration for poets and writers alike since time began.

Good food and fine wine served in a relaxed, unstuffy atmosphere and unpretentious surroundings combine to give you a rewarding break in the heart of the Lake District.

There are 26 rooms, some with lakeview, and a garden suite with separate lounge. Each has en suite bath/shower, bathrobes, direct-dial telephone, radio, trouser press, hairdryer, tea/coffee making facilities and stereo/CD player.

Whatever the occasion, whatever the season, Linthwaite House will be there to pamper you.

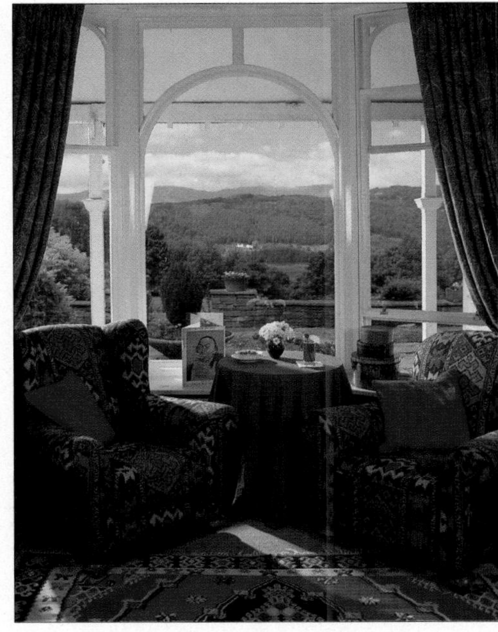

LOCATION

On eastern side of Lake Windermere. Exit 36/M6 and A591 for 8 miles; first left at roundabout onto B5284 to Crook. Hotel is 7 miles on left (1 mile past Windermere Golf Club).

Crook Road, Windermere, The Lake District LA23 3JA

Telephone 015394 88600
Fax 015394 88601

E-mail: linthwaite@bestloved.com

OWNER

Mike Bevans

ROOM RATES

1 Single	£85 - £115
9 Doubles/Twins	£90 - £150
3 Superior Doubles/Twins	£160 - £180
12 Lake/Garden view	£185 - £210
1 Suite	£235 - £260

Includes full breakfast and VAT

CHARGE/CREDIT CARDS

• DC • JCB • MC • VI

RATINGS & AWARDS

E.T.C. ★★★ Gold Award
R.A.C. ★★★ Dining Award 3
A.A. ★★★ ❀❀ 81%
England for Excellence Award
A.A. Courtesy & Care Award

FACILITIES

On site: Gardens, croquet, fly fishing, bicycles, Licensed for weddings
3 meeting rooms/max 60 people
Nearby: Golf, riding, tennis, watersports, leisure spa

RESTRICTIONS

No children under 7 years in restaurant after 7 pm
No pets

ATTRACTIONS

Beatrix Potter's Home & Museum, Wordsworth's Dove Cottage, Lake Windermere, Sizergh Castle, Levens Hall & Topiary Gardens

AFFILIATIONS

The Celebrated Hotels Collection

NEAREST

MAJOR CITY:
Manchester - 95 miles/1¾ hrs
MAJOR AIRPORT:
Manchester - 95 miles/1¾ hrs
RAILWAY STATION:
Windermere - 3 miles/10 mins

RESERVATIONS

Toll free in US: 800-322-2403
Quote **Best Loved**

ACCESS CODES

AMADEUS UI CAXLHH
APOLLO/GALILEO UI 48735
SABRE/ABACUS UI 35752
WORLDSPAN UI 40645

A keen Angler? Refer to page 472 for our Fishing Index

• Map p.496 ref: C5

"I have stayed in many small highly rated hotels in Europe and at home. I have never found any to better this one"

Harold Goodman, Shropshire

LOVELADY SHIELD

Georgian country house

Nenthead Road, Alston, Cumbria CA9 3LF

Telephone 01434 381203
Fax 01434 381515

E-mail: lovelady@bestloved.com

OWNERS
Peter and Marie Haynes

RATES PER PERSON
9 Doubles/Twins £53 - £103
1 Four-poster £68 - £103
Includes full breakfast, dinner and VAT

CHARGE/CREDIT CARDS

• MC • VI

RATINGS & AWARDS
E.T.C. ★★
A.A. ★★ ❀❀ 74%

FACILITIES
On site: Garden, croquet, heli-pad
Licensed for weddings
2 meeting rooms/max 45 people
Nearby: Golf, fishing, hunting/shooting, riding, walking

RESTRICTIONS
No facilities for disabled guests
£5 surcharge for pets
No children under 7 years in restaurant after 7.30pm
Closed 3 Jan – 4 Feb

ATTRACTIONS
Lake District, Hadrian's Wall, Holy Island, High Force Waterfall, Barnard Castle, Durham Cathedral

AFFILIATIONS
Fine Individual Hotels

NEAREST
MAJOR CITY:
Penrith - 19 miles/30 mins

MAJOR AIRPORT:
Newcastle - 42 miles/1 hr

RAILWAY STATION:
Penrith - 19 miles/30 mins

RESERVATIONS
Toll free in US: 800-544-9993
Quote **Best Loved**

ACCESS CODES
Not applicable

NORTH

Hidden atop the Pennine moors is a guest book swelling with compliments

At Alston, you are at a watershed. As England's highest market town, it stands amongst the moors and fells of the North Pennines; located in a heatherclad wilderness with a choice of The Lake District, The Yorkshire Dales or the Border Forest to explore. Indecision has its own rewards: simply by staying put, you will discover a prolific wildlife you might think had long since gone the way of the Dodo. And heritage galore: for example, the South Tyneside narrow-gauge railway starts here.

If this whets your appetite for surprises, try to find Lovelady Shield. If the name has the ring of romance, the house and the location certainly live up to it. It lies in three acres of garden upon a wooded hillside on the banks of the Nent.

First impressions are to be trusted. Lovelady looks an absolute gem of a place - and it is. The guest book positively swells with compliments particularly about the friendliness of the owners, Peter and Marie Haynes and their staff. So, too, does the food which owes everything to Master Chef Barrie Gordon whose efforts are enhanced by an interesting list of 100 wines.

Alas, Lovelady Shield is a secret that's hard to keep; but who could deny a friend such pleasure?

LOCATION

2¼ miles east of Alston. The entrance to the drive is at the junction of the A689 and the B6294.

"Food worth driving 100 miles for"

Derek Cooper, radio presenter

• *Map p.496 ref: E7*

19th century retreat

THE MANOR HOUSE

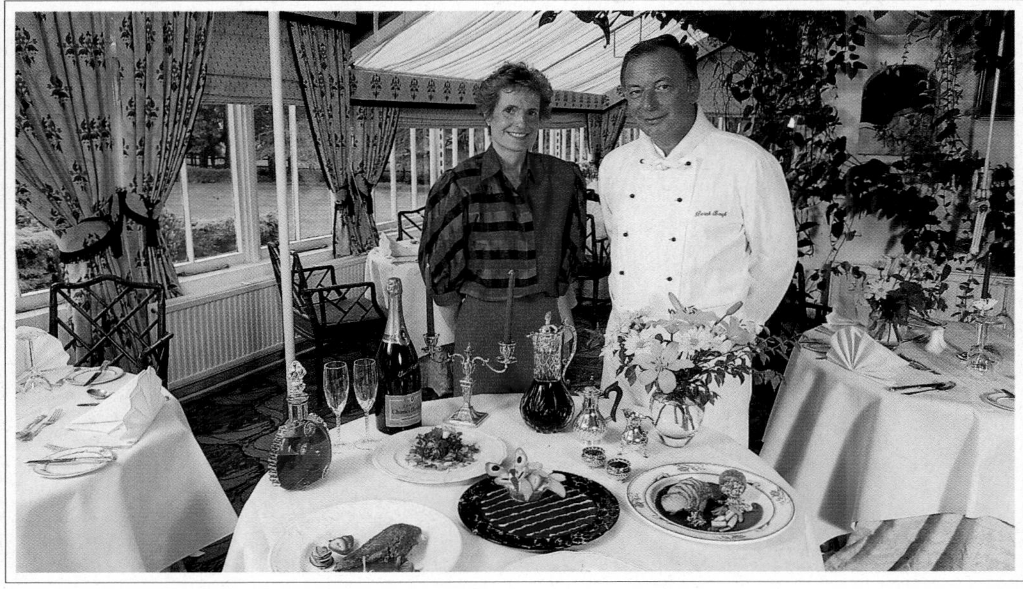

A civilised retreat surrounded by rolling wooded countryside

Overlooking horse paddocks and parkland, and set in three acres of tree-lined grounds, The Manor House occupies a tranquil position on the rolling Yorkshire Wolds. This 19th-century retreat is perfect for those seeking relaxation and luxury. Lee and Derek Baugh maintain a high standard in all aspects of entertaining.

The bedrooms have open, attractive views; guests will find themselves pampered with unexpected personal comforts. Relax in the drawing room with an aperitif as you anticipate the delights being prepared for you by Chef-patron Derek Baugh, formerly of The Dorchester.

Through his inspired culinary approach, there has evolved a distinctive, creative style of cuisine. Lee Baugh's confections are irresistible. The wine list reflects an informed interest in the best European wines. As an alternative to the restaurant, the conservatory is an ideal place to wine and dine on a summer evening.

A wealth of activities lies on the doorstep – the vastness of the North Yorkshire Moors, the rugged grandeur of the coastline from Bridlington to the old whaling port of Whitby and the many stately homes and villages.

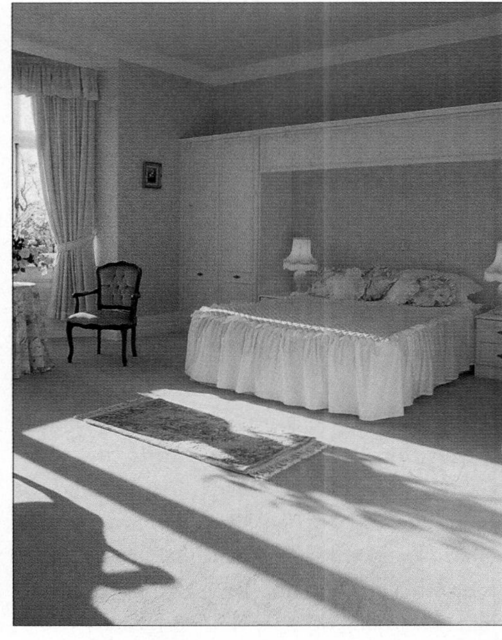

LOCATION

Exit 38/M62 to North Cave and then B1230 to Beverley. After passing through Walkington turn left at traffic lights. At first minor cross-roads, turn left again. Hotel is 400 yards on left.

Northlands, Walkington, Beverley, East Yorkshire HU17 8RT

Telephone 01482 881645
Fax 01482 866501

E-mail: *manoryorks@bestloved.com*

OWNERS

Derek and Lee Baugh

ROOM RATES

Single occupancy *£70 - £80*
7 Doubles/Twins *£80 - £100*
Includes VAT

CHARGE/CREDIT CARDS

• *MC* • *VI*

RATINGS & AWARDS

E.T.C. ★★
R.A.C. ★★ *Dining Award 3*
A.A. ★★ ❀❀ *73%*

FACILITIES

On site: *Garden, heli-pad*
Licensed for weddings
1 meeting room/max 20 people
Nearby: *Golf, riding, clay pigeon shooting*

RESTRICTIONS

No facilities for disabled guests
Small dogs only

ATTRACTIONS

Beverley Minster, Museum of Army Transport, Lincoln Cathedral, York, Thornton Abbey

AFFILIATIONS

Independent

NEAREST

MAJOR CITY:
Hull - 9 miles/12 mins

MAJOR AIRPORT:
Humberside - 20 miles/30 mins

RAILWAY STATION:
Hull - 9 miles/12 mins

RESERVATIONS

Direct with hotel
*Quote **Best Loved***

ACCESS CODES

Not applicable

"My guests were very impressed with the hotel, the food, the high standards of the rooms but more especially the helpfulness of the staff"

Chris Hara, Lincoln Financial Group

MATFEN HALL

Regency mansion

Matfen,
Near Newcastle-upon-Tyne,
Northumberland NE20 ORH

Telephone 01661 886500
Fax 01661 886055

E-mail: *matfenhall@bestloved.com*

NORTH

OWNERS

Sir Hugh and Lady Blackett

GENERAL MANAGER

Simon Bath

ROOM RATES

Single occupancy	£95 - £135
28 Doubles/Twins	£120 - £220
1 Four-poster	£220
1 Suite	£220

Includes full breakfast and VAT

CHARGE/CREDIT CARDS

• MC • VI

RATINGS & AWARDS

E.T.C. ★★★

A.A. ★★★ *70%*

FACILITIES

On site: *Garden, croquet, golf, fishing, heli-pad*
Licensed for weddings
7 meeting rooms/max 200 people
Nearby: *Riding*

RESTRICTIONS

Pets by arrangement

ATTRACTIONS

Alnwick Castle, Holy Island, Centre of Life, Angel of the North, Newcastle United Football Club, Bamburgh Castle

AFFILIATIONS

Independent

NEAREST

MAJOR CITY:
Newcastle - 15 miles/20 mins

MAJOR AIRPORT:
Newcastle - 18 miles/15 mins

RAILWAY STATION:
Newcastle - 15 miles/20 mins

RESERVATIONS

Direct with hotel
*Quote **Best Loved***

ACCESS CODES

AMADEUS HK NCLMAT
APOLLO/GALILEO HT 22362
SABRE/ABACUS HK 49495
WORLDSPAN HK MATFE

A magnificent Northumberland landmark

As soon as you enter the impressive two mile driveway, you just know that you are going to find something special at the end. Sir Hugh and Lady Blackett have carefully restored the Hall into a magnificent country house hotel, set in some of Northumberland's most stunning countryside.

Nestled alongside the extremely pretty village of Matfen with an equally pretty pub where guests can become temporary 'regulars', Matfen Hall is finished to exacting standards. Each of the 30 bedrooms are wonderfully opulent, but traditionally so. At the same time, all the modern amenities are there. Great care has been taken to preserve many original features such as the ornate ceilings, the Drawing Room fireplace, and the Library, now a cosy, book-lined dining room. The quite magnificent Great Hall with its massive pillars is breathtaking and unique as a venue for private dining, wedding receptions and corporate use.

You don't have to be a golfer to enjoy Matfen, but if you are then the highly-rated course boasts a variety of teasing water features and several holes where dry stone 'ha ha' walls add a distinctly local note to the proceedings. Around Matfen, take time out to visit Hadrian's Wall and Durham Cathedral to the south, and the glorious Northumberland National Park to the north.

LOCATION

From A1 take the A69 signposted Hexham and Carlisle. At Heddon on the Wall take the B6318 towards Chollerford. The hotel is on the right hand side after 7 miles.

“Hotel of dreams, it's that extra special care that has given Mere Court such a first class reputation”

Living Edge Magazine

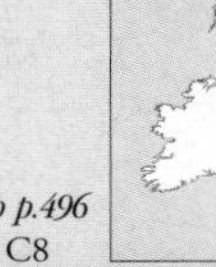

• Map p.496 ref: C8

Edwardian country house

MERE COURT HOTEL

A heritage home making a dramatic entrance into the realms of hospitality

Right in the middle of the vale that sweeps between Roman Chester and the picturesque peaks and stately homes of Derbyshire is Mere Court. It was built as an Edwardian Country House in an area famous for its 'Magpie Houses', those half-timbered cottages you will have seen charicatured in story books. Set in seven acres of delightful gardens that include an ornamental lake, it is hard to believe that Manchester, its airport and its affluent neighbourhoods like Altrincham and Knutsford all lie so close.

Mere Court has recently been given a new lease of life by Lesley Hampson who has put her heart and soul, not to mention many of her own family treasures, into recreating the grandeur of this fine, listed building. She has a natural eye for design: subtle colours harmonise with luxuriant fabrics; the ample bedrooms are attended by stately bathrooms graced with double Jacuzzis. One restaurant, fine food, light lunches in the lounge bar and afternoon tea continue a theme that is as elegant as the period setting in which it all comes so delightfully together.

This is a meeting place par excellence: within a year, it has become the place to celebrate a wedding and, with its state-of-the-art facilities, an ideal conference venue. A fine achievement well patronised by the locals and deserving of wider recognition.

LOCATION

On the A50, Knutsford to Warrington Road, 1 mile west of junction with A556 on the right-hand side.

Warrington Road, Mere, Knutsford, Cheshire WA16 ORW

Telephone 01565 831000
Fax 01565 831001

E-mail: *merecourt@bestloved.com*

NORTH

OWNERS

Les and Lesley Hampson

ROOM RATES

Single occupancy	£70 - £110
31 Doubles/Twins	£80 - £130
2 Four-poster suites	£140 - £180
1 Suite	£140 - £180

Includes full breakfast and VAT

CHARGE/CREDIT CARDS

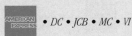

• DC • JCB • MC • VI

RATINGS & AWARDS

E.T.C. ★★★★
R.A.C. ★★★★ *Dining Award 2*
A.A. ★★★★ ❀ *69%*

FACILITIES

On site: *Garden, croquet, fishing*
10 meeting rooms/max 120 people
Nearby: *Golf, tennis, fitness, fishing, riding*

RESTRICTIONS

None

ATTRACTIONS

Tatton Park, Chester, North Wales Coastline, Manchester, Peak District, Liverpool, Trafford Centre

AFFILIATIONS

Independent

NEAREST

MAJOR CITY:
Manchester - 8 miles/15 mins

MAJOR AIRPORT:
Manchester - 5 miles/10 mins

RAILWAY STATION:
Manchester - 5 miles/10 mins
Knutsford - 2 miles/5 mins

FERRY PORT:
Liverpool - 30 miles/30 mins

RESERVATIONS

Direct with hotel
Quote ***Best Loved***

ACCESS CODES

Not applicable

• Map p.496 ref: B5

“ This is a wonderful place, treasure it! ”

James Seff, San Francisco, USA

MICHAELS NOOK

Victorian house

Grasmere, Ambleside, Cumbria LA22 9RP

Telephone 015394 35496
Fax 015394 35645

E-mail: *nook@bestloved.com*

OWNER

Reg Gifford

ROOM RATES

Single occupancy	*£148*
11 Doubles	*£192 - £300*
1 Four-poster	*£300*
2 Suites	*£370 - £410*

Includes full breakfast, 4-course dinner and VAT

CHARGE/CREDIT CARDS

 *• DC • MC • VI*

RATINGS & AWARDS

A.A. ★★★ ❀❀❀❀

FACILITIES

On site: *Garden, croquet, heli-pad, Licensed for weddings*
1 meeting room/max 30 people
Nearby: *Riding, fishing, indoor pool, sauna, solarium, jacuzzi in nearby sister hotel*

RESTRICTIONS

No children under 7 years allowed in restaurant
No facilities for disabled guests
No pets

ATTRACTIONS

Wordsworth's Dove Cottage and Rydal Mount, Beatrix Potter's Hill Top, Sawrey, John Ruskin's Brantwood, Coniston

AFFILIATIONS

The Celebrated Hotels Collection

NEAREST

MAJOR CITY:
Carlisle - 45 miles/50 mins

MAJOR AIRPORT:
Manchester - 100 miles/2 hrs

RAILWAY STATION:
Windermere - 9 miles/15 mins

RESERVATIONS

Toll free in US: 800-322-2403
*Quote **Best Loved***

ACCESS CODES

SABRE/ABACUS HK 35650
APOLLO/GALILEO HT 41204
WORLDSPAN HK MICHA

NORTH

At the heart of English lakeland, an hotel cherished worldwide

Michaels Nook is a fine, early Victorian Lakeland house, with a wealth of mahogany panelling and elegant plasterwork. It derives its name from William Wordsworth's poem 'Michael', about a humble shepherd who spent his long life in the immediate vicinity.

It was opened as an hotel in 1969 by Reg Gifford, a former antique dealer, who has personally brought together the predominantly English embellishments, and it enjoys an international reputation for the excellence of its furnishings, food and service. There are two suites and 12 very comfortable bedrooms. Dishes which combine artistry with flavour are created from fine fresh produce for the restaurant, recently awarded a Michelin Star, and the outstanding wine list reflects another of Reg Gifford's special interests.

With open fires, an abundance of flowers and plants, Great Danes and exotic cats, Michaels Nook remains a home, with an atmosphere of intimacy and warmth – and just a hint of eccentricity. Magnificent walks start from the doorstep, as do spectacular drives through some of Britain's most impressive scenery. Dove Cottage, Wordsworth's home, is nearby, and Beatrix Potter's home at Sawrey is only a short drive away.

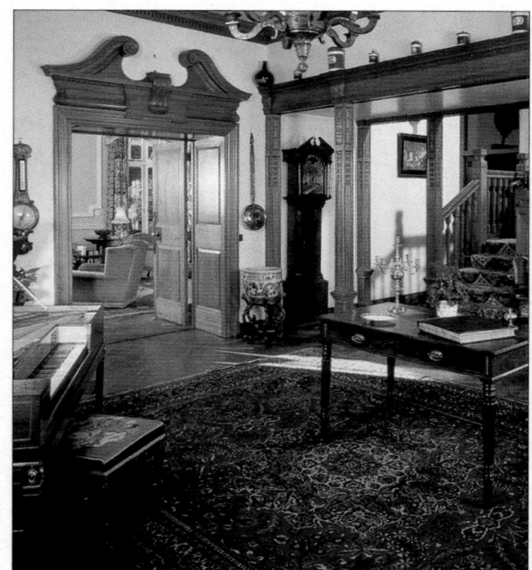

LOCATION

Turn uphill off the A591 just north of Grasmere at The Swan Hotel, and bear left with the lane for 400 yards.

" Diners are treated more like friends at Miller Howe "

OK Magazine

Country house hotel & restaurant

MILLER HOWE HOTEL

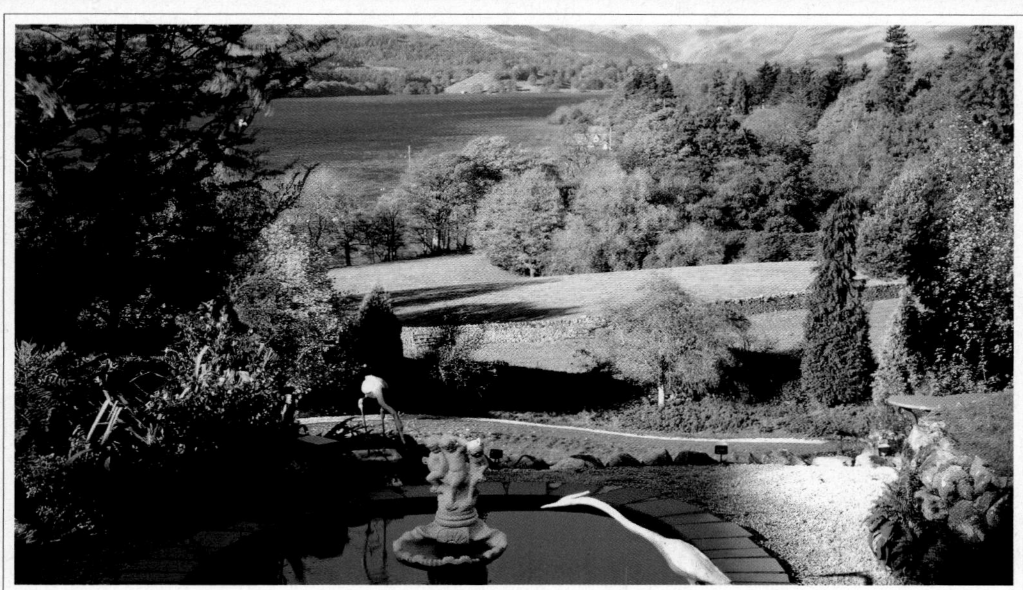

Country House Hotel with a very famous restaurant

The revolution continues on the slopes above Lake Windermere: Charles Garside, former Editor-in-Chief of The European and a former Deputy Editor of the Sunday Express, has done wonders for Miller Howe in the past year.

Regulars will be glad to know that the food that made Miller Howe famous continues to go from strength to strength; the introduction of Editions, has proved a great success with bon viveurs as has the modest lunch menu at £17.50 per person. Last year, a Director's Choice was introduced to the formidable wine list making the choice easier and adding greater value. Another welcome innovation that is here to stay.

Although the hotel's reputation is built around its dining room, the complete refurbishment of the house since our last edition has considerably enhanced the hotel's standing amongst its peers. A restaurant with rooms? Or a country house hotel? Take your pick, Miller Howe combines the best of both worlds without a trace of compromise.

The fact you can enjoy all this within a 4½-acre estate which reaches down to Lake Windermere, with gorgeous views every step of the way, makes this a very special place indeed. Add to that the exemplary service from a very charming and willing team, together with Charles' effortless ability to entertain and amuse, and you have the perfect recipe for a time to remember.

LOCATION

A592 between Windermere and Bowness.

Rayrigg Road, Windermere, Cumbria LA23 1EY

Telephone 015394 42536
Fax 015394 45664

E-mail: *millerhowe@bestloved.com*

OWNER

Charles Garside

RATES PER PERSON

Single occupancy	*£95 - £165*
5 Standard Doubles/Twins	*£80 - £135*
1 Mini suites	*£95 - £125*
6 Master Doubles/Twins	*£99 - £135*

Includes full breakfast, dinner and VAT

CHARGE/CREDIT CARDS

• DC • MC • VI

RATINGS & AWARDS

A.A. ★★ ❀❀
Courvoisier's Book of the Best

FACILITIES

On site: *Garden, croquet, heli-pad*
Licensed for weddings
2 meeting rooms/max 40 people
Nearby: *Golf, riding, fishing (permits provided)*
complimentary use of leisure club

RESTRICTIONS

No children under 8 years
No facilities for disabled guests
No pets in public rooms

ATTRACTIONS

Lake District National Park, Beatrix Potter's home and museum, Steamboat Museum, Dove Cottage, Holehird Gardens

AFFILIATIONS

Independent

NEAREST

MAJOR CITY:
Manchester - 90 miles/1½ hrs

MAJOR AIRPORT:
Manchester - 100 miles/1½ hrs

RAILWAY STATION:
Windermere - 1 mile/5 mins

RESERVATIONS

Direct with hotel
Quote ***Best Loved***

ACCESS CODES

Not applicable

NORTH

• Map p.496 ref: C7

"The food was so fantastic that the Palace would have approved and the atmosphere so relaxed I kicked off my shoes"

Carol Chester, travel writer

NORTHCOTE MANOR

Victorian manor house

Northcote Road, Langho, Near Blackburn, Lancashire BB6 8BE

Telephone 01254 240555
Fax 01254 246568

E-mail: *northcote@bestloved.com*

OWNERS

Craig Bancroft and Nigel Haworth

ROOM RATES

Single occupancy	*£90 - £110*
13 Doubles/Twins	*£110 - £130*
1 Four-poster	*£130*

Includes full breakfast and VAT

CHARGE/CREDIT CARDS

• *MC* • *VI*

RATINGS & AWARDS

E.T.C. ★★★ Gold Award
A.A. ★★★ ❀❀❀ 70%
Caterer & Hotelkeeper 'Independent Hotel of the Year 1999'

FACILITIES

On site: *Garden, heli-pad, Licensed for weddings*
1 meeting room/max 40 people
Nearby: *Golf, fishing*

RESTRICTIONS

No pets

ATTRACTIONS

Ribble Valley, Clitheroe, Stonyhurst College, Whalley Abbey, Pendle Witches, Ribchester

AFFILIATIONS

Independent

NEAREST

MAJOR CITY:
Manchester - 28 miles/40 mins

MAJOR AIRPORT:
Manchester - 40 miles/45 mins
Blackpool - 29 miles/35 mins

RAILWAY STATION:
Preston - 11 miles/20 mins

RESERVATIONS

Direct with hotel
*Quote **Best Loved***

ACCESS CODES

Not applicable

NORTH

Where lovers of fine food and wine may want to stay forever

Northcote Manor in the Ribble Valley, one of the great beauty spots of England, is owned and run, with great talent, by partners Craig Bancroft and Nigel Haworth. Together they have built up this small hotel in fifteen years to become one of the most successful in the country.

Northcote Manor is best known for its outstanding food and award-winning restaurant and was awarded its first Michelin star in 1996. Nigel Haworth, holder of the 1999 'Wedgwood Chef & Potter Trophy' for Britain's Top Chef, has a special love of traditional Lancashire cooking and he has recreated many of those dishes in a very different style, including a sticky toffee pudding that has been voted one of the best in the country.

While Nigel cooks and presides over the kitchen, Craig looks after the guests' needs in the restaurant and rooms. His special love is wine and he delights in personally matching food and wine for the guests. There are fourteen bedrooms, all en suite, and one four-poster. Games, books, interesting ornaments and tea and coffee making facilities add to the home-from-home atmosphere. The very comfortable beds have prompted many visitors to ask where they can buy them. In 1999 Northcote Manor was proud to have been voted 'Independent Hotel of the Year' by the Caterer & Hotelkeeper - an 'Oscar' of the hospitality industry.

LOCATION

M6 Exit 31. Take A59 towards Clitheroe. Langho is close to junction with A666.

"Many hotels try what you have achieved - well done!"

Mr and Mrs R Lewis, London

Map p.496 ref: C8

Country house hotel

NUNSMERE HALL

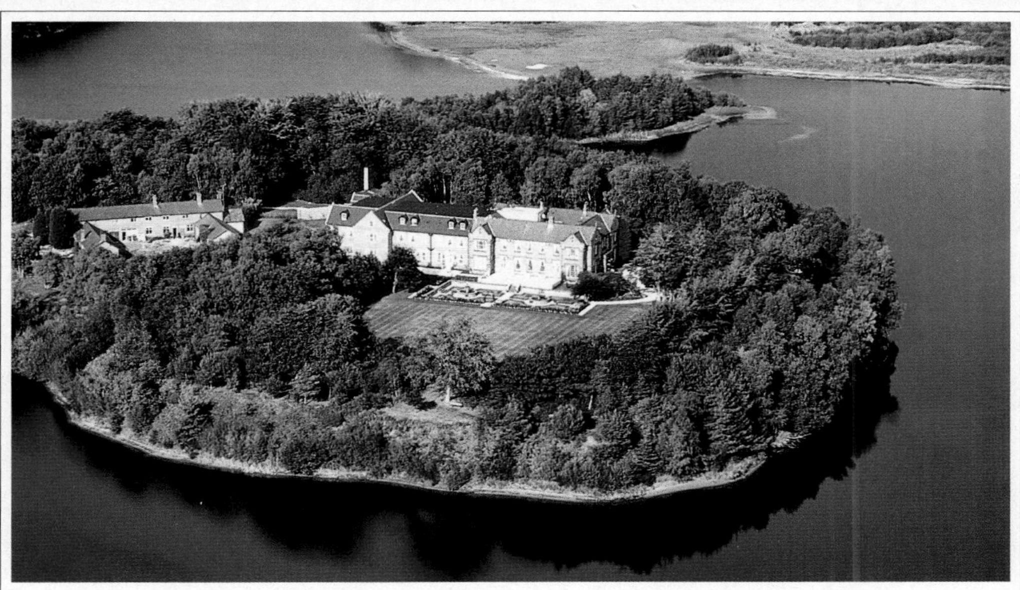

The style of a great transatlantic liner in the idyllic Cheshire countryside

The Brocklebanks' shipping company dates back to the early 1700s. In the 20th century, Sir Aubrey designed the Queen Mary. His son Sir John designed the QEII and became chairman of Cunard. It was Sir Aubrey who built Nunsmere Hall as his family home in 1898. Today, Nunsmere Hall echoes the style and eminence of the great transatlantic liners.

The setting is idyllic. This exquisite manor house is surrounded on three sides by a lake in its own wooded grounds. It has 36 comfortable bedrooms, an elegant lounge, a fine wood-panelled cocktail bar and a library.

The Garden Restaurant overlooks the sunken garden and in every way matches the quality of the house. Owners Malcolm and Julie McHardy are determined to achieve excellence. They have won a high reputation for exceptional country house food with a modern Mediterranean influence. Service by their young team is impeccable and the wine list is a classic.

Nunsmere Hall is close to North Wales, the historic Roman city of Chester and Manchester Airport. Liverpool, the Lake District, Stoke and the other Potteries towns are all easily reached by motorway.

LOCATION

On the A49 at Oakmere, near Northwich. From the north, leave M6 at Exit 19. From the south, leave M6 at Exit 18.

Tarporley Road, Oakmere, Near Northwich, Cheshire CW8 2ES

Telephone 01606 889100
Fax 01606 889055

E-mail: *nunsmere@bestloved.com*

OWNERS

Malcolm and Julie McHardy

ROOM RATES

3 Singles	*£98 - £118*
26 Doubles/Twins	*£150 - £160*
3 Four-posters	*£250 - £325*
4 Suites	*£250 - £325*

Includes VAT

CHARGE/CREDIT CARDS

• DC • MC • VI

RATINGS & AWARDS

A.A. ★★★ ❀❀
A.A. Romantic Hotel

FACILITIES

On site: *Garden, croquet, snooker*
Licensed for weddings
3 meeting rooms/max 80 people
Nearby: *Golf, riding, fitness, tennis*

RESTRICTIONS

No children under 12 years in restaurant after 7 pm
No pets

ATTRACTIONS

Chester, The Potteries, Stapeley Water Gardens, Lake District, North Wales, Delamere Forest

AFFILIATIONS

The Celebrated Hotels Collection

NEAREST

MAJOR CITY:
Chester - 12 miles/20 mins

MAJOR AIRPORT:
Manchester - 20 miles/30 mins

RAILWAY STATION:
Hartford - 5 miles/10 mins

RESERVATIONS

Toll free in US: 800-322-2403
*Quote **Best Loved***

ACCESS CODES

AMADEUS HK CEGNUN
APOLLO/GALILEO HT 26042
SABRE/ABACUS HK 51639
WORLDSPAN HK NUNSM

"This hotel far exceeded our expectations. It is also nice to feel so at home in a foreign country. We will surely be back"

Bill & Marianne Jackson, Houston, USA

PARSONAGE COUNTRY HOUSE *19th century parsonage*

Escrick, York, Yorkshire YO19 6LF

Telephone 01904 728111
Fax 01904 728151

E-mail: parsonage@bestloved.com

OWNERS
Paul and Karen Ridley

OPERATIONS DIRECTOR
Frank McCarten

ROOM RATES

Single occupancy	£75 - £115
17 Doubles/Twins	£75 - £125
2 Four-posters	£95 - £130
1 Family room	£75 - £125
1 Suite	£110 - £140

Includes full breakfast and VAT

CHARGE/CREDIT CARDS

• DC • MC • VI

RATINGS & AWARDS
E.T.C. ★★★
R.A.C. ★★★ *Dining Award 3*
A.A. ★★★ ❀❀ *75%*

FACILITIES
On site: *Garden, heli-pad*
Licensed for weddings
4 meeting rooms/max 150 people
Nearby: *Golf, tennis, fishing, riding, fitness, shooting*

RESTRICTIONS
No pets

ATTRACTIONS
York Minster, Jorvik Centre, Railway Museum, Castle Howard, Selby Abbey, The Yorkshire Moors and Dales

AFFILIATIONS
Grand Heritage Hotels

NEAREST
MAJOR CITY:
York - 5 miles/15 mins
MAJOR AIRPORT:
Leeds/Bradford - 34 miles/45 mins
RAILWAY STATION:
York - 5 miles/15 mins

RESERVATIONS
Toll free in US: 888-93-GRAND
Quote **Best Loved**

ACCESS CODES
AMADEUS UI QQY640
APOLLO/GALILEO UI 15537
SABRE/ABACUS UI 47567
WORLDSPAN UI 41481

The traditional idea of elegance counter-poised with an artist of modern cuisine

The essence of art is contrast - whatever its form: architecture, painting, poetry … In music, it's the combination of different rhythms in a single verse. In cooking, it's that squeeze of lemon on a perfectly grilled sole.

The Parsonage at Escrick possesses this quality. To look at, it is your archetypal country house sitting comfortably in its well-manicured garden; elegant, relaxed, aloof from the bustle of life; the rooms are delightfully furnished. A definitive statement about luxury, tranquillity and refined good taste. But, wait, that's only the half of it!

Step into the kitchen and you encounter the other: the fast moving, high-tension, colourful world of Chef Kenny Noble and his brigade.

One look at the menu suggests you are in for a surprise or two; the first taste whirls you to epicurean heights from which you will make a long, lingering descent. No question: Kenny is an artist and deserving of the second rosette recently gained for the hotel's Lascelles Restaurant - with more to come, no doubt. There seems no end to his invention or the panache with which it is presented. Fortunately, the wine list recognises his talent; the selection is particularly apt.

The local area will help you work up a good appetite with the attractions of York, nearby, and the romance of the Yorkshire Dales beyond.

By the way, do you believe in ghosts?

LOCATION

4 miles south of York on the A19, York to Selby road.

"** The skies were grey, the wind blew cold, but the warmth and comfort of the Pheasant's welcome shined on us throughout our short stay **"

J & M Wix, Hessle

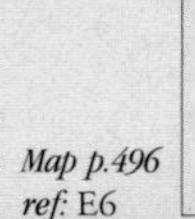

• *Map p.496 ref: E6*

17th century blacksmith's forge

PHEASANT HOTEL

Harome, Helmsley, North Yorkshire YO62 5JG

Telephone 01439 771241
Fax 01439 771744

***E-mail:** pheasant@bestloved.com*

OWNERS
The Binks Family

RATES PER PERSON

2 Singles	*£60 - £66*
8 Doubles/Twins	*£60 - £66*
1 Thatched Cottage	*£63 - £69*

Includes full breakfast, dinner and VAT

CHARGE/CREDIT CARDS

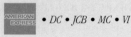

• DC • JCB • MC • VI

RATINGS & AWARDS
E.T.C. ★★★
R.A.C. ★★★
A.A. ★★★ *70%*

FACILITIES
***On site:** Indoor pool, gardens, ground floor room for the disabled*
***Nearby:** Golf, riding, swimming, fishing*

RESTRICTIONS
Pets by arrangement

ATTRACTIONS
Castle Howard, Rievaulx Abbey, North York Moors National Park, Byland Abbey, Nunnington Hall

AFFILIATIONS
Independent

NEAREST
MAJOR CITY:
York - 22 miles/40 mins

MAJOR AIRPORT:
Manchester - 90 miles/2½ hrs
Leeds/Bradford - 55 miles/1½ hrs

RAILWAY STATION:
York - 22 miles/40 mins

RESERVATIONS
Direct with hotel
*Quote **Best Loved***

ACCESS CODES
Not applicable

NORTH

A picturesque hotel by the mill stream and village pond

The hotel, established from what was at one time the village blacksmith's two cottages and the shop, has been renovated and extended to make a very comfortable country hotel with 12 bedrooms, all with private bathroom. All bedrooms face either south or south-west, some overlooking the village pond and mill stream, the remainder, the courtyard and walled garden.

There is a small oak-beamed bar with log fire, a large drawing room which, together with the dining room, opens onto the stone-flagged terrace looking over the mill stream.

A large garden and paddock provide fresh eggs, vegetables and fruit to the hotel kitchen where the best of English food is produced under the supervision of Mrs Tricia Binks. Ample car parking is provided.

Harome is a small village less than three miles from the attractive market town of Helmsley and the North York Moors National Park; it is unspoilt, still retaining six thatched cottages (probably more than any village in North Yorkshire). There are seven farms, an inn and both a church and chapel.

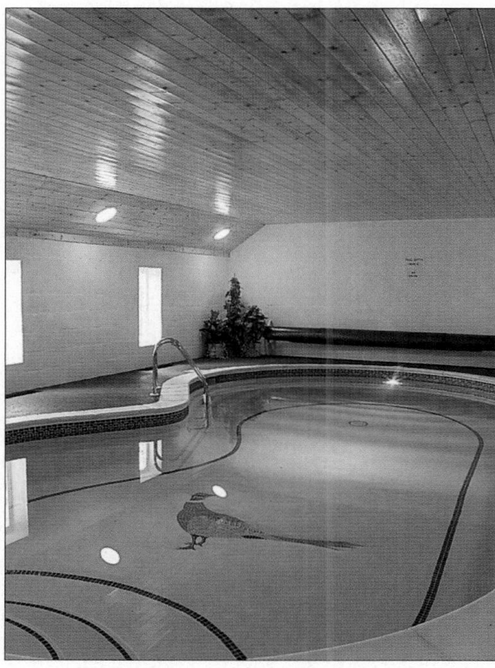

LOCATION

Leave Helmsley A170 direction Scarborough, after ¼ mile turn right for Harome. The hotel is near the church in centre of village.

Map p.496
ref: B5

" We were made so welcome and nothing was too much trouble "

Susan Vaux, Kent

THE PHEASANT

400 year old inn

Bassenthwaite Lake
Near Cockermouth
Cumbria CA13 9YE

Telephone 017687 76234
Fax 017687 76002

E-mail: thepheasant@bestloved.com

NORTH

GENERAL MANAGER
Matthew Wylie

ROOM RATES

Single occupancy	£70
3 Singles	£60
13 Doubles/Twis	£100 - £130

Including full breakfast and VAT

CHARGE/CREDIT CARDS
MC • VI

RATINGS & AWARDS
Independent

FACILITIES
On site: *Garden*
1 meeting room/max 30 people
Nearby: *Fishing, riding*

RESTRICTIONS
Limited facilities for disabled guests
Dogs not permitted in bedrooms

ATTRACTIONS
Wordsworth's Dove Cottage, Carlisle Castle, Rum Museum at Whitehaven, Maryport, Lake District National Park, Muncaster Castle RSBP Reserve

AFFILIATIONS
Independent

NEAREST
MAJOR CITY:
Carlisle - 28 miles/40 mins

MAJOR AIRPORT:
Manchester - 120 miles/2½ hrs

RAILWAY STATION:
Carlisle - 23 miles/30 mins

RESERVATIONS
Direct with hotel
Quote **Best Loved**

ACCESS CODES
Not applicable

Peace and tranquillity in a blissfully secluded corner of Cumbria

A brace of humble cottages before the discovery of a natural spring precipitated its transformation into a coaching inn, The Pheasant lies close to pristine Lake Bassenthwaite. This centuries-old institution is a rare old-style Cumbrian hostelry and a genuine 'get away from it all' escape where the bedrooms are television-free zones and few guests bother to take up the offer of a complimentary daily newspaper.

A sense of tradition is readily apparent in the welcoming lounges, where antiques, period prints and log fires create the relaxed and cosy atmosphere beloved of regular visitors. The bedrooms are bright and airy and the hotel will complete a total refurbishment in spring 2001. Everything from new linen to dining chairs hand-carved from English oak from the estate of Lord Inglewood has been carefully selected to compliment the period feel of the hotel.

The Pheasant's location, set against a backdrop of conifer woodlands at the foot of Skiddaw, appears enviably remote, yet the whole Lake District is easily explored from here. Outdoor pursuits such as walking and fishing, even a busy day's sightseeing are bound to work up an appetite and the restaurant is well-prepared for ravenous diners.

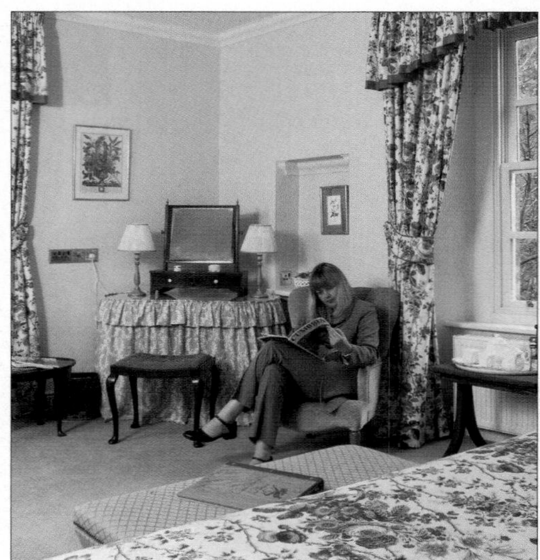

LOCATION

From M6 Exit 40, take the A66 to Keswick. At Keswick continue on the A66 towards Cockermouth. Signposted from the A66, after the dual carriageway, take the slip road to the left. The hotel is a short way down on the left.

“ In theory, you should be just like other hotels with high standards, but you’re not. You must be doing something different, I just like it here ”

J J Hammond, Winchester

• *Map p.496 ref: B6*

Regency manor house

ROTHAY MANOR

Relax and enjoy a Regency gem in the heart of Wordsworth country

William Wordsworth described the Lake District as “the loveliest spot that man has ever known”. He shared his passion for its inspirational landscape of rugged mountains and reflective lakes, doughty stone villages and valleys with fellow poets and artists, as well as generations of visitors who come here to hike, sail, fish or just admire their surroundings from a lake cruise.

A quarter of a mile from the head of Lake Windermere, and within a short walk of Ambleside, Rothay Manor is a wonderful base for exploring the region. The elegant Regency house is set in its own peaceful grounds and has been personally managed by the Nixon family for over 30 years (brothers Nigel and Stephen are currently at the helm). There is a real sense of family pride in the hotel’s warm and welcoming style, the thoughtfully decorated bedrooms and imaginative and beautifully presented food in the restaurant. Guests can pick up a free fishing permit or use the pool, sauna and steam room at a nearby leisure club without charge. The Nixons also offer a programme of special interest breaks between October and May ranging from painting and photography to walking, gardening and bridge.

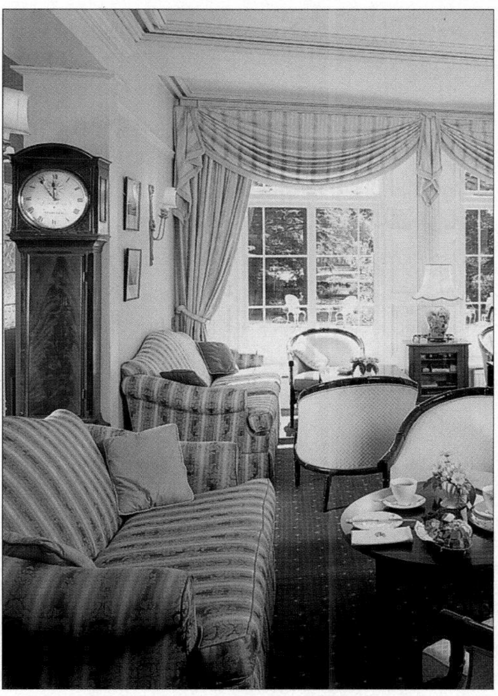

LOCATION

½ mile from Ambleside on the road to Coniston.

Rothay Bridge, Ambleside, Cumbria LA22 0EH

Telephone 015394 33605
Fax 015394 33607

E-mail: *rothay@bestloved.com*

OWNERS

Nigel and Stephen Nixon

ROOM RATES

2 Singles	*£65 - £75*
13 Doubles/Twins	*£120 - £135*
3 Suites	*£150 - £170*

Includes full breakfast and VAT

CHARGE/CREDIT CARDS

• DC • MC • VI

RATINGS & AWARDS

E.T.C. ★★★ Silver Award
R.A.C. ★★★
A.A. ★★★ ❀ 75%
The Good Food Guide Restaurant of the Year 1999

FACILITIES

On site: *Croquet, gardens*
1 meeting room/max 22 people
Nearby: *Golf, fishing, free use of leisure club*

RESTRICTIONS

No pets
No children under 8 years in dining room for dinner

ATTRACTIONS

Wordsworth’s Homes - Rydal Mount & Dove Cottage, Beatrix Potter’s House & Exhibition, The Bridge House, Lake Windermere, The Lake District

AFFILIATIONS

Fine Individual Hotels

NEAREST

MAJOR CITY:
Carlisle - 50 miles/1 hr

MAJOR AIRPORT:
Manchester - 95 miles/1½ hrs

RAILWAY STATION:
Windermere - 4 miles/10 mins

RESERVATIONS

Toll free in US: 800-544-9993
Quote ***Best Loved***

ACCESS CODES

Not applicable

• Map p.496 ref: D7

"Whether for business or pleasure a stay at the Studley is like visiting old friends"

L Ackerman, London

STUDLEY HOTEL

Contemporary hotel

Swan Road, Harrogate, North Yorkshire HG1 2SE

Telephone 01423 560425
Fax 01423 530967

E-mail: studleyhtl@bestloved.com

NORTH

OWNER

Bokmun Chan

ROOM RATES

15 Singles	£68 - £85
19 Doubles/Twins	£85 - £110
2 Suites	£100 - £120

Includes full breakfast and VAT

CHARGE/CREDIT CARDS

• DC • MC • VI

RATINGS & AWARDS

E.T.C. ★★★
A.A. ★★★ ❀ 66%
Les Routiers Casserole Award for Food
Les Routiers Corps d'Elite Award for the Wine List

FACILITIES

On site: Le Breton Restaurant
1 meeting room/max 15 people
Nearby: Golf, swimming

RESTRICTIONS

No facilities for disabled guests
Pets by arrangement

ATTRACTIONS

Fountains Abbey, Harewood House, Ripley Castle, Horse racing

AFFILIATIONS

Independent

NEAREST

MAJOR CITY:
Leeds - 16 miles/30 mins

MAJOR AIRPORT:
Manchester - 78 miles/1½ hrs
Leeds - 15 miles/30 mins

RAILWAY STATION:
Harrogate - 3 miles/5 mins

RESERVATIONS

Direct with hotel
Quote **Best Loved**

ACCESS CODES

Not applicable

Stylish comfort and good food on the doorstep of Yorkshire's greatest sights

Adjacent to the beautiful 120-acre Valley Gardens and a convenient stone's throw from the International Conference Centre, popular sightseeing and boutique shopping opportunities, the Studley rejoices in one of the best locations in town. The hotel is well-known to discerning travellers and offers comfortable and relaxing lounges brightened by potted greenery and fresh flowers on the tables, plus a choice of two bars. The attractive bedrooms all have thoughtful extras designed to ensure a memorable stay. The Studley's pride and joy is its restaurant, Le Breton, which has established itself as one of the most desirable eateries in and around Harrogate. A special feature is the charcoal grill and diners can watch the chef at work while making their selection from the well-priced wine list.

A spa town since the discovery of the Terwit Well in the latter part of the 16th century, Harrogate offers a busy year-round calendar of events from antiques and crafts shows to music and flower festivals. Curists can still enjoy a Turkish bath in the Royal Baths, and around the town there are many places of interest from abbeys and stately homes to golf and horse-racing courses.

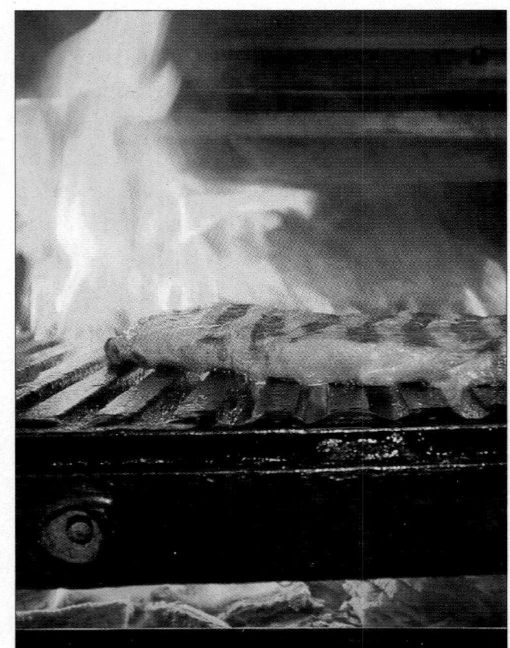

LOCATION

30 minutes from York, Leeds, the M1 and M62, and 20 minutes from the A1 (main north/south route).

"The whole of the Swinside experience has been magic"

Paddy Burt, Daily Telegraph

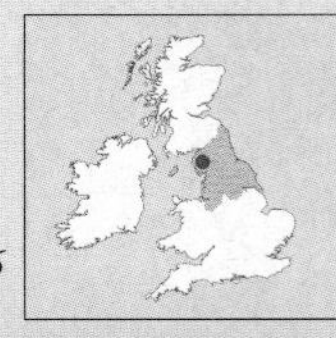

• Map p.496 ref: B5

Victorian house

SWINSIDE LODGE HOTEL

A real discovery just a stroll away from the 'Queen of the Lakes'

Swinside Lodge is a delightful Victorian house within one of the most beautiful and tranquil corners of the English Lakes. It stands in its own grounds at the foot of 'Cat Bells', one of many favourite mountain walks and is a mere five minutes stroll from the shores of Derwentwater – 'Queen of the Lakes'. A regular launch service operates on the lake, providing a leisurely mode of travel to the nearby bustling market town of Keswick and other local beauty spots.

Wild life abounds and the area is a paradise for birdwatchers and for walkers of all ages. Others will find it an ideal base from which to explore the natural beauty of the countryside.

Swinside Lodge is fast gaining a reputation for its very comfortable and well-appointed accommodation and, in particular, for its award-winning cuisine served in the intimate ambience of the candlelit dining room by friendly and attentive staff. For your added comfort the hotel has a no smoking policy.

You are invited to share in the relaxing and hospitable atmosphere of Swinside Lodge where caring staff will help to make your stay an enjoyable and memorable experience.

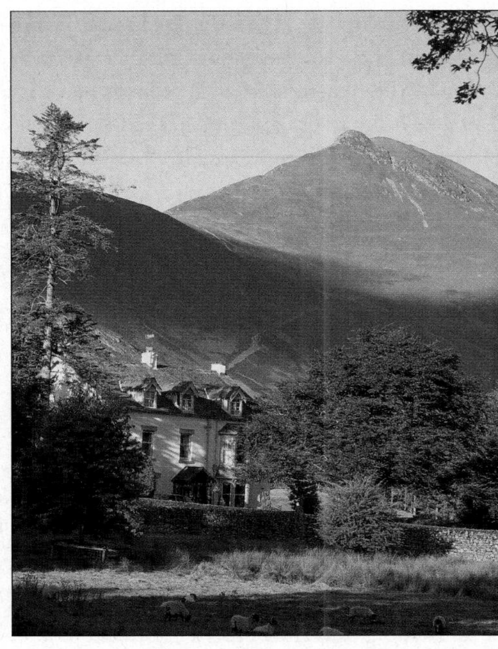

LOCATION

M6 Exit 40. Take A66 bypassing Keswick. Over main roundabout take 2nd left. Go through Portinscale, towards Grange. Hotel is 2 miles further on the right.

Grange Road, Newlands, Keswick, Cumbria CA12 5UE

Telephone 017687 72948
Fax 017687 72948

E-mail: *swinside@bestloved.com*

NORTH

OWNERS
Kevin and Susan Kniveton

ROOM RATES

Single occupancy	£77 - £90
7 Doubles/Twins	£67 - £85

Includes full breakfast, dinner and VAT

CHARGE/CREDIT CARDS
JCB • MC • VI

RATINGS & AWARDS
E.T.C. ★ Gold Award
R.A.C. Blue Ribbon ★ Dining Award 3

FACILITIES
On site: *Garden*
Nearby: *Golf, riding, fishing*

RESTRICTIONS
No children under 10 years
No facilities for disabled guests
No smoking
No pets

ATTRACTIONS
Lake District, Brough Castle, Beatrix Potter's House, Dove Cottage, Rydal Mount, Arthur's Round Table, Castlerigg Stone Circle

AFFILIATIONS
Independent

NEAREST
MAJOR CITY:
Carlisle - 38 miles/45 mins

MAJOR AIRPORT:
Newcastle - 100 miles/2 hrs
Carlisle - 38 miles/45 mins

RAILWAY STATION:
Penrith - 17 miles/20 mins

RESERVATIONS
Direct with hotel
Quote **Best Loved**

ACCESS CODES
Not applicable

" We have spent many happy holidays at Swinton "

Neville Chamberlain

Swinton Park

Stately home

Masham, Near Ripon, North Yorkshire HG4 4JH

Telephone 01765 680900
Fax 01765 680901

E-mail: *swintonpark@bestloved.com*

OWNERS
The Cunliffe-Lister family

ROOM RATES

Single occupancy	£95
17 Doubles/Twins	£95 - £250
3 Suites	£275 - £350

Includes full breakfast and VAT

CHARGE/CREDIT CARDS

• DC • MC • VI

RATINGS & AWARDS
Awards Pending

FACILITIES
On site: *Garden, croquet, fishing, riding, shooting, quad trekking, walking trails heli-pad, Licensed for weddings 7 meeting rooms/max 140 people*
Nearby: *Golf, leisure centre*

RESTRICTIONS
No children in dining room after 7 pm
No smoking in bedrooms
Pets by arrangement

ATTRACTIONS
Brewery Tours, Wensleydale, Ripon Cathedral, Herriot Centre, Fountains Abbey, Jervaulx Abbey, York Minster, Racing Stables

AFFILIATIONS
The Celebrated Hotels Collection

NEAREST
MAJOR CITY:
York - 37 miles/50 mins

MAJOR AIRPORT:
Leeds/Bradford - 33 miles/50 mins

RAILWAY STATION:
North Allerton - 14 miles/25 mins

RESERVATIONS
Toll free in US: 800-322-2403
Quote ***Best Loved***

ACCESS CODES
Not applicable

NORTH

A new lease of life for the family seat in the glorious Yorkshire Dales

Sir Abstrupus Danby, memorably but inaccurately christened by a befuddled parson, founded the first residence at Swinton Park in 1695. The parklands and a chain of five ornamental lakes were created in the 1760s, and the house metamorphosed into a 'castle' in the early 1800s with the addition of a tower, turrets and entirely fanciful battlements. In 1882, the castle was bought by Samuel Cunliffe-Lister, and his great-great-great grandson, Mark, together with wife Felicity, have recently transformed the family seat into a luxurious country house hotel.

Last year major renovations took place throughout Swinton as rooms were restored to their original proportions, an historic ceiling was discovered in the library, and Felicity teamed up with Mark's mother, Susan, to supervise the decorations while Mark concentrated on the beer cellar (famous Yorkshire brewers Theakstons and Black Sheep are based down the road in the market town of Masham). A spa and sauna offer health and beauty treatments and guests can relax in the bar, snooker room, and private cinema or take part in a wide range of country pursuits such as trout fishing, shooting, stalking and riding over the 20,000-acre estate. Nearby diversions include the Dales, York and Fountains Abbey.

LOCATION

From the A1 take B6267 to Masham. Drive through town and follow signs for Swinton.

"A very fine hotel indeed"

Mr Holloway, Cumbria

• Map p.496 ref: C3

Victorian mansion

TILLMOUTH PARK HOTEL

Cornhill-on-Tweed, Northumberland TD12 4UU

Telephone 01890 882255
Fax 01890 882540

E-mail: tillmouth@bestloved.com

GENERAL MANAGER
Ian Lang

ROOM RATES

1 Single	£90 - £125
9 Doubles/Twins	£130 - £160
4 Staterooms	£170

Includes full breakfast and VAT

CHARGE/CREDIT CARDS

• DC • MC • VI

RATINGS & AWARDS
E.T.C. ★★★ Silver Award
A.A. ★★★ ❀ 71%
Les Routiers Gold Key Award 2000

FACILITIES
On site: Garden, croquet, heli-pad
Licensed for weddings
3 meeting rooms/max 100 people
Nearby: Golf, riding, fishing, shooting

RESTRICTIONS
No facilities for disabled guests
No pets in public rooms

ATTRACTIONS
Bamburgh Castle, Scottish Borders, Holy Island and Lindisfarne Priory, Flodden Field Abbey, Farne Islands, Paxton House, Northumberland National Park

AFFILIATIONS
Grand Heritage Hotels

NEAREST
MAJOR CITY:
Edinburgh - 54 miles/2 hrs
MAJOR AIRPORT:
Edinburgh - 58 miles/2 hrs
Newcastle - 60 miles/2 hrs
RAILWAY STATION:
Berwick-upon-Tweed - 12 miles/20 mins

RESERVATIONS
Direct with hotel
Quote **Best Loved**

ACCESS CODES
AMADEUS UI XQGTIL
APOLLO/GALILEO UI 73276
SABRE/ABACUS UI 605
WORLDSPAN UI 40705

NORTH

Galleried elegance of a bygone era

Tillmouth Park was built by architect Charles Barry in 1882, using stones from nearby Twizel Castle. Sit in its galleried lounge and you'll feel yourself relax into a more leisured bygone age. Admire the spring daffodils and rhododendrons or fine autumnal colours, and the hustle of modern life slips away. Tillmouth Park offers the same warm welcome today as it did when it was a private house.

All 14 bedrooms are generous in size and have been refurbished in a distinctive old fashioned style with period furniture. Most have lovely views of the surrounding countryside.

The kitchen prides itself on traditional country fare. The chef takes fresh local produce, prepares it to a high standard, and presents it imaginatively. There is a well chosen wine list, and a vast selection of malt whiskies.

Tillmouth Park is an ideal centre for country pursuits, field sports, fishing, hillwalking, riding, birdwatching and golf. There are many stately homes such as Floors, Manderston and Paxton to visit. Ruined abbeys, Flodden Field, Lindisfarne and Holy Island are nearby – the coast is only 15 minutes away.

LOCATION

From the East Ord roundabout on the A1 at Berwick-upon-Tweed, take the A698 to Cornhill and Coldstream. The hotel is 9 miles along the road on the left hand side.

For route planning map of the North see page 496

• Map p.496 ref: B5

“We were staying in a real English home in another more peaceful and serene century”

Janet & George Railey, New York

UNDERSCAR MANOR

Country house

Applethwaite, Near Keswick, Cumbria CA12 4PH

Telephone 017687 75000
Fax 017687 74904

E-mail: *underscar@bestloved.com*

OWNERS
Pauline and Derek Harrison
Gordon Evans

ROOM RATES

Single occupancy	*£105 - £125*
11 Doubles/Twins	*£170 - £250*

Includes full breakfast, dinner and VAT

CHARGE/CREDIT CARDS

• *MC* • *VI*

RATINGS & AWARDS
Which? Hotel of the Year 2000

FACILITIES
On site: *Gardens, indoor pool, health & beauty*
1 meeting room/max16 people
Nearby: *Golf, riding, fishing, walking*

RESTRICTIONS
No facilities for disabled guests
No children under 12 years
No pets

ATTRACTIONS
Lake District National Park, Castlerigg Stone Circle, Beatrix Potter's House, Wordsworth's Dove Cottage, Brougham Castle, Penrith Castle

AFFILIATIONS
Independent

NEAREST
MAJOR CITY:
Manchester - 120 miles/2 hrs

MAJOR AIRPORT:
Manchester - 120 miles/2 hrs

RAILWAY STATION:
Penrith - 17 miles/20 mins

RESERVATIONS
Direct with hotel
Quote ***Best Loved***

ACCESS CODES
Not applicable

The jewel of the Lakes

“Today my companion and I took tea with the Oxleys at their exquisite house, Underscar. The house has been constructed on one of the most breathtaking locations that I have ever seen; set against the slopes of Skiddaw, and overlooking the tranquil Derwentwater. A lush garden surrounds the house filled with flowers and shrubs; with places to sit and admire the view. As I sipped my tea in the drawing room, a gem with its ornate plaster-work ceiling, I gazed down towards the lake and watched the sun setting on the water; it was a moment of rare, joyous beauty and I wish I could have stayed at Underscar forever.”

‘The Diary of a Victorian Country Gentlewoman’ – 11th May 1860

Today, 140 years on, Underscar Manor is a family owned and operated country house in the experienced and caring hands of Pauline and Derek Harrison. This breathtaking location is now in the Lake District National Park, designated an Area of Outstanding Natural Beauty.

The house is surrounded by forty acres of gardens and woodland walks, by a cascading stream. Its beautiful Victorian restaurant provides award-winning fine cuisine.

LOCATION

M6 Exit 40 towards Workington on A66 for 17 miles. At large roundabout, take 3rd exit and turn immediately right up lane signposted ‘Underscar’. Entrance to drive ¾ mile on right.

“ This is a beautiful home. Thank you for allowing us to have a share ”

R M Newton, Leicester

• Map p.496 ref: D3

Country house

WAREN HOUSE HOTEL

A gem of a country house amongst the treasures of the North East

One of England's most northerly Best Loved Hotels might well be summed up, 'we kept the best till last'. Waren House is the home of Anita and Peter Laverack who, during the last eleven years, have renovated and restored this lovely old house into an elegant 'Country Inn'. Set in six acres of mature grounds and walled garden, the hotel looks out over Budle Bay towards the Holy Island of Lindisfarne, only reached by causeway at low water.

This is the least populated part of the United Kingdom and even at the height of summer you can walk on miles of deserted golden beaches; visit ancient castles including Bamburgh, Alnwick, Lindisfarne and the ruins at Dunstanburgh; clamber over battlements including Hadrian's Wall; or have a round of golf on one of the numerous nearby courses before returning to Waren House, where a warm welcome, elegant accommodation, excellent food and a choice of over 250 wines awaits. For an extended stay there are two suites and one, the Edwardian, looks out over the walled garden and Cheviot Hills.

Waren House is within five miles of Northumberland's three main attractions: Farne Islands, Bamburgh Castle and Holy Island.

LOCATION

2 miles east of A1 on coast just south of Holy Island. There are advance signs from both north and south. Take B1342 to Waren Mill. The hotel (floodlit at night) is 2 miles from Bamburgh.

Waren Mill, Belford, Northumberland NE70 7EE

Telephone 01668 214581
Fax 01668 214484

E-mail: *warenhse@bestloved.com*

NORTH

OWNERS
Anita and Peter Laverack

ROOM RATES

8 Doubles/Twins	*£115 - £135*
1 Four-poster	*£135 - £155*
2 Suites	*£155 - £185*

Includes full breakfast and VAT

CHARGE/CREDIT CARDS

• DC • JCB • MC • VI

RATINGS & AWARDS
E.T.C. ★★★
R.A.C. ★★★
A.A. ★★★ *68%*
A.A. Romantic Hotel

FACILITIES
On site: *Gardens*
1 meeting room/max 30 people
Nearby: *Golf, riding*

RESTRICTIONS
No children under 14 years
No pets in public rooms
Smoking permitted in Library only

ATTRACTIONS
Bamburgh Castle, Holy Island, Alnwick Castle, Farne Islands

AFFILIATIONS
Fine Individual Hotels

NEAREST
MAJOR CITY:
Edinburgh - 70 miles/1½ hrs
Newcastle-upon-Tyne - 45 miles/1 hr

MAJOR AIRPORT:
Newcastle - 45 miles/45 mins

RAILWAY STATION:
Berwick-upon-Tweed - 15 miles/20 mins

RESERVATIONS
Toll free in US: 800-544-9993
Quote ***Best Loved***

ACCESS CODES
Not applicable

• Map p.496 ref: B6

"From the lovely room and friendly staff, to the beautiful setting and the excellent food, everything has been perfect"

Alan & Hayley Henshall, Toddington

WATEREDGE HOTEL

17th century waterside hotel

Waterhead Bay, Ambleside, Cumbria LA22 0EP

Telephone 015394 32332
Fax 015394 31878

E-mail: wateredge@bestloved.com

NORTH

OWNERS
Derek and Pamela Cowap

ROOM RATES

3 Singles	£30 - £50
5 Doubles/Twins	£60 - £100
11 Superior rooms	£80 - £120

Includes full breakfast and VAT

CHARGE/CREDIT CARDS

• MC • VI

RATINGS & AWARDS
E.T.C. ★★★ Silver Award
R.A.C. ★★★ Dining Award 1
A.A. ★★★ ❀ 72%
A.A. Courtesy & Care Award

FACILITIES
On site: Garden, private jetty, boat launch, rowing boat
Nearby: Fishing, lake cruises, riding, complimentary use of leisure club

RESTRICTIONS
No facilities for disabled guests
Dogs by arrangement

ATTRACTIONS
Lake District National Park, Beatrix Potter's home, steamer trips, Hardknott Roman Fort, Stott Park Bobbin Mill

AFFILIATIONS
Independent

NEAREST
MAJOR CITY:
Manchester - 100 miles/1¾ hrs

MAJOR AIRPORT:
Manchester - 100 miles/1¾ hrs

RAILWAY STATION:
Windermere - 4 miles/10 mins

RESERVATIONS
Direct with hotel
Quote **Best Loved**

ACCESS CODES
Not applicable

At the water's edge – eat well, relax and melt into Ambleside's beauty

Wateredge is a delightfully situated, family-run hotel nestling on the shores of Windermere. The building was originally two 17th-century fishermen's cottages, which have been warmly converted and extended.

The well maintained gardens with spectacular views of the lake and hills run down to the water's edge; alongside is a pleasant promenade leading to the 'Steamer Pier', the embarkation for cruising around the lake. Adjacent is Borrans Park and within strolling distance the tranquillity of the nearby fells.

Guests can relax in the comfortable lounges overlooking the lake or on the lawn, where light lunches, afternoon teas or drinks are served.

Dining at Wateredge is an occasion in itself. The dining area, set within the original cottages, creates its own particular ambience under oak-beamed ceilings. Here guests enjoy excellent cuisine prepared with flair and imagination using only fresh produce of the highest quality. Bread, pastries and jams are all homemade. A carefully chosen wine list complements the cuisine.

Pretty bedrooms offer the best of lakeland comfort and hospitality, many with lake views.

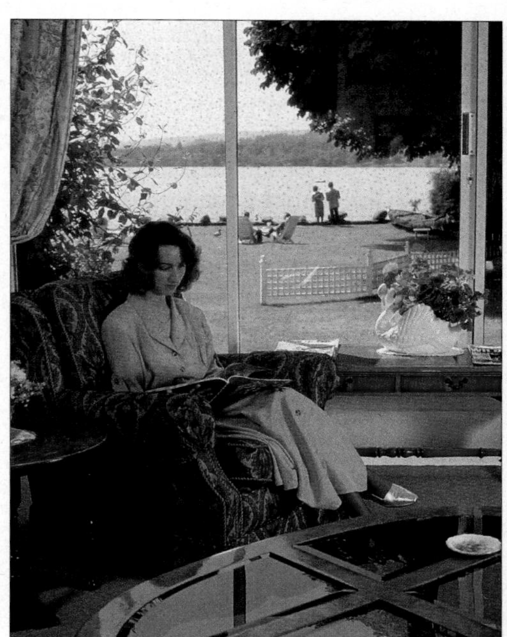

LOCATION

Travelling northwards on the A591, turn left at traffic lights just after the Ambleside sign, skirt the lake for a few hundred yards and look for Wateredge on your left.

“A pleasant surprise for a weary traveller”

David Roberts, New York

• Map p.496 ref: C5

Country hotel

WESTMORLAND HOTEL

An inspiration amongst the Yorkshire moors and Lake District mountains

As far ahead as the eye can see lie moors and mountains, and this is the setting, where the Yorkshire Dales meet the mountains of the Lake District, in which the Westmorland Hotel lies. The hotel is both a convenient stop-off and an ideal base for exploring the surrounding countryside. Access to the picturesque village of Orton or, via the Westmorland Service Station one mile north of junction 38 of the M6.

By using Cumberland stone and reclaimed timber to stunning effect, and harmonising it with coloured furnishings, a wonderfully welcoming interior has been created. It is the landscape outside the hotel, however, that is always the focal point. The lounge and all the guest rooms are simply but comfortably furnished. All have glorious views and the dining room is no exception with a truly spectacular panorama. Immediately outside the huge picture windows is a stream with a waterfall; beyond are the fells and valleys where sheep and rabbits graze, curlew and buzzards swoop and swirl overhead. Meanwhile, the award-winning food features local produce on an enterprising menu.

You will find the Westmorland is an excellent base from which to explore this stunning landscape. Bring your camera and sketch book.

LOCATION

Easily approached from exits 38 and 39 of the M6 motorway. At the Westmorland Service Station, follow the 'Hotel' signs.

Orton, Penrith, Cumbria CA10 3SB

Telephone 015396 24351
Fax 015396 24354

E-mail: *westmorland@bestloved.com*

MANAGER
Clive Watts

ROOM RATES

Single occupancy	£50 - £75
43 Doubles/Twins	£60 - £85
4 Suites	£75 - £85
6 Family rooms	£60 - £85

Includes VAT

CHARGE/CREDIT CARDS

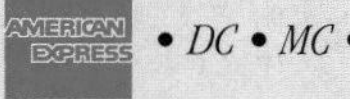

• DC • MC • VI

RATINGS & AWARDS
E.T.C. ★★★
R.A.C. ★★★
A.A. ★★★ ❀ 71%

FACILITIES
On site: *Licensed for weddings*
5 meeting rooms/max 200 people
Nearby: *Riding, fishing*

RESTRICTIONS
Limited facilities for disabled guests
No pets in public rooms

ATTRACTIONS
Rheged Discovery Centre, The World of Beatrix Potter, Wetheriggs Pottery, Dalemain House, Lake Cruises, Yorkshire Dales, Lake District

AFFILIATIONS
Independent

NEAREST
MAJOR CITY:
Carlisle - 40 miles/45 mins

MAJOR AIRPORT:
Manchester - 95 miles/2¼ hrs

RAILWAY STATION:
Penrith - 17 miles/20 mins

RESERVATIONS
Direct with hotel
Quote ***Best Loved***

ACCESS CODES
Not applicable

NORTH

• Map p.496 ref: D7

"To invite a person into your house is to take charge of his happiness for as long as he is under your roof"

Brillat Savarin, USA

THE WHITE HOUSE

Victorian town house

10 Park Parade, Harrogate, Yorkshire HG1 5AH

Telephone 01423 501388
Fax 01423 527973

E-mail: *whiteyorks@bestloved.com*

NORTH

OWNER
Jennie Forster

GENERAL MANAGER
Colin Allard

ROOM RATES

2 Singles	*£95*
10 Doubles/Twins	*£135*

Includes full breakfast, newspaper and VAT

CHARGE/CREDIT CARDS

 • *JCB • MC • VI*

RATINGS & AWARDS
R.A.C. ★★★ Dining Award 2
A.A. ★★★ ❀ 72%

FACILITIES
On site: *Garden*
2 meeting rooms/max 75 people
Nearby: *Golf, tennis, fitness*

RESTRICTIONS
No facilities for disabled guests
No pets

ATTRACTIONS
Harrogate, Castle Howard, Fountains Abbey, York Minster, Turkish spa, Yorkshire dales & moors

AFFILIATIONS
Independent

NEAREST
MAJOR CITY:
Leeds - 15 miles/25 mins

MAJOR AIRPORT:
Leeds/Bradford - 12 miles/20 mins

RAILWAY STATION:
Harrogate - ¼ mile/5 mins

RESERVATIONS
Direct with hotel
Quote ***Best Loved***

ACCESS CODES
Not applicable

Acclaimed good food in a Venetian setting

The spa town of Harrogate was popular in the 18th and, especially, the 19th centuries, when Londoners would come here to 'take the waters' for the treatment of lumbago, gout, the liver or simply the nerves. The White House was built in 1836 as the private home of the Mayor (also doctor of water cures) a few years before the Royal Pump Room was constructed to house the town's first public baths and the town began to be developed in earnest. The demand for the spa waters may have diminished, but Harrogate remains an attractive town, proud of its dignified Victorian architecture, its lavish flowerbeds and green spaces.

Overlooking the 200-acre stretch of grassland that probes the city centre, called The Stray, the White House would make the perfect setting for a private house party or an elegant wedding. The house was built as a replica of a Venetian villa and it still retains all the original touches of elegance. Enter the lounge or the library, both furnished with antiques, and you step back into an age where life was taken at a more gentle pace. Some of the ten bedrooms have four-poster or half-tester beds; all are individually furnished in traditional fabrics. Step forward again, and into the dining room now redesigned in Brasserie style, serving modern English food and renamed 'No 10'.

If you have a soft spot for nostalgia The White House will oblige you handsomely.

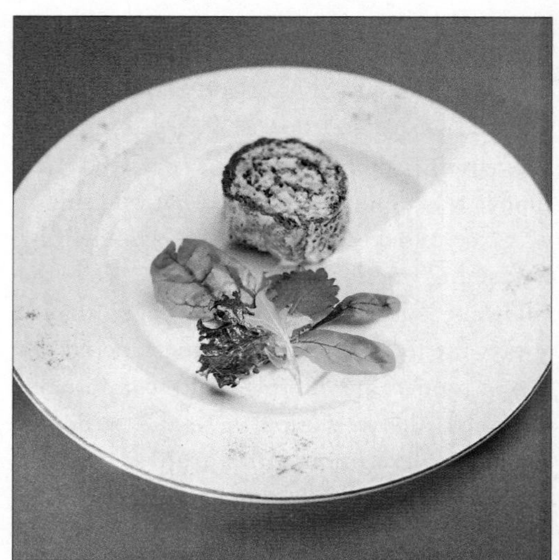

LOCATION

Overlooking The Stray. From the A59, Skipton Road, take Coach Road into Park Parade.

For a portrait of this region see page 90

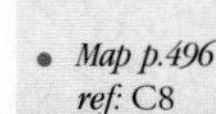

"An intimate jewel. Warm and sophisticated with the gracious personal touch of Judith and Ryland"

Olysia Tresznewsky, Wilmington, Delaware, USA

• Map p.496 ref: C8

Georgian town house

THE WHITE HOUSE MANOR

An entertaining hotel themed for the Millennium

Three reasons spring to mind for travelling to this part of Cheshire: Great antiques, superb stately homes and The White House Manor.

On entering The White House Manor, a beautifully restored Georgian house, you immediately realise that something different is afoot. For this Georgian shell has been transformed into a luxurious private sanctuary. The Wakeham's vision has given this small prosperous village a hotel of 21st century sophistication that defies its quaint rural setting. To call the 11 bedrooms 'individually furnished' is an understatement. Each of the themed bedrooms exhibit an imagination, humour and laser sense of detail. Rich fabrics and fine antiques mingle comfortably with space-age bathrooms with Turkish steam room, whirlpool baths, and power showers with body jets. Last year saw the addition of the Millennium suite, the Wakeham's idea of the year 2000. Natural fabrics and colours form the backdrop for an ultra-modern glass bed.

The hotel provides breakfast and room service, other meals are taken at the award-winning White House Restaurant a short walk (and well worth the trip) to the village centre. The location also makes it a great first or last night stop before flying out of nearby Manchester Airport.

LOCATION

From M6, exit 17 take A534 to Congleton then left on to A536 to Prestbury. Passing Prestbury Golf Course, take right at first roundabout. Go over bridge and the hotel is on the right.

New Road, Prestbury, Macclesfield, Cheshire SK10 4HP

Telephone 01625 829376
Fax 01625 828627

E-mail: *whitehsemanor@bestloved.com*

OWNERS

Ryland and Judith Wakeham

ROOM RATES

3 Singles	*£40 - £95*
6 Doubles/Twins	*£70 - £120*
2 Four-posters	*£110 - £120*

Includes VAT

CHARGE/CREDIT CARDS

• DC • MC • VI

RATINGS & AWARDS

E.T.C. ★★★★ Silver Award
A.A. ★★★★ Town House

FACILITIES

On site: *Garden*
4 meeting rooms/max 60 people
Nearby: *Golf, riding*

RESTRICTIONS

No facilities for disabled guests
No children under 10 years
No pets

ATTRACTIONS

Tatton Hall, Trafford Centre, Styal Mill and Park, Chatsworth, Staffordshire Potteries, Lowry Centre, Manchester United Museum

AFFILIATIONS

Independent

NEAREST

MAJOR CITY:
Manchester - 13 miles/30 mins

MAJOR AIRPORT:
Manchester - 7 miles/20 mins

RAILWAY STATION:
Macclesfield - 3 miles/10 mins

RESERVATIONS

Direct with hotel
Quote ***Best Loved***

ACCESS CODES

Not applicable

NORTH

"I don't know how you people manage it, but that which has always seemed perfect just keeps on getting better"

Edward B Catton, Michigan

WHITE MOSS HOUSE

18th century country house

Rydal Water, Grasmere, Cumbria LA22 9SE

Telephone 015394 35295
Fax 015394 35516

E-mail: whitemoss@bestloved.com

OWNERS
Sue and Peter Dixon

ROOM RATES

Single occupancy	£64 - £90
5 Doubles/Twins	£128 - £180
1 Four-poster	£128 - £180

Includes full breakfast, 5-course dinner and VAT

CHARGE/CREDIT CARDS

• MC • VI

RATINGS & AWARDS
A.A. ★ ❀❀

FACILITIES
On site: Garden, fishing
Nearby: Fell walking, riding, fishing, use of leisure club

RESTRICTIONS
Children under 8 years by arrangement
No facilities for disabled guests
No pets

ATTRACTIONS
Wordsworth's Dove Cottage & Rydal Mount, Hilltop - Beatrix Potter's home, Brantwood - Ruskin's home, Coniston, Hardknott Roman Fort, Ravenglass Roman Bath House

AFFILIATIONS
Independent

NEAREST
MAJOR CITY:
Carlisle - 40 miles/1 hr

MAJOR AIRPORT:
Manchester - 80 miles/2 hrs

RAILWAY STATION:
Windermere - 8 miles/15 mins

RESERVATIONS
Direct with hotel
Quote **Best Loved**

ACCESS CODES
Not applicable

Imagine, gourmet food and wine with a view that inspired the poets

White Moss House was bought by William Wordsworth for his son, and the poet often rested and wrote poetry there. Built in 1730, it overlooks Rydal Water in the heart of the Lake District. Many famous walks and drives, by lakes and over hills, begin from the front door.

Proprietors Sue and Peter Dixon have created an intimate family atmosphere. Personal care for the guests, and attention to detail are hallmarks of this charming hotel. There are five rooms in the main house and two situated in Brockstone Cottage Suite, whose isolated beauty makes it a truly romantic spot.

The value-for-money wine list of over 300 bins offers distinguished bottles from around the world. The restaurant has been continuously in The Good Food Guide for the last 28 years. Comments include:

Peter Dixon is a maestro of British cooking - The Sunday Times

Peter Dixon is an intuitive cook, with a deep understanding of ingredients and flavours. He uses wonderful local produce for his five course dinners - Bon Appetit

Lovers of good food and wine, who appreciate the beautiful scenery immortalised by the romantic poets, will love White Moss House.

LOCATION

On A591 at north end of Rydal Water, one mile south of Grasmere.

“ The food, the service and the rooms were all excellent, thank you for making our wedding day a memorable one ”

S Hudson, Chester

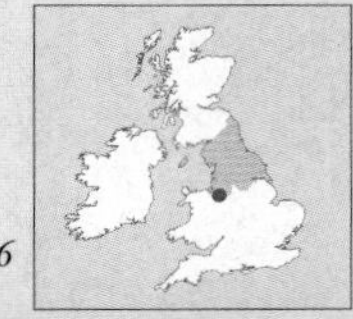

Elizabethan-style manor house

WILLINGTON HALL

The personal touch creates a memorable stay

Willington Hall enjoys a truly wonderful position at the foot of the Willington Hills with views that stretch across miles of unspoilt Cheshire countryside to the Welsh mountains in the distance. The Elizabethan-style brick house was actually founded in 1829, and remained in the same family for over 170 years before it was bought recently by Diana and Stuart Begbie.

The Begbie's have done a splendid job of rejuvenating the interior while preserving the integrity of the house. The traditionally decorated and comfy bedrooms offer oodles of space and large windows allow the light to pour in (together with those lovely views). The restaurant is open for lunch and dinner and there are bars in the Study and Drawing Room, or drinks can be taken out on the terrace. One of Willington Hall's chief charms is the relaxed and friendly atmosphere created by the Begbie's and their staff, which makes it a particular favourite with guests who value the personal touch.

Peace and quiet is ensured by the rural setting and 17 acres of gardens and parkland, but Willington is also conveniently located for road, rail and air connections. The historic city of Chester is nearby, and North Wales and the Peak District are easily accessible for a day trips, as are Beeston Castle, Liverpool, Manchester, Staffordshire and The Potteries.

LOCATION

Take the A51 from Tarporley to Chester and turn right at the Bull's Head at Clotton. Willington Hall is 1 mile ahead on the left.

Willington, Tarporley, Cheshire CW6 0NB

Telephone 01829 752321
Fax 01829 752596

***E-mail:** willington@bestloved.com*

OWNERS

Stuart and Diana Begbie

ROOM RATES

1 Single	*£68*
9 Doubles/Twins	*£100*

Includes full breakfast and VAT

CHARGE/CREDIT CARDS

 *• DC • MC • VI*

RATINGS & AWARDS

E.T.C. ★★★
A.A. ★★★
R.A.C. ★★★ *Dining Award 1*

FACILITIES

***On site:** Garden, tennis, riding*
Licensed for weddings
3 meeting rooms/max 60 people
***Nearby:** Golf*

RESTRICTIONS

Limited facilities for disabled guests
No dogs permitted in public areas
No smoking in public rooms

ATTRACTIONS

Chester, Beeston Castle, Tatton Park, Erdigg Hall, Delamere Forest, Staveley Water Gardens

AFFILIATIONS

Independent

NEAREST

MAJOR CITY:
Chester - 7 miles/15 mins

MAJOR AIRPORT:
Manchester - 28 miles/40 mins

RAILWAY STATION:
Chester - 7 miles/15 mins

RESERVATIONS

Direct with hotel
*Quote **Best Loved***

ACCESS CODES

Not applicable

NORTH

• *Map p.496 ref: B8*

"Different from even the best run hotel in the south"

Sir Peregrine Worsthorne, Sunday Telegraph

WOOLTON REDBOURNE HOTEL

Victorian mansion

Acrefield Road, Woolton, Liverpool, Merseyside L25 5JN

Telephone 0151 421 1500
Fax 0151 421 1501

E-mail: *woolton@bestloved.com*

NORTH

OWNER
Paul Collins

GENERAL MANAGER
Debbie Owen

ROOM RATES

5 Singles	*£63 - £103*
12 Doubles/Twins	*£92*
3 Four-posters	*£92 - £150*
2 Suites	*£120 - £150*

Includes VAT

CHARGE/CREDIT CARDS

• *DC* • *JCB* • *MC* • *VI*

RATINGS & AWARDS
E.T.C. ◆◆◆◆ Silver Award
City of Liverpool Vase Award Winner 1999
Merseyside Tourism Small Hotel of the Year 1999

FACILITIES
On site: *Garden*
1 meeting room/max 20 people
Nearby: *Golf*

RESTRICTIONS
No facilities for disabled guests
No smoking in dining room or lounge

ATTRACTIONS
Beatles Museum and Tour, St George's Hall, Merseyside Waterfront and Albert Dock, Catholic and Anglican Cathedrals, Speke Hall National Trust Property

AFFILIATIONS
Independent

NEAREST
MAJOR CITY:
Liverpool - 7 miles/20 mins

MAJOR AIRPORT:
Manchester - 24 miles/30 mins

RAILWAY STATION:
Liverpool - 7 miles/20 mins

RESERVATIONS
Direct with hotel
Quote ***Best Loved***

ACCESS CODES
Not applicable

Entertaining the entertainers in The Beatles home ground

Woolton is recorded in the Domesday Book and surviving reminders of its past are to be seen in 15th century houses and a sandstone cross in the centre of the village. It has also survived the urban grip of Liverpool's expansion by being declared a Conservation Area. Of its many listed buildings is The Woolton Redbourne Hotel, built by Sir Henry Tate in 1884.

The conversion from home to hotel is never easy and the wishful cliché, home away from home, not always completes what the imagination couldn't grasp. But here, we have an exception, not just because the transition has been very cleverly achieved, but because the rooms include the random clutter you find in your own home - albeit the clutter has class and comes from various antiquaria specialising in Victoriana. There are 20 luxury bedrooms including the Redbourne Suite which features a four-poster bed and a four-poster jacuzzi no less.

The service is exceptional: one guest reported that, on arriving late one evening, dinner was served in his room by the chef himself and a retinue of staff. You cannot get better than that!

And the food? Like the eclectic contents of the house, an entertainment to be savoured and appreciated by the connoisseur. No wonder visiting celebrities to Liverpool choose the Woolton Redbourne above any ordinary hotel.

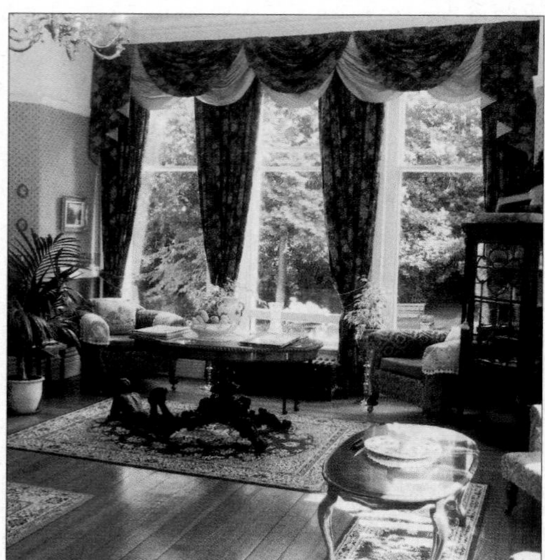

LOCATION

From the M62 take Exit 4 and turn left onto the A5058. After roundabout turn left at traffic lights, the hotel is 2 miles further on.

"Gracious service, courtesy, consideration and attention to detail"

P Heal

• Map p.496 ref: B5

Village hotel

THE WORDSWORTH HOTEL

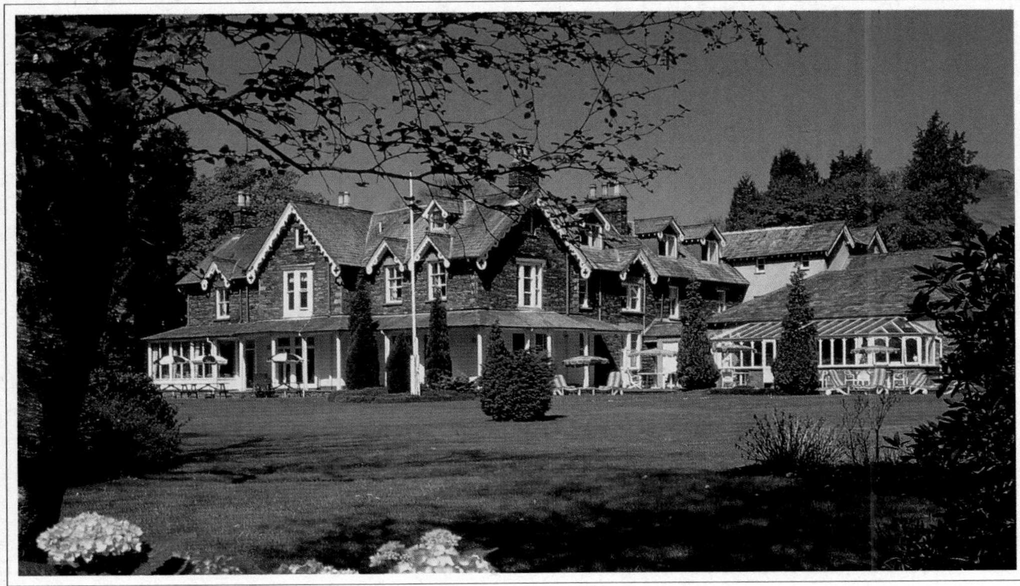

You'll wax poetic after staying at this lovely Lakeland beauty

In the very heart of English Lakeland, and the centre of one of its loveliest villages, The Wordsworth combines the sophistication of the first-class hotel with the magnificence of the surrounding countryside. Situated in two acres of landscaped grounds, next to the churchyard where William Wordsworth is buried, its name honours the memory of the area's most famous son. The scenery that so inspired the Lake Poets can be enjoyed from the peaceful lounges, furnished with fine antiques, or in the conservatory and cocktail bar, with the aid of a favourite aperitif or specially mixed drink.

The two suites and 37 bedrooms combine great character with comfort. There is an attractive indoor pool with jacuzzi and mini-gym.

The Prelude Restaurant named after Wordsworth's well-known poem, is the place to enjoy lighter or more substantial meals, skillfully prepared from a variety of fresh produce. 24-hour room service is available and the hotel has its own charming pub, The Dove and Olive Branch, a friendly meeting place for a traditional beer or tasty snacks.

The Wordsworth, known for its welcome, is very convenient for Lakeland's principal beauty spots and places of interest.

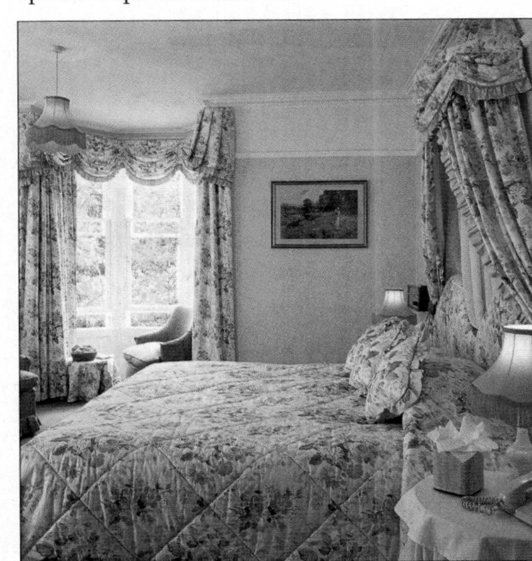

LOCATION

Exit 36/M6 northbound, (A591). Follow A591 past Kendal, Windermere and Ambleside. 4 miles north of Ambleside, turn left into Grasmere and hotel is on right next to church.

Grasmere, Cumbria LA22 9SW

Telephone 015394 35592
Fax 015394 35765

E-mail: *wordsworth@bestloved.com*

GENERAL MANAGER

J G van Stripriaan

ROOM RATES

4 Singles	£49 - £53
28 Doubles/Twins	£135 - £145
3 Four-posters	£152 - £165
2 Suites	£210 - £240

Includes full breakfast and VAT

CHARGE/CREDIT CARDS

• *DC* • *MC* • *VI*

RATINGS & AWARDS

R.A.C. ★★★★ *Dining Award 2*
A.A. ★★★★ ❀❀ *67%*

FACILITIES

On site: *Garden, croquet, indoor pool, solarium, gym, sauna, jacuzzi, fishing, heli-pad*
Licensed for weddings
3 meeting rooms/max 120 people
Nearby: *Golf, riding, sailing, walking, fishing*

RESTRICTIONS

Limited facilities for disabled guests
No pets

ATTRACTIONS

Wordsworth's Dove Cottage and museum, John Ruskin's home, Levens Hall, Hilltop - Beatrix Potter's home, Castlerigg Stone Circle, Keswick, Brougham, Penrith and Sizergh Castles

AFFILIATIONS

Preston's Global Hotels

NEAREST

MAJOR CITY:
Manchester - 95 miles/1½ hrs

MAJOR AIRPORT:
Manchester - 100 miles/2 hrs

RAILWAY STATION:
Windermere - 9 miles/20 mins

RESERVATIONS

Toll free in US: 800-544-9993
Quote ***Best Loved***

ACCESS CODES

Not applicable

NORTH

• Map p.496
ref: D6

"Wonderful food, charming host, comfy bed - perfect"

Dan & Moyra Robinson, Johannesburg, South Africa

THE YORKE ARMS

18th century shooting lodge

**Ramsgill-in-Nidderdale,
Pateley Bridge, Near Harrogate,
North Yorkshire HG3 5RL**

**Telephone 01423 755243
Fax 01423 755330**

E-mail: yorke@bestloved.com

OWNERS
Bill and Frances Atkins

RATES PER PERSON

3 Singles	£85 - £100
4 Doubles/Twins	£85 - £95
4 Suites	£100 - £150
1 Four-poster	£105 - £150
1 Family room	£95 - £105

Includes full breakfast, dinner and VAT

CHARGE/CREDIT CARDS

• DC • MC • VI

RATINGS & AWARDS
E.T.C. ★★ Silver Award
A.A. ★★ ❀❀ 73%
Yorkshire Life Magazine
Restaurant of the Year 2000

FACILITIES
On site: *Garden, heli-pad*
2 meetings rooms/max 18 people
Nearby: *Tennis, fitness, riding, hunting/shooting*

RESTRICTIONS
Limited facilities for disabled guests
No pets in hotel, kennels available

ATTRACTIONS
Ripon Cathedral, Harrogate, Ripley Castle, The Nidderdale Reservoirs, Fountains Abbey, Yorkshire Dales

AFFILIATIONS
Independent

NEAREST
MAJOR CITY:
Leeds - 30 miles/1¼ hrs
MAJOR AIRPORT:
Leeds -25 miles/45 mins
RAILWAY STATION:
Harrogate - 14 miles/25 mins

RESERVATIONS
Direct with hotel
Quote ***Best Loved***

ACCESS CODES
Not applicable

An inn of great renown in the Dales - one of the top 50 restaurants in Britain

The Yorke Arms promises to be one of the biggest surprises in this book. You cannot deny its picturesque charm but it blends so perfectly into the village of Ramsgill, nestling in one of the most beautiful of the Yorkshire Dales, that it does not exactly smack the consciousness.

It looks like, and purports to be, an unpretentious North Yorkshire inn. Accompanied by the aroma of wood smoke, you pass through the warren of downstairs rooms: the bar, the simple brasserie and the restaurant whose principal feature is a dresser gleaming with pewter. Upstairs is very civilised: a delightful choice of comfortable en suite bedrooms. All very cosy, you're thinking.

Now for the surprise: The Yorke Arms is an altar in the temple of gastronomy. Its praises have been sung across the land; The Good Food Guide puts it among the top 50 restaurants in the country. And all because Frances Atkins came home! With a successful career behind her, she returned to her native Yorkshire bringing an attitude of joy to cooking (unlike the histrionics of personality chefs). Her all-woman team is a deliberate choice - friends, she calls them. "I don't view produce as just something to eat but something so lovely you want to do something with it", she says. Husband Bill, chooses the wine list and it is a very fine compliment he pays her!

Wherever you are, do make this pilgrimage!

LOCATION

In Ramsgill on the north western tip of Gouthwaite Reservoir on the Low Wath Road 4 miles north of Pateley Bridge.

wales

Call to Arms: Cardiff's state-of-the-art Millennium Stadium is the new bastion of Welsh rugby rising phoenix-like from the site of the old Arms Park ground. Action of a different kind was once anticipated at the formidable 14th-century Marcher fortress of Chirk Castle (inset) which is softened by topiary and rose gardens.

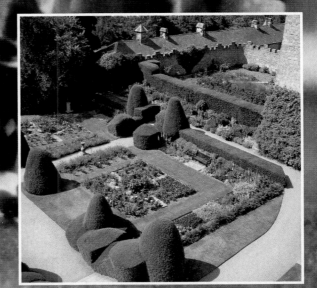

wales

Snowdon's rocky peaks rise to 3560 ft and dominate the north of Wales. From there, it slopes gently to the Lleyn peninsula and the Isle of Anglesey. South lies a sea of mountain ranges of remote moorland's, ancient drovers' routes, deep dark forests, lakes and waterfalls, the spectacular lakes and dams of the Elan Valley and the dramatic Aberswesyn Pass across the Roof of Wales.

Sheep dog trials are popular. There are World Heritage Sites at Beaumaris and Harlech Castles. Elegant Victorian architecture that sweeps round Llandudno. Picturesque Betws-y-Coed has its famous Swallow Falls.

At Knighton, is the 30-foot Offas's Dyke built by the King of Mercia in 784 to keep out marauders. South Wales too offers huge contrasts, encompassing the gentle rolling hills and peaks of the Brecon Beacons, the wooded glory of the Wye Valley and the bays and beaches of Pembrokeshire and the Gower peninsula. Cardiff is Britain's newest capital city, and home to the Welsh Rugby Team.

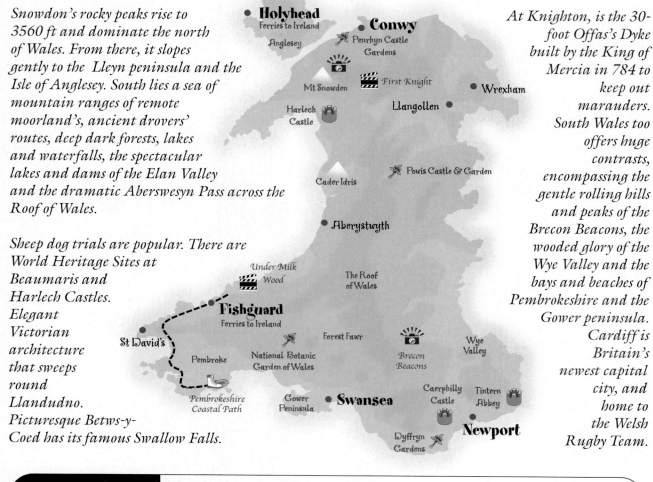

Holyhead
Ferries to Ireland
Anglesey
Conwy
Penrhyn Castle Gardens
Mt Snowden
First Knight
Wrexham
Harlech Castle
Llangollen
Cader Idris
Powis Castle & Garden
Aberystwyth
Under Milk Wood
The Roof of Wales
Fishguard
Ferries to Ireland
St David's
Pembroke
National Botanic Garden of Wales
Forest Fawr
Brecon Beacons
Wye Valley
Pembrokeshire Coastal Path
Gower Peninsula
Swansea
Caerphilly Castle
Tintern Abbey
Newport
Dyffryn Gardens

Map Symbols

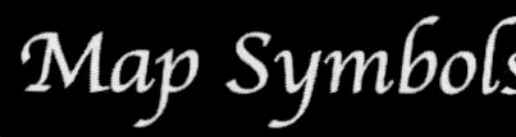

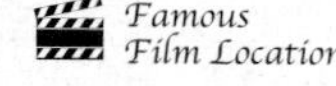

Take to the hills

Wales's three national parks encompass some of the most fantastic walking country in Britain from Snowdonia's peaks to the valleys of the Brecon Beacons and cliff-top paths of the Pembrokeshire Coast. The Offa's Dyke Path runs 168 miles down the Welsh-English border.

Capacity crowds

The Welsh Rugby Team line up to receive the cheers of a 72,500 capacity crowd at the Millennium Stadium where Six Nations Championship home games and rugby Internationals are keenly supported.

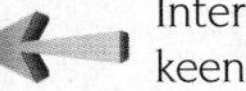

Gothick glory

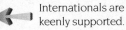

The Marquesses of Anglesey picked a lovely spot to build Plas Newydd, an 18th-century Gothic style mansion with stupendous views of Snowdonia in North Wales. A highlight of the house is Rex Whistler's 58ft-long scenic mural. The gardens are a real treat too, famous for their rhododendrons (late March to early June) and there is a pretty woodland walk leading down to the Menai Strait, where boat trips depart from the dock.

Tranquil terraces

The terraced Bodnant Garden, perched high above the River Conwy, is a horticultural paradise famed for its dramatic seasonal colours and glorious 180ft-long golden laburnum arch (May).

What the butler saw

One of the chief charms of Erdigg Hall, near Wrexham, is a rare look behind the scenes of a period country house at life in the servants' quarters and outbuildings including the laundry, bakehouse and smithy. There is also plenty to interest keen gardeners in the restored walled garden with its yew walk and Victorian parterre, as well as the National Collection of Ivies. Gentle walks explore the the home park and woodlands.

Garden Guide

The National Botanic Garden of Wales
Llanarthne, Carmarthenshire SA32 8HG
Tel: 01558 668 768
The UK's first National Botanic Garden

Dyffryn Gardens
St Nicholas, Cardiff CF5 6SU
Tel: 029 2059 3328
An Edwardian garden with features and displays throughout all seasons

Penrhyn Castle
Bangor LL57 4HN
Tel: 01248 353084
Located just outside Bangor, the castle and gardens are certainly worth a visit

Powis Castle & Garden
Nr Welshpool SY21 8RF
Tel: 01938 554338
A truly fascinating and world famous garden of Italian and French design

Find out more. There are many more attractions listed on the Best Loved Website: **www.bestlovedhotels.com**
Further information about Wales can be found by contacting: **Wales Tourist Board.** Brunel House, 2 Fitzalan Road, Cardiff, CF24 0UY, Tel: +44 029 2049 9909

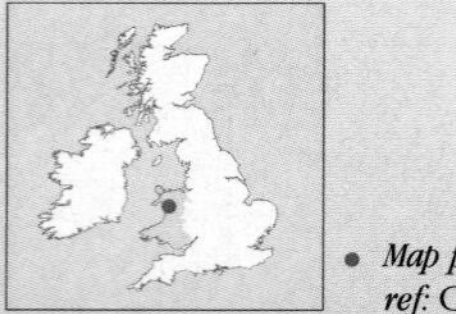

• Map p.498 ref: C3

“ A haven of tranquillity within a haven of tranquillity. We left with a great deal more than we came ”

Phil Jupituse, comedian

BAE ABERMAW

Contemporary country house

**Panorama Hill,
Barmouth,
Gwynedd LL42 1DQ**

**Telephone 01341 280550
Fax 01341 280346**

E-mail: baeabermaw@bestloved.com

OWNER
Simon Atkinson

GENERAL MANAGER
John Clarke

ROOM RATES

Single occupancy	£46 - £60
10 Doubles/Twins	£81 - £110
2 Suites	£81 - £120
3 Family rooms	£81 - £120

Includes full breakfast and VAT

CHARGE/CREDIT CARDS

• MC • VI

RATINGS & AWARDS
W.T.B. ★★★★ Hotel

FACILITIES
On site: Garden, croquet
Licensed for weddings
4 meeting rooms/max 120 people
Nearby: Golf, fishing, cycling trails, walking, climbing

RESTRICTIONS
No facilities for disabled guests
Smoking permitted in bar only
No pets

ATTRACTIONS
Snowdonia & Cader Idris,
Harlech & Caernarfon Castles,
Portmeirion Italianate village,
Ffestiniog Railway & Slate Mine,
Mawwdach Estuary & bird sanctuary

AFFILIATIONS
Independent

NEAREST
MAJOR CITY:
Chester - 69 miles/1¾ hrs
MAJOR AIRPORT:
Manchester - 100 miles/2¼ hrs
RAILWAY STATION:
Barmouth - ¼ mile/5 mins

RESERVATIONS
Direct with hotel
Quote **Best Loved**

ACCESS CODES
Not applicable

WALES

Contemporary style overlooking Cardigan Bay and Snowdonia

Architects Simon Atkinson and Robin Abrams (he is British, she American) have brought their considerable skill and vision to bear on transforming this old Victorian hotel into a superbly stylish contemporary property with a spectacular position above Cardigan Bay. Enormous care has gone into restoring (and replacing where necessary) the handsomely proportioned rooms, highly polished wood floors, and marble and slate open fireplaces. The colour scheme is white on white, but far from being intimidating it is chic and fresh, and guests are positively encouraged to get out and explore Snowdonia National Park or the beach, returning muddy (or sandy) and relaxed to enjoy deep baths and great food.

Food is a compelling reason to discover Bae Abermaw. The chefs are passionate about this corner of the world and bake their own traditional Welsh lava bread, catch local fish such as sea bass, grow herbs in the garden, and the new vegetable patch is coming on a treat. On rainy days, guests might find a spontaneous cookery class in the kitchen.

The national park literally begins at the back door, and all the staff will be very eager to pass on tips as to the best local walks from gentle potters to challenging hikes up mountainous Cader Idris. Golfers can sample notable courses at Aberdovey and Royal St David's, while other sporting activities range from sailing, sport fishing and mountain biking to rock climbing.

LOCATION

From Dolgellau take the A496 to Barmouth. At Barmouth turn right, signposted Bae Abermaw. The hotel is 100 yards up the hill on the right.

"We look forward to future visits with eager anticipation"

Tony & Judy Asbury, Buckinghamshire

• *Map p.498 ref: C3*

Victorian mansion

BONTDDU HALL HOTEL

An historic home that has played host to three great Prime Ministers

This Victorian mansion is set in 14 acres of grounds with a profusion of azaleas, camellias, and rhododendrons against a backdrop of mountains and a river estuary. The magical views are amongst the finest in Wales. The house was built by Charles Beale in 1873, father-in-law of Joseph Chamberlain, a Victorian politician, whose son, Neville Chamberlain, became Prime Minister in the 1930s.

Bontddu Hall has a well-earned reputation for high standards and attention to detail. There are 19 well-appointed en suite bedrooms and three suites–Churchill, Chamberlain, and Lloyd George – named after previous guests. There is also some self-catering accommodation for two to six people.

The cuisine is classic in style, using the best of fresh local produce – Welsh mountain lamb, Mawddach salmon, Cardigan Bay lobster. A fine wine cellar complements the food.

Bontddu Hall is in Snowdonia National Park. There are championship links golf courses at Harlech and Aberdyfi and historic castles in all directions. The locality provides for hillwalking, pony trekking, exploring slate and gold mines, bird watching, sea and river fishing and even narrow gauge steam railways.

LOCATION

Turn off A470 north of Dolgellau, on to A496 (direction Barmouth). 2 miles to village of Bontddu, hotel is on the right as you come into the village.

Bontddu, Near Barmouth, Gwynedd LL40 2UF

Telephone 01341 430661
Fax 01341 430284

E-mail: *bontddu@bestloved.com*

OWNERS

Mike and Gretta Ball

ROOM RATES

2 Singles	*£61 - £71*
13 Doubles/Twins	*£110 - £130*
1 Four-poster	*£160*
3 Suites	*£160*

Includes full breakfast and VAT

CHARGE/CREDIT CARDS

• DC • JCB • MC • VI

RATINGS & AWARDS

W.T.B. ★★★★ Hotel
R.A.C. ★★★ Dining Award 3
A.A. ★★★ ❀❀ 71%

FACILITIES

On site: *Garden*
Licensed for weddings
Nearby: *Golf, riding, mountain walking, fishing, dry ski slope*

RESTRICTIONS

No children under 3 years
No facilities for disabled guests
Pets by arrangement
Closed Jan - Feb

ATTRACTIONS

Snowdon Mountain Railway, Harlech Castle, Caernarfon Castle, Dinas Oleu, Bala Lake

AFFILIATIONS

Independent

NEAREST

MAJOR CITY:
Chester - 70 miles/1½ hrs

MAJOR AIRPORT:
Manchester - 120 miles/2 hrs

RAILWAY STATION:
Barmouth - 5 miles/10 mins

RESERVATIONS

Direct with hotel
Quote ***Best Loved***

ACCESS CODES

Not applicable

Planning a wedding reception? Turn to 'Meeting Facilities' on page 476

• Map p.498 ref: B6

" Service, food and facilities are all superb. We've had a great weekend "

Clive Benham, Ilminster, Somerset

COURT HOTEL

Country house hotel

Lamphey, Pembroke SA71 5NT

Telephone 01646 672273
Fax 01646 672480

E-mail: *courthotel@bestloved.com*

OWNER
Tony Lain

MANAGER
Rene Koomen

ROOM RATES

2 Singles	£69 - £79
20 Doubles/Twins	£69 - £110
15 Suites	£100 - £130

Includes full breakfast and VAT

CHARGE/CREDIT CARDS

• MC • VI

RATINGS & AWARDS
W.T.B. ★★★★ Hotel
A.A. ★★★ 74%

FACILITIES
On site: *Garden, tennis, sauna, indoor pool, jacuzzi, health & beauty, gym, heli-pad*
3 meeting rooms/max 100 people
Nearby: *Golf, riding, fishing, water skiing*

RESTRICTIONS
Limited facilities for disabled guests
Pets by arrangement

ATTRACTIONS
Pembrokeshire Coast, Oakwood Leisure Park, St David's Cathedral, Pembroke Castle, Tenby, Dylan Thomas Boatyard

AFFILIATIONS
Best Western

NEAREST
MAJOR CITY:
Cardiff - 95 miles/1½ hrs

MAJOR AIRPORT:
Cardiff - 95 miles/1½ hrs

RAILWAY STATION:
Lamphey - ½ mile/5 mins

RESERVATIONS
Toll free in US/Canada: 800-528-1234
Quote ***Best Loved***

ACCESS CODES
AMADEUS BW HAW424
APOLLO/GALILEO BW 13378
SABRE/ABACUS BW 12484
WORLDSPAN BW 83424

WALES

Georgian charm and modern comfort in Pembrokeshires National Park

The Lamphey Court Hotel is a magnificent mansion built in 1823 and carefully restored by the Lain family. Idyllically located in its own spacious grounds, it is bordered by the Pembrokeshire National Park and the coast. From the moment you step past the classic Ionic colonnade and portico entrance, you are treated as an important guest. The furnishings and decor are sumptuous. All bedrooms are beautifully appointed, and very comfortable indeed.The mouthwatering cuisine in the candlelit Georgian restaurant is prepared from local produce which includes Teifi salmon and Freshwater Bay lobster. The superb leisure centre has an indoor heated swimming pool, gymnasium, sauna, solarium and jacuzzi.

Nearby you can play golf, fish, sail, surf, ride or charter the hotel's private yacht. The area is a treasure house of places worth visiting in Wales. Within easy reach are St David's Cathedral (the country's largest church, built 1180), Oakwood Leisure Park, Pembroke Castle, birthplace of Henry VII, and the seaside town of Tenby. Dylan Thomas lived in the Boat House at Laugharne; the village was the model for all those famous and infamous Welsh voices in Under Milk Wood.

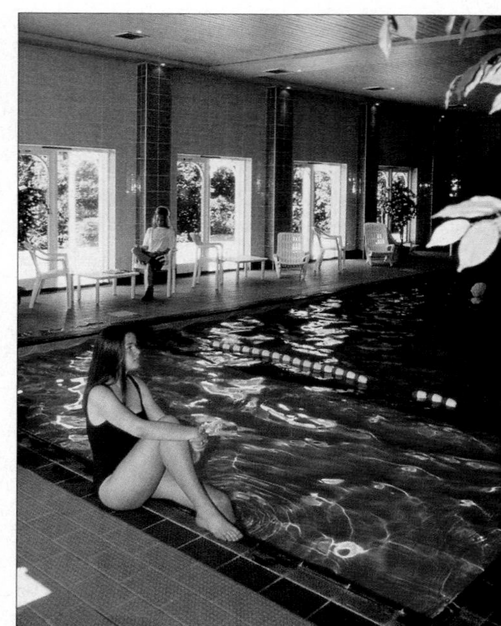

LOCATION

M4 to Carmarthen, A477 towards Pembroke. Turn left at Milton village for Lamphey. The hotel is well sign-posted both from M4 and the Irish ferry.

Looking for an hotel with a golf course on site? See our 'Golf Guide' on page 478

"The sort of place we hoped to find but thought we never would"

Dr Alan Scott, New York

Map p.498 ref: E5

17th century inn

THE CROWN AT WHITEBROOK

A delectable auberge transported to the depths of the Wye Valley

A mile from the River Wye, a tiny lane burrows between steep green banks into the remote heart of the Whitebrook Valley. Here, all but enveloped in the leafy embrace of Tintern Forest and a silence so profound it is almost unnerving (no mobile phone signal either - joy!), the Crown is essentially a restaurant with rooms, an unpretentious, intimate haven of tranquillity in an unspoilt Area of Outstanding Natural Beauty.

The Crown's front door opens into a comfortable lounge where guests can relax, or gather for chat over after-dinner drinks and coffee. The informal atmosphere encouraged by proprietors (and sisters) Angela and Elizabeth Barbara is one of the hotel's great strengths. However, the food is the main draw and the French-inspired menu employs the very best Welsh ingredients from new season lamb to delicious cheeses such as Harlech flavoured with parsley and horseradish, yet still surprisingly mild.

The bedrooms are comfortable, fastidiously clean and utterly peaceful with thoughtful little touches like home baked Welsh cakes.

Working up an appetite is no problem. Walkers can join the Lower Wye Valley Walk or the Offa's Dyke Path to Tintern Abbey direct from the hotel grounds. Interesting local towns include Monmouth and the antique book capital of Hay-on-Wye and South Wales offers a veritable embarrassment of historic castles and keeps.

LOCATION

From Heathrow: M4 & M48 west, take first exit after crossing Severn Bridge & A466 (to Monmouth). At Bigsweir Bridge bear left for Whitebrook, hotel is 2 miles up on left.

Whitebrook, Monmouth, Monmouthshire NP25 4TX

Telephone 01600 860254
Fax 01600 860607

E-mail: *crownwales@bestloved.com*

OWNERS

Angela and Elizabeth Barbara

ROOM RATES

Single occupancy	£53
10 Doubles/Twins	£85
1 Four-poster	£90

Includes full breakfast and VAT

CHARGE/CREDIT CARDS

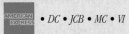

• DC • JCB • MC • VI

RATINGS & AWARDS

W.T.B. ★★★ Restaurant with Rooms
A.A. ★★ ❀❀ 70%

FACILITIES

On site: *Gardens*
1 meeting room/max 10 people
Nearby: *Golf, riding, fishing*

RESTRICTIONS

No facilities for disabled guests

ATTRACTIONS

Tintern Abbey, Chepstow Castle, Forest of Dean, Raglan Castle, Brecon Beacons, Wye Valley, Clearwell Caves, Chepstow Racecourse

AFFILIATIONS

Welsh Rarebits

NEAREST

MAJOR CITY:
Cardiff - 20 miles/40 mins

MAJOR AIRPORT:
London Heathrow - 100 miles/1½ hrs

RAILWAY STATION:
Chepstow - 12 miles/15 mins

RESERVATIONS

Direct with hotel
Quote ***Best Loved***

ACCESS CODES

Not applicable

• Map p.498 ref: C2

"We enjoyed your lovely hotel and found Wales to be filled with delightful attractions and great people like yourselves"

Louis and Molly Webber, New York

THE EMPIRE

Victorian resort hotel

Church Walks, Llandudno, Conwy LL30 2HE

Telephone 01492 860555
Fax 01492 860791

E-mail: *empire@bestloved.com*

OWNERS
Len and Elizabeth Maddocks

MANAGERS
Elyse and Michael Waddy

ROOM RATES

Single occupancy	£50 - £70
51 Doubles/Twins	£85 - £100
7 Suites	£100 - £250

Includes full breakfast and VAT

CHARGE/CREDIT CARDS

• DC • JCB • MC • VI

RATINGS & AWARDS
W.T.B. ★★★★ Hotel
A.A. ★★★ ❀ 75%
A.A. Courtesy & Care Award

FACILITIES
On site: *Indoor/outdoor heated pools, sauna, whirlpool & spa bath, steamroom, beauty treatments, roof garden & patio*
1 meeting room/max 40 people
Nearby: *Golf, riding, fishing, sailing*

RESTRICTIONS
No facilities for disabled guests
No pets, guide dogs only

ATTRACTIONS
Snowdonia National Park, Conwy and Caernarfon Castles, Bodnant Gardens, Portmeirion Italianate village, Great Little Trains of Wales

AFFILIATIONS
Independent

NEAREST
MAJOR CITY:
Chester - 50 miles/50 mins

MAJOR AIRPORT:
Manchester - 84 miles/1½ hrs

RAILWAY STATION:
Llandudno Junction - 3 miles/10 mins

RESERVATIONS
Direct with hotel
Quote ***Best Loved***

ACCESS CODES
Not applicable

WALES

Affordable luxury for that special occasion

The Empire is privately owned and has been run by the Maddocks family for over 50 years. Helping Len and Elizabeth, are daughter Elyse and her husband Michael Waddy who, between them, offer some of the kindest hospitality in the region. Amongst the family treasures are wonderful antiques and one of the largest private collections of artists' prints by Sir William Russell Flint. You will feel at home here: the generously appointed bedrooms are complete with jacuzzi in the marbled bathrooms, TV and VCR (the videos are free) and modem connections for the traveller who wants to keep up to the minute.

There is an indoor heated pool with sauna, steam room and spa bath. Outside, there is another heated pool around which you can recline on sun loungers amongst the flowers. If you feel the need for greater relaxation, the therapist has a range of beauty treatments, aromatherapy, reflexology and Indian head massage.

Michael, with a gifted team of young chefs at his elbow, serves innovative fresh food daily in the award-winning Watkins & Co restaurant. Do not overlook the home-made bread and wicked desserts.

The Empire, set on the picturesque Victorian promenade and near the pier, offers special two-night breaks. From here, you can take a bracing walk among the estuary dunes and marvel at the views from Caernarfon Castle to Snowdonia.

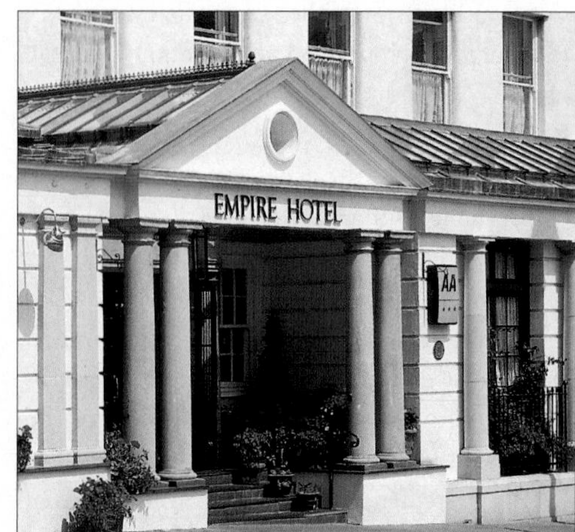

LOCATION

Exit the A55 at the A470 intersection for Llandudno. Follow signs for town centre, drive down the main street (Mostyn Street). The hotel is at the end and faces the town.

Thinking of pampering yourself? See the 'Health & Beauty' index on page 472

" Peace, beauty and wonderful food and a great welcome "

P D James

• Map p.498 ref: C6

Georgian manor house

FAIRYHILL

'Midst woods and valleys there's a kitchen of delightful surprises

Fairyhill is a haven of peace and tranquillity, nestling in the heart of the Gower peninsular. A delightful mansion built in 1720 and still the epitome of relaxed country living. Here, in 24 acres of park and woodland alongside the beautiful valley through which the little Burry trout stream meanders, you can be at peace!

The pleasantly furnished bedrooms offer all the essentials for an enjoyable stay. Each is equipped with remote controlled TV and CD stereo systems and you will be welcome to enjoy the music from an extensive library.

Chefs, Paul Davies and Adrian Coulthard, have achieved recognition in all major food guides. The menus are designed around the seasons and the locality with regular use of sewin, lobster and, if the fancy takes you, laverbread and cockles – famous delicacies to be found in these parts.

The surrounding scenery will be an added pleasure to your stay. The famous beaches and spectacular Worms Head are a few minutes away. For the golfing enthusiast there is a choice of five golf courses (parkland and links) within eight miles and for the garden enthusiast, the National Botanical Garden of Wales and the gardens of Aberglasney are but a short drive away.

LOCATION

Take Exit 47 off M4 and follow signs to Gower/Gowerton. From Gowerton go through Penclawdd, signposted Llanridian and Crofty. Fairyhill is 1 mile past Greyhound Inn.

Reynoldston, Gower, Swansea SA3 1BS

Telephone 01792 390139
Fax 01792 391358

E-mail: *fairyhill@bestloved.com*

OWNERS

Andrew Hetherington, Peter Camm, Jane Camm and Paul Davies

ROOM RATES

Single occupancy	*£110 - £210*
8 Doubles	*£125 - £225*

Includes early morning tea, newspaper, full breakfast and VAT

CHARGE/CREDIT CARDS

• JCB • MC • VI

RATINGS & AWARDS

W.T.B. ★★★★★ Country Hotel

A.A. ★★ ❀❀❀

A.A. Wine List of the Year Wales 2000

FACILITIES

On site: *Croquet, gardens, heli-pad*
1 meeting room/max 24 people
Nearby: *Riding, fishing*

RESTRICTIONS

No children under 8 years
No facilities for disabled guests
No pets

ATTRACTIONS

The Gower Peninsula, Swansea, Weobley Castle, National Botanical Garden of Wales, Aberglasney Gardens

AFFILIATIONS

Welsh Rarebits

NEAREST

MAJOR CITY:
Swansea - 12 miles/25 mins

MAJOR AIRPORT:
London Heathrow - 170 miles/2½ hrs
Cardiff - 50 miles/1 hr

RAILWAY STATION:
Swansea - 12 miles/25 mins

RESERVATIONS

Direct with hotel
Quote ***Best Loved***

ACCESS CODES

Not applicable

A keen Angler? Refer to page 472 for our Fishing Index

"Of all the hotels that I stay at in the world, The George is where I choose to spend my leisure, pleasure and peace"

Graham Smith, Toyota GB Ltd

• Map p.498 ref: C3

17th century inn

GEORGE III HOTEL

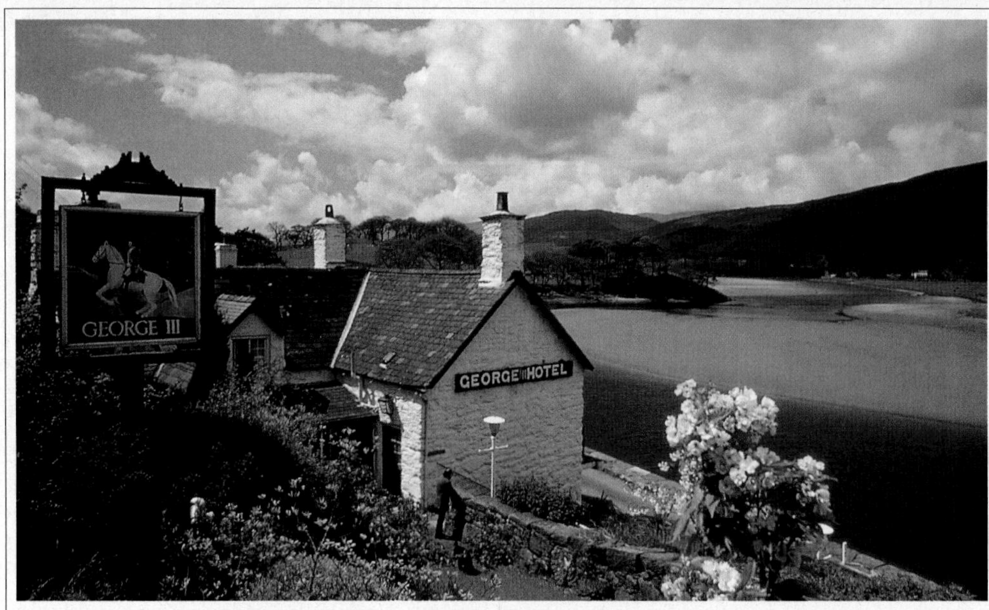

A house of great character in a wonderful location

The George III Hotel is situated on the magnificent Mawddach Estuary. The main hotel was built around 1650 as two separate buildings, pub and ship chandlers. The adjacent Lodge is a Victorian building built as a Waiting Room, Ticket Office and Station Master's house for the railway station, now closed.

The hotel is owned and personally run by John and Julia Cartwright and their family. Guests may choose between accommodation in the hotel or in the lodge. Every room is full of character, comfortably furnished and has a wonderful view of the estuary.

Great emphasis is placed on the food with Welsh lamb and seafood being the specialities. On fine days, bar lunches are served on the balcony and the non-smoking cellar bar is ideal for families.

The area is packed with romantic ruins and fairytale castles so the hotel's mountain bikes make a change from the usual form of sightseeing. Or you can fish for salmon and trout, go clay pigeon shooting or power trekking or take a ride on one of the little railways in the area.

LOCATION

Turn left off A470 signposted Tywyn, approximately 2 miles, turn right for toll bridge, then first left for hotel.

Penmaenpool, Dolgellau, Gwynedd LL40 1YD

Telephone 01341 422525
Fax 01341 423565

E-mail: *george3@bestloved.com*

OWNERS

John and Julia Cartwright

ROOM RATES

Single occupancy £40 - £55
11 Doubles/Twins £70 - £94
Includes full breakfast and VAT

CHARGE/CREDIT CARDS

MC • JCB • VI

RATINGS & AWARDS

W.T.B. ★★★ Country Hotel
R.A.C. ★★
A.A. ★★ 72%

FACILITIES

On site: *Gardens, fishing, mountain bike hire*
1 meeting room/max 20 people
Nearby: *Golf, pony trekking, walking, clay pigeon shooting*

RESTRICTIONS

Pets by arrangement
Limited facilities for disabled guests

ATTRACTIONS

Snowdonia National Park, Cymer Abbey, Harlech Castle, Ffestiniog Railway, Difi Furnace, Dinas Oleu, Cader Idris

AFFILIATIONS

Independent

NEAREST

MAJOR CITY:
Chester - 70 miles/1½ hrs

MAJOR AIRPORT:
Manchester - 90 miles/2 hrs

RAILWAY STATION:
Barmouth - 8 miles/15 mins

RESERVATIONS

Direct with hotel
Quote ***Best Loved***

ACCESS CODES

Not applicable

For route planning map of Wales see page 498

• Map p.498 ref: C2

"Absolutely wonderful - accommodation lovely and food delicious. Staff incredibly nice"

Mr & Mrs Kay, Clitheroe, Lancashire

THE GROES INN

16th century inn

Tyn-y-Groes,
Near Conwy LL32 8TN

Telephone 01492 650545
Fax 01492 650855

E-mail: groesinn@bestloved.com

OWNERS

Dawn, Tony and Justin Humphreys

ROOM RATES

Single occupancy	£63 - £95
11 Doubles/Twins	£80 - £101
1 Family room	£85 - £105
2 Junior suites	£114

Includes full breakfast and VAT

CHARGE/CREDIT CARDS

• DC • MC • VI

RATINGS & AWARDS

W.T.B. ★★★★ Hotel
R.A.C. ★★★ Dining Award 1
A.A. ★★★ 71%

FACILITIES

On site: *Garden*
2 meeting rooms/max 20 people
Nearby: *Golf, fishing, yachting, tennis, fitness centre, riding*

RESTRICTIONS

No children under 10 years in main restaurant
Limited facilities for disabled guests

ATTRACTIONS

Snowdonia National Park, Conwy and Caernarfon castles, Portmeirion, Bodnant Gardens, Ffestiniog and Llanberis railways, hill and mountain walks

AFFILIATIONS

Welsh Rarebits

NEAREST

MAJOR CITY:
Chester - 50 miles/1 hr

MAJOR AIRPORT:
Manchester - 75 miles/1½ hrs

RAILWAY STATION:
Llandudno Junction - 5 miles/7 mins

FERRY PORT:
Holyhead - 30 miles/40 mins

RESERVATIONS

Direct with hotel
Quote ***Best Loved***

ACCESS CODES

Not applicable

WALES

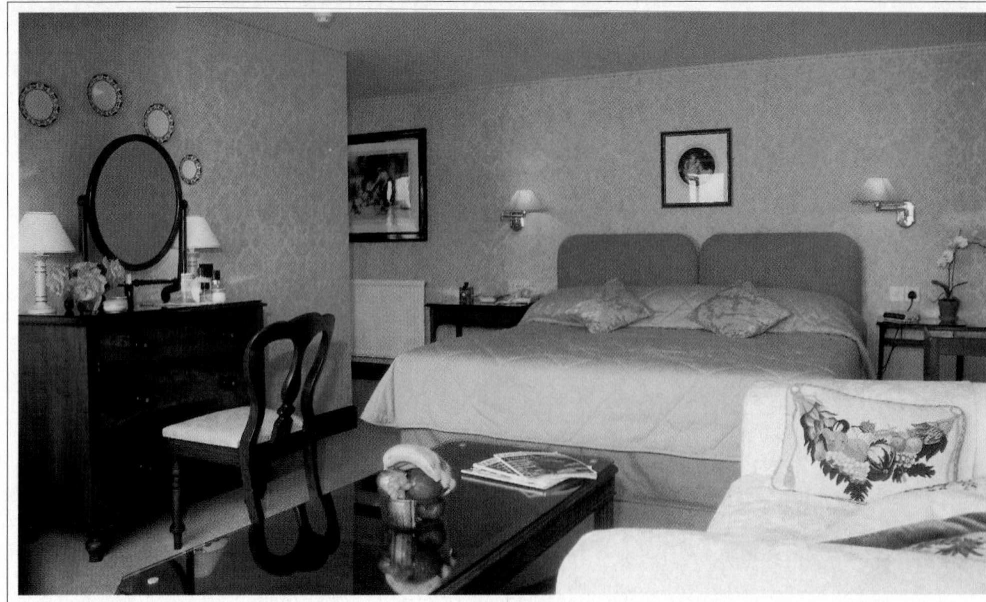

The fine art of inn keeping at its best in the foothills of Snowdonia

The Groes Inn is a revelation for those who mourn the passing of the great British inn - a traditional refuge of travellers blending the warm welcome of a local pub with the homely comforts of a good bed and wholesome food. These words, taken from The Groes' brochure, are something of an understatement. There is a much deeper satisfaction in prospect here and it starts with the proprietors who have the fine art of innkeeping bred into them for three generations.

The inn is just two miles south of the walled town of Conwy, set in the Conwy River valley amongst the foothills of Snowdonia. It first had its licence in 1573 and, ever since, has kept the spirit of hospitality alive. Today's visitors will be reassured to find there have been subtle changes to hoist the facilities to present-day standards. Its character, however, remains unchanged. A recent addition to these facilities is the Gallery Suite, comprising of two elegantly furnished rooms which are not only ideal for weddings and private dinner parties but also make an incredible setting for a small meeting or conference.

The area is well-known for the excellence of its produce: beef, home cured ham and of course Welsh lamb and lovely fresh vegetables, too. From Anglesey comes crab, wild salmon, plaice, oysters and mussels, all fresh as the day. The Groes Inn gets its pick and works wonders with it! And if you can manage it, do try the puddings.

LOCATION

From Conwy Castle, take the B5106 towards Trefriw passing under the double arches of the town walls. The inn is about 2 miles further on the right.

"You've bought a hotel and turned it into a home"

John J Howells, Cardiff

• Map p.498 ref: D5

Victorian country house

THE LAKE COUNTRY HOUSE

If you can't relax here, you can't relax anywhere!

An air of elegance and calm informality pervades this exquisitely furnished Welsh country house. Warmly welcoming, this award-winning retreat stands serenely in 50 acres of parkland including a large trout lake, a haven for fascinating wildlife. In such a setting, guests experience the true feeling of Wales.

One may enjoy a mouth-watering, traditional Welsh afternoon tea in front of log fires in the lounge or in the garden in summer. Dining by candlelight in the restaurant is a memorable experience; the cuisine has been winning prestigious awards for its excellence.

Suites and bedrooms are delightfully appointed, each having a private bathroom, television, direct-dial telephone, period furniture and fine pictures and books.

Excellent salmon and trout fishing is available on the rivers Wye and Irfon and the hotel's own picturesque lake which regularly yields trout of five pounds and over and has no closed season. There is tennis, croquet, clay pigeon shooting and a nine-hole golf course within the grounds. The hotel's billiards room is a popular evening venue. There are four 18-hole courses in the vicinity and pony trekking can be arranged.

LOCATION

A40 to Abergavenny-Brecon; after Brecon veer left onto B4519, then left for Llangammarch Wells. Cross Mount Eppynt (6 miles) & turn left at foot of hill. Hotel is one mile along on right.

Llangammarch Wells, Powys LD4 4BS

Telephone 01591 620202
Fax 01591 620457

E-mail: *lakecountry@bestloved.com*

OWNERS

Jean-Pierre and Janet Mifsud

ROOM RATES

Single occupancy	*£90 - £205*
8 Luxury doubles	*£145*
11 Suites	*£175 - £205*

Includes full breakfast and VAT

CHARGE/CREDIT CARDS

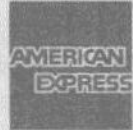

• *DC* • *JCB* • *MC* • *VI*

RATINGS & AWARDS

W.T.B. ★★★★ Country Hotel
R.A.C. Blue Ribbon ★★★ Dining Award 2
A.A. ★★★ ❀❀
A.A. Courtesy & Care Award
A.A. Inspectors Selected Hotel

FACILITIES

On site: *Garden, croquet, tennis, snooker, heli-pad, clay pigeon shooting, salmon/trout fishing, 9 hole par 3 golf course, putting area*
Licensed for weddings
1 meeting room/max 65 people

RESTRICTIONS

No children under 7 years in dining room after 7.30 pm
£6 surcharge per dog per night

ATTRACTIONS

Powis Castle, The Elan Valley, Brecon Beacons, Hay-on-Wye's bookshops

AFFILIATIONS

Pride of Britain
Welsh Rarebits

NEAREST

MAJOR CITY:
Hereford - 40 miles/45 mins

MAJOR AIRPORT:
Cardiff - 60 miles/1¼ hrs

RAILWAY STATION:
Llangammarch Wells - 1 mile/5 mins

RESERVATIONS

Toll free in US: 800-98-PRIDE
Quote ***Best Loved***

ACCESS CODES

Not applicable

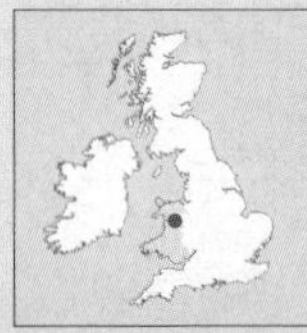

• Map p.498 ref: D3

"It was indeed splendid. Everything was absolute perfection - the staff were wonderful and the food excellent"

Kate Dunkley, Cheshire

LAKE VYRNWY HOTEL

Victorian country house

Lake Vyrnwy, Llanwddyn, Montgomeryshire SY10 0LY

Telephone 01691 870692
Fax 01691 870259

E-mail: *vyrnwy@bestloved.com*

OWNERS
The Bisiker Family

ROOM RATES

34 Doubles/Twins	£110 - £182
1 Suite	£182

Includes full breakfast and VAT

CHARGE/CREDIT CARDS

• DC • MC • VI

RATINGS & AWARDS
W.T.B. ★★★★ *Country Hotel*
R.A.C. ★★★ *Dining Award 1*
A.A. ★★★ ❀❀ *73%*

FACILITIES
On site: *Garden, tennis, fly fishing, shooting, cycling, walking trails, RSPB Reserve, rowing, sailing, clay pigeon shooting, heli-pad, quad trekking, Licensed for weddings*
3 meeting rooms/max 120 people
Nearby: *White water rafting, RSPB hides, canoeing, walking trails*

RESTRICTIONS
No facilities for disabled guests
No pets in public rooms

ATTRACTIONS
Powis Castle, Great Little Trains of Wales, Vyrnwy Visitor Centre, Lake Vyrnwy

AFFILIATIONS
Independent

NEAREST
MAJOR CITY:
Shrewsbury - 32 miles/45 mins
Chester - 43 miles/1 hr

MAJOR AIRPORT:
Birmingham/Manchester - 90 miles/1¾ hrs

RAILWAY STATION:
Welshpool - 22 miles/30 mins
Shrewsbury - 32 miles/45 mins

RESERVATIONS
Direct with hotel
Quote ***Best Loved***

ACCESS CODES
Not applicable

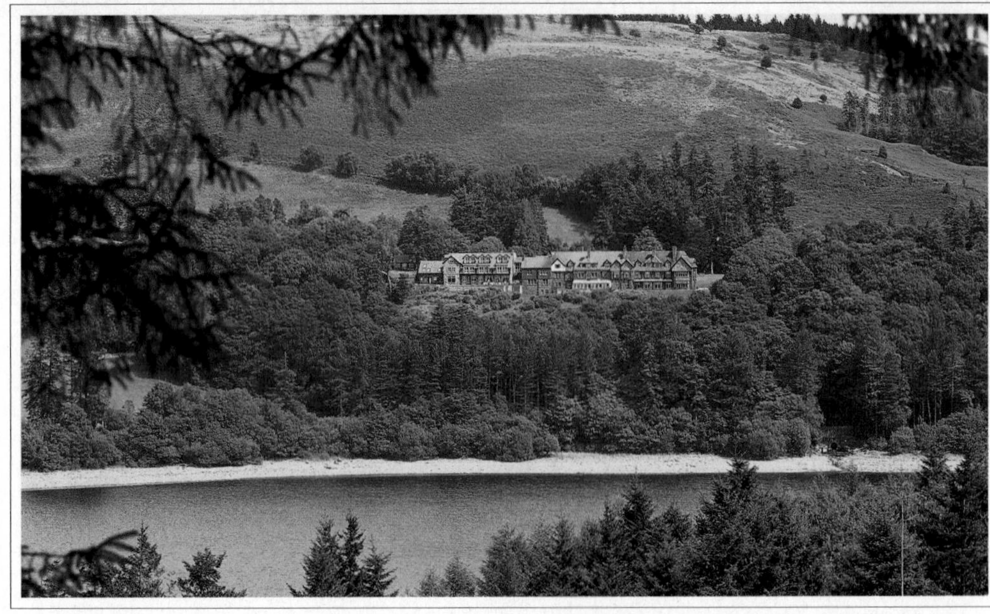

The sheer magnetism of this place makes it almost impossible to leave!

This hotel is situated high on the hillsides within the 24,000 acres of the Vyrnwy Estate, commanding breathtaking views of mountains, lake and moorland. The hotel is surrounded by lawns and fringed with an abundance of rhododendrons, woods and meadowlands. Built in 1890, its heritage has been maintained for 100 years as a retreat for all country lovers.

Each bedroom is individually furnished and decorated, many with antiques; some have jacuzzis, four-posters, suites or private balconies. The public rooms are all warm and welcoming with log fires. The elegant drawing room has cosy chintz sofas, a grand piano and oil paintings, whilst the cocktail bar has a club atmosphere, with deep leather chairs, sporting prints and pitch pine.

The award-winning restaurant's menu changes seasonally. Everything from the marmalade at breakfast to the bread rolls and petitfours at dinner are created in the Vyrnwy kitchens.

The hotel owns sole sporting rights on the estate together with the fishing rights on the five-mile long lake. 16,000 acres are also a nature sanctuary providing a wealth of wildlife and beautiful walks. Other activities include tennis, cycling, boating and sailing. Peace and tranquillity reign. Special two-day breaks are available.

LOCATION

Follow brown tourist signs for Lake Vyrnwy from Shrewsbury A458 or from Oswestry A5.

" What a delightful retreat! Thank you for the wonderful hospitality and kind service. We truly did feel as if we were in someone's beautiful home "

Janis and Jeffrey Rubin, Canfield, Ohio

• Map p.498 ref: D5

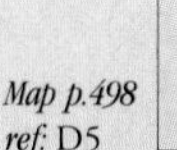

Country house

LLANGOED HALL

Designed by a distinguished architect, recreated by a great designer

Llangoed Hall may have been the legendary White Palace, home of the first Parliament at the dawn of Welsh history. In AD 560, Prince Iddon donated it to the church in expiation of his sins. A mansion was built here in 1632. The great architect Sir Clough Williams-Ellis designed it as a gracious country house in 1912, retaining the surviving Jacobean porch as part of the south wing.

Sir Bernard Ashley saw it as the place where he could fulfil his ambition to recreate the atmosphere of an Edwardian house party. There is no reception desk, just friendly staff to carry the bags. In summer the Great Hall's French windows are open so that guests can enjoy the garden. In winter, the huge stone fireplace has a merry log blazing. In the Picture Gallery are fine portraits and works by Whistler and the Edwardians. The handsome dining room offers modern classical cooking. It makes the most of fresh local produce, such as Welsh lamb, Wye salmon and laverbread.

The secluded Wye Valley and the Black Mountains are all around; the Brecon Beacons, Cardiff, the bookshops of Hay-on-Wye, Caerphilly, Raglan and Powis Castles and Wordsworth's Tintern Abbey are nearby.

LOCATION

On A470. 11 miles south east of Builth Wells; 11 miles north east of Brecon.

Llyswen, Brecon, Powys LD3 0YP

Telephone 01874 754525
Fax 01874 754545

E-mail: *llangoed@bestloved.com*

OWNER

Sir Bernard Ashley

ROOM RATES

2 Singles	*£110 - £280*
11 Doubles/Twins	*£145 - £270*
7 Four-posters	*£145 - £270*
3 Suites	*£295 - £320*

Includes full breakfast and VAT

CHARGE/CREDIT CARDS

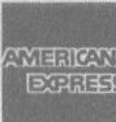

• DC • JCB • MC • VI

RATINGS & AWARDS

W.T.B. ★★★★★ Country Hotel
R.A.C. Blue Ribbon ★★★★
Dining Award 3
A.A. ★★★★ ❀❀

FACILITIES

On site: *Garden, croquet, fishing, snooker, mountain bikes, clay pigeon shooting, tennis, heli-pad, Licensed for weddings*
3 meeting rooms/max 50 people

Nearby: *Golf, hunting/shooting, riding, 4x4, canoeing, gliding*

RESTRICTIONS

No facilities for disabled guests
No children under 8 years
No pets in main building - heated kennels available

ATTRACTIONS

Brecon Beacons, Cardiff, Hay-on-Wye, Tintern Abbey, Powis & Raglan Castles

AFFILIATIONS

The Celebrated Hotels Collection
Welsh Rarebits

NEAREST

MAJOR CITY:
Cardiff - 55 miles/55 mins
MAJOR AIRPORT:
Cardiff - 65 miles/1½ hrs
RAILWAY STATION:
Newport - 48 miles/1 hr

RESERVATIONS

Toll free in US: 800-322-2403
Toll free in UK: 0321 ASHLEY
Quote ***Best Loved***

ACCESS CODES

Not applicable

WALES

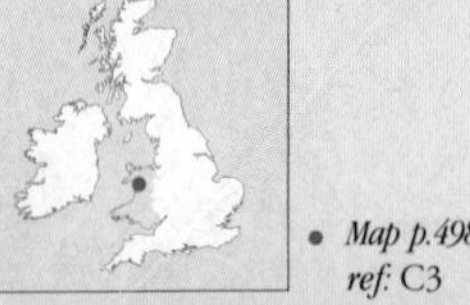

• Map p.498 ref: C3

"Comfortable rooms, beautiful gardens, delicious cuisine, and consummate hosts. We look forward to our return"

Norman & Kathryn Kinney, Michigan

HOTEL MAES-Y-NEUADD

600-year old manor house

Talsarnau, Near Harlech, Gwynedd LL47 6YA

Telephone 01766 780200
Fax 01766 780211

E-mail: maes@bestloved.com

OWNERS

June and Michael Slatter
Lynn and Peter Jackson

ROOM RATES

1 Single	£69
12 Doubles/Twins	£144 - £177
1 Four-poster	£155
2 Suites	£155 - £177

Includes full breakfast and VAT

CHARGE/CREDIT CARDS

• DC • JCB • MC • VI

RATINGS & AWARDS

W.T.B. ★★★★ Country Hotel
R.A.C. Gold Ribbon ★★ Dining Award 3
A.A. ★★ ❀❀❀
The Good Food Guide Restaurant of the Year 2000

FACILITIES

On site: Croquet, gardens, heli-pad
Licensed for weddings
1 meeting room/max 20 people
Nearby: Golf, riding, fishing, walking, shooting

RESTRICTIONS

No children under 8 years at dinner after 7 pm
Limited facilities for disabled guests

ATTRACTIONS

Mount Snowdon, Portmeirion, Caernarfon and Harlech Castles, Royal St David's Golf Course

AFFILIATIONS

The Celebrated Hotels Collection
Welsh Rarebits

NEAREST

MAJOR CITY:
Bangor - 35 miles/1 hr

MAJOR AIRPORT:
Manchester - 100 miles/2 hrs

RAILWAY STATION:
Harlech - 3 miles/10 mins

RESERVATIONS

Toll free in US: 800-322-2403
or 800-98-PRIDE
Quote **Best Loved**

ACCESS CODES

Not applicable

WALES

Elegance and serenity in the midst of magnificent Snowdonia

Deep in Snowdonia, amongst some of the most beautiful scenery in Britain, the manor house of Maes-y-Neuadd has watched over this timeless, magnificent scene for more than 600 years. For centuries the home of one family, the house is now owned by two couples, Lynn and Peter Jackson and June and Michael Slatter. They have lovingly restored and refurbished the house, creating a warm and welcoming haven for travellers from all over the world. The rooms are furnished using the best of modern craftsmanship, filled with fine antiques and many paintings by local artists. The eight acres of grounds reflect the beauty of the seasons, nurtured by the mild Gulf Stream climate.

Chef proprietor Peter Jackson revels in the quality of the 'natural larder' on his doorstep. To complement the fine lamb, cheese, fish and game for which Wales is renowned, many vegetables, fruit and herbs are grown in the kitchen garden. Through the hotel's associate company, 'Steam & Cuisine' all this can also be enjoyed on the famous Ffestiniog Railway.

The ancient language, culture and music set this area of Wales apart from the rest of Britain. Above all the welcome, 'Croeso', for which Wales is so famous, is nowhere warmer than at Maes-y-Neuadd.

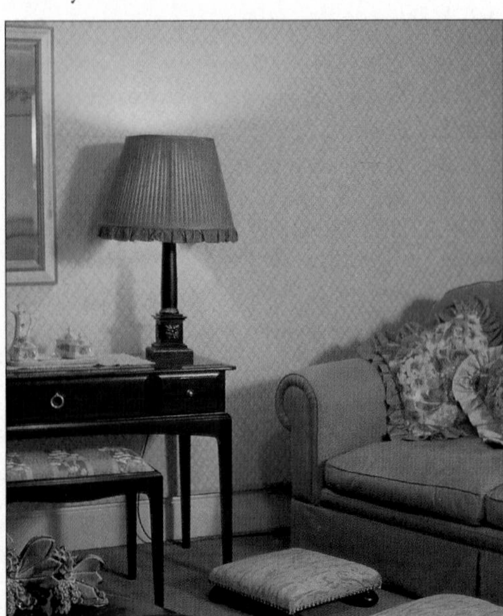

LOCATION

Located ½ mile off B4573, 3½ miles north of Harlech. Hotel sign on corner of lane.

“ I can't remember the last occasion on which we enjoyed such a skillfully crafted and thoroughly delicious dinner. Enthusiasm for the culinary arts shon through every mouthful ”

Ruth & Richard Shearn, Cheshir

11th century manor

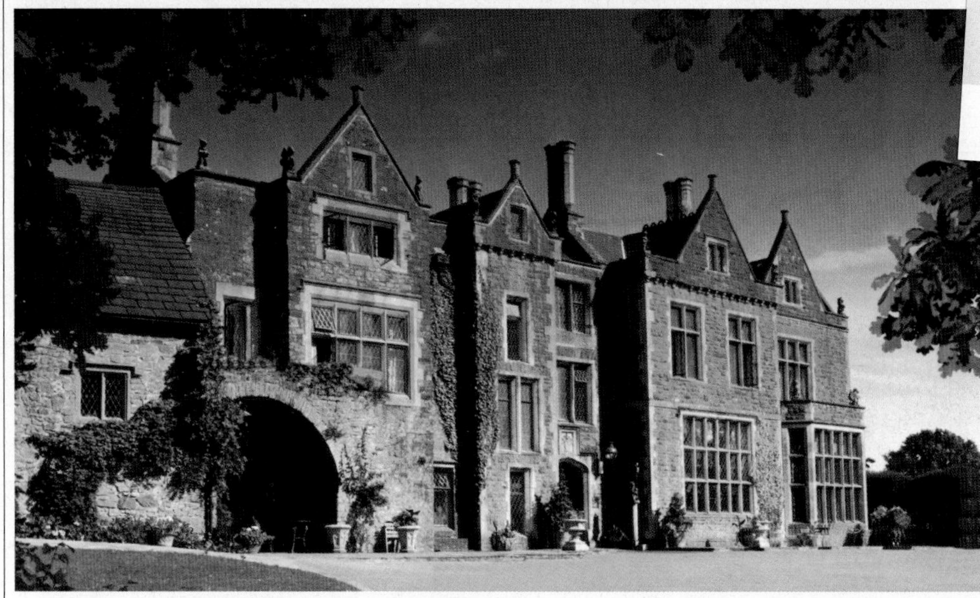

It would be difficult to find a more beautiful building in Wales

The beauty of Wales depends on where the beholder is. The Vale of Glamorgan, at the foot of the Cambrian Mountains, is a case in point. A thousand years ago, when the principality was divided into Cwmwds (sections) this part was called 'Miscin' or 'lovely plain' (hence Miskin Manor) and it remains as lovely as ever.

Since the 10th century, Miskin Manor has been a family home. It was rebuilt in 1857, survived two fires and became a country house hotel in 1985. Colin and Leah Rosenberg bought it in 1997 and, after much loving restoration, put back what the years wore away and added the comforts and conveniences consistent with the new age and a grand old historic house .

Miskin's most striking feature is its graceful use of space: the bedrooms are superbly appointed (Edward, Prince of Wales, stayed in one of them back in the 1920s). One of the most impressive rooms is the baronial Minstrel's Hall used for meetings, weddings and banquets. The Maesgyn Restaurant is similarly touched by elegance and serves its own interpretation of a Taste of Wales, a wonderful blend of culinary expertise and the Welsh wonders of field and farm nearby.

The 22-acre landscaped estate includes a fully equipped Health & Leisure Club, complete with pool, squash and badminton courts, gym, creche, restaurant and bar - all available to guests.

LOCATION

¾ miles from Exit 34 off the M4.
8 miles from Cardiff on the A4119.

E-mail: *miskin@bestloved.com*

OWNERS

Leah and Colin Rosenberg

ROOM RATES

4 Singles	*£95*
31 Doubles/Twins	*£126*
2 Four-posters	*£150*
7 Junior suites	*£205*

Includes full breakfast and VAT

CHARGE/CREDIT CARDS

• *DC* • *MC* • *VI*

RATINGS & AWARDS

W.T.B. ★★★★ *Country Hotel*
R.A.C. ★★★★
A.A. ★★★★ ❀ *69%*
Welsh Tourist Board Welcome Host Gold Award

FACILITIES

On site: *Garden, croquet, indoor pool, squash, badminton, snooker, sauna, jacuzzi, health & beauty, gym, creche, heli-pad, Licensed for weddings*
5 meeting rooms/max 200 people
Nearby: *Golf, riding*

RESTRICTIONS

Limited facilities for disabled guests

ATTRACTIONS

Cardiff Castle, Cardiff Bay, Castle Coch, Swansea, Gower Peninsula, Heritage Museum, Brecon Beacons, Big Pit Mining, Caerphilly Castle, Millennium Stadium

AFFILIATIONS

Welsh Rarebits
Preston's Global Hotels

NEAREST

MAJOR CITY:
Cardiff - 8 miles/15 mins

MAJOR AIRPORT:
Cardiff - 8 miles/20 mins

RAILWAY STATION:
Pontyclun - 1½ miles/5 mins

RESERVATIONS

Toll free in US: 800-544-9993
*Quote **Best Loved***

ACCESS CODES

Not applicable

" The torch for cooking on the North Wales coast is carried by Wendy Vaughan. Faultless throughout! "

Vogue Magazine

• Map p.498
ref: C2

...ECTORY COUNTRY HOUSE

Georgian country house

...sanffraid Glan Conwy,
Near Conwy,
Conwy LL28 5LF

Telephone 01492 580611
Fax 01492 584555

E-mail: orectconwy@bestloved.com

OWNERS

Michael and Wendy Vaughan

ROOM RATES

Single occupancy	*£79 - £129*
5 Doubles/Twins	*£99 - £149*
1 Four-poster	*£99 - £149*

Includes full breakfast and VAT

CHARGE/CREDIT CARDS

MC • JCB • VI

RATINGS & AWARDS

W.T.B. ★★★★★ Country House
R.A.C. Gold Ribbon ★★ Dining Award 4
A.A. ★★ ❀❀❀

FACILITIES

On site: *Gardens*
Nearby: *Golf, riding, fishing*

RESTRICTIONS

No children under 5 years
(does not apply to babes-in-arms)
No facilities for disabled guests
Pets by arrangement
No smoking throughout

ATTRACTIONS

Conwy Castle, Llandudno, Bodnant Gardens, Snowdonia National Park

AFFILIATIONS

Welsh Rarebits
Selected British Hotels

NEAREST

MAJOR CITY:
Chester - 40 miles/45 mins

MAJOR AIRPORT:
Manchester - 70 miles/1½ hrs

RAILWAY STATION:
Llandudno Junction - 1½ miles/5 mins

FERRY PORT:
Holyhead - 35 miles/1 hr

RESERVATIONS

Toll free in US: 800-323-5463
*Quote **Best Loved***

ACCESS CODES

AMADEUS HK CEGOLD
APOLLO/GALILEO HK 25905
SABRE/ABACUS HK 31998
WORLDSPAN HK OLDRE

WALES

"Outstanding comfort, welcome, service and food" – lovely place, too!

The charming Old Rectory Country House, idyllically set in beautiful gardens, panoramically overlooks the grand sweep of Conwy estuary, historic Conwy Castle and the Snowdonia Mountains. There are many things to delight the eye in this elegant Georgian country house. Its highly polished rooms are decorated with old paintings, antiques and porcelain.

The Vaughans have created a calm, relaxing, unfussy atmosphere and have received an award for 'Welsh Hospitality at its Best'. They have also been granted Red Star status by the A.A. and a coveted Gold Ribbon by the R.A.C. for 'outstanding comfort, welcome, service and food'. Indeed, this six-bedroom country house is deserving of its many accolades. Wendy Vaughan's acclaimed cuisine – she is a 'Master Chef of Great Britain' – is complemented by an award-winning wine cellar.

Situated midway between Chester and Caernarfon and near Betwys-Y-Coed, it is an ideal centre for touring North Wales. Within three miles there are three championship golf courses. Michael's help with touring routes and his knowledge of all things Welsh, guarantee a memorable stay. You are assured of personal attention at this 'beautiful haven of peace'.

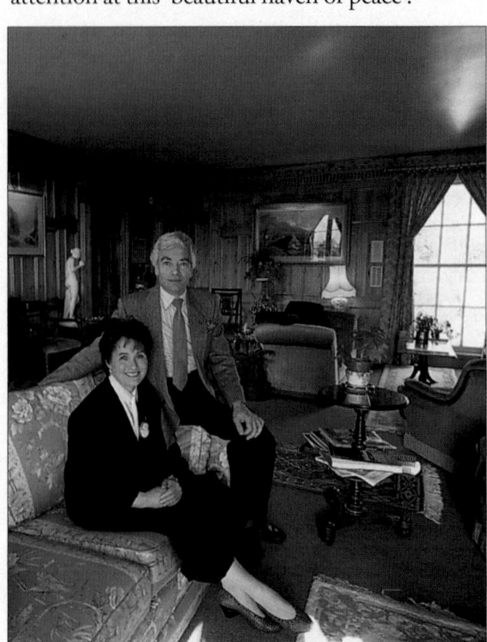

LOCATION

On the A470, ½ mile south of its junction with the A55.

"We found Palé Hall a haven of peace and tranquillity . . . Good food and accommodation"

Mr & Mrs Holmes, Derbyshire

• Map p.498 ref: D3

Manor house

PALÉ HALL COUNTRY HOUSE

Pale Estate, Llandderfel, Bala, Gwynedd LL23 7PS

Telephone 01678 530285
Fax 01678 530220

E-mail: pale@bestloved.com

OWNERS

Saul and Judith Nahed

ROOM RATES

1 Single	£69 - £120
16 Doubles/Twins	£95 - £155

Includes full breakfast and VAT

CHARGE/CREDIT CARDS

• JCB • MC • VI

RATINGS & AWARDS

W.T.B. ★★★★ Country Hotel
A.A. ★★★ ❀❀ 75%

FACILITIES

On site: Garden, croquet, clay pigeon shooting, salmon and trout fishing, game shooting, heli-pad
Licensed for weddings
2 meeting rooms/max 40 people

RESTRICTIONS

No facilities for disabled guests
Children by arrangement
No pets

ATTRACTIONS

Snowdonia, Powis Castle & Gardens, Bodnant Gardens, Conwy and Penrhyn Castles, Lechwedd Slate Caverns, Portmeirion, Erddig House, Chirk Castle, Pistyll Rhaeadr water fall

AFFILIATIONS

Independent

NEAREST

MAJOR CITY:
Chester - 38 miles/50 mins

MAJOR AIRPORT:
Manchester - 77 miles/1¾ hrs
Liverpool - 55 miles/1½ hrs

RAILWAY STATION:
Welshpool - 30 miles/40 mins
Wrexham - 32 miles/45 mins

RESERVATIONS

Direct with hotel
Quote **Best Loved**

ACCESS CODES

Not applicable

WALES

A magnificent house once graced by the presence of Queen Victoria

Palé Hall, a luxurious Victorian mansion set in acres of parkland, was built in 1870 for a wealthy Scottish gentleman and railway engineer. His brief to the architects was that "no expense should be spared" in building this family home.

This splendid house has stunning interiors including exquisite features like the magnificent entrance hall with its lofty vaulted ceiling and galleried oak staircase, the boudoir with its handpainted ceiling, the marble bar and fireplaces. The public rooms express a quiet confidence reflecting the more leisured times in which they were built.

All bedrooms are individually decorated and en suite with television, direct dial telephone, luxury toiletries and hospitality tray. They all enjoy a commanding view of the gardens and surrounding panoramic scenery, including the entrance to the Queen's Walk named after a stay by Queen Victoria in 1889. The original bath and half tester bed used by Her Majesty during her stay are still available for the comfort of guests.

The restaurant is acclaimed for its food, including vegetarian and other diets, the emphasis on the fresh and natural with a regular change of menu. The restaurant possesses a restful intimate atmosphere for dinner by candlelight. Palé Hall is easily accessible by road and is an excellent base for touring.

LOCATION

The house is situated just off the B4401 Corwen to Bala road 4 to 5 miles from Llandrillo. Hotel is signposted from main road.

"We raise our wine glasses to toast the magnificent south Pembrokeshire coast. What better way to end a perfect day in this enchanting place, the Riviera of Wales"

P Wyman, Calgary Herald

• Map p.498 ref: B6

17th century abbey

PENALLY ABBEY

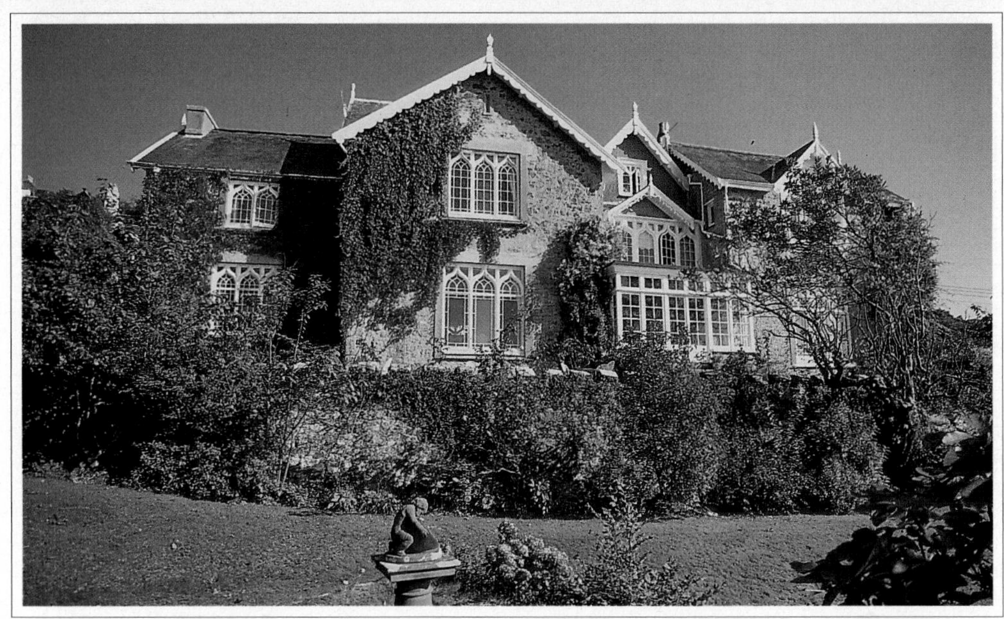

Panache and a leisurely pace, high above an incomparable coastline

Penally Abbey is, quite simply, one of Pembrokeshire's loveliest listed country houses. Elegant but not imposing, its very name conjures up an air of tranquillity, where the emphasis is on relaxation. The five acres of gardens and woodland, wishing well and a ruined chapel, the last surviving link with its monastic past.

The elegant lounge and dining room, overlooking the gardens and terrace, enjoy spectacular sea views across the golf course and Carmarthen Bay. Sympathetically furnished and decorated, the effect is romantic without being sentimental. Dinner is a candlelit affair, with mouthwatering dishes of fresh seasonal delicacies, complemented by excellent wines from the cellar.

The bedrooms are exquisitely furnished and decorated with antiques and period furniture. Many have four-poster beds and all have en suite bathrooms, tea and coffee making facilities, telephones, colour television and hairdryers. Whether in the main building or the adjoining converted coach-house you will be delighted with their old world charm. After an exciting day, you can unwind in the warm indoor pool; play snooker, or just sip cocktails on the terrace before dinner.

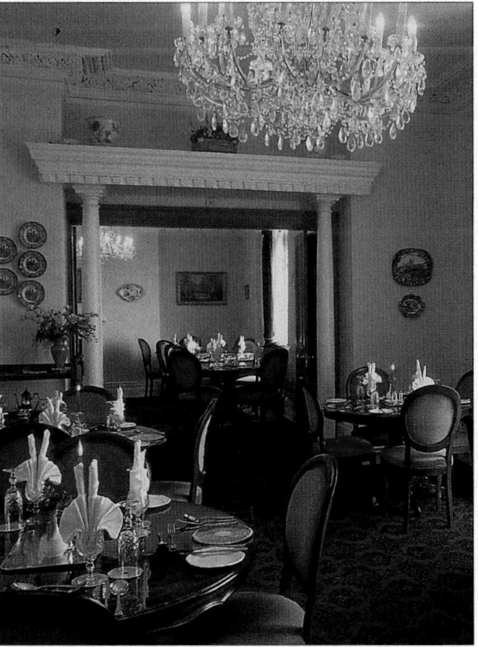

LOCATION

Penally Abbey is situated adjacent to the 12th century church on the village green in the village of Penally, 1½ miles from Tenby. Off the A4139 Tenby-Pembroke coast road.

Penally, Near Tenby, Pembrokeshire SA70 7PY

Telephone 01834 843033
Fax 01834 844714

E-mail: *penally@bestloved.com*

OWNERS

Stephen and Elleen Warren

ROOM RATES

Single occupancy	*£90*
5 Doubles/Twins	*£100*
7 Four-posters	*£120*

Includes full breakfast, newspaper and VAT

CHARGE/CREDIT CARDS

• *MC* • *VI*

RATINGS & AWARDS

W.T.B. ★★★★ Country Hotel
A.A. ★★★ ❀ 77%

FACILITIES

On site: *Garden, croquet, indoor pool, snooker, Licensed for weddings*
1 meeting room/max 12 people
Nearby: *Golf, riding, fishing*

RESTRICTIONS

No children under 7 years allowed in restaurant for dinner
No facilities for disabled guests
No pets

ATTRACTIONS

Tenby, Dylan Thomas Boathouse, Pembroke Castle, Manorbear Castle, Pembokeshire National Park

AFFILIATIONS

Welsh Rarebits

NEAREST

MAJOR CITY:
Cardiff - 90 miles/1¾ hrs

MAJOR AIRPORT:
Cardiff - 90 miles/1¾ hrs
London Heathrow - 150 miles/4 hrs

RAILWAY STATION:
Tenby - 1¼ miles/5 mins

RESERVATIONS

Direct with hotel
*Quote **Best Loved***

ACCESS CODES

Not applicable

• Map p.498
ref: C3

“ Every now and then life does you a good turn, you find a ‘gem’; something you want to keep to yourself. I cannot be that selfish about my stay at Penmaenuchaf Hall ”

Mr Alan T Mumby, Welsh Design Advisory Service, Cardiff

PENMAENUCHAF HALL

Victorian mansion

Penmaenpool, Dolgellau, Gwynedd LL40 1YB

Telephone 01341 422129
Fax 01341 422787

E-mail: *penhall@bestloved.com*

OWNERS

Mark Watson and Lorraine Fielding

ROOM RATES

Single occupancy	*£70 - £110*
14 Doubles/Twins	*£110 - £170*

Includes full breakfast and VAT

CHARGE/CREDIT CARDS

• *DC* • *JCB* • *MC* • *VI*

RATINGS & AWARDS

W.T.B. ★★★★ *Country Hotel*
A.A. ★★★ ❀❀ *72%*

FACILITIES

On site: *Garden, croquet, snooker, fishing*
Licensed for weddings
2 meeting rooms/max 50 people
Nearby: *Riding, golf, clay pigeon shooting, quad biking*

RESTRICTIONS

No children under 6 years
(does not apply to babes-in-arms)
Pets by arrangement

ATTRACTIONS

Portmeirion, Harlech Castle, Ffestiniog Railway, Llechwedd Slate Caverns, Celtica: a celtic experience

AFFILIATIONS

Welsh Rarebits

NEAREST

MAJOR CITY:
Chester - 69 miles/1¼ hrs

MAJOR AIRPORT:
Manchester - 100 miles/2 hrs

RAILWAY STATION:
Fairbourne - 6 miles/10 mins

RESERVATIONS

Direct with hotel
Quote ***Best Loved***

ACCESS CODES

Not applicable

Award-winning food in the romantic foothills of Snowdonia

Cader Idris, the Chair of Arthur, stands 2927ft high amongst the peaks of Snowdonia where folklore and legend intertwine with history told in romantic ruins that grace this spectacular part of Britain. Iron Age forts, Roman roads and fortresses and splendid Norman castles gather in haphazard profusion. A fascinating place to come for pony-trekking, walking and fishing.

And especially for the food! This stunning countryside sets the scene for some of the most memorable cuisine to be had in Wales. Bass, lobster and crab; Welsh lamb, black beef and game; fresh fruit, vegetables and Welsh dairy products - all prepared with the authority and flair of an award-winning chef.

Penmaenuchaf Hall was built in 1860 and is set amidst 21 extensive acres of landscaped gardens and woodland with views of the Mawddach Estuary and the mountains beyond. Its dedicated owners have kept a family home atmosphere whilst indulging their guests in every way they can. Your room will be luxurious and well-appointed and the hospitality as warm as the glowing oak and mahogany interiors and the crackling log fires of winter.

It's said that he who sleeps the night on Cader Idris will wake blind, mad or a poet. Not here; you will awake refreshed, wiser too for having stayed at Penmaenuchaf Hall.

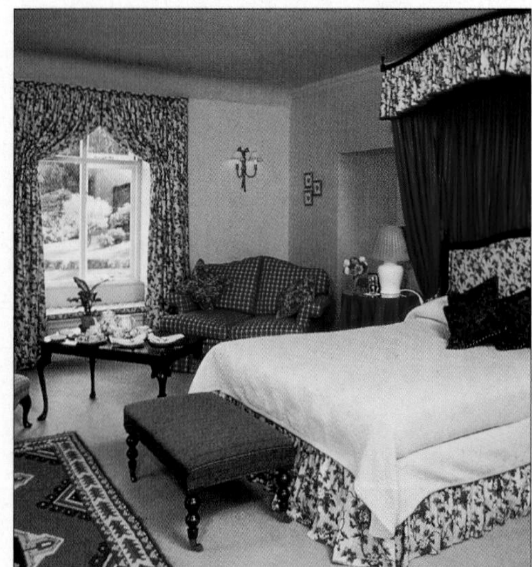

LOCATION

From Dolgellau by-pass (A470) take A493 towards Tywyn and Fairbourne. The entrance is ¾ mile on left.

Planning a wedding reception? Turn to 'Meeting Facilities' on page 476

"Plas Dinas is a very romantic house with stunning views over Snowdon to the east and a distant view of Ireland to the west"

Peregrine Armstrong-Jones, previous owner

• Map p.498 ref: C2

17th century country house

PLAS DINAS HOTEL

A few days could add colour to your life and focus to your dreams of achievement

This hotel is about living life to the hilt: Good food? - the chefs are a wizz with blas ar Cymru, New Welsh Cuisine. Fine wine? - the list, with helpful commentary, has been chosen by TV's Master of Wine, Jonathan Pedley. Art? Until recently, the house belonged to the Armstrong-Jones family (of which Lord Snowdon is a famous son) and much of the family furniture, portraits and memorabilia will interest the connoisseur. Sport? The Dunn's can arrange riding around the slopes of Snowdonia, shooting on the estate of the Marquis of Angelsey; fishing in waters famed for record-breaking catches: golf, kayaking, sailing and much more. Scenery? It's inspiring and you can see it on foot, from the quaint Welsh Highland Railway or on the hotel's bicycles. Flying? Yes, flying! Novices are welcome at reasonable cost. Shopping? Dublin is a cheap and easy day trip away aboard the high speed Stena Seacat!

Plas Dinas opened in May 1999 under the practised hands of the owners, David and Marlene Dunn. Together they have created a cultured refuge with bags of character (that Gun Room really is quite something) and all without pretension - even the price is modest. An escapists dream - and you're welcome to it!

LOCATION

In Bontnewydd, off the A487, the Caernarfon to Porthmadog road.

Bontnewydd, Caernarfon, Gwynedd LL54 7YF

Telephone 01286 830214
Fax 01286 830308

E-mail: *plasdinas@bestloved.com*

OWNERS

David and Marlene Dunn

ROOM RATES

Single occupancy	*£50*
9 Doubles/Twins	*£55*

Includes full breakfast and VAT

CHARGE/CREDIT CARDS

• JCB • MC • VI

RATINGS & AWARDS

W.T.B. ★★★ Hotel

FACILITIES

On site: *Garden, croquet, bicycles, heli-pad*
One room equipped for disabled
2 meeting rooms/max 40 people
Nearby: *Golf, fitness, yachting, riding, fishing, hunting/shooting, flying*

RESTRICTIONS

Well-behaved dogs only
No smoking in bedrooms

ATTRACTIONS

Electric Mountain, Portmeirion, Snowdon Mountain Railway, Caernarfon, Beaumaris and Conwy Castles, Snowdonia National Park, Llechwedd Slate Caverns

AFFILIATIONS

Independent

NEAREST

MAJOR CITY:
Bangor - 9 miles/15 mins

MAJOR AIRPORT:
Manchester - 99 miles/2¼ hrs

RAILWAY STATION:
Bangor - 9 miles/15 mins

FERRY PORT:
Holyhead - 22 miles/45 mins

RESERVATIONS

Direct with hotel
Quote ***Best Loved***

ACCESS CODES

Not applicable

WALES

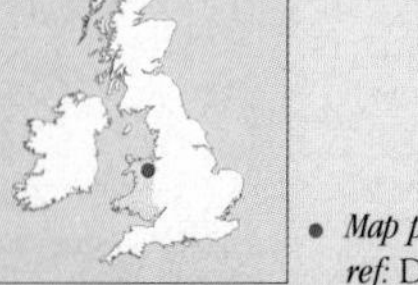

• Map p.498 ref: D3

“ Found on a stormy night we have returned again and again . . . it's a special treat at all times of the year ”

Jill Tweedie & Alan Brien, Authors

TYDDYN LLAN COUNTRY HOUSE *Georgian country house*

Llandrillo, Near Corwen, Denbighshire LL21 0ST

Telephone 01490 440264
Fax 01490 440414

E-mail: *tyddyn@bestloved.com*

OWNERS
Peter and Bridget Kindred

ROOM RATES
10 Doubles/Twins £105 - £140
Includes full breakfast and VAT

CHARGE/CREDIT CARDS

• DC • JCB • MC • VI

RATINGS & AWARDS
W.T.B. ★★★★ Country Hotel
A.A. ★★ ❀❀

FACILITIES
***On site:** Garden, croquet, health & beauty, fishing*
Licensed for weddings
2 meeting rooms/max 50 people
***Nearby:** Golf, riding, shooting, windsurfing, sailing, canoeing*

RESTRICTIONS
Limited facilities for disabled guests
Pets by arrangement

ATTRACTIONS
Snowdonia National Park, Bodnant Gardens, Portmeirion Village, Harlech, Chirk and Caernarfon Castles, Erdigg Hall, Chester, Golf at Bala and Llangollen courses

AFFILIATIONS
Welsh Rarebits

NEAREST
MAJOR CITY:
Chester - 35 miles/50 mins

MAJOR AIRPORT:
Manchester - 65 miles/1¼ hrs

RAILWAY STATION:
Chester - 35 miles/50 mins
Wrexham - 28 miles/45 mins

RESERVATIONS
Direct with hotel
*Quote **Best Loved***

ACCESS CODES
Not applicable

WALES

A stylish oasis in the midst of this magical Welsh valley

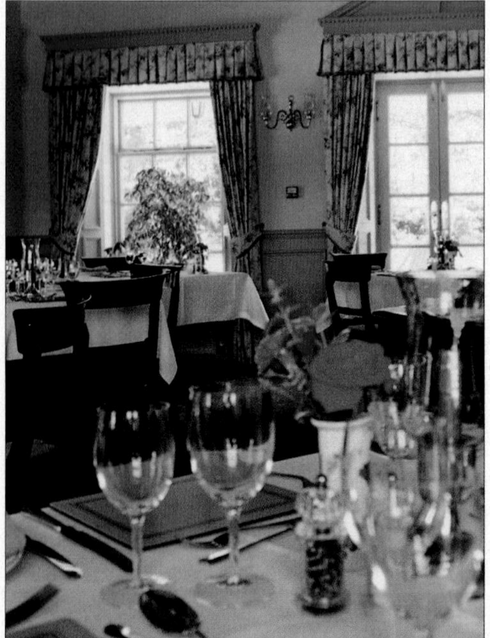

Tyddyn Llan is a lovely Georgian country house surrounded by some of the most magnificent countryside in Wales. A one-time shooting lodge for the Dukes of Westminster, it was converted in 1983 by Peter and Bridget Kindred into an hotel that they, after much travelling, would like to stay in. Peter's career as a set designer in television and films has been used to advantage to create the elegant decor and Bridget's knowledge and love of food has established a much acclaimed restaurant.

Friendly and informal with antiques, interesting paintings, some by Peter himself, comfortable furniture and encircled by its own beautiful gardens, it is an oasis amidst the mountains, rivers and the great outdoors. This unspoilt valley of the River Dee provides excellent walking over the Berwyn Mountains, fishing (with a ghillie if required), horseriding and shooting in season.

The hotel is also well placed to explore the splendour of Snowdonia with its many castles and monuments and it is not far from the Roman City of Chester and the majestic Mawddach and Dyfi Estuaries. The Kindreds look forward to wishing you 'Croeso I Cymru' – 'Welcome to Wales'.

LOCATION

From A5 in Corwen, take 1st left turning to Llandrillo – B4401 for 41/2 miles. Tyddyn Llan is on the right side on the way out of the village to Bala.

"Ty'n Rhos has set the standard that all other hotels will have to live up to"

Visitors' book

• *Map p.498 ref: C2*

17th century farm

TY'N RHOS COUNTRY HOTEL

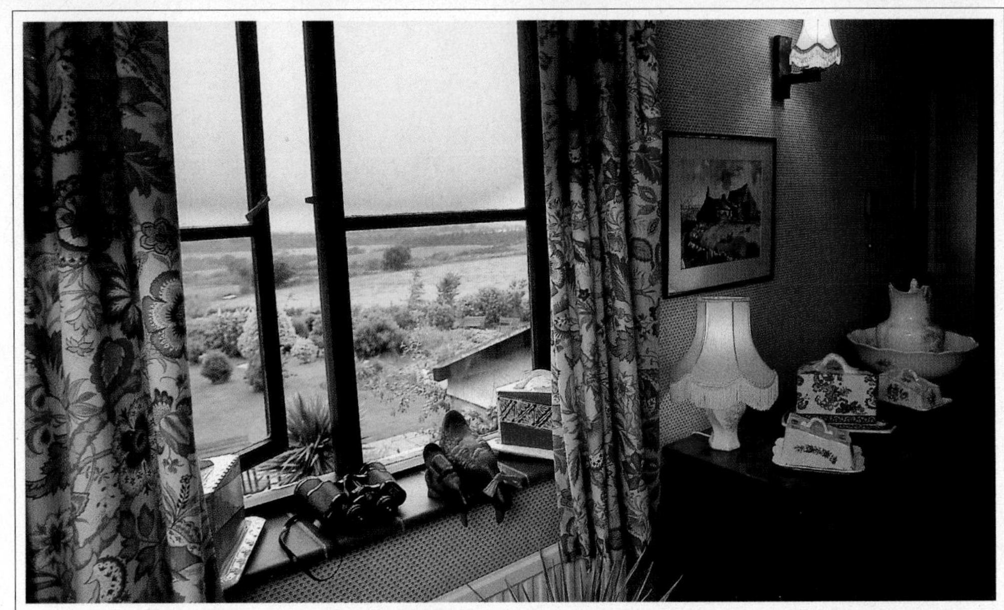

An ancient farm that's grown into a fine country house and restaurant

Ty'n Rhos (the house on the heath) started life as a humble working farm. In 1695, it was described as a single storey cottage with a thatched roof. Over the years, it has changed considerably and is now a country house of distinction offering the finest accommodation to discerning travellers and lovers of good food.

All the bedrooms are en suite and are decorated and furnished to the highest standards. Each room is individual in character and all have tea/coffee making facilities, colour television and direct-dial telephones.

There is a lovely dining room with wonderful views across farmland to the Isle of Anglesey. This is where their talented chefs present high quality dishes using the finest fresh local ingredients to promote a Taste of Wales.

Situated in a land of legend, castles and mountains, Ty'n Rhos is an ideal touring base as it stands between Snowdonia and the sea. It lies close to the mighty castle of Caernarfon, the wonderful beaches of Anglesey and the beauty of the Lleyn peninsula.

Quality allied to value for money are the keynotes at Ty'n Rhos.

LOCATION

Take the B4366 (signposted Bethel) from Caernarfon. Pass through Bethel and after passing the Gors Bach Inn take the first left signposted Seion. Ty'n Rhos is on the left.

Seion, Llanddeiniolen, Caernarfon, Gwynedd LL55 3AE

Telephone 01248 670489
Fax 01248 670079

E-mail: *tynrhos@bestloved.com*

OWNERS
Nigel and Lynda Kettle

GENERAL MANAGER
Nigel Hughes

ROOM RATES

1 Single	*£55*
9 Doubles/Twins	*£80 - £98*

Includes full breakfast and VAT

CHARGE/CREDIT CARDS

• JCB • MC • VI

RATINGS & AWARDS
W.T.B. ★★★★ Country Hotel
A.A. ★★ ❀❀ 77%
Which? Hotel of the Year 2000

FACILITIES
On site: *Gardens, croquet, heli-pad*
1 meeting room/max 20 people
Nearby: *Golf, riding, fishing, leisure centre*

RESTRICTIONS
No children under 6 years
No smoking in bedrooms or restaurant
No pets

ATTRACTIONS
Lleyn Peninsular, Anglesey, Portmeirion Village, Bodnant Gardens, Snowdon, Caernarfon, Beaumaris and Conwy Castles

AFFILIATIONS
Welsh Rarebits

NEAREST
MAJOR CITY:
Manchester - 90 miles/1½ hrs
Chester - 50 miles/1 hr

MAJOR AIRPORT:
Manchester - 90 miles/1½ hrs

RAILWAY STATION:
Bangor - 4½ miles/15 mins

RESERVATIONS
Direct with hotel
Quote ***Best Loved***

ACCESS CODES
Not applicable

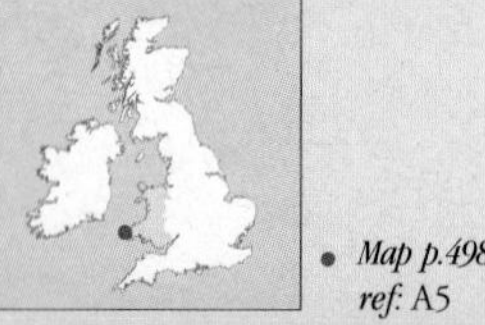

• Map p.498 ref: A5

"We found an historic but friendly country house which combines peace, unsurpassed views and excellence in every way"

T H Davies, LVO

WARPOOL COURT HOTEL

Country house

St Davids, Pembrokeshire SA62 6BN

Telephone 01437 720300
Fax 01437 720676

E-mail: warpool@bestloved.com

GENERAL MANAGER
Rupert Duffin

ROOM RATES

2 Singles	£74 - £90
23 Doubles/Twins	£122 - £180

Includes full breakfast and VAT

CHARGE/CREDIT CARDS

• DC • MC • VI

RATINGS & AWARDS
W.T.B. ★★★★ Country House
R.A.C. ★★★ Dining Award 2
A.A. ★★★ ❀❀ 77%

FACILITIES
On site: Garden, croquet, gym, sauna, indoor heated pool, tennis
Licensed for weddings
2 meeting rooms/max 150 people
Nearby: Riding, sea fishing, surfing, windsurfing

RESTRICTIONS
No facilities for disabled guests
£5 surcharge per dog per night

ATTRACTIONS
St Davids' Cathedral, Pembroke Castle, St Davids' Bishops Palace, Pembrokeshire Coast National Park

AFFILIATIONS
Welsh Rarebits

NEAREST
MAJOR CITY:
Swansea - 75 miles/1½ hrs

MAJOR AIRPORT:
Cardiff - 115 miles/2 hrs

RAILWAY STATION:
Fishguard - 15 miles/30 mins
Haverfordwest - 15 miles/30 mins

RESERVATIONS
Direct with hotel
Quote **Best Loved**

ACCESS CODES
Not applicable

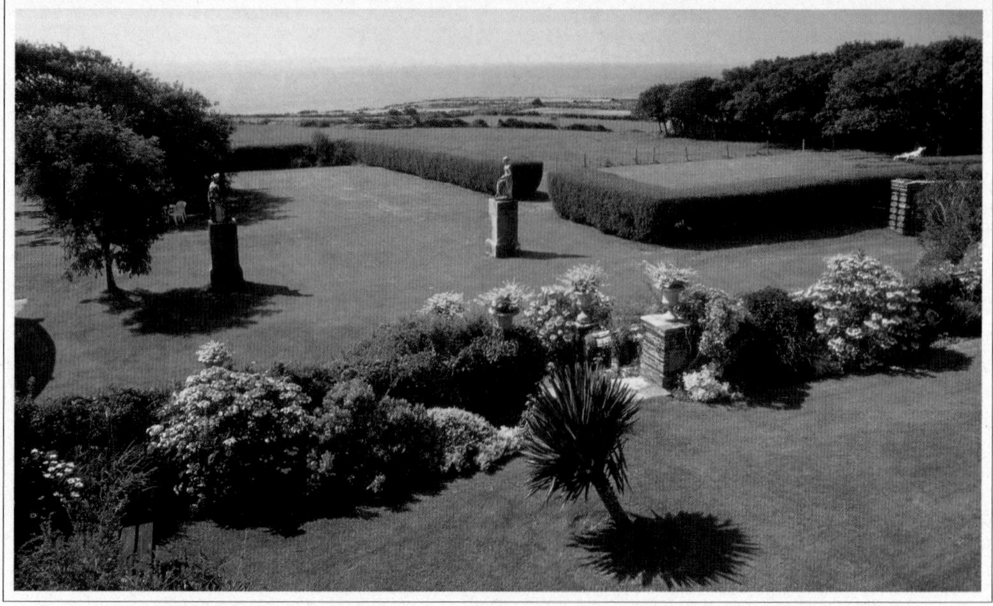

Some of the most spectacular sea views you'll find in this book

Originally built as St Davids' Cathedral choir school in the 1860s this privately owned hotel enjoys spectacular scenery at the heart of the Pembrokeshire National Park, with views over the coast and St Brides Bay to the islands beyond.

First converted to an hotel 30 years ago, the Court offers a unique antique tile collection and 25 comfortable and individually decorated bedrooms, many of which have glorious sea-views.

The dining room enjoys a splendid reputation offering imaginative menus, and vegetarian dishes, using local produce – crab, lobster, sewin and seabass are caught just off the coast and the hotel smokes its own salmon and mackerel.

Set in seven acres, the tranquil gardens offer pre-dinner drinks on the lawns or peaceful strolls. For those wishing for a more active pursuit, the covered heated pool (open April to October), exercise rooms, sauna or tennis court beckon – croquet, pool and table tennis are also available.

A five minute walk will take you either to the coastal path with its spectacular scenery or the Cathedral and Bishops Palace in St Davids. The area boasts many sandy beaches, and offers a wealth of history and natural beauty.

LOCATION

From Cross Square in St Davids, bear left between Cartref Restaurant and Midland Bank. Go down Goat Street. At bottom, fork left and follow hotel signs.

Thinking of pampering yourself? See the 'Health & Beauty' index on page 472

midshires

Vroom vroom: Home of the British Grand Prix, Silverstone is one of Europe's fastest F1 circuits and home turf to motor-racing greats from Stirling Moss to David Coulthard. On a more peaceful note, the 1,000-acres of landscaped turf at Chatsworth (inset) is the work of Capability Brown.

midshires

The fertile land of central England has been of great importance in the shaping of the nation's history. At Bosworth Field, Henry Tudor slew Richard III and took the crown. In 1651 the Battle of Worcester confirmed Cromwell in power. The drama of the Gunpowder Plot has strong connections with Broughton Castle. Shakespeare was born at Stratford-upon-Avon. The industrial heartlands of Birmingham and the Black Country mass-produced everything from chocolate to cars. Music lovers come to concerts at Snape Maltings in Suffolk. Nearby are the Constable landscapes and Flatford Mill. The Norfolk Broads are known among boat lovers and as a bird sanctuary. Derbyshire has the rugged Peak District. In Staffordshire you can visit the potteries. Adjacent is A E Housman's Shropshire and Telford's Ironbridge. Further south, you can almost hear the lyrical music of Edward Elgar amongst the Malvern Hills. The Cotswolds are the home of the dreaming spires of Oxford and the mellow stone villages of Gloucestershire. The other famous seat of learning is to the east at Cambridge on the edge of the fens.

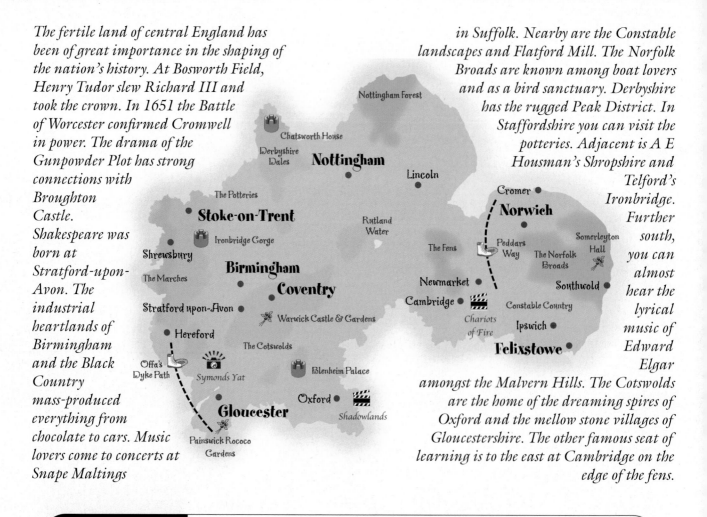

Map Symbols

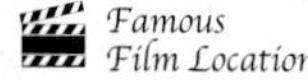

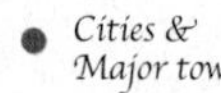

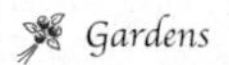

National treasure

These superb formal Italian gardens are just one of the treasures in store at Blenheim Palace in the Oxfordshire village of Woodstock. The Woodstock estate was a gift to the warring Duke of Marlborough from Queen Anne and a grateful nation. The monumental Baroque masterpiece was also the birthplace of the Duke's famous descendent and Britain's World War II leader, Sir Winston Churchill, in 1874.

Life's a breeze

If unspoilt rural England and the wind in your hair sounds like fun discover East Anglia by bicycle. Generally as flat as a pancake, this is ideal cycling country.

Charting the ancient world

The historic cathedral city of Hereford is famous for the 1275 Mappa Mundi which depicted the extent of the known world radiating from Jerusalem. Also the Chained Library (pictured) housing hundreds of rare books and manuscripts dating back to the 8th century, many of them firmly secured by metal chains.

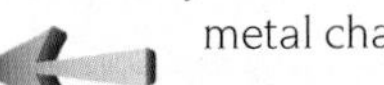

Deer, deer

Palladian-style Holkham Hall in Norfolk is surrounded by a 3,000-acre deer park laid out on reclaimed land in 1722. It once stretched as far as the sea before the coastline receded.

Gold Cup fever

A gracious Regency spa in the Cotswolds popularised by a visit from George III in 1788, Cheltenham is a festival city with celebrated music, cricket and literary events spread throughout the year. In March, it is the turn of the horse-racing fraternity who gather in droves for one of Britain's premier steeple-chasing events, the Cheltenham Gold Cup.

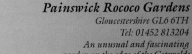

Crowning glory

Just north of Grantham, Belton House is widely regarded as the apogee of Restoration architecture set like a jewel in elegantly landscaped gardens and park-land. It was designed by Sir Christopher Wren for the influential Brownlow family, whose portraits line the walls of the Marble Hall.

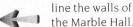

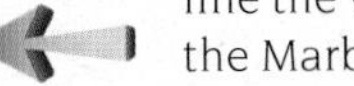

Garden Guide

Hodnet Hall Gardens

Hodnet, Market Drayton, Shropshire TF9 3NN
Tel: 01630 685202
Extensive acreage of lakeside gardens and woodlands, located just north of Telford

Painswick Rococo Gardens

Gloucestershire GL6 6TH
Tel: 01452 813204
An unusual and fascinating garden on the edge of the Cotswolds

Somerleyton Hall & Gardens

Somerleyton, Lowerstoft, Suffolk NR32 5QQ
Tel: 01502 730224
A towering pergola and a maze are among the gardens many features

Warwick Castle

Warwick CV34 4QU
Tel: 01926 401692
A Capability Brown designed landscape surrounding this medieval stronghold

Find out more. There are many more attractions listed on the Best Loved Website: **www.bestlovedhotels.com**
Further information about the Midshires can be found by contacting: **Heart of England Tourist Board.** Tel: +44 (0)1905 763 436. **East of England Tourist Board.** Tel: +44 (0)1473 822922

"You have a hotel to be proud of. Congratulations to you all"

Mrs J S Arnold, Kent

THE ANGEL HOTEL

Market town hotel

**Angel Hill, Bury St Edmunds,
Suffolk IP33 1LT**

**Telephone 01284 714000
Fax 01284 714001**

E-mail: *theangel@bestloved.com*

OWNERS

The Gough Family

ROOM RATES

9 Singles	£69
51 Doubles/Twins	£89 - £150
4 Four-posters	£133
1 Mini suite	£133
1 Suite	£150

Includes VAT

CHARGE/CREDIT CARDS

• DC • MC • VI

RATINGS & AWARDS

E.T.C. ★★★
R.A.C. ★★★
A.A. ★★★ ❀ 71%

FACILITIES

On site: *Licenced for weddings
3 meeting rooms/max 80 people*
Nearby: *Gardens, riding, golf, fishing, tennis, shooting*

RESTRICTIONS

None

ATTRACTIONS

Bury St Edmunds Cathedral & Abbey Gardens, Lavenham, Long Melford, Ickworth House, Newmarket Racecourse, Cambridge

AFFILIATIONS

Selected British Hotels

NEAREST

MAJOR CITY:
Cambridge - 28 miles/40 mins

MAJOR AIRPORT:
Stansted - 50 miles/1 hr
London Heathrow - 98 miles/2 hrs

RAILWAY STATION:
Bury St Edmunds - 1½ miles/5 mins

RESERVATIONS

Toll free in US: 800-323-5463
Quote **Best Loved**

ACCESS CODES

SABRE/ABACUS RW 28668
GALILEO RW 16366
AMADEUS RW BEQ62E
WORLDSPAN RW 28668

Experience the same traditional pleasures enjoyed by Charles Dickens

Who can explain why an area made famous by John Constable, whose acres of grazing sheep and timbered and thatch villages remind one of The Cotswolds, should be so ignored by tourism? At its centre is picturesque Bury St Edmunds. And dominating the centre of the town is The Angel all clad in Ivy demurely hiding its great age!

In 1452, The Angel was three separate inns. You can tell as you pick your way through the maze of polished corridors and stairs that creek with history; the presence of 500 years of tradition and hospitality hangs in the air. King Louis Phillippe and his sister, Princess Amelia, stayed here whilst escaping from the French. So did Charles Dickens; and you can sleep in his bed in the room named after him. That you can stay in this privately-owned treasure of English heritage is a rare privilege, indeed!

The public rooms are comfortably furnished with antiques many of which were bought locally (Suffolk is an antique hunters paradise). More bedrooms have recently been added but which-ever one you find yourself in, rest assured it will be comfortable with every modern facility.

The dining room has two AA rosettes for excellence. The food is the very best of British with local speciality dishes and succulent roasts cooked to perfection. "Just the thing!", Mr Pickwick would have enthused in expectation!

LOCATION

From the A14 eastbound, take second exit to Bury St Edmunds. At second roundabout veer left and turn right at the second set of lights. The Angel is on the right.

" Warwickshire's best kept secret, anything but run of the mill ... "

Sue & Wes Anson, La Jolla, CA, USA

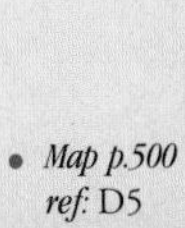

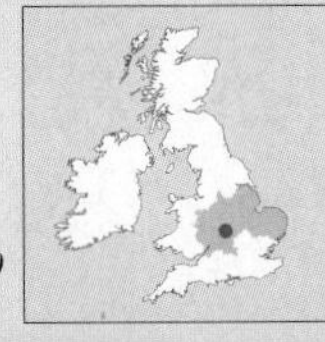

• Map p.500
ref: D5

Ancient mill

ARROW MILL HOTEL

An ancient mill at the heart of England's culture and history

Arrow Mill was valued in the Domesday Book in 1086 at three shillings and sixpence (17pence), a severe underestimate. It continued as a working flour mill for centuries. Arrow Mill's supremely beautiful, secluded riverside setting in its own 60 acre grounds has hardly changed. There is still the same panoramic vista across the mill pond. The mill building retains its historic character. Ancient oak beams and roaring log fires recall England's countryside of long ago. The bedrooms are tastefully furnished, and the modern facilities are discreetly unobtrusive.

The Millstream Restaurant incorporates the original floor of the mill. The River Arrow continues to turn the wheel. The à la carte menu depends on high quality local ingredients from this garden area of England, as well as the excellent team of chefs. Lunches from the Miller's Table are similarly delectable.

Alcester is close to the centre of England, and to its historic and cultural heart. The North Warwickshire mines and Birmingham's smiths produced over 15,000 swords to arm Cromwell's army. Warwick, Leamington, Kenilworth and Shakespeare's Stratford-upon-Avon are all nearby and make Arrow Mill an enviable spot from which to base a holiday.

LOCATION

Set back from the A435 1 mile south of Alcester.

Arrow, Alcester, Warwickshire B49 5NL

Telephone 01789 762419
Fax 01789 765170

E-mail: *arrowmill@bestloved.com*

OWNERS

The Woodhams Family

ROOM RATES

3 Singles	£65
9 Doubles/Twins	£80 - £96
5 Family rooms	£90
1 Four-poster	£140

Includes full breakfast and VAT

CHARGE/CREDIT CARDS

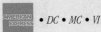

• DC • MC • VI

RATINGS & AWARDS

Independent

FACILITIES

On site: *Garden, fishing*
2 meeting rooms/max 60 people
Nearby: *Golf, shooting*

RESTRICTIONS

No facilities for disabled guests
Pets by arrangement

ATTRACTIONS

Stratford-upon-Avon, Warwick Castle, The Cotswolds, National Exhibition Centre, Coughton Court

AFFILIATIONS

Independent

NEAREST

MAJOR CITY:
Stratford-upon-Avon - 8 miles/20 mins

MAJOR AIRPORT:
Birmingham - 25 miles/40 mins

RAILWAY STATION:
Stratford-upon-Avon - 8 miles/20 mins

RESERVATIONS

Direct with hotel
*Quote **Best Loved***

ACCESS CODES

Not applicable

MIDSHIRES

Looking for an hotel with a golf course on site? See our 'Golf Guide' on page 478

• Map p.500 ref: E6

"Staff care and surroundings made this stay feel like a perfect retreat from the fast pace"

Dr Daily, Question of Service

THE BAY TREE HOTEL

Tudor manor house

Sheep Street, Burford, Oxfordshire OX18 4LW

Telephone 01993 822791
Fax 01993 823008

E-mail: baytree@bestloved.com

GENERAL MANAGER

Jason Wolverson

ROOM RATES

Single occupancy	£99
12 Doubles/Twins	£135
5 Suites	£185 - £210
4 Four-posters	£185

Includes full breakfast and VAT

CHARGE/CREDIT CARDS

• DC • JCB • MC • VI

RATINGS & AWARDS

E.T.C. ★★★
A.A. ★★★ ❀ 67%

FACILITIES

On site: Garden, croquet
Licensed for weddings
3 meeting rooms/max 60 people
Nearby: Golf, tennis, fitness, fishing

RESTRICTIONS

No facilities for disabled guests
Pets by arrangement

ATTRACTIONS

Blenheim Palace, Oxford, Stratford-upon-Avon, Bourton-on-the-Water, Cotswold Wildlife Park, antiques hunting

AFFILIATIONS

Grand Heritage Hotels

NEAREST

MAJOR CITY:
Oxford - 18 miles/20 mins

MAJOR AIRPORT:
London Heathrow - 60 miles/1½ hrs

RAILWAY STATION:
Charlbury - 5 miles/10 mins

RESERVATIONS

Toll free in US: 888-93-GRAND
Quote **Best Loved**

ACCESS CODES

AMADEUS UI OXFBTH
APOLLO/GALILEO UI 86803
SABRE/ABACUS UI 31078
WORLDSPAN UI 40769

MIDSHIRES

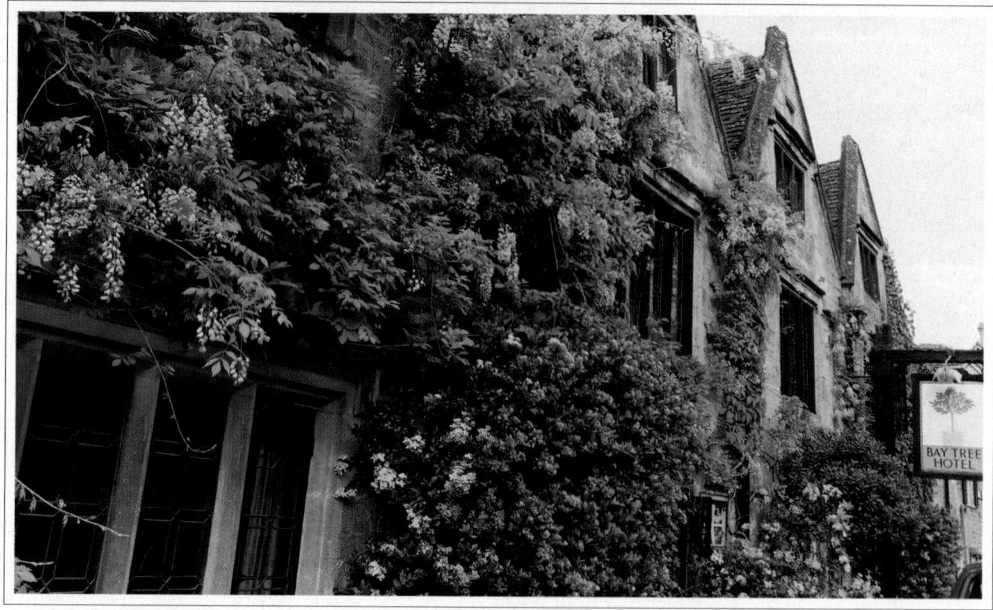

500 years ago Elizabeth I visited. The reception is as royal as ever.

History has reserved a special place for Burford, though seeing it now weathered by the winds of time, politics and agrarian change, it's hard to see. 500 years ago, it was the capital of England's wool production. Today the commercial cut and thrust has long gone and only the mellow stones can fill in the gaps of history and recall lost legends.

The Bay Tree was once the home of the Baron of the Exchequer to Elizabeth I; it's said she stayed here herself en passant. And if you should be travelling on the same road, you, too, can enjoy the hospitality of this meandering old manor house albeit in far greater comfort than was fit for Her Majesty. The creak and must of history blend happily with the scent of fresh flowers and the discreetly installed comforts of today. The reception rooms are oak-beamed and flagstoned and include an impressive raftered hall. The country bar offers delicious light meals at the counter that auger the promise of greater rewards in the candlelit restaurant; a promise that will be fulfilled by an excellent wine list.

In summer, the terraced garden at the back is a sun-trap, shielded by Cotswold stone walls, trees and flowering shrubs. A delightful place to take coffee after lunch or a scone with afternoon tea.

Stepping through the Wisteria at the front door, you set out on an enchanted journey through the centuries; once made, never forgotten.

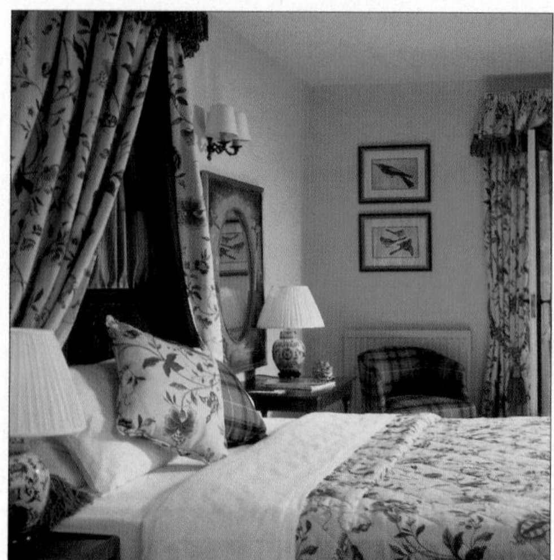

LOCATION

Location Burford is less than a mile off the A40 Oxford to Cheltenham road and well marked. In Burford, turn into Sheep Street halfway down the steep main street. The hotel is on the right.

" The quality of the food was mouth-watering, along with the selection of wine "

Tony Parish, Question of Service

• Map p.500 ref: D6

17th century ale house

THE BEAR OF RODBOROUGH HOTEL

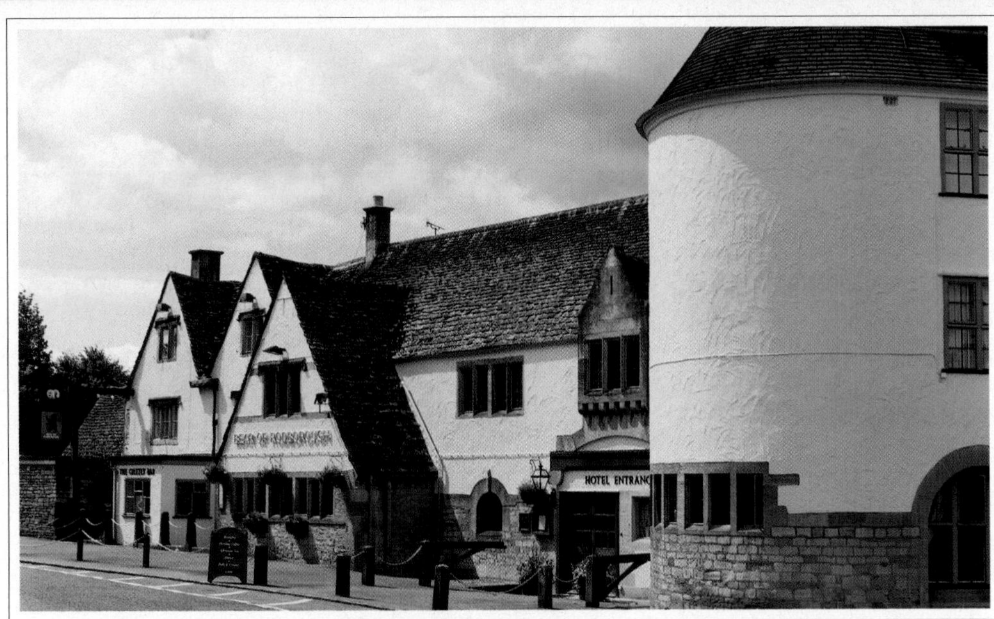

An oasis of comfort and cuisine in a lost world of countryside romance

It's amazing how pockets of England have remained untouched by progress until so recently. Remember Cider with Rosie, Laurie Lee's delicious autobiography published in 1959? One such area lies south of Stroud largely oblivious of the world for centuries until Lee wrote of it. Not fifty years ago, charcoal burners made a living in the woods, traction engines and horses helped with the harvest. The Bear of Rodborough, a name derived from bearbaiting outlawed back in 1835, is set amongst hundreds of acres of National Trust parkland and nicely poised to introduce you to the area's picturesque charms and (legal) customs!

Time was, some 300 years ago, when The Bear was a coaching inn; today, the warm welcome is the same but the hotel aims to satisfy the creature comforts of latter day 'travellers'- (those living beyond the next village!). The rooms are romantically furnished, some with four-posters or half testers, and decorated with sumptuous fabrics. The reception rooms glow from the honeyed Cotswold stone walls. In the best old English fashion, The Mulberry Restaurant depends on seasonal fresh vegetables for what it calls *Modern* British Cooking - and jolly good it is, too! But the first thing that strikes one in the dining room is the astonishing view of the deep Woodchester valley beyond the picture windows. It is the lost world of Laurie Lee. And the romance survives.

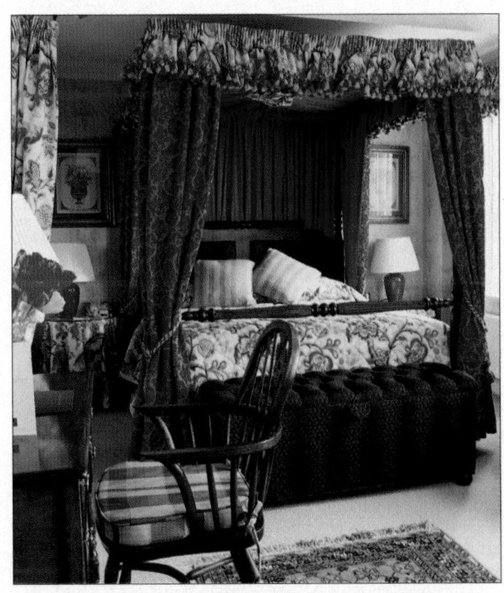

LOCATION

On Rodborough Common, 2 miles south of Stroud, off the A46.

Rodborough Common, Stroud, Gloucestershire GL5 5DE

Telephone 01453 878522
Fax 01453 872523

E-mail: *bear@bestloved.com*

GENERAL MANAGER

Chris Ashby

ROOM RATES

6 Singles	*£75 - £95*
38 Doubles/Twins	*£120 - £130*
1 Four-poster	*£145*
1 Suite	*£160*

Includes full breakfast and VAT

CHARGE/CREDIT CARDS

• *DC* • *JCB* • *MC* • *VI*

RATINGS & AWARDS

E.T.C. ★★★

A.A. ★★★ ❀ *70%*

FACILITIES

On site: *Garden, croquet*
Licensed for weddings
5 meeting rooms/max 80 people
Nearby: *Golf, tennis, fitness, fishing, riding*

RESTRICTIONS

No facilities for disabled guests
Pets by arrangement

ATTRACTIONS

Cheltenham, Cirencester, Berkeley Castle, Painswick Rococo Gardens, Westonbirt Arboretum

AFFILIATIONS

Grand Heritage Hotels

NEAREST

MAJOR CITY:
Cheltenham - 14 miles/25 mins

MAJOR AIRPORT:
London Heathrow - 96 miles/1¾ hrs

RAILWAY STATION:
Stroud - 1½ miles/5 mins

RESERVATIONS

Toll free in US: 888-93-GRAND
Quote ***Best Loved***

ACCESS CODES

AMADEUS UI GLOBEA
APOLLO/GALILEO UI 13614
SABRE/ABACUS UI 47205
WORLDSPAN UI 40759

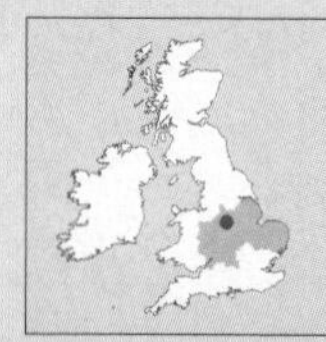

" We had a very good meal and a great time. It's a great place to stay and very comfortable "

Sarah Ferguson, Duchess of York

BEECHES RESTAURANT

Restaurant with rooms

Waldley, Doveridge,
Near Ashbourne,
Derbyshire DE6 5LR

Telephone 01889 590288
Fax 01889 590559

E-mail: *beeches@bestloved.com*

OWNERS

Barbara and Paul Tunnicliffe

ROOM RATES

Single occupancy	*£48*
3 Doubles/Twins	*£64 - £74*
7 Family rooms	*£64 - £74*

(Sharing child rate £10.50)
Includes full breakfast and VAT

CHARGE/CREDIT CARDS

 • *MC* • *VI*

RATINGS & AWARDS

E.T.C. ★★★★
A.A. ❀❀
Derbyshire Life Golden Goblet Award

FACILITIES

On site: *Garden*
1 meeting room/max 12 people
Nearby: *Golf, riding, fishing, hunting/shooting*

RESTRICTIONS

Limited facilities for disabled guests
No pets

ATTRACTIONS

Alton Towers, Abraham Heights, Potteries Museums, Uttoxeter Race Course, Chatsworth, Sudbury Hall, Dovedale Walking and Cycle Hire

AFFILIATIONS

Independent

NEAREST

MAJOR CITY:
Derby/Stoke - 15 miles/20 mins

MAJOR AIRPORT:
East Midlands - 20 miles/25 mins
Manchester - 40 miles/1 hr

RAILWAY STATION:
Uttoxeter - 5 miles/10 mins

RESERVATIONS

Direct with hotel
Quote ***Best Loved***

ACCESS CODES

Not applicable

A gourmet treat amidst the glorious Derbyshire Dales

Just south of the Peak District National Park (a good place to build up an appetite if ever there was one), this convivial little restaurant with rooms inhabits an attractive old family farmhouse.

The interior is cosy, with a wealth of exposed beams, chintzy wallpapers and fabrics, and a thoroughly relaxed and informal air, which Paul Tunnicliffe describes as "unstarchy".

Paul's wife, Barbara, is renowned for her culinary expertise and is something of a local celebrity with numerous radio and television appearances to her credit. Supported by a talented head chef, she oversees a brace of menus: the gourmet à la carte menu and a more robust brasserie menu. One of the favourite dishes from the former is pan-fried turbot with spiced cabbage, foie gras, lobster and almonds - quite sublime. The hearty brasserie menu offers exceptionally good food for as little as £12 with dishes like Gloucester Old Spot sausages with chive mash.

A place truly full of character, it is ideal for business and family travellers alike. Its location offers easy access to the M1, M6 and A50 and is one of those discoveries worth heading off the motorway for.

LOCATION

From M6 Jct 15, A50 towards Derby. At Doveridge left. Follows signs to Waldley. From M1 Jct 24, A50 towards Stoke. At Doveridge left. In village, right at roundabout for Waldley.

" Hugely enjoyable stay. Loved the communal ambience of dinner and the quality of the food and wine "

Mr & Mrs C D King, East Sussex

• Map p.500 ref: D3

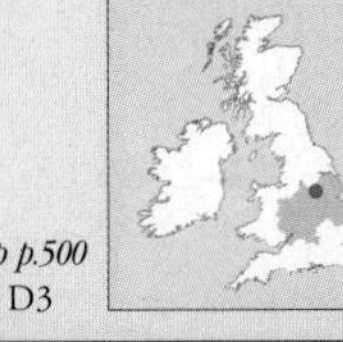
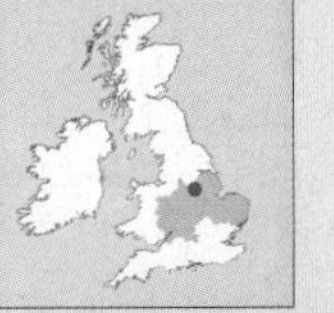

17th century hall

BIGGIN HALL

Traditional farmhouse cooking in the peace of the Peak District

Biggin Hall is a 17th century house standing in its own spacious eight acres in open countryside at the heart of the Peak District National Park. It has been renovated in keeping with its original character. Its stone mullioned windows saw daylight again only recently after being obliterated to save paying the 18th century window tax. All the spacious bedrooms are attractively furnished with antiques. The sitting rooms offer colour TV and a crackling open fire.

The dinners have to be eaten to be believed. Traditional home cooking and fine wines create a highly convivial atmosphere. The emphasis is on local free range wholefoods and natural flavours, with a seasonal selection of vegetables. Menus change every day to give a wide choice of farmhouse fare.

At 1,000 feet above sea level, the area is a delight to tour especially for cyclists who can roam the traffic-free trails of Tissington and High Peak, Manifold Valley, too. It is wonderful country: drystone walling, deep wooded valleys, heather clad moorlands and timeless market towns. The diverse Derbyshire landscape provides a perfect setting for relaxation. Stately homes at Chatsworth, Haddon Hall and Keddleston Hall are all within 20 miles. For an occasional urban variation, the famous potteries at Stoke-on-Trent are a short drive away.

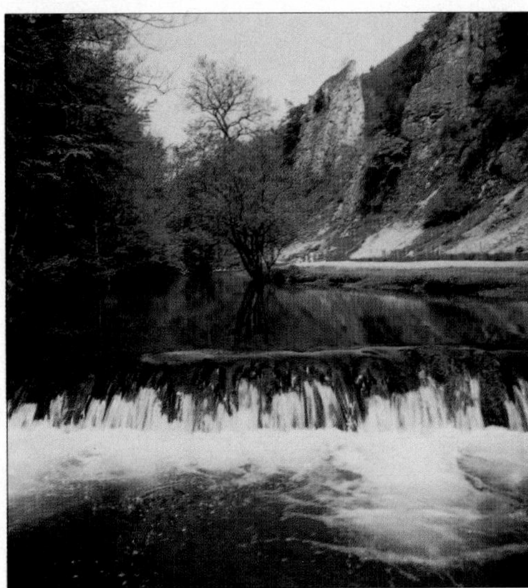

LOCATION

Hotel's drive starts next to Waterloo Pub in Biggin, ½ mile off the A515 between Ashbourne and Buxton.

Biggin-by-Hartington,
Buxton,
Derbyshire SK17 0DH

Telephone 01298 84451
Fax 01298 84681

E-mail: biggin@bestloved.com

OWNER

James Moffett

ROOM RATES

Single occupancy	*£40 - £65*
16 Doubles/Twins	*£49 - £90*
1 Four-poster	*£80 - £110*

Includes continental breakfast and VAT

CHARGE/CREDIT CARDS

• *MC* • *VI*

RATINGS & AWARDS

E.T.C. ★★

FACILITIES

On site: *Garden, croquet, heli-pad*
1 meeting room/max 20 people
Nearby: *Walking, cycling*

RESTRICTIONS

No facilities for disabled guests
No children under 12 years
Pets by arrangement

ATTRACTIONS

Chatsworth, Haddon Hall, Blue John Mines, Industrial Archeology, Keddleston Hall, The Potteries

AFFILIATIONS

Independent

NEAREST

MAJOR CITY:
Derby - 23 miles/40 mins

MAJOR AIRPORT:
Manchester - 30 miles/1¼ hrs

RAILWAY STATION:
Buxton/Matlock - 10 miles/20 mins

RESERVATIONS

Direct with hotel
Quote ***Best Loved***

ACCESS CODES

Not applicable

• Map p.500 ref: E6

"We wanted you to know how much we enjoyed our stay. You have made it into a fantastic place. We will be back"

Anthony & Vicky Smee, London

BIGNELL PARK HOTEL

18th century country house

Chesterton, Bicester, Oxfordshire OX26 1UE

Telephone 01869 241444/241192
Fax 01869 241444

E-mail: *bignell@bestloved.com*

OWNERS
E K Sorensen and M A Young

ROOM RATES

Single occupancy	£60 - £90
20 Doubles/Twins	£85 - £100
3 Four-posters	£105 - £145

Includes full breakfast and VAT

CHARGE/CREDIT CARDS

• DC • MC • VI

RATINGS & AWARDS
E.T.C. ★★ Silver Award
A.A. ★★ ❀ 60%

FACILITIES
On site: *Garden*
2 meeting rooms/max 50 people
Nearby: *Golf, fishing*

RESTRICTIONS
No children under 6 years in restaurant
Pets by arrangement

ATTRACTIONS
Oxford Colleges, Blenheim Palace, The Cotswolds, Warwick Castle, Kirtlington Polo Club, Silverstone Circuit, Bicester Shopping Village

AFFILIATIONS
Independent

NEAREST
MAJOR CITY:
Oxford - 10 miles/25 mins

MAJOR AIRPORT:
London Heathrow - 40 miles/1 hr

RAILWAY STATION:
Bicester North - 2 miles/10 mins

RESERVATIONS
Direct with hotel
Quote **Best Loved**

ACCESS CODES
Not applicable

A cosy and characterful retreat close to Blenheim and Oxford

Originally an 18th-century Cotswold stone farmhouse, Bignell Park Hotel combines traditional, old-world charm with the easy grace of a beautifully-run country house. The hotel is set in 2½ acres of secluded informal gardens and orchard close to the renowned Kirtlington Polo Club. It is also ideally situated for side trips to Blenheim Palace, ancestral home of the Dukes of Marlborough, the dreaming spires of Oxford, Warwick Castle, Stratford-upon-Avon, and a clutch of enchanting honey-coloured Cotswold villages.

Recently refurbished, each of the hotel's 23 en suite bedrooms (including three with four-poster beds) has been attractively decorated and furnished with care. The comfortably elegant drawing room overlooks the garden and guests relax beside log fires in the colder months. The food at Bignell Park has never been better and the atmospheric candlelit restaurant with its wood beamed ceiling, open fire and minstrels' gallery is a wonderful setting to enjoy it. An extensive and carefully compiled wine list includes both fine New and Old World wines which complement the English/French menu perfectly. A private dining room offers the perfect answer for small, intimate gatherings.

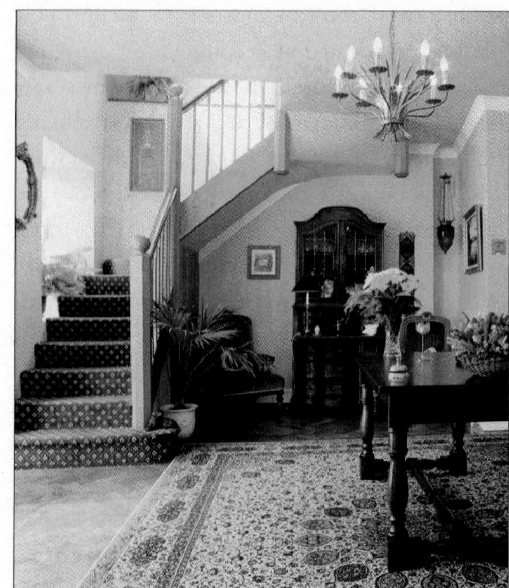

LOCATION

From M40 Junction 9, take the A41 towards Bicester. After about 1½ miles, turn left to Chesterton. Leaving Chesterton towards Bicester, Bignell Park is on the A4095.

"This hotel has to be the nicest we know. The treatment we receive each time from the staff could not be bettered - please don't change anything"

Mrs S Barker, Question of Service

• Map p.500 ref: D5

15th century abbot's retreat

THE BROADWAY HOTEL

The Broadway descent to the temptations of good living

Broadway lays claim to be the prettiest village in England and, to heighten the excitement of its discovery, you have to sneak up on it - from Oxford. The road has been straight for miles riding across the undulating Cotswold hills when, suddenly, it arrives at a steep escarpment to reveal a vast panorama, The Vale of Evesham, aka The Garden of England. On a clear day you can see Wales, Worcester Cathedral, the Malvern Hills and 13 counties. At the base of the hairpin descent, is Broadway and you begin to understand why it's called broad way and how it earned its picturesque title.

The Broadway Hotel is set back on the green at the bottom of the village. It used to be a retreat for the Abbots of Pershore 600 years ago and it still has an aura of tranquillity though the monastic privations have given way to the sinful luxuries and comforts expected by today's travellers. It has all the low-beamed, mellow Cotswold charm of a traditional inn with attractive, modern fabrics and furnishings.

On race days, the Jockey Bar can get a bit lively but there is a secluded garden if you prefer. The Courtyard Restaurant will also entertain you with its à la carte dishes that earn the right to be accompanied by a decent bottle of wine.

Altogether, something surprisingly special.

LOCATION

On the A44 on the village green at the bottom of Broadway.

The Green, Broadway, Worcestershire WR12 7AA

Telephone 01386 852401
Fax 01386 853879

E-mail: *broadway@bestloved.com*

GENERAL MANAGER

Noel Linington

ROOM RATES

3 Singles	*£74 - £80*
12 Doubles/Twins	*£115*
4 Superior doubles	*£130*
1 Four-poster	*£130*

Includes full breakfast and VAT

CHARGE/CREDIT CARDS

• DC • JCB • MC • VI

RATINGS & AWARDS

E.T.C. ★★★ Silver Award
A.A. ★★★ 65%

FACILITIES

On site: *Garden, Licensed for weddings*
2 meeting rooms/max 40 people
Nearby: *Golf, tennis, fitness, riding*

RESTRICTIONS

No facilities for disabled guests
Pets by arrangement

ATTRACTIONS

Bourton-on-the-Water, Sudeley and Warwick Castles, Stratford-upon-Avon, walking

AFFILIATIONS

Grand Heritage Hotels

NEAREST

MAJOR CITY:
Birmingham - 35 miles/45 mins

MAJOR AIRPORT:
London Heathrow - 90 miles/1¾ hrs
Birmingham - 40 miles/45 mins

RAILWAY STATION:
Evesham - 5 miles/10 mins

RESERVATIONS

Toll free in US: 888-93-GRAND
Quote ***Best Loved***

ACCESS CODES

AMADEUS UI BHXBDH
APOLLO/GALILEO UI 10139
SABRE/ABACUS UI 40453
WORLDSPAN UI 40734

• Map p.500 ref: D5

"Tranquillity and beauty only surpassed by the excellence of the food and service"

Henry Blofeld, cricket commentator

BROCKENCOTE HALL

Victorian country mansion

Chaddesley Corbett, Near Kidderminster, Worcestershire DY10 4PY

Telephone 01562 777876
Fax 01562 777872

E-mail: brockencote@bestloved.com

OWNERS

Alison and Joseph Petitjean

ROOM RATES

Single occupancy	£99 - £130
15 Doubles/Twins	£135 - £170
2 Four-posters	£170

Includes full breakfast and VAT

CHARGE/CREDIT CARDS

• DC • MC • VI

RATINGS & AWARDS

E.T.C. ★★★ Gold Award
R.A.C. Blue Ribbon ★★★ Dining Award 3
A.A. ★★★ ❀❀❀

FACILITIES

On site: Garden, croquet, fishing, tennis
2 meeting rooms/max 30 people
Nearby: Golf, riding, fishing, water sports

RESTRICTIONS

No pets

ATTRACTIONS

Warwick Castle, Worcester, Hereford Cathedral, Stratford-upon-Avon, Black Country Museum, Cotswolds, Ironbridge, Cadbury World

AFFILIATIONS

Grand Heritage Hotels

NEAREST

MAJOR CITY:
Birmingham - 18 miles/30 mins

MAJOR AIRPORT:
Birmingham - 20 miles/30 mins

RAILWAY STATION:
Kidderminster - 4 miles/10 mins

RESERVATIONS

Toll free in US: 888-93-GRAND
Toll free in UK: 0800 056 0457
Quote **Best Loved**

ACCESS CODES

AMADEUS UI BHXBHC
APOLLO/GALILEO UI 27837
SABRE/ABACUS UI 52406
WORLDSPAN UI 41367

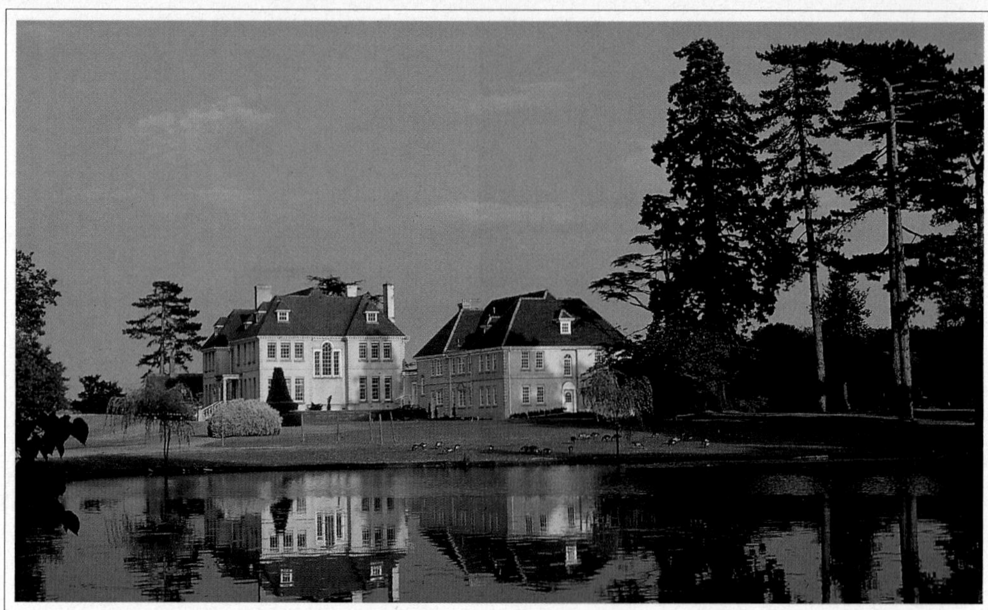

Authentic French enclave in the heart of the Worcestershire countryside

The builders of the original Victorian mansion that is now the beautiful Brockencote Hall Hotel, certainly knew a thing or two about finding a perfect place for relaxation.

Nestling in the heart of the Worcestershire countryside, Brockencote Hall is set in 70 acres of private parkland yet is close to the motorway network, just half an hour from Birmingham – the perfect location for touring the sites of an area rich in history and culture. From here, you are equally well-placed to visit Shakespeare's Stratford-upon-Avon, Warwick Castle, the idyllic Cotswolds and the wonders of Wales.

Guests at Brockencote Hall will experience something else that is unique in the area: the hotel is renowned for its authentic French ambience. Proprietors Joseph and Alison Petitjean have created a charming Gallic oasis in the heart of England, combining traditional French comfort and friendliness with superb French cuisine.

The hotel offers a choice of 17 superb bedrooms, all with en suite facilities, including one that has been especially designed to make stays comfortable for disabled guests.

LOCATION

Exit 1 (M42), westbound only, or Exit 4 (M5). Go into Bromsgrove and take the A448 towards Kidderminster. The hotel is 5 miles along on the left.

“ I am sure that when you decide to stay at the Brookhouse you will find comfort and relaxation ”

D Fotheringham-Kidd

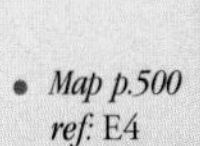

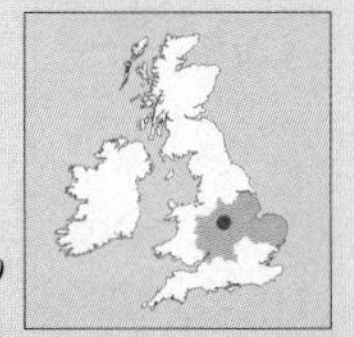

• Map p.500 ref: E4

17th century farmhouse

THE BROOKHOUSE

House of character, where dining is a pleasure and the beds amazing

After the River Dove abandons the cascades of the Derbyshire Dales, it winds languorously through the fertile flatlands between Burton-on-Trent and Derby. The area has a pastoral beauty scarcely known and barely touched by modern times. Rolleston-on-Dove is the quintessential Old English village complete with thatched cottages and a babbling brook, The Dove no less, running through it. This is the setting for The Brookhouse, not just posing postcard-pretty by the river but a charming village character.

The Brookhouse has woven a kind of magic over the people who work there. They are all local and as loyal as can be, two of the staff have been there 20 years and the only new boy is the owner, John Westwood, who has been there only 11 years! The service is nimble and comes wreathed in smiles and a winning country accent.

The restaurant has an excellent reputation for good food. Soft lights and candlelight reflect in silver and crystal; fresh flowers are everywhere. Freshness is the order of the day and your food is cooked to order. The wine list offers imaginative, rare and unusual wines.

The bedrooms are splendidly appointed but do ask to see the other bedrooms; you will find a truly remarkable collection of antique beds, all gorgeously caparisoned. Comfortable, too!

One of the great 'finds' in this book.

LOCATION

Rolleston is just outside Burton-upon-Trent between the A50 to Stoke-on-Trent and the A38 to Derby.

Brookside, Rolleston-on-Dove, Burton-upon-Trent, Staffordshire DE13 9AA

Telephone 01283 814188
Fax 01283 813644

E-mail: *brookhouse@bestloved.com*

OWNER

John Westwood

ROOM RATES

7 Singles	*£72 - £79*
12 Doubles/Twins	*£95 - £105*

Includes full breakfast, complimentary newspaper and VAT

CHARGE/CREDIT CARDS

• DC • JCB • MC • VI

RATINGS & AWARDS

Independent

FACILITIES

On site: *Garden*
1 meeting room/max 18 people
Nearby: *Golf, riding*

RESTRICTIONS

No children under 12 years
Dogs by arrangement

ATTRACTIONS

Tutbury Castle, Derbyshire Dales, Calke Abbey, Haddon and Keddleston Halls

AFFILIATIONS

Independent

NEAREST

MAJOR CITY:
Derby - 8 miles/15 mins

MAJOR AIRPORT:
Birmingham - 25 miles/40 mins
Manchester - 70 miles/1½ hrs

RAILWAY STATION:
Burton-upon-Trent - 3 miles/10 mins

RESERVATIONS

Direct with hotel
Quote ***Best Loved***

ACCESS CODES

Not applicable

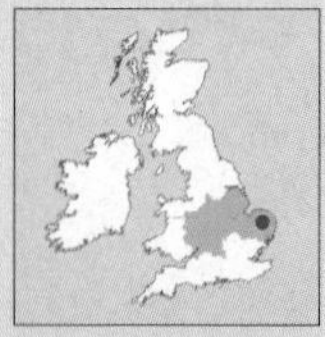

• Map p.500
ref: H4

"Very relaxing and tranquil stay. Recommend to others"

Mr Remington, Scunthorpe

BROOM HALL COUNTRY HOTEL

Country house

**Richmond Road,
Saham Toney, Near Thetford,
Norfolk IP25 7EX**

**Telephone 01953 882125
Fax 01953 882125**

E-mail: broomhall@bestloved.com

OWNERS
Nigel, Angela and Simon Rowling

ROOM RATES

1 Single	£38 - £45
7 Doubles/Twins	£67 - £79
1 Four-poster	£90

Includes full breakfast and VAT

CHARGE/CREDIT CARDS
MC • VI

RATINGS & AWARDS
A.A. ★★ 63%

FACILITIES
On site: Garden, indoor pool, snooker, heli-pad
Licensed for weddings
1 meeting room/max 30 people
Nearby: Golf, fishing, cycling, clay pigeon shooting

RESTRICTIONS
No facilities for disabled guests
Smoking permitted in bar only
No pets, guide dogs only

ATTRACTIONS
Sandringham Royal Residence, Holkham Hall, Blickling Hall, Norwich, Heacham Lavender Farm, Cambridge, Ely

AFFILIATIONS
Independent

NEAREST
MAJOR CITY:
Norwich - 22 miles/40 mins

MAJOR AIRPORT:
Stansted - 60 miles/1 hr

RAILWAY STATION:
Thetford - 13 miles/20 mins

RESERVATIONS
Direct with hotel
Quote **Best Loved**

ACCESS CODES
Not applicable

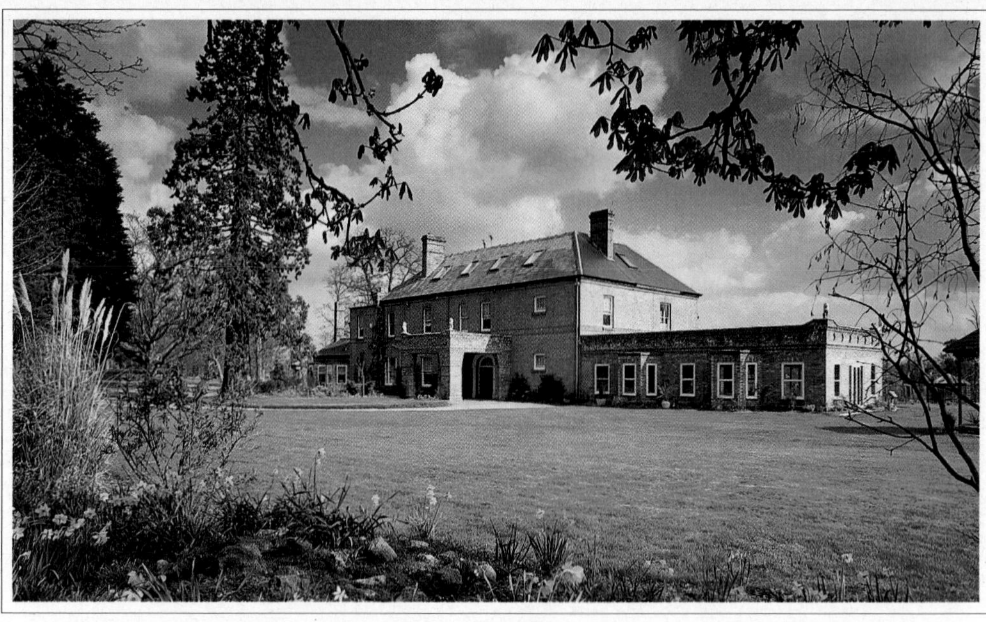

A charming family-run country home close to the Norfolk Broads

Broom Hall is a real family concern run by Nigel, Angela and Simon Rowling - and, of course, Hector the dog, who doubles as chief greeter and PR officer. The comfortable Victorian house lies at the end of a winding driveway flanked by lime trees in traditional English gardens planted with flourishing herbaceous borders. The gardens in turn are surrounded by 13 acres of paddocks and parkland ensuring utter peace and quiet.

This is a great place to wind down and relax, enjoy Angela and Simon's generous home cooking, and contemplate the views from the terrace or snuggle up to an open fire in the winter months. Telephones are banned from the bedrooms to further allow the setting to work its magic, but there is gentle exercise to be had in the heated indoor pool, or perhaps a game of snooker.

While staying at Saham Toney, you are in easy reach of the Norfolk Broads, the beaches and nature reserves of the North Norfolk Coast, and the royal Sandringham, where the Queen traditionally spends Christmas. The Jacobean glories of Blickling Hall are also nearby, and walkers can stretch their legs along the trans-Norfolk Peddars Way.

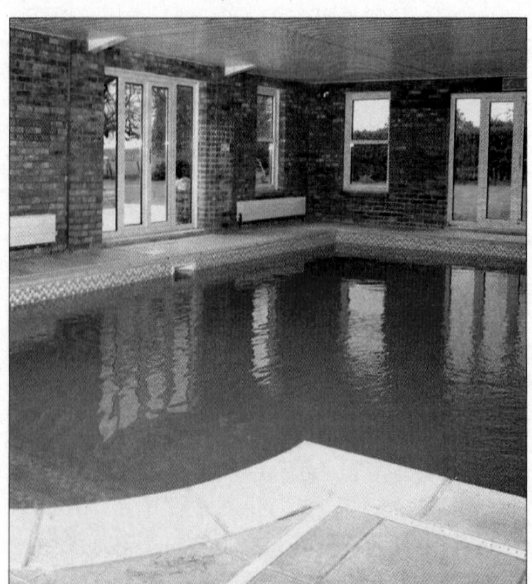

LOCATION

From A11 take A1075. At Watton turn left and then at next roundabout turn right to Saham Toney on B1077. Continue into Richmond Road and hotel entrance is on the left hand side.

For route planning map of the Midshires see page 500

"Such a stylish and welcoming house; such friendly and professional hosts - what a combination"

Michael Thompson, Canford Cliffs, Dorset

• Map p.500 ref: E6

Tudor town house

BURFORD HOUSE

Bed and breakfast in unashamed luxury

Said to be the 'Gateway to The Cotswolds' in the 'most beautiful countryside in England' Burford just goes on getting prettier and prettier as time matures the same golden Cotswold stone that built Blenheim Palace and St Paul's Cathedral. In the centre of town, built on a steeply sloping High Street, amongst the quaint antique shops, tea rooms and traditional butchers and grocers is Burford House. It is a focal point in a scene of rural peace and plenty.

Though the house dates back to Tudor times, Simon and Jane Henty bring a freshness to their special kind of hospitality and already, this gift has made many friends. It appears effortless but that is the hallmark of professionals. Burford House is fast becoming a Cotswold landmark

Described as a luxury Bed and Breakfast Town House Hotel, it is, indeed, very attractively furnished and decorated. Simon and Jane have made this their home - and it shows. The welcome is warm and friendly; the whole atmosphere is that of a private house. Four-poster beds and gleaming luxury bathrooms are there to indulge you. A flower-filled courtyard and cosy sitting rooms refresh the flagging spirit.

LOCATION

Burford is situated just north of the junction of the A424 and the A40 Oxford to Cheltenham road. The hotel is on the High Street in the middle of the town.

99 High Street, Burford, Oxfordshire OX18 4QA

Telephone 01993 823151
Fax 01993 823240

E-mail: *burford@bestloved.com*

OWNERS

Simon and Jane Henty

ROOM RATES

Single occupancy	*£75 - £95*
3 Doubles/Twins	*£90 - £110*
4 Four-posters	*£95 - £120*

Includes full breakfast and VAT

CHARGE/CREDIT CARDS

• *MC* • *VI*

RATINGS & AWARDS

E.T.C. ◆◆◆◆◆ *Silver Award*
A.A. ◆◆◆◆◆

FACILITIES

On site: *Garden*
Nearby: *Golf, fishing, riding*

RESTRICTIONS

No facilities for disabled guests
No smoking in bedrooms
No pets

ATTRACTIONS

Oxford, Bath, Stratford-upon-Avon, Blenheim Palace, Warwick Castle, Barnsley House & Gardens

AFFILIATIONS

Cotswolds Finest Hotels
Preston's Global Hotels

NEAREST

MAJOR CITY:
Oxford - 18 miles/20 mins

MAJOR AIRPORT:
London Heathrow - 60 miles/1½ hrs

RAILWAY STATION:
Kingham - 5 miles/10 mins
Charlbury - 5 miles/10 mins

RESERVATIONS

Toll free in US: 800-544-9993
Quote ***Best Loved***

ACCESS CODES

Not applicable

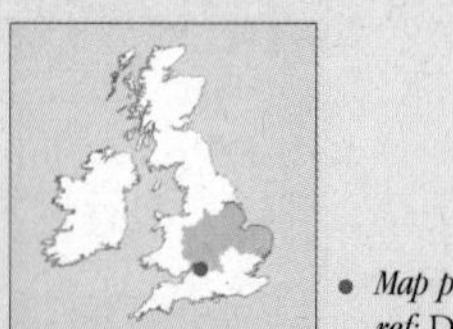

• Map p.500 ref: D6

"We don't come on holiday to England ... we come on holiday to Calcot"

Paul & Lynda Steggada, Phoenix, USA

CALCOT MANOR

14th century manor house

Near Tetbury, Gloucestershire GL8 8YJ

Telephone 01666 890391
Fax 01666 890394

E-mail: *calcot@bestloved.com*

MANAGING DIRECTOR

Richard J G Ball

ROOM RATES

24 Doubles/Twins/Family £135 - £180
4 Family suites £185 - £190
Includes full breakfast and VAT

CHARGE/CREDIT CARDS

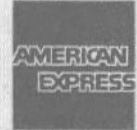
• DC • MC • VI

RATINGS & AWARDS

E.T.C. ★★★ Gold Award
R.A.C. Blue Ribbon ★★★
Dining Award 3
A.A. ★★★ ❀❀

FACILITIES

On site: *Heated outdoor pool, tennis, croquet, gardens, jacuzzi, heli-pad*
Licensed for weddings
1 meeting room/max 60 people
Nearby: *Golf, riding, clay pigeon shooting, health & beauty*

RESTRICTIONS

No pets

ATTRACTIONS

Westonbirt Arboretum, Bath, Cotswold villages, Berkeley Castle, Badminton

AFFILIATIONS

Pride of Britain
Selected British Hotels
Preston's Global Hotels

NEAREST

MAJOR CITY:
Bath - 22 miles/35 mins
MAJOR AIRPORT:
London Heathrow - 100 miles/1½ hrs
Bristol - 30 miles/45 mins
RAILWAY STATION:
Kemble - 15 miles/10 mins

RESERVATIONS

Toll free in US: 800-544-9993
or 800-98-PRIDE
*Quote **Best Loved***

ACCESS CODES

SABRE/ABACUS HK 34714
APOLLO/GALILEO HT 41198
AMADEUS HK LHRCAL
WORLDSPAN HK CALCO

Ancient and modern ... an enduring family favourite

Calcot was originally converted in 1984 and is now run by Richard Ball. The hotel is located in an unspoilt part of the Cotswold Hills, well-placed for visiting Bath and within reach of the country's finest antique centres. There is a heated swimming pool, two tennis courts and a croquet lawn in the grounds and bicycles can be provided for touring the famous Cotswold villages.

This charming Cotswold manor house was originally a farmhouse dating back to the 15th century. Its beautiful stone barns and stables, now converted into further superb bedrooms, include a 14th century tithe barn that was built by Cistercian Monks in 1300 and is amongst the oldest in Britain.

The hotel is beautifully furnished and the service is friendly and unobtrusive. In the award-winning restaurant, guests can linger over delicious meals whilst enjoying wonderful views of the countryside.

Calcot welcomes families and has a number of suites with sofa beds, toys, child-listening facilities, a playroom and an outdoor play area.

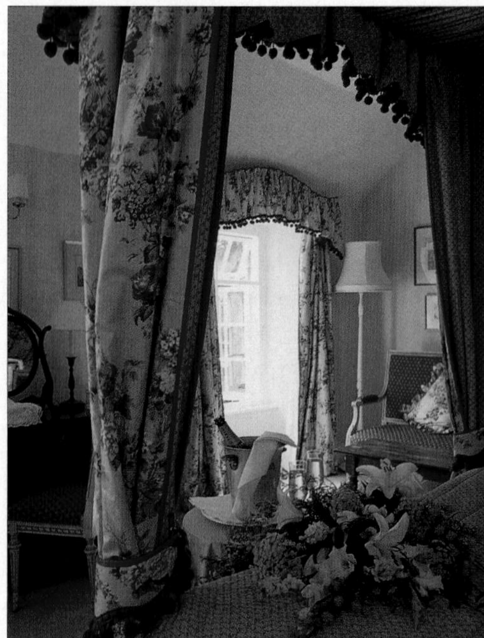

LOCATION

Ideally situated on the edge of the Cotswolds, only 35 minutes north of Bath. Exit 18 off M4, Calcot is 4 miles west of Tetbury at junction of A46 and A4135.

A keen Angler? Refer to page 472 for our Fishing Index

" Congratulations on the best hotel west of Kensington "

Derek Parker, Kensington, London

• *Map p.500*
ref: C5

Luxury hotel

CASTLE HOUSE

Castle Street, Hereford,
Herefordshire HR1 2NW

Telephone 01432 356321
Fax 01432 365909

E-mail: *castlehse@bestloved.com*

OWNERS

Dr and Mrs Albert Heijn

GENERAL MANAGER

Ben Jager

ROOM RATES

4 Singles	*£90*
1 Double	*£155*
10 Suites	*£165 - £210*

Includes continental breakfast and VAT

CHARGE/CREDIT CARDS

• *MC* • *VI*

RATINGS & AWARDS

R.A.C. Gold Ribbon ★★★★
Dining Award 4
A.A. ★★★★ ❀❀❀❀ *87%*
A.A. Hotel of the Year 2001

FACILITIES

On site: *Garden*
Nearby: *Golf, swimming, tennis, riding, fishing*

RESTRICTIONS

None

ATTRACTIONS

Hereford Cathedral, Mappa Mundi, Offa's Dyke, Eastnor Castle, Cider Museum, Black and White Village Trail

AFFILIATIONS

The Celebrated Hotels Collection
Pride of Britain
Small Luxury Hotels

NEAREST

MAJOR CITY:
Hereford
MAJOR AIRPORT:
Birmingham International - 65 miles/1½ hrs
RAILWAY STATION:
Hereford - 1 mile/5 mins

RESERVATIONS

Toll free in US: 800-322-2403 or 800-525-4800 or 800-98-PRIDE
Quote ***Best Loved***

ACCESS CODES

AMADEUS LX BHXCAS
APOLLO/GALILEO LX 30262
SABRE/ABACUS LX 55135
WORLDSPAN LX BHXCH

MIDSHIRES

One of the most talked about hotels in the country

Close to the cathedral and its famed exhibition, this gracious small hotel occupies a handsome Grade II-listed mansion fashioned out of a pair of 18th-century Georgian villas over 100 years ago. A sensitive restoration programme has preserved many of the original features and the elegant décor and discrete, well-polished service recreate the feel of a timeless and hospitable private home.

Attention to detail is a watchword at Castle House. The lovely bedrooms are thoughtfully equipped with mini hi-fi's and fridges stocked to guests' requirements. Late arrival suppers can be pre-ordered so that late check-in's can find a light supper - maybe smoked salmon and chilled white wine - waiting in their rooms. There is also a decanter of Hereford apple brandy for a night cap. Guests have use of a fully-equipped office suite and dining in is essential. Noted chef Stuart McLeod (ex-Savoy and Gleneagles Hotel) has created a series of delicious menus with a regional flavour including the seven-course Taste of the Marches gourmet experience. The hotel is very fortunate to have its own farm, Ford Abbey, which keeps the Kitchen supplied with Hereford beef and Gloucester Old Spot pork and bacon.

On first impressions, Hereford may appear slow and sleepy, but think again. You would need to extend your stay indefinitely to sample a fraction of the local attractions on offer, including the Mappa Mundi and chained library.

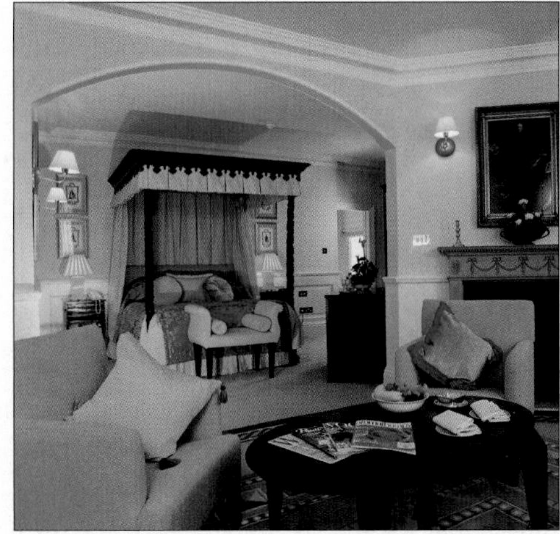

LOCATION

In the centre of Hereford. Follow signs for City Centre and then City Centre East. From St Owen's Street turn right into St Ethelbert Street, then veer right into Castle Street.

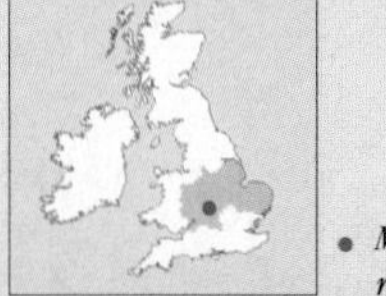

• Map p.500 ref: D5

"Charingworth Manor stands for unadulterated pleasure and I am not ashamed to enjoy it"

Patrick Maclagan, Berkshire

Charingworth Manor

14th century manor

Near Chipping Campden, Gloucestershire GL55 6NS

Telephone 01386 593555
Fax 01386 593353

E-mail: charingworth@bestloved.com

GENERAL MANAGER
Trevor Nicholl

ROOM RATES

Single occupancy	£115 - £180
21 Doubles/Twins	£150 - £235
2 Four-posters	£250
3 Suites	£275

Includes full breakfast, early morning tea or coffee, newspaper and VAT

CHARGE/CREDIT CARDS

• DC • MC • VI

RATINGS & AWARDS
E.T.C. ★★★ Gold Award
R.A.C. ★★★
A.A. ★★★ ❀ 75%

FACILITIES
On site: Garden, croquet, indoor pool, sauna, steam room, solarium, gymnasium, heli-pad, Licensed for weddings
2 meeting rooms/max 70 people
Nearby: Clay shooting, archery

RESTRICTIONS
No facilities for disabled guests
No pets

ATTRACTIONS
The Cotswolds, Broadway, Warwick Castle, Oxford, Chipping Campden, Stratford-upon-Avon

AFFILIATIONS
English Rose Hotels

NEAREST
MAJOR CITY:
Stratford-upon-Avon - 12 miles/30 mins
MAJOR AIRPORT:
Birmingham - 36 miles/1 hr
RAILWAY STATION:
Moreton-in-Marsh - 8 miles/10 mins

RESERVATIONS
Toll free in US: 800-HERITAGE or 800-322-2403
Toll free in UK: 0800 282811
Quote **Best Loved**

ACCESS CODES
AMADEUS GH GLOCWM
APOLLO/GALILEO GH 84371
SABRE/ABACUS GH 38652
WORLDSPAN GH BHXCW

The perfect retreat from the twentieth century

The ancient manor of Charingworth lies amidst the gently rolling Cotswold countryside, three miles from Chipping Campden, described as having "the most beautiful High Street in the whole of England". The 14th century manor house is set in its own gardens and grounds of fifty acres and offers peace, tranquillity and breathtaking views.

Inside Charingworth is an historic patchwork of intimate public rooms with log fires burning during the colder months. The atmosphere is warm and relaxed, the service friendly and attentive. There are 26 bedrooms, all furnished with antiques and fine fabrics. The chefs create imaginative dishes where great emphasis is placed on the finest produce available. Recognition has come in the form of a rosette from the A.A.

To enhance your stay there is an elegant romanesque leisure spa, entirely in keeping with the relaxed comfort found throughout Charingworth. It offers an indoor heated pool, sauna, steam room, solarium and billiards room, there is also a tennis court in the grounds.

The lovely Cotswold villages, Warwick Castle and famous gardens of Hidcote and Kiftsgate are very close by. Also easily reached are the historic Stratford-upon-Avon and Oxford.

LOCATION

Charingworth is situated on the B4035 between Chipping Campden and Shipston-on-Stour. 2½ miles from the A429.

“ It was lovely to get personal attention and you and your colleagues made the evening a great success ”

Jeremy Budden, Willis National, London

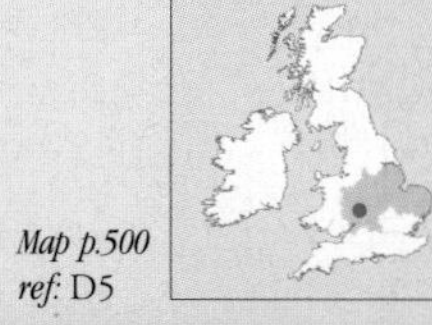
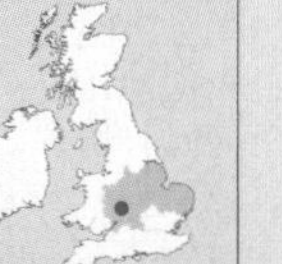

• Map p.500 ref: D5

Country house

COLWALL PARK HOTEL

Inspirational surroundings on the sunny side of the Malvern Hills

Long celebrated as one of Britain's most alluring landscapes, the Malvern Hills have inspired generations of artists and writers, most notably the composer Sir Edward Elgar. From the undulating ridge of the hills, the views stretch over 10 counties, east across the Cotswolds, and west over the Severn Valley to the Welsh Mountains. This is wonderful countryside to explore, virtually untainted by tourism and full of interest.

Nestled on the western flanks of the hills, Colwall Park combines high standards of traditional comfort and noticeably professional, and efficient service, in equal measure. Indeed, the hotel has been voted 'English Hotel of the Year' by the Automobile Association.

The 24 bedrooms and suites are comfortable and prettily furnished. Downstairs guests can curl up in deep armchairs in the Lounge or play a round of cards or a boardgame in the Library. The oak panelled Edwardian Restaurant offers an excellent, well priced menu whilst simpler dishes, particularly good for the business traveller, are available from the bar.

Colwall Park offers instant access to the hills that inspired Elgar's Pomp and Circumstance and the Enigma Variations and the Elgar Route leads you to both his birthplace and grave. Other popular side trips include Malvern, the Royal Worcester Porcelain Factory, and Eastnor Castle.

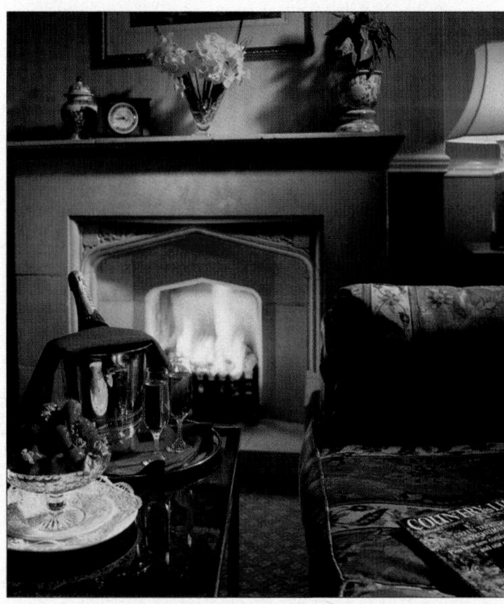

LOCATION

Situated in the centre of Colwall Village on the B4218 between Malvern and Ledbury.

Colwall, Malvern, Worcestershire WR13 6QG

Telephone 01684 540000
Fax 01684 540847

E-mail: *colwallpark@bestloved.com*

OWNERS

Iain and Sarah Nesbitt

ROOM RATES

3 Singles	*£65 - £80*
15 Doubles/Twins	*£110 - £130*
4 Suites	*£150*

Includes full breakfast and VAT

CHARGE/CREDIT CARDS

• MC • VI

RATINGS & AWARDS

E.T.C. ★★★ Gold Award
R.A.C. ★★★
A.A. ★★★ ❀❀ 78%
A.A. Courtesy & Care Award 2000

FACILITIES

On site: *Garden, croquet, boules*
4 meeting rooms/max 150 people
Nearby: *Golf, riding, health club*

RESTRICTIONS

No facilities for disabled guests

ATTRACTIONS

Eastnor Castle, The Cotswolds, Cheltenham, Worcester, Gloucester, Hereford

AFFILIATIONS

Independent

NEAREST

MAJOR CITY:
Worcester - 12 miles/20 mins

MAJOR AIRPORT:
Birmingham International - 40 miles/1 hr

RAILWAY STATION:
Colwall - 20 yds/½ min

RESERVATIONS

Direct with hotel
Quote ***Best Loved***

ACCESS CODES

Not applicable

• Map p.500 ref: H4

“ The epitome of the English country hotel ”

Hilary Rubinstein, The Good Hotel Guide

CONGHAM HALL

Georgian country house

Grimston, Kings Lynn,
Norfolk PE32 1AH

Telephone 01485 600250
Fax 01485 601191

E-mail: congham@bestloved.com

OWNER
Countess Von Essen

GENERAL MANAGER
Andrew Chantrell

ROOM RATES

1 Single	£90 - £140
15 Doubles/Twins	£130 - £175
4 Suites	£205 - £230

Includes full breakfast and VAT

CHARGE/CREDIT CARDS

• DC • MC • VI

RATINGS & AWARDS
E.T.C. ★★★ Gold Award
R.A.C. Gold Ribbon ★★★ Dining Award 4
A.A. ★★★ ❀❀

FACILITIES
On site: Garden, croquet, tennis, outdoor pool, heli-pad
Licensed for weddings
2 meeting rooms/max 50 people
Nearby: Golf, fishing, riding, hunting/shooting

RESTRICTIONS
No children under 7 years
No dogs in hotel - kennels available
Smoking permitted in lounge & bar only

ATTRACTIONS
Holkham Hall, Sandringham, Houghton Hall, RSPB Bird Reserves, Newmarket Racecourse, ballooning

AFFILIATIONS
Pride of Britain
Von Essen Hotels

NEAREST
MAJOR CITY:
Norwich - 43 miles/1 hr
MAJOR AIRPORT:
London Stansted - 76 miles/1½ hrs
RAILWAY STATION:
Kings Lynn - 6 miles/15 mins

RESERVATIONS
Toll free in US: 800-98-PRIDE
Quote **Best Loved**

ACCESS CODES
AMADEUS HK STNCON
APOLLO/GALILEO HK CONGH
SABRE/ABACUS HK 34243
WORLDSPAN HT 41199

Norfolk's finest country house experience

Not enough has been written extolling the virtues of Norfolk. In summer, acres of golden fields give way to the wilds of the Broads, a paradise to wildlife enthusiasts. In winter, its rugged coastline provides the perfect backdrop for reflective walks.

Another Norfolk virtue must be Congham Hall, the very essence of the country house experience. Its 40 acres of parkland include one of England's finest herb gardens. For Congham throws up romantic images of a seemingly vanishing rural England but here it is, thankfully, as fresh as ever.

The atmosphere can be described as relaxed luxury. A member of staff is never far away to attend your every need. Whether enjoying a book in the pot pourri-scented lounges or enjoying the heated pool, all has been designed to achieve an air of ‘no hassle, no pressure, no noise!’, as a guest put it. The spotless bedrooms are prettily furnished and exude a warmth and homeliness throughout.

If you come to Congham Hall in need of a good rest, your expectations will be met and exceeded. As a touring base for Norfolk and East Anglia you will find no better choice of hotel. Pilots should note the following heli-pad grid reference: 132 (TF) N 5246.8 E 3031.8.

LOCATION

From the A148/A149 interchange north east of Kings Lynn, follow the A148 towards Cromer for 100 yards. Turn right towards Grimston and the hotel is 2½ miles on left hand side.

For information about hotel affiliations see page 14

“ A stay here is worthwhile for Baba Hine's food, Denis Hine's wine list and the air of bonhomie they create ”

Vogue magazine

• *Map p.500 ref: D6*

18th century house

CORSE LAWN HOUSE HOTEL

Grace and flavour between the Malverns and Cotswolds

A Rip van Winkle style hamlet dozing peacefully amidst rolling Gloucestershire farmland, Corse Lawn appears blissfully unaware that the 21st century has arrived. It is hard to believe that the M5 and M50 motorways are just six miles away, and you can be in Cheltenham, Gloucester or Worcester within 20 minutes.

At the heart of the tiny settlement, a graceful Queen Anne house set in mature gardens overlooks the village green and the large duck pond which once served as a drive-in coach wash for a stage-and-four. Corse Lawn House has been the home of the Hine family, of cognac fame, and an intimate country house hotel for over 20 years.

Denis, Baba and Giles Hine are superlative hosts and have a natural ability to make you feel like one of their guests, rather than a hotel guest. Baba's renowned culinary skills have inspired several of today's leading modern British chefs. The varied menu, including seasonal grouse and partridge and a wine selection to drool over are all part and parcel of a great stay. As you would expect, the house cognac has been specially selected for Mr Hine and the cellar stocks many rare Hine vintages.

Winter or summer, this is a place to really unwind and enjoy, and a great location for exploring the Cotswolds, the Malvern Hills and the Forest of Dean.

LOCATION

On B4211, 1 mile off A438. 5 miles from Tewkesbury and 9 miles from Ledbury.

Corse Lawn, Gloucestershire GL19 4LZ

Telephone 01452 780771
Fax 01452 780840

E-mail: *corselawn@bestloved.com*

OWNERS
Baba and Denis Hine

GENERAL MANAGER
Giles Hine

ROOM RATES

1 Single	*£75*
16 Doubles/Twins	*£90 - £140*
2 Suites	*£155*

Includes full breakfast and VAT

CHARGE/CREDIT CARDS

• DC • JCB • MC • VI

RATINGS & AWARDS
E.T.C. ★★★ Silver Award
A.A. ★★★ ❀❀ 75%
A.A. Half Bottle Wine List of the Year

FACILITIES
On site: *Garden, croquet, indoor pool, tennis, heli-pad*
Licensed for weddings
2 meeting rooms/max 100 people
Nearby: *Golf, riding, fishing*

RESTRICTIONS
None

ATTRACTIONS
Berkeley Castle, Tewkesbury Abbey, Slimbridge Wildfowl Trust, Royal Forest of Dean, Wye Valley, Malvern Hills

AFFILIATIONS
Preston's Global Hotels

NEAREST
MAJOR CITY:
Gloucester - 9 miles/10 mins

MAJOR AIRPORT:
Birmingham - 30 miles/45 mins

RAILWAY STATION:
Gloucester - 9 miles/15 mins

RESERVATIONS
Toll free in US: 800-544-9993
*Quote **Best Loved***

ACCESS CODES
Not applicable

• Map p.500 ref: E5

"Thank you for making our first visit to England so very memorable"

James Lamberti, Vermont, USA

COTSWOLD HOUSE HOTEL

Regency house

Chipping Campden, Gloucestershire GL55 6AN

Telephone 01386 840330
Fax 01386 840310

E-mail: cotswoldhouse@bestloved.com

OWNERS

Ian and Christa Taylor

ROOM RATES

1 Single £80
13 Doubles/Twins £120 - £170
1 Four-poster £180
Includes full breakfast and VAT

CHARGE/CREDIT CARDS

• MC • VI

RATINGS & AWARDS

R.A.C. Blue Ribbon ★★★ Dining Award 3
A.A. ★★★ ❀❀

FACILITIES

On site: Croquet, garden
1 meeting room/max 30 people
Nearby: Golf, riding, fishing, clay shooting, walking, hot air ballooning

RESTRICTIONS

No facilities for disabled guests

ATTRACTIONS

The Cotswolds, Hidcote & Kiftsgate Gardens, Stratford-upon-Avon, Warwick, Berkeley & Sudeley Castles, Snowshill Manor, Batsford Arboretum

AFFILIATIONS

Preston's Global Hotels

NEAREST

MAJOR CITY:
Oxford - 33 miles/45 mins
Stratford - 10 miles/15 mins

MAJOR AIRPORT:
London Heathrow - 78 miles/1¾ hrs
Birmingham - 30 miles/30 mins

RAILWAY STATION:
Moreton-in-Marsh - 7 miles/10 mins

RESERVATIONS

Toll free in US: 800-544-9993
Quote **Best Loved**

ACCESS CODES

AMADEUS HK BHXCOT
APOLLO/GALILEO HT 14869
SABRE/ABACUS HK 30593
WORLDSPAN HK COTSW

Exquisite style and good taste in the heart of the Cotswolds

A prosperous wool centre in the Middle Ages, Chipping Campden is one of the loveliest and most perfectly preserved old Cotswold towns richly endowed with elegant patrician architecture dating from the 15th and 16th centuries, interesting shopping and splendid views from Dover's Hill on the Cotswold Way. The best time to explore is late afternoon when the day trippers have departed and the evening light turns the mellow local stone buildings to a rich gold - a perfect excuse, if one were needed, for an overnight stop.

Cotswold House is an architectural gem in its own right, an elegantly proportioned 17th-century mansion fronting onto the town square. Recently refurbished to exacting standards by Christa and Ian Taylor, the interior deftly blends the antique furnishings, period paintings and roaring log fires of a Regency past with modern comforts such as state-of-the-art bathrooms and luxurious outsize beds made up with crisp linen. The Garden Room Restaurant and informal Hicks Brasserie feature the intelligent cuisine of talented young chef, Alan Dann. Cotswold House is also a convenient base for excursions to Oxford and Stratford-upon-Avon, the Cheltenham races, and a slew of historic homes and gardens scattered throughout the Cotswolds.

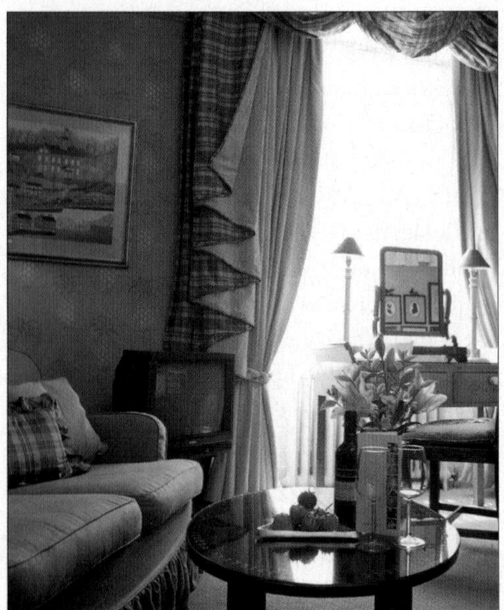

LOCATION

On B4081, 2 miles north of A44 between Moreton-in-Marsh and Broadway.

“ The welcome, comfort, service and food were second to none and I now have a new yardstick by which to judge other hotels ”

A Pollard, Salisbury

• Map p.500 ref: E4

17th century cottages — THE COTTAGE COUNTRY HOUSE HOTEL

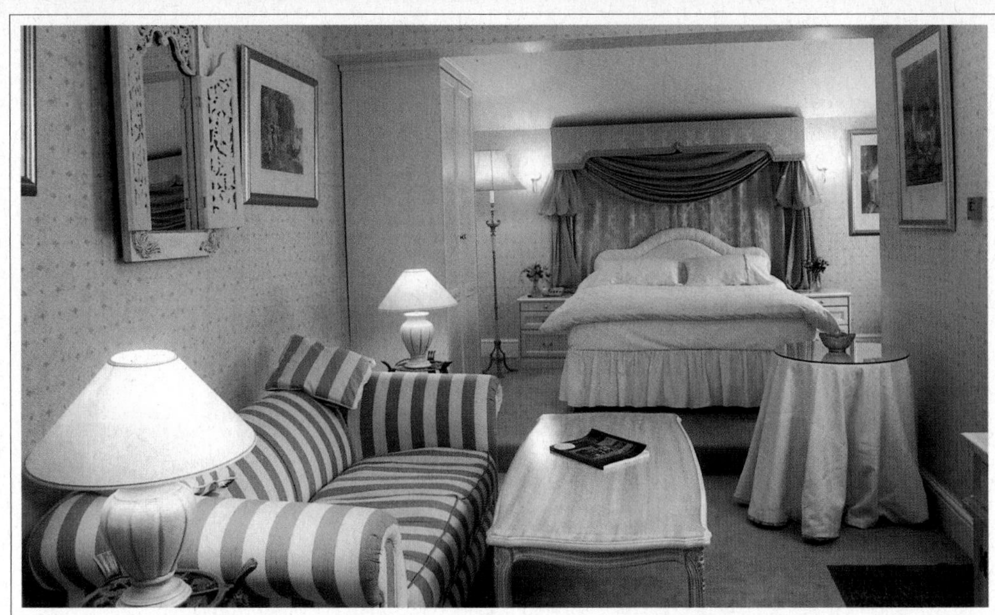

Impeccable hospitality with a touch of the Med

Such is the welcome at The Country Cottage House Hotel that you are greeted as soon as you pull up and escorted straight to your room without the usual form-filling formalities. And, while drinks or light snacks are offered, your luggage is portered and your car parked.

Having settled into your room, all en-suite with direct dial telephones, colour TV's and tea and coffee making facilities, you begin to appreciate the hotel's unique personality created by its owners Tim and Christina Ruffell. Mediterranean influences are everywhere (both lived and worked in the region for some years) from the yacht cabin-style single room to the eclectic menu and the many ornaments and pictures collected over the years. The hotel, renovated by local craftsmen to the Ruffell's design (winning three conservation awards), is formed by 17th century cottages around a private, gated courtyard and walled garden. Inside, a superb Inglenook fireplace and a well-stocked barrel-vaulted wine cellar heighten its authentic character.

Should you wish to get to know the area, Christina loves Nottingham and its environs and happily shares her vast local knowledge with you.

'The Cottage' is aptly named: small, cosy, full of character, old-fashioned values and boundless hospitality. Don't miss it!

LOCATION

3 miles south of Nottingham in Ruddington. Turn right off main A60. Turn right into High Street and right again into Easthorpe St. The hotel is 150 metres on right.

Easthorpe Street, Ruddington, Nottinghamshire NG11 6LA

Telephone 0115 984 6882
Fax 0115 921 4721

E-mail: cottage@bestloved.com

OWNERS
Tim and Christina Ruffell

GENERAL MANAGER
David Swift

ROOM RATES

1 Single	£80
12 Doubles/Twins	£95 - £145
2 Suites	£150

Includes full breakfast and VAT

CHARGE/CREDIT CARDS

• JCB • MC • VI

RATINGS & AWARDS
Awards pending

FACILITIES
On site: *Garden*
4 meeting rooms/max 60 people
Nearby: *Golf, tennis, water skiing, yachting, fishing, riding, hunting/shooting, go-karting*

RESTRICTIONS
Children by arrangement
No smoking in bedrooms or restaurant
Limited facilities for disabled guests
No pets

ATTRACTIONS
Nottingham City and Castle, Belvoir Castle, Newstead Abbey, Holmepierrepoint National Watersports Centre, Wollaton Hall, Robin Hood Experience

AFFILIATIONS
Independent

NEAREST
MAJOR CITY:
Nottingham - 5 miles/10 mins
MAJOR AIRPORT:
London Heathrow - 130 miles/2½ hrs
East Midlands - 13 miles/20 mins
RAILWAY STATION:
Nottingham - 5 miles/10 mins

RESERVATIONS
Direct with hotel
Quote ***Best Loved***

ACCESS CODES
Not applicable

• Map p.500 ref: 15

"With a wine list that possesses magnitude and a notable self-effacing policy where pricing is concerned"

Fay Maschler, London Evening Standard

THE CROWN HOTEL

250-year old inn

90 High Street, Southwold, Suffolk IP18 6DP

Telephone 01502 722275
Fax 01502 727263

E-mail: crownsuffolk@bestloved.com

MANAGER
Michael Bartholomew

DEPUTY MANAGER
Angie Brown

ROOM RATES

2 Singles	£50
10 Doubles/Twins	£60 - £75
2 Family rooms	£80 - £100

Includes morning tea, continental breakfast, newspapers and VAT

CHARGE/CREDIT CARDS

• DC • MC • VI

RATINGS & AWARDS
E.T.C. ★★
A.A. ★★ ❀ 69%

FACILITIES
On site: 2 meeting rooms/max 20 people
Nearby: Golf, tennis, shooting, fishing, sailing, fitness, riding

RESTRICTIONS
No children under 5 years in restaurant
No facilities for disabled guests
No pets

ATTRACTIONS
Suffolk Wildlife Park, Earsham Otter Trust, Saxtead Green Post Mill, Aldeburgh Festival, Snape Maltings, Minsmere Bird Sanctuary

AFFILIATIONS
Adnams Hotels

NEAREST
MAJOR CITY:
Norwich - 36 miles/50 mins

MAJOR AIRPORT:
Stansted - 90 miles/2 hrs

London Heathrow - 150 miles/3½ hrs

RAILWAY STATION:
Darsham - 5 miles/15 mins

RESERVATIONS
Direct with hotel
Quote **Best Loved**

ACCESS CODES
Not applicable

MIDSHIRES

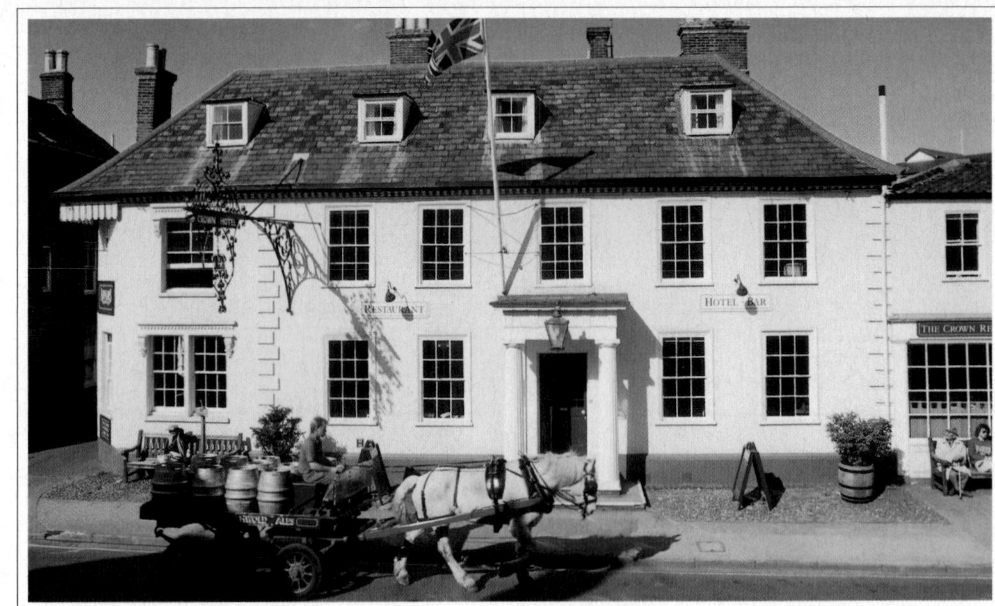

Great value, good food and fine wine at the Suffolk seaside

In this part of Suffolk, the pretty village of Southwold is plainly different. In many ways it displays the characteristics of an island. Bounded on three sides by creeks, marshes and the River Blyth and on the fourth by the sea, the effect has been to isolate the town from change. Here, the locals display a certain joie de vivre and natural inclination toward good times, hospitality and fine food.

One of the town's central places for dining is the Crown Inn owned by local brewer and wine-merchant, Adnams. It has given the 250-year-old inn a thorough face-lift. Bedrooms are simply furnished, comfortable and offer very good value.

At the heart of the small hotel is the bustling restaurant, a combination of pub, wine bar and brasserie, serving up imaginative cuisine with an obvious emphasis on fresh seafood which goes down a treat. As you might expect, the choice of award-winning beers, ales, and wines is extensive and the perfect complement to any meal. Every evening the restaurant is filled with locals, holiday-makers and visitors vying for tables. It is best to book ahead.

As an antidote to eating, lying on the beach, walking or exploring the nearby historic area, rich in churches and castles, is just as satisfying.

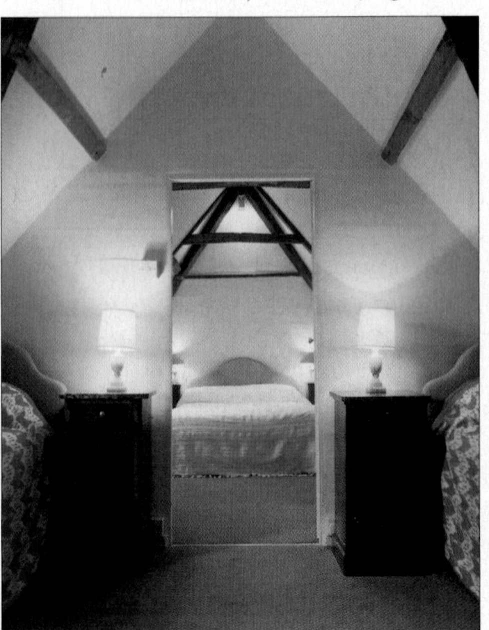

LOCATION

In the centre of Southwold.

"Superb food, good wine, even forgot the weather"

Patrick Dewitt

• *Map p.500 ref: E6*

16th century coaching inn **THE CROWN INN & HOTEL**

A comfortable and traditional inn with an award-winning restaurant

This charming, award-winning, mellow-stoned 16th century coaching inn, with its trademark archways, is set in a picturesque village in the heart of the Cotswolds. The friendly staff are always on hand to make your stay memorable. The 19 well-equipped and tastefully furnished bedrooms are all en suite and include colour television and tea making facilities.

In summer, the Crown provides the perfect setting to enjoy a drink and fine food under a cooling parasol on the patio or in the garden. On colder days you can relax and enjoy the home comforts of the friendly atmosphere of this family-run hotel in front of a log fire.

The Brasserie has a fine menu of traditional English and European cuisine but the selection of fresh fish is a speciality of the talented brigade. The mussels are a must. The Bar offers a lighter meal and chance to meet one of the many local characters.

For smaller business meetings, there is a conference room making a pleasant change from the office environment.

The Crown Hotel reflects the tranquil nature of the Cotswolds with walks along tree-lined footpaths and horse riding from local stables. There is a golf club nearby.

LOCATION

2 miles off the A44 Evesham to Moreton-in-Marsh road.

High Street, Blockley, Moreton-in-Marsh, Gloucestershire GL56 9EX

Telephone 01386 700245
Fax 01386 700247

E-mail: *crownmoreton@bestloved.com*

OWNERS

Paul Clayton-Smith and Jim Fraser

GENERAL MANAGER

Virginia Piper

ROOM RATES

Single occupancy	*£70*
13 Doubles/Twins	*£99 - £135*
2 Four-posters	*£120*
4 Suites	*£135*

Includes full breakfast and VAT

CHARGE/CREDIT CARDS

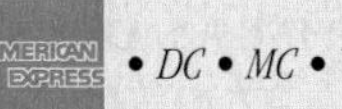

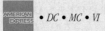

• *DC* • *MC* • *VI*

RATINGS & AWARDS

R.A.C. ★★★
A.A. ★★★ ❀ *67%*

FACILITIES

On site: *1 meeting room/max 50 people*
Nearby: *Golf, leisure centre, riding, clay pigeon shooting, archery, quad-biking*

RESTRICTIONS

No facilities for disabled guests
Pets by arrangement

ATTRACTIONS

Broadway, Stratford-upon-Avon, Warwick Castle, Oxford, Cotswold villages

AFFILIATIONS

Independent

NEAREST

MAJOR CITY:
Oxford - 25 miles/30 mins

MAJOR AIRPORT:
Birmingham - 40 miles/1 hr

RAILWAY STATION:
Moreton-in-Marsh - 5 miles/10 mins

RESERVATIONS

Direct with hotel
*Quote **Best Loved***

ACCESS CODES

Not applicable

• Map p.500 ref: D5

“Everything and everyone was wonderful. We feel fortunate to have happened upon you”

Freling and Linda Smith, NY, USA

DORMY HOUSE

17th century farmhouse

Willersey Hill, Broadway, Worcestershire WR12 7LF

Telephone 01386 852711
Fax 01386 858636

E-mail: dormy@bestloved.com

MANAGING DIRECTOR
Ingrid Philip-Sorensen

GENERAL MANAGER
David Field

ROOM RATES

3 Singles	£75 - £100
42 Doubles/Twins	£150 - £180
3 Suites	£192 - £243

Includes full breakfast and VAT

CHARGE/CREDIT CARDS

• DC • MC • VI

RATINGS & AWARDS
E.T.C. ★★★ Silver Award
R.A.C. ★★★ Dining Award 3
A.A. ★★★ 74%

FACILITIES
On site: *Croquet, gardens, putting green, sauna, gym, billiards*
Licensed for weddings
5 meeting rooms/max 170 people
Nearby: *Golf, riding, fishing, clay pigeon shooting, archery*

RESTRICTIONS
Limited facilities for disabled guests

ATTRACTIONS
Warwick Castle, Blenheim Palace, Stratford-upon-Avon, The Cotswolds, Broadway, Chipping Campden, Gardens of Hidcote and Kiftsgate

AFFILIATIONS
Selected British Hotels

NEAREST
MAJOR CITY:
Oxford - 40 miles/1 hr
MAJOR AIRPORT:
Birmingham - 40 miles/1 hr
London Heathrow - 90 miles/2 hrs
RAILWAY STATION:
Moreton-in-Marsh - 6 miles/10 mins

RESERVATIONS
Toll free in US: 800-323-5463
Quote ***Best Loved***

ACCESS CODES
Not applicable

MIDSHIRES

A haven for Stratford-upon-Avon, The Cotswolds and Broadway itself

Dormy House is set high in the beautiful Cotswold countryside amid picturesque, medieval villages. Originally a 17th century farmhouse, the hotel blends its historic past with 21st century facilities and personalised service. Each of the 48 bedrooms is beautifully decorated and provides every comfort for a good night's rest.

The charming lounges, enhanced with bowls of fresh flowers, have deep armchairs in which to relax. In winter, roaring log fires provide a welcoming atmosphere. The candlelit Tapestries Restaurant offers diners the choice of cosy alcoves in the old farmhouse or the elegant conservatory style dining room. The food is of a truly international standard; the freshest ingredients of the highest quality ensure an unforgettable experience. Lunch and evening meals are also served in the oak-beamed Barn Owl bar.

Surrounding the hotel on three sides is the Broadway Golf Club where guests can play by arrangement. Cheltenham's shops and Stratford's theatres are within easy reach and the friendly staff are a mine of information on the surrounding Cotswold villages, sporting facilities, country homes and gardens.

LOCATION

On the A44, at the top of Fish Hill 1½ miles from Broadway Village, take the turn signposted Saintbury and Picnic Area. After ½ mile fork left and Dormy House is on the left.

“ The house smiles at you ”

John Hunter, Indianapolis

• Map p.500 ref: E6

Victorian country house

FALLOWFIELDS COUNTRY HOUSE HOTEL

A fine country retreat with Oxford on your doorstep

Originally part of the Kingston Estate, Fallowfields was once the home of the Begum Aga Khan and dates back over 300 years. It has been in private hands for about a century and was extended during that time. Today, whilst its southern aspect is early Victorian Gothic, the northern elevation is a magnificent late Victorian facade.

Fallowfields is set in 12 acres of grounds, two of which are given over to formal gardens and prolific vegetable and herb gardens. Chef Alan Jefferson Mackney makes good use of the home-produce for his imaginative fare.

Personal attention is assured in this intimate establishment which has a croquet lawn and tennis facilities.

Situated ten miles to the west of Oxford, Fallowfields is an ideal centre for touring. It is convenient for Stratford-upon-Avon, the Cotswolds, Blenheim Palace, Oxford University, Bath and Bristol. The surrounding Vale of the White Horse, named after the White Horse at Uffington which was carved out of the chalk downs in pre-Saxon times, is worth exploring too.

LOCATION

In Kingston Bagpuize with Southmoor. From Oxford take A420 towards Faringdon. Turn left at roundabout where A415 crosses A420, then first right. Fallowfields is 1 mile on left.

Faringdon Road, Kingston Bagpuize, Near Oxford, Oxfordshire OX13 5BH

Telephone 01865 820416
Fax 01865 821275

E-mail: *fallowfields@bestloved.com*

OWNERS

Peta and Anthony Lloyd

ROOM RATES

Single occupancy	*£116*
2 Four-posters	*£145 - £155*
8 King size	*£122 - £165*

Includes full breakfast and VAT

CHARGE/CREDIT CARDS

• *MC* • *VI*

RATINGS & AWARDS

E.T.C. ★★★
A.A. ★★★ ❀ *69%*

FACILITIES

On site: *Garden, croquet, tennis, heli-pad*
Licensed for weddings
3 meeting rooms/max 120 people
Nearby: *Riding, fishing, golf, windsurfing, water-skiing*

RESTRICTIONS

No facilities for disabled guests
Pets by arrangement
Smoking very restricted

ATTRACTIONS

Oxford, Cotswolds, Blenheim Palace, River Thames

AFFILIATIONS

Preston's Global Hotels

NEAREST

MAJOR CITY:
Oxford - 10 miles/15 mins

MAJOR AIRPORT:
London Heathrow - 50 miles/1 hr

RAILWAY STATION:
Oxford - 8 miles/10 mins

RESERVATIONS

Toll free in US: 800-544-9993
Quote ***Best Loved***

ACCESS CODES

Not applicable

A keen Angler? Refer to page 472 for our Fishing Index

• Map p.500 ref: E5

"Not since Château de Bagnols in France has there been such attention to detail in an historic house hotel. It should be an inspiration to English hoteliers"

Lyn Middlehurst, Gallivanter's Guide

FAWSLEY HALL

15th century manor

**Fawsley,
Northamptonshire NN11 3BA**

Telephone 01327 892000
Fax 01327 892001

E-mail: fawsley@bestloved.com

GENERAL MANAGER
Jeffrey Crockett

ROOM RATES

Single occupancy	£135 - £295
21 Doubles/Twins	£175 - £199
6 Four-posters	£225 - £255
3 Suites	£255 - £495

Includes full breakfast and VAT

CHARGE/CREDIT CARDS

• DC • JCB • MC • VI

RATINGS & AWARDS
A.A. ★★★★ ❀❀

FACILITIES
On site: Garden, outdoor tennis, heli-pad
Licensed for weddings
4 meeting rooms/max 120 people
Nearby: Golf, fishing, hunting/shooting, riding

RESTRICTIONS
Limited facilities for disabled guests
Pets by prior arrangement

ATTRACTIONS
Althorp, Sulgrave Manor, Warwick Castle, Silverstone, Stratford-upon-Avon, Towcester Racecourse

AFFILIATIONS
The Celebrated Hotels Collection
Pride of Britain

NEAREST
MAJOR CITY:
Birmingham - 40 miles/ 1 hr

MAJOR AIRPORT:
Birmingham - 35 miles/50 mins
Coventry - 24 miles/40 mins

RAILWAY STATION:
Northampton - 15 miles/25 mins

RESERVATIONS
Toll free in US: 800-322-2403 or 800-98-PRIDE
Quote **Best Loved**

ACCESS CODES
Not applicable

MIDSHIRES

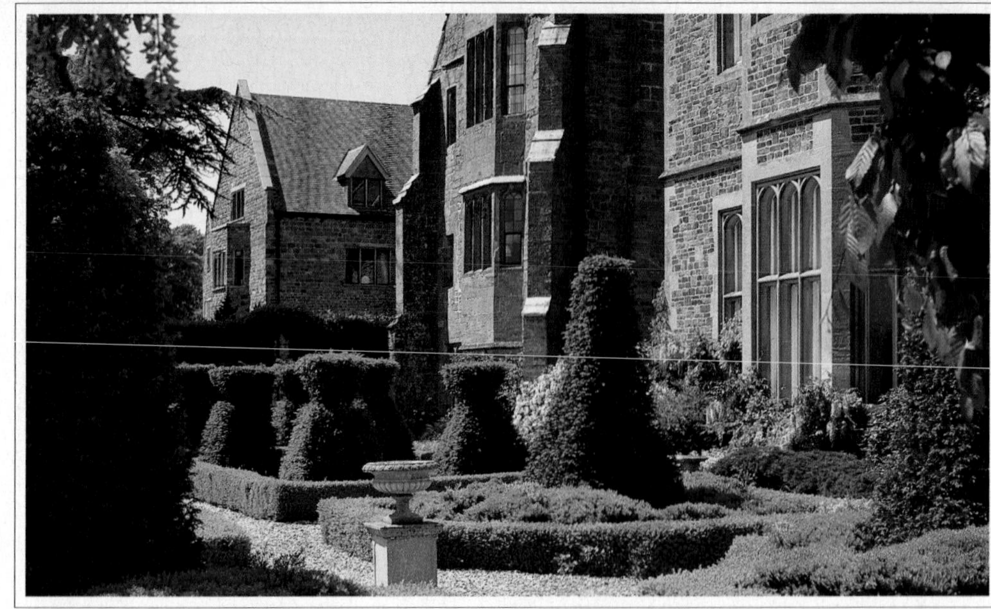

Spend a little time living in the lap of history

Shakespeare's Cottage at Stratford-upon-Avon, the ancestral homes Sulgrave Manor (George Washington), and Althorp, (Diana, Princess of Wales) form a triangle (all within 30 minutes drive) whose heart is Fawsley Hall. Each place marks an important aspect of England's colourful heritage.

Fawsley Hall in many respects is as historically and architecturally important - better yet you can stay here! This 500 year old stately house consists of three expertly and sensitively restored Tudor, Georgian, and Victorian wings allowing the guest ample choice of historic accommodation. Topping off the house are the glorious Capability Brown designed views. A more idyllic setting has rarely been realised. Luxury pervades every aspect of the Hall. From the decorative features to the staff's enthusiastic attentiveness you can easily begin to believe that you too are the Lord of the Manor.

While the decor is left to history, the restaurant provides a refreshing contemporary contrast. Here you will find serious cutting edge European cuisine excellently prepared and lovingly served. This is a great place for an intimate romantic getaway or a grand memorable gathering. In any event, Fawsley Hall should not be missed.

LOCATION

Take exit 11 off the M40 and follow the A361 signposted for Daventry. The hotel is situated between Charwelton and Badby.

Thinking of pampering yourself? See the 'Health & Beauty' index on page 472

"Comfortable, charming and unpretentious . . . it is one of the places to which I keep coming back"

Elizabeth Ortiz, Gourmet Magazine

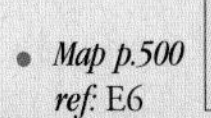
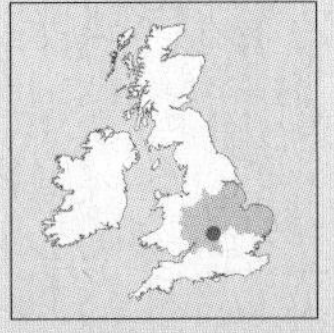

• Map p.500 ref: E6

17th century town house hotel

THE FEATHERS

Warmth and charm next to Sir Winston Churchill's birthplace

This privately owned 17th century town hotel is located in the heart of picturesque Woodstock which nestles by the gates of Blenheim Palace, the home of the 11th Duke of Marlborough and birth place of Sir Winston Churchill. The Feathers offers the ideal base from which to explore the dreaming spires of the university city of Oxford and the beautiful Cotswolds, yet it is only 1½ hours from London.

The hotel has 17 individually designed rooms and five suites all with antiques, books and interesting pictures. All rooms have private bathrooms, colour televisions with satellite channels and direct dial telephones.

In winter, log fires blaze in all the sitting rooms and the bar. In warmer months, the courtyard garden provides the ideal location to take a light meal or refreshment.

The well renowned restaurant has received much critical acclaim. The interesting dishes on the menu are carefully but simply created using only the finest ingredients. Guests may select from the constantly changing à la carte menu.

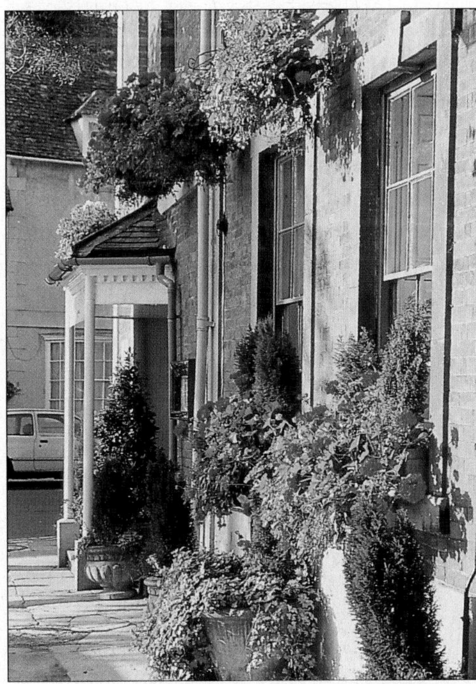

LOCATION

From the south, take the A44 to Woodstock. After Blenheim Palace gates take first left after traffic lights – the hotel is on left.

Market Street, Woodstock, Oxfordshire OX20 1SX

Telephone 01993 812291
Fax 01993 813158

E-mail: *feathers@bestloved.com*

RESIDENT MANAGER

Peter Bate

ROOM RATES

1 Single	*£98 - £170*
16 Doubles/Twins	*£120 - £185*
5 Suites	*£210 - £295*

Includes tea on arrival, newspaper, early morning tea, full breakfast and VAT

CHARGE/CREDIT CARDS

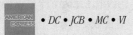

• DC • JCB • MC • VI

RATINGS & AWARDS

A.A. ★★★ ❀❀❀ *79%*

FACILITIES

On site: *Courtyard garden, mountain bikes*
2 meeting rooms/max 60 people
Nearby: *Golf, riding, fishing*

RESTRICTIONS

No facilities for disabled guests
Guests to provide dog's bedding and food

ATTRACTIONS

Blenheim Palace, Broughton Castle, Oxford, Stratford-upon-Avon, The Cotswold, Silverstone

AFFILIATIONS

The Celebrated Hotels Collection
Selected British Hotels

NEAREST

MAJOR CITY:
Oxford - 8 miles/15 mins

MAJOR AIRPORT:
London Heathrow - 40 miles/1 hr

RAILWAY STATION:
Oxford - 8 miles/15 mins

RESERVATIONS

Toll free in US: 800-322-2403
or 800-323-5463
Quote ***Best Loved***

ACCESS CODES

AMADEUS HK OXFFEA
APOLLO/GALILEO HK 25900
SABRE/ABACUS HK 30576
WORLDSPAN HK FEATH

• Map p.500 ref: E2

"A well kept hotel, innovative and stylish in every way. Wonderful food and service, can't wait to come again!"

Mr and Mrs Todd, Buckinghamshire

THE GEORGE IN HATHERSAGE

Coaching inn

Main Road, Hathersage, Derbyshire S32 1BB

Telephone 01433 650436
Fax 01433 650099

E-mail: georgederbys@bestloved.com

OWNER
Eric Marsh

GENERAL MANAGER
Gerald Chislett

ROOM RATES

4 Singles	£60 - £80
14 Doubles/Twins	£90 - £100
1 Four-poster	£120

Includes full breakfast and VAT

CHARGE/CREDIT CARDS

• DC • MC • VI

RATINGS & AWARDS
A.A. ★★★ ❀ 70%
R.A.C. ★★★ Dining Award 2

FACILITIES
On site: *Courtyard*
2 meeting rooms/max 150 people
Nearby: *Golf, pool, riding, tennis, fishing, walking, hill climbing*

RESTRICTIONS
No facilities for disabled guests
Pets by arrangement

ATTRACTIONS
Chatsworth, Haddon Hall, Eyam Plague Village, Buxton & Bakewell, Blue John Mine

AFFILIATIONS
Independent

NEAREST
MAJOR CITY:
Sheffield - 12 miles/30 mins

MAJOR AIRPORT:
East Midlands - 50 miles/1 hr

RAILWAY STATION:
Hathersage - 1/4 mile/5 mins

RESERVATIONS
Direct with hotel
Quote **Best Loved**

ACCESS CODES
Not applicable

Literary connections and oodles of character in the Derbyshire Peak District

The little town of Hathersage lies in the middle of the Peak District National Park surrounded by the rugged beauty of some of Britain's most spectacular scenery. It makes a great base for outdoor pursuits from walking and cycling to pot-holing and climbing, but for some visitors, Hathersage is a place of literary pilgrimage famous as the setting for 19th-century novelist Charlotte Brontë's masterpiece, Jane Eyre.

This traditional old Derbyshire alehouse has now been thoughtfully renovated while retaining its antique character in bare stone walls, hefty oak beams and open fires. The bedrooms are bright and comfy (some have four poster beds) with power showers in the bathrooms. In the restaurant, chef Benjamin Handley (locally-trained at the award-winning Cavendish Hotel on the Chatsworth Estate) has established a reputation for good food at affordable prices.

There is so much to see you will certainly want to stay longer than you originally planned. Chatsworth, the plague village of Eyam, Bakewell – famous for the tart, Blue John mines of Castleton, The Lady Bower Dam (used as a training ground for the Dam Busters) and in Hathersage's own Churchyard 'Little' John, one of Robin Hood's merrymen is buried.

LOCATION

On the A625, Sheffield to Chapel-en-le-Frith road. The hotel is in the centre of the village opposite the junction with the B6001.

Looking for an hotel with a golf course on site? See our 'Golf Guide' on page 478

" I'm hard pressed to name any family enterprise, in France or Britain, that can match the remarkable efforts of the Morris team "

Richard Binns, travel writer

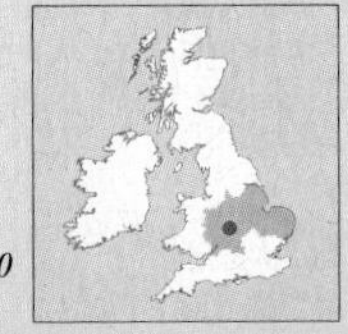

• Map p.500 ref: D5

Manor house

GRAFTON MANOR

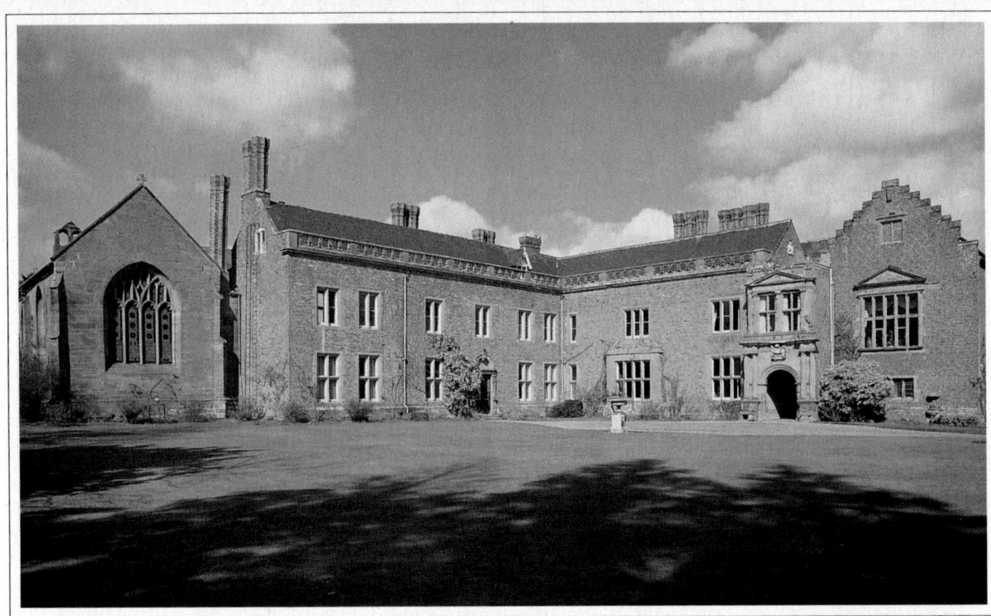

A great house with an illustrious past now the epitome of modern elegance

The Manor of Grafton has an illustrious history; from its foundation before the Norman Conquest, Grafton has been recognised as one of Worcestershire's great historic houses. This splendid house, for centuries the home of king makers, was opened as an hotel in 1980 by the present owners John (now The Lord of Grafton) and June Morris who, together with their family, ensure guests receive attentive, friendly service.

The elegant 17th century dining room is the focal point of a visit to Grafton, with imaginative menus created by Simon Morris who aims to produce only the best for guests, complemented by a fine wine list. Damask-rose petal and mulberry sorbets are indicative of the inspired style of cuisine. The guest bedrooms have been painstakingly restored, introducing the comforts demanded today while retaining the grace and elegance of another age.

There is much to enjoy at Grafton: a superb formal Herb Garden in 26 acres of beautiful grounds, a two-acre lake, a 16th century fish stew (brick building in the stream), and a 15th century private chapel. Grafton Manor is an ideal base from which to explore the Worcestershire countryside.

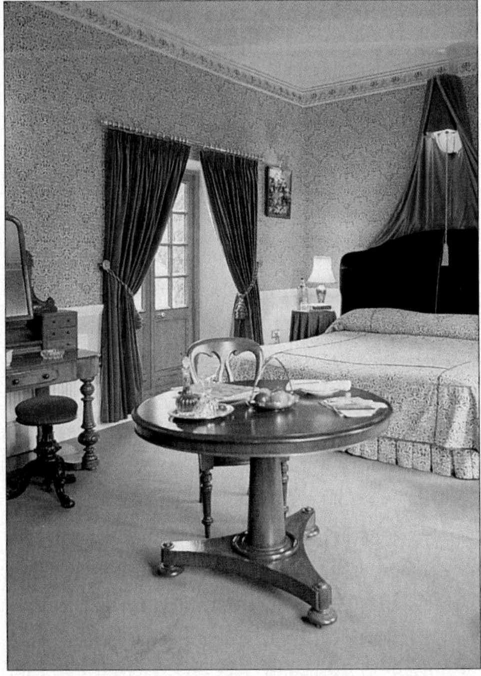

LOCATION

From M5 Exit 5 proceed via A38 towards Bromsgrove. Bear left at first roundabout; Grafton Lane is first left after half a mile.

Grafton Lane, Bromsgrove, Worcestershire B61 7HA

Telephone 01527 579007
Fax 01527 575221

E-mail: grafton@bestloved.com

OWNER
The Lord of Grafton

MANAGER
Stephen Morris

ROOM RATES

1 Single	£85 - £95
5 Doubles/Twins	£105 - £125
1 Four-poster	£125 - £150
2 Suites	£150

Includes full breakfast and VAT

CHARGE/CREDIT CARDS

• DC • MC • VI

RATINGS & AWARDS
A.A. ❀❀
Member of Master Chefs Institute

FACILITIES
On site: Croquet, gardens, special wedding marquee, fishing, heli-pad
Licensed for weddings
2 meeting rooms/max 170 people
Nearby: Golf, riding

RESTRICTIONS
No facilities for disabled guests
No pets

ATTRACTIONS
Stratford-upon-Avon, Worcester, The Cotswolds, Warwick Castle, Stourbridge Glass, Welsh Marches

AFFILIATIONS
Independent

NEAREST
MAJOR CITY:
Birmingham - 17 miles/30 mins

MAJOR AIRPORT:
Birmingham - 25 miles/25 mins

RAILWAY STATION:
Bromsgrove - 2 miles/5 mins

RESERVATIONS
Direct with hotel
Quote **Best Loved**

ACCESS CODES
AMADEUS HK BHXGRA
SABRE/ABACUS HK 36237
WORLDSPAN HK GRAFT

Planning a wedding reception? Turn to 'Meeting Facilities' on page 476

• Map p.500 ref: D6

"It was a delight to be able to return to such a pleasant hotel"

The Rt Hon John Major, former Prime Minister

THE GREENWAY

Elizabethan country manor

Shurdington, Cheltenham, Gloucestershire GL51 5UG

Telephone 01242 862352
Fax 01242 862780

E-mail: greenway@bestloved.com

GENERAL MANAGER
Andrew MacKay

ROOM RATES
1 Single £79
21 Doubles/Twins £120 - £200
Includes full breakfast and VAT

CHARGE/CREDIT CARDS

 • DC • MC • VI

RATINGS & AWARDS
R.A.C. Blue Ribbon ★★★ Dining Award 3
A.A. ★★★ ❀❀❀

FACILITIES
On site: *Garden, croquet, heli-pad*
Licensed for weddings
2 meeting rooms/max 45 people
Nearby: *Golf, fishing, walking, clay pigeon shooting, tennis, swimming, riding*

RESTRICTIONS
No children under 7 years
No pets

ATTRACTIONS
The Cotswolds, Stratford-upon-Avon, Bath, Cheltenham Spa, Painswick, Wye Valley, Sudeley Castle, Forest of Dean, Cirencester Polo Park

AFFILIATIONS
The Celebrated Hotels Collection
Pride of Britain
Selected British Hotels

NEAREST
MAJOR CITY:
Cheltenham - 2½ miles/5 mins
Gloucester - 5 miles/15 mins

MAJOR AIRPORT:
Birmingham - 60 miles/1¼ hrs
Bristol - 45 miles/50 mins

RAILWAY STATION:
Cheltenham - 2½ miles/5 mins

RESERVATIONS
Toll free in US: 800-322-2403
or 800-323-5463
*Quote **Best Loved***

ACCESS CODES
Not applicable

A long-standing reputation for excellence in the Cotswolds

One of Britain's first country house hotels, The Greenway retains an enviable reputation for its peerless style and welcoming atmosphere. Guests can enjoy a genuine country house experience with all the personalised attention to detail you would expect from the hostess of an elegant private home. The setting is glorious, too, with the Cotswold Hills for a backdrop and extensive gardens where the huge old yew hedges look like a scene straight out of Alice in Wonderland.

Recently, The Greenway's public rooms have been classically refurbished in fresh and pretty yellow and green tones. Gleaming antique furniture adds a mellow note and there are cosy log fires in winter. In summer there is a lovely indoor-outdoor feel as the bar opens onto the lawn, while the restaurant overlooks a sunken garden and lily pond. Bedrooms are generously proportioned and traditionally furnished. They are divided between the main house and a Georgian coach house where original elements such as the wooden beams and stalls have been cleverly incorporated in the design.

The Greenway is ideally placed for visiting the Cotswolds' numerous beauty spots, quaint villages and the spa town of Cheltenham, as well as Shakespeare's home town, Stratford-upon-Avon.

LOCATION

Leave M5 at Exit 11A and join A417 towards Cirencester. At A46 turn left direction Cheltenham. Hotel is 1 mile on the right.

“I would recommend it to my friends as a lovely stay, in a wonderful hotel, whose staff are exceptionally customer focused”

Julie Young, Barnes

• Map p.500 ref: D6

17th century manor house

HATTON COURT

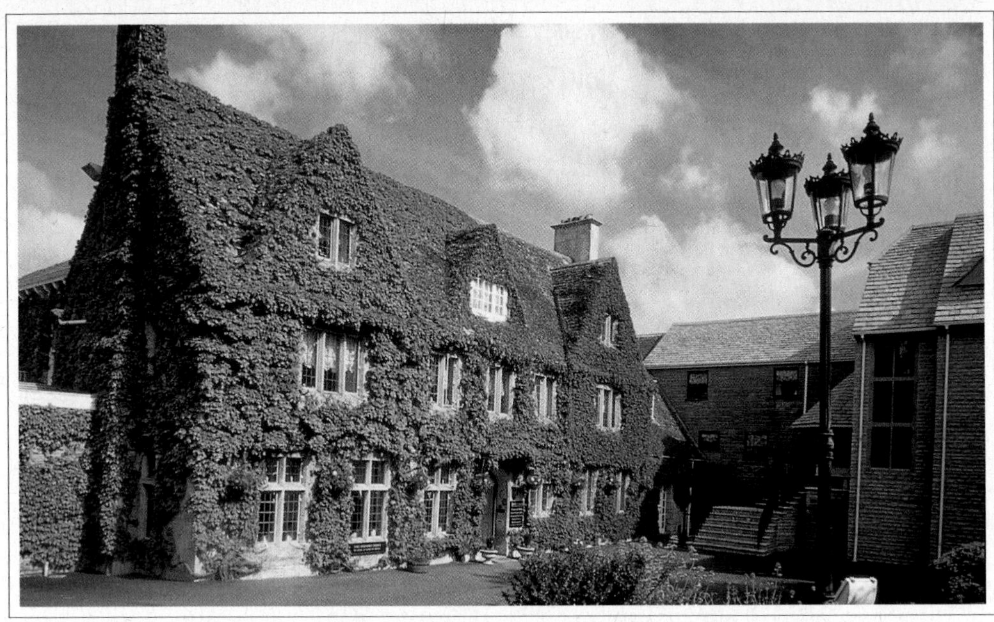

You will think you've died and gone to Hatton

Hatton Court's creeper-covered façade fronts one of the most stupendous views in the Cotswolds. The hotel nestles in the protective lee of a 400-foot escarpment, which rises majestically from the Severn Valley, and from Hatton Court's elevated terrace you can see for miles across a patchwork of open fields and woodlands to the far horizon.

Thoughtfully extended from the original 17th-century manor house, the hotel is both relaxed and unassuming. Personal touches in the bedrooms include fresh fruit, cuddly toys and a resident rubber duck in the bathroom. Several of the superior and executive rooms feature four-posters and jacuzzis. Guests can drink in the view as well as enjoy traditional English and classic French cuisine in Carringtons Restaurant, and to work off the pounds, there is a small Health Suite with sauna, whirlpool spa and mini-gym.

Hatton Court is well-placed for sightseeing outings to the nearby cathedral city of Gloucester and its award-winning dockside development, or Bath and Stratford-upon-Avon further afield. The hotel's helpful staff can also arrange activities ranging from fishing, golf and squash to dry slope skiing and clay pigeon shooting. Walking the hills behind the hotel is often as far as you need to go!

LOCATION

Exit M4 at junction 13 and follow A419 and A46 towards Cheltenham. At Painswick take the B4073 to Upton St Leonards. The hotel is 4 miles along on the left hand side

Upton Hill, Upton St Leonards, Gloucestershire GL4 8DE

Telephone 01452 617412
Fax 01452 612945

E-mail: *hattoncourt@bestloved.com*

DIRECTOR

Russell Pendregaust

ROOM RATES

Single occupancy £85 - £131
31 Doubles/Twins £105 - £116
14 Jacuzzi rooms £115 - £151
Includes full breakfast, newspaper and VAT

CHARGE/CREDIT CARDS

• DC • JCB • MC • VI

RATINGS & AWARDS

E.T.C. ★★★ Silver Award
A.A. ★★★ 69%
Investors in People

FACILITIES

On site: *Garden, croquet, health & beauty*
Licensed for weddings
6 meeting rooms/max 60 people
Nearby: *Golf, riding, laser shooting, dry skiing, swimming, bowling*

RESTRICTIONS

No facilities for disabled guests

ATTRACTIONS

Gloucester Docks, Sudeley Castle, Cheltenham, The Cotswolds, Slimbridge Wildfowl Trust, Stratford-upon-Avon

AFFILIATIONS

Hatton Hotels

NEAREST

MAJOR CITY:
Gloucester - 4 miles/10 mins

MAJOR AIRPORT:
Birmingham International - 63 miles/1 hr

RAILWAY STATION:
Gloucester - 4 miles/10 mins

RESERVATIONS

Direct with hotel
Quote **Best Loved**

ACCESS CODES

AMADEUS HK GLOHAC
APOLLO/GALILEO HT 14847
SABRE/ABACUS HK 30137
WORLDSPAN HK HATTO

• Map p.500 ref: H3

“ Our 27th favourite hotel in the world ”

The Times, London

THE HOSTE ARMS

17th century manor house

*The Green,
Burnham Market,
Norfolk PE31 8HD*

*Telephone 01328 738777
Fax 01328 730103*

E-mail: *hostearms@bestloved.com*

OWNER
Paul Whittome

GENERAL MANAGER
Emma Tagg

ROOM RATES

3 Singles	*£64 - £122*
13 Doubles/Twins	*£86 - £160*
4 Four-posters	*£102 - £140*

Includes full breakfast and VAT

CHARGE/CREDIT CARDS
MC • VI

RATINGS & AWARDS
E.T.C. ★★ Silver Award
A.A. ★★ ❀❀ 71%

FACILITIES
On site: *Garden*
3 meeting rooms/max 80 people
Nearby: *Golf, yachting, tennis, fitness centre, hunting/shooting, riding*

RESTRICTIONS
None

ATTRACTIONS
Caithness Crystal, Holkham Hall, Sealife Centre, Pensthorpe Waterfowl Park, Sandringham, Norfolk Broads

AFFILIATIONS
The Great Inns of Britain

NEAREST
MAJOR CITY:
Norwich - 35 miles/45 mins

MAJOR AIRPORT:
Norwich - 35 miles/45 mins
Stansted - 75 miles/1½ hrs

RAILWAY STATION:
Kings Lynn - 22 miles/35 mins

RESERVATIONS
Direct with hotel
Quote ***Best Loved***

ACCESS CODES
Not applicable

MIDSHIRES

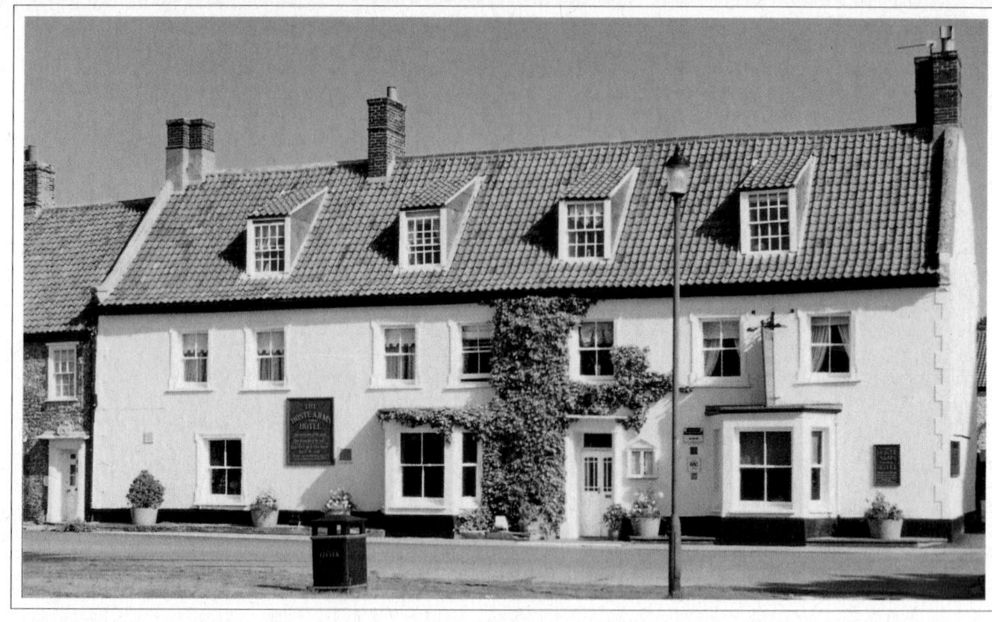

Good food, drink, music and art in one of England's most beautiful villages

Since the railways abandoned North Norfolk, its treasures (of which there are many) and its character happily co-exist in unhurried peace. For example, of all Britain's villages, Burnham Market is arguably the most beautiful. It was built in an area now designated as of Outstanding Natural Beauty containing a fascinating coastline of reed-beds, marshes and sand-duned beaches, nature reserves full of wildlife, historic houses, ancient churches, working windmills and craft centres.

In the centre of Burnham Market, known also for its variety of shops, is the Hoste Arms, whose colourful history pre-dates the village. Once frequented by Lord Nelson, the inn now thrives on its restoration by Paul Whittome, who clearly adores the place, and the regulars who come as much for the company as for a jug of their preference. But its renaissance is also due to a well-established reputation for good food; the menu revels in temptation with more than a teasing influence from the Orient. Wonderful!

The bedrooms are pretty, well-appointed, full of character and as comfortable as you could wish.

“My aim has been to develop the Hoste to the most popular inn in England combining my love of people, food, drink, music and art”, says Paul. What a success he has made of it!

LOCATION

Located approximately 2 miles from the A149 between Brancaster and Wells-next-the-Sea.

"The guide didn't do it justice! Perfection"

Mr & Mrs Taylor, Pennsylvania

• *Map p.500*
ref: D6

Regency town house

HOTEL ON THE PARK

Regency elegance in the centre for the Cotswolds

This beautifully restored Regency building is the finest town house hotel in the Cheltenham area and is perfectly located for touring the Cotswolds and surrounding towns of interest such as Stratford-upon-Avon and Bath. It is in a superb position overlooking Pittville Park yet only a short walk from the town centre and the National Hunt Racecourse.

This exclusive privately-owned hotel offers the discerning traveller unparalleled comfort and luxury with friendly and courteous staff to assist with every need. The bedrooms are individually designed and dressed with traditional fabrics, crisp Egyptian cotton sheets, fine antiques and porcelain with original paintings adorning the walls.

All rooms feature en suite bathrooms, some with ball and claw baths. Facilities include complimentary hot and cold drinks. There is an elegant, candlelit drawing room and bar or an intimate library with crackling log fire to read and relax in. The hotel is privileged to have as its restaurant, The Bacchanalian, with food prepared by Simon Hulstone, whose modern British food reveals its European influences.

LOCATION

In the Regency spa town of Cheltenham. Take A435 signposted Evesham from town centre. Hotel on left opposite Pittville Park.

Evesham Road, Cheltenham, Gloucestershire GL52 2AH

Telephone 01242 518898
Fax 01242 511526

E-mail: *onthepark@bestloved.com*

OWNER
Darryl Gregory

ROOM RATES

Single occupancy	*£77 - £140*
10 Doubles/Twins	*£98 - £118*
1 Junior suite	*£128*
1 Four-poster	*£158*

Includes VAT

CHARGE/CREDIT CARDS

• *DC* • *MC* • *VI*

RATINGS & AWARDS
E.T.C. ★★★ *Gold Award*
R.A.C. ★★★ *Blue Ribbon Dining Award 3*
A.A. ★★★ ❀❀

FACILITIES
On site: *Garden, 'The Bacchanalian' Restaurant, 1 meeting room/max 18 people*
Nearby: *Golf, riding, fishing*

RESTRICTIONS
No children under 8 years
No facilities for disabled guests
No pets

ATTRACTIONS
The Cotswolds, Pittville Pump Room, Gustav Holst birthplace, Sudeley Castle, Cheltenham Races

AFFILIATIONS
Fine Individual Hotels

NEAREST
MAJOR CITY:
Birmingham - 49 miles/1 hr

MAJOR AIRPORT:
Birmingham - 49 miles/1 hr

RAILWAY STATION:
Cheltenham - 2 miles/10 mins

RESERVATIONS
Toll free in US: 800-544-9993
Toll free fax UK: 0800 7311053
Quote ***Best Loved***

ACCESS CODES
Not applicable

“ The fare is more than fair at this Inn ”

Paddy Burt, Daily Telegraph

KINGS HEAD

15th century inn

The Green, Bledington, Oxfordshire OX7 6XQ

Telephone 01608 658365
Fax 01608 658902

E-mail: *kingshead@bestloved.com*

OWNERS

Archie and Nicola Orr-Ewing

ROOM RATES

Single occupancy	*£45*
11 Doubles/Twins	*£65 - £75*
1 Four-poster	*£90*

Includes VAT

CHARGE/CREDIT CARDS

• *MC* • *VI*

RATINGS & AWARDS

E.T.C. ◆◆◆◆
A.A. ◆◆◆◆

FACILITIES

On site: *Garden*
Nearby: *Golf, riding, fishing, archery, tennis, hunting/shooting, quad biking*

RESTRICTIONS

No facilities for disabled guests
, No smoking in bedrooms
No pets

ATTRACTIONS

Blenheim Palace, Oxford, Stratford-upon-Avon, Bath, Warwick Castle, Cotswold villages

AFFILIATIONS

Independent

NEAREST

MAJOR CITY:
Oxford - 25 miles/30 mins

MAJOR AIRPORT:
Birmingham - 40 miles/50 mins
London Heathrow - 60 miles/1½ hrs

RAILWAY STATION:
Kingham - ½ mile/5 mins

RESERVATIONS

Direct with hotel
Quote ***Best Loved***

ACCESS CODES

Not applicable

Where history comes hot buttered

This quintessentially 15th century inn was last year's runner up in the Sunday Times 'Pub of the Year' competition. The family inn occupies an idyllic setting on the village green and the small brook running through it is home to a friendly gaggle of ducks, which are never very far away. The King's Head has always been a hostelry. Prince Rupert of the Rhine, leader of the Cavaliers, lodged here before the battle of Stow in 1642. Much of the medieval character remains today: exposed stone walls, original beams, and inglenook fireplace with trestles and pews.

There is a residents' lounge and a private sun patio. The bedrooms are furnished to a very high standard with full modern facilities and thoughtful personal extras. The inn has earned a high reputation and many recent awards for its fine cuisine. Everything is prepared in house and to order, using fresh local produce.

In summer, visiting Morris dancers and musicians perform the well-known 'Bledington Dances' in the Inn courtyard. The traditional Cotswold game of 'Aunt Sally' is played in the Inn's rear garden. Bledington consecutively won the Bledisloe cup for best kept village. It is in the heart of the Cotswolds, within easy reach of Stratford upon Avon, Oxford, Blenheim Palace and Warwick. Rarely is English history served up with such relish.

LOCATION

On B4450, 6 miles from Stow-on-the-Wold. From M40 Exit 8 take A40 west and A424. From M5 Exit 11 take A40 east and A429.

"Once in a blue moon it is still possible to come across a country house that makes one want to jump for joy"

Craig Brown, Sunday Times

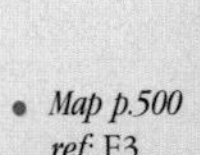

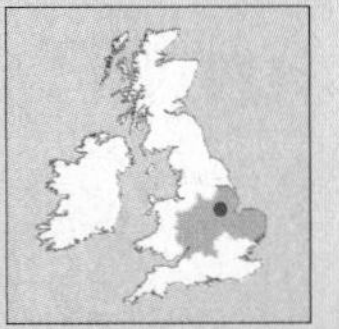

• Map p.500 ref: F3

George IV mansion

LANGAR HALL

A house of special charm in the beautiful Vale of Belvoir

Langar Hall was built in 1837 on the site of a great historic house, the home of Admiral Lord Howe. It stands in quiet seclusion overlooking lovely gardens beyond which sheep graze among the ancient trees in the park. Below the croquet lawn, lies a romantic network of medieval fishponds stocked with carp.

This charming hotel is the family home of Imogen Skirving, who combines the standards of good hotel keeping with the hospitality of an informal country house where children are welcome. Most of the bedrooms enjoy lovely views and every one is quiet, comfortable and well-equipped particularly for guests who have business in Nottingham.

Downstairs, you will find the study, a quiet room for reading and meetings, the white sitting room, for afternoon tea and drinks before dinner, the Indian room, ideal for private parties and conferences and the dining room. This elegant pillared hall is open every day for lunch and dinner, a popular neighbourhood restaurant serving fresh seasonal food with an emphasis on game in winter and fish in summer.

We can recommend Langar Hall as being particularly suited to exclusive house parties.

LOCATION

Langar is on A52 between Nottingham and Grantham - turn at Bingham. Between Newark and Leicester on A46 - drive through Cropwell Bishop. Both roads are sign-posted.

Langar,
Nottinghamshire NG13 9HG

Telephone 01949 860559
Fax 01949 861045

E-mail: *langar@bestloved.com*

OWNER

Imogen Skirving

ROOM RATES

Single occupancy	*£65 - £98*
8 Doubles/Twins	*£100 - £130*
1 Four-poster	*£150 - £175*
1 Suite	*£175*

Includes full breakfast and VAT

CHARGE/CREDIT CARDS

• DC • MC • VI

RATINGS & AWARDS

E.T.C. ★★★ Silver Award
A.A. ★★ ❀ 70%

FACILITIES

On site: *Garden, children's adventure play area, croquet, coarse fishing, heli-pad*
Licensed for weddings
2 meeting rooms/max 20 people
Nearby: *Golf, riding, fitness, fishing, hunting/shooting, parachuting/parascending/hang-gliding*

RESTRICTIONS

No facilities for disabled guests
Pets by arrangement

ATTRACTIONS

Newark antique fairs, Trent Bridge cricket, Nottingham Forest football, Belvoir Castle, Chatsworth House, Southwell and Lincoln Cathedrals, Sherwood Forest, Hardwick Hall, Belton House

AFFILIATIONS

Independent

NEAREST

MAJOR CITY:
Nottingham - 12 miles/20 mins
MAJOR AIRPORT:
East Midlands - 20 miles/30 mins
RAILWAY STATION:
Grantham/Bingham - 4 miles/15 mins

RESERVATIONS

Direct with hotel
Quote ***Best Loved***

ACCESS CODES

Not applicable

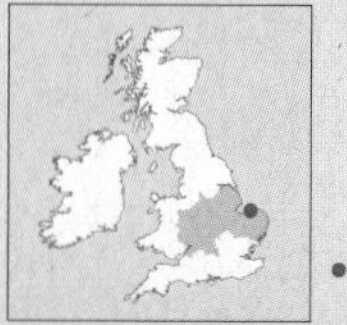

• Map p.500 ref: H3

" The welcome is warm and genuine; the staff friendly and helpful; and the food is excellent. What more could you want? "

Brenda and Kevin Davis, Norfolk & Suffolk Life

THE LIFEBOAT INN

16th century inn

Ship Lane, Thornham, Norfolk PE36 6LT

Telephone 01485 512236
Fax 01485 512323

E-mail: *lifeboat@bestloved.com*

OWNERS

Charles and Angie Coker

GENERAL MANAGER

Julia Galligan

ROOM RATES

Single occupancy	*£40 - £60*
13 Doubles/Twins	*£68 - £86*

Includes VAT

CHARGE/CREDIT CARDS

• *MC* • *VI*

RATINGS & AWARDS

E.T.C. ★★

A.A. ★★ ❀ 67%

FACILITIES

On site: *Patio garden, children's area, ancient game of penny in the hole 2 meeting rooms/max 60 people*

Nearby: *Golf, fishing, water skiing, yachting, tennis, fitness centre, riding, hunting/shooting*

RESTRICTIONS

Limited facilities for disabled guests
No smoking in bedrooms

ATTRACTIONS

Sandringham House, Burnham Thorpe, Holkham Hall, Blakeney Point, Titchwell Marsh Nature Reserve, Thursford Steam Museum, golf courses

AFFILIATIONS

Independent

NEAREST

MAJOR CITY:
Norwich - 40 miles/1 hr

MAJOR AIRPORT:
Norwich - 40 miles/1 hr
Stansted - 65 miles/1½ hrs

RAILWAY STATION:
Kings Lynn - 20 miles/30 mins

RESERVATIONS

Direct with hotel
Quote ***Best Loved***

ACCESS CODES

Not applicable

Wonderful seafood in the haunt of smugglers near Royal Sandringham

If you have not yet fallen for the lure of North Norfolk, now's the time to make amends. The seafood here is not only different but a delight and the crustacea are sensational. The game that thrives off the marshes has a richness fit for royalty (this is Sandringham country). And, of course, Norfolk is the nation's kitchen garden.

Hooked? Well, if you are, you will need to find a place to stay. Somewhere inexpensive, plenty of character, comfortable and, most important, knows what Norfolk cooking is all about. May we suggest The Lifeboat Inn. It packs in the locals on a Saturday night; many for the company, some for a drink but most for the pleasure of sampling the latest catch. It's worth making the pilgrimage for the famed Lifeboat mussels alone!

The Inn looks out to sea hunched against the gales of winter or pretty as a picture peeping through the softly-singing reeds in summer. Either way, its inner warmth is deeply satisfying. The ancient game of Pennies is still played here and the smugglers of old who once made this their haven seem, in spirit, loath to depart!

All the bedrooms are en suite and pleasantly furnished with modern comforts. Most look over Thornham Harbour and out to sea. A great big breakfast that will start your day spent walking the dunes, playing golf or discovering the hidden pleasures of another England! Not to be missed.

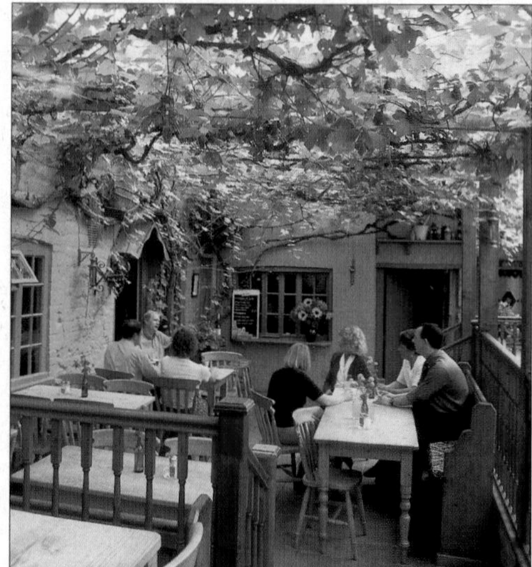

LOCATION

Follow the A149 coast road from Kings Lynn towards Thornham. Take the first left after the sign for Thornham and the hotel is on the right.

"A veritable haven of peace and tranquillity"

Anthony Donaldson, London

• Map p.500
ref: D6

17th century manor

LORDS OF THE MANOR

Paradise found in the heart of The Cotswolds

The Lords of the Manor is a 17th Century country house hotel in the heart of the Cotswolds. Built in 1650, this former rectory stands in eight acres of secluded gardens and parkland in Upper Slaughter, one of the Cotswolds' prettiest and most unspoilt villages.

Comfortable surroundings and big roaring fires, beautifully tended well-loved gardens and croquet on the lawn create an idyllic setting.

The award-winning restaurant at the Lords of the Manor has a fine reputation for modern English cooking and uses only the best local produce. The rambling cellar produces a wine list to complement even the most diverse palate. All the bedrooms are furnished with period pieces giving each room its individual character.

For leisure activities, guests can enjoy a game of croquet or coarse fishing on the lake. Riding, golf, game and clay pigeon shooting can be arranged locally.

The Lords of the Manor is ideally situated to explore many of the honey-stoned villages which have made the Cotswolds an ideal area for a truly memorable stay.

LOCATION

2 miles off the A429 between Stow-on-the-Wold and Bourton-on-the-Water. Signed to 'The Slaughters'.

Upper Slaughter, Near Bourton-on-the-Water, Gloucestershire GL54 2JD

Telephone 01451 820243
Fax 01451 820696

E-mail: *lords@bestloved.com*

GENERAL MANAGER

Iain Shelton

ROOM RATES

2 Singles	*£99*
16 Doubles/Twins	*£149 - £189*
6 Old Rectory rooms	*£229 - £299*
3 Suites	*£259 - £299*

Includes full breakfast and VAT

CHARGE/CREDIT CARDS

• *DC* • *JCB* • *MC* • *VI*

RATINGS & AWARDS

E.T.C. ★★★ Gold Award
R.A.C. Gold Ribbon ★★★ Dining Award 4
A.A. ★★★ ❀❀❀❀

FACILITIES

On site: *Croquet, gardens, fishing*
Licensed for weddings
1 meeting room/max 20 people
Nearby: *Clay pigeon shooting, archery, golf, riding, fishing, quad-biking*

RESTRICTIONS

No facilities for disabled guests
No pets

ATTRACTIONS

The Cotswolds, Blenheim Palace, Oxford, Stratford-upon-Avon, Sudeley Castle, Hidcote Gardens

AFFILIATIONS

The Celebrated Hotels Collection
Small Luxury Hotels

NEAREST

MAJOR CITY:
Oxford - 35 miles/40 mins
MAJOR AIRPORT:
London Heathrow - 80 miles/1¾ hrs
Birmingham - 45 miles/1¼ hrs
RAILWAY STATION:
Moreton-in-Marsh - 8 miles/20 mins

RESERVATIONS

Toll free in US: 800-322-2403
or 800-872-4564
Quote ***Best Loved***

ACCESS CODES

AMADEUS LX BRSLOM
APOLLO/GALILEO LX 32333
SABRE/ABACUS LX 31994
WORLDSPAN LX GLOLM

"A symphony of comfort and a vacation for the senses! Lower Slaughter Manor is our family's little slice of heaven"

Ron F Docksai, West Virginia

• Map p.500 ref: D6

17th century manor

LOWER SLAUGHTER MANOR

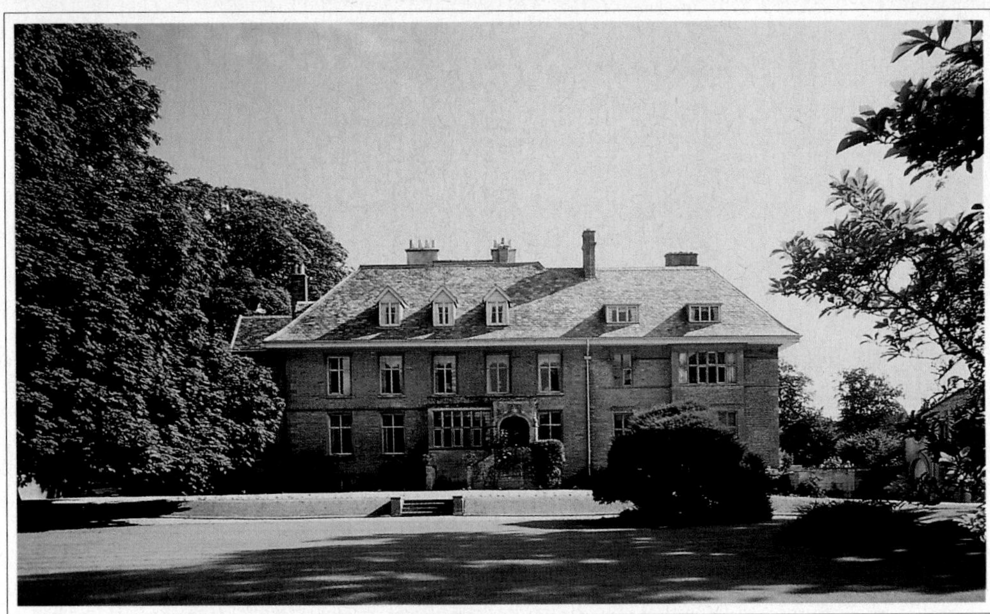

A grand old English country home where food is taken very seriously

Off the beaten track in the heart of the Cotswolds runs the River Eye under small stone bridges and between honey coloured houses. A tiny part of England that the rapacious path of progress seems to have left alone. In this Elysian scene, stands Lower Slaughter Manor. It was built in 1658 by Valentine Strong for the High Sheriff of Gloucestershire, in whose family it remained for the next 300 years.

Lower Slaughter Manor is a true country house hotel with a wonderful feeling of spaciousness, style and dignity where the experienced staff tend the needs of visitors in the good old fashioned manner. The family home atmosphere persists in a warm and welcoming fashion as in days gone by.

The Manor is furnished with antiques and four-poster beds that blend happily with elegant china, beautiful paintings and sumptuous soft furnishings. Every bedroom has its own personality with home-made biscuits and English toffees to welcome you.

All this is a good enough reason to enjoy this home-from-home but there is a much more compelling purpose to this grand old Manor: the food - above all, the food! The restaurant has delighted the critics leaving them bereft of superlatives.

LOCATION

From traffic lights on A424 (Burford to Stow-on-the-Wold) take A429 towards Cirencester. After 1½ miles turn right at signpost for 'The Slaughters'. After two bends, hotel is on right.

Lower Slaughter, Gloucestershire GL54 2HP

Telephone 01451 820456
Fax 01451 822150

E-mail: slaughter@bestloved.com

OWNERS
Roy and Daphne Vaughan

GENERAL MANAGER
Robert Tether

ROOM RATES

Single occupancy	£150 - £325
11 Doubles/Twins	£175 - £325
2 Four-posters	£325
3 Suites	£325 - £375

Includes early morning tea, full breakfast and VAT

CHARGE/CREDIT CARDS

• DC • MC • VI

RATINGS & AWARDS
E.T.C. ★★★ Gold Award
R.A.C. Gold Ribbon ★★★ Dining Award 3
A.A. ★★★ ❀❀❀
Recommended Hotel & Restaurant - Andrew Harper's Hideaway Report

FACILITIES
On site: Garden, croquet, tennis, indoor pool, heli-pad
2 meeting rooms/max 40 people
Nearby: Golf, fishing, riding, clay pigeon shooting

RESTRICTIONS
No facilities for disabled guests
No children under 12 years
No pets

ATTRACTIONS
The Cotswolds, Bath, Oxford, Stratford-upon-Avon, Blenheim Palace

AFFILIATIONS
The Celebrated Hotels Collection

NEAREST
MAJOR CITY:
Cheltenham - 18 miles/30 mins
MAJOR AIRPORT:
London Heathrow - 80 miles/1¾ hrs
RAILWAY STATION:
Kingham - 4 miles/10 mins

RESERVATIONS
Toll free in US: 800-322-2403
Quote **Best Loved**

ACCESS CODES
Not applicable

MIDSHIRES

• Map p.500
ref: D5

"The hay is so good and everything so neat, and the dogs so fat!"

The fifth Viscount Torrington, The Torrington Diaries

THE LYGON ARMS

16th century coaching inn

High Street, Broadway, Worcestershire WR12 7DU

Telephone 01386 852255
Fax 01386 858611

E-mail: lygon@bestloved.com

GENERAL MANAGER

Barry Hancox

ROOM RATES

2 Singles	£115
52 Doubles/Twins	£155 - £285
6 Four-posters	£285 - £325
5 Suites	£325 - £510

Includes newspaper, continental breakfast and VAT

CHARGE/CREDIT CARDS

 • DC • JCB • MC • VI

RATINGS & AWARDS

E.T.C. ★★★★ Gold Award
R.A.C. Blue Ribbon ★★★★ Dining Award 4
A.A. ★★★★ ❀❀

FACILITIES

On site: *Garden, croquet, outdoor tennis, gym, indoor pool, health & beauty, sauna, solarium, jacuzzi, billiards, heli-pad*
Licensed for weddings
5 meeting rooms/max 100 people
Nearby: *Hot air ballooning, golf, riding, clay pigeon shooting, archery*

RESTRICTIONS

No children under 8 years in dining room for dinner

ATTRACTIONS

Stratford-upon-Avon, Oxford, Blenheim Palace, Warwick Castle, Hidcote Gardens, the Cotswolds

AFFILIATIONS

The Savoy Group

NEAREST

MAJOR CITY:
Birmingham - 35 miles/45 mins
MAJOR AIRPORT:
London Heathrow - 90 miles/1¼ hrs
Birmingham - 40 miles/45 mins
RAILWAY STATION:
Moreton-in-Marsh - 8 miles/12 mins

RESERVATIONS

Toll free in US: 800-637-2869
Quote **Best Loved**

ACCESS CODES

AMADEUS VY BHXLYG
APOLLO/GALILEO VY 18902
SABRE/ABACUS VY 48744
WORLDSPAN VY LYG

MIDSHIRES

A 16th century coaching inn of quite stunning proportions

The Lygon Arms has been welcoming visitors for over 450 years, listing both Charles I and Oliver Cromwell amongst its guests. Centrepiece of picturesque Broadway, in the heart of the Cotswolds, the Inn is filled with fresh flowers, antiques, country furnishings and roaring log fires.

The bedrooms range from magnificent four-posters to award-winning contemporary rooms, decorated in country house style. Guests can choose to dine in the Great Hall, with its heraldic friezes and minstrels' gallery, or in summer al fresco on The Patio. Each offers traditional English dishes with innovative touches, whilst Olivers Brasserie provides a less formal alternative.

The Inn is also the perfect setting for small conferences and top-level board meetings, being located just two hours from London and 45 minutes from Birmingham Airport. The five meeting rooms, accommodating up to 80 delegates, include fully air-conditioned rooms, with the very latest AV technology including video-conference capability.

You can enjoy the adjoining Spa with its galleried pool, spa bath, sauna, solaria, steam room, beauty treatment rooms and billiards room, or stroll in the delightful garden with its all-weather tennis court and heli-pad.

Further afield are Stratford-upon-Avon, Warwick and a cornucopia of enchanting mellow-stone villages. Outings and activities can be arranged from riding and hot-air ballooning, to Shakespeare at Stratford and visits to private houses and gardens.

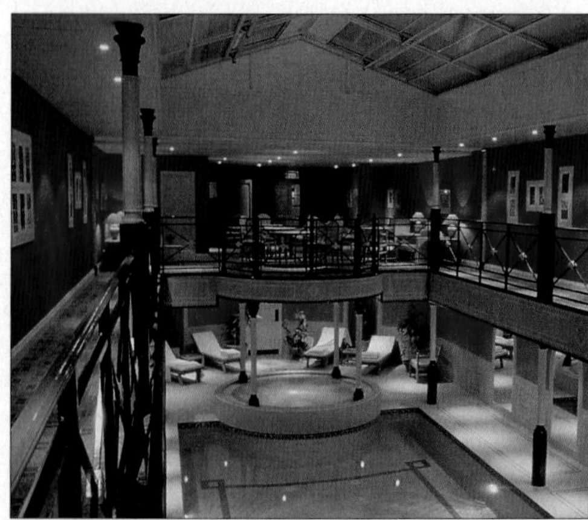

LOCATION

Take Exit 8 off the M40 from London. Broadway is off the A44 and The Lygon Arms is in the centre of the village.

"Full of ambience, full of charm, full of lovely food - full of regrets at leaving"

Mr & Mrs B, Ashby de la Zouch

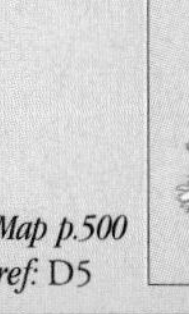

• Map p.500 ref: D5

16th century malting house

THE MALT HOUSE

Enjoy good food and feel like part of the family at this Cotswolds home

Broad Campden is one of the many tiny honey-coloured villages in the picture postcard area of the Cotswolds.Within the village is a small, charming hotel, formally a malt house from which it takes its name, owned by the Brown family. As you enter the house, you are struck by the relaxed, easy going atmosphere the Brown's have achieved due entirely to their gift for making friends with their guests. It is a most comfortable environment; sitting rooms have blazing open fires and are furnished with antiques softened by beautiful fresh flowers.

The large comfortable bedrooms, most with views overlooking the gardens, are tastefully furnished and have modern bathrooms.

Their son, Julian, oversees the kitchen and open-beamed, well-appointed dining room, producing award-winning cooking enhanced by produce grown in their own kitchen garden. What better way to enjoy an evening than sitting down to a fine supper ending with coffee and after dinner drinks in the lounge. Working up the appetite is no problem with so much to do in the Cotswolds.

LOCATION

In the village of Broad Campden off the B4081 just one mile west of Chipping Campden.

Broad Campden, Gloucestershire GL55 6UU

Telephone 01386 840295
Fax 01386 841334

E-mail: *malt@bestloved.com*

OWNERS

Nick and Jean Brown

ROOM RATES

6 Doubles/Twins	£90 - £105
1 Four-poster	£90 - £105
1 Suite	£107 - £150

Includes full breakfast and VAT

CHARGE/CREDIT CARDS

• DC • JCB • MC • VI

RATINGS & AWARDS

Independent

FACILITIES

On site: *Garden, croquet*
Nearby: *Golf, riding, fishing*

RESTRICTIONS

No facilities for disabled guests

ATTRACTIONS

Stratford-upon-Avon, Cotswold villages, Warwick Castle, Chipping Campden, Cheltenham Races, Oxford, Bath

AFFILIATIONS

Independent

NEAREST

MAJOR CITY:
Oxford - 35 miles/1¼ hrs

MAJOR AIRPORT:
Birmingham - 32 miles/1 hr

RAILWAY STATION:
Moreton-in-Marsh - 6 miles/15 mins

RESERVATIONS

Direct with hotel
Quote ***Best Loved***

ACCESS CODES

Not applicable

For information about hotel affiliations see page 14

• Map p.500 ref: D5

"We can pay for accommodation anywhere, but it is not possible to buy the care you have shown us while we have been here"

Dr J Coates, Cumbria

THE MILL AT HARVINGTON

18th century mill

Anchor Lane, Harvington, Evesham, Worcestershire WR11 5NR

Telephone 01386 870688
Fax 01386 870688

E-mail: millharv@bestloved.com

OWNERS

Simon and Jane Greenhalgh

ROOM RATES

Single occupancy	£63 - £85
21 Doubles/Twins	£86 - £121

Includes full breakfast and VAT

CHARGE/CREDIT CARDS

• JCB • MC • VI

RATINGS & AWARDS

E.T.C. ★★★ Silver Award
R.A.C. Blue Ribbon ★★ Dining Award 2
A.A. ★★ ❀❀ 80%

FACILITIES

On site: Garden, croquet, tennis, outdoor pool, fishing
1 meeting room/max 40 people
Nearby: Golf, riding

RESTRICTIONS

No children under 10 years
No facilities for disabled guests
No pets, guide dogs only

ATTRACTIONS

Stratford, The Cotswolds, Warwick Castle, Ragley Hall, Sudeley Castle, The Malverns

AFFILIATIONS

Independent

NEAREST

MAJOR CITY:
Birmingham - 30 miles/50 mins

MAJOR AIRPORT:
Birmingham - 32 miles/40 mins

RAILWAY STATION:
Evesham - 4 miles/5 mins

RESERVATIONS

Direct with hotel
Quote **Best Loved**

ACCESS CODES

Not applicable

MIDSHIRES

Delights aplenty twixt Stratford and Broadway

The village of Harvington in the Vale of Evesham is recorded in the Domesday Book. The Mill, the old Bakery and the Georgian house beside it have served the village since before 1750 and are now sensitively converted into a delightful hotel and an excellent restaurant.

The 21 comfortable bedrooms, some separate from the main house, face the morning sun and overlook the garden and river. Each has en suite bathroom, colour TV, radio, tea and coffee-making facilities and telephone.

Menus are changed frequently to take advantage of the freshest foods available through the seasons. Full use is made of local Evesham produce; fruit, vegetables, meat, fish and game with fresh herbs from the hotel garden.

The hotel is set in eight acres of wooded parkland with splendid willows shading its 600 feet of River Avon frontage. Fishing is available directly from the grounds. Heron stalk the shallows of the weir. There is a hard tennis court and a heated outdoor swimming pool.

Harvington is an ideal holiday centre for Shakespeare's England. Stratford-upon-Avon is only ten miles away. For history lovers there are the medieval castles of Warwick, Kenilworth, Berkeley and Sudeley. There are stone-age burial mounds, Roman villas, Saxon villages, palaces, churches and cathedrals in plenty!

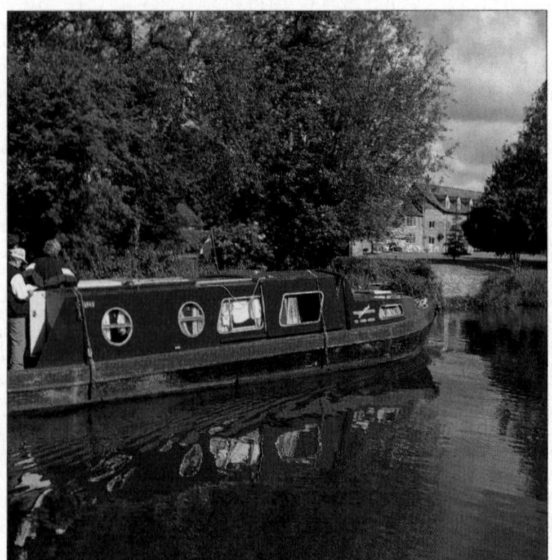

LOCATION

Exit 15/M40. Follow A46 towards Evesham. Exit 7/M5. Follow A44 to Evesham. Hotel off A46 & signed between Abbots Salford and Norton.

"One of the most romantic hotels in England"

Jeff Banks, fashion designer & TV presenter

• Map p.500
ref: E5

17th century manor

NAILCOTE HALL

An idyllic country retreat near to Warwick and Stratford-upon-Avon

Nailcote Hall is a charming country house hotel set in 15 acres of gardens and surrounded by Warwickshire countryside. Built around 1640, the house was used by Cromwell during the Civil War and damaged by troops prior to the assault on Kenilworth Castle.

In the intimate Tudor surroundings of the Oak Room restaurant, the chef will delight you with superb cuisine, while the cellar boasts an extensive choice of international wines. Alternatively dine 'under the stars' in Rick's Mediterranean style bistro.

38 en suite bedrooms offer luxury accommodation. Leisure facilities include indoor swimming pool, gymnasium, solarium and steam room. Outdoors, guests can enjoy the all-weather tennis courts, petanque, croquet and the championship nine-hole par three golf course (each year host venue to The British Professional Short Course Championship) - or those nearby at The Belfry, Forest of Arden and The Warwickshire.

Ideally located in the heart of England, Nailcote Hall is within 15 minutes' drive of the castle towns of Kenilworth and Warwick, Coventry Cathedral, Birmingham International Airport and the National Exhibition Centre. Shakespeare's Stratford-upon-Avon is just 20 minutes away.

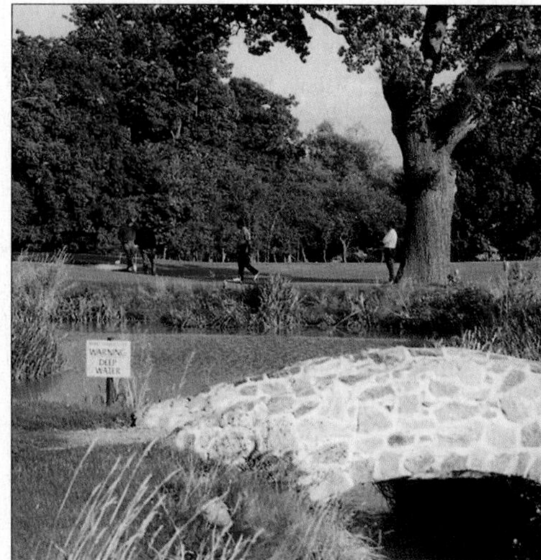

LOCATION

Situated 6 miles south of Birmingham International Airport on the B4101 Balsall Common-Coventry road within 10 minutes of the Midlands motorway network.

Nailcote Lane, Berkswell, Warwickshire CV7 7DE

Telephone 024 7646 6174
Fax 024 7647 0720

E-mail: nailcote@bestloved.com

OWNER

Rick Cressman, Lord of Baswich

ROOM RATES

Single occupancy £145
30 Doubles/Twins £155
3 Four-posters £190
5 Named rooms £190 - £270
Includes full breakfast and VAT

CHARGE/CREDIT CARDS

• *DC* • *MC* • *VI*

RATINGS & AWARDS

E.T.C. ★★★★ Silver Award
R.A.C. ★★★★ Dining Award 3
A.A. ★★★★ ❀❀ 67%

FACILITIES

On site: *Indoor pool, gardens, croquet, tennis, championship 9-hole par 3 golf course, petanque, steam room, beauty salon, solarium, gym, heli-pad*
Licensed for weddings
7 meeting rooms/max 100 people
Nearby: *Golf*

RESTRICTIONS

No pets

ATTRACTIONS

Warwick Castle, Kenilworth Castle, Stratford-upon-Avon, National Exhibition Centre, Coventry Cathedral

AFFILIATIONS

Independent

NEAREST

MAJOR CITY:
Coventry - 4 miles/10 mins

MAJOR AIRPORT:
Birmingham - 6 miles/10 mins

RAILWAY STATION:
Berkswell - 2 miles/5 mins
Birmingham Intl - 6 miles/10 mins

RESERVATIONS

Direct with hotel
Quote ***Best Loved***

ACCESS CODES

Not applicable

For route planning map of the Midshires see page 500

• Map p.500 ref: E6

“ Heaven on earth! We'll be back ”

Susie and Nigel Green, Bradford, West Yorkshire

THE NEW INN AT COLN

16th century inn

Coln-St-Aldwyns,
Near Circencester,
Gloucestershire GL7 5AN

Telephone 01285 750651
Fax 01285 750657

E-mail: newinn@bestloved.com

OWNERS

Brian and Sandra-Anne Evans

ROOM RATES

1 Single	£68 - £70
Single occupancy	£80 - £99
12 Doubles/Twins	£96 - £115
1 Four-poster	£96

Includes full breakfast, newspaper and VAT

CHARGE/CREDIT CARDS

• MC • VI

MIDSHIRES

RATINGS & AWARDS

R.A.C. Blue Ribbon ★★ Dining Award 3
A.A. ★★ ❀❀
A.A. Courtesy & Care Award 1999

FACILITIES

On site: 1 meeting room/max 12 people
Nearby: Golf, riding, fishing, water skiing

RESTRICTIONS

No children under 10 years
No facilities for disabled guests
Pets by arrangement

ATTRACTIONS

Oxford, Bath, Westonbirt Arboretum, Cotswold villages, Barnsley House, Hidcote Gardens, Sudeley & Berkeley Castles

AFFILIATIONS

The Great Inns of Britain
Cotswolds Finest Hotels

NEAREST

MAJOR CITY:
Oxford - 30 miles/40 mins

MAJOR AIRPORT:
London Heathrow - 70 miles/1¼ hrs
Birmingham - 70 miles/1¼ hr

RAILWAY STATION:
Swindon - 18 miles/30 mins

RESERVATIONS

Direct with hotel
Quote **Best Loved**

ACCESS CODES

Not applicable

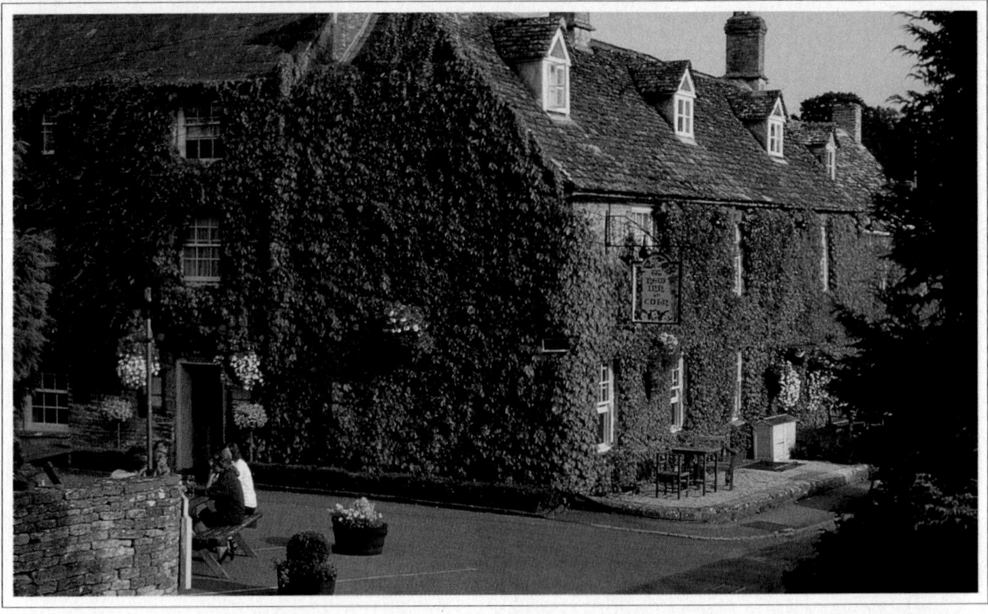

Founded in the reign of Elizabeth I - honoured in the reign of Elizabeth II

The New Inn at Coln was built 400 years ago when Queen Elizabeth I decreed there should be a coaching inn within a day's travel of every major centre of population, for the comfort and security of her subjects. It is still a great place to stay: in 1999 it gained a Courtesy and Care award from the AA. Owners Brian and Sandra-Anne Evans and staff welcome guests as friends, willingly providing any help needed to enjoy the Cotswolds.

Each bedroom is a private castle of comfort, richly adorned with floral prints and English chintz curtains. The renowned restaurant serves food with flair: the emphasis is on local produce and fresh ingredients. Old English recipes, long forgotten are now triumphantly revived. Real ales and fine malt whiskies are there to be savoured beneath the ancient beams in the bar.

Away from the ivy-covered stone walls and the Dovecote, lie some of England's finest attractions. Dreamy cottages and lazy streams are on every Cotswold trail. Oxford's quadrangles, Bath's regal squares and crescents and Cheltenham's racecourse are all within a short drive.

LOCATION

A40 to Burford, take the B4425 towards Bibury, turn left shortly after Aldsworth.

" The whole experience of having dinner in the restaurant was the perfect end to our honeymoon "

Mr & Mrs Schonhut, Question of Service

• Map p.500 ref: E5

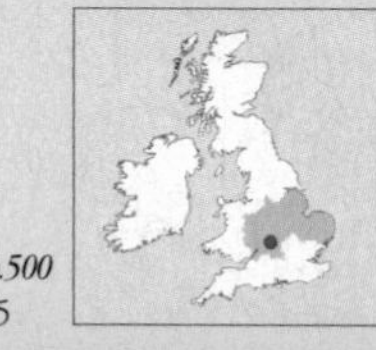

Ancient inn

THE NOEL ARMS HOTEL

An historic inn with an ancient tradition of comfort and good food

The 15th century church of St James in Chipping Campden, like so many across the country, is a treasury of history whose sacred stones bear the names of the good and the great. One of the finer monuments is that of the Noel family whose name is also carved above the door of The Noel Arms in the centre of this ancient market town in the heart of the Cotswolds.

Pass beneath the sign and you tread the footsteps of King Charles II who came here to recover from his defeat by Oliver Cromwell at the Battle of Worcester in 1651. It was a fine old hostelry then, fit for a king no less, and it still is although there have been quite a few reassuring changes consistent with our age.

Despite its size, The Noel Arms has two bars - one for smokers and the other smoke-free except for a resplendent fireplace to warm heart and soul in winter months. The dining room continues a long tradition of excellence with a fine wine list on hand. For those who would settle for a lighter meal at the bar (either of them), the chef obliges with a mouth-watering snack made on the premises to your order. Don't mention fast food!

The quaint bedrooms have every modern comfort particularly appreciated by transatlantic visitors! Definitely a place to write home about.

LOCATION

Chipping Campden is signposted off the A44 Oxford to Evesham road, 5 miles from Broadway. The hotel is in the High Street.

High Street, Chipping Campden, Gloucestershire GL55 6AT

Telephone 01386 840317
Fax 01386 841136

E-mail: *noel@bestloved.com*

GENERAL MANAGER

Ellie Jobson

ROOM RATES

Single occupancy	*£75*
23 Doubles/Twins	*£115*
2 Four-posters	*£125 - £135*

Includes full breakfast and VAT

CHARGE/CREDIT CARDS

• DC • JCB • MC • VI

RATINGS & AWARDS

E.T.C. ★★★

A.A. ★★★ ❀❀ *73%*

FACILITIES

On site: *Licensed for weddings*
2 meeting rooms/max 80 people
Nearby: *Golf, fishing, riding*

RESTRICTIONS

No facilities for disabled guests
Pets by arrangement

ATTRACTIONS

Bourton-on-the-Water, Blenheim Palace, Hidcote Gardens, Kiftsgate Gardens, Warwick Castle, Stratford-upon-Avon, antiques hunting, walking

AFFILIATIONS

Grand Heritage Hotels

NEAREST

MAJOR CITY:
Oxford - 33 miles/45 mins
Cheltenham - 30 miles/40 mins

MAJOR AIRPORT:
London Heathrow - 78 miles/1¾ hrs
Birmingham - 30 miles/30 mins

RAILWAY STATION:
Moreton-in-Marsh - 7 miles/10 mins

RESERVATIONS

Toll free in US: 888-93-GRAND
Quote ***Best Loved***

ACCESS CODES

AMADEUS UI BHXNOE
APOLLO/GALILEO UI 15074
SABRE/ABACUS UI 33097
WORLDSPAN UI 40776

• Map p.500 ref: 14

" Paradise found "

Vogue Magazine

THE NORFOLK MEAD HOTEL

Georgian manor

Coltishall, Norwich, Norfolk NR12 7DN

Telephone 01603 737531
Fax 01603 737521

E-mail: norfolkmead@bestloved.com

OWNERS

Jill and Don Fleming

ROOM RATES

Single occupancy	£65 - £90
7 Doubles/Twins	£70 - £120
1 Four-poster	£120
1 Family room	£95 - £120

Includes full breakfast and VAT

CHARGE/CREDIT CARDS

 • DC • MC • VI

RATINGS & AWARDS

E.T.C. ★★ Silver Award
A.A. ★★ ❀ 77%

FACILITIES

On site: Garden, croquet, outdoor pool, health & beauty, fishing, heli-pad, marina, rowing boat
2 meeting rooms/max 40 people
Nearby: Golf, sea fishing, water skiing, yachting, tennis, fitness centre, hunting/shooting, riding

RESTRICTIONS

No smoking in bedrooms or restaurant
No pets in public rooms

ATTRACTIONS

Sandringham, Blickling Hall, Norwich, Norfolk Broads, North Norfolk coast, nature reserves

AFFILIATIONS

Independent

NEAREST

MAJOR CITY:
Norwich - 7 miles/15 mins

MAJOR AIRPORT:
Stansted - 80 miles/2 hrs
Norwich - 5 miles/15 mins

RAILWAY STATION:
Norwich - 7 miles/15 mins

RESERVATIONS

Direct with hotel
Quote **Best Loved**

ACCESS CODES

Not applicable

MIDSHIRES

As fine a place for rest and relaxation as you will find on the Norfolk Broads

The villages surrounding Norwich are the essence of East Anglian life: Thatched roofs, white-washed characterful pubs, friendly easy-going folk and, as a bonus, the untamed beautiful Norfolk Broads. This is definitely 'R & R country'. An area of great tranquillity and peace where you can cruise along a latticework of rivers or lounge by a pool enjoying a Pimms.

One such place is situated only 15 minutes north of Norwich; The Norfolk Mead Hotel is a real find. The day we arrived, the scene looked like something straight out of a travel programme: boats cruising up the River Bure and a Labrador playing on the sunlit lawn. All very idyllic. On entering this fine Georgian House, lunch was over, clearly an enjoyable affair as contented diners were singing its praises as they took their coffee. Meanwhile, tanning themselves by the pool, were other guests working up an appetite for dinner, occasionally sauntering over to the convivial bar overlooking the walled garden.

Jill and Don Fleming have put a lot of work into the hotel and it shows. The bedrooms are comfortable and tastefully decorated with views of the pool, the garden, and, of course the river.

The Norfolk Mead makes an excellent place to explore the Broads, or to escape from doing business in town. Thoroughly recommended!

LOCATION

From Norwich: take ring road to B1150, head for North Walsham. At Coltishall turn right at petrol station and right again in front of church.

Looking for an hotel with a golf course on site? See our 'Golf Guide' on page 478

" Sheer perfection . . . faultless "

Olwyn and Bill Payne, California

• *Map p.500 ref: D5*

Country house

NUTHURST GRANGE

Unashamed luxury in the very heart of England

A long tree-lined drive takes you to Nuthurst Grange nestling in 7½ acres of gardens and woodlands. The restaurant is the centrepiece of the hotel, providing an intimate and relaxing setting for luncheon or dinner. Chef/Patron David Randolph and his team of chefs have won many ratings & awards for their imaginative menus which feature the freshest seasonal produce. Complemented by a fine wine list, the cuisine embraces the best of modern and classical French/British cooking. The pre-meal canapes, the selection of bread, biscuits and petits fours are all home-made.

All 15 spacious bedrooms are furnished and decorated in soft country house style. Each has superb rural views through traditional leaded windows and private bathrooms with air-spa baths.

The seclusion of the hotel belies its easy accessibility. Just off the Stratford-upon-Avon to Birmingham road, the hotel is within 15 minutes of Birmingham International Airport and the heart of England's motorway network.

LOCATION

M42, Exit 4 and M40 Exit 16.
½ mile south of Hockley Heath on A3400, turning by hotel signboard into Nuthurst Grange Lane.

Nuthurst Grange Lane,
Hockley Heath,
Warwickshire B94 5NL

Telephone 01564 783972
Fax 01564 783919

E-mail: *nuthurst@bestloved.com*

OWNER
David Randolph

MANAGER
Karen Seymour

ROOM RATES

Single occupancy	*£135*
13 Doubles/Twins	*£155 - £170*
1 Four-poster	*£185*
1 Suite	*£185*

Includes full breakfast and VAT

CHARGE/CREDIT CARDS

• DC • MC • VI

RATINGS & AWARDS
E.T.C. ★★★ Gold Award
A.A. ★★★ ❀❀

FACILITIES
On site: *Garden, croquet, heli-pad*
Licensed for weddings
3 meeting rooms/max 150 people
Nearby: *Golf, riding, fishing, tennis, gym, pool*

RESTRICTIONS
Pets by arrangement

ATTRACTIONS
Stratford-upon-Avon, Warwick Castle, Kenilworth Castle, National Exhibition Centre, The Cotswolds

AFFILIATIONS
Independent

NEAREST
MAJOR CITY:
Birmingham - 12 miles/25 mins
MAJOR AIRPORT:
Birmingham - 7 miles/15 mins
RAILWAY STATION:
Birmingham Intl - 7 miles/15 mins

RESERVATIONS
Direct with hotel
*Quote **Best Loved***

ACCESS CODES
AMADEUS HK LGWNUT
APOLLO/GALILEO HT 41205
SABRE/ABACUS HK 34903
WORLDSPAN HK NUTF1

A keen Angler? Refer to page 472 for our Fishing Index

• Map p.500 ref: E6

"Few people have added more to the sum of human happiness in Oxford than hotelier Jeremy Mogford"

The Oxford Times

OLD BANK HOTEL

Georgian banking house

92-94 High Street, Oxford, Oxfordshire OX1 4BN

Telephone 01865 799599
Fax 01865 799598

E-mail: oldbank@bestloved.com

OWNER
Jeremy Mogford

GENERAL MANAGER
Ian Hamilton

ROOM RATES

Single occupancy	£135
40 Doubles/Twins	£155 - £225
2 Luxury rooms	£255
1 Suite	£300

Includes VAT

CHARGE/CREDIT CARDS

• DC • JCB • MC • VI

RATINGS & AWARDS
E.T.C. ★★★★ Gold Award
A.A. ★★★★ ❀ Town House

FACILITIES
On site: *Garden, air conditioned bedrooms, fax/modem links, CD player, private car park*
Nearby: *Golf, tennis, fitness, punting*

RESTRICTIONS
No pets

ATTRACTIONS
Blenheim Palace, Oxford Botanical Gardens, The Cotswolds, Waddesdon, Oxford University Colleges

AFFILIATIONS
Preston's Global Hotels
Design Hotels
The European Connection

NEAREST
MAJOR CITY:
Oxford

MAJOR AIRPORT:
London Heathrow - 50 miles/1 hr
Birmingham - 40 miles/45 mins

RAILWAY STATION:
Oxford - 1 mile/5 mins

RESERVATIONS
Toll free in US: 800-544-9993
Quote **Best Loved**

ACCESS CODES
Not applicable

MIDSHIRES

A sophisticated luxury hotel in Oxford, a landmark for the new millennium

Oxford has had to wait far too long for a deluxe contemporary hotel being, as it is, first stop out of London on the tourist circuit. In November 1999, The Old Bank, a familiar sight amongst the city's landmarks, opened its doors to reveal a metamorphosis as exciting as it is imaginative.

The Georgian facade masks an older building, parts of which are Elizabethan. Having bought the bank premises, it was to French designer Gladys Wagner that Jeremy Mogford, the owner, looked for his interiors. Her smart, clean-cut style is completely in step with the new millennium. The bedrooms look over the famous Oxford sky line of cupolas and spires; muted colours and contrasting textures create a relaxing ambience. Linen bed covers are trimmed with velvet and shantung silk that blend with green, red, blue and beige colour schemes. There are original Stanley Spencer sketches in every bedroom which also have a TV and a CD player as well as UK/US modem links for business travellers!

The Quod Bar & Grill has become the focal point for eating and meeting in Oxford. The decor is sleek (stone floors, zinc-topped bar and leather banquette seating) and there's an Italian accent to the food which, in summer, can be enjoyed on a sunny terrace overlooking the garden. The Old Bank is as cool as they come with a welcome as warm as can be.

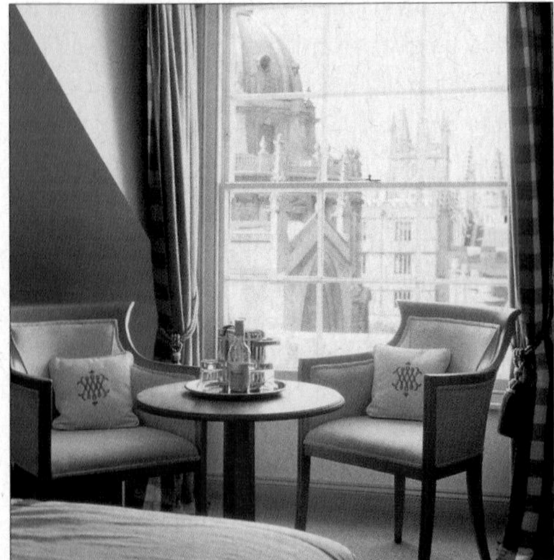

LOCATION

Exit M40 at Exit 8. Aim for the city centre. Cross Magdalen Bridge and turn left after the traffic lights into Merton Street then right into Magpie Lane. Parking is clearly marked.

"My wife and I have spent some of our happiest times, outside our own home, at The Old Parsonage. We feel the Parsonage has been one of our real finds"

James Nelson, Cumbria

• Map p.500 ref: E6

17th century town house

OLD PARSONAGE

The spirit of Oxford in the heart of this famous university city

The Old Parsonage site dates back to 1308. The building is a much-loved Oxford landmark. It played its part in the city's history; as a sanctuary for persecuted clergy in the Middle Ages, as a stronghold for Royalists in the Civil War of the 1640s, and as a home for 19th century literati including Oscar Wilde. The historic character of the building has been preserved. The hotel is small, individually run, with a distinct personality.

Each of the 30 bedrooms is furnished in a style of its own. Many enjoy views over the secluded walled garden or the unique roof garden. Each has a luxurious marble bathroom.

The much praised Parsonage Bar serves as a combined bar and restaurant. Open for breakfast until late, the restaurant has an imaginative menu complemented by a well-researched wine list. The Parsonage Restaurant and Bar has become famous amongst residents and the local Oxford community for a quiet cappuccino, a glass of champagne or sumptuous cream teas. Meals are served on the terrace in fine weather. Gee's Restaurant, housed in a spectacular Victorian conservatory and owned by the hotel, is less than five minutes walk along the Banbury Road. Located between Keble and Somerville Colleges, the hotel is a short walk from Oxford's shops, theatres, museums and art galleries.

LOCATION

Leave northern ring road at roundabout at top of Banbury Road. Follow Banbury Road through Summertown towards city centre. Hotel is on right, next to St Giles Church.

1 Banbury Road, Oxford, Oxfordshire OX2 6NN

Telephone 01865 310210
Fax 01865 311262

E-mail: *oldparsoxon@bestloved.com*

GENERAL MANAGER

Philip Mason-Gordon

ROOM RATES

1 Single	*£130*
25 Doubles/Twins	*£150 - £175*
4 Suites	*£200*

Includes full breakfast and VAT

CHARGE/CREDIT CARDS

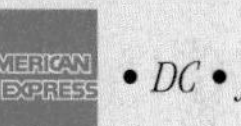

• *DC* • *JCB* • *MC* • *VI*

RATINGS & AWARDS

E.T.C. ★★★ *Silver Award*
A.A. ★★★★ *Town House*

FACILITIES

On site: *Garden, private parking*
Nearby: *Golf, flying, fishing*

RESTRICTIONS

No facilities for disabled guests
No pets

ATTRACTIONS

Oxford University, Ashmolean Museum, Botanical Gardens, Sheldonian Theatre

AFFILIATIONS

The European Connection
Preston's Global Hotels

NEAREST

MAJOR CITY:
London - 53 miles/1 hr

MAJOR AIRPORT:
London Heathrow - 47 miles/1 hr

RAILWAY STATION:
Oxford - 2 miles/5 mins

RESERVATIONS

Toll free in US: 800-544-9993
Quote ***Best Loved***

ACCESS CODES

AMADEUS HK OXFOLD
WORLDSPAN HK OLDPA
SABRE/ABACUS HK 30442
APOLLO/GALILEO HT 14857

• Map p.500 ref: H3

"A unique and restful place – delightful"

D Corbett, Indiana

THE OLD RECTORY

500-year old manor house

**Barsham Road,
Great Snoring, Fakenham,
Norfolk NR21 0HP**

**Telephone 01328 820597
Fax 01328 820048**

E-mail: orectfaken@bestloved.com

OWNER
Rosamund M Scoles

ROOM RATES

Single occupancy	£70 - £79
6 Doubles/Twins	£95 - £101
Sheltons Cottages	£130

Includes early morning tea, full breakfast and VAT

CHARGE/CREDIT CARDS

• JCB • MC • VI

RATINGS & AWARDS
Independent

FACILITIES
On site: *Walled garden, heli-pad*
1 meeting room/max 8 people
Nearby: *Riding, fishing*

RESTRICTIONS
Children by arrangement
No facilities for disabled guests
No pets

ATTRACTIONS
Norfolk Heritage Coast, Sandringham House, Holkham Hall, Norwich, Cambridge

AFFILIATIONS
Independent

NEAREST
MAJOR CITY:
Norwich - 22 miles/30 mins

MAJOR AIRPORT:
London Heathrow - 115 miles/3 hrs
Stansted - 90 miles/2½ hrs

RAILWAY STATION:
King's Lynn - 22 miles/40 mins

RESERVATIONS
Direct with hotel
Quote **Best Loved**

ACCESS CODES
Not applicable

An historic home cradled in the timeless serenity of rural Norfolk

The Old Rectory at Great Snoring, a former manor house, noted for its architectural history, stands in 1½ acres of walled garden and nestles contentedly beside the village church. This secluded haven, which dates from 1500, promises the discerning traveller old fashioned charm with a homely warmth and friendliness.

Relaxed informality is assured, given the size of the 'hotel' – just six bedrooms, each one different from the other as governed by the unique architecture of the house. The dining room has stone mullion windows and heavy oak beams. It is a versatile room where guests enjoy delicious dinners and hearty breakfasts.

For those who relish the idea of independence together with service, 'The Sheltons' provide the answer. These self-contained cottages, serviced on a daily basis, allow the guest complete freedom and flexibility. The Sheltons, named after the family responsible for the manor house, have been sympathetically constructed in the grounds of the house, which with the neighbouring church, provide a majestic back-drop for this unique development.

The Old Rectory is well placed for those visiting this special part of Norfolk.

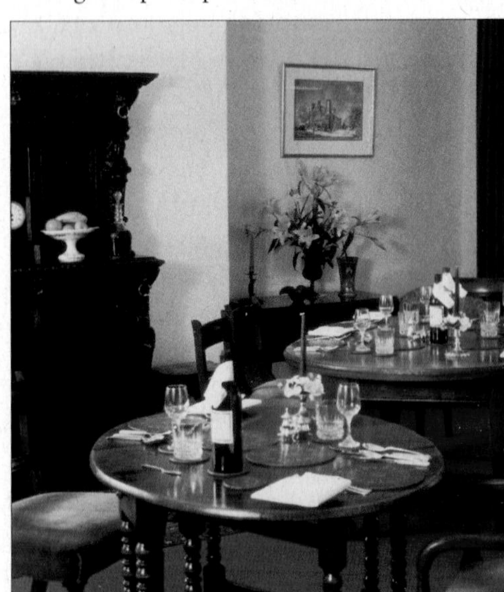

LOCATION

Great Snoring is situated 3 miles north east of Fakenham from the A148. The Old Rectory is behind the church on the road signposted to Barsham from the village street.

“Owlpen is a Gloucestershire Shangri-la where those in the know come year after year for absolute peace and seclusion”

The Sunday Times

• Map p.500 ref: D6

15th century manor

OWLPEN MANOR

Your own historic cottage in one of the most romantic estates in the country

HRH The Prince of Wales described Owlpen as the epitome of the English village. Set in its own peaceful wooded valley, Owlpen is one of the most romantic, historic estates in the country. Its Tudor manor house remains a family home; Queen Margaret, Henry VI's queen, slept in its Great Chamber, during the Wars of the Roses in 1471 and it is famed for its 16th and 17th century formal gardens and the great yew trees. The medieval Cyder House with its huge oak cider press serves as a restaurant and reception area for visitors who stay in the distinctive, historic cottages. The cottages include a medieval barn, a watermill restored in 1464, the 1620 Court House and weavers' and keepers' cottages. Several are listed buildings in their own right.

The cottages are furnished and decorated in the style of an English country house where family possessions have accumulated over the generations. Modern comforts are discreetly and fully provided. The cottages have their own gardens providing a sheltered spot in which to relax and breathe the scents of flowers.

Owlpen is in the Royal Triangle in the heart of the Cotswolds. Limestone villages, prehistoric barrows, quiet lanes and antique shops are all here to be explored. Bath, Cheltenham, Cirencester and Gloucester are all about 20 miles away.

LOCATION

Situated half a mile east of Uley, off the B4066. From the M4 take exit 18 and follow the signs from the A4135.

Owlpen, Near Uley, Gloucestershire GL11 5BZ

Telephone 01453 860261
Fax 01453 860819

E-mail: *owlpen@bestloved.com*

OWNERS

Nicholas and Karin Mander

ROOM RATES

9 Self-catering cottages £40 - £120
Includes VAT

CHARGE/CREDIT CARDS

• DC • MC • VI

RATINGS & AWARDS

E.T.C. 3-4 Stars

FACILITIES

On site: *Garden, fly fishing, heli-pad, shooting*
3 meeting rooms/max 35 people
Nearby: *Golf, riding, gliding*

RESTRICTIONS

No facilities for disabled guests
Pets by arrangement

ATTRACTIONS

Owlpen Manor House, The Cotswolds, Berkeley Castle, Slimbridge Wildfowl Trust, Roman City of Bath, Westonbirt Arboretum

AFFILIATIONS

Independent

NEAREST

MAJOR CITY:
Bath - 25 miles/40 mins

MAJOR AIRPORT:
London Heathrow - 105 miles/2 hrs

RAILWAY STATION:
Stroud - 7 miles/20 mins

RESERVATIONS

Direct with hotel
Quote ***Best Loved***

ACCESS CODES

Not applicable

• Map p.500 ref: D6

"My sister and I had a truly memorable stay. Dinner was sumptous, breakfast a pleasure. In all a wonderful experience . Oh! And the views! And the luxurious accommodation! And the service! And...!" *The Contarino Sisters, USA*

THE PAINSWICK HOTEL

18th century country house

Kemps Lane, Painswick, Gloucestershire GL6 6YB

Telephone 01452 812160
Fax 01452 814059

E-mail: *painswick@bestloved.com*

OWNERS

Gareth and Helen Pugh

ROOM RATES

2 Singles	*£75 - £90*
15 Doubles/Twins	*£120 - £170*
2 Four-posters	*£195*

Includes full breakfast, newspaper and VAT

CHARGE/CREDIT CARDS

 • *JCB • MC • VI*

RATINGS & AWARDS

E.T.C. ★★★ Silver Award
R.A.C. ★★★ Dining Award 3
A.A. ★★★ ❀❀ 78%

FACILITIES

On site: *Garden, croquet*
Licensed for weddings
3 meeting rooms/max 75 people
Nearby: *Golf, riding, gliding, hot air ballooning*

RESTRICTIONS

No facilities for disabled guests

ATTRACTIONS

Sudeley Castle, Berkeley Castle, Bath, Stratford-upon-Avon, Rococco gardens, The Cotswolds

AFFILIATIONS

Preston's Global Hotels
The European Connection

NEAREST

MAJOR CITY:
Gloucester - 5 miles/10 mins

MAJOR AIRPORT:
London Heathrow - 90 miles/1¾ hrs

RAILWAY STATION:
Stroud - 3 miles/5 mins

RESERVATIONS

Toll free in US: 800-544-9993
Quote ***Best Loved***

ACCESS CODES

AMADEUS HK GLOPAI
SABRE/ABACUS HK 50497

"Sheer poetry", said His Majesty. A sentiment as true today as ever it was

"The valleys around Painswick are sheer poetry, in this Paradise" – King Charles I's words. The village comprises medieval cottages lying cheek-by-jowl with the 17th and 18th century merchants' houses and has been accorded the title: The Queen of the Cotswolds. The former rectory, built in 1790 in the Palladian style is today The Painswick Hotel.

The hotel has 19 luxury bedrooms, all with luxury toiletries, baskets of fresh fruit, mineral water, books, magazines and other amenities. The stunning fabrics, soft furnishings, antique furniture, period engravings and objets d'art all contribute to the sense of well-being. In the pine panelled dining room, simply delicious and tempting food is served with an emphasis on seafood, local game and Gloucestershire cheeses.

The public rooms, all with distinct elegance and character, have antique furniture and fine pictures, together with open fires. They express a quiet confidence reflecting the more leisured times in which they were built.

Painswick is a superb touring, sporting and cultural centre. All the pleasures of The Cotswolds, Regency Cheltenham and Bath, Gloucester and Stratford-upon-Avon are within an easy drive.

LOCATION

In the centre of Painswick behind Parish church. 8 miles off M5 Exit 13 take A419 to A46 north. 28 miles off M4 Exit 15 take A419 to A46 north.

For information about hotel affiliations see page 14

"Easy going atmosphere and unpretentious comfort ... great food ... people come again and again"

Alisdair Sawdey, Alisdair Sawdey Publishing

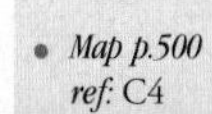

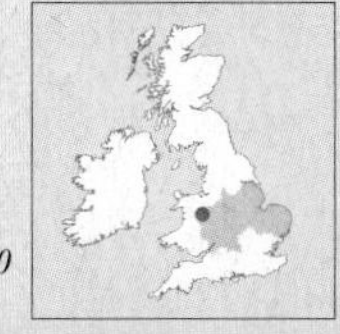

Georgian rectory

PEN-Y-DYFFRYN COUNTRY HOTEL

A spectacular setting at this idyllic retreat near Chester

Pen-y-Dyffryn was built as a rectory during the last century for an eccentric Celtic scholar and spiritual and mental refreshment are certainly high on the menu at this beautiful country hotel.

With its quite magnificent setting almost a thousand feet up on the last hill in Shropshire and facing all the splendour of the Welsh mountains, the hotel offers a superb retreat from all the stress and bustle of everyday life. It's the ideal place to clear the mind, fill the lungs with clear country air and recharge the batteries. Nearby, castles and medieval towns such as Chester and Shrewsbury offer plenty of interest, or guests can simply walk amidst the breathtaking scenery, go fishing, play golf at the picturesque Mile End course, or just allow the soul to bathe in the truly unspoilt natural beauty of the hotel's wonderful surroundings.

People return again and again to enjoy the easy going atmosphere, the delicious and imaginative country cooking and the unpretentious comfort of this beautiful country house. The interior exudes a cosy warmth and tranquillity whilst views in all directions are out of this world. Once visited never forgotten.

LOCATION

Leave the A5 and drive towards Oswestry town centre then follow signs for Llansilin on the B4580. The hotel is 3 miles from Oswestry, set back from the road on the left hand side.

Rhydycroesau, Nr Oswestry
Shropshire SY10 7JD

Telephone 01691 653700
Fax 01691 650066

E-mail: *penydyff@bestloved.com*

OWNERS

Miles and Audrey Hunter

ROOM RATES

Single occupancy	£60 - £65
9 Doubles/Twins	£76 - £100
1 Family room	£116 - £126

Includes full breakfast and VAT

CHARGE/CREDIT CARDS

• DC • MC • VI

RATINGS & AWARDS

E.T.C. ★★★ Silver Award
A.A. ★★★ ❀❀ 74%
A.A. Romantic Hotel

FACILITIES

On site: *Garden, fishing*
Nearby: *Golf, tennis, riding, hunting/shooting*

RESTRICTIONS

Limited facilities for disabled guests
Smoking very restricted
Closed 20 Dec - 20 Jan

ATTRACTIONS

Powis Castle, Erddig Castle, Chirk Castle & Aquaduct, Pistyll Rhaeadr, Waterfall, Snowdonia, Ironbridge Gorge

AFFILIATIONS

Independent

NEAREST

MAJOR CITY:
Chester - 22 miles/30 mins

MAJOR AIRPORT:
Manchester - 60 miles/1 hr

RAILWAY STATION:
Gobowen - 5 miles/15 mins

RESERVATIONS

Direct with hotel
Quote ***Best Loved***

ACCESS CODES

Not applicable

• Map p.500 ref: E6

“ Neither of us have experienced such discreet and polite hospitality. So, for ‘running such a beautiful ship’ and for your friendliness, thank you very much ”

Richard White, High Wycombe

THE PLOUGH AT CLANFIELD

16th century manor house

**Bourton Road, Clanfield,
Oxfordshire OX18 2RB**

**Telephone 01367 810222
Fax 01367 810596**

E-mail: *plough@bestloved.com*

OWNERS

John and Rosemary Hodges

ROOM RATES

Single occupancy	*£80 - £95*
9 Doubles/Twins	*£115*
2 Four-posters	*£125*
1 Suite	*£135*

Includes continental or full breakfast and VAT

CHARGE/CREDIT CARDS

• DC • JCB • MC • VI

RATINGS & AWARDS

R.A.C. ★★★ Dining Award 3
A.A. ★★★ ❀❀ 71%

FACILITIES

On site: *Garden*
2 meeting rooms/max 35 people
Nearby: *Golf, fishing, tennis, fitness centre, hunting/shooting, riding*

RESTRICTIONS

No children under 12 years
No pets, guide dogs only
No smoking in rooms or restaurant
Closed from 25 - 29 Dec

ATTRACTIONS

Blenheim Palace, Rousham House, Kelmscott Manor, Stonor Park, Oxford, Waterperry Gardens

AFFILIATIONS

Independent

NEAREST

MAJOR CITY:
Oxford - 18 miles/25 mins

MAJOR AIRPORT:
London Heathrow - 65 miles/1½ hrs

RAILWAY STATION:
Oxford - 18 miles/25 mins

RESERVATIONS

Direct with hotel
Quote ***Best Loved***

ACCESS CODES

Not applicable

Deep-piled comfort and wonderful country food in a classic manor

In Cirencester, a short drive from Clanfield there is a marvellously intact Roman amphitheatre which is said to date from 1BC. The structure is a symbol of ancient Roman ingenuity. And if, in a 1,000 years, you stumbled upon the honey-coloured Cotswolds manor house that is The Plough, you might be similarly struck with respect for Elizabethan architecture. This is a classic in every respect!

John and Rosemary Hodges have lovingly turned this graceful old house into a welcoming hostelry renowned throughout the region for fine food. The Plough is very much the ideal of the country house experience. Voluminous sofas and oversized armchairs invite you to sink into comfort and pass an afternoon with a good book. In the evening, candle-lit tables with proper napery beckon the guest to enjoy a wonderful repast.

The bedrooms, in keeping with the rest of the house, have been tastefully and traditionally decorated and and include lovely little extras like a decanter of sherry and plush bathrobes.

The Plough is the perfect base from which to explore Oxford, Bath, Stratford-upon-Avon and the pretty Cotswold villages.

LOCATION

Located on the edge of the village of Clanfield, at the junction of the A4095 and the B4020 between Witney and Faringdon.

MIDSHIRES

"I was most impressed on my visit at the amazing attention to detail on such a busy occasion. Your staff showed equanable service to everyone that crossed the portals of your hotel"

Anonymous, Argyll, Scotland

229

• Map p.500 ref: E6

Georgian hotel

THE RANDOLPH

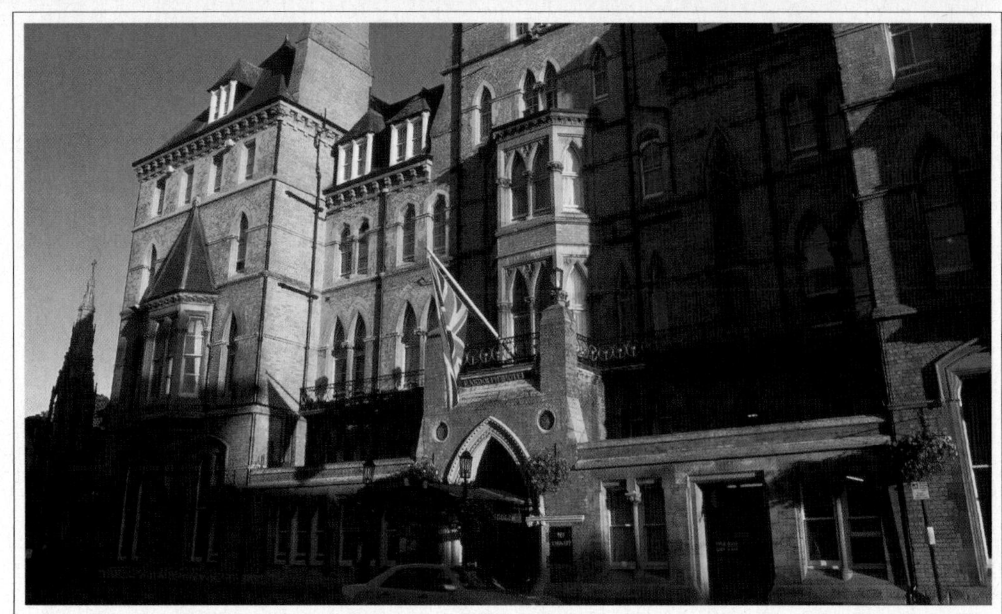

Classic true blue pedigree in the city of dreaming spires

A famous landmark since its grand 19th-century neo-Gothic outline first graced the heart of the city, the Randolph is a veritable local institution within a stone's throw of ancient colleges, museums, shops and theatres. It has hosted the good and the great from Hollywood stars such as Elizabeth Burton and Richard Taylor, who used a private passageway between the hotel and the Oxford Playhouse to avoid attention during a 1960s production of Faustus, to literary creations such as the academic sleuth Inspector Morse.

The hotel is currently undergoing a major refurbishment programme which will upgrade every corner of the property from the bedrooms to the traditional public rooms and Spires Restaurant with its impressive collection of college coats-of-arms. Where once taking afternoon tea at the Randolph was considered the height of good taste (this is where English author C.S. Lewis and American poet Joy Gresham first meet in the film Shadowlands), the new look Randolph will boast a chic oyster and champagne bar. In between sips, note the renowned series of paintings by Osbert Lancaster depicting the infamous Zuleika Dobson who created havoc in the city in Sir Max Beerbohm's novel of the same name.

LOCATION

In the centre of Oxford, opposite the Ashmolean Museum.

Beaumont Street, Oxford, Oxfordshire OX1 2LN

Telephone 0870 4008200
Fax 01865 791678

E-mail: *randolph@bestloved.com*

GENERAL MANAGER

James Stewart

ROOM RATES

32 Singles	£89 - £152
77 Doubles/Twins	£149 - £170
1 Four-poster	£169 - £210
7 Junior suites	£169 - £250
2 Deluxe suites	£214 - £400

Includes full breakfast and VAT

CHARGE/CREDIT CARDS

• DC • JCB • MC • VI

RATINGS & AWARDS

R.A.C. ★★★★ Dining Award 2
A.A. ★★★★ 67%

FACILITIES

On site: *Licensed for weddings*
6 meeting rooms/max 400 people
Nearby: *Golf, tennis, leisure centre*

RESTRICTIONS

Pets by arrangement

ATTRACTIONS

Oxford University Colleges, Oxford Story Museum, Ashmolean Museum, Blenheim Palace, The Cotswolds, Waddesdon

AFFILIATIONS

Heritage Hotels

NEAREST

MAJOR CITY:
Oxford

MAJOR AIRPORT:
London Heathrow - 46 miles/1 hr

RAILWAY STATION:
Oxford - 1 mile/10 mins

RESERVATIONS

Toll free in US: 800-225-5843
*Quote **Best Loved***

ACCESS CODES

AMADEUS FE OXF170
APOLLO/GALILEO FE 5476
SABRE/ABACUS FE 11170
WORLDSPAN FE 0170

MIDSHIRES

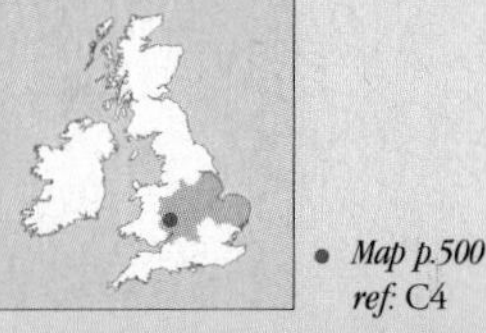

• Map p.500 ref: C4

"What a special, special place. Super surroundings, staff and service. Thanks ever-so"

Sue & Christopher Bedwell-Smith, Harrogate, Yorkshire

RAVEN HOTEL & RESTAURANT *15th century coaching inn*

Barrow Street, Much Wenlock, Shropshire TF13 6EN

Telephone 01952 727251
Fax 01952 728416

E-mail: ravenhotel@bestloved.com

OWNER
Kirk Heywood

ROOM RATES

Single occupancy	£65
12 Doubles/Twins	£95
1 Four-poster	£105
1 Family room	£115
1 Suite	£125

Includes full breakfast and VAT

CHARGE/CREDIT CARDS

• DC • JCB • MC • VI

RATINGS & AWARDS
A.A. ★★★ ❀❀ 73%

FACILITIES
On site: *Garden, health & beauty*
1 meeting room/max 16 people
Nearby: *Golf, tennis, fishing, riding, swimming*

RESTRICTIONS
No facilities for disabled guests
No pets

ATTRACTIONS
Ironbridge, Dudmaston Hall, Coalport Pottery, Stokesay Castle, Wenlock Priory, Wroxeter Roman City, Wenlock Edge, Attingham Park

AFFILIATIONS
Independent

NEAREST
MAJOR CITY:
Telford - 10 miles/15 mins
Shrewsbury - 13 miles/20 mins

MAJOR AIRPORT:
Birmingham - 53 miles/1 hr

RAILWAY STATION:
Shrewsbury - 13 miles/25 mins

RESERVATIONS
Direct with hotel
Quote ***Best Loved***

ACCESS CODES
Not applicable

MIDSHIRES

Much praised in Much Wenlock on the gourmet circuit of Shropshire

The modern Olympic Games owe much to a certain Dr Penny Brookes who lived in Much Wenlock. He founded the Wenlock Olympian Society in 1850 and, years later, worked with Baron Coubertin to found the modern Olympic movement. In 1890, the Baron wrote: "And of the Olympic Games … it is not a Greek to whom one is indebted but rather to Dr W P Brookes".

Since the games began the Raven has been the haunt of spectators and competitors alike. Then, as now, the traditional welcome is as warm as a 500-year old coaching inn can muster. The place has immense character. The flower-filled courtyard gives access to a number of bedrooms which have been delightfully furnished and provided with every modern comfort. There are four-poster rooms and an imaginatively designed galleried suite, a good example of a blend of old and new.

Before you dine, have a look at the Olympian memorabilia on display in the public rooms, then prepare yourself for a treat. The two rosette AA rating is a clue but a look at the menu, and you will agree with Paddy Burt of the Daily Telegraph, "This is what I call serious food". It's imaginative and delicious with a good choice of something traditional or much higher up the culinary scale.

On this 150th anniversary of the Wenlock Games, it's a racing certainty that the Raven will be a centre of attraction - as it is at any time!

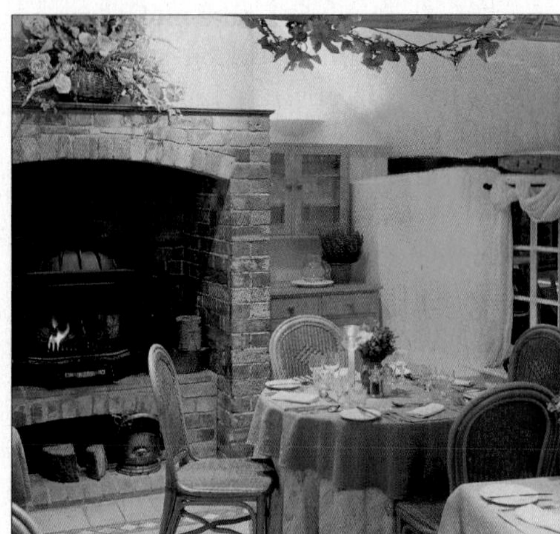

LOCATION

10 miles from Telford between Shrewsbury and Bridgnorth where the A4169 meets the A458. Proceed down Much Wenlock High St, turn right, hotel is 100 yards on right.

A keen Angler? Refer to page 472 for our Fishing Index

“The hotel is very impressive, the food was first class (definitely “compliments to the chef”) and the bedrooms a delight”

Pat Hague, British Railways

• *Map p.500 ref: E3*

Victorian manor

RISLEY HALL

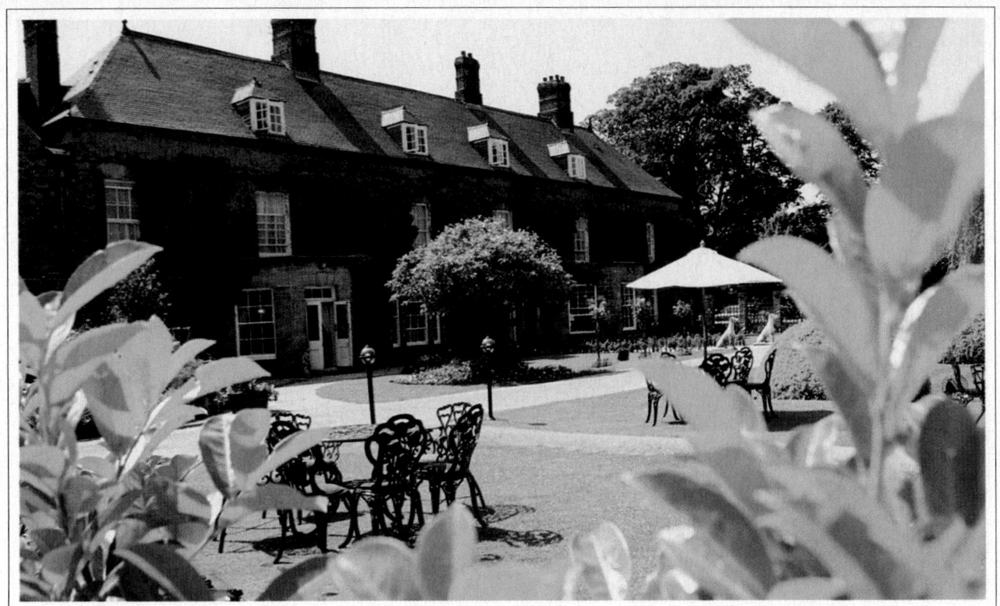

A Victorian home purpose-built for the pleasures of good living

This is Saxon country whose prosperity grew with the lace industry in the last century. Risley Hall itself has a history that goes back to the 11th century. It prospered into the grand house it is in Victorian times under the ownership of a flamboyant entrepreneur called Ernest Terah Hooley.

Today, the splendours of this baronial hall have been restored; the house and its gardens once again receive guests intent on the pleasures of good food and amusing company in luxury surroundings. A country retreat offering fine cuisine, luxurious bedchambers and outstanding service in a majestic setting.

There are 16 double bedrooms. Tasteful colour schemes, elegant furnishings, beautiful brocades and original oak beams create a relaxing environment with a character of its own. From soft sophistication to a cosy cottage feel or a dramatic four-poster style, there's a room to suit every mood and occasion.

The chef de cuisine indulges his diners in his own distinctive style. They can opt for the à la carte or menu du jour menus. Whatever the choice, Abbey's restaurant could not be a more beautiful place in which to enjoy it.

LOCATION

Exit 25 off M1, take Sandiacre exit from Bostock Lane. At cross roads, turn left towards Risley. Follow A5010 Derby road for half a mile. Risley Hall is on left hand side.

Derby Road, Risley, Derbyshire DE72 3SS

Telephone 0115 939 9000
Fax 0115 939 7766

E-mail: *risley@bestloved.com*

OWNER
Mike Crosbie

GENERAL MANAGER
Julie Dunkley

ROOM RATES

Single occupancy	*£85 - £100*
13 Doubles/Twins	*£95 - £115*
2 Four-posters	*£95 - £115*
1 Suite	*£140*

Includes VAT

CHARGE/CREDIT CARDS

• *MC* • *VI*

RATINGS & AWARDS
E.T.C. ★★★ *Silver Award*
R.A.C. ★★★ *Dining Award 1*
A.A. ★★★ ❀❀ *72%*

FACILITIES
On site: *Garden, croquet, indoor pool, jacuzzi, snooker*
Licensed for weddings
4 meeting rooms/max 150 people
Nearby: *Golf, tennis, fitness, riding*

RESTRICTIONS
Limited facilities for disabled guests
No pets

ATTRACTIONS
Nottingham Castle, Sherwood Forest, Peak District National Park, Chatsworth House, Belvoir Castle

AFFILIATIONS
Independent

NEAREST
MAJOR CITY:
Nottingham - 7 miles/15 mins
Derby - 7 miles/15 mins
MAJOR AIRPORT:
East Midlands - 10 miles/15 mins
RAILWAY STATION:
Long Eaton - 3 miles/5 mins

RESERVATIONS
Direct with hotel
*Quote **Best Loved***

ACCESS CODES
Not applicable

• Map p.500 ref: D6

"This has everything that makes an enjoyable break away - lovely rooms, warm welcome and amazing food and drink. Can't wait to come back"

Charlotte West, London

THE ROYALIST HOTEL

10th century inn

Digbeth Street, Stow-on-the-Wold, Gloucestershire GL54 1BN

Telephone 01451 830670
Fax 01451 870048

E-mail: royalist@bestloved.com

OWNERS

Alan and Georgina Thompson

ROOM RATES

Single occupancy	*£50 - £130*
4 Cottage rooms	*£90*
5 Doubles/Twins	*£130*
1 Superior Four-poster	*£150*
1 Luxury Superior suite	*£160*

Includes full breakfast and VAT

CHARGE/CREDIT CARDS

• DC • JCB • MC • VI

RATINGS & AWARDS

Awards Pending

FACILITIES

On site: *Bar*
1 meeting room/max 25 people
Nearby: *Riding, fishing, quad biking, clay pigeon shooting*

RESTRICTIONS

Smoking in residents lounge only
No children under 8 years in the restaurant for dinner
Limited facilities for disabled guests

ATTRACTIONS

Warwick Castle, Cotswolds, Oxford, Blenheim Palace, Hidcote Gardens, Stratford-upon-Avon

AFFILIATIONS

Independent

NEAREST

MAJOR CITY:
Oxford - 35 miles/40 mins

MAJOR AIRPORT:
Birmingham - 43 miles/1¼ hrs

RAILWAY STATION:
Kingham - 4 miles/10 mins

RESERVATIONS

Direct with hotel
Quote ***Best Loved***

ACCESS CODES

Not applicable

MIDSHIRES

A restaurant, an hotel and an inn. Three into one does go!

The Royalist is the oldest inn in England dating back to 947 AD when it was a hospice and almshouse owned by the Knights of St John. It is truly atmospheric with antique beams and spooky marks to ward off witches, leper holes and a Babylonian frieze dating from the Crusades.

While it would be hard to improve on this hospitable landmark, new owners of The Royalist, Alan and Georgina Thompson, have completed a superb major refurbishment of the hotel. Behind the mellow 17th-century Cotswold stone façade, there are a dozen bedrooms, each different and inspired by top British designers. For something really unusual, check out the jewel-like Porch House Room created out of the 1615 porch and glassed-in on three sides.

A noted chef, Alan presides over the excellent 947 AD Restaurant. As an Australian he and Georgina are determined to keep the atmosphere relaxed. For those seeking draught ale and great pub food, take a stroll over the flagstones to the 'Eagle and Child'. This is a real find, so book now before word gets out.

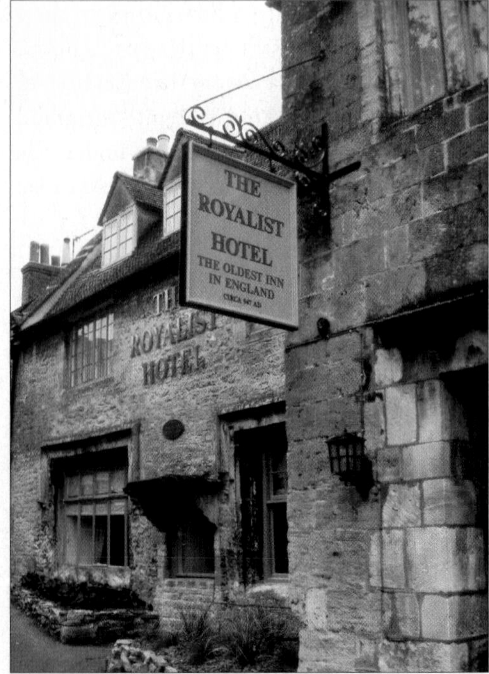

LOCATION

At Stow-on-the-Wold turn off A429 for Chipping Norton. The hotel is 300 yards on left, behind The Green.

“ The Shakespeare is like a home from home ”

J E Nichols, Ashton-under-Lyme

• Map p.500 ref: E5

Tudor town houses

THE SHAKESPEARE HOTEL

Another Shakespearean inheritance enjoyed by thespians

We have much to be grateful to Shakespeare for, not least for the preservation of Stratford-upon-Avon as a superb living exhibition of Tudor architecture. The Shakespeare, with its nine great wooded gables probably did not become an inn until the early 18th century but it was swiftly attracting many well-known thespians as well as writers and artists. David Garrick, the greatest actor of the 18th century, often stayed at the hotel when touring, staying in rooms, then as now, named after Shakespearian characters.

As one might expect from an hotel made up of three separate buildings, all of ancient lineage, the interior is fascinating with oak beams in abundance, open fires and antique furnishings. Many of the rooms are oak panelled, three have four-posters and one suite has twin beds of solid oak. The decor of the David Garrick restaurant is characteristically Elizabethan and offers award-winning cuisine of the highest standard. The hotel also has a bistro and wine bar called Othellos. It offers a wide range of beers, wines and exciting and award-winning cuisine in a relaxed setting with a terrace for summer.

Stratford-upon-Avon contains many treasures such as Shakespeare's birthplace, the splendid Hall's Croft, the home of his eldest daughter and Anne Hathaway's cottage at Shottery. The lovely Warwickshire countryside, too is much the same as Shakespeare would have known it.

LOCATION

In the centre of Stratford-upon-Avon, some ten miles south west of Exit 15 on the M40.

Chapel Street, Stratford-upon-Avon, Warwickshire CV37 6ER

Telephone 0870 4008182
Fax 01789 415411

E-mail: *shakespeare@bestloved.com*

GENERAL MANAGER

John Reynolds

ROOM RATES

12 Singles	*£110*
50 Doubles/Twins	*£150*
2 Four-posters	*£180*
8 Mini suites	*£180*
1 Suite	*£240*

Includes newspaper, service and VAT

CHARGE/CREDIT CARDS

• DC • JCB • MC • VI

RATINGS & AWARDS

R.A.C. ★★★★

A.A. ★★★★ ❀ *66%*

FACILITIES

On site: *Licensed for weddings*
6 meeting rooms/max 120 people

Nearby: *Golf, fishing, tennis, fitness, riding*

RESTRICTIONS

No facilities for the disabled

ATTRACTIONS

Shakespeare's birthplace properties, Royal Shakespeare Theatre, Warwick Castle, Cotswold villages, Blenheim Palace, Oxford

AFFILIATIONS

Heritage Hotels

NEAREST

MAJOR CITY:
Birmingham - 25 miles/40 mins

MAJOR AIRPORT:
Birmingham - 25 miles/40 mins

RAILWAY STATION:
Stratford-upon-Avon - 1 mile/10 mins

RESERVATIONS

Toll free in US/Canada: 800-225-5843
Toll free in UK: 0800 404040
Toll free in Australia: 008 222446
Quote ***Best Loved***

ACCESS CODES

AMADEUS FE BHX210
APOLLO/GALILEO FE 5479
SABRE/ABACUS FE 11210
WORLDSPAN FE 6089

" I want to share a wonderful discovery with your readers . . . "

Patricia Morris, Readers Write column, Los Angeles Times

• Map p.500 ref: E6

14th century abbey THE SHAVEN CROWN

600 years of history, a medieval hall and a family welcome

The Shaven Crown hotel is beautifully situated in the heart of the Cotswolds. Originally a 14th century hospice to Bruern Abbey, it is built of local honey-coloured stone around a central medieval courtyard garden. It has the mellowed charm of 600 years of hospitality. The hotel is owned by the Burpitt family who are actively engaged in its daily running.

The pride of the Shaven Crown Hotel, in addition to its original 14th century gateway, is the medieval hall - now the residents' lounge. All the bedrooms have tea and coffee-making facilities, TV and private bathrooms. The hotel is centrally heated throughout.

An intimate candlelit restaurant serves food fresh every day. The bar offers an imaginative array of bar meals, beside the log fire, at lunch and dinner seven days a week. You may eat al fresco in the courtyard when you choose to.

The area is justly renowned for antiques-hunting. Cheltenham and the other towns and villages of the Cotswolds are within easy reach, as are Oxford, Stratford-upon-Avon and Cirencester. Blenheim Palace, birthplace of Sir Winston Churchill, is one of the many great stately homes in the district.

LOCATION

On the A361, 4 miles north of Burford and 6 miles south of Chipping Norton.

High Street, Shipton-under-Wychwood, Oxfordshire OX7 6BA

Telephone 01993 830330
Fax 01993 832136

E-mail: *shaven@bestloved.com*

OWNERS
Robert and Jane Burpitt

ROOM RATES

Single occupancy	*£55*
8 Doubles/Twins	*£95 - £120*
1 Four-poster	*£120*

Includes full breakfast and VAT

CHARGE/CREDIT CARDS

• *MC* • *VI*

RATINGS & AWARDS
A.A. ★★ ❀ *66%*

FACILITIES
On site: *Garden, bowling green*
1 meeting room/max 30 people
Nearby: *Golf, fishing, riding*

RESTRICTIONS
None

ATTRACTIONS
The Cotswolds, Blenheim Palace, Burford, Bourton-on-the-Water, Stow-on-the-Wold

AFFILIATIONS
Independent

NEAREST
MAJOR CITY:
Oxford - 26 miles/30 mins

MAJOR AIRPORT:
London Heathrow - 70 miles/1½ hrs
Birmingham - 55 miles/1¼ hrs

RAILWAY STATION:
Charlbury - 6 miles/10 mins

RESERVATIONS
Direct with hotel
*Quote **Best Loved***

ACCESS CODES
Not applicable

For route planning map of the Midshires see page 500

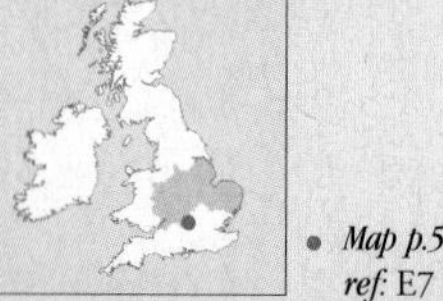

• Map p.500 ref: E7

"A wonderful retreat from the hustle and bustle of London life, being only a short distance away"

Claire & Mark Grabiner, London

THE SPRINGS HOTEL & GOLF CLUB

Country house

Wallingford Road, North Stoke, Oxfordshire OX10 6BE

Telephone 01491 836687
Fax 01491 836877

E-mail: *springs@bestloved.com*

DIRECTOR

Svenia Wolf

ROOM RATES

Single occupancy	*£90 - £155*
29 Doubles/Twins	*£100 - £140*
2 Suites	*£165*

Includes VAT

CHARGE/CREDIT CARDS

• *DC* • *JCB* • *MC* • *VI*

RATINGS & AWARDS

R.A.C. ★★★

A.A. ★★★ ❀❀ *72%*

FACILITIES

On site: *Garden, 18-hole golf course, croquet, outdoor heated pool, sauna, jacuzzi, fishing*
Licensed for weddings
4 meeting rooms/max 50 people
Nearby: *Riding*

RESTRICTIONS

Limited facilities for disabled guests
Pets by arrangement

ATTRACTIONS

Blenheim Palace, Oxford, Windsor, Henley-on-Thames, The Chilterns, The Cotswolds

AFFILIATIONS

Independent

NEAREST

MAJOR CITY:
Oxford - 12 miles/20 mins
Reading - 12 miles/20 mins

MAJOR AIRPORT:
London Heathrow - 30 miles/1 hr

RAILWAY STATION:
Reading - 12 miles/20 mins

RESERVATIONS

Direct with hotel
Quote ***Best Loved***

ACCESS CODES

Not applicable

A secret hideaway by The Thames for peace and relaxation

The Springs lies in a small Thames-side village midway between the M40 and M4. Its proximity to Oxford, Windsor and Henley makes it an ideal base to explore the wonderful countryside and villages of the Chilterns and Cotswolds or for a relaxing and peaceful break.

The Springs, one of the first mock-tudor houses to be built in England, lies in six acres of wooded grounds and formalised gardens, overlooking a spring-fed lake from which it takes its name. In the panelled lounge, traditional furnishings and glowing log fires in winter reinforce a warm and friendly atmosphere. The bedrooms are attractively decorated and complete with every luxury. Some rooms have balconies overlooking the lake and a few have jacuzzi baths.

The magical setting of the balcony restaurant overlooking the floodlit lake with swans and ducks makes up a very English scene. The imaginative executive chef bases his cooking on English culinary heritage.

For the sporty, there is use of a guitar shaped outdoor swimming pool (open May to September), croquet, putting and the newly opened 18 hole, par 72 golf course.

LOCATION

Just outside the market town of Wallingford on B4009, 20 minutes drive from Oxford.

"I greatly enjoyed the time I spent there and I trust you will experience the same pleasures at one of the most wonderful stately homes in Britain"

The Earl of Lichfield

• Map p.500 ref: F4

Stately home

STAPLEFORD PARK

An historic stately home with a sumptuously unique lifestyle

Stapleford is one of England's finest stately homes. It was held by Henry de Ferrers, who fought alongside William the Conqueror at the Battle of Hastings in 1066. In the 14th century, it belonged to John O'Gaunt. For 484 years it was the home of the Sherard family, descendants of the Conqueror himself. William Sherard restored what is now the Old Wing in 1633 - his name is carved in the stone.

In 1996, Peter de Savary purchased Stapleford Park which is affiliated to Skibo Castle, home of the Carnegie Club in Scotland. Many millions of pounds of refurbishment has created a unique, luxurious, welcoming environment. 51 wonderfully furnished bedrooms, sumptuous reception rooms, a health spa and private 18-hole championship golf course designed by Donald Steel are part of a lifestyle surpassing even the best hotels.

The main dining room is decorated with 17th century carvings by Grinling Gibbons. Stapleford prides itself on its culinary skills, with interesting, varied menus that change daily, and feature an adult nursery dish. In the Grand Hall, murals by Jenny Bell interpret the Spanish Riding School in Vienna.

Within the magnificent woodlands is a profusion of formal walled and natural gardens. Nearby are Burghley House, Chatsworth, Belvoir Castle, Belton House and Rutland Water.

LOCATION

4 miles east of Melton Mowbray on B676 towards Colsterworth and the A1.

Stapleford Park, Near Melton Mowbray, Leicestershire LE14 2EF

Telephone 01572 787522
Fax 01572 787651

E-mail: *stapleford@bestloved.com*

CHAIRMAN
Peter de Savary

GENERAL MANAGER
Alan Thomas

ROOM RATES

1 Single	*£205*
48 Doubles/Twins	*£205 - £425*
2 Suites	*£595*

Includes breakfast, newspaper and VAT

CHARGE/CREDIT CARDS

• DC • MC • VI

RATINGS & AWARDS
R.A.C. Gold Ribbon ★★★★
Dining Award 4
A.A. ★★★★ ❀❀

FACILITIES
On site: *Garden, croquet, tennis, archery, sauna, jacuzzi, indoor pool, Clarins Spa, gym, snooker, riding, fishing, 18-hole golf course, falconry, pétanque, boule, mountain bikes, clay pigeon shooting, off-road driving, heli-pad*
10 meeting rooms/max 300 people
Nearby: *Hunting/shooting*

RESTRICTIONS
None

ATTRACTIONS
Burghley House, Belvoir Castle, Rutland Water, Chatsworth House, Belton House, Stamford

AFFILIATIONS
The Celebrated Hotels Collection
Preferred Hotels & Resorts

NEAREST
MAJOR CITY:
Leicester - 18 miles/35 mins
MAJOR AIRPORT:
East Midlands - 20 miles/45 mins
RAILWAY STATION:
Grantham - 15 miles/25 mins

RESERVATIONS
Toll free in US: 800-322-2403
*Quote **Best Loved***

ACCESS CODES
Not applicable

• Map p.500 ref: F7

“ All of our friends wrote to say how much they enjoyed the setting, your hospitality and the memorable food ”

J Pimkin, Berkshire

THE STONOR ARMS

Georgian inn

Stonor, Near Henley-on-Thames, Oxfordshire RG9 6HE

Telephone 01491 638866
Fax 01491 638863

E-mail: stonor@bestloved.com

GENERAL MANAGER
Sophia Williams

ROOM RATES
Single occupancy £99
10 Doubles/Twins £125 - £155
Includes full breakfast and VAT

CHARGE/CREDIT CARDS

• MC • VI

RATINGS & AWARDS
E.T.C. ★★★ Silver Award
A.A. ★★★ ❀❀ 73%

FACILITIES
***On site:** Garden, room for the disabled*
Licensed for weddings
2 meeting rooms/max 16 people
***Nearby:** Golf, fishing, tennis, shooting, fitness, riding, boating, hot air ballooning*

RESTRICTIONS
None

ATTRACTIONS
Oxford, Windsor Castle, Ascot Racecourse, Henley-on-Thames, Chiltern Valley, Old Luxters Vineyard

AFFILIATIONS
The Great Inns of Britain

NEAREST
MAJOR CITY:
Oxford - 20 miles/30 mins

MAJOR AIRPORT:
London Heathrow - 40 miles/45 mins

RAILWAY STATION:
Henley - 5 miles/10 mins

RESERVATIONS
Direct with hotel
*Quote **Best Loved***

ACCESS CODES
Not applicable

A small hotel with a great reputation for good food

The high points in the British sporting calendar and the social diary are Wimbledon, Royal Ascot and Henley Royal Regatta. Two of these, Ascot and Henley, take place within easy reach of Stonor, a picturesque hamlet hidden in the Thames Valley. Here you will find the Stonor Arms, a small hotel with a reputation for good food that is out of all proportion to its size.

The hotel was built as an inn in Georgian times and, as you enter, you can almost feel the centuries of hospitality it has extended to its visitors. Today, it is privately owned and it shows; the wealth of French and English antiques, the fabrics and furniture bear the hallmarks of someone who really loves the place. Each of the spacious bedrooms has a character all of its own. The ground floor bedrooms have direct access to the garden.

But possibly the most compelling reason to visit this delightful hotel is its food which, under the imaginative skills of chef, Steven Morris, has earned itself two well-deserved rosettes. If you prefer something lighter, Blades, the flagstoned bar, serves mouthwatering snacks which, in summer, you can enjoy in the traditional walled garden.

LOCATION

From the M25, take M40 to Oxford. Take exit 6, follow signs to Watlington and, from there, to Henley-on-Thames. On your way to Henley from Watlington, take road to Stonor.

“A bird worth flying east for”

Michael Palin, actor

• *Map p.500 ref: 15*

300 year old inn

SWAN HOTEL

Continuing an ancient tradition of hospitality, good food and fine wines

The secluded seaside town of Southwold, has, for a long time, been a popular spot for Londoners fleeing the routine of city life. Its stunning stony beach is as attractive in summer as it is in winter.

At the 300 year old Swan Hotel, appearances can be deceiving. Outwardly, a typical coaching inn, inside it is a bustling centre of activity. Situated in the town's centre it is the happy meeting place of locals, travelling businessman, and holiday-makers. Adnams, the famed regional brewer, has clearly placed its mark of quality on this characterful establishment.

The relaxed bar and reading room vie for your attention. The hotel's bedrooms are comfortable and fitted out with all the necessary amenities. Even more attractive are the series of garden rooms overlooking the old bowling green which appeal to those on an extended holiday. The hotel's elegant restaurant is the pride of Southwold. Here memories are created; business deals concluded, anniversaries and birthdays celebrated. As you walk down the narrow streets the sea's pull is as strong as the tide. “You can watch the fisherman bringing in their catch or simply stand on Gun Hill as the sea pounds the shingle and cargo boats drift across the horizon”, as the hotel most aptly puts it!

LOCATION

In the centre of Southwold.

Market Place, Southwold, Suffolk IP18 6EG

Telephone 01502 722186
Fax 01502 724800

E-mail: *swansouthwold@bestloved.com*

MANAGER

Carole Ladd

ROOM RATES

4 Singles	*£60 - £65*
36 Doubles/Twins	*£99 - £130*
2 Suites	*£150 - £165*
1 Four-poster	*£175*

Includes early morning tea, full breakfast, newspaper and VAT

CHARGE/CREDIT CARDS

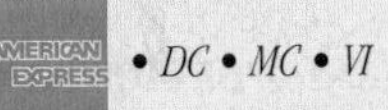

• *DC* • *MC* • *VI*

RATINGS & AWARDS

E.T.C. ★★★ *Silver Award*
A.A. ★★★ ❀ *71%*

FACILITIES

On site: *Garden, croquet*
1 meeting room/max 20 people
Nearby: *Golf, tennis, fitness, riding, sea fishing*

RESTRICTIONS

No children under 5 years in restaurant for dinner
Limited facilities for disabled guests

ATTRACTIONS

Suffolk Wildlife Park, Eastern Otter Trust, Saxtead Green Post Mill, Snape Maltings, Minsmere Bird Reserve, Aldeburgh Festival

AFFILIATIONS

Adnams Hotels

NEAREST

MAJOR CITY:
Norwich - 36 miles/50 mins

MAJOR AIRPORT:
London Heathrow - 140 miles/4 hrs
Stansted - 100 miles/2 hrs

RAILWAY STATION:
Darsham - 5 miles/15 mins

RESERVATIONS

Direct with hotel
Quote ***Best Loved***

ACCESS CODES

Not applicable

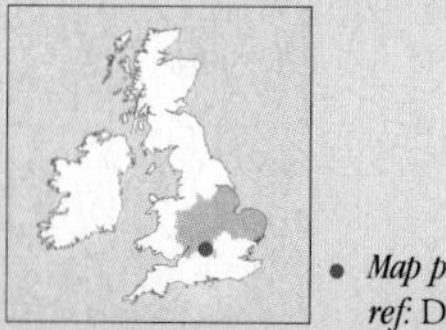

• Map p.500 ref: D6

"... we stay in many different hotels, but without exception your standards of friendliness far exceeded any either of us have been to"

Dave & Rachel Archer, Theale, Berkshire

SWAN HOTEL AT BIBURY

Historic Cotswold hotel

Bibury, Near Cirencester, Gloucestershire GL7 5NW

Telephone 01285 740695
Fax 01285 740473

E-mail: swanbibury@bestloved.com

OWNER
Miss E A Rose

GENERAL MANAGER
John P Stevens

ROOM RATES

Single occupancy	£105
14 Doubles/Twins	£165 - £200
3 Four-posters	£220 - £250
1 Family room	£250

Includes full breakfast, early morning tea, newspaper and VAT

CHARGE/CREDIT CARDS

 • DC • JCB • MC • VI

RATINGS & AWARDS
E.T.C. ★★★ Gold Award
A.A. ★★★ ❀❀ 79%

FACILITIES
On site: Garden, fishing
3 meeting rooms/max 50 people
Nearby: Golf, riding

RESTRICTIONS
No pets

ATTRACTIONS
Roman Baths, Stratford-upon-Avon, Black Mountains, Barnsley House Gardens, Westonbirt Arboretum, Cotswold villages

AFFILIATIONS
Selected British Hotels

NEAREST
MAJOR CITY:
Cheltenham - 12 miles/20 mins

MAJOR AIRPORT:
London Heathrow - 68 miles/1½ hrs

RAILWAY STATION:
Kemble - 9 miles/20 mins

RESERVATIONS
Toll free in US: 800-323-5463
Quote **Best Loved**

ACCESS CODES
Not applicable

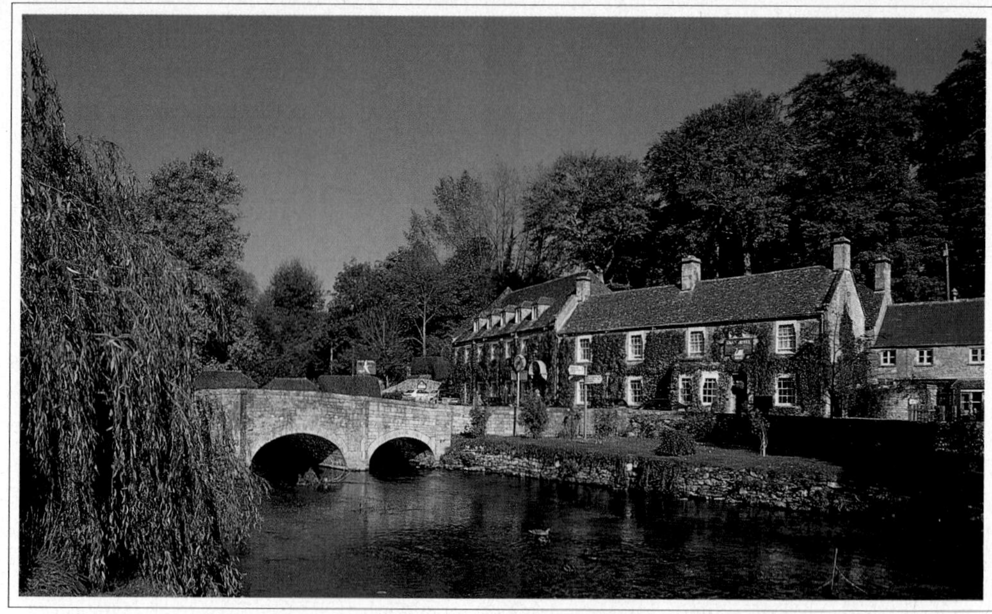

A pride of Cotswold villages with English cooking to be proud of

William Morris, great Victorian aesthete and founder of the Society for the Preservation of Ancient Buildings, listed Bibury as one of the prettiest of Cotswold villages. The Swan was the showpiece of the village when Morris came there. Restored to private ownership and run by a handpicked team of staff, the Swan offers a most splendid base for the Cotswolds.

Guests relax and are cosseted in the parlour with its cosy sofas, or the writing room with a delightful watercolour of the Swan as it was in 1630. Each bedroom is stylishly and comfortably furnished with fluffy white towels and robes, and modern facilities.

The richly decorated dining room with its glittering chandelier is the home of great English cooking. Dinner menus change daily and are complemented by a fine wine selection. Alternatively, you can try the more informal Jankowski's Brasserie offering crisp, healthy, traditionally styled cuisine.

Roman and Georgian Bath, Stratford-upon-Avon, the Black Mountains of Brecon, Westonbirt Arboretum and Barnsley House gardens are within easy reach. Bibury and other soft yellow limestone Cotswold villages are on the doorstep.

LOCATION

On B4425, 7 miles north of Cirencester, 9 miles south of Burford. ½ hour from M4 Swindon and M5 Cheltenham. Easily accessible from M40 via A40 Oxford.

"We would sincerely like to thank yourself, Claire and the rest of your wonderful staff for everything you did to make the wedding day such a memorable one"

Liz and John Puddick, Suffolk

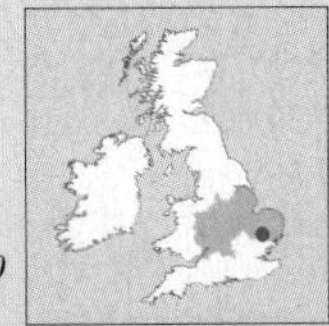

• Map p.500 ref: G5

Country mansion

SWYNFORD PADDOCKS

A classy thoroughbred handily placed for Cambridge and Newmarket

Swynford Paddocks' racing connection is not just confined to its name. There is a working stud farm within the 62-acre grounds, and the hotel's address at Six Mile Bottom refers to its excellent location six miles as the crow flies from the historic university city of Cambridge and Newmarket, the headquarters of British horseracing for over 300 years.

An elegant country mansion surrounded by its namesake paddocks, Swynford also has a notorious past. In 1813, the Romantic poet Lord Byron conducted a passionate affair with his married half-sister Augusta Leigh, who lived at Swynford. Later the house was owned by Lord and Lady Halifax before it was sympathetically converted into a comfortable country hotel.

Swynford Paddocks makes a great base for exploring East Anglia's diverse attractions. Take a day trip to Cambridge for its medieval churches and ancient colleges, punting on the River Isis or a gentle stroll along the 'Backs' as the riverbanks are known. For fans of the turf, the flat racing at Newmarket is a major draw and there are visits to the National Stud and National Horseracing Museum. The hotel can also arrange behind-the-scenes tours. Other popular side trips include magnificent Ely Cathedral, the picturesque old wool towns of Lavenham and Long Melford, and the Imperial War Museum at Duxford.

LOCATION

From M11 Exit 9, take A11 towards Newmarket. After 10 miles take A1304 signposted Newmarket. The hotel is 3/4 mile on the left.

Six Mile Bottom, Newmarket, Suffolk CB8 OUE

Telephone 01638 570234
Fax 01638 570283

E-mail: swynford@bestloved.com

GENERAL MANAGERS
Ian and Jenni MacKenzie

ROOM RATES

Single occupancy	£110 - £140
13 Doubles/Twins	£135 - £165
2 Four-posters	£155 - £195

Includes full breakfast and VAT

CHARGE/CREDIT CARDS

 • DC • MC • VI

RATINGS & AWARDS
E.T.C. ★★★
R.A.C. ★★★ Dining Award 2
A.A. ★★★ ❀ 73%

FACILITIES
On site: Garden, croquet, tennis, putting green, heli-pad
Licensed for weddings
1 meeting room/max 120 people
Nearby: Golf, riding

RESTRICTIONS
No facilities for disabled guests
No pets in public rooms

ATTRACTIONS
Newmarket Racecourse, Museum & National Stud, Ely Cathedral, Cambridge, Lavenham & Long Melford, Duxford Imperial War Museum, Ickworth House

AFFILIATIONS
Independent

NEAREST
MAJOR CITY:
Cambridge - 12 miles/20 mins

MAJOR AIRPORT:
Stansted - 20 miles/30 mins

RAILWAY STATION:
Cambridge - 12 miles/20 mins

RESERVATIONS
Direct with hotel
Quote **Best Loved**

ACCESS CODES
Not applicable

• Map p.500 ref: C6

"Everything was wonderful. (I don't know if I will be able to get my wife to leave.)"

Andrew Greenspan, USA

THORNBURY CASTLE

Tudor castle

Thornbury,
South Gloucestershire BS35 1HH

Telephone 01454 281182
Fax 01454 416188

E-mail: thornbury@bestloved.com

OWNER
Countess Von Essen

GENERAL MANAGER
Brian Jarvis

ROOM RATES

2 Singles	£85 - £105
9 Doubles/Twins	£105 - £270
13 Four-posters	£170 - £270
3 Suites	£195 - £350

Includes continental or buffet breakfast, early morning tea, newspaper and VAT

CHARGE/CREDIT CARDS

• DC • MC • VI

RATINGS & AWARDS
R.A.C. Gold Ribbon ★★★ Dining Award 3
A.A. ★★★ ❀❀
'Super Star Hotel' Reed Travel Group, USA

FACILITIES
On site: *Garden, croquet, heli-pad*
Licensed for weddings
3 meeting rooms/max 80 people
Nearby: *Golf, tennis, shooting, riding, ballooning*

RESTRICTIONS
No facilities for disabled guests
No pets

ATTRACTIONS
Berkeley Castle, Chepstow Castle, Slimbridge Wildfowl Trust, The Cotswolds, Bath, Bristol, Wye Valley, Tintern Abbey

AFFILIATIONS
The Celebrated Hotels Collection
Von Essen Hotels
Pride of Britain

NEAREST
MAJOR CITY:
Bristol - 15 miles/20 mins
Bath - 23 miles/45 mins
MAJOR AIRPORT:
Bristol - 21 miles/35 mins
RAILWAY STATION:
Bristol Parkway - 12 miles/15 mins

RESERVATIONS
Toll free in US: 800-322-2403
or 800-98-PRIDE
Quote ***Best Loved***

ACCESS CODES
APOLLO/GALILEO HT 41651
SABRE/ABACUS HK 36355
WORLDSPAN HK THORN

MIDSHIRES

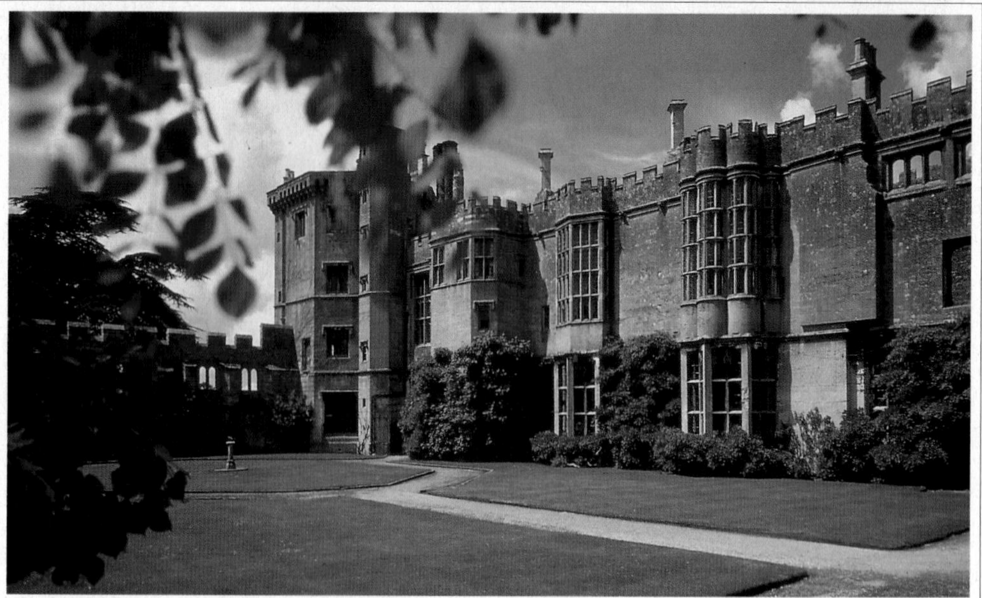

'The top hotel in Europe' says Conde Nast Traveler Magazine

The building of Thornbury Castle, started in 1511 by Edward Stafford, 3rd Duke of Buckingham, ended in 1521 when he was beheaded by Henry VIII. Buckingham's vast estates, including Thornbury, were confiscated by the King who stayed here with Anne Boleyn in 1535. Henry's daughter, Mary Tudor, lived here as a princess and when she became Queen she returned the Castle to the descendants of the late Duke.

Today, this Tudor castle-palace stands serenely in 15 acres, with distant views of the Severn Estuary and the hills of South Gloucestershire and Wales. Fine old panelling, tapestries and paintings enrich the interiors. There are 27 carefully restored bedchambers, most overlooking the oldest Tudor garden in England or the vineyard. Many have sumptuous four-poster beds and huge Tudor fireplaces.

The three intimate dining rooms have a gracious ambience to suit the superb cuisine.

Thornbury is an ideal base from which to discover the many historic sites, villages and towns located within an hour's drive of the castle, or cross the Severn Bridge into Wales and explore that beautiful country. Pilots should note the following heli-pad grid reference: 172 - N 6340 E 9060 05162.

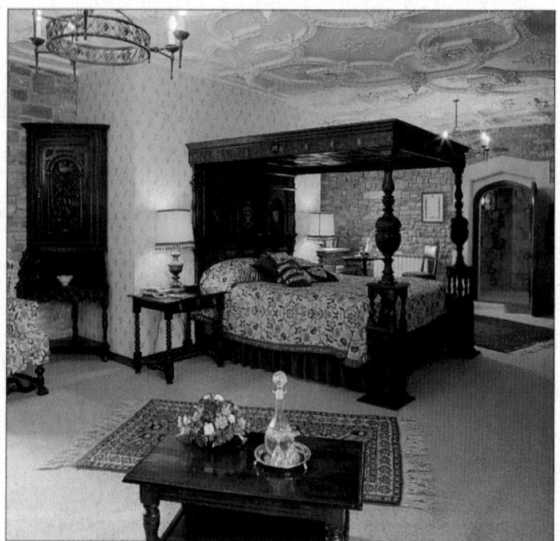

LOCATION

Exit 20 off M4 and A38 north for 6 miles, turn left at sign for Thornbury. At bottom of High Street bear left into Castle Street. After 300 yards, Castle entrance is on left of church. Follow brown historic castle signs.

"It's not like staying in an hotel - it's better"

Chris Jowsey, Scotland

• Map p.500 ref: C6

13th century farmhouse

TUDOR FARMHOUSE HOTEL

High Street, Clearwell, Near Coleford, Gloucestershire GL16 8JS

Telephone 01594 833046
Fax 01594 837093

E-mail: *tudorfarm@bestloved.com*

OWNERS

Colin and Linda Gray

ROOM RATES

Single occupancy	£50 - £55
13 Doubles/Twins	£65 - £85
4 Four-posters	£85
2 Bedroom suites	£90 - £125

Includes full breakfast and VAT

CHARGE/CREDIT CARDS

• JCB • MC • VI

RATINGS & AWARDS

E.T.C. ★★★
A.A. ★★★ ❀ 72%

FACILITIES

On site: Garden
2 meeting rooms/max 60 people
Nearby: Golf, riding, canoeing, cycling, fishing

RESTRICTIONS

No children under 12 years in restaurant after 7.30 pm

ATTRACTIONS

Tintern Abbey, Chepstow Castle, Forest of Dean, Clearwell Caves, Raglan Castle, Wye Valley

AFFILIATIONS

Independent

NEAREST

MAJOR CITY:
Bristol - 25 miles/45 mins

MAJOR AIRPORT:
Birmingham - 80 miles/1¼ hrs
Bristol - 25 miles/45 mins

RAILWAY STATION:
Chepstow - 12 miles/20 mins

RESERVATIONS

Toll free in UK: 0800 7835935
Quote **Best Loved**

ACCESS CODES

Not applicable

Hospitality with a smile beside the historic Forest of Dean

The house was built in the 13th century, some time before the Tudors! Original oak beams and panelling, a wide oak spiral staircase, open stonework and a large roughstone fire, ready to roar whenever toes feel chilly, give the Tudor Farmhouse Hotel a cosy, intimate and friendly atmosphere that makes it the perfect retreat from the hustle and bustle of working or touring life.

Colin and Linda Gray place great emphasis on quality hospitality and comfort for guests. The candlelit Restaurant has a deserved reputation for its food. The chef uses only the finest seasonal produce to create a varied, imaginative menu that changes regularly. There is a grill menu and vegetarian choice. The bedrooms have been extensively refurbished to a very high standard.

Clearwell is an historic village dominated by the ramparts of its Neo-Gothic castle. Clearwell caves, once the site of early iron working, are now an award-winning museum. The Forest of Dean is one of Britain's few remaining ancient Forests, with an estimated 20 million trees and marvellous woodland walks. Tintern Abbey, Chepstow and Raglan Castles, and the Wye valley, designated as an Area of Outstanding Beauty, are all nearby.

LOCATION

From M4 Exit 21 take M48. Leave M48 at Exit 2 to Chepstow, then follow A48 and B4231.

• Map p.500 ref: D6

"We found your staff, facilities and overall atmosphere excellent, and will most certainly recommend The Unicorn"

Mr & Mrs R W F Mundy, Question of Service

THE UNICORN HOTEL

Tudor town house

Sheep Street,
Stow-on-the-Wold,
Gloucestershire GL54 1HQ

Telephone 01451 830257
Fax 01451 831090

E-mail: unicorn@bestloved.com

GENERAL MANAGER

Stephen Wilson

ROOM RATES

2 Singles £60 - £70
17 Doubles/Twins £105 - £120
1 Four-poster £120
Includes full breakfast and VAT

CHARGE/CREDIT CARDS

• DC • JCB • MC • VI

RATINGS & AWARDS

E.T.C. ★★★
A.A. ★★★ 68%

FACILITIES

On site: *Licensed for weddings*
1 meeting room/max 70 people
Nearby: *Golf, fishing, riding, tennis*

RESTRICTIONS

No facilities for disabled guests
Pets by arrangement

ATTRACTIONS

Bourton-on-the-Water, Blenheim Palace, Warwick Castle, Stratford-upon-Avon, antiques hunting, walking

AFFILIATIONS

Grand Heritage Hotels

NEAREST

MAJOR CITY:
Oxford - 29 miles/40 mins
Cheltenham - 19 miles/20 mins

MAJOR AIRPORT:
London Heathrow - 75 miles/1½ hrs
Birmingham - 40 miles/45 mins

RAILWAY STATION:
Moreton-in-Marsh - 5 miles/10 mins

RESERVATIONS

Toll free in US: 888-93-GRAND
Quote ***Best Loved***

ACCESS CODES

AMADEUS UI GLOUNH
APOLLO/GALILEO UI 13389
SABRE/ABACUS UI 43640
WORLDSPAN UI 40752

The seductions of "the bath, the lounge and the well-appointed dinner table"

Pax Romana lasted 300 years from 47AD and drew its strength from the building of great roads that flew as true as arrows between strategic cities and, what Tacitus described as the seduction of the Celtic aristocracy with "the bath, the lounge and the well-appointed dinner table!" The Unicorn stands in the centre of Stow-on-the-Wold, four-square on Fosse Way, the Roman road connecting Exeter and Lincoln, seducing the traveller in true Taciturn fashion - and has been doing so for these past three hundred years!

The comfort levels include facilities fit for the new millennium subtly blended with the old world charm and ancient fabric of the building.

At the heart of The Unicorn is a great flagstone hearth whose flame sets aglow the polished antique bric-a-brac, warming the hand of friendship. Lounging one's way through a drink or two with, perhaps, a delicious light meal if the fancy takes you, the mantle of peace descends irresistibly. The bedrooms enjoy an individuality spun from the contrast between the Jacobean furniture and modern fabrics; the adjoining bathrooms are fit for a Caesar!

The Restaurant has, indeed, a well-appointed dinner table serving honest-to-goodness English fare and fine wines.

But equally seductive are the antique shops of Stow and the myriad delights of the Cotswolds.

LOCATION

In Sheep Street near the Market Square in the centre of Stow-on-the-Wold on the A429.

❝ A once in a lifetime hotel for our once in a lifetime trip. You made us feel so welcome. Thank you ❞

The MacIntosh family, Minnesota

• Map p.500 ref: D6

Country house

WASHBOURNE COURT HOTEL

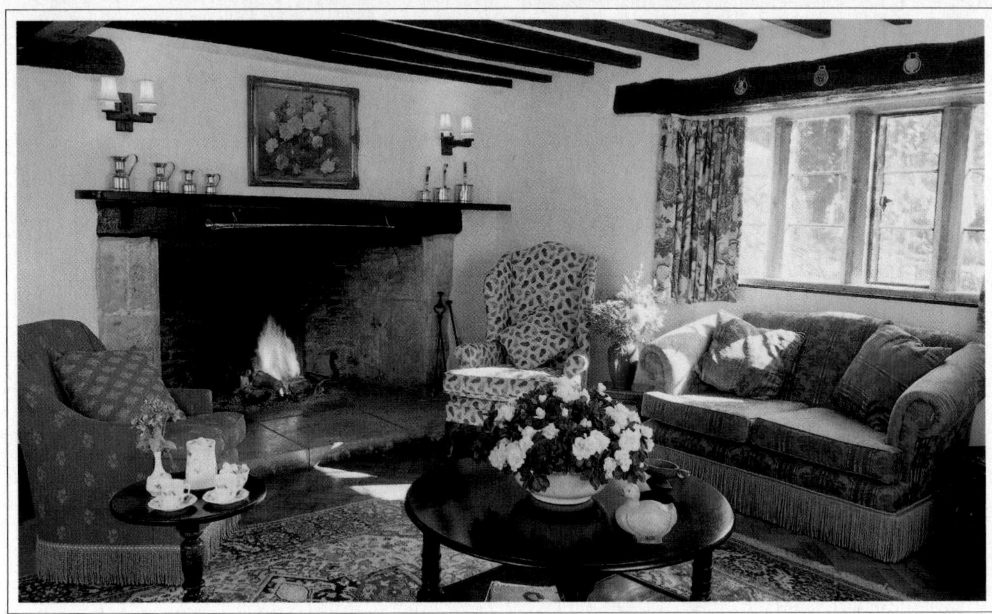

A true gem right in the heart of the Cotswolds

Washbourne Court is a truly magnificent hotel, partly housed in a 17th century building, standing in four acres of grounds alongside the River Eye in the centre of Lower Slaughter - undoubtedly one of the most beautiful and unspoilt of all the Cotswold villages. Whatever the season, the building retains all the original charm and character that has been gently acquired over the last 400 years.

The hotel continues a tradition of being family-owned and run; Roy and Daphne have the happy knack of easy going hospitality. The bedrooms are comfortable, each with its own character and very well appointed - some even have their own jacuzzis. For choice, there is also cottage accommodation that somehow helps you to feel part of village life.

The intimate riverside restaurant offers the finest of modern English cuisine and only the best of fresh local produce is used. The ambience and atmosphere is one to be savoured.

Lower Slaughter is famous for its outstanding scenic beauty, and is the perfect location for exploring the beautiful north Cotswolds and nearby villages.

If you are in search of peace, tranquillity and the epitome of English country life then Washbourne Court is your style of hotel.

LOCATION

About half a mile off the A429 between Stow-on-the-Wold and Bourton-on-the-Water. (Signed to The Slaughters).

Lower Slaughter, Gloucestershire GL54 2HS

Telephone 01451 822143
Fax 01451 821045

E-mail: *washbourne@bestloved.com*

OWNERS
Roy and Daphne Vaughan

GENERAL MANAGER
Adam Smith

ROOM RATES

Single occupancy	*£100 - £170*
14 Doubles/Twins	*£145 - £165*
10 Cottages	*£185*
4 Deluxe rooms	*£215*

Includes VAT

CHARGE/CREDIT CARDS

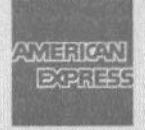

• DC • MC • VI

RATINGS & AWARDS
E.T.C. ★★★ Silver Award
A.A. ★★★ ❀❀ 76%

FACILITIES
On site: *Garden, tennis, heli-pad*
2 meeting rooms/max 80 people
Nearby: *Golf, riding, quad biking, clay pigeon shooting, ballooning*

RESTRICTIONS
No facilities for disabled guests
No children under 12 years in dining room
No smoking throughout
No pets

ATTRACTIONS
Blenheim Palace, Oxford, Stratford-upon-Avon, Old Roman Fosseway, Bath, The Cotwolds

AFFILIATIONS
Independent

NEAREST
MAJOR CITY:
Oxford - 25 miles/40 mins

MAJOR AIRPORT:
London Heathrow - 80 miles/1¾ hrs
Birmingham - 55 miles/45 mins

RAILWAY STATION:
Kingham - 5 miles/10 mins

RESERVATIONS
Toll free in US: 800-544-9993
Quote ***Best Loved***

ACCESS CODES
Not applicable

• Map p.500 ref: E5

"Truly a haven of peace and tranquillity - with superb service"

Howard Cragg, Sussex

WELCOMBE HOTEL

Country mansion with golf course

Warwick Road,
Stratford-upon-Avon,
Warwickshire CV37 0NR

Telephone 01789 295252
Fax 01789 414666

E-mail: welcombe@bestloved.com

MANAGING DIRECTOR

Richard Eden

ROOM RATES

1 Single	£120 - £150
48 Doubles/Twins	£155 - £185
5 Suites	£275
8 Gallery/Four-posters	£310
1 Lady Caroline Suite	£750

Includes full breakfast and VAT

CHARGE/CREDIT CARDS

• DC • JCB • MC • VI

RATINGS & AWARDS

E.T.C. ★★★★ Silver Award
R.A.C. ★★★★ Dining Award 3
A.A. ★★★★ ❀❀ 74%

FACILITIES

On site: *18-hole golf course, health & beauty salon, fitness room, tennis, gardens, heli-pad, Licensed for weddings*
7 meeting rooms/max 140 people
Nearby: *Boating, riding, swimming*

RESTRICTIONS

Limited facilities for disabled guests
No children under 12 in restaurant after 7pm
No pets, guide dogs only

ATTRACTIONS

Royal Shakespeare Theatre, Shakespeare's Birthplace, Warwick Castle, Anne Hathaway's Cottage, Blenheim Palace

AFFILIATIONS

Fine Individual Hotels
Small Luxury Hotels
The European Connection

NEAREST

MAJOR CITY:
Birmingham - 28 miles/35 mins
MAJOR AIRPORT:
Birmingham - 25 miles/30 mins
RAILWAY STATION:
Stratford-upon-Avon - 3 miles/5 mins

RESERVATIONS

Toll free in US: 800-525-4800
or 800-544-9993
Toll free in UK: 0500 203 022
Quote ***Best Loved***

ACCESS CODES

AMADEUS LX BHXWG
APOLLO/GALILEO LX 62380
SABRE/ABACUS LX 17115
WORLDSPAN LX BHXWH

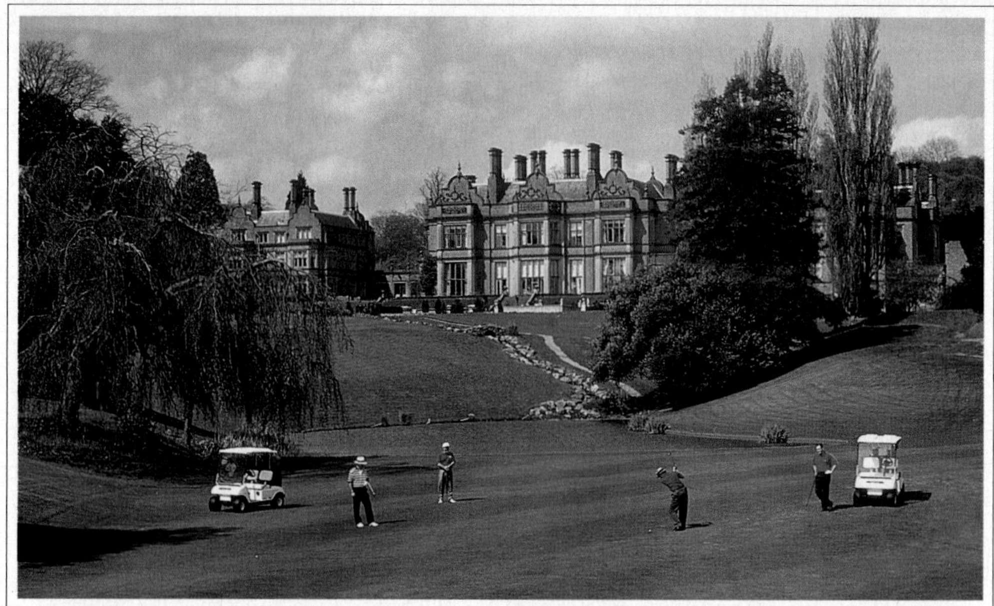

Shakespeare once owned the grounds. Theodore Roosevelt stayed here

This magnificent Jacobean-style mansion stands within its own 157-acre parkland estate, much of which was owned by William Shakespeare. The Welcombe was built in 1869 as a country house. Theodore Roosevelt was a guest here in 1910.

Today, the Welcombe has a reputation for maintaining the very highest international standards. There are 63 double rooms of which many are suites or luxuriously-appointed superior doubles that feature marble bathrooms and four-posters. The award-winning restaurant has large bay windows overlooking the gardens. Before or after dining, drinks can be taken either in the Trevelyan Terrace Bar or the magnificent oak-panelled lounge.

Leisure facilities include an excellent 18-hole golf club with two resident PGA professionals, a health and beauty salon, gym and all-weather floodlit tennis courts. The grounds include extensive formal gardens with lakes and a waterfall. Horse riding and other country pursuits may be arranged in the vicinity.

The Welcombe provides the perfect base for visiting the picturesque Cotswolds, famous castles and all that is Shakespeare.

LOCATION

1 mile from centre of Stratford-upon-Avon on A439. 5 miles from Exit 15 on the M40.

For a portrait of this region see page 172

"Tina and Dino are two of the most welcoming and hospitable hosts in the Cotswolds"

Drew Smith, Editor of Taste magazine, Wiltshire

• Map p.500 ref: D6

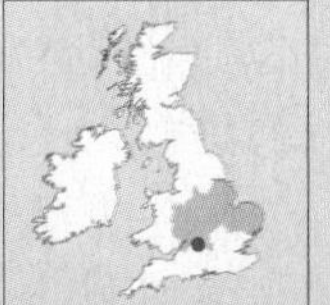

Elizabethan inn

THE WILD DUCK

An attractive 15th century inn of great character

The Wild Duck is a mellow Cotswold stone Elizabethan Inn. A typical local English inn, warm and welcoming, rich in colours and hung with old oil portraits of English ancestors. Large open log fires burn in the bar and the oak panelled residents' lounge in wintertime.

The garden is secluded, delightful and perfect for al fresco dining in the summer. The bar offers six real ales and the wine list is extensive and innovative.

The country-style dining room offers fresh seasonal food; game in winter and fresh fish delivered overnight from Brixham in Devon, which can include such exotic fare as parrot fish and tilapia.

There are nine bedrooms, two of which have four-poster beds and overlook the garden. All rooms have direct-dial telephone, colour TV and tea/coffee-making facilities.

Within a mile, The Wild Duck is surrounded by the Cotswold Water Park, with 80 lakes providing fishing, swimming, sailing, water and jet-skiing. Polo at Cirencester Park is a regular event. Every March, Cheltenham holds the Gold Cup Race Meeting. Horse trials at Gatcombe Park and Badminton are held annually.

LOCATION

From M4 take Exit 17 and follow Cirencester signs. Before Cirencester, turn right at Kemble and follow signs to Ewen.

Drakes Island, Ewen, Cirencester, Gloucestershire GL7 6BY

Telephone 01285 770310
Fax 01285 770924

E-mail: *wildduck@bestloved.com*

OWNER
Tina Mussell

ROOM RATES

Single occupancy	£55
8 Doubles	£75
2 Four-posters	£90
1 Directors double	£90

Includes continental breakfast and VAT

CHARGE/CREDIT CARDS

• MC • VI

RATINGS & AWARDS
E.T.C. ★★
R.A.C. ★★
A.A. ★★ ❀ 70%

FACILITIES
Nearby: *Sailing, jet skiing, golf, riding, fishing*

RESTRICTIONS
No facilities for disabled guests
£5 surcharge for dogs

ATTRACTIONS
Slimbridge Wild Fowl Sanctuary, Badminton and Gatcombe Horse Trials, Bath, The Cotswolds, Stratford-upon-Avon

AFFILIATIONS
Independent

NEAREST
MAJOR CITY:
Bath - 25 miles/35 mins

MAJOR AIRPORT:
London Heathrow - 70 miles/1¾ hrs
Bristol - 40 miles/45 mins

RAILWAY STATION:
Kemble - 3 miles/3 mins

RESERVATIONS
Direct with hotel
Quote ***Best Loved***

ACCESS CODES
Not applicable

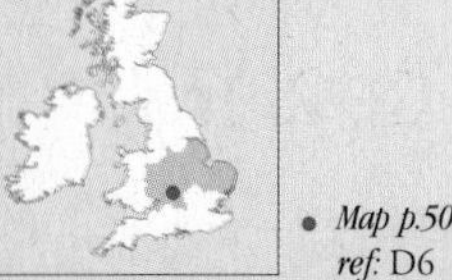

• Map p.500 ref: D6

"Our short stay at Wyck Hill was very pleasing and therapeutic as well - what a beautiful place to escape from our hectic lives"

Stephen Anderson, Texas, USA

WYCK HILL HOUSE

18th century mansion

Stow-on-the-Wold, Gloucestershire GL54 1HY

Telephone 01451 831936
Fax 01451 832243

E-mail: *wyckhill@bestloved.com*

GENERAL MANAGER
Colin Heaney

ROOM RATES

Single occupancy	£105 - £150
21 Doubles/Twins	£155 - £205
3 Four-posters	£190 - £255
6 Suites	£255
2 Family rooms	£255

Includes full breakfast and VAT

CHARGE/CREDIT CARDS

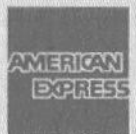

• DC • MC • VI

RATINGS & AWARDS
R.A.C. ★★★★ Dining Award 3
A.A. ★★★★ ❀❀ 71%

FACILITIES
On site: *Garden, croquet, heli-pad*
Licensed for weddings
4 meeting rooms/max 100 people
Nearby: *Golf, tennis, riding, hunting/shooting, fishing, quad bikes, ballooning*

RESTRICTIONS
No facilities for disabled guests
No pets in public rooms

ATTRACTIONS
Stratford-upon-Avon, Bath, Warwick, Blenheim Palace, Bourton-on-the-Water, Burford

AFFILIATIONS
The Celebrated Hotels Collection
The Wren's Hotel Group

NEAREST
MAJOR CITY:
Cheltenham - 16 miles/35 mins
MAJOR AIRPORT:
Birmingham - 50 miles/1 hr
RAILWAY STATION:
Moreton in Marsh - 5 miles/12 mins

RESERVATIONS
Toll free in US: 800-322-2403
*Quote **Best Loved***

ACCESS CODES
SABRE/ABACUS UI 45327
APOLLO/GALILEO UI 74265
AMADEUS UI GLOWHH
WORLDSPAN UI 40713

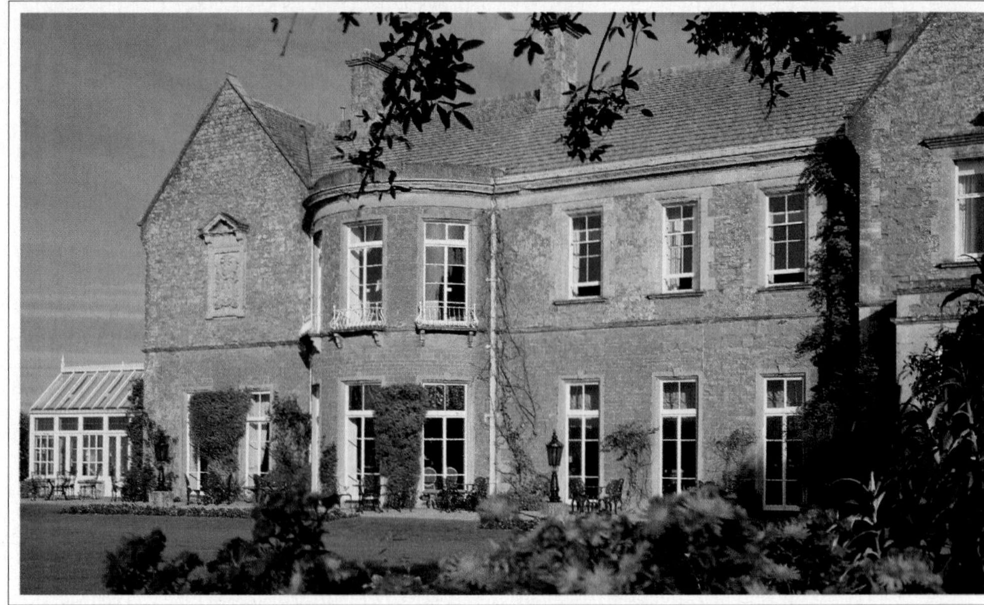

Mansion house living in the heart of the Cotswolds

This luxurious 18th century mansion has recently been completely refurbished and restored to a truly magnificent standard. Step into the interior and you step into all the opulence and grandeur of mansion house style in its most elegant expression. No detail has been spared in providing the richest of furnishings and decor to recreate the peaceful ambience and traditional luxury of country house life. Oak and mahogany panelling, pillars and woodwork have been used throughout and afternoon tea in the refined atmosphere of the library is a must.

All the picturesque charm and splendour of the Cotswolds are met in the hotel's spectacular hilltop setting amidst 100 acres of beautifully landscaped woodlands and gardens, all laid out on different levels. There's a most attractive courtyard with pretty fountain set within the old stable block and some of the rooms are also located in the charming coach house and orangery.

The bedrooms are very special, ornately furnished and each with a brand new luxury bathroom. With excellent conference and meeting facilities and the highest standards of international cuisine, Wyck Hill offers the perfect escape for business or pleasure.

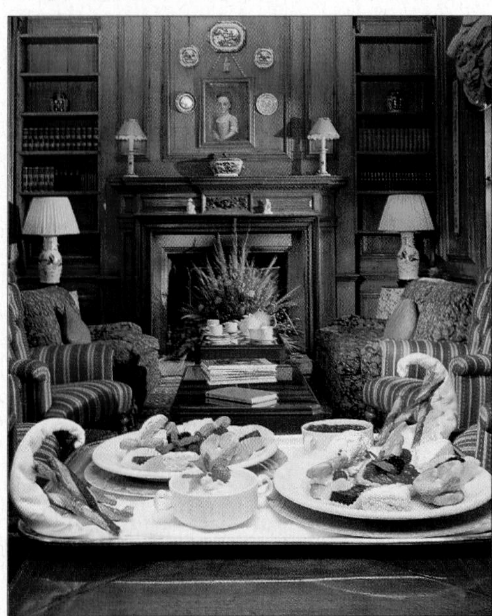

LOCATION

From London - north on M25 to M40. Go west on M40 leaving exit 8 and take A40 to Burford and A424 to Stow. Hotel is 8 miles on the left.

the west

Westward Ho!: Once smugglers' havens, the hidden creeks, secluded bays and river ports of the West Country are a yachtsmen's paradise. The warming effects of the Gulf Stream are largely responsible for Cornwall's tropical gardens, such as Trebah (inset) on the Helford River.

the west

The West Country lives up to its reputation as an inspiration for romantic tales: Lorna Doone, Hounds of the Baskervilles, Westward Ho!, Pirates of Penzance, Cider with Rosie - titles that, if you have read the books, gone to the theatre or seen the films, give a fair idea of the nature of this stretch of England with the longest shoreline and the fairest weather. And there's a wealth of heritage that takes in the haunted medieval castle of Berry Pomeroy and the legendary Tintagel Castle and Merlin's Cave on the dramatic Cornish coast. At Glastonbury Abbey in Somerset the seeds of Christianity were sown in England. Wells has England's first Gothic cathedral and nearby is the historic port of Bristol and elegant Bath Spa.

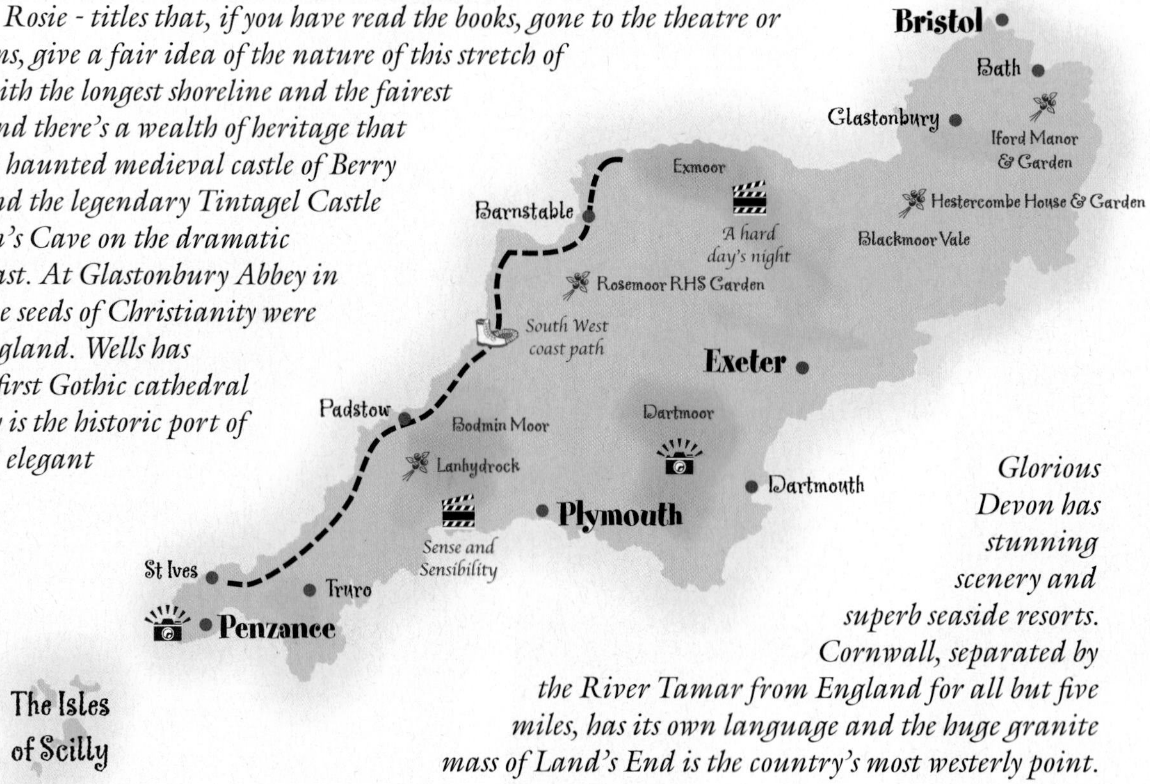

Bristol
Bath
Glastonbury
Iford Manor & Garden
Exmoor
Barnstable
A hard day's night
Hestercombe House & Garden
Blackmoor Vale
Rosemoor RHS Garden
South West coast path
Exeter
Padstow
Bodmin Moor
Dartmoor
Lanhydrock
Dartmouth
Plymouth
Sense and Sensibility
St Ives
Truro
Penzance
The Isles of Scilly

Glorious Devon has stunning scenery and superb seaside resorts. Cornwall, separated by the River Tamar from England for all but five miles, has its own language and the huge granite mass of Land's End is the country's most westerly point.

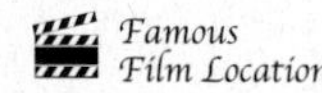

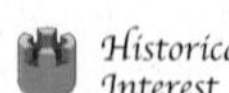

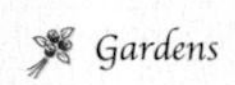

Arthurian legend

Wild and windswept Tintagel Head is believed to be the legendary birthplace of King Arthur. However, the castle ruins are the remnants of a 13th-century Norman fortress balanced precariously above the crashing Atlantic surf.

Botanical bubble

Opening in spring 2001, the Eden Project in Cornwall is described as 'a gateway to the world of plants and people'. Three giant biomes have been erected in an abandoned china clay pit near St Austell to house exotic rainforest, warm temperate and native species.

First line of defence

Dartmouth Castle has guarded the entrance to the River Dart since the 15th century. In those days a chain would have been stretched across the river mouth to a companion fort at Kingswear on the opposite bank.

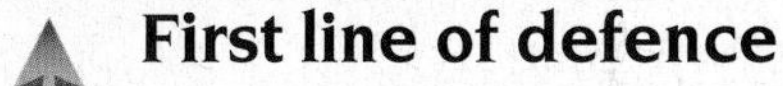

Of water babies and wetsuits

The West Country is a magnet for watersports enthusiasts of all descriptions. Sailing schools for beginners and dinghy and yacht charter are big business along the south coast, while Atlantic rollers attract increasing numbers of surfers to the north coast of Devon and Cornwall from Bude due southwest to hip Newquay.

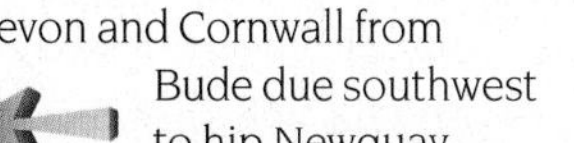

Garden Guide

Medieval romance

Knightshayes Court, near Tiverton, was designed by William Burges in the mid-19th century and combines the richness of high Victorian ornamentation with a medieval romanticism that also found its outpouring in the pre-Raphaelite movement. Knightshayes' gardens are equally captivating and decorative with spectacular topiary, rare trees and shrubs, a lily pond and woodland walks.

Iford Manor
Bradford-on-Avon, Wiltshire BA15 2BA
Tel: 01622 765400
Italian style garden which was the former home of famous landscape architect Harold Peto

Hestercombe Gardens
Cheddon Fitzpaine, Taunton, Somerset TA2 8LG
Tel: 01823 413923
A grade I listed garden with formal gardens planted by Gertrude Jekyll

Lanhydrock
Lanhydrock, Bodmin, Cornwall PL30 5AD
Tel: 01208 73320
One of a number of fascinating gardens for which Cornwall has now become world famous

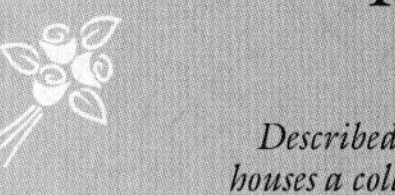

Rosemoor RHS Garden
Great Torrington, Devon
Tel: 01805 624067
Described as a garden for 'gardeners' which houses a collection of over 200 varieties of roses

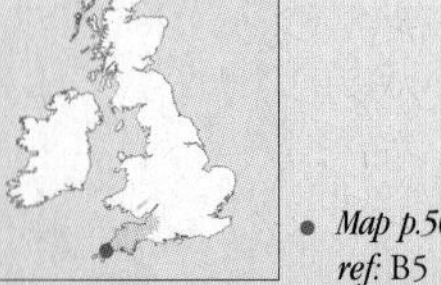

• Map p.502 ref: B5

"A really excellent hotel. The meals and service equal the Waldorf Astoria, New York"

Frank & Margaret Blatchford, Victoria, Australia

ALVERTON MANOR

Cornish country manor

Tregolls Road, Truro, Cornwall TR1 1ZQ

Telephone 01872 276633
Fax 01872 222989

E-mail: alverton@bestloved.com

OWNER
Michael Sagin

ROOM RATES

6 Singles	£67
16 Doubles/Twins	£99
8 Deluxe Doubles/Twins	£114
4 Suites	£139

Includes full breakfast and VAT

CHARGE/CREDIT CARDS

 • DC • JCB • MC • VI

RATINGS & AWARDS
E.T.C. ★★★ Silver Award
R.A.C. ★★★ Dining Award 1
A.A. ★★★ ❀❀ 72%

FACILITIES
On site: Garden, snooker, fishing
Licensed for weddings
5 meeting rooms/max 200 people
Nearby: Fishing, sailing, riding, 18-hole golf course

RESTRICTIONS
None

ATTRACTIONS
Truro and Truro Cathedral, Isles of Scilly, Pendennis Castle, St Mawes Castle, Gardens of Cornwall

AFFILIATIONS
Independent

NEAREST
MAJOR CITY:
Truro - ½ mile/3 mins

MAJOR AIRPORT:
Exeter - 90 miles/1½ hrs
Newquay - 12 miles/20 mins

RAILWAY STATION:
Truro - 1 mile/5 mins

RESERVATIONS
Direct with hotel
Quote **Best Loved**

ACCESS CODES
Not applicable

WEST COUNTRY

The charm and character of another age

Alverton Manor is a truly impressive sight. Built during the early 19th century, the manor was for many years occupied by the Sisters of the Epiphany. Located on a hillside, the hotel boasts fine period sandstone walls, attractive mullioned windows and an original Cornish Delabole slate roof. The building is Grade II listed, and considered of special historical interest.

Outstandingly comfortable in a discreetly elegant way, it has been lovingly restored and is well appointed, retaining the character and charm of another age. All 34 bedrooms are furnished with all the amenities one expects from a modern luxury hotel. The hotel is renowned in the West Country for its contemporary English and French cuisine and the restaurant boasts two A.A. Rosettes.

For the golf enthusiast, the hotel offers concessions on its own golf course within the historic Killiow estate situated in over 400 acres of rolling parkland, only five minutes away by car.

Truro has some of the best-preserved Georgian houses in Britain and its own three-spired cathedral. The many reminders from Cornwall's stirring history include Henry VIII's castles at Pendennis and St Mawes.

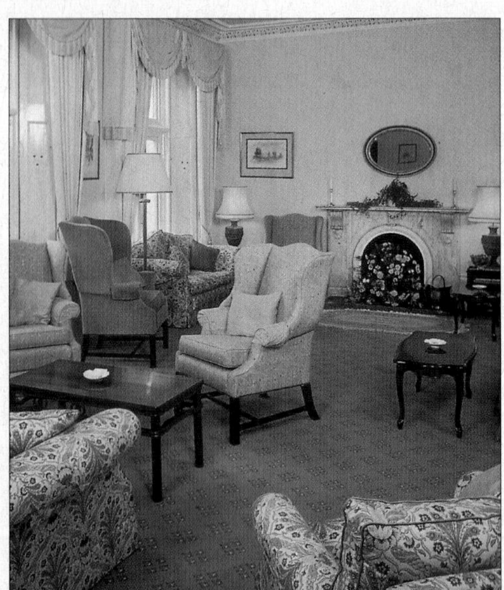

LOCATION

Situated on the A390 approach road to Truro from St Austell, the hotel is located on your right hand side as you approach the first major roundabout on entering Truro.

Planning a wedding reception? Turn to 'Meeting Facilities' on page 476

"Perfect in every way"

Paul Dirratte, Dix Hills, NY, USA

• Map p.502 ref: F2

Stately home

APSLEY HOUSE HOTEL

Make yourself at home in Bath - in the house of the Duke of Wellington

Apsley House is one of Britain's finest small hotels. Originally built as a country house in 1830 for the Duke of Wellington, victor of the Battle of Waterloo when he was Prime Minister. Today the house is furnished with fine antiques and original oil paintings, and the interior includes many period features.

Owned and run by David and Annie Lanz, Apsley House offers a very warm welcome and personal care. The atmosphere is more in keeping with a private house than an hotel. Guests relax in the stylish comfort of the Duke of Wellington's drawing room, and in the intimate bar.

The hotel recognises the wealth of good food to be enjoyed in Bath's many restaurants, wine bars and bistros so it concentrates on a feast of a breakfast served in the sumptuously appointed dining room. You have a choice of traditional English to Apsley House specials. Thoughtfully, there is also a vegetarian selection.

A leisurely twenty minutes' walk takes you into the heart of Bath, with its magnificent Abbey, Pump Room and Georgian streets and squares. Despite its proximity to the city centre, Apsley House has a delightful garden that preserves the feeling of living in a 19th century country house. It also has, fortunately, its own car park.

LOCATION

Just over 1 mile west of the city centre on the A431, which branches off the A4.

Newbridge Hill, Bath, Somerset BA1 3PT

Telephone 01225 336966
Fax 01225 425462

E-mail: *apsley@bestloved.com*

OWNERS

David and Annie Lanz

ROOM RATES

Single occupancy	*£60 - £85*
9 Doubles/Twins	*£70 - £120*

Includes full breakfast and VAT

CHARGE/CREDIT CARDS

• MC • VI

RATINGS & AWARDS

A.A. ◆◆◆◆◆

FACILITIES

On site: *Garden*

Nearby: *Golf, fishing, tennis, fitness, hunting/shooting, hot air ballooning*

RESTRICTIONS

No children under 5 years
No facilities for disabled guests
No pets

ATTRACTIONS

Roman Baths and Pump Room, Costume Museum, Stonehenge, Wells Cathedral, the Cotswolds, Stourhead Gardens, Avebury

AFFILIATIONS

Independent

NEAREST

MAJOR CITY:
Bath

MAJOR AIRPORT:
London Heathrow - 90 miles/1½ hrs

RAILWAY STATION:
Bath Spa - 2 miles/10 mins

RESERVATIONS

Direct with hotel
Quote ***Best Loved***

ACCESS CODES

Not applicable

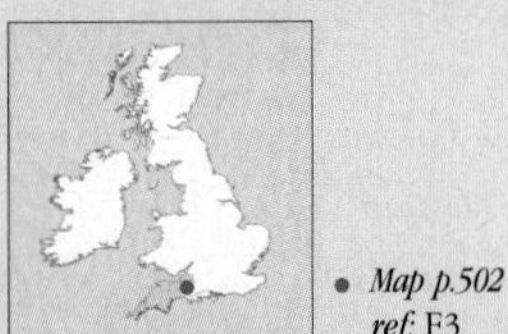

• Map p.502 ref: F3

"Some places on earth can't be beaten, you've created one of those places"

John & Ann Wright, Cambridge

BATH LODGE HOTEL

Georgian estate lodge

Norton St Philip, Bath, Somerset BA3 6NH

Telephone 01225 723040
Fax 01225 723737

E-mail: bathlodge@bestloved.com

OWNERS
Graham and Nicola Walker

ROOM RATES

1 Single	£45 - £85
7 Doubles/Twins	£65 - £85
3 Four-posters	£75 - £105

Includes full breakfast and VAT

CHARGE/CREDIT CARDS

• MC • VI

RATINGS & AWARDS
A.A. ◆◆◆◆◆

FACILITIES
On site: Garden, clay pigeon shooting
Nearby: Golf, riding, hunting/shooting

RESTRICTIONS
No children under 10 years
Limited facilities for the disabled
Smoking in conservatory only
Pets by arrangement
Dinner served Friday & Saturday only

ATTRACTIONS
Bath Abbey, Roman Baths, American Museum, Stonehenge, Longleat, Stourhead, Wells, Glastonbury

AFFILIATIONS
Wessex Historic Hotels

NEAREST
MAJOR CITY:
Bath - 7 miles/15 mins

MAJOR AIRPORT:
London Heathrow - 100 miles/2 hrs
Bristol - 29 miles/45 mins

RAILWAY STATION:
Bath - 7 miles/15 mins

RESERVATIONS
Direct with hotel
Quote **Best Loved**

ACCESS CODES
Not applicable

WEST COUNTRY

Castle comforts amidst the romance of an ancient deer forest

Originally called Castle Lodge, the Bath Lodge Hotel has all the appearance of a pocket-sized medieval castle from its impressive stone structure, portcullis and heraldic shields right up to the battlements and towers above. In fact, the Lodge was built between 1806 and 1813 as the principal of six gate lodges to the Farleigh estate.

The building boasts the original oak beams, natural masonry, a log-burning fireplace and mullioned windows. All the rooms are beautifully decorated and furnished to a high standard with elegant antique furniture happily co-existing with contemporary comforts and facilities. The original lodge rooms benefit from four- poster or brass bedsteads, showers in the turrets and balconies overlooking the grounds.

There's a stream that cascades through the natural garden that clandestinely merges into the ancient deer forest where kings and barons once hunted. All very romantic.

Situated only seven miles outside Bath, the hotel is also ideally located for visiting the heritage sites of Stonehenge, Longleat, Stourhead and Wells with its magnificent cathedral as well as many other attractions of the area. That's why Bath Lodge likes to set its guests up for the day with an excellent breakfast which has no doubt contributed to the hotel's five diamond A.A. rating. In the evening, the romantic and relaxed atmosphere provides the perfect end to the day.

LOCATION

From Bath take A36 Warminster Road. The hotel is approximately 7 miles along this road on left.

For a portrait of this region see page 250

" I rate The Priory the best hotel in town "

David Wickers, The Sunday Times

• Map p.502
ref: F2

Victorian houses

THE BATH PRIORY HOTEL & RESTAURANT

Utter Sumptuousness in the Roman City of Bath

Set in four acres of award-winning landscaped gardens on the edge of the city, The Bath Priory Hotel was built in 1835 as a private residence and remains one of the finest examples of Gothic architecture of its time. Now beautifully converted, it offers visitors comfort, peace and privacy as well as luxurious health spa facilities.

Overlooking the stunning gardens are two restaurants under the direction of Restaurant Manager, Vito Scaduto, where guests can enjoy modern French and Mediterranean cuisine from Head Chef, Robert Clayton.

International Designer, Penny Morrison, has created The Priory's 28 sumptuous bedrooms all of which are equipped with ISDN line, voice mail, US/UK modem points, remote control TV with satellite channels, marble bathrooms, fine antique furniture, traditional British fabrics and objets d'art.

Guests are free to use the health club which features a fully equipped gymnasium, heated indoor and outdoor swimming pools, spa, steamroom and solarium.

Theatres, museums, antique shops, and the Roman Baths are within a pleasant walk.

LOCATION

From London: exit 18 off M4, A46 to Bath. Follow signs to Bristol (A4) until Victoria Park. Turn right at Park Lane and left at Weston Road. The Priory is 300 yards on left.

Weston Road, Bath, Somerset BA1 2XT

Telephone 01225 331922
Fax 01225 448276

E-mail: *priorybath@bestloved.com*

GENERAL MANAGER

Tim Pettifer

ROOM RATES

Single occupancy	*£170*
23 Doubles/Twins	*£285*
3 Junior suites	*£345*
2 Four-posters	*£375*

Includes breakfast, dinner, service and VAT

CHARGE/CREDIT CARDS

• DC • MC • VI

RATINGS & AWARDS

R.A.C. Blue Ribbon ★★★★ Dining Award 4
A.A. ★★★★ ❀❀❀ 78%

FACILITIES

On site: *Indoor and outdoor pool, gym, sauna, steam room, croquet, gardens*
3 meeting rooms/max 60 people
Nearby: *Golf*

RESTRICTIONS

No pets, guide dogs only

ATTRACTIONS

Bath, Lacock, Roman Baths, Royal Crescent, Botanic Gardens, Castle Combe, Royal Victoria Park, Costume Museum, Longleat, Stourhead

AFFILIATIONS

The Celebrated Hotels Collection

NEAREST

MAJOR CITY:
Bath - 1 mile/5 mins

MAJOR AIRPORT:
London Heathrow - 90 miles/1½ hrs
Bristol - 15 miles/25 mins

RAILWAY STATION:
Bath Spa - 1 mile/5 mins

RESERVATIONS

Toll free in US: 800-322-2403
*Quote **Best Loved***

ACCESS CODES

Not applicable

"This beautiful hotel has made our special week in Bath quite perfect"

Joanna Lumley, actress

THE BATH SPA HOTEL

19th century Georgian mansion

**Sydney Road, Bath,
Somerset BA2 6JF**

**Telephone 0870 4008222
Fax 01225 444006**

E-mail: *bathspa@bestloved.com*

GENERAL MANAGER

Michael Grange

ROOM RATES

91 Doubles/Twins	£174 - £265
6 Four-posters	£254 - £315
5 Suites	£294 - £385

Includes VAT

CHARGE/CREDIT CARDS

• DC • JCB • MC • VI

RATINGS & AWARDS

R.A.C. ★★★★★ *Dining Award 3*
A.A. ★★★★★ ❀❀ *64%*

FACILITIES

On site: *Garden, croquet, tennis, sauna, indoor pool, creche, jacuzzi, gym, health & beauty, valet and chauffeur service*
5 meeting rooms/max 120 people
Nearby: *Golf, riding*

RESTRICTIONS

None

ATTRACTIONS

Roman Baths, Museum of Costume, Georgian crescents, antique markets, Bath, Longleat, American Museum

AFFILIATIONS

Heritage Hotels

NEAREST

MAJOR CITY:
Bath

MAJOR AIRPORT:
London Heathrow - 90 miles/2 hrs

RAILWAY STATION:
Bath - 1 mile/5 mins

RESERVATIONS

Toll free in US/Canada: 800-543-4300
Quote **Best Loved**

ACCESS CODES

AMADEUS FE BRS026
APOLLO/GALILEO FE 5645
SABRE/ABACUS FE 21430
WORLDSPAN FE 0026

Georgian style and splendour in the 20th century

An immaculately restored 19th century mansion, The Bath Spa is a handsome hotel set amidst seven acres of tranquil gardens. Panoramic views of the formal gardens, ponds and gentle fountains surround you.

The Bath Spa has two restaurants providing excellent variety for the most sophisticated of palates. Modern British cooking is set off to advantage in the elegant surroundings of The Vellore, while the conservatory style of The Alfresco showcases the more Mediterranean feel to the menu.

There are 102 bedrooms including suites. The hotel offers all the modern amenities you would expect of a five star Hotel, while still retaining the character of a homely country house.

Guests receive complimentary membership of The Laurels Health and Leisure Spa during their stay. Qualified staff are on hand to arrange exercise programmes, relaxing massages and pampering beauty treatments. There is a swimming pool and a jacuzzi to help soothe the nerves, a tennis court for the energetic and a croquet lawn for the dastardly. Quality golf is a mere three iron drive away at Sham Castle.

LOCATION

The hotel is on Sydney Road, 10 minutes walk from the centre of Bath.

Planning a wedding reception? Turn to 'Meeting Facilities' on page 476

"Your home is the epitome of warmth and elegance"

Bungey Travel Inc, California, USA

• Map p.502 ref: E3

Gothic mansion

BINDON COUNTRY HOUSE HOTEL

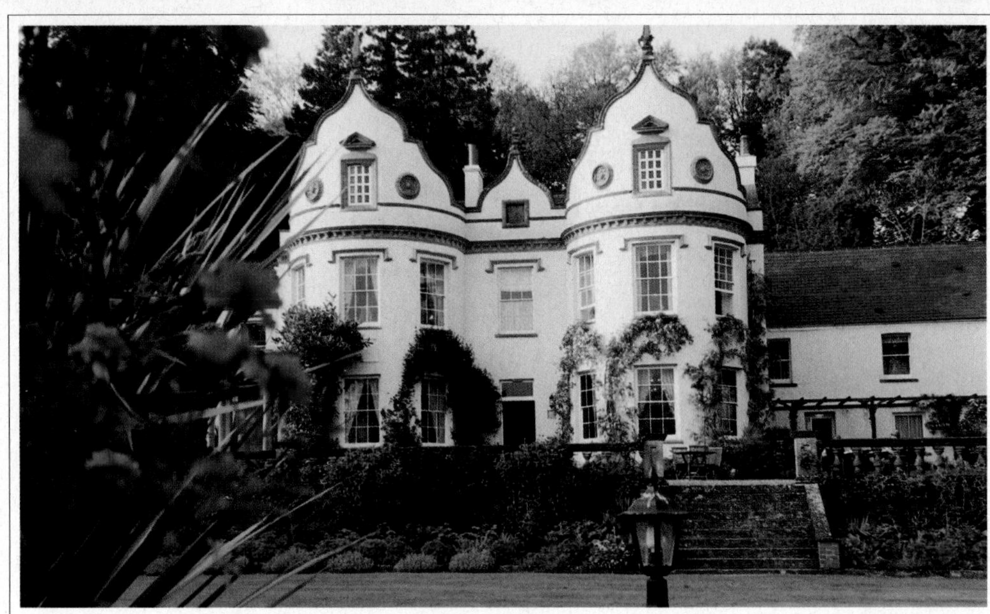

An inspired blend of French and English cuisine and seven acres of tranquillity

Meticulously restored Bindon House is one of Somerset's finest country house hotels with a Grade II listing and an inscription 'Je trouve bien' (I find well) above the west wing entrance. The historic oak panelled Wellington Bar, with its open fireplace, is the place to relax with an after dinner drink with coffee and petit fours or play a game of chess.

Amongst the seven acres of stunning formal and woodland gardens are a heated outdoor swimming pool, tennis court, croquet lawn, a rediscovered rose garden and a Victorian Orangery. The 180-acre Langford Heath Nature Reserve is a mere five minutes walk away.

In the hotel's Wellesley Restaurant, gifted French chef, Patrick Robert, has created an integration of classical French cuisine with imaginative modern British cookery. The restaurant has already won a reputation for excellent food and wines.

Unspoiled countryside, 18th century Gothic splendours, a genuinely innovative hotel, superb food. If you are looking for these things, at Bindon you will find them well.

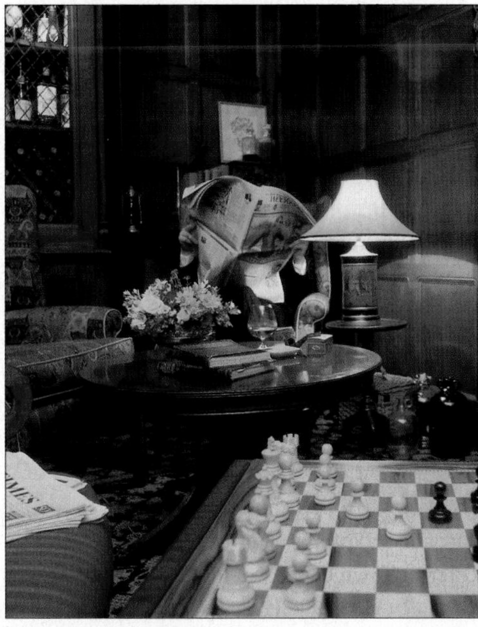

LOCATION

Exit 26 /M5; A38 & then B3187 to Wellington. At second traffic lights, at sharp 's' bend turn right to Langford Budville and, after village, right to Wiveliscombe and right again. Hotel is 1½ miles on right.

Langford Budville, Wellington, Somerset TA21 0RU

Telephone 01823 400070
Fax 01823 400071

E-mail: bindon@bestloved.com

OWNERS

Mark and Lynn Jaffa

ROOM RATES

1 Single	£85
8 Doubles/Twins	£95 - £185
2 Suites	£125 - £155
1 Four-poster	£185

Includes newspaper, full breakfast and VAT

CHARGE/CREDIT CARDS

• DC • MC • VI

RATINGS & AWARDS

R.A.C. Blue Ribbon ★★★ Dining Award 3
A.A. ★★★ ❀❀ 78%

FACILITIES

On site: Garden, croquet, tennis, outdoor heated pool, heli-pad
Licensed for weddings
2 meeting rooms/max 100 people
Nearby: Golf, riding, shooting, fishing

RESTRICTIONS

Limited facilities for disabled guests
Pets by arrangement

ATTRACTIONS

Exeter & Wells Cathedrals, Hestercombe & National Trust Gardens, Exmoor & Dartmoor, Dunster Castle, Bath, Glastonbury

AFFILIATIONS

Pride of Britain
Preston's Global Hotels

NEAREST

MAJOR CITY:
Taunton - 8 miles/15 mins

MAJOR AIRPORT:
Bristol - 50 miles/45 mins
Exeter - 25 miles/25 mins

RAILWAY STATION:
Tiverton Parkway - 8 miles/15 mins
Taunton - 8 miles/15 mins

RESERVATIONS

Toll free in US: 800-544-9993
or 800-98-PRIDE
Quote **Best Loved**

ACCESS CODES

Not applicable

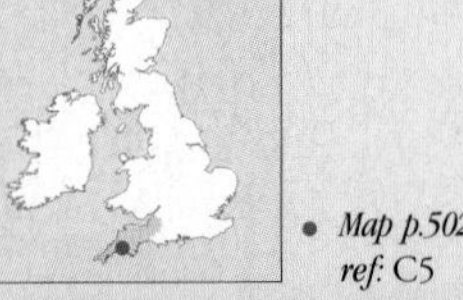

• Map p.502 ref: C5

"We felt like guests of considerate, discriminating and charming friends – we wish we had had the foresight to have stayed longer – a wonderful place"

Professor Clayton, Massachusetts

BOSCUNDLE MANOR

18th century manor house

Tregrehan, St Austell, Cornwall PL25 3RL

Telephone 01726 813557
Fax 01726 814997

E-mail: *boscundle@bestloved.com*

OWNERS

Andrew and Mary Flint

ROOM RATES

2 Singles	£65 - £85
5 Doubles	£110 - £130
3 Suites	£140 - £160

Includes full breakfast and VAT

CHARGE/CREDIT CARDS

• MC • VI

RATINGS &AWARDS

E.T.C. ★★

R.A.C. ★★ *Dining Award 2*

A.A. ★★ ❀ *78%*

FACILITIES

On site: *Garden, indoor and outdoor pools, croquet, snooker, golf practice area, gym, heli-pad*

Nearby: *Golf, riding, tennis, fishing*

RESTRICTIONS

No facilities for disabled guests
No pets in public rooms

ATTRACTIONS

Eden Project, Lanhydrock Gardens, Lost Gardens of Heligan, Fowey, Charlestown and Mevagissey villages, St Mawes and Restormel Castles, Coastal walks

AFFILIATIONS

Preston's Global Hotels

NEAREST

MAJOR CITY:
Truro - 14 miles/30 mins

MAJOR AIRPORT:
London Heathrow - 280 miles/4 hrs
Newquay - 19 miles/40 mins

RAILWAY STATION:
St Austell - 2 miles/5 mins

RESERVATIONS

Toll free in US: 800-544-9993
Quote **Best Loved**

ACCESS CODES

Not applicable

Cornish magic just west of Eden

The magic of Cornwall is here at Boscundle Manor, a beautiful small 18th century manor house set in 12 acres of secluded grounds just ½ mile from the sea and 1 mile from the fascinating Eden Project. All rooms are attractively furnished with antiques, pictures and family possessions. The bedrooms are extremely comfortable, the double rooms having spa baths and showers. The grounds include two practice golf holes (for guests' use only) and the remains of the main Engine House and chimney of the Wheal Eliza tin mine.

Andrew and Mary Flint bought the property on the first day they saw it and have now been here for over 20 years. They aim to provide their guests with fresh local food, cooked with loving care and served as imaginatively as possible. The extensive wine list of over 150 wines is particularly strong on clarets.

Although the Flints do not attempt to provide a formal hotel service, their personal involvement and enthusiasm create a relaxed and happy atmosphere. Many of their guests return time and time again. They are always delighted to help guests make the best use of their time in Cornwall and to discover some of its unique magic.

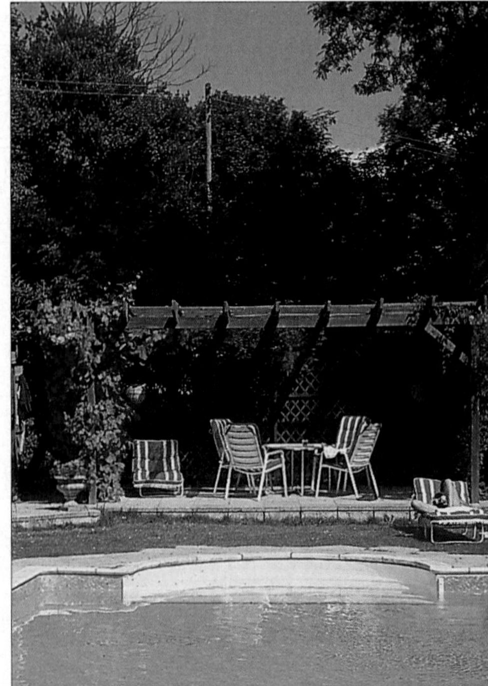

LOCATION

2 miles east of St Austell off the A390 on road signposted to Tregrehan.

“ We will never return to England without visiting Buckland-Tout-Saints ”

Franco Ghezzi, California

• Map p.502
ref: D5

300-year old mansion

BUCKLAND-TOUT-S

Heavenly - undoubtedly one of the West Country's finest

Once upon a time you might have been lucky enough to own a dolls' house modelled on the elegant William and Mary symmetry of Buckland-Tout-Saints. Steeply pitched slate roof pierced by dormers and matching chimneys, neat rows of freshly painted sash windows arranged in a mellow stone façade, yet this gorgeous Grade II listed building is for real and it welcomes visitors.

The house was built in 1690, and set in an idyllic fold of green and wooded hills. Mark and Julia Trumble bought the property in 1998, and set about a 'simple spring clean' which extended over nine months and cost something in the region of £1 million (Mark still doesn't like to think about it). The result is a triumph of luxury tempered by good taste, fine antiques, romantic bedrooms and a brace of splendid original fireplaces discovered during renovations, one of which measures some 16ft across.

Buckland's restaurant serves the best of English and French cuisine devised by head chef Jean-Philippe Bidart. There are set lunch and dinner menus as well as a la carte options and a superb wine list with an impressive selection of half-bottles and house wines by the glass.

LOCATION

Take the A381 to Kingsbridge. The hotel is situated 2 miles north of Kingsbridge. After Halwell and The Mounts, turn left at the hotel sign.

Goveton, Kingsb
Devon TQ7 2D

Telephone 01548 8530
Fax 01548 856261

E-mail: *buckland@bestloved.com*

OWNERS
Mark and Julia Trumble

MANAGER
Julie Hudson

ROOM RATES

1 Single	*£75 - £95*
3 Doubles/Twins	*£150 - £240*
4 Superior doubles	*£170 - £240*
2 Suites	*£200 - £260*

Includes full breakfast and VAT

CHARGE/CREDIT CARDS
MC • VI • JCB

RATINGS & AWARDS
A.A. ★★★ ❀❀❀ 79%

FACILITIES
On site: *Garden, croquet, heli-pad*
Licensed for weddings
2 meeting rooms/max 200 people
Nearby: *Golf, health centre, tennis, sea fishing, yachting, riding*

RESTRICTIONS
Limited facilities for disabled guests

ATTRACTIONS
Dartmouth, Salcombe Estuary, Berry Pomeroy Castle, Dartmoor, Dartington Hall Gardens, Mayflower sailing, Plymouth

AFFILIATIONS
Independent

NEAREST
MAJOR CITY:
Plymouth - 20 miles/45 mins

MAJOR AIRPORT:
Exeter - 40 miles/45 mins
London Heathrow - 220 miles/3½ hrs

RAILWAY STATION:
Totnes - 12 miles/25 mins

RESERVATIONS
Toll free in US: 800-435-8281
*Quote **Best Loved***

ACCESS CODES
Not applicable

“ Perfection is a very hard commodity to find, and should be cherished. ...ank you at Budock for coming so close ”

The St John Family, Stratford-upon-Avon

...E HOTEL ON THE RIVER **Resort hotel**

...SAINTS

...ridge,

...S

...55

...ed.com

OWNERS

The Barlow family

RATES PER PERSON

5 Singles £49 - £97
50 Doubles/Twins £49 - £97
1 Four-poster £59 - £97
1 Suite £124 - £162

Includes full breakfast, dinner, service and VAT

CHARGE/CREDIT CARDS

DC • MC • VI

RATINGS & AWARDS

E.T.C. ★★★★

R.A.C. ★★★★ Dining Award 2

A.A. ★★★★ ❀❀ 73%

FACILITIES

On site: Garden, golf course, tennis, indoor pool, health & beauty, snooker, fishing, motor boat, heli-pad

Licensed for weddings

4 meeting rooms/max 80 people

Nearby: Water skiing, yachting, riding

RESTRICTIONS

No facilities for disabled guests

No children under 7 years in restaurant

No pets in public rooms

Closed 1 - 21 Jan

ATTRACTIONS

The Lost Gardens of Heligan, Trebah Gardens, The Seal Sanctuary, Minack Open Air Theatre, St Michael's Mount, Tate Gallery

AFFILIATIONS

Grand Heritage Hotels

NEAREST

MAJOR CITY:

Truro - 15 miles/20 mins

MAJOR AIRPORT:

Newquay - 30 miles/45 mins

RAILWAY STATION:

Falmouth - 6 miles/10 mins

RESERVATIONS

Toll free in UK: 0800 833 927

Quote **Best Loved**

ACCESS CODES

AMADEUS UI PZEBVC

APOLLO/GALILEO UI 24799

SABRE/ABACUS UI 49775

WORLDSPAN UI 41000

WEST COUNTRY

Indulgent living and superb sports facilities in a beautiful location

Budock Vean is an elegant, unspoilt retreat on the banks of the Helford River, a designated area of Outstanding Natural Beauty. Beside Britain's most dramatic coastline, it is ideal for a range of country pursuits, including fishing, shooting, golf, tennis, walking, riding and sailing. The climate is so mild that the golf course plays well for the whole year. A spectacular indoor heated pool opens out on to the terrace in summer or, in winter, has its own log fire

There is a feeling of privacy and exclusivity within the 65 acres of gardens and parkland. Many bedrooms have private sitting rooms with open views across the hotel's golf course and gardens towards the river. Old world cottages in the grounds can be rented. Seafood is a speciality of the award-winning restaurant, with local Helford oysters and mussels. Less formal meals are served in the Country Club restaurant whose large picture windows overlook the estate.

Cornwall has a unique identity rich in ancient heritage, rites and customs. With breathtaking coastal scenery, picturesque fishing villages and country footpaths, the area has stunning woodland walks beside the estuary. The superb gardens of Glendurgan and Trebah are a short stroll away.

LOCATION

From the A39 Truro to Falmouth road, follow brown signs to Trebah Gardens, then continue for ½ mile to Budock Vean.

"Gosh, they really have got it all just right, haven't they?"

Paddy Burt, The Daily Telegraph

• Map p.502 ref: F2

Country inn

THE CARPENTERS ARMS

In the tradition of a country inn, enjoy good food, real ales and fine company

This charming inn lies in the hamlet of Stanton Wick on the edge of the Mendip Hills and overlooks the Chew Valley. The Carpenters Arms is a unique combination of a traditional English pub, superb food and twelve delightful bedrooms, all with their own bathrooms.

Ideally situated for touring Bath, Bristol and Wells, The Carpenters Arms offers a relaxing environment for those seeking the peace of the countryside. The business executive, keen to escape the tedium of large impersonal hotels, will also find a haven of rest and relaxation.

Good food, real ales and fine wines make The Carpenters Arms a very popular venue. Guests have a choice of two dining rooms and, from the menu in the restaurant, you can choose from a varied and interesting selection of freshly prepared dishes in a warm and inviting atmosphere. If you wish to enjoy the 'olde world' atmosphere on a less expensive scale, dine in the Coopers Parlour where the quality of fayre is just as high and the manner less formal.

The nearby theatres, the antique shops, the museums, the cathedrals and the stately homes make The Carpenters Arms the perfect location for touring.

LOCATION

In the beautiful Chew Valley countryside, close to Bath. Turn off the A37 Wells to Bristol road at Pensford. Alternatively turn off the A368 Bath to Weston-super-Mare road.

Stanton Wick,
Near Pensford,
Somerset BS39 4BX

Telephone 01761 490202
Fax 01761 490763

E-mail: *carpenters@bestloved.com*

OWNERS

Michael Ruthven and Simon Pledge

ROOM RATES

Single occupancy	*£53 - £63*
12 Doubles/Twins	*£70 - £80*

Includes full breakfast, newspaper and VAT

CHARGE/CREDIT CARDS

• DC • MC • VI

RATINGS & AWARDS

E.T.C. ◆◆◆◆

FACILITIES

On site: *Terrace*
2 meeting rooms/max 50 people
Nearby: *Golf, riding, fishing, hot air ballooning, clay pigeon shooting*

RESTRICTIONS

No facilities for disabled guests
No smoking in bedrooms or dining room
No pets

ATTRACTIONS

Bath, Bristol, Longleat, Cheddar Gorge, Wookey Hole, Wells, Glastonbury

AFFILIATIONS

Independent

NEAREST

MAJOR CITY:
Bristol - 7 miles/20 mins

MAJOR AIRPORT:
London Heathrow - 120 miles/2 hrs
Bristol - 5 miles/10 mins

RAILWAY STATION:
Bristol Temple Meads - 7 miles/20 mins

RESERVATIONS

Direct with hotel
Quote ***Best Loved***

ACCESS CODES

Not applicable

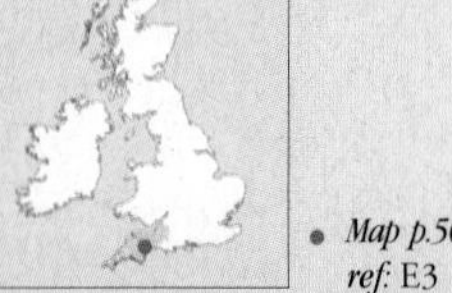

• Map p.502 ref: E3

"Everything at the Castle was perfection; the courtesy and attention of all the staff, the accommodation and not to be forgotton, the food"

Dr and Mrs P Minc, Canada

CASTLE AT TAUNTON

12th century castle

Castle Green, Taunton, Somerset TA1 1NF

Telephone 01823 272671
Fax 01823 336066

E-mail: castle@bestloved.com

OWNERS
The Chapman Family

GENERAL MANAGER
Kevin McCarthy

ROOM RATES

12 Singles	£95
27 Doubles/Twins	£150 - £165
5 Suites	£240

Includes full breakfast and VAT

CHARGE/CREDIT CARDS

• DC • MC • VI

RATINGS & AWARDS
R.A.C. Gold Ribbon ★★★
A.A. ★★★ ❀❀❀

FACILITIES
On site: *Garden*
4 meeting rooms/max 120 people
Nearby: *Golf, leisure centre, health and beauty*

RESTRICTIONS
Limited facilities for disabled guests
Pets by arrangement

ATTRACTIONS
Bath, Exmoor, Longleat Safari Park, Blackdown Hills, Forde Abbey, Wells Cathedral, Quantocks, Dunster

AFFILIATIONS
Independent

NEAREST
MAJOR CITY:
Bristol - 50 miles/1 hr

MAJOR AIRPORT:
Bristol - 40 miles/45 mins
Exeter - 35 miles/40 mins

RAILWAY STATION:
Taunton - 1mile/5 mins

RESERVATIONS
Direct with hotel
Quote ***Best Loved***

ACCESS CODES
Not applicable

WEST COUNTRY

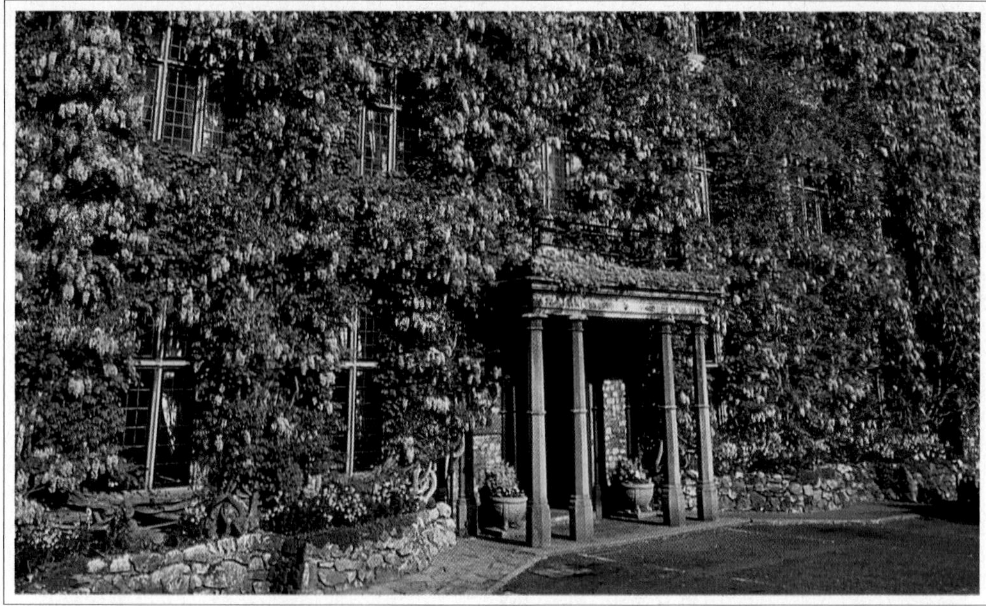

Twelve centuries of fascinating history and West Country hospitality

The Castle at Taunton is steeped in the drama and romance of English history. As exemplified by the Duke of Monmouth's officers, who in 1685 were heard "roistering at the Castle Inn" before they were defeated by the forces of King James II. Today the Castle lives at peace with its turbulent past but preserves the atmosphere of its ancient tradition, and having withstood this test of time visitors today can enjoy those very same pleasures.

The Chapman family have been running the hotel for 50 years and in that time it has acquired a worldwide reputation for the warmth of its hospitality. Diners have the choice of gracious and award winning, refined dining or the more relaxed yet innovative Brazz restaurant.

Located in the heart of England's beautiful West Country, the Castle is the ideal base for exploring a region rich in history. This is the land of King Arthur, King Alfred, Lorna Doone's Exmoor and the monastic foundations of Glastonbury and Wells. Roman and Regency Bath, Longleat House and the majestic gardens of Stourhead and Hestercombe. All this and much more can be discovered within easy driving distance of Taunton.

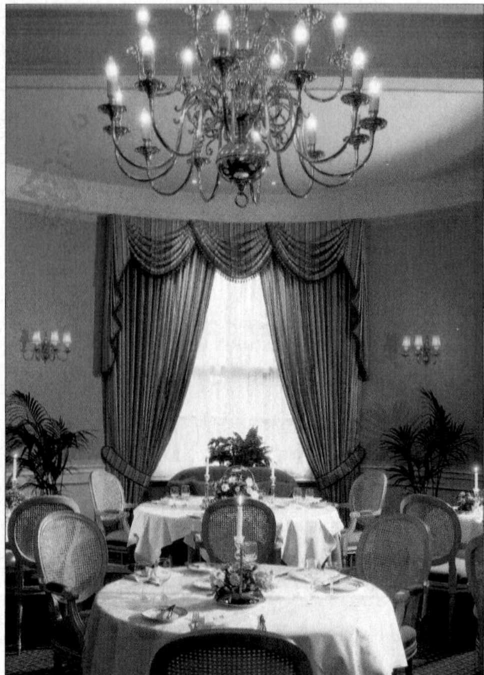

LOCATION

Exit Junction 25 of M5 and follow signs for Taunton town centre. Once in town centre follow signs for The Castle.

Looking for an hotel with a golf course on site? See our 'Golf Guide' on page 478

"The food was magnificent, the rooms superb and everyone was so friendly and helpful"

Jane O'Neill, IPC Magazines

• Map p.502 ref: F3

17th century manor

CHARLTON HOUSE

The Mulberry makeover - the perfect country house

To restore, refurbish and revitalise Charlton House into a dream hotel was quite simply a labour of love for Roger and Monty Saul, founders of the internationally famous Mulberry label. Their place in the country has become a luxurious hotel and restaurant that serves as the perfect setting for the Mulberry Home Collection.

The Manor of Charlton was first mentioned in the Domesday Book of 1086. Merchant Roger Ames built Charlton House for his bride in 1630, and the Ames family lived there for almost 200 years. Each generation added its individual touch, and the imposing Georgian-fronted house has unique character.

The Mulberry makeover lives up to the sense of theatre. The main hall is rich burgundy rolled with gold. The dining room has inspirational textural-effect walls and hooded caftan chairs. From the kitchen comes a unique style, blending traditional and exotic. The wine-cellar does justice to Roger Saul's passion for the grape.

Particular care has been lavished on the 16 bedrooms. Each reflects character, originality and wit. Items are created specifically to meet the needs of today's travellers. For the discerning traveller the 'Charlton House experience' is a must.

LOCATION

From Exit 17 of the M4, follow A350 south on to A361. Proceed past Frome. Charlton House is on the right, one mile from Shepton Mallet.

Shepton Mallet, Near Bath, Somerset BA4 4PR

Telephone 01749 342008
Fax 01749 346362

E-mail: charlton@bestloved.com

OWNERS
Mr and Mrs R J Saul

GENERAL MANAGER
Ian Jupp

ROOM RATES

Single occupancy	£105 - £235
13 Doubles/Twins	£140 - £210
3 Suites	£235 - £340

Includes continental breakfast, newspaper and VAT

CHARGE/CREDIT CARDS

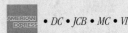

 • DC • JCB • MC • VI

RATINGS & AWARDS
E.T.C. ★★★ Gold Award
R.A.C. ★★★
A.A. ★★★ ❀❀❀

FACILITIES
On site: Garden, croquet, tennis, sauna, indoor pool, fishing, heli-pad Licensed for weddings
3 meeting rooms/max 120 people
Nearby: Golf, riding, hunting/shooting

RESTRICTIONS
No facilities for disabled guests
Pets by arrangement

ATTRACTIONS
Bath, American Museum, Longleat House, Glastonbury, Stourhead, Wells Cathedral, Mulberry Factory Shop

AFFILIATIONS
Preston's Global Hotels
Grand Heritage Hotels

NEAREST
MAJOR CITY:
Bath - 18 miles/30 mins
MAJOR AIRPORT:
Bristol - 19 miles/30 mins
RAILWAY STATION:
Castle Cary - 6 miles/15 mins

RESERVATIONS
Toll free in US: 800-544-9993 or 888-93-GRAND
Quote **Best Loved**

ACCESS CODES
AMADEUS UI BRSCHH
APOLLO/GALILEO UI 83676
SABRE/ABACUS UI 24964
WORLDSPAN UI 40672

• Map p.502 ref: F2

"This has been a wonderful home from home: we've felt like house-party guests"

Peter Baillie and Sarah Mitchener, Farnham, Surrey

CLIFFE HOTEL

19th century country house hotel

Crowe Hill, Limpley Stoke, Bath, Somerset BA3 6HY

Telephone 01225 723226
Fax 01225 723871

E-mail: *cliffe@bestloved.com*

OWNERS

John and Carol Hawken

ROOM RATES

Single occupancy	*£75 - £95*
8 Doubles/Twins	*£95 - £115*
3 Four-posters	*£115 - £125*

Includes full breakfast and VAT

CHARGE/CREDIT CARDS

• *DC* • *MC* • *VI*

RATINGS & AWARDS

E.T.C. ★★★ *Silver Award*

A.A. ★★★ ❀ *73%*

FACILITIES

On site: *Garden, outdoor pool*
Licensed for weddings
1 meeting room/max 30 people
Nearby: *Golf, tennis, fitness, riding*

RESTRICTIONS

No pets in public rooms

ATTRACTIONS

Roman Baths, Bath Abbey, Longleat, Wells Cathedral, Stonehenge, Glastonbury

AFFILIATIONS

Best Western

NEAREST

MAJOR CITY:
Bath - 4½ miles/10 mins

MAJOR AIRPORT:
London Heathrow - 105 miles/1¾ hrs
Bristol - 25 miles/45 mins

RAILWAY STATION:
Bath - 5 miles/10 mins

RESERVATIONS

Direct with hotel
Quote ***Best Loved***

ACCESS CODES

SABRE/ABACUS BW 10374
AMADEUS BW BRS041
APOLLO/GALILEO BW 13347
WORLDSPAN BW 83041

WEST COUNTRY

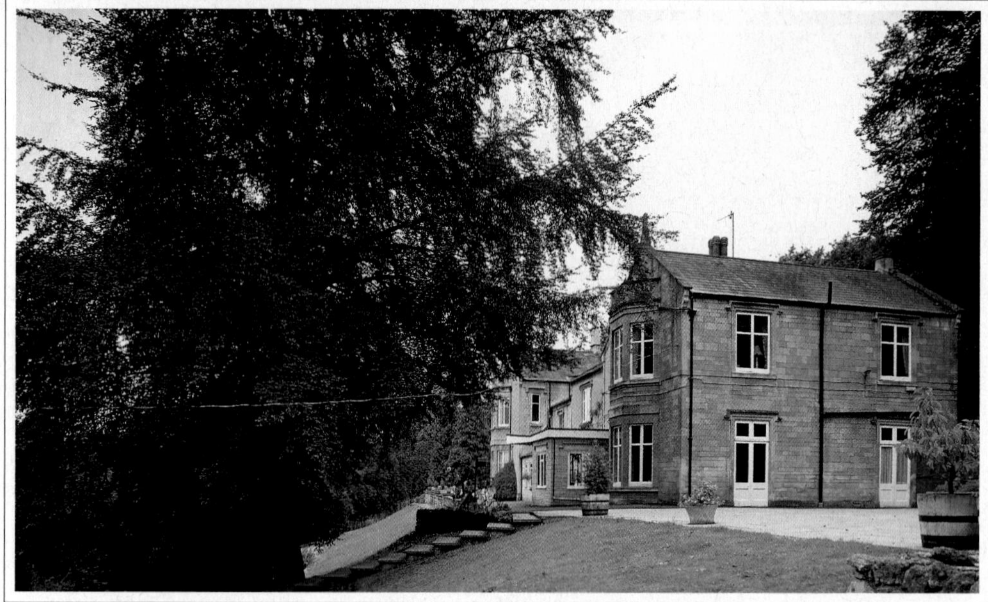

Feel like house-party guests at this popular haven just outside Bath

The owners of this charming country house style hotel set such great store at being the perfect hosts that they would claim the hotel recently hosted the perfect wedding - their own!

Overlooking spectacular views across the Avon valley, including a wonderful old viaduct, the hotel strikes a perfect balance between the highest standards of service and hospitality expected from a large city hotel, and all the homely comforts and relaxed, friendly atmosphere of a country house.

The hotel is much in demand by people visiting Bath for its many attractions or as a base to visit picturesque Wiltshire villages, nearby Longleat House with its Safari Park, or historic Wells and Glastonbury. It is also ideally situated for business people needing to visit the commercial centres of Bristol and Bath and who also need easy access to South Wales and the South West.

Landscaped, terraced gardens, spacious, individually styled bedrooms and a local reputation as one of the places to dine, all combine to make The Cliffe Hotel the perfect venue for any celebration, romantic break or for a wonderfully relaxing weekend when comfort, peace and privacy are all you require.

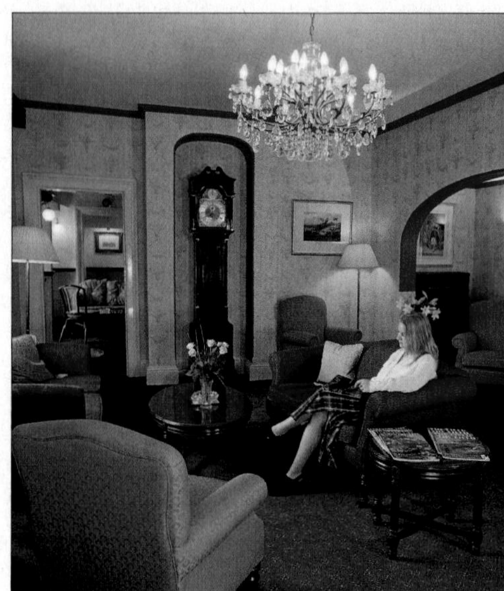

LOCATION

Follow A36 from Bath to Limpley Stoke; at traffic lights turn left; follow road for ½ mile, turn right before railway bridge, through village. Cliffe Hotel is 800 metres on right.

"The most delightful situation in the vicinity of Bath"

John Wesley, 1781

• Map p.502
ref: F2

Country house COMBE GROVE MANOR HOTEL & COUNTRY CLUB

Something for everyone on the very edge of Bath

Named after the large fir groves surrounding the house and gardens, Combe Grove Manor was entertaining visitors long before it became an hotel and country club. Built on a hillside site of a Roman settlement, this historic encounter of 18th century elegance with unrivalled 21st century sports and leisure facilities is encompassed by 82 acres of private gardens and woodland which command a spectacular view over the Limpley Stoke.

Situated just two miles from the Georgian splendours of Bath, Combe Grove Manor offers a choice of 40 individually designed bedrooms, nine in the main house, and 31 in the Garden Lodge, from deluxe to four-poster suites, the Manor House boasts two restaurants, the Georgian Restaurant offers superb cuisine from both a Table d'Hôte and A La Carte Menu whilst the Manor Vaults offers bistro fare in a more relaxed atmosphere.

Guests have unlimited access to the leisure facilities including four tennis courts, Nautilus gymnasium, indoor and outdoor heated swimming pools, sauna, steam room, solaria and beauty rooms featuring a range of therapeutic treatments using exclusive Clarins skincare products.

LOCATION

Two miles south of the city of Bath. For detailed directions guests are advised to contact hotel reception.

Brassknocker Hill,
Monkton Combe, Bath,
Somerset BA2 7HS

Telephone 01225 834644
Fax 01225 834961

E-mail: *combegrove@bestloved.com*

ASSISTANT DIRECTOR

James Parker

ROOM RATES

Single occupancy	£99 - £320
36 Doubles	£99 - £185
2 Four-posters	£185 - £320
2 Suites	£225 - £270

Includes full breakfast, use of sports and leisure facilities and VAT

CHARGE/CREDIT CARDS

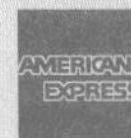

• DC • MC • VI

RATINGS & AWARDS

E.T.C. ★★★★ Silver Award
R.A.C. ★★★★ Dining Award 3

FACILITIES

On site: *Indoor/outdoor pool, solaria, sauna, steam room, gym, tennis, heli-pad, practice golf/driving range, croquet, jogging trail, crèche, health & beauty*
Licensed for weddings
4 meeting rooms/max 80 people
Nearby: *Golf, riding, fishing, shooting*

RESTRICTIONS

No pets
No facilities for disabled guests

ATTRACTIONS

Bath, Wells, Longleat, the Cotswolds, Stonehenge

AFFILIATIONS

Independent

NEAREST

MAJOR CITY:
Bath - 2 miles/5 mins

MAJOR AIRPORT:
London Heathrow - 100 miles/2 hrs

RAILWAY STATION:
Bath Spa - 2 miles/5 mins

RESERVATIONS

Direct with hotel
Quote ***Best Loved***

ACCESS CODES

Not applicable

• Map p.502 ref: E4

" At last we've found it – the perfect hotel! A very special house owned and staffed by very special people "

Linda and Nigel Carver, Cambridge

COMBE HOUSE AT GITTISHAM

Elizabethan manor

Gittisham, Honiton, Near Exeter, Devon EX14 3AD

Telephone 01404 540400
Fax 01404 46004

E-mail: combehouse@bestloved.com

OWNERS

Ken and Ruth Hunt

ROOM RATES

Single occupancy	£120 - £180
8 Doubles/Twins	£130
3 Superior rooms	£190
1 Four-poster	£225
3 Suites/Master rooms	£245

Includes full breakfast and VAT

CHARGE/CREDIT CARDS

• DC • MC • VI

RATINGS & AWARDS

E.T.C. ★★★
R.A.C. ★★★ Dining Award 3
A.A. ★★★ ❀❀ 73%

FACILITIES

On site: *Garden, croquet, heli-pad, Chauffeured transfer car service Licensed for weddings 2 meeting rooms/max 90 people*
Nearby: *Golf, private fishing, shooting, riding*

RESTRICTIONS

No facilities for disabled guests

ATTRACTIONS

Powderham Castle, Killerton House and Garden, Exeter Racecourse, Exeter Cathedral, Exmoor, Dartmoor, Lyme Regis, antique hunting, fossiling

AFFILIATIONS

Pride of Britain

NEAREST

MAJOR CITY:
Exeter - 16 miles/20 mins
Taunton - 19 miles/40 mins

MAJOR AIRPORT:
Exeter - 12 miles/10 mins
London Heathrow - 145 miles/3½ hrs

RAILWAY STATION:
Honiton - 4 miles/5 mins

RESERVATIONS

Toll free in US: 800-98-PRIDE
Quote ***Best Loved***

ACCESS CODES

Not applicable

Friendship and informality in a stately Elizabethan manor

Combe House is a gracious manor built in the reign of Queen Elizabeth I and situated in one of the finest settings in England. Its interior and many treasured antiques and works of art date back to the 16th century. Secluded from modern hustle in over 3,500 acres of ancient woodland, it is ideally placed as the gateway to the West Country – a little over two hours from London, Waterloo.

The elegantly understated bedrooms have unparalled views across the gardens and estate. For all the grandeur of this classic house, hosts Ken and Ruth Hunt have created a uniquely relaxed and informal atmosphere. Chef Philip Leach, a Master Chef of Great Britain, produces contemporary British cuisine and is noted for his fine combinations of flavours and the stunning presentation of all his dishes.

On the Combe estate are walks in rich, broad-leaved woodland, enchanting gardens, and paddocks of beautiful Arabian horses. Working farms trace their history back into the early Middle Ages, as does the charming Devon village of Gittisham, with its pretty thatch cottages and Saxon church, described by Prince Charles as 'the ideal English village'. Also close by is Honiton, a treasure trove of antiques, rare books and lace and the World Heritage coast line from Lyme Regis to Sidmouth.

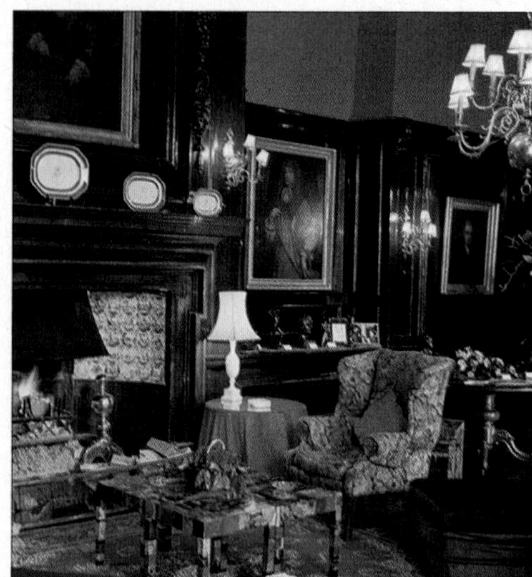

LOCATION

Travelling south exit 28/M5 onto A373, or (from London) A303/A30, Honiton/Heath Park. Travelling north exit 29/M5 Honiton/Fenny Bridges. Follow signs to Gittisham.

"Came for one week and stayed for three - hospitality in every respect just unbelievable"

Lyndon & Kate Hawkins, Thornbury, South Gloucestershire

• Map p.502 ref: C5

Farm house COOMBE FARM COUNTRY HOUSE HOTEL

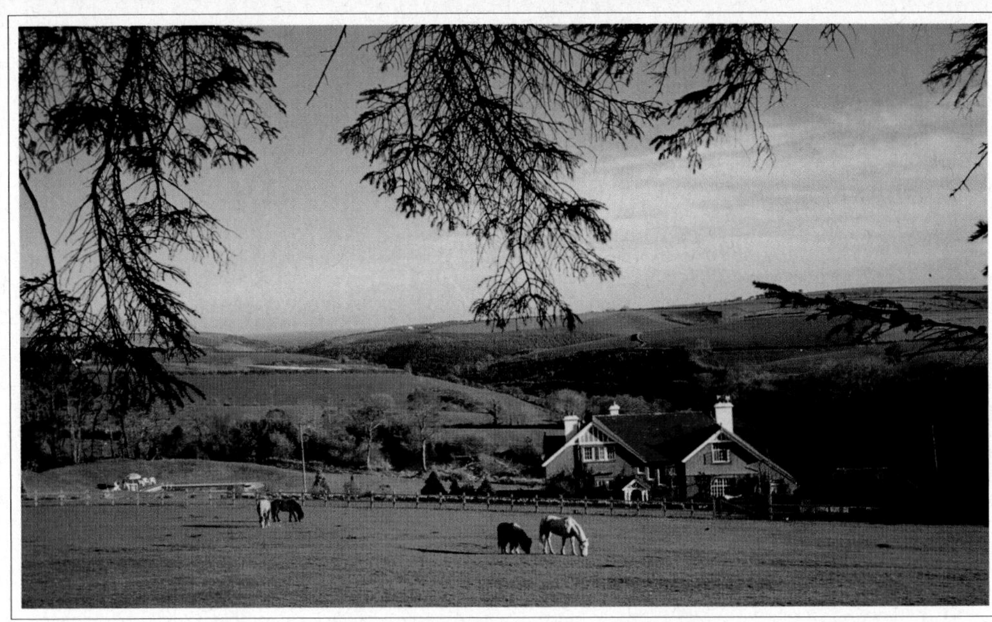

An award-winning small hotel of rare character with a tale to tell from the East

Coombe Farm was built in 1925, by a Colonel Hext on his retirement from the British Army in India. Modelled on an Indian Hill Station bungalow, with extra rooms added in the deep roof it began as a working farm. In 1979, the house was completely renovated and began the second phase of its life as an hotel. Within two years, it was an acclaimed guest house which, in 1996, was presented with the RAC Small Hotel of the Year Award for the West of England.

Now Martin and Sylvia Eades have taken over and continue the high standard for which Coombe Farm is already well-established and have received various accolades to prove it.

The house has been lovingly furnished with antiques, paintings and interesting old objects. A variety of board games are available in the lounge and a stone barn has been converted into a games room for snooker and table tennis. The ten bedrooms all have lovely country views and are centrally heated. All have shower with WC, satellite TV, direct-dial telephone, radio, hair drier and tea and coffee making facilities.

The full English breakfast includes a choice of eggs and delicious kippers. In the evening, a four-course candlelit diner costs just £16 per person.

Outside are ten acres of grounds with superb views down a wooded valley to the sea. Close by are glorious walks, beaches and splendid National Trust properties.

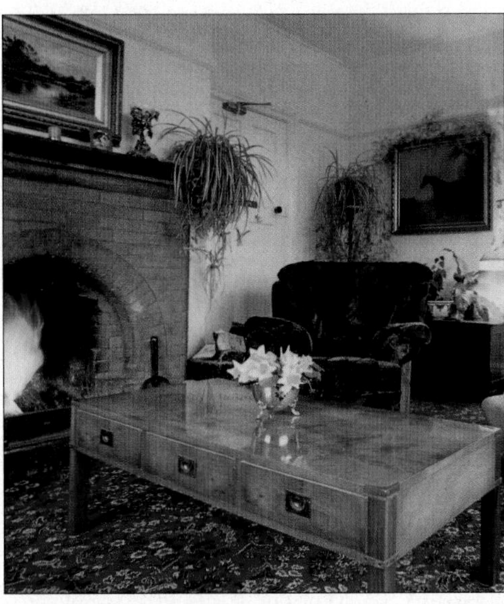

LOCATION

On the B3253 from Hessenford to Looe.

Widegates, Near Looe, Cornwall PL13 1QN

Telephone 01503 240223
Fax 01503 240895

E-mail: *coombefarm@bestloved.com*

OWNERS

Martin and Sylvia Eades

MANAGERS

Sally Wickes and Val Hoare

RATES PER PERSON

6 Doubles/Twins £28 - £36
4 Family suites £28 - £36
25% discount for children under 16 sharing with parents
Includes full breakfast and VAT

CHARGE/CREDIT CARDS

• *MC* • *VI*

RATINGS & AWARDS

E.T.C. ◆◆◆◆ *Silver Award*
R.A.C. ◆◆◆◆
Sparkling Diamond & Warm Welcome Awards
A.A. ◆◆◆◆

FACILITIES

On site: *Garden, croquet, outdoor pool, snooker, table tennis*
Nearby: *Golf, tennis, riding, fitness, water skiing, fishing*

RESTRICTIONS

Pets by arrangement
No smoking
Closed 1 Nov - 28 Feb

ATTRACTIONS

Lanhydrock House, Polperro, Tintagel, Cotehele, Lost Gardens of Heligan, St Michaels Mount, Fowey, The Eden Project

AFFILIATIONS

Independent

NEAREST

MAJOR CITY:
Plymouth - 15 miles/25 mins

MAJOR AIRPORT:
London Heathrow - 220 miles/3½ hrs

RAILWAY STATION:
Liskeard - 7 miles/10 mins

RESERVATIONS

Direct with hotel
*Quote **Best Loved***

ACCESS CODES

Not applicable

• Map p.502 ref: C5

"Absolutely idyllic combination of gourmet food, real hospitality, comfort and stunning views"

A Carter, Somerset

CORMORANT ON THE RIVER

Riverside hotel

Golant-by-Fowey, Cornwall PL23 1LL

Telephone 01726 833426
Fax 01726 833574

E-mail: cormorant@bestloved.com

OWNERS
Colin and Carrie King

ROOM RATES

Single occupancy	£38 - £59
11 Doubles/Twins	£76 - £92

Includes full breakfast, service and VAT

CHARGE/CREDIT CARDS

 • JCB • MC • VI

RATINGS & AWARDS
E.T.C. ★★
R.A.C. ★★ Dining Award 1
A.A. ★★ 70%

FACILITIES
On site: Garden, indoor pool
Nearby: Golf, river and sea fishing, yachting and riding

RESTRICTIONS
No facilities for disabled guests
Pets by arrangement
No smoking in bedrooms

ATTRACTIONS
Lanhydrock House, Heligan Gardens, St Michael's Mount, St Ives Tate Gallery, Trelissick, The Eden Project

AFFILIATIONS
Independent

NEAREST
MAJOR CITY:
Truro - 25 miles/40 mins

MAJOR AIRPORT:
Exeter - 83 miles/1¾ hrs
London Heathrow - 300 miles/4 hrs

RAILWAY STATION:
Par - 5 miles/10 mins

RESERVATIONS
Direct with hotel
Quote **Best Loved**

ACCESS CODES
Not applicable

WEST COUNTRY

Whether you come for the view or the good food, you'll be happy!

There was a time when the Fowey was a bustling commercial port, and, even today, the deep-water inlet guarded by the narrow heads provides safe haven to ships and occasional visits from the Royal Navy. Smugglers, too, have played a role in the area's history. Of all Britain's natural harbours, the Fowey Estuary must be one of the loveliest. Surveying this magnificent seascape from a hillside up river is a restaurant of repute, The Cormorant on the River.

It is a wonderful vantage point that the hotel exploits to the full. All the bedrooms, the lounge, the dining room, the indoor swimming pool and the terrace have views of the estuary.

Colin and Carrie King, the hotel's new owners, have a great enthusiasm for this corner of the world and it comes as no surprise that their own hobbies include sailing, riding and walking. Ask either of them, and they will gladly tell you the best places to go to take full advantage of all these pursuits.

The many famous Cornish gardens are all within easy reach and the regions latest and most adventurous attraction, The Eden Project, is only 5 miles away. Colin and Carrie's specially created 'Garden Break' is worth asking about as well.

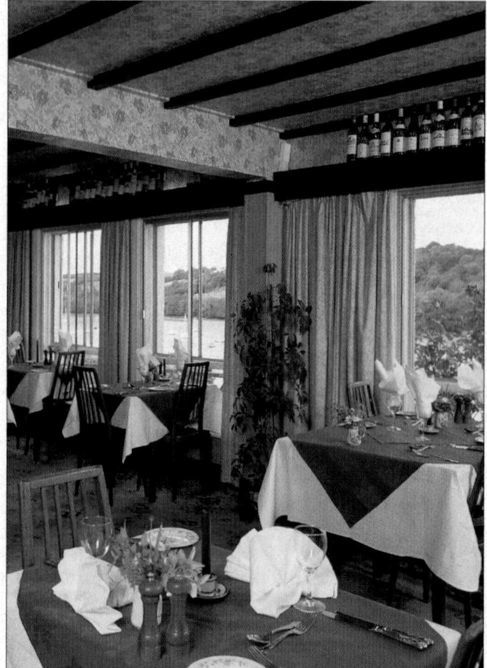

LOCATION

After leaving Lostwithiel on the A390 towards St Austell, turn left on to the B3269. After three miles, turn left at the sign for Golant.

" What a lovely peaceful place! "

Lulu, London

• *Map p.502 ref: C4*

Victorian country house

COURT BARN

Crackling log fires, good food and wine in a romantic Devon hideaway

Built as the 'Sanctuary' around the 16th century, the present house was partly rebuilt in 1853, and had its own chapel. It is a small, but delightful country house, set in park-like grounds with an aura of peace amidst glorious Devon countryside.

The hotel has great charm. Attractive and individually furnished en suite bedrooms, most with bath and shower, offer a wide range of facilities. Cracking log fires and the cosy, well stocked bar, create a warm relaxed atmosphere in which to unwind. For the duller days there is a well stocked library, board games, bridge and perhaps indulgence in an award-winning cream tea.

Robert and Susan are justifiably proud of their reputation for hospitality and good food. A selection of 350 wines accompany the mouth-watering four-course dinner created from fresh, quality produce. While the breakfast room looks over the croquet lawns, the restaurant, candlelit in the evenings and decorated with antiques, fresh flowers and crisp linen, has views of the garden.

You will find good, old-fashioned values of service and hospitality at Court Barn, the perfect base from which to discover this delightful part of unexplored Devon and Cornwall.

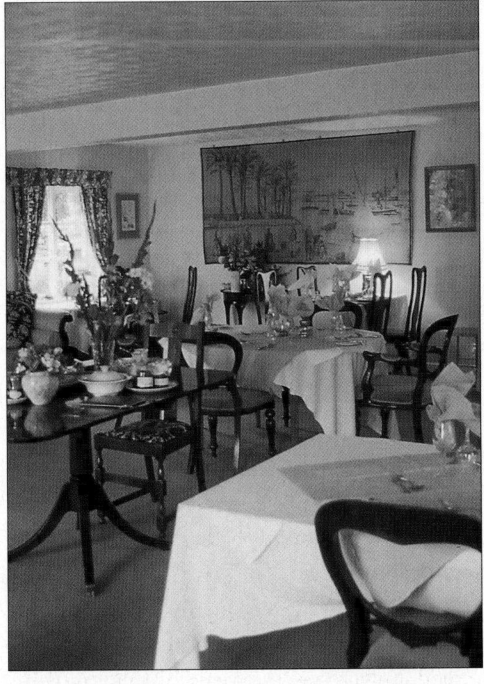

LOCATION

2½ miles south of Holsworthy off A388, turn towards North Tamerton for ½ mile. Hotel is next to 12th century Clawton Church.

Clawton, Holsworthy, Devon EX22 6PS

Telephone 01409 271219
Fax 01409 271309

E-mail: *courtbarn@bestloved.com*

PROPRIETORS

Robert and Susan Wood

ROOM RATES

Single occupancy	*£38 - £55*
6 Doubles/Twins	*£60 - £80*
1 Four-poster	*£90*
1 Small Suite	*£100*

Includes full breakfast and VAT

CHARGE/CREDIT CARDS

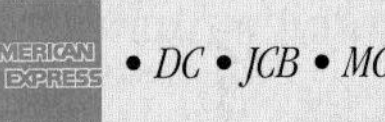

• DC • JCB • MC • VI

RATINGS & AWARDS

E.T.C. ★★ Silver Award
R.A.C. ★★
Tea Council 'Best Teas' in Britain
Taste of the West Guide

FACILITIES

On site: *Garden, croquet, badminton, lawn tennis, 4-hole pitch & putt*
2 meeting rooms/max 25 people
Nearby: *Golf, riding, fishing, sailing, archery, clay shooting, indoor pool, leisure centre*

RESTRICTIONS

No facilities for disabled guests
Smoking in bar and TV room only

ATTRACTIONS

Boscastle, Clovelly, Tintagel, Docton Mill, Hartland Abbey, Tamar Cycle Trail, Exmoor, Bodmin Moor, Dartmoor, Tate Gallery St Ives, RHS Rosemoor

AFFILIATIONS

Independent

NEAREST

MAJOR CITY:
Exeter - 35 miles/50 mins

MAJOR AIRPORT:
London Heathrow - 240 miles/4 hrs

RAILWAY STATION:
Exeter - 35 miles/50 mins

RESERVATIONS

Direct with hotel
Quote ***Best Loved***

ACCESS CODES

Not applicable

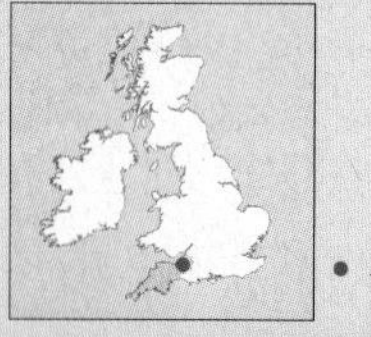

• Map p.502 ref: F3

"Thank you for such enjoyable sojourns"

John Cleese, actor

DANESWOOD HOUSE HOTEL

Country house hotel

Cuck Hill, Shipham,
Near Winscombe,
Somerset BS25 1RD

Telephone 01934 843145
Fax 01934 843824

E-mail: *daneswood@bestloved.com*

OWNERS

David and Elise Hodges

ROOM RATES

Single occupancy	*£75 - £95*
8 Doubles/Twins	*£80 - £95*
1 Four-poster	*£110*
3 Suites	*£135*

Includes full breakfast, service and VAT

CHARGE/CREDIT CARDS

• *DC* • *MC* • *VI*

RATINGS & AWARDS

E.T.C. ★★★

R.A.C. ★★★

A.A. ★★★ ❀❀ *73%*

FACILITIES

On site: *Garden*

2 meeting rooms/max 80 people

Nearby: *Golf, fishing, tennis, riding, dry ski slope*

RESTRICTIONS

Pets by arrangement

No facilities for disabled guests

ATTRACTIONS

Cheddar Gorge,
Clarks Village,
Wells, Glastonbury,
Stonehenge, Bath

AFFILIATIONS

Independent

NEAREST

MAJOR CITY:
Bristol - 12 miles/30 mins

MAJOR AIRPORT:
Bristol - 7 miles/10 mins

RAILWAY STATION:
Weston-Super-Mare - 7 miles/20 mins

RESERVATIONS

Direct with hotel

Quote ***Best Loved***

ACCESS CODES

Not applicable

A secluded Somerset gem perched in the Mendip Hills

Handsomely positioned above a steep, wooded valley, Daneswood House enjoys tremendous views across Somerset's rolling Mendip Hills to the Bristol Channel and beyond. The hotel was originally built as an Edwardian homeopathic health hydro and has been thoughtfully transformed into an intimate small hotel.

Owners David and Elise Hodges have taken every care to anticipate their guests needs and hone Daneswood's relaxed and comfortable style to perfection over their 22-year tenure. Generously proportioned bedrooms are decorated with charming floral fabrics and a smattering of antique furnishings and ornaments. The attractive dining room, adorned with dark William Morris wallpaper, has a fine reputation for exemplary service.

Daneswood is ideally situated for exploring a variety of local attractions. The hotel grounds offer direct access to the Mendip Walkway, there is horse riding nearby, and Cheddar Gorge is just two miles from the front gate. Within a short drive, golf, trout fishing and clay pigeon shooting provide further possibilities. A little further afield are Bristol, Bath, Wells and Glastonbury. Conveniently located for Bristol Airport and the M5, the hotel is both a 'get away from it all' retreat and useful meetings/conference centre for the South West.

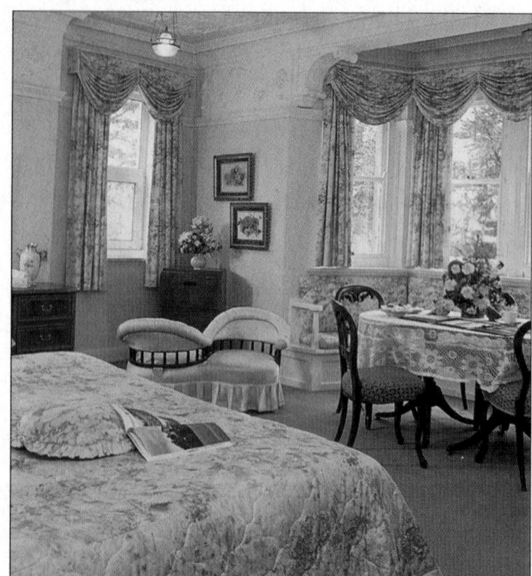

LOCATION

South of Bristol off A38 towards Cheddar. Go through Shipham - hotel is on left as you drive out of the village.

" Thank you very much for making our trip to historic Bath an enjoyable one. Everyone was so helpful and friendly that it made our visit extra special "

Maria Mammes, Germany

• *Map p.502 ref: F2*

Georgian townhouse

DUKES HOTEL

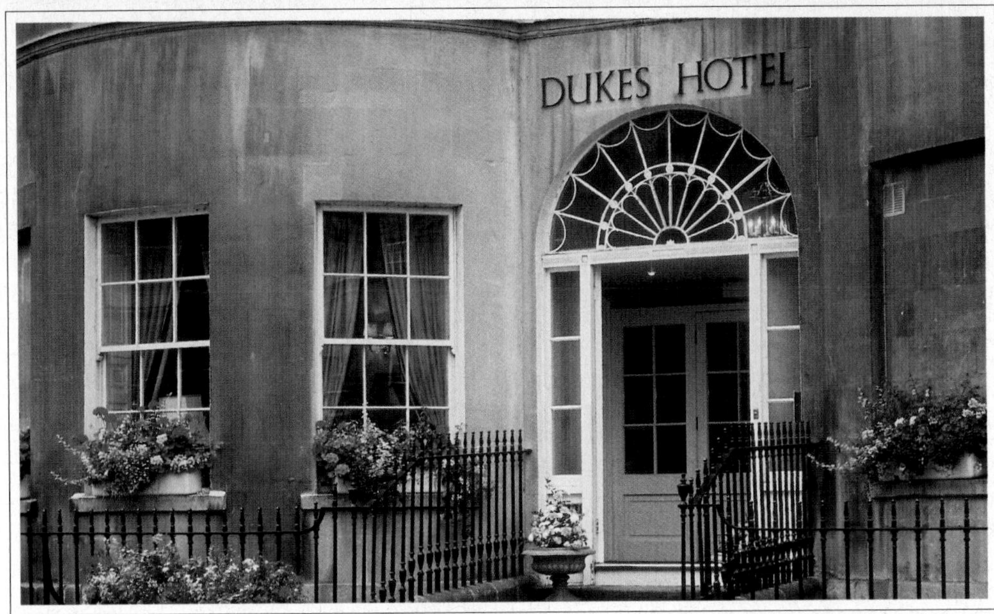

Very special value in the very special city of Bath

Dukes' Hotel was built in about 1780 and is an architecturally important Grade I listed building. It stands proud in Europe's most elegant Georgian boulevard, Great Pulteney Street. It has been fully restored, refurbished and modernised for comfort. Original mouldings, cornices and the magnificent staircase are retained to give a very special feeling of Georgian elegance.

The food is unpretentious, English and excellent. A Master of Wine has chosen the list on quality and price. Despite its aristocratic origins, Dukes' Hotel offers good old fashioned English comfort and service.

Bath is one of England's most beautiful and interesting cities. Many streets that feature so prominently in Jane Austen's novels of high society are almost unchanged. Bath Abbey, Roman Baths, Royal Circus, Pump Room, Assembly Rooms, Museum of Costume and the Theatre Royal are within close walking distance. So is the superb modern shopping centre and the exclusive shops, restaurants and tea rooms.

The famous Lions of Longleat, Lord Mountbatten's stately home at Broadlands and the American Museum and Gardens are all within easy reach. This is a sister property to Holne Chase Hotel, Devon and shares with it the same traditional comfort and hospitality.

LOCATION

Situated just 5 minutes walk from the centre of Bath and 5 minutes by taxi from the station.

Great Pulteney Street, Bath, Somerset BA2 4DN

Telephone 01225 463512
Fax 01225 483733

E-mail: *dukesbath@bestloved.com*

OWNERS

Sebastian and Philippa Hughes

OPERATIONS MANAGER

Theresa Vickery

ROOM RATES

3 Singles from £85
20 Doubles/Twins from £110
1 Family room £130
Includes full breakfast and VAT

CHARGE/CREDIT CARDS

• MC • VI

RATINGS & AWARDS

E.T.C. ★★★
R.A.C. ★★★ *Dining Award 1*
A.A. ★★★ *63%*

FACILITIES

On site: *1 meeting room/max 20 people*
Nearby: *Golf, swimming pool, leisure centre*

RESTRICTIONS

No facilities for disabled guests

ATTRACTIONS

Roman Baths, American Museum, Museum of Costume, Wells, Wells Cathedral, The Crescent, Stonehenge

AFFILIATIONS

Selected British Hotels

NEAREST

MAJOR CITY:
Bath

MAJOR AIRPORT:
London Heathrow - 90 miles/1½ hrs
Bristol - 15 miles/30 mins

RAILWAY STATION:
Bath Spa - ½ mile/10 mins

RESERVATIONS

Toll free in the US: 800-323-5463
Quote ***Best Loved***

ACCESS CODES

Not applicable

" At last, enchanting England. We've found heaven! "

Max Malden, Calgary

• Map p.502 ref: D5

Manor house

GABRIEL COURT HOTEL

500 years of heritage and a sunny disposition

For nearly 500 years this was the home of the Churchward family, the Squires of Stoke Gabriel. In 1928 the house was converted into an hotel and since then has earned an excellent reputation for hospitality and comfort. Appealing essentially to those who like peace and quiet it is, nevertheless, a wonderful base for exploring the tourist attractions which abound in a 30 mile radius. Dartmoor, the Heritage Coast, National Trust properties, Totnes and Dartmouth, to name but a few.

The hotel overlooks the very pretty village of Stoke Gabriel which stands by the River Dart. From ancient records it would appear that there has been a church in the village since the tenth century.

Set in its own grounds and surrounded by a high stone wall, the hotel faces south and enjoys all available sunshine.

The food is English cooking at its best with salmon from the Dart, sea fish landed at Brixham and game from nearby estates. Vegetables are often from the hotel's own garden. The table d'hôte menu is changed daily and offers an excellent choice. The Beacom family will warmly welcome you to Gabriel Court.

LOCATION

Leave A38 at Buckfastleigh. Take A384 to Totnes, then A385 towards Paignton. Turn right towards village at Parker's Arms.

Stoke Gabriel, Near Totnes, Devon TQ9 6SF

Telephone 01803 782206
Fax 01803 782333

E-mail: *gabriel@bestloved.com*

OWNER

Mr O M Beacom

ROOM RATES

2 Singles £59
17 Doubles/Twins £86
Includes full breakfast and VAT

CHARGE/CREDIT CARDS

 • *DC • MC • VI*

RATINGS & AWARDS

R.A.C. ★★★ Dining Award 1
A.A. ★★★ 71%

FACILITIES

On site: *Garden, croquet, tennis, outdoor pool*
1 meeting room/max 20 people
Nearby: *Golf, riding, walking, fishing*

RESTRICTIONS

No facilities for disabled guests

ATTRACTIONS

Dartmoor National Park, Totnes, River Dart, Dartmouth Castle, Coleton Fishacre, South Devon coastline

AFFILIATIONS

Independent

NEAREST

MAJOR CITY:
Plymouth - 28 miles/40 mins

MAJOR AIRPORT:
Exeter - 28 miles/40 mins
London Heathrow - 190 miles/3¾ hrs

RAILWAY STATION:
Totnes - 4 miles/15 mins

RESERVATIONS

Direct with hotel
Quote ***Best Loved***

ACCESS CODES

Not applicable

A keen Angler? Refer to page 472 for our Fishing Index

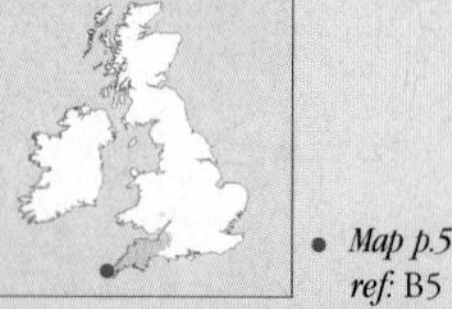

• Map p.502 ref: B5

"As usual everything, especially the cuisine, was superb, outshone only by Kilby hospitality"

Joyce & Bob Hinze, USA

THE GARRACK HOTEL

Cornish coastal hotel

Burthallan Lane, St Ives, Cornwall TR26 3AA

Telephone 01736 796199
Fax 01736 798955

E-mail: *garrack@bestloved.com*

OWNERS

The Kilby Family (Frances, Michael, Stephen)

ROOM RATES

1 Single	£58 - £62
16 Doubles/Twins	£116 - £148
1 Four-poster	£116 - £148

Includes full breakfast and VAT

CHARGE/CREDIT CARDS

• DC • MC • VI

RATINGS & AWARDS

E.T.C. ★★★

A.A. ★★★ ❀❀ *67%*

FACILITIES

On site: *Garden, indoor pool, spa, sauna, solarium, gym, licensed coffee shop, special facilities for the disabled 1 meeting room/max 30 people*

Nearby: *Golf, riding, walking, fishing*

RESTRICTIONS

Pets by arrangement

ATTRACTIONS

St Ives Tate Gallery, Newlyn, Land's End, Orion Gallery, St Michael's Mount, Cornish coastal path

AFFILIATIONS

Relais du Silence

NEAREST

MAJOR CITY:
Truro - 25 miles/45 mins

MAJOR AIRPORT:
Exeter - 110 miles/ 2¼ hrs
London Heathrow - 300 miles/6 hrs

RAILWAY STATION:
St Ives - 1 mile/3 mins

RESERVATIONS

Toll free in UK: 08000 197393
Quote ***Best Loved***

ACCESS CODES

Not applicable

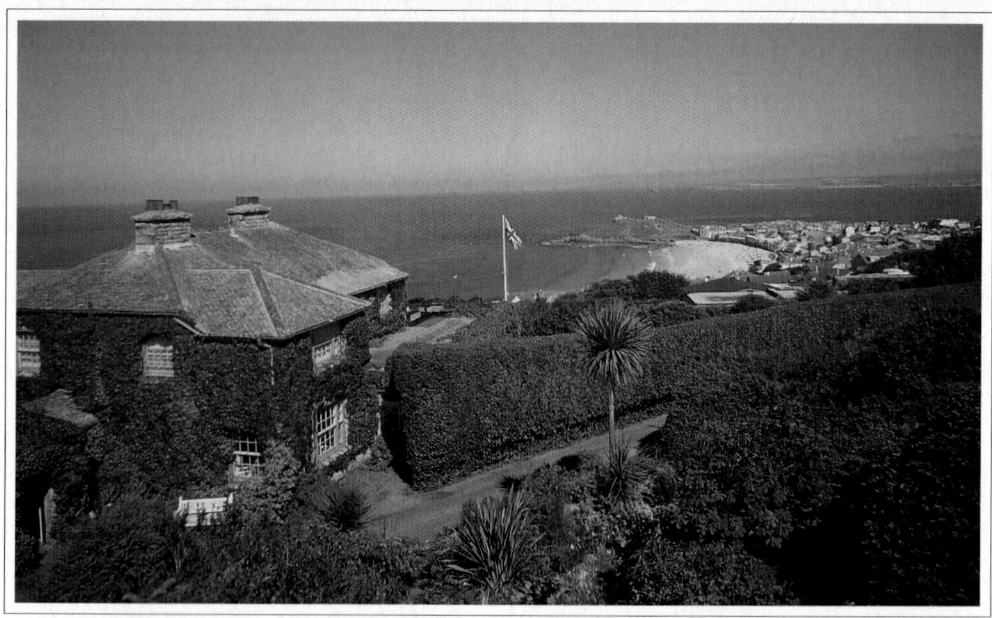

The connoisseur's choice for seeing Cornwall and south-west England

Cornwall is unique, both for its history and its scenery. It is a land of contrasts from its rugged coastline, precipitous cliffs and often angry seas, to lazy wooded creeks, small fishing harbours and sandy coves.

Originally a private house known in the Cornish language as Chy-an-Garrack, which translates into English as The House on the Rock, it was the home of Lady Ebury prior to becoming a hotel in 1947. Since then the Kilby family has made many changes: new bedrooms have been added and a small leisure centre with swimming pool, sauna and solarium.

It is now a secluded, vine covered granite building standing in two acres of gardens high above Porthmeor Beach with fabulous views of St Ives Bay and the coastal landscape beyond. Of the 18 bedrooms, some have four-poster beds and some have personal spa baths. The hotel is proud of its reputation for good culinary standards, recognised by an award of two rosettes by the A.A., and for an extensive wine list. The hotel is dedicated to providing comfort in tranquil and beautiful surroundings, accompanied by good food, good service and good company where the customers' interests are paramount. As a base for visiting the many attractions including the renowned Tate Gallery, St Ives and the Garrack have no equal.

LOCATION

From the A30, take 2nd exit to St Ives. Take B3311 then join B3306 towards St Ives. Take third left after petrol station,after 400 yards the hotel is signposted.

"Your kindness and consideration was exceptional. Thank you for making our time with you so enjoyable"

John Major, former Prime Minister

• Map p.502 ref: D4

Country house hotel

GLAZEBROOK HOUSE HOTEL

Tradition, comfort and conviviality in the heart of Dartmoor Park

Glazebrook House is a family-owned hotel in the best tradition of comfort and affability. It is set on an elevated site in Dartmoor Park itself amidst landscaped grounds containing a profusion of colour throughout the year. The original building dates back to around 1600 and was extended in 1879 into a mid-Victorian country house.

The interior of the hotel exhibits a splendidly carved fireplace depicting the events which led to the execution of the Duke of Hamilton. Modern convenience has been added to the grace and elegance of the building's old fabric. There are three honeymoon suites, each with a four-poster bed and all bedrooms have en suite facilities, remote control TV, direct dial telephone and tea/coffee making equipment.

Dinner is prepared by chef David Merriman using fresh local ingredients and the cellar comes to the aid of the party with a wide range of fine wines. Afterwards, in the bar, you will meet your host, Fred Heard, whose easy way encourages everyone in pleasant conversation.

Buckfast Abbey and the River Dart Country Park are nearby. The beauty of Dartmoor is all around. For golfers, Wrangaton Golf Course deserves a special mention: the front nine holes are on Dartmoor, and the back nine cross stunning parkland.

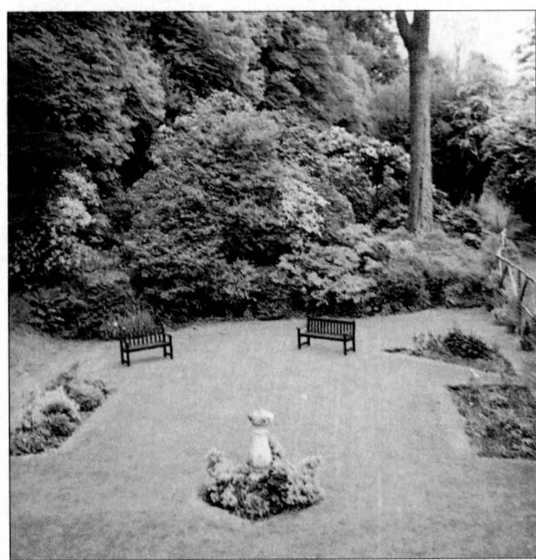

LOCATION

From Exeter take A38. Take South Brent/Avonwick turnoff. Take left lane, follow hotel signs through village, turn right at bottom of village.

Glazebrook, South Brent, South Devon TQ10 9JE

Telephone 01364 73322
Fax 01364 72350

E-mail: *glazebrook@bestloved.com*

OWNERS

Fred and Christine Heard

ROOM RATES

2 Singles	£48
5 Doubles/Twins	£68
3 Four-posters	£88 - £125

Includes full breakfast and VAT

CHARGE/CREDIT CARDS

• JCB • MC • VI

RATINGS & AWARDS

A.A. ★★ ❀ 74%

FACILITIES

On site: *Garden*
2 meeting rooms/max 200 people
Nearby: *Golf, fishing, tennis, fitness, riding, hunting/shooting, walking on Dartmoor*

RESTRICTIONS

Limited facilities for disabled guests
No smoking in bedrooms
Pets by arrangement

ATTRACTIONS

Saltram House, River Dart Country Park, Yealmpton Shire Horse Centre, Buckfast Abbey, Dartmoor National Park, Dartmoor Castle

AFFILIATIONS

Independent

NEAREST

MAJOR CITY:
Plymouth - 12 miles/15 mins

MAJOR AIRPORT:
London Heathrow - 190 miles/3½ hrs
Plymouth - 12 miles/15 mins

RAILWAY STATION:
Totnes - 6 miles/15 mins

RESERVATIONS

Direct with hotel
Quote ***Best Loved***

ACCESS CODES

Not applicable

278

• Map p.502 ref: F2

“ Bursting with hospitality ”

Judith Chalmers, “100 Irresistible Weekends”

HAYDON HOUSE

Edwardian town house

9 Bloomfield Park, Bath, Somerset BA2 2BY

Telephone 01225 444919
Fax 01225 427351

E-mail: haydon@bestloved.com

OWNERS

Gordon and Magdalene Ashman-Marr

ROOM RATES

Single occupancy	£50 - £65
3 Doubles/Twins	£70 - £95
1 Four-poster	£85 - £98
1 Suite	£85 - £98

Includes full breakfast and VAT

CHARGE/CREDIT CARDS

• JCB • MC • VI

RATINGS & AWARDS

E.T.C. ◆◆◆◆◆ Silver Award
A.A. ◆◆◆◆◆
WHICH? Hotel of the Year 1999

FACILITIES

On site: *Garden, sun terrace*
Nearby: *Golf, riding, health club*

RESTRICTIONS

Children by arrangement
No facilities for disabled guests
No smoking throughout
No pets

ATTRACTIONS

Bath, Wells Cathedral, Glastonbury, Cotswolds, Avebury, Salisbury, Stonehenge

AFFILIATIONS

Independent

NEAREST

MAJOR CITY:
Bath

MAJOR AIRPORT:
London Heathrow - 90 miles/1½ hrs
Bristol - 15 miles/30 mins

RAILWAY STATION:
Bath Spa - 1 mile/5 mins

RESERVATIONS

Direct with hotel
*Quote **Best Loved***

ACCESS CODES

Not applicable

WEST COUNTRY

Jane Austen wrote about the secrets of Bath … here's another

Bath needs little introduction as one of the loveliest cities in the world with so much more to enjoy than simply taking the waters, as in Roman times, or the wider range of secret pleasures available in Jane Austen's day. Nowadays, it holds one more secret … a secret you should know – Haydon House.

It looks like any other Edwardian house, so typical of the residential streets of Bath. Inside, however, an oasis of tranquillity and elegance awaits you, where high standards of hospitality prevail.

The reception rooms are tastefully furnished with antiques, whilst the five guest bedrooms are decorated to a very high standard. All rooms have private facilities, colour television and direct-dial telephone and a generous hospitality tray offering complimentary home-made shortbread and a decanter of sherry.

Innovative breakfasts are stylishly served and there is a lovely garden in which to relax.

The hosts' aim at Haydon is to make your stay, however short or long, truly happy and memorable by providing a secluded retreat from which you can readily enjoy all the pleasures of Georgian Bath, yet escape the throng.

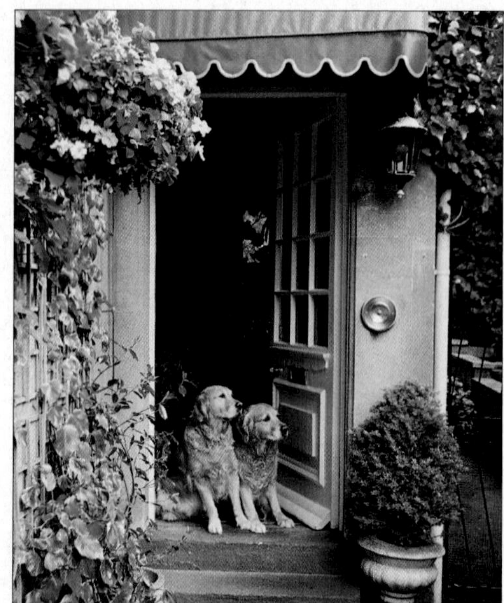

LOCATION

Half a mile south of the city centre on the A367, fork right off Wellsway then turn second right.

“A glimpse of paradise at Heddon's Gate”

Paddy Burt, The Daily Telegraph

• *Map p.502 ref: D3*

Country house

HEDDON'S GATE HOTEL

An Exmoor hideaway!

Romantic Exmoor, home of the legendary Lorna Doone, is the stunning location of Heddon's Gate Hotel. Set high above the beautiful wooded Heddon Valley, the hotel enjoys unrivalled views across the western hills of Exmoor. An unspoilt landscape of high rolling moorland and deep valleys, this North Western area of the Exmoor National Park has the most dramatic coastal scenery. The famous South Western Peninsula Footpath can be accessed directly from the hotel.

This Edwardian house, which has a quintessentially English atmosphere, has been run as an hotel for over 30 years by proprietor and cook, Bob Deville. He uses the very best of Exmoor's produce – locally-reared beef and lamb, Devon and Somerset cheeses as well as Devonshire clotted cream.

Heddon's Gate is a very comfortable place, with en suite bedrooms, peaceful lounges with log fires, and outside, terraced lawns and gardens. Every day a complimentary traditional English afternoon tea is offered to all guests. Heddon's Gate is for those seeking to experience Exmoor hospitality at its best.

Please note: the approach is via steep and winding lanes and may not be suitable for just a one night stay!

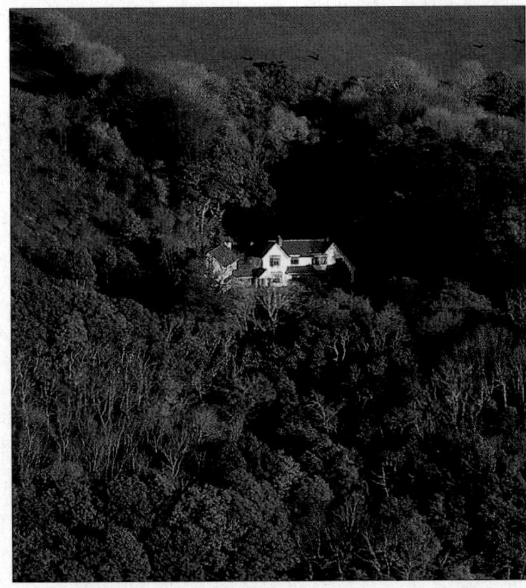

LOCATION

From A39, 3 miles west of Lynton, take unclassified road signposted 'Martinhoe and Woody Bay'. Left at next crossroads, go downhill for 2 miles – private drive on right.

Heddon's Mouth, Parracombe, Barnstaple, Devon EX31 4PZ

Telephone 01598 763313
Fax 01598 763363

E-mail: *heddons@bestloved.com*

OWNER
Bob Deville

MANAGER
Heather Deville

ROOM RATES

1 Single	*£34 - £43*
9 Doubles/Twins	*£60 - £86*
1 Four-poster	*£65 - £86*
3 Suites	*£71 - £107*

Includes full breakfast, afternoon tea and VAT

CHARGE/CREDIT CARDS

• *MC* • *VI*

RATINGS & AWARDS
E.T.C. ★★ Silver Award
A.A. ★★ ❀ 76%

FACILITIES
On site: *Gardens*
Nearby: *Riding, coastal walks*

RESTRICTIONS
Children by arrangement
No facilities for disabled guests

ATTRACTIONS
Lynton & Lynmouth Cliff Railway, Arlington Court, Lorna Doone Country, South Western Peninsula Footpath, Exmoor National Park, Marwood Gardens

AFFILIATIONS
Independent

NEAREST
MAJOR CITY:
Exeter - 45 miles/1½ hrs

MAJOR AIRPORT:
London Heathrow - 200 miles/4½ hrs
Bristol - 95 miles/2½ hrs

RAILWAY STATION:
Barnstaple - 16 miles/40 mins

RESERVATIONS
Direct with hotel
Quote ***Best Loved***

ACCESS CODES
Not applicable

For information about hotel affiliations see page 14

"A haven of tranquillity and comfort, the highlight of our British visit"

Dan Elinghausen, Chicago

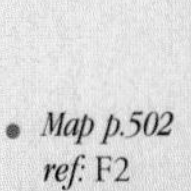

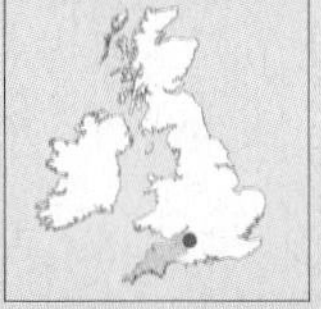

Map p.502
ref: F2

Victorian town house

HOLLY LODGE

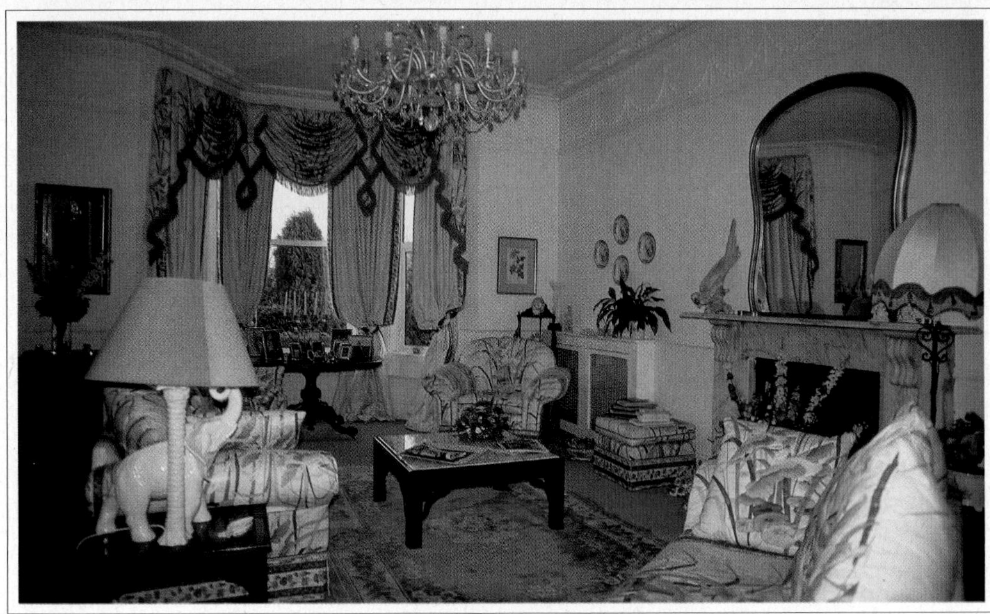

So much of England's heritage on your award-winning doorstep!

Holly Lodge is a large Victorian town house set in its own grounds and enjoys magnificent views over the world heritage city of Bath. It was rescued from semi-dereliction in 1986 by Carrolle Sellick and George Hall and now boasts seven individually designed rooms, some with queen size beds and others with specially built four-posters. All the rooms have luxury bathrooms, TV and satellite movies, direct-dial telephones, hot drink facilities and a host of extras.

You can enjoy imaginative breakfasts in the conservatory and relax in the beautiful lounge or the floodlit gazebo in the evenings. Holly Lodge is strictly no smoking.

Past winners of an 'England for Excellence' Award, Holly Lodge is graded five diamonds by the English Tourism Council.

Holly Lodge is conveniently placed for touring a wide variety of attractions – Stonehenge, the Cotswolds, Southern Wales, Wells and the Mendip Hills, all within a 40 mile radius of Bath. The magnificent architecture, Roman remains and fine shops of central Bath are on the doorstep.

LOCATION

½ mile south west of Bath city centre off A367 Wells Road.

8 Upper Oldfield Park, Bath, Somerset BA2 3JZ

Telephone 01225 424042
Fax 01225 481138

E-mail: *hollylodge@bestloved.com*

OWNER

George Hall

ROOM RATES

1 Single	*£55 - £65*
6 Doubles	*£79 - £97*

Includes full breakfast and VAT

CHARGE/CREDIT CARDS

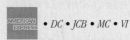

• *DC* • *JCB* • *MC* • *VI*

RATINGS & AWARDS

E.T.C. ◆◆◆◆◆ *Silver Award*
A.A. ◆◆◆◆◆

FACILITIES

On site: *Gardens*
Nearby: *Golf, riding, health spas*

RESTRICTIONS

Limited facilities for disabled guests
No smoking throughout
No pets

ATTRACTIONS

Castle Combe, Bath, Cotswolds, Wells Cathedral, Stonehenge

AFFILIATIONS

Independent

NEAREST

MAJOR CITY:
Bath - ½ mile/5 mins

MAJOR AIRPORT:
London Heathrow - 90 miles/2¼ hrs
Bristol - 13 miles/40 mins

RAILWAY STATION:
Bath Spa - ½ mile/5 mins

RESERVATIONS

Direct with hotel
Quote ***Best Loved***

ACCESS CODES

Not applicable

• Map p.502 ref: D4

"We came for peace and tranquillity and found it in abundance"

David and Sarah Boulay, Ipswich

HOLNE CHASE HOTEL

Victorian country house

Ashburton, Devon TQ13 7NS

Telephone 01364 631471
Fax 01364 631453

E-mail: *holnechase@bestloved.com*

OWNERS

Sebastian and Philippa Hughes

ROOM RATES

Single occupancy	*£95*
9 Doubles/Twins	*£125 - £145*
1 Four-poster	*£165*
7 Suites	*£165*

Includes full breakfast and VAT

CHARGE/CREDIT CARDS

DC • MC • VI

RATINGS & AWARDS

E.T.C. ★★★
R.A.C. ★★★
A.A. ★★★ ❀❀❀ *74%*

FACILITIES

On site: *Garden, croquet, fishing, putting green, heli-pad*
1 meeting room/max 20 people
Nearby: *Riding*

RESTRICTIONS

No facilities for disabled guests
No children under 10 years in restaurant
No smoking in bedrooms

ATTRACTIONS

Dartmoor National Park, Buckfast Abbey, Dartington Hall, Totnes Castle, Plymouth, Dartmouth Castle

AFFILIATIONS

Selected British Hotels
Preston's Global Hotels

NEAREST

MAJOR CITY:
Exeter/Plymouth - 22 miles/30 mins

MAJOR AIRPORT:
Exeter - 22 miles/30 mins
Bristol - 90 miles/1¾ hrs

RAILWAY STATION:
Newton Abbot - 10 miles/20 mins

RESERVATIONS

Toll free in US: 800-544-9993
or 800-323-5463
Quote ***Best Loved***

ACCESS CODES

Not applicable

WEST COUNTRY

"A peculiarly secluded and romantic situation"

Remarkably, the above description from White's Directory of Devon of 1850, still rings true today. Holne Chase nestles in a woodland clearing,s overlooking a pocket of sloping lawns within the Dartmoor National Park. Its origins lie back in the 11th century, when the abbots of Buckfast Abbey kept a hunting lodge here, and the present Victorian era country house is very much a sporting retreat as well as a restorative escape from everyday stresses and strains.

Sebastian and Philippa Hughes run the hotel like a private home with the loyal assistance of Batty, the bassett hound, who maintains her own web site and is particularly keen to welcome animal lovers and canine visitors to her patch. The four handsomely converted Stable Suites are ideally suited to sporting visitors keen to fish, ride, shoot, or hike on the moors, and all the rooms in the main hotel have been recently refurbished with pretty English fabrics mirroring fresh flowers from the garden.

Holne Chase's walled garden also provides fruit and vegetables for the kitchen, and the chef's enthusiasm for good food made with top quality local ingredients embraces seafood from Brixham and Looe, and seasonal game dishes.

LOCATION

From M5, join A38 towards Plymouth. Take 2nd turning for Ashburton at Pear Tree Cross, following signs for Dartmeet. The hotel entrance is on the right, 300 metres after Holne Bridge.

For a portrait of this region see page 250

"The Hotel du Vin is the very best sort of mid-range hotel"

Walter F Stowry, The Sunday Times

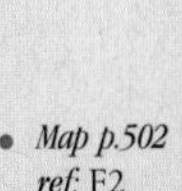

18th century warehouse

HOTEL DU VIN & BISTRO

The Sugar House,
Narrow Lewins Mead,
Bristol BS1 2NU

Telephone 0117 925 5577
Fax 0117 925 1199

E-mail: duvinbris@bestloved.com

DIRECTOR

Charles Morgan

ROOM RATES

Single occupancy	£99 - £125
35 Doubles/Twins	£99 - £125
5 Suites	£150 - £195

Includes VAT

CHARGE/CREDIT CARDS

• DC • MC • VI

RATINGS & AWARDS

A.A. ★★★★ ❀

FACILITIES

On site: Billiard room
3 meeting rooms/max 100 people
Nearby: Golf, fitness

RESTRICTIONS

No pets

ATTRACTIONS

S.S. Great Britain, @Bristol, Harvey's Wine Museum, Bristol Cathedral, Bath, Clifton Suspension Bridge, Somerset, South Wales

AFFILIATIONS

The Alternative Hotel Co Ltd
Preston's Global Hotels
The European Connection

NEAREST

MAJOR CITY:
Bristol

MAJOR AIRPORT:
London Heathrow - 107 miles/2 hrs
Bristol - 9 miles/30 mins

RAILWAY STATION:
Bristol Temple Meads - 1 mile/10 mins

RESERVATIONS

Toll free in US: 800-544-9993
Quote **Best Loved**

ACCESS CODES

Not applicable

WEST COUNTRY

New to the centre of Bristol preceded by an impeccable reputation

A neat place, indeed, to open a new restaurant let alone a new hotel. Nice timing, too! Showing a now familiar skill, the owners of Hotel du Vin & Bistro (see pages 333 and 334) have converted an old warehouse near the Bristol heritage docks and a short walk from its Millennium centre-piece, '@Bristol', a state-of-the-art electronic odyssey into the worlds of science and nature.

The Sugar House dates from the 1700's and has been used in a number of ways including the manufacture of clay pipes and tobacco and, more recently, sugar refining. It is fitting, therefore, that the decor of Hotel du Vin draws for inspiration on the city's industrial past and the space age, clean cut design of today. Simple white washed rubble walls contrast with steel columns; a fountain plays in the centre of the flagged courtyard reminiscent of French hostelries often designed in similar manner. The rooms are bright and comfortable with the functionality of a first class hotel designed for the international traveller.

From the opulence of the Lanson Room to the cigar-festooned walls of the Jeanneau Room with its full-size antique billiard table, the Hotel du Vin Bristol is already catching the eye of the cognoscente. With its sister hotels having already established their reputations for the excellence and good value of their cuisine, this newcomer comes with impeccable credentials.

LOCATION

From the end of the M32 into Bristol, aim city centre. 200 yards past Bentalls Department Store, turn right at traffic lights and follow carriageway. The hotel is on the corner of Lewins Mead and Narrow Lewins Mead.

• Map p.502 ref: F2

"One of the most completely satisfying evenings we have enjoyed for some time. An impeccable example of the marriage of kitchen, cellar, service and setting"

N H Bagot, Bristol

HUNSTRETE HOUSE

18th century country estate

Hunstrete,
Chelwood, Near Bath,
Somerset BS39 4NS

Telephone 01761 490490
Fax 01761 490732

E-mail: hunstrete@bestloved.com

DIRECTOR
Major R H Gillis

HOUSE MANAGER
David Hennigan

ROOM RATES

1 Single	£100 - £125
16 Doubles/Twins	£125 - £195
2 Four-posters	£135 - £265
3 Suites	£240 - £265

Includes full breakfast and VAT

CHARGE/CREDIT CARDS

• DC • MC • VI

RATINGS & AWARDS
A.A. ★★★ ❀❀❀ 78%
The Good Food Guide Restaurant of the Year 2000

FACILITIES
On site: Garden, croquet, outdoor pool, tennis, heli-pad
3 meeting rooms/max 50 people
Licensed for weddings
Nearby: Golf, fishing, riding, paint balling, orienteering

RESTRICTIONS
No facilities for disabled guests
No pets

ATTRACTIONS
Bath, Wells Cathedral, Longleat, Glastonbury, Stonehenge, Avebury

AFFILIATIONS
The Celebrated Hotels Collection
Grand Heritage Hotels

NEAREST
MAJOR CITY:
Bath - 7 miles/15 mins
MAJOR AIRPORT:
London Heathrow - 90 miles/2 hrs
Bristol - 11 miles/30 mins
RAILWAY STATION:
Bath - 7 miles/15 mins

RESERVATIONS
Toll free in US: 800-322-2403
Quote **Best Loved**

ACCESS CODES
AMADEUS UI BRSHUN
APOLLO/GALILEO UI 22206
SABRE/ABACUS UI 49148
WORLDSPAN UI 40925

WEST COUNTRY

A top restaurant, a stately house and garden near Roman Bath

The 'Houndstreet' estate has a colourful history dating back to 963AD. The diarist, John Evelyn, referred to "Old Sir Francis (Popham), he lived like a hog at Hownstret in Somerset, with a moderate pittance". Rest assured guests will find some welcome changes.

Hunstrete House was a private home from the mid-18th century and only became an hotel 20 years ago. In that time, it has established itself as a first rate restaurant and a splendid country house hotel. Although they play the hotel bit down: one is encouraged to treat the place as your own.

Some invitation! The drawing room and library are splendidly furnished with antiques, original paintings and collections of fine porcelain. They look out onto six acres of formal gardens and beyond to the 90-acre park complete with fallow deer and horse paddocks. The dining room opens into the flower-filled courtyard where al fresco dining makes the best of summer.

The 22 princely bedrooms are an exhibition of romantic design; fairytale settings for very special occasions. And part of the joy is the friendly, efficient way the staff care for you.

The grounds will delight and surprise you with the sweeping lawns, intimate bowers, walled garden with its astonishing botanic variety and woodland walks.

Once you have experienced the Hunstrete magic, it will be calling you back. Count on it!

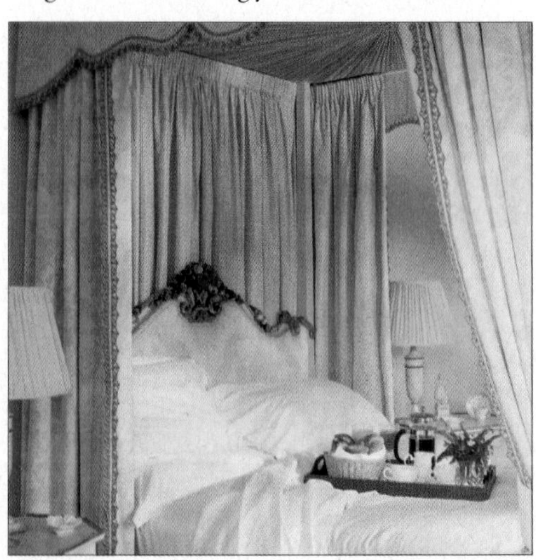

LOCATION

From M4/Exit 18 take A46 to Bath. Leave Bath on A4 to Bristol then take A39 to Wells and Weston. Hunstrete is 5 miles on right.

“ In a lifetime of travel, I do not remember more beautiful surroundings or more gracious treatment ”

Cordelia May, Pennsylvania

• Map p.502 ref: D4

17th century manor house

LEWTRENCHARD MANOR

Grandeur and good living in a Jacobean manor

Built by the Monk family, on the site of an earlier house, this Jacobean manor was embellished by the Victorian hymn writer Sabine Baring Gould. There are granite mullion windows with 19th century stained glass and high ceilings with decorative plasterwork set off by rich oak panelling. Bedrooms, some with four-posters, are tastefully decorated and the views are of formal and informal gardens.

The grand oak staircase descends from the long gallery to the imposing entrance hall that gleams with brass. In the panelled lounge, you will find the proprietors, James and Sue Murray who love to chat to guests. There are log fires and fresh flowers everywhere.

In the dining room, with its crisp white linen, you can enjoy classic English cooking with modern interpretations.

The Murrays offer clay pigeon shooting, fishing and croquet in the grounds and there are riding, golf and tennis facilities nearby. Guests can be met at both Exeter and Plymouth stations and airports.

Lewtrenchard Manor is well placed for National Trust properties, Dartmoor and the Devon or Cornish coasts.

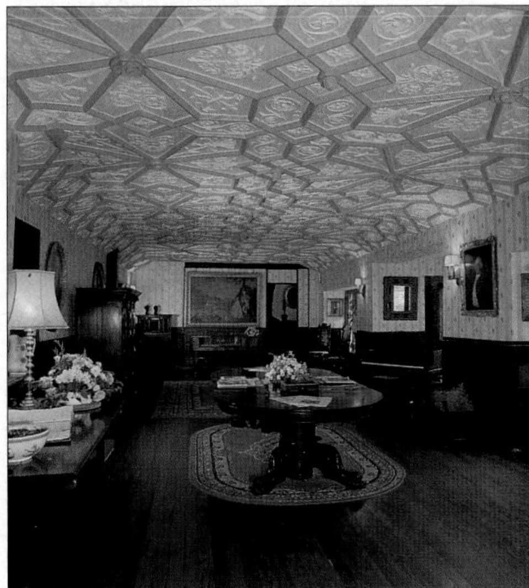

LOCATION

A30 (Okehampton – Bodmin) from Exeter. After 25 miles, road to Tavistock/Plymouth. Follow signs to Lewdown and then Lewtrenchard. Hotel is signposted.

Lewdown,
Near Okehampton,
Devon EX20 4PN

Telephone 01566 783256
Fax 01566 783332

E-mail: *lewtrenchard@bestloved.com*

OWNERS

James and Sue Murray

ROOM RATES

2 Doubles	*£115*
4 Superior twins	*£160*
2 Four-posters	*£160*
1 Suite	*£170*

Includes full breakfast and VAT

CHARGE/CREDIT CARDS

• DC • MC • VI

RATINGS & AWARDS

A.A. ★★★ ❀❀

FACILITIES

On site: *Garden, croquet, heli-pad, fishing*
Licensed for weddings
2 meeting rooms/max 100 people
Nearby: *Riding*

RESTRICTIONS

Children under 8 years by arrangement
Limited facilities for disabled guests
No pets in public rooms

ATTRACTIONS

Dartmoor National Park, Lydford Gorge, Cotehele House, Buckland Abbey, RHS Rosemoor Gardens, Devon & Cornwall coastline

AFFILIATIONS

Pride of Britain

NEAREST

MAJOR CITY:
Exeter/Plymouth - 30 miles/45 mins

MAJOR AIRPORT:
Exeter/Plymouth - 30 miles/45 mins
London Heathrow - 195 miles/3½ hrs

RAILWAY STATION:
Exeter/Plymouth - 30 miles/45 mins

RESERVATIONS

Toll free in US: 800-98-PRIDE
Quote ***Best Loved***

ACCESS CODES

Not applicable

WEST COUNTRY

Looking for an hotel with a golf course on site? See our 'Golf Guide' on page 478

"One of the prettiest small hotels in Devon"

Val Hennessy, Daily Mail

THE LITTLE ADMIRAL

Town house

Victoria Road, Dartmouth, Devon TQ6 9RT

Telephone 01803 832572
Fax 01803 835815

E-mail: *littleadmiral@bestloved.com*

OWNERS
Sebastian and Philippa Hughes

GENERAL MANAGER
Kevin Chapman

ROOM RATES

Single occupancy	*£40 - £60*
9 Doubles/Twins	*£50 - £100*
1 Four-poster	*£90 - £120*

Includes breakfast and VAT

CHARGE/CREDIT CARDS
MC • VI

RATINGS & AWARDS
E.T.C. ★★

FACILITIES
On site: *Car park*
1 meeting room/max 15 people
Nearby: *Riding, golf, fishing, sailing, health & beauty*

RESTRICTIONS
No facilities for disabled guests
£10 supplement for dogs
No smoking in bedrooms

ATTRACTIONS
Dartmouth Castle, Dartmoor National Park, Coleton Fishacre Gardens, Greenways - home of Agatha Christie, Totnes Castle, Buckfast Abbey, Britannia Royal Naval College

AFFILIATIONS
Preston's Global Hotels

NEAREST
MAJOR CITY:
Exeter - 40 miles/45 mins

MAJOR AIRPORT:
Exeter - 50 miles/1 hr

RAILWAY STATION:
Totnes - 14 miles/25 mins

RESERVATIONS
Toll free in US: 800-544-9993
Quote ***Best Loved***

ACCESS CODES
Not applicable

WEST COUNTRY

An inviting port of call in an historic maritime setting

The picturesque old port of Dartmouth lies on the banks of the River Dart steeped in naval history. Beneath the monumental outline of Britannia Naval College on the hillside, the town's cosy huddle of narrow cobbled streets leads down towards the waterfront where The Little Admiral sits 150 yards back from the yacht-packed harbour.

The hotel takes its name from a teak statue that once marked a specialist compass and quadrant maker's premises founded by an ancestor of hotel owner Sebastian Hughes. There is a distinct nod in the direction of things nautical in the shipshape elegance of this delightful town house and considerable care has gone into creating a soothing and supremely comfortable environment furnished with antiques and maritime art. The maritime theme continues through into the restaurant where dishes make the very best use of local produce, especially locally caught fish.

Around Dartmouth the South Hams countryside rolls back from the coast in a patchwork of green fields, woodlands and deep-set lanes. Popular diversions include coastal walks, the gardens and beaches of the English Riviera, and boat trips upriver. Fishing and sailing can be arranged by the hotel, as can fly-fishing at sister hotel Holne Chase on the edge of Dartmoor.

LOCATION

From M5 join the A38 and then the A384 signposted to Totnes. Follow signs to Dartmouth. The hotel is in the town centre just opposite the covered market.

"This is quite the most enjoyable stay that I've had in an hotel and I've travelled and stayed worldwide!"

L M Deuchar, Wiltshire

• Map p.502 ref: C5

17th century seaside inn

THE LUGGER HOTEL

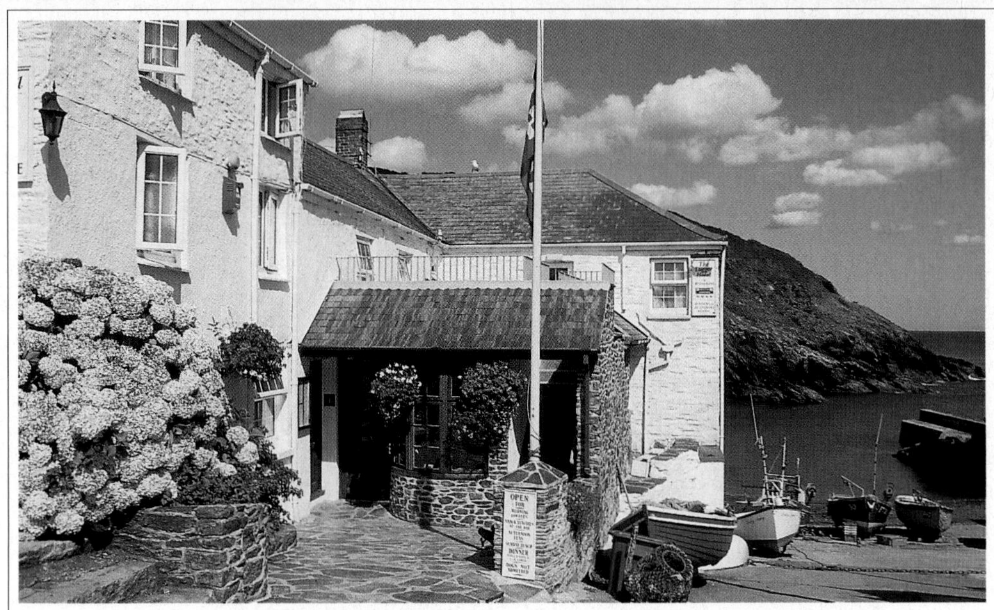

Complete relaxation in a romantic setting

The Lugger Hotel sits at the very water's edge of the picturesque fishing village of Portloe in a great unspoilt part of Cornwall. Untouched by time, this quiet community lies in the heart of the beautiful Roseland Peninsula, and is close to the attractive villages of St Mawes and Veryan, famous for their round thatched cottages.

A 17th century inn reputed to have been the haunt of smugglers, The Lugger has been in the Powell Family for three generations and is now a comfortable, well-appointed hotel. There are 19 tastefully furnished bedrooms, all with en suite facilities.

The cocktail bar, once used by fishermen and smugglers, overlooks the harbour. Here one can enjoy a delicious fresh crab sandwich for lunch or perhaps afternoon tea. The restaurant has panoramic views and offers varied and exciting menus of anglo-continental dishes specialising in local seafood. The extensive wine list includes a locally produced Cornish wine. An oak-beamed lounge adjoins the bar and restaurant.

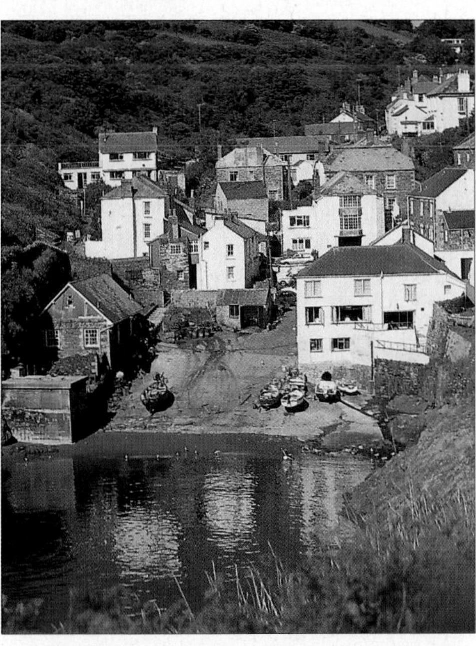

LOCATION

Turn off A390 St Austell to Truro road on to B3287 to Tregony. Then take A3078 (St Mawes road) and after two miles, fork left for Veryan and Portloe, turning left at T-junction for Portloe.

Portloe, Near Truro, Cornwall TR2 5RD

Telephone 01872 501322
Fax 01872 501691

E-mail: lugger@bestloved.com

OWNERS
The Powell Family

GENERAL MANAGER
Stephen Powell

RATES PER PERSON

3 Singles	£63 - £80
14 Doubles/Twins	£79
2 Mini suites	£84

Includes full breakfast, dinner and VAT

CHARGE/CREDIT CARDS

• DC • JCB • MC • VI

RATINGS & AWARDS
E.T.C. ★★★

FACILITIES
On site: *Sauna*
Nearby: *Riding, tennis, bowls, cliff walks*

RESTRICTIONS
No children under 12 years
No facilities for disabled guests
No pets

ATTRACTIONS
St Just in Roseland, St Mawes Castle, Lands' End, Penzance, Pendennis Castle, Trelissick Gardens

AFFILIATIONS
Preston's Global Hotels

NEAREST
MAJOR CITY:
Truro - 12 miles/25 mins

MAJOR AIRPORT:
Newquay - 20 miles/35 mins
London Heathrow - 220 miles/5 hrs

RAILWAY STATION:
Truro - 12 miles/25 mins

RESERVATIONS
Toll free in US: 800-544-9993
Quote **Best Loved**

ACCESS CODES
Not applicable

WEST COUNTRY

• Map p.502 ref: D4

" Great food, great service, great find! "

Nicholas Granger, London

MILL END HOTEL

18th century mill

Sandy Park, Chagford,
Newton Abbot,
Devon TQ13 8JN

Telephone 01647 432282
Fax 01647 433106

E-mail: *millend@bestloved.com*

OWNER
Keith Green

ROOM RATES

2 Singles	*£50 - £79*
13 Doubles/Twins	*£80 - £100*
2 Family rooms	*£100 - £150*

Includes full breakfast and VAT

CHARGE/CREDIT CARDS

• *JCB* • *MC* • *VI*

RATINGS & AWARDS
E.T.C. ★★★ *Silver Award*
A.A. ★★★ ❀❀ *70%*

FACILITIES
On site: *Garden, croquet, fishing*
3 meeting rooms/max 20 people
Nearby: *Golf, riding, fishing*

RESTRICTIONS
No facilities for disabled guests
No pets in public rooms

ATTRACTIONS
Drogo Castle, Rosemoor Gardens, Dartmoor National Park, Exeter Cathedral, Teign Gorge

AFFILIATIONS
Independent

NEAREST
MAJOR CITY:
Exeter - 20 miles/35 mins

MAJOR AIRPORT:
Exeter - 25 miles/50 mins

RAILWAY STATION:
Exeter - 20 miles/35 mins

RESERVATIONS
Direct with hotel
Quote ***Best Loved***

ACCESS CODES
Not applicable

WEST COUNTRY

Mill End is quintessentially English - and proud of it

Think cream teas and cricket, chintz and homemade jam, log fires in winter and the lazy buzz of bumblebees in summer and you will have conjured up an image of an almost forgotten Britain, which we are happy to report is alive and well at Mill End. The term 'country house hotel' does not do justice to this wonderful time capsule housed in an 18th-century former flour mill on the River Teign. The experience is far more cosy and personal, rather like staying with a favourite, rather old-fashioned and slightly eccentric branch of the family.

Mill End has been an hotel since 1929, but has preserved all manner of nooks and crannies where guests can hole up with a good book and relax. Upstairs bedrooms have lovely views, while downstairs rooms enjoy private stone-flagged patios. The fine award winning cuisine in the restaurant is augmented by an impressive cheese board laden with local specialities and regular guests rave about the dangerously tempting desserts.

There are plenty of ways to work off the calories around and about. Hiking in the Dartmoor National Park, pony trekking and golf are easily arranged. Mill End also offers private salmon and trout fishing. Local attractions include Castle Drogo, the Sir Edwin Lutyens-designed National Trust property. The north and south Devon coasts are also within striking distance.

LOCATION

Located on the A382 which is just off the A30, Exeter to Okehampton road, at Whiddon Down. The hotel is not in Chagford village so do not turn into Chagford from A382.

" There is no greater luxury than to feel at home "

Chris Markiewicz, Barnet

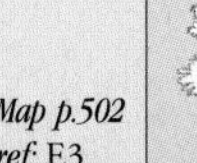

• *Map p.502 ref: E3*

Regency country house THE MOUNT SOMERSET

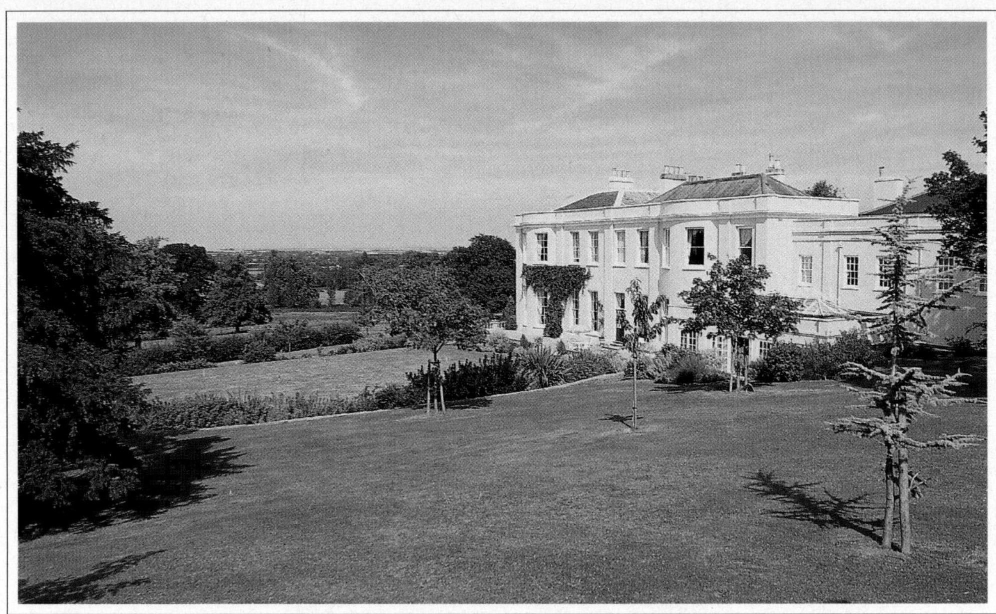

Arrive as a guest - leave as a friend

High on the slopes of the Blackdown Hills, stands The Mount Somerset. It was built in 1805 by an Italian architect and much of its original plasterwork has been preserved to blend with the decor, antiques and lavish furnishings giving a feeling of maturity, elegance and great character. It is very much more a home than an hotel and every encouragement is given to make you feel at ease.

Both the dining room and garden room, with its French doors opening on to a sunny terrace, create the perfect setting for some grand repast. Inspired dishes make the most of local produce as well as delicacies from home and abroad. A well-chosen wine list completes a truly delightful experience.

There are 23 sumptuously furnished bedrooms and suites rich in colour co-ordinated fabrics and carpeting including the Barrington Suite which, with its elaborately carved and decorated Queen-sized bed, is palatial both in size and decor. The luxurious bathrooms, most with double whirlpool spa baths and twin hand basins set in marble are a perfect complement to the bedrooms.

The local area is rich in places to visit and things to do: sport, wildlife, natural phenomena, museums, churches, stately homes and lots more. Pilots should note the following heli-pad grid reference: ST. 2732 31.

LOCATION

Exit 25 off M5, A358 towards Chard. After passing through Henlade, turn right towards Stoke St Mary. Turn left at T-junction and hotel's drive is 100 yards on the right.

Henlade, Taunton, Somerset TA3 5NB

Telephone 01823 442500
Fax 01823 442900

E-mail: *somerset@bestloved.com*

OWNER
Countess Von Essen

GENERAL MANAGER
Scott Leeming

ROOM RATES

Single occupancy	*£85 - £105*
16 Doubles/Twins	*£100 - £125*
5 Suites	*£145*
2 Four-poster suites	*£170*

Includes newspaper, full breakfast and VAT

CHARGE/CREDIT CARDS

• DC • JCB • MC • VI

RATINGS & AWARDS
A.A. ★★★ ❀ 78%

FACILITIES
On site: *Garden, croquet, heli-pad*
3 meeting rooms/max 100 people
Nearby: *Riding, fishing, tennis, health and fitness club*

RESTRICTIONS
Limited facilities for disabled guests
No pets

ATTRACTIONS
Somerset County Cricket ground, Cheddar Gorge, Bath, Wells Cathedral, Exmoor and Dartmoor, Stonehenge

AFFILIATIONS
Von Essen Hotels

NEAREST
MAJOR CITY:
Taunton - 2 miles/10 mins
Exeter - 30 miles/30 mins

MAJOR AIRPORT:
Bristol - 40 miles/45 mins
London Heathrow - 120 miles/2 hrs

RAILWAY STATION:
Taunton - 2 miles/10 mins

RESERVATIONS
Direct with hotel
Quote ***Best Loved***

ACCESS CODES
Not applicable

• Map p.502 ref: E4

❝ This 16th century inn is heaven; unspoilt, an excellent wine list and the largest selection of whiskies I have seen outside Scotland. There is life outside the metropolis ❞

Fiona Fullerton

THE NOBODY INN

16th century inn

Doddiscombsleigh, Near Exeter, Devon EX6 7PS

Telephone 01647 252394
Fax 01647 252978

E-mail: nobody@bestloved.com

OWNER
Nick Borst-Smith

ROOM RATES

Single occupancy	£23 - £38
7 Doubles/Twins	£33 - £70

Includes continental breakfast and VAT

CHARGE/CREDIT CARDS

• MC • VI

RATINGS & AWARDS
Whisky Pub of the Year 1999
Wine Pub of the Year 1999/2000

FACILITIES
On site: *Garden*
1 meeting room/max 30 people
Nearby: *Golf, tennis, shooting, fitness, riding, fishing*

RESTRICTIONS
No children under 14 years
No facilities for disabled guests
No pets

ATTRACTIONS
Dartmoor National Park, Teignmouth, Castle Drogo, The cob cottages of Devon, Great Fulford, University Arboretum

AFFILIATIONS
Independent

NEAREST
MAJOR CITY:
Exeter - 6 miles/15 mins

MAJOR AIRPORT:
London Heathrow - 200 miles/3 hrs
Exeter - 10 miles/20 mins

RAILWAY STATION:
Exeter - 6 miles/15 mins

RESERVATIONS
Direct with hotel
Quote ***Best Loved***

ACCESS CODES
Not applicable

WEST COUNTRY

Traditional ales, local ciders, 850 wines, 240 whiskies - and a bed for the night!

Long ago, this curiously named inn locked its doors to weary travellers and became known as the Nobody Inn. Visitors now receive a friendlier welcome as they cross the threshold into the centuries-old building.

The bar and cellar rank with the finest in the land. Traditionally-brewed beer, local cider, 240 whiskies, 850 wines, fine ports and brandies and home-made mulled wine will spoil you for choice. Whilst this astonishing variety makes this inn outstandingly different, it also has a reputation for excellent food. The restaurant menu takes full advantage of the finest fresh local produce including game, fish and vegetables in season. The asparagus is home-grown! Cheeses, another 'speciality of the house', all come from local farms. You can enjoy all this in the bar or in the relaxed atmosphere of the dining room.

The oak-beamed bedrooms, mostly en suite, are full of character and furnished with all the usual modern comforts. Breakfast is served in your room and if you want a television or telephone, all you have to do is ask. The Nobody Inn is an ideal base for visiting Exeter, Dartmoor and the South Devon Coast and for sporting or more gentle pursuits. Be warned, you may find the inn's gourmet attractions inhibit straying too far!

LOCATION

A38 south to Plymouth. Exit at Haldon Racecourse. Follow signs to Dunchideock & then (before Dunchideock) signs for Doddiscombsleigh. Hotel is in centre of village.

For information about hotel affiliations see page 14

" Perfect service, perfect food, perfect setting; what more could we want? - Just more time to enjoy it "

Muriel & Peter Harris, Hetchingham, Sussex

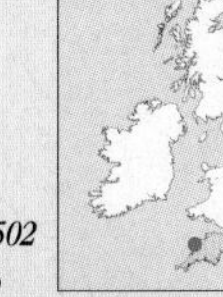

17th century manor NORTHCOTE MANOR

Burrington,
Near Umberleigh, Barnstaple,
Devon EX37 9LZ

Telephone 01769 560501
Fax 01769 560770

E-mail: *northcotedevon@bestloved.com*

OWNER
David Boddy

HOUSE MANAGER
Karen Dawson

ROOM RATES

Single occupancy	£124 - £188
6 Doubles/Twins	£165
1 Four-poster	£200
2 Junior suites	£220
2 Master suites	£250

Includes full breakfast and VAT

CHARGE/CREDIT CARDS

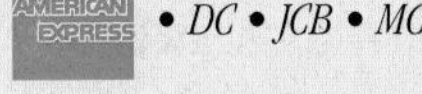

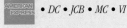

• DC • JCB • MC • VI

RATINGS & AWARDS
E.T.C. ★★★ Silver Award
R.A.C. Blue Ribbon ★★★
A.A. ★★★ ❀❀ 81%

FACILITIES
On site: *Garden, croquet, tennis*
Licensed for weddings
1 meeting room/max 60 people
Nearby: *Golf, riding, fishing, gliding, parachuting, heli-pad*

RESTRICTIONS
No facilities for disabled guests
Pets by arrangement

ATTRACTIONS
Dartmoor, Lydford Gorge, Exmoor, Devon and Cornish coast, RHS Rosemoor Gardens

AFFILIATIONS
Pride of Britain

NEAREST
MAJOR CITY:
Exeter - 28 miles/40 mins
MAJOR AIRPORT:
Bristol - 85 miles/1½ hrs
RAILWAY STATION:
Umberleigh - 6 miles/10 mins

RESERVATIONS
Toll free in US: 800-98-PRIDE
Quote ***Best Loved***

ACCESS CODES
Not applicable

WEST COUNTRY

Possibly the most exciting hotel in North Devon

We should be grateful to people like David and Marian Boddy; whereas most of us might make a gesture to conservation, they have committed heart and soul to it; Northcote Manor is assured of a place in the annals of the new millennium.

As the Boddy's vision approaches fruition (only the revival of the water garden feature remains to be completed), Northcote Manor is already recognised as a paragon of country houses by national and regional media as well as the local tourist boards. Eleven luxury bedrooms and suites have been splendidly created which, together with the sumptuous interiors, have attracted much acclaim and the hotel is delighted to have retained their Blue Ribbon Award from the RAC. Chef Chris Dawson has been awarded two rosettes for his cuisine and the hotel also features in the Good Food Guide and the 2001 edition of the Good Hotel Guide.

The location, too, takes some beating: close to Exmoor and Dartmoor, next door to a golf club, a stretch of the Taw at the bottom of the drive where you can fish (gilly provided) and some of the best shooting in the country. It's quiet and beautiful surpassing all superlatives.

If you choose to come for the luxury of the accommodation or the unrivalled cuisine or the country lifestyle, you will not be disappointed but you might be missing the point. Northcote Manor will embrace you in its history.

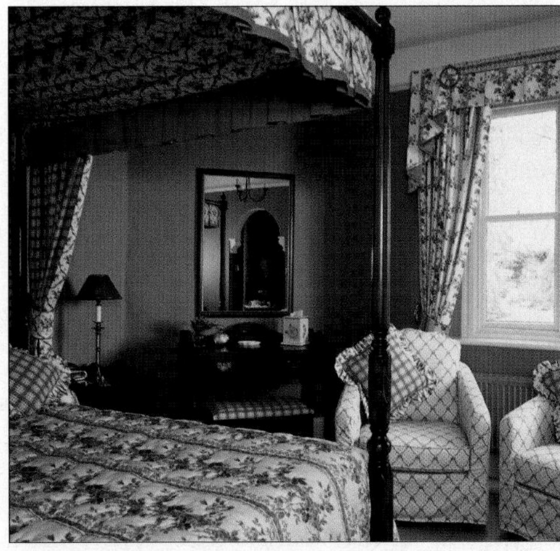

LOCATION

From South Molton town centre, fork left on B3226 to A377, and right to Barnstaple. Do not enter Burrington village. Hotel is situated 100 yards past Portsmouth Arms railway station.

• *Map p.502 ref: F3*

"If there is any place we would come back to, it is here!"

Mr & Mrs Anderson, Dundee

THE OLD PRIORY

12th century priory

Church Square, Midsomer Norton, Near Bath, Somerset BA3 2HX

Telephone 01761 416784
Fax 01761 417851

E-mail: *oldpriory@bestloved.com*

OWNER
Terri Knight

ROOM RATES

Single occupancy	*£60*
3 Doubles/Twins	*£90*
2 Family rooms	*£100*
2 Four-poster	*£120*

Includes full breakfast and VAT

CHARGE/CREDIT CARDS

• *JCB* • *MC* • *VI*

RATINGS & AWARDS
E.T.C. ★★
A.A. ★★★ ❀ *73%*

FACILITIES
On site: *Garden*
2 meeting rooms/max 40 people
Nearby: *Golf, riding, tennis*

RESTRICTIONS
No facilities for disabled guests
Pets by arrangement
No smoking in bedrooms or restaurant

ATTRACTIONS
Bath, Wells Cathedral, Glastonbury, Longleat, Chew Valley Lakes, Cheddar Gorge

AFFILIATIONS
Independent

NEAREST
MAJOR CITY:
Bath - 10 miles/20 mins

MAJOR AIRPORT:
Bristol - 16 miles/30 mins

RAILWAY STATION:
Bath - 10 miles/20 mins

RESERVATIONS
Direct with hotel
Quote ***Best Loved***

ACCESS CODES
Not applicable

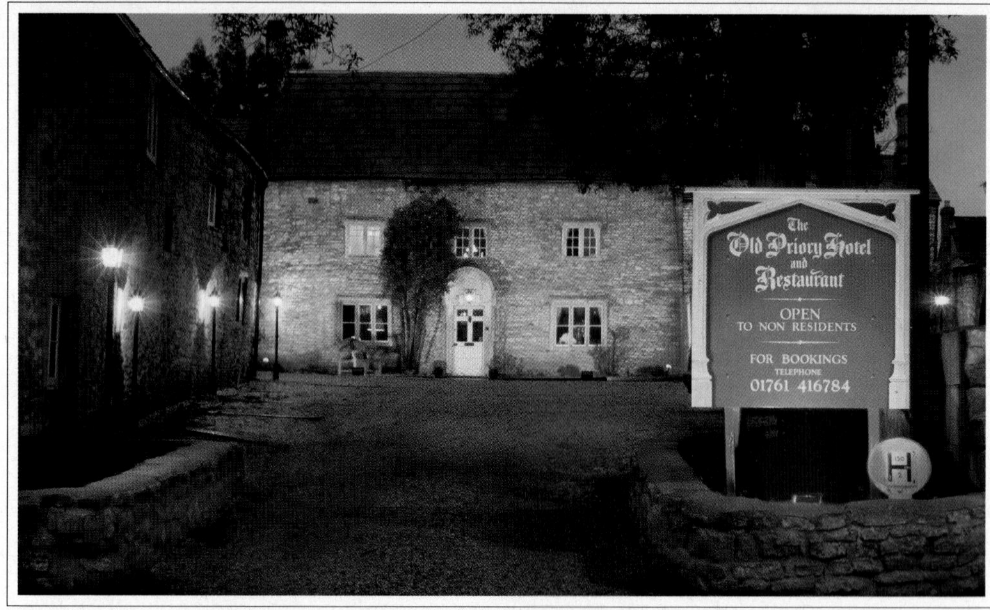

A stunning small hotel in a fascinating corner of the South West

Visitors to the Old Priory are apt to fall head-over-heels in love at first sight. At the end of the neat gravel driveway, and behind a tidy row of box hedges, one of the prettiest old stone buildings imaginable awaits.

The front door swings open into the hall with its tracery of Gothic wood panelling rescued from the church. In the ox-blood red lounge, an eclectic collection of plump sofas and chairs in rich complimentary fabrics are arranged around the huge fireplace that has a tiny loveseat tucked away in the corner of the hearth.

A spiral staircase and uneven landings lead to beautifully renovated bedrooms decorated in bold colours and well chosen furnishings which suit the age and style of the house. Original features have been enhanced and cleverly incorporated into the décor and there are many thoughtful touches throughout like the old fashioned children's prints on the walls in the family room.

The dining room has a distinctly Tuscan feel and an intimate private dining room-cum-meeting room opens out on to the prettily kept walled garden.

This is a truly wonderful small hotel which is perfectly situated for exploring the many mystical delights of Somerset.

LOCATION

From Bath take A367 towards Exeter. At Radstock turn right to Midsomer Norton. At mini-roundabout turn left into High Street, at the end set of lights turn right, then right at the next mini-roundabout. The hotel is straight ahead.

"We had such a wonderful time here! Orestone Manor is so beautiful and relaxing! Thank you for your hospitality"

Marla Blank and Ross Meridith, California, USA

• Map p.502 ref: E4

Georgian country house

ORESTONE MANOR

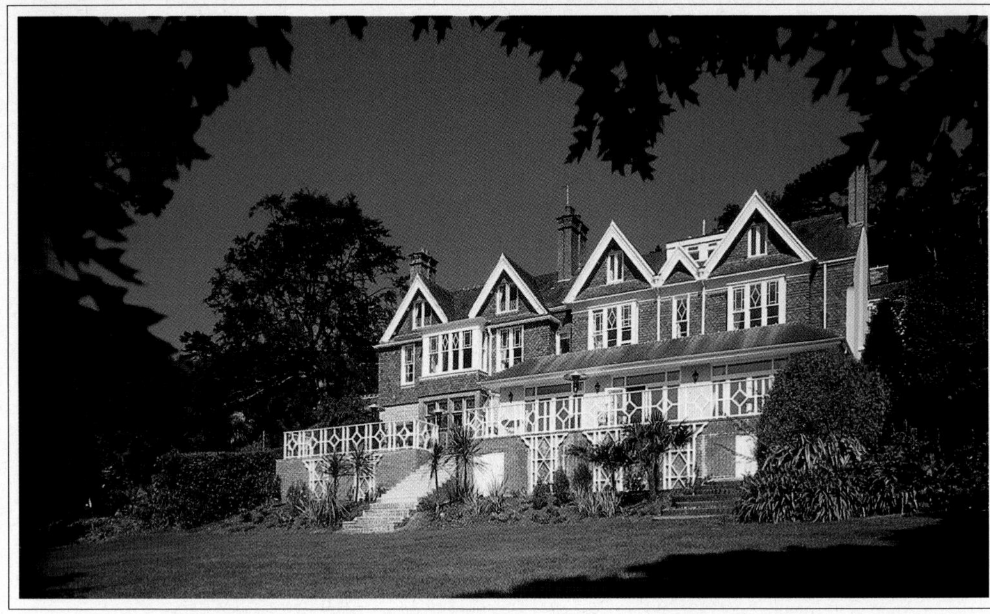

Rockhouse Lane, Maidencombe, Torquay, Devon TQ1 4SX

Telephone 01803 328098
Fax 01803 328336

E-mail: orestone@bestloved.com

GENERAL MANAGER
Rosemary Dallas

ASSISTANT MANAGERS
Rachael Miller
Patrica Dallas

ROOM RATES

1 Single	£50
11 Doubles/Twins	£100 - £160

Includes full breakfast and VAT

CHARGE/CREDIT CARDS

• MC • VI

RATINGS & AWARDS
E.T.C. ★★★
A.A. ★★★ ❀❀ 75%

FACILITIES
On site: Garden, heated outdoor pool, snooker
1 meeting room/max 20 people
Nearby: Golf, fishing, water skiing, yachting, tennis, shooting, riding

RESTRICTIONS
Pets by arrangement
Closed 2 - 14 Jan

ATTRACTIONS
Dartmoor, Berry Pomeroy and Dartmouth Castles, Buckfast Abbey, beaches and coastal walks

AFFILIATIONS
Independent

NEAREST
MAJOR CITY:
Exeter - 20 miles/30 mins

MAJOR AIRPORT:
Exeter - 25 miles/45 mins
London Heathrow - 190 miles/3½ hrs

RAILWAY STATION:
Newton Abbot - 6 miles/15 mins

RESERVATIONS
Direct with hotel
Quote **Best Loved**

ACCESS CODES
Not applicable

WEST COUNTRY

A delightful clifftop eyrie head and shoulders above the English Riviera

Strategically perched on the South Devon cliffs, Orestone Manor commands fabulous views down over the treetops to the glittering expanse of Lyme Bay. The house was built in 1809, and was once the home of painter John Horsley RA, whose celebrated portrait of Isambard Kingdom Brunel hangs in the National Gallery.

Orestone has recently received an inspired makeover from the new owners Peter Morgan and Friederike Etessami. The overall style is Seaside Victorian from the white Lloyd loom garden furniture in the splendidly palm-fringed conservatory to the cosy drawing room with its winter season open fire. Each of the very generously sized bedrooms have been designed around a unique theme and the Chinese room and Master bedroom are certainly worth a peek. Up in the gables the rooms have even had their windows enlarged to improve the view.

On the atmosphere front, think country house not hotel. The welcome is relaxed and friendly, and the excellent restaurant is a real focus for foodies, where chef Tony Hetherington's contemporary English cuisine has garnered numerous plaudits. If you need to work up an appetite, the South Devon Heritage Coast footpath is just 300 yards away and takes in spectacular scenery as well as access to glorious beaches and coves.

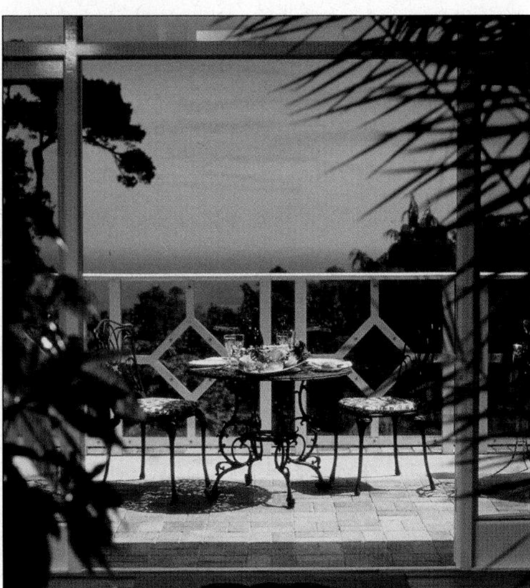

LOCATION

Located 4 miles from Torquay on the A379 (formerly B3199) coastal road. The hotel is opposite Brunel Manor on the coastal side.

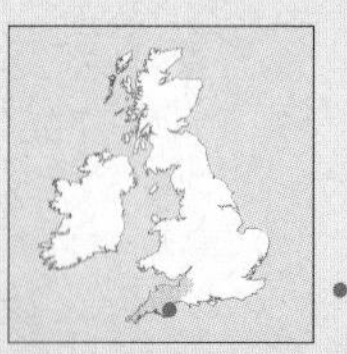

• Map p.502 ref: E4

“ From the magnificent views to the friendly and professional service, everything is first class ”

Mrs Jill Wood, Caversham, Reading

THE OSBORNE HOTEL & LANGTRY RESTAURANT

Seaside hotel

Hesketh Crescent, Meadfoot
Torquay, Devon TQ1 2LL

Telephone 01803 213311
Fax 01803 296788

E-mail: osborne@bestloved.com

OWNER

Ian Davies

ROOM RATES

1 Single	£52 - £102
20 Doubles/Twins	£124 - £168
8 Suites	£154 - £198

Sea view supplement
Includes full breakfast and VAT

CHARGE/CREDIT CARDS

• MC • VI

RATINGS & AWARDS

E.T.C. ★★★ Silver Award
R.A.C. ★★★ Dining Award 2
A.A. ★★★ ❀ 75%
A.A. Courtesy & Care Award 1999

FACILITIES

On site: *Garden, tennis, gym, sauna, indoor/outdoor pools, snooker, putting lawn*
1 meeting room/max 60 people
Nearby: *Fishing, water skiing, yachting, golf*

RESTRICTIONS

Limited facilities for disabled guests
No pets

ATTRACTIONS

Dartmoor National Park, Plymouth, Dartmouth, Dartmouth & Totnes Castles, Exeter Cathedral

AFFILIATIONS

Independent

NEAREST

MAJOR CITY:
Exeter - 22 miles/35 mins

MAJOR AIRPORT:
London Heathrow - 190 miles/3½ hrs
Exeter - 25 miles/45 mins

RAILWAY STATION:
Torquay - 2 miles/10 mins

RESERVATIONS

Direct with hotel
*Quote **Best Loved***

ACCESS CODES

Not applicable

Elegant Regency grandeur and a panoramic view over Tor Bay

The Osborne Hotel is situated in its own five acres of beautiful gardens at the centre of an elegant Regency terrace, looking straight out across the vivid, wide, blue panorama of Tor Bay. The Osborne has often been described as 'Bath by the Sea'. For grace, grandeur, peace and quiet, it matches that Regency showplace, but nowhere in Bath will you find the golden sands, tropical palm trees and luxuriant vegetation that delight the Osborne's guests.

The public rooms and some of the bedrooms benefit from magnificent views that rank high among Britain's most spectacular land and seascapes. In Langtry's Restaurant Head Chef Wayne Maddern consistently produces interesting and imaginative dishes, and the less formal brasserie provides appetising meals and refreshments throughout the day.

Torquay is renowned for its leisure facilities, and the Osborne has a good range of its own. A heated swimming pool, putting green and hard tennis courts are in the grounds. The indoor choices include heated swimming pool, satellite TV, full size snooker table, pool table, gymnasium, plunge pool and solarium - outdoors too there is generally a good supply of sunshine.

LOCATION

A38 to centre of Torquay. Follow Torbay Road along harbour. Turn left at clock tower and right at traffic lights. Follow road over hill and down to Meadfoot Beach. Hotel is on right.

A keen Angler? Refer to page 472 for our Fishing Index

"A good bet if you can find it"

Paddy Burt, Daily Telegraph

• Map ref

296

16th century estate PERCY'S COUNTRY HOTEL &

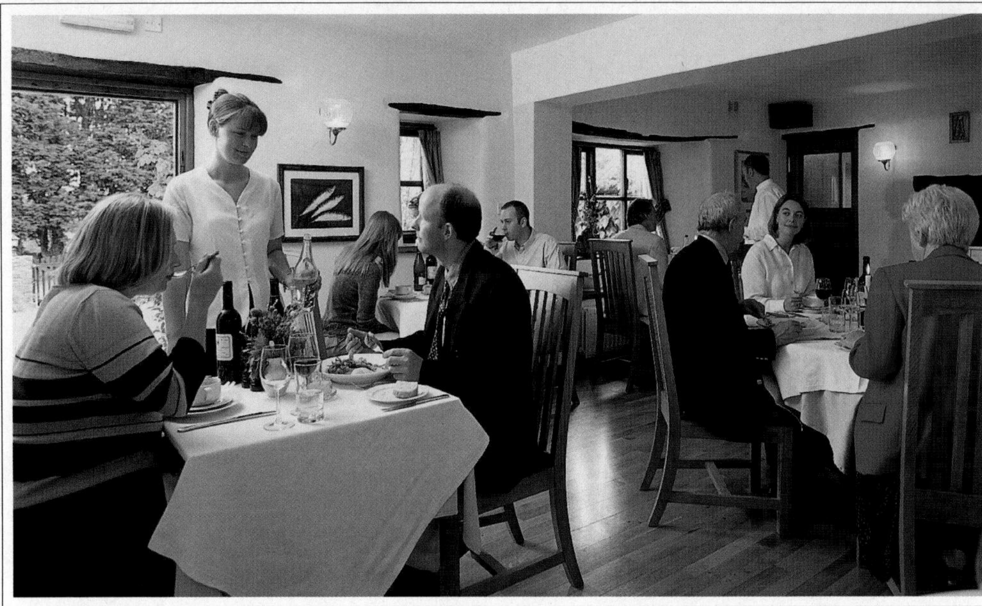

A successful London restaurant sets up with rooms in the middle of Devon

The Bricknell-Webbs wanderlust is over. They seem to have found journey's end, a trail that has taken them via the world of bookmaking and their first restaurant venture, Percy's in North London, which attracted generous applause from the food guides and even a nod from a Michelin inspector. But, now, here they are, in the middle of Devon, not just running a restaurant, but a small hotel, a farm (which has just quadrupled in size to 130 acres) and a butchery producing its own sausages and home-cured ham and bacon.

"It was blood, sweat, toil and tears." says Tony. And it must have been; it has all come together in three short years but the result justifies all.

It is almost the perfect place to have a country restaurant: the sea is only 20 miles away at most and the famous red Devon soil is especially fertile. So, the seafood is still bright as it goes into the pan, the herbs and vegetables are picked from the farm and the Jacob's lamb comes straight from the restaurant's pastures. Tastes have that special piquancy you rarely find in cities; it s not just fresher, the food has been organically grown. Percy's has awards for that, too.

The bedrooms are huge, unfussily furnished, have grand views and big, big beds. There is luxury in every detail with nice touches like a cafetiere with real coffee and a bowl of fresh fruit.

Bring walking shoes, there are other attractions!

LOCATION

Leave the A30 at Launceston and take the A388 towards Holsworthy. At St Giles-on-the-Heath, turn right to Virginstowe. The hotel is signposted.

Virginstow, N... Devon EX21 5E...

Telephone 01409 211236
Fax 01409 211275

E-mail: *percy@bestloved.com*

OWNERS

Tony and Tina Bricknell-Webb

ROOM RATES

Single occupancy	*£60 - £80*
8 Doubles/Twins	*£80 - £100*

Includes full breakfast and VAT

CHARGE/CREDIT CARDS

• *DC* • *MC* • *VI*

RATINGS & AWARDS

E.T.C. ◆◆◆◆◆ *Gold Award*
R.A.C. ◆◆◆◆◆ *Dining Award 3*
Sparkling Diamond Award
A.A. ❀❀
Taste of the West Best Restaurant in the South West Award 2000

FACILITIES

On site: *Garden, heli-pad*
Licensed for weddings
Nearby: *Golf, water skiing, yachting, fishing, riding*

RESTRICTIONS

Smoking permitted in bar only

ATTRACTIONS

Rosemoor RHS Garden, Eden Project, Dartmoor National Park, Bodmin Moor, Roadford Lake, National Trust Properties

AFFILIATIONS

Independent

NEAREST

MAJOR CITY:
Exeter - 40 miles/50 mins

MAJOR AIRPORT:
London Heathrow - 250 miles/4 hrs
Plymouth - 25 miles/30 mins

RAILWAY STATION:
Plymouth - 25 miles/30 mins
Exeter - 40 miles/50 mins

RESERVATIONS

Direct with hotel
Quote ***Best Loved***

ACCESS CODES

Not applicable

"*What a find! Excellent accommodation, good company and friendly, helpful hosts. Best of all, fine quality horses and excellent riding*"

Helen Curtin, Toronto, Canada

ORLOCK VALE HOUSE

Country house

Porlock Weir,
Somerset TA24 8NY

Telephone 01643 862338
Fax 01643 863338

E-mail: *porlock@bestloved.com*

OWNERS

Helen and Kim Youd

ROOM RATES

Single occupancy £40 - £65
15 Doubles/Twins £70 - £90
Includes full breakfast and VAT

CHARGE/CREDIT CARDS

• *MC* • *VI*

RATINGS & AWARDS

E.T.C. ★★ Silver Award
A.A. ★★ 71%

FACILITIES

On site: *Garden, riding, fishing*
1 meeting room/max 20 people
Nearby: *Golf, tennis, hunting, shooting*

RESTRICTIONS

No facilities for disabled guests
No children under 12 years
No pets allowed in hotel, kennels available
No smoking in bedrooms

ATTRACTIONS

Dunster Castle and Gardens, Lorna Doone Valley, Devon Coast, RHS Rosemoor Gardens, Exmoor & Tarr Steps, Arlington Court

AFFILIATIONS

Independent

NEAREST

MAJOR CITY:
Taunton - 30 miles/50 mins

MAJOR AIRPORT:
London Heathrow - 180 miles/3½ hrs
Bristol - 70 miles/1½ hrs

RAILWAY STATION:
Taunton - 30 miles/50 mins

RESERVATIONS

Direct with hotel
*Quote **Best Loved***

ACCESS CODES

Not applicable

Informal and comfortable - an idyllic setting by the sea

Fringed by the sea and sheltered from the winds that can blow across Exmoor, is Porlock Vale House standing in 25 acres of grounds. It started life as a hunting lodge and its equestrian links are as thriving today as ever. Indeed, it was once the training centre of the British Event team for the 1952 Olympics. Today, it is a charming small hotel with an unusually friendly atmosphere and a superbly equipped and professionally-run stable within its estate.

The hotel's many comforts are the perfect foil to days of fresh air and fun. The sitting rooms open onto a terrace that overlooks Porlock Bay, a view shared by some of the bedrooms, while others look over the extensive grounds. All are prettily furnished and well-appointed with en suite bathrooms. There is a bar for a relaxing drink before dinner. Enjoy good food prepared in traditional style with all the flavours of Somerset's coast and country.

If you can tear yourself away from the horses, the area is rich in things to see and do; this is Lorna Doone country, there are some lovely walks from the house and all sorts of country sports like shooting and fishing to be pursued.

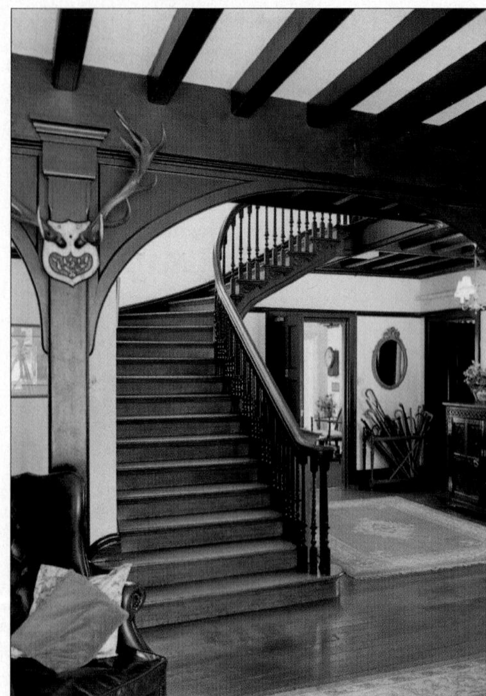

LOCATION

11/2 miles out of the village of Porlock (A39) on Porlock Weir Road, by the sea.

“Just exactly what we were looking for - imagine such elegance in the middle of a wild place”

Mr B Lewis, Minnesota, USA

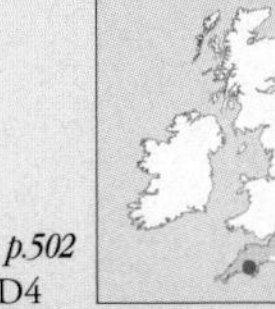

• *Map p.502 ref: D4*

Georgian country house

PRINCE HALL HOTEL

The joy of the great outdoors combined with conviviality and good food

What was a former stable and hunting lodge of the Duke of Cornwall (aka The Prince of Wales) Prince Hall, hence the name, is today an elegantly and attractively furnished country house hotel. A perennial favourite of those seeking a few days rest and relaxation in magnificent Dartmoor, Prince Hall combines peace and quiet with fresh air, stunning scenery, comfort, good food and unfussy hospitality.

You will find no nicer nor more easy-going hosts than Adam and Carrie Southwell who bought Prince Hall in 1995. Their insistence on everyone having a good time is evident in the relaxed and friendly atmosphere where their commitment and caring approach play an important part.

If you enjoy outdoor activities look no further. Once you deposit your car you need not think about it until you leave. From walking and shooting, to fishing, riding and mountain biking Dartmoor is the perfect setting for working up a hearty appetite. Fortunately, Adam obliges with creative menus reflecting his passion for Dartmoor and West Country produce. An ample wine list rounds out what is, no doubt, a truly memorable off-the- beaten-track experience.

LOCATION

From the M5, take the A38 towards Plymouth, then the B3357 towards Princetown. The hotel is 10 miles further on, on the left, a mile before Two Bridges Junction.

Near Two Bridges, Dartmoor, Devon PL20 6SA

Telephone 01822 890403
Fax 01822 890676

E-mail: *princehall@bestloved.com*

OWNERS

Adam and Carrie Southwell

RATES PER PERSON

1 Single	*£65 - £90*
6 Doubles/Twins	*£69 - £85*
2 Four-posters	*£72*

Includes full breakfast, dinner, service and VAT

CHARGE/CREDIT CARDS

• DC • MC • VI

RATINGS & AWARDS

E.T.C. ★★ Silver Award
A.A. ★★ ❀❀ 78%
West Country Cooking Awards
'Best Hotel Restaurant' 2000

FACILITIES

On site: *Garden, croquet, clay pigeon shooting*
1 meeting room/max 20 people
Nearby: *Golf, fishing, hunting/shooting, riding, walking trails*

RESTRICTIONS

No children
No facilities for disabled guests
Closed mid Dec - mid Feb

ATTRACTIONS

Dartmoor, Merrivale Prehistoric Settlement, Buckland Abbey, Cotehele House, Castle Drogo, Lanhydrock

AFFILIATIONS

Independent

NEAREST

MAJOR CITY:
Plymouth - 12 miles/30 mins
MAJOR AIRPORT:
Plymouth - 12 miles/30 mins
London Heathrow - 150 miles/3 hrs
RAILWAY STATION:
Plymouth - 12 miles/30 mins
FERRY PORT:
Plymouth - 12 miles/30 mins

RESERVATIONS

Direct with hotel
Quote ***Best Loved***

ACCESS CODES

Not applicable

• Map p.502 ref: F2

“ Our stay at the Queensberry ranks as our most memorable hotel stay in England ”

Heather Cameron, New York

QUEENSBERRY HOTEL

Regency house

Russel Street, Bath, Somerset BA1 2QF

Telephone 01225 447928
Fax 01225 446065

E-mail: queensberry@bestloved.com

OWNERS
Stephen and Penny Ross

ROOM RATES

Single occupancy	£100 - £145
29 Doubles	£120 - £220

Includes continental breakfast and VAT

CHARGE/CREDIT CARDS

• MC • VI

RATINGS & AWARDS
E.T.C. ★★★ Gold Award
R.A.C. Blue Ribbon ★★★ Dining Award 3
A.A. ★★★ ❀❀
WHICH? 'Town House Hotel of the Year 2000'

FACILITIES
On site: *Courtyard garden*
1 meeting room/max 30 people
Nearby: *Golf, riding*

RESTRICTIONS
No facilities for disabled guests
No pets

ATTRACTIONS
Bath, Roman Baths, Stonehenge, Wells, Longleat, Stourhead Gardens

AFFILIATIONS
Selected British Hotels
Preston's Global Hotels

NEAREST
MAJOR CITY:
Bath

MAJOR AIRPORT:
London Heathrow - 90 miles/1¾ hrs
Bristol - 15 miles/30 mins

RAILWAY STATION:
Bath Spa - 1 mile/5 mins

RESERVATIONS
Toll free in US: 800-323-5463
or 800-544-9993
Quote ***Best Loved***

ACCESS CODES
Not applicable

WEST COUNTRY

An architecturally acclaimed house in the Roman city of Bath

The Queensberry – luxurious, decorative and intimate – a few minutes' walk from the Roman Baths but itself in the heart of Georgian Bath. Built by John Wood of Royal Crescent fame, for the Marquis of Queensberry in 1772, the house retains its splendid period plasterwork and fireplaces, all now complemented by Penny Ross's interiors. There is a delightful courtyard garden, drawing room and cocktail bar.

The focal point of the hotel is The Olive Tree Restaurant which Patron Stephen Ross describes as a contemporary restaurant – informal, modestly priced, with English cooking that combines excellent local produce with the robust flavours of the Mediterranean.

The Queensberry could not be better placed for visiting the highlights of Bath; the Roman Baths, Theatre Royal, Assembly Rooms and Royal Crescent are close to the hotel. A meander downhill takes you past the antiques markets, the best shops outside London and on to Bath Abbey. The famous spa waters are there to be tested.

LOCATION

Exit 18/M4, A46 to Bath. Turn right at T-junction, right at mini-roundabout to next lights, sharp right at Lansdown Road, 2nd left into Bennet Street and Russell Street is 1st right.

" Unsurpassed in service and friendliness . . . superb cuisine . . . The Riviera is truly lovely in every respect and continues to be one of our favourite hotels "

Patricia Polidor, New York

• Map p.502 ref: E4

Georgian seaside hotel

HOTEL RIVIERA

The charm of a unique hotel set in an 18th century seaside resort

Is there any finer place in Devon to sit and watch the world go by than the terrace at the Hotel Riviera, on Sidmouth's famous Georgian esplanade? With the beach a stone's throw across the broad promenade, here is the perfect place to drink coffee, take tea or sip a sundowner. Welcome to the Which? Hotel Guide Hotel of the Year, 1999 - and one of the few hotels in Britain with the coveted Courtesy and Care award from the Automobile Association. Little wonder then that Peter Wharton's Hotel Riviera, with its fine, Regency façade and bow fronted windows, handsome public rooms and beautifully appointed en suite bedrooms - many with sea views - is arguably one of the most comfortable and certainly the most welcoming in this ancient and beautiful South West corner of England. Perfectly located in the town which England's Poet Laureate and lover of architecture, Sir John Betjeman, called his favourite holiday place, the Riviera enjoys four-star categories of both the AA and the RAC. Here is superb cuisine, prepared by Swiss and French trained chefs, a fine cellar and elegant dining in a handsome salon overlooking Lyme Bay. Close by are gardens, coastal walks, golf, bowling, croquet, putting, tennis, fishing, sailing and riding, whilst the cathedral city of Exeter is nearby and everywhere around, lush countryside and stunning coastline to explore.

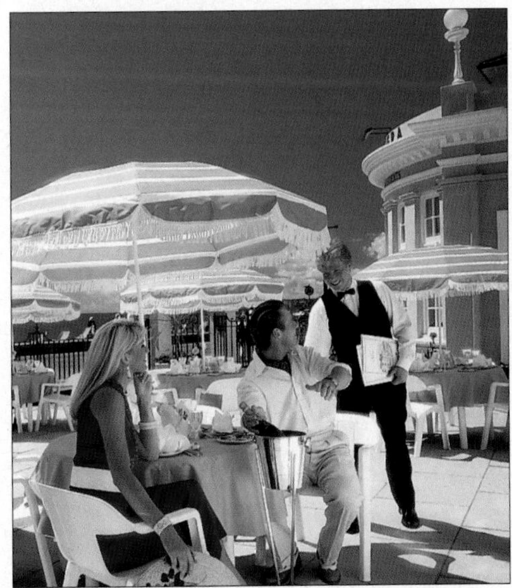

LOCATION

Sidmouth is 13 miles from M5, Exit 30 (then follow A3052).

The Esplanade, Sidmouth, Devon EX10 8AY

Telephone 01395 515201
Fax 01395 577775

E-mail: *riviera@bestloved.com*

OWNER

Peter S Wharton

RATES PER PERSON

7 Singles	*£87 - £113*
18 Doubles/Twins	*£77 - £103*
2 Suites	*£103 - £113*

Includes full breakfast, 7-course dinner and VAT

CHARGE/CREDIT CARDS

• DC • MC • VI

RATINGS & AWARDS

E.T.C. ★★★★ Gold Award
R.A.C. ★★★★ Dining Award 2
A.A. ★★★★ ❀ 74%
A.A. Courtesy and Care Award
WHICH? Hotel Guide 'Hotel of the Year 1999'

FACILITIES

On site: *Patio*
1 meeting room/max 85 people
Nearby: *Golf, riding, fishing, tennis, croquet, game shooting*

RESTRICTIONS

No pets in public rooms

ATTRACTIONS

Killerton House, Exeter Cathedral, Bicton Park and Gardens, Dartmoor and Exmoor

AFFILIATIONS

Independent

NEAREST

MAJOR CITY:
Exeter - 13 miles/30 mins
London - 165 miles/3½ hrs

MAJOR AIRPORT:
London Heathrow - 153 miles/3½ hrs
Exeter - 10 miles/30 mins

RAILWAY STATION:
Exeter - 13 miles/30 mins

RESERVATIONS

Direct with hotel
Quote ***Best Loved***

ACCESS CODES

Not applicable

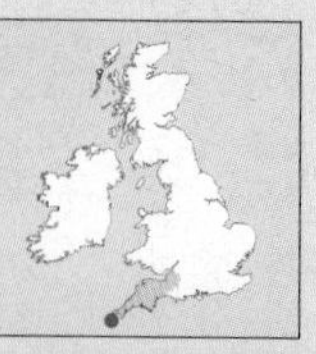

• Map p.502 ref: B6

"In 1492 Columbus discovered America, in 1992 my husband and I discovered the Isles of Scilly"

Denise & Frank Lucibello Paramus, New Jersey

ST MARTIN'S ON THE ISLE

Island hotel

The Island of St Martin, Isles of Scilly, Cornwall TR25 0QW

Telephone 01720 422090
Fax 01720 422298

E-mail: stmartin@bestloved.com

OWNERS

Peter and Penny Sykes

GENERAL MANAGER

Keith Bradford

ROOM RATES

Single occupancy	£85 - £125
28 Doubles/Twins	£170 - £270
2 Suites	£270 - £330

Includes full breakfast, dinner and VAT

CHARGE/CREDIT CARDS

 • DC • MC • VI

RATINGS & AWARDS

R.A.C. Blue Ribbon ★★★
Dining Award 4
A.A. ★★★ ❀❀❀

FACILITIES

On site: *Garden, tennis, private beach, indoor pool, snooker, fishing, sailing, clay pigeon shooting*
3 meeting rooms/max 60 people
Nearby: *Golf, riding*

RESTRICTIONS

No smoking in restaurant
Closed Nov - Mar

ATTRACTIONS

Naturalist's Paradise, Botanical gardens, uninhabited islands & beaches, bird watching, Tresco Abbey

AFFILIATIONS

Pride of Britain

NEAREST

MAJOR CITY:
Penzance - 40 miles/2½ hrs (ferry)

MAJOR AIRPORT:
London Heathrow - 320 miles/2 hrs (by air via Newquay or Plymouth)

RAILWAY STATION:
Penzance - 40 miles/2½ hrs (ferry)

RESERVATIONS

Toll free in US: 800-98-PRIDE
Quote ***Best Loved***

ACCESS CODES

Not applicable

WEST COUNTRY

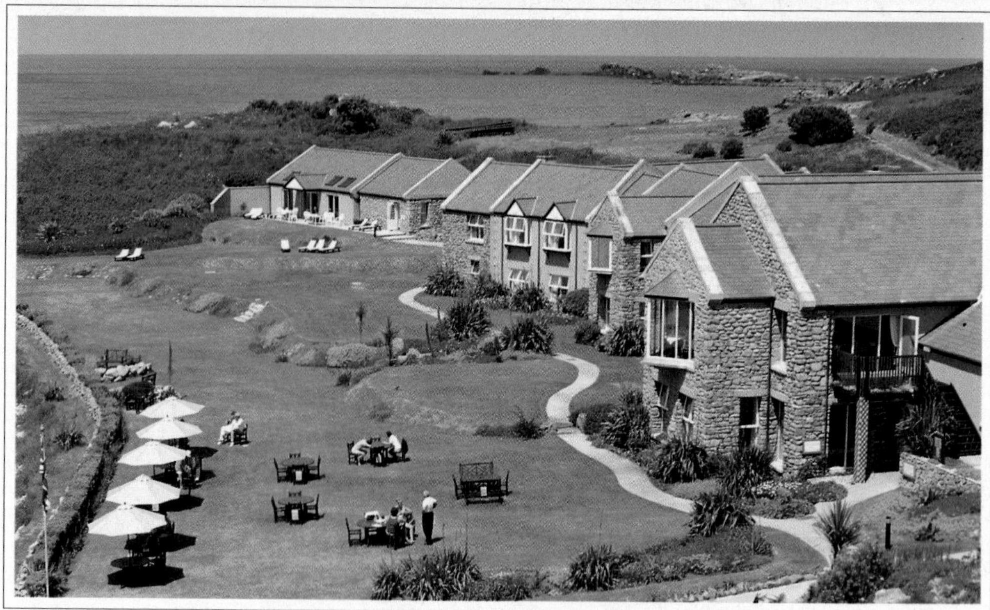

Everything on St Martin's is unspoilt - except the guests!

St Martin's is one of the Isles of Scilly, just two miles long and half a mile wide, pitched into the Atlantic 28 miles off Land's End. Ocean rollers and the warming Gulf Stream have created one of the loveliest settings you will find in this book. Part of the fun at staying at St Martin's on the Isle, is in the getting there, the fastest way is by helicopter from Penzance to St Mary's (the largest of the Isles) followed by a launch which leaves you at the hotel's private quay. This is a true island getaway whether for a weekend or a week. It is like stepping back in time; no noise but the sea and the gulls, no pollution and none of the leftovers of tourism. Marvellous.

You may feel moved to come for the rare beauty of the place. But there is another siren song: the hotel has undoubtedly the best restaurant in the islands and possibly one of the finest views you could wish for. The speciality is seafood (of course) but the crustacia are divine. Opting for the local crab salad is a must! The Tean Restaurant and the Round Island Bar are the focus of the islands' social life. The rooms, named after local legends, can be described as 'world-class island resort', very comfortable and prettily furnished.

This secluded idyll is home to Atlantic seals and an abundance of bird-life. The hotel is a perfect base for fishing, snorkelling and diving, and for visiting the famous gardens at Tresco. But no doubt the best part will be simply doing absolutely nothing on one of the many solitary beaches, except perhaps of dreaming of your next visit.

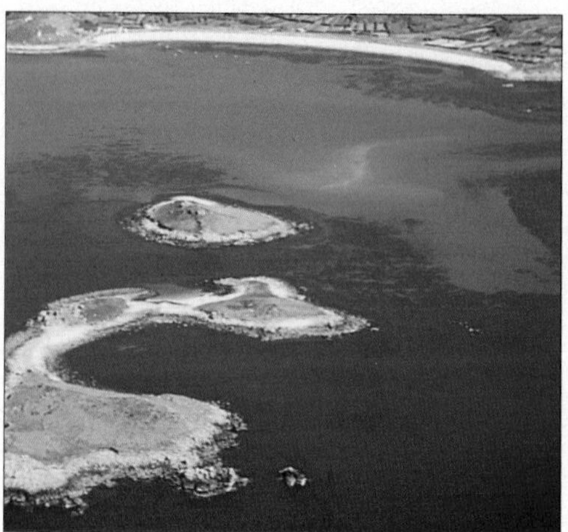

LOCATION

On the island of St Martin, one of the Isles of Scilly.

At the time of printing the exchange rate for £1.00 was US$1.55

“ An oasis of calm in the heart of the city ”

Mr Mitchell, London

• Map p.502 ref: E4

Georgian town house

ST OLAVES HOTEL

Mary Arches Street, Exeter, Devon EX4 3AZ

Telephone 01392 217736
Fax 01392 413054

E-mail: stolaves@bestloved.com

OWNERS
Sebastian and Philippa Hughes

ROOM RATES

1 Single	£90
14 Doubles/Twins	£95 - £105
3 Suites	from £120

Includes breakfast and VAT

CHARGE/CREDIT CARDS
DC • MC • VI

RATINGS & AWARDS
E.T.C. ★★★
R.A.C. ★★★ Dining Award 2
A.A. ★★★ ❀❀ 67%

FACILITIES
On site: Secluded walled gardens
3 meeting rooms/max 80 people
Nearby: Golf, riding

RESTRICTIONS
No facilities for disabled guests

ATTRACTIONS
Exeter Cathedral, North Devon coast, Dartmoor National Park

AFFILIATIONS
Preston's Global Hotels

NEAREST
MAJOR CITY:
Exeter

MAJOR AIRPORT:
Exeter - 7 miles/12 mins
London Heathrow - 180 miles/3 hrs

RAILWAY STATION:
Exeter - 1 mile/5 mins

RESERVATIONS
Toll free in US: 800-544-9993
Quote **Best Loved**

ACCESS CODES
Not applicable

A gracious town house hotel within the sound of cathedral bells

Just 400 yards from Exeter Cathedral, this lovely Georgian property boasts a private walled garden right in the heart of the city as well as a long-standing reputation for its welcoming home-from-home atmosphere and fine dining. New owners, Sebastian and Philippa Hughes, who also run the delectable Holne Chase country house hotel in the wilds of Dartmoor (see page 282), have carried out a complete refurbishment downstairs, creating a new dining room, drawing room and bar whilst carefully preserving the elegant period style of the building. The Hughes' love of the English countryside and traditional pursuits can be seen in the sporting prints decorating the drawing room, and upstairs they have introduced a real breath of country air in the fresh and prettily decorated bedrooms which now include three spacious suites.

St Olaves is a handy touring base for the South Devon coastline, which leads down from the mouth of the River Exe to the seaside towns and beaches of the English Riviera. If you like your scenery rugged, head inland for the windswept beauty of Dartmoor National Park; if you prefer nature tamed, plan a trip to the Killerton or Coleton Fishacre National Trust gardens.

LOCATION

From Exeter city centre follow signs to 'Mary Arches P'. Hotel entrance is directly opposite.

WEST COUNTRY

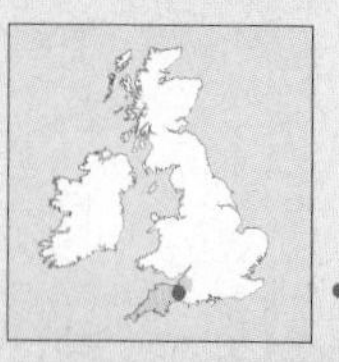

• Map p.502
ref: F3

"A stately home with elegance yet a most comfortable country house"

John Taylor, Cricket St Thomas

STON EASTON PARK

Palladian mansion

Ston Easton, Near Bath,
Somerset BA3 4DF

Telephone 01761 241631
Fax 01761 241377

E-mail: stoneaston@bestloved.com

OWNER
Countess Von Essen

GENERAL MANAGER
Nicholas Romano

ROOM RATES

12 Doubles/Twins	£185 - £195
3 Superior Doubles/Twins	£265 - £315
6 Four-posters	£225
3 Suites	£320 - £405

Includes early morning tea, newspaper and VAT

CHARGE/CREDIT CARDS

• DC • MC • VI

RATINGS & AWARDS
E.T.C. ★★★★
R.A.C. Blue Ribbon ★★★★ Dining Award 4
A.A. ★★★★ ❀❀

FACILITIES
On site: Garden, fishing, tennis, croquet, hot-air ballooning, laser shooting, hunting, off-road driving, falconry display, billiards, heli-pad
Licensed for weddings
1 meeting room/max 150 people
Nearby: Clay pigeon shooting, riding

RESTRICTIONS
No facilities for disabled guests
No children under 7 years (does not apply to babes in arms),
No pets in hotel, kennels provided

ATTRACTIONS
Bath, Longleat House, Glastonbury, Wells Cathedral, American Museum, Stourhead

AFFILIATIONS
Von Essen Hotels
Relais and Chateaux
The Celebrated Hotels Collection

NEAREST
MAJOR CITY:
Bath - 15 miles/25 mins
MAJOR AIRPORT:
Bristol - 12 miles/20 mins
RAILWAY STATION:
Castle Cary - 4 miles/10 mins

RESERVATIONS
Direct with hotel
Quote **Best Loved**

ACCESS CODES
Not applicable

Grand in style and effervescent in spirit

One of Britain's most glorious Palladian mansions, Ston Easton Park epitomises the very essence of the aristocratic English country house set in grounds created by the 18th century landscape supremo, Humphry Repton.

Ston Easton is at once ineffably elegant and stately, yet surprisingly human in scale. A private home until recently, many of its furnishings, paintings and objects d'art have been amassed over the years and are intrinsic to the overall effect. Opulent stucco decorations and trompe-l'oeil murals are highlights of the magnificent Saloon, and Regency mahogany furnishings can be found in the Library and Yellow Dining Room. The bedrooms are delicate and pretty with fine antique beds and garden views. For guests wanting utter privacy, the 17th century Gardener's Cottage is an idyllic retreat on the wooded banks of the River Norr.

Ston Easton's atmosphere mirrors the grand yet human feel of the house. On the one hand, impeccably trained staff squeeze the lemon and stir the sugar into your tea in the manner of an old school butler. On the other, the General Manager and Sorrel the friendly spaniel, materialise, as if by magic, to greet guests as they pull into the drive, adding that elusive personal touch which gives Ston Easton such a special sense of ease. Pilots should note the following heli-pad grid reference: 6225 5375 51 17N 0732W OS.65-75.

LOCATION

Exit junction 18 of the M4 on to the A46 to Bath. From Bath follow signs for Bristol (A4). At Globe Inn roundabout follow signs for Corston (A39). At T junction with A37 turn left and follow the signs for the hotel.

"The food was excellent, neither 'gourmet' nor home-cooking, with menus suited for a long stay - different every night"

The Good Hotel Guide

• Map p.502 ref: C5

Cornish manor house

TALLAND BAY HOTEL

A rare example of a country house hotel by the sea

Hidden down a sunken lane that leads to the sea, the Talland Bay Hotel is a real charmer. The stylishly converted old manor, parts of which date back to the 16th century, is nestled in two acres of glorious gardens and enjoys splendid views of the twin headlands flanking its namesake bay.

Comfort and quiet are two key components in Talland Bay's unpretentious and relaxing atmosphere. The Library and sitting room open onto a pool terrace, where palm trees add a distinctly Mediterranean air in summer. The bright and airy bedrooms are decorated with pretty chintzes, and nine have sea views. Two cottages in the walled garden offer an appealing alternative.

Cornwall's bracing sea air is bound to build up an appetite and menus display a healthy bias in favour of traditional local ingredients. Fresh crab and lobster from the fish markets of Looe, Cornish lamb and West Country cheeses are staples, while the wine list runs to around 100 choices from around the world.

Local explorations range from coastal walks to visits to the famous Lost Gardens of Heligan and the spectacular glasshouses of the Eden Project due to open in 2001. Sporting types can try their hand at golf, riding, sailing, and sea fishing. Talland Bay also offers four-day painting holidays with a tutor in the off-season (spring and autumn).

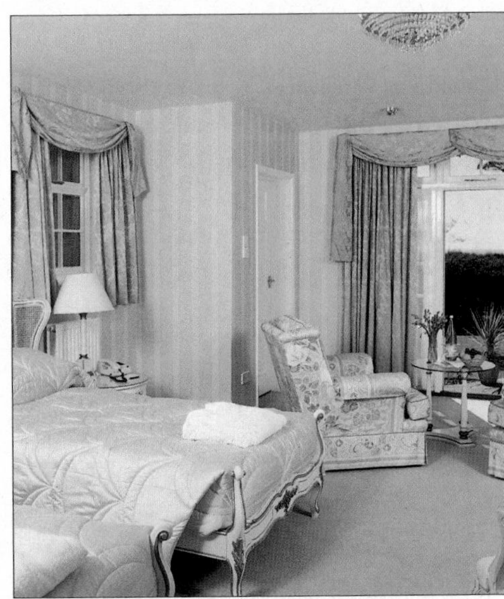

LOCATION

From Plymouth take the A38 south. Then the B3251 to Looe. Head towards Polperro for 2 miles. Left at crossroads.

Talland-by-Looe, Cornwall PL13 2JB

Telephone 01503 272667
Fax 01503 272940

E-mail: *tallandbay@bestloved.com*

OWNERS

Barry and Annie Rosier

GENERAL MANAGER

Maureen La Page

ROOM RATES PER PERSON

2 Singles	*£47 - £79*
15 Doubles/Twins	*£94 - £158*
2 Four-posters	*£94 - £158*

Includes full breakfast, afternoon tea and VAT

CHARGE/CREDIT CARDS

• DC • MC • VI

RATINGS & AWARDS

A.A. ★★★ ❀ 71%

FACILITIES

On site: *Garden, croquet, sauna, outdoor pool, putting green, table tennis*
1 meeting room/max 20 people
Nearby: *Golf, riding, sailing, boating, sea fishing, tennis*

RESTRICTIONS

No facilities for disabled guests
Pets by arrangement

ATTRACTIONS

Restormel Castle, Bodmin Moor, St Catherine's Castle, Fowey, Dupath Well House, Callington, St Michael's Mount, Lanhydrock, Lost Gardens of Heligan, Eden Project

AFFILIATIONS

Independent

NEAREST

MAJOR CITY:
Plymouth - 25 miles/30 mins

MAJOR AIRPORT:
Plymouth - 25 miles/30 mins

RAILWAY STATION:
Liskeard - 10- miles/15 mins

RESERVATIONS

Direct with hotel
Quote ***Best Loved***

ACCESS CODES

Not applicable

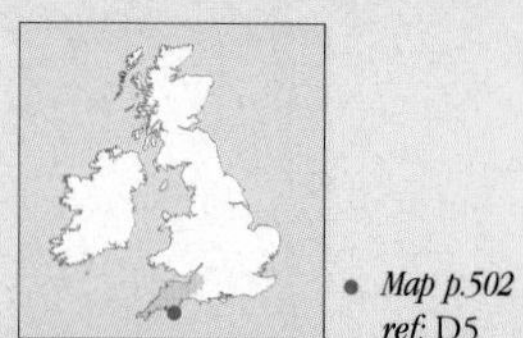

• Map p.502 ref: D5

"Completely relaxed, wholly pampered and now totally addicted"

George Turner III, Washington

TIDES REACH HOTEL

Beachside resort

South Sands, Salcombe, Devon TQ8 8LJ

Telephone 01548 843466
Fax 01548 843954

E-mail: tidesreach@bestloved.com

OWNER
Roy Edwards

MANAGER
John Edwards

RATES PER PERSON

Single occupancy	£64 - £100
32 Doubles/Twins	£55 - £115
3 Family suites	£90 - £100

Includes full breakfast, dinner and VAT

CHARGE/CREDIT CARDS

• DC • MC • VI

RATINGS & AWARDS
E.T.C. ★★★ Silver Award
R.A.C. ★★★ Dining Award 2
A.A. ★★★ ❀❀ 80%

FACILITIES
On site: Garden, indoor pool, squash, snooker, fitness centre, sauna, hair & beauty salon, windsurfing, sailing, water skiing
Nearby: Golf, riding, beaches

RESTRICTIONS
No children under 8 years
No facilities for disabled guests

ATTRACTIONS
National Marine Aquarium, Dartmoor, Dartmouth & Totnes Castles, Plymouth, Overbeck Museum, South Devon coast

AFFILIATIONS
Independent

NEAREST
MAJOR CITY:
Plymouth - 24 miles/40 mins
MAJOR AIRPORT:
London Heathrow - 220 miles/4½ hrs
Plymouth - 24 miles/40 mins
RAILWAY STATION:
Totnes - 20 miles/30 mins

RESERVATIONS
Direct with hotel
Quote **Best Loved**

ACCESS CODES
Not applicable

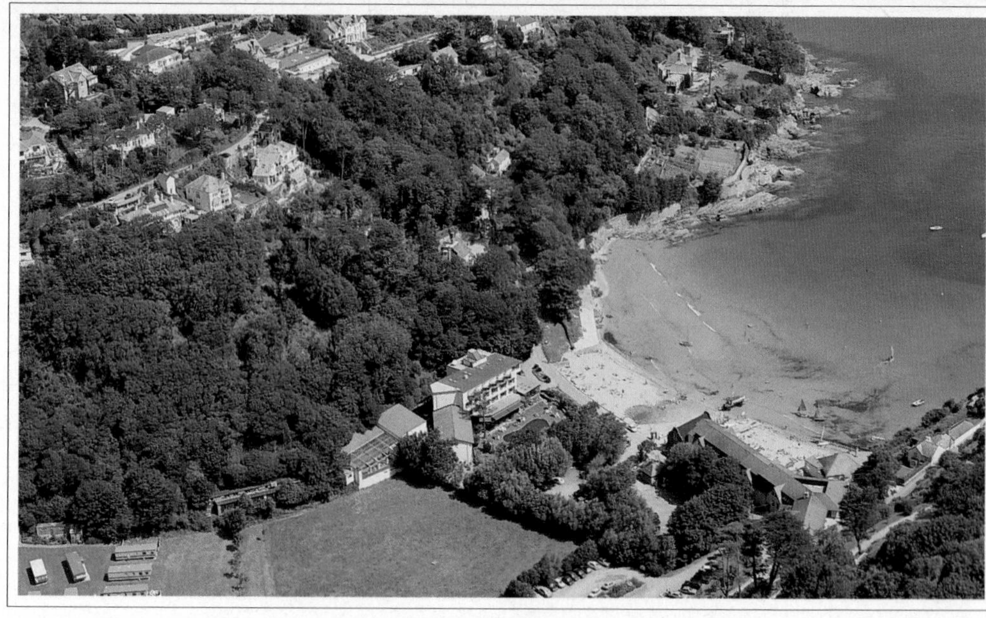

An ideal holiday location for total relaxation

Elegant and luxuriously appointed the Tides Reach Hotel has been under the personal supervision of the owners, Mr and Mrs Roy Edwards, for more than 30 years. They have built up an enviable reputation for cuisine and standards of service complementing the hotel's situation which must be one of the most naturally beautiful in the British Isles.

Set in a commanding position, facing south in the tree-fringed sandy cove of South Sands, it is the ideal location for a short break or relaxing holiday. The hotel stands just inside the mouth of the outstandingly scenic Salcombe Estuary.

At Tides Reach, one of the most important ingredients is the service. Highly trained staff, carefully chosen for their caring and courteous service, are dedicated to making your stay a pleasant and memorable one. In the Garden Room Restaurant the connoisseur of fine food and wine will find great satisfaction. Fresh fish and carefully selected local produce are expertly prepared to uphold the hotel's international reputation.

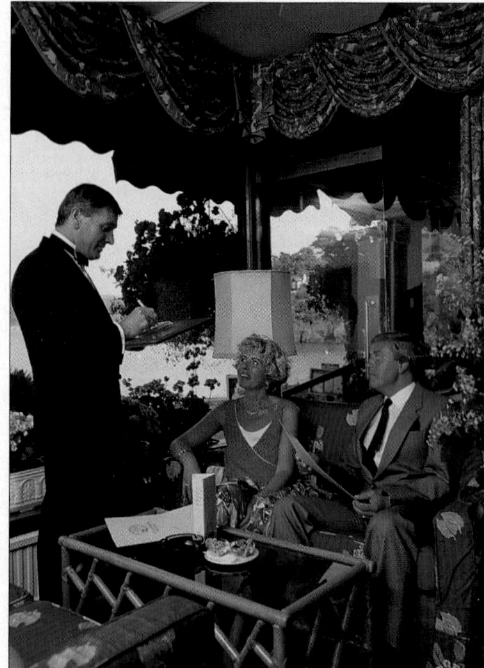

LOCATION

Leave A38 at Totnes, then follow A381 to Kingsbridge and thereafter to Salcombe as signposted.

Looking for an hotel with a golf course on site? See our 'Golf Guide' on page 478

“ After leaving you, we went on to stay at another hotel. We paid twice as much and didn't enjoy it half as much. You are the best innkeeper in the UK ”

Name withheld, USA

• *Map p.502 ref: C5*

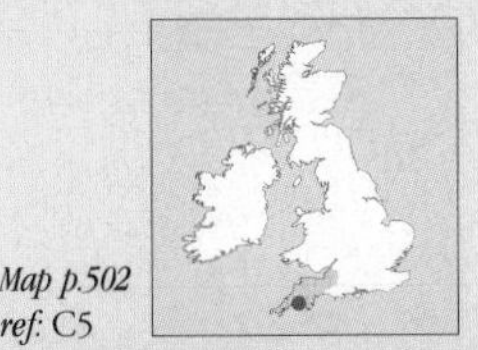

Victorian country manor — THE WELL HOUSE

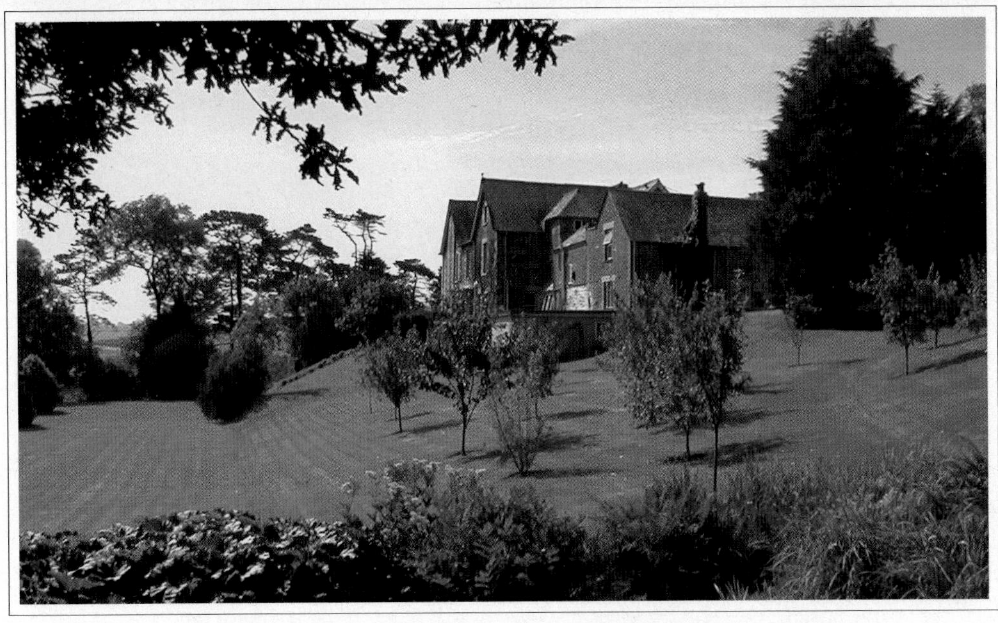

Discover Cornwall from this delightful secluded manor

An intimate nine-bedroomed Victorian country manor, The Well House is tucked away down a country lane deep in Cornwall's Looe Valley, just beyond the River Tamar. Its facade, wrapped in rambling wisteria and jasmine trailers, is just one of the hotel's continuous series of delights that include top quality service, modern luxury and impeccable standards of comfort.

The dining room, with its magnificent bay windows and sun terrace overlooking the lawns, has a contemporary style which is echoed in the cooking though the traditions of the area are clearly in evidence. Cornish fish soup and freshly caught sea bass, turbot or lobster, along with wild boar, partridge and local English cheeses are all a feature of the daily changing menu at this internationally acclaimed restaurant.

The hotel is set in four acres of gardens, with an all-weather tennis court, swimming pool and croquet lawn – in a spectacular setting. Excellent fishing, riding and golf can be found nearby and the coastline offers matchless scenery and walking territory.

LOCATION

From Liskeard, take the B3254 to St Keyne, 3 miles south of Liskeard. Take the left fork by the church and the hotel is ½ mile from there.

St Keyne, Liskeard, Cornwall PL14 4RN

Telephone 01579 342001
Fax 01579 343891

E-mail: *wellhouse@bestloved.com*

OWNERS

Nick Wainford and Ione Nurdin

MANAGER

Denise Manning

ROOM RATES

Single occupancy £75 - £95
9 Doubles/Twins £100 - £175
Includes full breakfast and VAT

CHARGE/CREDIT CARDS

• *DC* • *JCB* • *MC* • *VI*

RATINGS & AWARDS

A.A. ★★ ❀❀❀

West Country Cooking 'Best Hotel in Cornwall'
WHICH? 'Secluded Charm Award 2000'
Courvoisier's Book of the Best

FACILITIES

On site: *Garden, croquet, tennis, outdoor pool*
1 meeting room/max 20 people
Nearby: *Golf, riding, fishing*

RESTRICTIONS

No children under 8 years at dinner
No facilities for disabled guests

ATTRACTIONS

The Eden Project, Heligan and 70 other gardens, Restormel and Cothele Castles, Land's End, St Michael's Mount, fishing villages of Looe, Polperro and Fowey

AFFILIATIONS

Independent

NEAREST

MAJOR CITY:
Plymouth - 16 miles/25 mins

MAJOR AIRPORT:
London Heathrow - 220 miles/3½ hrs
Plymouth - 16 miles/25 mins

RAILWAY STATION:
Liskeard - 3 miles/5 mins

RESERVATIONS

Direct with hotel
Quote ***Best Loved***

ACCESS CODES

Not applicable

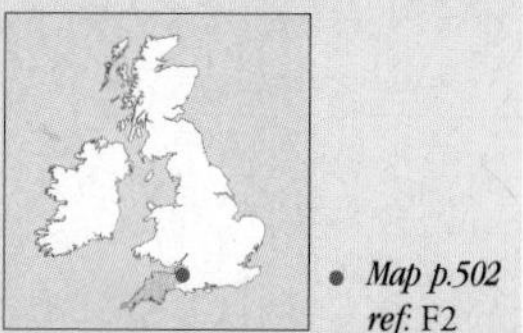

• Map p.502 ref: F2

" Top drawer, splendid stay, thanks very much "

Jerry & Conny Cuthbert, USA

THE WINDSOR

Town centre hotel

69 Great Pulteney Street, Bath, Somerset BA2 4DL

Telephone 01225 422100
Fax 01225 422550

E-mail: *windsor@bestloved.com*

OWNERS

Cary and Sachiko Bush

GENERAL MANAGER

Beverley Blunt

ROOM RATES

2 Executive singles	*£85 - £115*
7 Doubles/Twins	*£135 - £175*
2 Four-posters	*£195*
2 Junior suites	*£195*

Includes full breakfast, tea or coffee on arrival, newspaper, morning tea and VAT

CHARGE/CREDIT CARDS

• *DC* • *JCB* • *MC* • *VI*

RATINGS & AWARDS

Awards Pending

FACILITIES

On site: *Restaurant, Internet access*
Nearby: *Golf*

RESTRICTIONS

No children under 12 years
No facilities for disabled guests
No smoking

ATTRACTIONS

Roman Baths, American Museum, Museum of Costume, Wells, Wells Cathedral, Royal Crescent, Stonehenge

AFFILIATIONS

Independent

NEAREST

MAJOR CITY:
Bath

MAJOR AIRPORT:
Bristol - 15 miles/30 mins
London Heathrow - 90 miles/1½ hrs

RAILWAY STATION:
Bath Spa - ½ mile/10 mins

RESERVATIONS

Direct with hotel
Quote ***Best Loved***

ACCESS CODES

Not applicable

Gracious Georgian Bath infused with a delicate touch of the Orient

Bath's latest town house hotel offers a beguiling take on the traditional English hotel one generally expects to find in this world-famous spa town. Cary and Sachiko Bush have taken on a splendid Grade I listed terraced house in one of the town's most handsome Georgian carriageways and refurbished it to the highest standard whilst retaining many original period features. They have used finest quality English fabrics and antique furnishings throughout. The Georgian Drawing Room is the perfect setting for afternoon tea or after dinner drinks, and the luxurious and romantic bedrooms conceal essential modern comforts from Internet access to thoughtfully designed bathrooms. It is worth noting that the rooms at the back of the house have uninterrupted views over the playing fields of the Bath recreation ground to the hills beyond.

Now here is the surprise: Sachiko's Japanese background has inspired Bath's first Japanese restaurant, Sakura, in the hotel. Here the décor is traditionally Japanese with views out onto a small but perfectly formed Japanese garden decorated in bamboo and stone, and the menu features sukiyaki and shabu shabu. All this lies minutes away from Bath's main sightseeing attractions, tempting shopping and dining options.

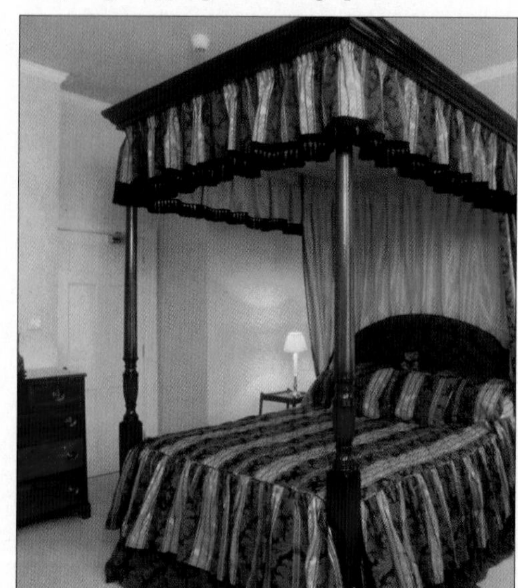

LOCATION

From the South and West approach the City on the A36 and follow signs for London and the M4. The hotel is just off Walcot Street on Great Pulteney Street..

Thinking of pampering yourself? See the 'Health & Beauty' index on page 472

"Nearest place to heaven (outside Scotland)"

Jim & Christine Riddle, Galashiels, Scotland

• Map p.502
ref: E3

Victorian country house WOODLANDS COUNTRY HOUSE HOTEL

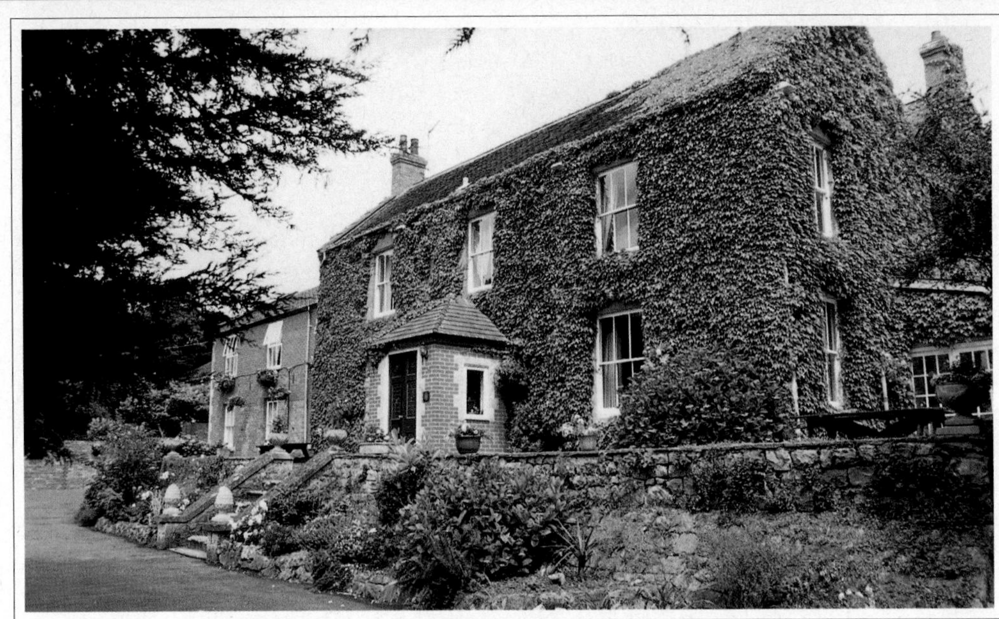

Relax and unwind in the shadow of history

This mellow country house hotel nestles at the foot of Brent Knoll, a strategic hillock once crowned by an Iron Age hill fort and later a Roman encampment, in an extraordinarily peaceful corner of West Somerset. The area is steeped in history and legend. Nearby is the small but lovely cathedral city of Wells, Cheddar Gorge, the wilds of Exmoor, the Quantock Hills, and Glastonbury with its heady mixture of religious and mystical connections ranging from the Holy Grail to Arthurian legend.

Woodlands is a rare escape set deep in the countryside yet only 5 minutes from the M5, and ideal for business travellers in search of the personal touch. Hosts Colin and Angie Lapage have undertaken an extensive refurbishment programme, which has already seen the majority of the comfy rooms redecorated with pretty fabrics, pine furniture and new bathrooms (some with double showers), and will continue to ensure guests' every comfort. Breakfast is taken in the Garden Room overlooking the patio and swimming pool, while a modern British menu is served in the Victorian-style dining room, with highly polished mahogany tables and lots of fresh flowers. Woodlands really is a great spot for a few days retreat.

LOCATION

Exit the M5 at Exit 22 and then take the A38 north for ½ mile. Turn left following the signs to Brent Knoll.

Hill Lane, Brent Knoll, Somerset TA9 4DF

Telephone 01278 760232
Fax 01278 769090

E-mail: *woodlands@bestloved.com*

OWNERS

Colin and Angie Lapage

ROOM RATES

6 Doubles/Twins	*£60 - £75*
1 Four-poster	*£80*
1 Deluxe Bridal Suite	*£115*

Includes full breakfast and VAT

CHARGE/CREDIT CARDS

• *MC* • *VI*

RATINGS & AWARDS

A.A. ★★ *68%*

FACILITIES

On site: *Garden, swimming pool*
2 meeting rooms/max 75 people
Nearby: *Golf, fishing, water skiing, tennis, shooting, yachting, fitness, riding, para-gliding*

RESTRICTIONS

No facilities for disabled guests

ATTRACTIONS

Cheddar Gorge, Wookey Hole, Wells, Glastonbury, Bath, Stonehenge

AFFILIATIONS

Independent

NEAREST

MAJOR CITY:
Bristol - 30 miles/45 mins

MAJOR AIRPORT:
Bristol - 15 miles/25 mins

RAILWAY STATION:
Highbridge - 3 miles/10 mins

RESERVATIONS

Direct with hotel
Quote ***Best Loved***

ACCESS CODES

Not applicable

the south

Mad hatters: Royal Ascot is the glossiest event in the British racing calendar and a fabulous excuse for English roses to sport extravagant headgear. Summer roses also flourish at Polesden Lacey (inset), where George VI and the Queen Mother honeymooned.

the south

The South encircles London and its the most populated and prosperous area of Britain - even as long ago as Roman times. And, just as the Thames divides the capital, so it severs the Chiltern Hills of Hertfordshire and the Bedfordshire Flats from the Surrey Hills and South Downs of Sussex. As it flows towards its estuary, it changes from the whimsy of Jerome K Jerome's Three Men in a Boat, the commercial imperatives of Docklands to the oyster beds of Colchester and Whitstable where it is lost to the salt of the North Sea.

Many of the major cities and attractions of the area are about an hour from Central London; you will find Nelson's flagship Victory at Portsmouth, a bizarre Pavilion in Brighton and Thomas a Becket's cathedral in Canterbury. Slightly further afield, but still within easy reach, is Stonehenge, the New Forest and the county of Dorset whose stunning landscape is strewn with many fascinating historical sites.

The Vale of Aylesbury
Whipsnade Zoo
Aylesbury
Four Weddings and a Funeral
Colchester
The Chiltern Hills
Henley-on-Thames
Newbury
Highclere Castle
London
Ascot
Pilgrim's Way
RHS Gardens Wisley
Canterbury
Alton (Jane Austen's House)
Epsom
Leeds Castle & Gardens
Winchester
Dover
Ferries to France
Ashdown Forest
Folkestone
Ferries to France
Leonardslee Gardens
Stonehenge
South Downs Way
The New Forest
Glyndebourne
Heritage Coast
The Giant of Cerne Abbas
Southampton
Hastings
Lyme Regis
Mrs Brown
Cowes
Chichester
Brighton
Corfe Castle
Isle Of Wight
The French Lieutenant's Woman
Abbotsbury Sub-tropical Gardens
The Channel Islands

Map Symbols

 Great Trails
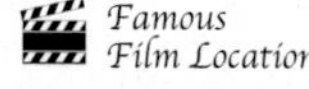 Famous Film Locations
 Scenic Views
 Historical Interest
 Cities & Major towns
 Gardens

Sport of kings...

...And queens. Elizabeth II and HRH Queen Elizabeth, the Queen Mother, are both avid horse-racing fans and expert judges of horseflesh adding an undoubted cachet to events such as Royal Ascot. Major South of England racecourses include Epsom (home of the Derby), Newbury, and summer season flat-racing favourite 'glorious' Goodwood, in the gentle shadow of the South Downs.

High drama

Jutting out to sea from the popular resort of Lyme Regis, the stone pier known as The Cobb marks the border between Dorset and Devon. It is also a literary landmark playing a vital role in The French Lieutenant's Woman, and also Jane Austen's Persuasion.

Revolutionary thinking

Shortly after his marriage, 19th-century naturalist Charles Darwin settled at Down House in Kent. Today visitors to Down can see the study where he penned On the Origin of Species, the revolutionary treatise which exploded the Biblical story of Creation and threw open the debate on evolution.

Fair stood the wind

Henry V, the Mayflower and Lord Nelson all set sail from the Solent. Today it is a haven for yachtsmen and setting for August's Cowes Week regattas and galas on the Isle of Wight.

Temples of delight

Celebrated British landscape specialists Capability Brown, William Kent and Charles Bridgeman worked on the Stowe Landscape Gardens, now in the grounds of a famous public school. An 18th-century owner, Sir Richard Temple, whose motto was Templa Quam Delecta (How Delightful Are Your Temples) commissioned the 32 temples adorning the gardens today.

Abbotsbury Sub-Tropical Gardens
Abbotsbury, Weymouth, Dorset DT3 4JT
Tel: 01305 871387
A coastal, tropical garden dating back to 1765 and situated on the edge of Lyme Bay

Leeds Castle
Maidstone, Kent ME17 1PL
Tel: 01622 765400
A fairytale setting with park and grounds extending to over 500 acres

Leonardslee Gardens
Lower Beeding, Horsham, West Sussex RH13 6PP
Tel: 01403 891212
An extensive garden with Alpine House, Rock Garden and Bonsai display

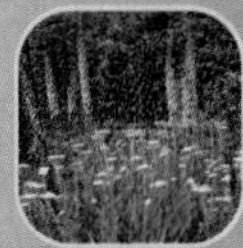

RHS Garden Wisley
Nr Woking, Surrey GU23 6QB
Tel: 01483 224234
A centre of great importance to the gardening world, loved by novices and enthusiasts alike

Historic den for a literary lion

Nobel Prize-winning author of The Jungle Book and The Just So Stories, Rudyard Kipling, lived at Bateman's in the Sussex village of Burwash from 1902-36. The lovely Jacobean house has been preserved much as it was in Kipling's day full of books and mementoes and the pretty garden borders a riverbank.

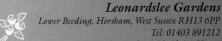

Find out more. There are many more attractions listed on the Best Loved Website: **www.bestlovedhotels.com**
Further information about the South can be found by contacting: **STB.** Tel: +44 (0)23 8062 0006. **SETB.** Tel: +44 (0)1892 540 766. **WTB.** Tel: +44 (0)1394 276 351.

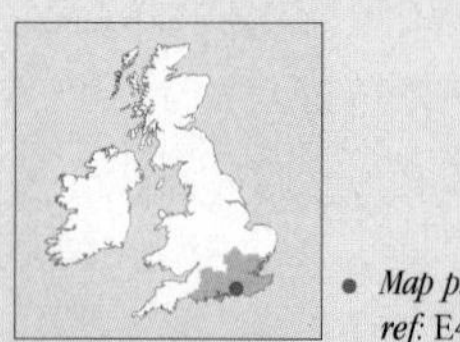

• Map p.504 ref: E4

"Our congratulations to you and your staff for being one of the best and most organised hotels we have had the pleasure to experience"

Geoff & Penny Sider, Guernsey

ALEXANDER HOUSE HOTEL

17th century country house

Turners Hill, West Sussex RH10 4QD

Telephone 01342 714914
Fax 01342 717328

E-mail: alexander@bestloved.com

GENERAL MANAGER

Mark Fagan

ROOM RATES

1 Single	£115 - £135
8 Doubles	£139 - £165
4 Twins/Suites	£189 - £235
2 Four-posters	£239 - £310

Includes full breakfast and VAT

CHARGE/CREDIT CARDS

 • DC • MC • VI

RATINGS & AWARDS

R.A.C. Blue Ribbon ★★★ Dining Award 3

A.A. ★★★ ❀❀❀

FACILITIES

On site: Garden, croquet, health & beauty, tennis, snooker, clay shooting, heli-pad

Licensed for weddings

6 meeting rooms/max 100 people

Nearby: Golf, fishing, rifle shooting, archery, team building activities, riding

RESTRICTIONS

No children under 7 years

No facilities for disabled guests

No pets

ATTRACTIONS

Hever Castle, Chartwell, Glyndebourne, Wakehurst Place, Brighton

AFFILIATIONS

Small Luxury Hotels

NEAREST

MAJOR CITY:

Brighton - 24 miles/35 mins

MAJOR AIRPORT:

London Gatwick - 9 miles/15 mins

RAILWAY STATION:

London Gatwick - 9 miles/15 mins

East Grinstead - 4 miles/10 mins

RESERVATIONS

Toll free in US: 800-525-4800

Quote **Best Loved**

ACCESS CODES

AMADEUS LX LGWALE

APOLLO/GALILEO LX 64741

SABRE/ABACUS LX 20136

WORLDSPAN LX ALEXT

Comfort and dedicated service in Shelley's historic home

The Alexander House estate has a recorded history dating back to 1332. Some of England's most important families have made it their home, including Percy Bysshe Shelley the famous romantic poet, and William Campbell, Governor of the Bank of England.

Today Alexander House is an exclusive country house hotel set in 135 acres of private parkland. With 15 bedrooms and a wealth of public rooms and meeting rooms, it successfully combines tradition with all the modern comforts and amenities. From the moment guests arrive, the dedicated staff attend to their every wish.

Superb Table d'Hôte and à la Carte meals are served in the dining room. The chef has established a fine reputation for particularly delicious classic English and French cuisine. Menus emphasise fresh natural foods carefully prepared and artistically presented.

The hotel has a range of amenities for those of an active disposition: croquet, tennis and a snooker room. Other activities on the estate include clay pigeon shooting and archery. The area is rich in places of interest, from the opera at Glyndebourne, racing at Lingfield to National Trust properties at Wakehurst Place, and Chartwell, the home of Sir Winston Churchill.

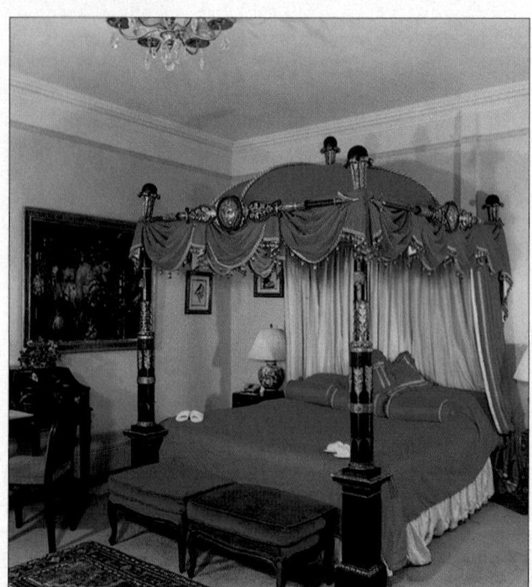

LOCATION

Exit 10 off M23 for East Grinstead. At 2nd roundabout follow signs for Turners Hill (B2028). At Turners Hill turn left (B2110) for East Grinstead. Hotel is 1½ miles along on left.

“ Amberley Castle – the friendliest castle in the world ”

Mrs R Simpson

12th century castle

AMBERLEY CASTLE

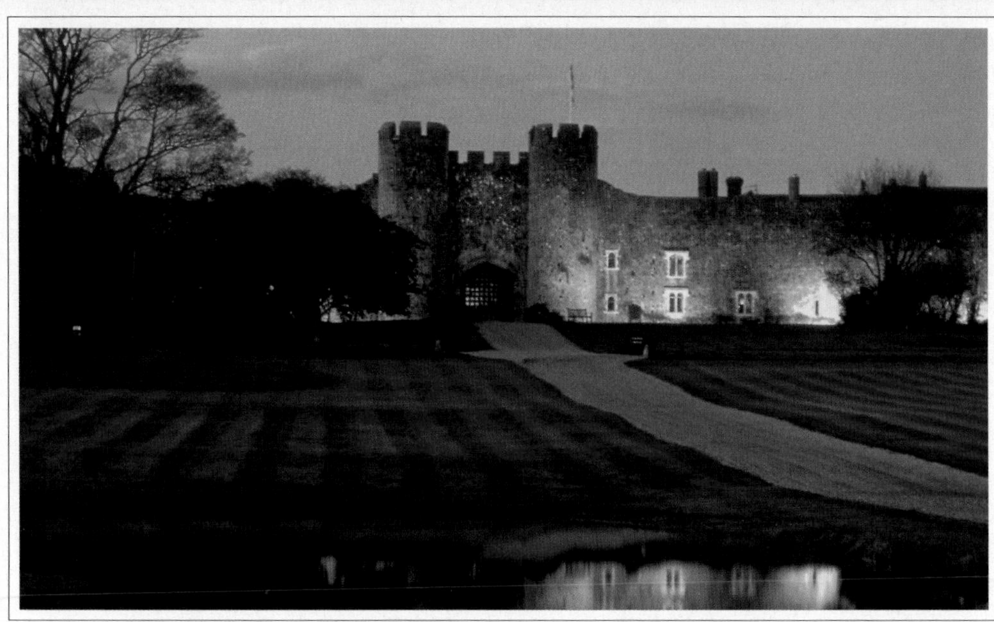

Peace and serenity within the 60 foot walls of a 900-year-old castle

For more than 900 years, Amberley Castle has stood in its serene landscape of undulating downland and hauntingly beautiful water meadows. Built originally by Bishop Luffa of Chichester as a country retreat, the magnificent building has extended hospitality to Henry VIII, Elizabeth I and Charles II.

Lovingly restored by its resident owners, Joy and Martin Cummings, Amberley Castle was transformed into England's only medieval castle hotel in 1988. With its 20 rooms, each with jacuzzi bath en suite, Amberley Castle offers superb luxury and every convenience, while retaining all its authentic grandeur.

The 12th century Queen's Room, with its barrel vaulted ceiling and 17th century mural, and the Great Room offer a splendid setting for award-winning castle cuisine based on English culinary heritage with a modern-day interpretation.

Just 60 miles from London and convenient for air and channel ferry ports, Amberley Castle lies beside one of the prettiest Sussex downland villages, amidst a host of historic landmarks such as Arundel Castle and Petworth House. There is shopping and theatre in Brighton and Chichester, Glorious Goodwood for horse racing, Cowdray Park for polo and much more besides.

LOCATION

Amberley Castle is on the B2139, off the A29 between Fontwell and Bury.

Amberley, Near Arundel, West Sussex BN18 9ND

Telephone 01798 831992
Fax 01798 831998

E-mail: *amberley@bestloved.com*

OWNERS
Joy and Martin Cummings

GENERAL MANAGER
Clive Cummings

ROOM RATES

6 Doubles/Twins	*£145 - £275*
7 Four-posters	*£195 - £300*
6 Suites	*£275 - £300*

Includes VAT

CHARGE/CREDIT CARDS

• DC • MC • VI

RATINGS & AWARDS
A.A. ★★★ ❀❀
Courvoisier's Book of the Best

FACILITIES
On site: *Garden, croquet, tennis, en suite jacuzzis, heli-pad, Licensed for weddings*
2 meeting rooms/max 50 people
Nearby: *Golf, riding, shooting, fishing*

RESTRICTIONS
No facilities for disabled guests
No children under 13 years
No smoking in bedrooms
No pets

ATTRACTIONS
Arundel Castle, Petworth, Brighton Royal Pavillion, Amberley Chalk Pits, Goodwood House, Chichester, Parham House

AFFILIATIONS
The Celebrated Hotels Collection
Small Luxury Hotels
Pride of Britain

NEAREST
MAJOR CITY:
London - 55 miles/1¼ hrs
MAJOR AIRPORT:
London Gatwick - 30 miles/45 mins
RAILWAY STATION:
Amberley - 1 mile/5 mins

RESERVATIONS
Toll free in US: 800-322-2403
or 800-98-PRIDE
Quote ***Best Loved***

ACCESS CODES
AMADEUS LX LONAMB
WORLDSPAN LX ESHAC
SABRE/ABACUS LX 26404
APOLLO/GALILEO LX 4517

• Map p.504 ref: E4

"Again, thank you all for making our weekend so specially wonderful. We felt to be part of the family ..."

Dr Loveday

ASHDOWN PARK HOTEL

Victorian mansion

Wych Cross, Forest Row, East Sussex RH18 5JR

Telephone 01342 824988
Fax 01342 826206

E-mail: ashdown@bestloved.com

MANAGING DIRECTOR
Graeme Bateman

GENERAL MANAGER
Michael Purtill

ROOM RATES

6 Singles	£125 - £189
65 Doubles/Twins	£159 - £219
30 Suites	£270 - £355
6 Four-posters	£340 - £355

Includes full breakfast and VAT

CHARGE/CREDIT CARDS

• DC • MC • VI

RATINGS & AWARDS
E.T.C. ★★★★ Gold Award
R.A.C. Blue Ribbon ★★★★
Dining Award 3
A.A. ★★★★ ❀❀
Investors in People

FACILITIES
On site: *Garden, croquet, snooker, indoor pool, sauna, jacuzzi, gym, health & beauty, hair salon, tennis, 18-hole golf course, heli-pad*
Licensed for weddings
16 meeting rooms/max 200 people
Nearby: *Golf, riding*

RESTRICTIONS
No pets

ATTRACTIONS
Hever Castle, Sheffield Park, Wakehurst Place, Tunbridge Wells, Glyndebourne Opera, Pooh Corner

AFFILIATIONS
Small Luxury Hotels

NEAREST
MAJOR CITY:
Tunbridge Wells - 12 miles/20 mins
MAJOR AIRPORT:
London Gatwick - 15 miles/20 mins
RAILWAY STATION:
East Grinstead - 5 miles/10 mins

RESERVATIONS
Toll free in US/Canada: 800-525-4800
*Quote **Best Loved***

ACCESS CODES
AMADEUS LX LGWAPH
APOLLO/GALILEO LX 44666
SABRE/ABACUS LX 38628
WORLDSPAN LX LGWAD

Much to see and do from this Victorian showpiece

Built in 1867 and restored in the 1990s, this impressive mansion is set in 186 acres of beautiful countryside in the heart of Ashdown Forest. The gilt and embossed ceilings of the lounges, the tranquil view from the leaded windows and open fires complete the friendly and welcoming atmosphere. In these beautiful surroundings you can relax and enjoy a drink before or after a delectable meal in the award-winning Anderida Restaurant.

Great thought has gone into the design of the 107 bedrooms and every room is beautifully decorated. From the elegance of the four-poster bedrooms the views of Ashdown Park stretch out, providing the perfect setting for honeymooners and romantics.

Relaxation is assured; the swimming pool, sauna, snooker and gentle walks are invitingly at hand. The beauty salon offers a good range of up-to-the-minute treatments for which it has recently won 'Matis Salon of the Year 1999/2000'. For the more energetic there is a gym, tennis courts and a 18-hole, par 3, golf course. Ashdown Park is ideally situated for a wide variety of interests and activities. Historic Hever Castle, Penshurst Place and Tunbridge Wells are within easy reach, as are the Bluebell Railway, Brighton with its exotic Pavilion, Pooh Corner, Glyndebourne Opera House and Lingfield and Brighton Racecourses.

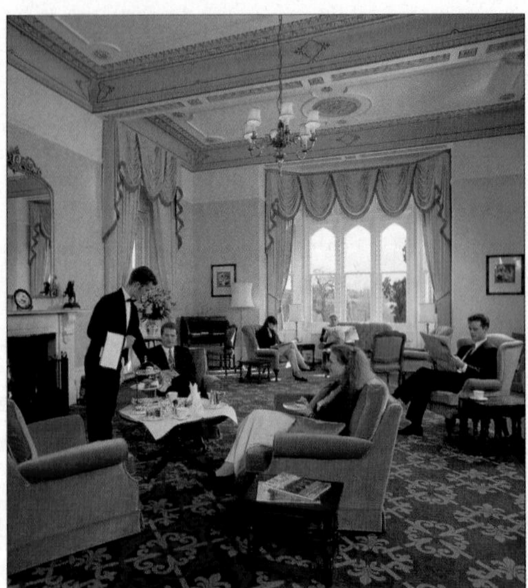

LOCATION

Exit 10 off M23, A264 to East Grinstead then the A22 to Eastbourne. 2 miles south of Forest Row, turn left at the traffic lights at Wych Cross to Hartfield. Ashdown Park is on the right after half a mile.

"Hard to believe it's 1998 when here! Absolutely charming!"

Alan & Sandy Werft, Sarasota, Florida

• Map p.504
ref: C3

15th century inn — AT THE SIGN OF THE ANGEL

The quintessential English inn in a National Trust village

In the 15th century, a wool merchant built a house for his family in the Wiltshire village of Lacock. The oak panelled lounge reflects the warmth of his family home. The beautiful old staircase looks down on courtyard and gardens. Crackling, log fires, squeaky floor boards, oak panels and beams add up to the quintessential English inn. Since 1953 the Levis family has run it with enthusiasm and friendship.

The restaurant is renowned for traditional English cooking. Breakfasts feature the inn's own eggs, locally cured bacon, home-made bread and Mrs Levis's marmalade. Lunch and dinner concentrate on traditional roasts, fish fresh from Cornwall and herbs, vegetables and asparagus from the kitchen garden. All the puddings are made on the premises.

Lacock is the archetypal English village, with winding streets, Gothic-arched grey-stone houses and half-timbered cottages. William Fox-Talbot, maker of the world's first photographic prints in 1833, lived here and his house is now a world-famous Museum of Photography. The Roman city of Bath, Stonehenge and Avebury are within 40 minutes' drive, as are historic houses in Wiltshire, Somerset and Gloucestershire and the cathedral cities of Salisbury and Wells.

LOCATION

From M4 Exit 17 take A350 towards Chippenham. Then follow signs into Lacock. The hotel is in Church Street.

6 Church Street, Lacock, Chippenham, Wiltshire SN15 2LB

Telephone 01249 730230
Fax 01249 730527

E-mail: *atthesign@bestloved.com*

OWNERS

George Hardy and Lorna Levis

ROOM RATES

Single occupancy	*£68 - £85*
8 Doubles/Twins	*£99 - £125*
2 Four-posters	*£116 - £138*

Includes full breakfast and VAT

CHARGE/CREDIT CARDS

• *DC* • *JCB* • *MC* • *VI*

RATINGS & AWARDS

A.A. ◆◆◆◆◆

WHICH? Hotel of the Year 2000

FACILITIES

On site: *Garden*

3 meeting rooms/max 18 people

Nearby: *Golf, riding*

RESTRICTIONS

Limited facilities for disabled guests

No pets in public rooms

Closed Christmas week

ATTRACTIONS

Lacock Abbey and village, Bath, Stonehenge, Avebury, Corsham Hall, Fox-Talbot Museum of Photography

AFFILIATIONS

Independent

NEAREST

MAJOR CITY:
Bath - 15 miles/30 mins

MAJOR AIRPORT:
London Heathrow - 90 miles/2 hrs

RAILWAY STATION:
Chippenham - 4 miles/15 mins

RESERVATIONS

Direct with hotel

Quote ***Best Loved***

ACCESS CODES

Not applicable

Planning a wedding reception? Turn to 'Meeting Facilities' on page 476

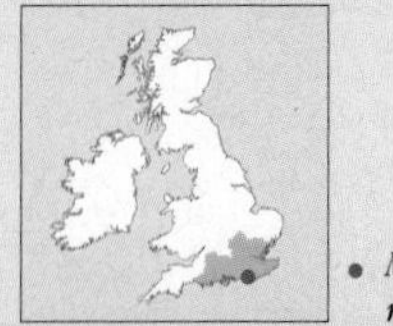

• Map p.504 ref: E4

"This is our favourite place on earth"

Mark Elliott, London

BAILIFFSCOURT HOTEL

Medieval manor house

Climping, Near Arundel, West Sussex BN17 5RW

Telephone 01903 723511
Fax 01903 723107

E-mail: *bailiffscourt@bestloved.com*

DIRECTORS
Sandy and Anne Goodman

GENERAL MANAGER
Martin Harris

ROOM RATES

1 Single	£125
26 Doubles/Twins	£140 - £310
4 Suites	£285 - £335

Includes full breakfast and VAT

CHARGE/CREDIT CARDS

• DC • MC • VI

RATINGS & AWARDS
A.A. ★★★ ❀❀ 76%

FACILITIES
On site: *Garden, outdoor heated pool, croquet, tennis, heli-pad*
Licensed for weddings
2 meeting rooms/max 70 people
Nearby: *Golf, riding, fishing*

RESTRICTIONS
No facilities for disabled guests
No children under 8 years in restaurant for dinner

ATTRACTIONS
Arundel Castle, Petworth, Chichester, Brighton, Goodwood House

AFFILIATIONS
Selected British Hotels
Grand Heritage Hotels

NEAREST
MAJOR CITY:
Chichester - 8 miles/15 mins
MAJOR AIRPORT:
London Gatwick - 35 miles/45 mins
RAILWAY STATION:
Littlehampton - 3 miles/5 mins

RESERVATIONS
Toll free in USA: 800-323-5463 or 888-93-GRAND
Quote ***Best Loved***

ACCESS CODES
AMADEUS UI BSHBHH
APOLLO/GALILEO UI 48856
SABRE/ABACUS UI 5271
WORLDSPAN UI 40640

A luxurious and magnificent caprice with the pleasures of the seaside nearby

Gothic mullioned windows wink through the trees along the approach to Bailiffscourt. As you walk under the gnarled 15th century beams you can sense the dignity of the Middle Ages. Yet Bailiffscourt is an extraordinary architectural fantasy – a medieval manor built in the 1930s at immense cost to satisfy a caprice of the late Lord Moyne, from materials dating as far back as the 13th century.

Bailiffscourt has a unique atmosphere and specially captivating charm. The 31 bedrooms are luxuriously furnished, many with four-poster beds, oak beams and log fires for winter nights. There is a truly magnificent master suite with cathedral ceiling, four-poster bed, open log fire and two baths side-by-side.

A special feature is the walled-courtyard filled with climbing roses, occasionally visited by the peacocks who have made Bailiffscourt their home for many years. Thatched cottages and mellow stone buildings are grouped around the courtyard and surrounded by 32 acres of idyllic parkland bordering the beach.

The innovative young head chef is receiving the highest accolades for his imaginative cuisine and the restaurant is renowned for its superb food accompanied by the finest wines.

LOCATION

Off the A259 at Climping, near Arundel, 'next to the sea'.

"...superb comfort and decor accompanied by the excellent food served in your delightful conservatory more than justify the awards and acclaim of your hotel"

Mr & Mrs G Jay, Isle of Wight

317

• Map p.504 ref: C4

Georgian town house

BEECHLEAS HOTEL & RESTAURANT

Georgian elegance with Anglo-French cuisine in Thomas Hardy country

Beechleas is a delightful Georgian Grade II listed town house hotel, five minutes' walk from the centre of Wimborne Minster. It offers the traditional welcome of a good family hotel. The Lodge and Coach House feature cosy beamed rooms with the atmosphere of yesteryear and the comforts of today while the Georgian rooms offer a spacious and elegant ambience.

The charming restaurant, overlooking a pretty walled garden, features genuine English cooking, with some French influence. It has a prestigious Red Rosette from the A.A. Welcoming log fires during the chillier months enhance a warm, friendly atmosphere as does the conservatory in spring and summer.

Beechleas is perfectly situated for visiting the beautiful Thomas Hardy countryside. National Trust properties within easy reach include Kingston Lacy House, Corfe Castle and the Iron Age defensive earthworks of Badbury Rings. Walking, riding, fishing and golf are close by. Sailing can be arranged from Poole Harbour on the hotel's own yacht to coves such as Lulworth, Old Harry Rocks or The Needles. Sandy beaches, shopping at Poole and Bournemouth, the New Forest and Purbeck Hills are all within 20 minutes' drive.

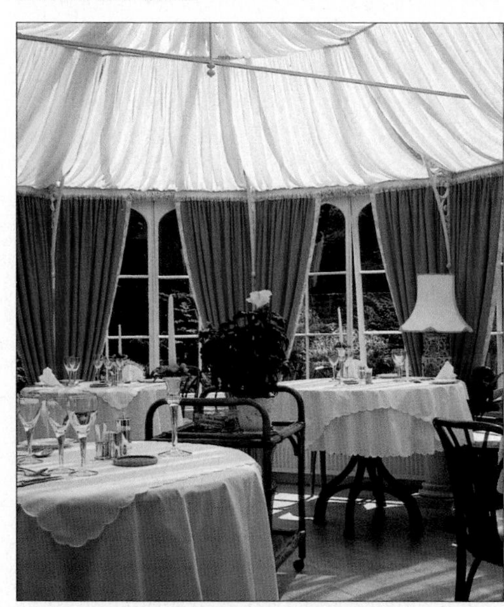

LOCATION

From London: A31 to Wimborne. From large roundabout take B3073 which becomes Leigh Road after 2 miles. At next roundabout turn left (A349). Beechleas is on right hand side.

17 Poole Road, Wimborne Minster, Dorset BH21 1QA

Telephone 01202 841684
Fax 01202 849344

E-mail: beechleas@bestloved.com

OWNER

Josephine McQuillan

ROOM RATES

Single occupancy	£69 - £89
9 Doubles/Twins	£79 - £109

Includes newspaper, early morning tea, breakfast and VAT

CHARGE/CREDIT CARDS

RATINGS & AWARDS

E.T.C. ★★ Silver Award
R.A.C. Blue Ribbon ★★ Dining Award 1
A.A. ★★ ❀ 75%

FACILITIES

On site: *Garden, parking*
1 meeting room/max 40 people
Nearby: *Fishing, golf, sailing, riding, tennis, swimming*

RESTRICTIONS

Limited facilities for disabled guests
Pets by arrangement

ATTRACTIONS

Kingston Lacy House, Purbecks, New Forest, Poole Harbour, Brownsea Island, Wimborne Minster

AFFILIATIONS

Independent

NEAREST

MAJOR CITY:
Bournemouth/Poole - 6 miles/15 mins

MAJOR AIRPORT:
London Heathrow - 85 miles/1½ hrs

RAILWAY STATION:
Poole - 6 miles/15 mins
Bournemouth - 6 miles/15 mins

RESERVATIONS

Direct with hotel
*Quote **Best Loved***

ACCESS CODES

Not applicable

• Map p.504 ref: E4

"My home . . . away from home"

F A Barber, Gloucestershire

CHEQUERS HOTEL

16th century historic house

Old Rectory Lane, Pulborough, West Sussex RH20 1AD

Telephone 01798 872486
Fax 01798 872715

E-mail: *chequers@bestloved.com*

OWNERS
Pandora and Martin Pellett

ROOM RATES

6 Doubles/Twins	£85 - £95
1 Four-poster	£99
2 Family rooms	£95

Includes full breakfast and VAT

CHARGE/CREDIT CARDS

• MC • VI

RATINGS & AWARDS
E.T.C. ★★ Silver Award
A.A. ★★ ❀❀ 73%

FACILITIES
On site: *Garden, conservatory*
1 meeting room/max 20 people
Nearby: *Golf, shooting, fishing, riding*

RESTRICTIONS
No facilities for disabled guests

ATTRACTIONS
Brighton Pavillion, Arundel Castle, Goodwood House, Petworth House, Glyndebourne, Chichester, bird watching, horse racing, wine tasting at local vineyards

AFFILIATIONS
Independent

NEAREST
MAJOR CITY:
Brighton - 20 miles/35 mins

MAJOR AIRPORT:
London Gatwick - 23 miles/30 mins

RAILWAY STATION:
Pulborough - ½ mile/2 mins

RESERVATIONS
Direct with hotel
Quote ***Best Loved***

ACCESS CODES
Not applicable

SOUTH

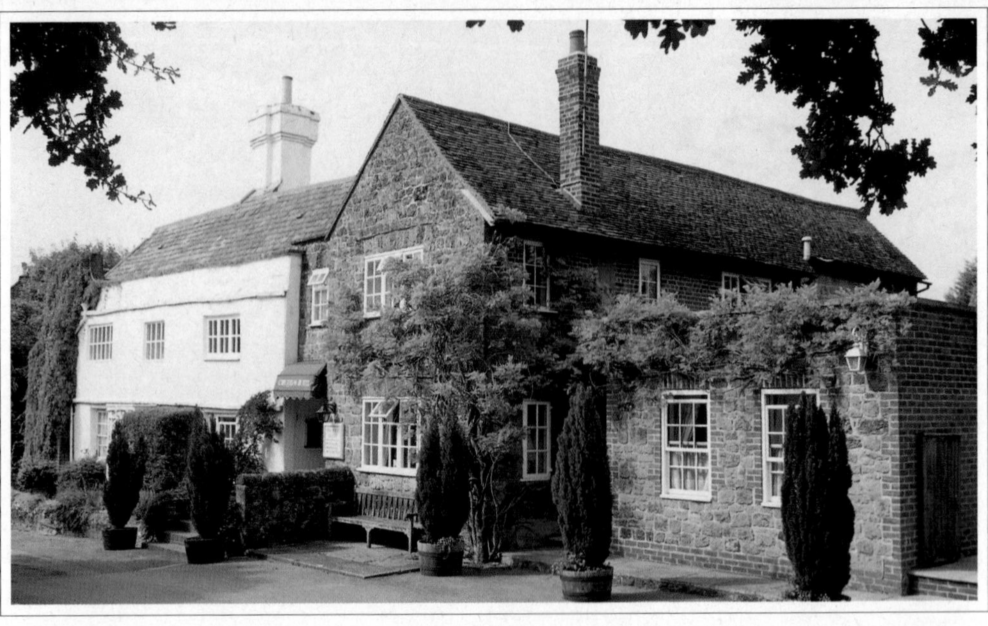

The quintessential small English hotel in the heart of rural West Sussex

The Chequers is first recorded as changing hands in 1548, and its most recent change of ownership occurred just three years ago when Pandora and Martin Pellett took up the reins. In a short time, they have worked wonders with this lovely old Sussex home. Great hosts of real character, they have created a cosy and charming hotel with an intimate atmosphere that offers exceptional value for money. Guests are cosseted in comfortable and attractively decorated bedrooms furnished with thoughtful little extras, and good food is an essential ingredient in the hotels' success. Both the well-regarded Chequers Restaurant and less formal conservatory dining area are the domain of master chef Geoffrey Welch.

Only an hour from London, Pulborough is surrounded by glorious countryside and the hotel stands within a conservation area with views over the water meadows and meandering River Arun to the South Downs. Entertaining side trips range from walking on the Downs and birdwatching by the river to strolling along the Brighton seafront. Nearby, 17th-century Petworth House is set in glorious grounds designed by Capability Brown and displays the National Trust's finest picture collection, featuring the works of Turner, while the town itself is a renowned antiques centre.

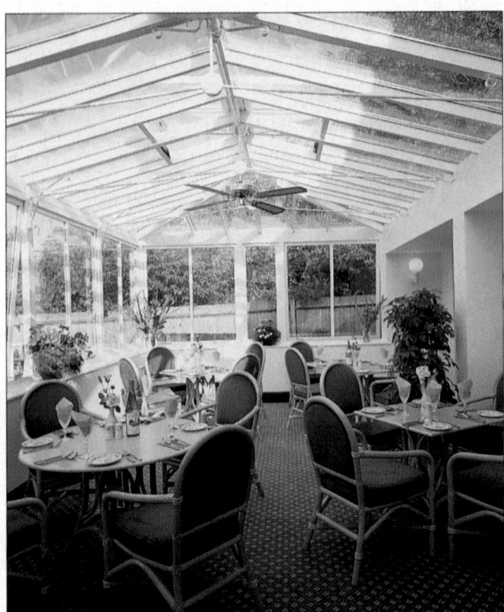

LOCATION

The hotel is just north of the village centre at the top of the hill, opposite the church.

Looking for an hotel with a golf course on site? See our 'Golf Guide' on page 478

"It was our wedding day. The service and friendliness made our stay a complete success"

John & Rosemary Rodd

• Map p.504 ref: E3

16th century coaching inn — THE CHRISTOPHER HOTEL

Irresistible to future prime ministers and their parents!

Since 1511, there has been a Christopher Hotel situated in the heart of Eton's High Street. This old coaching inn for many years had a rather racy reputation. Eton College, nearby on the High Street, declared The Christopher strictly out of bounds. This was an irresistible recommendation for the pupils, many of whom went on to reach the very highest levels on the ladder of success in Britain. Their parents came too.

It has 31 comfortably furnished and fully equipped bedrooms. The hotel's atmospheric Lilly Langtry Restaurant is an excellent place to meet friends either for lunch or dinner. The à la carte menu changes regularly to take advantage of the very best organic produce the market has to offer. Alternatively, the Victoria Bar serves lighter food and snacks and offers a fine selection of drinks.

Eton is a paradise for shoppers and visitors. Famous shops sell antique furniture, rare books, toys, clothing and items of special interest. 200 yards away across the river is Royal Windsor where William the Conqueror built his fortified castle. A royal residence for over 900 years, it houses the sumptuous State Apartments, St George's Chapel and The Queen's Collection of Master Drawings. Local attractions include the Windsor Royal Horse Show, Henley Regatta, Royal Ascot and Legoland. London, Oxford and the Cotswolds are all within reach.

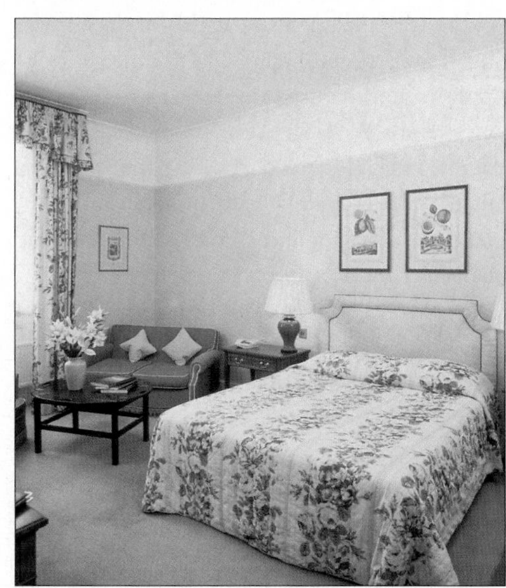

LOCATION

5 minutes from Windsor's two railway stations. 5 minutes from M4, 10 minutes from M25.

110 High Street, Eton, Windsor, Berkshire SL4 6AN

Telephone 01753 852359/811677
Fax 01753 830914

E-mail: *christopher@bestloved.com*

OWNER

Carol Martin

ROOM RATES

7 Singles	£100 - £120
10 Doubles/Twins	£115 - £125
11 Executive rooms	£120 - £140
3 Family rooms	£120

Includes service and VAT

CHARGE/CREDIT CARDS

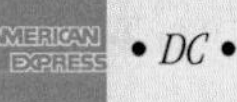

• *DC* • *MC* • *VI*

RATINGS & AWARDS

E.T.C. ★★★
A.A. ★★★ *69%*

FACILITIES

On site: *Patio*
1 meeting room/max 50 people
Nearby: *Golf, riding, tennis, fitness*

RESTRICTIONS

No facilities for disabled guests
Pets by arrangement

ATTRACTIONS

Eton College, Legoland, Windsor Castle, Royal Windsor Theatre, Hampton Court, Henley-on-Thames, Savill Gardens, Windsor and Ascot Racecourses

AFFILIATIONS

Best Western

NEAREST

MAJOR CITY:
London - 15 miles/35 mins

MAJOR AIRPORT:
London Heathrow - 10 miles/15 mins

RAILWAY STATION:
Windsor/Eton Riverside - ¼ mile/5 mins
Hatton Cross Underground - 8 miles/20 mins

RESERVATIONS

Direct with hotel
*Quote **Best Loved***

ACCESS CODES

SABRE/ABACUS BW 47102
AMADEUS BW LHR675
APOLLO/GALILEO BW 1580
WORLDSPAN BW 83675

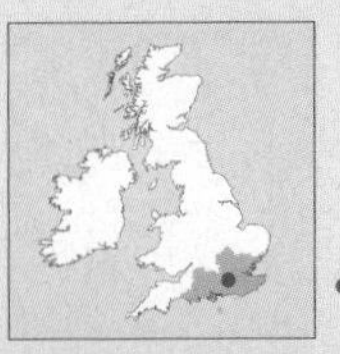

• Map p.504 ref: E3

"Having stayed in many fine hotels, this one in my opinion excels. It is perhaps of note that this is the first occasion I have felt strongly enough to write"

Giles Harvey, Metheringham

Coppid Beech Hotel

Unique alpine design

John Nike Way, Bracknell, Berkshire RG12 8TF

Telephone 01344 303333
Fax 01344 301200

***E-mail:** coppidbeech@bestloved.com*

MANAGING DIRECTOR
Alan Blenkinsopp

ROOM RATES

44 Executive singles	£80 - £155
117 Doubles/Twins	£95 - £165
25 Superior doubles	£115 - £175
19 Suites	£165 - £295

Includes full breakfast and VAT

CHARGE/CREDIT CARDS

• DC • JCB • MC • VI

RATINGS & AWARDS
E.T.C. ★★★★ Silver Award
R.A.C. ★★★★ Dining Award 1
A.A. ★★★★ ❀❀ 76%
Best Restaurant Wine Menu of the Year - Hotel & Restaurant Show

FACILITIES
***On site:** Health & beauty, gym, indoor pool, jacuzzi, sauna, heli-pad, ice skating rink, dry ski slope, Licenced for weddings*
11 meeting rooms/max 350 people
***Nearby:** Golf, fishing, riding*

RESTRICTIONS
No pets in public rooms

ATTRACTIONS
Windsor Castle, Legoland, Ascot Racecourse, Wisley Gardens, Hampton Court Palace

AFFILIATIONS
Thames Valley Hotels

NEAREST
MAJOR CITY:
London - 34 miles/45 mins
MAJOR AIRPORT:
London Heathrow - 26 miles/35 mins
RAILWAY STATION:
Bracknell - 2 miles/5 mins

RESERVATIONS
Direct with hotel
*Quote **Best Loved***

ACCESS CODES
APOLLO/GALILEO HT 83777
SABRE/ABACUS HK 34706
WORLDSPAN HK LHRCOB
AMADEUS HK COPPI

An hotel? Or a resort? It's worth finding out!

The Coppid Beech likes to present itself as something completely different - and it is! Even at first glance, the Alpine architecture set in a 48-acre estate that includes an Olympic-size ice rink and a dry ski slope is a surprising find in the middle of Berkshire. Another is the huge range of facilities and the expansive way they are all set out; the space and its use are impressive. Waves Health and Fitness Club includes a large pool (see picture) and gym along with sauna, steam room, spa bath, solarium and a beauty room offering manicures and all sorts of relaxing treatments.

For these reasons and many more, the Coppid Beech is a natural venue for conferences and corporate events. But not exclusively: it is also a popular rendezvous for families and friends.

Besides being a resort in the fullest sense, The Coppid Beech is also a very good hotel. There are 205 well-appointed bedrooms (including mini bar and TV etc) and excellent round-the-clock room service. For entertainment (and the food certainly qualifies for this category), there are two restaurants, Rowans (two AA rosettes and on the formal side) and Brasserie at the Keller (casual with live music on Fridays and Saturdays); and Apres Nightclub appealing to the hyperactive set.

The resort's other great asset is its location: just off the M4 close to London and a short distance from Windsor Castle, Legoland and the racecourses at Windsor and Ascot.

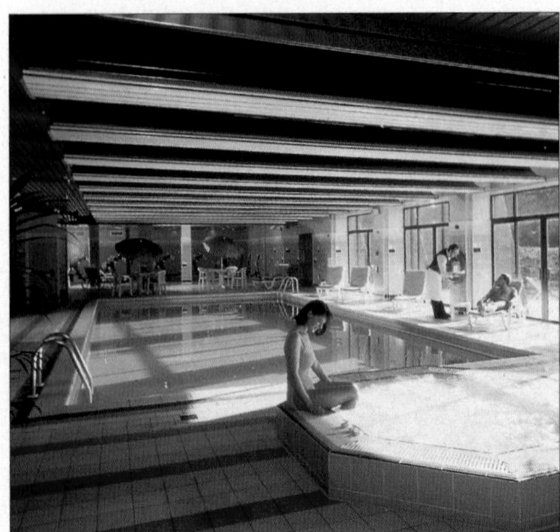

LOCATION

Exit 10 off M4 take Wokingham/Binfield exit on to the A329. At Coppid Beech roundabout take first exit left for Binfield and right at mini-roundabout. The hotel is on right.

"Danesfield was the highlight of our trip to Europe"

Mrs S Ralston, New York

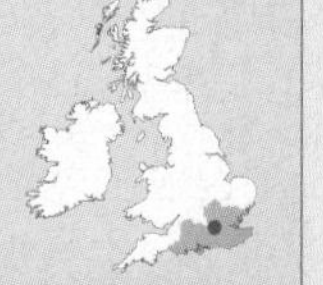

• Map p.504
ref: E3

Stately country house

DANESFIELD HOUSE

65 acres of magnificent gardens looking down on the River Thames

Danesfield House is set within 65 acres of gardens and parkland overlooking the River Thames and offering panoramic views across the Chiltern Hills. It is the third house since 1664 to occupy this lovely setting and was designed and built in the sumptuous style of the late 19th century. After years of neglect, the house is now fully restored, combining its Victorian splendour with the very best in modern hotel facilities.The 87 luxury bedrooms are all beautifully decorated and furnished and offer extensive facilities. These include two telephone lines (one of which may be used for personal fax), satellite TV, mini bar, trouser press, hair dryer, bath robes and toiletries.

Guests may relax in the magnificent drawing room with its galleried library, or in the sunlit atrium. There is a choice of two restaurants: the acclaimed Oak Room and The Orangery brasserie, both offering a choice of international cuisine with a distinguished wine list.

Leisure facilities include an outdoor pool, croquet, tennis court and jogging and walking trails. Guests will be able to pamper themselves further when the much awaited Danesfield Spa opens in 2001. Fishing, golf, horseriding, gliding, sailing and shooting are available, as are activities on the River Thames with a picnic hamper from the hotel's kitchens. Within easy reach are Windsor Castle, Henley-on- Thames, the dreaming spires of Oxford and Blenheim Palace.

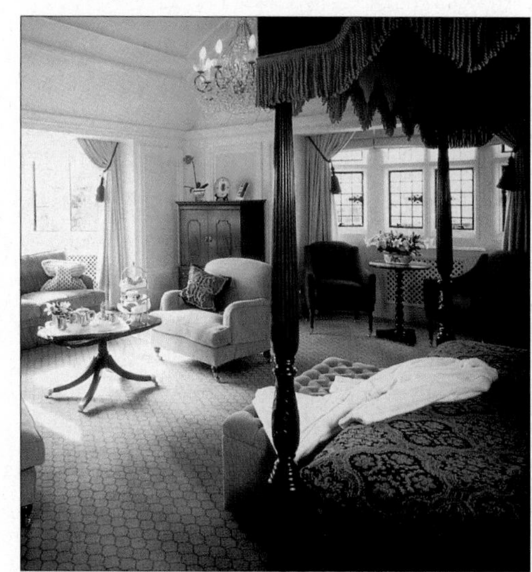

LOCATION

M4 Exit 8/9. 3 miles from Marlow on the A4155 travelling towards Henley.

Marlow,
Near Henley-on-Thames,
Buckinghamshire SL7 2EY

Telephone 01628 891010
Fax 01628 890408

E-mail: *danesfield@bestloved.com*

GENERAL MANAGER

Brian Miller

ROOM RATES

9 Singles	£155 - £165
53 Doubles/Twins	£165 - £205
14 Executive doubles	£205 - £225
11 Suites	£245 - £300

Includes VAT

CHARGE/CREDIT CARDS

• DC • JCB • MC • VI

RATINGS & AWARDS

E.T.C. ★★★★ Silver Award
R.A.C. ★★★★
A.A. ★★★★ ❀❀ 74%

FACILITIES

On site: *Garden, croquet, tennis, outdoor pool, snooker, heli-pad*
5 meeting rooms/max 150 people
Nearby: *Golf, fishing, riding*

RESTRICTIONS

Limited facilities for disabled guests
No pets

ATTRACTIONS

Windsor Castle, Henley-on-Thames, Blenheim Palace, Oxford

AFFILIATIONS

Small Luxury Hotels

NEAREST

MAJOR CITY:
London - 29 miles/45 mins

MAJOR AIRPORT:
London Heathrow - 25 miles/35 mins
London Gatwick - 60 miles/1¼ hrs

RAILWAY STATION:
Maidenhead - 8 miles/12 mins

RESERVATIONS

Toll free in US: 800-525-4800
Quote ***Best Loved***

ACCESS CODES

SABRE/ABACUS LX 18631
APOLLO/GALILEO LX 72012
WORLDSPAN LX LHRDH
AMADEUS LX LHRDFH

• Map p.504
Inset map

“A quiet state of grace”

Marianne Curphey, The Times

DIXCART HOTEL

16th century farmhouse

Isle of Sark GY9 0SD, Channel Islands

Telephone 01481 832015
Fax 01481 832164

***E-mail:** dixcart@bestloved.com*

OWNERS
Mr and Mrs J Brannam

ROOM RATES
3 Singles £30 - £50
12 Doubles/Twins £60 - £100
Includes full breakfast

CHARGE/CREDIT CARDS

• DC • MC • VI

RATINGS & AWARDS
A.A. ★★ 69%
Les Routiers Gold Key Award 1999/2000

FACILITIES
***On site:** Garden*
1 meeting room/max 150 people
***Nearby:** Snooker, fishing, caving, cycling, walking, swimming*

RESTRICTIONS
No facilities for disabled guests
Pets by arrangement
No cars or motorbikes

ATTRACTIONS
La Seigneurie Gardens, Woodturner, glassblower, potters, silversmith, Venus pool, La Coupée Isthmus, Horse and cart travel, VAT exempt

AFFILIATIONS
Independent

NEAREST
MAJOR CITY:
St Peter Port - 9 miles by boat

MAJOR AIRPORT:
Guernsey - 15 miles by boat and taxi

FERRY PORT:
Guernsey - 9 miles by boat

RESERVATIONS
Direct with hotel
*Quote **Best Loved***

ACCESS CODES
Not applicable

An old fashioned welcome to peaceful life on the feudal island of Sark

Family owned and managed, Dixcart is the oldest hotel on the Isle of Sark and has played an important part in the island's history. The hotel occupies the original 16th century farm 'longhouse' of La Jaspellerie Ténément which still holds a seat in the Sark Parliament. It has 40 acres of land including gardens, medieval hand-dug terraces, woodlands, fields and Dixcart Bay - a sheltered beach used as a landing place since Roman Times. Over the years, visitors to Dixcart have included Prince Henry and Edward VII as well as writers Victor Hugo, AC Swinburne and Mervyn Peake.

All the single, double and family bedrooms are en suite, centrally heated with coffee making facilities, televisions and direct dial telephones. There are three comfortable lounges and a residents' diners' bar with log fires. The candlelit restaurant offers beautifully presented 'value for money' food and wines. The Public Bar serves a wide range of snacks and seafood dishes.

Sark is the smallest independent state in the British Commonwealth. Cars are banned. This magical, feudal island is almost untouched by the 20th century. Your luggage arrives by tractor, you on foot, bike or horse and cart. You experience peace and quiet as nowhere else in the world and you receive the warmest of welcomes from the people at Dixcart and Sark's 600 other residents.

LOCATION

Left at end of main avenue, past old prison on outskirts of the village.

For information about hotel affiliations see page 14

" Having had tea at the Mandarin in Hong Kong, Singapore Slings at Raffles in Singapore and tea at the Ritz, none of them come close to Donnington Valley Hotel "

H S, Newbury

• Map p.504 ref: D3

Hotel and golf course

DONNINGTON VALLEY HOTEL

Old Oxford Road, Donnington, Newbury, Berkshire RG14 3AG

Telephone 01635 551199
Fax 01635 551123

E-mail: donnington@bestloved.com

MANAGING DIRECTOR
Andrew McKenzie

GENERAL MANAGER
Frank Adams

ROOM RATES

Single occupancy	£139 - £169
53 Doubles/Twins	£139 - £169
5 Suites	from £199

Includes VAT

CHARGE/CREDIT CARDS

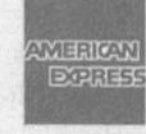

• DC • MC • VI

RATINGS & AWARDS
E.T.C. ★★★★ Gold Award
R.A.C. Blue Ribbon ★★★★ Dining Award 2
A.A. ★★★★ ❀❀ 80%

FACILITIES
On site: Garden, 18-hole golf, heli-pad
Licensed for weddings
9 meeting rooms/max 140 people
Nearby: Fishing, tennis, hunting/shooting, riding

RESTRICTIONS
No pets

ATTRACTIONS
Oxford, Bath, London, Highclere Castle, Newbury Racecourse

AFFILIATIONS
Independent

NEAREST
MAJOR CITY:
Oxford - 25 miles/30 mins

MAJOR AIRPORT:
London Heathrow - 50 miles/50 mins

RAILWAY STATION:
Newbury - 2 miles/5 mins

RESERVATIONS
Toll free in US: 800-856-5813
Quote **Best Loved**

ACCESS CODES
AMADEUS HK EWYDON
APOLLO/GALILEO HK 25903
SABRE/ABACUS HK 30972
WORLDSPAN HK DONNI

Set in Royal Berkshire with historic cities in every direction

In the beautiful countryside of Royal Berkshire, Donnington Valley Hotel blends charm and elegance with the luxury and personal service expected from a privately owned hotel.

As well as having its own 18-hole par 71 golf course, the hotel is a 40 minute drive from England's top championship courses of Sunningdale and Wentworth.

Inside, uncompromising quality extends to each of the 58 guest rooms and suites which all enjoy peaceful views and ensure total comfort.

The Wine Press Restaurant offers an intimate, yet informal atmosphere where guests can enjoy superb cuisine complemented by wines from an excellent cellar, whilst the uniquely designed 'Greens' is the perfect setting for exclusive private parties and gourmet dinners.

A host of activities are available on the estate offering any combination of golfing, clay pigeon shooting or a day at Newbury Races.

Being at the crossroads of England, you have the perfect touring base for visits to the historic cities of Oxford, Windsor and Bath, and still are only an hour's drive from central London. Personal service, and attention to detail will ensure a warm welcome and a memorable stay.

LOCATION

Exit 13/M4, A34 southbound to Newbury. Leave A34 at first exit signed Donnington Castle. Turn right then left towards Donnington. Donnington Valley Hotel is 1 mile on right.

SOUTH

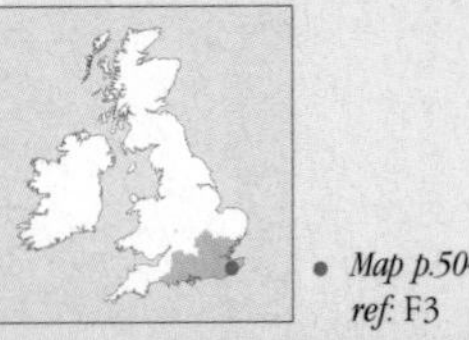

• Map p.504
ref: F3

“ I thought I was in heaven - great welcome, great food, great staff, thank you ”

Peggy Hulcombe

EASTWELL MANOR

19th century manor

Eastwell Park, Boughton Lees, Ashford, Kent TN25 4HR

Telephone 01233 213000
Fax 01233 635530

E-mail: eastwell@bestloved.com

OWNER

Turrloo Parrett

ROOM RATES

Single occupancy	£160 - £320
55 Doubles/Twins	£190 - £350
2 Four-posters	£230
5 Suites	£260 - £350

Includes newspaper, full breakfast and VAT

CHARGE/CREDIT CARDS

• DC • MC • VI

RATINGS & AWARDS

E.T.C. ★★★★ Gold Award
R.A.C. ★★★★ Dining Award 4
A.A. ★★★★ ❀❀❀ 78%

FACILITIES

On site: *Garden, croquet, indoor and outdoor pools, tennis, heli-pad, Pavilion Club & Spa*
Licensed for weddings
7 meeting rooms/max 250 people
Nearby: *Golf, fishing, riding*

RESTRICTIONS

None

ATTRACTIONS

Leeds Castle, Canterbury Cathedral, Sissinghurst Gardens, Hever Castle, Penshurst Place, the Channel Tunnel

AFFILIATIONS

Pride of Britain
Small Luxury Hotels

NEAREST

MAJOR CITY:
Canterbury - 10 miles/30 mins

MAJOR AIRPORT:
London Gatwick - 70 miles/1½ hrs

RAILWAY STATION:
Ashford - 4 miles/10 mins

RESERVATIONS

Toll free in US: 800-98-PRIDE
Toll free in UK: 0500 526735
Quote ***Best Loved***

ACCESS CODES

Not applicable

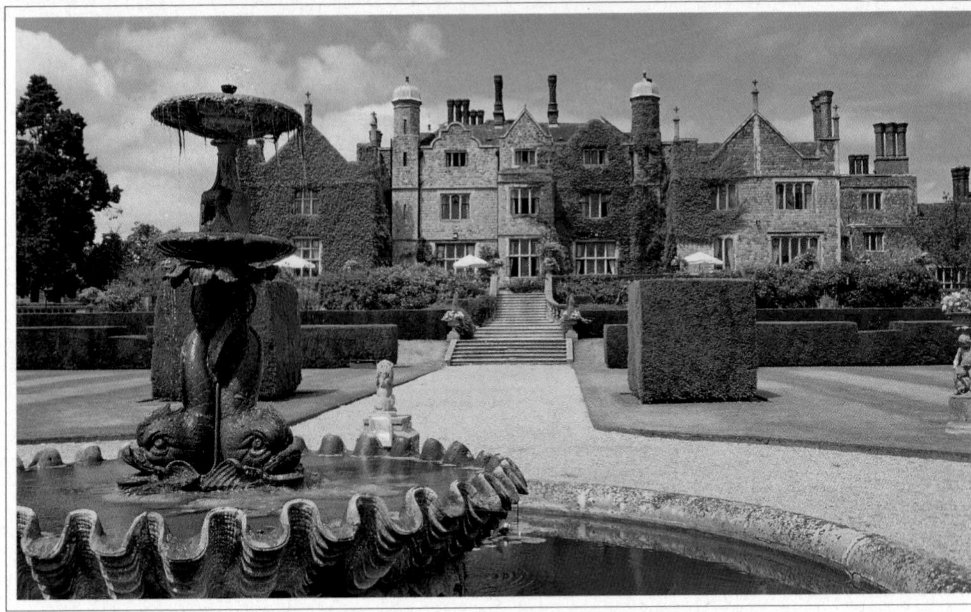

Quality is a hallmark of this beautiful manor in the Garden of England

Gloriously positioned in the tranquil Kent countryside, Eastwell Manor's sunny terraces, manicured lawns and trickling fountains overlook 62 acres of landscaped gardens set within a 3,000-acre working estate. The manor is an independent and family-owned country house hotel offering an appealing combination of luxurious surroundings, exceptional service and fine traditional and contemporary cuisine.

Eastwell's 62 guest bedrooms and suites include 19 courtyard apartments of one, two, and three bedrooms (ideal for families and groups). Being a luxury establishment, guests can expect to indulge in every possible comfort to make their stay especially memorable. Among the hotel's excellent facilities are a heated outdoor swimming pool, tennis court, pétanque terrains and a croquet lawn. The Eastwell Pavilion health and beauty spa features a 20m indoor pool, hydrotherapy pool, sauna, steam room and solarium, plus a state-of-the-art gymnasium, hair and beauty salon, and 12 fully-equipped treatment rooms for wet and dry therapies.

Romantic Leeds Castle (frequently judged 'The most beautiful castle in the world'), Canterbury and its famous cathedral, and Vita Sackville-West's glorious Sissinghurst Gardens are just a sample of the local attractions, or hop aboard the Eurostar train to Paris for an extra special day out.

LOCATION

Take the M20 to Exit 9 at Ashford, then follow the A251 Faversham Road.

" The immense fun of our stay was second only to the warmth of hospitality "

Mr & Mrs Hollingsworth, California

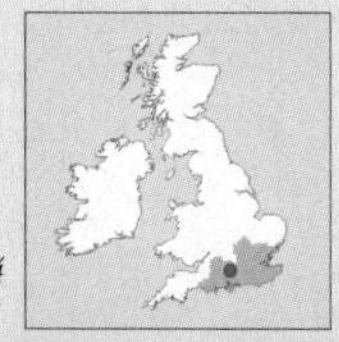

• Map p.504 ref: D3

Country house hotel

ESSEBORNE MANOR

Close by Stonehenge in the heart of southern England

Esseborne Manor, set in rich farmland high on the north Wessex Downs, is an ideal location for exploring the South with Highclere Castle, mystical Stonehenge, Avebury and the Iron Age Danebury Rings, famous gardens and the great cathedral cities of Salisbury and Winchester close by. London and the historic towns of Bath and Oxford are within an hour and a half's drive. Altogether one of the finest places to discover an aspect of Britain's heritage that goes back over almost 4,000 years!

Privately owned, the hotel, once described as "invitingly snug", has 15 individually designed bedrooms with comfortable sitting rooms that complement the elegant dining room, which itself reflects the importance placed by the owners on their cuisine and celebrated cellar.

The gardens are for enjoying and lazing and traffic free walks abound. The more energetic may in summer play croquet on the finely manicured lawns, tennis year round on the all weather court or golf on a nearby course.

Esseborne Manor is essentially a centre for staying and touring where every comfort is provided by hospitable hosts and caring staff.

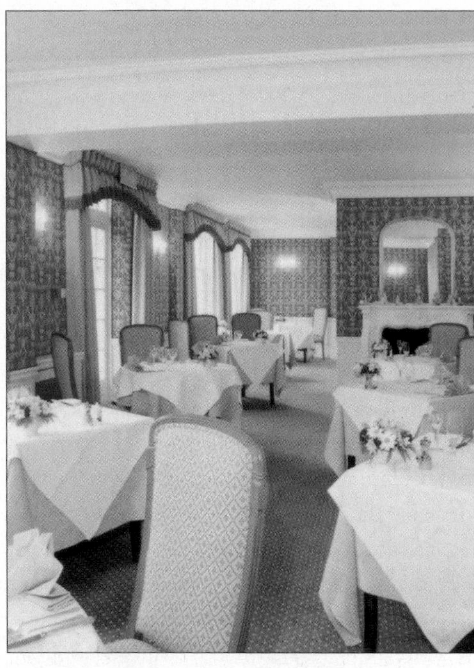

LOCATION

Leave the M4 at Exit 13 to Newbury. Take A343 towards Andover. The hotel is 1½ miles north of Hurstbourne Tarrant on A343, (or M3/A303 to Andover).

Hurstbourne Tarrant, Andover, Hampshire SP11 0ER

Telephone 01264 736444
Fax 01264 736725

E-mail: esseborne@bestloved.com

OWNERS

Ian and Lucilla Hamilton

ROOM RATES

Single occupancy	£88 - £95
15 Doubles/Twins	£100 - £160

Includes full breakfast and VAT

CHARGE/CREDIT CARDS

• DC • MC • VI

RATINGS & AWARDS

R.A.C. ★★★ Dining Award 1
A.A. ★★★ ❀❀ 73%

FACILITIES

On site: *Garden, croquet, tennis, heli-pad*
Licensed for weddings
2 meeting rooms/max 50 people
Nearby: *Golf, riding, fitness centre*

RESTRICTIONS

None

ATTRACTIONS

Stonehenge, Highclere Castle, Broadlands, Windsor, Salisbury Cathedral, Winchester Cathedral

AFFILIATIONS

Independent

NEAREST

MAJOR CITY:
Andover - 6 miles/15 mins

MAJOR AIRPORT:
London Heathrow - 55 miles/1 hr

RAILWAY STATION:
Andover - 6 miles/15 mins

RESERVATIONS

Direct with hotel
Quote ***Best Loved***

ACCESS CODES

Not applicable

SOUTH

• Map p.504 ref: F4

" Wonderful hotel . . . unpretentious, warm and friendly "

Barry D Jones, Singapore

FLACKLEY ASH HOTEL

Georgian country house

Peasmarsh, Rye,
East Sussex TN31 6YH

Telephone 01797 230651
Fax 01797 230510

E-mail: flackley@bestloved.com

OWNERS
Clive and Jeanie Bennett

GENERAL MANAGER
Colin Smith

ROOM RATES

Single occupancy	£75 - £90
35 Doubles/Twins	£119 - £159
3 Four-posters	£139
4 Suites	£159 - £169

Includes full breakfast and VAT

CHARGE/CREDIT CARDS

• DC • MC • VI

RATINGS & AWARDS
E.T.C. ★★★
R.A.C. ★★★
A.A. ★★★ 74%

FACILITIES
On site: Garden, putting green, croquet, indoor pool, sauna, spa, steam-room, mini-gym, health and beauty, heli-pad
Licensed for weddings
2 meeting rooms/max 100 people
Nearby: Riding

RESTRICTIONS
Limited access for disabled guests

ATTRACTIONS
Cinque Port of Rye, Bodiam Castle, Sissinghurst Castle, Canterbury Cathedral

AFFILIATIONS
Best Western
Marston Hotels

NEAREST
MAJOR CITY:
London - 60 miles/2 hrs
MAJOR AIRPORT:
London Heathrow - 50 miles/1¾ hrs
London Gatwick - 40 miles/1¼ hrs
RAILWAY STATION:
Rye - 4 miles/10 mins

RESERVATIONS
Direct with hotel
Quote **Best Loved**

ACCESS CODES
AMADEUS BW VLW138
APOLLO/GALILEO BW 13106
SABRE/ABACUS BW 11492

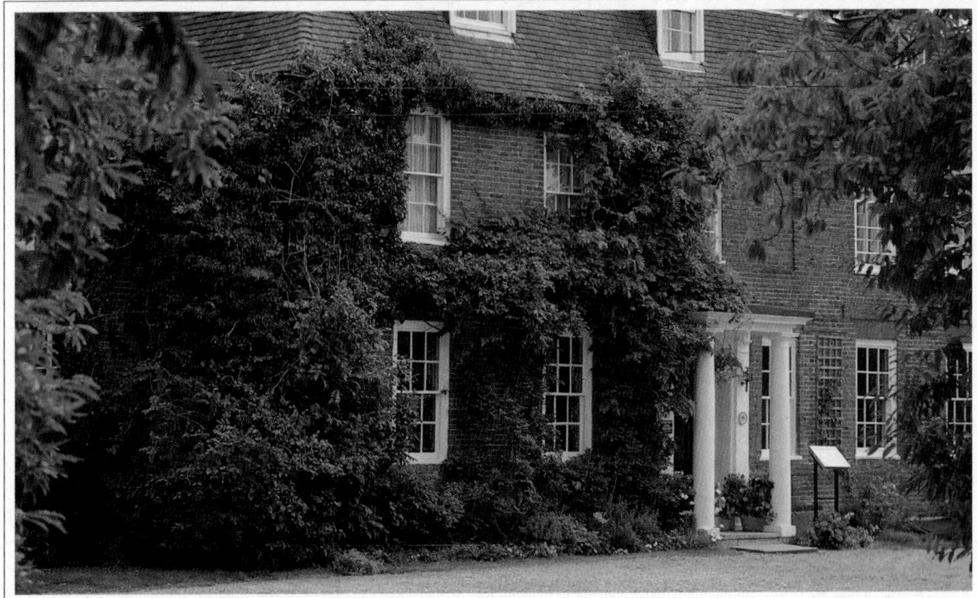

A Georgian country house near Rye, the perfect place to relax

Deep in the Sussex countryside nestles the pretty village of Peasmarsh near Rye and the delightful Flackley Ash Hotel. A far cry from the hustle and bustle of modern city life, this attractive Georgian country house is the ideal place to enjoy a relaxing holiday.

The fine traditions of comfort and service are retained by Clive and Jeanie Bennett, the owners, who for over twenty years have provided a warm and friendly welcome for their guests. The bedrooms are furnished in the style of a traditional country home and have all the modern facilities. In the friendly lounge you can read the morning paper, meet other guests or relax with coffee after a dinner in the candle-lit restaurant.

In such a place it is easy to drift back in time. Wander the cobbled streets of medieval Rye with its potteries, antique shops, taverns and tea shops. Discover the enchantingly beautiful Bodiam Castle and Bateman's, the house where Kipling lived. Follow in the footsteps of William the Conqueror, visit the fields where the first 'Battle of Britain' was fought and see the abbey built to mark his victory.

You can relax with croquet or putting in the pretty gardens, and in the indoor swimming pool and leisure centre with its mini-gym, sauna, whirlpool spa, steam room and beauty parlour.

LOCATION

From M25 Exit 5 (signposted A21 Hastings). Turn left on to A268 at Flimwell traffic lights. Proceed through Hawkhurst and Northiam to Peasmarsh.

SOUTH

“ The best spit-roasted duck I have ever tasted ”

Kevin Brant, Berkshire

• Map p.504
ref: D3

Riverside hotel

FRENCH HORN HOTEL

Peace and plenty on the banks of the River Thames

At the foot of the Chilterns, beside the tranquil River Thames, is a very special English country house – The French Horn at Sonning. For over 150 years the hotel has provided a riverside retreat from the cares of the world. Today it offers comfortable rooms and outstanding cooking in the most beautiful of settings.

By day the sunny restaurant is the perfect rendezvous for an enjoyable lunch. At night the graceful weeping willows fringing the Thames are romantically floodlit. The cuisine is a traditional mixture of French and English cooking using the freshest ingredients, many local. The French Horn's wine list is amongst the finest in Europe and includes many rare and unusual bottles. In the old panelled bar, ducks roast on a spit before an open fire. Upstairs, the beautifully decorated suites and rooms look out over landscaped grounds.

The French Horn has five luxury suites and 15 well-appointed suites and double rooms. Each has a TV, alarm radio and direct dial telephone.

The Emmanuels continue the tradition of family ownership at the French Horn, ensuring that the standard of excellence is maintained throughout.

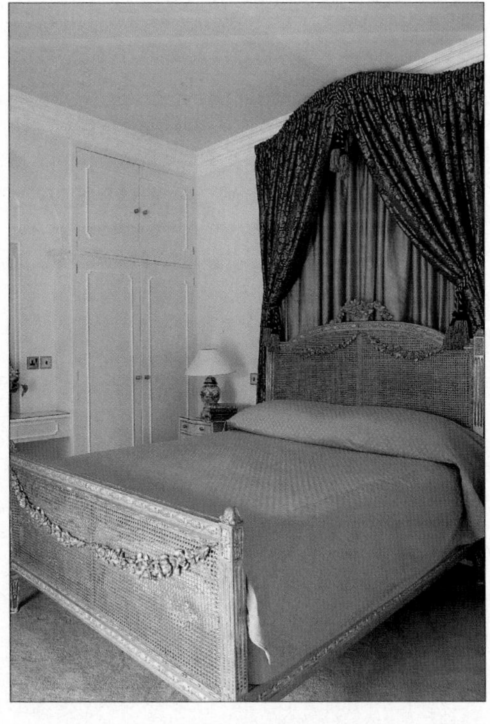

LOCATION

Take the A4 to Reading then turn off for Sonning.

Sonning on Thames,
Berkshire RG4 6TN

Telephone 01189 692204
Fax 01189 442210

E-mail: *frenchhorn@bestloved.com*

OWNERS

The Emmanuel family

ROOM RATES

10 Doubles/Twins	*£110 - £130*
10 Suites	*£145 - £175*

Includes full breakfast and VAT

CHARGE/CREDIT CARDS

• DC • MC • VI

RATINGS & AWARDS

R.A.C. ★★★★ Dining Award 3
A.A. ★★★ ❀❀ 77%

FACILITIES

On site: *Garden, fishing, heli-pad*
1 meeting room/max 16 people
Nearby: *Golf, riding, health centre*

RESTRICTIONS

No pets

ATTRACTIONS

Blenheim Palace, Windsor Castle, Mapledurham House, Stratfield Saye House, Ascot Racecourse, Windsor, Newbury

AFFILIATIONS

Pride of Britain

NEAREST

MAJOR CITY:
London - 36 miles/1 hr

MAJOR AIRPORT:
London Heathrow - 20 miles/45 mins

RAILWAY STATION:
Reading - 4 miles/15 mins

RESERVATIONS

Toll free in US: 800-98-PRIDE
*Quote **Best Loved***

ACCESS CODES

Not applicable

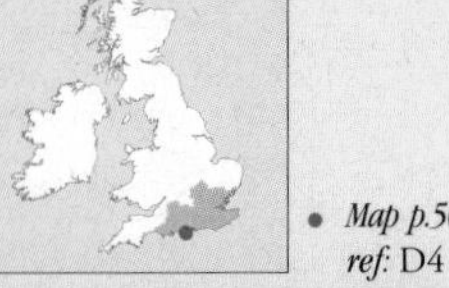

• Map p.504 ref: D4

" It's my dream hotel because it's so rare to find food, service, character and wonderful harbour views in the same place "

Jean-Christophe Novelli

THE GEORGE

17th century mansion

Quay Street, Yarmouth, Isle of Wight PO41 0PE

Telephone 01983 760331
Fax 01983 760425

***E-mail:** georgeiow@bestloved.com*

GENERAL MANAGERS

Jeremy Willcock & Jackie Everest

ROOM RATES

2 Singles	*£115*
12 Doubles/Twins	*£155 - £175*
1 Four-poster	*£205*
2 Balcony doubles	*£205*

Includes full breakfast and VAT

CHARGE/CREDIT CARDS

• JCB • MC • VI

RATINGS & AWARDS

R.A.C. ★★★ Dining Award 3

A.A. ★★★ ❀❀❀

FACILITIES

***On site:** Garden, Licensed for weddings 2 meeting rooms/max 30 people*

***Nearby:** Golf, riding, fitness centre, tennis, fishing, hunting/shooting, water skiing*

RESTRICTIONS

No children under 12 years

Pets by arrangement

ATTRACTIONS

Osborne House, Cowes Marina, Beaulieu, Carisbrooke Castle, The Needles, New Forest

AFFILIATIONS

Independent

NEAREST

MAJOR CITY:
Southampton - 25 miles/45 mins

MAJOR AIRPORT:
Southampton - 25 miles/45 mins

RAILWAY STATION:
Lymington Pier - 4 miles/35 mins

FERRY PORT:
Lymington Pier - 4 miles/35 mins

RESERVATIONS

Direct with hotel

*Quote **Best Loved***

ACCESS CODES

Not applicable

An historic waterside inn just bursting with character and charm

The old town of Yarmouth is almost 900 years old with a history as chequered as it comes. It was burnt down at least twice by the French, suffered the Black Death and, due to its strategic position, was not only the capital of the Isle of Wight but much favoured by English monarchs until the Hanovarians. Central to the town's fortunes was its most prestigious building now known as The George standing on the town quay.

The 17th century building was influenced by the style of Sir Christopher Wren and has since been enlarged, though its charm and character still echo the robust entertainment enjoyed by its owners and visiting dignitaries over the centuries.

Plus ça change… nothing changes; The George remains a house of social and gastronomic entertainment situated by the little port crammed in summer by visiting yachts. Dining here is the big attraction; the menu is well-balanced, appetising, very good value and supported by a varied and well-priced wine list.

Staying a night or so in one of the comfortable bedrooms completes the pleasure of a visit to this picturesque little town; after an enjoyable day sightseeing and the indulgence of good food, a bed in such romantic surroundings is bliss!

LOCATION

Take Exit 1 off M27, follow signs to Lyndhurst then Lymington. Follow signs to Isle of Wight Ferry.

" I cannot speak too highly of the hotel. The staff and facilities are outstanding. We will certainly recommend both the hotel and the Mirabelle Restaurant to our friends "

Mrs A Morgan, London

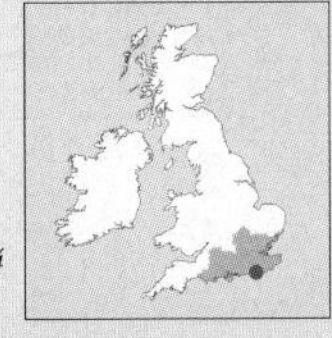

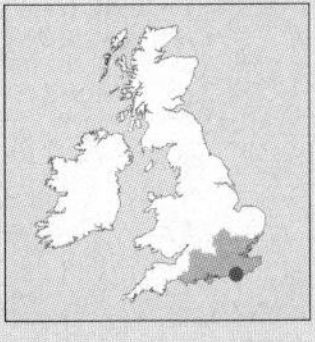

• Map p.504 ref: F4

Victorian seaside hotel

GRAND HOTEL

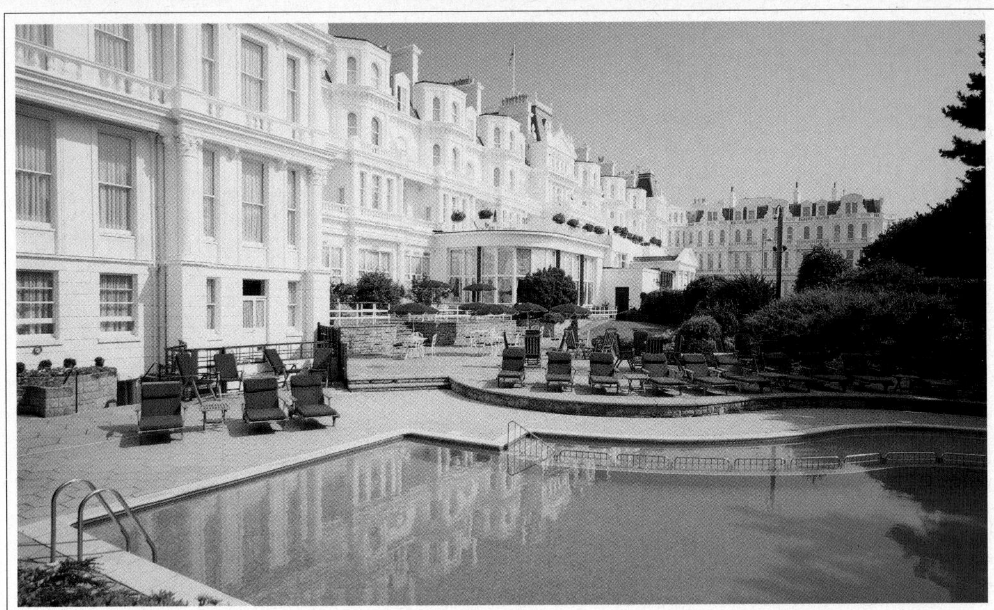

Known as The Palace - the choice of kings, statesmen, the rich and famous

Anna Pavlova, Dame Nellie Melba, several members of the British Royal family, Emperor Haile Selassie of Abyssinia, Sir Winston Churchill, Sir Edward Elgar, Sir Alec Guinness and many other luminaries have stayed at the Grand Hotel, The Palace as it is affectionately known. The Duke of Devonshire, whose family had a house nearby, wrote: "If I were asked to describe Eastbourne's outstanding quality, I would choose the word excellence and if this can be used to describe the borough as a whole it can certainly be used to describe the Grand Hotel".

The hotel dominates the western promenade with its classic white façade. The bedrooms are nothing less than majestic in design, decor and facilities - perhaps why royalty felt so comfortable here. It was, and still is, a sanctuary from worldly pressures. Music was, and still is, a part of the hotel's ethos. Readers may recall Sunday evenings with the BBC's Palm Court Orchestra; they were broadcast from the Great Hall. A touch of nostalgia? Sure, but, whilst age has added lustre to this great lady, she remains as spritely as ever. The vast health club with spa, indoor pool, gym and array of beauty treatments has added immeasurably to the hotel's youthful appeal. And there's many a conference organiser who will know The Grand by name, if not, by heart. A truly grand hotel in the finest tradition.

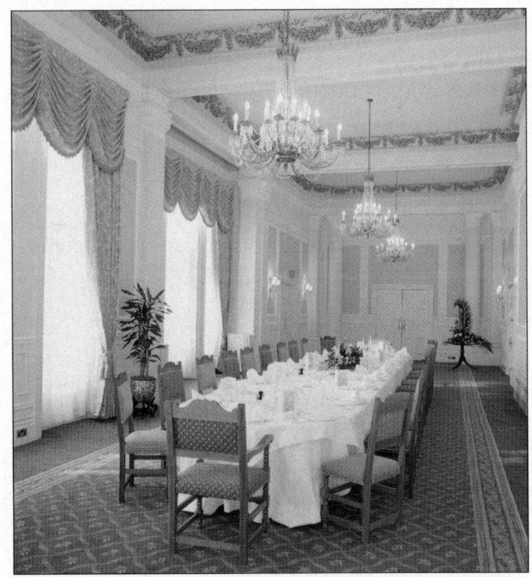

LOCATION

From A22 follow signs to the seafront (west). Turn right, The Grand Hotel is situated opposite the Western Lawns.

King Edwards Parade, Eastbourne, East Sussex BN21 4EQ

Telephone 01323 412345
Fax 01323 412233

E-mail: *grand@bestloved.com*

GENERAL MANAGER

Jonathan Webley

ROOM RATES

Single occupancy	£105 - £389
106 Doubles/Twins	£135 - £219
7 Four-posters	£149 - £420
46 Suites	£189 - £420

Includes full breakfast, newspaper and VAT

CHARGE/CREDIT CARDS

• DC • MC • VI

RATINGS & AWARDS

E.T.C. ★★★★★ Gold Award
R.A.C. ★★★★★ Dining Award 3
A.A. ★★★★★ ❀❀ 73%
South East England Tourist Board Hotel of the Year 2000

FACILITIES

On site: *Garden, indoor & outdoor pool, gym, sauna, health & beauty, jacuzzi, snooker, live entertainment*
Licensed for weddings
17 meeting rooms/max 350 people
Nearby: *Golf, water skiing, yachting, fishing*

RESTRICTIONS

No pets

ATTRACTIONS

Battle Abbey, Hever Castle, Penhurst Place, Rye, Hastings, Herstmonceux Castle & Science Centre

AFFILIATIONS

Small Luxury Hotels

NEAREST

MAJOR CITY:
Eastbourne
MAJOR AIRPORT:
London Gatwick - 47 miles/1 hr
RAILWAY STATION:
Eastbourne - 1 mile/10 mins

RESERVATIONS

Toll free in US: 800-525-4800
Quote ***Best Loved***

ACCESS CODES

AMADEUS LX BSHGHE
APOLLO/GALILEO LX 16662
SABRE/ABACUS LX 17113
WORLDSPAN LX LGWGH

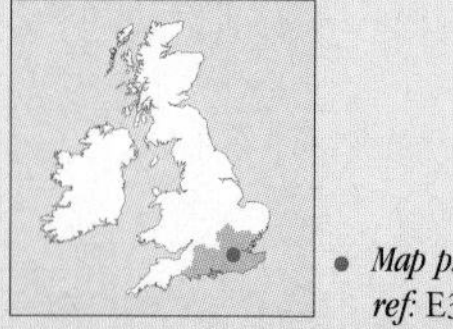

• Map p.504 ref: E3

"To find an hotel with such a balance of comfort and historical integrity is rare, but to stumble across one within such a short distance of London and its airport must be unique"

A Salisbury-Jones, Boston, USA

GREAT FOSTERS

Elizabethan manor house

Stroude Road, Egham, Surrey TW20 9UR

Telephone 01784 433822
Fax 01784 472455

E-mail: greatfosters@bestloved.com

GENERAL MANAGER

Richard Young

ROOM RATES

17 Singles	£88 - £125
22 Doubles/Twins	£115 - £295
1 Four-poster	£265
2 Suites	£265

Includes early morning tea, newspaper and VAT

CHARGE/CREDIT CARDS

• DC • MC • VI

RATINGS & AWARDS

E.T.C. ★★★★
R.A.C. ★★★★

FACILITIES

On site: Garden, croquet, health & beauty, outdoor tennis, outdoor pool, heli-pad
Licensed for weddings
5 meeting rooms/max 200 people
Nearby: Golf, riding, boating, windsurfing

RESTRICTIONS

No pets

ATTRACTIONS

Garden, croquet, outdoor tennis, outdoor pool, sauna, heli-pad
Licensed for weddings

AFFILIATIONS

The Celebrated Hotels Collection

NEAREST

MAJOR CITY:
London - 25 miles/40 mins

MAJOR AIRPORT:
London Heathrow - 7 miles/20 mins

RAILWAY STATION:
Egham - 1 mile/5 mins

RESERVATIONS

Toll free in US: 800-322-2403
Quote **Best Loved**

ACCESS CODES

Not applicable

SOUTH

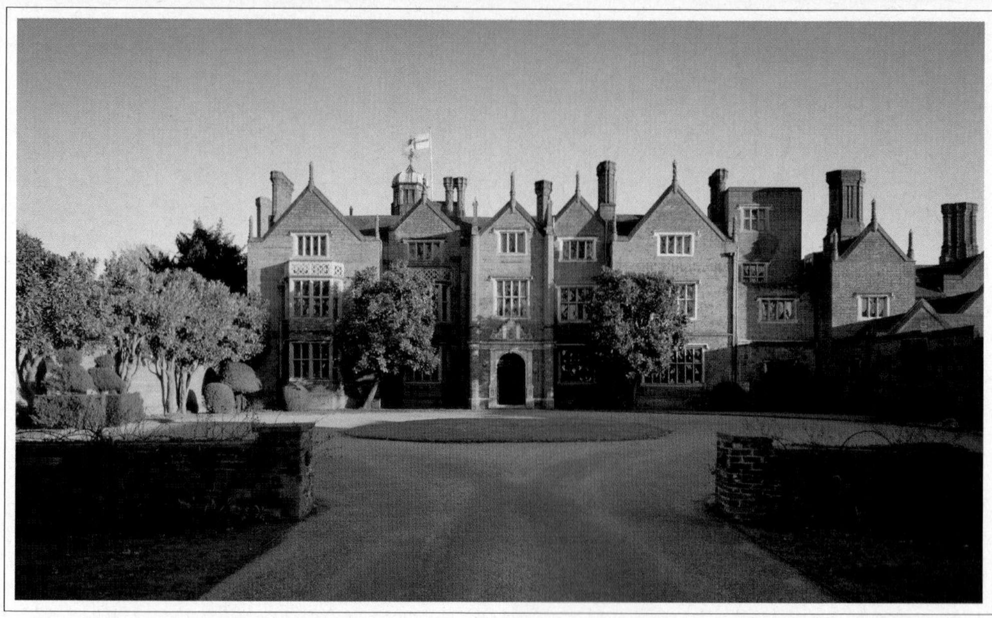

An illustrious historical pedigree spanning four centuries

Great Fosters can genuinely claim to offer the best of both worlds. An atmospheric former manor house, where Elizabethan courtiers once strolled the corridors and warmed themselves beside roaring log fires, it has one foot in an enviably rich and fascinating past. Meanwhile, the other foot is firmly planted in the present, conveniently close to the M25, and within half an hour of Central London and Heathrow airport.

This unusual combination offers an alluring opportunity to travel-weary visitors keen to experience a side of England only usually found deep in the distant shires. Great Fosters is a scheduled historic monument which still displays a plethora of original features in the grand public rooms, the dining room and lavishly decorated bedrooms. The hotel's magnificent gardens cover some 50 landscaped acres liberally adorned with topiary and statuary. A highlight is the intricate Knot Garden, which is surrounded by a Saxon moat and despite its Tudor overtones actually dates from the early 20th-century Arts and Crafts Movement era. There are rose gardens and a lily pond as well, and guests can take a little gentle exercise on the croquet lawn, in the swimming pool, or on the tennis court.

LOCATION

7 miles from Heathrow Airport. Exit 13 on M25 and take A30 for Egham. From Egham head towards Virginia Water and hotel is in Stroude Road on left.

"We felt so at home, we forgot we would have to pay"

Peter Goulandris

• Map p.504
ref: F4

Country house hotel

HORSTED PLACE

A grand place to indulge your most trivial pursuit or gourmet desire

Horsted Place and its surrounding 1,100-acre estate represents a way of life which has now largely disappeared. It is a magnificent Victorian manor house designed by Augustus Pugin and overlooks the tenth tee of the West Course of East Sussex National Golf Club - arguably one of the most challenging and picturesque holes in England. In the recent past, when the estate was privately owned, the Royal Family were regular guests but they could not have been better cared for than today's guests, all of whom are treated royally.

The gracious living of Victorian times is nicely balanced with modern amenities like the indoor swimming pool, all weather tennis court and full conference facilities for up to 100 people. Both the Pugin Dining Room and the private dining room have the warmth and intimacy which is impossible to capture in a larger establishment, whilst the cuisine is of a standard worth travelling some distance to experience.

With its rich woods, beautiful furnishings, individually decorated bedrooms and suites, Horsted Place is a country house hotel of distinction. Stay for a night or two and you'll carry the memory with you for a long time.

LOCATION

45 miles from Central London, 2 miles south of Uckfield on A26 to Lewes.

Little Horsted, Uckfield, East Sussex TN22 5TS

Telephone 01825 750581
Fax 01825 750459

E-mail: *horsted@bestloved.com*

GENERAL MANAGER

Harvey Pascoe

ROOM RATES

Single occupancy	*£110 - £270*
6 Doubles/Twins	*£110 - £155*
14 Suites	*£155 - £300*

Includes full breakfast and VAT

CHARGE/CREDIT CARDS

• DC • MC • VI

RATINGS & AWARDS

E.T.C. ★★★ Gold Award
A.A. ★★★ ❀❀ 77%

FACILITIES

On site: *Garden, indoor heated pool, croquet, all weather tennis, holistic massage, health & beauty, golf, heli-pad*
Licensed for weddings
5 meeting rooms/max 100 people
Nearby: *Riding*

RESTRICTIONS

No facilities for disabled guests
No children under 7 years in the restaurant
No pets

ATTRACTIONS

Glyndebourne, Sheffield Park, The Bluebell Railway, Wakehurst Place, Lewes Castle

AFFILIATIONS

Independent

NEAREST

MAJOR CITY:
London - 45 miles/1¼ hrs

MAJOR AIRPORT:
London Gatwick - 25 miles/35 mins

RAILWAY STATION:
Lewes - 7 miles /10 mins

RESERVATIONS

Direct with hotel
Quote ***Best Loved***

ACCESS CODES

Not applicable

"Every town in England should have an Hotel du Vin"

Janis Miller, San Rafael, USA

• *Map p.504*
ref: F4

Georgian town house — HOTEL DU VIN & BISTRO

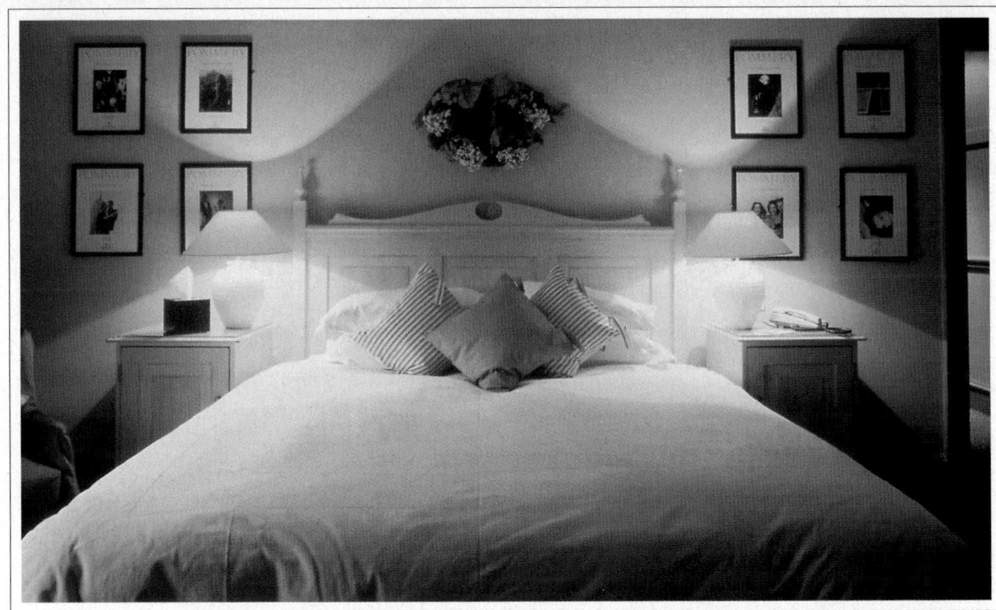

A 'must visit' hotel in the centre of historic and scenic Kent

This sandstone Grade-II listed building in the heart of the historic spa town of Royal Tunbridge Wells was built as a private residence for the Earl of Egremont in 1762, and converted into an hotel in the mid-19th century. Princess Victoria was a frequent visitor. The latest conversion came in 1997 following the acclaimed success of its sister hotel in Winchester (see next page).

Hotel du Vin continues a theme of an easy-going life style within an ambience of sophisticated luxury; where the attention to detail is fastidiously attended to by the friendly staff. The bistro presents reasonably priced, high-quality food and wine, now becoming the signature of all Hotel du Vin establishments. The Burgundy Bar features a selection of exceptional but affordable vintages chosen personally by Henri Chapon (1995 UK Wine Waiter of the Year), and the Havana Room has an antique billiard table and a range of fine Cuban cigars.

Since its opening, the Tunbridge Wells Hotel du Vin has caught the eye of food critics, all of whom have awarded it full marks. The concept is a good one and deserves its growing reputation.

LOCATION

In town centre, on Crescent Road across from Town Council and Assembly Hall.

Crescent Road, Tunbridge Wells, Kent TN1 2LY

Telephone 01892 526455
Fax 01892 512044

***E-mail:** duvinton@bestloved.com*

DIRECTORS
Peter Chittick & Henri Chapon

GENERAL MANAGER
Matthew Callard

ROOM RATES
32 Doubles/Twins £85 - £139
Includes VAT

CHARGE/CREDIT CARDS

• DC • MC • VI

RATINGS & AWARDS
A.A. ★★★★ ❀❀ Town House
The Good Food Guide Restaurant of the Year 1999

FACILITIES
***On site:** Garden, snooker*
2 meeting rooms/max 75 people
***Nearby:** Golf, tennis*

RESTRICTIONS
No facilities for disabled guests
No pets

ATTRACTIONS
The Pantiles, Hever Castle, Chartwell, Groombridge, Scotney Castle, Sissinghurst Gardens

AFFILIATIONS
The Alternative Hotel Company Ltd
Preston's Global Hotels
Selected British Hotels

NEAREST
MAJOR CITY:
Tunbridge Wells

MAJOR AIRPORT:
London Gatwick - 27 miles/40 mins

RAILWAY STATION:
Tunbridge Wells - ¼ mile/2 mins

RESERVATIONS
Toll free in US: 800-544-9993
or 800-323-5463
*Quote **Best Loved***

ACCESS CODES
Not applicable

• Map p.504
ref: D4

“The best bed I've ever slept in”

Emma Thompson, actress

HOTEL DU VIN & BISTRO

Georgian town house

Southgate Street, Winchester, Hampshire SO23 9EF

Telephone 01962 841414
Fax 01962 842458

E-mail: duvinwin@bestloved.com

GENERAL MANAGER
Nigel Buchanan

ROOM RATES

22 Doubles/Twins	£95 - £125
1 Suite	£185

Includes VAT

CHARGE/CREDIT CARDS

• DC • MC • VI

RATINGS & AWARDS
A.A. ★★★★ ❀❀ Town House
A.A. Best Dessert Wine List in the UK 2000

FACILITIES
On site: *Garden, petanque*
2 meeting rooms/max 50 people
Nearby: *Golf, riding, fishing*

RESTRICTIONS
Limited facilities for disabled guests
No pets, guide dogs only

ATTRACTIONS
Winchester Cathedral, Portsmouth Naval Base, New Forest, Stonehenge, King Alfred's Round Table

AFFILIATIONS
The Alternative Hotel Co Ltd
Preston's Global Hotels
Selected British Hotels

NEAREST
MAJOR CITY:
Winchester

MAJOR AIRPORT:
London Heathrow - 50 miles/45 mins
Southampton - 10 miles/15 mins

RAILWAY STATION:
Winchester - ½ mile/2 mins

RESERVATIONS
Toll free in US: 800-544-9993 or 800-323-5463
Quote **Best Loved**

ACCESS CODES
Not applicable

A 'total experience' just minutes away from Winchester Cathedral

In the heart of Winchester, near the Cathedral, is Hotel du Vin & Bistro. The red brick Georgian Grade II listed building was built as a private house in 1715; and was first converted to an hotel about 70 years ago.

After distinguished careers in the world's top hotels, Robin Hutson and Gerard Basset have made Hotel du Vin & Bistro a remarkable Town House Hotel. Emphasis is on casual comfort at sensible prices. This is a relaxed establishment with a true warmth of welcome in an unpretentious way. Great attention has been paid to detail and the wine theme is evident throughout. Each bedroom has been sponsored by a leading wine house. They all feature top quality essentials such as excellent beds, deep baths and power showers.

Basset has been Britain's leading sommelier for many years, and has won countless national and international competitions. The food and wine, which are carefully prepared and chosen, offer really great value for money. The chef has a passion for fresh local produce, which shows in the simple yet innovative style of food.

LOCATION

M3 to Winchester. Southgate Street is between city centre and St. Cross.

" From the moment we arrived the service was outstanding, the food was simply superb and the welcome second to none "

Mr & Mrs McDermont, Redhill, Surrey

• Map p.504 ref: E3

16th century manor house

LANGSHOTT MANOR

Such antiquity, style and seclusion next door to Gatwick ... astonishing!

Cocooned by the centuries and a three-acre award-winning garden, complete with moat, is Langshott Manor. As if by some historical sleight of hand it stands just eight minutes drive from Gatwick airport but once within its embrace, the strident sounds of today ebb in diminuendo; only far, far away might you catch the occasional reminder of our age.

The illusion of time in reverse continues inside the house. Two cottages dating from the 1500's, were joined by the Victorians, adding a bell tower and a mews. The eccentricities of the building give great character to the rooms which a recent refurbishment has exploited to great effect. The picturesque bedrooms, despite their great age, have a fresh individuality given greater charm by posies of flowers in every nook and cranny. Concessions are made, however, to the modern world, so the facilities are luxuriously right up to the minute!

The dining room will tempt you to an array of classic delights and a tempting wine list that is a wonderful compliment to the chef's gastronomic inspirations.

An enchanted place, so near and yet so far from London, Brighton and the South East.

LOCATION

From the A23 in Horley, take Ladbroke Road to Langshott. The hotel is situated ¾ of a mile further on.

Horley, Near Gatwick, Surrey RH6 9LN

Telephone 01293 786680
Fax 01293 783905

E-mail: *langshott@bestloved.com*

OWNERS

Peter and Deborah Hinchcliffe

GENERAL MANAGER

Kenneth Sharp

ROOM RATES

Single occupancy	*£125 - £220*
12 Doubles/Twins	*£155 - £210*
2 Four-posters	*£210*
1 Suite	*£250*

Includes full breakfast, newspaper service, taxi to the airport and VAT

CHARGE/CREDIT CARDS

• DC • MC • VI

RATINGS & AWARDS

R.A.C. Gold Ribbon ★★★ Dining Award 3

A.A. ★★ ❀❀

FACILITIES

On site: *Garden, croquet*
Licensed for weddings
2 meeting rooms/max 60 people

Nearby: *Golf, fishing, fitness centre, hunting/shooting, riding*

RESTRICTIONS

No facilities for disabled guests
Smoking permitted in lounges only

ATTRACTIONS

Windsor, Brighton, Chartwell, Glyndebourne, Wisley, London

AFFILIATIONS

The Celebrated Hotels Collection
Small Luxury Hotels

NEAREST

MAJOR CITY:
London - 28 miles/30 mins

MAJOR AIRPORT:
London Gatwick - 3 miles/8 mins

RAILWAY STATION:
Horley - ½ mile/5 mins

RESERVATIONS

Toll free in US: 800-322-2403
or 800-525-4800
Quote ***Best Loved***

ACCESS CODES

AMADEUS LX LGW249
APOLLO/GALILEO LX 92710
SABRE/ABACUS LX 42115
WORLDSPAN LX 11674

• Map p.504 ref: C4

“ Very occasionally you stumble upon a rare gem of an hotel where the building, food, service and history blend to form something quite exceptional – such is Langtry Manor ”

Out & About Magazine

LANGTRY MANOR

Victorian country house

Derby Road, Bournemouth, Dorset BH1 3QB

Telephone 01202 553887
Fax 01202 290115

E-mail: *langtry@bestloved.com*

OWNER

Pamela Hamilton Howard

GENERAL MANAGERS

Tara Howard and James Tonry

RATES PER PERSON

Single occupancy	£90
10 Doubles/Twins	£70
2 Four-posters	£80
3 Suites	£90
King Edward VII suite	£110

Includes full breakfast, dinner and VAT

CHARGE/CREDIT CARDS

• DC • JCB • MC • VI

RATINGS & AWARDS

A.A. ★★★ ❀ 73%

FACILITIES

On site: *Gardens*
Licensed for weddings
3 meeting rooms/max 100 people
Nearby: *Golf, riding, fishing, beaches*

RESTRICTIONS

Children by arrangement
No pets in public rooms

ATTRACTIONS

Beaulieu Motor Museum, Palace House, Hardy Country, Lord Mountbatten's Broadlands, New Forest, Isle of Wight

AFFILIATIONS

Independent

NEAREST

MAJOR CITY:
Bournemouth - 1 mile/5 mins

MAJOR AIRPORT:
London Heathrow - 98 miles/1½ hrs

RAILWAY STATION:
Bournemouth - ½ mile/3 mins

RESERVATIONS

Direct with hotel
Quote ***Best Loved***

ACCESS CODES

Not applicable

History and elegance in the romantic love nest of a king

Built in 1877 by the then Prince of Wales (later King Edward VII) for his favourite Lillie Langtry as a love nest; this beautiful home is located on a quiet tree-lined avenue. Langtry Manor has been lovingly restored by the Howard family in the style of the finest country house hotels. Intertwined hearts bearing the initials of Lillie and Prince Edward are scratched into a window pane.

All bedrooms and suites are individually designed for your comfort, some with a four-poster bed and/or jacuzzi. You can even stay in the King's own suite.

The magnificent Dining Hall with its Minstrels' Gallery and stained glass windows is complemented by delicious food and fine wines. Weekend stays include an Edwardian Banquet at which all six mouth-watering courses are displayed for your choice by staff in Edwardian dress. A short 'Life & Times of Lillie Langtry' in words and music gives a flavour of the history of this lovely house and its famous occupants. Langtry Manor is justly famous for its Anniversary and Birthday Celebration Weekends at no extra cost. Midweek and weekly bookings offer considerable reductions on published rates.

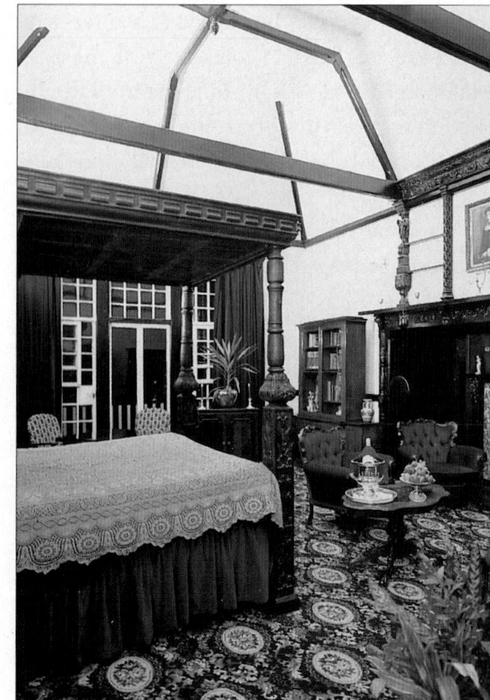

LOCATION

5 minutes walk from Bournemouth Central Station and East Cliff Sands.

"It has been a wonderful introduction to unexpected delights"

Peter Ustinov

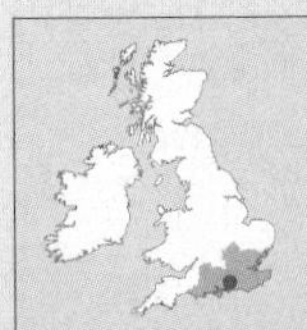

• Map p.504 ref: E4

Tudor country house

LYTHE HILL HOTEL

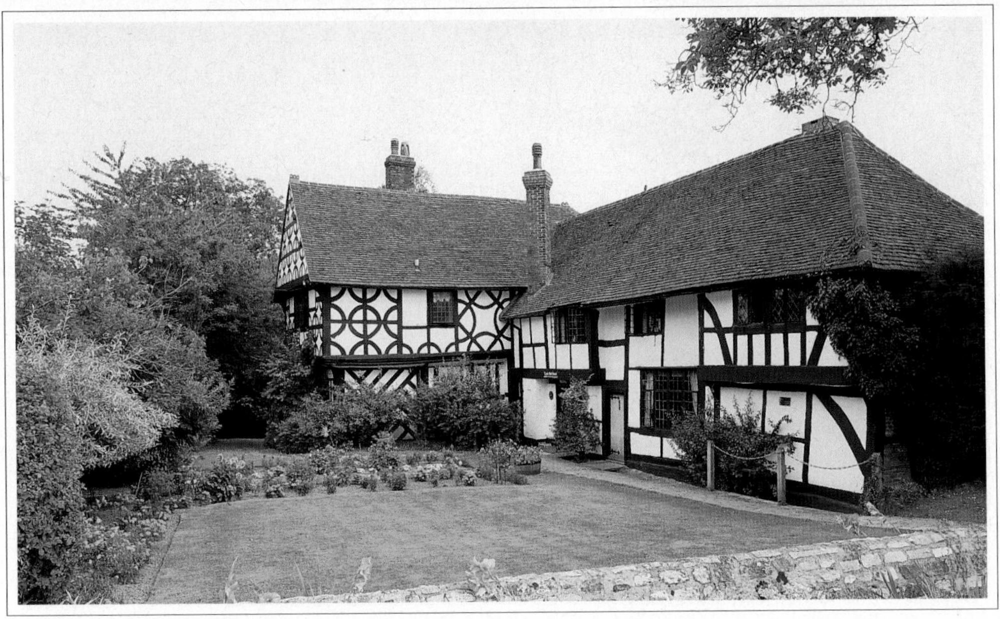

In the heart of Surrey - England's Secret Garden

Cradled by the Surrey foothills in a tranquil Wealden setting, is the enchanting Lythe Hill Hotel. It is an unusual cluster of ancient buildings, parts of which date from the 14th century.

Five charming rooms in the Tudor house complement a wide choice of more modern rooms across the courtyard, including two luxury garden suites overlooking the lake. In the main hotel dining room, the cooking is in the English tradition. Superb French cuisine is served in the Auberge de France, the oak-panelled dining room which overlooks the lake and parklands. An exceptional wine list offers over 200 wines from over a dozen countries.

Less than an hour from Heathrow, Gatwick and London and easily accessible from the Channel ports, Lythe Hill is ideal for touring the South of England. National Trust hillsides adjoining the hotel grounds provide delightful walking and views over the surrounding countryside. The area is rich in historic country houses and castles. There is horse-racing at Goodwood and Fontwell Park and polo at Cowdray Park. Beautiful gardens such as Wisley Royal Horticultural Gardens and Winkworth Arboretum are nearby. Local villages offer all the charms of the village pub and antique shop by the village green. It is an area of truly unspoilt rural England.

LOCATION

Leave the A3 at Hindhead and head towards Haslemere. Lythe Hill is 1½ miles east of Haslemere on the B2131.

Petworth Road, Haslemere, Surrey GU27 3BQ

Telephone 01428 651251
Fax 01428 644131

E-mail: *lythe@bestloved.com*

GENERAL MANAGER

Kevin Lorimer

ROOM RATES

Single occupancy	*£98*
24 Doubles/Twins	*£120*
2 Four-posters	*£180*
12 Luxury suites	*£140 - £180*
2 Garden suites	*£225*

Includes VAT

CHARGE/CREDIT CARDS

• DC • JCB • MC • VI

RATINGS & AWARDS

E.T.C. ★★★★ Silver Award
R.A.C. ★★★★ Dining Award 2
A.A. ★★★★ ❀❀ 65%

FACILITIES

On site: *Garden, croquet, tennis, fishing, games room, heli-pad*
Licensed for weddings
6 meeting rooms/max 125 people
Nearby: *Golf*

RESTRICTIONS

None

ATTRACTIONS

Arundel Castle, Petworth House, Clandon Park, Chichester Cathedral, Uppark, Yvonne Arnaud Theatre, Goodwood House and racecourse

AFFILIATIONS

Selected British Hotels

NEAREST

MAJOR CITY:
Guildford - 12 miles/20 mins

MAJOR AIRPORT:
London Heathrow - 35 miles/50 mins
London Gatwick - 35 miles/50 mins

RAILWAY STATION:
Haslemere - 1 mile/5 mins

RESERVATIONS

Toll free in US: 800-323-5463
Quote ***Best Loved***

ACCESS CODES

Not applicable

Looking for an hotel with a golf course on site? See our 'Golf Guide' on page 478

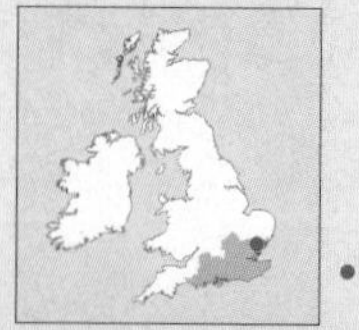

• Map p.504 ref: F2

" The Ritz of the East "

Beverley Byrne, The Lady Magazine

MAISON TALBOOTH

Riverside restaurant & Victorian hotel

Dedham, Colchester, Essex CO7 6HN

Telephone 01206 322367
Fax 01206 322752

E-mail: talbooth@bestloved.com

OWNERS

Gerald and Paul Milsom

ROOM RATES

Single occupancy	£120 - £150
5 Doubles/Twins	£155 - £175
5 Suites	£195

Includes continental breakfast and VAT

CHARGE/CREDIT CARDS

• DC • MC • VI

RATINGS & AWARDS

R.A.C. Blue Ribbon ★★★ Dining Award 3
A.A. ★★★ ❀❀

FACILITIES

On site: Garden, croquet, garden chess, heli-pad
Licensed for weddings
2 meeting rooms/max 50 people
Nearby: Golf, river fishing, hunting/shooting, riding

RESTRICTIONS

No pets

ATTRACTIONS

Constable country, Flatford and Willy Lott's cottages, Lavenham, Colchester Castle Museum, Cambridge, Beth Chatto's Gardens

AFFILIATIONS

Pride of Britain

NEAREST

MAJOR CITY:
Colchester - 6 miles/10 mins

MAJOR AIRPORT:
London Heathrow - 90 miles/1½ hrs
Stansted - 45 miles/50 mins

RAILWAY STATION:
Colchester - 10 miles/15 mins

RESERVATIONS

Toll free in US: 800-98-PRIDE
Quote **Best Loved**

ACCESS CODES

Not applicable

Fine art and great cooking in beautiful Constable country

A Victorian country house blessed with a superb position overlooking the Stour river valley and the medieval church of Stratford St. Mary, Maison Talbooth is the hotel arm of the renowned Le Talbooth restaurant which lies just a short distance along the riverbank. The hotel is a charmer, with ten spacious and appealing bedrooms decorated with a real eye for colour and thoughtful touches which emphasise the Milsom family's dedication to guests comfort. A courtesy car is on hand to whisk guests between the hotel and restaurant at lunch and dinner (breakfast and light meals are available at the hotel).

Le Talbooth itself occupies a delightful 16th-century timber framed house with a riverside terrace that is transformed into a glorious outdoor dining room in summer. A gourmet pilgrimage of note, Le Talbooth's other claim to fame is that the building featured in John Constable's famous painting of Dedham Vale. Do make time to explore around Dedham and Flatford admiring the scenery which inspired England's greatest landscape painter. There is another artistic connection at Sudbury, where the great portraitist Gainsborough's family home can be visited, conveniently close to the old wool towns and antiques centres of Lavenham and Long Melford.

LOCATION

Follow the A12 to Ipswich bypassing Colchester. Take the exit signposted for Stratford St Mary. Turn right at the bottom of the hill to Dedham. The hotel is situated after the bridge 300 yards further on.

SOUTH

" This is a wonderful, wonderful hotel. I can't fault it "

Jilly Cooper, author

• Map p.504 ref: C4

18th century town house

THE MANSION HOUSE HOTEL

Premier hospitality beside the world's second largest natural harbour

The Mansion House Hotel is the original 'Mayoral House' of Old Poole dating back to the Georgian era.

Poole has great links with the New World and the Lester family, who built the Mansion House around 1780. They made their fortune from their maritime ties with the Newfoundland cod-fish traders. The famous 'cod fillet fireplace' commemorates their transatlantic connection. Poole itself is the world's second largest natural harbour and is at the heart of Dorset's Thomas Hardy country and near William the Conqueror's New Forest.

So The Mansion House, a country house in an historic town, exemplifies that link with the past. Its converted 32 bedrooms, whilst containing all modern amenities, are furnished sympathetically and many are named after a famous Georgian figure.

The hotel is privately owned by the Leonard family. Their Dining Club, to which hotel guests enjoy temporary membership, is the premier 'eating house' in Poole and naturally specialises in local seafood. Terms are modest and quality is not diminished. A short stay at The Mansion House will linger in the memory!

LOCATION

In Poole follow signs to Channel Ferry. Take inside lane on approaching Poole Bridge & turn left into Poole Quay. Turn left after 200 yards into Thames Street - hotel is on left.

Thames Street, Poole, Dorset BH15 1JN

Telephone 01202 685666
Fax 01202 665709

E-mail: *mansionpoole@bestloved.com*

OWNER
Robert J Leonard

MANAGING DIRECTOR
Jackie Godden

ROOM RATES

9 Singles	*£65 - £90*
21 Doubles/Twins	*£95 - £130*
2 Four-posters	*£130*

Includes full breakfast, early morning tea, newspaper and VAT

CHARGE/CREDIT CARDS

• *DC* • *JCB* • *MC* • *VI*

RATINGS & AWARDS
A.A. ★★★ *80%*

FACILITIES
On site: *Private dining club, Bistro Licensed for weddings 3 meeting rooms/max 50 people*
Nearby: *Golf, riding, fishing*

RESTRICTIONS
No facilities for disabled guests
No pets

ATTRACTIONS
Poole Old Town, Corfe Castle, Hurst Castle, Hardy Country, The New Forest, Abbotsbury Abbey

AFFILIATIONS
Best Western

NEAREST
MAJOR CITY:
Poole

MAJOR AIRPORT:
London Heathrow - 100 miles/2¼ hrs

RAILWAY STATION:
Poole - 1 mile/5 mins

RESERVATIONS
Toll free in US: 800-528-1234
Quote ***Best Loved***

ACCESS CODES
AMADEUS BW BOH382
APOLLO/GALILEO BW 58155
SABRE/ABACUS BW 14103
WORLDSPAN BW 83382

Thinking of pampering yourself? See the 'Health & Beauty' index on page 472

• Map p.504 ref: D4

"The facilities were excellent, the rooms all very comfortable, and the countryside magnificent. Your staff treated us with unfailing courtesy and helpfulness"

Rt Rev J Gledhill, Bishop of Southampton

MASTER BUILDER'S HOUSE

18th century country house

Bucklers Hard,
Beaulieu,
Hampshire SO42 7XB

Telephone 01590 616253
Fax 01590 616297

E-mail: master@bestloved.com

OWNERS
Jeremy Willcock and John Illsley

GENERAL MANAGER
Christine Bayley

ROOM RATES

Single occupancy	from £115
19 Doubles/Twins	from £155
6 Superior Doubles/Twins	from £205

Includes full breakfast and VAT

CHARGE/CREDIT CARDS

• JCB • MC • VI

RATINGS & AWARDS
A.A. ★★★ ❀❀ 79%

FACILITIES
On site: *Garden, fishing*
1 meeting room/max 50 people
Nearby: *Golf, tennis, riding*

RESTRICTIONS
No pets
Limited facilities for disabled guests
No children under 7 years

ATTRACTIONS
Beaulieu Village and Motor Museum, Buckler's Hard, Exbury Gardens, New Forest

AFFILIATIONS
Best Western

NEAREST
MAJOR CITY:
Southampton - 14 miles/25 mins
MAJOR AIRPORT:
London Heathrow - 80 miles/2½ hrs
Southampton - 20 miles/30 mins
RAILWAY STATION:
Brockenhurst - 8 miles/15 mins

RESERVATIONS
Direct with hotel
*Quote **Best Loved***

ACCESS CODES
AMADEUS BW SOU725
SABRE BW 32059
GALILEO BW 87954
WORLDSPAN BW 83725

Historic maritime house in idyllic New Forest village

The Master Builder's House Hotel stands in a beautiful location in the idyllic New Forest, right on the banks of the Beaulieu River. It is part of the estate owned by Lord Montagu's family since 1538. Once it was the home of Henry Adams, Master Shipbuilder. Adams built many famous ships of the English fleet, including Nelson's favourite Agamemnon. The house is in the maritime village of Buckler's Hard, which retains much atmosphere from its shipbuilding days.

The 18th century house has a character and charm all of its own. It has been sympathetically converted and extended to provide high quality accommodation. All bedrooms have en-suite or private bathrooms, with full modern facilities.

The restaurant offers superb English cuisine and the finest of wines. The Yachtsman's Bar evokes the lively atmosphere of an 18th century inn, with traditional fare. The Residents' Lounge offers quiet views across the water and an inglenook fireplace. Tea can be taken on the terrace overlooking the harbour.

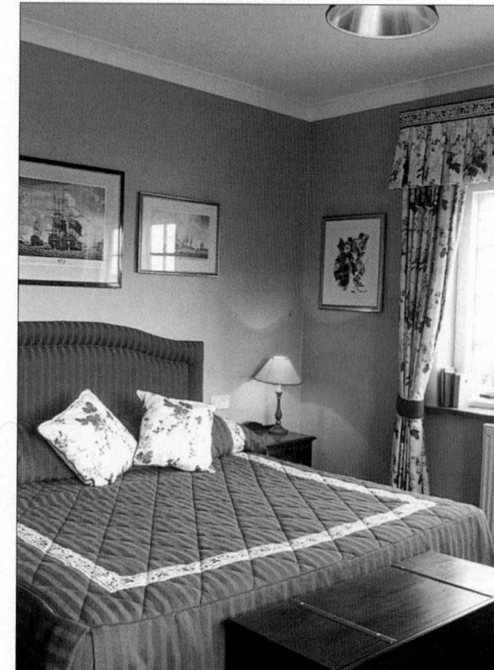

LOCATION

From London take M3, M27 West, exit 2 for Beaulieu. In Beaulieu turn left and 1st left again following signs for Buckler's Hard and hotel.

"Even better than last year. Exceptional in every way"

Debbie and Josiah Macie, English Harbour, Antigua

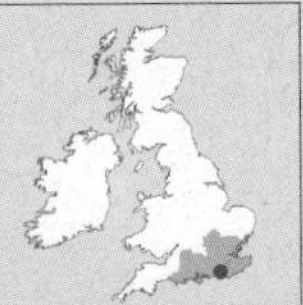

• Map p.504
ref: E4

17th century country house

THE MILL HOUSE

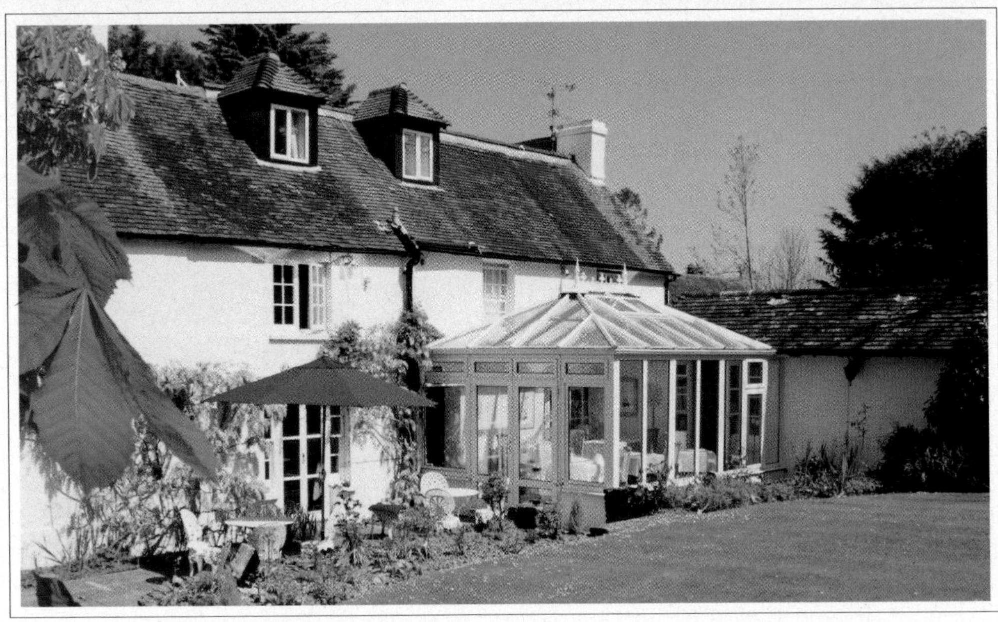

A private house? A restaurant? So much more than meets the eye

The South Downs harbour a colourful history, which occasionally reveals itself in dramatic contrast to the gentle pastoral landscape and sleepy lassitude of its grazing South Wold sheep (now a world-famous breed). Arundel Castle, for example, built just after the Norman Conquest, was devastated by cannon fire from Oliver Cromwell. During the brief period of his republic, the Mill House was built and, in character with its surroundings, has much more to offer than its demure appearance suggests.

This charming small country house hotel is run by Simon and Maria Hudson, a multi-talented husband-and-wife team who are equally at home either in the kitchen or at front of house. As a rule, Simon oversees the kitchen while Maria tends the guests, but roles swap and the couple's complementary talents make the art of hotel keeping look disarmingly simple. The atmosphere at the Mill House combines elegance with an appealing air of informality and the Hudson's convivial approach is to share their treasures, pleasures, and garden with you. The comfy bedrooms are like those of a private home, while the dining room and conservatory offer imaginative cuisine worthy of an independent restaurant complemented by a notably well-chosen wine list.

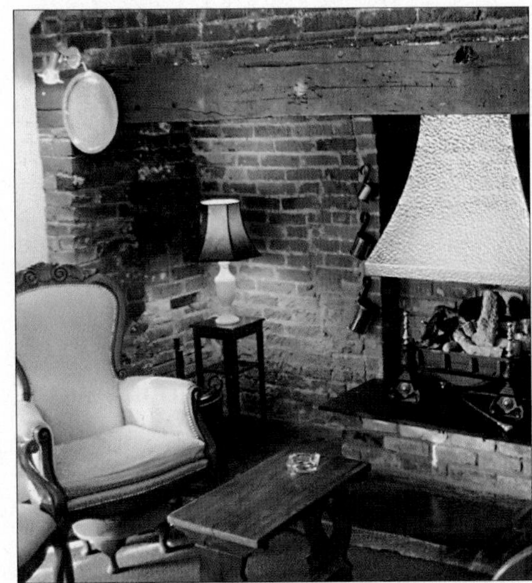

LOCATION

From London, leave the A24 following the signs for Ashington. Turn right at the Red Lion and follow Mill Lane past Muddle Feeds to the hotel which is on the left.

Mill Lane, Ashington, West Sussex RH20 3BX

Telephone 01903 892426
Fax 01903 892855

E-mail: *millsussex@bestloved.com*

OWNERS

Simon and Maria Hudson

ROOM RATES

3 Singles	*£49 - £57*
6 Doubles/Twins	*£79 - £89*
1 Four-poster	*£89*

Includes full breakfast, service and VAT

CHARGE/CREDIT CARDS

• *MC* • *VI*

RATINGS & AWARDS

E.T.C. ★★★ Silver Award

FACILITIES

On site: *Garden*
2 meeting rooms/max 40 people
Nearby: *Golf, tennis, fitness, water skiing, yachting, fishing, riding*

RESTRICTIONS

No facilities for disabled guests

ATTRACTIONS

Arundel Castle, South Downs, Goodwood, Leonardslee Gardens, Parham House, Bluebell Steam Railway

AFFILIATIONS

Independent

NEAREST

MAJOR CITY:
Brighton - 12 miles/20 mins

MAJOR AIRPORT:
London Gatwick - 17 miles/30 mins

RAILWAY STATION:
Pulborough - 6 miles/15 mins

RESERVATIONS

Direct with hotel
Quote **Best Loved**

ACCESS CODES

Not applicable

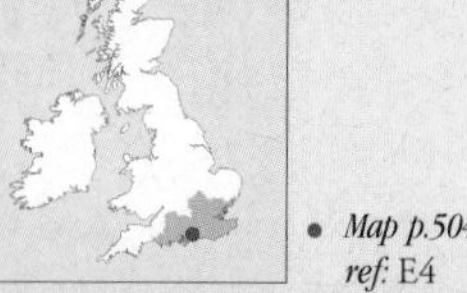

• Map p.504 ref: E4

"As always the food was excellent, nothing is too much trouble, and the friendliness of everyone makes a stay with you such a joy"

Mr & Mrs Miller, Farnham

MILLSTREAM HOTEL AND RESTAURANT *18th century manor house*

Bosham Lane, Bosham, Chichester, West Sussex PO18 8HL

Telephone 01243 573234
Fax 01243 573459

E-mail: millstream@bestloved.com

GENERAL MANAGER
Antony Wallace

ROOM RATES

5 Singles	£72 - £99
27 Doubles/Twins	£115 - £130
3 Suites	£145 - £170

Includes full breakfast and VAT

CHARGE/CREDIT CARDS

• DC • MC • VI

RATINGS & AWARDS
E.T.C. ★★★ Silver Award
R.A.C. ★★★ Dining Award 2
A.A. ★★★ ❀ 72%
South East England Tourist Board Hotel of the Year - Runner Up 1999

FACILITIES
On site: *Gardens*
Licenced for weddings
1 meeting room/max 20 people
Nearby: *Golf, riding, fishing*

RESTRICTIONS
No pets in public rooms

ATTRACTIONS
Chichester Festival Theatre, Fishbourne Roman Palace, Arundel Castle, Portsmouth Historic Ships, Goodwood House, Weald & Downland Open Air Museum

AFFILIATIONS
Independent

NEAREST
MAJOR CITY:
Chichester - 4 miles/10 mins

MAJOR AIRPORT:
London Gatwick - 48 miles/1 hr

RAILWAY STATION:
Bosham - 1 mile/5 mins

RESERVATIONS
Direct with hotel
Quote ***Best Loved***

ACCESS CODES
Not applicable

Turn back the tides of the modern world and take life at a gentler pace

They say King Canute, regally enthroned on the shingle beach, tried to turn back the tide somewhere in the vicinity of Bosham (pronounced Bozum). It was not a success. However, while any attempt to force the English Channel into retreat from the shores of West Sussex will undoubtedly prove futile, it is possible to escape the nerve-fraying assaults of the modern world at a little place called the Millstream in Old Bosham.

Old Bosham is an outrageously picturesque village gathered around a Saxon church on the shores of Chichester Harbour. The clatter of rigging down in the marina identifies it as a popular sailing centre, but there is little but the quacking of ducks to disturb guests ensconced in the peaceful gardens of the Millstream. Housed in an 18th-century malthouse reached by a bridge over its namesake waterway, the Millstream is perfect for a romantic weekend or an out-of-town break by the sea, offering the character and intimate appeal of a small country house. Floral motifs seem to have gravitated organically from the garden into the fabrics and botanical prints of the sitting room and delectably pretty bedrooms. Fresh flowers adorn the tables in the restaurant where the mixed English and continental menu might include a fillet of home-smoked trout with horseradish cream and pan-fried and honey-roasted duck served with a plum and brandy compote.

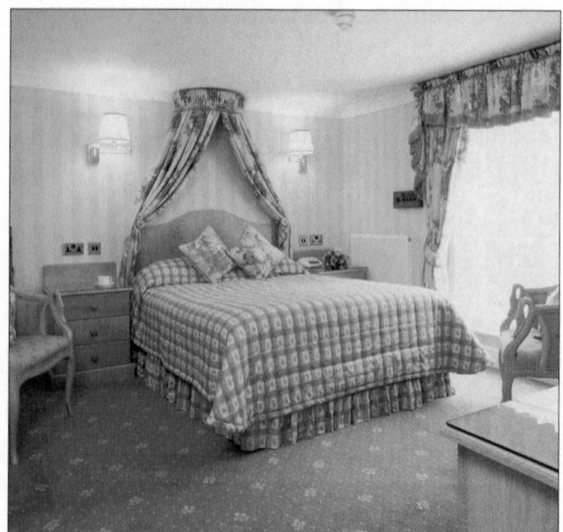

LOCATION

From the A259 Portsmouth to Chichester road, turn off at the small roundabout towards Bosham. The hotel is very well signposted from here.

“ Tout a été parfait ”

Salmon Yvah, Rennes, France

• *Map p.504* Inset map

19th century town house

MOORE'S HOTEL

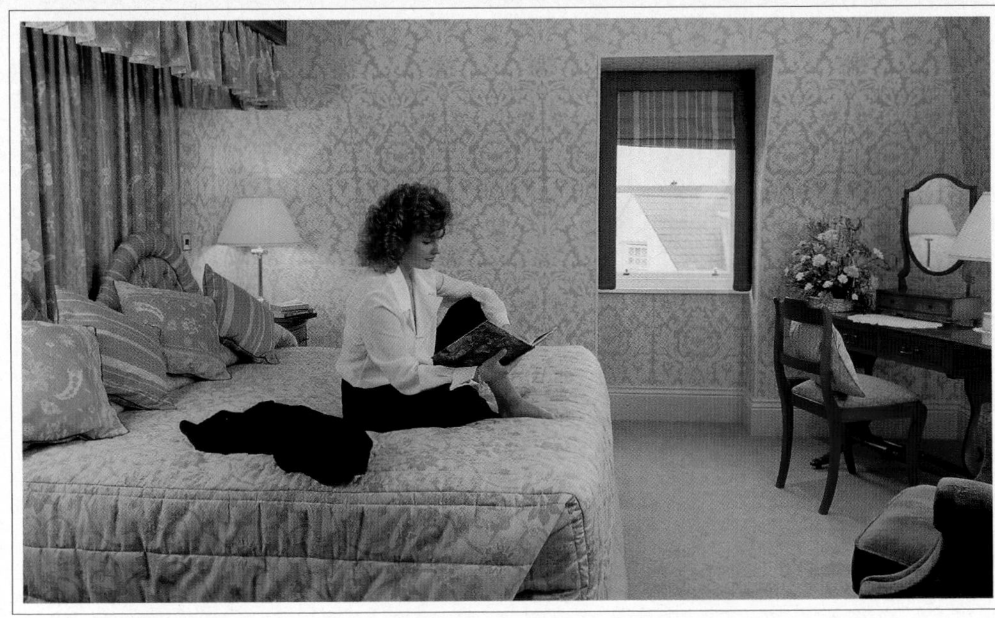

Where too much of a good thing can be simply wonderful

In the heart of St Peter Port stands Moore's Central Hotel, an elegant blue granite building which was once the home of the de Saumarez's, one of Guernsey's oldest families. Parts of the building date back to the middle of the 18th century. Moore's lives up to its slogan that 'Too much of a good thing can be simply wonderful'.

The 49 bedrooms each have private bathroom and toilet. All rooms have colour TV with teletext, radio, tea-making facilities, trouser press, hair-dryer and direct-dial telephone.

The main restaurant is the Conservatory, part of which is under glass. Full English breakfast is served here each morning. In the evening you can select from a five-course dinner menu, or from an extensive à la carte menu where the specialities are fresh fish and seafood. The Austrian-style Patisserie offers home-baked gateaux and light lunches and there is also a Library Bar and Carvery. The cocktail bar has a blazing log fire on winter days, but spring and summer come early to Guernsey.

The almost traffic-free shopping streets of Guernsey's capital are near at hand. Just a few minutes' stroll brings you on to the sea front. From here ferries frequently depart to St Malo, Jersey and the smaller islands.

LOCATION

In the town centre of St Peter Port.

Le Pollet, St Peter Port, Guernsey GY1 1WH, Channel Islands

Telephone 01481 724452
Fax 01481 714037

E-mail: *moores@bestloved.com*

OWNERS

André and Sheila Sendlhofer
Karel and Mike Harris

ROOM RATES

2 Singles	*£40 - £80*
44 Doubles/Twins	*£68 - £108*
3 Suites	*£120 - £166*

Includes full breakfast

CHARGE/CREDIT CARDS

• *DC • MC • VI*

RATINGS & AWARDS

G.T.B. ♛♛♛♛ Highly Commended
R.A.C. ★★★ Dining Award 1
A.A. ★★★ 70%

FACILITIES

On site: *Terrace garden, sauna, jacuzzi, solarium, gym*
2 meeting rooms/max 120 people
Nearby: *Golf, fishing, riding, sailing, surfing, windsurfing, water skiing*

RESTRICTIONS

No facilities for disabled guests
No pets

ATTRACTIONS

St Peter Port, Military Museum, Guernsey Museum, Castle Cornet, Maritime Museum, Victor Hugo's house, Sculpture Trail at Sausmauez Manor, VAT exempt

AFFILIATIONS

Best Western

NEAREST

MAJOR CITY:
Southampton - 120 miles/40 mins by air
MAJOR AIRPORT:
Guernsey - 5 miles/15 mins
FERRY PORT:
St Peter Port - ½ mile/3 mins

RESERVATIONS

Direct with hotel
*Quote **Best Loved***

ACCESS CODES

AMADEUS BW GCI 731
APOLLO/GALILEO BW 47143
SABRE/ABACUS BW 5319
WORLDSPAN BW 83731

Planning a wedding reception? Turn to 'Meeting Facilities' on page 476

• Map p.504 ref: D4

"We celebrated our wedding here and the whole experience was something of a lovely dream. Superb staff and management"

Mr & Mrs Michael Bower

NEW PARK MANOR

16th century hunting lodge

Lyndhurst Road, Brockenhurst, Hampshire SO42 7QH

Telephone 01590 623467
Fax 01590 622268

E-mail: newparkmanor@bestloved.com

OWNER
Countess Von Essen

GENERAL MANAGER
Sue Plaisted

ROOM RATES

Single occupancy	£85
8 New Forest rooms	£110
12 Superior New Forest rooms	£140
2 Junior suites	£150
2 Four-poster rooms	£160

Includes full breakfast and VAT

CHARGE/CREDIT CARDS

• DC • MC • VI

RATINGS & AWARDS
E.T.C. ★★★ Silver Award
R.A.C. ★★★ Dining Award 4
A.A. ★★★ ❀❀ 75%

FACILITIES
On site: Garden, croquet, tennis, horse riding, heated outdoor swimming pool (June-Sept), heli-pad
3 meeting rooms/max 150 people
Nearby: Golf, fishing

RESTRICTIONS
No children under 7 years
No smoking in the bedrooms
Pets by arrangement

ATTRACTIONS
New Forest, Exbury Gardens, Beaulieu Motor Museum, Highcliffe Castle, Stonehenge, Broadlands at Romsey, Isle of Wight

AFFILIATIONS
Von Essen Hotels

NEAREST
MAJOR CITY:
Southampton - 10 miles/20 mins
MAJOR AIRPORT:
London Heathrow - 80 miles/1½ hrs
London Gatwick - 93 miles/2 hrs
RAILWAY STATION:
Brockenhurst - 1½ miles/5 mins
FERRY PORT:
Southampton - 10 miles/20 mins

RESERVATIONS
Direct with hotel
Quote **Best Loved**

ACCESS CODES
Not applicable

SOUTH

Once King Charles II's favourite hunting lodge

The New Forest is one of England's oldest forests, and New Park's origins go way back to its earliest days. In 1070 William the Conqueror made the Forest his hunting preserve. King Charles II named New Park his favourite hunting lodge on his return from exile in France in 1666, when he used it in the company of Nell Gwyn. His carved Royal Coat of Arms stands proud in the dining room.

New Park Manor is one of the New Forest's finest country house hotels. The 24 bedrooms have private bathrooms, and most overlook forest parklands. The historic, oak-panelled Rufus Bar, with its open fireplace, includes a library stocked with old and rare books. The New Forest Suite complements the colours of the New Forest, and conveys the atmosphere of the area. The Stag restaurant has upgraded its classical/modern European influenced cuisine with excellent table d'hôte and à la carte menus and a fine wine list. Afternoon teas are also served daily.

The hotel has its own stables with BHS trained stablecrew and well-schooled horses. It also has an outdoor swimming pool, tennis court and croquet lawn. There are some marvellous walks into the New Forest. Golf, forest biking, hot air ballooning, helicopter trips and even flying lessons can all be arranged. Pilots should note the following heli-pad grid reference: N.50.50.46 W.01.34.99.

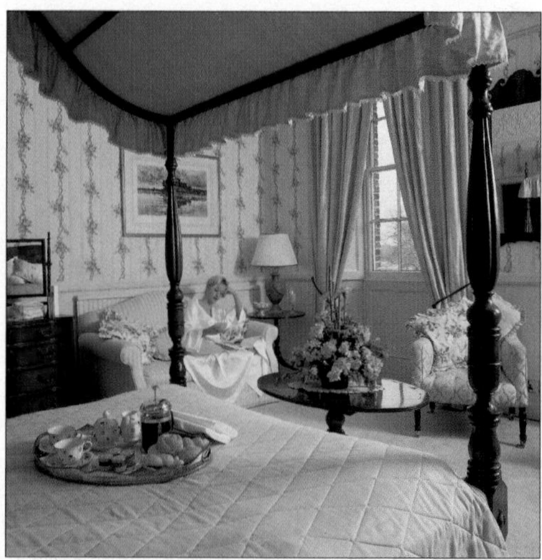

LOCATION

From M27, follow A337 for 6 miles south past Lyndhurst. Turn right at sign for New Park Manor. The hotel is ¼ mile into the forest.

"Fabulous food, fabulous people, fabulous place. We will return"

The Kaufmans, New Jersey, USA

Map p.504 ref: E4

18th century estate

NEWICK PARK COUNTRY ESTATE

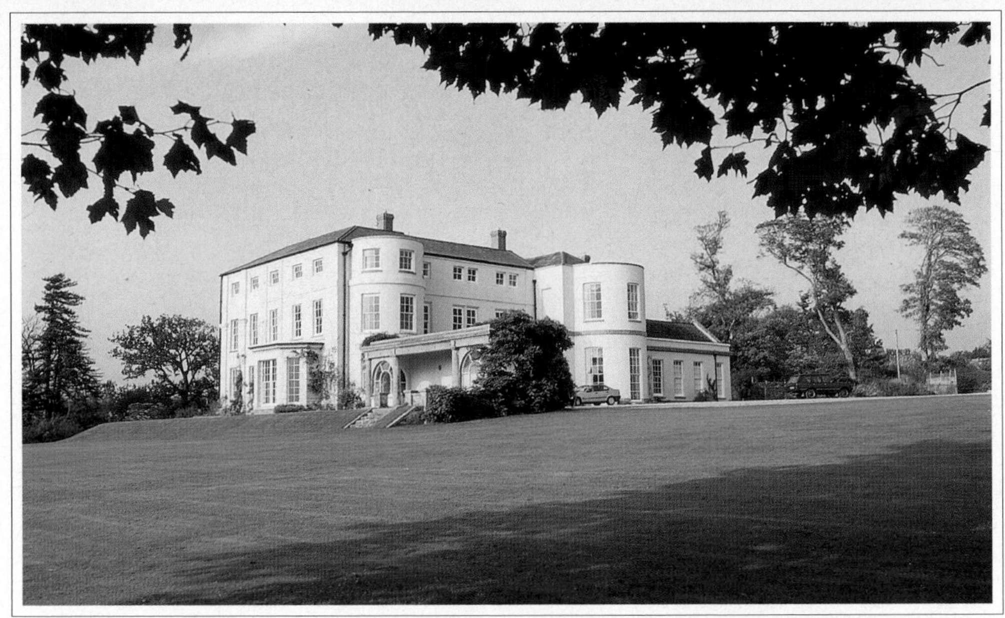

The Ironmaster's home where you will be enveloped in luxury

Visiting East Sussex today, it is hard to imagine that here, in the 17th century, the iron industry reached its zenith. Ironworks needed oak and the largest oak forest was at Ashdown. Today the area is a mix of wild heaths, rocky outcrops and woodlands, a great place for walking and hiking

Newick Park Country Estate, is very much a part of this early industrial history. The oldest part of the house was built as an Ironmaster's home. Additions were made in the 18th century but it was not until 1990 when the Childs family rescued and restored it to the grand country house it now is.

From the comfortable log fires in the sitting room to the beautiful bedrooms an air of understated elegance pervades and envelops everyone. This is a home rather than an hotel. The atmosphere carries over into the dining room where the chef prepares beautifully presented modern British cuisine.

Another grand aspect of Newick Park are the beautiful Dell Gardens which include a rare collection of 100 year old Royal Ferns.

Newick is a great place to get away but should you wish to sightsee, Brighton with its Royal Pavilion is an easy 20 minutes away.

LOCATION

From Newick village turn south on The Green and continue down lane until you come to a T-junction. Turn left and Newick Park is on the right after ¼ mile.

Newick, Lewes, East Sussex BN8 4SB

Telephone 01825 723633
Fax 01825 723969

E-mail: *newick@bestloved.com*

OWNERS
Virginia and Mike Childs

ROOM RATES

1 Single	*£95 - £120*
10 Doubles/Twins	*£165 - £235*
2 Four-posters	*£235*
3 Suites	*£165 - £235*

Includes full breakfast and VAT

CHARGE/CREDIT CARDS

• JCB • MC • VI

RATINGS & AWARDS
E.T.C. ★★★★
A.A. ★★★ ❀❀ *80%*

FACILITIES
On site: *Garden, croquet, tennis, outdoor pool, quad bikes, tanks, hunting/shooting, clay pigeon shooting, fishing, riding, heli-pad*
Licensed for weddings
2 meeting rooms/max 120 people
Nearby: *Golf, fitness*

RESTRICTIONS
Smoking very restricted

ATTRACTIONS
Brighton Marina, Sheffield Park, Bluebell Railway, Borde Hill Gardens, Ashdown Forest, Chartwell, Glyndebourne, Michelham Priory

AFFILIATIONS
Independent

NEAREST
MAJOR CITY:
Brighton - 15 miles/25 mins

MAJOR AIRPORT:
London Gatwick - 20 miles/35 mins

RAILWAY STATION:
Lewes - 7 miles/10 mins

RESERVATIONS
Direct with hotel
Quote ***Best Loved***

ACCESS CODES
Not applicable

• Map p.504 ref: E4

"Adored the food, loved the bed, and appreciated the fine service after a long day's travel"

Mr & Mrs William Morris, Dallas, TX, USA

OCKENDEN MANOR

16th century manor house

Ockenden Lane, Cuckfield, West Sussex RH17 5LD

Telephone 01444 416111
Fax 01444 415549

E-mail: ockenden@bestloved.com

OWNERS
Mr and Mrs Sandy Goodman

MANAGER
Mr Kerry Turner

ROOM RATES

1 Single	£99 - £105
15 Doubles/Twins	£132 - £205
6 Four-posters	£240 - £275

Includes continental breakfast and VAT

CHARGE/CREDIT CARDS

• DC • MC • VI

RATINGS & AWARDS
A.A. ★★★ ❀❀ 75%

FACILITIES
On site: *Garden, croquet*
Licensed for weddings
1 meeting room/max 100 people
Nearby: *Golf, riding, fishing*

RESTRICTIONS
No facilities for disabled guests
No pets

ATTRACTIONS
Brighton, Bluebell Railway, Leonardslee Gardens, Chartwell, Wakehurst Place, Hever Castle, Charleston, Penshurst Place, Sheffield Park Gardens

AFFILIATIONS
The Celebrated Hotels Collection
Pride of Britain

NEAREST
MAJOR CITY:
London - 40 miles/1 hr
MAJOR AIRPORT:
London Gatwick - 13 miles/20 mins
RAILWAY STATION:
Haywards Heath - 2 miles/10 mins

RESERVATIONS
Toll free in US: 800-322-2403
or 800-98-PRIDE
Quote ***Best Loved***

ACCESS CODES
AMADEUS HK LGWOCK
APOLLO/GALILEO HK OCKEN
SABRE/ABACUS HK 36354
WORLDSPAN HT 4164

Gastronomic excellence in a 400 year-old family manor

Ockenden Manor is a 16th century manor house set in the tranquil Tudor village of Cuckfield, just 20 minutes away from Gatwick Airport. The setting offers peace and quiet but is in easy reach of major cities such as London and Brighton.

The 22 bedrooms, of which six have four-poster beds, either overlook the splendid nine-acre gardens surrounding the manor, or over to the rolling South Downs. The public rooms offer log fires in the winter and superb views all year round.

Ockenden Manor is well known for its Elizabethan oak panelled dining room with its unique gold leaf painted ceiling. Chef Martin Hadden uses only the finest local produce and ingredients such as fresh crab from Chichester. His cuisine has a delicate but excellent touch and this is borne out by the many return visits from satisfied guests! The wine cellar is extensive with over 200 bins of both New World and the more traditional French varieties available.

Ockenden Manor is well situated for visits to the opera at Glyndebourne and antique hunting in many of the nearby villages. National Trust properties abound within easy reach, as do golf courses. The seaside is close by, as well as the countryside for walking and outdoor pursuits.

LOCATION

Take A23 south of Crawley towards Brighton. Proceed east at exit B2115 marked Cuckfield. Drive 3½ miles to village.

“ Forest is great: it is true old wild English Nature, and then the fresh heath-sweetened air is so delicious. The Forest is grand ”

Alfred Lord Tennyson

• Map p.504 ref: D4

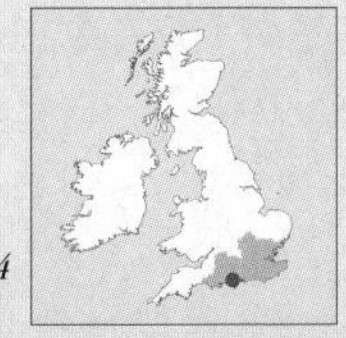

Country house hotel

PASSFORD HOUSE HOTEL

A rather special country house on the edge of the New Forest

Passford House Hotel, the former home of Lord Arthur Cecil, is situated on the edge of the New Forest in nine acres of grounds and beautifully maintained gardens. The hotel boasts a compact leisure centre featuring indoor and outdoor pools, a sauna, solarium, gym, a hard tennis court and a croquet lawn.

The informal charm of the panelled oak lounge and bar is matched by the deluxe bedrooms all with private bathroom, some of which are on the ground floor. The elegant restaurant offers an imaginative and tempting menu complemented by fine wines.

Two miles away, the old Georgian town of Lymington has a superb shopping centre, thriving Saturday market, two impressive marinas and superior yachting facilities. A short drive away are Beaulieu, the cathedral cities of Winchester and Salisbury, and ferry ports to the Isle of Wight and France.

There are numerous golf courses within easy driving distance, horse riding stables, the glorious New Forest on the very doorstep, cycling paths, beautiful walks and, of course, sailing on the Solent.

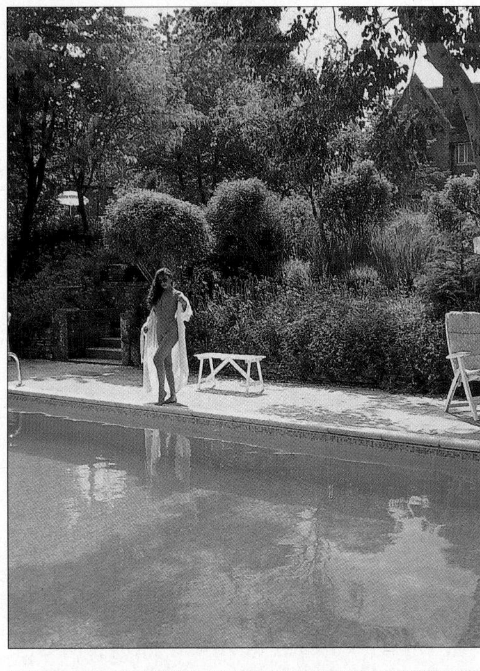

LOCATION

Exit 1/M27 (West), A337 to Brockenhurst. After railway bridge & mini roundabout, right at Tollhouse Pub & bear right into Mount Pleasant Lane. Hotel is 1 mile past garden centre.

Mount Pleasant Lane,
Lymington,
Hampshire SO41 8LS

Telephone 01590 682398
Fax 01590 683494

E-mail: *passford@bestloved.com*

OWNER

Ian Hudleston

ROOM RATES

4 Singles	*£65 - £85*
47 Doubles/Twins	*£60 - £130*
1 Four-poster	*£120*

Includes full breakfast and VAT

CHARGE/CREDIT CARDS

• DC • MC • VI

RATINGS & AWARDS

E.T.C. ★★★
R.A.C. ★★★ *Dining Award 1*
A.A. ★★★ *72%*

FACILITIES

On site: *Garden, indoor/outdoor pool, croquet, tennis, petanque, heli-pad, gym, sauna, table tennis*
4 meeting rooms/max 100 people
Nearby: *Golf, riding, fishing, sailing*

RESTRICTIONS

No facilities for disabled guests

ATTRACTIONS

Salisbury and Winchester Cathedrals, New Forest, Beaulieu Motor Museum, Exbury Gardens, Isle of Wight, Broadlands, Wilton House

AFFILIATIONS

Independent

NEAREST

MAJOR CITY:
Southampton - 17 miles/30 mins
Bournemouth -15 miles/25 mins

MAJOR AIRPORT:
London Heathrow - 80 miles/1¾ hrs
Southampton - 17 miles/30 mins

RAILWAY STATION:
Brockenhurst - 4 miles/10 mins

RESERVATIONS

Direct with hotel
Quote ***Best Loved***

ACCESS CODES

Not applicable

Looking for an hotel with a golf course on site? See our 'Golf Guide' on page 478

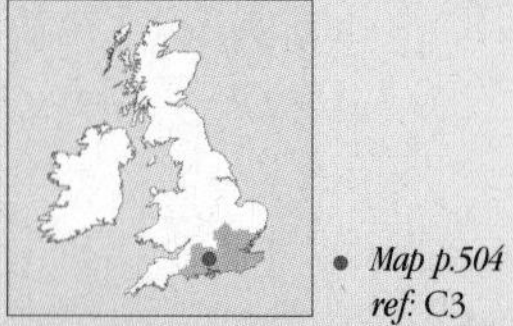

• Map p.504 ref: C3

"Pretty, Polished, Professional, Perfect"

Paddy Burt, The Daily Telegraph

THE PEAR TREE AT PURTON

Former vicarage

Church End, Purton, Wiltshire SN5 4ED

Telephone 01793 772100
Fax 01793 772369

E-mail: peartree@bestloved.com

OWNERS

Francis and Anne Young

ROOM RATES

1 Single	£110
10 Doubles/Twins	£110
7 Executive Doubles/Twins	£130
2 Suites	£140 - £150

Includes breakfast and VAT

CHARGE/CREDIT CARDS

• DC • JCB • MC • VI

RATINGS & AWARDS

R.A.C. Blue Ribbon ★★★ Dining Award 3
A.A. ★★★ ❀❀ 78%

FACILITIES

On site: Garden, croquet, heli-pad
Licensed for weddings
4 meeting rooms/max 60 people
Nearby: Leisure centre, riding, shooting, jet-skiing

RESTRICTIONS

None

ATTRACTIONS

The Cotswolds, Bowood House, Cirencester, GWR Steam Railway Museum, Cotswold Water Park, Designer Outlet Village

AFFILIATIONS

Pride of Britain

NEAREST

MAJOR CITY:
Swindon - 5 miles/10 mins

MAJOR AIRPORT:
Bristol - 30 miles/30 mins

RAILWAY STATION:
Swindon - 5 miles/10 mins

RESERVATIONS

Toll free in the US: 800-98-PRIDE
Quote **Best Loved**

ACCESS CODES

AMADEUS HK SWIPEA
APOLLO/GALILEO HT 14848
SABRE/ABACUS HK 30135
WORLDSPAN HK PEART

SOUTH

Peaceful retreat in the lovely Vale of the White Horse

Not far from the source of the River Thames in the gently rolling landscape of north Wiltshire, The Pear Tree's rural surroundings belie its convenient location minutes from the M4 with easy access to Heathrow and four-star sightseeing attractions such as Oxford and Bath. For those of a more mystical persuasion, the ancient Avebury Stone Circle and even Stonehenge are within striking distance, as are the white horses carved into the chalk hills of the Vale of the White Horse and Vale of Pewsey.

The Pear Tree occupies a handsome 16th-century former vicarage moved brick by brick from its original position next to the unusual twin-towered church of St. Mary's 400 yards away in 1912. Each of the pretty and extremely comfortable rooms are named after famous local characters from Anne Hyde, mother of Queen Mary and Queen Anne, to cricketer E.H. Budd. The conservatory restaurant is a key feature with lovely views of the traditional English gardens scented with roses and fragrant stocks in summer. The hotel has a charmingly relaxed family-run air lent by hosts Francis and Anne Young, and the service is memorable for its genuine consideration and care towards guests.

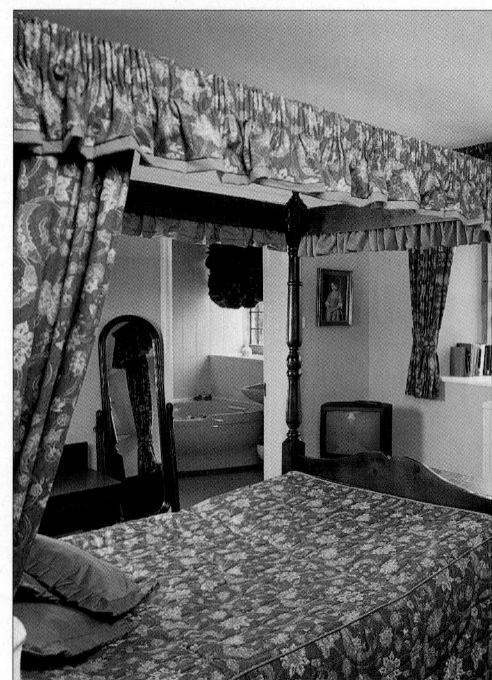

LOCATION

From M4 Exit 16 follow signs to Purton. At Spar Grocers turn right. The hotel is ¼ mile along on the left hand side.

"You have managed to find the perfect mix of great service, marvellous accommodation and magnificent dining"

Sarah Lomas, Colchester

• *Map p.504 ref: G2*

Harbourside hotel — THE PIER AT HARWICH

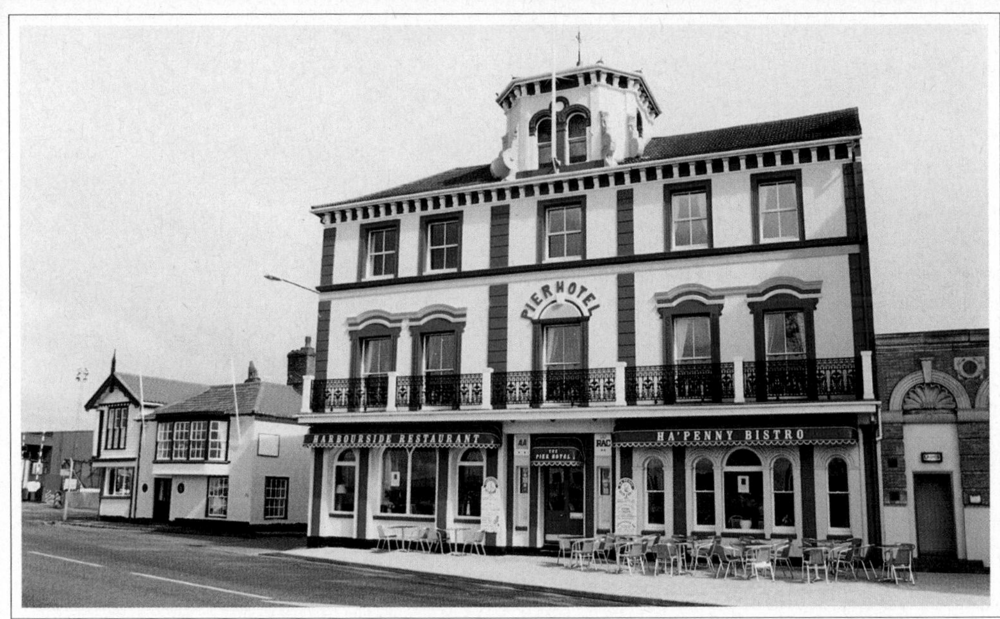

Quayside seafood restaurants with rooms and bustling harbour views

The Harbourside Restaurant and its more casual little sister, The Ha-Penny Bistro, sit right on recently restored Old Harwich Quay. Over the years, they have established an enviable reputation for the quality and variety of their seafood menus, which will come as no surprise to foodies when they realise that the owners are the Milsom family of Le Talbooth fame (a watchword for fine dining in East Anglia).

Adjacent to the restaurants, one of The Pier's chief charms is its harbour views constantly enlivened by the coming and going of yachtsmen and traditional fishing boats. The 14 bedrooms breathe a distinctly nautical chic of their own after a fresh and modern seaside themed redecoration programme completed under the talented guidance of Geraldine Milsom. The imaginative use of seashells and rope, weatherboarding and natural fibre floor coverings augmented by marine paintings and photographs lends a wonderfully briny air and there are numerous creative touches to amuse and entertain throughout the hotel. The Pier makes a welcome overnight stop en route to the continent, or take advantage of the hotel's great value sailing weekends. There are also short break offers in conjunction with Maison Talbooth (see page 338).

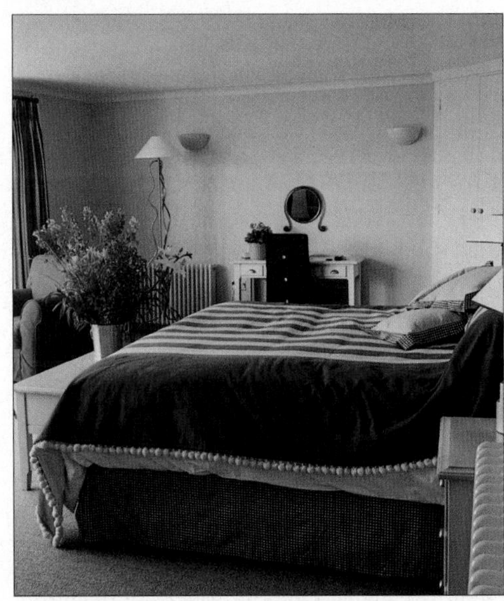

LOCATION

Take the A120 to Harwich and continue straight on this road until it comes to an end on the quayside of Old Harwich. The Pier is on the right, opposite the Life Boat Station.

The Quay, Harwich, Essex CO12 3HH

Telephone 01255 241212
Fax 01255 551922

E-mail: *pier@bestloved.com*

OWNERS
Gerald and Paul Milsom

CHEF DIRECTOR
Chris Oakley

ROOM RATES

Single occupancy	*£62 - £100*
13 Doubles/Twins	*£80 - £100*
1 Suite	*£150*

Includes continental breakfast and VAT

CHARGE/CREDIT CARDS

• *DC* • *MC* • *VI*

RATINGS & AWARDS
E.T.C. ★★★
R.A.C. ★★★ *Dining Award 3*
A.A. ★★★ ❀❀ *72%*

FACILITIES
On site: *Licensed for weddings*
1 meeting room/50 people
Nearby: *Pool, golf, tennis, boating, fishing, sailing*

RESTRICTIONS
No pets

ATTRACTIONS
Harwich Maritime & Lifeboat Museums, Kentwell Hall & Lavenham, Beth Chatto's Gardens, Flatford Mill & Constable Country, Colchester Castle

AFFILIATIONS
Great Inns of Britain

NEAREST
MAJOR CITY:
Harwich

MAJOR AIRPORT:
Stansted - 60 miles/50 mins

RAILWAY STATION:
Harwich - ½ mile/2 mins
FERRY PORT:
Harwich International Port - 1 mile/3 mins

RESERVATIONS
Direct with hotel
*Quote **Best Loved***

ACCESS CODES
Not applicable

• Map p.504 ref: C4

" The most comfortable, friendly and relaxing 'restaurant with rooms' in which we have had the good fortune to stay - and you have a magician in the kitchen "

Mrs D E Raymond, Haywards Heath

PLUMBER MANOR

17th century manor

Sturminster Newton, Dorset DT10 2AF

Telephone 01258 472507
Fax 01258 473370

E-mail: *plumber@bestloved.com*

OWNER
Richard Prideaux-Brune

ROOM RATES
Single occupancy £80 - £90
16 Doubles/Twins £95 - £145
Includes full breakfast, newspaper, service and VAT

CHARGE/CREDIT CARDS

• DC • MC • VI

RATINGS & AWARDS
A.A. ★★★ ❀❀ 71%

FACILITIES
On site: *Garden, croquet, outdoor tennis, heli-pad*
1 meeting room/max 15 people
Nearby: *Golf, fishing, hunting/shooting, riding, clay pigeon shooting*

RESTRICTIONS
No pets in public rooms
Closed Feb

ATTRACTIONS
Dorset villages, Kingston Lacy, Corfe Castle, Cerne Abbas, Lulworth Cove, Poole Harbour, Brownsea Island

AFFILIATIONS
Pride of Britain

NEAREST
MAJOR CITY:
Salisbury - 30 miles/1 hr

MAJOR AIRPORT:
London Heathrow - 100 miles/2½ hrs

RAILWAY STATION:
Gillingham - 10 miles/20 mins

RESERVATIONS
Toll free in US: 800-98-PRIDE
Quote **Best Loved**

ACCESS CODES
Not applicable

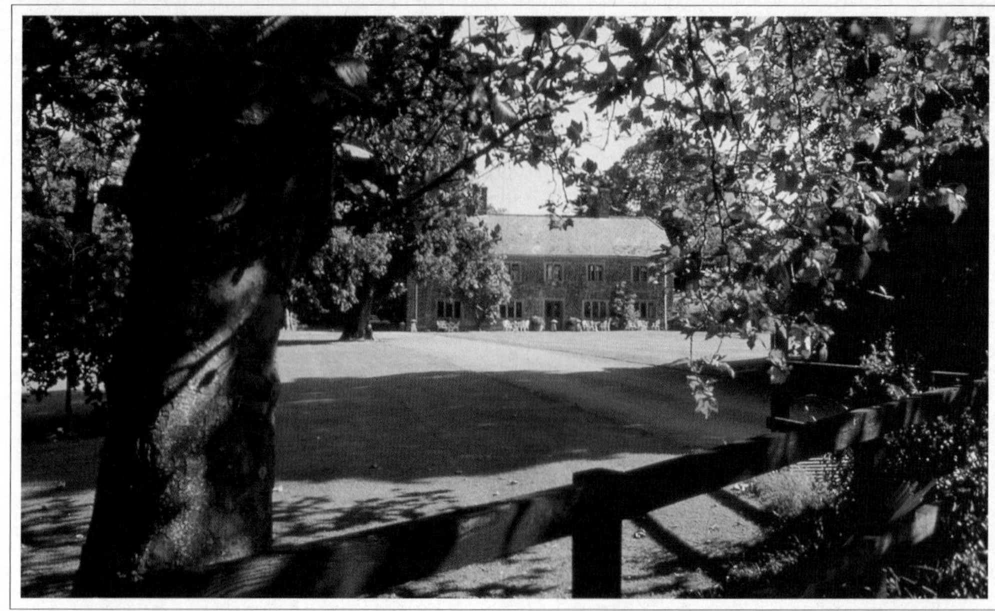

A Devilish place to satisfy the senses

Plumber Manor is a wonderful Jacobean manor house lost in the lush green countryside of Thomas Hardy's Dorset. The five-acre lawns are edged by the Devilish Stream, an idyllic picture of sublime peace in pastoral bliss.

Inside the house there are homely touches like family heirlooms and jars of homemade shortbread that refute any notion that this is an hotel! One look at the plumped-up, oversized furniture tells you comfort is the keynote here. There are six rooms in the original manor and another ten in the stable courtyard across the lawn. The original drawing room is now a part of a trio of richly decorated dining rooms. The bar is what used to be the dining room.

The Prideaux-Brunes still live here and that's what gives the place such an authentic feeling of home. Richard attends to front of house duties while his younger brother, Brian, is the chef whose unfussy style of cuisine fits the Plumber philosophy like a rind to its fruit. His imaginative menu based on the goodness of Dorset has won a loyal following and well-earned recognition from the major guides.

The world seems oblivious of little Dorset's huge inheritance; making Plumber Manor your base, your senses, all of them, will be in for a treat.

LOCATION

Located 11/2 miles south west of Sturminster Newton on the Hazelbury Bryan road. Turn off the A357 towards Hazelbury Bryan and the hotel is situated 2 miles further on.

“ A style uniquely its own, tremendous hospitality. It's the hosts that make the inn ”

General K Israel, US Air Force

• Map p.504
ref: F4

Country house

POWDER MILLS HOTEL

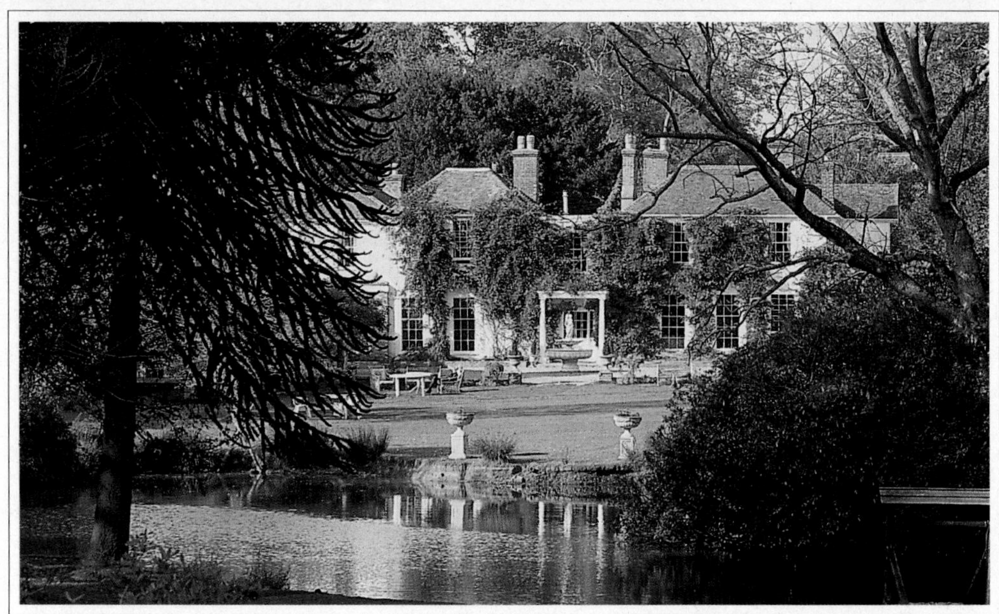

Many would argue British history started here back in 1066 AD

Powder Mills is a stunning 18th century country house hotel set in 150 acres of parks and woodland just outside the historic town of Battle. This is '1066 country' – where William the Conqueror fought and killed King Harold. The hotel, with its historic atmosphere and legendary surroundings, is ideally located for exploring the most beautiful and ancient parts of Sussex and Kent.

A seven-acre specimen fishing lake and three smaller lakes are available to guests. There are plenty of opportunities to relax and wander around the grounds. Proprietors Douglas and Julie Cowpland and their staff are on hand to make you feel at home in warm and friendly surroundings.

This corner of the country is like a treasure trove to the antique enthusiast, and the hotel itself has been richly furnished with antiques from many of the local shops.

The Orangery Restaurant has received glowing ratings and awards for its fine classical cooking prepared under the direction of Chef Daniel Ayton. It is open to residents and non-residents for lunch, afternoon tea and dinner.

LOCATION

Through town of Battle on A2100, direction Hastings. First turning right into Powdermill Lane. After 1 mile Hotel is on right-hand side of lane after sharp bend.

Powdermill Lane, Battle, East Sussex TN33 0SP

Telephone 01424 775511
Fax 01424 774540

E-mail: *powdermills@bestloved.com*

OWNERS
Douglas and Julie Cowpland

MANAGER
Nick Walker

ROOM RATES

2 Singles	*£70 - £85*
17 Doubles/Twins	*£95 - £120*
10 Four-posters	*£95 - £160*
6 Junior suites	*£160*

Includes full breakfast and VAT

CHARGE/CREDIT CARDS

• DC • MC • VI

RATINGS & AWARDS
R.A.C. ★★★ Dining Award 1
A.A. ★★★ ❀ 70%

FACILITIES
On site: *Garden, fishing, outdoor pool*
Licensed for weddings
3 meeting rooms/max 300 people
Nearby: *Golf, riding*

RESTRICTIONS
None

ATTRACTIONS
Battle Abbey, Rye, Hastings, local antique shops

AFFILIATIONS
Grand Heritage Hotels

NEAREST
MAJOR CITY:
Hastings - 6 miles/10 mins

MAJOR AIRPORT:
London Gatwick - 48 miles/1 hr

RAILWAY STATION:
Battle - 1 mile/2 mins

RESERVATIONS
Toll free in US: 888-93-GRAND
*Quote **Best Loved***

ACCESS CODES
AMADEUS UI LGWPMP
APOLLO/GALILEO UI 94007
SABRE/ABACUS UI 43023
WORLDSPAN UI 40664

• Map p.504
ref: C4

“ The Priory is the sort of hotel I'd recommend other hoteliers to stay in ”

Paddy Burt, Daily Telegraph

PRIORY HOTEL

16th century priory

Church Green, Wareham, Dorset BH20 4ND

Telephone 01929 551666
Fax 01929 554519

E-mail: *prioryware@bestloved.com*

OWNERS
Stuart and John Turner

ROOM RATES

3 Singles	£80 - £135
12 Doubles/Twins	£110 - £250
2 Four-posters	£210 - £220
2 Suites	£250

Includes full breakfast, early morning tea or coffee, newspaper and VAT

CHARGE/CREDIT CARDS

• DC • JCB • MC • VI

RATINGS & AWARDS
E.T.C. ★★★ Gold Award
R.A.C. ★★★ Blue Ribbon Dining Award 3
A.A. ★★★ ❀❀

FACILITIES
On site: *Croquet, garden*
1 meeting room/max 20 people
Nearby: *Fishing, sailing, riding, cycling, golf*

RESTRICTIONS
Children by prior arrangement
No pets

ATTRACTIONS
Corfe, Purbeck, Hurst and Portland Castles, Lulworth Cove, Kingston Lacey, Poole Harbour, Wareham, Dorchester, Hardy Country

AFFILIATIONS
Independent

NEAREST
MAJOR CITY:
Salisbury - 35 miles/45 mins

MAJOR AIRPORT:
London Heathrow - 100 miles/1½ hrs

RAILWAY STATION:
Wareham - 1 mile/3 mins

RESERVATIONS
Direct with hotel
Quote ***Best Loved***

ACCESS CODES
Not applicable

SOUTH

Steeped in history, an idyllic sanctuary for the world-weary

Dating from the early 16th century, the one-time Lady St Mary Priory has offered sanctuary for years. Far from the hustle and bustle of city life, The Priory stands in four acres of immaculate gardens on the banks of the River Frome, surrounded by idyllic Dorset countryside.

Steeped in history, The Priory has undergone a sympathetic conversion to a charming yet unpretentious hotel. Each bedroom is distinctively styled with family antiques lending character. Many rooms have commanding views of the Purbeck Hills. A 16th century clay barn has been transformed into the Boathouse, consisting of four spacious luxury suites at the river's edge.

Tastefully furnished, the drawing room, residents' lounge and intimate bar, together create a convivial atmosphere. The 'Garden Room' is open for breakfast and lunch, while dinner is served in the 'Abbots Cellar Restaurant'. There are moorings for guests arriving by boat.

Dating back to the 9th century, the market town of Wareham has more than 200 listed buildings. Corfe Castle, Lulworth Cove, Poole and Swanage are all close by.

LOCATION

Wareham is on the A351 to the west of Bournemouth and Poole. The hotel is beside the River Frome to the east of Wareham.

For route planning map of the South see page 504

"Delicious food, excellent service, wonderful atmosphere"

Donna Dawson, Boston

• Map p.504 ref: E3

Georgian mansion

RICHMOND GATE HOTEL

All the amenities of a country house pleasantly close to London

A Georgian country house, The Richmond Gate Hotel stands on the crest of Richmond Hill close to the Royal Park and Richmond Terrace. The 68 stylishly furnished, en suite bedrooms combine every comfort of the present with the elegance of the past. Several luxury four-poster rooms with a traditional ambience add the perfect touch to any stay.

Award-winning cuisine is presented at lunch and dinner in the 'Gates On The Park Restaurant' whilst breakfast is served in the less formal Victorian style conservatory which opens out onto the hotel's walled garden. Guests can also enjoy an English afternoon tea here or in the Club Lounge. Cedars Health and Leisure Club offers a wide range of facilities: 20-metre pool, spa, gym, aerobics studio, sauna, steam, health and beauty suite.

Richmond is close to central London and the West End yet in a pleasant country setting. You can shop for antiques in the narrow lanes, visit the Victorian theatre, take a boat along the Thames or walk through the Royal Park with its herds of deer.

Health and Beauty Weekends and Heritage Breaks including one attraction cost from £198.

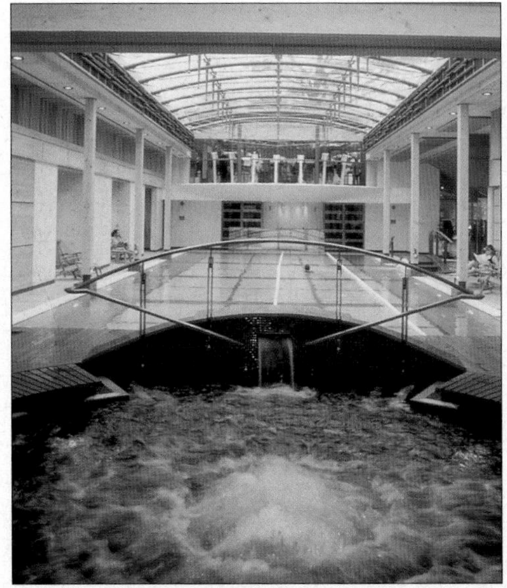

LOCATION

7 miles from London Heathrow Airport. From the M25, via the M4 motorway and Kew Bridge (or M3 and A316), into Richmond. First left up Richmond Hill.

Richmond Hill, Richmond-upon-Thames, Richmond, Surrey SO41 8LR

Telephone 020 8940 0061
Fax 020 8332 0354

E-mail: *richmond@bestloved.com*

GENERAL MANAGER
Graham Marskell

ROOM RATES

9 Singles	£145
58 Doubles/Twins	£172
1 Suite	£202

Includes full breakfast, use of adjoining leisure club and VAT

CHARGE/CREDIT CARDS

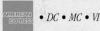

• DC • MC • VI

RATINGS & AWARDS
R.A.C. ★★★★
A.A. ★★★★ ❀❀ 74%

FACILITIES
On site: *Gardens, croquet, indoor pool, gym, sauna, jacuzzi, steam room, aerobics, health & beauty, crèche, Licensed for weddings*
4 meeting rooms/max 80 people
Nearby: *Boating, golf, riding, fishing*

RESTRICTIONS
No facilities for disabled guests
No pets

ATTRACTIONS
Hampton Court Palace, Kew Palace & Botanical Gardens, Richmond Royal Park, Twickenham, Wimbledon

AFFILIATIONS
Corus & Regal Hotels

NEAREST
MAJOR CITY:
London - 7 miles/30 mins

MAJOR AIRPORT:
London Heathrow - 7 miles/30 mins

RAILWAY STATION:
Richmond - 1 mile/5 mins

RESERVATIONS
Toll free fax in UK: 0800 387546
Quote ***Best Loved***

ACCESS CODES
APOLLO/GALILEO UI 22152
SABRE/ABACUS UI 25533

• Map p.504 ref: E2

" A wonderful place - wonderful people - wonderful time, not far from home in miles but a different peaceful world. Thank you "

R D Higgis, Bank of England, London

ST MICHAEL'S MANOR

16th century lakeside hotel

St Michael's Village, Fishpool Street, St Albans, Hertfordshire AL3 4RY

Telephone 01727 864444
Fax 01727 848909

E-mail: *stmichaels@bestloved.com*

OWNERS
Newling Ward Family

GENERAL MANAGER
Richard Newling Ward

ROOM RATES

3 Singles	*£110 - £145*
18 Doubles/Twins	*£145 - £195*
1 Four-poster	*£235*
1 Suite	*£295*

Includes full breakfast, newspaper and VAT

CHARGE/CREDIT CARDS

• MC • VI

RATINGS & AWARDS
E.T.C. ★★★ Silver Award
R.A.C. ★★★ Dining Award 2
A.A. ★★★ ❀ 76%

FACILITIES
On site: *Garden, croquet, fishing*
Licensed for weddings
3 meeting rooms/max 20 people
Nearby: *Golf, fitness, tennis, riding, fishing, water skiing, yachting*

RESTRICTIONS
Limited facilities for disabled guests
No pets

ATTRACTIONS
Abbey, Knebworth House, Roman Museum, Hatfield House, RAF Museum, Whipsnade Zoo

AFFILIATIONS
Independent

NEAREST
MAJOR CITY:
St Albans - 1/4 mile/10 mins
MAJOR AIRPORT:
London Heathrow - 25 miles/45 mins
RAILWAY STATION:
St Albans City - 1 mile/10 mins

RESERVATIONS
Toll free in US: 800-544-9993

ACCESS CODES
AMADEUS HK LTMSTH
APOLLO/GALILEO HT 69464
SABRE/ABACUS HK 25783
WORLDSPAN HK STMIS

Village charm and hidden lakeside gardens in historic St Albans

In the shadow of Verulamium, ancient Roman heart of St Albans, and the imposing abbey and cathedral named for the Roman soldier who became Britain's first Christian martyr in 209 AD, the gentle curve of Fishpool Street winds through the picturesque heritage district of St Michael's Village. Here, St Michael's Manor fronts five acres of beautiful gardens arranged around a peaceful lake and shaded by mature trees.

The original manor was built on medieval foundations for the Gape family in around 1512, and the site of the family's tannery business was discovered at the bottom of the lake during the drought of 1976. The manor has been harmoniously altered and extended over the centuries but remains rich in character and architectural detail while offering an enviable degree of comfort and unparalleled service to leisure and business travellers alike. The charming bedrooms have been thoughtfully supplied with games, books and magazines, many feature fine antiques and some have views over the garden. The notable Terrace Room restaurant with its ornate Victorian conservatory specialises in seasonally-influenced British regional cooking, and guests will find one of the finest selections of malt whiskys outside Scotland in the Garden Bar.

LOCATION

By road, M1/M25 or M4/M40 motorways. By train 20 minutes from London's Kings Cross - short taxi ride from St Albans station.

Planning a wedding reception? Turn to 'Meeting Facilities' on page 476

" A delightful experience 'oft to be repeated "

Nina Howe, Basingstoke

• *Map p.504 ref: C4*

Waterside hotel

SALTERNS HOTEL

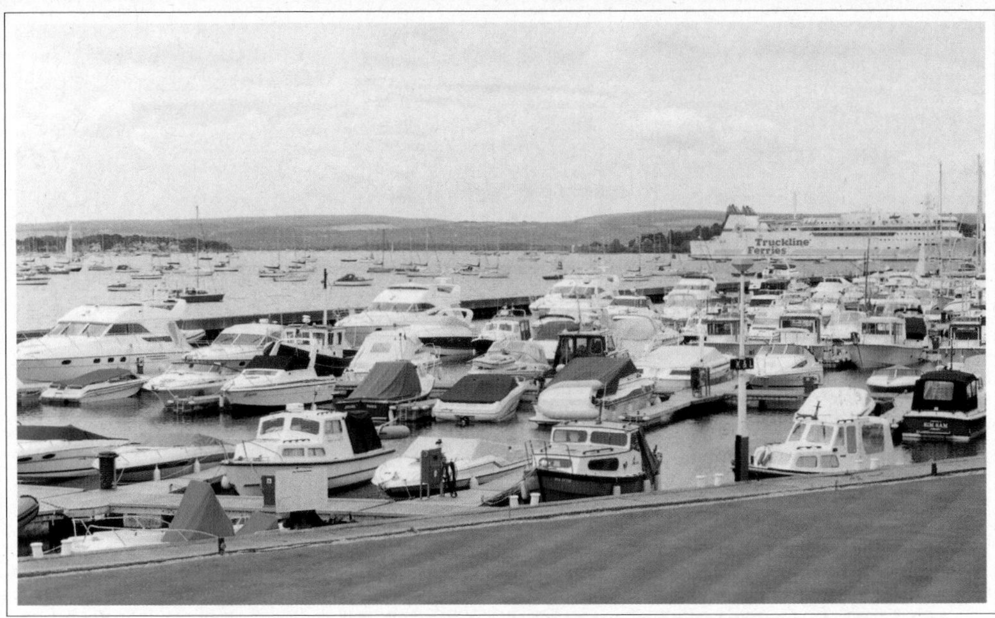

Romantic dining and a room with a glorious view of Poole Harbour

Salterns Hotel has certainly picked a glorious location: right on the edge of Poole Harbour. As if this isn't enough to tempt you, it also ranks as one of the top three star hotels in the country.

You are made welcome from the moment you enter the hotel and you soon begin to appreciate what makes it such an attractive place to visit. It has its own waterside patio, lawn and pretty borders of carefully kept shrubs.

At its heart is the waterside bar in which to enjoy not just the drink or the company but the compelling view of the harbour. There are 20 themed bedrooms offering high standards of comfort with all the extras to enhance your stay and, of course, they all enjoy that stunning view.

Dinner in the candlelit restaurant is a romantic affair; peachy table cloths, fluted peach starched napkins and food that has earned two AA Rosettes for the past seven years. Shellies Bistro is more informal where the emphasis is on seafood caught daily by the hotel's own fishing boat.

But, at the end of the day, as you gaze at the sunset across the harbour, you have to reflect on your good fortune at having found such a place.

LOCATION

Leave Poole in the direction of Sandbanks, B3369. After approximately 1½ miles turn right into Salterns Way at Lilliput.

Salterns Way, Poole, Dorset BH14 8JR

Telephone 01202 707321
Fax 01202 707488

***E-mail:** salterns@bestloved.com*

OWNERS

Beverley Helliwell-Smith and John Smith

ROOM RATES

10 Singles £86
10 Doubles/Twins £106
Includes VAT

CHARGE/CREDIT CARDS

• DC • MC • VI

RATINGS & AWARDS

R.A.C. ★★★ Dining Award 2
A.A. ★★★ ❀❀ 80%

FACILITIES

***On site:** Garden, heli-pad*
Licensed for weddings
3 meeting rooms/max 120 people
***Nearby:** Golf, fishing*

RESTRICTIONS

No facilities for disabled guests
Pets by arrangement

ATTRACTIONS

Corfe Castle, Stonehenge, Thomas Hardy country, Poole pottery

AFFILIATIONS

Best Western

NEAREST

MAJOR CITY:
Poole

MAJOR AIRPORT:
London Heathrow - 100 miles/2½ hrs
Hurn - 8 miles/30 mins

RAILWAY STATION:
Poole - 2 miles/10 mins

RESERVATIONS

Direct with hotel
*Quote **Best Loved***

ACCESS CODES

SABRE/ABACUS BW 16339

SOUTH

• Map p.504 ref: E3

“ The porter was a prince. The night manager was equally fantastic. You prepared a special late night meal and drinks for us. Truly magnificent service, above and beyond! ”

David, Nancy and Emily Takashima, Frankfort, IL, USA

SIR CHRISTOPHER WREN'S HOUSE

Historic house

Thames Street, Windsor, Berkshire SL4 1PR

Telephone 01753 861354
Fax 01753 860172

E-mail: *wren@bestloved.com*

HOTEL MANAGER

Rupert Spurgeon

ROOM RATES

11 Singles	£155
33 Doubles/Twins	£205
21 Executive rooms	£250
5 Suites	£305
7 Apartments	£305

Includes service and VAT

CHARGE/CREDIT CARDS

• DC • MC • VI

RATINGS & AWARDS

E.T.C. ★★★ Gold Award
R.A.C. ★★★
A.A. ★★★ ❀❀ 75%

FACILITIES

On site: *Riverside gardens, terrace*
Licensed for weddings
11 meeting rooms/max 90 people
Nearby: *Golf, riding, fishing, fitness, tennis, water skiing, Thames River cruises*

RESTRICTIONS

No facilities for disabled guests
No pets

ATTRACTIONS

Windsor Castle, Eton, Legoland, Thorpe Park, Henley on Thames, Royal Ascot Races, London

AFFILIATIONS

The Wren's Hotel Group
Preston's Global Hotels
Grand Heritage Hotels

NEAREST

MAJOR CITY:
Windsor - ¼ mile/3 mins
MAJOR AIRPORT:
London Heathrow - 7 miles/20 mins
RAILWAY STATION:
Windsor Central - ½ mile/5 mins

RESERVATIONS

Toll free in US: 800-544-9993
Quote ***Best Loved***

ACCESS CODES

AMADEUS UI LHR300
APOLLO/GALILEO UI 95105
SABRE/ABACUS UI 243762
WORLDSPAN UI 40753

SOUTH

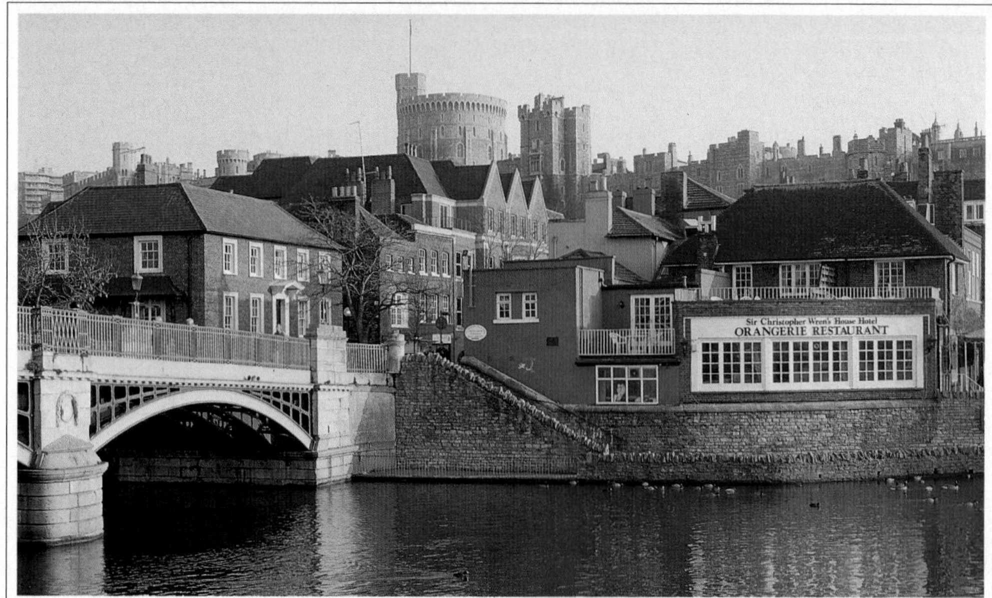

Architect-designed, and what an architect!

In 1676 Sir Christopher Wren, architect of St Paul's Cathedral, built this house. Wren was born in Windsor; his father was Dean of Windsor. This house was Wren's own private retreat. Many original features are still proudly visible, among them a fine alabaster fireplace in the drawing room.

Within the past year, all 71 bedrooms have been refurbished in keeping with Wren's original style and 7 fully serviced, self catering apartments have been added. The house is fascinating to explore. Elegant public rooms lead to a light, leafy conservatory and out on to the river terrace. The conservatory houses the hotel's restaurant where meals are prepared freshly and imaginatively.

Just a stone's throw away is a towpath along an attractive stretch of the River Thames. The regal skyline of Windsor Castle towers above. There are plenty of interesting sights and shops within strolling distance, with the antiques centres of Eton just across the bridge. Within a short drive are Henley on Thames, Legoland, Royal Ascot races and Thorpe Park. So is London, with the 51 churches that Wren built after the 1666 Great Fire, and Oxford with Wren's Sheldonian Theatre.

LOCATION

In the heart of Windsor. 20 minutes from London, the hotel is close to M4 (exit 6) and within easy reach of M40, M3 and M25 motorways. The M25 links to M1, M2, M11, M20 and M23.

“ The Spread Eagle of Midhurst, that oldest and most revered of all the prime inns of this world ”

Hilaire Belloc

• Map p.504 ref: E4

Hotel and Health Spa THE SPREAD EAGLE HOTEL & SPA

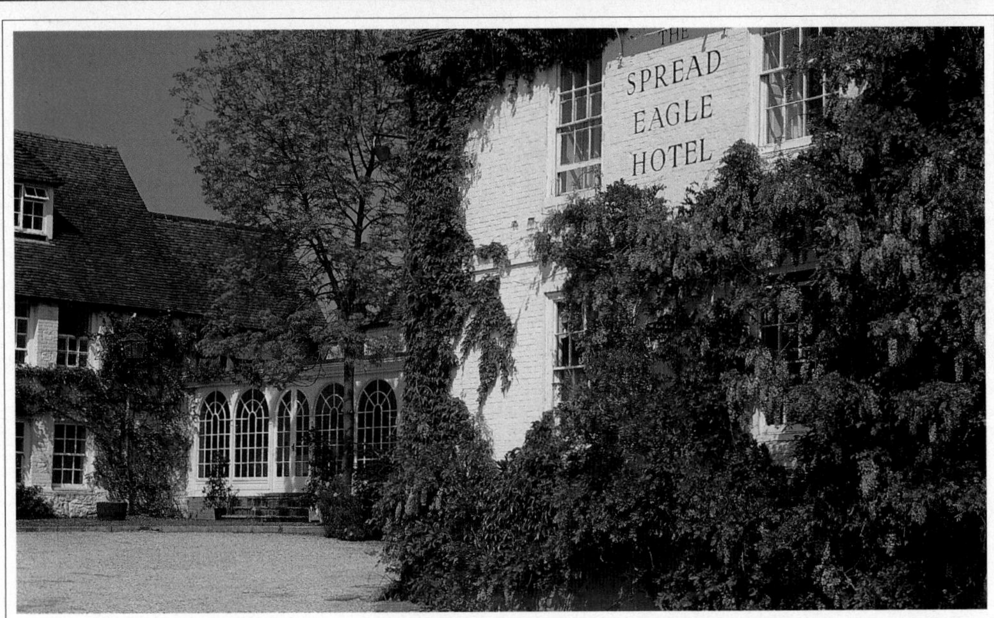

This famous and historic hotel has been welcoming guests since 1430

The Spread Eagle is one of England's oldest hotels, dating back to 1430. Successive influences have been reflected both in the architecture and the decorative features; superb, heavy polished timbers, Flemish stained glass windows and Tudor bread ovens are amongst them. Whilst the past makes this hotel the venerable character it is, recent changes have dramatically increased its appeal: a conservatory lounge has been added along with two new bedroom suites. There is now an outdoor terrace and a conference centre but the pride of the Spread Eagle is the Aquila Club which, eschewing tradition, offers the very latest in health, beauty and fitness facilities.

For all that, history lives here; you get British cooking at its traditional best served in the restaurant with its coppered inglenook fireplace and dark oak beams. The bedrooms match the mood with co-ordinated fabrics and antique furnishings but with modern facilities added.

The 17th century Jacobean Hall is available for meetings or maybe a medieval banquet with minstrels and all! There is a secluded courtyard flanked by climbing roses and clematis.

There are many stately homes in the area, Chawton, Jane Austen's home, and the attractions of Chichester are within easy reach.

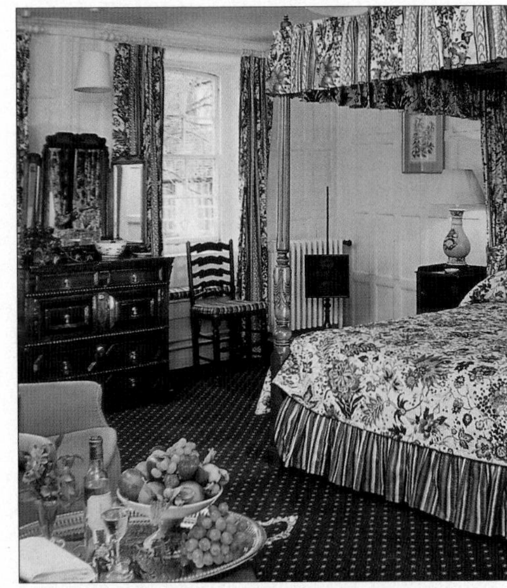

LOCATION

Situated in the old and historic town of Midhurst, The Spread Eagle can be found just off the A272 near the old market square.

South Street, Midhurst, West Sussex GU29 9NH

Telephone 01730 816911
Fax 01730 815668

E-mail: *spread@bestloved.com*

OWNERS

Sandy and Anne Goodman

GENERAL MANAGER

Andrew Brockett

ROOM RATES

Single occupancy	*£80 - £180*
31 Doubles/Twins	*£110 - £210*
6 Four-posters	*£180 - £210*
2 Suites	*£180 - £210*

Includes full breakfast and VAT

CHARGE/CREDIT CARDS

• DC • MC • VI

RATINGS & AWARDS

A.A. ★★★ ❀❀ 74%

FACILITIES

On site: *Garden, indoor pool, health spa*
Licensed for weddings
5 meeting rooms/max 80 people
Nearby: *Golf, riding*

RESTRICTIONS

No facilities for disabled guests

ATTRACTIONS

Chawton, Goodwood House, Petworth, Cowdray polo, Arundel town and castle, Uppark Country House

AFFILIATIONS

Grand Heritage Hotels

NEAREST

MAJOR CITY:
London - 52 miles/1½ hrs

MAJOR AIRPORT:
London Gatwick - 40 miles/50 mins
London Heathrow - 46 miles/1 hr

RAILWAY STATION:
Haslemere - 8 miles/10 mins

RESERVATIONS

Toll free in US: 888-93-GRAND
*Quote **Best Loved***

ACCESS CODES

AMADEUS UI PMESEH
APOLLO/GALILEO UI 48885
SABRE/ABACUS UI 38367
WORLDSPAN UI 40636

• Map p.504 ref: E3

"We were very pleased with all the arrangements and in particular with the meal. The service, setting and ambience were all first class"

Aidan McKeon, Allied Irish Bank

STOKE PARK CLUB

Palladian clubhouse

Park Road, Stoke Poges, Buckinghamshire SL2 4PG

Telephone 01753 717171
Fax 01753 717181

E-mail: *stokepark@bestloved.com*

GENERAL MANAGER

Mark Godfrey

ROOM RATES

Single occupancy	£245 - £595
13 Doubles/Twins	£245
4 Executive Doubles/Twins	£285
3 Suites	£365 - £1,100

Includes service and VAT

CHARGE/CREDIT CARDS

 • DC • JCB • MC • VI

RATINGS & AWARDS

Independent

FACILITIES

On site: *Garden, croquet, golf, tennis, fishing, snooker, 27-hole golf course, heli-pad*
Licensed for weddings
8 meeting rooms/max 250 people
Nearby: *Water skiing, fitness, riding*

RESTRICTIONS

No facilities for disabled guests
No pets, guide dogs only

ATTRACTIONS

Ascot and Windsor Race Courses, Windsor Castle, Henley and Marlow, Hampton Court, Stanley Spencer Museum, Eton, London's West End

AFFILIATIONS

Leading Small Hotels of the World

NEAREST

MAJOR CITY:
London - 23 miles/35 mins

MAJOR AIRPORT:
London Heathrow - 8 miles/15 mins

RAILWAY STATION:
Slough - 3 miles/5 mins

RESERVATIONS

Toll free in US: 800-223-6800
Quote ***Best Loved***

ACCESS CODES

AMADEUS LW LON418
APOLLO/GALILEO LW 22782
SABRE/ABACUS LW 49565
WORLDSPAN LW 0418

Sybaritic luxury and 27 championship holes add up to a golfer's dream

The Stoke Park estate was first mentioned in the Domesday Book in 1086. It numbers Elizabeth I amongst its former owners, and the unfortunate Charles I was imprisoned here in 1647. Over a century later, the magnificent Palladian mansion seen today was designed by George III's architect, James Wyatt, for John Penn, grandson of the founder of Pennsylvania. The landscaped parkland was the work of 'Capability' Brown and Humphry Repton in the late-18th century.

In 1908, 'Pa' Lane Jackson, founder of the renowned Corinthian Sporting Club, purchased the estate and set about creating Britain's finest parkland golf course with designer Harry Colt (of Wentworth and Muirfield fame). Stoke Park Club was firmly established long before James Bond played his high stakes game against Goldfinger here, and 007 made a repeat visit in Tomorrow Never Dies.

Stoke Park Club has just 20 bedrooms offering a sumptuous degree of comfort. Marble bathrooms, huge beds and fabulous views are just the beginning; some rooms boast open fires and terraces too. Guests enjoy the same exacting standards of service, food and wine offered to club members, and the use of meeting rooms, tennis courts, and the 250-year-old fishing lake. Golfer or not, your stay here will be unforgettable.

LOCATION

From M4 junction 6 take A355 towards Beaconsfield. After 2½ miles turn right at double mini-roundabout on to B416 (Park Road). Stoke Park is 1¼ miles on the right.

"The staff could not have been more helpful. Nothing we have asked for has caused any problems. We have been treated with friendly efficiency throughout our stay"

Margaret Hawkes, Bristol

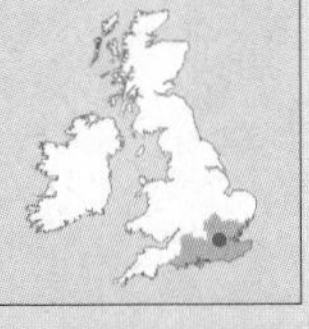

• Map p.504 ref: E3

Stately Home

TAPLOW HOUSE

A stately welcome and princely comfort not an hour from London

American readers might be amused to know that 22 years before the Pilgrim Fathers landed on Plymouth Rock (1620), the Taplow House estate was given by King James I to the first Governor of Virginia. Its splendid six acres include a tree said to have been planted by Queen Elizabeth I and Europe's tallest tulip tree. The park is virtually unchanged since it was originally landscaped.

The mansion stands out of earshot, but within 15 minutes, of Heathrow Airport so providing a fitting welcome and a convenient home-from-home for our newly-arrived New World cousins. It is a fine example of Georgian classicism with Doric columns, high decorative ceilings, chandeliers and chiselled brass balusters. A recent refurbishment programme has rejuvenated the old fabric and installed the latest technology so that the period design is subtly combined with contemporary amenities and creature comforts.

This is no ordinary hotel. All the 32 luxury bedrooms could happily feature in a mega-budget period drama. And to be seated in the dining room, enjoying award-winning cuisine, is quite the stately occasion. Memories are made of this!

As you stroll like a lord through your very own estate, it is hard to believe you are so close to the capital - within an hour of London's West End. And so near Windsor, Oxford, Henley and other Royal beauty spots along the Thames Valley.

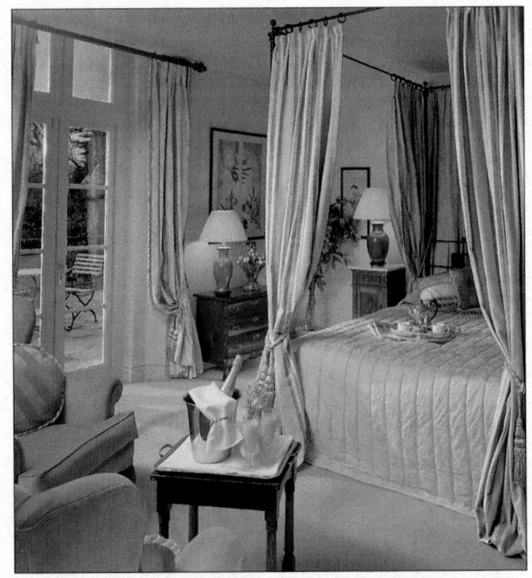

LOCATION

Exit 7/M4 on to A4 (signposted Maidenhead). Take B476 (signposted Taplow). The hotel is two hundred yards down B467 on right hand side.

Berry Hill, Taplow, Berkshire SL6 0DA

Telephone 01628 670056
Fax 01628 773625

E-mail: *taplow@bestloved.com*

GENERAL MANAGER

Hayri Alpcan

ROOM RATES

7 Singles	*£130*
18 Doubles/Twins	*£160 - £220*
3 Four-posters	*£200*
4 Suites	*£220 - £425*

Includes VAT

CHARGE/CREDIT CARDS

• DC • MC • VI

RATINGS & AWARDS

E.T.C. ★★★★

A.A. ★★★ *74%*

FACILITIES

On site: *Garden, croquet, putting green, river cruises*
Licensed for weddings
5 meeting rooms/max 150 people
Nearby: *Golf*

RESTRICTIONS

No facilities for disabled guests
No smoking in bedrooms or restaurant
No pets

ATTRACTIONS

Windsor Castle, Legoland, Royal Ascot, Henley-on-Thames, Thorpe Park, Windsor Races, boating on the Thames

AFFILIATIONS

The Wren's Hotel Group
Preston's Global Hotels

NEAREST

MAJOR CITY:
London - 20 miles/45 mins

MAJOR AIRPORT:
London Heathrow - 15 miles/30 mins

RAILWAY STATION:
Maidenhead - 3 miles/5 mins

RESERVATIONS

Toll free in US: 800-544-9993
Quote ***Best Loved***

ACCESS CODES

AMADEUS UI LHR100
GALILEO UI 94922
SABRE UI 19742
WORLDSPAN UI 40754

Thinking of pampering yourself? See the 'Health & Beauty' index on page 472

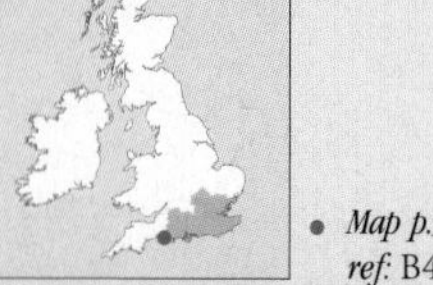

• Map p.504 ref: B4

“The perfect small hotel...I have had the good fortune to eat at some of the world’s best restaurants, and I have never tasted a soufflé as delicious as Andrea’s”

Val Hennessy, Daily Mail

THATCH LODGE HOTEL

Thatched cottage

The Street, Charmouth, Near Lyme Regis, Dorset DT6 6PQ

Telephone 01297 560407
Fax 01297 560407

E-mail: *thatchlodge@bestloved.com*

OWNERS

Christopher J Worsfold and Andrea Ashton-Worsfold

ROOM RATES

3 Doubles/Twins	£78 - £94
1 Half-tester	£100
1 Four-poster	£100
1 Suite	£120

Includes full breakfast and VAT

CHARGE/CREDIT CARDS

JCB • MC • VI

RATINGS & AWARDS

E.T.C. ◆◆◆◆◆ *Gold Award*

A.A. ◆◆◆◆◆ ❀❀

The Sunday Times Golden Pillow Award ’99

FACILITIES

On site: *Garden*

Nearby: *Golf, sea fishing, fossil hunting, tennis, coastal walking, riding*

RESTRICTIONS

No smoking throughout hotel
No children or pets
Closed Jan - mid Mar
Office open all year

ATTRACTIONS

Lyme Regis, Dorset Heritage Coast, Thomas Hardy’s Cottage, Forde Abbey, Parnham House, Abbotsbury Gardens, Athelhampton House

AFFILIATIONS

Independent

NEAREST

MAJOR CITY:
Exeter - 31 miles/45 mins

MAJOR AIRPORT:
London Heathrow - 140 miles/3 hrs
Exeter - 31 miles/40 mins

RAILWAY STATION:
Axminster - 3 miles/5 mins

RESERVATIONS

Direct with hotel
Quote ***Best Loved***

ACCESS CODES

Not applicable

SOUTH

Lyme Regis, the delight of the film makers, harbours this divine surprise!

Thatch Lodge Hotel was built in 1320 as a monk’s retreat for nearby Forde Abbey. Its thatch roof, pink cobb walls, hanging baskets and oak beams make it as pretty as a picture postcard within this Area of Outstanding Natural Beauty. Lovingly restored by resident owners, it boasts antiques and family art. Each of the six bedrooms proudly displays an identity all of its own with quality and comfort the only features in common. The health conscious will appreciate the no smoking policy making Thatch Lodge the perfect place to unwind.

The food is outstanding. Andrea, a talented chef, cooks modern English cuisine with a dedication to fresh local produce. In late summer and autumn, guests can indulge in grapes hand-picked from the hotel’s 200-year-old vine - the perfect complement to a well-ripened blue-veined Stilton.

Charmouth, a coastal village dating back to the Iron Age, is a World Heritage Site. In 1811, the skeleton of a 100-million year-old ichtyosaurus was discovered and is now in London’s Science Museum. To this day its jurassic fossil strewn beach and cliffs still yield exceptional finds. Nearby is Lyme Regis with its romantic Cobb Harbour made famous by Jane Austen’s Persuasion and John Fowles’ French Lieutenant’s Woman. Frequently used in films for its unspoilt Dorset charm, productions include: Emma, Tom Jones, Tess and Restoration.

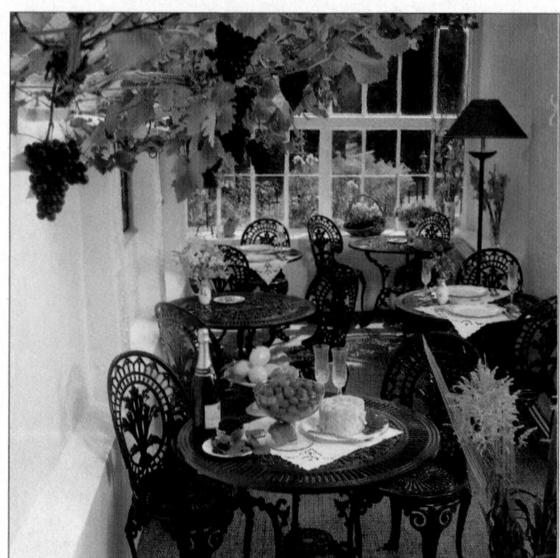

LOCATION

Charmouth is clearly signposted off the A35, 2 miles east of Lyme Regis.

Looking for an hotel with a golf course on site? See our ‘Golf Guide’ on page 478

"The place is so magical that I was unable to resist proposing to my girlfriend"

M Thompson, Addlestone, Surrey

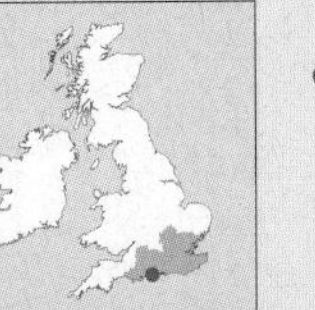

• *Map p.504 ref: D4*

17th century cottage

THATCHED COTTAGE HOTEL

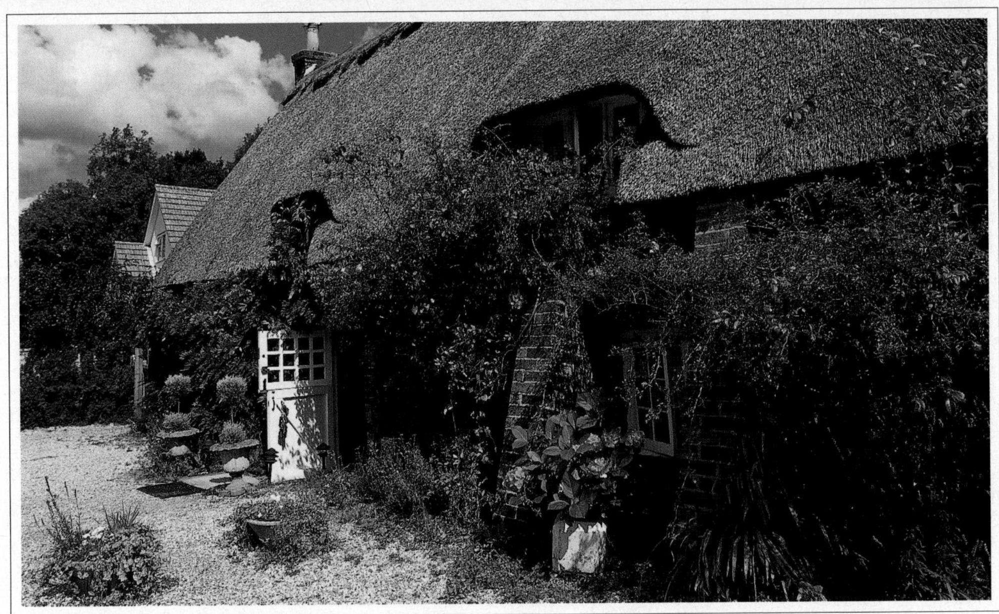

A cottage for the happy few

The Thatched Cottage nestles in a pretty village in the heart of the New Forest. Built in 1629 it is today one of Britain's most romantic small hotels. It is run by the Matysik family who bring well over a century's combined experience of managing top hotels to the personal care of their guests. The five bedrooms, decorated with antiques and objets d'art, combine old world charm with the modern essentials.

The quality and individuality of the dinners have won numerous awards, and are much acclaimed by the British and international press. Local specialities include New Forest venison and mushrooms. The newest recruit to the Matysik family is a leading chef from Japan, she adds Japanese flare to the signature dishes. Gastronomic highlights are late breakfast in bed and wicker picnic hampers. The hotel with its tea garden was recently named as one of England's top 50 establishments for afternoon tea.

The New Forest is the oldest of England's great forests, but it was new to William the Conqueror when he decreed it as his hunting ground in 1079. The Forest verderers look after its unique wildlife. The Conqueror's red deer and the protected New Forest ponies stroll freely when you walk through the beautiful 200 square miles of forest and heath land.

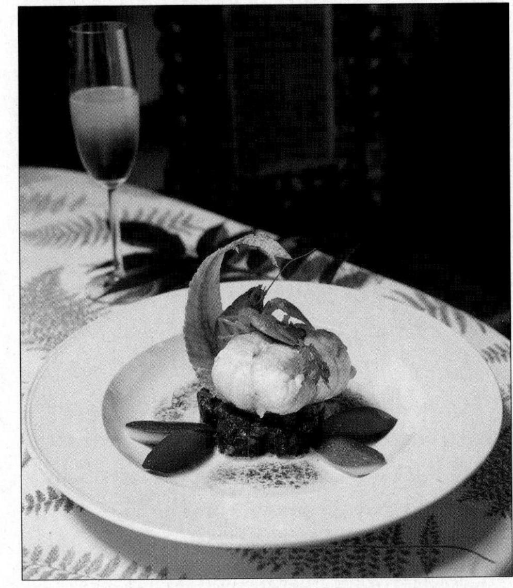

LOCATION

Take exit 1 from the M27 and drive south on the A337 to Brockenhurst. Turn right onto Brookley Road just before the level crossing.

16 Brookley Road, Brockenhurst, Hampshire SO42 7RR

Telephone 01590 623090
Fax 01590 623479

***E-mail:** thatchedcottage@bestloved.com*

OWNERS

The Matysik Family

ROOM RATES

2 Doubles/Twins	*£90 - £115*
2 Four-posters	*£120 - £145*
1 Suite	*£135 - £155*

Includes full breakfast, complimentary newspaper and VAT

CHARGE/CREDIT CARDS

JCB • MC • VI

RATINGS & AWARDS

A.A. ◆◆◆◆◆ ❀❀

FACILITIES

***On site:** Garden*

***Nearby:** Golf, fishing, yachting, riding, mountain biking*

RESTRICTIONS

No children under 10 years
Closed 3 Jan - 12 Feb

ATTRACTIONS

New Forest, Stonehenge, Beaulieu Motor Museum, Winchester, Salisbury, Exbury Gardens, Isle of Wight

AFFILIATIONS

Independent

NEAREST

MAJOR CITY:
Southampton - 12 miles/20 mins

MAJOR AIRPORT:
London Heathrow - 76 miles/1½ hrs

RAILWAY STATION:
Brockenhurst - ½ mile/5 mins

RESERVATIONS

Direct with hotel
*Quote **Best Loved***

ACCESS CODES

Not applicable

For a portrait of this region see page 308

Map p.504 ref: C4

"Very cosy and comfortable rooms and the cooking was exquisite"

Mr & Mrs A Conway

THE THREE LIONS

19th century farmhouse

Stuckton, Fordingbridge, Hampshire SP6 2HF

Telephone 01425 652489
Fax 01425 656144

E-mail: threelions@bestloved.com

OWNERS

Mike and Jayne Womersley

ROOM RATES

Single occupancy	£59 - £70
3 Doubles/Twins	£70 - £85

Includes continental breakfast and VAT

CHARGE/CREDIT CARDS

• MC • VI

RATINGS & AWARDS

E.T.C. ♦♦♦♦♦ Gold Award

A.A. ♦♦♦♦♦ ❀❀❀

FACILITIES

On site: Garden, jacuzzi/hot tub

Nearby: Golf, river and sea fishing, water skiing, yachting, tennis, fitness centre, hunting/shooting, riding, cycling

RESTRICTIONS

No pets, guide dogs only
No children under 3 years
No smoking in dining room or bedrooms
Closed end Jan - early Feb

ATTRACTIONS

Salisbury Cathedral, Avebury, Stonehenge, Brockenhurst, Burley, New Forest, Beaulieu Motor Museum, Exbury Gardens, Broadlands

AFFILIATIONS

Independent

NEAREST

MAJOR CITY:
Salisbury - 14 miles/20 mins

MAJOR AIRPORT:
London Heathrow - 83 miles/1½ hrs

RAILWAY STATION:
Salisbury - 16 miles/20 mins

RESERVATIONS

Direct with hotel
Quote **Best Loved**

ACCESS CODES

Not applicable

Stunning gourmand cooking on the edge of the New Forest

Built in 1863 as a farmhouse in the hamlet of Stuckton on the edge of the New Forest, the Three Lions is now a destination for enthusiasts of good food. It is personally owned and run by Mike and Jayne who live on the premises. Mike learnt his craft over ten years in two and three-star Michelin restaurants in France and Britain. His personal style of cuisine is based on the best local produce available most of it organically grown and reared in the vicinity. They succeeded well enough to be named Restaurant of the Year a few years ago by The Times. The 180 bin wine list is compiled from personally tasted and selected wines from all over the world.

The rooms are very comfortable and quiet having views over the manicured gardens in which there is a Catalina whirlpool spa open all year round for your enjoyment. The Three Lions is a comfortable environment in which to relax, a place where you can come and go as you please without the formality of an hotel.

The Three Lions is ideally situated for exploring the New Forest. The inviting sandy beaches of the South Coast or Studland's nature reserve are half an hour away. A little further afield are Salisbury, Poole, Rockbourne, Winchester and many picturesque Dorset villages which you can visit in a day and still be back for dinner.

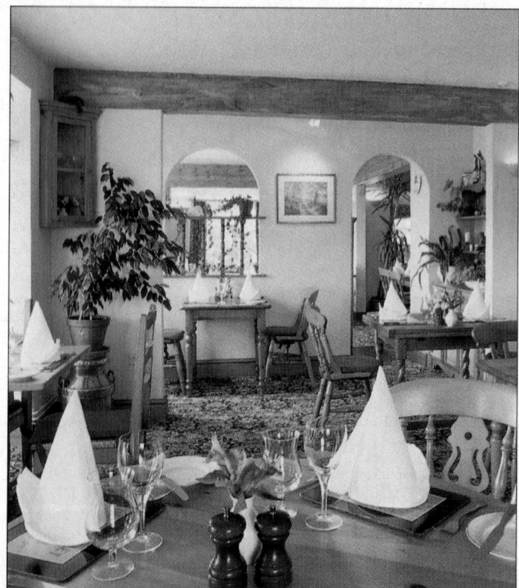

LOCATION

Located ½ mile east of Fordingbridge on the A338 or B3078. From the Q8 garage follow the brown tourists signs marked Three Lions.

"As luxurious as we had hoped but much more friendly than we'd ever expected"

Mr & Mrs Poppy, England

• Map p.504 ref: D3

Country mansion

TYLNEY HALL

A luxurious private party awaits all those who enter this stately home

Arriving at Tylney Hall in the evening, you can imagine that you are arriving to a party at a private stately home. This gracious country manor, set in 66 acres of stunning landscaped gardens, typifies the great houses of the past.

Originally built in 1561, the present mansion dates from the beginning of this century when no expense was spared in creating a highly-prized country seat with panelling of Italian walnut and a Rococo ceiling from the Gramini Palace. At the same time, the famous Gertrude Jekyll 'Water Gardens' and Weir Schulz 'arches' transformed the grounds. Little has changed and today, aperitifs are taken in the oak-panelled library bar and award-winning cuisine is served in the Oak Room restaurant, complemented by fine wines and conscientious service.

An 18-hole golf course borders the hotel and exclusive leisure facilities include indoor and outdoor heated swimming pools, multi-gym, sauna, tennis, croquet, snooker, hot air ballooning, archery and clay pigeon shooting. These facilities are being extended in early 2001 to include a new beauty treatment room and hair salon. Horse-riding is offered locally. The wooded trails are ideal for rambling or jogging. The cathedral town of Winchester, the country home of the Duke of Wellington and the picturesque village of Hartley Wintney are nearby. London and Windsor are an hour's drive away.

LOCATION

5 minutes from Exit 5 of the M3.
15 minutes from Exit 11 of the M4.
30 minutes from the M25.

**Rotherwick, Hook,
Hampshire RG27 9AZ**

**Telephone 01256 764881
Fax 01256 768141**

E-mail: *tylney@bestloved.com*

GENERAL MANAGER

Rita Mooney

ROOM RATES

Single occupancy	*£125 - £385*
83 Doubles/Twins	*£159 - £210*
20 Suites	*£270 - £410*
7 Four-posters	*£270 - £410*

Includes full breakfast, newspaper service and VAT

CHARGE/CREDIT CARDS

• *DC* • *JCB* • *MC* • *VI*

RATINGS & AWARDS

E.T.C. ★★★★ Gold Award
R.A.C. Gold Ribbon ★★★★
Dining Award 3
A.A. ★★★★ ❀❀
A.A. Courtesy & Care Award
Southern Tourist Board
Hotel of the Year Award 2000

FACILITIES

On site: *Garden, croquet, tennis, sauna, indoor/outdoor pools, snooker, gym, golf, clay pigeon shooting, archery, ballooning, heli-pad*
Licensed for weddings
12 meeting rooms/max 100 people
Nearby: *Riding*

RESTRICTIONS

No facilities for disabled guests
No pets

ATTRACTIONS

Winchester, Windsor Castle, Stonehenge, Salisbury, Jane Austen's House, Highclere Castle, Sandham Memorial Chapel

AFFILIATIONS

Small Luxury Hotels

NEAREST

MAJOR CITY:
Winchester - 30 miles/30 mins
MAJOR AIRPORT:
London Heathrow - 35 miles/40 mins
Eastleigh - 35 miles/40 mins
RAILWAY STATION:
Basingstoke - 6 miles/10 mins

RESERVATIONS

Toll free in US/Canada: 800-525-4800
Quote ***Best Loved***

ACCESS CODES

AMADEUS LX LONTHH
APOLLO/GALILEO LX 21653
SABRE/ABACUS LX 19817
WORLDSPAN LX SOUTH

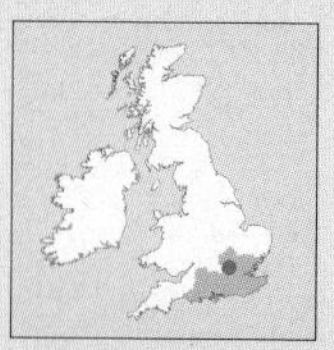

• Map p.504 ref: D2

" The accommodation and food were excellent. Nothing was too much trouble for any of the staff and the whole weekend couldn't have been any better "

Barbara & Peter Flowers, Hemel Hempstead

VILLIERS HOTEL

17th century coaching inn

3 Castle Street, Buckingham, Buckinghamshire MK18 1BS

Telephone 01280 822444
Fax 01280 822113

E-mail: *villiers@bestloved.com*

GENERAL MANAGER

Henry Scrase

ROOM RATES

3 Singles	£105
31 Doubles/Twins	£120
8 Premium doubles	£138
4 Suites	£160

Includes full breakfast, service and VAT

CHARGE/CREDIT CARDS

• DC • MC • VI

RATINGS & AWARDS

E.T.C. ★★★ Silver Award
R.A.C. ★★★ Dining Award 1
A.A. ★★★ ❀❀ 72%

FACILITIES

On site: *Licensed for weddings*
6 meeting rooms/max 250 people
Nearby: *Complimentary use of local leisure club*

RESTRICTIONS

None

ATTRACTIONS

Althorpe, Sulgrave Manor, Stowe Gardens, Woburn Abbey, Claydon House, Silverstone

AFFILIATIONS

Independent

NEAREST

MAJOR CITY:
Milton Keynes - 10 miles/20 mins

MAJOR AIRPORT:
London Heathrow - 50 miles/1¾ hrs

RAILWAY STATION:
Milton Keynes - 10 miles/20 mins

RESERVATIONS

Direct with hotel
Quote **Best Loved**

ACCESS CODES

Not applicable

A 400-year tradition of hospitality continues unabated

The antique walls of the Villiers Hotel literally ooze history - and a few ghostly visitors if the stories are to be believed. In Cromwellian times, this 400-year-old hostelry was Buckingham's most important coaching inn, and Cromwell himself is reputed to have billeted his troops here during a visit in 1643. Perhaps one of these guests stayed behind, as an expert in the supernatural detected the presence of a large bearded man with a sword and red sash after a series of unexplained incidents in an upstairs bedroom! A ghostly grey-suited gentleman has also been spotted in the library bar.

While steeped in history, the Villiers is up to the minute when it comes to guests' comfort. Warm pastel tones, soft fabrics, and fresh flowers create a restful ambience in the main building. Across the courtyard is Henry's Restaurant and the splendid old Swan & Castle bar, where the dark oak panelling, flagstone floor and large inglenook fireplace hark back to the inn's Jacobean origins.

Around Buckingham, sightseeing opportunities range from the grandeur of Blenheim Palace and the dreaming spires of Oxford to Sulgrave Manor, home of George Washington's ancestors. Just four miles from Buckingham, the Stowe Landscape Gardens are renowned for their 32 temples. Now in the grounds of an exclusive private school, the gardens are open in the summer holidays. For motor racing enthusiasts, a few miles further on lies Silverstone Race Circuit.

LOCATION

In the town centre. Castle Street is to the right of the Old Town Hall.

"You really do have a 'gem' in The Vineyard"

Raymond Blanc

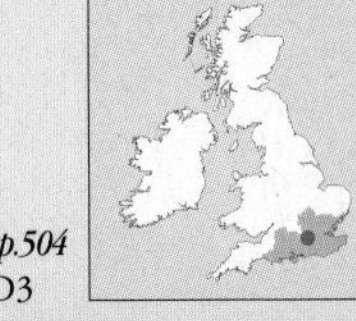

Map p.504 ref: D3

Restaurant with suites

THE VINEYARD AT STOCKCROSS

Stockcross, Newbury, Berkshire RG20 8JU

Telephone 01635 528770
Fax 01635 528398

E-mail: *vineyard@bestloved.com*

OWNER
Sir Peter Michael

MANAGING DIRECTOR
Andrew McKenzie

ROOM RATES

11 Singles	£158
9 Doubles/Twins	£188 - £276
11 Suites	£276 - £393
2 Four-posters	£511

Includes soft drinks, early morning tea, newspaper and VAT

CHARGE/CREDIT CARDS

 • DC • MC • VI

RATINGS & AWARDS
E.T.C. ★★★★★ Gold Award
R.A.C. Gold Ribbon ★★★★ Dining Award 4
A.A. ★★★★ ❀❀❀
A.A. Wine Award

FACILITIES
On site: *Garden, indoor pool, sauna, spa bath, steam room, gym*
Licensed for weddings
2 meeting rooms/max 60 people
Nearby: *Golf, fishing, tennis, hunting/shooting, riding*

RESTRICTIONS
No children under 5 years in restaurant
No facilities for disabled guests
No pets

ATTRACTIONS
Oxford, Cotswolds, Bath, Newbury Racecourse, Highclere Castle, Windsor Castle

AFFILIATIONS
The Celebrated Hotels Collection
Small Luxury Hotels

NEAREST
MAJOR CITY:
Oxford - 29 miles/30 mins
MAJOR AIRPORT:
London Heathrow - 50 miles/1 hr
RAILWAY STATION:
Newbury - 2 miles/15 mins

RESERVATIONS
Toll free in US: 800-322-2403
Toll free in UK: 0800-VINEYARD
Quote **Best Loved**

ACCESS CODES
AMADEUS LX EWYVST
APOLLO/GALILEO LX 18934

A fusion of sublime food and wine in an elegant environment

The Vineyard at Stockcross was opened in 1998 by Sir Peter Michael, founder of Classic FM radio. This restaurant with suites is a showcase for the finest Californian wines, including those from his renowned Peter Michael Winery. Head Sommelier, Edoardo Amadi, has created a Burke's Peerage of wines in a wide, innovative wine list. Awarded four red stars and three rosettes by the AA, the classic French cuisine has a British twist with pure flavours, fresh ingredients and subtle design to match the excellence of the wine list.

The Vineyard at Stockcross is more than a fusion of sublime food and wine. It was built in the 19th century as the country retreat of the Lords of the Manor of Stanford Dingley. The purpose-built restaurant matches the original warm Bath stone, featuring full-length windows set between contemporary pillars. Suites and rooms provide an elegant, spacious and well-appointed environment. They have been designed in French provincial style with both authentic French and contemporary furniture. Another stimulating feature of The Vinyard, is the collection of paintings and sculptures.

The new Vineyard Spa is a paragon of luxury and tranquillity in which to relax or exercise. Altogether an indulgence for all the senses.

LOCATION

From Exit 13 of the M4, take A34 to Newbury. At first roundabout, take Hungerford exit (A4), at the second head for Stockcross. The hotel is on the right.

SOUTH

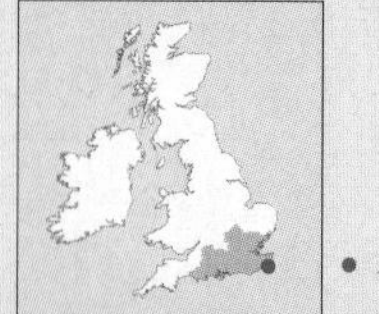

• Map p.504 ref: G3

" A peaceful haven in a hectic world "

Viscount Richard Girling, Battersea

WALLETT'S COURT

Country house hotel

Westcliffe, St Margaret's-At-Cliffe, Dover, Kent CT15 6EW

Telephone 01304 852424
Fax 01304 853430

E-mail: *walletts@bestloved.com*

OWNERS
Christopher, Leonora and Gavin Oakley

GENERAL MANAGER
Colin Kirkwood

ROOM RATES

Single occupancy	£70 - £110
11 Doubles/Twins	£80 - £100
2 Four-posters	£100 - £130
4 Suites	£130 - £150

Includes VAT

CHARGE/CREDIT CARDS

• DC • JCB • MC • VI

RATINGS & AWARDS
E.T.C. ★★★ Silver Award
R.A.C. ★★★ Dining Award 2
A.A. ★★★ ❀❀ 76%

FACILITIES
On site: *Garden, croquet, tennis, sauna, indoor pool, jacuzzi, gym, steam room, golf practice area, heli-pad*
3 meeting rooms/max 60 people
Nearby: *Golf, fishing, hunting/shooting, yachting, windsurfing, surfing*

RESTRICTIONS
No facilities for disabled guests
No pets

ATTRACTIONS
Dover Castle, Canterbury, Leeds Castle, Eurostar to Paris

AFFILIATIONS
Independent

NEAREST
MAJOR CITY:
Canterbury - 15 miles/20 mins
MAJOR AIRPORT:
London Gatwick - 60 miles/1 hr
RAILWAY STATION:
Dover Priory - 3 miles/10 mins
FERRY PORT:
Dover - 3 miles/10 mins

RESERVATIONS
Direct with hotel
Quote **Best Loved**

ACCESS CODES
Not applicable

Historic connections and inspired cooking on Europe's doorstep

Wallett's Court is owned and run by the Oakley family. They first discovered it, near derelict, on a summer's day in 1975. It was listed as the Manor of Westcliffe in the Domesday Book and its history embraces such luminaries as Bishop Odo of Bayeux, Queen Eleanor of Castille, historian Edward Gibbon, Admiral Lord Aylmer and Prime Minister William Pitt.

Today it is a family home and country house hotel with 17 large, comfortable bedrooms. The style is homely: you can settle in the old leather sofa by a blazing fire, hear the grandfather clock ticking, or relax in the conservatory.

The indoor pool, sauna, steam and fitness rooms, as well as the luxurious health spa, housed within a Kentish barn, add an attractive dimension to the hotel. As indeed, does its location: close to Canterbury and on the doorstep of the continent - the ever expanding Cruise Terminal is only 4 miles away.

The surrounding area is designated as being of Outstanding Natural Beauty. A mile away is St Margaret's Bay and on a clear day you can see France. On others, you can visit Leeds Castle, Canterbury Cathedral and the secret wartime tunnels of Dover Castle.

LOCATION

From M2/A2 or M20/A20 follow signs for A258 Deal. After Swingate Inn take right turn to Westcliff, St Margaret's. Hotel is 1 mile down road on the right.

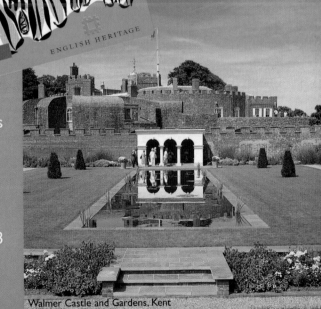

london

Centre of attention: For two weeks each summer, Centre Court at the All England Lawn Tennis Club in Wimbledon is the focus of the tennis world. Kew Gardens (inset) has been the focus of the botanical world since the 1840s.

london

For a thousand years, London has been the centre of England's government, finance and culture. The list of things to see and do is endless: museums, galleries, palaces, parks, shops, stores and bargain basements. The places that are 'in' this year won't be next year - and that's part of the excitment. Once it was Carnaby Street, now it is Covent Garden with its newly opened Opera House. London takes on a fresh lease of life every evening. A slice of history comes alive with just about any ticket you buy for a West End theatre. And there's another world of alternative music and theatre, all in Time Out magazine - gigs, concerts, little theatres and pubs. There are the thousands of places to eat from cafes, diners, bistros, brasseries and everything to the classiest of restaurants on earth. And they offer culinary styles as diverse as the world serving fresh food from as far away as the Pacific. Sport, too, is important in London. Lawn Tennis at Wimbledon; football at Wembley Stadium; Cricket at Lords and The Oval, the Oxford and Cambridge boat race on the Thames. London's many famous parks and gardens provide a welcome respite from the excitement and noise of the country's capital.

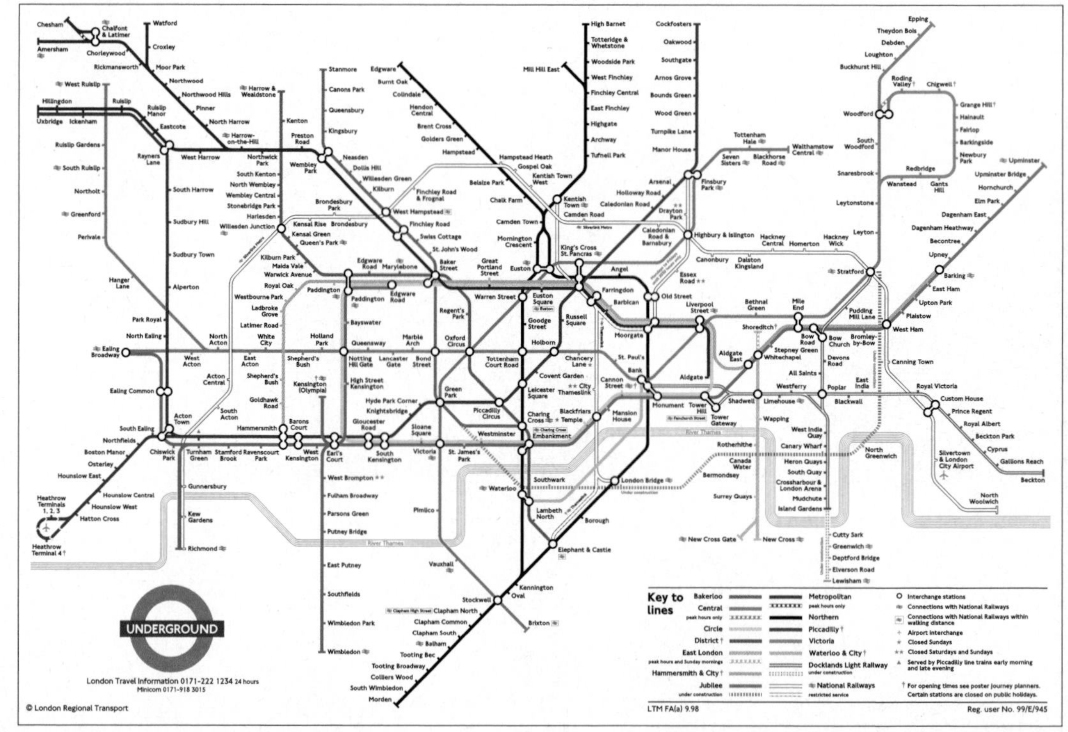

All mapped out: The award-winning London Underground map was designed in the early 1930's and still has the freshness of contemporary design.

Rare plantsmen

Two of England's most famous gardeners are buried in the churchyard of St Mary-at-Lambeth, which now houses the Museum of Garden History in their honour. John Tradescant father and son spearheaded a horticultural revolution in the 17th century, introducing plants from their travels to Russia, America and southern Europe, many of which can be admired in the period style garden.

Howzat!

First contested in 1876, the England v. Australia Ashes Test Cricket Series returns to north London's Lord's Ground in July.

Messing about on the river

In the wake of ultimate Olympian Steve Redgrave's rowing gold in Sydney, the River Thames is entitled to share a little glory as the hero's training ground. It is also the setting for the traditional Oxford v. Cambridge University Boat Race each spring between the bridges at Putney and Barnes.

Secret garden

Tucked away down a quiet side street, the Chelsea Physic Garden was founded in 1673, making it the second oldest botanical garden in England. Cotton seeds from Chelsea were first sent to the Americas back in 1732.

Cultural beacon

The wide open spaces, terrific views, woodlands and ponds of Hampstead Heath offer a real escape from the bustle of the city. Here, Kenwood House sits on a rise above the Lake and harbours the exceptional Old Master paintings of the Iveagh Bequest including works by Rembrandt, Gainsborough and Vemeer. Summer concerts are held in the grassy amphitheatre.

An Italianate idyll

Chiswick House in west London is probably England's finest Palladian building inspired by Palladio's own Villa Rotunda outside Vicenza. The classical landscaped gardens reflect a similarly graceful Italian influence ornamented with statues from the Emperor Hadrian's villa at Tivoli, a temple and sunken garden.

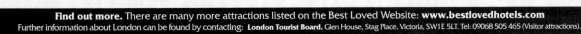

Garden Guide

Eltham Palace
Eltham SE9 5QE
Tel: 020 8294 2548
An intriguing garden in the grounds of the stylish and elegant Eltham Palace

Hampton Court Palace
Surrey KT8 9AU
Tel: 020 8781 9500
One of Britain's greatest and most important treasures housing the world famous maze

Museum of Garden History
Lambeth Palace Road, London SE1 7LB
Tel: 020 7401 8865
Fascinating museum, well worth going out your way for. Open from early Mar to mid Dec

Syon Park
Brentford TW8 8JF
Tel: 020 8560 0883
The home of the Duke of Northumberland with landscaping by Capability Brown

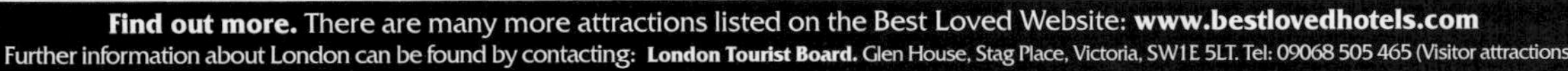

Find out more. There are many more attractions listed on the Best Loved Website: **www.bestlovedhotels.com**
Further information about London can be found by contacting: **London Tourist Board.** Glen House, Stag Place, Victoria, SW1E 5LT. Tel: 09068 505 465 (Visitor attractions).

“The entire staff was gracious and the facilities were impeccable”

Kim & Mark Riley, Englewood, NJ, USA

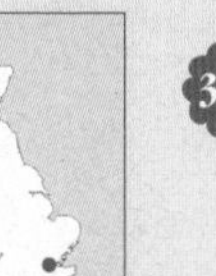

• Map p.506
ref: H3

Georgian town house

THE ACADEMY TOWN HOUSE

Top marks and top value in the bookish quarter of central London

Mention Bloomsbury and the mind conjures up names like Virginia Woolf, Lytton Strachey and J M Keynes; English writers, aesthetes and philosophers whose contribution to 20th-century British culture is widely acknowledged today. The presence of the British Museum lends the area the hush of a library, but the bright lights of Covent Garden and the West End are within a few minutes' walk.

The Academy, The Bloomsbury Town House, occupies five Georgian terraced houses in the heart of this secluded yet accessible corner of London. At the rear, there are private gardens where guests can take tea or drinks in summer, a conservatory for cooler days, and the newly refurbished hotel has a delightful country feel that is both welcoming and elegant. There is a choice of cosy lounges and an informal basement restaurant. Luxurious bedrooms benefit from gleaming new bathrooms, pure linen bedsheets, carefully chosen ornaments and prints, and Internet access. Each one is completely different so regular guests develop particular favourites.

The Academy has one very special trick up its sleeve: it can devote one whole house with eight guest bedrooms and exclusive use of a garden and the library for a private party. It is the only hotel in London to offer this unique feature, perfect for a corporate 'do' or a wedding party.

LOCATION

The hotel is in Bloomsbury on Gower Street equidistant from Tottenham Court Road and Goodge Street underground stations.

21 Gower Street,
London WC1E 6HG

Telephone 020 7631 4115
Fax 020 7636 3442

E-mail: *academy@bestloved.com*

GENERAL MANAGER
Margaret Kavanagh

ROOM RATES

12 Singles	*£153*
26 Doubles/Twins	*£179*
11 Studio suites	*£240*

Includes full breakfast, newspaper and VAT

CHARGE/CREDIT CARDS

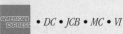

• DC • JCB • MC • VI

RATINGS & AWARDS
Independent

FACILITIES
On site: *Courtyard gardens*
1 meeting room/max 25 people
Nearby: *Leisure centre*

RESTRICTIONS
No pets, guide dogs only
No facilities for disabled guests

ATTRACTIONS
British Museum, Theatreland, Covent Garden, National Gallery, Bloomsbury squares

AFFILIATIONS
Utell International

NEAREST
MAJOR CITY:
London

MAJOR AIRPORT:
London Heathrow - 15 miles/45 mins
London Gatwick - 40 miles/1 hr

RAILWAY STATION:
King's Cross/Euston - ½ mile/5 mins
Goodge Street Underground

RESERVATIONS
Toll free in US: 800-678-3096
*Quote **Best Loved***

ACCESS CODES
AMADEUS UI LONACA
APOLLO/GALILEO UI 62068
SABRE/ABACUS UI 20496
WORLDSPAN UI 41062

“ Ascott Mayfair is ranked among the top three serviced apartments in London ”

Janet Ho, Sunday Times

ASCOTT MAYFAIR

Mayfair apartments

49 Hill Street, Mayfair, London W1J 5NB

Telephone 020 7499 6868
Fax 020 7499 0705

E-mail: *ascott@bestloved.com*

GENERAL MANAGER
Christine Malcolm

ROOM RATES

7 Studios	£195 - £230
27 1 Bedroom apts	£285 - £335
21 2 Bedroom apts	£415 - £488
1 3 Bedroom apts	£580 - £680

Includes continental breakfast and VAT

CHARGE/CREDIT CARDS

• DC • JCB • MC • VI

RATINGS & AWARDS
Awards Independent

FACILITIES
On site: *Garden, gym, steam room, solarium, sauna, business services, use of The Hothouse Health Club*
2 meeting rooms/max 50 people
Nearby: *Riding, boating, tennis, squash, parking*

RESTRICTIONS
No facilities for disabled guests
No pets

ATTRACTIONS
Hyde Park, Piccadilly Circus, Harrods, Leicester Square, Selfridges, Oxford Street, Buckingham Palace, Covent Garden

AFFILIATIONS
The Celebrated Hotels Collection

NEAREST
MAJOR CITY:
London
MAJOR AIRPORT:
London Heathrow - 15 miles/40 mins
London Gatwick - 30 miles/1¼ hrs
RAILWAY STATION:
Victoria - 2 miles/10 mins
Green Park Underground

RESERVATIONS
Toll free in US: 800-322-2403
Quote **Best Loved**

ACCESS CODES
AMADEUS UI LONASC
APOLLO/GALILEO UI 75023
SABRE/ABACUS UI 14921
WORLDSPAN UI 25130

Your residence in stylish Mayfair

With high quality accommodation, a wide range of facilities and excellent service, the Ascott Mayfair is a very desirable address in London. You will enjoy all the facilities and services of a luxury hotel, with the privacy, comfort and relaxed environment of a home.

The studios and the one, two and three-bedroom apartments are all luxuriously furnished. Each has a lounge, dining and study area, kitchen and bathroom, satellite TV and computer games, video, music system, and telephone. Breakfasts, concierge and daily maid service are all included. The building's Art Deco heritage achieves an elegant and refined style that is welcoming and relaxing. Original artworks in the Ascott's exclusive Club will delight you.

Mayfair's attractions stem from the elegance of its Georgian architecture and its central location. It is bound by Hyde Park, the department stores of Oxford Street and Regent Street and Piccadilly. It is a perfect place for shopping; international fashion houses rub shoulders with small specialist shops. Almost every kind of cuisine is available around Shepherd's Market. The Royal Academy, the Museum of Mankind and, of course, the West End theatres are close at hand.

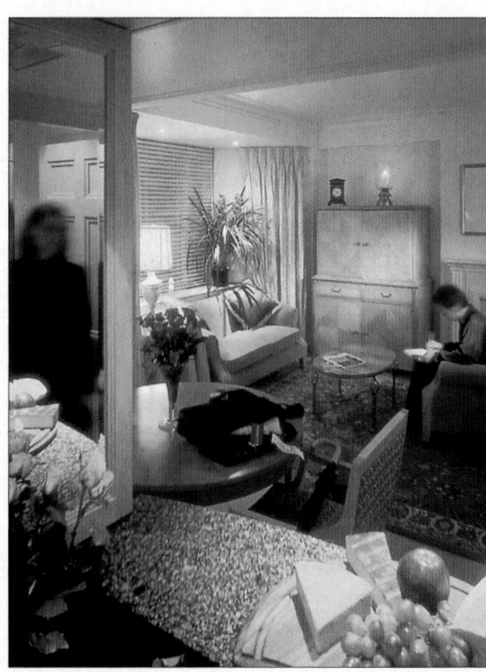

LOCATION

Between Berkeley Square and Park Lane.

" It's my personal perfection "

Omar Sharif

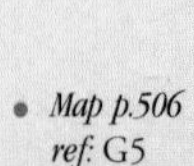

Luxury hotel & apartments

ATHENÆUM HOTEL

An hotel of distinctive charm with a warm and friendly welcome

The Athenæum Hotel & Apartments is unusual in that it is not only in private hands so that it has a distinct personality all of its own, it commands possibly the finest location in central London: on Piccadilly, right opposite Green Park, close to the fashionable shops of Bond Street and Mayfair and a pleasant stroll from the city's vibrant theatre and restaurant scene.

The whole property has recently undergone a refurbishment programme. Nothing has escaped the attention of the designers from the luxurious furnishings to the discreet installation of IT wizardry enabling the international traveller to keep in touch with affairs around the world.

Discretion! Now there's a word that epitomises The Athenæum. Appreciated by those who need to escape the attention of the world media, the hotel is a kind of sanctuary and nothing expresses this better than the restaurant, Bullochs at 116. Here, even the recluse can feel at home dining as well as in any of the voguish eateries nearby.

In addition to a choice between bedrooms and suites, The Athenæum offers a number of unique luxury apartments which benefit from 24-hour room service and all the other facilities of the hotel including the free use of the excellent health spa which has a gym, sauna and steam room.

Your first stay will not be the last.

LOCATION

On Piccadilly, in Mayfair overlooking Green Park.

116 Piccadilly, Mayfair, London W1J 7BJ

Telephone 020 7499 3464
Fax 020 7493 1860

E-mail: *athenaeum@bestloved.com*

GENERAL MANAGER

Jonathan Critchard

ROOM RATES

27 Singles	*£280 - £320*
84 Doubles/Twins	*£300 - £350*
12 Suites	*£425*
34 Apartments	*£425 - £575*

Includes VAT

CHARGE/CREDIT CARDS

• DC • MC • VI

RATINGS & AWARDS

R.A.C. Gold Ribbon ★★★★
Dining Award 3
A.A. ★★★★ ❀

FACILITIES

On site: *Health & beauty, gym, jacuzzi, sauna*
4 meeting rooms/max 50 people
Nearby: *Riding*

RESTRICTIONS

No facilities for disabled guests
No pets

ATTRACTIONS

Buckingham Palace, Royal Parks, Harrods, Westminster Abbey, Houses of Parliament, Theatreland, Bond Street, Tower of London

AFFILIATIONS

Small Luxury Hotels

NEAREST

MAJOR CITY:
London

MAJOR AIRPORT:
London Heathrow - 15 miles/45 mins
London Gatwick - 30 miles/1¼ hrs

RAILWAY STATION:
Victoria - ¼ mile/10 mins
Green Park Underground

RESERVATIONS

Toll free in US: 800-335-3300
or 800-525-4800
Quote ***Best Loved***

ACCESS CODES

AMADEUS LX LONATH
APOLLO/GALILEO LX 61396
SABRE/ABACUS LX 871
WORLDSPAN LX LONTA

Looking for an hotel with a golf course on site? See our 'Golf Guide' on page 478

• Map p.506 ref: E6

"It is so nice to keep seeing familiar faces amongst the staff and to be recognised"

Clare Fellows, Kingston, Ontario

BASIL STREET HOTEL

Traditional English hotel

Basil Street, Knightsbridge, London SW3 1AH

Telephone 020 7581 3311
Fax 020 7581 3693

E-mail: basil@bestloved.com

GENERAL MANAGER

David Brockett

ROOM RATES

29 Singles	from £150
44 Doubles/Twins	from £223
5 Family rooms	from £294

Includes VAT

CHARGE/CREDIT CARDS

• JCB • MC • VI

RATINGS & AWARDS

E.T.C. ★★★ Silver Award
R.A.C. ★★★ Dining Award 1
A.A. ★★★ 70%
Investors in People

FACILITIES

On site: *Restaurant, business centre, The Parrot Club for women*
3 meeting rooms/max 40 people
Nearby: *Pool, gym, riding, tennis*

RESTRICTIONS

Limited facilities for disabled guests
No pets in public rooms

ATTRACTIONS

Harrods, Buckingham Palace, Victoria & Albert Museum, Royal Academy of Art

AFFILIATIONS

Preston's Global Hotels

NEAREST

MAJOR CITY:
London
MAJOR AIRPORT:
London Heathrow - 18 miles/45 mins
London Gatwick - 30 miles/1¼ hrs
RAILWAY STATION:
Victoria - 1¼ miles/15 mins
Knightsbridge Underground

RESERVATIONS

Toll free in US: 800-544-9993
or 800-448-8355
Quote **Best Loved**

ACCESS CODES

AMADEUS UI LONBAS
APOLLO/GALILEO UI 18513
SABRE/ABACUS UI 264
WORLDSPAN UI 3896

The Basil - an excellent hotel steeped in tradition

The Basil is an island of hospitality in an increasingly brusque, modern life, and that is why their guests come back again and again. Many of their returning guests have said that The Basil is just like coming home. Tradition is respected, nothing is contrived and there is warmth and friendliness in the air. The interior is full of English and Oriental antiques, and at every turn there is something to delight the eye. Plants and flowers are in abundance.

Each of the 78 comfortable bedrooms is different in shape and decor and regular visitors are given their favourites whenever possible.

Fully furnished rooms are available for private parties. The Basil is large enough to contain all the amenities expected in a cosmopolitan hotel, yet not too large to become impersonal.

General Manager David Brockett and his colleagues, carry on the traditions which have become synonymous with The Basil. They will do their utmost to ensure that your visit is an enjoyable one. Few world class hotels in a city centre are so perfectly situated for both business and pleasure.

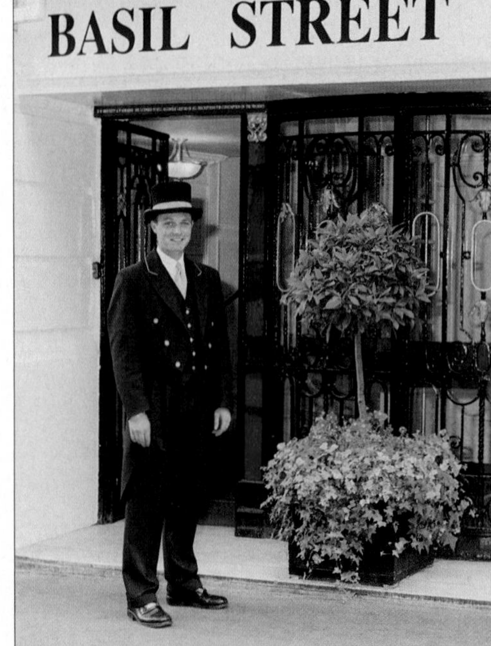

LOCATION

In Knightsbridge, a few steps away from Harrods, Harvey Nichols and Knightsbridge Underground Station.

"If you want to be treated as an individual, stay with the people who know how"

Dyan Cannon

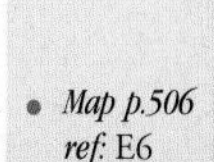

• *Map p.506 ref: E6*

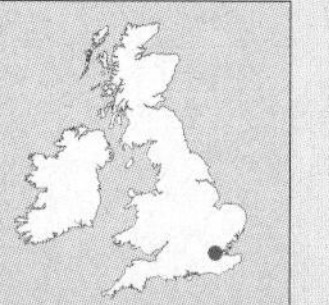

Private house hotel — THE BEAUFORT

Great value, service and much more awaits you in London's Knightsbridge

High quality, individual attention, the best value for money and of course wonderful staff are what makes The Beaufort so successful. 100 yards from Harrods in a quiet tree-lined Victorian square, The Beaufort offers everything it can to make guests feel comfortable and at home.

Complimentary breakfast in the rooms is served on fine bone Wedgwood china with solid silver cutlery – hot croissants and rolls, fresh orange juice and steaming coffee. The rooms are beautifully decorated in bright colours – and are air-conditioned. Each room is provided with Swiss chocolates, shortbread and a decanter of brandy.

A complimentary limousine is available to and from the airport for guests booking junior suites. The hotel's direct dial telephone service provides guests with their own private number plus the use of a personal fax. All rates include service, and there is no tipping. There is CNN, a video and cassette library, and portable CD player. There is a closed front door – only guests have front door keys.

The Beaufort is home to the world's largest collection of over 400 original English floral watercolours. All drinks including champagne and cream teas are served free of charge in the drawing room.

LOCATION

Quietly situated in the heart of Knightsbridge.

33 Beaufort Gardens, Knightsbridge, London SW3 1PP

Telephone 020 7584 5252
Fax 020 7589 2834

E-mail: *beaufort@bestloved.com*

GENERAL MANAGER

Jackie Kennedy

ROOM RATES

3 Singles	*£182 - £212*
5 Superior singles	*£194 - £212*
13 Doubles/Twins	*£253 - £306*
7 Junior suites	*£347 - £376*

Includes breakfast, afternoon tea, all drinks (including champagne) and VAT

CHARGE/CREDIT CARDS

• DC • MC • VI

RATINGS & AWARDS

A.A. Town House
Courvoisier's Book of the Best
Zaget - Highest Rated Hotel in London for Service (26/30)

FACILITIES

On site: *Guest's private bar*
1 meeting room/max 6 people
Nearby: *Health club & pool, riding*

RESTRICTIONS

No facilities for disabled guests
No pets

ATTRACTIONS

Harrods, Victoria & Albert Museum, Buckingham Palace

AFFILIATIONS

Independent

NEAREST

MAJOR CITY:
London

MAJOR AIRPORT:
London Heathrow - 14 miles/45 mins
London Gatwick - 30 miles/1¼ hrs

RAILWAY STATION:
Victoria - 1 mile/20 mins
Knightsbridge Underground

RESERVATIONS

Toll free fax in US: 800-548-7764
Quote ***Best Loved***

ACCESS CODES

APOLLO/GALILEO RW 16376
SABRE/ABACUS RW 31342
WORLDSPAN RW 31342

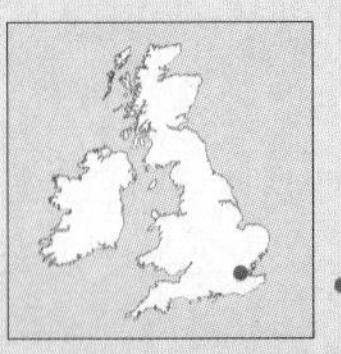

• Map p.506 ref: D7

" If ever dreams can become reality, then Blakes is where it will happen "

Nina Prommer, London

BLAKES HOTEL

Victorian mansion

33 Roland Gardens, South Kensington, London SW7 3PF

Telephone 020 7370 6701
Fax 020 7373 0442

E-mail: *blakes@bestloved.com*

OWNER
Anouska Hempel

GENERAL MANAGER
Edward Wauters

ROOM RATES

20 Doubles	*£282 - £382*
9 Suites	*£605 - £934*

Includes service and VAT

CHARGE/CREDIT CARDS

• *DC* • *MC* • *VI*

RATINGS & AWARDS
Andrew Harper's Hideaway Report
Courvoisier's Book of the Best

FACILITIES
On site: *Blakes Restaurant*
Licensed for weddings
1 meeting room/max 10 people
Nearby: *health club*

RESTRICTIONS
No facilities for disabled guests
No pets

ATTRACTIONS
South Kensington Museums, Harrods and Knightsbridge, antique shops, Christies Auction Room

AFFILIATIONS
Preferred Hotels & Resorts
The Hempel & Blakes Amsterdam

NEAREST
MAJOR CITY:
London

MAJOR AIRPORT:
London Heathrow - 15 miles/45 mins
London Gatwick - 30 miles/1¼ hrs

RAILWAY STATION:
Victoria - 1 mile/20 mins
South Kensington Underground

RESERVATIONS
Toll free in US: 800-926-3173
Quote ***Best Loved***

ACCESS CODES
APPOLLO/GALILEO PH 87401
SABRE/ABACUS PH 21718

Exclusive and stylish - the haunt of the famous

Blakes was created just over ten years ago out of two Victorian mansions in South Kensington by Anouska Hempel, the London hotelier and internationally renowned designer.

Blakes is a statement about what good design can achieve; daring and dramatic, each of the rooms are individually designed to provide the ideal blend of colour, texture and atmosphere. Respected for protecting the privacy of its clients, it's the London base for film stars, musicians and top designers. Blakes is now established as unique, the model for 'the fashionable small hotel'.

To the international business man or woman, it is convenience and efficiency: private faxes, telephone and all the other high-tech paraphernalia for modern living.

Blakes Restaurant, 'an opium den managed by Coco Chanel' has an unrivalled reputation for the originality and contents of its superb menu devised and designed by Anouska Hempel, classic cooking with oriental twists, stunning presentation and spectacular tastes ensures Blakes continues to attract critical acclaim as one of the top three restaurants in London.

LOCATION

A few minutes' walk from South Kensington tube station.

"We were made to feel so special by everyone at Blooms and this made our stay in London even more enjoyable"

A O'Hanlon, New York

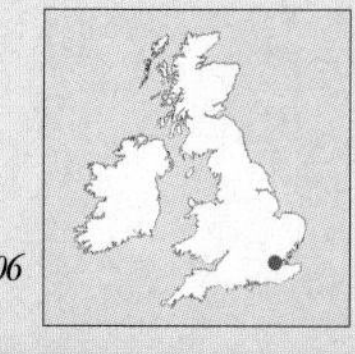
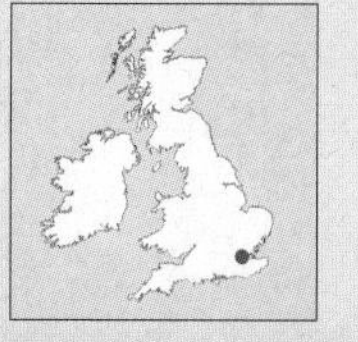

• Map p.506 ref: H3

18th century town house

BLOOMS TOWN HOUSE HOTEL

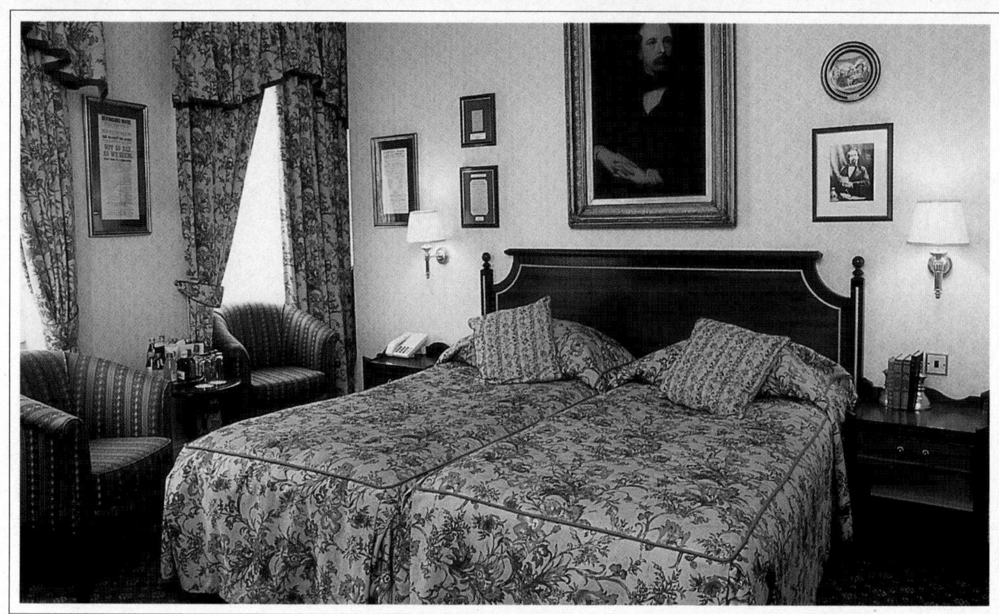

Rich heritage in the cultural heart of London

Blooms is a four-star town house hotel in an elegant 18th century house in Bloomsbury, the literary heart of London. The 27 bedrooms are individually designed to reflect the rich heritage of the hotel. All have private bathroom, satellite TV, telephone, radio, hair dryer, trouser press, tea and coffee making facilities, butler tray and 24-hour room service. The period style lounge combines comfort with the ambience of a bygone era, where guests may relax with the daily papers, select material from the library, or enjoy one of the many board games available.

Overlooking the British Museum is the hotel's own pretty walled garden, where guests can take refreshments during the summer. A breakfast buffet is available each morning, and the famous traditional English breakfast is cooked to order. Throughout the day both light snacks and a full menu are available along with an excellent wine list to complement the home style food. Bloomsbury has genteel architecture, antiquarian bookshops, London University and the splendid British Museum. Blooms Hotel is ideally situated for the department stores of Oxford Street, the historic City of London, the West End, theatreland, Covent Garden and the good food restaurants of Soho and Charlotte Street.

LOCATION

Blooms is only minutes away from Euston, King's Cross & St Pancras railway stations, and Russell Square & Holborn Underground stations - on Piccadilly line direct from Heathrow.

7 Montague Street, Bloomsbury, London WC1B 5BP

Telephone 020 7323 1717
Fax 020 7636 6498

E-mail: *blooms@bestloved.com*

MANAGER

Oliver Brown

ROOM RATES

5 Singles *£130 - £175*
22 Doubles/Twins *£195 - £205*
Includes welcome drink, newspaper, full breakfast and VAT

CHARGE/CREDIT CARDS

• *DC* • *JCB* • *MC* • *VI*

RATINGS & AWARDS

E.T.C. ★★★★
A.A. ★★★★ *Town House*

FACILITIES

On site: *Patio*
Licensed for weddings
1 meeting room/max 40 people
Nearby: *Health Club*

RESTRICTIONS

No facilities for disabled guests
No pets

ATTRACTIONS

British Museum, Theatreland, Oxford Street, Soho, Covent Garden

AFFILIATIONS

Independent

NEAREST

MAJOR CITY:
London

MAJOR AIRPORT:
London Heathrow - 16 miles/40 mins
London Gatwick - 30 miles/1¼ hrs

RAILWAY STATION:
King's Cross/Euston - ¾ mile/15 mins
Russell Square Underground

RESERVATIONS

Direct with hotel
Quote ***Best Loved***

ACCESS CODES

APOLLO/GALILEO UI 58898
SABRE/ABACUS UI 23881
WORLDSPAN UI 21436

"Friendly staff, a great location - and perfect for Harrods!"

Gloria Kenny, New York

BURNS HOTEL

Victorian house

18 - 26 Barkston Gardens,
Kensington,
London SW5 0EN

Telephone 020 7373 3151
Fax 020 7370 4090

E-mail: *burns@bestloved.com*

GENERAL MANAGER
Suzanne Martin

ROOM RATES

37 Singles	£100 - £112
63 Doubles/Twins	£124 - £138
3 Family rooms	£132 - £147
2 Deluxe Doubles/Twins	£150 - £168

Includes full breakfast and VAT

CHARGE/CREDIT CARDS

• DC • MC • VI

RATINGS & AWARDS
E.T.C. ★★★

FACILITIES
Nearby: *Fitness centre*

RESTRICTIONS
No facilities for disabled guests
No pets in public rooms

ATTRACTIONS
Royal Albert Hall, Buckingham Palace, Science Museum, Hyde Park, Natural History Museum, Knightsbridge

AFFILIATIONS
Utell International

NEAREST
MAJOR CITY:
London

MAJOR AIRPORT:
London Heathrow - 10 miles/45 mins

RAILWAY STATION:
Victoria - 2 miles/15 mins
Earls Court Underground

RESERVATIONS
Direct with hotel
Quote ***Best Loved***

ACCESS CODES
AMADEUS UI LONBUR
APOLLO/GALILEO UI 26742
SABRE/ABACUS UI 31698
WORLDSPAN UI 3260

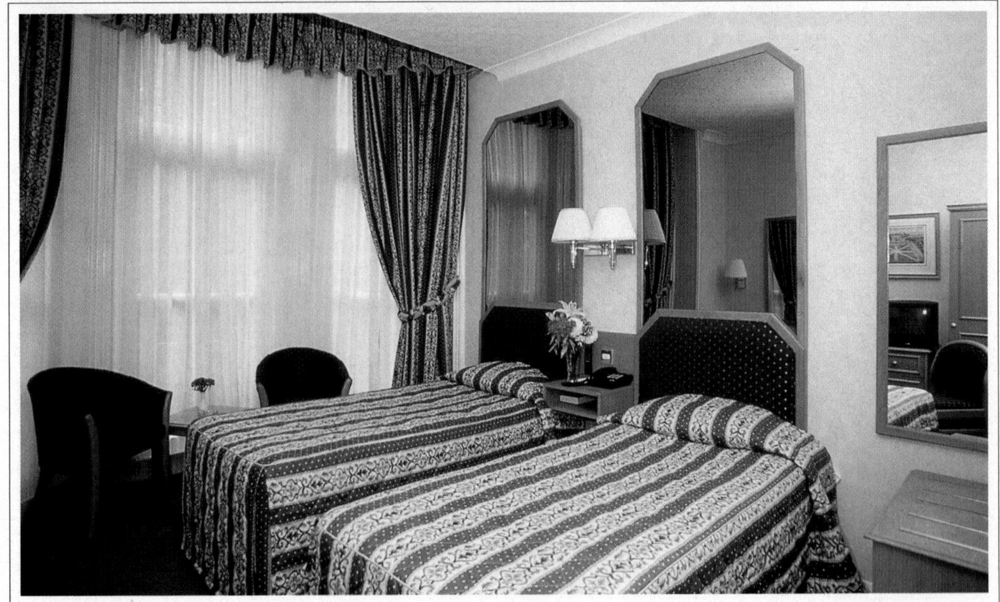

A great location and four star quality - at three star prices

For the travel weary, finding good value accommodation in major cities is an ever-increasing problem. London is no different in this regard and when you finally find a great place then it seems to lie on the very outskirts of where you want to be. Look no further, because Burns delivers on both counts, value and location.

Situated in a quiet leafy square in South Kensington, around the corner from a main line Underground Station the hotel delivers four-star quality at three star prices. The bedrooms are attractively decorated in various combinations of bright blues and vibrant yellows. The high ceilings, innovative use of mirrors and the long elegant windows give a feeling of spaciousness and light. Many generous little touches add to the overall feeling of comfort, and being exceptionally well equipped, the frequent traveller is left wanting for nothing.

Business people will enjoy its proximity to the Earls Court and Olympia Exhibition Centre. Holiday travellers or those wanting to shop London's major High Streets will find getting to and from all major attractions and museums is either a simple hop on the Tube or a short walk away.

LOCATION

Turn right out of Earls Court Tube Station and Barkston Gardens is the first road on the left.

“ It’s lovely to stay in an hotel where guests are referred to by name and not by number ”

D Theobald, New York

• Map p.506 ref: G5

Deluxe hotel

THE CHESTERFIELD MAYFAIR

Gracious living just off Berkeley Square

Named after the third Earl of Chesterfield, a noted Mayfair resident in the 18th century, this hotel combines the gracious living standards of an elegant past with every modern comfort, service and convenience.

Traditional fabrics and exquisite furnishings are featured in the nine suites, four themed rooms and 97 deluxe guest rooms, all fully air-conditioned. Guests are pampered with thoughtful personal comforts that include nightly turndown service, plush bathrobes, hairdryer, potpourri sachets, bottled mineral water and deluxe toiletries. As for technology, you can relax while watching full cable TV or see one of the many movies on demand. Great care has been taken in providing for the needs of the business traveller including generous desk space, modem/fax facilities and Internet access in most rooms.

The Restaurant's seasonal menus place emphasis on both English specialities, like table carved roasts, as well as the finest international cuisine. A highly enjoyable feature of the hotel is the resident pianist who plays nightly in the hotel's club-style Terrace Bar.

The Chesterfield is close to the famous West End theatres and nightlife, and a short stroll to famous shops, museums and landmarks. You can jog through Hyde Park or walk across Green Park to Buckingham Palace. The Chesterfield is a perfect choice for a stay in the Capital.

LOCATION

In the heart of exclusive Mayfair.

35 Charles Street, Mayfair, London W1J 5EB

Telephone 020 7491 2622
Fax 020 7491 4793

E-mail: *chesterfield@bestloved.com*

GENERAL MANAGER

Andrew Colley

ROOM RATES

11 Singles	£170 - £230
56 Doubles/Twins	£185 - £255
30 King bedded	£235 - £280
4 Themed rooms	£280 - £375
5 Junior suites	£280 - £375
4 Executive suites	£395 - £575

Includes service and VAT

CHARGE/CREDIT CARDS

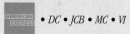

• DC • JCB • MC • VI

RATINGS & AWARDS

R.A.C. ★★★★

A.A. ★★★★ ❀ 71%

FACILITIES

On site: *Valet, 24 hour room service*
Licensed for weddings
6 meeting rooms/max 150 people
Nearby: *Use of leisure facilities*

RESTRICTIONS

No facilities for disabled guests
Pets by arrangement

ATTRACTIONS

Buckingham Palace, Bond Street, Regent Street, Piccadilly, Harrods, Royal Academy of Art

AFFILIATIONS

Red Carnation Hotels
The European Connection

NEAREST

MAJOR CITY:
London
MAJOR AIRPORT:
London Heathrow - 15 miles/45 mins
London Gatwick - 30 miles/1¼ hrs
RAILWAY STATION:
Victoria - ½ mile/10 mins
Green Park Underground

RESERVATIONS

Toll free in US: 877-955-1515
Quote ***Best Loved***

ACCESS CODES

AMADEUS UI LONCHE
APOLLO/GALILEO UI 5219
SABRE/ABACUS UI 274
WORLDSPAN UI 0327

"Beautiful and charming - lovely place, we highly recommend it"

Mr & Mrs C Ramin, San Francisco, USA

THE COLONNADE TOWN HOUSE

Victorian town house

2 Warrington Crescent, London W9 1ER

Telephone 020 7286 1052
Fax 020 7286 1057

E-mail: *colonnade@bestloved.com*

GENERAL MANAGER
Mette Cooper

ROOM RATES

17 Doubles/Twins	£165
16 Deluxe Doubles/Twins	£205
3 Four-posters	£205 - £259
7 Suites	from £259

Includes full breakfast and VAT

CHARGE/CREDIT CARDS

• DC • JCB • MC • VI

RATINGS & AWARDS
E.T.C. ★★★★ Silver Award
London Tourist Board Hotel of the Year

FACILITIES
On site: *Garden*
Nearby: *Golf, tennis, riding, squash*

RESTRICTIONS
No pets, guide dogs only
Limited facilities for disabled guests

ATTRACTIONS
Little Venice, Regents Park, Camden Market, Lords Cricket Ground, Portobello Road, London Zoo

AFFILIATIONS
The Celebrated Hotels Collection
Utell International

NEAREST
MAJOR CITY:
London

MAJOR AIRPORT:
Heathrow - 15 miles/25 mins

RAILWAY STATION:
Paddington - 1 mile/5 mins
Warwick Avenue Underground

RESERVATIONS
Toll free in US: 800-322-2403
or 800-44-UTELL
Quote ***Best Loved***

ACCESS CODES
AMADEUS UI LONMCO
APOLLO/GALILEO UI 82381
SABRE/ABACUS UI 41050

Indulgent luxury in leafy Little Venice - relaxed, convenient and good value

Contrary to expectations, five-star luxury does not have to be in the city centre - and The Colonnade, The Little Venice Town House, is the exception that proves the rule; it stands amongst the leafy gardens of Little Venice within easy reach of Piccadilly and Heathrow (25 minutes) yet it competes room-for-room on equal terms with the highest standards of service and luxury you will find anywhere in central London.

The Colonnade is new, the result of a £1.75 million conversion of an elegant Victorian mansion frequented by Sigmund Freud and birthplace of Alan Turing, breaker of the Enigma Code in WW2. The furnishings are lavish, the fabrics sumptuous, the objets d'art genuinely antique. There are only 43 bedrooms many with a four-poster bed and even a private terrace (not one central London hotel can make such a boast) and all of them have the latest e-facilities to delight the international business traveller.

The breakfast at the Colonnade is deserving of a mention. The buffet is truly a feast, for the eyes as much as the appetite, for which the hotel receives as much praise as it does for its rooms. Whilst the hotel does not serve lunch or dinner their room service menu is varied and substantial and there are at least 5 restaurants that come highly recommended within 5 minutes walk.

And the price of such indulgent luxury? Like its location - a breath of fresh air!

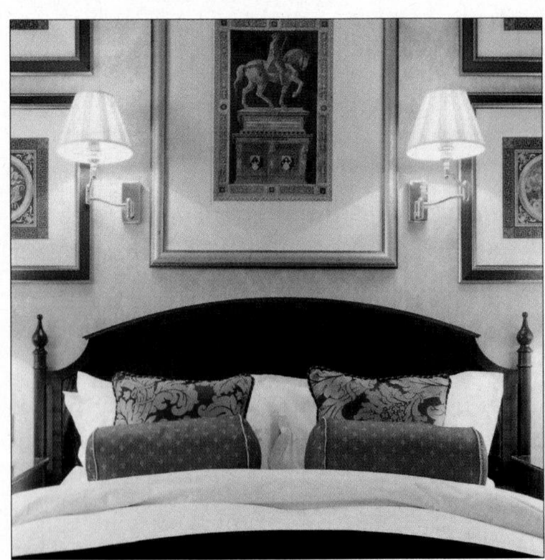

LOCATION

50 yards to Warwick Avenue Underground with direct trains to central London. 5 minutes from Paddington and the Heathrow Express.

Planning a wedding reception? Turn to 'Meeting Facilities' on page 476

"This second visit confirms my first thought, that after ten years of looking, I've finally found my London hotel"

Brent Stevens, Beverly Hills, California

THE CRANLEY

Victorian mansion

10-12 Bina Gardens, South Kensington, London SW5 0LA

Telephone 020 7373 0123
Fax 020 7373 9497

E-mail: *cranley@bestloved.com*

GENERAL MANAGER

Karen Dukes

ROOM RATES

3 Singles	*£182*
24 Doubles/Twins	*£212 - £223*
3 Four-posters	*£259*
3 Junior suites	*£247*
2 Executive suites	*£294*

Includes service and VAT

CHARGE/CREDIT CARDS

• DC • JCB • MC • VI

RATINGS & AWARDS

A.A. ★★★★

FACILITIES

On site: *Air conditioning, honesty bar, patio, internet TV's*
Nearby: *Use of local health club, pool*

RESTRICTIONS

No facilities for disabled guests
No pets

ATTRACTIONS

Harrods, Museums of South Kensington, King's Road, Chelsea, Royal Albert Hall, Buckingham Palace, Kensington Gardens, Westminster, House of Commons

AFFILIATIONS

Argyll Townhouse Hotels

NEAREST

MAJOR CITY:
London

MAJOR AIRPORT:
Heathrow - 15 miles/40 mins

RAILWAY STATION:
Victoria - 3 miles/15 mins
Gloucester Road Underground

RESERVATIONS

Toll free in US & Canada: 800-44-UTELL
*Quote **Best Loved***

ACCESS CODES

AMADEUS UI LONCRA
APOLLO/GALILEO UI 61263
SABRE UI 32652
WORLDSPAN UI 21563

An enviable pied-à-terre in Royal Kensington and Chelsea

Most first-time visitors do a double-take and recheck the address when they arrive outside The Cranley. It looks so quiet, so private, blending seamlessly into one of London's smartest residential neighbourhoods. However, closer inspection reveals the discrete gold plaque confirming that these three elegant mansion houses are indeed a hotel.

The captivating first impression is created by the bold Prussian blue lounge, where the reception arrangements are confined to an unobtrusive desk next to the honour bar. Already, you feel at home, and tempted to sink gratefully into the depths of a comfy sofa after your journey. Relieved of luggage by enthusiastic staff (who, miraculously, appear to know your name already), you'll be offered a complimentary glass of sherry or whisky, or the opportunity to relax in your room first. Most of the bedrooms have been recently refurbished in soft gold, beige and cream tones, and equipped with custom-built desks, ISDN and Internet access; some luxurious suites also boast four-posters and seating/breakfasting areas in bay windows.

A short step beyond The Cranley's front door, several excellent restaurants serve lunch and dinner, and the celebrated Victoria & Albert, Science and Natural History museums vie for your attention with world-class shopping.

LOCATION

2 minutes walk south of Gloucester Road Underground Station, just north of the Old Brompton Road.

For route planning map of London see page 506

" Your hotel was a real 'find' for us and we look forward to making The Darlington our regular home away from home "

Phil Lewis, Dallas, Texas

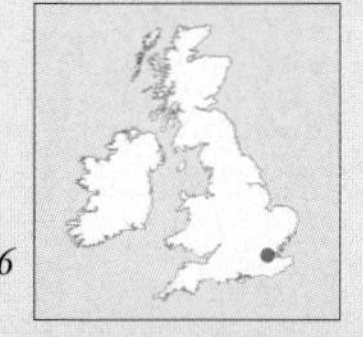

• Map p.506 ref: D4

Victorian town house

THE DARLINGTON HYDE PARK

20 minutes from Heathrow, in the centre of London, earning top marks for value

The fastest way to and from London Heathrow these days is the high speed, high tech, non-stop Heathrow Express linking the airport with Paddington Station in 15 minutes, every 15 minutes. Paddington to The Darlington is so close, you'll earn a derisory quip from a cabbie if you stop him; it's not five minutes on foot.

The other feature about The Darlington is that it is one of a new breed of places to stay in London: clean and comfortable, simple without being stark, and provisioned with all the facilities you need as a business or leisure traveller. It is centrally located but in a quieter part of town, living up to the highest standards of hotel keeping but without the frills. Result: great value! You are free to enjoy your stay without the need of paramedical support when you check out.

The Conservatory Restaurant serves a freshly cooked traditional breakfast or you can help yourself to a Continental Buffet. For lunch and dinner, there are many excellent places on the doorstep with a cosmopolitan choice of cuisine. If you are more ambitious, the glitter of the West End and the World's highest concentration of theatres, concert halls and galleries are about 20 minutes away by cab. The Darlington may well appeal beyond the budget-conscious traveller, its convenience and comfort factors get top marks.

LOCATION

5 minutes walk from both Paddington Station (Heathrow Express Terminal) and Lancaster Gate Underground Station next to Hyde Park.

111-117 Sussex Gardens, London W2 2RU

Telephone 020 7460 8800
Fax 020 7460 8828

E-mail: *darlington@bestloved.com*

GENERAL MANAGER

Jo Douch

ROOM RATES

5 Singles	£90 - £130
27 Doubles/Twins	£120 - £140
6 Suites	£145 - £155
2 Family rooms	£135 - £145

Includes continental breakfast and VAT

CHARGE/CREDIT CARDS

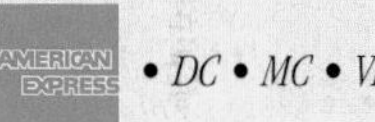

• DC • MC • VI

RATINGS & AWARDS

A.A. ★★★★ Town House

FACILITIES

On site: *Self-service guest laundry*
Nearby: *Tennis, fitness*

RESTRICTIONS

No facilities for disabled guests
No pets

ATTRACTIONS

Hyde Park, Knightsbridge, Windsor Castle, Oxford Street shopping, Theatreland, Hampton Court

AFFILIATIONS

Preston's Global Hotels

NEAREST

MAJOR CITY:
London

MAJOR AIRPORT:
London Heathrow - 15 miles/45 mins
London Gatwick - 30 miles/1½ hrs

RAILWAY STATION:
Paddington - ¼ mile/5 mins
Paddington Undergound

RESERVATIONS

Toll free in US: 800-544-9993
*Quote **Best Loved***

ACCESS CODES

Not applicable

For route planning map of London see page 506

• Map p.506 ref: H8

"The hotel in the square is London's best kept secret"

Lord Peter Graves

DOLPHIN SQUARE HOTEL

Luxury suites

Dolphin Square, Pimlico, London SW1V 3LX

Telephone 020 7798 8890
Fax 020 7798 8896

E-mail: dolphin@bestloved.com

HOTEL MANAGER

Clare Stewart

ROOM RATES

Single occupancy	£140 - £255
110 1 Bedroom suites	£165 - £300
35 2 Bedroom suites	£235 - £290
3 3 Bedroom suites	£400

Includes newspapers (excluding Sunday), service and VAT

CHARGE/CREDIT CARDS

• DC • MC • VI

RATINGS & AWARDS

E.T.C. ★★★★

FACILITIES

On site: Garden, indoor pool, croquet, tennis, gym, squash, shops, health & beauty, bureau de change, business centre,
Licensed for weddings
3 meeting rooms/max 100 people

RESTRICTIONS

No pets, guide dogs only

ATTRACTIONS

Houses of Parliament, Westminster, Tate Gallery, West End Theatres, Knightsbridge, Buckingham Palace, London Eye

AFFILIATIONS

Preston's Global Hotels

NEAREST

MAJOR CITY:
London

MAJOR AIRPORT:
London Heathrow - 15 miles/45 mins
London Gatwick - 30 miles/40 mins
London City - 8 miles/30 mins

RAILWAY STATION:
Victoria - ½ mile/10 mins
Pimlico Underground

RESERVATIONS

Toll free in US: 800-544-9993
Toll free in UK: 0800-616607

ACCESS CODES

AMADEUS UI LONDSH
APOLLO/GALILEO UI 96713
SABRE UI 32611
WORLDSPAN UI 40411

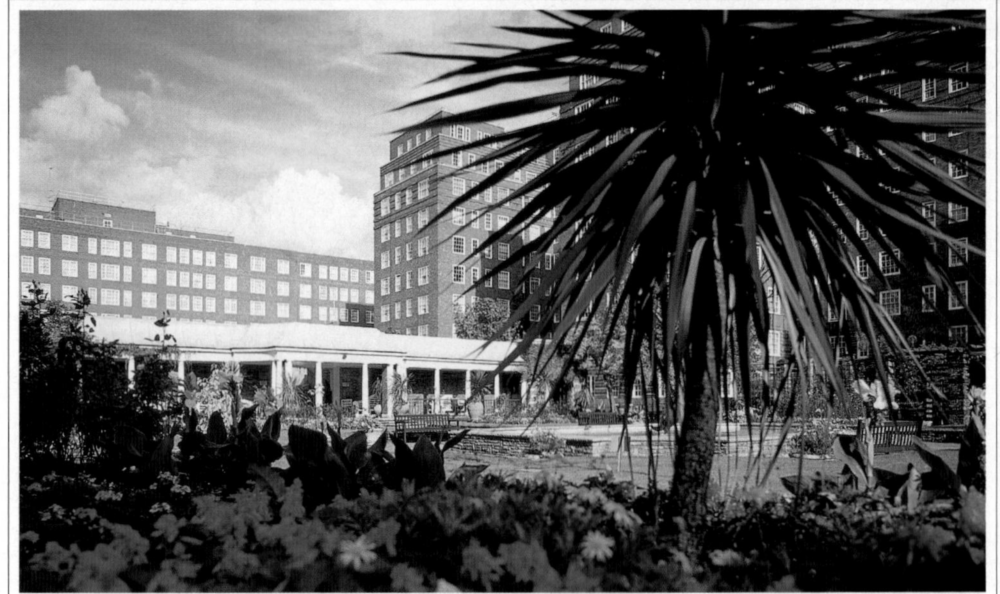

A unique property by the river with its own shops, bar and restaurants

Despite its size and prominent position on the Embankment, the exclusive Dolphin Square complex maintains a remarkably low profile - a fact much appreciated by residents and visitors, many of whom are public figures. The complex is, in effect, a self-contained village with its own security system, small shopping area, health spa, and 3½-acre garden which surprises everyone who discovers it. At the risk of penetrating the Square's well-guarded cloak of anonymity, let us introduce the Dolphin Square Hotel.

Located on the north side of the Square, the hotel offers apartment-style accommodation in studios, one-, two- and three-bedroom suites ideal for short or long lets for singles, couples, families or a group of friends. Guests can enjoy the facilities at the Zest! Health and Fitness Spa, which include an extensively equipped gymnasium, 18-metre swimming pool, aerobics classes, squash and tennis courts. There are pampering treatments, too, from a simple facial to advanced reflexology.

Also within the hotel, sample celebrity chef Gary Rhodes' modern British cuisine at the Rhodes in the Square restaurant, or dine in the less formal surroundings of the Brasserie, and guests can relax over a drink with friends at the nautically-themed Clipper Bar.

LOCATION

Central London beside the Thames off Grosvenor Road.

"The total ambience of the hotel is delightful, and the staff really caring and sensitive to the needs of the guests"

John C Groome, Hull

• Map p.506 ref: G5

Mayfair hotel & apartments

FLEMINGS MAYFAIR

A high quality hotel with London on your doorstep

The elegance of the Georgian age, together with the best of English hospitality, can be found in the heart of London's exclusive Mayfair, where Flemings Hotel has been welcoming guests since the early 1900s. Its location is superb. It is within a couple of minutes walk of Green Park underground station, within easy reach of all the West End's attractions, yet it is in a quiet street tucked away from the bustle of Piccadilly.

The opulent lounge is a pleasant place for afternoon tea, and the magnificent restaurant offers a fine à la carte menu of traditional British and Continental cuisine.

There are ten luxury self contained apartments, which have been recently refurbished to a five star standard, in addition to the 121 bedrooms. Flemings has full 24 hour room service, and the experience of the concierge team is there to help you make the most of your visit.

London really does belong to you when you stay at Flemings. Buckingham Palace, Regent Street, Bond Street, Piccadilly Circus, West End theatreland, the Royal Academy of Arts and Trafalgar Square are all within easy walking distance.

LOCATION

Turn right out of the Piccadilly north side exit at Green Park station and walk for two minutes down Piccadilly past Bolton Street towards Hyde Park Corner.

7-12 Half Moon Street, London W1Y 7BB

Telephone 020 7499 2964
Fax 020 7499 1817

E-mail: *flemings@bestloved.com*

GENERAL MANAGER

Robert Savage-Hanford

ROOM RATES

30 Deluxe singles	£217
69 Doubles/Twins	£229
19 Executive studios	£247
3 Junior suites	£299
10 Apartments	£382 - £499

Including VAT

CHARGE/CREDIT CARDS

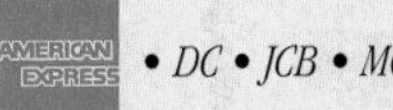

• DC • JCB • MC • VI

RATINGS & AWARDS

R.A.C. ★★★★ Dining Award 1
A.A. ★★★★ 63%

FACILITIES

On site: *3 meeting rooms/max 55 people*
Nearby: *Tennis, riding, golf*

RESTRICTIONS

No facilities for disabled guests
No pets

ATTRACTIONS

Buckingham Palace, Bond Street, Regents Street, Piccadilly Circus, Trafalgar Square

AFFILIATIONS

Independent

NEAREST

MAJOR CITY:
London

MAJOR AIRPORT:
London Heathrow - 15 miles/45 mins
London Gatwick - 30 miles/1¼ hrs

RAILWAY STATION:
Victoria - 2 miles/15 mins
Green Park Underground

RESERVATIONS

Toll free in US: 800-348-4685
or 800-44-UTELL
Quote ***Best Loved***

ACCESS CODES

AMADEUS UI LONFLE
APOLLO/GALILEO UI 5265
SABRE/ABACUS UI 13258
WORLDSPAN UI 0393

Planning a wedding reception? Turn to 'Meeting Facilities' on page 476

• Map p.506 ref: G6

"The Goring is that great rarity, a smart, privately owned one-off hotel"

Craig Brown, The Sunday Times

THE GORING HOTEL

Luxury hotel

15 Beeston Place, London SW1W 0JW

Telephone 020 7396 9000
Fax 020 7834 4393

E-mail: goring@bestloved.com

OWNER
George Goring

GENERAL MANAGER
William Cowpe

ROOM RATES

19 Singles	£203
37 Doubles/Twins	£247
11 Deluxe doubles	£306
7 Suites	£376

Includes service and VAT

CHARGE/CREDIT CARDS

• DC • MC • VI

RATINGS & AWARDS
E.T.C. ★★★★ Gold Award
R.A.C. Gold Ribbon ★★★★
Dining Award 3
A.A. ★★★★ ❀❀

FACILITIES
On site: *Garden*
Licensed for weddings
4 meeting rooms/max 100 people
Nearby: *Golf, riding, free use of local health club*

RESTRICTIONS
No pets

ATTRACTIONS
Buckingham Palace, Royal Parks, West End, Houses of Parliament

AFFILIATIONS
Pride of Britain
Selected British Hotels

NEAREST
MAJOR CITY:
London
MAJOR AIRPORT:
London Heathrow - 16 miles/45 mins
RAILWAY STATION:
Victoria - 100 yards/2 mins

RESERVATIONS
Toll free in US: 800-98-PRIDE
Quote ***Best Loved***

ACCESS CODES
AMADEUS HK LONGOR
APOLLO/GALILEO HK 14860
SABRE/ABACUS HK 30136
WORLDSPAN HK GORIN

Charm and efficiency characterise the Goring

For three generations the Goring family has harmonised traditional standards of hotel keeping with progressive management. George Goring, the grandson of the founder and present managing director, is proud to operate one of London's most prestigious hotels.

The 75 bedrooms are individually designed with every modern facility. All have air conditioning and the marble bathrooms are in a class of their own. The elegant lounge, new bar and the terrace overlook The Goring's own private garden, each in its own way the perfect rendezvous to enjoy lavish bar snacks and afternoon tea. The traditional style and opulence of the restaurant make it popular for both lunch and dinner. Traditional food is accompanied by some of the best wines personally selected by George Goring and William Cowpe.

The Goring is located in a quiet haven in the centre of London. It is adjacent to Buckingham Palace within walking distance of the Royal Parks; also close by are London's principal shopping areas, the West End, theatreland, The Houses of Parliament and Westminster Abbey.

George Goring, William Cowpe and their faithful, experienced staff will ensure a warm welcome to your London 'home from home'.

LOCATION

Beeston Place is a small, quiet street between Grosvenor Gardens and Buckingham Palace. It is very close to Victoria British Rail and Underground stations.

• Map p.506 ref: F5

"The staff were superb, the accommodation outstanding and the facilities good. Please convey my appreciation to everyone involved in making my visit so memorable"

Doug Rhymes, Scottsdale, USA

LE MÉRIDIEN GROSVENOR HOUSE

City centre hotel

Park Lane,
London W1K 7TN

Telephone 020 7499 6363
Fax 020 7493 3341

E-mail: grosvenorhse@bestloved.com

EXECUTIVE DIRECTOR

Paolo Biscioni

ROOM RATES

185 Superior Doubles/Twins	£195 - £225
36 Deluxe Doubles/Twins	£225 - £255
40 Superior Suites	£690 - £720
187 Le Royal Club rooms	£255 - £820
139 Apartments	£310 - £1,665

Includes service and VAT

CHARGE/CREDIT CARDS

• DC • JCB • MC • VI

RATINGS & AWARDS

E.T.C. ★★★★★

R.A.C. ★★★★★

A.A. ★★★★★ ❀❀❀❀❀ 73%

FACILITIES

On site: *Indoor pool, gym, sauna, health & beauty, hairdresser, business centre*

Licensed for weddings

29 meeting rooms/max 1,500

Nearby: *Golf, riding*

RESTRICTIONS

No pets, guide dogs only

ATTRACTIONS

Royal Parks, Victoria & Albert Museum, Knightsbridge, Bond Street, Oxford Street, Theatreland, National Gallery, Buckingham Palace, Hyde Park

AFFILIATIONS

Forte & Le Méridien Hotels

NEAREST

MAJOR CITY:
London

MAJOR AIRPORT:
London Heathrow - 15 miles/40 mins
London Gatwick - 30 miles/1¼ hrs

RAILWAY STATION:
Victoria - 2 miles/10 mins
Marble Arch Underground

RESERVATIONS

Toll free in US/Canada: 800-543-4300
Toll free in UK: 0800 40 40 40
*Quote **Best Loved***

ACCESS CODES

APOLLO/GALILEO FE 5455
AMADEUS FE LON250
SABRE/ABACUS FE 11250
WORLDSPAN FE 5932

Luxury, comfort and style in Mayfair, London's best address

In 1929 Le Méridien Grosvenor House opened as the first hotel on prestigious Park Lane. It was built on the site of the 18th century residence of the Duke of Westminster. The facade was designed by Sir Edwin Lutyens, creator of the imperial city of Delhi. He designed the building to capture natural light and provide extensive views of Hyde Park. The hotel won a reputation for high quality and exclusivity. Its huge ice rink became The Great Room, Europe's largest hotel ballroom, hosting grand gala balls from the 1930s on.

Le Méridien Grosvenor House continues to supply the accommodation and services that international high-fliers require. It was the first hotel in the world to provide high-speed access to the Internet in all guest bedrooms. In 1995 it opened the first all day, everyday dining restaurant, run by award-winning restaurateur Nico Ladenis. £multi-million refurbishments have provided private rooms for hire, a unique library facility and an executive floor, called Le Royal Club.

At the heart of Mayfair, Le Méridien Grosvenor House is minutes away from haute couture shopping in Bond Street and the West End theatres. For travellers who value the opportunity to mingle with leaders in business, fashion and society, the hotel offers a winning combination of luxury and comfort, with flawless service.

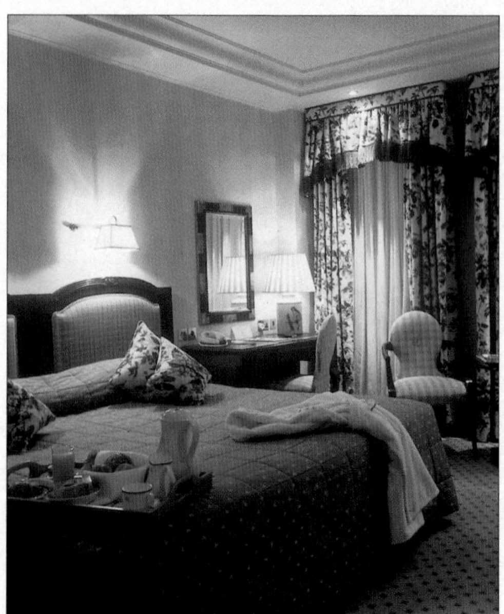

LOCATION

Situated on Park Lane between Hyde Park Corner and Marble Arch.

"There are few homes and even fewer hotels that can boast the services of The Halcyon"

European Travel & Life

• Map p.506 ref: A5

Victorian mansion

THE HALCYON

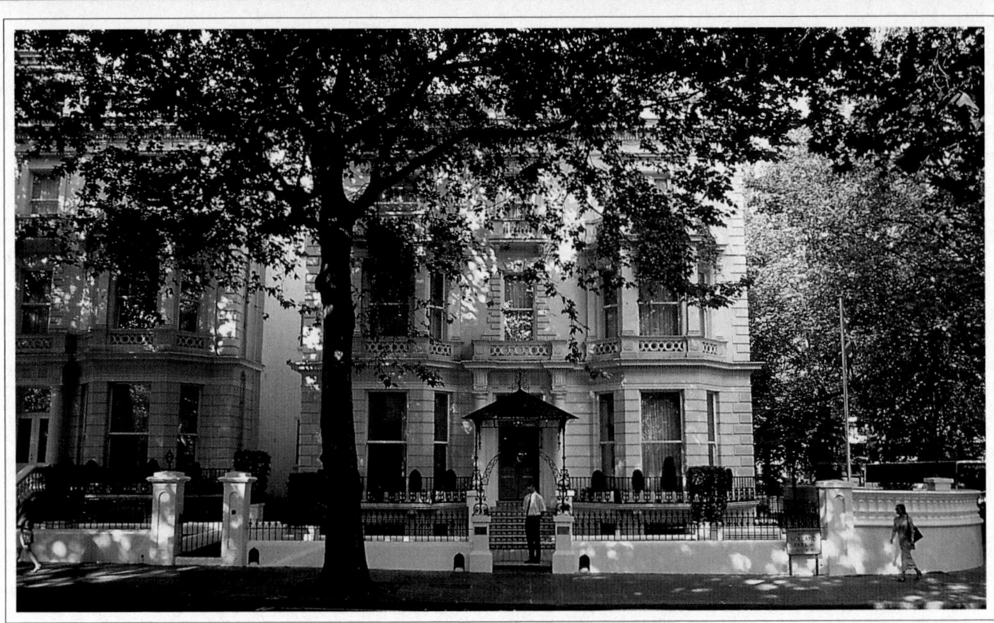

A country house in Holland Park - diplomatic heart of London

The Halcyon, the exclusive Holland Park hotel once dubbed 'the city's best kept secret' by the Los Angeles Times, achieves the impossible by being the ultimate luxurious hideaway, but only a couple of miles from the bustle of the West End and the city's most fashionable shopping areas and restaurants.

An elegant stuccoed building, meticulously restored to blend with the many ambassadorial residences in the area, The Halcyon is full of surprises. The first is the electrification of the apparently classical doors which swing open as you climb the steps. Entering The Halcyon is like walking into the country house of your dreams.

The large, beautifully lit rooms offer modern comfort in the best classical traditions. Some have four-poster beds, jacuzzis or corner baths, others gloriously tented ceilings. Everywhere, the colour schemes are impeccably conceived, with well chosen antiques lending a tasteful depth to the decor. Guests, for whom maintaining a low profile is a priority, will be relieved to hear that the entire menu from The Halcyon's upbeat restaurant, The Room, can be served in the comfort of their suite.

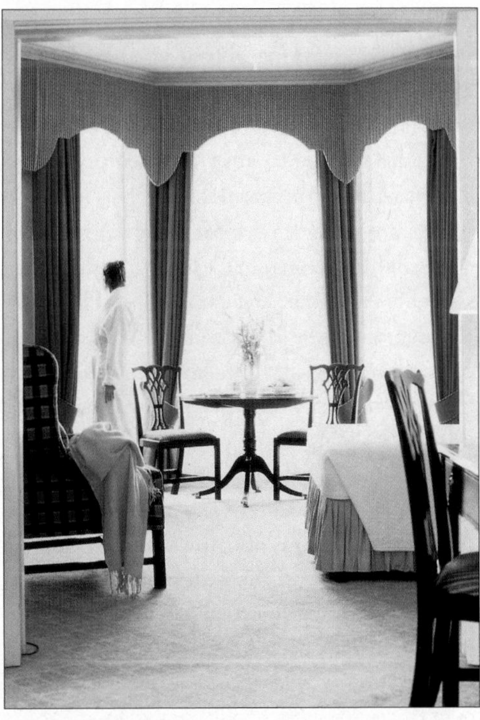

LOCATION

Leafy, diplomatic, residential area with easy access to central London (10 minutes).

81 Holland Park, London W11 3RZ

Telephone 020 7727 7288
Fax 020 7229 8516

E-mail: halcyon@bestloved.com

HOTEL DIRECTOR

Robin Sheppard

ROOM RATES

3 Singles	£217 - £276
20 Doubles	£329
20 Suites	£376 - £823

Includes VAT

CHARGE/CREDIT CARDS

• DC • JCB • MC • VI

RATINGS & AWARDS

A.A. ★★★★ ❀❀❀ 78%

Best Modern British Restaurant in London - Carlton TV

FACILITIES

On site: Garden

1 meeting room/max 12 people

Nearby: Private health club, tennis, riding

RESTRICTIONS

No facilities for disabled guests

ATTRACTIONS

Portobello antiques market, Holland Park, Kensington Palace

AFFILIATIONS

The Celebrated Hotels Collection

Summit Hotels

NEAREST

MAJOR CITY:
London

MAJOR AIRPORT:
London Heathrow - 14 miles/50 mins
London Gatwick - 30 miles/1¼ hrs

RAILWAY STATION:
Paddington - ¾ mile/10 mins
Holland Park Underground

RESERVATIONS

Toll free in US: 800-322-2403 or 800-457-4000

Quote **Best Loved**

ACCESS CODES

AMADEUS XL LONHAL
APOLLO/GALILEO XL 24553
SABRE/ABACUS XL 28259
WORLDSPAN XL 16458

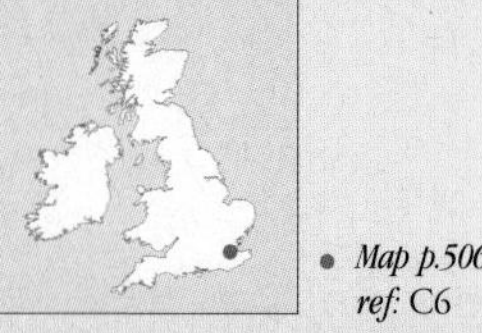

• Map p.506 ref: C6

“We were very happily surprised and thrilled at the reasonable rates, lovely location, the beauty of the hotel and the fabulous service”

Beth Sobel, USA

KENSINGTON HOUSE

Contemporary town house

15-16 Prince of Wales Terrace, Kensington, London W8 5PQ

Telephone 020 7937 2345
Fax 020 7368 6700

E-mail: *kensingtonhse@bestloved.com*

GENERAL MANAGER
Samantha Fitzgerald

ROOM RATES

11 Singles	£135
8 Doubles/Twins	£155
20 Executive doubles	£175
2 Junior suites	£195

Includes continental breakfast and VAT

CHARGE/CREDIT CARDS

• DC • JCB • MC • VI

RATINGS & AWARDS
Independent

FACILITIES
Nearby: *Fitness, riding, tennis*

RESTRICTIONS
None

ATTRACTIONS
Natural History Museum, Science Museum, Royal Albert Hall, Knightsbridge, Kensington Gardens, Hyde Park, Victoria & Albert Museum

AFFILIATIONS
Independent

NEAREST
MAJOR CITY:
London

MAJOR AIRPORT:
London Heathrow - 15 miles/40 mins

RAILWAY STATION:
Victoria - 3 miles/15 mins
High Street Kensington Underground

RESERVATIONS
Direct with hotel
Quote ***Best Loved***

ACCESS CODES
AMADEUS LM LON907
APOLLO/GALILEO LM 26891
SABRE/ABACUS LM 51957
WORLDSPAN LM 05907

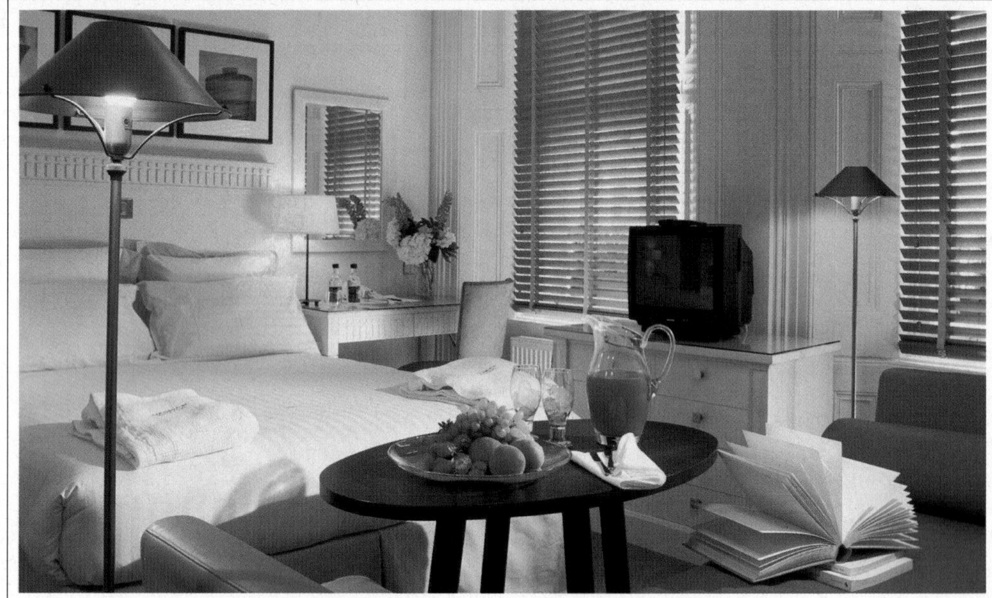

Understatement is the key to this modern take on hospitality

A brand new name on the capital's boutique hotel scene, Kensington House opened its doors in April 2000. This is a thoroughly modern hotel created with an understated but distinctive style within the traditional setting of a quiet 19th-century site off fashionable High Street Kensington.

The aim of any city centre hotel is to provide guests with a respite from the hurly-burly of urban street life - no minor feat in the heart of London. Kensington House achieves this enviable state of calm through what appears to be an effortless blend of simplicity, sophistication and a sense of informality that relaxes guests, yet standards of service never fall short of utter professionalism. Guest bedrooms are light and airy, decorated in restful combinations of oatmeal and white with sleek contemporary fittings and communications facilities including voicemail/modem. The hotel has its own bar, open throughout the day serving anything from a coffee to a 3 course meal with the menu reflecting its own individual style.

Kensington House is a terrific base for exploring London. Just a short step from a whole range of fine shops and restaurants, Kensington Palace and the wide green spaces of Hyde Park, it is also well-placed for the West End, museums, galleries, and nightlife.

LOCATION

The turning into Prince of Wales Terrace is off Kensington Road, opposite Kensington Gardens. The hotel is a short way down on the right.

" For more than ten years, Knightsbridge Green has been my 'home' in London . . . it is a very nice place to come back to "

Mr Peter Yeo

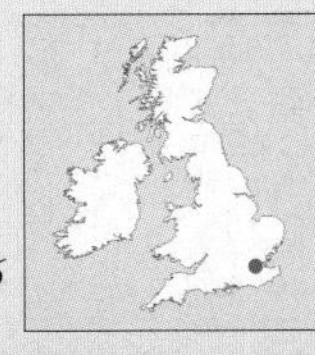

• *Map p.506 ref: E6*

Town house

KNIGHTSBRIDGE GREEN HOTEL

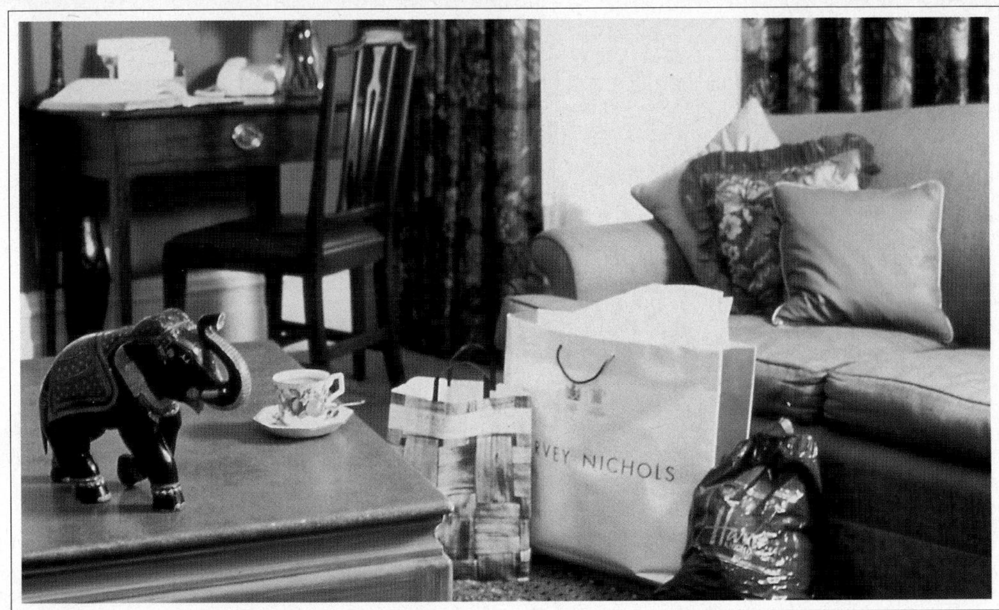

A family-owned hotel with a personal touch

Knightsbridge Green is a small hotel with a big difference: with Harrods just across the street and Hyde Park virtually on your doorstep, it is hard to believe that, these days, a family-owned establishment could exist in such a wonderfully central position. And yet, here it is combining the comforts and pleasures of the larger consortia hotels with the personality and friendliness you can only find in a privately-owned business.

The hotel has recently been transformed: new furnishings, new lighting, new colours; new marbled bathrooms with top quality fittings and fixtures. Double glazing keeps the peace in one of London's busiest areas and air-conditioning in all the bedrooms and suites allows you to find your own comfort level. The rooms are exceptionally large, a single at the Knightsbridge Green being the size of many a double anywhere else.

The area is blessed with a great range of cafés, restaurants, pubs, wine bars and bistros offering all kinds of cuisine. So a restaurant in the hotel is superfluous although a hearty breakfast will be served in your room as you wish.

When you want help in booking a restaurant, theatre tickets, limousine or hire car, all you have to do is ask.

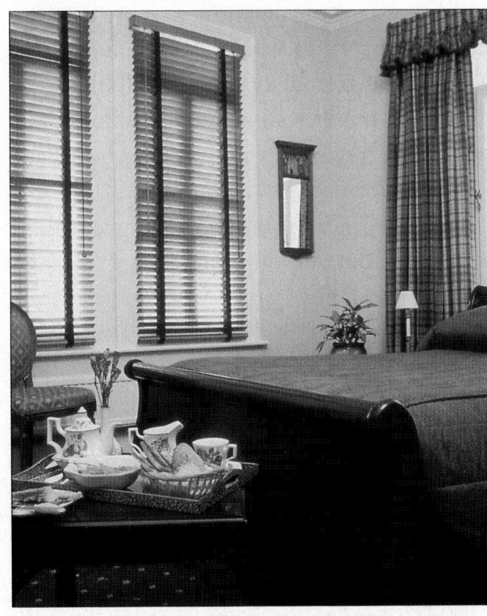

LOCATION

In Knightsbridge, central London, adjacent to Hyde Park.

159 Knightsbridge, London SW1X 7PD

Telephone 020 7584 6274
Fax 020 7225 1635

E-mail: *knightsbridge@bestloved.com*

OWNERS
The Marler Family

MANAGER
Paul Fizia

ROOM RATES

7 Singles	*£105*
9 Doubles/Twins	*£140*
12 Suites	*£165*

Includes service and VAT

CHARGE/CREDIT CARDS

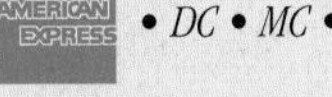

• *DC* • *MC* • *VI*

RATINGS & AWARDS
E.T.C. ◆◆◆◆
B&B Award Scheme
Commended past winner of BTA London - Certificate of Distinction

FACILITIES
On site: *Suites with reception rooms*
Nearby: *Riding*

RESTRICTIONS
No facilities for disabled guests
No smoking throughout
No pets

ATTRACTIONS
Harrods, Kensington Palace, Natural History Museum, Victoria & Albert Museum

AFFILIATIONS
Preston's Global Hotels

NEAREST
MAJOR CITY:
London

MAJOR AIRPORT:
London Heathrow - 15 miles/45 mins
London Gatwick - 30 miles/1¼ hrs

RAILWAY STATION:
Victoria - ½ mile/10 mins
Knightsbridge Underground

RESERVATIONS
Toll free in US: 800-544-9993
Quote ***Best Loved***

ACCESS CODES
Not applicable

• Map p.506
ref: E7

"Simply wonderful. Why can't other hotels be run this way?"

Quentin Wilson, BBC, London

THE LONDON OUTPOST OF THE CARNEGIE CLUB *Town house*

69 Cadogan Gardens, Near Sloane Square, London SW3 2RB

Telephone 020 7589 7333
Fax 020 7581 4958

E-mail: *outpost@bestloved.com*

GENERAL MANAGER
Caroline Nolan

ROOM RATES
11 Doubles £180 - £300
Includes VAT

CHARGE/CREDIT CARDS

• DC • MC • VI

RATINGS & AWARDS
Independent

FACILITIES
On site: *24 hour room service, conservatory, private garden*
Nearby: *Access to health & fitness club, riding*

RESTRICTIONS
None

ATTRACTIONS
Harrods, Knightsbridge, Buckingham Palace, Victoria & Albert Museum, Sloane Street

AFFILIATIONS
The Celebrated Hotels Collection
Small Luxury Hotels

NEAREST
MAJOR CITY:
London

MAJOR AIRPORT:
London Heathrow - 15 miles/45 mins
London Gatwick - 30 miles/1¼ hrs
London City - 7 miles/25 mins

RAILWAY STATION:
Victoria - ¾ mile/15 mins
Sloane Square Underground

RESERVATIONS
Toll free in US/Canada: 800-322-2403 or 800-525-4800
Quote **Best Loved**

ACCESS CODES
AMADEUS LX LONFEN
APOLLO/GALILEO LX 8216
SABRE/ABACUS LX 14795
WORLDSPAN LX LONTF

Once a grand home, now an elegant boutique hotel in the heart of London

Peace and quiet are difficult to find in a great capital city but The London Outpost has achieved a unique level of privacy and exclusivity, which transcends that found at even the very best hotels in the world. It is a small, unique, and luxurious place, dedicated to offering the discerning traveller all of the friendliness and impeccable personal service of the legendary Carnegie Club at Skibo Castle, Scotland.

Pure elegance pervades throughout the property, from the airy conservatory to the comfortable library where you can relax and enjoy your favourite drink.

Once a grand private residence, The Outpost is elegantly decorated with priceless antiques and fine works of art. The eleven air-conditioned bedrooms, some having attractive views overlooking private gardens, provide every convenience including entertainment and business facilities.

What distinguishes The Outpost is its emphasis on thoughtful personal service by Caroline and her team, from the evening champagne reception to the traditional breakfast that is served in your room until a decadent 2pm. When you have discovered London Outpost you will have found your London home.

LOCATION

From Sloane Square, take Symons Street, which leads into Cadogan Gardens. The London Outpost is 50 yards on the left hand side.

Looking for an hotel with a golf course on site? See our 'Golf Guide' on page 478

" The Milestone is one of the great hotels of the world "

Roger Collis, International Herald Tribune

• Map p.506 ref: C6

19th century town house THE MILESTONE HOTEL & APARTMENTS

Hallmark of elegance and luxury overlooking Kensington Gardens

The Milestone Hotel is one of London's more exclusive small hotels. Built in the late 19th century as two private residences, the hotel is a Victorian showpiece which has recently been completely refurbished and restored to its original architectural splendour. It is attractively set in the most fashionable part of London overlooking Kensington Palace.

All the hotel's suites and bedrooms are fully air-conditioned and most overlook Kensington Gardens. They are all surprisingly spacious and magnificently furnished emphasising the architectural detail of the building. The renovations have brought with them all the wizardry of this electronic age; modems, voicemail and suchlike as well as a multi-facetted entertainment centre. When it comes to luxury, even the most fastidious of travellers will feel happily at home.

Another convenience is the round-the-clock service available, not just in your room but also in the Park Lounge, Conservatory and Stables Bar. What's more the service is prompt, courteous and attentive. For those who like to exercise body as well as mind, the health and fitness centre will satisfy the needs of most.

For secluded indulgence at a good address in central London, make it The Milestone.

LOCATION

The Milestone is centrally located, a short walk from Kensington High Street Underground and a few minutes by taxi to Knightsbridge and the West End.

1 Kensington Court, London W8 5DL

Telephone 020 7917-1000
Fax 020 7917-1010

E-mail: milestone@bestloved.com

GENERAL MANAGER

Caroline King

ROOM RATES

Single occupancy	£294 - £882
45 Doubles/Twins	£294 - £470
12 Suites	£411 - £882
6 Apartments (per week)	£2,527

Includes VAT

CHARGE/CREDIT CARDS

• DC • MC • VI

RATINGS & AWARDS

E.T.C. ★★★★★ Gold Award
R.A.C. ★★★★★ Dining Award 3
A.A. ★★★★★ ❀
American Academy of Hospitality Sciences Five Star Diamond Award

FACILITIES

On site: Air conditioning, private fax, modem and DVD player in all rooms, health and fitness
Licensed for weddings
2 meeting rooms/max 25 people
Nearby: Riding

RESTRICTIONS

Pets by arrangement

ATTRACTIONS

Kensington Palace, Harrods, Kensington Gardens, Hyde Park, Royal Albert Hall, Victoria & Albert Museum, Knightsbridge shopping

AFFILIATIONS

Red Carnation Hotels
Leading Hotels of the World

NEAREST

MAJOR CITY:
London
MAJOR AIRPORT:
London Heathrow - 15 miles/45 mins
London Gatwick - 30 miles/1¼ hrs
RAILWAY STATION:
Victoria/Paddington - 3 miles/20 mins
Kensington High Street Underground

RESERVATIONS

Toll free in US: 800-223-6800
Quote **Best Loved**

ACCESS CODES

AMADEUS LW LONMIL
APOLLO/GALILEO LW 48252
SABRE LW 30954
WORLDSPAN LW LONMI

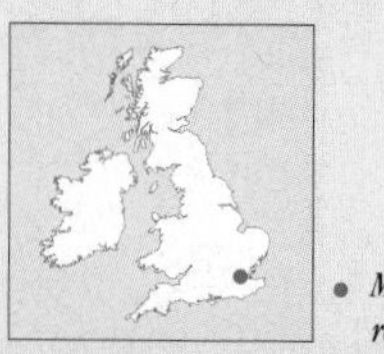

• Map p.506 ref: C7

"Victorian splendour with modern values"

Richard G Nixon, USA

MILLENNIUM BAILEY'S

Victorian town house

140 Gloucester Road, London SW7 4QH

Telephone 020 7373 6000
Fax 020 7370 3760

E-mail: *baileys@bestloved.com*

GENERAL MANAGER
Simon Pearce

ROOM RATES

36 Singles	£145 - £240
149 Doubles/Twins	£240 - £295
25 Junior suites	£295
2 Junior penthouses	£411

Includes VAT

CHARGE/CREDIT CARDS

• DC • JCB • MC • VI

RATINGS & AWARDS
A.A. ★★★★ 65%

FACILITIES
On site: *Car park, gym*
6 meeting rooms/max 20 people
Nearby: *Riding*

RESTRICTIONS
No facilities for disabled guests
No pets

ATTRACTIONS
Royal Albert Hall, Museums of South Kensington, Hyde Park, Knightsbridge, Harrods, Earls Court & Olympia Exhibition Centres

AFFILIATIONS
Millennium Hotels and Resorts

NEAREST
MAJOR CITY:
London

MAJOR AIRPORT:
London Heathrow - 12 miles/40 mins
London Gatwick - 30 miles/1½ hrs

RAILWAY STATION:
Victoria - 1 mile/10 mins
Gloucester Road Underground

RESERVATIONS
Toll free in US: 800-465-6486
Toll free in UK: 800 414741
Quote ***Best Loved***

ACCESS CODES
AMADEUS MU LONMBH
APOLLO/GALILEO MU 3852
SABRE/ABACUS MU 263
WORLDSPAN MU 3656

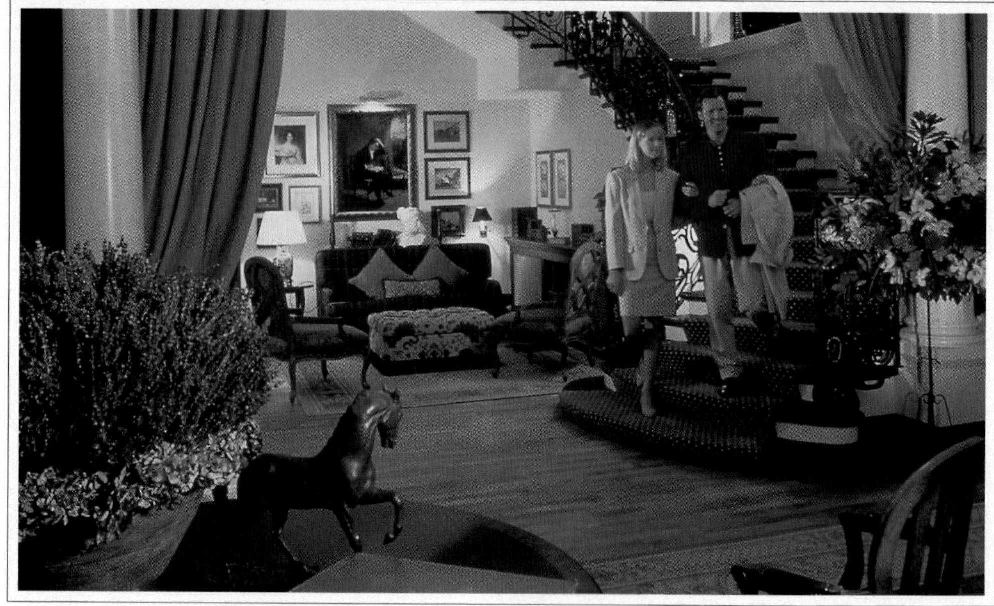

A grand residence in a fashionable residential area

The Millennium Bailey's Hotel, originally opened in 1876, has been renovated and carefully restored to its original glory. Complemented by its elegant Victorian façade, the Bailey's now offers the comforts of a luxurious home with the convenience of modern hotel facilities and traditional service. All the bedrooms and suites have their own character and provide international visitors with the convenience of satellite television and compatible electrical sockets.

Olives restaurant and bar offers distinctive cuisine in informal surroundings with modern furnishings sitting comfortably with the 19th century architectural features of Bailey's.

This first class hotel is located in a most favoured residential area in the Royal Borough of Kensington and Chelsea and, unusually for central London, has its own car park. It is only a short walk from the Royal Albert Hall, Natural History, Science and Victoria & Albert Museums. Knightsbridge, with its elegant stores, including Harrods, is nearby.

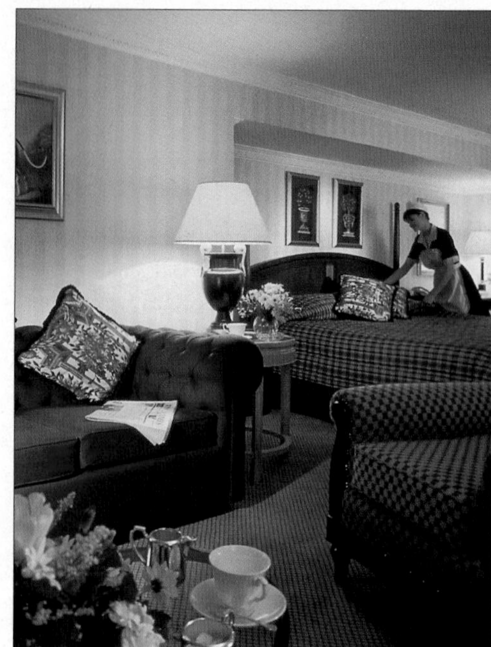

LOCATION

Directly opposite Gloucester Road Underground where the Circle, District and Piccadilly lines provide a direct link with the West End and the City, as well as with Earl's Court.

" We came here on business and now consider The Montague our home in London "

Mr & Mrs Charles Bond, Charles Bond & Associates

• Map p.506 ref: 13

Luxury Georgian hotel THE MONTAGUE ON THE GARDENS

Comfort and personal service in a unique London setting

In Georgian times, Bloomsbury was the home of rich merchants and aristocrats. It later was famed for the Bloomsbury group of writers that included Virginia Woolf. From the Montague's garden setting beside the British Museum, the attractions of London's West End theatres are a stroll away and the Tower of London and The City are within easy reach.

The townhouse style Montague on the Gardens has been completely refurbished for modern business and leisure. Its 104 guest rooms are fully air-conditioned and include 11 split-level and deluxe suites. 'Business ready' rooms provide office supplies, speaker phones, fax machines on request, good desk space and lighting. Laptop users will find hooking up to each bedroom's UK/US modem lines a snap. And, for relaxation, you can take advantage of the hotels in-room movies on demand capability or work out in the recently installed gym and fitness centre.

Montague staff members proudly wear red carnations, symbolising personal service and attention to detail. Traditional afternoon tea is served daily. The Blue Door Bistro offers a gastronomic treat with superb lunchtime selections and à la carte dinner menu. You can relax on the terrace, wood-deck or in the conservatory overlooking the private garden and be 200 years away from today's pressures.

LOCATION

In Bloomsbury, close to Russell Square Underground and Airbus A1 stop. Convenient parking facilities nearby.

15 Montague Street, Bloomsbury, London WC1B 5BJ

Telephone 020 7637 1001
Fax 020 7637 2516

E-mail: *montague@bestloved.com*

GENERAL MANAGER

Tricia Fitzsimons

ROOM RATES

26 Singles	*£140 - £200*
44 Doubles/Twins	*£160 - £215*
23 King bedded rooms	*£180 - £225*
5 Junior suites	*£210 - £330*
6 Executive suites	*£270 - £420*

Includes service and VAT

CHARGE/CREDIT CARDS

• DC • JCB • MC • VI

RATINGS & AWARDS

E.T.C. ★★★★ Silver Award
R.A.C. ★★★★
A.A. ★★★★ 69%

FACILITIES

On site: *Garden terrace, bar-b-que, health suite, conservatory*
Licensed for weddings
5 meeting rooms/max 150 people

RESTRICTIONS

No facilities for disabled guests

ATTRACTIONS

The British Museum, Theatre district, Trafalgar Square, Tower of London, Covent Garden, Westminster

AFFILIATIONS

Red Carnation Hotels
The European Connection

NEAREST

MAJOR CITY:
London

MAJOR AIRPORT:
London Heathrow - 18 miles/45 mins
London Gatwick - 30 miles/1¼ hrs

RAILWAY STATION:
Euston/King's Cross - ½ mile/6 mins
Holborn/Russell Square Underground

RESERVATIONS

Toll free in US: 877-955-1515
*Quote **Best Loved***

ACCESS CODES

AMADEUS VP LONMON
APOLLO/GALILEO VP 18505
SABRE VP 10896
WORLDSPAN VP 0366

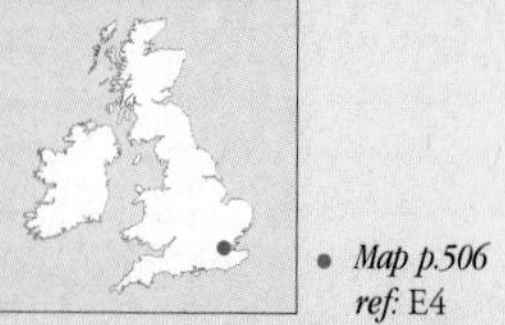

• Map p.506 ref: E4

" I have been frequenting The Montcalm for over twenty years. It has changed little - it is small, private, discreet and with friendly impeccable service "

Frederick Forsyth, Author

THE MONTCALM

Georgian town house

Great Cumberland Place, London W1A 2LF

Telephone 020 7402 4288
Fax 020 7724 9180

E-mail: *montcalm@bestloved.com*

GENERAL MANAGER

Jonathan Orr-Ewing

ROOM RATES

43 Singles	*£180 - £260*
63 Doubles/Twins	*£180 - £290*
14 Suites	*£370 - £705*

Includes VAT

CHARGE/CREDIT CARDS

• *DC* • *JCB* • *MC* • *VI*

RATINGS & AWARDS

R.A.C. ★★★★ Dining Award 3

A.A. ★★★★ ❀❀ 77%

FACILITIES

***On site:** In-room fax machines & voice mail, bicycles*

3 meeting rooms/max 120 people

***Nearby:** Jogging, riding*

RESTRICTIONS

Limited facilities for disabled guests

No pets, guide dogs by arrangement

ATTRACTIONS

Buckingham Palace, London Diamond Centre, The Wallace Collection, Bond Street, Madame Tussaud's

AFFILIATIONS

Nikko Hotels International

NEAREST

MAJOR CITY: London

MAJOR AIRPORT: London Heathrow - 15 miles/50 mins
London Gatwick - 30 miles/1¼ hrs

RAILWAY STATION: Paddington - ½ mile/10 mins
Marble Arch Underground

RESERVATIONS

Toll free in US: 800-645-5687
Toll free in UK: 0800 282502
*Quote **Best Loved***

ACCESS CODES

AMADEUS NK LON001
APOLLO/GALILEO NK 26211
SABRE/ABACUS NK 14527
WORLDSPAN NK 14527

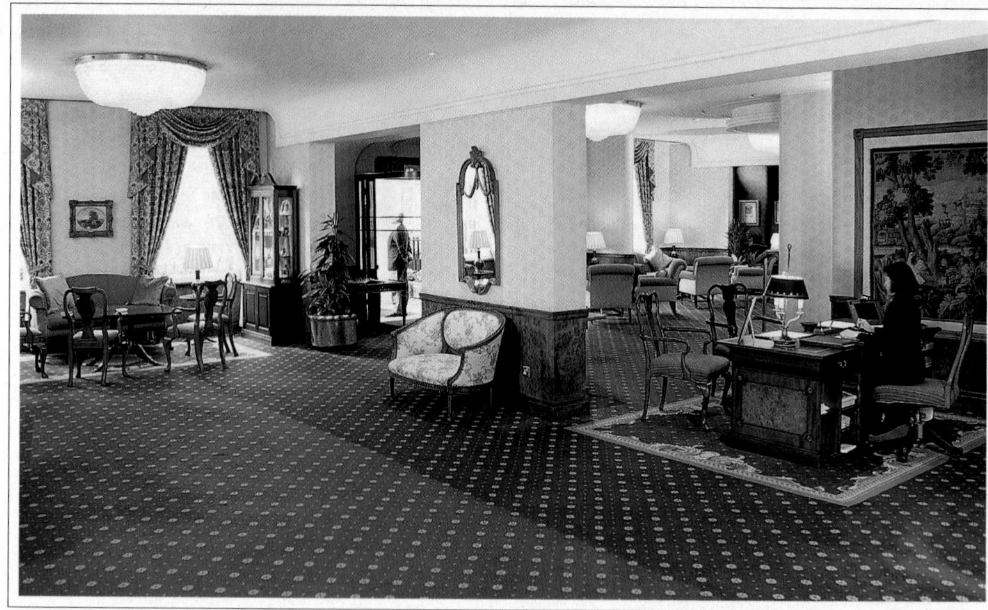

An oasis of sophisticated charm in the heart of London

Tucked away in a quiet, tree-lined crescent behind Marble Arch and the bustling Oxford Street shopping district, The Montcalm makes an exceptional base for the discerning traveller in one of the greatest cities in the world.

The hotel was named after an 18th-century general, the Marquis de Montcalm, who was renowned for his dignity and style. These two qualities are admirably reflected in the surroundings and atmosphere of this London outpost of the highly-regarded Nikko Hotel group. Behind the discreet Georgian façade, comfortable traditional bedrooms and duplex suites feature modern conveniences from private fax machines and voicemail to satellite and CNN television channels. The spacious lobby is an ideal meeting point for friends and business colleagues, or there is the wood panelled bar where afternoon tea is served, and an open fire provides a cosy focus in winter.

The Montcalm's elegant Crescent Restaurant has a light and airy feel with tall windows and an Arcadian mural of a formal English garden stretching off into distant countryside. The menu features the inspired modern British cuisine of talented chef Stephen Whitney (ex-Mosimann's and the Savoy). A typical offering would be the delice of salmon on spinach and wild rice with a caviar and vodka butter.

LOCATION

Two minutes walk from Marble Arch and Oxford Street.

“ '41' is a unique concept and is already surpassing all expectations of even the most discerning traveller ”

Joseph Cinque, The American Academy of Hospitality Sciences

Map p.506 ref: G6

All-inclusive luxury hotel

NUMBER 41

Club style comfort and service, IT wizardry and all-inclusive rates

London's first all-inclusive luxury club hotel, '41' is aiming to create new standards in service and facilities within the boutique hotel industry. The motivating force behind '41', and founder of the Red Carnation Hotel Collection, is Bea Tollman, who has employed her considerable expertise to recruit an international coterie of highly-experienced staff. She has also lavished considerable attention on the décor and creature comforts that transform a hotel stay into a memorable experience.

'41' enjoys a prime location on Buckingham Palace Road, convenient for the West End and the City financial district. The discreet entrance leads into a handsome traditional interior with a distinctly clubbable feel, but the revolutionary guest room facilities owe more to the space age. Each room doubles as a personal communications centre equipped with all-in-one interactive TV/CD/DVD player and personal computer featuring e-mail and high-speed Internet access. Business travellers can also make use of the state-of-the-art boardroom facilities including video conferencing.

The hotel's all-inclusive pricing structure includes a full breakfast, afternoon tea and buffet meals throughout the day and evening, all drinks, mobile phone and laptop rental, business cards, valet/butler service, laundry, and a knowledgeable Guest Host on call 24-hours a day.

LOCATION

Directly opposite the Royal Mews of Buckingham Palace, just a few minutes walk from Victoria Station and Westminster.

41 Buckingham Palace Road, London SW1W OPS

Telephone 020 7300 0041
Fax 020 7300 0141

E-mail: *number41@bestloved.com*

GENERAL MANAGER

Paul Hemmings

ROOM RATES

Single occupancy	*£382 - £617*
16 King size	*£382*
3 Suites	*£470*
1 Master suite	*£617*

Includes food & beverage, dry cleaning, national calls and VAT

CHARGE/CREDIT CARDS

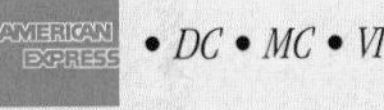

• *DC* • *MC* • *VI*

RATINGS & AWARDS

American Academy of Hospitality Sciences Five Star Diamond Award

FACILITIES

On site: *Fully air-conditioned, cyber-centre, executive lounge 2 meeting rooms/max 20 people*
Nearby: *Tennis, fitness centre, riding*

RESTRICTIONS

Pets by arrangement

ATTRACTIONS

Buckingham Palace, National Portrait Gallery, Queens Gallery, Westminster Abbey, Green Park, West End theatres

AFFILIATIONS

Red Carnation Hotels
VIP International
The European Connection

NEAREST

MAJOR CITY:
London

MAJOR AIRPORT:
London Heathrow - 15 miles/45 mins

RAILWAY STATION:
Victoria - 190 metres/2 mins

RESERVATIONS

Toll free in US: 877-955-1515
Quote ***Best Loved***

ACCESS CODES

AMADEUS VP LON751
APOLLO/GALILEO VP19844
SABRE VP 07911
WORLDSPAN VP 00751

• Map p.506 ref: G6

"We felt every detail needed to be addressed for comfort, pleasure and lasting memories of our parents' 50th wedding anniversary. The Rubens was truly a highlight of their trip and memories"

The Pelton family, Olympia, USA

THE RUBENS AT THE PALACE

Victorian luxury

39 Buckingham Palace Road,
London SW1W 0PS

Telephone 020 7834 6600
Fax 020 7233 6037

E-mail: rubens@bestloved.com

GENERAL MANAGER

Paul Hemmings

ROOM RATES

40 Singles	£155 - £199
75 Doubles/Twins	£185 - £225
46 King-bedded rooms	£205 - £299
7 Junior suites	£275 - £299
6 Executive/Master suites	£295 - £500

Includes VAT

CHARGE/CREDIT CARDS

• DC • JCB • MC • VI

RATINGS & AWARDS

R.A.C. ★★★★ Dining Award 2
A.A. ★★★★ ❀ 73%

FACILITIES

On site: Fully air-conditioned
5 meeting rooms/max 80 people
Nearby: Tennis, fitness centre, riding

RESTRICTIONS

Pets by arrangement

ATTRACTIONS

Buckingham Palace, Hyde Park, Houses of Parliament, Westminster Abbey, Tower of London, Royal Mews

AFFILIATIONS

Red Carnation Hotels
The European Connection

NEAREST

MAJOR CITY:
London

MAJOR AIRPORT:
London Heathrow - 15 miles/45 mins

RAILWAY STATION:
Victoria - 200 metres/2 mins

RESERVATIONS

Toll free in US: 877-955-1515
Quote **Best Loved**

ACCESS CODES

AMADEUS VP LONRUB
APOLLO/GALILEO VP 10977
SABRE VP 10687
WORLDSPAN VP LONRB

Luxurious sanctuary in a Royal neighbourhood

An old rule suggests that an hotel's location is essential to its success. The Rubens at the Palace goes a long way to proving this rule. Look out your bedroom window and directly across the street are the grounds of Buckingham Palace. Westminster is a short stroll and Victoria Station provides easy access in and around town.

Red Carnation Hotels has invested heavily in upgrading this landmark to a luxury standard. Lush fabrics and furnishings throughout create a calm mood. In the Cavalry Bar and Palace Lounge, you can enjoy a traditional tea or in the evening listen to a live piano while sipping a night-cap. Dining options include the elegant Library Restaurant serving superb international cuisine or the more relaxed Carvery, where the obvious emphasis is on mouth-watering roasts.

Bedrooms have received serious attention and redecorating has meant sparing no expense in creating comfortable and luxurious environments. Suites and bedrooms include king and queen-sized beds. Often overlooked details aren't missed and include flowers, magazines, and in the suites, evening canapés. Business travellers will appreciate their needs have been properly addressed with bedrooms that can be transformed into virtual offices with ample workspace and state-of-the-art communication facilities.

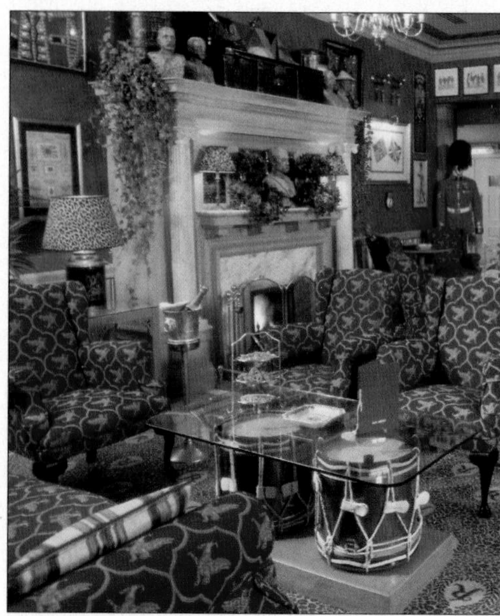

LOCATION

Opposite the Royal Mews of Buckingham Palace. Only 200 metres from Victoria Station.

"Superb decor, excellent staff, my home away from home in London"

Jim Kent, Florida

• Map p.506 ref: E7

Luxury town house — THE SLOANE HOTEL

Hi-technology and modern service within Victorian pastiche

London may not be the most beautiful city in the world but, in common with other capitals, it has its landmarks that slide into cliché at the click of a camera. What is so fascinating about London are its curiosities, thousands of them, many never even making it to the guide books, vestiges of past times, memorials to eccentrics. The Sloane Hotel comfortably fits into this category. It audaciously demonstrates a certain ambivalence by being an hotel, a museum and a showroom all in one. One thing for certain is that it is no cliché but it has to have the most photogenic interiors in this book.

It is a pastiche of Victoriana, the invention of interior designer Sue Rogers who has traipsed the antiquarians and auction rooms to furnish her ideas. Says Sue Rogers: 'It may seem incredible but you can sleep in one of our wonderful four-poster beds and, if you like it, you can buy it and have it delivered to your home.' In fact, you can buy almost anything you see - at a price - but don't ask about the reception desk; it was specially made for the hotel by Viscount Linley and it's not for sale.

There is a rooftop reception room and terrace, which on sunny days, gives you a bird's eye view of the Royal Borough of Chelsea and a greyer, more mundane world than the flights of fancy you will find in this jewel of an hotel.

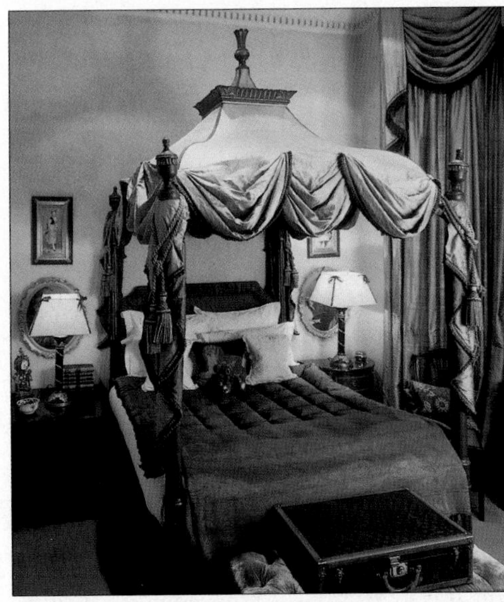

LOCATION

Off Sloane Square on Draycott Place, running north parallel to the Kings Road, on the left side when coming from Sloane Square.

29 Draycott Place, Chelsea, London SW3 2SH

Telephone 020 7581 5757
Fax 020 7584 1348

E-mail: *sloanehotel@bestloved.com*

GENERAL MANAGER
Xavier Colin

MANAGER
Miguel Pita

ROOM RATES

2 Doubles/Twins	*£164*
7 Deluxe doubles	*£217*
3 Four-poster suites	*£264*

Includes VAT

CHARGE/CREDIT CARDS

• DC • JCB • MC • VI

RATINGS & AWARDS
WHICH? Hotel of the Year 2000
Lovable Lodgings in London' - Vogue
'Most Romantic Room in London' - W Magazine

FACILITIES
On site: *Roof-top reception room, technical and secretarial support*
Nearby: *Fitness club*

RESTRICTIONS
No facilities for disabled guests
No pets

ATTRACTIONS
Harrods, Hyde Park, Buckingham Palace, Christies, Victoria & Albert Museum

AFFILIATIONS
The European Connection

NEAREST
MAJOR CITY:
London

MAJOR AIRPORT:
London Heathrow - 15 miles/40 mins
London Gatwick - 30 miles/1¼ hrs

RAILWAY STATION:
Victoria - 2 miles/5 mins
Victoria Underground

RESERVATIONS
Toll free in US: 800-324-9960
Quote ***Best Loved***

ACCESS CODES
APOLLO/GALILEO HT 25927
SABRE/ABACUS HK 32477

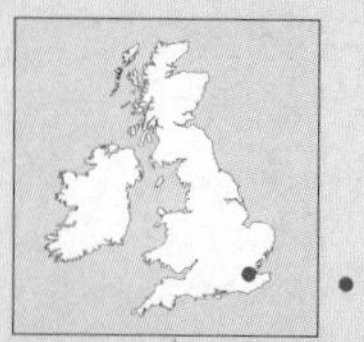

• Map p.506 ref: B7

" Without doubt, the best small hotel we've ever stayed at "

Anonymous, Kuala Lumpur

TWENTY NEVERN SQUARE

Town house hotel

20 Nevern Square, London SW5 9PD

Telephone 020 7565 9555
Fax 020 7565 9444

E-mail: *twentynevern@bestloved.com*

GENERAL MANAGER
Faisel Saloojee

ROOM RATES

Single occupancy	*£110 - £140*
16 Doubles/Twins	*£140 - £175*
3 Four-posters	*£195*
Pasha Suite	*£275*

Includes buffet breakfast, service and VAT

CHARGE/CREDIT CARDS

• *DC • JCB • MC • VI*

RATINGS & AWARDS
E.T.C. ★★★★ *Town House Hotel*

FACILITIES
On site: *Car parking on request*
1 meeting room/max 25 people
Nearby: *Tennis, leisure centre, business centre*

RESTRICTIONS
No facilities for disabled guests
No pets

ATTRACTIONS
Natural History Museum, Science Museum, Knightsbridge, Theatre district, Earls Court & Olympia

AFFILIATIONS
Small & Select Hotels of the World
Small Hotel Company

NEAREST
MAJOR CITY:
London

MAJOR AIRPORT:
London Heathrow - 15 miles/45 mins
London Gatwick - 30 miles/1½ hrs

RAILWAY STATION:
Victoria - 1 mile/20 mins
Earls Court Underground

RESERVATIONS
Direct with hotel
*Quote **Best Loved***

ACCESS CODES
AMADEUS SB LON742
APOLLO/GALILEO SB 13426
SABRE/ABACUS SB 47371
WORLDSPAN SB 00742

A contemporary touch of the East

A tall, terraced 1880s town house facing a leafy garden square, Twenty Nevern Square is a surprising find minutes from the Earls Court exhibition centre in West London. Its discreet redbrick façade gives barely a hint of the warm and vibrant interior within, but glance down at the mosaic patterned steps leading up to the front door and you will see the inspiration for what lies beyond.

Once across the threshold, guests are greeted by a striking contemporary blend of Eastern and European influences reflected in Oriental furnishings, luxurious fabrics and unusual objets d'art. The bedrooms feature an eclectic fusion of handcrafted furniture from Indonesia, natural materials such as cotton, linen and silk, and marble bathrooms, and there are individual themes such as the elegant Chinese Room or the Pasha Suite with silken peacock bedcovers and a tiny private terrace. Creature comforts include modem connections, CD players and wide screen digital TVs. All guests are offered a glass of champagne on arrival and unlimited tea and coffee is served downstairs throughout the day.

Nevern Square is a short walk from Earls Court underground station with direct services to Heathrow (under 30 minutes) and the shopping and dining opportunities of Knightsbridge and the West End. A special feature is the early evening drinks and canapes with an Eastern twist.

LOCATION

Just off the Warwick Road. The 2nd turning on the right from the Earls Court tube going up to Cromwell Road.

ireland

Freewheeling: Explore the beautiful west coast at your own pace and experience the charm of its countryside and people. Also take time to enjoy the magnificent gardens at Mount Stewart House (inset) in Co. Down, created by Edith, Lady Londonderry.

ireland

There's a special place for Ireland in people's hearts throughout the world. Maybe it is the wit of the Irish, the way they express themselves in prose, verse and music, the legendary beauty of its women or the impish philosophy of its menfolk. Ireland is always entertaining.

Dublin traces its history back to Ptolemy in 140 AD. In the 9th century, the Vikings named it Dubh Linn, meaning Dark Pool. Today it is a city of Georgian beauty. Whilst Belfast, framed against Ben Madigan and the distant blue hills, has more commercial origins and, today, finds it renaissance amongst the wharves of Laganside.

From the mountains of Mourne and Giant's Causeway in the north to the Ring of Kerry in the far southwest, you will find varied landscapes: rugged mountains, lush green fields, deep blue lakes and uncrowded sandy beaches. You can trace the history from monuments older than the Pyramids, through hundreds of prehistoric stone shelters, ancient Celtic castles, Roman forts, and medieval churches and towers.

This is the land of a hundred thousand welcomes - Cead Miele Failte.

Map Symbols

Great Trails

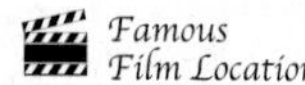
Famous Film Locations

Scenic Views

Historical Interest

Cities & Major towns

Gardens

Tight lines

With more than 2,000 miles of coastline, 920,000 acres of lakes and 9,000 miles of rivers and streams, Ireland is packed with opportunities for anglers. Most sea fishing takes place off the south and west coasts, while dry-fly fishermen ply the inland loughs and rivers for freshwater salmon and brown trout.

Saddle up and set forth

Not surprisingly for an island that is horse-mad, there are numerous equestrian centres offering pony-trekking and riding experiences.

A grand day at the races

The Irish love a wager almost as much as they love horses, so an Irish race meeting is a felicitous combination of the two. The Curragh, in Co. Kildare, is the HQ of Irish racing and host to summer season classics including the Oaks and the Irish Derby, while across the border in Co. Meath, Fairytown packs in the spectators for Easter's Irish Grand National.

Off the beaten track

Whether you decide to paddle your own canoe, venture by car or bicycle into the intriguing maze of country lanes behind the main roads, or hike into the hills on foot, getting off the beaten track is a thoroughly rewarding experience in Ireland.

Lovely Lismore

Laid out beside the Blackwater River in a peaceful valley, the Lismore Castle Gardens surround the Irish home of the Duke of Devonshire. The Duke's residence is a romantic reconstruction of a Tudor era castle dating from the 19th century, but a medieval fort did once stand here. The split-level gardens include walled and woodland gardens, and the Yew Walk is a highlight.

Garden Guide

Antrim Castle Gardens
Randalstown Road, Antrim BT41 4LH
Tel: 028 9442 8000
Anglo-Dutch water gardens, dating back to the 17th century, on the shores of Lough Neagh

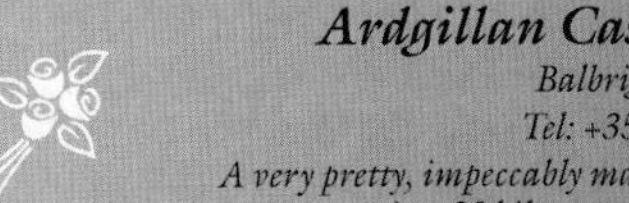

Ardgillan Castle Garden
Balbriggan, Co Dublin
Tel: +353 (0)1 849 2212
A very pretty, impeccably maintained garden just 30 kilometres north of Dublin

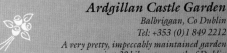

Bantry House & Gardens
Bantry, Co Cork
Tel: +353 (0)27 50795
A magnificent garden of great note with sweeping views over the expansive bay

Powerscourt Estate
Enniskerry, Co Wicklow
Tel: +353 (0)1 204 6000
World renowned garden where great terraces open out to a panorama of the Wicklow mountains

The height of hurley-burley

Fast and furious, the native sport of hurling bears a passing resemblance to both hockey and lacrosse but these two more modern games appear positively pedestrian by comparison. Players employ a wooden stick to control the ball, which can also be handled, and hurl it over the H-shaped goal posts.

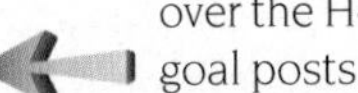

Find out more. There are many more attractions listed on the Best Loved Website: **www.bestlovedhotels.com**
Further information about Ireland can be found by contacting: **Bord Failte (Irish Tourist Board).** Tel: +353 (0)1 676 5871. **Northern Ireland Tourist Board.** Tel: +44 028 90231221

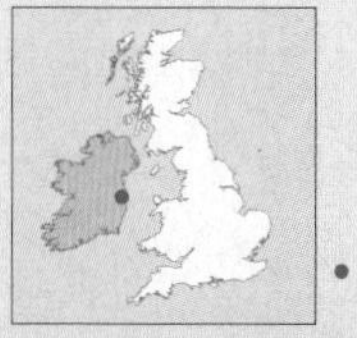

• Map p.508 ref: G7

" This is truly all that one expects of a private hotel, the Edwardian features, the personal service and the surroundings "

Brian Sanker, Los Gatos, California

ABERDEEN LODGE

Edwardian town house

53 Park Avenue, off Ailesbury Road, Ballsbridge, Dublin 4, Republic of Ireland

Telephone +353 (0)1 283 8155
Fax +353 (0)1 283 7877

E-mail: *aberdeen@bestloved.com*

OWNER

Pat Halpin

ROOM RATES *(Irish Punts)*

3 Singles	£84 - £99
10 Doubles/Twins	£99 - £145
2 Four-posters	£115 - £165
2 Suites	£127 - £195

Includes full breakfast, newspaper and VAT

CHARGE/CREDIT CARDS

• DC • JCB • MC • VI

RATINGS & AWARDS

I.T.B. ★★★★
Galtee Breakfast Award

FACILITIES

On site: *Garden, health & beauty, car park*
2 meeting rooms/max 30 people
Nearby: *Golf, riding, fitness centre, tennis, hunting/shooting, fishing, water skiing*

RESTRICTIONS

No children under 2 years
No pets

ATTRACTIONS

Trinity College, National Art Gallery, Christchurch, Gardens of Wicklow, New Grange, Powerscourt Gardens

AFFILIATIONS

Green Book of Ireland
Relais du Silence
Preston's Global Hotels

NEAREST

MAJOR CITY:
Dublin
MAJOR AIRPORT:
Dublin - 6 miles/20 mins
RAILWAY STATION:
Sydney Parade - ¼ mile/5 mins

RESERVATIONS

Toll free in US: 800-544-9993
or 800-223-6510
*Quote **Best Loved***

ACCESS CODES

AMADEUS UI DUBABE
APOLLO/GALILEO UI 1400
SABRE/ABACUS UI 35428
WORLDSPAN UI 19689

IRELAND

A peaceful, private address in Dublin's fashionable embassy district

Dublin's elegance has many facets: wide streets and Georgian facades, parks and gardens, the vibrant city centre with its bright lights, shops and night life … and the quiet, secluded leafy areas just off the city centre. In one of these more exclusive areas, world's embassies are located. So is the Aberdeen Lodge.

Aberdeen Lodge, a converted Edwardian house, is an affordable, well-located option for any visitor, providing high standards of comfort and service within the generous proportions of its rooms. Each bedroom is en suite, and lists multichannel TV, direct dial telephone, trouser press and hairdryer amongst its facilities. The suites additionally include a whirlpool spa and fine period furniture.

The hotel is owned and run by the Halpin family who, as well established hoteliers, know the needs of their guests and how to indulge them. This particularly applies to the dining room where, overlooking the garden, you can dine on good food and wine. Indeed, the hotel has enjoyed excellent reviews from the Irish Tourist Board, the AA and the RAC.

In short, the Aberdeen Lodge can match most of the qualities of Dublin's city centre hotels but adds to them greater seclusion and great value.

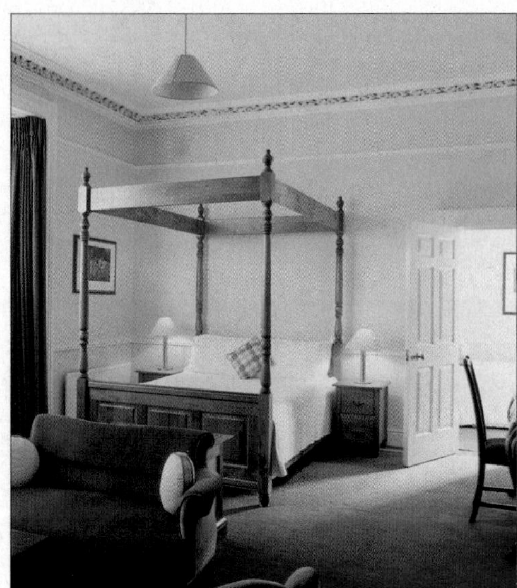

LOCATION

From city centre take Merrion Road towards Sydney Parade DART station and then first left into Park Avenue.

“They are surrounded by the finest fish in the sea”

The Guardian

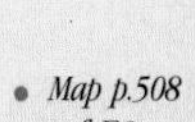

• Map p.508 ref: E9

Hotel and restaurant

AHERNES

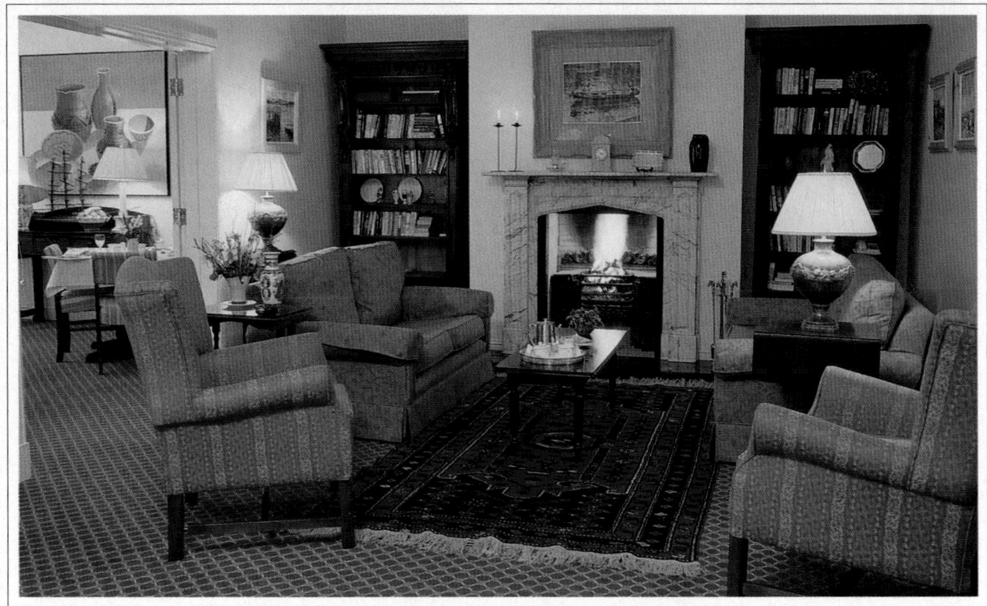

Luxury rooms with a 'seafood view'

Ahernes is in the heart of the picturesque Youghal (pronounced Yawl), the old historic walled port at the mouth of the River Blackwater. It is a family pub that the Fitzgibbons (3rd generation) have changed into a renowned restaurant that specialises in the freshest local seafood. Lobsters, crab, sole, salmon, monkfish, mussels, clams all feature on menus that change daily.

The twelve luxurious bedrooms, generous in size, have been tastefully decorated and furnished. They combine modern features (six-foot beds, hairdryer, TV, direct-dial telephone and trouser press) with carefully chosen antiques that blend perfectly together.

East Cork is a primary tourist area on the splendid south coast of Ireland. Ancient historic buildings include the still used 12th century Collegiate Church, the unique Clock Tower and Ireland's first post-Norman University, founded in 1464.

Close by are an 18-hole golf course, deep sea and river angling, riding, two Blue Flag beaches and superb walks through beautiful countryside. From the moment you are first greeted by the family, you will find Ahernes is a marvellous place to relax and enjoy yourself.

LOCATION

On the N25, on Youghal's main street.

163 North Main St, Youghal, Co Cork, Republic of Ireland

Telephone +353 (0)24 92424
Fax +353 (0)24 93633

E-mail: *ahernes@bestloved.com*

OWNERS

The Fitzgibbon Family

ROOM RATES *(Irish Punts)*

Single occupancy £80 - £85
12 Doubles/Twins £116 - £160
Includes full breakfast and VAT

CHARGE/CREDIT CARDS

• *DC* • *MC* • *VI*

RATINGS & AWARDS

I.T.B. ★★★★
R.A.C. ◆◆◆◆◆ ❀❀
Dining Award 2
Sparkling Diamond & Warm Welcome Awards

FACILITIES

On site: *1 meeting room/max 20 people*
Nearby: *Golf, fishing, riding, hill walking*

RESTRICTIONS

No pets
Closed 24 - 28 Dec

ATTRACTIONS

Jameson Heritage Centre, Cork, Waterford Crystal, Blarney Castle, Queenstown Heritage Centre

AFFILIATIONS

Ireland's Blue Book
Preston's Global Hotels

NEAREST

MAJOR CITY:
Cork - 30 miles/45 mins

MAJOR AIRPORT:
Cork - 30 miles/45 mins

RAILWAY STATION:
Cork - 30 miles/45 mins

RESERVATIONS

Toll free in US: 800-544-9993
or 800-323-5463
Quote ***Best Loved***

ACCESS CODES

Not applicable

• Map p.508 ref: B9

“ The days at Ard na Sidhe are the highlight of our visit in Ireland ”

Hans Jürgen Linschind

ARD NA SIDHE

Victorian country house

Caragh Lake,
Killorglin, Co Kerry,
Republic of Ireland

Telephone +353 (0)66 9769105
Fax +353 (0)66 9769282

E-mail: ardnasidhe@bestloved.com

RESIDENT MANAGER
Kathleen Dowling

ROOM RATES *(Irish Punts)*

2 Singles	£80
15 Doubles/Twins	£126 - £150
3 Superiors	£176

Includes full breakfast, service and VAT

CHARGE/CREDIT CARDS

• DC • MC • VI

RATINGS & AWARDS
I.T.B. ★★★★
National Garden Competition Winner

FACILITIES
On site: *Garden, fishing, boating*
Nearby: *Golf*

RESTRICTIONS
No facilities for disabled guests
No children
No pets
Closed 1 Oct - 30 Apr

ATTRACTIONS
Ring of Kerry, Caragh Lake, Killarney National Park, Dingle Peninsula

AFFILIATIONS
Killarney Hotels Ltd
Preston's Global Hotels

NEAREST
MAJOR CITY:
Cork - 91 miles/2¼ hrs

MAJOR AIRPORT:
Shannon - 95 miles/2½ hrs
Cork - 70 miles/2¼ hrs

RAILWAY STATION:
Killarney - 17 miles/40 mins

RESERVATIONS
Toll free in US: 800-544-9993
or 800-537-8483
Quote ***Best Loved***

ACCESS CODES
Not applicable

The house of your dreams in an award-winning garden

Ard na Sidhe translates as 'the Hill of the Fairies'. This 20-bedroom mansion hotel on the edge of Caragh Lake has modern facilities, high standards of cuisine and service you would expect from Killarney Hotels, one of Ireland's leading leisure groups. It stands in an award-winning garden. Yet it also has a mystic history that reaches deep into the country's distant and magical past.

Lady Gordon, a lady of titled Irish lineage, built the house in 1913. It is long and low and gabled, with casement windows set in stone mullions, "and never", said Lady Gordon, "looked new." The ghost of her ancestor, Bess Stokes, is said to haunt the grounds, but it was 'The Hill of the Fairies' long before Bess.

The house fits harmoniously into superbly romantic scenery, beside Ireland's highest mountain, McGillicuddy's Reeks. All around is magnificently beautiful countryside for fishing, cycling and boating on the lakes. Several of the country's finest golf courses are within an easy and delightful drive away.

At the Ard na Sidhe you will enjoy the full range of holiday leisure and historical touring attractions that have made Killarney one of the best-loved places in the world. And there is an extra special something in the unique and mystical history of The Hill of the Fairies.

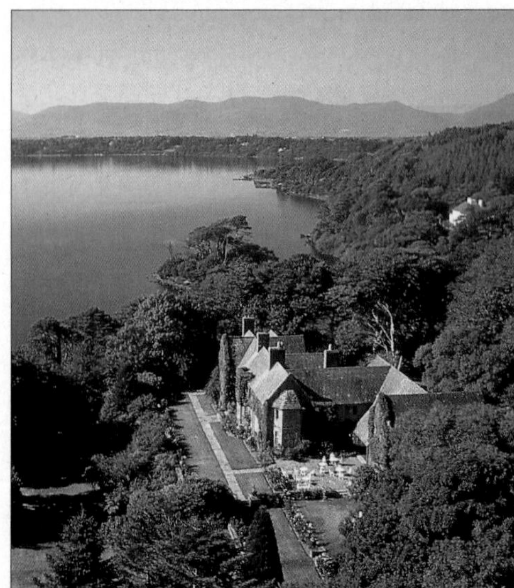

LOCATION

Right at the edge of the beautiful Caragh Lake at Killarney.

“ The beauty of not only the castle but the surrounding grounds and lough evoke a restful and peaceful feeling that is hard to describe ”

Sidney Sheldon, author

• Map p.508 ref: C6

13th century castle

ASHFORD CASTLE

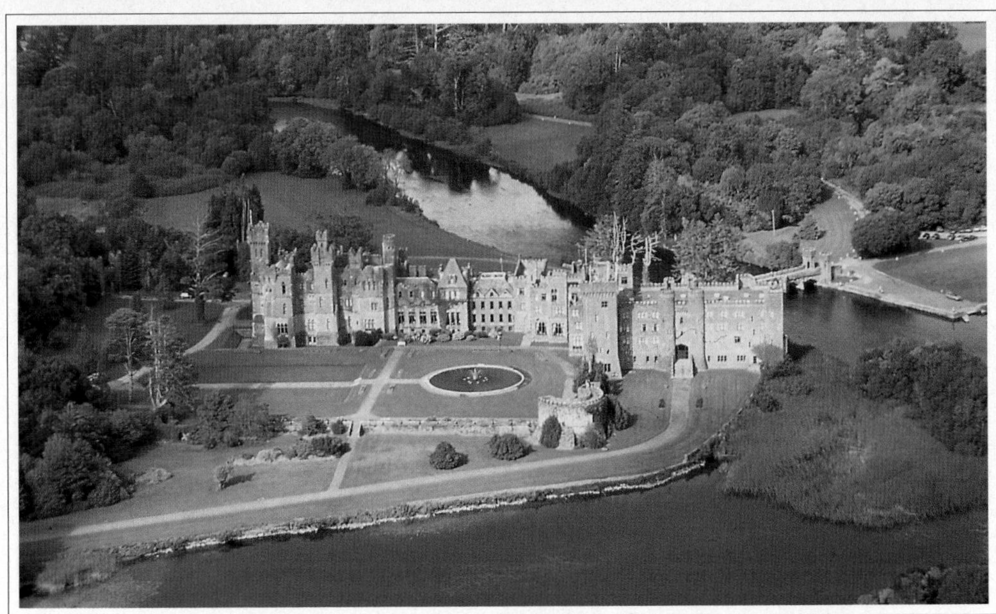

A stately home, sporting complex and the best of the West of Ireland

Until 1939, Ashford Castle was part of an estate owned by the Guinness family and the residence of Lord Ardilaun. It was transformed into a luxury hotel and many of its lavish furnishings, the rich panelling of the Great Hall, the objets d'art and masterpiece paintings came into the domain of those guests fortunate enough to stay there.

The estate provides an almost inexhaustable array of sporting pleasures: a nine-hole golf course, indoor equestrian centre, clay pigeon shooting, archery, fishing, a fully equipped gymnasium, a health centre and some of the most magnificent walks in Ireland.

Everything about Ashford Castle reflects its aristocratic antecedents: the comfort, the service and, not least, the food. This area of Ireland is famous for the quality of its produce especially the seafood which comes from the cleanest waters in Europe. You have a choice between traditional and French cuisine dining in either the George V or The Connaught restaurants. An evening drink in the Dungeon Bar is accompanied by a resident pianist and harpist.

The lordly bedrooms are sumptuously furnished to the highest standards and most overlook the lough or the river.

LOCATION

From Galway take the N84 north to Headford then the R334 forking left onto the R346 to Cong. At a village called Cross, turn left at the church and drive through the castle gates.

Cong, Co Mayo, Republic of Ireland

Telephone +353 (0)92 46003
Fax +353 (0)92 46260

E-mail: *ashford@bestloved.com*

GENERAL MANAGER

Rory Murphy

ROOM RATES *(Irish Punts)*

Single occupancy	*£136 - £665*
40 Standard Doubles/Twins	*£146 - £295*
32 Deluxe Doubles/Twins	*£227 - £350*
5 State rooms	*£388 - £490*
6 Suites	*£467 - £675*

Includes service and VAT

CHARGE/CREDIT CARDS

• DC • MC • VI

RATINGS & AWARDS

I.T.B. ★★★★★

R.A.C. ★★★★★ *Dining Award 3*

FACILITIES

On site: *Garden, tennis, golf, archery, snooker, clay pigeon shooting, gym, health & beauty, riding, fishing, walking, heli-pad*

1 meeting room/max 110 people

RESTRICTIONS

No facilities for disabled guests

No pets

ATTRACTIONS

Westport, Clifden, Connemara, Kylemore Abbey, Galway, Ceidhe Fields

AFFILIATIONS

Relais & Châteaux

NEAREST

MAJOR CITY:
Galway - 35 miles/45 mins

MAJOR AIRPORT:
Shannon - 90 miles/1½ hrs

RAILWAY STATION:
Galway - 35 miles/45 mins

RESERVATIONS

Toll free in US: 800-346-7007

Quote ***Best Loved***

ACCESS CODES

Not applicable

A keen Angler? Refer to page 472 for our Fishing Index

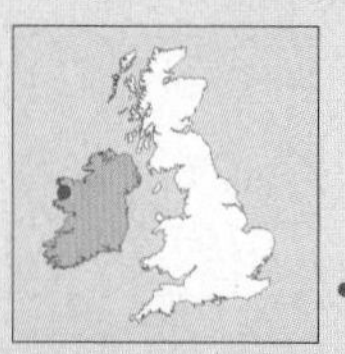

"We have stayed at most of the world's top ten hotels and I would consider this hotel to have the best staff we have yet encountered"

David Everetts, Greenwood, Indiana, USA

BALLYNAHINCH CASTLE HOTEL

16th century castle

**Ballinafad, Recess,
Connemara, Co Galway,
Republic of Ireland**

**Telephone +353 (0)95 31006
Fax +353 (0)95 31085**

E-mail: ballynahinch@bestloved.com

GENERAL MANAGER
Patrick O'Flaherty

ROOM RATES (Irish Punts)

Single occupancy	£80 - £160
18 Doubles/Twins	£115 - £145
10 Superior Doubles/Twins	£125 - £165
9 Luxury Doubles/Twins	£155 - £210
3 Suites	£245 - £275

Includes full breakfast and VAT

CHARGE/CREDIT CARDS

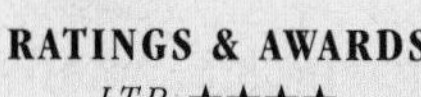

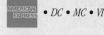

• DC • MC • VI

RATINGS & AWARDS
I.T.B. ★★★★
A.A. ★★★★ ❀❀ 74%

FACILITIES
On site: Garden, croquet, outdoor tennis, fishing, heli-pad, narrated walks, shooting, mountain bikes, wild salmon, fishery, clay shooting (by arrangement)
Nearby: Golf, sea fishing, yachting, fitness centre, riding

RESTRICTIONS
No pets
Closed Christmas week and Feb

ATTRACTIONS
Connemara National Park, The Aran Islands, Kylemore Abbey, the Sky Road, hill walking, beaches,

AFFILIATIONS
Manor House Hotels of Ireland

NEAREST
MAJOR CITY:
Galway - 45 miles/1 hr
MAJOR AIRPORT:
Shannon - 99 miles/2½ hrs
RAILWAY STATION:
Galway - 45 miles/1 hr

RESERVATIONS
Toll free in US/Canada: 800-44-UTELL
Quote **Best Loved**

ACCESS CODES
AMADEUS UI GWYBAL
APOLLO/GALILEO UI 91700
SABRE/ABACUS UI 8116
WORLDSPAN UI 40028

A grand and beautiful castle on a famous wild salmon river

"In the wild grandeur of her mien, erect and high, she dauntless stood." So they wrote of pirate queen Grace O'Malley when she wed the warlike Donal O'Flaherty and came to Ballynahinch Castle in 1529. Hospitality at the grand castle, rebuilt in the 18th century, has a long history. Distinguished owners include the Indian cricketer, Maharajah Ranjitsinhji. Recent guests include celebrities and statesman. Manager Patrick O'Flaherty peacefully welcomes them to the full service of a four star hotel that combines high quality with personal friendliness.

The soul of Ballynahinch lies in its setting on its renowned wild salmon river in the heart of Connemara. Most rooms have views of the mountains, the river or both and the addition of a luxury riverside wing with four-poster beds and beautiful suites completes the picture. Casual country elegance is the style with the very best of Irish Country House and French cuisine.

With vast wooded grounds and walks, fishing rights on its own river and an extensive prime woodcock shoot, the castle offers all the attractions of a large private estate. At the heartland of Irish culture, it is close to Connemara National Park, the Heather Island of James Joyce and W B Yeats, the Aran Islands and so much that encapsulates Gaelic Ireland.

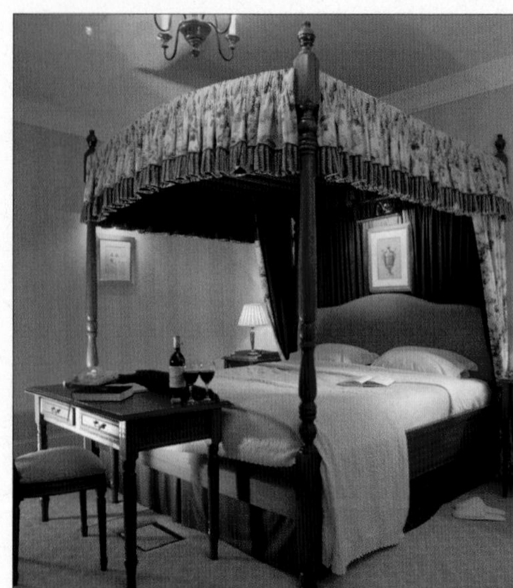

LOCATION

From Galway City take the N59 west towards Clifden. After Recess take the third turn left, signposted Roundstone and Ballynahinch Castle.

"You have created an oasis of peace"

Chihuly Studios, Seattle, USA

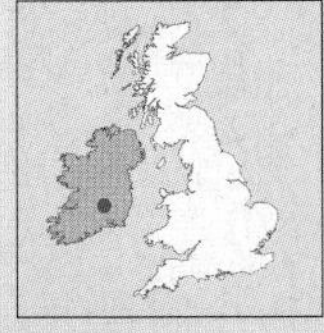

• Map p.508 ref: E9

Georgian country house

BALLYRAFTER HOUSE HOTEL

Relaxing hospitality and good food in the famous valley of the Blackwater Salmon

Many of the finest estates in the counties of Cork and Waterford were founded during the 17th and 18th centuries along the picturesque Blackwater valley - and for good reason: this is a particularly lush, fertile part of Ireland.

Ballyrafter House was originally part of the Duke of Devonshire's estate and was converted to a hotel in 1966 by the Willoughby family. The hotel, standing in its own secluded garden, retains all the old-world charm and character of the ancestoral manor that it is. But make no mistake the facilities are right up-to-date. You will find it elegantly comfortable with many individual touches that express the genuine warmth of the Willoughby's hospitality.

Given that the river has so many stretches of Prime Salmon fishing, it will come as no surprise that oak smoked Blackwater Salmon makes a daily appearance on the imaginative menu that blends the best of traditional Irish with European cuisines. For good food, a perfect setting and a friendly, relaxed atmosphere, Ballyrafter House has a great deal to offer.

The hotel is beautifully placed for exploring the area's many attractions: Lismore and its castle, Cork, Waterford Crystal factory, The Rock of Cashel, Kilkenny and Killarney; not to mention the Jameson Old Midleton Distillery where you'll be given a drop of the real thing.

LOCATION

½ mile east of Lismore just off the N72. Travelling west, turn right at the signpost to the Vee by the service station.

Lismore, Co Waterford, Republic of Ireland

Telephone +353 (0)58 54002
Fax +353 (0)58 53050

E-mail: ballyrafter@bestloved.com

OWNERS

Joe and Noreen Willoughby

ROOM RATES (*Irish Punts*)

9 Doubles/Twins £70 - £90

Includes full breakfast and VAT

CHARGE/CREDIT CARDS

• DC • MC • VI

RATINGS & AWARDS

I.T.B. ★★

A.A. ★★ ❀ 64%

FACILITIES

On site: *Garden, croquet*

2 meeting rooms/max 100 people

Nearby: *Golf, tennis, fishing, riding*

RESTRICTIONS

No dogs in bedrooms, kennels available

No smoking in bedrooms

ATTRACTIONS

Lismore Heritage Town, Lismore Castle Gardens, Waterford Crystal, Jameson Heritage Centre, Cobh Heritage Centre, Rock of Cashel

AFFILIATIONS

Independent

NEAREST

MAJOR CITY:
Cork - 34 miles/1 hr

MAJOR AIRPORT:
Dublin - 140 miles/3½ hrs
Cork - 40 miles/1 hr

RAILWAY STATION:
Cork - 34 miles/1 hr

RESERVATIONS

Direct with hotel

Quote **Best Loved**

ACCESS CODES

Not applicable

• Map p.508 ref: D10

"Significant parts of my life are spent in four and five star hotels. The atmosphere and presentation of the Bayview matches the best of them"

Peter Maxwell, Hampshire

BAYVIEW HOTEL

Seaside hotel

Ballycotton, Co Cork, Republic of Ireland

Telephone +353 (0)21 4646746
Fax +353 (0)21 4646075

E-mail: bayview@bestloved.com

OWNER

Mr John O'Brien

GENERAL MANAGER

Stephen Belton

ROOM RATES (Irish Punts)

Single occupancy	£77 - £89
33 Doubles/Twins	£113 - £138
2 Suites	£163 - £188

Includes full breakfast and VAT

CHARGE/CREDIT CARDS

• DC • MC • VI

RATINGS & AWARDS

I.T.B. ★★★★
R.A.C. ★★★ Dining Award 2
A.A. ★★★ ❀❀ 73%

FACILITIES

On site: Garden, sea fishing, table tennis
2 meeting rooms/max 40 people
Nearby: Golf, fishing, tennis, riding

RESTRICTIONS

Limited facilities for disabled guests
No pets

Closed Nov - Easter

ATTRACTIONS

Cobh Heritage Centre, Youghal Cathedral, Titanic Trail, Fota Wildlife Park, Jameson Heritage Centre

AFFILIATIONS

Manor House Hotels of Ireland

NEAREST

MAJOR CITY:
Midleton - 12 miles/30 mins

MAJOR AIRPORT:
Cork - 23 miles/45 mins

RAILWAY STATION:
Cork - 23 miles/45 mins

RESERVATIONS

Toll free in US/Canada: 800-44-UTELL
Quote **Best Loved**

ACCESS CODES

AMADEUS UI ORKBAY
APOLLO/GALILEO UI 91672
SABRE/ABACUS UI 27287

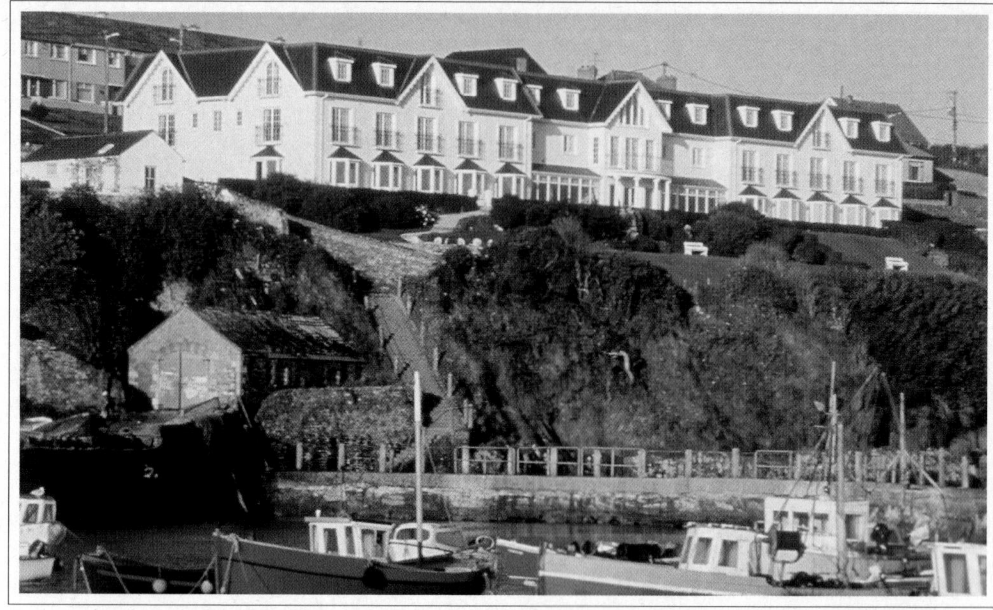

Superb food and marvellous views of a spectacular coastline

Bayview Hotel at Ballycotton overlooks a small, unspoilt, fishing harbour. Every bedroom is a room with a view over miles of spectacular coastline. The hotel was caringly restored in 1991, and now combines modern luxury with the charm and warmth of bygone days. The style is informal and friendly. The dinners are superb, based on the best use of fresh local produce to provide dishes with the right balance of flavour, texture and presentation to make them truly delightful. The hotel's original garden offers invigorating air and an insight into the work of a traditional fishing harbour.

The hotel is excellently placed for sea angling, especially for warm water fish such as shark and conger, and for bird watching, coastal walking and swimming. Six golf courses, links and woodland, are within 30 minutes' drive.

Ballycotton is a traditional fishing village dating back to 1250. It is ideally located for exploring the many treasures of East Cork and the wider environs of counties Cork and Waterford. Close at hand are Fota Wildlife Park, Jameson Whiskey Heritage Centre, Queenstown Harbour with its Titanic connections, and the Queenstown Story at Cobh, where many Irish emigrants set sail for America from the mid 19th century to the 1950s.

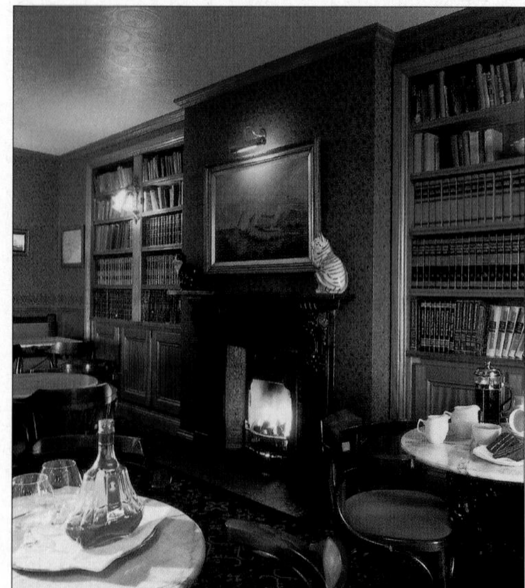

LOCATION

At Castlemartyr on the A25 turn onto the R632 towards Garryvoe. From Garryvoe follow signs for Shanagarry and Ballycotton.

"In great appreciation to you both for providing hours of pleasure in your wonderful cooking and very beautiful restaurant"

A devoted fan (name witheld)

• Map p.508 ref: B10

Georgian country house

BLAIR'S COVE HOUSE

Self-catering, b-and-b, and an acclaimed restaurant in 4½ tropical acres by the sea

Blairs Cove House is a beautiful Georgian country house set on the shores of Dunmanus Bay in four and a half acres of lawns and sub-tropical gardens. The old stone buildings that are arranged around the cobbled courtyard have been converted into two houses, a duplex apartment and a studio, all of which can be rented year round on either a self-catering or a bed-and-breakfast basis (This is not an hotel). There are also two cottages, one in its own grounds with direct access to the sea, the other on Dunmanus Pier, both self-catering. All are delightful.

Local craftsmen have been employed to blend old and new in the conversion of the very different living spaces, making the best of spectacular views over the cove or the hills and valleys. The owners have furnished each one in an individual style, with a good eye for colour, using carefully chosen fabrics and floor coverings, antiques and locally made modern furniture, works of art and choice pieces of bric-à-brac. Facilities include washing machine/driers or use of a laundry, and some of the suites have a video and stereo system. In the old stable block, with high stone walls and lofty, beamed roof, is the much-acclaimed restaurant (open March to late October for dinner only).

Plan to stay for as long as you can.

LOCATION

1½ miles from Durrus along the Coleen/Barleycove Road. The hotel's entrance (blue gates) is on the right hand side.

Near Bantry, Durrus, Co Cork, Republic of Ireland

Telephone +353 (0)27 61127
Fax +353 (0)27 61487

E-mail: blairs@bestloved.com

OWNERS
Philippe and Sabine De Mey

ROOM RATES *(Irish Punts)*

Single occupancy	£45 - £85
3 Suites	£70 - £150

Includes continental breakfast, service and VAT

CHARGE/CREDIT CARDS

• DC • MC • VI

RATINGS & AWARDS
Independent

FACILITIES
On site: *Garden*
Nearby: *Golf, tennis, fitness, yachting, fishing, riding*

RESTRICTIONS
No facilities for disabled guests
Restaurant closed 31 Oct - 31 Mar
No pets

ATTRACTIONS
Bantry House, Ring of Beara, Garnish Island Italian Gardens, Mizenhead Lighthouse, Ring of Kerry, Schull Planetarium

AFFILIATIONS
Ireland's Blue Book

NEAREST
MAJOR CITY:
Cork - 80 miles/1¼ hrs

MAJOR AIRPORT:
Cork - 80 miles/1¼ hrs

RAILWAY STATION:
Cork - 80 miles/1¼ hrs

RESERVATIONS
Toll free in US: 800-323-5463
*Quote **Best Loved***

ACCESS CODES
Not applicable

For information about hotel affiliations see page 14

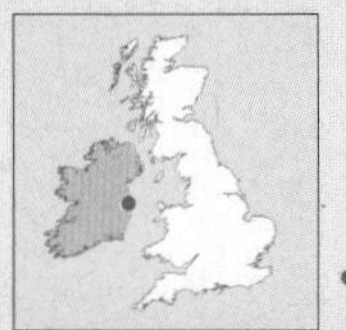

• Map p.508 ref: G7

"A wonderful town house, can't wait to come back"

Margaret Clarke, New Jersey, USA

BLAKES TOWNHOUSE

Town house

50 Merrion Road, Ballsbridge, Dublin 4, Republic of Ireland

Telephone +353 (0)1 6688324
Fax +353 (0)1 6684280

E-mail: blakestown@bestloved.com

OWNER

Pat Halpin

ROOM RATES (*Irish Punts*)

Single occupancy	£84 - £99
5 Doubles/Twins	£99 - £145
5 Superior Doubles/Twins	£119 - £165
2 Four-posters	£129 - £195

Includes full breakfast, service and VAT

CHARGE/CREDIT CARDS

• DC • JCB • MC • VI

RATINGS & AWARDS

Awards pending

FACILITIES

On site: *Garden, car park*
1 meeting room/max 30 people
Nearby: *Complimentary use of nearby leisure centre, riding, fishing*

RESTRICTIONS

Limited facilities for disabled guests
No children under 2 years
No pets, guide dogs only

ATTRACTIONS

Trinity College, National Art Gallery, Christchurch, St Stephen's Green, Grafton Street, Powerscourt Gardens

AFFILIATIONS

Green Book of Ireland
Luxe Boutique Hotels

NEAREST

MAJOR CITY:
Dublin

MAJOR AIRPORT:
Dublin - 6 miles/20 mins

RAILWAY STATION:
Sandymount - ¼ mile/5 mins

RESERVATIONS

Toll free in US: 800-888-1199
Toll free in UK: 0800 371 425
Quote ***Best Loved***

ACCESS CODES

AMADEUS LE DUB987
APOLLO/GALILEO LE 27207
SABRE/ABACUS LE 52264
WORLDSPAN LE 52264

Small is beautiful (and affordable) in the fair city of Dublin

If you are looking for a home-from-home that won't break the bank in Eire's increasingly fashionable capital city, Blakes' Townhouse is a very useful address to know. One of a row of three-storey Edwardian homes in the quiet residential quarter of Ballsbridge (also known as the Embassy District for the proliferation of foreign embassies that have established themselves here), Blakes' combines century-old style and an intimate ambience with modern facilities. Easy access to the city centre is a major attraction - it is close enough to walk - yet without the inflated prices.

Friendly, welcoming staff are essential to the success of a small private hotel and the staff at Blakes make every effort to put guests at their ease.

The very comfortable bedrooms are equipped with the latest in-room technology to suit the most discerning professional and leisure traveller, while the executive rooms and four-poster suites also feature whirlpool spas. Guests can also enjoy full use of leisure facilities including a sauna and fitness centre at Blakes's adjacent sister property Merrion Hall. And if you are keen to escape the city for the day, the hotel can arrange golfing packages and scenic country tours.

LOCATION

From City Centre take Merrion Road, hotel is on left side opposite RDS Convention Centre.

“ The Blue Haven stands out from the crowd as being a most charming hotel where food and good hospitality go hand in hand ”

Georgina Campbell, food writer, Irish Country Cooking

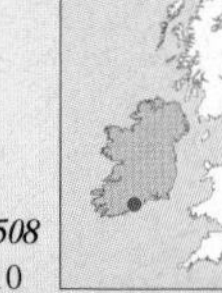

Traditional hotel

BLUE HAVEN HOTEL

A founder member of the International Gourmet Festival

Back in 1334, Kinsale was an important port for both fishing and shipping. In 1703, a London merchant, taking refuge from the heavy weather at sea, wrote: “We thought ourselves in a land of plenty with fine large salmon and very good French claret, we did not a little indulge ourselves”. This observation had a prophetic ring to it because, today, Kinsale's International Gourmet Festival is now in its 26th year.

In the centre of the town, and central to the festivities, is the Blue Haven Hotel, one of the founder members of the Festival.

Food critics from far and wide are unanimous in their praise. Standing on the site of the old fish market, it is appropriate that the speciality of the house is seafood and shellfish. Elle magazine voted the Hot Smoked Salmon one of their Top Ten Dream Meals of the World.

The hotel itself is a small, cosy town house with 17 comfortable bedrooms. The standards are fastidiously high and maintained by an enthusiastic staff blessed with Irish charm. Like so many before you, a stay at The Blue Haven is one to be savoured and remembered.

The town, aptly described as ‘rich in history’, is as picturesque as you could wish with its medieval buildings, forts, churches and castles.

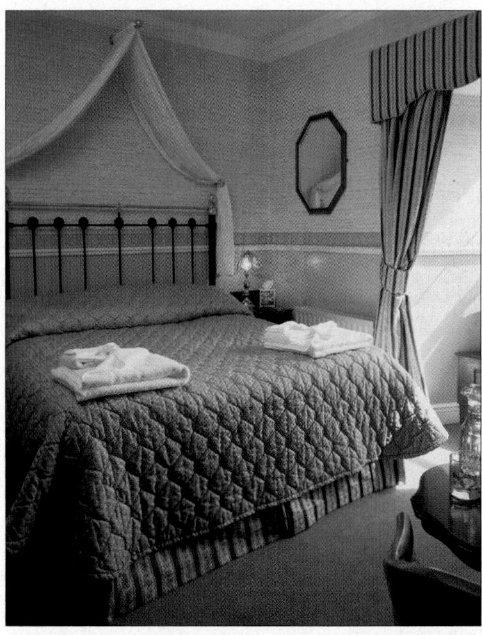

LOCATION

In the town centre.

Kinsale, Co Cork, Republic of Ireland

Telephone +353 (0)21 772209
Fax +353 (0)21 774268

E-mail: *bluehaven@bestloved.com*

OWNER

Avril Greene

ROOM RATES *(Irish Punts)*

1 Single	*£65 - £95*
16 Doubles/Twins	*£100 - £160*

Includes full breakfast, service and VAT

CHARGE/CREDIT CARDS

• DC • MC • VI

RATINGS & AWARDS

I.T.B. ★★★

FACILITIES

On site: *Restaurant*
Nearby: *Golf, tennis, fishing, water skiing, yachting*

RESTRICTIONS

No facilities for disabled guests
No pets
Closed 24 - 26 Dec

ATTRACTIONS

International Museum of Wine, Desmond Castle, Charles Fort, West Cork Scenic Drive, Clonakilty Model Village, Cobh Heritage Centre, Fota Wildlife Park, Action Pak Outdoor Activity Centre

AFFILIATIONS

Independent

NEAREST

MAJOR CITY:
Cork - 18 miles/30 mins

MAJOR AIRPORT:
Cork - 15 miles/25 mins

RAILWAY STATION:
Cork - 18 miles/30 mins

RESERVATIONS

Direct with hotel
Quote ***Best Loved***

ACCESS CODES

Not applicable

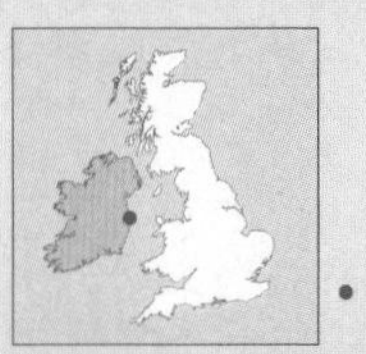

• Map p.508 ref: G7

"I would rate Brooks and the attitude of the staff as one of the best I have experienced. The willingness to help and friendly manner was evident without being overbearing"

Adrian Norman, Dow Jones, London

BROOKS HOTEL

Contemporary town house hotel

59 - 62 Drury Street,
Dublin 2,
Republic of Ireland

Telephone +353 (0)1 670 4000
Fax +353 (0)1 670 4455

E-mail: brookshotel@bestloved.com

GENERAL MANAGER

Anne McKiernan

ROOM RATES

6 Singles	£130 - £160
64 Doubles/Twins	£175 - £195
3 Executive rooms	£220
2 Family (triple) rooms	£195

Includes full breakfast and VAT

CHARGE/CREDIT CARDS

• DC • MC • VI

RATINGS & AWARDS

I.T.B. ★★★★

FACILITIES

On site: *3 meeting rooms/max 70 people*
Nearby: *Golf, fitness*

RESTRICTIONS

No pets

ATTRACTIONS

Dublin Castle, National Gallery, National Museum, St Stephen's Green, Trinity College, Book of Kells

AFFILIATIONS

Sinnott Hotels Group

NEAREST

MAJOR CITY:
Dublin

MAJOR AIRPORT:
Dublin - 6 miles/30 mins

RAILWAY STATION:
Pearse Street - 1 mile/15 mins

FERRY PORT:
Dun Loaghaire - 6 miles/30 mins

RESERVATIONS

Toll free in US: 800-537-8483
Toll free in UK: 0800 894351
Quote **Best Loved**

ACCESS CODES

AMADEUS LM DUB779
APOLLO/GALILEO LM 88312
SABRE/ABACUS LM 7498
WORLDSPAN LM 02779

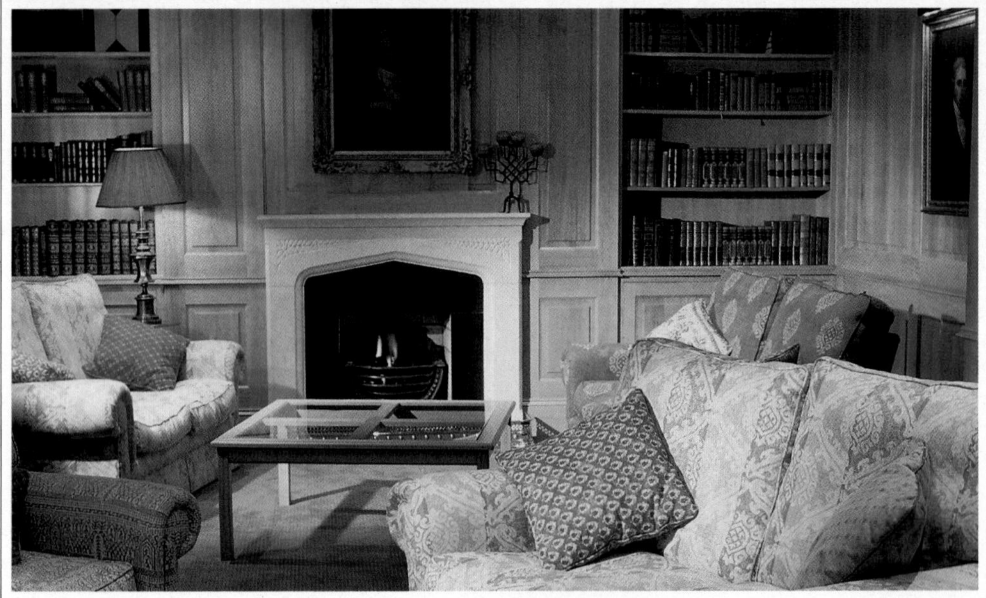

An oasis in the fashionable heart of Dublin City

Brooks has a clubby, residential feel about it. Within the husk of this contemporary building, there's a soft centre of luxury. A pleasing mix of traditional comfort, classic style and chic colour schemes. The sort of place that puts you at your ease as soon as you arrive. The hotel has a bar, a sumptuous drawing room where you can enjoy a post-theatre drink, perhaps, and a cosy restaurant which features international cuisine. The food is good, innovative and certainly merits Brooks' place on Dublin's gastronomic map.

Converts to the e-world of correspondence and the Web will find themselves right at home: the spacious bedrooms have been designed for both sleeping and working and there are modem points and telephones with ISDN connections.

For the technophobes who wish to remain aloof from such mysteries, the colour TV, video and sophisticated sound systems provide a range of in-room entertainment which can be 'piped' to the bathrooms. Air conditioning is a feature in all the bedrooms.

Whether you visit Dublin on business or pleasure, you will find Brooks is in just the right place: tucked away in Drury Street but within the business centre of the city and near its famous landmarks - Trinity College, Grafton Street and Georgian St Stephen's Green.

A boutique hotel if ever there was one.

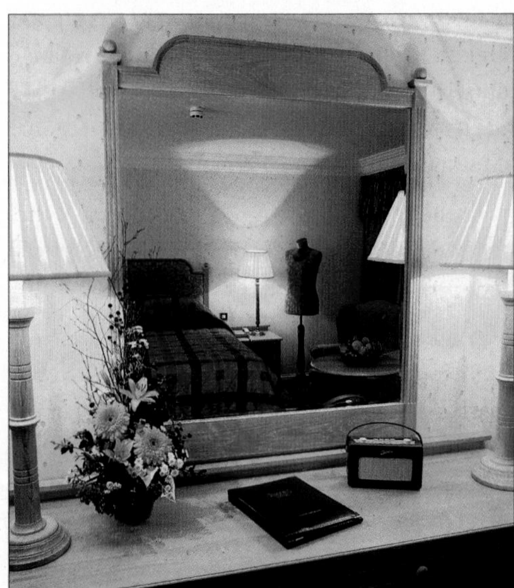

LOCATION

In Drury Street, midway between St Stephen's Green, Trinity College and Dublin Castle.

Planning a wedding reception? Turn to 'Meeting Facilities' on page 476

" Sumptuous food in splendid surroundings "

Lucinda O'Sullivan, Irish Independent

• Map p.508
ref: G7

Georgian town house

BROWNES TOWNHOUSE

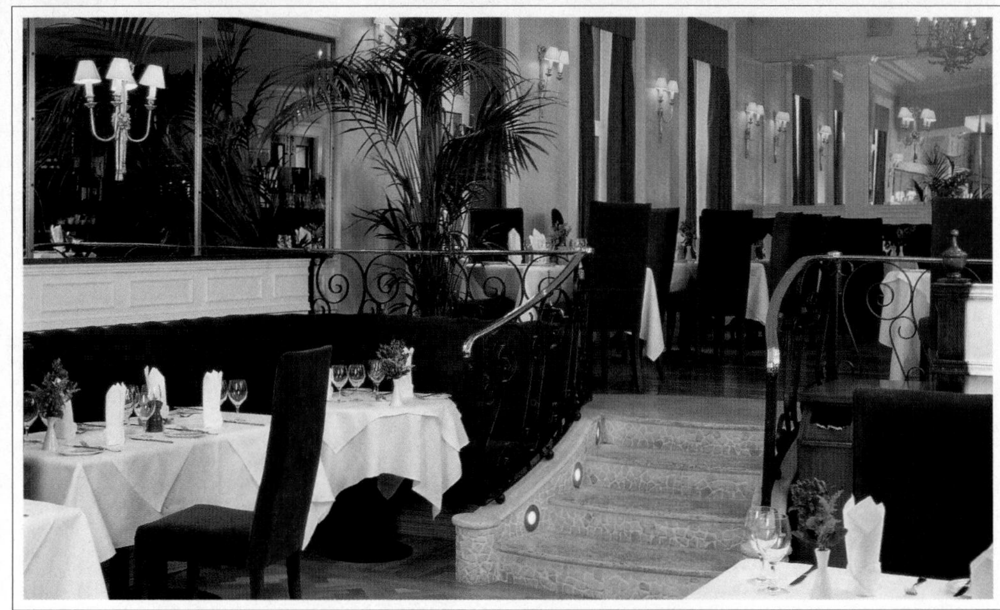

The talk of Dublin stylishly set in its cultural centre

Sophisticated but relaxed - this is the atmosphere that pervades this Georgian town house whose tall windows overlook St Stephen's Green, the spacious and prestigious park right in the heart of Dublin. Close by are the buildings of Trinity College and the National Museum, Grafton Street's fashionable shopping district, many of the city's most popular pubs and all the gathering places of trendy Temple Bar.

Brownes is a city-centre hotel, yet it has the intimacy and warmth of a country house. The twelve bedrooms and suites are equipped with all the facilities a business guest requires (including ISDN and a direct fax line), but each is individually designed and traditionally decorated and furnished with comfort and luxury in mind.

Brownes Brasserie is a gracious, split-level dining room whose plush deep-red seating is set off by the crisp white table linen. Known by locals for its sumptuous cuisine, the Brasserie is, like the townhouse, stylish in a traditional manner with a contemporary, relaxed ambience. It prides itself on being the perfect setting for a casual meal with friends, a lunch with business colleagues, or a romantic dinner à deux. There is a suite for small, private meetings, and a private dining room with view of St Stephen's Green.

Full of life. A place to see and be seen.

LOCATION

From the airport follow the signs to 'City Centre' and then 'St Stephen's Green'. Brownes is on the North side of St Stephen's Green.

22 St Stephen's Green, Dublin 2, Republic of Ireland

Telephone +353 (0)1 638 3939
Fax +353 (0)1 638 3900

E-mail: brownes@bestloved.com

OWNER
Barry Canny

GENERAL MANAGER
Ronan Branigan

ROOM RATES (Irish Punts)

2 Singles	£90 - £165
8 Doubles/Twins	£145 - £165
1 Four-poster	£165
2 Suites	£295 - £350

Includes full breakfast and VAT

CHARGE/CREDIT CARDS

• MC • VI

RATINGS & AWARDS
I.T.B. ★★★★ Town House

FACILITIES
On site: *1 meeting room/max 40 people*
Nearby: *Golf, tennis, fitness, water skiing, fishing, riding, hunting/shooting*

RESTRICTIONS
No pets

ATTRACTIONS
St Stephen's Green, Trinity College, National Museum, Grafton Street, Temple Bar

AFFILIATIONS
Manor House Hotels of Ireland

NEAREST
MAJOR CITY:
Dublin

MAJOR AIRPORT:
Dublin - 15 miles/30 mins

RAILWAY STATION:
Heuston - 6 miles/15 mins

RESERVATIONS
Toll free in US: 800-44-UTELL
Quote **Best Loved**

ACCESS CODES
Not applicable

"It's one of those places where you hope it rains all day so you have an excuse to snuggle indoors"

Ian Cruikshank, Journalist, Canada

THE BUSHMILLS INN

Coaching inn and restaurant

9 Dunluce Road, Bushmills, Co Antrim BT57 8QG Northern Ireland

Telephone +44 (0)28 207 3 2339
Fax +44 (0)28 207 3 2048

E-mail: bushmills@bestloved.com

MANAGERS

Alan Dunlop and Stella Minogue

ROOM RATES

4 Singles	£68 - £78
28 Doubles/Twins	£88 - £128

Includes full breakfast and VAT

CHARGE/CREDIT CARDS

• MC • VI

RATINGS & AWARDS

N.I.T.B. ★★★
R.A.C. ★★★ Dining Award 2
Taste of Ulster

FACILITIES

On site: Garden, fishing, heli-pad
3 meeting rooms/max 50 people
Nearby: Golf, riding, fishing, walking

RESTRICTIONS

No pets, guide dogs only

ATTRACTIONS

Giant's Causeway, Dunluce Castle, Old Bushmills Distillery, Carrick-a-Rede rope bridge, Royal Portrush Golf Club

AFFILIATIONS

Ireland's Blue Book
Northern Ireland's Best Kept Secrets

NEAREST

MAJOR CITY:
Belfast - 60 miles/1¼ hrs

MAJOR AIRPORT:
Belfast International - 48 miles/1 hr
Londonderry - 32 miles/45 mins

RAILWAY STATION:
Coleraine - 9 miles/15 mins

RESERVATIONS

Toll free in US: 800-323-5463
Quote **Best Loved**

ACCESS CODES

Not applicable

An intriguing inn by the world's oldest distillery near The Giant's Causeway

The Giant's Causeway Coast is reckoned the most spectacular in Europe - wide sandy beaches washed by Atlantic rollers, neat fishing harbours nestling between craggy cliffs and grassy dunes supporting a wealth of wildlife. The area is a golfer's paradise with no less than eight courses, including Royal Portrush, within easy driving range while, for anglers, the River Bush is within casting distance of the hotel gardens.

The welcoming glow of, not one but four, turf fires is just one of many features that give this historic inn its unique and intriguing character. There is a secret room, if you can find it and, in the bar, still lit by gaslight, you can treat yourself to a glass of 25 year old Bushmills malt whiskey from the hotel's private cask before anticipating the pleasures of the Taste of Ulster Restaurant. Within its white washed walls and intimate snugs you can enjoy excellent, freshly prepared dishes and a glass (or two) of expertly chosen wines.

Bedrooms in the Coaching Inn are individually furnished in comfortable cottage style. The oak-beamed Loft is the gateway to the Mill House on the banks of the River Bush and here the spacious bedrooms have their own sitting room area.

Since its re-opening in 1987, the inn has come to epitomise the true spirit of Ulster hospitality and is regularly featured by television presenters and travel writers from all over the world.

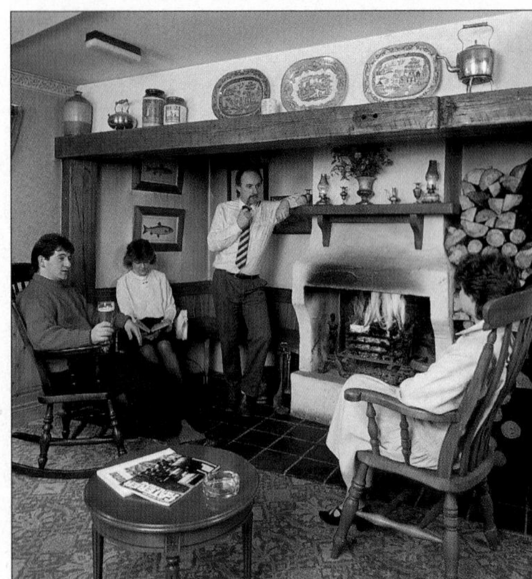

LOCATION

On the A2 Antrim coast road. From Ballymoney take the B62 turning right on to the B17 from Coleraine. Follow the Giant's Causeway signs.

Looking for an hotel with a golf course on site? See our 'Golf Guide' on page 478

“ Even before I leave I cherish the thought of returning to your magical house ”

Bruce & Noreen Finnamore, Bath

• Map p.508 ref: G7

Dublin town house

BUTLERS TOWN HOUSE

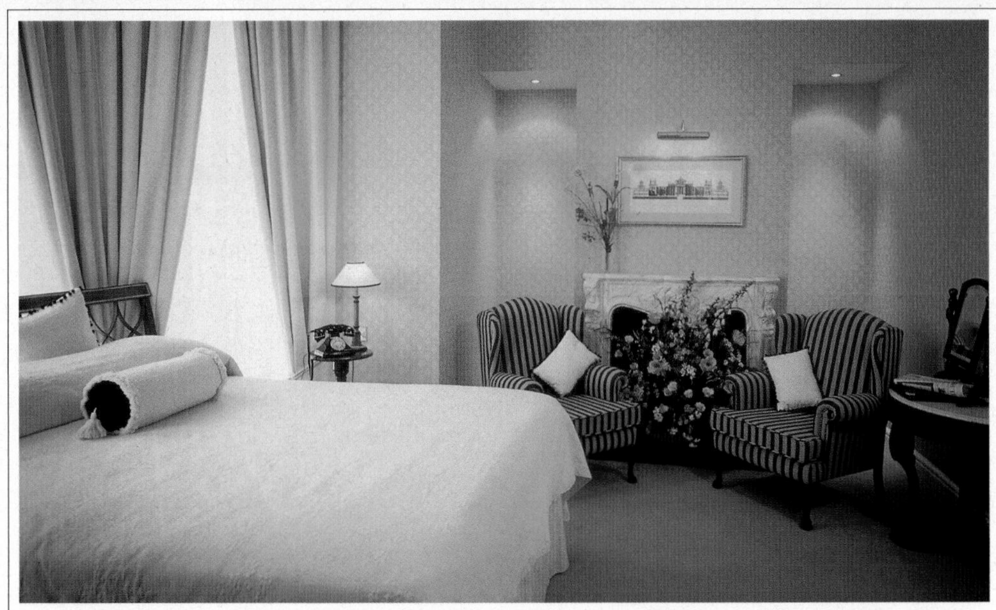

Behind the blue door, a haven of calm in the heart of cosmopolitan Dublin

On a quiet, leafy avenue in the Victorian quarter of Ballsbridge, the red brick façade of Butlers Town House is pierced by one of the city's characteristic painted doors. In this case it is a handsome deep blue and a gentle reflection on the peaceful and stylish surroundings and superior service that regular visitors to Butlers value so highly.

This elegant town house has retained many of its original features imaginatively interwoven with 21st-century conveniences from air-conditioning and modem points in the bedrooms to a computer for guests' use in the reception area. The ambience is intimate, even clubby, with a degree of personalised service that belongs to another more leisured age and the skilled staff appear positively telepathic in their ability to anticipate your needs.

The gourmet Irish breakfast is designed to set up the most demanding appetite for the day. Menu choices include traditional favourites such as black and white puddings and scrambled eggs with Irish cheddar and tomatoes, as well as more exotic fare from poached eggs with salmon and hollandaise sauce to French toast with maple syrup. There is also a light room service menu and a plethora of excellent restaurants nearby.

LOCATION

Travel along the M1 to the City, follow signs for East Link Toll Bridge. Drive to the top of Bath Avenue and take a left - Butlers is 100 yards on the right.

44 Lansdowne Road, Ballsbridge, Dublin 4, Republic of Ireland

Telephone +353 (0)1 667 4022
Fax +353 (0)1 667 3960

E-mail: *butlers@bestloved.com*

GENERAL MANAGER

Chris Vos

ROOM RATES *(Irish Punts)*

Single occupancy	*£110 - £130*
16 Doubles/Twins	*£110 - £150*
4 Deluxe doubles	*£130 - £170*

Includes buffet breakfast, 24 hour complimentary tea and coffee, service and VAT

CHARGE/CREDIT CARDS

• *DC* • *MC* • *VI*

RATINGS & AWARDS

I.T.B. ★★★★
R.A.C. ◆◆◆◆◆ *Town House*
Sparkling Diamond & Warm Welcome Awards
A.A. ◆◆◆◆◆ *89%*

FACILITIES

On site: *Garden*
1 meeting room/max 22 people
Nearby: *Golf, tennis, fitness, riding, sea fishing*

RESTRICTIONS

Limited facilities for disabled guests
No pets
Closed 23 Dec - 8 Jan

ATTRACTIONS

Trinity College, National Museum, St Stephen's Green, National Gallery, Christchurch, Grafton Street, Royal Dublin Society

AFFILIATIONS

Manor House Hotels of Ireland
The Charming Hotels

NEAREST

MAJOR CITY:
Dublin
MAJOR AIRPORT:
Dublin - 8 miles/25 mins
RAILWAY STATION:
Heuston - 3 miles/15 mins

RESERVATIONS

Toll free in US: 800-44-UTELL
Quote ***Best Loved***

ACCESS CODES

SABRE/ABACUS UI 3779
AMADEUS UI DUBBUT
APOLLO/GALILEO UI 82012
WORLDSPAN UI 26133

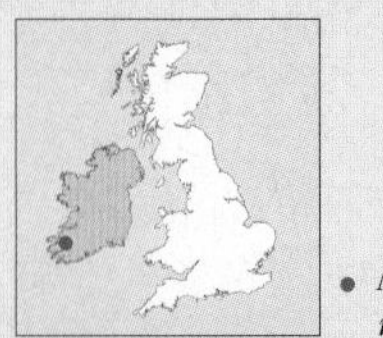

• Map p.508 ref: B9

" Paradise on earth, can't wait 'til next time "

Captain John Pettit, Senior Training Captain, British Airways

Caragh Lodge

Country house

Caragh Lake, Co Kerry, Republic of Ireland

Telephone +353 (0)66 9769115
Fax +353 (0)66 9769316

E-mail: *caragh@bestloved.com*

OWNER

Mary Gaunt

ROOM RATES *(Irish Punts)*

1 Single	*£85*
13 Doubles/Twins	*£125 - £160*
1 Suite	*£220*

Includes full breakfast, service and VAT

CHARGE/CREDIT CARDS

 • *DC* • *MC* • *VI*

RATINGS & AWARDS

I.T.B. ★★★★
R.A.C. Gold Ribbon ★★ *Dining Award 3*
A.A. ◆◆◆◆◆
Karen Brown Recommended

FACILITIES

On site: *Garden, tennis, sauna, fishing*
Nearby: *Golf, riding, beaches*

RESTRICTIONS

No children under 12 years
Limited facilities for disabled guests
No pets
Closed mid Oct - mid Apr

ATTRACTIONS

Ring of Kerry, Dingle Peninsula, Killarney, Skelligs Rock

AFFILIATIONS

Ireland's Blue Book
Preston's Global Hotels

NEAREST

MAJOR CITY:
Cork - 70 miles/2 hrs

MAJOR AIRPORT:
Shannon/Cork - 70 miles/2 hrs

RAILWAY STATION:
Killarney - 16 miles/30 mins

RESERVATIONS

Toll free in US: 800-544-9993
or 800-323-5463
Quote ***Best Loved***

ACCESS CODES

AMADEUS LM SNN598
APOLLO/GALILEO LM 22778
SABRE/ABACUS LM 49607
WORLDSPAN LM 05598

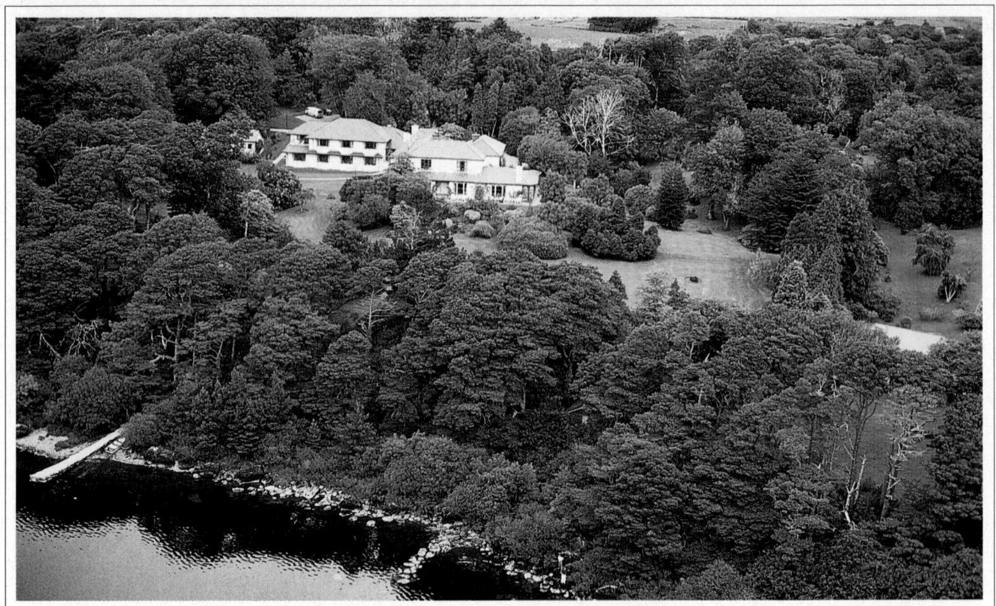

A gracious house a stone's throw from the spectacular Ring of Kerry

Less than one mile from the spectacular Ring of Kerry and four miles from the golden beaches of Dingle Bay, Caragh Lodge sits on the shore of Caragh Lake, looking towards the breathtaking slopes of the McGillycuddy Reeks, Ireland's highest mountains.

The rooms are sumptuously decorated with period furnishings and antiques. The converted garden rooms offer spectacular views. Each looks on to stunning displays of magnolias, rhododendrons, azaleas, camelias and many rare shrubs. Exquisite furnishings and welcoming log fires in the main house's lounges provide the perfect place to end the day.

Overlooking the lake, the dining room features only the finest Irish cuisine, freshly caught wild salmon, succulent Kerry lamb, garden grown vegetables and home baked breads, all personally prepared by Mary Gaunt.

Golfers will find Caragh Lodge the perfect base. With eight courses nearby, tee-off times can be easily arranged prior to your stay. Salmon and brown trout fishing are on the doorstep and two boats are available for guests. Ghillies or any necessary permits for fishing in the two local rivers can be arranged.

LOCATION

Caragh Lodge is situated just off N70. Travelling from Killorglin to Glenbeigh, take road signposted 'Caragh Lodge 1 mile'. Turn left at lake, lodge is on right.

“ Cashel House is undoubtedly the loveliest place we have stayed in. Our greatest disappointment is that we couldn't stay long enough ”

Gene Ray and Michell Clandos, LA, USA

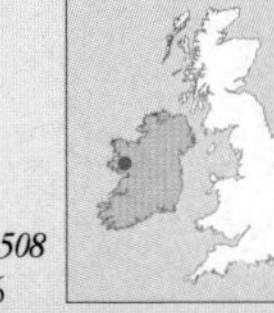

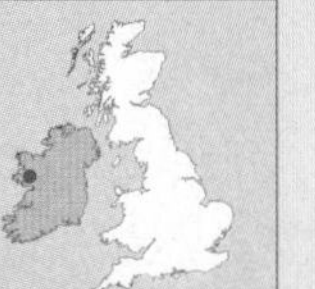

• Map p.508 ref: B6

Country house

CASHEL HOUSE HOTEL

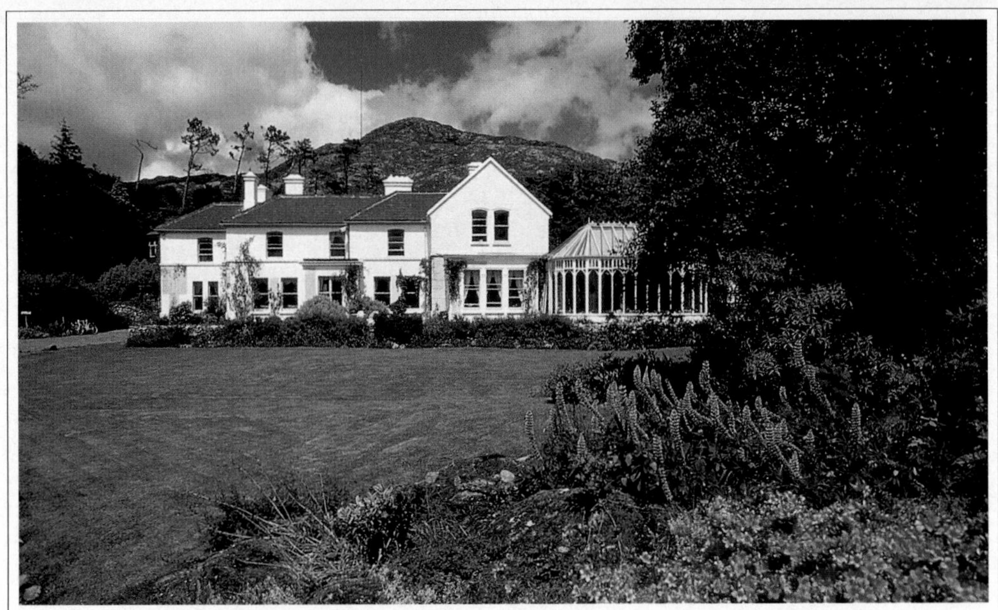

A magnificent garden setting on Ireland's blustery Atlantic Coast

You do not have to be a hot house flower to benefit from a stay at Cashel House, but the utter peace, fresh Connemara sea air and the McEvilly family's total dedication to their guests' enjoyment will leave you feeling as cosseted and resplendent as any prize horticultural bloom.

Cashel is a wonderful base for getting to know Ireland's blustery Atlantic coast, but it can be hard to tear oneself away from the truly spectacular gardens which date back to the first owners of the house in the mid-19th century. Himalayan shrubs such as rhododendrons, azaleas and camellias flourish here alongside native heathers and ferns. The floral influence extends to the warm and welcoming house with its colourful chintzes and antique furnishings glowing in the light of traditional turf and log fires. Connemara's lakes and coastline stock the chef's larder with fresh lobster, salmon and shellfish, while the garden provides many of the fresh vegetables served in the dining room. To build up an appetite do take the opportunity to explore the grounds on foot or on horseback, borrow a rowing boat to navigate the bay, or venture a little further afield for golf and fishing.

LOCATION

From Galway head towards Recess on the N59, the hotel is in the village of Cashel.

Cashel, Co Galway, Republic of Ireland

Telephone +353 (0)95 31001
Fax +353 (0)95 31077

E-mail: *cashelhouse@bestloved.com*

OWNERS

Dermott and Kay McEvilly

ROOM RATES *(Irish Punts)*

2 Singles	*£59 - £85*
15 Doubles/Twins	*£110 - £190*
13 Suites	*£158 - £210*

Includes full breakfast and VAT

CHARGE/CREDIT CARDS

• DC • MC • VI

RATINGS & AWARDS

R.A.C. Gold Ribbon ★★★

A.A. ★★★ ❀❀

FACILITIES

On site: *Gardens, riding, tennis, private beach, heli-pad*

Nearby: *Health & fitness centre, fishing*

RESTRICTIONS

No children under 6 years

No dogs in public rooms

ATTRACTIONS

Beach walks, Kylemore Abbey, Connemara National Park, Inish Boffin Island, Aran Islands

AFFILIATIONS

Ireland's Blue Book

The Celebrated Hotels Collection

Relais & Châteaux

NEAREST

MAJOR CITY:
Galway - 40 miles/1 hr

MAJOR AIRPORT:
Shannon - 110 miles/2½ hrs

RAILWAY STATION:
Galway - 40 miles/1 hr

RESERVATIONS

Toll free in US: 800-322-2403 or 800-323-5463

Quote ***Best Loved***

ACCESS CODES

AMADEUS WB GWYCAS

APOLLO/GALILEO WB 14720

SABRE/ABACUS WB 11321

For a portrait of this region see page 404

• Map p.508 ref: D9

" A beautiful, secluded, unique and special experience "

J & B Shallat, New York

CastleHyde Hotel

17th century country house

Castlehyde, Fermoy,
Co Cork,
Republic of Ireland

Telephone +353 (0)25 31865
Fax +353 (0)25 31485

E-mail: *castlehyde@bestloved.com*

OWNERS

Erik and Helen Speekenbrink

ROOM RATES ***(Irish Punts)***

Single occupancy £75 - £170
14 Doubles/Twins £100 - £150
5 Self-catering cottages £147 - £251
Includes full breakfast, service and VAT

CHARGE/CREDIT CARDS

• *DC* • *MC* • *VI*

RATINGS & AWARDS

Awards Pending

FACILITIES

On site: *Garden, outdoor pool*
1 meeting room/max 40 people
Nearby: *Golf, river and sea fishing*

RESTRICTIONS

Limited facilities for disabled guests
No smoking in bedrooms
No pets

ATTRACTIONS

Mitchelstown Caves,
Jameson Heritage Centre,
Rock of Cashel, Cahir Castle,
Lismore Castle and gardens,
Cobh Heritage Centre,
Lusitania - Titanic trail

AFFILIATIONS

Preston's Global Hotels

NEAREST

MAJOR CITY:
Cork - 25 miles/40 mins

MAJOR AIRPORT:
Cork - 30 miles/30 mins

RAILWAY STATION:
Mallow - 18 miles/30 mins

FERRY PORT:
Cork - 35 miles/45 mins

RESERVATIONS

Toll free in US: 800-544-9993
Quote ***Best Loved***

ACCESS CODES

Not applicable

From pre-Raphaelite ruins to a sanctuary of luxury. The stuff of legend.

The transformation of CastleHyde is a tribute to the vision, energy and enterprise of Erik and Helen Speekenbrink. In two years, its decaying pre-Raphaelite ruins have been converted into a grand house with every contemporary comfort and indulgence hidden discretely within its stone walls. It is an amazing feat made all the more remarkable by the fact that the haunting romance remains strong as ever. Full marks go to Helen. Her inate ability to spot a treasure in a builder's tip has provided the 200-year old Pitchpine columns supporting the walkways, the Chinese slate floor in the reception area and the wood floors in the dining room. She also has an eagle eye for colour and contrasting materials. Tensions simply melt just to look at the harmony of it all.

Erik is a professional hotelier making his debut as an owner/manager. He is well aware of what satisfies guests and has ensured the amenities live up to their expectations: a choice between well-appointed bedrooms and luxurious self-catering cottage suites, a heated outdoor swimming pool set in the sanctuary of beautiful gardens and a dining room which will inevitably find honour in the good food guides. Erik is supported by a cheerful, attentive staff who enjoy meeting and looking after his guests.

The Blackwater Valley is an angler's paradise and a horse breeding centre; a magical place where legends are made - like CastleHyde!

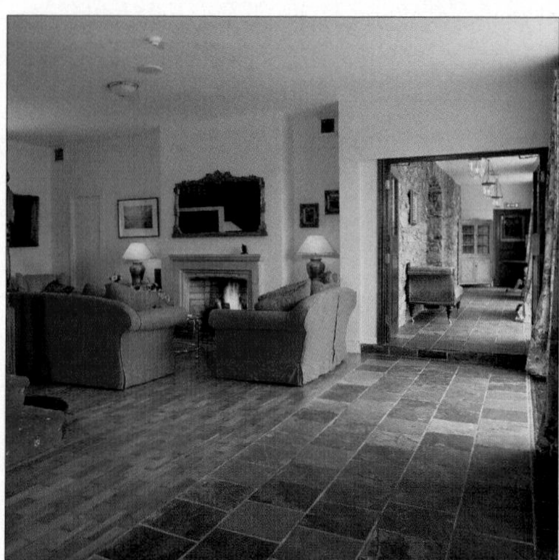

LOCATION

On the Dublin side of Fermoy take the N72 to Mallow. The hotel is by the N72, between Ballyhooly and 3 kms from Fermoy.

"101%"

Richard King, London

• *Map p.508 ref: G9*

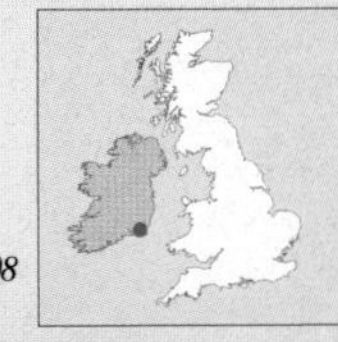

Irish farmhouse

CHURCHTOWN HOUSE

A sense of tranquillity

Churchtown House was built circa 1703. Set in its own eight-acre estate of mature trees and shrubbery, this charming period house is characterised by 'a sense of tranquillity'. It has recently been refurbished to provide high standards of comfort in elegant surroundings. It is lovingly run by its owners, Patricia and Austin Cody. They personally greet guests, making sure that traditional country house hospitality is in place and the log fires blaze on cold days.

Churchtown House, four miles from Rosslare Ferryport and very close to the main Rosslare/Wexford road, is a natural stopover on arrival or departure. It is suitable for a longer stay because this is an excellent area for sea-fishing, swimming, riding or golf on three good local courses. Wexford traces its history back 3,000 years and is a Bord Failte Heritage Town. Wexford is rich in music and friendship. Each October Wexford Opera Festival is the jewel in the crown of Ireland's arts. In easy visiting reach are the JFK Arboretum, Johnstown Castle, Our Lady's Island, Carne, Old Wexford Town and miles of sandy beaches. There is also wonderful bird life including the winter haven of the Brent, and canada geese in autumn and spring. This is an historic, beautiful and charming part of Ireland.

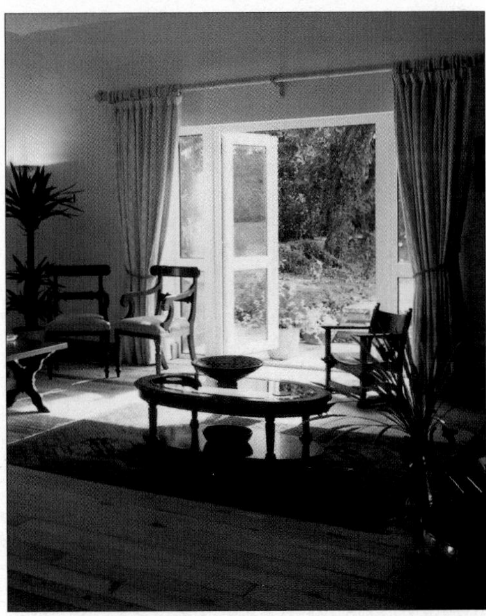

LOCATION

Take the N25 for 2½ miles from Rosslare Harbour. At Tagoat turn right onto the R736. The hotel is situated ½ mile on the left.

Tagoat, Rosslare, Co Wexford, Republic of Ireland

Telephone +353 (0)53 32555
Fax +353 (0)53 32577

E-mail: *churchtown@bestloved.com*

OWNERS

Austin and Patricia Cody

ROOM RATES *(Irish Punts)*

1 Single	*£65*
10 Doubles/Twins	*£110 - £140*
1 Mini-suite	*£170*

Includes VAT

CHARGE/CREDIT CARDS

• MC • VI

RATINGS & AWARDS

A.A. ◆◆◆◆◆

R.A.C. ◆◆◆◆◆ *Dining Award 1*

Sparkling Diamond & Warm Welcome Awards

FACILITIES

On site: *Garden, croquet*

Nearby: *Golf, sea fishing, yachting, tennis, riding, bird watching*

RESTRICTIONS

Limited facilities for disabled guests
No children
No pets, guide dogs only
Smoking permitted in lounge only
Closed mid Nov - 1 Mar

ATTRACTIONS

Wexford, North Slob Bird Sanctuary, Wexford Way Coastal Walk, JFK Arboretum, National Heritage Centre, Waterford Crystal, Wexford Festival of Opera

AFFILIATIONS

Manor House Hotels of Ireland

NEAREST

MAJOR CITY:
Waterford - 50 miles/1 hr

MAJOR AIRPORT:
Waterford - 50 miles/1 hr
Dublin - 95 miles/2½ hrs

RAILWAY STATION:
Rosslare - 2 miles/4 mins

FERRY PORT:
Rosslare - 4 miles/10 mins

RESERVATIONS

Toll free in US/Canada: 800-44-UTELL
*Quote **Best Loved***

ACCESS CODES

Not applicable

• Map p.508 ref: D5

"Dinner by candlelight and beech wood fire. Bushmills Malt, Bordeaux and Burgundy; roast lamb, roast duck and Sheila's chocolate mousse. Thank you for the last two weeks"

Lucy Tan and Christof Geyer, Zurich, Switzerland

COOPERSHILL

Georgian mansion

Riverstown, Co Sligo, Republic of Ireland

Telephone +353 (0)71 65108
Fax +353 (0)71 65466

E-mail: coopershill@bestloved.com

OWNERS

Brian and Lindy O'Hara

ROOM RATES *(Irish Punts)*

Single occupancy	£66 - £73
6 Doubles/Twins	£112 - £126
2 Four-posters	£112 - £126

Includes full Irish breakfast and VAT

CHARGE/CREDIT CARDS

• DC • JCB • MC • VI

RATINGS & AWARDS

Independent

FACILITIES

On site: Garden, croquet, tennis, fishing
1 meeting room/max 24 people
Nearby: Fishing, riding

RESTRICTIONS

No smoking in bedrooms and dining room
No facilities for disabled guests
No pets
Closed 1 Nov - 31 Mar

ATTRACTIONS

Lissadell House,
King House & Boyle Abbey,
Slieve League Donegal,
Strokes Townhouse & Famine Museum,
Keide Fields - Mayo, Megalithic Monuments

AFFILIATIONS

Ireland's Blue Book

NEAREST

MAJOR CITY:
Sligo - 13 miles/25 mins

MAJOR AIRPORT:
Knock - 24 miles/45 mins
Dublin - 125 miles/2½ hrs

RAILWAY STATION:
Ballymote - 7 miles/15 mins

RESERVATIONS

Toll free in US/Canada: 800-544-9993
or 800-323-5463
Quote **Best Loved**

ACCESS CODES

Not applicable

IRELAND

A fine Georgian mansion, a family welcome and sumptuous cooking

The fine Georgian mansion Coopershill has been home to seven generations of the O'Hara family since it was built in 1774. Six of its bedrooms have four-poster or canopy beds, and all have their own private bathrooms. The furniture dates from the 18th century.

Brian and Lindy O'Hara welcome guests to their home. Candle-lit dinners with family silver and crystal glass, a wide choice of wines and Lindy's sumptuous cooking make a Coopershill holiday memorable.

There are delightful walks and abundant wildlife on the 500 acres of farm and woodland. Facilities include an all-weather tennis court, trout and coarse fishing on the River Arrow which flows through the estate, and a croquet lawn. A boat for fishing or exploring is available on nearby Lough Arrow. Uncrowded beaches, the top-ten rated County Sligo championship golf course and the spectacular mountains and lakes of WB Yeats country are in the vicinity. Lissadell House, the Famine Museum at Strokestown, the Abbey and historic King House at Boyle, and Ireland's largest collection of megalithic tombs are part of the district's fascinating history.

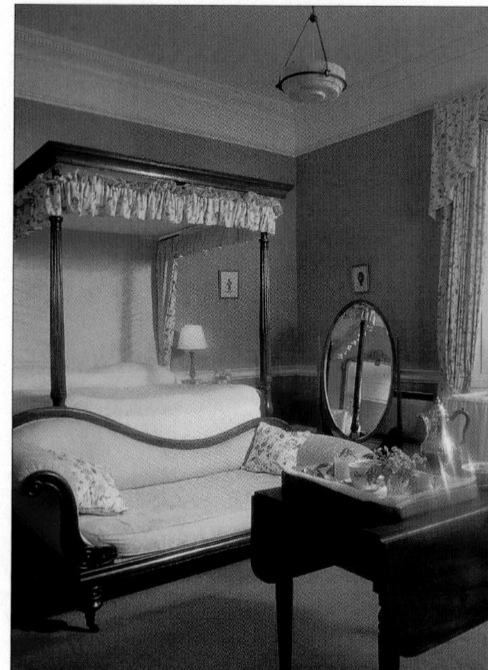

LOCATION

Coopershill is 2 miles from Riverstown and 12 miles from Sligo town, clearly signposted on the N4 Sligo-Dublin road.

Planning a wedding reception? Turn to 'Meeting Facilities' on page 476

“Everyone is so eager to please - this alone makes you world class”

Dr James Van Ness, Laguna Beach, California

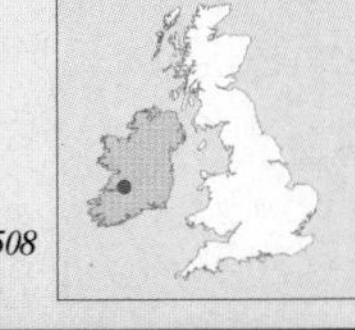

Map p.508 ref: C8

16th century castle

DROMOLAND CASTLE

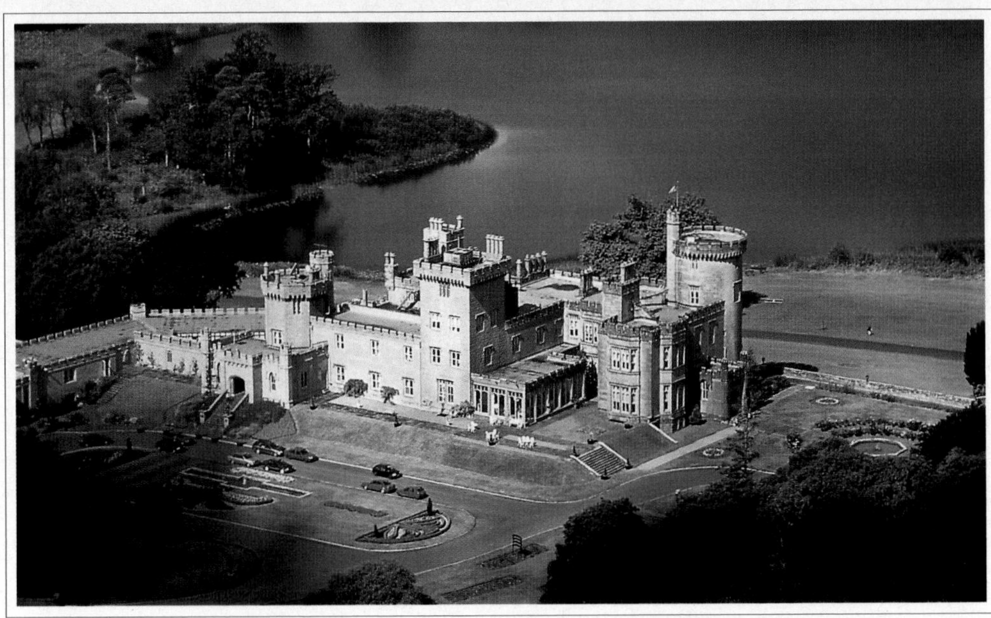

Supreme comfort in a castle on an historic estate

In the 16th century, the Dromoland Estate became the seat of the O'Brien clan, descendants of 'Brian Boru', High King of Ireland. Today the castle is one of Europe's top luxury hotels. Its rooms and suites blend period pieces with modern comfort. Its gallery has one of Ireland's largest collections of portraits, most notably Lucius O'Brien painted by the Swedish artist Michael Dahl. The 17th Baron Inchiquin gave musical recitals in the drawing room where guests take tea or coffee. His study is now the Library Bar.

The 375 acre estate is supremely beautiful. There are many private facilities for guests. Fine trout have been caught on the lake and the Castle has its own 18-hole championship golf course and club house with a brassiere restaurant and health and beauty spa. Fishing, shooting, horse riding, jogging trails and tennis are all on the estate.

The splendid dining room gives panoramic views of the lake and golf course. David McCann, Head Chef of international repute, presents house specialities such as lamb with foie gras, and steamed fillets of turbot in fennel. There is an outstanding list of wines from the cellar, which guests are welcome to visit. Dromoland sets out to provide the highest standard of personal service. Your home will be your castle when you make Dromoland Castle your home.

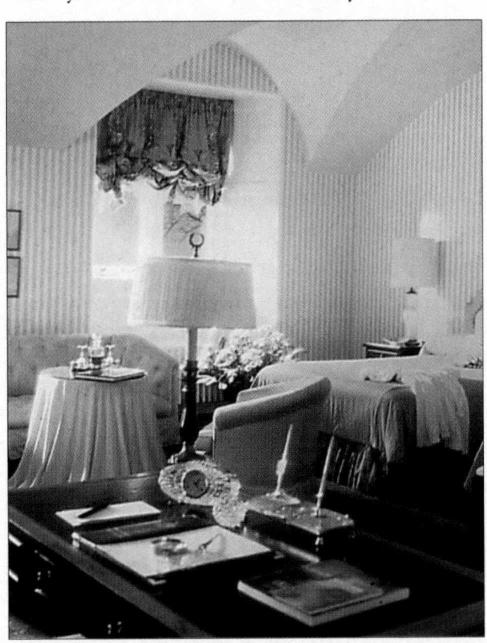

LOCATION

8 miles north of Shannon airport.

Newmarket-on-Fergus, Co Clare, Republic of Ireland

Telephone +353 (0)61 368144
Fax +353 (0)61 363355
Republic of Ireland

E-mail: *dromoland@bestloved.com*

GENERAL MANAGER

Mark Nolan

ROOM RATES *(Irish Punts)*

Single occupancy	£146 - £264
29 Doubles/Twins	£146 - £264
26 Deluxe rooms	£200 - £328
24 Club rooms	£353
15 Staterooms	£280 - £630
6 Suites	£392 - £850

Includes VAT

CHARGE/CREDIT CARDS

• DC • MC • VI

RATINGS & AWARDS

I.T.B. ★★★★★

R.A.C. ★★★★★ *Dining Award 2*

A.A. ★★★★★ ❀❀ *73%*

Conde Nast Best Resort in Ireland 1999/2000

FACILITIES

On site: *Garden, tennis, snooker, gym, indoor pool, sauna, health & beauty, golf, fishing, riding, heli-pad*
6 meeting rooms/max 350 people

Nearby: *Hunting*

RESTRICTIONS

No pets

ATTRACTIONS

Cliffs of Moher, The Burren, Bunratty Castle, King John's Castle, Craggaunowen Project, Aran Islands, Hunt Museum, Ballybunion & Lahinch golf courses

AFFILIATIONS

Preferred Hotels & Resorts

NEAREST

MAJOR CITY:
Limerick - 17 miles/25 mins

MAJOR AIRPORT:
Shannon - 8 miles/15 mins

RAILWAY STATION:
Limerick - 18 miles/30 mins

RESERVATIONS

Toll free in US: 800-346-7007
*Quote **Best Loved***

ACCESS CODES

Not applicable

• Map p.508 ref: F9

"We had the most wonderful time, wonderful food, amazing wine, exceptional company ... both you and your staff have created a very special place"

Noel McSweeney, Senator Windows

DUNBRODY COUNTRY HOUSE

Georgian country house

Arthurstown, Co Wexford, Republic of Ireland

Telephone +353 (0)51 389 600
Fax +353 (0)51 389 601

E-mail: dunbrody@bestloved.com

OWNERS
Kevin and Catherine Dundon

ROOM RATES (Irish Punts)

Single occupancy	£79 - £96
15 Doubles/Twins	£138 - £164
4 Suites	£196 - £240

Includes full breakfast and VAT

CHARGE/CREDIT CARDS

 • DC • MC • VI

RATINGS & AWARDS
I.T.B. ★★★★
A.A. ★★★ ❀❀ 77%
Bridgestone Top 100 Places to Stay in Ireland

FACILITIES
On site: *Garden, croquet, clay pigeon shooting*
3 meeting rooms/max 150 people
Nearby: *Golf, fishing, polo cross*

RESTRICTIONS
No children in restaurant after 8 pm
Pets accommodated in stables
Closed 24 Dec - 31 Jan

ATTRACTIONS
Waterford Crystal, Tintern Abbey, Hook Peninsula and Lighthouse, JFK Arboretum, shark fishing, beaches

AFFILIATIONS
Ireland's Blue Book

NEAREST
MAJOR CITY:
Waterford - 10 miles/15 mins

MAJOR AIRPORT:
Dublin - 100 miles/2 hrs

RAILWAY STATION:
Waterford - 10 miles/20 mins

FERRY PORT:
Rosslare - 40 miles/45 mins

RESERVATIONS
Toll free in US: 800-323-5463
*Quote **Best Loved***

ACCESS CODES
Not applicable

All the attributes of a fine country house with a restaurant to grace any great city

Epicures amongst you who reckon they can tell the difference between a restaurant in a country hotel and its modish city counterpart, may have to adjust their mind sets. Dunbrody House is your archetypal country house alright with big, spacious bedrooms all beautifully appointed, a 20-acre woodland and manicured garden setting etc, etc ... but there the cliché ends. Its restaurant has the gastronomic authority you will find in any European capital and a discerning, well-travelled, appreciative clientele to prove it. Gone is that ghastly hush; this place buzzes with enthusiasm - as true of the diners as of the cheerful young staff who attend them.

The amazing thing, is that all this happened so recently. Three years ago the house was a ruin in an overgrown estate. Its renaissance is due to the ambition and skills of Kevin and Catherine Dundon. Kevin acquired star-status as a Master Chef in Canada before returning as the Executive Chef at the Shelbourne in Dublin. The 'Front of House' is managed by Catherine whose marketing background blends perfectly with Kevin's creative talents. They must be very happy with their achievement; their welcome says it all.

The garnish on this unexpected pleasure is the hotel's gorgeous location: on Ireland's Sunshine Coast on a long promontory in historic and luscious Co Wexford.

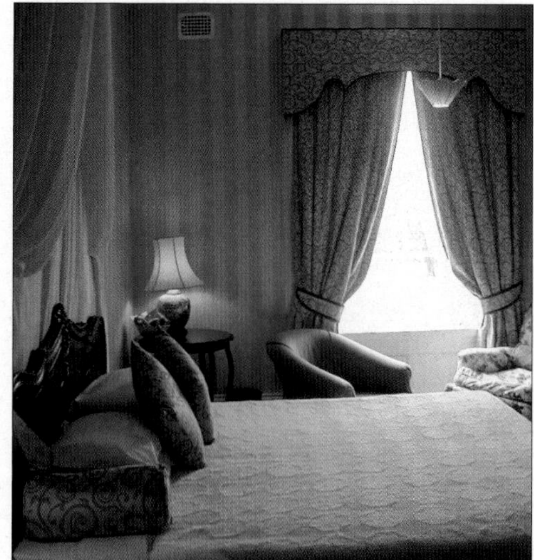

LOCATION

From Wexford take the R733 to Duncannon and Arthurstown. Dunbrody is located on the left coming into Arthurstown village.

" A Georgian gem in stunning Irish countryside with a fantastic golf course "

Anonymous

• Map p.508 ref: D8

Georgian manor

DUNDRUM HOUSE

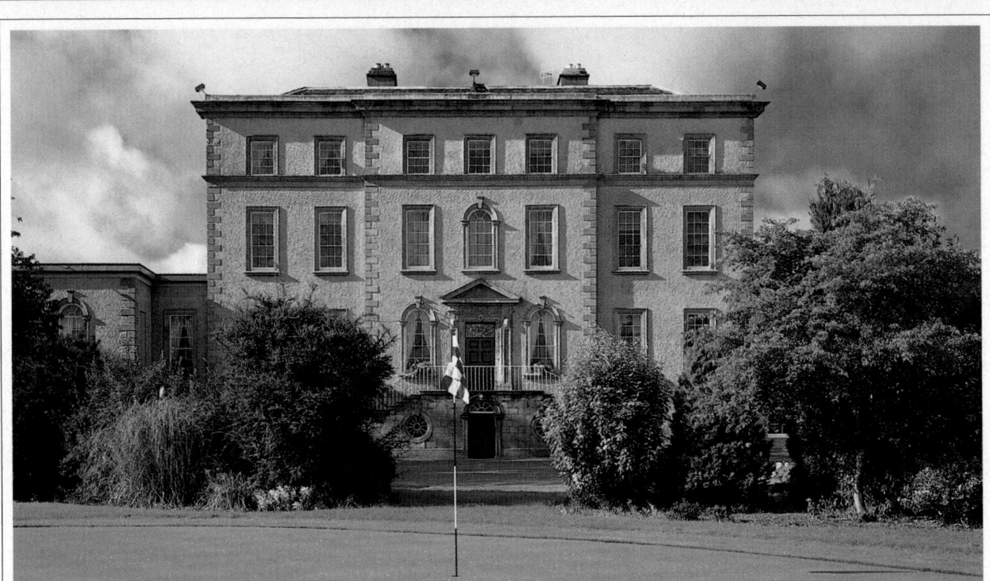

Ancient and modern, there is something for everyone here

Looking for a touring base in the southwest of Ireland? Interested in local history or golf? Travelling with children or organising a conference? If the answer to any of these questions is 'yes', then the solution could lie at Dundrum House.

A splendid grey stone Georgian manor, Dundrum House was built by the Earl of Montalt in 1730. It stands on land formerly held by ancient Irish chieftains just six miles from the Rock of Cashel, historic seat of the Kings of Munster. The kings held court here for some seven centuries, and it is said that St. Patrick was visiting Cashel when he picked the shamrock used to explain the doctrine of the Holy Trinity, which in turn became an Irish symbol.

The manor has been handsomely restored and remodelled as a hotel retaining many of its gracious period features. The range of bedrooms and suites includes several self-contained luxury apartments. In addition to 18 holes of championship golf, sports enthusiasts can enjoy the 20m swimming pool, jacuzzi, solarium and fitness centre in the Health and Leisure Club. And, for families, there are crèche facilities, a kiddy pool, and a summer season children's activities club.

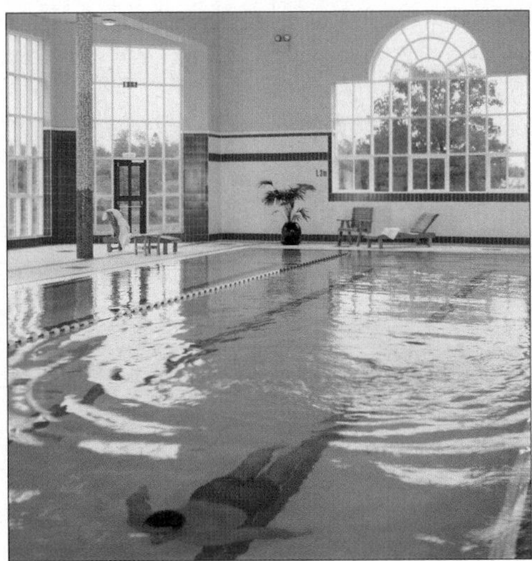

LOCATION

Take the N8, Dublin to Cork Road, to Cashel. At Cashel take the N74 signposted for Tipperary and Dundrum. Drive through Dundrum and take a right at the end of the village. The hotel is at the top of this road.

Dundrum, Co Tipperary, Republic of Ireland

Telephone +353 (0)62 71116
Fax +353 (0)62 71366

E-mail: *dundrum@bestloved.com*

OWNER
Austin Crowe

GENERAL MANAGER
Joe Kelly

ROOM RATES *(Irish Punts)*

Single occupancy	*£64 - £85*
84 Doubles/Twins	*£98 - £140*

Includes full breakfast and VAT

CHARGE/CREDIT CARDS

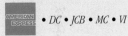

• DC • JCB • MC • VI

RATINGS & AWARDS
I.T.B. ★★★

FACILITIES
On site: *Garden, croquet, indoor pool, golf, health & beauty, fishing, heli-pad*
3 meeting rooms/max 600 people
Nearby: *Riding, fishing, shooting*

RESTRICTIONS
No pets

ATTRACTIONS
Rock of Cashel, Cashel Heritage Town, Waterford Crystal factory, Tipperary Crystal factory, Limerick

AFFILIATIONS
Manor House Hotels of Ireland

NEAREST
MAJOR CITY:
Limerick - 30 miles/40 mins

MAJOR AIRPORT:
Shannon - 45 miles/50 mins

RAILWAY STATION:
Limerick Junction - 10 miles/15 mins

RESERVATIONS
Toll free in US: 800-44-UTELL
Quote ***Best Loved***

ACCESS CODES
AMADEUS UI SNNDUH
APOLLO/GALILEO UI 91683
SABRE/ABACUS UI 8118
WORLDSPAN UI 40019

"Your property is outstanding; its pastoral setting, magnificent"

Lynn Dixson, North Carolina

DUNLOE CASTLE

Luxury hotel

Killarney, Co Kerry,
Republic of Ireland

Telephone +353 (0)64 44111
Fax +353 (0)64 44583

E-mail: dunloe@bestloved.com

RESIDENT MANAGER
Michael Brennan

ROOM RATES (Irish Punts)

74 Doubles/Twins	£132
19 Superior Doubles/Twins	£176
9 Executive superiors	£186
1 Suite	£220

Includes full breakfast, service and VAT

CHARGE/CREDIT CARDS

• DC • MC • VI

RATINGS & AWARDS
I.T.B. ★★★★★
R.A.C. ★★★★ *Dining Award 1*

FACILITIES
On site: *Garden, tennis, indoor pool, steam room, sauna, riding, putting green, fishing*
6 meeting rooms/max 250 people
Nearby: *Golf*

RESTRICTIONS
No facilities for disabled guests
Closed 1 Oct - 20 Apr
No pets

ATTRACTIONS
Gap of Dunloe, Dunloe Castle, Ring of Kerry, Dingle Peninsula

AFFILIATIONS
Killarney Hotels Ltd

NEAREST
MAJOR CITY:
Cork - 57 miles/1¼ hrs

MAJOR AIRPORT:
Cork - 60 miles/1¼ hrs

RAILWAY STATION:
Killarney - 7 miles/20 mins

RESERVATIONS
Toll free in US: 800-537-8483
Quote **Best Loved**

ACCESS CODES
Not applicable

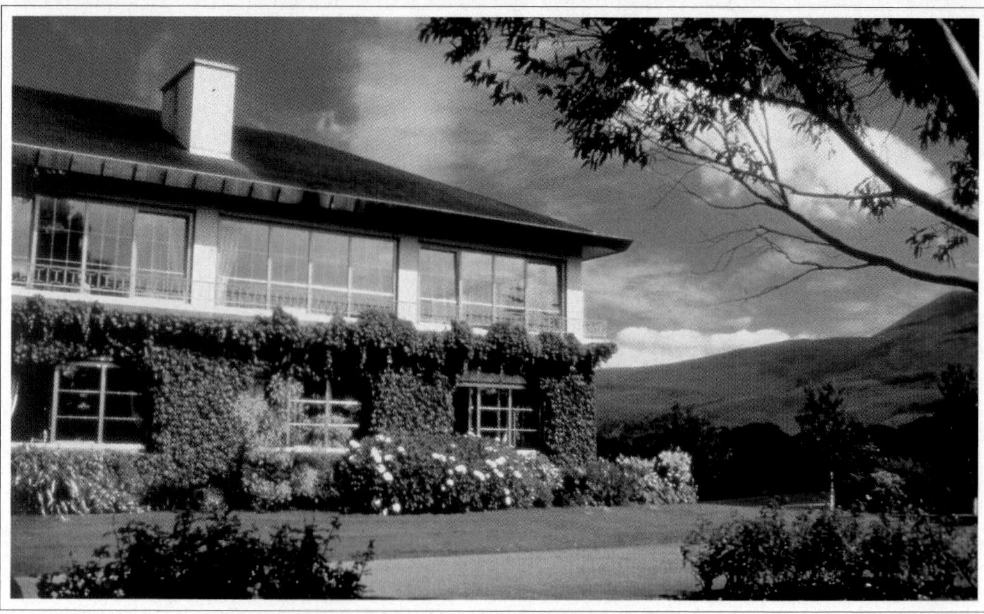

Peace and birdsong in a historic Killarney setting

The five-star Hotel Dunloe Castle is in the midst of a fascinating park landscape. The Green Isle's magic is reflected in the hotel park, an award-winning botanic collection of international renown. An unbelievable assortment of flowers and plants flourish here, and there are Haflinger horses grazing nearby. The park looks out to the famous Gap of Dunloe, and the beauties of unspoilt nature. The hotel is a member of the Historic Houses and Gardens Association.

The hotel's furnishings are elegant and comfortable. Its decor is stylish with exquisite details. The 103 rooms and mini-suites, have each been designed to include world class deluxe appointments.

In the most beautiful natural settings, you can enjoy the best of international and Irish cuisine in the gourmet restaurant. A magnificent list of wines is there to complement your meal, and you can have a Guinness, an Irish whiskey or anything else you fancy in the cocktail bar. The countless opportunities for leisure activities within easy reach include no fewer than ten golf courses.

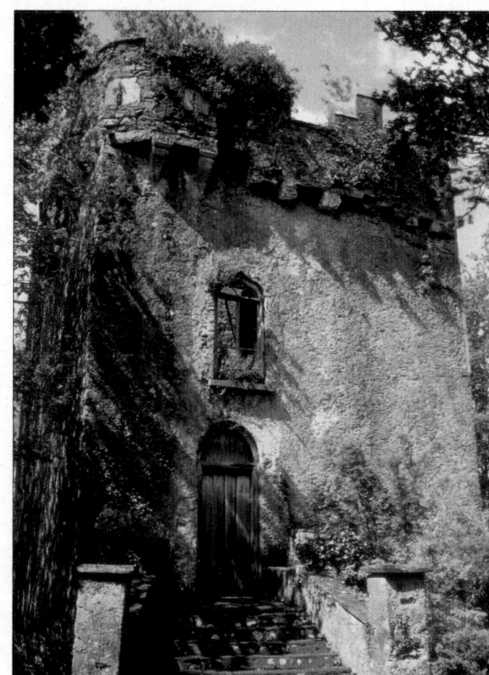

LOCATION

From Killarney take N72 Killorglin road. After 4½ miles take a left turn towards Gap of Dunloe. Hotel is then signposted.

" Wonderful hotel, warm people, beautiful setting "

Jean Kennedy Smith, US Ambassador to Ireland, Dublin

• Map p.508 ref: C6

18th century manor

GLENLO ABBEY HOTEL

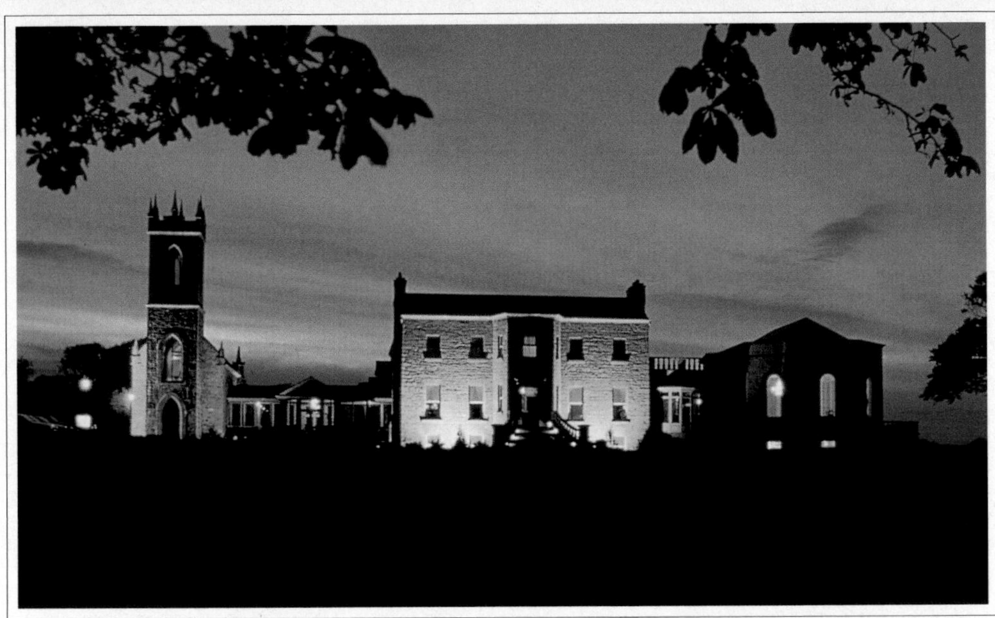

The Orient Express awaits you at Galway's most luxurious hotel

Built in 1740, Glenlo Abbey was the ancestral home of the Ffrench family one of the fourteen tribes that ruled Galway for five centuries. Set on 138 acres on the shores of Lough Corrib, the estate has a nine-hole golf course, driving range, fishing rights and opportunities for boating.

After eight years of painstaking restoration, owners Peggy and John Bourke turned it into a luxury hotel but an hotel with a difference. The skilled plasterwork and hand woven carpets are by local craftsmen with particularly fine examples in The French Room. Three centuries of antiques furnish the house and recent works by local artists hang up on its walls. The overall effect is very stylish without being overbearing, and comfortably grand.

But what gives the hotel its novelty is the newly acquired Pullman Restaurant - two of the original carriages from The Orient Express. One of them, Leona, has quite a provenance: it starred in Murder on the Orient Express but long before that, carried many a celebrity such as Sir Winston Churchill and Sir Lawrence Olivier. The food served in The Pullman Restaurant is themed on some of the famous train's destinations: Paris, St Petersburg, Istanbul …

You might enjoy the walk to the medieval city of Galway, it's less than three miles, and discover its infinite pleasures not least the pubs, boutiques and heritage shops that line the streets.

LOCATION

The hotel is located on the N59, just 2½ miles from Galway.

Bushypark, Galway, Co Galway, Republic of Ireland

Telephone +353 (0)91 526666
Fax +353 (0)91 527800

E-mail: glenlo@bestloved.com

OWNER

John Bourke

ROOM RATES *(Irish Punts)*

Single occupancy	£100 - £192
43 Doubles/Twins	£147 - £235
3 Suites	£350

Includes VAT

CHARGE/CREDIT CARDS

• DC • MC • VI

RATINGS & AWARDS

I.T.B. ★★★★★
R.A.C. Blue Ribbon ★★★★
Dining Award 3
A.A. ★★★★ ❀❀
A.A. Romantic Hotel

FACILITIES

On site: *Garden, golf, fishing, putting green, boating, clay pigeon shooting, business centre, heli-pad*
12 meeting rooms/max 220 people
Nearby: *Yachting, tennis, fitness centre, hunting/shooting, riding, watersports*

RESTRICTIONS

No pets, guide dogs only

ATTRACTIONS

Lough Corrib, Aran Islands, The Burren, Cliffs of Moher, Connemara, Galway City

AFFILIATIONS

Small Luxury Hotels

NEAREST

MAJOR CITY:
Galway - 2½ miles/10 mins
MAJOR AIRPORT:
Shannon - 56 miles/1½ hrs
RAILWAY STATION:
Galway - 2 miles/10 mins

RESERVATIONS

Toll free in US: 800-525-4800
Toll free in UK: 00800-4536-5666
Quote ***Best Loved***

ACCESS CODES

AMADEUS LX GWYGAH
APOLLO/GALILEO LX 58443
SABRE/ABACUS LX 13705
WORLDSPAN LX GWYGA

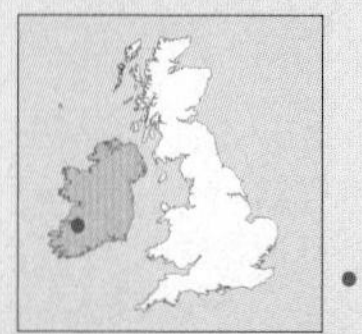

• Map p.508 ref: C8

"One of the truly outstanding private houses of the world"

Andrew Harper's Hideaway Report

GLIN CASTLE

Historic house

Glin, Co Limerick, Republic of Ireland

Telephone +353 (0)68 34173
Fax +353 (0)68 34364

E-mail: *glin@bestloved.com*

OWNERS
Desmond FitzGerald, Knight of Glin and Madam FitzGerald

GENERAL MANAGER
Bob Duff

ROOM RATES (*Irish Punts*)

1 Single	£190
13 Doubles/Twins	£190 - £300
1 Four-poster	£300

Includes breakfast and VAT

CHARGE/CREDIT CARDS

• DC • MC • VI

RATINGS & AWARDS
R.A.C. ★★★ Dining Award 2

FACILITIES
On site: *Garden, croquet, tennis*
1 meeting room/max 20 people
Nearby: *Golf, riding, fishing, yachting*

RESTRICTIONS
No children under 10 years
No facilities for disabled guests
No pets allowed in hotel, kennels available
Closed 5 Nov – 1 Apr

ATTRACTIONS
Cliffs of Moher, The Burren, Ring of Kerry, Dingle Peninsula, Birr Castle and Demesne, Adare and Limerick

AFFILIATIONS
The Celebrated Hotels Collection
Ireland's Blue Book

NEAREST
MAJOR CITY:
Limerick - 32 miles/45 mins

MAJOR AIRPORT:
Shannon - 45 miles/1 hr

RAILWAY STATION:
Limerick - 32 miles/45 mins

RESERVATIONS
Toll free in US: 800-322-2403 or 800-323-5463
Quote ***Best Loved***

ACCESS CODES
Not applicable

IRELAND

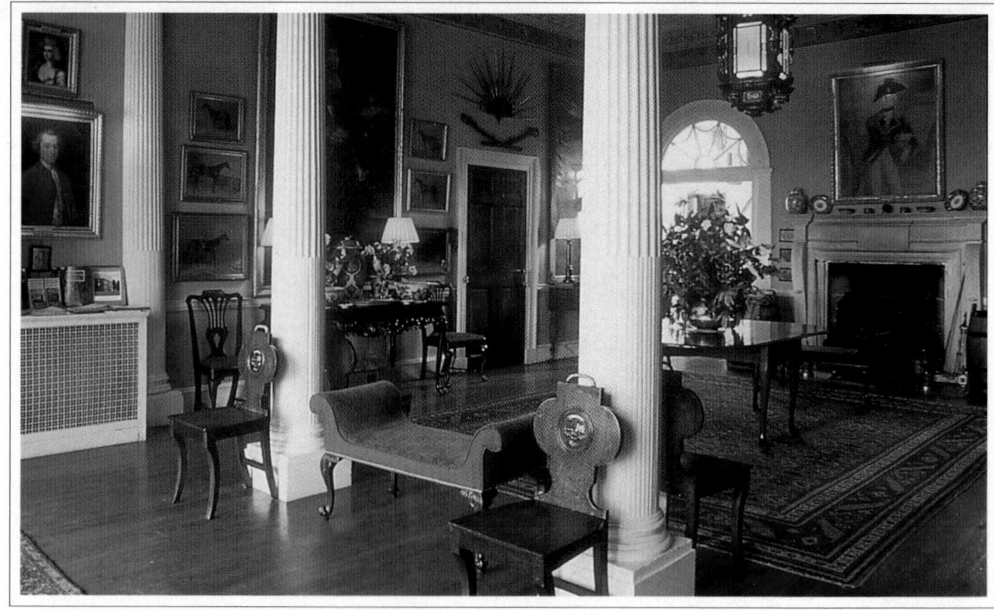

Art and architecture in a unique, historic home

Glin Castle took pride of place in a recent exhibition of Irish Country Houses. The 29th Knight of Glin and Madam FitzGerald welcome visitors in style. The present Glin Castle succeeds the medieval ruin in the village of Glin and was built in the late 18th century with entertaining in mind. It is steeped in Ireland's history and its architectural pleasures. The entrance hall has a screen of Corinthian pillars, a superb neo-classical plaster ceiling and a unique collection of Irish mahogany furniture. Family portraits and Irish pictures line the walls. The library bookcase has a secret door. The hall has a rare flying staircase.

The drawing room is a superb setting for coffee and conversation. It has an Adam period ceiling, a beautiful Bossi chimney piece and six long windows looking out to the croquet lawn. Upstairs are sets of bedrooms, bathrooms and dressing rooms with wall-to-wall carpets, chaises longues and comfortable chintz-covered beds.

The cooking is good Irish country house, using vegetables from the walled garden, fresh local fish, poultry and meats. The castle garden grows its own flowers and fruit, bees for honey and hens for free-range eggs. The staff take great care to welcome visitors, and make sure they enjoy their visit to a unique, historic home.

LOCATION

Off N69, 32 miles to the west of Limerick.

Thinking of pampering yourself? See the 'Health & Beauty' index on page 472

" A perfect find! "

Lisa Duff, Automobile Association, Ireland

• *Map p.508 ref: A9*

Guesthouse & restaurant GORMANS CLIFFTOP HOUSE & RESTAURANT

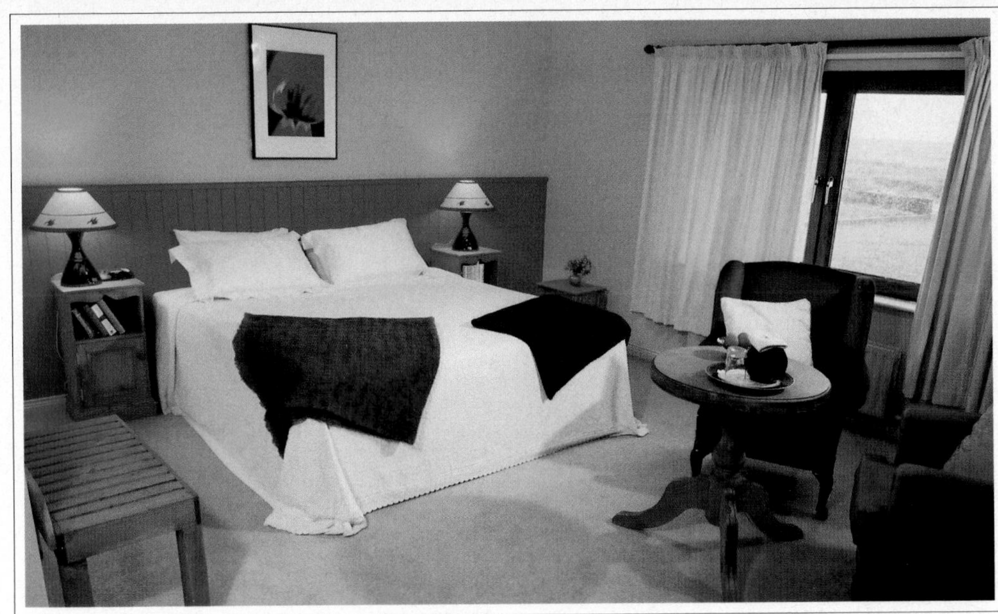

A welcoming clifftop refuge at the tip of the glorious Dingle Peninsula

Gorman's Clifftop is surely one of the most westerly establishments in Europe. The house looks out over Smerwick Harbour to the Three Sisters and the vastness of the Atlantic beyond. Vincent Gorman's family settled this land in the 1700s, and his wife, Sile (pronounced Sheila), proudly proclaims that she came here on holiday over 20 years ago and if anything loves it more than ever.

Dingle is all about long sandy beaches and tall cliffs peppered with little coves and harbours. There are mountains in the background, and hedgerows burgeoning with wild fuschias. Irish is the first language of the local people, and traditional culture is very much part of everyday life from the fishermen hauling in lobster pots to spontaneous outbreaks of music and dance. Around and about there are walks, golf, and archaeological sites to visit.

Every room at Gorman's Clifftop pays homage to the landscape offering breathtaking views of mountains or the ocean. The spacious bedrooms are furnished in pine offset by hand-thrown pottery lamps and tapestry wall hangings. Downstairs guests can gather around the fire to read or chat, dine handsomely, and sit out in the garden to watch the sun set behind Ballydavid Head on a summer's evening.

LOCATION

The hotel is exactly 8 miles from the roundabout on the western side of Dingle on the road signposted for Feoghanach. When the road forks keep to the left.

Glaise Bheag, Ballydavid, Dingle Peninsula, Co Kerry, Republic of Ireland

Telephone + 353 (0)66 9155162
Fax + 353 (0)66 9155162

E-mail: *gormans@bestloved.com*

OWNERS

Sile and Vincent Gorman

ROOM RATES *(Irish Punts)*

Single occupancy	*£45 - £50*
5 Doubles/Twins	*£70 - £90*
2 Mini suites	*£80 - £100*
2 Family rooms	*£85 - £105*

Includes full breakfast and VAT

CHARGE/CREDIT CARDS

MC • VI

RATINGS & AWARDS

A.A. ◆◆◆◆◆

FACILITIES

On site: *Garden, cycle hire*
Nearby: *Golf, fishing, riding*

RESTRICTIONS

Limited facilities for disabled guests
Smoking permitted in lounge only
No pets, guide dogs only
Closed mid Jan - Feb

ATTRACTIONS

Gallerus Oratory, Blasket Islands, Inch Strand, Killarney National Park, Ring of Kerry

AFFILIATIONS

Independent

NEAREST

MAJOR CITY:
Cork - 105 miles/2½ hrs

MAJOR AIRPORT:
Shannon - 150 miles/3 hrs
Cork - 105 miles/2½ hrs

RAILWAY STATION:
Tralee - 40 miles/1 hr

RESERVATIONS

Direct with hotel
*Quote **Best Loved***

ACCESS CODES

Not applicable

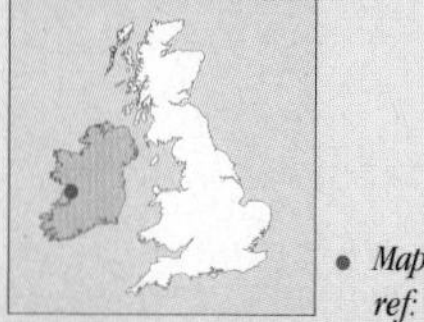

• Map p.508 ref: C7

" Like The Burren itself, Gregans Castle is one of the quiet treasures of Ireland. First among its charms are the owners, whose superb management is matched only by the warmth of their welcome " *Gibbons & Kay Ruark, Pennsylvania*

GREGANS CASTLE

18th century country house

Ballyvaughan, Co Clare, Republic of Ireland

Telephone +353 (0)65 707 7005
Fax +353 (0)65 707 7111

E-mail: *gregans@bestloved.com*

OWNERS
The Haden Family

ROOM RATES *(Irish Punts)*

Single occupancy	*£126 - £178*
14 Doubles/Twins	*£146 - £198*
4 Suites	*£250 - £290*

Includes full breakfast, service and VAT

CHARGE/CREDIT CARDS

• MC • VI

RATINGS & AWARDS
I.T.B. ★★★★
R.A.C. Blue Ribbon ★★★
A.A. ★★★ ❀❀

FACILITIES
On site: *Garden, croquet*
1 meeting room/max 35 people
Nearby: *Riding, fishing*

RESTRICTIONS
No pets
Closed Nov - Easter

ATTRACTIONS
The Burren, Cliffs of Moher, Galway Bay, Aran Islands

AFFILIATIONS
Ireland's Blue Book
Preston's Global Hotels

NEAREST
MAJOR CITY:
Galway - 33 miles/45 mins

MAJOR AIRPORT:
Shannon - 36 miles/1 hr

RAILWAY STATION:
Gort - 22 miles/25 mins

RESERVATIONS
Toll free in US: 800-544-9993
or 800-323-5463
Quote ***Best Loved***

ACCESS CODES
AMADEUS LM SNNGRG
APOLLO/GALILEO LM 5417
SABRE/ABACUS LM 27478

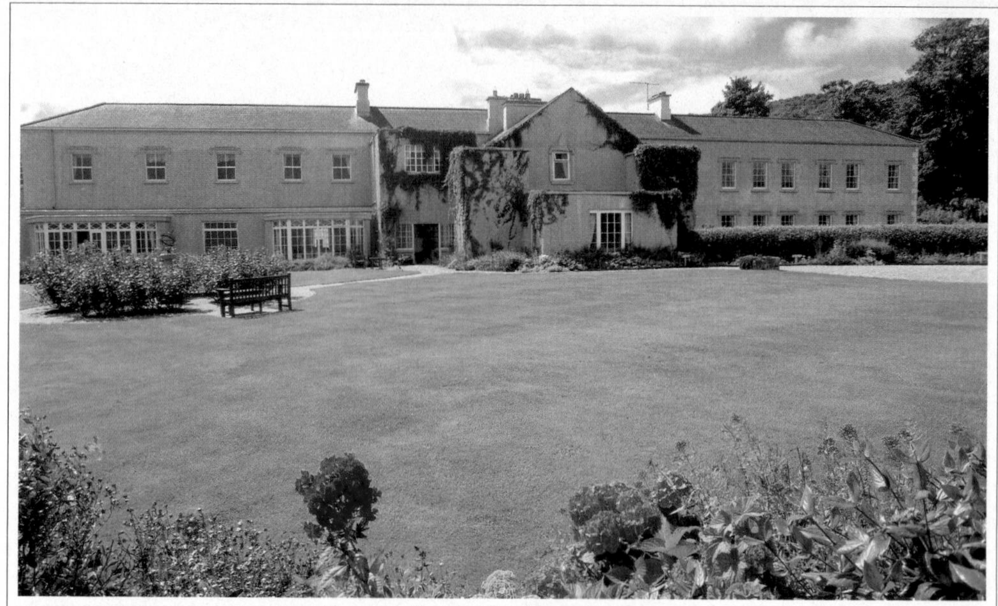

A solitaire in The Burren's majestic wilderness

Gregans Castle Hotel is a welcome surprise in a remote part of the West of Ireland. Nestling at the foot of the Corkscrew Hill with majestic views of bare limestone mountains and Galway Bay, this country house offers warmth, welcome and every possible comfort.

This area of only ten miles square is called The Burren and is known worldwide for its wild flowers and distinctive scenery. A rich legacy of ancient monuments tells the story of inhabitants as far back as 5,000 years. The seascapes are dramatic: Atlantic Ocean, Galway Bay, the famous Cliffs of Moher, two golden beaches and several small local fishing harbours of character.

Gregans Castle Hotel was built as a private house more than 150 years ago for the Martyn family to replace their home in the old castle nearby. Recently converted into an hotel, it is now one of the most comfortable hostelries on the west coast of Ireland.

Dinner is an essential part of the day and a special emphasis is placed on local produce. The expert cooking has earned the hotel many ratings & awards in all the better travel guide books. Gregans Castle Hotel is owner-managed by the Haden family, and is an elected member of the prestigious Ireland's Blue Book.

LOCATION

On the west coast of Ireland, near the village of Ballyvaughan in County Clare.

Looking for an hotel with a golf course on site? See our 'Golf Guide' on page 478

"What an experience again, the rugged coastline, the resort of Kilkee and then the warmth of Halpin's"

Professor Trevor Elliott, University of Liverpool

• Map p.508 ref: B8

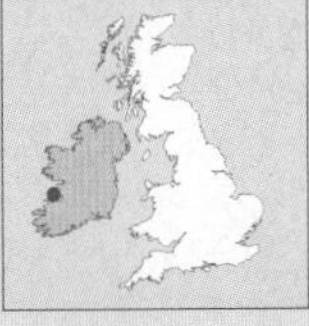

Town house hotel

HALPIN'S HOTEL

Welcoming, friendly, the place to find the true taste of Ireland

Western Ireland has many attractions but two in particular are fundamental to the others: the rugged beauty of its coast and the warm, unpolluted waters of the gulf stream that wash over it. Kilkee stands in a pretty horseshoe bay midway between the awesome Cliffs of Moher and the picturesque Ring of Kerry. There is plenty of scenic variety and all sorts of attractions - one of them being the well-known, privately owned and managed Halpin's Hotel & Vittles Restaurant.

Modestly priced and as unpretentious as the town it stands in, its looks belie its true character. It is a haven for the world weary. The bedrooms are comfortable and offer every facility. You will meet many of the locals in the atmospheric bar with its open hearth fireplace and flag-stoned floor. But the real delight can be found in the dining room. The seafood from the waters of the Atlantic and the rich harvest from the fields of County Clare provide opportunities that Vittles Restaurant turns into mouthwatering cuisine. The wine list is well-chosen and adds greatly to one's pleasure of good food attentively served in the most hospitable surroundings.

Local attractions include scenic drives, heritage sites, cliffs, beaches and caves and all kinds of sports on land and sea including golf. Halpin's is surely a place to discover the true taste of Ireland.

LOCATION

50 minutes from Shannon Airport on the N67. The hotel is in the centre of Kilkee.

Erin Street, Kilkee, Co Clare, Republic of Ireland

Telephone +353 (0)65 9056032
Fax +353 (0)65 9056317

E-mail: *halpins@bestloved.com*

OWNER
Pat Halpin

MANAGER
Ann Keane

ROOM RATES *(Irish Punts)*

2 Singles	*£45 - £70*
8 Doubles/Twins	*£70 - £108*
2 Executive rooms	*£80 - £125*

Includes full breakfast, newspaper and VAT

CHARGE/CREDIT CARDS

• *DC* • *JCB* • *MC* • *VI*

RATINGS & AWARDS
I.T.B. ★★★
A.A. ★★ *60%*

FACILITIES
On site: *Garden*
Nearby: *Golf, riding, fitness centre, tennis, fishing, water skiing*

RESTRICTIONS
No pets
Closed 15 Nov - 15 Mar

ATTRACTIONS
Cliffs of Moher, The Burren, Bunratty Castle, Aran Islands, Lakes of Killarney, Lahinch and Ballybunion golf courses

AFFILIATIONS
Green Book of Ireland
Preston's Global Hotels

NEAREST
MAJOR CITY:
Limerick - 50 miles/1 hr
MAJOR AIRPORT:
Shannon - 40 miles/50 mins
BUS STATION:
Kilkee - ¼ mile/5 mins

RESERVATIONS
Toll free in US: 800-544-9993 or 800-223-6510
Quote ***Best Loved***

ACCESS CODES
AMADEUS UI SNNHAL
APOLLO/GALILEO UI 1437
SABRE/ABACUS UI 35170
WORLDSPAN UI 19690

IRELAND

• Map p.508 ref: D10

"A superb union of country house charm and elegance, only minutes from the city centre"

Ann Cahill, writer, Ireland

HAYFIELD MANOR

Country house in the city

Perrott Avenue, College Road, Cork, Co Cork, Republic of Ireland

Telephone +353 (0)21 4315600
Fax +353 (0)21 4316839

E-mail: *hayfield@bestloved.com*

OWNERS
Margaret and Joseph Scally

DEPUTY GENERAL MANAGER
Margaret Naughton

ROOM RATES (*Irish punts*)

Single occupancy	*£140 - £170*
70 Doubles/Twins	*£200 - £240*
17 Suites	*£245 - £700*

Includes full breakfast, service and VAT

CHARGE/CREDIT CARDS

• DC • MC • VI

RATINGS & AWARDS
I.T.B. ★★★★★
R.A.C. Blue Ribbon ★★★★
Dining Award 3
A.A. ★★★★ ❀

FACILITIES
On site: *Garden, gym, indoor pool, steam room, health & beauty, jacuzzi*
4 meeting rooms/max 80 people
Nearby: *Riding, golf, tennis, fishing, water skiing*

RESTRICTIONS
No pets

ATTRACTIONS
Midleton Distillery, Kinsale, Waterford Crystal, Ring of Kerry/Killarney, Blarney Castle, Cobh Heritage Centre

AFFILIATIONS
The Celebrated Hotels Collection
Small Luxury Hotels

NEAREST
MAJOR CITY:
Cork - 1 mile/10 mins
MAJOR AIRPORT:
Cork - 6 miles/20 mins
RAILWAY STATION:
Cork (Kent station) - 2 miles/15 mins

RESERVATIONS
Toll free in US: 800-322-2403
or 800-525-4800
*Quote **Best Loved***

ACCESS CODES
AMADEUS LX ORKHMR
APOLLO/GALILEO LX 78411
SABRE/ABACUS LX 31327
WORLDSPAN LX ORKHM

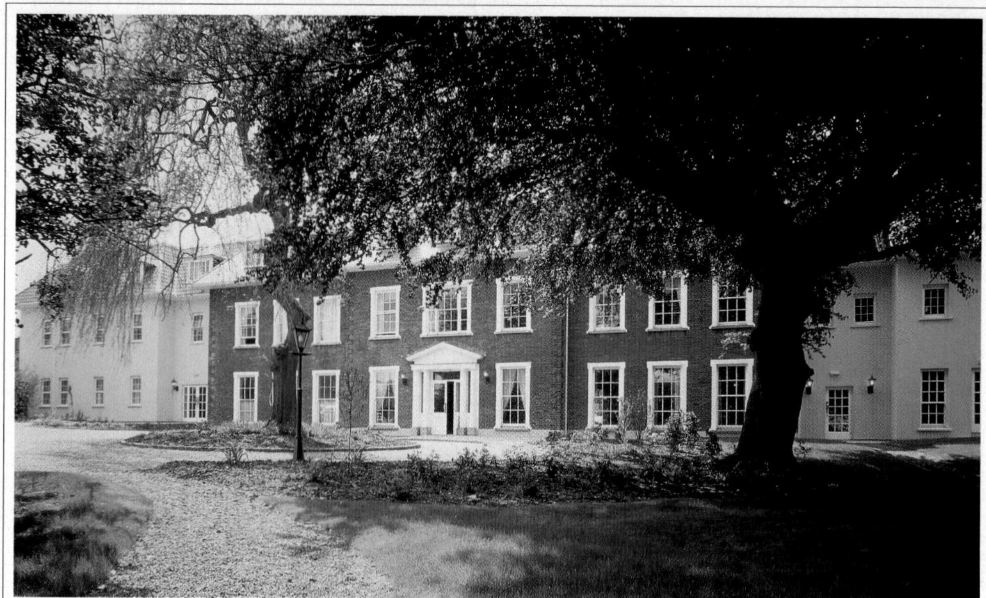

The best of town and country, of traditional and modern

Hayfield Manor offers the best of both worlds in several respects. It is an elegant 19th century mansion, yet it is Cork's only five-star hotel with every modern comfort. It is a country house standing among the old parkland trees of its own quiet, two-acre mature gardens with its private well-concealed car park, yet it is within a mile of the city centre.

The spacious guest rooms are matched by luxurious marble bathrooms. The grandeur and style of the Manor Room restaurant combine with superb cuisine to create a magnificent gourmet experience.

From your room, you have direct access to an executive health club where even the pool has views across the formal garden. Whether you wish to work out in the fitness suite, enjoy the steam room or simply relax in the outdoor jacuzzi, Hayfield is the complete health facility.

Cork has much to commend it as a touring centre. Hayfield Manor is well placed for the Cobh Heritage Centre and Midleton Distillery and within easy reach of Killarney, the Ring of Kerry, Kinsale, Blarney Castle and Waterford, famous for its glass.

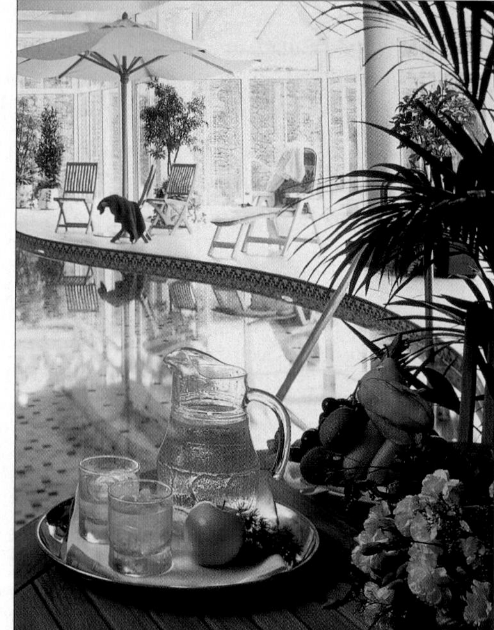

LOCATION

Travelling west from City Centre, take N70 for Killarney. Turn left at University Gates off Western Rd, at top of road turn right and immediate left - hotel is at top of avenue.

"The rooms were spacious and spotless, the staff exceptionally friendly; the service outstanding and the food first class"

John Walker, Walker Travel Group, Virginia

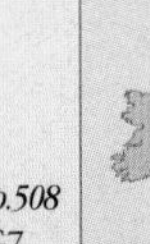

• Map p.508 ref: G7

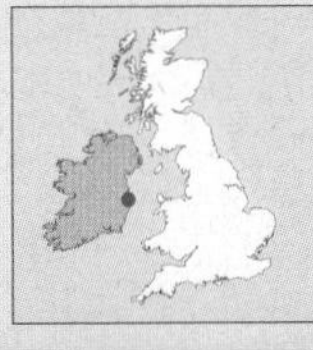

Contemporary hotel

HERBERT PARK HOTEL

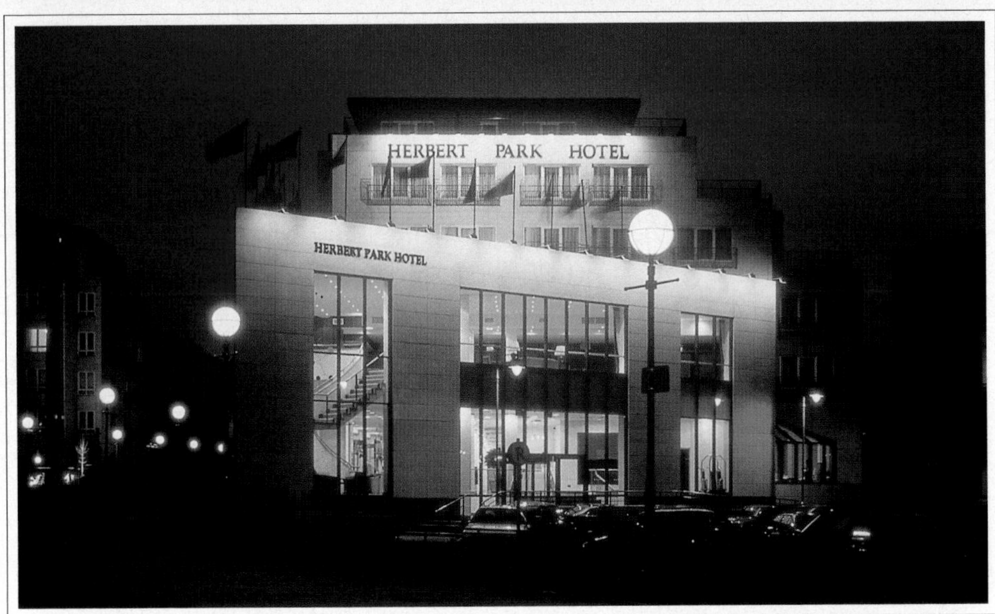

Contemporary Irish design finds a spectacular showcase in vibrant Dublin

Cocooned in the leafy parklands of the Embassy District, the Herbert Park is a very special modern Irish hotel. Its warm honey-coloured stone and glass façade has been purposely designed as a continuation of the park and bathes the striking two-storey public areas in natural light. Vistas range over trees and city to the countryside and mountains beyond, and the view west from the Mezzanine is spectacular at sunset.

A sense of calm and space is intrinsic to the airy inside-out design of the hotel. The style is clean and contemporary, but softened by clever use of colour and collections of Irish abstract art and portraiture. Facilities are excellent from the king size double beds and outstanding dining options to the fully-equipped health spa and meeting rooms. And let's not forget the all-important human touch evident in the superb service.

As well as offering a grand base for exploring Dublin, Herbert Park is a favourite with golfers, ideally placed for all the major links and parkland courses to the south and west of the city. Druids Glen, home to the Irish Open, is also easily accessible, and the hotel is delighted to arrange tee times for guests.

LOCATION

From the City Centre follow signs to Ballsbridge. Take the first right after the Ball's Bridge down Anglesea Road and next right again into the hotel.

Ballsbridge, Dublin 4, Republic of Ireland

Telephone +353 (0)1 667 2200
Fax +353 (0)1 667 2595

E-mail: *herbertpark@bestloved.com*

GENERAL MANAGER

Ewan Plenderleith

ROOM RATES *(Irish Punts)*

9 Singles	*£170*
103 Doubles/Twins	*£205*
11 Superior Doubles	*£225*
27 Executive Doubles/Twins	*£250*
3 Suites	*£320*

Includes service and VAT

CHARGE/CREDIT CARDS

• DC • MC • VI

RATINGS & AWARDS

I.T.B. ★★★★
R.A.C. ★★★★ *Dining Award 2*
A.A. ★★★★ *74%*

FACILITIES

On site: *Gym*
5 meeting rooms/max 150 people
Nearby: *Golf, tennis, fitness, fishing, yachting, water skiing*

RESTRICTIONS

No pets

ATTRACTIONS

Tours of Dublin City, National Art Gallery, National Library, Guinness Hopstore, Horseracing, Wicklow Mountains

AFFILIATIONS

Utell International

NEAREST

MAJOR CITY:
Dublin - 1½ miles/10 mins

MAJOR AIRPORT:
Dublin - 8 miles/30 mins

RAILWAY STATION:
Lansdowne Road - ½ mile/5 mins

RESERVATIONS

Toll free in US: 800-44-UTELL
Quote ***Best Loved***

ACCESS CODES

AMADEUS UI DUBHER
APOLLO/GAILILEO UI 76888
SABRE/ABACUS UI 23542
WORLDSPAN UI 25224

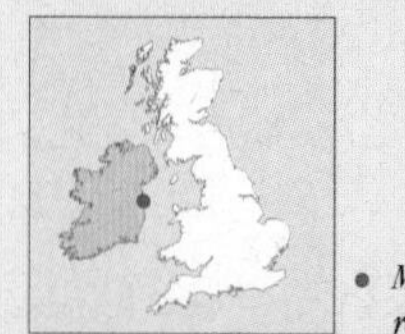

• Map p.508 ref: G7

"One of the five most stylish hotels in the Irish capital"

Conde Nast, Traveller Magazine

HIBERNIAN HOTEL

Victorian town house

Eastmoreland Place, Ballsbridge, Dublin 4, Republic of Ireland

Telephone +353 (0)1 668 7666
Fax +353 (0)1 660 2655

***E-mail:** hibernian@bestloved.com*

DIRECTOR
David Butt

GENERAL MANAGER
Niall Coffey

ROOM RATES *(Irish Punts)*

Single occupancy	*from £110*
30 Doubles/Twins	*from £150*
10 Junior suites	*£190*

Includes service and VAT

CHARGE/CREDIT CARDS

• *DC • MC • VI*

RATINGS & AWARDS
R.A.C. ★★★ Dining Award 3
A.A. ★★★ ❀❀❀ 77%
A.A. Courtesy & Care Award 1999

FACILITIES
***On site:** Restaurant*
1 meeting room/max 35 people
***Nearby:** Golf, health centre, riding*

RESTRICTIONS
No pets
Closed 24 - 27 Dec

ATTRACTIONS
National Art Gallery,
Shopping on Grafton Street, Trinity College

AFFILIATIONS
Manor House Hotels of Ireland
The Celebrated Hotels Collection
Small Luxury Hotels

NEAREST
MAJOR CITY:
Dublin
MAJOR AIRPORT:
Dublin - 7 miles/30 mins
RAILWAY STATION:
Connolly - 2 miles/15 mins

RESERVATIONS
Toll free in US/Canada: 800-322-2403
or 800-525-4800
Toll free in UK: 00800 525 48000
*Quote **Best Loved***

ACCESS CODES
AMADEUS LX DUBTHH
APOLLO/GALILEO LX 58480
SABRE/ABACUS LX 35282
WORLDSPAN LX DUBHH

A taste of gracious city living, an experience to be savoured

Awarded Hotel of the Year 1997 by Small Luxury Hotels of the World, the Hibernian Hotel is a tranquil haven of true hospitality in bustling downtown Dublin. This splendid Victorian building, built at the end of the 19th century, offers a very warm welcome with friendly smiles and an impeccable service.

Each of the hotel's 40 elegant and luxurious bedrooms is individually decorated in true historic style. Professionalism and care prevail throughout, creating, for the guest, a 'home-away-from-home' feeling. The drawing room, library and sun lounge are graced by antiques, original oil paintings, fresh flowers and rich furniture, recreating an inviting atmosphere of relaxation and times past. For business meetings and private gatherings the wood-panelled boardroom is the ideal setting.

The hotel's gourmet restaurant, 'The Patrick Kavanagh Room' with adjoining conservatory serves mouth-watering culinary masterpieces prepared from only the very best of Irish produce.

The Hibernian is classical and enchanting and offers the ultimate in relaxation, intimacy and professional care. The Hibernian is a taste of gracious city living, an experience to be savoured.

LOCATION

Turn right from Mespil Road into Baggot Street Upper; then left into Eastmoreland Place. The Hibernian is at the end on the left.

" Lovely hotel, lovely and friendly staff "

Donal and Fidelma Jennings

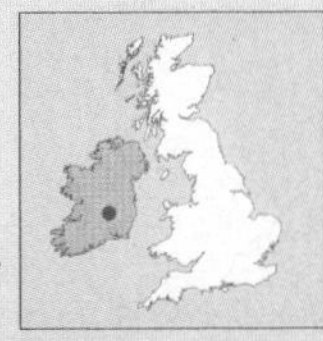

• Map p.508
ref: F8

City centre hotel

HIBERNIAN HOTEL

Bank on a comfortable stay in the 'Marble City'

Large tracts of County Kilkenny in the southeast of Ireland are formed of a limestone rock which turns black when polished. Much of the historic city of Kilkenny is built with this characteristic local stone hence the 'Marble City'. Marble is no stranger to the handsome purlieus of the Hibernian Hotel. This gracious old Victorian bank has been sympathetically transformed and substantially extended into a welcoming hotel with a grand lobby area and many original features, such as the marble fireplaces in the bedrooms, which survive from an even earlier incarnation as a private residence.

The Hibernian's comfortable bedrooms feature generous king-size beds, sleek bathrooms and Irish fabrics in soft, warm tones with floral touches. Guests can relax over a drink or a cup of coffee and the daily newspapers in the traditional Hibernian Bar, or sample the more lively ambience of Morrissons Bar. The Jacobs Cottage restaurant offers an eclectic menu of Irish and international cuisine including the ubiquitous but utterly delicious sticky toffee pudding. If you need to work off a surfeit of pudding, guests enjoy complimentary membership of an adjacent health and leisure centre with pool, gym, sauna and steam room.

LOCATION

Situated on main crossroad in Kilkenny town centre, on the corner of Ormonde Street and Patrick Street. Parking available in Ormonde Street.

1 Ormonde Street,
Kilkenny, Co Kilkenny,
Republic of Ireland

Telephone +353 (0)56 71888
Fax +353 (0)56 71877

E-mail: *ckhibernian@bestloved.com*

OWNERS

Gerry Byrne and David Lawlor

ROOM RATES *(Irish Punts)*

Single occupancy	*£70 - £104*
35 Doubles/Twins	*£110 - £138*
4 Junior suites	*£130 - £158*
3 Penthouse suites	*£150 - £178*

Includes full breakfast and VAT

CHARGE/CREDIT CARDS

• DC • MC • VI

RATINGS & AWARDS

Awards Pending

FACILITIES

On site: *2 meeting rooms/max 80 people*
Nearby: *Golf, riding tennis, fishing, health & leisure centre*

RESTRICTIONS

Closed 24 - 26 Dec

ATTRACTIONS

Kilkenny Castle, Waterford Crystal, Rock of Cashel, Smithicks Brewery, Craft Trail, Walking Tours

AFFILIATIONS

Independent

NEAREST

MAJOR CITY:
Waterford - 30 miles/40 mins

MAJOR AIRPORT:
Dublin - 85 miles/2 hrs

RAILWAY STATION:
Kilkenny - 1 mile/5 mins

RESERVATIONS

Direct with hotel
Quote ***Best Loved***

ACCESS CODES

Not applicable

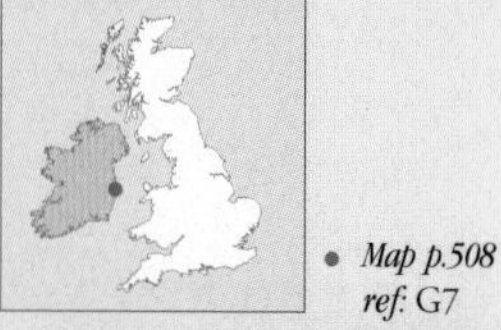

• Map p.508 ref: G7

"I have been to many places in the south of Ireland but I find this lovely spot the most peaceful and charming of them all"

W D Doherty FRCS, London

HUNTER'S HOTEL

18th century coaching inn

Newrath Bridge, Rathnew, Co Wicklow, Republic of Ireland

Telephone +353 (0)404 40106
Fax +353 (0)404 40338

E-mail: *hunters@bestloved.com*

OWNERS

The Gelletlie Family

ROOM RATES ***(Irish Punts)***

2 Singles £65 - £80
14 Doubles/Twins £130 - £150
Includes full breakfast and VAT

CHARGE/CREDIT CARDS

 • *DC* • *MC* • *VI*

RATINGS & AWARDS

I.T.B. ★★★
A.A. ★★★ ❀ *67%*

FACILITIES

On site: *Garden*
1 meeting room/max 30 people
Nearby: *Golf, riding, fishing, walking*

RESTRICTIONS

No pets
Closed 24 - 26 Dec

ATTRACTIONS

Mount Usher Gardens, Powerscourt Gardens and Waterfall, Glendalough, Russborough House

AFFILIATIONS

Ireland's Blue Book

NEAREST

MAJOR CITY:
Dublin - 28 miles/45 mins

MAJOR AIRPORT:
Dublin - 40 miles/1¼ hrs

RAILWAY STATION:
Wicklow - 3 miles/5 mins

RESERVATIONS

Toll free in US: 800-323-5463
*Quote **Best Loved***

ACCESS CODES

Not applicable

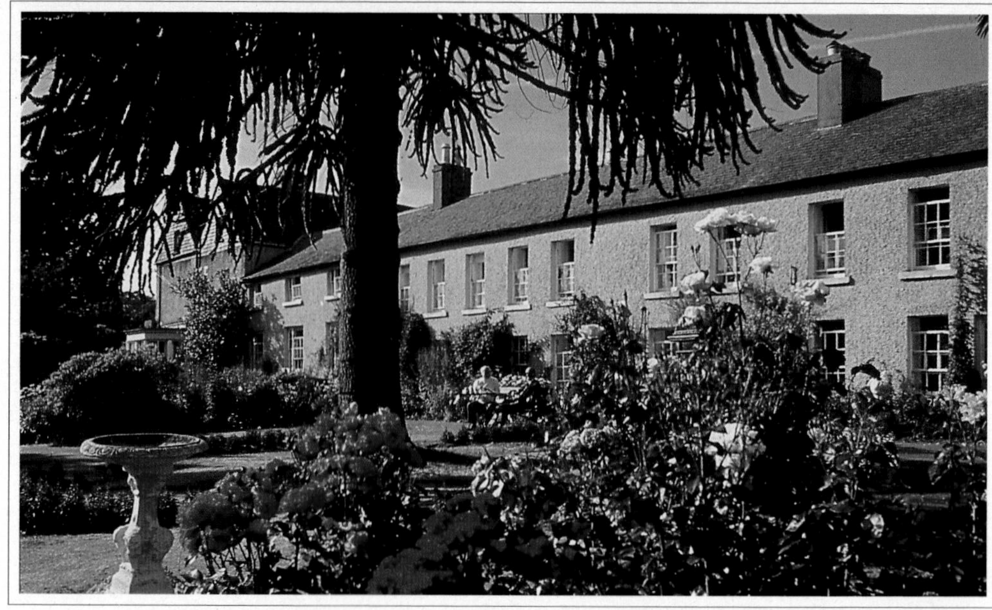

Good food and old-world charm – a family tradition of five generations

Hunter's Hotel, one of Ireland's oldest coaching inns, has been established for over 270 years, since the days of post horses and carriages. Run by the same family for five generations, the hotel has built up a strong tradition based on good food, comfortable surroundings and unique, old world charm.

Set in one of Ireland's most beautiful counties, the hotel stands in gardens bordering the River Vartry. All the rooms retain the character of bygone days, with antique furniture, open fires, fresh flowers and polished brass. Most of the 16 attractive bedrooms overlook the gardens.

Sea angling, riding, hunting, tennis, swimming and hiking are all in the immediate locality. There are 18 golf courses within 30 minutes' drive including Druids Glen and The European Club. The beautiful Wicklow countryside, known as 'Garden of Ireland', lies at your doorstep. Lovely sandy beaches, breathtaking mountain scenery, quiet glens and well known beauty spots such as Mount Usher Gardens, Powerscourt, Russborough House, Avondale House, Glendalough, the Devil's Glen and Roundwood are all within easy reach.

Whether you want a country base from which to visit Dublin, a peaceful rural holiday or a pleasant overnight stop after the ferry, Hunter's Hotel is the ideal location.

LOCATION

Take N11 to Rathnew village. Turn left just before the village on Dublin side.

"Whatever happened to the rush hour?"

Michael Gorda, Cheadle, Cheshire

• *Map p.508 ref: G5*

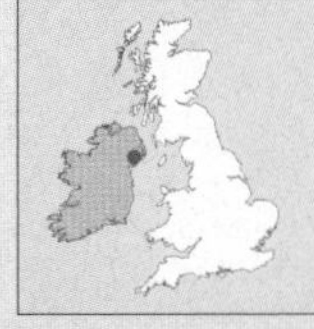

Restaurant with rooms

JORDAN'S TOWNHOUSE

Spaciousness, tranquillity and finest foods from land and sea

Jordan's was built in the 16th century as a row of fishermen's cottages in the then thriving fishing port of Carlingford. It has served as a salt and barrelling house and a cold store. It has to be one of the most elegant townhouses of any village. The five guest bedrooms are huge: about 400 square feet each, compared to the 320 required for a five-star hotel. Antique Irish pine takes pride of place in the sumptuous furnishings.

Jordan's was opened as a restaurant in the early 1980s. It has won many ratings & awards, and is currently ranked in Ireland's top 100 restaurants. It offers the best of seasonal local produce. True to its history and the high quality at nearby East Coast ports, Jordan's is renowned for fish, lobsters and oysters. In winter, game comes into its own. Irish lamb from the mountains is a delight in all seasons.

Tranquil Carlingford is a heritage village. Prehistoric remains at Newgrange date back 8,000 years. In the Middle Ages it was strategically important; medieval treasures include King John's Castle, the Mint, Taaffe's Castle, Thosel old town hall, and the ruined Dominican abbey. Navan Fort, Dublin, Belfast and five top golf courses are within easy reach.

LOCATION

1¼ miles north of Dundalk - turn right at intersection.

Newry Street, Carlingford, Co Louth, Republic of Ireland

Telephone +353 (0)42 9373223
Fax +353 (0)42 9373827

E-mail: *jordans@bestloved.com*

OWNERS

Ambrose and Marion Ferguson

ROOM RATES (*Irish Punts*)

5 Doubles/Twins £80 - £110
Includes full breakfast and VAT

CHARGE/CREDIT CARDS

• *MC* • *VI*

RATINGS & AWARDS

I.T.B. ★★★★
R.A.C. ◆◆◆◆◆
A.A. ◆◆◆◆◆

FACILITIES

On site: *Tennis*
Nearby: *Golf, water skiing, fishing, riding*

RESTRICTIONS

No smoking in bedrooms and dining room
No pets

ATTRACTIONS

Newgrange 6000 B.C., Dublin, Navan Fort, Carlingford Heritage Village, Belfast, 5 Golf Courses within 20 minutes

AFFILIATIONS

Independent

NEAREST

MAJOR CITY:
Dublin - 63 miles/1½ hrs

MAJOR AIRPORT:
Belfast - 55 miles/1 hr
Dublin - 63 miles/1½ hrs

RAILWAY STATION:
Dundalk - 15 miles/20 mins

RESERVATIONS

Direct with hotel
*Quote **Best Loved***

ACCESS CODES

Not applicable

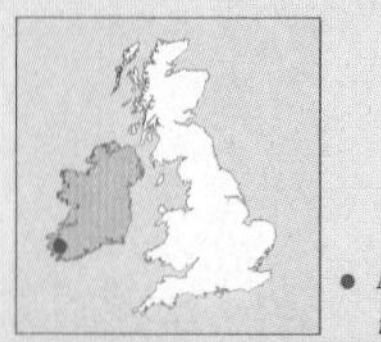

• Map p.508 ref: C9

"The hotel is beautiful and impeccably maintained, but it is the consistent willingness and helpfulness of every member of staff which makes my guests stay in Ireland such a memorable experience"

Jerry Quinlan, Jerry Quinlan's Celtic Golf

KILLARNEY PARK HOTEL

Luxury hotel

Kenmare Place,
Killarney, Co Kerry,
Republic of Ireland

Telephone +353 (0)64 35555
Fax +353 (0)64 35266

E-mail: killarneypark@bestloved.com

OWNERS

Padraig and Janet Treacy

GENERAL MANAGER

Donagh Davern

ROOM RATES (Irish Punts)

Single occupancy	£170 - £500
56 Deluxe Doubles/Twins	£170 - £250
17 Junior suites	£250 - £350
3 Superior suites	£400 - £500

Includes full breakfast and VAT

CHARGE/CREDIT CARDS

• DC • MC • VI

RATINGS & AWARDS

I.T.B. ★★★★★

R.A.C. Blue Ribbon ★★★★ Dining Award 3

A.A. ★★★★ ❀ 78%

CIE Tours National Award of Excellence 1999

FACILITIES

On site: Indoor pool, health & beauty 3 meeting rooms/max 150 people

Nearby: Fishing, golf, cycling, shooting, riding, hill & mountain walking

RESTRICTIONS

No pets

ATTRACTIONS

Killarney National Park, Muckross House, Ring of Kerry, Gap of Dunloe, Ross Castle, Torc Waterfalls

AFFILIATIONS

The Celebrated Hotels Collection

NEAREST

MAJOR CITY:
Cork - 54 miles/1½ hrs

MAJOR AIRPORT:
Kerry - 15 miles/20 mins
Cork - 54 miles/1½ hrs

RAILWAY STATION:
Killarney - ¼ mile/1 min

RESERVATIONS

Toll free in US: 800-322-2403 or 800-537-8483

Quote **Best Loved**

ACCESS CODES

AMADEUS LM KIR744
APOLLO/GALILEO LM 25271
SABRE/ABACUS LM 50359
WORLDSPAN LM 05744

Old-world courtesy and charm honed to perfection by three generations of expertise

Marrying together the many and varied vital ingredients that make a successful hotel is a complex art form. To start from scratch with a new building and create a gracious Victorian-style country house hotel takes a minor miracle. Fortunately Janet and Padraig Treacy can call on three generations of expertise in the hotel industry, and they have indeed performed miracles at the Killarney Park.

The Treacys' attention to detail is phenomenal from traditional fabrics and furnishings to the oh-so-Victorian potted plants. Soft, relaxing colour schemes lend a restful air to the bedrooms, and there are splendid antique beds and open fires in the generously proportioned suites. The quiet, half-panelled Library actually contains books you want to read, and the clubby Billiards Room almost demands a fat cigar and snifter of brandy for accompaniment. The ladies' preserve is the elegant Drawing Room, though gentlemen are certainly welcome. Meanwhile, everybody appreciates the warm welcome in the Garden Bar with its choice of newspapers, sheltered outdoor terrace, and a barman who can concoct the most delicious Irish coffee imaginable.

However, Killarney Park is far from locked in the amber of the Victorian era. Queen Victoria herself might have been impressed by the lavishly-equipped Health Spa. She would also have heartily endorsed the horse-riding, golf, fishing, and other country sports available, perhaps interspersed with a spot of sightseeing.

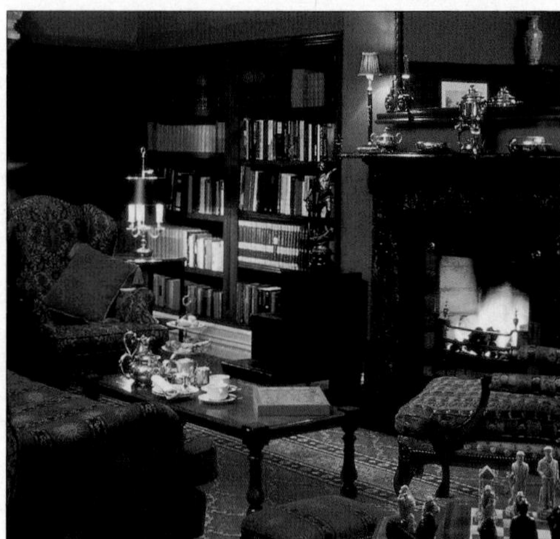

LOCATION

Situated in the centre of Killarney town. Kenmare Place is a continuation of Main Street and the hotel is on the right hand side.

"The wonderful service, the great accommodation, your fantastic dining room and staff make the Royal a truly first class establishment"

Mrs Desmond, London

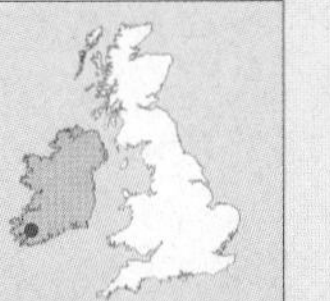

• Map p.508 ref: B9

Victorian town house

KILLARNEY ROYAL HOTEL

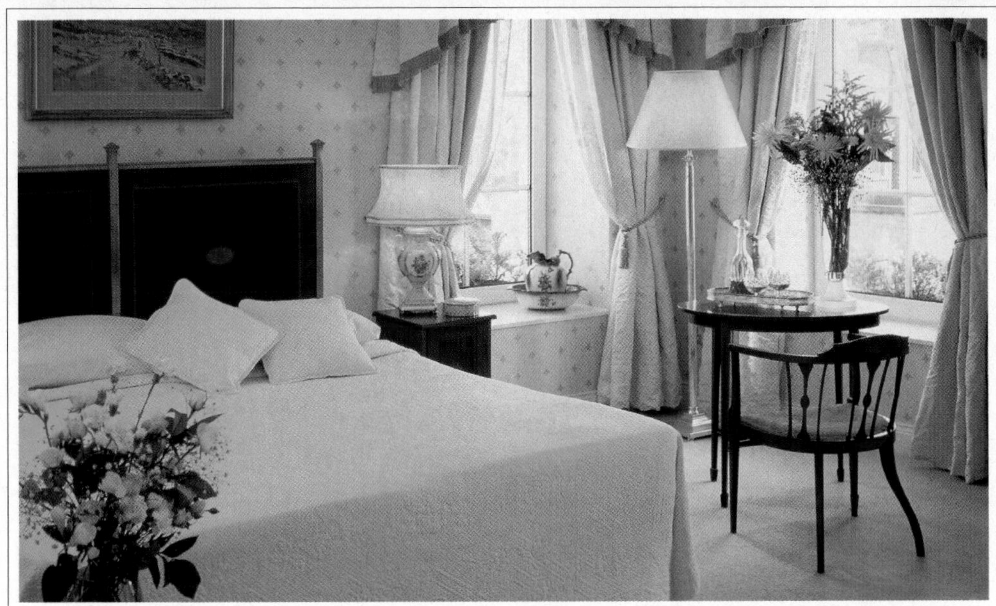

Right royal hospitality and good food in Ireland's romantic south west

Killarney is a popular touring base for the southwest of Ireland: visitors come to explore the legendary Ring of Kerry, the scenic Dingle Peninsula or beautiful, 21-mile long Bantry Bay; to walk in the 25,000 acres of Killarney National Park where native Irish red deer roam, to play golf on the town's two championship courses or to taste the excellent local brown trout; to visit Victorian Muckross House and Gardens and Kate Kearney's Cottage, an illegal drinking house for mid-19th century travellers. Yet many visitors have said the highlight of their trip was their stay at the Killarney Royal, in the centre of town.

The Scally family pride themselves on the excellent, personal service they offer their guests. They have recently completed a major refurbishment, redesigning the bedrooms, decorating them with antiques (all personal treasures) and installing air-conditioning. Comfort is the key to their brand of hospitality; from the upholstered dining chairs in the graceful dining room to the airy bedrooms and the marble bathrooms.

The dining room attracts a big local following - its traditional, fine-dining menu offers good Irish beef, lamb and salmon. The bar has a homely, local feel to it, and in the lounge you can take tea and scones by an open fire.

A touch of pure luxury in Ireland's wild west!

LOCATION

Kilarney Royal is situated in the centre of Killarney on College Street off the N22.

College Street, Killarney, Co Kerry, Republic of Ireland

Telephone +353 (0)64 31853
Fax +353 (0)64 34001

E-mail: *killarney@bestloved.com*

OWNERS

Margaret and Joseph Scally

ROOM RATES *(Irish Punts)*

Single occupancy	*£90 - £140*
24 Doubles/Twins	*£140 - £210*
5 Junior suites	*£190 - £260*

Includes full breakfast and VAT

CHARGE/CREDIT CARDS

• *DC* • *MC* • *VI*

RATINGS & AWARDS

Awards Pending

FACILITIES

On site: *1 meeting room/max 50 people*
Nearby: *Golf, tennis, fitness, fishing, riding*

RESTRICTIONS

No pets
Closed 22 - 28 Dec

ATTRACTIONS

Ring of Kerry, Dingle Peninsula, Gap of Dunloe, Lakes of Killarney, Muckross House & Gardens, Torc Waterfall

AFFILIATIONS

Independent

NEAREST

MAJOR CITY:
Cork - 55 miles/1¼ hrs

MAJOR AIRPORT:
Kerry - 9 miles/15 mins

RAILWAY STATION:
Killarney

RESERVATIONS

Toll free in UK: 00800 4748 4748
Quote ***Best Loved***

ACCESS CODES

Not applicable

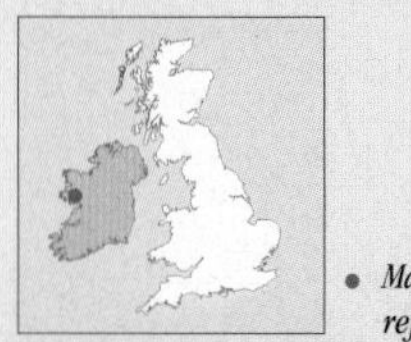

• Map p.508 ref: C5

"Our first visit to Westport has been brilliant, largely due to our choice of accommodation which has been splendid in every respect"

Annette, Martin & Claire Murphy, Belfast

KNOCKRANNY HOUSE

Victorian style house

Westport, Co Mayo, Republic of Ireland

Telephone +353 (0)98 28600
Fax +353 (0)98 28611

E-mail: knockranny@bestloved.com

OWNERS

Adrian and Geraldine Noonan

ROOM RATES (Irish Punts)

Single occupancy	£130
42 Doubles/Twins	£170
9 Deluxe Doubles/Twins	£200
3 Four-posters	£220

Includes full breakfast and VAT

CHARGE/CREDIT CARDS

• MC • VI

RATINGS & AWARDS

I.T.B. ★★★★

A.A. ★★★★ ❀ 69%

FACILITIES

On site: *Garden*

3 meeting rooms/max 700 people

Nearby: *Golf, riding, fishing, tennis, complimentary leisure facilities, blue flag beaches*

RESTRICTIONS

No pets

ATTRACTIONS

Westport House, Clare Island, Croagh Patrick Mountain, Kylemore Abbey, Connemara National Park, Ceide Fields

AFFILIATIONS

Independent

NEAREST

MAJOR CITY:
Galway - 55 miles/1 hr

MAJOR AIRPORT:
Shannon - 125 miles/1¾ hrs

RAILWAY STATION:
Westport - ½ mile/5 mins

RESERVATIONS

Direct with hotel
*Quote **Best Loved***

ACCESS CODES

Not applicable

Irish hospitality and an island for every day of the year in Clew Bay

Locals claim there is an island for every day of the year anchored in the broad and peaceful embrace of Clew Bay. On the shore, the seaside town of Westport, often described as the cultural capital of Mayo, is a marvellous touring base for Co. Mayo and neighbouring Co. Galway. One of the great charms of Knockranny House is its enviable position above Westport with views over the Bay and of Croagh Patrick, Ireland's famous pilgrimage mountain. St Patrick is reputed to have spent the Lentern retreat of AD441 on its summit and each year on the last Sunday in July pilgrims make the trek to the mountaintop chapel.

Knockranny House is a classic Victorian-built hotel successfully combining period style with modern comforts and very friendly and efficient staff headed by welcoming hosts Adrian and Geraldine. From the moment you walk into the reception area, the animated hub of the hotel with large windows overlooking the town, there is a sense of spaciousness and brightness which extends throughout. The dining room enjoys yet more wonderful views and at dinner the mainly seafood menu is accompanied by a classical pianist. Knockranny also offers excellent conference facilities for up to 700 delegates.

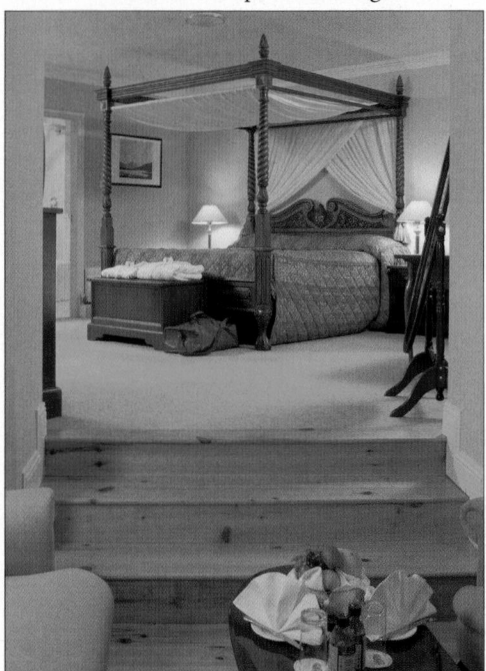

LOCATION

Take N5/N60 from Castlebar. Hotel is on left before entering Westport.

A keen Angler? Refer to page 472 for our Fishing Index

"Longfield's has proved to be a tranquil haven in an active city. Wonderful to have been cared for by an excellent team of staff"

Mrs Sandra Hamilton, London

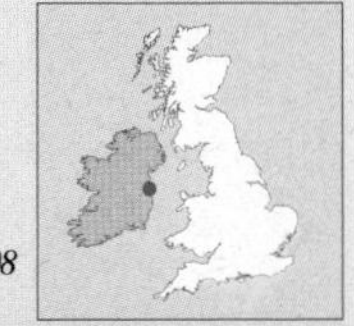

• Map p.508 ref: G7

18th century Georgian house

LONGFIELD'S

A home in the centre of Dublin you could almost call your own

"During this morning walk in Dublin, I continued to believe that no matter where I looked I would find traces of the faces, the laughter and the voices which gave birth to this city and whose buildings and streets had a way of making you feel they belonged to you". This is how J P Donleavy, the Irish-American novelist described one of Europe's smallest cities and, arguably, its most endearing and entertaining.

Within walking distance of the principal attractions of the city is Longfield's gracing one of the many elegant Georgian terraces for which this part of Dublin is famous. If you were not staying there, you might be tempted by Number Ten, the below stairs restaurant, whose intimate ambience, excellent cuisine and splendid cellar entice and satisfy its business and residential neighbours.

If you find the acquaintance of the restaurant to your liking, you will surely fall for the other pleasures of this erstwhile home of Lord Longfield. The high-ceilinged rooms have all the refinements of which his lordship would have thoroughly approved and many he could never have dreamed of, introduced as some were, in an ongoing major refurbishment of the property.

Indeed, as the charming staff put you at your ease, you may reflect, like Donleavy, that this haven in some way belongs to you.

LOCATION

Only 10 minutes (¼ mile) from Grafton Street and the City Centre.

9 - 10 Fitzwilliam Street Lower, Dublin 2, Republic of Ireland

Telephone +353 (0)1 676 1367
Fax +353 (0)1 676 1542

E-mail: longfield@bestloved.com

GENERAL MANAGER

Philip Ryan

ROOM RATES (Irish Punts)

2 Singles	£80 - £125
17 Twins	£110 - £135
5 Superior Doubles	£125 - £160
2 Four-posters	£140 - £180

Includes full breakfast and VAT

CHARGE/CREDIT CARDS

• DC • MC • VI

RATINGS & AWARDS

I.T.B. ★★★

R.A.C. ★★★ Dining Award 2

FACILITIES

On site: No 10 Restaurant

Nearby: Tennis, fishing, fitness, riding, golf

RESTRICTIONS

No facilities for disabled guests

Closed 24 - 26 Dec

No pets

ATTRACTIONS

Trinity College, National Library, St Stephen's Green, National Art Gallery, Grafton Street, Christchurch Cathedral

AFFILIATIONS

Manor House Hotels of Ireland

NEAREST

MAJOR CITY: Dublin

MAJOR AIRPORT: Dublin - 7 miles/30 mins

RAILWAY STATION: Dublin - ½ mile/15 mins

RESERVATIONS

Toll free in US: 800-44-UTELL

Quote **Best Loved**

ACCESS CODES

AMADEUS UI DUBLON

APOLLO/GALILEO UI 91673

SABRE/ABACUS UI 33792

WORLDSPAN UI 40025

• Map p.508 ref: D9

"If you are seeking a romantic interlude on a gracious country estate, you can do no better than to choose Longueville House"

Karen Brown, USA

LONGUEVILLE HOUSE

Georgian manor

Mallow, Co Cork, Republic of Ireland

Telephone +353 (0)22 47156
Fax +353 (0)22 47459

***E-mail:** longueville@bestloved.com*

OWNERS
O'Callaghan family

MANAGER
Kate Murphy

ROOM RATES *(Irish Punts)*

Single occupancy	*£125 - £240*
8 Superior Doubles/Twins	*£160 - £180*
3 Mini suites	*£170 - £190*
1 Suite	*£200 - £250*

Includes full breakfast and VAT

CHARGE/CREDIT CARDS

• DC • MC • VI

RATINGS & AWARDS
I.T.B. ★★★★
R.A.C. Blue Ribbon ★★★ *Dining Award 3*
A.A. ★★★ ❀❀❀

FACILITIES
***On site:** Garden, fishing, heli-pad*
2 meeting rooms/max 45 people
***Nearby:** Golf, lake and river fishing, hiking*

RESTRICTIONS
No facilities for disabled guests
Pets not permitted in hotel

ATTRACTIONS
Blarney Castle & village, Rock of Cashel, Kinsale fishing village, Ring of Kerry, Waterford Glass Factory, Adare village

AFFILIATIONS
Ireland's Blue Book
Relais & Châteaux

NEAREST
MAJOR CITY:
Cork City - 21 miles/40 mins

MAJOR AIRPORT:
Cork - 25 miles/45 mins

RAILWAY STATION:
Mallow - 3 miles/10 mins

RESERVATIONS
Toll free in US: 800-323-5463
*Quote **Best Loved***

ACCESS CODES
AMADEUS WB ORKLON
APOLLO/GALILEO WB 14724
SABRE/ABACUS WB 52018
WORLDSPAN WB 1E04

The history of Longueville is that of Ireland in miniature

Cork is the gateway to Ireland's dramatic southwest coast, which draws visitors like bees to a honey pot. Take the time to stop and savour the beauties of inner Cork, its gentle, green countryside dotted with megalithic forts and grand estate gateways that often lead to modest homes, ruins or even open fields. These lands were once occupied by the early settler families, such as the O'Callaghans of Dromineen Castle, which was demolished in the Cromwellian Confiscation and its ruins lie in full view of the present O'Callaghan seat, Longueville House.

Lovely Longueville is a listed Georgian manor dating from 1720, and set in 500 acres of gardens, woods and farmland overlooking the Blackwater River Valley. The O'Callaghan family has created a truly elegant and charming country house hotel with a very special feature in the fabulous Victorian conservatory constructed by master glasshouse designer Richard Turner of Kew Gardens fame. Apart from the exquisite bedrooms, The Presidents' Restaurant is another highlight of Longueville, where chef William O'Callaghan comes into his own preparing delicious and deceptively simple dishes inspired by the freshest produce from the estate's farm, gardens and river and there is a remarkable wine list from the Old and New Worlds.

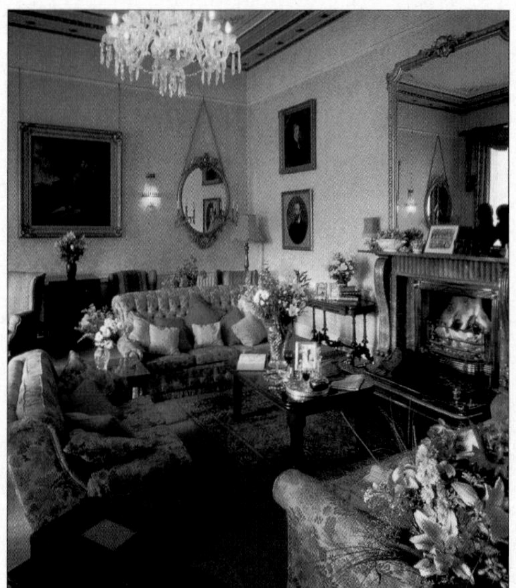

LOCATION

3 miles west of Mallow via N72 Killarney Road. Turn right at Ballyclough junction and follow sign.

“ Addiction is the word that springs to mind. Had a fabulous weekend. Thanks a million again. See you next time ”

Colman Finlay & Claire Bolan, Ireland

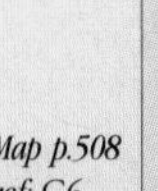

• Map p.508 ref: C6

Victorian lodge

LOUGH INAGH LODGE HOTEL

The most beautiful place to go hill walking and see Connemara

The lodge is set on the shores of Lough Inagh, one of Connemara's most beautiful lakes. Amidst the most spectacular scenery in Ireland, visitors can fish, shoot, pony trek, cycle, play golf or simply relax. Sturdily built in the 1880s, Lough Inagh Lodge combines the comforts and pleasures of a modern hotel with its own old-world charm. The original lodge record books make fascinating reading for fishermen, and everyone else can take in Ireland's finest panoramic views that accompany morning coffee or afternoon tea in the sitting room. Each bedroom has a separate dressing room, and fabulous vistas over the lake and The Twelve Bens mountains. Open log fires in the library and the oak-panelled bar symbolise the warmth of Inagh hospitality. Seafood and wild game dishes are specialities of the house, and are complemented by an excellent wine list.

Outdoor action is unlimited. There is game fishing on Lough Inagh, sea fishing within ten miles, driven woodcock shooting, riding and golf. All Irish craftware is available in the many shops at Recess, Kylemore and Clifden.

The lodge is the ideal base for a tour of Connemara. It is surrounded by noted beauty spots, including the Connemara National Park. Kylemore Abbey is nearby.

LOCATION

Take the N59 towards Clifden as far as Recess. Turn right onto the R344 just after Recess and head towards Letterfrack. The hotel is situated approximately 7 kms from this junction.

Recess, Connemara, Co Galway, Republic of Ireland

Telephone +353 (0)95 34706
Fax +353 (0)95 34708

E-mail: loughinagh@bestloved.com

OWNER

Maire O'Connor

ROOM RATES (Irish Punts)

10 Doubles/Twins	£121 - £143
2 Four-posters	£132 - £165

Includes full breakfast and VAT

CHARGE/CREDIT CARDS

• DC • MC • VI

RATINGS & AWARDS

I.T.B. ★★★
A.A. ★★★ ❀❀ 77%
A.A. Romantic Hotel

FACILITIES

On site: Garden, fishing, heli-pad, shooting, walking, cycle hire
1 meeting room/max 24 people
Nearby: Golf, sea fishing, riding, scuba diving

RESTRICTIONS

Limited facilities for disabled guests
Closed mid Dec - mid Mar

ATTRACTIONS

Connemara National Park, Twelve Bens Mountain Range, Kylemore Abbey, Letterfrack Furniture College, local craft shops

AFFILIATIONS

Manor House Hotels of Ireland

NEAREST

MAJOR CITY:
Galway - 42 miles/1 hr
MAJOR AIRPORT:
Shannon - 99 miles/2½ hrs
Knock - 75 miles/2½ hrs
RAILWAY STATION:
Galway - 42 miles/1 hr

RESERVATIONS

Toll free in US/Canada: 800-44-UTELL
Quote **Best Loved**

ACCESS CODES

SABRE/ABACUS UI 33759
AMADEUS UI GWYLOU
WORLDSPAN UI 40027
APOLLO/GALILEO UI 91711

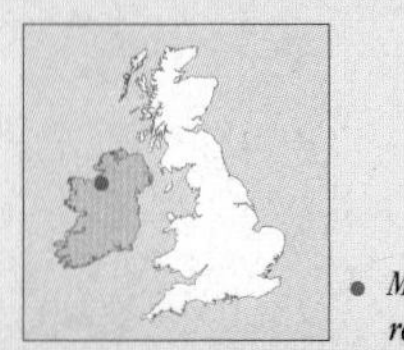

• Map p.508 ref: D5

“ Ireland's finest castle of its period ”

Lord Clark, 'Civilisation' television programme

MARKREE CASTLE

17th century castle

Collooney, Co Sligo, Republic of Ireland

Telephone +353 (0)71 67800
Fax +353 (0)71 67840

E-mail: markree@bestloved.com

OWNERS
Charles and Mary Cooper

MANAGER
Bill Chambers

ROOM RATES (*Irish Punts*)

Single occupancy	£68 - £74
25 Doubles/Twins	£116 - £130
5 Suites	£156 - £170

Includes full breakfast and VAT

CHARGE/CREDIT CARDS

• DC • MC • VI

RATINGS & AWARDS
I.T.B. ★★★
R.A.C. ★★★
A.A. ★★★ ❀❀ 62%
Bewley's Best Coffee Award
Bridgestone Top 100 Best Hotels

FACILITIES
On site: Garden, fishing, riding
Nearby: Golf, fishing

RESTRICTIONS
Closed 24 - 26 Dec

ATTRACTIONS
Yeats Country, Lough Gill, Carrowmore megalithic remains, Parke's Castle

AFFILIATIONS
Independent

NEAREST
MAJOR CITY:
Galway - 80 miles/2 hrs

MAJOR AIRPORT:
Dublin/Shannon - 125 miles/3 hrs
Knock - 40 miles/30 mins

RAILWAY STATION:
Collooney - 1½ miles/5 mins

RESERVATIONS
Direct with hotel
Quote **Best Loved**

ACCESS CODES
Not applicable

IRELAND

The Coopers have lived here for 350 years – the welcome is as warm as ever

Home of the Cooper family for over 350 years, Markree Castle is now run as a small family hotel by Charles and Mary Cooper, the 10th generation of the Coopers to live at Markree.

Set in a large estate with lovely gardens, the original house has been altered many times over the years, the main addition being in 1802 by the architect Francis Johnston. The enormous oak staircase is overlooked by a stained glass window depicting the Cooper family tree going back 20 generations, and the Louis Philippe style plasterwork in the dining-room makes it one of Ireland's most spectacular rooms.

Charles Cooper worked in hotels in many other countries before returning to Markree in 1989. Since then much has been restored creating a family hotel of character. The bedrooms all have private bathrooms, telephones, and efficient heating, yet great care has been taken to retain the character of the old building and the family atmosphere, rather than the formal, impersonal atmosphere of more luxurious hotels.

The restaurant has also become well known for carefully prepared meals of a high standard.

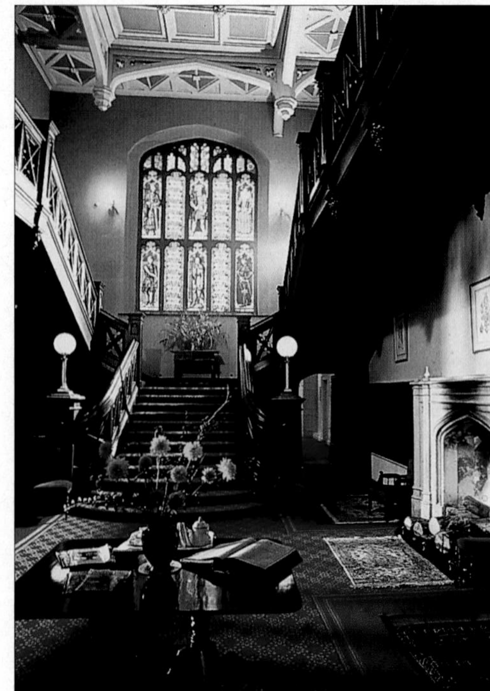

LOCATION

8 miles south of Sligo town, just off N4 and N17 junction.

" Sublime "

Robert Redford, Sundance, Utah

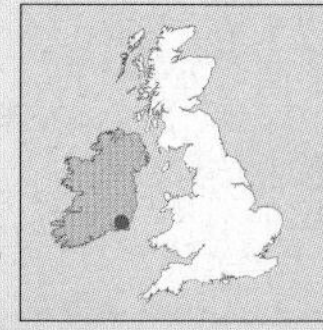

• *Map p.508 ref: G8*

Regency country house — MARLFIELD HOUSE

One of the treasures of Ireland's countryside heritage

Marlfield House is a fine Regency house set in 35 acres of woodlands and gardens and was the residence in Ireland of the Earl of Courtown. Just an hour from Dublin, it provides an ideal setting for touring the beauty spots of Wicklow and the south-east of Ireland.

The 20 bedrooms include five State Rooms and one magnificent Master Suite. The whole house is lavishly decorated with sumptuous fabrics, period fireplaces and numerous antiques. Bathrooms feature highly polished marble and free-standing bathtubs.

Eating in the curved Turner conservatory dining room is a memorable experience; the cuisine is modern Irish with a strong classical influence. The gardens provide the vegetables, herbs and fruits necessary for a kitchen to maintain its excellent reputation which has earned it numerous awards, including the Relais & Châteaux Worldwide Best Breakfast Award.

The house has been converted by its present owners, Ray and Mary Bowe, whose aim is to meet the demands of the more discerning guest looking for the best country house atmosphere.

LOCATION

The hotel is situated 57 miles south of Dublin Ferry Port; 63 miles south of Dublin Airport; 50 miles south of Dun Laoghaire Ferry Port; 39 miles north of Rosslare Ferry.

Gorey, Co Wexford, Republic of Ireland

Telephone +353 (0)55 21124
Fax +353 (0)55 21572

E-mail: *marlfield@bestloved.com*

OWNERS

Ray and Mary Bowe

ROOM RATES

2 Singles	*£85 - £105*
12 Doubles/Twins	*£165 - £180*
5 State rooms	*£290 - £365*
1 Master suite	*£530*

Includes full breakfast and VAT

CHARGE/CREDIT CARDS

• DC • MC • VI

RATINGS & AWARDS

I.T.B. ★★★★
R.A.C. Gold Ribbon ★★★
Dining Award 3
A.A. ★★★ ❀❀

FACILITIES

On site: *Tennis, croquet, sauna, heli-pad, garden and woodland, wildlife reserve*
2 meeting rooms/max 60 people
Nearby: *Golf, riding*

RESTRICTIONS

No children under 8 years allowed in restaurant for dinner
Limited facilities for disabled guests
Pets by arrangement
Closed 17 Dec - 1 Feb

ATTRACTIONS

Co Wicklow's lakes & mountains, gardens & historic houses, sandy beaches, Waterford Crystal, Kilkenny Castle and Cathedral

AFFILIATIONS

Ireland's Blue Book
The Celebrated Hotels Collection
Relais & Châteaux

NEAREST

MAJOR CITY:
Dublin - 57 miles/1¼ hrs
MAJOR AIRPORT:
Dublin - 63 miles/1¾ hrs
RAILWAY STATION:
Gorey - 1½ miles/5 mins

RESERVATIONS

Toll free in US: 800-322-2403
or 800-323-5463
*Quote **Best Loved***

ACCESS CODES

AMADEUS UI WEXMAR
APOLLO/GALILEO UI 67960
SABRE/ABACUS UI 22790
WORLDSPAN UI 6592

For route planning map of Ireland see page 508

• Map p.508 ref: G4

"A stylish hotel, an oasis of comfortable calm"

Karen Brown's, Charming Inns & Itineraries, Ireland

THE McCAUSLAND HOTEL

19th century warehouse

34 - 38 Victoria Street, Belfast BT1 3GH, Northern Ireland

Telephone +44 (0)28 9022 0200
Fax +44 (0)28 9022 0220

E-mail: *mccausland@bestloved.com*

DIRECTOR
David Butt

GENERAL MANAGER
Joseph Hughes

ROOM RATES

Single occupancy	from £110
51 Doubles/Twins	from £120
9 Suites	from £170

Includes service and VAT

CHARGE/CREDIT CARDS

• DC • JCB • MC • VI

RATINGS & AWARDS
R.A.C. ★★★★ Dining Award 1
A.A. ★★★★ 61%

FACILITIES
On site: *3 meeting rooms/max 100 people*
Nearby: *Golf, fishing, water skiing, yachting, tennis, fitness centre, riding*

RESTRICTIONS
No pets
Closed 24 - 27 Dec

ATTRACTIONS
Waterfront Hall, The Grand Opera House, Castle Court, The Odyssey, Ulster Museum, Botanical Gardens

AFFILIATIONS
The Celebrated Hotels Collection
Small Luxury Hotels
Manor House Hotels of Ireland

NEAREST
MAJOR CITY:
Belfast
MAJOR AIRPORT:
Belfast International - 14 miles/20 mins
Belfast City - 3 miles/10 mins
RAILWAY STATION:
Belfast Central - ⅔ mile/5 mins

RESERVATIONS
Toll free in US: 800-322-2403
or 800-525-4800
Toll free in UK: 00800 525 48000
Quote **Best Loved**

ACCESS CODES
AMADEUS LX BFSTMH
APOLLO/GALILEO LX 96467
SABRE/ABACUS LX 44462
WORLDSPAN LX BFSMH

Belfast's hotel of the future with traditional standards of luxury

The area of Belfast known as Laganside was once a busy port whose great warehouses were built by eminent Victorian architects. Its recent and dramatic rejuvenation has been spearheaded by the Waterfront Hall entertainment centre. Laganside heralds a resurgence of the good times with bistros, restaurants, bars, boutiques, galleries and penthouse apartments. The McCausland Hotel, built as two warehouses in the 1850s, is an integral part of this exciting renaissance.

The hotel is Italianate in concept. Behind the splendid four-storey Victorian façade, is an elegant blend of technology, imagination and contemporary design. When its doors opened in late 1998, a luxury hotel was revealed providing 60 rooms with every possible facility launching it into world class exclusivity.

Conceptually, it is an hotel of tomorrow: there are IT options to satisfy the technophile, bedrooms specifically designed for the lady traveller and rooms that cater for wheelchairs. Guests can enjoy a drink in Café Marco Polo and sample the contemporary Irish dishes of Merchants Brasserie. Business meetings are also catered for in the well-equipped conference rooms. This is a sister property to The Hibernian Hotel, Dublin, and shares with it a provenance of excellence.

This is a place to come, see and be conquered!

LOCATION

Located on Victoria Street between Anne Street and the Albert Clock Tower.

"The longer we stay the harder it is for us to leave"

Alan and Olga Jones, California, USA

• *Map p.508 ref: G7*

Town house hotel

MERRION HALL

Secluded, comfortable and great value close to downtown Dublin

Within minutes of downtown Dublin, the Embassy district of Ballsbridge combines the virtues of a great location with the peace and tranquillity of a well-established and fashionable residential quarter. Here, in an Edwardian-style town house, Merrion Hall, lies close by the RDS Convention Centre and is linked to the business district and major tourist sites by the DART electric train.

For such a central location the bedrooms are generously spacious and are thoughtfully well equipped for the modern traveller with fax and modem facilities. The four-poster and executive suites have air-conditioning and whirlpool spas. In keeping with Dublin's rich literary history the Merrion has a library, which is well stocked with a wide selection of classic and contemporary literature including plenty of Irish titles. In addition to the library, there is a drawing room which provides a quiet corner for afternoon tea or a nightcap.

Breakfast is the only meal served, and as you would expect of a past winner of the Galtee Irish Breakfast Award, it is an extensive affair with kippers and scrambled eggs with smoked salmon among the temptations on offer. For lunch and dinner there are numerous restaurants within just a short stroll of the hotel leaving guests utterly spoilt for choice. Merrion Hall and its neighbouring sister hotel Blakes Townhouse are examples of the art of good hotelkeeping.

LOCATION

From City Centre take Merrion Road, hotel is on left side opposite RDS Convention Centre.

54 Merrion Road, Ballsbridge, Dublin 4 Republic of Ireland

Telephone +353 (0)1 668 1426
Fax +353 (0)1 668 4280

E-mail: *merrionhall@bestloved.com*

OWNER

Pat Halpin

ROOM RATES *(Irish Punts)*

Single occupancy	*£84 - £99*
8 Doubles/Twins	*£99 - £145*
12 Superior Doubles/Twins	*£119 - £165*
4 Four-posters	*£127 - £195*

Includes full breakfast and VAT

CHARGE/CREDIT CARDS

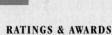

• DC • JCB • MC • VI

RATINGS & AWARDS

I.T.B. ★★★★

A.A. ◆◆◆◆◆

Galtee Breakfast Award

FACILITIES

On site: *Garden, car park*
2 meeting rooms/max 40 people
Nearby: *Complimentary use of nearby leisure club, riding, fishing*

RESTRICTIONS

Limited facilities for disabled guests
No children under 2 years
No pets, guide dogs only

ATTRACTIONS

Trinity College, National Art Gallery, Christchurch, Gardens of Wicklow, New Grange, Powerscourt Gardens

AFFILIATIONS

Green Book of Ireland
Preston's Global Hotels

NEAREST

MAJOR CITY:
Dublin
MAJOR AIRPORT:
Dublin - 6 miles/20 mins
RAILWAY STATION:
Sydney Parade - ¼ mile/5 mins
FERRY PORT:
Dun Laoghaire - ½ mile/10 mins

RESERVATIONS

Toll free in US: 800-544-9993 or 800-223-6510
*Quote **Best Loved***

ACCESS CODES

AMADEUS UI DUBMHH
APOLLO/GALILEO UI 25226
SABRE/ABACUS UI 50151
WORLDSPAN UI 41063

Planning a wedding reception? Turn to 'Meeting Facilities' on page 476

Dúchas Heritage Card

...the way to explore Ireland's heritage

Adult	£15	€19.04
Senior Citizen	£10	€12.69
Child/Student	£6	€7.61
Family	£36	€45.71

** Prices in IR£*

Free admission for one year
to over 65 heritage sites

For more information...

Tel: +353 1 6472461
Callsave: 1850 600 601 (within Ireland only)
Fax: +353 1 6616764
email: heritagecard@ealga.ie
Web: www.heritageireland.ie

Dúchas The Heritage Service

An Roinn Ealaíon, Oidhreachta, Gaeltachta agus Oileán
Department of Arts, Heritage, Gaeltacht and the Islands

National Heritage Week: 2nd-9th September, 2

"It is rare to find such an esprit de corps and positive helpful attitude throughout the entire staff"

K G Nelson, Pittston, PA, USA

• Map p.508 ref: G7

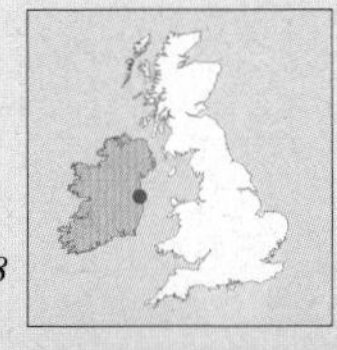

Deluxe hotel

MERRION HOTEL

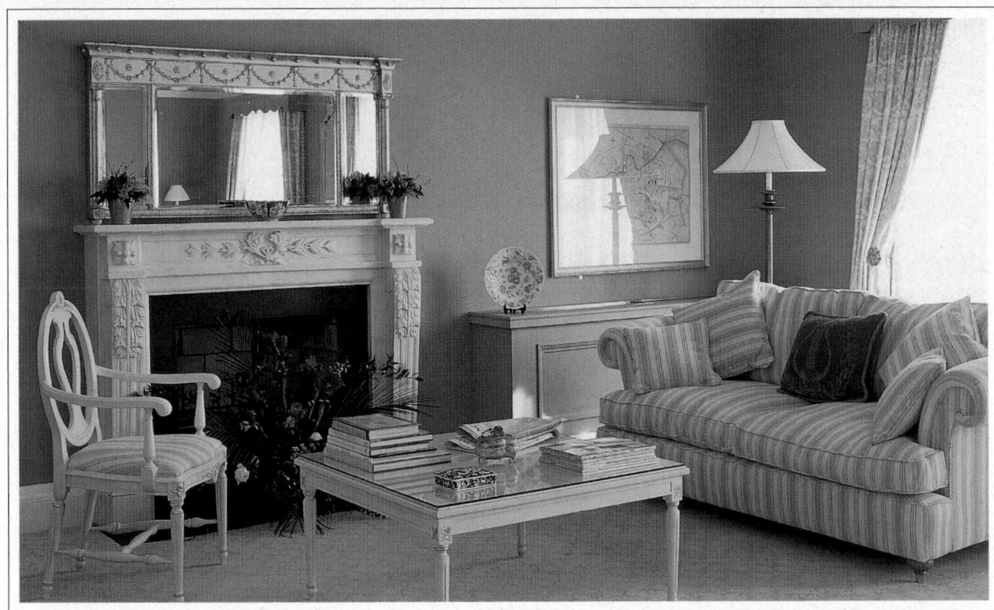

Dublin's most gracious Georgian hotel with 5-star modern facilities

Four Georgian houses were sensitively restored and two magnificent 18th century formal landscaped gardens combined to create The Merrion, Dublin's most gracious hotel. It opened in autumn 1997, an oasis of tranquillity close to exclusive Grafton Street and even closer to the leafy walks and shady lawns of Merrion Square.

The 145 rooms and suites are designed to recall the elegance of the Georgian era and achieve five-star standards of luxury. Each has individually controllable air conditioning, in-room safe and 24-hour valet and room service. The splendid salons are in authentic period style. Contemporary Irish art from the country's finest collection is on display.

Restaurant Patrick Guilbaud presents a renowned gastronomic menu in classical style. Mornington's Brasserie offers superb contemporary Irish cuisine in a more relaxed environment. The Cellar Bar is graced by the vaulted ceilings of the original Georgian wine cellars.

In the heart of Dublin, the Merrion is directly opposite Government Buildings. Trinity College, the National Museum and National Gallery are among its nearest neighbours. Yet, such is the peace in the gardens that the only sounds are the songs of the birds.

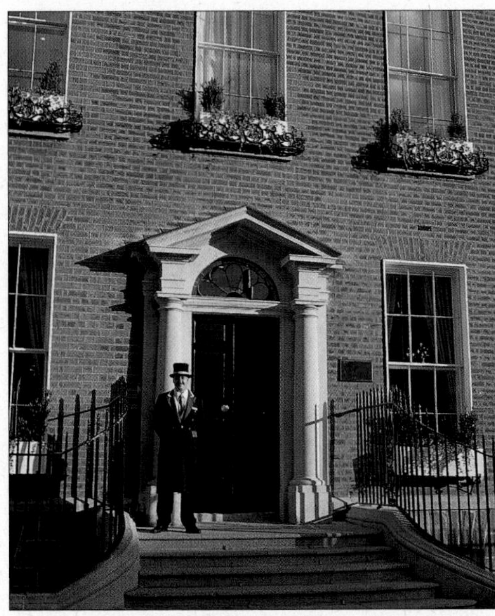

LOCATION

In the heart of Dublin.

Upper Merrion St, Dublin 2, Republic of Ireland

Telephone +353 (0)1 603 0600
Fax +353 (0)1 603 0700

E-mail: *merrion@bestloved.com*

GENERAL MANAGER

Peter MacCann

ROOM RATES *(Irish Punts)*

45 Singles	*£210 - £250*
80 Doubles/Twins	*£230 - £275*
20 Suites	*£400 - £750*

Includes newspaper and VAT

CHARGE/CREDIT CARDS

• DC • JCB • MC • VI

RATINGS & AWARDS

I.T.C. ★★★★★
R.A.C. ★★★★★ Dining Award 5
A.A. ★★★★★ ❀❀❀❀ 79%
Dublin's Best Hotel Room - Fortune Magazine
The American Academy of Hospitality Science Five Star Diamond Award 2000

FACILITIES

On site: *Garden, gym, steam room, health & beauty, indoor pool*
6 meeting rooms/max 50 people
Nearby: *Golf, riding, fishing, tennis*

RESTRICTIONS

No pets, guide dogs only

ATTRACTIONS

Trinity College, National Art Gallery, Grafton St, Newgrange, Christchurch Cathedral, Powerscourt House & Gardens

AFFILIATIONS

Leading Hotels of the World
The European Connection

NEAREST

MAJOR CITY:
Dublin
MAJOR AIRPORT:
Dublin - 4 miles/25 mins
RAILWAY STATION:
Heuston Station - 2 miles/15 mins

RESERVATIONS

Toll free in US: 800-223-6800
Toll free in UK: 0800 181123
Quote ***Best Loved***

ACCESS CODES

SABRE/ABACUS LW 8715
AMADEUS LW DUB430
WORLDSPAN LW 8430
APOLLO/GALILEO LW 82598

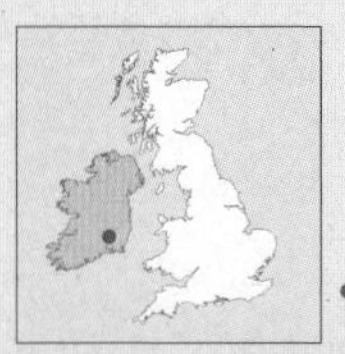

• Map p.508 ref: F8

"You too will be thankful that someone turned this serene place into a haven we can all enjoy"

Melanie Garrett, Editor - Golf World

MOUNT JULIET

Georgian mansion

Thomastown, Co Kilkenny, Republic of Ireland

Telephone +353 (0)56 73000
Fax +353 (0)56 73019

E-mail: mountjuliet@bestloved.com

GENERAL MANAGER

Richard Hudson

ROOM RATES (*Irish Punts*)

3 Singles	£150 - £200
43 Doubles/Twins	£140 - £310
1 Suite	£240 - £400
1 Four-poster suite	£300 - £400
11 2-bed apartments	£320 - £420

Includes service and VAT

CHARGE/CREDIT CARDS

• DC • MC • VI

RATINGS & AWARDS

I.T.B. ★★★★
R.A.C. Gold Ribbon ★★★★ Dining Award 3
A.A. ★★★★ ❀❀
A.A. Hotel of the Year 1999

FACILITIES

On site: *Garden, croquet, tennis, indoor pool, gym, sauna, health & beauty, snooker, golf tuition, 18 hole putting course, riding, fishing, archery, clay target shooting, heli-pad*
5 meeting rooms/max 150 people

RESTRICTIONS

No pets

ATTRACTIONS

Waterford Crystal, Wicklow Mountains, National Heritage Centre, Kilkenny, Rock of Cashel, Local craft trail

AFFILIATIONS

Independent

NEAREST

MAJOR CITY:
Dublin - 75 miles/2 hrs

MAJOR AIRPORT:
Dublin - 75 miles/2 hrs
Waterford - 30 miles/30 mins

RAILWAY STATION:
Thomastown - 2 miles/10 mins

RESERVATIONS

Toll free in US: 800-525-4800
Toll free in Ireland: 1850 49 49 49
Toll free in UK: 0800 964470
Quote ***Best Loved***

ACCESS CODES

Not applicable

Discover a sporting paradise on one of Europe's great estates

Mount Juliet Estate is one of Europe's last great historic estates. In the middle ages, the land was owned by Jerpoint Abbey and the Waltons, an ancient Norman family. In 1757 the first Earl of Carrick amalgamated the estate and built his mansion. He named it Mount Juliet in honour of his wife.

One of Ireland's finest Georgian houses, Mount Juliet has priceless hand-carved marble Adam fireplaces, with intricate stucco work decorating walls and ceilings of the main reception rooms. The Lady Helen Dining Room offers superb cuisine. The bedrooms have refined decor and modern facilities. Additional bedrooms on the estate are in the Hunters Yard and the Rose Garden two-bedroom lodges. The estate has 1,500 acres beside the River Nore.

Great golfing names have added to the estate's distinction within the past ten years. The Jack Nicklaus designed course went straight into the ranking of top-50 British courses when it opened in 1991. It hosted the Irish Open for three years consecutively from 1993 to 1995. Highly trained Golf Professionals are at hand if you desire tuition during your stay.

When you tire of golf, the hotel's ideal location makes it a perfect base from which to tour or simply enjoy the many outdoor pursuits and leisure facilities within the grounds of the hotel.

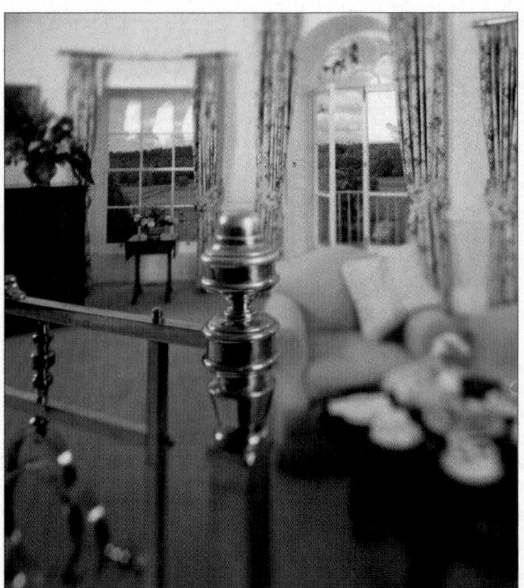

LOCATION

In Thomastown, on the Dublin to Waterford road, the N9.

" This is a unique hotel in a lovely setting "

David Young, AA Chief Hotel Inspector

• Map p.508 ref: G7

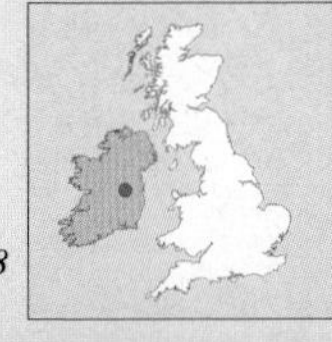

Georgian mansion

MOYGLARE MANOR

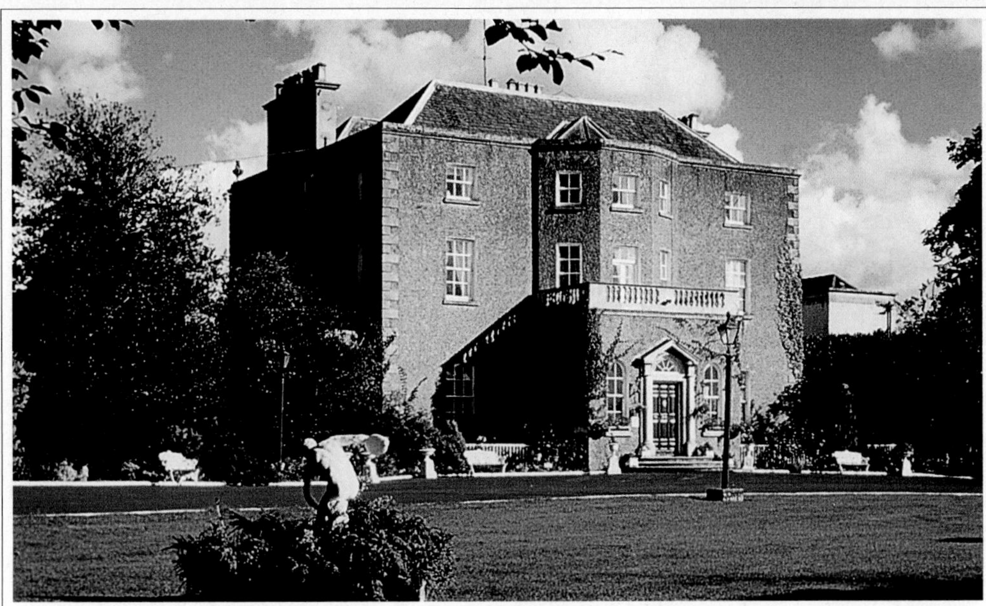

Maynooth, Co Kildare, Republic of Ireland

Telephone +353 (0)1 628 6351
Fax +353 (0)1 628 5405

E-mail: moyglare@bestloved.com

OWNER
Norah Devlin

MANAGER
Shay Curran

ROOM RATES (Irish Punts)

1 Single	£110
14 Doubles/Twins	£180
1 Suite	£395

Includes full breakfast and VAT

CHARGE/CREDIT CARDS

• DC • MC • VI

RATINGS & AWARDS
I.T.B. ★★★
R.A.C. ★★★ Dining Award 3
A.A. ★★★ ❀❀ 74%

FACILITIES
On site: Gardens, heli-pad
3 meeting rooms/max 40 people
Nearby: Golf, riding, fishing

RESTRICTIONS
No children under 12 years
No pets

ATTRACTIONS
Maynooth College, Castletown House, National Stud Farm, Carton House, Russborough House

AFFILIATIONS
Ireland's Blue Book

NEAREST
MAJOR CITY:
Dublin - 17 miles/30 mins

MAJOR AIRPORT:
Dublin - 20 miles/30 mins

RAILWAY STATION:
Maynooth - 3 miles/10 mins

RESERVATIONS
Toll free in US: 800-323-5463
Quote **Best Loved**

ACCESS CODES
Not applicable

Luxury and award-winning cuisine in an area famed for horse breeding

Moyglare Manor is a Georgian house set in beautiful parkland and evokes a splendid era of Irish country house living and hospitality.

At the top of an imposing Georgian staircase each bedroom is equipped with a spacious en suite bathroom. Period furniture blends perfectly with tasteful modern decor and convenience, creating an aura of elegance and old world charm. Cosy log fires in the lounges give an extra touch of warmth which is part of the hospitality that is Moyglare Manor.

Good food is an integral part of gracious living at Moyglare, and their award-winning chef ensures that the cuisine is both varied and excellent, with fresh vegetables and fruit from the hotel's own gardens and orchards.

Moyglare Manor is situated a mile and a half from the university town of Maynooth and is only 20 miles from Dublin city. The great limestone plain on which the town stands has been the breeding ground for some of the world's best horses and the area has many stud farms and race tracks where meetings occur on a regular basis. Castletown House is nearby and the area is rich in archaeological remains.

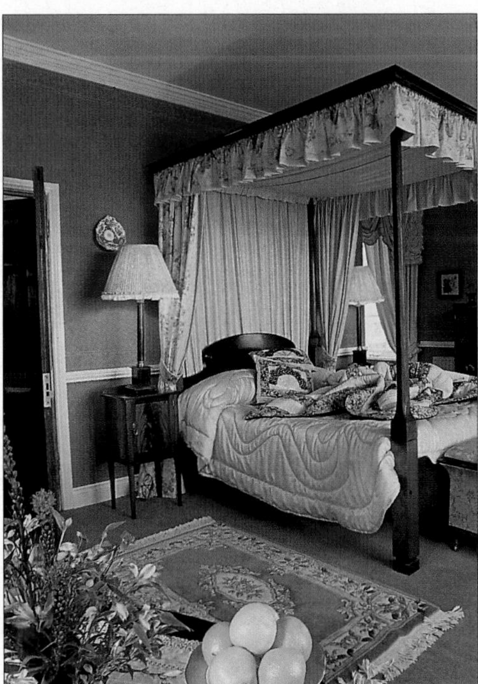

LOCATION

From Dublin, travelling west on M4 take exit for Maynooth. Keep right at Roman Catholic church for 1½ miles.

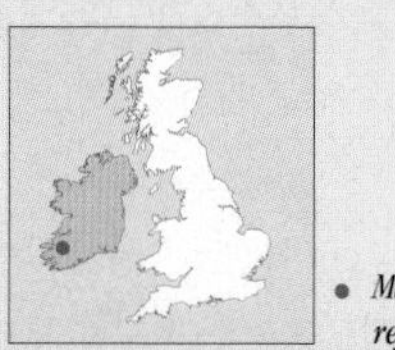

• Map p.508 ref: B9

"It is unusual to find such considerate and personal service as we have experienced here. A 'gem' of an hotel!"

Helen Young, UK

MUCKROSS PARK HOTEL

Country house

Muckross Village, Killarney, Co Kerry, Republic of Ireland

Telephone +353 (0)64 31938
Fax +353 (0)64 31965

E-mail: muckross@bestloved.com

MANAGER

Patricia Shanahan

ROOM RATES (Irish Punts)

Single occupancy	£65 - £85
25 Doubles	£90 - £130
2 Suites	£150 - £300

Includes full breakfast and VAT

CHARGE/CREDIT CARDS

 • DC • MC • VI

RATINGS & AWARDS

I.T.B. ★★★★
R.A.C. ★★★★ Dining Award 1
A.A. ★★★★ 64%

FACILITIES

On site: Gardens, fishing
3 meeting rooms/max 200 people
Nearby: Forest walks, golf, riding, boating

RESTRICTIONS

No facilities for disabled guests
No pets

ATTRACTIONS

Killarney National Park, Muckross House and gardens, Ross Castle, Torc Waterfall

AFFILIATIONS

Independent

NEAREST

MAJOR CITY:
Cork - 50 miles/1 hr

MAJOR AIRPORT:
Shannon - 80 miles/2 hrs
Cork - 55 miles/1½ hrs

RAILWAY STATION:
Killarney - 2½ miles/5 mins

RESERVATIONS

Toll free in US: 800-223-6510
Quote **Best Loved**

ACCESS CODES

Not applicable

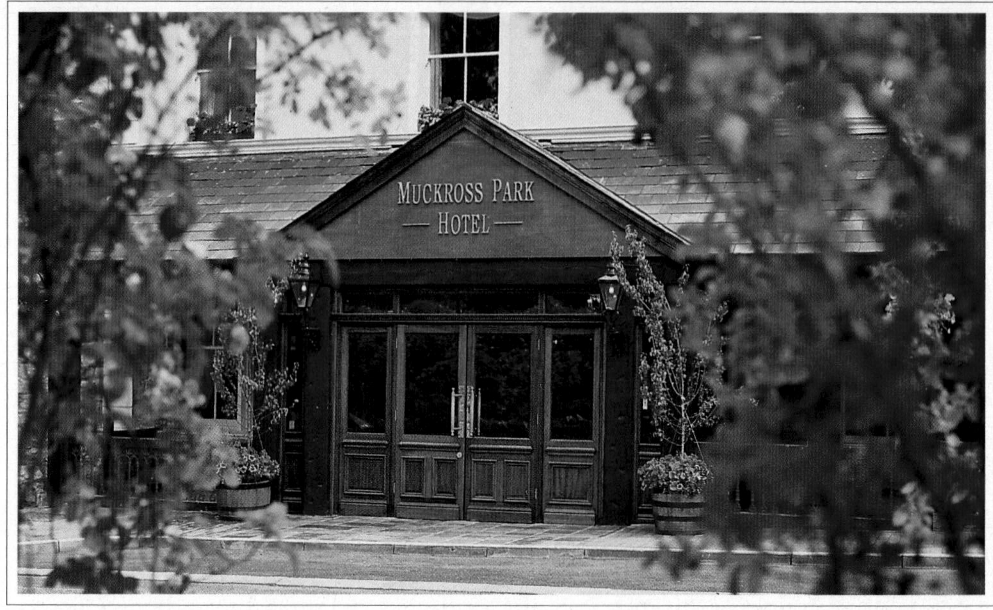

A luxury hotel with an award-winning traditional pub and restaurant

In the heart of Killarney's famous National Park, in the village of Muckross, the Muckross Park Hotel is a redevelopment of the oldest hotel in Killarney. Welcoming visitors since 1795, the hotel retains the luxurious ambience of a traditional Irish country house, but with the comfort of a modern four-star hotel.

All 25 guest bedrooms are exceptional and both suites are simply unique. The Bluepool Restaurant, where one can savour the delights from the country kitchen, overlooks two acres of landscaped gardens leading down to the hotel's river frontage and forest walks.

Adjacent to the hotel, you will find Molly's, an award-winning traditional Irish pub and restaurant, which was voted 'Pub of the Year' for both Kerry and Munster for three successive years. Its stone walls, wooden floors, beamed ceilings, open fires and live entertainment recreate the pleasures of bygone days.

Situated only 2½ miles outside Killarney town, the hotel is only minutes away from Muckross House and Gardens, Muckross Abbey and Killarney's world famous lakes. Golfing, hill walking, boating, fishing, tennis, clay pigeon shooting and horseriding can all be arranged through the hotel during your visit.

LOCATION

2½ miles outside Killarney town on road to Kenmare.

Thinking of pampering yourself? See the 'Health & Beauty' index on page 472

“ Fabulous decor, we felt like we were at home. The food was fantastic and service impeccable ”

G Lamson, Travel & Leisure, San Diego

• Map p.508 ref: C8

Country house restaurant MUSTARD SEED AT ECHO LODGE

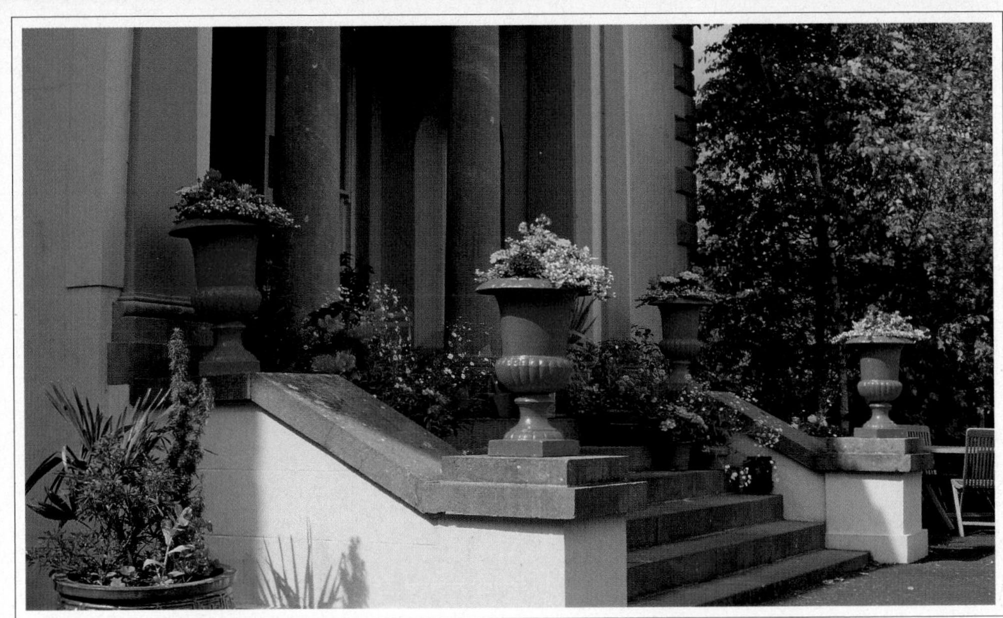

Share your Irish country home with a top Irish restaurant

Daniel Mullane's Mustard Seed Restaurant in Adare village became one of Ireland's most respected. In 1995 he bought Echo Lodge, a fine Victorian country house built in 1884 in the tranquil village of Ballingarry near Adare. Into it he has put his restaurant, his love for the space and elegance of a bygone age, plus today's comforts and amenities. Guests are welcomed for dinner with an overnight stay. The 12 bedrooms are beautifully decorated and furnished. There are seven acres of lawns, pleasure grounds and peace. The library has an unusually excellent book collection.

The restaurant is memorable. Great care is taken to source ingredients from the best of Ireland's organic farms and cheese makers. The herbs are grown in the garden. The menu is made up of the delightful flavour of the very best of Irish cuisine, both traditional and modern. It is complemented by a serious wine list.

Peaceful countryside with delightful walks is all around. The air is enchanting. Cycling, five golf courses, angling and horse riding are within the locality.

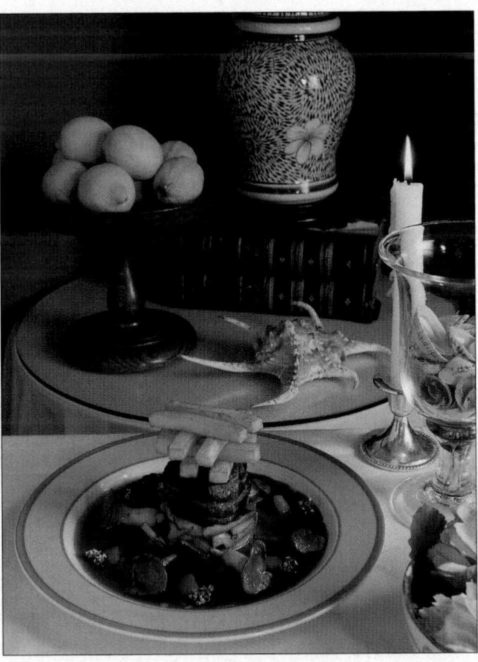

LOCATION

From the top of Adare Village, take the N21 Killarney Road for 1/4 mile. Turn left at the first junction and follow signs to Ballingarry where the hotel is signed as Mustard Seed.

Ballingarry, Co Limerick, Republic of Ireland

Telephone +353 (0)69 68508
Fax +353 (0)69 68511

E-mail: *mustard@bestloved.com*

OWNER

Daniel Mullane

ROOM RATES *(Irish Punts)*

2 Singles	*£90 - £105*
9 Doubles/Twins	*£130 - £200*
1 Four-poster	*£150 - £200*

Includes full breakfast and VAT

CHARGE/CREDIT CARDS

• *MC* • *VI*

RATINGS & AWARDS

I.T.B. ★★★★
Bridgestones 100 Best in Ireland
Gilbeys Gold medal for catering excellence in Ireland

FACILITIES

On site: *Garden, sauna, massage room, exercise room (opening Apr 2001)*
1 meeting room/max 30 people
Nearby: *Golf, riding, fishing*

RESTRICTIONS

No pets permitted in hotel - kennels available
Closed late Jan - 1 Mar

ATTRACTIONS

Glin Castle & Gardens, Islandmore Gardens, Ring of Kerry, Adare's antique shops, Clonshire Equestrian Centre, Cliffs of Moher, The Burren

AFFILIATIONS

Ireland's Blue Book
Preston's Global Hotels

NEAREST

MAJOR CITY:
Limerick - 20 miles/35 mins

MAJOR AIRPORT:
Shannon - 33 miles/1 hr

RAILWAY STATION:
Limerick - 20 miles/45 mins

RESERVATIONS

Toll free in US/Canada: 800-544-9993 or 800-323-5463
Quote ***Best Loved***

ACCESS CODES

Not applicable

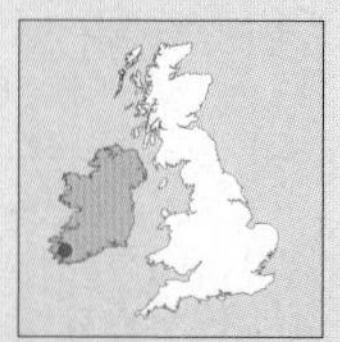

" Set fair to become the outstanding hotel in Ireland "

Travel & Leisure

PARK HOTEL KENMARE

Victorian country hotel

Kenmare, Co Kerry,
Republic of Ireland

Telephone +353 (0)64 41200
Fax +353 (0)64 41402

E-mail: *kenmare@bestloved.com*

OWNER
Francis Brennan

GENERAL MANAGER
John Brennan

ROOM RATES (*Irish Punts*)

4 Singles	£115 - £131
19 Standards	£200 - £250
17 Superiors	£250 - £300
9 Suites	£362 - £426

Includes VAT, excludes service charge of 15%

CHARGE/CREDIT CARDS

• DC • MC • VI

RATINGS & AWARDS
I.T.B. ★★★★★
R.A.C. Gold Ribbon ★★★★
A.A. ★★★★ ❀❀❀
Courvoisier's Book of the Best
Hideaway Report - Hotel of the Year

FACILITIES
On site: *Croquet, tennis, gardens, fitness, golf adjacent, heli-pad*
2 meeting rooms/max 30 people
Nearby: *Fishing, cycling, riding*

RESTRICTIONS
No children in restaurant after 6 pm
No pets in hotel, kennels available
Closed 4 Nov - Easter. Open Xmas & New Year

ATTRACTIONS
Ring of Kerry, Lakes of Killarney, World renowned gardens

AFFILIATIONS
The Celebrated Hotels Collection
Ireland's Blue Book
Small Luxury Hotels

NEAREST
MAJOR CITY:
Cork - 60 miles/1½ hrs
MAJOR AIRPORT:
Cork - 60 miles/1½ hrs
RAILWAY STATION:
Killarney - 20 miles/45 mins

RESERVATIONS
Toll free in US: 800-322-2403 or 800-323-5463
Quote ***Best Loved***

ACCESS CODES
AMADEUS LX KIRPHK
APOLLO/GALILEO LX 32328
SABRE/ABACUS LX 30947
WORLDSPAN LX KIRPH

Relaxation and luxury in the heart of Ireland's Lake District

The building was constructed in 1897 by the Great Southern and Western Railway Company to provide overnight accommodation for passengers travelling to Parknasilla 17 miles away. Ownership continued in the hands of the GS&W Company until 1977 when the hotel was sold. In 1980, refurbishment began and the hotel was re-opened in late 1980 under its new name 'The Park Hotel Kenmare'. Since then, it has become renowned for its splendid collection of antiques and interior furnishings.

In 1985, Mr Francis Brennan, the then manager, took complete control becoming the proprietor and managing director. In the quest for superior comfort, a refurbishment programme was undertaken to double the size of the bedrooms and to add balconies to some rooms to allow wonderful views of the river. This latest development has firmly established the hotel as one of Ireland's most luxurious. The hotel lays special emphasis on personalised service and has won many accolades to date.

Numerous outdoor activities are available, including an 18-hole golf course, fishing (sea and lake), horse riding, and many scenic walks. The pressures of modern living can easily be forgotten at the Park Hotel Kenmare where the staff are waiting to make your stay - whether for a holiday or on business - most memorable.

LOCATION

Southwest Ireland, off the N70 from Killarney on the 'Ring of Kerry'.

Looking for an hotel with a golf course on site? See our 'Golf Guide' on page 478

“My bedroom overlooked rolling lawns and ancient oaks. The bed was the size of a croquet lawn”

Alan Bestic - The Sunday Telegraph

• Map p.508 ref: F7

Queen Anne stables

RATHSALLAGH HOUSE

The most stylish and entertaining nineteenth hole you'll ever find!

Take 530 acres of gorgeous Irish parkland at the foot of the Wicklow Mountains, convert some ivy-covered Queen Anne stables into a country house and surround it with an 18-hole championship golf course and you have the prospect of a superb holiday - whether or not you play golf!

This is the home of Joe and Kay O'Flynn and their welcome is as big as the countryside around them. The house has a happy and relaxed atmosphere and is fully centrally heated. But nothing can match the genial warmth of the log and turf fires that blaze away in the well-proportioned reception rooms. Upstairs, the bedrooms are luxuriously appointed with views of the park.

The food is country house cooking at its best with a light modern influence from Head Chef Niall Hill; game in season, fresh fish from the Wexford coast and breakfasts to drool over! Rathsallagh has won the National Breakfast Awards three times! All this is a tribute to Kay's imagination and mastery of the culinary arts.

The championship golf course was designed by former world amateur champion, Peter McEvoy and leading Irish professional Christie O'Connor. Rathsallagh is set on lush parkland amidst mature trees and natural water hazards. Other facilities include a heated indoor pool, sauna, tennis court, billiard room and spa room.

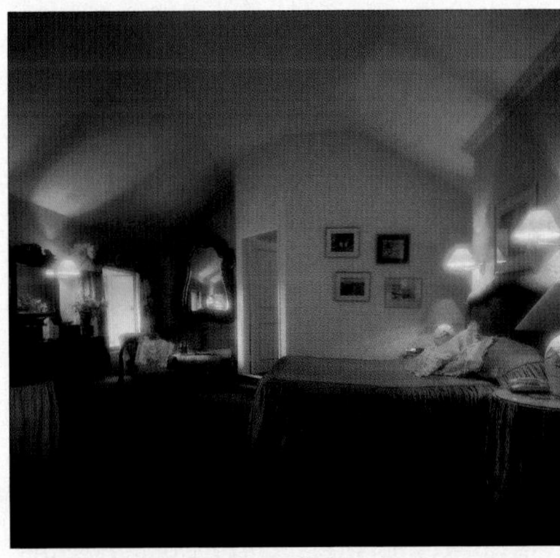

LOCATION

From Dublin Airport take the M50 to exit 9 then N7 and exit for the M8/N9 towards Carlow. After 6 miles pass Priory Inn on left. After 2 miles turn left for Rathsallagh.

Dunlavin, Co Wicklow, Republic of Ireland

Telephone +353 (0)45 403112
Fax +353 (0)45 403343

E-mail: *rathsallagh@bestloved.com*

OWNERS

The O'Flynn family

ROOM RATES *(Irish Punts)*

Single occupancy	*£110 - £160*
26 Doubles/Twins	*£110 - £210*
1 Four-poster	*£210*
2 Suites	*£210*

Includes full breakfast and VAT

CHARGE/CREDIT CARDS

• DC • JCB • MC • VI

RATINGS & AWARDS

I.T.B. ★★★★ Country House
R.A.C. ★★★ Dining Award 2
3 National Breakfast Awards
Bridgestone 100 Best Places to Stay in Ireland 2000
Georgina Campbells' Country House of the Year 2000

FACILITIES

On site: *Garden, croquet, tennis, indoor pool, health & beauty, snooker, clay shooting, archery, hunting, heli-pad, 18-hole championship golf course, 3 meeting rooms/max 100 people*
Nearby: *Fishing, riding*

RESTRICTIONS

No children under 12 years
Closed 24 - 27 Dec

ATTRACTIONS

Russborough House, National Stud, Curragh Racecourse, Glendalough, Punchestown Racecourse

AFFILIATIONS

Ireland's Blue Book

NEAREST

MAJOR CITY:
Dublin - 35 miles/1 hr
MAJOR AIRPORT:
Dublin - 45 miles/1½ hrs
RAILWAY STATION:
Kildare - 15 miles/30 mins

RESERVATIONS

Toll free in US: 800-323-5463
*Quote **Best Loved***

ACCESS CODES

Not applicable

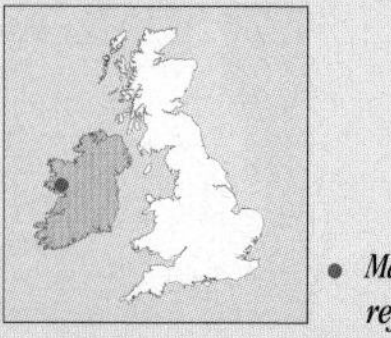

• Map p.508 ref: B6

"Thank you once more and most heartily for the unforgettable experience of your hospitality at Rosleague Manor"

Richard Weiszècker, President of former German Federal Republic

Rosleague Manor

Country house

Letterfrack, Co Galway, Republic of Ireland

Telephone +353 (0)95 41101
Fax +353 (0)95 41168
Republic of Ireland

E-mail: *rosleague@bestloved.com*

OWNER
Edmund Foyle

MANAGER
Mark Foyle

ROOM RATES *(Irish Punts)*

Single occupancy	*£90 - £105*
16 Doubles/Twins	*£100 - £150*
4 Junior suites	*£140 - £170*

Includes full breakfast and VAT

CHARGE/CREDIT CARDS

• *JCB* • *MC* • *VI*

RATINGS & AWARDS
I.T.B. ★★★★ Country House

FACILITIES
On site: *Garden, tennis, sauna*
Nearby: *Fishing, riding, swimming, gym*

RESTRICTIONS
No facilities for disabled guests
Pets by arrangement
Closed Nov - Mar

ATTRACTIONS
Connemara National Park, Kylemore Abbey, Cliffs of Moher, the Sky Road, scuba diving, hill walking

AFFILIATIONS
Ireland's Blue Book
Preston's Global Hotels

NEAREST
MAJOR CITY:
Galway - 50 miles/1¼ hrs

MAJOR AIRPORT:
Shannon - 110 miles/2½ hrs

RAILWAY STATION:
Galway - 50 miles/1¼ hrs

RESERVATIONS
Toll free in US: 800-544-9993
or 800-323-5463
Quote ***Best Loved***

ACCESS CODES
Not applicable

Character, charm and good food on the rugged Connemara coast

On the wild western shores of Co. Galway, romantic and evocative Connemara combines scenic grandeur with a strong folkloric tradition and genuine Irish hospitality. It is a land of extraordinary and constantly changing natural beauty, of sea and sky, blue mountains and peat-stained streams, doughty homesteads and sturdy little ponies. Here, sandwiched between sheltered Ballinakill Bay and the glories of the Connemara National Park, father and son Edmund and Mark Foyle preside over a delightful small hotel with a well-deserved reputation for wonderful food.

A Georgian country house with sympathetic later additions, Rosleague Manor is surrounded by 30 acres of landscaped gardens with a path leading down to the bay. There is an all-weather tennis court, the Connemara Golf Course nearby, and a host of beautiful and almost deserted beaches, plus numerous opportunities for hiking, horse riding and superb salmon and trout fishing. Another good way to work up an appetite is a spot of sea fishing or boat trip to the island of Inishbofin from the fishing village of Cleggan. Fresh seafood is speciality of the hotel restaurant, which prides itself on featuring the finest seasonal local produce from Connemara lamb to homegrown vegetables.

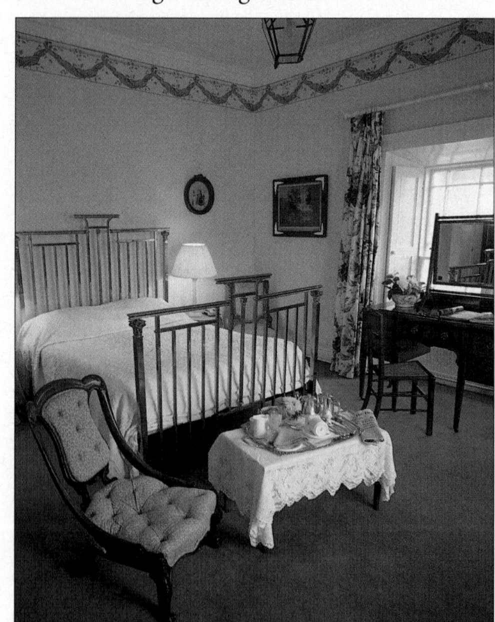

LOCATION

Letterfrack is 7 miles north of Clifden, the capital of Connemara off the N59.

"It is indeed a rare luxury today to experience such a warm, friendly and family atmosphere that you both so naturally provide at Ross Lake House"

Paddy & Clodagh Donovan, Dublin

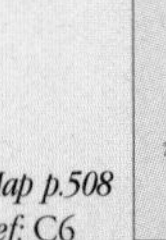

• Map p.508 ref: C6

Country house

ROSS LAKE HOUSE HOTEL

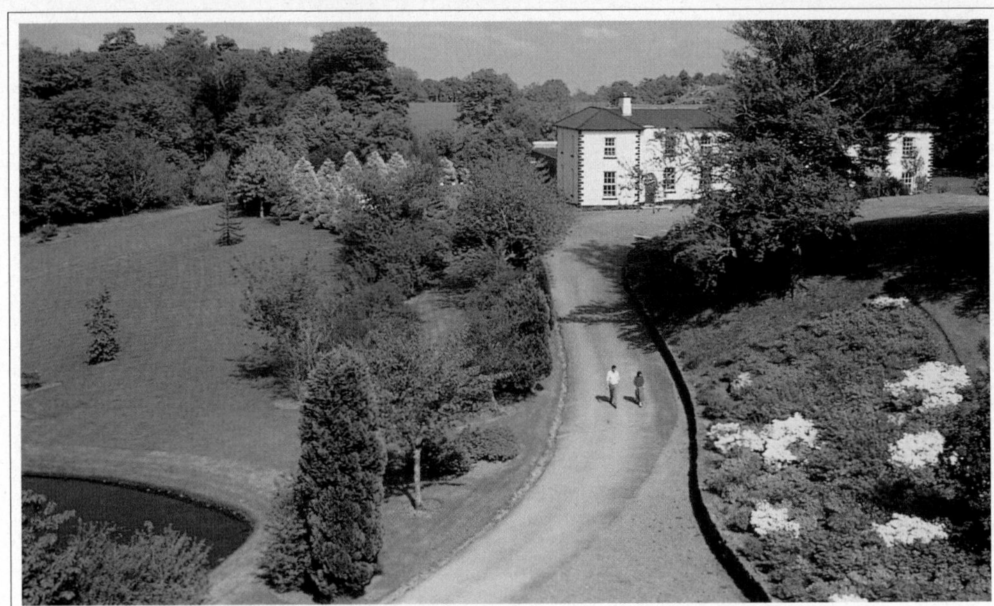

A wonderful old house at the gateway to Connemara

Ross Lake is a wonderful old country house whose former glory has been revived by owners Henry and Elaine Reid. This 19th century mansion was formerly an estate house of the landed gentry, who prized it for its serenity. It has one suite and twelve comfortable, well appointed double bedrooms.

From the moment you arrive, Henry and Elaine will make you feel at home. The intimate bar is ideal for a drink before dinner. A high quality Irish menu is delightfully prepared and presented featuring a tempting variety of fresh produce from the nearby Connemara hills, streams and lakes, as well as fish straight from the Atlantic.

Ross Lake House has its own magnificent gardens, with hardcourt tennis. Oughterard golf course is two miles away. Lough Corrib and local lakes are famous for game and coarse fishing. The surrounding countryside is rich in superb mountain walks and climbs. Nearby attractions include Aughnanure Castle, Kylemore Abbey, Connemara National Park, the Aran Islands, the Cliffs of Moher and the Burren.

LOCATION

The hotel is situated 14 miles from Galway City on the N59, the main Galway to Clifden road. Turn left after village of Rosscahill.

Rosscahill, Oughterard, Co Galway, Republic of Ireland

Telephone +353 (0)91 550109
Fax +353 (0)91 550184

E-mail: *rosslake@bestloved.com*

OWNERS

Henry and Elaine Reid

ROOM RATES *(Irish Punts)*

Single occupancy	*£65 - £100*
12 Doubles/Twins	*£100 - £170*
1 Suite	*£180*

Includes full breakfast and VAT

CHARGE/CREDIT CARDS

• *DC* • *MC* • *VI*

RATINGS & AWARDS

I.T.B. ★★★

R.A.C. ★★★ *Dining Award 1*

FACILITIES

On site: *Garden, tennis*
1 meeting room/max 150 people
Nearby: *Golf, fishing, riding*

RESTRICTIONS

No pets in public rooms
Closed 1 Nov - 15 Mar

ATTRACTIONS

Aughnanure Castle, Connemara National Park, Cliffs of Moher, Kylemore Abbey, Aran Islands, the Burren

AFFILIATIONS

Preston's Global Hotels
Green Book of Ireland

NEAREST

MAJOR CITY:
Galway - 14 miles/30 mins

MAJOR AIRPORT:
Shannon - 65 miles/2 hrs

RAILWAY STATION:
Galway - 14 miles/30 mins

RESERVATIONS

Toll free in US: 800-544-9993 or 800-888-1199
Toll free in UK: 0800 371 425
Quote ***Best Loved***

ACCESS CODES

AMADEUS LE GWY279
APOLLO/GALILEO LE 26193
SABRE/ABACUS LE 42799
WORLDSPAN LE 42799

• Map p.508 ref: D7

"A great home, superb staff and excellent dining... a winning combination"

Bill Power, Toronto, Canada

ST CLERANS

18th century manor house

Craughwell, Co Galway, Republic of Ireland

Telephone +353 (0)91 846555
Fax +353 (0)91 846600

E-mail: stclerans@bestloved.com

OWNER
Merv Griffin

GENERAL MANAGER
Seamus Dooley

ROOM RATES *(Irish Punts)*

Single occupancy	£230 - £380
12 Doubles/Twins	£230 - £380

Includes full breakfast and VAT

CHARGE/CREDIT CARDS

• MC • VI

RATINGS & AWARDS
I.T.B. ★★★★
A.A. ◆◆◆◆◆

FACILITIES
On site: Garden, croquet, putting green, driving range, fishing, riding, clay pigeon shooting, heli-pad
1 meeting room/max 50 people
Nearby: Golf, riding, hunting/shooting

RESTRICTIONS
No pets

ATTRACTIONS
Cliffs of Moher, The Burren, Connemara National Park, Kylemore Abbey, Aran Islands

AFFILIATIONS
Ireland's Blue Book
The Celebrated Hotels Collection
Relais & Châteaux

NEAREST
MAJOR CITY:
Galway - 20 miles/45 mins

MAJOR AIRPORT:
Shannon - 60 miles/1½ hrs
Galway - 20 miles/45 mins

RAILWAY STATION:
Athenry - 10 miles/15 mins

RESERVATIONS
Toll free in US: 800-322-2403
or 800-323-5463
Quote **Best Loved**

ACCESS CODES
Not applicable

The choice of Hollywood's best

Celebrated US film director John Huston once owned this delightful manor house and described it as one of the most beautiful houses in all of Ireland. As someone with an eye for the picturesque, he was undoubtedly drawn to the dramatic setting, unique character and magical atmosphere of this classic country house.

Now restored to its former splendour, the hotel is decorated in an exquisite and elegant manner and boasts twelve deluxe guest rooms that blend tradition, luxury and bold contemporary colours to create high style and great individuality. The richly furnished library with its dark volumes, open chessboard and art treasures from around the world, makes the perfect setting to imagine some great mystery or romance enfolding within the hotel's beautiful gardens and grounds. And the sumptuous dining room that once played host to kings, princes and the cream of Hollywood celebrities, has become renowned for its outstanding cuisine.

The hotel has its own putting green and driving range and is surrounded by the most breathtaking countryside. Once inside, the warmth of the interior is matched in full by the warmth of the welcome and the home-from-home friendliness of the hotels staff and owner.

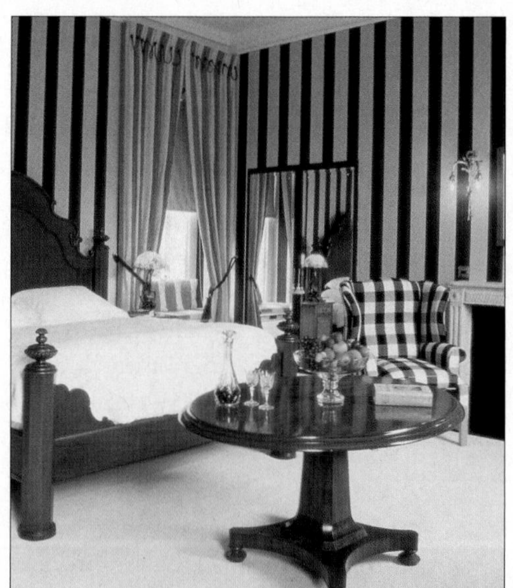

LOCATION

From the N6 between Loughrea and Craughwell, turn right 1 mile outside Loughrea to St. Clerans and athenry, drive 3½ miles, turn left to St. Clerans (signposted).

"I'm only too eager to return to St John's"

Janet Laudenslager, Vice President, City Bank, New York

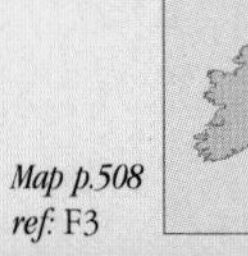

Georgian hotel

ST JOHN'S COUNTRY HOUSE

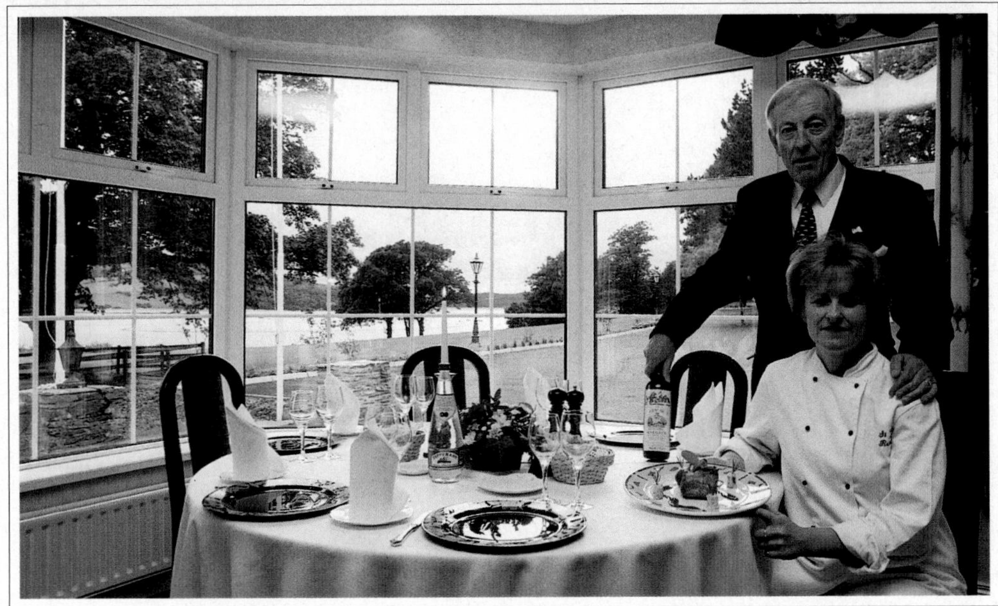

A little bit of Irish magic amidst the Donegal Highlands

However well they pack, guests always leave something of themselves behind at this totally captivating country house hotel! Little wonder that it has become frequented by many famous people from both home and abroad. Guests find they are so well looked after and their stay so enjoyable that many plan their return before they have even left.

Located in the remote northwest corner of Ireland by the shores of Lough Swilly, the hotel enjoys quite breathtaking and magical views of Inch Island and the Donegal Highlands. The area is rich in ancient myths and legends with the spectacular ring fort of Grianan of Aileach nearby dating back to around 1700 BC.

The golf clubs in the area are close to the hearts of golfers worldwide even if they have never played on them, Ballyliffen or Royal Portrush, for example; there's a motor launch available for guests' use, you can go salmon and trout fishing or just get away from it all. Every one a good reason for visiting this idyllic haven. Further enticement is provided by what many regard as one of the finest restaurants in the whole of Ireland. In fact, the hotel originally opened as a restaurant. Many leading Senators and speakers of the US Congress have dined in the restaurant which has won international acclaim and many awards. An unforgettable experience.

LOCATION

Situated in the village of Fahan on the main road from Derry to Boncrana R238.

Fahan, Inishowen,
Co Donegal,
Republic of Ireland

Telephone +353 (0)77 60289
Fax +353 (0)77 60612

E-mail: *stjohns@bestloved.com*

OWNERS

Reg Ryan and Phil McAfee

ROOM RATES

5 Doubles/Twins £110 - £150
Includes full breakfast and VAT

CHARGE/CREDIT CARDS

• DC • JCB • MC • VI

RATINGS & AWARDS

Independent

FACILITIES

On site: *Garden, fishing*
2 meeting rooms/max 30 people
Nearby: *Golf, tennis, fitness, water skiing, yachting, lake/river/sea fishing, riding, motor launch, hunting/shooting*

RESTRICTIONS

No smoking in dining room
Closed Jan - Feb

ATTRACTIONS

Irishowen 100 route,
Glenveagh National Park,
Giants Causeway, six golf courses,
Trout & Salmon fishing, sea angling

AFFILIATIONS

Ireland's Blue Book

NEAREST

MAJOR CITY:
Derry - 8 miles/30 mins

MAJOR AIRPORT:
Belfast - 68 miles/2 hrs
Derry - 9 miles/40 mins

RAILWAY STATION:
Derry - 7 miles/30 mins

FERRY PORT:
Larne - 60 miles/2 hrs

RESERVATIONS

Toll free in US: 847-251-4110
or 800-323-5463
Quote ***Best Loved***

ACCESS CODES

Not applicable

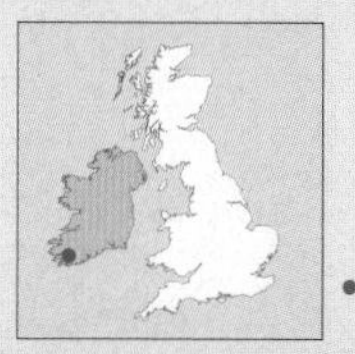

• Map p.508 ref: C10

"Thank you for such a lovely stay. Sea View House was utterly charming. It's just my kind of place - elegant but not pretentious"

Bill Sertl, Travel Editor, Saveur Garden Design, New York

SEA VIEW HOUSE HOTEL

19th century country house

Ballylickey,
Bantry, Co Cork,
Republic of Ireland

Telephone +353 (0)27 50462
Fax +353 (0)27 51555

E-mail: seaview@bestloved.com

OWNER

Kathleen O'Sullivan

ROOM RATES (*Irish Punts*)

Single occupancy	*£45 - £65*
15 Doubles/Twins	*£70 - £120*
2 Suites	*£115 - £130*

Includes newspaper, full breakfast and VAT

CHARGE/CREDIT CARDS

• *DC* • *MC* • *VI*

RATINGS & AWARDS

I.T.B. ★★★★
R.A.C. ★★★ *Dining Award 2*
A.A. ★★★ ❀❀ *75%*
I.T.B. Award for Excellence
Gilbeys Gold Medal Award for Catering Excellence in Ireland

FACILITIES

On site: *Garden*
1 meeting room/max 25 people
Nearby: *Golf, fishing, tennis, riding*

RESTRICTIONS

No pets in public rooms
Closed mid Nov - mid Mar

ATTRACTIONS

Gougane Barra, Killarney, Bantry House, Armada Centre, Garnish Island

AFFILIATIONS

Manor House Hotels of Ireland

NEAREST

MAJOR CITY:
Cork - 56 miles/1½ hrs

MAJOR AIRPORT:
Cork - 56 miles/1½ hrs
Shannon - 120 miles/3 hrs

RAILWAY STATION:
Cork - 56 miles/1½ hrs

RESERVATIONS

Toll free in US/Canada: 800-44-UTELL
*Quote **Best Loved***

ACCESS CODES

Not applicable

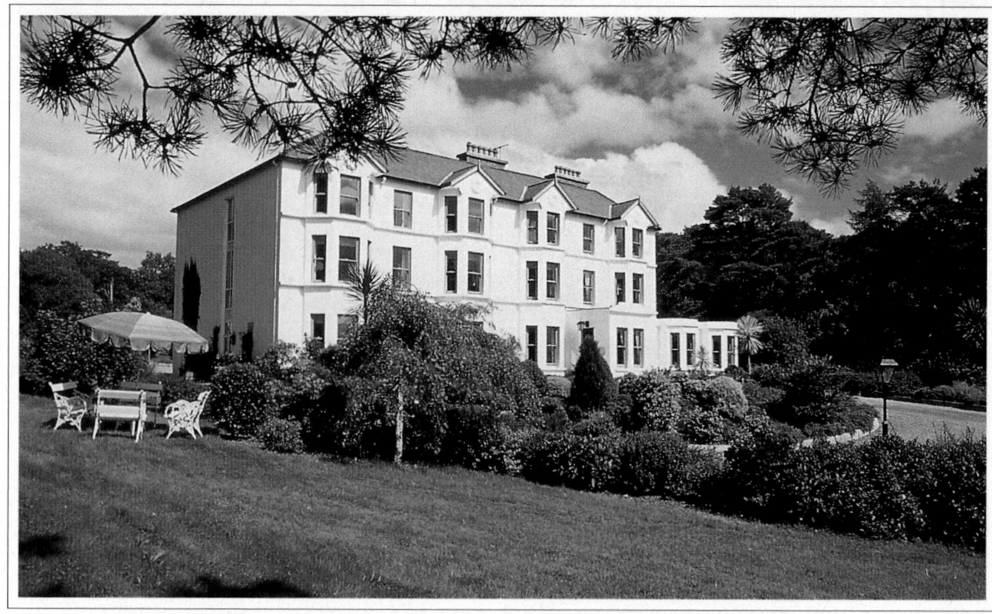

Resplendent and secluded amongst the delights of Ireland

This exceptional hotel offers perfect location and food which is worth going out of your way for. This is possibly one of the most romantic areas in the world; all mountains, lakes and a coast line praised in song that has passed down the generations across the world. Culturally, it is a rich seam of gold that spans prehistory, the Celts, the dawn of Christendom and modern history. Relics and remains are preserved for all to see.

Seashore and landscapes provide never-ending pleasure: golfing to walking, pony trekking, fishing. Whatever your interest, there is nowhere more beautiful in which to enjoy it.

Sea View House nestles comfortably into this idyllic picture. An elegant house that stands aloof from worldly pressures, basking in a reputation for good food that has spread far and wide. "It's really a country house with country house cooking" says Kathleen O'Sullivan, who owns and runs the hotel. She has a 'nose' for good wine so it stands to reason the cellar is a veritable treasure trove!

She also has an eye for beauty; her splendid collection of antiques is displayed throughout the house and in the charming well-appointed bedrooms. It is, after all, her home. What makes it so special is that so many of her guests have been encouraged to call it theirs, too!

LOCATION

70 yards off the N71 Bantry to Glengarriff road close by Ballylickey Bridge.

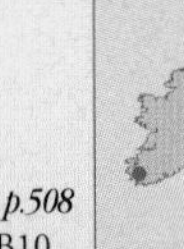

" I came to surprise her and ended up being surprised myself! Quite simply the most beautiful hotel I've ever stayed in "

David & Connie, Kentstown, Navan

• Map p.508 ref: B10

Luxury resort hotel

SHEEN FALLS LODGE

Kenmare, Co Kerry, Repbulic of Ireland

Telephone +353 (0)64 41600
Fax +353 (0)64 41386

E-mail: sheenfalls@bestloved.com

OWNER
Mr B Hoyer

GENERAL MANAGER
Adriaan Bartels

ROOM RATES (Irish Punts)

44 Deluxe rooms	£180 - £285
8 Superior deluxe rooms	£250 - £365
9 Suites	£310 - £440
Little Hay Cottage (per week)	£3,000 - £6,000

Includes VAT

CHARGE/CREDIT CARDS

• DC • MC • VI

RATINGS & AWARDS
I.T.B. ★★★★★ De Luxe
R.A.C. ★★★★ Gold Award
Dining Award 3
A.A. ★★★★ ❀❀
American Academy of Hospitality Sciences Five Star Diamond Award

FACILITIES
On site: Garden, croquet, health spa, indoor heated pool, tennis, riding, private fishing, clay shooting, billiards, heli-pad
3 meeting rooms/max 120 people
Nearby: Two 18-hole golf courses

RESTRICTIONS
No pets

ATTRACTIONS
Beara Peninsula and The Healy Pass, The Ring of Kerry, Killarney National Park

AFFILIATIONS
The Celebrated Hotels Collection
Relais & Châteaux

NEAREST
MAJOR CITY:
Cork - 60 miles/1½ hrs
MAJOR AIRPORT:
Kerry - 30 miles/50 mins
Cork - 60 miles/1½ hrs
RAILWAY STATION:
Killarney - 23 miles/30 mins

RESERVATIONS
Toll free in US: 800-735-2478 or 800-322-2403
Quote **Best Loved**

ACCESS CODES
AMADEUS LM KEH275
APOLLO/GALILEO LM 96346
SABRE/ABACUS LM 30264
WORLDSPAN LM 04275

Dedicated to your indulgence in Ireland's most lyrical landscape

If ever there was an hotel that existed to exploit the beauty of its surroundings, none does it better or with greater panache than Sheen Falls Lodge. Set amongst the lyrical beauty of south west Ireland is the resort's 300-acre estate complete with a 15 mile stretch of river that tumbles and sparkles in a picturesque cascade in front of the sub-tropical garden of this 17th century retreat.

The scene is set for all kinds of country pursuits: walking and horse riding through the woodlands, clay pigeon shooting and fishing for salmon in the Sheen River (rods supplied). The fully equipped Health Spa attends one's corporal needs with a heated swimming pool, extensive range of facial and body treatments, jacuzzi, steam room and gym. And there's a tennis court. In short, working up an appetite is not difficult.

La Cascade Restaurant is your reward. It's not enough to say it is award-winning, so many others make a similar claim. The food really is exceptional, an assembly of gorgeous Irish produce and terrific culinary flair. You can also dine at Oscar's Bistro where you will find a lighter bite in a less formal atmosphere. Now you begin to see why Sheen Falls is so highly rated. The rooms breathe quality from the rich, polished woods to the authentic Irish linen. This is a luxury hotel with irresistible Irish charm; famous in Ireland but for the rest of us, what a find!

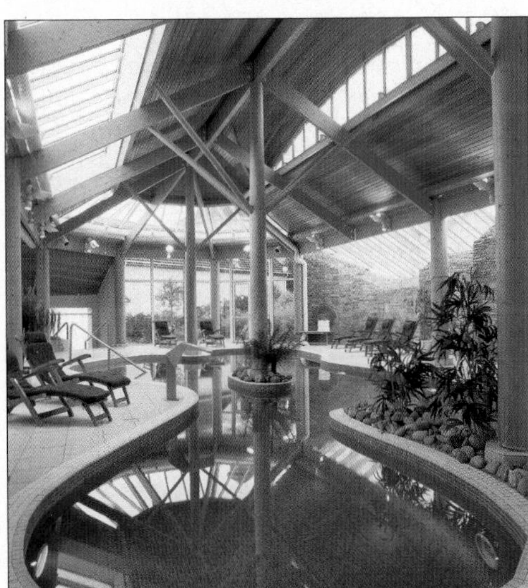

LOCATION

The hotel is 1 mile outside Kenmare. Follow the Glengarriff road, take first turn on left and hotel is ½ mile on the left.

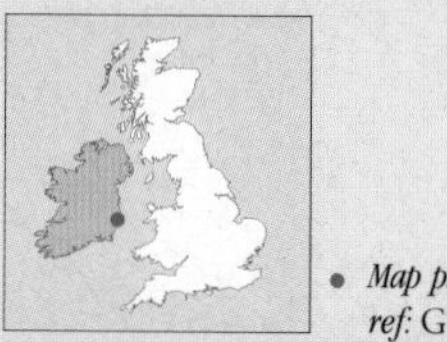

• Map p.508 ref: G7

"In a world of hotels where the anodyne and the anonymous are the norm, Tinakilly House is a beacon to restore hope to the traveller's heart"

1996 Bon Appetit Special Collector's Edition

TINAKILLY HOUSE

Victorian country house

Wicklow, (Rathnew),
Co Wicklow,
Republic of Ireland

Telephone +353 (0)404 69274
Fax +353 (0)404 67806

E-mail: *tinakilly@bestloved.com*

OWNERS

Raymond and Josephine Power

ROOM RATES ***(Irish Punts)***

Single occupancy	*£122 - £188*
12 Doubles/Twins	*£148 - £164*
10 Four-posters	*£184 - £208*
25 Junior suites	*£184 - £208*
5 Captain suites	*£248 - £280*

Includes full breakfast and VAT

CHARGE/CREDIT CARDS

 • *DC* • *MC* • *VI*

RATINGS & AWARDS

I.T.B. ★★★★

R.A.C. Blue Ribbon ★★★ *Dining Award 3*

A.A. ★★★ ❀❀

FACILITIES

On site: *Garden, health & beauty, croquet, tennis, heli-pad*

3 meeting rooms/max 80 people

Nearby: *Golf, riding, biking*

RESTRICTIONS

No facilities for disabled guests

No pets

ATTRACTIONS

Glendalough, Mount Usher, Powerscourt Gardens & Waterfall, Dublin City, Trinity College

AFFILIATIONS

Ireland's Blue Book

The Celebrated Hotels Collection

NEAREST

MAJOR CITY:
Dublin - 29 miles/45 mins

MAJOR AIRPORT:
Dublin - 35 miles/1½ hrs

RAILWAY STATION:
Wicklow - 2 miles/5 mins

RESERVATIONS

Toll free in US: 800-322-2403
or 800-323-5463
Quote ***Best Loved***

ACCESS CODES

SABRE/ABACUS LX 30077
APOLLO/GALILEO LX 67443
AMADEUS LX DUBTCH
WORLDSPAN LX DUBTC

Splendid fresh food in rich and elegant Victorian surroundings

Truly a romantic secret hideaway, Tinakilly is just south of Dublin. This gracious Victorian Italianate manor stands on seven acres of gardens that sweep down to the Irish Sea. Built for Captain Halpin, who laid the world's telegraph cables, the ornate interiors are rich in period furnishings, oil paintings and seafaring memorabilia. Tinakilly is now the home of the Power family, who together with their friendly staff bid you a warm welcome.

Each of the 52 bedrooms is a perfect blend of Victorian splendour and modern comfort. The Captain Suites and four-poster Junior Suites enjoy breathtaking sea and garden views.

Chef Chris Daly uses fresh local produce such as fish and Wicklow lamb flavoured with herbs from Tinakilly's own gardens, Chris's creations are complemented by an award-winning wine cellar. Brown bread is baked daily, which is especially delicious with the locally smoked Irish salmon.

Excellent local golf courses include the links European Club and parkland Druid's Glen, home of the 1996-1999 Irish Open. A host of nearby visitor attractions include the Wicklow Mountains and the 6th century monastic city Glendalough.

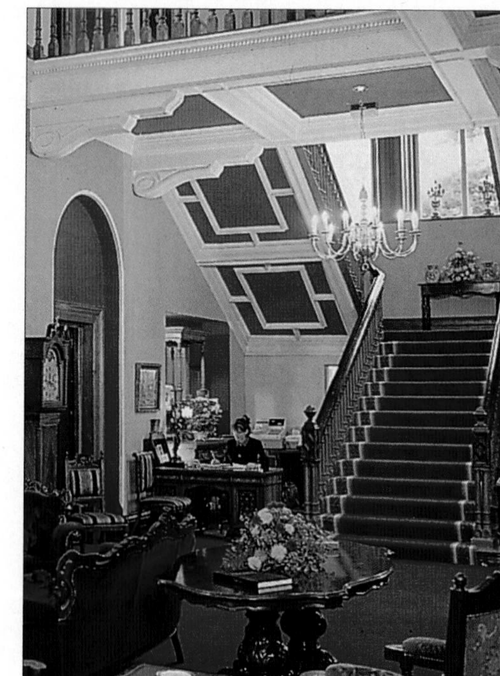

LOCATION

From Dublin follow the N11/M11 to Rathnew and then R570 towards Wicklow. Entrance is on the left, 500 metres outside of Rathnew.

“ I came tired and left relaxed. One of the best hotels in the world ”

Michael & Irene Dowd, New York

• Map p.508 ref: F9

15th century castle

WATERFORD CASTLE

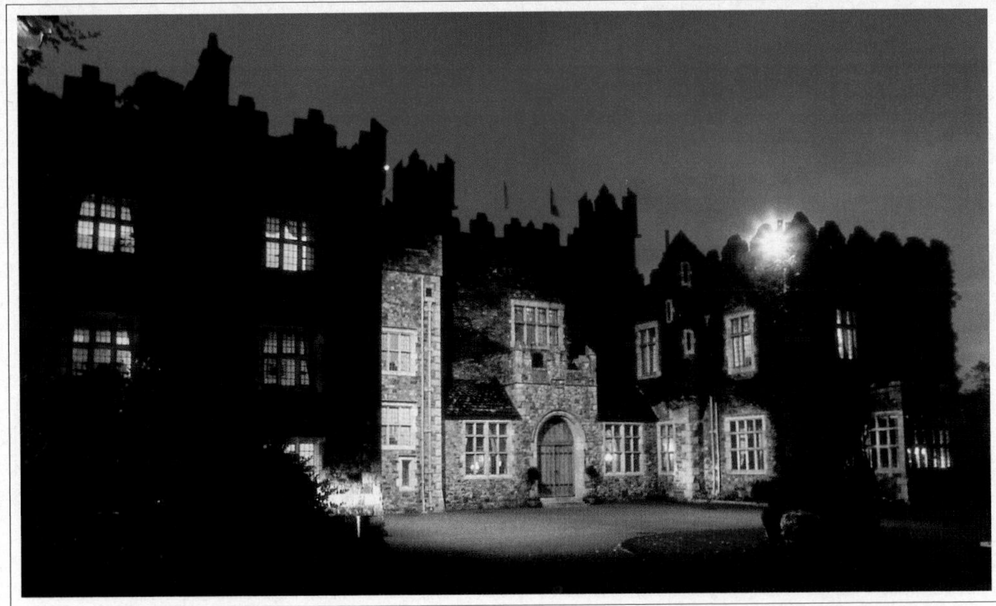

Take the ferry to a secluded island with luxury hotel and golf course

Waterford Castle, former home of the Fitzgerald family, dates back to the 15th century. To stay here is to pass into another world of legend and folklore. It starts as you take the car ferry across from reality onto this enchanted island. From there, the drive that a thousand years ago was a rough track carved out by medieval monks leads to the greystone castle, as proud and romantic as your imagination will allow. Pass through the carved granite arch with its studded oak doors and you arrive in the grand entrance hall dominated by a cavernous fireplace.

The fairy tale illusion is continued at dinner: With the menu as your guide book, crested plates bear culinary delights and confections dreamed up by the castle's gifted chefs. The food is divine, as bewitching as the castle itself.

The bedrooms are bright and airy with stunning views of the surrounding island estate.

Completing the picture, are the leisure facilities available to guests free of charge at the Waterford Castle Golf Club only 300 metres from the Castle. These include an indoor heated swimming pool and tennis courts.

There is nothing temporary about a visit here; the magic lingers for a lifetime.

LOCATION

Take N9 to Waterford. Cross bridge and stay by River Suir. At the Tower Hotel turn left into Dunmore Road for 3 miles passing Hospital, take 4th turn on left. Follow signs for ferry.

The Island, Ballinakill, Co Waterford, Republic of Ireland

Telephone +353 (0)51 878203
Fax +353 (0)51 879316

E-mail: *waterford@bestloved.com*

GENERAL MANAGER

Naill Edmondson

ROOM RATES *(Irish Punts)*

Single occupancy	*£140 - £245*
14 Doubles/Twins	*£140 - £315*
4 Deluxe four-poster suites	*£280 - £415*
1 Presidential Suite	*£340 - £450*

Includes VAT

CHARGE/CREDIT CARDS

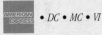

• DC • MC • VI

RATINGS & AWARDS

I.T.B. ★★★★★
R.A.C. ★★★★
A.A. ★★★★ ❀❀ *74%*

FACILITIES

On site: *Garden, croquet, tennis, 18-hole golf course, heli-pad*
2 meeting rooms/max 70 people
Nearby: *Fishing, riding*

RESTRICTIONS

No facilities for disabled guests
Pets by arrangement
Closed 2 Jan - 9 Feb

ATTRACTIONS

Waterford Crystal Showrooms, Waterford, Walking tours, Reginalds Tower Museum, Christ Church Cathedral, The Waterford Show, Waterford Treasures Museum

AFFILIATIONS

The Celebrated Hotels Collection

NEAREST

MAJOR CITY:
Waterford - 3 miles/10 mins

MAJOR AIRPORT:
Dublin - 109 miles/3 hrs

RAILWAY STATION:
Waterford - 3 miles/10 mins

RESERVATIONS

Toll free in US: 800-322-2403
Quote ***Best Loved***

ACCESS CODES

Not applicable

Ferries can make the crossing between Scotland and Ireland in 45 minutes

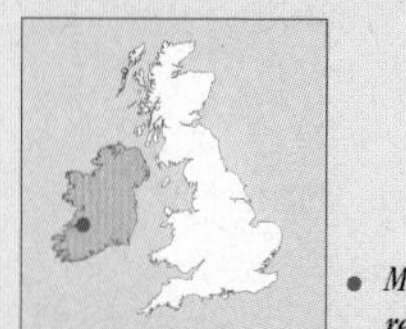

• Map p.508 ref: D8

"Don't change anything in this house, you can't make it better"

Grislind & Helmut Glaser, Munich, Bavaria

WATERMAN'S LODGE

Country house

Ballina/Killaloe, Co Clare, Republic of Ireland

Telephone +353 (0)61 376333
Fax +353 (0)61 375445

E-mail: *watermans@bestloved.com*

OWNER
Marcus McMahon

MANAGER
Tom Reilly

ROOM RATES *(Irish Punts)*

Single occupancy	*£50 - £80*
3 Standard Doubles/Twins	*£90 - £120*
7 Superior Doubles/Twins	*£110 - £140*

Includes full breakfast and VAT

CHARGE/CREDIT CARDS

• *MC* • *VI*

RATINGS & AWARDS
I.T.B. ★★★
Bridgestone 100 Best Places to Stay in Ireland

FACILITIES
On site: *Garden*
1 meeting room/max 20 people
Nearby: *Lake and river fishing - ghillie provided, walking, riding, golf, sailing, boat hire*

RESTRICTIONS
Limited facilities for disabled guests
No pets
Closed 20 Dec - 20 Jan

ATTRACTIONS
The Burren, Cliffs of Moher, Bunratty Castle, Kilkenny Castle & City, Birr Castle & Demesne, Galway, Shannon, Killaloe Cathedral

AFFILIATIONS
Manor House Hotels of Ireland

NEAREST
MAJOR CITY:
Limerick - 12 miles/30 mins
MAJOR AIRPORT:
Shannon - 20 miles/40 mins
RAILWAY STATION:
Bird Hill - 3 miles/5 mins

RESERVATIONS
Toll free in US: 800-44-UTELL
Quote ***Best Loved***

ACCESS CODES
Not applicable

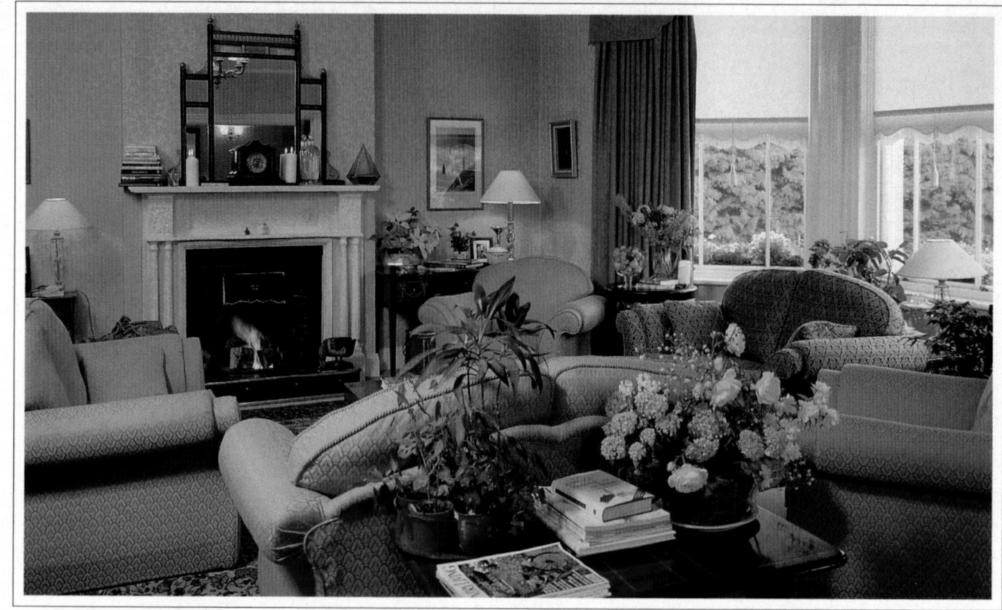

Become a part of village life - this is country living at its best

Perched on a hill overlooking the River Shannon, the Clare Hills and the lovely, unspoilt village of Killaloe, Waterman's Lodge oozes charm, peace and tranquillity. Old stone steps, high ceilings, timber floors, brass and cast iron beds, together with open fires and books add up to the perfect rural retreat. The ten bedrooms are all beautifully furnished with rugs, antiques and books.

The kitchen is the heart of this country house. Using organic produce and excellent cooking skills, it provides wonderful food for dinner guests in the converted courtyard restaurant with its high timbered ceiling.

The recently opened Lough Derg Bar completes the relaxed atmosphere while the village of Killaloe has some great pubs and people - no cars required, just stroll home. Fishing, boat hire, ghillies, rods etc are all available in the village. There are excellent golf courses within a short drive, and Cork, Galway and Kerry are all within easy reach.

The philosophy is simple - provide a beautiful rural retreat, good food, and a warm welcome. The ideal home-from-home, it is a real escape from the hurly burly and offers guests the chance to experience country village life at its best.

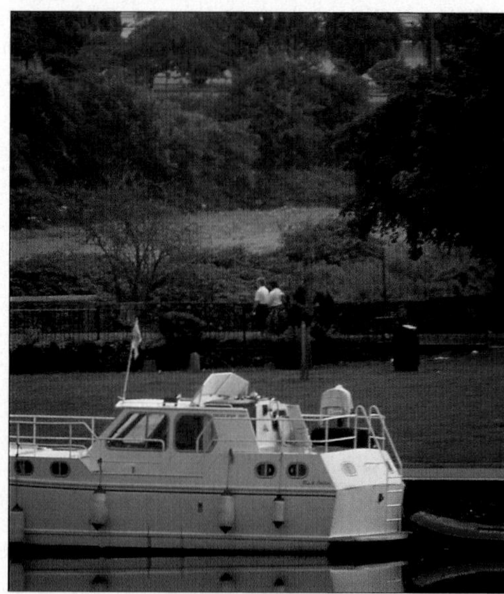

LOCATION

On the N7 Limerick to Dublin road, turn left in Birdhill on to a road signposted Killaloe/ Ballina. Drive through Ballina and the house is just outside the village on the left.

"I, for a short time, had the privilege of residing in its magic"

Margaret Johnson, Travel Writer, USA

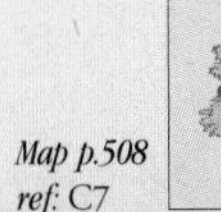

• Map p.508 ref: C7

Luxury hotel

WOODSTOCK HOTEL

Unadulterated luxury and superb golfing in Shannon

The Woodstock is one of the most exciting new Irish hotel developments of recent years. Opened in the spring of 2000, it is a luxurious country cousin of the highly acclaimed Hibernian Hotel in Dublin, and the McCausland Hotel in Belfast, two of Ireland's top addresses for discerning visitors.

For a start, the Woodstock's setting is glorious. Just off the West Coast tourist trail between Limerick and Galway, it revels in 155 acres of rolling green countryside and a championship standard golf course generously supplied with handsome vistas. The hotel's architecture is dynamic to say the least - an harmonious blend of modern and classical that is both striking and stylish. From the first view of the soaring reception area with its marble floors, stained glass windows and fabulous outsize chandelier, the Woodstock continues to impress. Charming bedrooms, delicious contemporary Irish cuisine, a well-equipped leisure club featuring swimming pool, sauna, and gym, and superb service are all an integral part of the Woodstock experience.

Difficult though it may be to tear yourself away from Woodstock's sybaritic charms, golfers will find another eight courses within a 45-minute drive, including the notable links course at Lahinch. There is also fishing and riding close by as well as good walking in the Burren. The many sightseeing attractions include the Cliffs of Moher and Bunratty Castle.

LOCATION

From Ennis, take the Lahinch Road (N85), turning left at the One Mile Inn. The hotel is half a mile on the left.

Shanaway Road, Ennis, (Near Shannon), Co Clare, Republic of Ireland

Telephone +353 (0)65 684 6600
Fax +353 (0)65 684 6611

E-mail: woodstock@bestloved.com

DIRECTOR
David Butt

GENERAL MANAGER
Siobhan Maher

ROOM RATES

Single occupancy	from £75
65 Doubles/Twins	from £145
2 Junior suites	from £175

Includes full breakfast, service and VAT

CHARGE/CREDIT CARDS

• DC • JCB • MC • VI

RATINGS & AWARDS
A.A. ★★★★ 70%

FACILITIES
On site: *Gardens, indoor pool, golf, health & beauty, fishing, heli-pad 4 meeting rooms/max 200 people*
Nearby: *Riding, hunting, fishing, tennis, cycling*

RESTRICTIONS
No pets
Closed 25 Dec

ATTRACTIONS
Cliffs of Moher, Bunratty Castle, The Burren, King John's Castle, Aran Islands

AFFILIATIONS
The Celebrated Hotels Collection
Small Luxury Hotels

NEAREST
MAJOR CITY:
Limerick - 22 miles/40 mins
MAJOR AIRPORT:
Shannon - 18 miles/30 mins
RAILWAY STATION:
Limerick - 22 miles/40 mins

RESERVATIONS
Toll free in US: 800-322-2403 or 800-525-4800
Toll free in UK: 00800 525 48000
Quote ***Best Loved***

ACCESS CODES
AMADEUS LX SNNWOO
APOLLO/GALILEO LX 28974
SABRE/ABACUS LX 54323
WORLDSPAN LX SNNWO

Quote Unquote

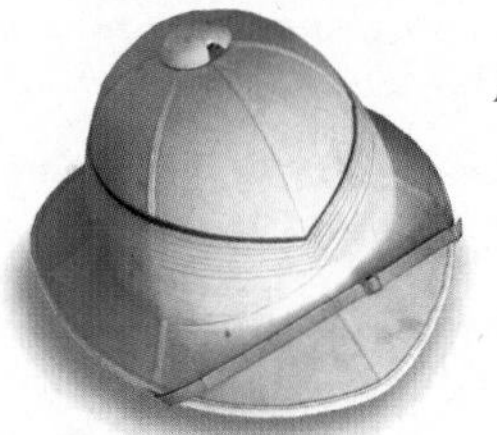

At the top of every hotel page in this book is a recommendation in the form of a "Best Loved" quotation. Our memories and experiences of travelling are pertinent and unique to each of us. What follows is a small collection of quotes, some of which are taken from this book, and others which we thought you might find entertaining.

"In 1492 Columbus discovered America, in 1992 my husband and I discovered the Isles of Scilly."

Denise & Frank Lucibello Paramus
New Jersey, on St Martin's Hotel

"The use of travelling is to regulate imagination by reality, and, instead of thinking how things maybe to see them as they are."

Johnson

"At last, enchanting England. We've found heaven!"

Max Malden
Calgary, on Gabriel Court, Devon

"Our England is a garden that is full of stately views. Of border beds and shrubberies and lawns and avenues. With statues on the terraces and peacocks strutting by; But the Glory of the Garden lies in more than meets the eye."

Rudyard Kipling
The Glory of the Gardens, 1911

"My bedroom overlooked rolling lawns and ancient oaks, the bed was the size of a croquet lawn."

Alan Bestic
Sunday Telegraph, on Rathsallagh House, Ireland

"The world is a great book of which they who never stir from home read only a page"

St Augustine

"Now we were arrived at Stonehenge. Indeed a stupendious Monument, how so many, & huge pillars of stone should have been brought together...and so exceedingly hard, that all my strength with a hammer, could not breake a fragment."

John Evelyn,
Diary, 1654

"One of the great pleasures of exploration is the contrast between extremes. I can think of nothing I have enjoyed more than eating at the superb Well House after a spell in the Wilderness."

Patricia Morris
Readers Write column, Los Angeles Times

"Yesterday...we went up Ben Nevis, the highest Mountain in Great Britain ...I am heartily glad it is done ...Imagine the task of mounting 10 St Pauls without the convenience of stair cases."

John Keats
Letter to Thomas Keats, 1818

"To invite a person into your house is to take charge of his happiness for as long as he is under your roof."

Brillat Savarin
USA, on the White House, Harrogate

If you have something to say about your favourite Best Loved Hotel, or indeed, your own personal travel experiences, we would love to hear from you.

We may decide to publish your quote in a future edition, in which case you will be sent a complimentary copy of Best Loved.

Best Loved Hotels of the World
Suite 11, The Linen House,
253 Kilburn Lane, London W10 4BQ

Tel: **020 8962 9555** ♦ *Fax:* **020 8962 9550**
E-mail: **mail@bestlovedhotels.com**

Maps & Indexes

Hotel Facilities

SWIMMING POOL

Definition: *Hotels reporting that they have either outdoor, indoor or heated swimming pools on their premises.*

HEALTH & BEAUTY

Definition: *Hotels reporting that they have health & beauty facilities on their premises.*

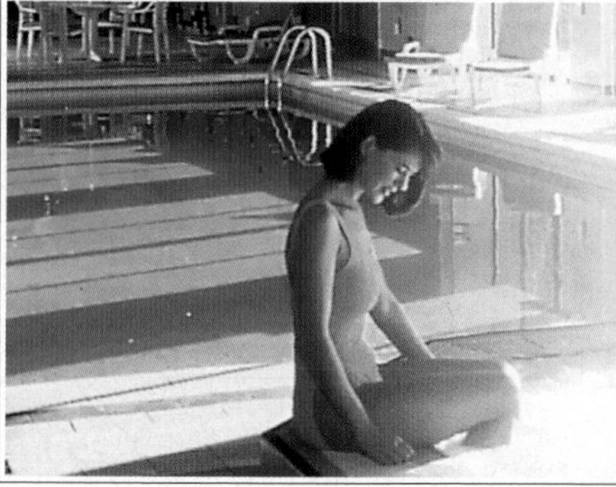

SOUTH

LONDON

IRELAND

TENNIS

Definition: *Hotels reporting that they have either indoor/outdoor or all weather tennis courts on their premises.*

HOTEL **PAGE**

SCOTLAND

NORTH

WALES

MIDSHIRES

WEST COUNTRY

SOUTH

LONDON

IRELAND

(Tennis/Ireland continued)

FISHING

Definition: *Hotels reporting fishing on, or adjacent to, their premises.*

HOTEL **PAGE**

RIDING

Definition: *Hotels who report that they have horseback riding available on site.*

HOTEL **PAGE**

— Licensed For Weddings —

A good number of **BEST LOVED HOTELS** throughout England and Wales are licensed to carry out civil marriages on their premise, so you can take your pick from the hotels listed below.

This list, however, is constantly growing as more and more hotels are granted licenses. Therefore, if a particular favourite of yours does not appear below it's still worth giving them a call.

Scotland has long had this facility (remember Gretna Green) and therefore civil ceremonies are permitted at all the Scottish hotels. This rule does not extend, however, to the Republic of Ireland.

NORTH

Armathwaite Hall Hotel	94
Chester Crabwall Manor, The	97
Devonshire Arms, The	101
Devonshire Fell, The	102
Grange Hotel, The	106
Haley's Hotel & Restaurant	109
Holbeck Ghyll Hotel & Spa	110
Judges at Kirklevington Hall	111
Lakeside Hotel	113
Leeming House	114
Linthwaite House	115
Lovelady Shield	116
Manor House, The	117
Matfen Hall	118
Mere Court Hotel	119
Michaels Nook	120
Miller Howe Hotel	121
Northcote Manor	122
Nunsmere Hall	123
Parsonage Country House	124
Swinton Park	130
Tillmouth Park Hotel	131
Westmorland Hotel	135
Willington Hall	139
Wordsworth Hotel, The	141

WALES

Bae Abermaw	148
Bontddu Hall Hotel	149
Maes-y-Neuadd, Hotel	160
Lake Country House, The	157
Lake Vyrnwy Hotel	158
Llangoed Hall	159
Miskin Manor	161
Pale Hall Country House	163
Penally Abbey	165
Penmaenuchaf Hall	166
Plas Dinas Hotel	167
Tyddyn Llan Country House	168
Warpool Court Hotel	170

MIDSHIRES

Angel Hotel, The	176
Bay Tree Hotel, The	178
Bear of Rodborough Hotel, The	179
Broadway Hotel, The	183
Broom Hall Country Hotel	186
Calcot Manor	188
Charingworth Manor	190
Congham Hall	192
Corse Lawn House Hotel	193
Dormy House	198
Fallowfields Country House	199
Fawsley Hall	200
Grafton Manor	203
Greenway, The	204
Hatton Court	205
Langar Hall	209
Lords of the Manor	211
Lygon Arms, The	214
Nailcote Hall	217
Noel Arms, The	219
Nuthurst Grange	221
Painswick Hotel, The	226
Randolph, The	229
Risley Hall	231
Shakespeare Hotel, The	233
Springs Hotel & Golf Club,The	236
Stapleford Park	237
Stonor Arms,The	238
Swan Hotel At Bibury	240
Swynford Paddocks	241
Thornbury Castle	242
Welcombe Hotel	246
Wyck Hill House, The	248

WEST COUNTRY

Alverton Manor	254
Bath Spa Hotel, The	258
Bindon Country House Hotel	259
Buckland-Tout-Saints	261
Budock Vean	262
Charlton House	265
Cliffe Hotel	266
Combe Grove Manor Hotel	267
Combe House at Gittisham	268
Court Barn	271
Hunstrete House	284
Lewtrenchard Manor	285
Northcote Manor	291
Percy's Country Hotel	295
Ston Easton Park	302

SOUTH

Alexander House Hotel	312
Amberley Castle	313
Ashdown Park Hotel	314
Bailiffscourt Hotel	316
Coppid Beech Hotel	320
Danesfield House	321
Donnington Valley Hotel	323
Eastwell Manor	324
Esseborne Manor	325
Flackley Ash Hotel	326
George, The	328
Grand Hotel	329
Great Fosters	330
Horsted Place	331
Langshott Manor	335
Langtry Manor	336
Lythe Hill Hotel	337
Maison Talbooth	338
Mansion House Hotel, The	339
Millstream Hotel	342
New Park Manor	344
Newick Park Country Estate	345
Ockenden Manor	346
Pear Tree at Purton, The	348
Pier at Harwich, The	349
Powder Mills Hotel	351
Richmond Gate Hotel	353
Salterns Hotel	355
Sir Christopher Wren's House	356
Spread Eagle Hotel & Spa, The	357
St Michael's Manor	354
Stoke Park Club	358
Taplow House	359
Tylney Hall	363
Villiers	364
Vineyard At Stockcross, The	365

LONDON

Blakes Hotel	378
Blooms Town House Hotel	379
Chesterfield Mayfair, The	381
Dolphin Square Hotel	386
Goring Hotel, The	388
Grosvenor House	390
Milestone Hotel & Apartments, The	395
Montague On The Gardens,The	397

Don't forget our Scottish hotels which can be found on pages 20 to 88.

Meeting Facilities

MOST BEST LOVED HOTELS *have facilities for meetings, conferences, receptions and weddings, some small and comfortable, some large and sophisticated. Take your choice from this list, get full details from the page on which your choice appears and telephone to find out more.*

Definition: *Hotels reporting the maximum number of individuals they could accommodate for a cocktail reception and the number of meeting and reception rooms they maintain.*

CAPACITY: UP TO 25 PEOPLE

HOTEL	MEETING ROOMS	PAGE
SCOTLAND		
Glenmoriston Arms Hotel	1	47
Inverlochy Castle	1	55
Kinloch House Hotel	1	60
Kirroughtree Hotel	1	64
Knipoch House Hotel	2	65
Lake of Menteith Hotel, The	2	69
Peat Inn, The	1	78
Taychreggan	2	85
NORTH		
Broxton Hall	1	96
Crosby Lodge	2	99
Eleven Didsbury Park	1	103
Leeming House	2	114
Manor House, The	1	117
Rothay Manor	1	127
Studley Hotel	1	128
Underscar Manor	1	132
Woolton Redbourne Hotel	1	140
Yorke Arms, The	2	142
WALES		
Crown at Whitebrook, The	1	151
Fairyhill	1	153
George III Hotel	1	155
Groes Inn, The	2	156
Maes-y-Neuadd, Hotel	1	160
Penally Abbey	1	165
Ty'n Rhos Country Hotel	1	169
MIDSHIRES		
Beeches Restaurant	1	180
Biggin Hall	1	181
Brookhouse, The	1	185
Crown Hotel, The	2	196
Hotel on the Park	1	207
Langar Hall	2	209
Lords of the Manor	1	211
New Inn At Coln, The	1	218
Old Rectory, The	1	224
Royalist Hotel, The	1	232
Stonor Arms, The	2	238
Swan Hotel	1	239
WEST COUNTRY		
Court Barn	2	271
Dukes Hotel	1	273
Gabriel Court Hotel	1	275
Holne Chase Hotel	1	282
Little Admiral, The	1	286
Mill End Hotel	3	288
Orestone Manor	1	293
Porlock Vale House	1	296
Prince Hall Hotel	1	297
Talland Bay Hotel	1	303
Well House, The	1	305
SOUTH		
At The Sign Of The Angel	3	315
Chequers Hotel	1	318
French Horn Hotel	1	327
Millstream Hotel and Restaurant	1	342
Plumber Manor	1	350
Priory Hotel	1	352
St Michael's Manor	3	354
LONDON		
Ahernes	1	409
Butlers Town House	1	421
Coopershill	1	426
Glin Castle	1	432
Lough Inagh Lodge Hotel	1	447
Sea View House Hotel	1	464
Waterman's Lodge	1	468
IRELAND		
Ahernes	1	409
Butlers Town House	1	421
Coopershill	1	426
Glin Castle	1	432
Lough Inagh Lodge Hotel	1	447
Sea View House Hotel	1	464
Waterman's Lodge	1	468

CAPACITY: 26 TO 50 PEOPLE

HOTEL	MEETING ROOMS	PAGE
SCOTLAND		
Ardanaiseig	1	20
Craigellachie Hotel	3	31
Cromlix House	3	33
Enmore Hotel	2	41
Flodigarry Country House Hotel	1	43
Glenapp Castle	3	45
Glenmorangie House	1	46
Green Craigs	1	48
Greywalls	1	49
Howard, The	3	50
Isle of Eriska	3	56
Kinkell House	2	59
Knockinaam Lodge	1	66
Knockomie Hotel	2	67
Loch Melfort	1	71
Mullardoch House Hotel	1	74
Old Mansion House	2	77
NORTH		
Fayrer Garden House Hotel	1	104
Gilpin Lodge Hotel	0	105
Graythwaite Manor Hotel	2	108
Lovelady Shield	2	116
Michaels Nook	1	120
Miller Howe Hotel	2	121
Northcote Manor	1	122
Pheasant, The	1	126
Waren House Hotel	1	133
WALES		
Empire, The	1	152
Llangoed Hall	3	159
Pale Hall Country House	2	163
Penmaenuchaf Hall	2	166
Plas Dinas Hotel	2	167
Tyddyn Llan Country House	2	168
MIDSHIRES		
Bignell Park Hotel	2	182
Broadway Hotel, The	2	183
Brockencote Hall	2	184
Broom Hall Country Hotel	1	186
Congham Hall	1	192
Cotswold House Hotel	1	194
Crown Inn & Hotel, The	1	197
Greenway, The	2	204
Lower Slaughter Manor	2	213
Mill at Harvington, The	1	216
Norfolk Mead Hotel, The	2	220
Owlpen Manor	3	225
Plough At Clanfield, The	2	228
Shaven Crown, The	1	235
Springs Hotel & Golf Club, The	4	236
Swan Hotel At Bibury	3	240
WEST COUNTRY		
Carpenters Arms, The	2	263
Cliffe Hotel	1	266
Garrack Hotel, The	1	276
Hunstrete House	3	284
Nobody Inn, The	1	290
Old Priory, The	2	292
Queensberry Hotel	1	298
SOUTH		
Amberley Castle	2	313
Beechleas Hotel & Restaurant	1	317
Christopher Hotel, The	1	319
Esseborne Manor	2	325
George, The	2	328
Hotel du Vin & Bistro	2	334
Langshott Manor	2	335
Maison Talbooth	2	338
Mansion House Hotel, The	3	339
Master Builder's House	1	340
Mill House, The	2	341
LONDON		
Ascott Mayfair	2	374
Athenæum Hotel	4	375
Basil Street Hotel	3	376
Blooms Town House Hotel	1	379
IRELAND		
Aberdeen Lodge	2	408
Bayview Hotel	2	414
Blakes Townhouse	1	416
Brownes Townhouse	1	419
Bushmills Inn, The	3	420
CastleHyde Hotel	1	424
Gregans Castle	1	434
Hibernian Hotel	1	438
Hunter's Hotel	1	440
Killarney Royal Hotel	1	443
Longueville House	2	446
Merrion Hall	2	451
Merrion Hotel	6	453
Moyglare Manor	3	455
Mustard Seed At Echo Lodge	1	457
Park Hotel Kenmare	2	458
St John's Country House	2	463

CAPACITY: 51 TO 75 PEOPLE

HOTEL	MEETING ROOMS	PAGE
SCOTLAND		
Auchterarder House	2	22
Coul House Hotel	2	30

Culloden House	3	35
Devonshire Hotel, The	2	37
Farleyer House	2	42
Inn At Lathones	1	53
Kinfauns Castle	3	58
NORTH		
Devonshire Fell, The	1	102
Grange Hotel, The	2	106
Holbeck Ghyll Hotel & Spa	2	110
Linthwaite House	3	115
White House, The	2	136
White House Manor, The	4	137
Willington Hall	3	139
WALES		
Lake Country House, The	1	157
MIDSHIRES		
Arrow Mill Hotel	2	177
Bay Tree Hotel, The	3	178
Calcot Manor	2	188
Charingworth Manor	2	190
Cottage Country House Hotel, The	4	195
Feathers, The	2	201
Hatton Court	6	205
Lifeboat Inn, The	2	210
Thornbury Castle	2	242
Tudor Farmhouse Hotel	2	243
Unicorn Hotel, The	1	244
WEST COUNTRY		
Bath Priory Hotel & Restaurant, The	3	257
Northcote Manor	1	291
Osborne Hotel, The	1	294
St Martin's On The Isle	3	300
Woodlands Country House Hotel	2	307
SOUTH		
Bailiffscourt Hotel	2	316
Hotel Du Vin & Bistro	2	333
Pear Tree at Purton, The	4	348
Vineyard At Stockcross, The	2	365
Wallett's Court	3	366
LONDON		
Flemings Mayfair	3	387
IRELAND		
Brooks Hotel	3	418
Marlfield House	2	449
Waterford Castle	2	467

CAPACITY: 76 TO 100 PEOPLE

HOTEL	MEETING ROOMS	PAGE
SCOTLAND		
Bonham, The	1	24
Bunchrew House Hotel	3	25
Channings	3	29
Cringletie House Hotel	4	32
Eilean Iarmain, Hotel	2	40
Ladyburn	1	68
Melvin House Hotel	4	73
Roman Camp Country House	2	81
Royal Marine Hotel	2	83
Three Chimneys, The	1	86
Woodside Hotel, The	2	88
NORTH		
Armathwaite Hall Hotel	4	94
Chester Crabwall Manor, The	5	97
Grants Hotel	5	107
Haley's Hotel & Restaurant	3	109
Nunsmere Hall	3	123
Tillmouth Park Hotel	3	131
WALES		
Court Hotel	3	150
MIDSHIRES		
Angel Hotel, The	3	176
Bear of Rodborough Hotel, The	5	179
Corse Lawn House Hotel	2	193
Hoste Arms, The	3	206
Lygon Arms, The	5	214
Nailcote Hall	7	217
Noel Arms, The	2	219
Painswick Hotel, The	3	226
Washbourne Court Hotel	2	245
Wyck Hill House, The	4	248
WEST COUNTRY		
Bindon Country House Hotel	2	259
Budock Vean - The Hotel on the River	4	262
Combe Grove Manor Hotel & Country Club	4	267
Combe House at Gittisham	2	268
Daneswood House Hotel	2	272
Hotel du Vin & Bistro	3	283
Riviera, Hotel	1	299
Lewtrenchard Manor	2	285
Mount Somerset, The	3	289
St Olaves Hotel	3	301
SOUTH		
Alexander House Hotel	6	312
Flackley Ash Hotel	2	326
Horsted Place	5	331
Langtry Manor	3	336
Ockenden Manor	1	346
Passford House Hotel	4	347
Pier at Harwich, The	1	349
Richmond Gate Hotel	4	353
Sir Christopher Wren's House	11	356
Spread Eagle Hotel & Spa, The	5	357
Tylney Hall	12	363
LONDON		
Dolphin Square Hotel	3	386
Goring Hotel, The	4	388
Rubens At The Palace, The	5	400
IRELAND		
Ballyrafter House Hotel	2	413
Hayfield Manor	4	436
Hibernian Hotel	2	439
McCausland Hotel, The	3	450
Rathsallagh House	3	459
Tinakilly House	3	466

CAPACITY: 101 TO 150 PEOPLE

HOTEL	MEETING ROOMS	PAGE
SCOTLAND		
Cairnbaan Hotel	2	26
Dalhousie Castle & Spa	5	36
Dryfesdale Country House Hotel, The	3	38
Four Seasons Hotel, The	3	44
Roxburghe Hotel & Golf Course	3	82
NORTH		
Devonshire Arms, The	4	101
Lakeside Hotel	7	113
Mere Court Hotel	10	119
Swinton Park	7	130
Wordsworth Hotel, The	3	141
WALES		
Bae Abermaw	4	148
Lake Vyrnwy Hotel	3	158
MIDSHIRES		
Colwall Park Hotel	4	191
Fallowfields Country House Hotel	3	199
Fawsley Hall	7	200
George in Hathersage, The	2	202
Nuthurst Grange	3	221
Risley Hall	4	231
Shakespeare Hotel, The	6	233
Swynford Paddocks	1	241
Welcombe Hotel	7	246
WEST COUNTRY		
Bath Spa Hotel, The	7	258
Castle at Taunton, The	4	264
Charlton House	3	265
Ston Easton Park	1	302
SOUTH		
Danesfield House	5	321
Dixcart Hotel	1	322
Donnington Valley Hotel	9	323
Lythe Hill Hotel	6	337
Moore's Hotel	2	343
New Park Manor	2	344
Newick Park Country Estate	2	345
Salterns Hotel	3	355
Taplow House	5	359
LONDON		
Chesterfield Mayfair, The	6	381
Montague On The Gardens, The	5	397
Montcalm Hotel, The	3	398
IRELAND		
Ashford Castle	1	411
Dunbrody Country House	3	428
Herbert Park Hotel	5	437
Mount Juliet	5	454
Ross Lake House Hotel	1	461
Sheen Falls Lodge	3	465

CAPACITY: OVER 150 PEOPLE

HOTEL	MEETING ROOMS	PAGE
SCOTLAND		
Balbirnie House Hotel	5	23
Cameron House	5	27
Carnoustie Golf Resort & Spa	6	28
Huntingtower Hotel	6	51
Letham Grange Hotel & Golf Course	5	70
North West Castle Hotel	2	75
Old Manor Hotel	3	76
Piersland House Hotel	3	79
Prestonfield House	6	80
NORTH		
Crewe Hall	16	98
Judges at Kirklevington Hall	3	111
Matfen Hall	7	118
Parsonage Country House	4	124
Westmorland Hotel	5	135
WALES		
Miskin Manor	5	161
Warpool Court Hotel	2	170
MIDSHIRES		
Dormy House	5	198
Grafton Manor	2	203
Randolph, The	6	229
Stapleford Park	10	237
WEST COUNTRY		
Alverton Manor	5	254
Buckland-Tout-Saints	2	261
Glazebrook House Hotel	2	277
SOUTH		
Ashdown Park Hotel	16	314
Coppid Beech Hotel	11	320
Eastwell Manor	3	324
Grand Hotel	17	329
Great Fosters	5	330
Powder Mills Hotel	3	351
Stoke Park Club	8	358
Villiers	6	364
LONDON		
Grosvenor House	29	390
IRELAND		
Dromoland Castle	6	427
Dundrum House Hotel	3	429
Dunloe Castle	6	430
Glenlo Abbey Hotel	12	431
Killarney Park	3	442
Knockranny House Hotel	3	444
Muckross Park Hotel	3	456
Woodstock Hotel	4	469

Golf Guide

SCOTLAND

HOTEL	COURSE	MILES AWAY	PAGE
Ardanaiseig	Taynuilt	10	20
Ardsheal House	Fort William	20	21
Auchterarder House	Auchterarder	2	22
Bonham, The	Murrayfield	3	24
Bunchrew House Hotel	Inverness	4	25
Cairnbaan Hotel	Lochgilphead	4	26
Channings	Braid Hills	3	29
Craigellachie Hotel	Dufftown	3	31
Cringletie House Hotel	Peebles	2½	32
Cromlix House	Dunblane New	4	33
Culdearn House	Grantown-on-Spey	1	34
Culloden House	Nairn	18	35
Dalhousie Castle & Spa	Broomieknowe	1	36
Devonshire Hotel, The	Dougalston	7	37
Dryfesdale Country House	Lockmaben	2	38
Dunain Park Hotel	Nairn	22	39
Enmore Hotel	Cowal	¼	41
Flodigarry Country House	Skeabost	20	43
Four Seasons Hotel, The	St Fillans	½	44
Glenapp Castle	Stranraer	18	45
Glenmorangie House	Tain	6	46
Glenmoriston Arms Hotel	Fort Augustus	5	47
Green Craigs	Kilspindie	1	48
Greywalls	Muirfield	½	49
Eilean Iarmain, Hotel	Sconcer	10	40
Howard, The	Murrayfield	5	50
Huntingtower Hotel	King James VI	3	51
Inn at Ardgour, The	Fort William	13	52
Inn At Lathones	Craighead Links	8	53
Inn On The Green, The	Dougalston	7	54
Inverlochy Castle	Fort William	½	55
Killiechronan House	Craignure	10	57
Kinfauns Castle	King James VI	2	58
Kinkell House	Muir of Ord	5	59
Kinloch House Hotel	Blairgowrie	4	60
Kinloch Lodge	Sconser	15	61
Kirkton House	Cardross	1	63
Kirroughtree Hotel	Newton Stewart	1	64
Knipoch House Hotel	Glencruitten	6	65
Knockinaam Lodge	Dunskey Port Patrick	3	66
Knockomie Hotel	Forres	2	67
Ladyburn	Brunston Castle	3	68
Lake of Menteith Hotel	Aberfoyle	2	69
Loch Melfort	Oban	20	71
Manor House, The	Glencruitten	3	72
Melvin House Hotel	Murrayfield	2	73
Mullardoch House Hotel	Algan	20	74
North West Castle Hotel	Stranraer	2	75
Old Manor Hotel	Lundin Links	¼	76
Old Mansion House	Downfield	5	77
Peat Inn, The	St Andrew's	6	78
Piersland House Hotel	Royal Troon	Adjacent	79
Roman Camp Country	Callander	⅓	81
Royal Marine Hotel	Brora	Adjacent	83
Summer Isles	Ullapool	25	84
Taychreggan	Taynuilt	2	85
Three Chimneys, The	Skeabost Hotel	20	86
Tigh an Eilean	Lochcarron	17	87
Woodside Hotel, The	Aberdour	¼	88

NORTH

HOTEL	COURSE	MILES AWAY	PAGE
Armathwaite Hall Hotel	Keswick	10	94
Borrowdale Gates	Keswick	7	95
Broxton Hall	Aldersley	2	96
Chester Crabwall Manor	Mollington Grange	Adjacent	97
Crewe Hall	Mere	12	98
Crosby Lodge	Eden	½	99
Dale Head Hall	Keswick	5	100
Devonshire Arms, The	Skipton	5	101
Devonshire Fell, The	Skipton	6	102
Eleven Didsbury Park	Didsbury	1	103
Fayrer Garden House	Windermere	1	104
Gilpin Lodge Hotel	Windermere	½	105
Grange Hotel, The	Fulford	4	106
Grants Hotel	Oakdale	½	107
Graythwaite Manor Hotel	Grange	1½	108
Haley's Hotel	Cookridge Hall	3	109
Holbeck Ghyll Hotel	Windermere	4	110
Judges at Kirklevington Hall	Eaglescliffe	8	111
Lakeside Hotel	Grange	6	113
Leeming House	Penrith	8	114
Linthwaite House	Windermere	1	115
Lovelady Shield	Alston Moor	2	116
Manor House, The	Beverley	2	117
Mere Court Hotel	Mere	¼	119
Michaels Nook	Keswick	12	120
Miller Howe Hotel	Windermere	2	121
Northcote Manor	Wilpshire	2	122
Nunsmere Hall	Sandiway	3	123
Parsonage Country House	Fulford	4	124
Pheasant, The	Cockermouth	4	126
Pheasant Hotel	Kirkbymoorside	4	125
Rothay Manor	Windermere	5	127
Studley Hotel	Pannal	3	128
Swinside Lodge Hotel	Keswick	6	129
Swinton Park	Masham	¼	130
Tillmouth Park Hotel	Hirsel	4	131
Underscar Manor	Keswick	4	132
Waren House Hotel	Bamburgh Castle	2	133
Wateredge Hotel	Windermere	7	134
Westmorland Hotel	Penrith	17	135
White House, The	Harrogate	1	136
White House Manor, The	Prestbury	1	137
White Moss House	Windermere	5	138
Willington Hall	Portal	3	139
Woolton Redbourne Hotel	Woolton	1	140
Wordsworth Hotel, The	Keswick	10	141
Yorke Arms, The	Knaresborough	18	142

WALES

HOTEL	COURSE	MILES AWAY	PAGE
Bae Abermaw	Royal St David's	18	148
Bontddu Hall Hotel	Royal St David's	15	149
Court Hotel	Tenby	6	150
Crown at Whitebrook	Royal Forest of Dean	5	151
Empire, The	North Wales	1	152
Fairyhill	Pennard	8	153
George III Hotel	Royal St David's	16	155
Groes Inn, The	Conwy	3	156
Maes-y-Neuadd, Hotel	Royal St David's	3	160
Lake Vyrnwy Hotel	Llanymnech	20	158
Llangoed Hall	Cradoc	11	159
Miskin Manor	Vale of Glamorgan	4	161
Old Rectory Country	Conwy	3	162
Pale Hall Country House	Bala Lake	4	163
Penally Abbey	Tenby	2	165
Penmaenuchaf Hall	Dolgellau	2	166
Plas Dinas Hotel	Morfa	15	167
Ty'n Rhos Country Hotel	Caenarfon	9	169
Tyddyn Llan Country	Llangollen	18	168
Warpool Court Hotel	St David's City	3	170

MIDSHIRES

HOTEL	COURSE	MILES AWAY	PAGE
Angel Hotel, The	Flempton	4	176
Arrow Mill Hotel	Stratford-upon-Avon	8	177
Bay Tree Hotel, The	Witney	6	178
Bear of Rodborough	Minchinhampton	4	179
Beeches Restaurant	Uttoxeter	5	180
Biggin Hall	Cavendish	12	181
Bignell Park Hotel	Chesterton	¼	182
Broadway Hotel, The	Broadway	2	183
Brockencote Hall	Ombersley	12	184
Brookhouse, The	Craythorne	½	185
Broom Hall	Richmond Park	½	186
Burford House	Burford	1	187
Calcot Manor	Cotswold Edge	3	188
Castle House	Belmont	4	189
Charingworth Manor	Broadway	3	190
Colwall Park Hotel	Worcestershire	3½	191
Congham Hall	Hunstanton	5	192
Corse Lawn House Hotel	Puckrup Hall	6	193
Cotswold House Hotel	Broadway	3	194
Cottage Country House	Ruddington Grange	1	195
Crown Hotel, The	Southwold	½	196
Crown Inn & Hotel, The	Broadway	3	197
Dormy House	Broadway	Adjacent	198
Fallowfields Country House	Frilford Heath	1	199
Fawsley Hall	Farthingstone	5	200
Feathers, The	Chesterton	5	201
George in Hathersage	Sickleholme	2	202

On Site

Best Loved Hotels

Ashdown Park Hotel	314
Ashford Castle	411
Balbirnie House Hotel	23
Budock Vean - The Hotel on the River	262
Cameron House	27
Carnoustie Golf Resort & Spa	28
Combe Grove Manor Hotel & Country Club	267
Coul House Hotel	30
Donnington Valley Hotel	323
Dromoland Castle	427
Dundrum House Hotel Golf and Leisure Club	429
Farleyer House	42
Glenlo Abbey Hotel	431
Horsted Place	331
Isle of Eriska	56
Lake Country House, The	157

HOTEL	COURSE	MILES AWAY	PAGE
Grafton Manor	Bromsgrove	6	203
Greenway, The	Lilley Brook	3	204
Hatton Court	Painswick	3	205
Hoste Arms, The	Royal West Norfolk	5	206
Hotel On The Park	Lilley Brook	3	207
Kings Head	Lyneham	1	208
Langar Hall	Cotgrave Place	3	209
Lifeboat Inn, The	Hunstanton	5	210
Lords of The Manor	Naunton Downs	4	211
Lower Slaughter Manor	Naunton Downs	4	213
Lygon Arms, The	Broadway	1	214
Malt House, The	Broadway Golf Club	4	215
Mill at Harvington, The	Evesham	4	216
New Inn At Coln, The	Cirencester	7	218
Noel Arms, The	Broadway	3	219
Norfolk Mead Hotel, The	Sprowston	3	220
Nuthurst Grange	Shirley	2	221
Old Bank, The	Studley Wood	4	222
Old Parsonage, The	Oxfordshire	8	223
Old Rectory, The	Royal West Norfolk	17	224
Owlpen Manor	Cotswold Edge	3	225
Painswick Hotel, The	Painswick	1	226
Pen-Y-Dyffryn Hotel	Mile End	5	227
Plough At Clanfield, The	Carswell	7	228
Randolph, The	Studley Wood	4	229
Raven Hotel	Shrewsbury	10	230
Risley Hall	Maywood	1	231
Royalist Hotel, The	Naunton Downs	5	232
Shakespeare Hotel, The	Stratford Oaks	2	233
Shaven Crown, The	Burford	5	235
Stonor Arms, The	Badgemore	5	238
Swan Hotel	Southwold	½	239
Swan Hotel At Bibury	Cirencester	7	240

HOTEL	COURSE	MILES AWAY	PAGE
Swynford Paddocks	Gog Magog	12	241
Thornbury Castle	Thornbury	1	242
Tudor Farmhouse Hotel	Coleford	2	243
Unicorn Hotel, The	Naunton Downs	5	244
Washbourne Court Hotel	Naunton Downs	2	245
Wild Duck, The	Cirencester	5	247
Wyck Hill House, The	Naunton Downs	7	248

WEST COUNTRY

HOTEL	COURSE	MILES AWAY	PAGE
Alverton Manor	Killiow	2	254
Apsley House Hotel	Lansdown	3	255
Bath Lodge Hotel	Orchardsleigh	5	256
Bath Priory Hotel, The	Sham Castle	½	257
Bath Spa Hotel, The	Sham Castle	¼	258
Bindon Country House	Oak Manor	3	259
Boscundle Manor	Carlyon Bay	½	260
Buckland-Tout-Saints	Dartmouth	7	261
Carpenters Arms, The	Farrington Gurney	5	263
Castle at Taunton, The	Oake Manor	4	264
Charlton House	Orchardsleigh	9	265
Cliffe Hotel	Cumberwell Park	3	266
Combe House at Gittisham	Woodbury Park	14	268
Coombe Farm	Looe Bindown	1	269
Cormorant On The River	Carlyon Bay	5	270
Court Barn	Holsworthy	2½	271
Daneswood House Hotel	Mendips Spring	4	272
Dukes Hotel	Sham Castle	2	273
Gabriel Court Hotel	Dainton Park	4	275
Garrack Hotel, The	West Cornwall	3	276
Glazebrook House Hotel	Wrangaton	1	277
Haydon House	Bath	2	278
Heddon 's Gate Hotel	Saunton	15	279
Holly Lodge	Bath	3	281
Holne Chase Hotel	Stover	6	282
Hotel du Vin & Bistro	Bath	12	283
Hotel Riviera	Woodbury Park	7	299
Hunstrete House	Farrington	10	284
Lewtrenchard Manor	Hurdwick	6	285
Little Admiral, The	Dartmouth Golf	5	286
Lugger Hotel, The	Truro	12	287
Mill End Hotel	Manor House	8	288
Mount Somerset, The	Taunton Vale	3	289
Nobody Inn, The	Teign Valley	1	290
Northcote Manor	Libbaton	3	291
Old Priory, The	Farrington	1	292
Orestone Manor	Torquay	½	293
Osborne Hotel	Dainton Park	6	294
Percy's Country Hotel	Holsworthy	3	295
Porlock Vale House	Minehead	10	296
Prince Hall Hotel	Tavistock	5	297
Queensberry Hotel	Sham Castle	2	298
St Martin's On The Isle	Isle of Scilly	3 (by boat)	300
St Olaves Hotel	Woodbury Park	10	301
Ston Easton Park	Farrington	2	302
Talland Bay Hotel	Looe Bindown	10	303
Tides Reach Hotel	Thurlestone	5	304
Well House, The	St Mellion	10	305
The Windsor, The	Sham Castle	2	306
Woodlands Country House	Burnham & Berrow	2	307

Golf Courses

with a golf course on site

Letham Grange Hotel & Golf Course	*70*
Matfen Hall	*118*
Mount Juliet	*454*
Nailcote Hall	*217*
Park Hotel Kenmare	*458*
Prestonfield House	*80*
Rathsallagh House	*459*
Roxburghe Hotel & Golf Course	*82*
Springs Hotel & Golf Club, The	*236*
Stapleford Park	*237*
Stoke Park Club	*358*
Tylney Hall	*363*
Waterford Castle	*467*
Welcombe Hotel	*246*
Woodstock Hotel	*469*

SOUTH

HOTEL	COURSE	MILES AWAY	PAGE
Alexander House Hotel	Chartham	4	312
Amberley Castle	West Chiltington	5	313
At The Sign Of The Angel	Bowood	3	315
Bailiffscourt Hotel	Littlehampton	2	316
Beechleas Hotel	Canford Magna	2	317
Chequers Hotel	Slinfold Park	8	318
Christopher Hotel, The	Farnham Park	10	319
Coppid Beech Hotel	Blue Mountain	3	320
Danesfield House	Harleyford	1	321
Dixcart Hotel	St Pierre	9	322
Eastwell Manor	Ashford	2	324
Esseborne Manor	Hampshire	10	325
Flackley Ash Hotel	Lydd	14	326
French Horn Hotel	Castle Royal	4	327
George, The	Cowes	12	328
Grand Hotel	Royal Eastbourne	1	329
Great Fosters	Wentworth	4	330
Hotel Du Vin & Bistro	Dale Hill	10	333
Hotel du Vin & Bistro	South Winchester	3	334
Langshott Manor	Lingfield	7	335
Langtry Manor	Queens Park	1	336
Lythe Hill Hotel	Chiddingfold	4	337
Maison Talbooth	Hintlesham Hall	20	338
Mansion House Hotel	Parkstone	4	339
Master Builder's House	Brockenhurst	6	340
Mill House, The	West Chiltington	5	341
Millstream Hotel	Chichester	8	342
Moore's Hotel	L'Ancresse	4	343
New Park Manor	Brockenhurst	1½	344
Newick Park Estate	East Sussex National	10	345
Ockenden Manor	Paxhill Park	3	346
Passford House Hotel	Brockenhurst	4	347
Pear Tree at Purton, The	Wrag Barn	5	348
Pier at Harwich, The	Harwich Dovercourt	2	349
Plumber Manor	Sherborne	10	350
Powder Mills Hotel	Battle	3	351
Priory Hotel	Wareham	½	352
Richmond Gate Hotel	Richmond Park	½	353
Salterns Hotel	Parkstone	½	355
Sir Christopher Wren's	Stoke Poges	9	356
Spread Eagle Hotel	Cowdray Park	1	357
St Michael's Manor	Batchwood	½	354
Taplow House	Stoke Poges	3	359
Thatch Lodge Hotel	Lyme Regis	1	360
Thatched Cottage Hotel	Brockenhurst	1	361
Three Lions, The	Brook	10	362
Villiers	Buckingham	2	364
Vineyard At Stockcross	Donnington Valley	4	365
Wallett's Court	Royal St Georges	6	366

LONDON

HOTEL	COURSE	MILES AWAY	PAGE
Academy, The	Old Thorns	46	373
Ascott Mayfair	Richmond	9	374
Athenæum Hotel	Richmond	10	375
Basil Street Hotel	Richmond	6	376
The Beaufort, The	Stoke Poges	20	377
Blakes Hotel	Richmond	9	378
Blooms Town House Hotel	Stoke Poges	25	379
Burns Hotel, The	Richmond Park	10	380
Chesterfield Mayfair, The	Richmond Park	10	381
Colonnade Town House, The	Stoke Poges	20	382
Cranley, The	Richmond	10	384
Darlington Hyde Park, The	Stoke Poges	25	385
Dolphin Square Hotel	Richmond Park	8	386
Flemings Mayfair	Richmond	10	387
Goring Hotel, The	Richmond	8	388
Grosvenor House	Stockley Park	15	390
Halcyon, The	Stoke Poges	20	391
Kensington House	Richmond	9	392
Knightsbridge Green Hotel	Stoke Poges	20	393
London Outpost	Wentworth	10	394
Milestone Hotel	Stoke Poges	9	395
Millennium Bailey's	Richmond	6	396
Montague On The Gardens	Richmond	10	397
Montcalm Hotel, The	Hendon	10	398
Number 41	Richmond Park	6½	399
Rubens At The Palace	Richmond	6½	400
Sloane Hotel, The	Richmond Park	3	401
Twenty Nevern Square	Stoke Poges	20	402

IRELAND

HOTEL	COURSE	MILES AWAY	PAGE
Aberdeen Lodge	Elm Park	3	408
Ahernes	Youghal	1	409
Ard na Sidhe	Dooks	4	410
Ballynahinch Castle Hotel	Connemara	12	412
Ballyrafter House Hotel	Lismore	¼	413
Bayview Hotel	East Cork	12	414
Blairs Cove House	Bantry	7	415
Blakes Townhouse	Elm Park	½	416
Blue Haven Hotel	Kinsale	3	417
Brooks Hotel	Port Marnock	8	418
Brownes Townhouse	Elm Park	2	419
Bushmills Inn, The	Royal Portrush	4	420
Butlers Town House	Elm Park	1	421
Caragh Lodge	Dooks	4	422
Cashel House Hotel	Connemara	18	423
CastleHyde Hotel	Fermoy	5	424
Churchtown House	Rosslare	3½	425
Coopershill	County Sligo	18	426
Dunbrody Country House	Waterford Castle	10	428
Dunloe Castle	Dunloe	¼	430
Glin Castle	Newcastle West	10	432
Gormans Clifftop House	Ceannsibeal	8	433
Gregans Castle	Lahinch	16	434
Halpin's Hotel	Kilkee	¼	435
Hayfield Manor	Fota Island	12	436
Herbert Park Hotel	Elm Park	1½	437
Hibernian Hotel	Kilkenny	1	439
Hibernian Hotel	Portmarnock	8	438
Hunter's Hotel	Wicklow	3	440
Jordan's Townhouse	Greenore	1½	441
Killarney Park	Killarney Golf Club	2½	442
Killarney Royal Hotel	Killarney	2	443
Knockranny House Hotel	Westport	2	444
Longfield's	Royal Dublin	7	445
Longueville House	Ballyellis	6	446
Lough Inagh Lodge Hotel	Connemara	18	447
Markree Castle	Strandhill	5	448
Marlfield House	Courtown	2	449
McCausland Hotel, The	Royal Belfast	5	450
Merrion Hall	Elm Park	½	451
Merrion Hotel	Portmarnock	8	453
Moyglare Manor	K Club	6	455
Muckross Park Hotel	Killarney	5	456
Mustard Seed At Echo Lodge	Adare Manor	8	457
Rosleague Manor	Connemara	14	460
Ross Lake House Hotel	Oughterard	2	461
Sea View House Hotel	Bantry Park	1	464
Sheen Falls Lodge	Ring of Kerry	5	465
St Clerans	Athenry	5	462
St John's Country House	Lisfannon	3	463
Tinakilly House	Wicklow	2	466
Waterman's Lodge	East Clare	12	468

– Hotels That Accept Pets –

ORDER CARD

AMERICAN EXPRESS

Best Loved Hotels of the World 2001 - PRICE LIST

	UK£	US$	EIRE£
UK & Ireland Directory	14.99	19.95	15.99
Amex cardholders price	**13.99**	**17.95**	**14.99**
Add for post and packing	*4.50*	*3.00*	*4.50*

Postage to Europe - £6; to any other country - £10

Orderlines

UK: 0870 586 2010 Fax: 01548 831074
US: 800-808-7682 Toll free fax: 800-572-8131
E-mail: bookorder@bestlovedhotels.com
or order on-line at www.bestlovedhotels.com

Order by post

Fill in your details and send this card to the **FREEPOST** address below:

Best Loved Hotels of the World
Clientbase Fulfilment Ltd
FREEPOST (SWB40527), IVYBRIDGE PL21 0ZZ (UK only)

Please send me Best Loved Hotels of the World 2001

Copies required ☐ @ ☐ each **£/$***
Add for post and packing per copy **£/$*** ....
TOTAL **£/$*** ....

* Please circle the currency you are using

Payment method

Charge/Credit Card ☐ Personal Cheque ☐*
*Cheques to be made out to "World Media Publishing Ltd"

Please charge my account

American Express ☐ Diners ☐ Mastercard ☐ Visa ☐

Expires end

☐ I enclose my order on company letterhead. Please invoice my company (UK only).

Name (Mr/Mrs/Ms) ____
Company ____
Address ____

Zip/Postcode ____ Country ____
Tel ____ Fax ____
E-mail ____

Signature ____

Please allow at least two weeks for delivery. BLD01/OF

ORDER CARD

AMERICAN EXPRESS

Best Loved Hotels of the World 2001 - PRICE LIST

	UK£	US$	EIRE£
UK & Ireland Directory	14.99	19.95	15.99
Amex cardholders price	**13.99**	**17.95**	**14.99**
Add for post and packing	*4.50*	*3.00*	*4.50*

Postage to Europe - £6; to any other country - £10

Orderlines

UK: 0870 586 2010 Fax: 01548 831074
US: 800-808-7682 Toll free fax: 800-572-8131
E-mail: bookorder@bestlovedhotels.com
or order on-line at www.bestlovedhotels.com

Order by post

Fill in your details and send this card to the **FREEPOST** address below:

Best Loved Hotels of the World
Clientbase Fulfilment Ltd
FREEPOST (SWB40527), IVYBRIDGE PL21 0ZZ (UK only)

Please send me Best Loved Hotels of the World 2001

Copies required ☐ @ ☐ each **£/$***
Add for post and packing per copy **£/$*** ....
TOTAL **£/$*** ....

* Please circle the currency you are using

Payment method

Charge/Credit Card ☐ Personal Cheque ☐*
*Cheques to be made out to "World Media Publishing Ltd"

Please charge my account

American Express ☐ Diners ☐ Mastercard ☐ Visa ☐

Expires end

☐ I enclose my order on company letterhead. Please invoice my company (UK only).

Name (Mr/Mrs/Ms) ____
Company ____
Address ____

Zip/Postcode ____ Country ____
Tel ____ Fax ____
E-mail ____

Signature ____

Please allow at least two weeks for delivery. BLD01/OF

ORDER CARD

AMERICAN EXPRESS

Best Loved Hotels of the World 2001 - PRICE LIST

	UK£	US$	EIRE£
UK & Ireland Directory	14.99	19.95	15.99
Amex cardholders price	**13.99**	**17.95**	**14.99**
Add for post and packing	*4.50*	*3.00*	*4.50*

Postage to Europe - £6; to any other country - £10

Orderlines

UK: 0870 586 2010 Fax: 01548 831074
US: 800-808-7682 Toll free fax: 800-572-8131
E-mail: bookorder@bestlovedhotels.com
or order on-line at www.bestlovedhotels.com

Order by post

Fill in your details and send this card to the **FREEPOST** address below:

Best Loved Hotels of the World
Clientbase Fulfilment Ltd
FREEPOST (SWB40527), IVYBRIDGE PL21 0ZZ (UK only)

Please send me Best Loved Hotels of the World 2001

Copies required ☐ @ ☐ each **£/$***
Add for post and packing per copy **£/$*** ....
TOTAL **£/$*** ....

* Please circle the currency you are using

Payment method

Charge/Credit Card ☐ Personal Cheque ☐*
*Cheques to be made out to "World Media Publishing Ltd"

Please charge my account

American Express ☐ Diners ☐ Mastercard ☐ Visa ☐

Expires end

☐ I enclose my order on company letterhead. Please invoice my company (UK only).

Name (Mr/Mrs/Ms) ____
Company ____
Address ____

Zip/Postcode ____ Country ____
Tel ____ Fax ____
E-mail ____

Signature ____

Please allow at least two weeks for delivery. BLD01/OF

BEST LOVED HOTELS 2001

Ordering copies of the Best Loved Hotels of the World is easy; you can telephone, fax, e-mail, order on-line or send us this card by **FREEPOST** (UK only; no stamp required) to the address below:

Best Loved Hotels of the World
Clientbase Fulfilment Ltd
FREEPOST (SWB40527),
IVYBRIDGE, PL21 0ZZ

For telephone or fax orders, call:

IN THE UK

Phone:	**0870 586 2010**
Fax:	**01548 831074**

IN THE US

Phone:	**800-808-7682**
Toll free fax:	**800-572-8131**

E-mail: **bookorder@bestlovedhotels.com**
or order on-line at www.bestlovedhotels.com

When ordering, quote your charge/credit card number and expiry date. Remember to allow for the cost of post and packing. Full details are on the previous page.

Use your American Express chargecard and save - see over

BEST LOVED HOTELS 2001

Ordering copies of the Best Loved Hotels of the World is easy; you can telephone, fax, e-mail, order on-line or send us this card by **FREEPOST** (UK only; no stamp required) to the address below:

Best Loved Hotels of the World
Clientbase Fulfilment Ltd
FREEPOST (SWB40527),
IVYBRIDGE, PL21 0ZZ

For telephone or fax orders, call:

IN THE UK

Phone:	**0870 586 2010**
Fax:	**01548 831074**

IN THE US

Phone:	**800-808-7682**
Toll free fax:	**800-572-8131**

E-mail: **bookorder@bestlovedhotels.com**
or order on-line at www.bestlovedhotels.com

When ordering, quote your charge/credit card number and expiry date. Remember to allow for the cost of post and packing. Full details are on the previous page.

Use your American Express chargecard and save - see over

BEST LOVED HOTELS 2001

Ordering copies of the Best Loved Hotels of the World is easy; you can telephone, fax, e-mail, order on-line or send us this card by **FREEPOST** (UK only; no stamp required) to the address below:

Best Loved Hotels of the World
Clientbase Fulfilment Ltd
FREEPOST (SWB40527),
IVYBRIDGE, PL21 0ZZ

For telephone or fax orders, call:

IN THE UK

Phone:	**0870 586 2010**
Fax:	**01548 831074**

IN THE US

Phone:	**800-808-7682**
Toll free fax:	**800-572-8131**

E-mail: **bookorder@bestlovedhotels.com**
or order on-line at www.bestlovedhotels.com

When ordering, quote your charge/credit card number and expiry date. Remember to allow for the cost of post and packing. Full details are on the previous page.

Use your American Express chargecard and save - see over

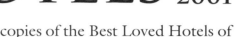

A-Z Index

A

ARDANAISEIG

B

COMBE GROVE MANOR HOTEL

C

D

E

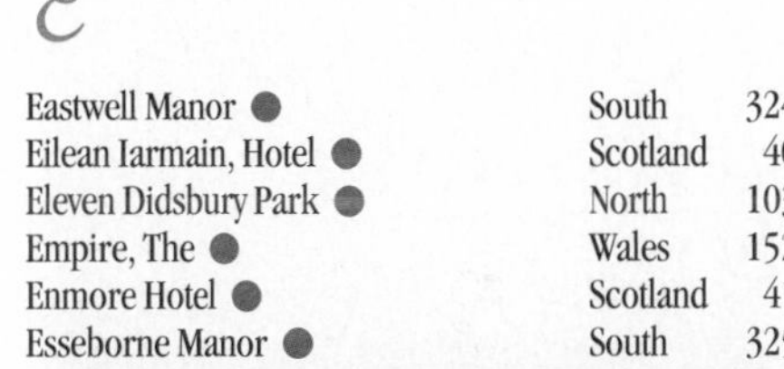

EMPIRE

F

● = Children Welcome. Please telephone hotels directly for any applicable restrictions

A-Z Index

G

GRAND HOTEL

H

I

J

K

KIRROUGHTREE HOUSE

L

M

MILESTONE HOTEL

N

● = Children Welcome. Please telephone hotels directly for any applicable restrictions

PENMAENUCHAF HALL

HOTEL RIVIERA

YORKE ARMS

● = Children Welcome. Please telephone hotels directly for any applicable restrictions

Bibliography

More Information

Listed below are various guides which have been helpful in our travels and in researching this book. All are available in good bookshops throughout the United Kingdom, Ireland and abroad.

Hotel Ratings

We have used the tourist board, RAC and AA ratings whenever any hotel featured in this book has merited them. In addition we have given acknowledgment to annual award recipients of the well-respected The Good Food Guide and Which? Hotel Guide. As indicators of quality and value, they speak for themselves but for more details, please refer to the appropriate tourist board listed in the introduction to every region in this book or the addresses on pages 490 and 491.

Which? Ltd

The Which? Hotel Guide 2000/2001
The Good Food Guide 2000/2001
Which? Ltd, 2 Marylebone Road,
London NW1 4DF

RAC Publications

RAC Hotel Guide Great Britain & Ireland
RAC Bartholomews Road Atlas
RAC Motoring Atlas of Great Britain & Ireland

United Kingdom:
West One Publishing
Portland House, 4 Great Portland St,
London W1N 5AA

AA Publications

AA Hotels in Britain and Ireland
Great Britain Road Atlas
Road Atlas of the British Isles
The Big Road Atlas of Britain
The Maxi Scale Atlas of Britain

United Kingdom:
Automobile Association Developments Limited,
Fanum House, Basingstoke, Hampshire RG21 4EA

United States:
Hunter Publishing Inc., 300 Raritan Center,
Parkway, Edison, NJ 08818

SCOTLAND (Map Page 494)

● *Double room: up to £95 per night* ● *Double room: £96 - £145 per night* ● *Double room: £146 - £195 per night* ● *Double room: £196+ per night*

Regional Index

WALES (Map Page 498)

MIDSHIRES (Map Page 500)

● *Double room: up to £95 per night* ● *Double room: £96 - £145 per night* ● *Double room: £146 - £195 per night* ● *Double room: £196+ per night*

Regional Index

THE WEST
(Map Page 502)

● *Double room: up to £95 per night* ● *Double room: £96 - £145 per night* ● *Double room: £146 - £195 per night* ● *Double room: £196+ per night*

Regional Index

THE SOUTH (Map Page 504)

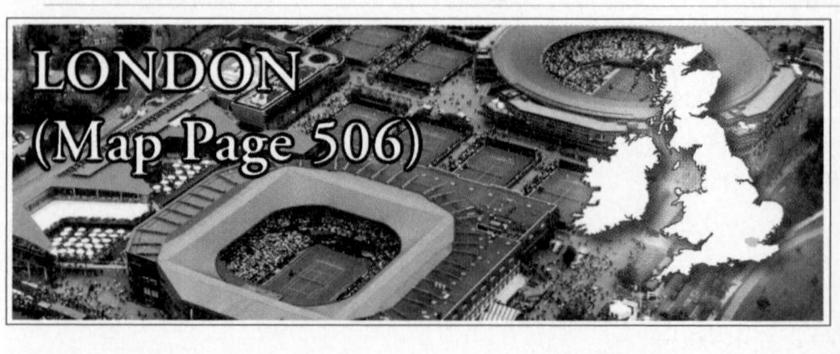

● *Double room: up to £95 per night* ● *Double room: £96 - £145 per night* ● *Double room: £146 - £195 per night* ● *Double room: £196+ per night*

County/ Hotel	Price range ●	●	●	●	Grid ref	Page
Beaufort, The				●	E6	377
Blakes Hotel				●	D7	378
Blooms Town House Hotel				●	H3	379
Burns Hotel, The		●			C7	380
Chesterfield Mayfair, The				●	G5	381
Colonnade Town House, The			●		A2	382
Cranley, The				●	C7	384
Darlington Hyde Park, The		●			D4	385
Dolphin Square Hotel			●		H8	386
Flemings Mayfair				●	G5	387
Goring Hotel, The				●	G6	388
Grosvenor House				●	F5	390
Halcyon, The				●	A5	391
Kensington House			●		C6	392
Knightsbridge Green Hotel		●			E6	393
London Outpost of the Carnegie Club, The				●	E7	394
Milestone Hotel & Apartments, The				●	C6	395
Millennium Bailey's				●	C7	396
Montague On The Gardens, The			●		I3	397
Montcalm Hotel, The				●	E4	398
Number 41				●	G6	399
Rubens At The Palace, The				●	G6	400
Sloane Hotel, The				●	E7	401
Twenty Nevern Square			●		B7	402

County/ Hotel	Price range ●	●	●	●	Grid ref	Page
BELFAST						
McCausland Hotel, The			●		G4	450
CO ANTRIM						
Bushmills Inn, The		●			G3	420
CO CLARE						
Dromoland Castle				●	C8	427
Gregans Castle			●		C7	434
Halpin's Hotel		●			B8	435
Waterman's Lodge		●			D8	468
Woodstock Hotel			●		C7	469
CO CORK						
Ahernes		●			E9	409
Bayview Hotel		●			D10	414
Blairs Cove House		●			B10	415
Blue Haven Hotel		●			D10	417
CastleHyde Hotel		●			D9	424
Hayfield Manor				●	D10	436
Longueville House			●		D9	446
Sea View House Hotel		●			C10	464
CO DONEGAL						
St John's Country House			●		F3	463
DUBLIN						
Aberdeen Lodge		●			G7	408
Blakes Townhouse		●			G7	416
Brooks Hotel			●		G7	418
Brownes Townhouse			●		G7	419
Butlers Town House		●			G7	421
Herbert Park Hotel				●	G7	437
Hibernian Hotel			●		G7	438
Longfield's		●			G7	445
Merrion Hall		●			G7	451
Merrion Hotel				●	G7	453
CO GALWAY						
Ballynahinch Castle Hotel		●			B6	412
Cashel House Hotel			●		B6	423
Glenlo Abbey Hotel			●		C6	431
Lough Inagh Lodge Hotel		●			C6	447
Rosleague Manor		●			B6	460
Ross Lake House Hotel		●			C6	461
St Clerans				●	D7	462
CO KERRY						
Ard na Sidhe		●			B9	410
Caragh Lodge		●			B9	422
Dunloe Castle			●		B9	430
Gormans Clifftop House & Restaurant	●				A9	433
Killarney Park				●	C9	442
Killarney Royal Hotel			●		B9	443
Muckross Park Hotel		●			B9	456
Park Hotel Kenmare				●	B9	458
Sheen Falls Lodge				●	B10	465
CO KILDARE						
Moyglare Manor			●		G7	455
CO KILKENNY						
Hibernian Hotel		●			F8	439
Mount Juliet				●	F8	454
CO LIMERICK						
Glin Castle			●		C8	432
Mustard Seed At Echo Lodge			●		C8	457
CO LOUTH						
Jordan's Townhouse		●			G5	441
CO MAYO						
Ashford Castle				●	C6	411
Knockranny House Hotel			●		C5	444
CO SLIGO						
Coopershill		●			D5	426
Markree Castle		●			D5	448
CO TIPPERARY						
Dundrum House Hotel		●			D8	429
CO WATERFORD						
Ballyrafter House Hotel	●				E9	413
Waterford Castle			●		F9	467
CO WEXFORD						
Churchtown House		●			G9	425
Dunbrody Country House			●		F9	428
Marlfield House			●		G8	449
CO WICKLOW						
Hunter's Hotel		●			G7	440
Rathsallagh House			●		F7	459
Tinakilly House			●		G7	466

● Double room: up to £95 per night   ● Double room: £96 - £145 per night   ● Double room: £146 - £195 per night   ● Double room: £196+ per night

Tourist Boards' overseas addresses

AUSTRALIA
Level 16, Gateway,
1 Macquarie Place,
Sydney NSW 2000
Tel 02 9377 4400
Fax 02 9377 4499

BELGIUM
Visit Britain Centre,
Avenue Louis 140,
Second Floor, 10 50 Brussels
Tel 02 626 25 80
Fax 02 646 27 26

BRAZIL
Rua da Assembleia 10, sala 3707,
Rio de Janeiro-RJ 20119-900
Tel 021 531 1717
Fax 021 531 0383

CANADA
5915 Airport Road, Suite 120,
Mississauga, Ontario L4V 1T1
Tel 905-405-1840
Fax 905-405-1835

DENMARK
Montergade 3,
1116 Copenhagen K
Tel 33 33 01 42
Fax 33 14 01 36

FRANCE
Maison de la Grande-Bretagne,
19 rue des Mathurins,
75009 Paris
Tel 01 44 51 56 22
Fax 01 44 51 56 38

GERMANY
Westendstr 16-22, 60325 Frankfurt
Tel 069 97 1123
Fax 069 97 112 444

GREAT BRITAIN
Thames Tower, Black's Road,
Hammersmith, London W6 9EL
Tel 020 8846 9000
Fax 020 8563 0302

HONG KONG
Room 1504, Eton Tower,
8 Hysan Avenue,
Causeway Bay, Hong Kong
Tel 2882 8724
Fax 577 1443

IRELAND
18-19 College Green, Dublin 2
Tel 01 670 8000
Fax 01 670 8244

ITALY
Via Nazionale 230,
00184 Rome
Tel 06 462 0221
Fax 02 7201 0086

JAPAN
Akasaka Twin Tower 1F,
2-17-22 Akasaka,
Minato-ku, Tokyo
Tel 03 5562 2550
Fax 03 5562 2551

NETHERLANDS
Aurora Gebouw (5e),
Stadhouderskade 2,
1054 ES Amsterdam
Tel 020 607 7705
Fax 020 618 6868

NEW ZEALAND
17th Fl, 151 Queen Street,
Auckland 1
Tel 09 303 1446
Fax 09 377 6965

NORWAY
Nedre Slottsgate 21,
4 Etasje, 0157 Oslo
Tel 022 39 68 39
Fax 022 42 48 74

SINGAPORE
01-01 Cecil Court,
138 Cecil Street,
Singapore 069 538
Tel 065 227 5400
Fax 065 227 5411

SOUTH AFRICA
Lancaster Gate,
Hyde Park Lane,
Hyde Park, 2196
Tel 011 325 0342
Fax 011 325 0344

SPAIN
Torre de Madrid 6/5,
Pza de Espana 18,
28008 Madrid
Tel 91 541 13 96
Fax 91 542 81 49

SWEDEN
Klara Norra Kyrkogata 29,
S 111 22 Stockholm
Tel 08 4401 700
Fax 08 21 31 29

SWITZERLAND
Limmatquai 78,
CH-8001 Zurich
Tel 01 261 42 77
Fax 01 251 44 56

USA - New York
7th Fl, 551 Fifth Avenue,
New York NY 10176 - 0799
Tel 212 986 2200
Fax 212 986 1188

Tourist Boards' overseas addresses

AUSTRALIA
Bord Fáilte
5th Level, 36 Carrington Street,
Sydney NSW 2000
Tel 02 9299 6177
Fax 02 9299 6323

BELGIUM
Irish Tourist Board
Avenue de Beaulieulaan 25,
1160 Brussels
Tel 02 673 99 40
Fax 02 672 1066

DENMARK
Det Irske Turistkontor
Klostergaarden, Amagertorv 29B,
3DK 1160 Copenhagen K
Tel 33 15 80 45
Fax 33 93 63 90

FINLAND
Irlannin Matkailutoimisto
Embassy of Ireland
Erottajankatu 7A,
PL33 00130 Helsinki
Tel 09 608 966
Fax 09 646 022

FRANCE
Office National du Tourisme Irlandais
33 Rue de Miromesnil,
75008 Paris
Tel 01 53 43 12 12
Fax 01 47 42 01 64

GERMANY
Irische Fremdenverkehrszentrale
Untermainanlage 7,
D 60329, Frankfurt/Main
Tel 069 92 31 85 50
Fax 069 92 31 85 88

GREAT BRITAIN
Bord Fáilte
150 New Bond Street,
London W1Y 0AQ
Tel 020 7493 3201
Fax 020 7493 9065

IRELAND
Bord Fáilte
Baggot Street Bridge, Dublin 2
Tel 01 602 4000
Fax 01 602 4100

ITALY
Ente Nazionale del Turismo Irlandese
Via S. Maria Segreta,
6, 20123 Milano
Tel 02 869 05 43
Fax 02 869 03 96

JAPAN
Irish Tourist Board
Ireland House 4F, 2-10-7
Kojimachi, Chiyodi-ku,
Tokyo 102-0083
Tel 03 52751611
Fax 03 52751623

NETHERLANDS
Iers National Bureau voor Toerisme
Spuistraat 104, 1012 VA,
Amsterdam
Tel 020 622 31 01
Fax 020 620 80 89

NEW ZEALAND
Walsches World, Sixth Floor,
18 Shortland Street,
Auckland 92136
Tel 09 379 8720
Fax 09 302 2420

NORWAY
Irlands Turistkontor
Drammensveien 126A,
PO Box 295 Skoyen, 0212 Oslo
Tel 022 56 33 10
Fax 022 12 20 71

SOUTH AFRICA
Irish Tourist Board
7th Flr, Everite House,
20 de Korte St, Braamfontein 2001,
Johannesburg
Tel 011 3394865
Fax 011 3392474

SWEDEN
Irlandska Turistbyran
P O Box 5292, Sibyllegatan 49,
10246 Stockholm
Tel 08 662 85 10
Fax 08 661 75 95

USA
Irish Tourist Board
345 Park Avenue,
New York, NY 10154
Tel 212 418 0800
Fax 212 371 9059

Finding your way about

This book has been designed to make finding your hotel easy whether you know what you are looking for or just want some inspiration. On these two pages, we explain how the cross referencing system works. Once you understand the system, the rest is easy.

Method One - Browsing.

You are simply thumbing through this book and you spot a picture that attracts you; you read about it, check the yellow fact column which tells you about the facilities of the hotel and some of the attractions nearby. You like what you see, but where is it?

The little thumbnail sketch at the top of the page has a locating red dot(●). You will see this on the miniature page below this paragraph and, in full size, on the right. The red dot tells you it is somewhere in the West Country.

Next to this little map is a Map Reference which tells you roughly where to find the hotel on the map. Our example, asks you to turn to page 502 and the grid reference D3.

If you turn to page 502 you will see the map has a grid on it. To save time, we have a detail from the same page opposite. Now, if you look at square "D" and "3" (both are circled in black), you will see two hotels, one is denoted with a pale blue rosette and one is red so your search has been narrowed down from 403 hotels to just two. Look for 291, the page number for Northcote Manor. We have circled the one you are looking for in white.

Now you have found it on the map, go back to page 291 and, at the bottom you will see a pale green box which provides detailed instructions on how to find your hotel by car.

291

• *Map p.502*
ref: D3

Northcote Manor

Burrington,
Near Umberleigh, Barnstaple,
Devon EX37 9LZ

Telephone 01769 560501
Fax 01769 560770

Best Loved Hotels of the World

"Perfect service, perfect food, perfect setting: what more could we want? - Just more time to enjoy it"

17th century manor

NORTHCOTE MANOR

Possibly the most exciting hotel in North Devon

LOCATION

LOCATION

From South Molton town centre, fork left on B3226 to A377, and right to Barnstaple. Do not enter Burrington village. Hotel is situated 100 yards past Portsmouth Arms railway station.

Method two - You know the name of the hotel, where is it?

Let's say a friend has recommended Northcote Manor in the West Country but you do not know where it is; first turn to the "A to Z" index this will give you the page number. Go to that page (the example will lead you to page 291) and you can then carry on from there as described above.

Method three - You want some ideas.

You could go straight to the map pages which start with Scotland on page 494. You are looking for ideas in the West. You will find the map on pages 502/503 but look at the detail of it on the opposite page. Having looked at the map, you get the idea that being halfway between Dartmoor and Devon's north coast looks interesting. It looks as if you have a choice of six hotels. This is when the colour coded rosettes start to play a role: The key (opposite) shows you the options to suit your pocket; the numbers refer to the page on which you will find full details of the hotels. Turn to each of the pages and choose the one that suits you best.

Finding Your Way About

The grid lines, north to south and east to west, are spaced 30 miles apart so you get a perspective of distances.

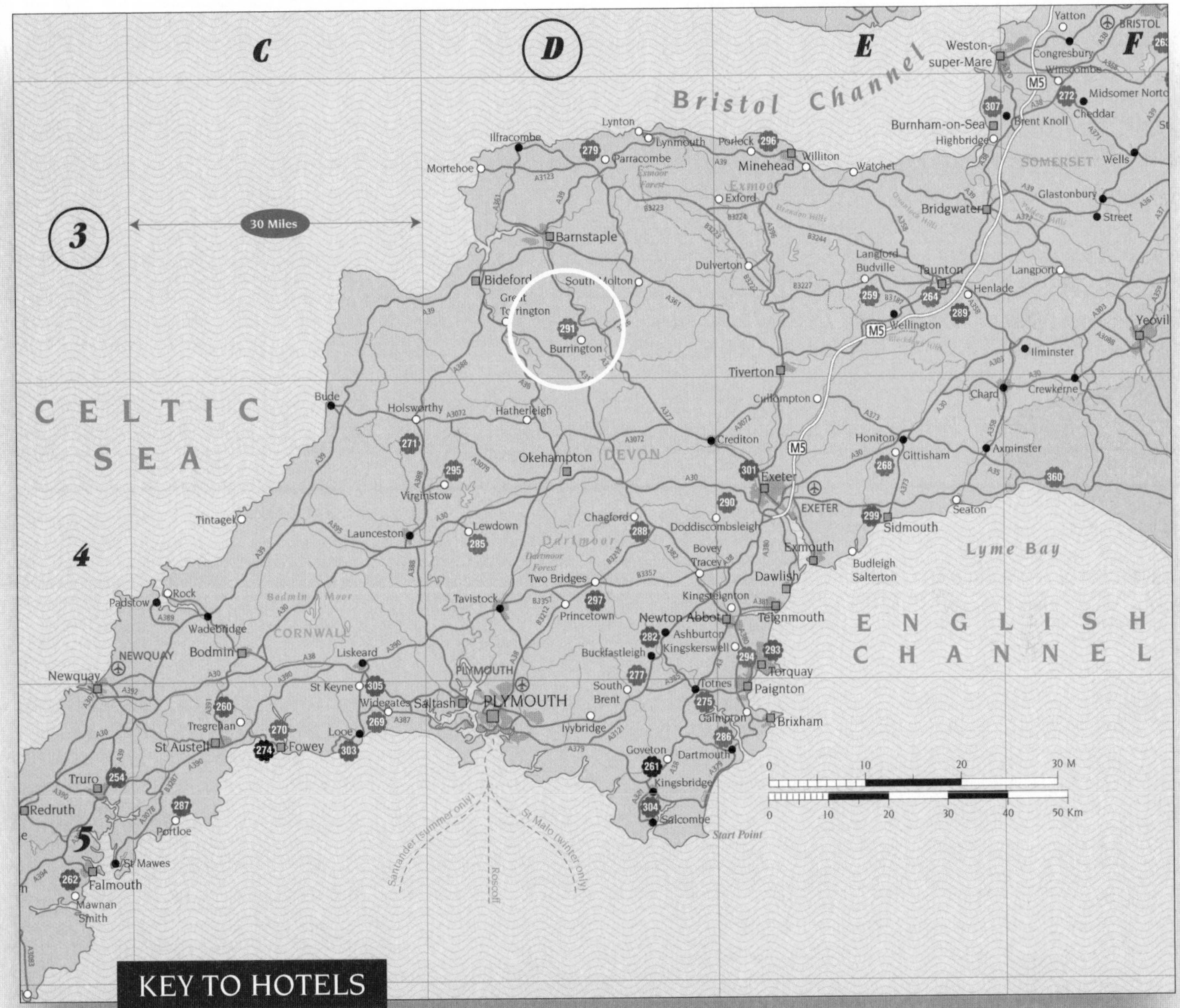

A detail from the map on page 502

KEY TO HOTELS

The rosettes indicate the page number of the hotel. The colour of the rosette is a rough guide to the price of a twin or double room (see colour key below).

- *Double room: up to £95 per night*
- *Double room: £96 - £145 per night*
- *Double room: £146 - £195 per night*
- *Double room: £196+ per night*

The coloured rosettes on the map show the location of the hotel. The colour is an indication of the cost of two people in a double room. The key (shown left) appears on every map page.

Taking our example of Northcote Manor, (circled in white above) the rosette is RED so expect an overnight stay to cost between £146 and £195. You can check this by turning to page 291 (the number in the centre of the rosette) and looking in the yellow fact column under "Room Rates".

Easy as that!

SCOTLAND

KEY TO HOTELS

The rosettes indicate the page number of the hotel. The colour of the rosette is a rough guide to the price of a twin or double room (see colour key below).

- *Double room: up to £95 per night*
- *Double room: £96 - £145 per night*
- *Double room: £146 - £195 per night*
- *Double room: £196+ per night*

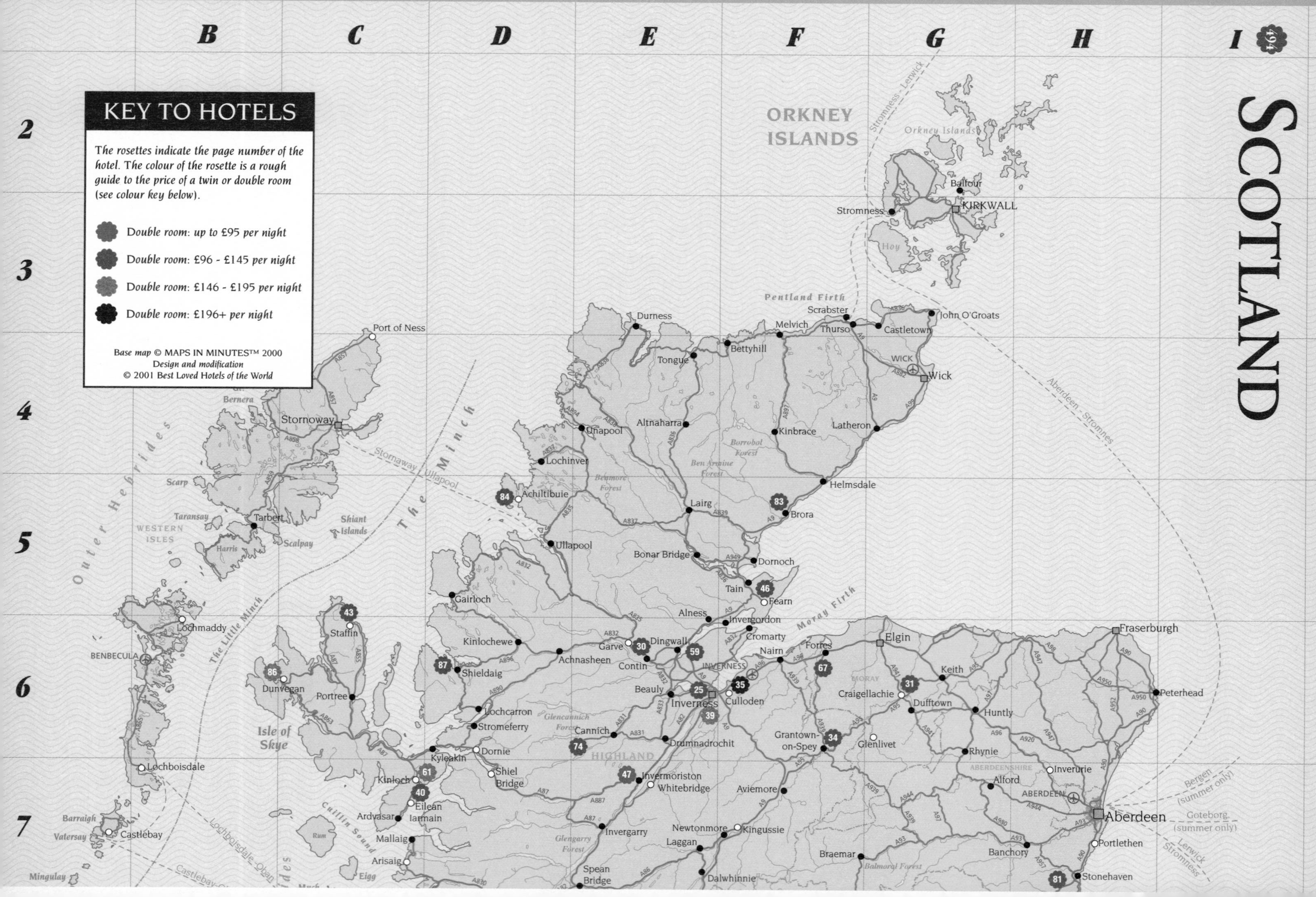

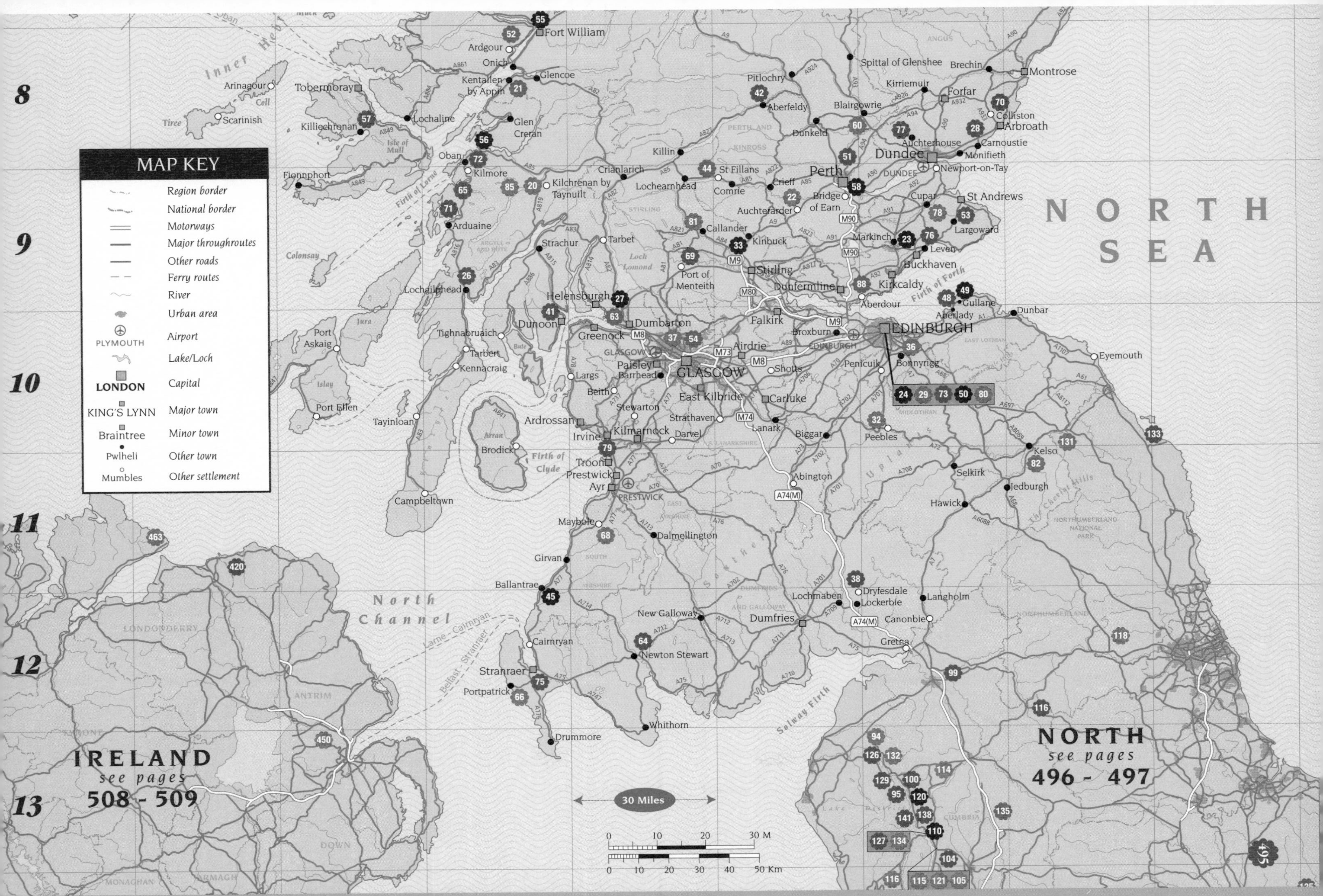

MAP KEY

	Region border
	National border
	Motorways
	Major throughroutes
	Other roads
	Ferry routes
	River
	Urban area
PLYMOUTH	Airport
	Lake/Loch
LONDON	Capital
KING'S LYNN	Major town
Braintree	Minor town
Pwlheli	Other town
Mumbles	Other settlement

NORTH SEA

North Channel

NORTH
see pages
496 - 497

IRELAND
see pages
508 - 509

30 Miles

0 10 20 30 M

0 10 20 30 40 50 Km

NORTH

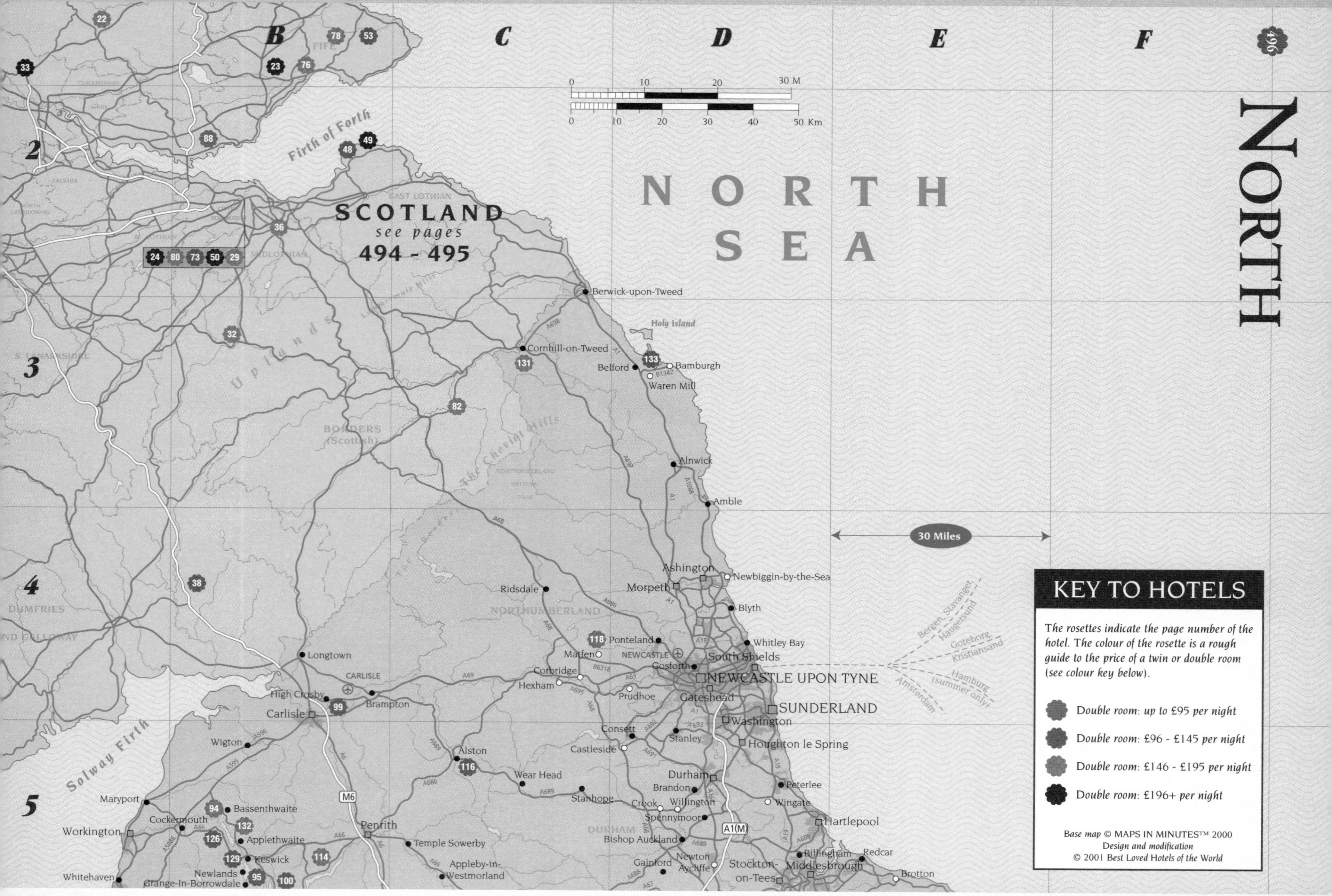

KEY TO HOTELS

The rosettes indicate the page number of the hotel. The colour of the rosette is a rough guide to the price of a twin or double room (see colour key below).

- Double room: *up to £95 per night*
- Double room: *£96 - £145 per night*
- Double room: *£146 - £195 per night*
- Double room: *£196+ per night*

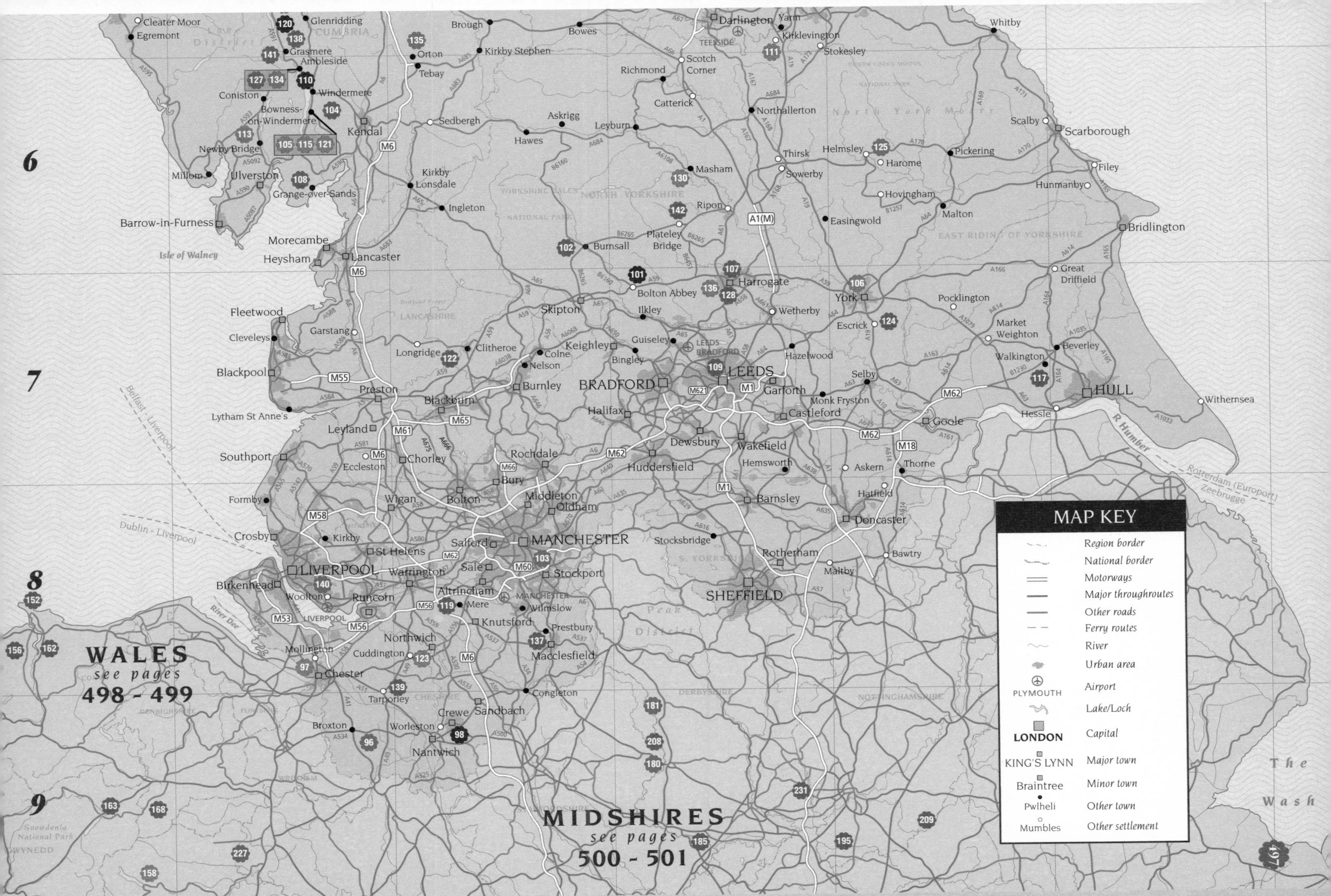

6

7

8

9

MAP KEY

	Region border
	National border
	Motorways
	Major throughroutes
	Other roads
	Ferry routes
	River
	Urban area
PLYMOUTH	Airport
	Lake/Loch
LONDON	Capital
KING'S LYNN	Major town
Braintree	Minor town
Pwllheli	Other town
Mumbles	Other settlement

WALES
see pages
498 - 499

MIDSHIRES
see pages
500 - 501

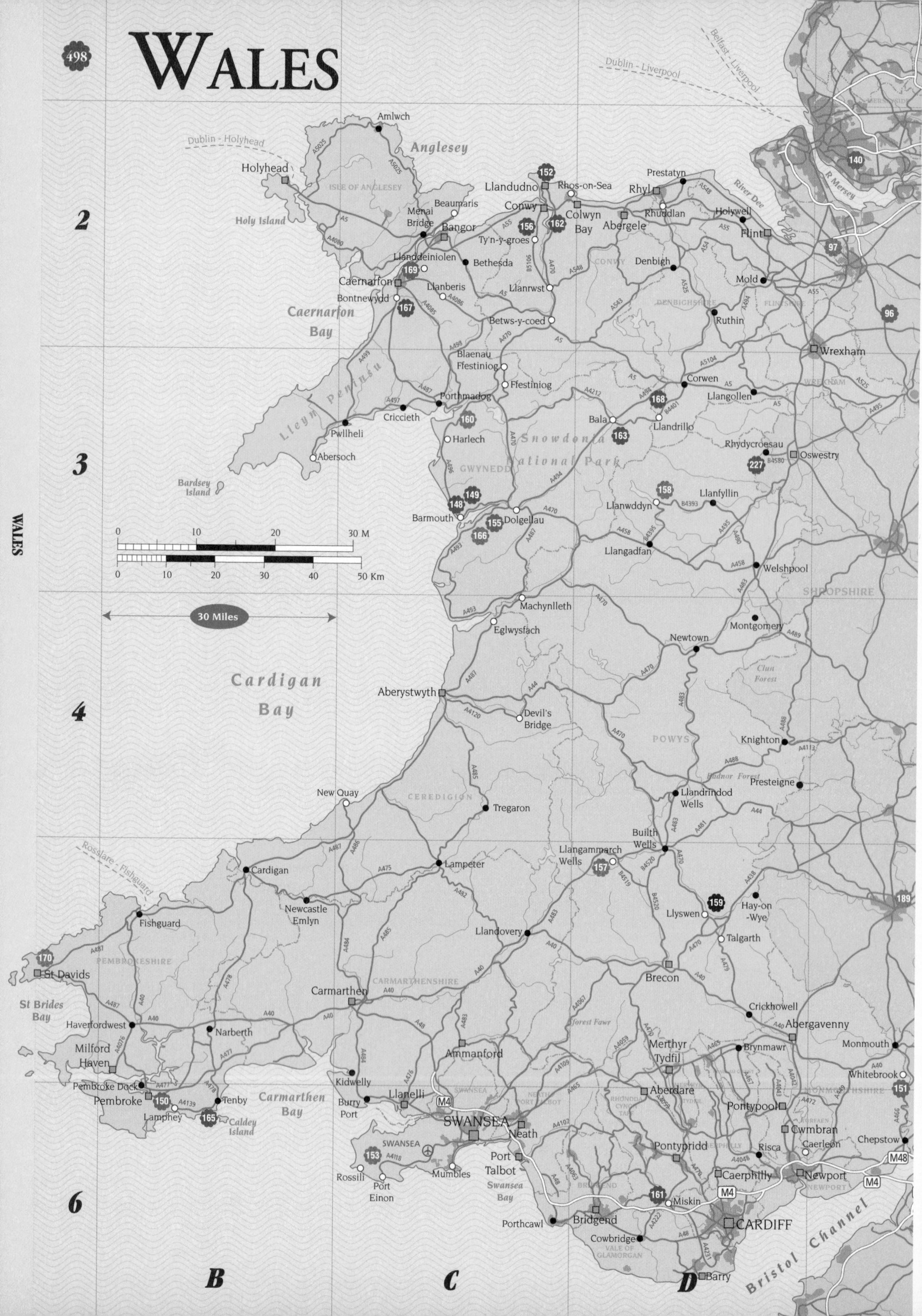

498
WALES
WALES
Dublin - Liverpool
Belfast - Liverpool
Dublin - Holyhead
Rosslare - Fishguard
Amlwch
Anglesey
Isle of Anglesey
Holyhead
Holy Island
Menai Bridge
Beaumaris
Bangor
Llanddeiniolen
Bethesda
Caernarfon
Bontnewydd
Llanberis
Caernarfon Bay
Llandudno
Rhos-on-Sea
Conwy
Colwyn Bay
Ty'n-y-groes
Llanrwst
Betws-y-coed
Abergele
Rhyl
Prestatyn
Rhuddlan
River Dee
Holywell
Flint
R Mersey
Denbigh
Conwy
Denbighshire
Flintshire
Mold
Ruthin
Wrexham
Blaenau Ffestiniog
Ffestiniog
Lleyn Peninsula
Porthmadog
Criccieth
Pwllheli
Abersoch
Bardsey Island
Harlech
Gwynedd
Snowdonia National Park
Corwen
Llangollen
Bala
Llandrillo
Rhydycroesau
Oswestry
Barmouth
Dolgellau
Llanwddyn
Llanfyllin
Llangadfan
Welshpool
Shropshire
Machynlleth
Eglwysfach
Newtown
Montgomery
Clun Forest
Cardigan Bay
Aberystwyth
Devil's Bridge
Powys
Knighton
Radnor Forest
Presteigne
New Quay
Ceredigion
Tregaron
Llandrindod Wells
Builth Wells
Llangammarch Wells
Cardigan
Lampeter
Newcastle Emlyn
Fishguard
Llyswen
Hay-on-Wye
Talgarth
Llandovery
Brecon
St Davids
Pembrokeshire
Carmarthenshire
Carmarthen
St Brides Bay
Haverfordwest
Narberth
Forest Fawr
Crickhowell
Abergavenny
Monmouth
Milford Haven
Ammanford
Merthyr Tydfil
Brynmawr
Whitebrook
Monmouthshire
Pembroke Dock
Pembroke
Lamphey
Tenby
Caldey Island
Carmarthen Bay
Kidwelly
Burry Port
Llanelli
Aberdare
Pontypool
Cwmbran
Caerleon
Chepstow
Swansea
Neath
Neath Port Talbot
Rhondda Cynon Taff
Torfaen
Rossili
Port Einon
Mumbles
Port Talbot
Swansea Bay
Pontypridd
Risca
Caerphilly
Newport
Porthcawl
Bridgend
Miskin
Cardiff
Cowbridge
Vale of Glamorgan
Barry
Bristol Channel
M4
M48
A5
A55
A470
A483
A487
A40
A44
A458
A494
A5104
2
3
4
6
B
C
D
0 10 20 30 M
0 10 20 30 40 50 Km
30 Miles
140 97 96 152 156 162 169 167 160 168 163 227 158 149 148 155 166 157 159 189 170 150 165 153 161 151

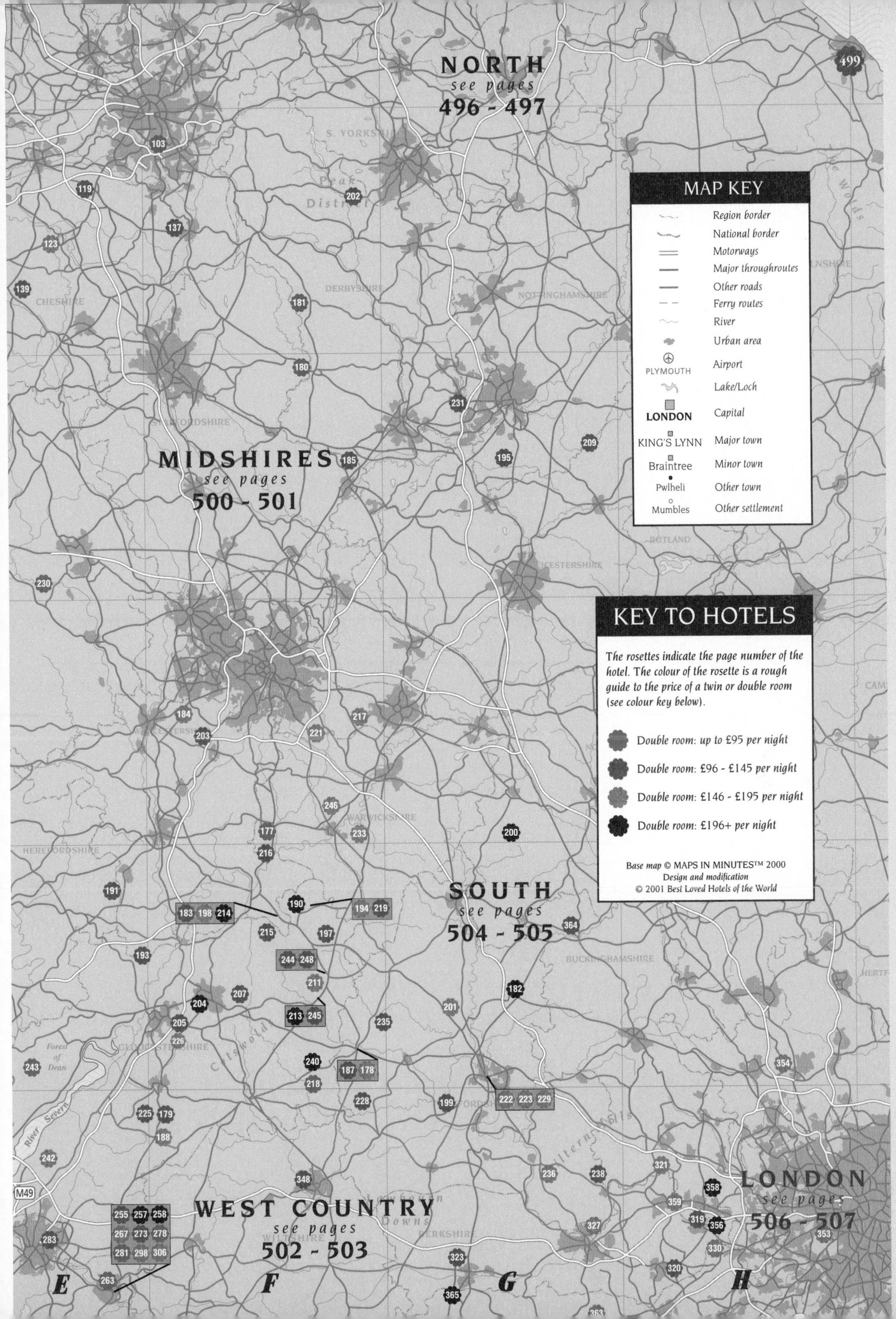

NORTH
see pages
496 - 497

MIDSHIRES
see pages
500 - 501

SOUTH
see pages
504 - 505

WEST COUNTRY
see pages
502 - 503

LONDON
see pages
506 - 507

MAP KEY

	Region border
	National border
	Motorways
	Major throughroutes
	Other roads
	Ferry routes
	River
	Urban area
PLYMOUTH	Airport
	Lake/Loch
LONDON	Capital
KING'S LYNN	Major town
Braintree	Minor town
Pwlheli	Other town
Mumbles	Other settlement

KEY TO HOTELS

The rosettes indicate the page number of the hotel. The colour of the rosette is a rough guide to the price of a twin or double room (see colour key below).

- *Double room: up to £95 per night*
- *Double room: £96 - £145 per night*
- *Double room: £146 - £195 per night*
- *Double room: £196+ per night*

S. YORKSHIRE
Peak District
DERBYSHIRE
NOTTINGHAMSHIRE
CHESHIRE
STAFFORDSHIRE
RUTLAND
LEICESTERSHIRE
WORCESTERSHIRE
WARWICKSHIRE
HEREFORDSHIRE
GLOUCESTERSHIRE
Cotswolds
Forest of Dean
River Severn
BUCKINGHAMSHIRE
WILTSHIRE
BERKSHIRE
Chiltern Hills
Lambourn Downs
M49

499 103 119 202 137 123 139 181 180 231 209 185 195 230 184 203 217 221 246 233 177 200 216 191 183 198 214 190 194 219 215 197 364 193 244 248 211 182 207 204 201 213 245 205 235 226 243 240 187 178 354 218 228 199 222 223 229 225 179 188 242 236 238 321 348 358 359 319 356 327 255 257 258 267 273 278 281 298 306 283 353 330 323 320 263 365 363

E F G H

MIDSHIRES

NORTH
see pages
496 - 497

WALES
see pages
498 - 499

WEST
COUNTRY
see pages
502 - 503

LANCASHIRE
GREATER MANCHESTER
MERSEYSIDE
S. YORKSHIRE
DERBYSHIRE
CHESHIRE
DENBIGHSHIRE
FLINTSHIRE
CONWY
WREXHAM
STAFFORDSHIRE
NOTTINGHAMSHIRE
LEICESTERSHIRE
SHROPSHIRE
POWYS
HEREFORDSHIRE
WARWICKSHIRE
NORTHAMPTONSHIRE
MONMOUTHSHIRE
OXFORDSHIRE
BERKSHIRE
WILTSHIRE
HAMPSHIRE
VALE OF GLAMORGAN
CAERPHILLY

Woodhead
Glossop
New Mills
Whaley Bridge
Hathersage
Buxton
Bakewell
Chesterfield
Clay Cross
Matlock
Sutton in Ashfield
Mansfield
Bawtry
Worksop
Retford
Biddulph
Leek
Kidsgrove
STOKE-ON-TRENT
Newcastle-under-Lyme
Dovedale
Ashbourne
Duffield
Ripley
NOTTINGHAM
Bingham
Langar
Whitchurch
Ellesmere
Oswestry
Market Drayton
Stone
Uttoxeter
DERBY
Risley
Long Eaton
Ruddington
EAST MIDLANDS
Eccleshall
Stafford
Burton upon Trent
Melton Mowbray
Newport
Rugeley
Ashby-de-la-Zouch
Loughborough
Coalville
Shrewsbury
Cannock
Lichfield
Telford
Tamworth
Much Wenlock
WOLVERHAMPTON
Sutton Coldfield
LEICESTER
Bridgnorth
Worfield
West Bromwich
Nuneaton
Hinckley
Dudley
BIRMINGHAM
Market Harborough
Clun Forest
Stourbridge
Halesowen
Solihull
Berkswell
COVENTRY
Binley
Rugby
Ludlow
Kidderminster
Kings Norton
Stourport-on-Severn
Bromsgrove
Hockley Heath
Redditch
Droitwich
Warwick
Leamington Spa
Daventry
Northampton
Presteigne
Studley
Kington
Leominster
Alcester
Bromyard
Worcester
Stratford upon Avon
Fawsley
Pershore
Alderminster
Great Malvern
Colwall
Chipping Campden
Evesham
Banbury
Hereford
Ledbury
Broadway
Broad Campden
Moreton-in-Marsh
Tewkesbury
Stow-on-the-Wold
Corse Lawn
Kingham
Cheltenham
Upper Slaughter
Bledington
Ross-on-Wye
Lower Slaughter
Withington
Chesterton
Bicester
Gloucester
Shurdington
Shipton-under-Wychwood
Woodstock
Kidlington
Coleford
Forest of Dean
Painswick
Burford
Witney
Lydney
Stroud
Cirencester
Bibury
Coln St-Aldwyns
OXFORD
Thame
Clanfield
Uley
Rodborough
Ewen
Kingston Bagpuize
Abingdon
River Severn
Tetbury
Didcot
Thornbury
Wallingford
Chipping Sodbury
North Stoke
Stonor
Hinton

M180
A1(M)
M1
M6
M54
M42
M5
M40
M45
M69
M50
M49
M4

122 109 103 140 119 137 162 97 123 139 96 98 181 202 180 163 168 231 209 227 158 185 195 230 184 203 221 217 246 177 233 216 200 157 191 189 190 159 183 198 214 215 197 194 219 193 364 207 232 244 248 211 204 208 235 201 182 205 213 245 226 240 218 187 178 243 151 228 199 222 223 229 225 179 188 247 242 236 238 161 255 257 258 267 273 278 281 298 306 283 327 284 263 365 323 325 363

B
C
D
E

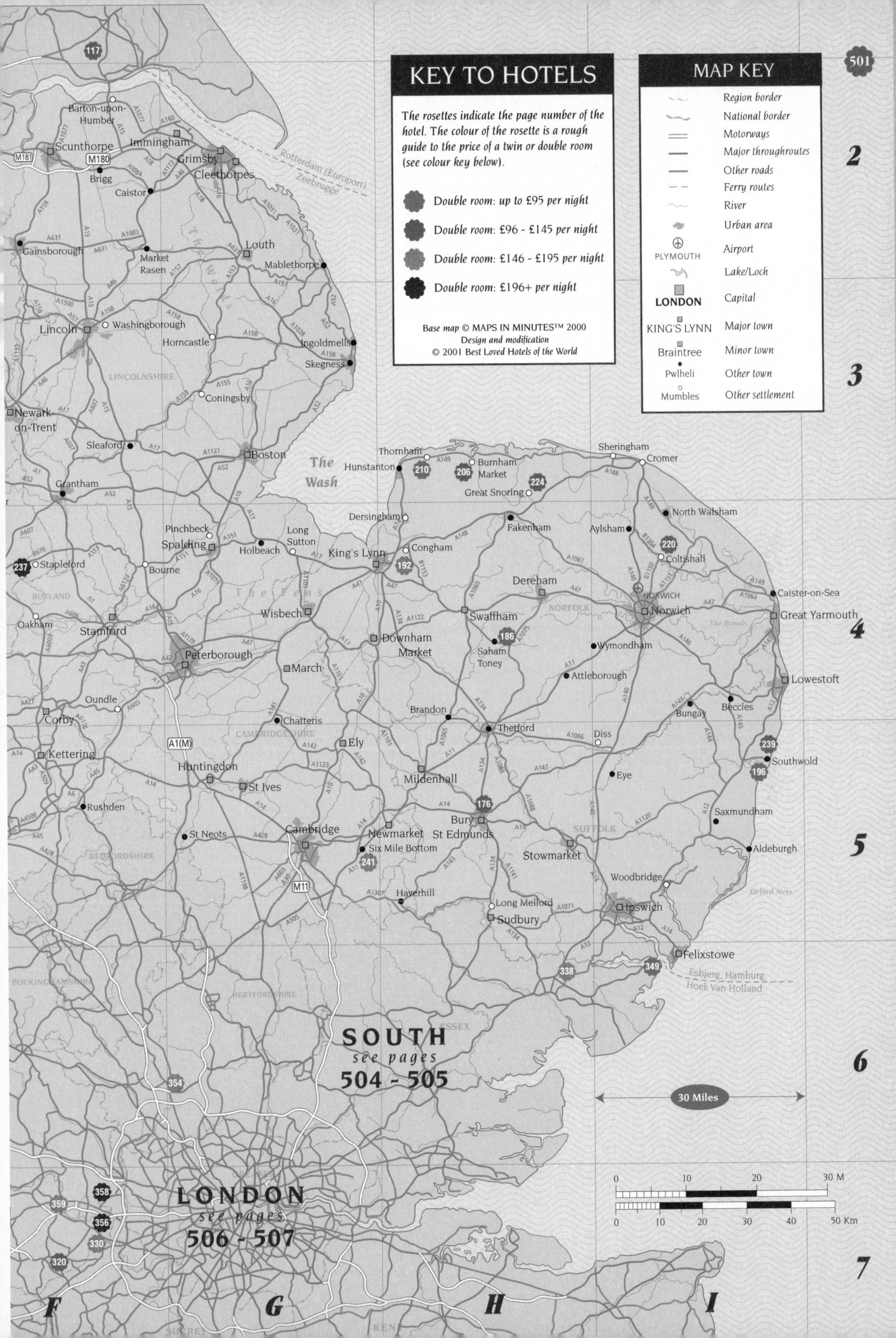
KEY TO HOTELS
The rosettes indicate the page number of the hotel. The colour of the rosette is a rough guide to the price of a twin or double room (see colour key below).
Double room: up to £95 per night
Double room: £96 - £145 per night
Double room: £146 - £195 per night
Double room: £196+ per night
Base map © MAPS IN MINUTES™ 2000
Design and modification
© 2001 Best Loved Hotels of the World
MAP KEY
Region border
National border
Motorways
Major throughroutes
Other roads
Ferry routes
River
Urban area
PLYMOUTH
Airport
Lake/Loch
LONDON
Capital
KING'S LYNN
Major town
Braintree
Minor town
Pwllheli
Other town
Mumbles
Other settlement
2
3
4
5
6
7
F
G
H
I
117
Barton-upon-Humber
Scunthorpe
Immingham
Grimsby
Cleethorpes
Brigg
Caistor
Rotterdam (Europort)
Zeebrugge
Gainsborough
Market Rasen
Louth
Mablethorpe
The Wolds
Lincoln
Washingborough
Horncastle
Ingoldmells
Skegness
LINCOLNSHIRE
Coningsby
Newark-on-Trent
Sleaford
Boston
The Wash
Grantham
Thornham
Hunstanton
210
206
Burnham Market
224
Great Snoring
Sheringham
Cromer
North Walsham
Dersingham
Fakenham
Aylsham
220
Coltishall
Pinchbeck
Spalding
Holbeach
Long Sutton
King's Lynn
Congham
192
237
Stapleford
Bourne
RUTLAND
The Fens
Dereham
NORWICH
Norwich
Caister-on-Sea
Great Yarmouth
The Broads
NORFOLK
Oakham
Stamford
Wisbech
Swaffham
Downham Market
186
Saham Toney
Wymondham
Peterborough
March
Attleborough
Lowestoft
Oundle
Corby
Chatteris
Brandon
Thetford
Bungay
Beccles
CAMBRIDGESHIRE
Ely
Diss
Kettering
A1(M)
239
Southwold
196
Huntingdon
St Ives
Mildenhall
Eye
Rushden
176
Bury St Edmunds
Saxmundham
St Neots
Cambridge
Newmarket
Six Mile Bottom
241
SUFFOLK
Stowmarket
Aldeburgh
BEDFORDSHIRE
M11
Haverhill
Long Melford
Sudbury
Woodbridge
Orford Ness
Ipswich
Felixstowe
338
349
Esbjerg, Hamburg
Hoek Van Holland
BUCKINGHAMSHIRE
HERTFORDSHIRE
ESSEX
SOUTH
see pages
504 - 505
354
30 Miles
358
359
356
330
320
LONDON
see pages
506 - 507
0 10 20 30 M
0 10 20 30 40 50 Km
KENT
SURREY

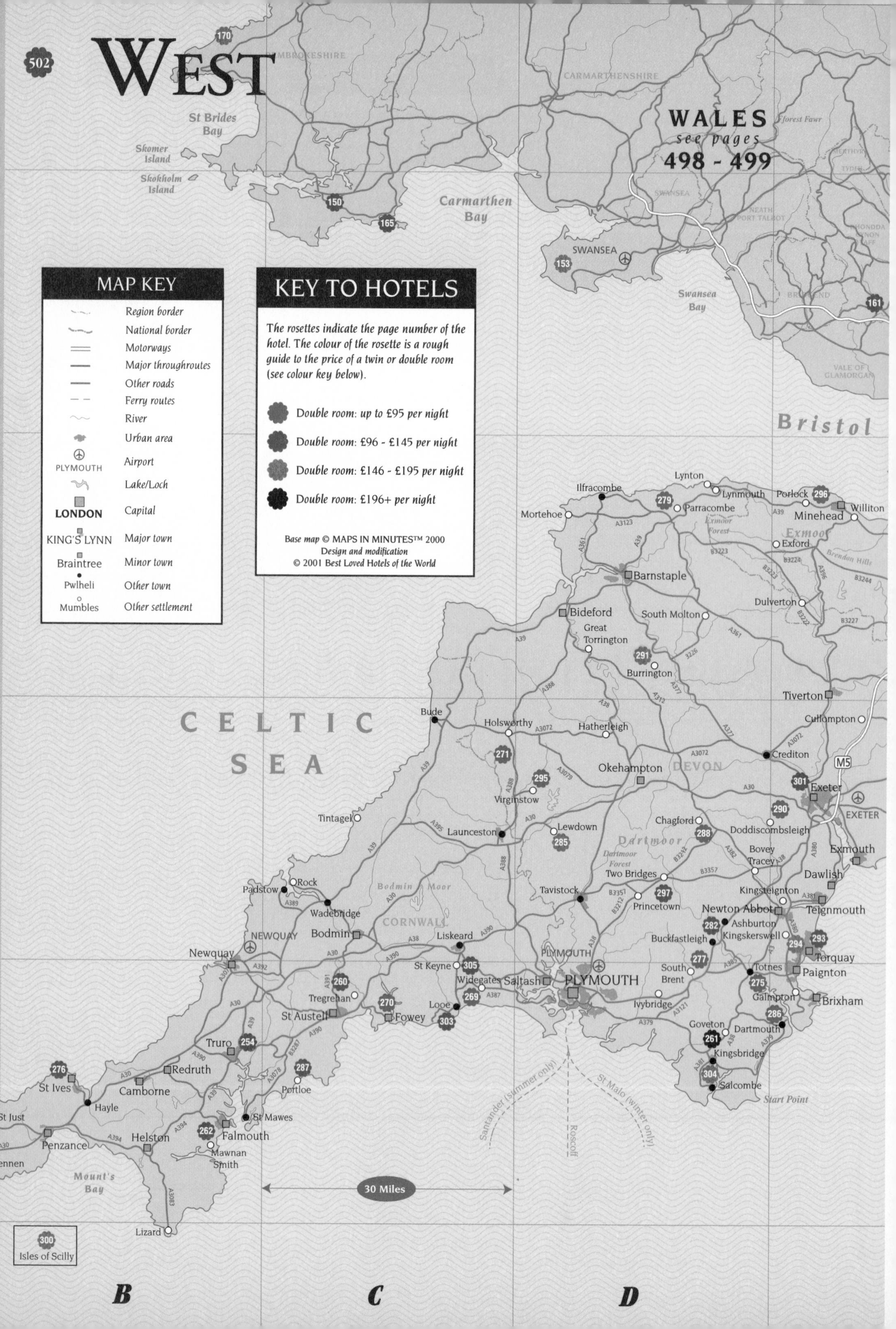

WEST

MAP KEY

	Region border
	National border
	Motorways
	Major throughroutes
	Other roads
	Ferry routes
	River
	Urban area
PLYMOUTH	Airport
	Lake/Loch
LONDON	Capital
KING'S LYNN	Major town
Braintree	Minor town
Pwlheli	Other town
Mumbles	Other settlement

KEY TO HOTELS

The rosettes indicate the page number of the hotel. The colour of the rosette is a rough guide to the price of a twin or double room (see colour key below).

- *Double room: up to £95 per night*
- *Double room: £96 - £145 per night*
- *Double room: £146 - £195 per night*
- *Double room: £196+ per night*

WALES
see pages
498 - 499

PEMBROKESHIRE
CARMARTHENSHIRE
St Brides Bay
Skomer Island
Skokholm Island
Carmarthen Bay
SWANSEA
Swansea Bay
NEATH PORT TALBOT
BRIDGEND
VALE OF GLAMORGAN
Forest Fawr
MERTHYR
Bristol
CELTIC SEA
Lynton
Lynmouth
Ilfracombe
Mortehoe
Parracombe
Porlock
Minehead
Williton
Exmoor
Exford
Barnstaple
Bideford
Great Torrington
South Molton
Dulverton
Burrington
Tiverton
Cullompton
Bude
Holsworthy
Hatherleigh
Crediton
Okehampton
DEVON
Exeter
EXETER
Virginstow
Tintagel
Launceston
Lewdown
Chagford
Doddiscombsleigh
Dartmoor
Bovey Tracey
Exmouth
Dawlish
Two Bridges
Padstow
Rock
Wadebridge
Bodmin Moor
Tavistock
Princetown
Kingsteignton
Teignmouth
Newton Abbot
Ashburton
Kingskerswell
Buckfastleigh
Torquay
Paignton
Totnes
NEWQUAY
Newquay
Bodmin
CORNWALL
Liskeard
St Keyne
Widegates
Saltash
PLYMOUTH
South Brent
Ivybridge
Galmpton
Brixham
Tregrehan
Fowey
Looe
St Austell
Dartmouth
Goveton
Kingsbridge
Salcombe
Start Point
Truro
Redruth
Camborne
Portloe
St Ives
Hayle
St Mawes
St Just
Penzance
Helston
Falmouth
Mawnan Smith
Sennen
Mount's Bay
Lizard
Santander (summer only)
Roscoff
St Malo (winter only)
30 Miles
Isles of Scilly

170 150 165 153 161 279 296 291 271 295 301 290 285 288 297 282 293 294 277 305 269 260 270 303 275 286 261 304 254 287 276 262 300

B C D

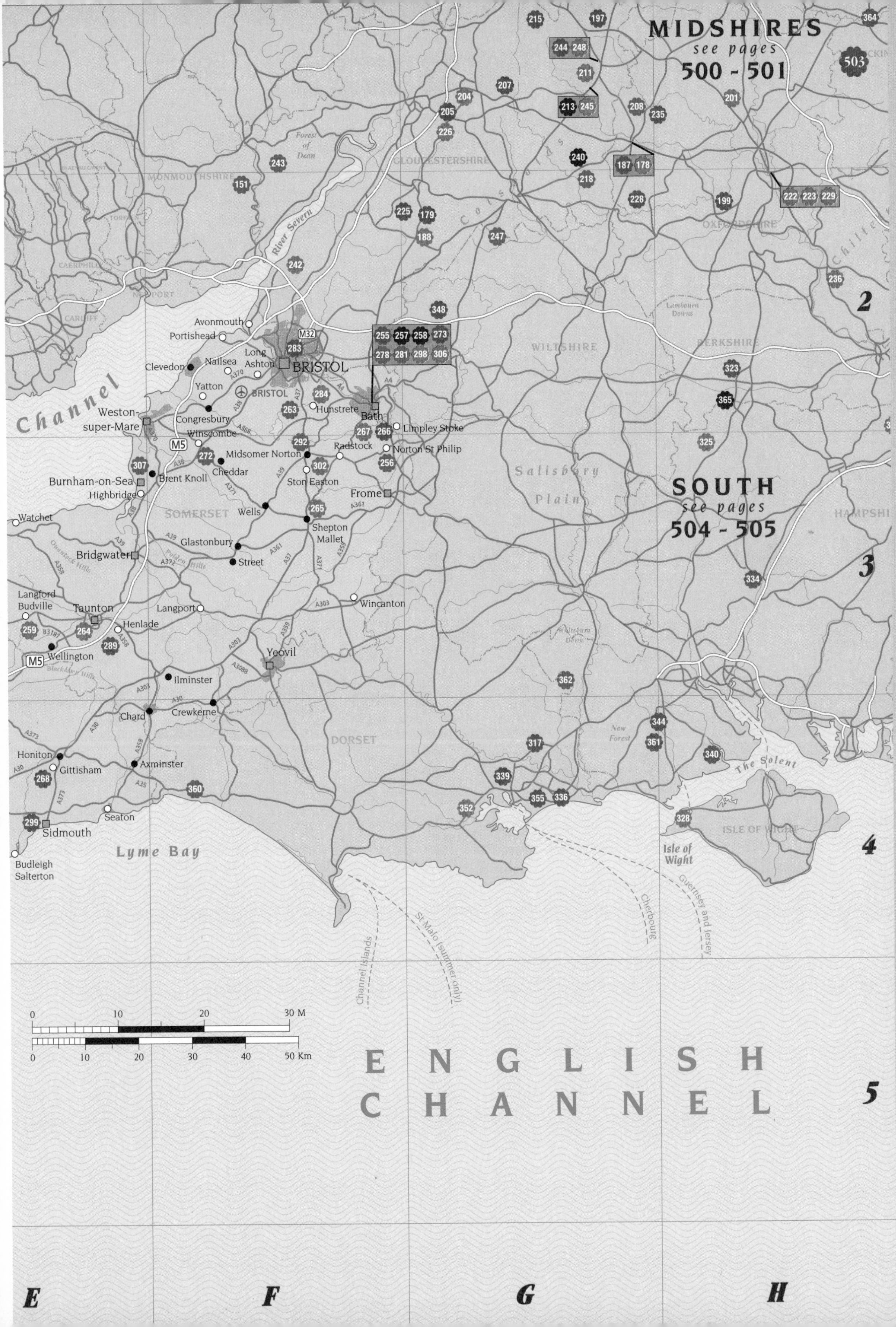
MIDSHIRES
see pages
500 - 501
SOUTH
see pages
504 - 505
ENGLISH CHANNEL
Channel
Lyme Bay
The Solent
Isle of Wight
ISLE OF WIGHT
MONMOUTHSHIRE
GLOUCESTERSHIRE
OXFORDSHIRE
WILTSHIRE
BERKSHIRE
HAMPSHIRE
SOMERSET
DORSET
Forest of Dean
River Severn
Cotswolds
Salisbury Plain
Lambourn Downs
New Forest
Quantock Hills
Polden Hills
Blackdown Hills
CAERPHILLY
NEWPORT
CARDIFF
TORFAEN
Avonmouth
Portishead
Clevedon
Nailsea
Long Ashton
BRISTOL
Yatton
Congresbury
Weston-super-Mare
Winscombe
Hunstrete
Bath
Limpley Stoke
Radstock
Norton St Philip
Midsomer Norton
Cheddar
Brent Knoll
Burnham-on-Sea
Highbridge
Ston Easton
Frome
Watchet
Wells
Shepton Mallet
Glastonbury
Street
Bridgwater
Langford Budville
Taunton
Langport
Wincanton
Henlade
Wellington
Yeovil
Ilminster
Chard
Crewkerne
Honiton
Gittisham
Axminster
Seaton
Sidmouth
Budleigh Salterton
Channel Islands
St Malo (summer only)
Cherbourg
Guernsey and Jersey
M5
M32
A4
A30
A35
A37
A38
A39
A303
A358
A361
A370
A371
A372
A373
A3088
B3187
215
197
364
244
248
211
503
207
204
205
213
245
208
235
201
226
243
240
187
178
151
218
228
199
222
223
229
225
179
188
247
242
236
348
255
257
258
273
278
281
298
306
283
323
284
263
365
267
266
292
325
272
302
256
307
265
334
259
264
289
362
344
361
317
340
339
355
336
352
328
268
360
299
0 10 20 30 M
0 10 20 30 40 50 Km
2
3
4
5
E
F
G
H

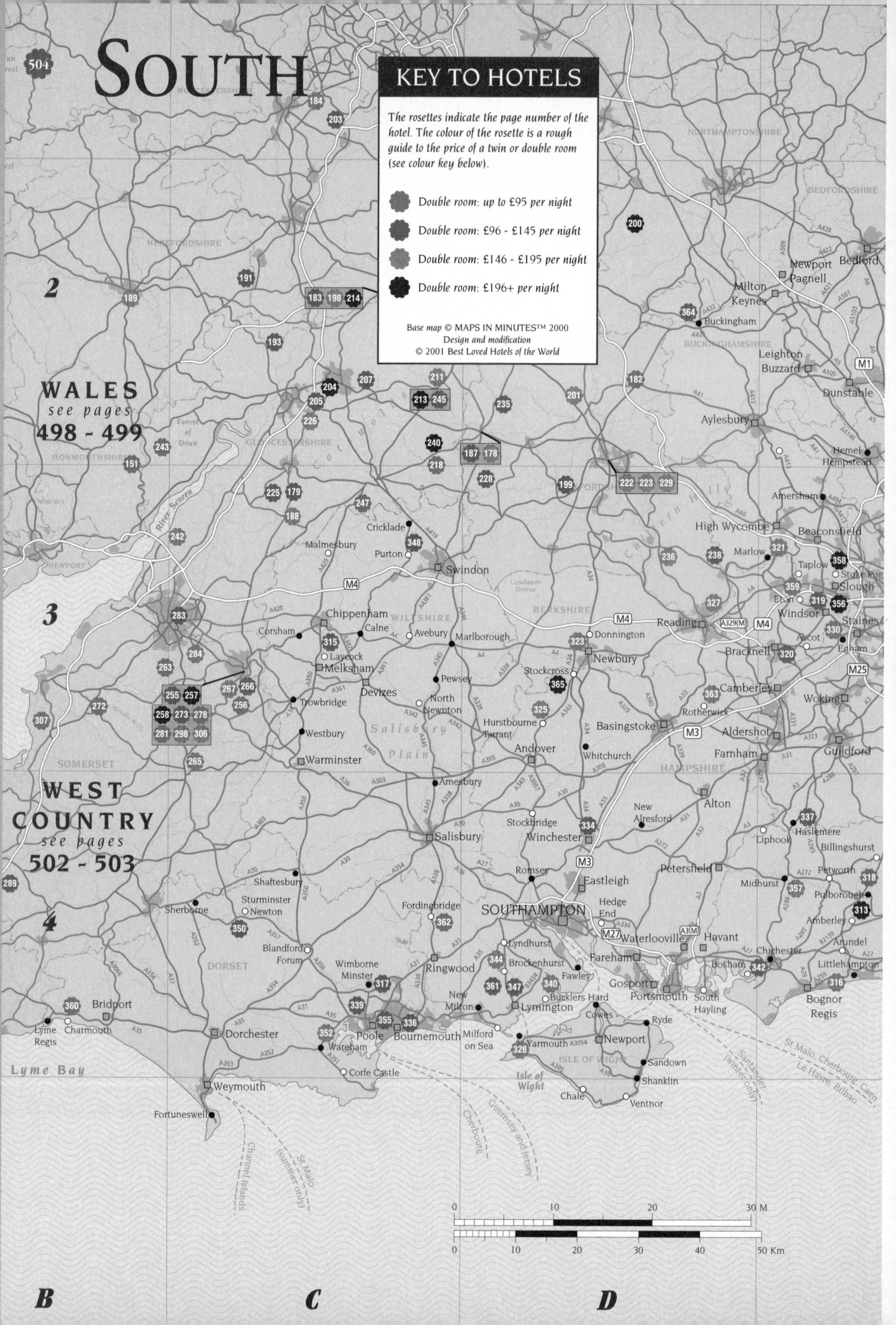

SOUTH

KEY TO HOTELS

The rosettes indicate the page number of the hotel. The colour of the rosette is a rough guide to the price of a twin or double room (see colour key below).

- *Double room: up to £95 per night*
- *Double room: £96 - £145 per night*
- *Double room: £146 - £195 per night*
- *Double room: £196+ per night*

WALES
see pages
498 - 499

WEST COUNTRY
see pages
502 - 503

2

3

4

B C D

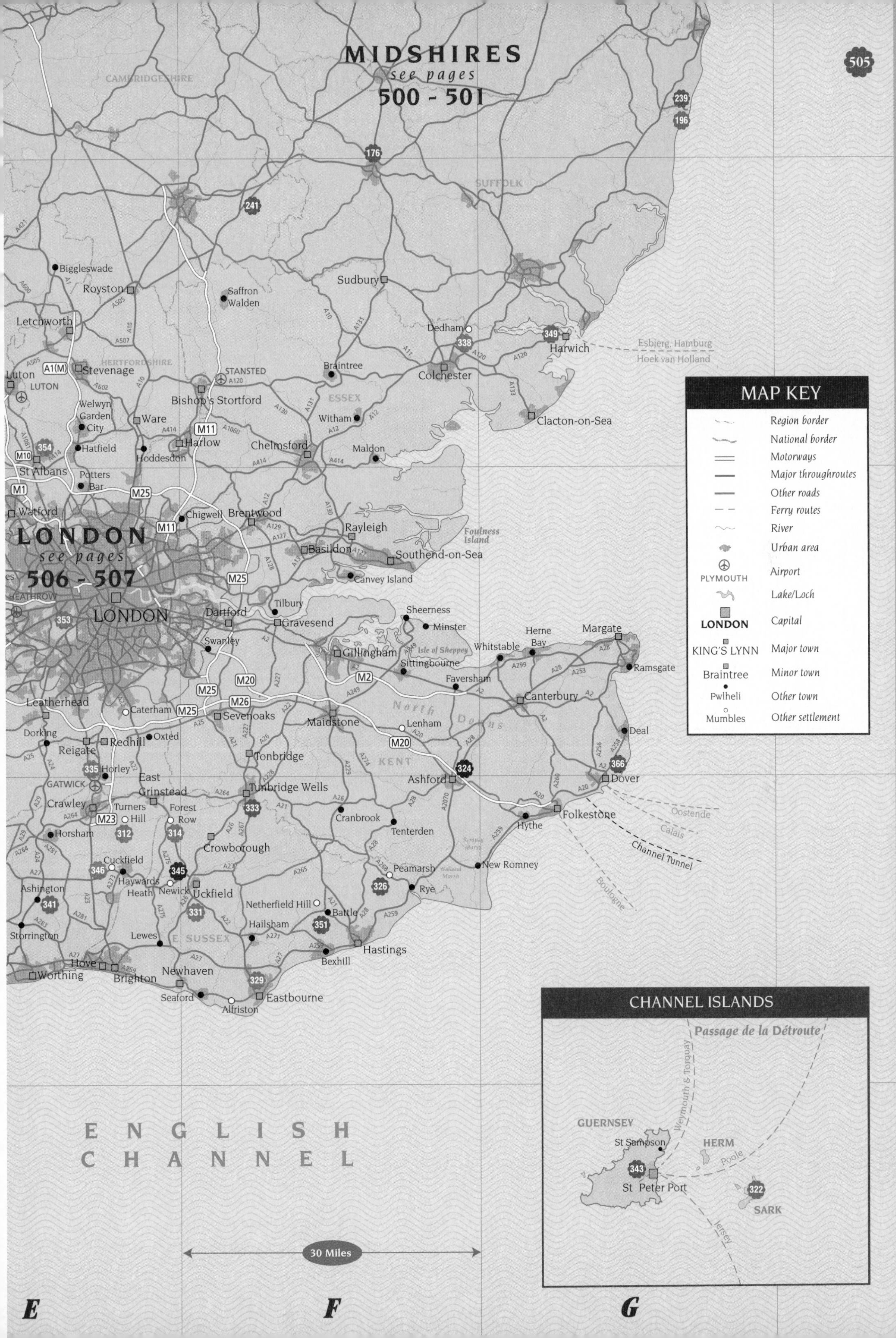

MIDSHIRES
see pages
500 - 501

CAMBRIDGESHIRE
SUFFOLK
HERTFORDSHIRE
ESSEX
KENT
E. SUSSEX

Biggleswade
Royston
Saffron Walden
Sudbury
Letchworth
Dedham
Harwich
Esbjerg, Hamburg
Hoek van Holland
Luton
LUTON
Stevenage
STANSTED
Braintree
Colchester
Bishop's Stortford
Welwyn Garden City
Ware
Witham
Clacton-on-Sea
Hatfield
Harlow
Chelmsford
Maldon
Hoddesdon
St Albans
Potters Bar
Watford
Chigwell
Brentwood
Rayleigh
Foulness Island
Basildon
Southend-on-Sea
Canvey Island

LONDON
see pages
506 - 507

HEATHROW
LONDON
Dartford
Tilbury
Gravesend
Sheerness
Minster
Isle of Sheppey
Whitstable
Herne Bay
Margate
Ramsgate
Swanley
Gillingham
Sittingbourne
Faversham
Canterbury
Leatherhead
Caterham
Sevenoaks
Maidstone
North Downs
Lenham
Deal
Dorking
Reigate
Redhill
Oxted
Tonbridge
Horley
East Grinstead
GATWICK
Tunbridge Wells
Ashford
Dover
Crawley
Turners Hill
Forest Row
Cranbrook
Tenterden
Folkestone
Hythe
Oostende
Calais
Channel Tunnel
Boulogne
Horsham
Crowborough
Romney Marsh
New Romney
Cuckfield
Haywards Heath
Newick
Uckfield
Peamarsh
Walland Marsh
Rye
Ashington
Netherfield Hill
Battle
Storrington
Lewes
Hailsham
Hastings
Bexhill
Hove
Worthing
Brighton
Newhaven
Seaford
Alfriston
Eastbourne

MAP KEY

	Region border
	National border
	Motorways
	Major throughroutes
	Other roads
	Ferry routes
	River
	Urban area
PLYMOUTH	Airport
	Lake/Loch
LONDON	Capital
KING'S LYNN	Major town
Braintree	Minor town
Pwlheli	Other town
Mumbles	Other settlement

CHANNEL ISLANDS

Passage de la Déroute
Weymouth & Torquay
GUERNSEY
St Sampson
HERM
Poole
St Peter Port
SARK
Jersey

ENGLISH CHANNEL

30 Miles

E F G

SOUTH

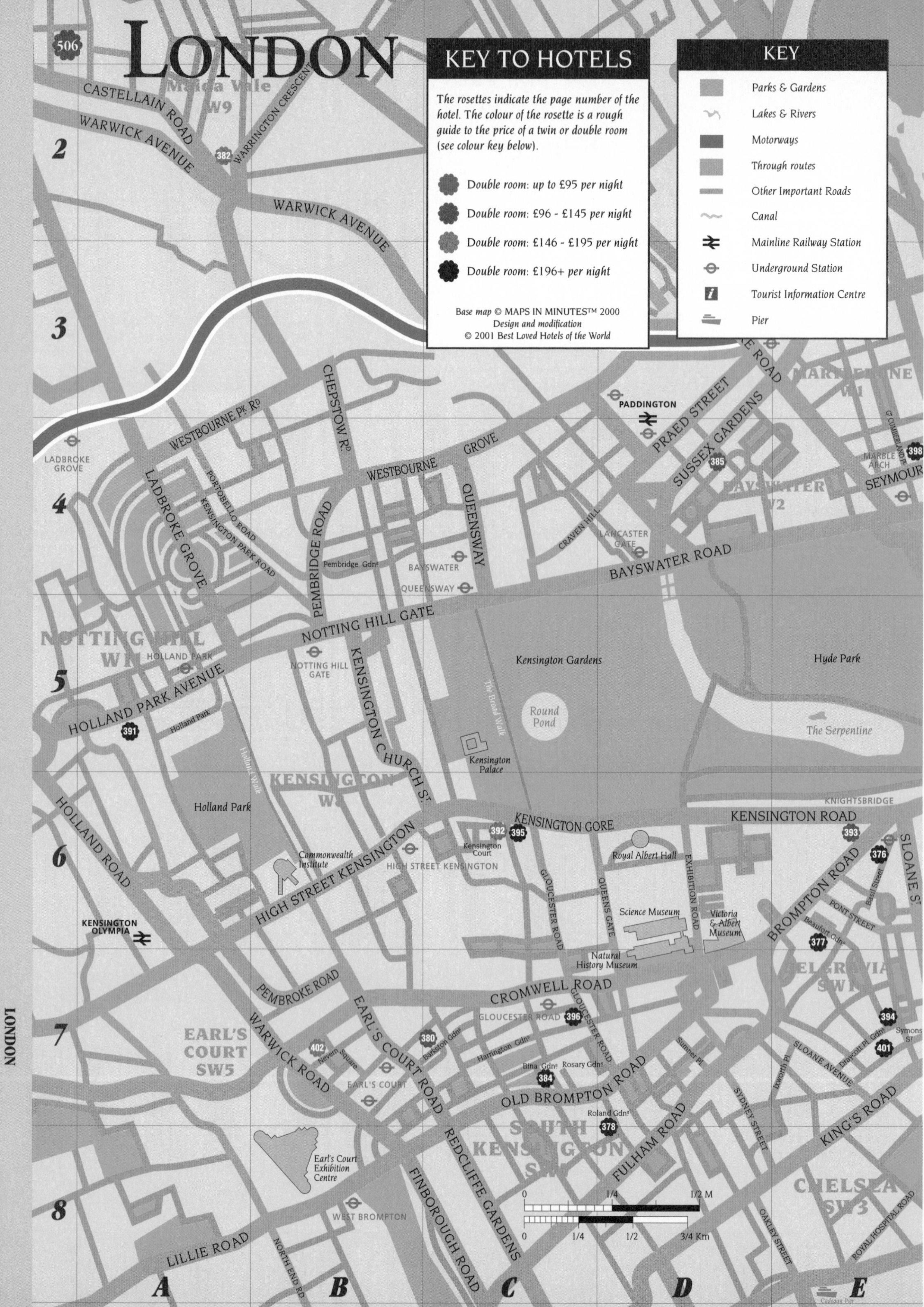
LONDON
KEY TO HOTELS
The rosettes indicate the page number of the hotel. The colour of the rosette is a rough guide to the price of a twin or double room (see colour key below).
Double room: up to £95 per night
Double room: £96 - £145 per night
Double room: £146 - £195 per night
Double room: £196+ per night
Base map © MAPS IN MINUTES™ 2000
Design and modification
© 2001 Best Loved Hotels of the World
KEY
Parks & Gardens
Lakes & Rivers
Motorways
Through routes
Other Important Roads
Canal
Mainline Railway Station
Underground Station
Tourist Information Centre
Pier
Maida Vale
W9
CASTELLAIN ROAD
WARWICK AVENUE
WARRINGTON CRESCENT
382
WARWICK AVENUE
2
3
4
5
6
7
8
A
B
C
D
E
LADBROKE GROVE
WESTBOURNE PK RD
CHEPSTOW RD
PADDINGTON
PRAED STREET
SUSSEX GARDENS
385
MARYLEBONE
W1
GT CUMBERLAND PL
398
MARBLE ARCH
SEYMOUR
BAYSWATER
W2
WESTBOURNE GROVE
LADBROKE GROVE
PORTOBELLO ROAD
KENSINGTON PARK ROAD
PEMBRIDGE ROAD
Pembridge Gdns
QUEENSWAY
BAYSWATER
QUEENSWAY
CRAVEN HILL
LANCASTER GATE
BAYSWATER ROAD
NOTTING HILL GATE
NOTTING HILL
W11
HOLLAND PARK
NOTTING HILL GATE
KENSINGTON CHURCH ST
Kensington Gardens
Hyde Park
The Broad Walk
Round Pond
The Serpentine
HOLLAND PARK AVENUE
391
Holland Park
Holland Walk
Kensington Palace
KENSINGTON
W8
Holland Park
HOLLAND ROAD
KNIGHTSBRIDGE
KENSINGTON ROAD
393
KENSINGTON GORE
392
395
Kensington Court
Commonwealth Institute
HIGH STREET KENSINGTON
HIGH STREET KENSINGTON
Royal Albert Hall
376
SLOANE ST
BROMPTON ROAD
Basil Street
PONT STREET
Beaufort Gdns
377
GLOUCESTER ROAD
QUEENS GATE
EXHIBITION ROAD
Science Museum
Victoria & Albert Museum
Natural History Museum
KENSINGTON OLYMPIA
BELGRAVIA
SW1
PEMBROKE ROAD
CROMWELL ROAD
GLOUCESTER ROAD
396
GLOUCESTER ROAD
394
Symons St
401
EARL'S COURT
SW5
WARWICK ROAD
402
Nevern Square
EARL'S COURT ROAD
380
Barkston Gdns
Harrington Gdns
Sumner Pl
Draycott Pl
Gdns
SLOANE AVENUE
Ixworth Pl
Bina Gdns
Rosary Gdns
384
EARL'S COURT
OLD BROMPTON ROAD
Roland Gdns
378
SYDNEY STREET
KING'S ROAD
SOUTH KENSINGTON
SW7
FULHAM ROAD
Earl's Court Exhibition Centre
REDCLIFFE GARDENS
FINBOROUGH ROAD
0
1/4
1/2 M
0
1/4
1/2
3/4 Km
CHELSEA
SW3
OAKLEY STREET
ROYAL HOSPITAL ROAD
WEST BROMPTON
LILLIE ROAD
NORTH END RD
Cadogan Pier

King's Cross
Pentonville Road
St Pancras
Pancras Rd
York Way
Eversholt Street
Hampstead Rd
Euston
Euston Road
Judd Street
Swinton St
Albany Street
Regent's Park
Regent's Park
Marylebone Road
Warren Street
Gt Portland St
Great Portland Street
Tottenham Court Road
Gower Street
Russell Square
Bernard Street
Guilford Street
Russell Square
Bloomsbury WC1
Gray's Inn Road
Farringdon Road
St. John Street
Clerkenwell
Theobalds Road
Hatton Garden
Charterhouse
Southampton Row
Montague St
Bedford Sq
Goodge Street
Goodge Street
Paddington St
Baker St.
373
379
397
The British Museum
Holborn
Chancery Lane
Fetter Lane
Holborn Viaduct
Shoe Lane
New Bridge St
New Oxford Street
Kingsway
Wigmore St.
Cavendish Sq.
Street
Oxford Street
Oxford Street
Bond Street
Tottenham Court Road
Charing Cross Rd
Avenue
Monmouth Av
Endell St
Bow St
Aldwych
Soho W1
Wardour Street
Regent Street
New Bond Street
Conduit St
Brewer Street
Shaftesbury
Leicester Square
St Martins La
Long Acre
Covent Garden
Theatre Museum
British Transport Museum
The Strand
Temple
Blackfriars
Victoria Embankment
Waterloo Bridge
Blackfriars Bridge
Grosvenor Sq
Upper Grosvenor
Carlos Pl
390
Mount Street
Hill Street
374
Park Lane
Park Lane
Museum of Mankind
Old Bond Street
Albemarle St
Royal Academy of Arts
National Gallery & National Portrait Gallery
British Travel Centre
Piccadilly Circus
Trafalgar
Charing Cross
Stratton St
Charles St
381
Mayfair SW1
Half Moon St
387
375
Piccadilly
Northern Ireland
Green Park
Pall Mall
Scotland
Square
Embankment
Northumberland Av
Charing Cross Pier
South Bank Festival Pier
Green Park
Hyde Park Corner
Constitution Hill
Buckingham Palace
Royal Mews
Grosvenor Place
Wilton Pl
Grosvenor Cr
Belgrave Square
Buckingham Gate
400
Beeston Pl
388
399
Westminster Cathedral
Pont Street
Belgrave Pl
Eaton Square
Eccleston St
Palace Road
Wilton Rd
Victoria
Buckingham
Belgrave Road
Ebury Street
Sloane Square
Pimlico Road
Warwick Way
Ebury Bridge Rd
Chelsea Bridge Road
Pimlico SW1
Dolphin Sq
386
Vauxhall Bridge
River
Grosvenor Road
1/2 Mile
Chelsea Bridge
Battersea Power Station
Nine Elms Lane
The Oval Cricket Ground
Battersea Park
F G H I J

GREATER LONDON

A1M
M11
M1
A1
A10
South see pages 502 - 503
A41
A406
M25
A412
A417
A1180
A404
A1
A12
A118
Hampstead
A13
358
M40
A4020
A5
Millennium Dome
M4
319
356
A4
A4
Heathrow
A30
A316
362
South see pages 504 - 505
A207
A2
A205
A20
330
M3
M20
M25
A3
A243
A24
A21
M26
A217
M23
A22
M25

IRELAND

MAP KEY

	Region border
	National border
	Motorways
	Major throughroutes
	Other roads
	Ferry routes
	River
	Urban area
PLYMOUTH	Airport
	Lake/Loch
LONDON	Capital
KING'S LYNN	Major town
Braintree	Minor town
Pwlheli	Other town
Mumbles	Other settlement

KEY TO HOTELS

The rosettes indicate the page number of the hotel. The colour of the rosette is a rough guide to the price of a twin or double room (see colour key below).

- Double room: up to £95 per night
- Double room: £96 - £145 per night
- Double room: £146 - £195 per night
- Double room: £196+ per night

Base map © MAPS IN MINUTES™ 2000
Design and modification

SCOTLAND
see pages
494 - 495

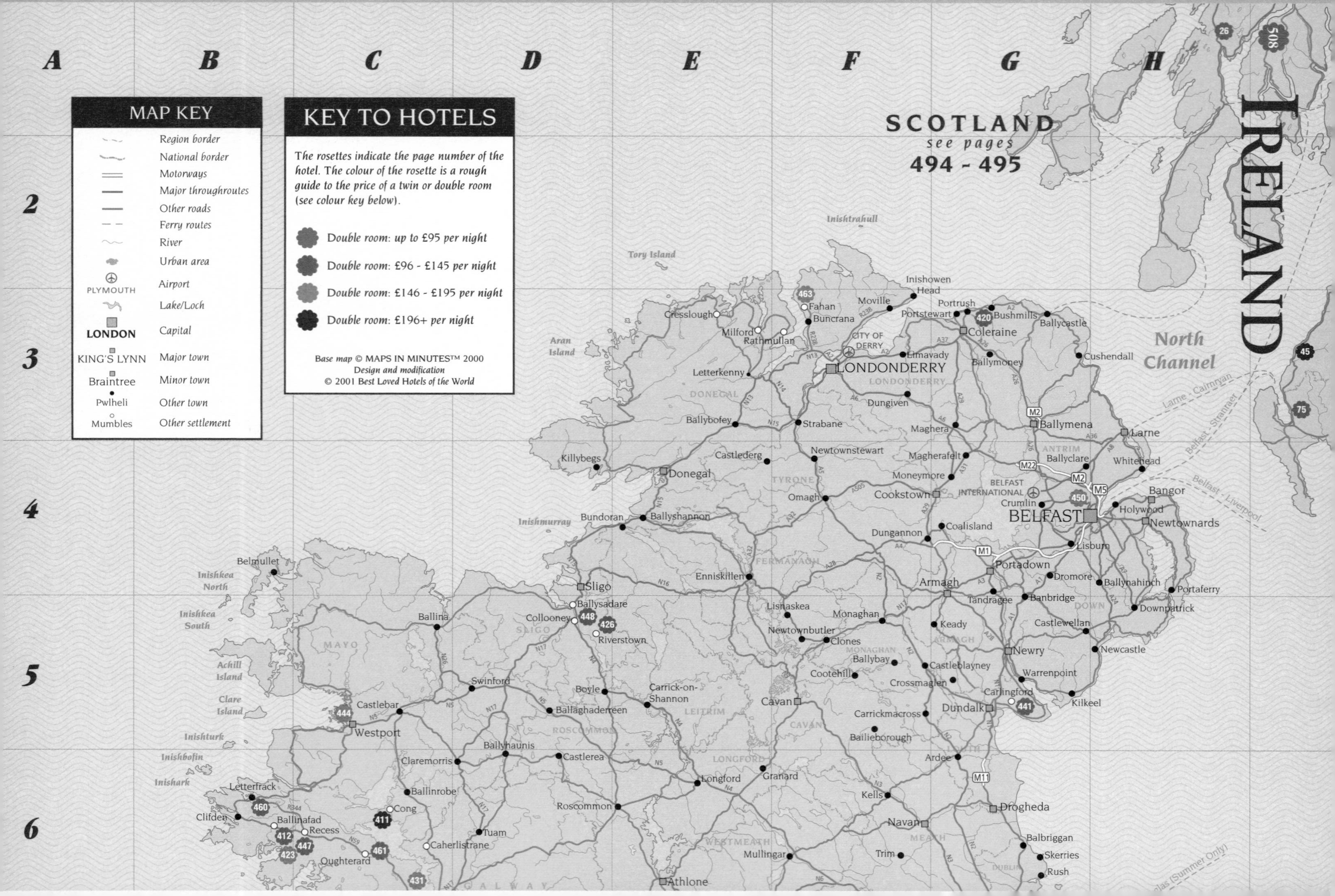

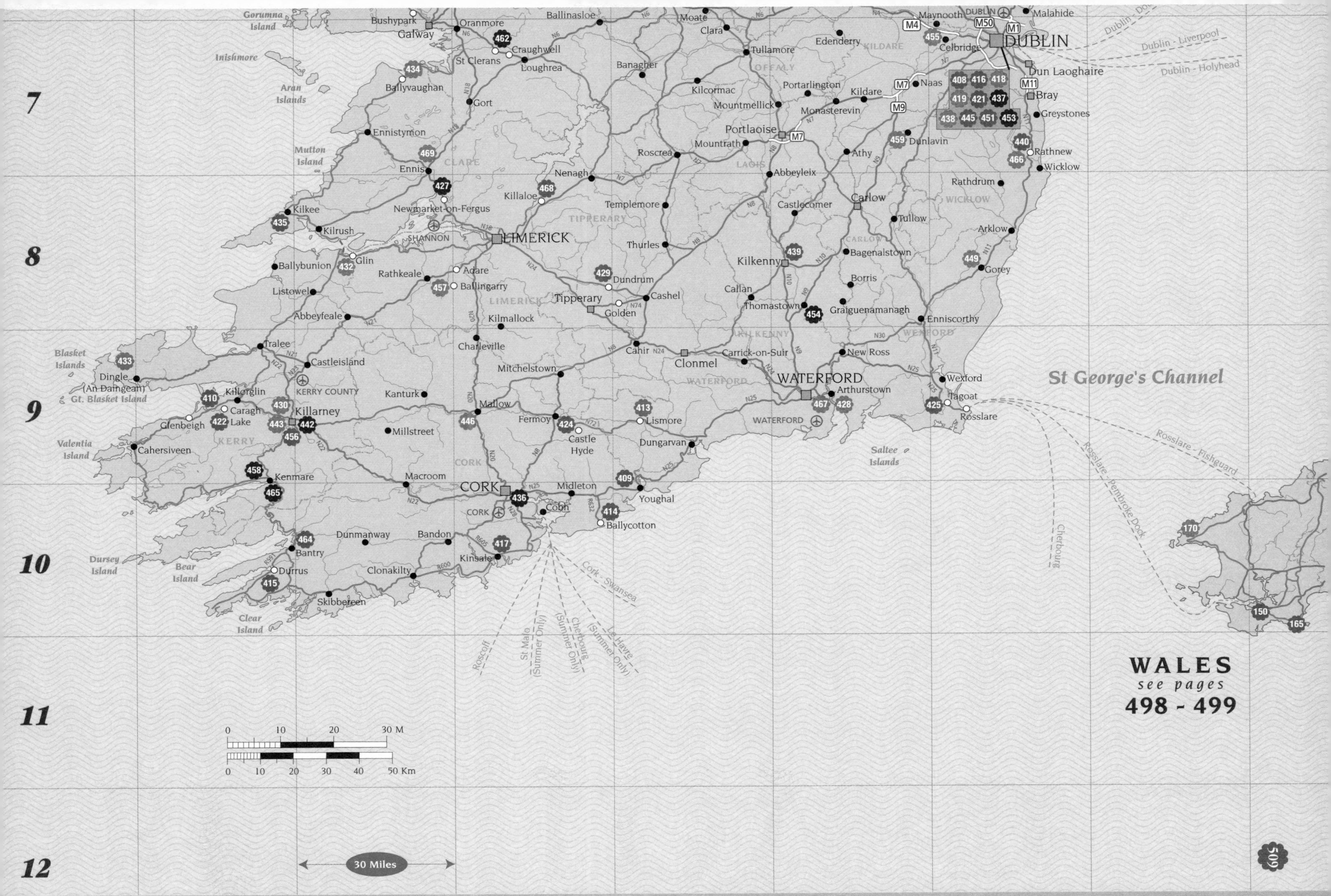

St George's Channel

WALES
see pages
498 - 499

Dublin - Liverpool
Dublin - Holyhead
Rosslare - Fishguard
Rosslare - Pembroke Dock
Cherbourg
Cork - Swansea
Le Havre (Summer Only)
Cherbourg (Summer Only)
St Malo (Summer Only)
Roscoff

DUBLIN
Malahide
Maynooth
Celbridge
Dun Laoghaire
Bray
Greystones
Naas
Kildare
Edenderry
Tullamore
Moate
Clara
Ballinasloe
Banagher
Portarlington
Monasterevin
Mountmellick
Kilcormac
Portlaoise
Mountrath
Athy
Dunlavin
Rathnew
Wicklow
Rathdrum
Arklow
Gorey
Tullow
Carlow
Castlecomer
Abbeyleix
Roscrea
Nenagh
Templemore
Thurles
Kilkenny
Bagenalstown
Borris
Graiguenamanagh
Enniscorthy
Wexford
Tagoat
Rosslare
New Ross
Arthurstown
WATERFORD
Thomastown
Callan
Carrick-on-Suir
Clonmel
Cashel
Dundrum
Tipperary
Golden
Cahir
Lismore
Dungarvan
Castle Hyde
Fermoy
Mitchelstown
Youghal
Midleton
Cobh
Ballycotton
CORK
Kinsale
Bandon
Clonakilty
Skibbereen
Dunmanway
Macroom
Millstreet
Mallow
Kanturk
Charleville
Kilmallock
LIMERICK
Adare
Ballingarry
Rathkeale
Killaloe
Newmarket-on-Fergus
Shannon
Ennis
Ennistymon
Gort
Ballyvaughan
Galway
Bushypark
Oranmore
Craughwell
St Clerans
Loughrea
Kilkee
Kilrush
Glin
Ballybunion
Listowel
Abbeyfeale
Tralee
Castleisland
Kerry County
Killarney
Killorglin
Caragh Lake
Glenbeigh
Cahersiveen
Kenmare
Bantry
Durrus
Dingle (An Daingean)

Gorumna Island
Inishmore
Aran Islands
Mutton Island
Blasket Islands
Gt. Blasket Island
Valentia Island
Dursey Island
Bear Island
Clear Island
Saltee Islands

KILDARE
OFFALY
LAOIS
WICKLOW
CARLOW
KILKENNY
WEXFORD
WATERFORD
TIPPERARY
LIMERICK
CLARE
KERRY
CORK

7
8
9
10
11
12

0 10 20 30 M
0 10 20 30 40 50 Km
30 Miles

BEST LOVED HOTELS.com

Corporate Event Planning

Over 400 characterful places from Stately Homes & Country Houses to Golf Resorts & City Centre hotels, matched with a dedicated Corporate Planner with advanced dynamic search capabilities to give the professional corporate planner a fast, efficient on-line venue finding solution.

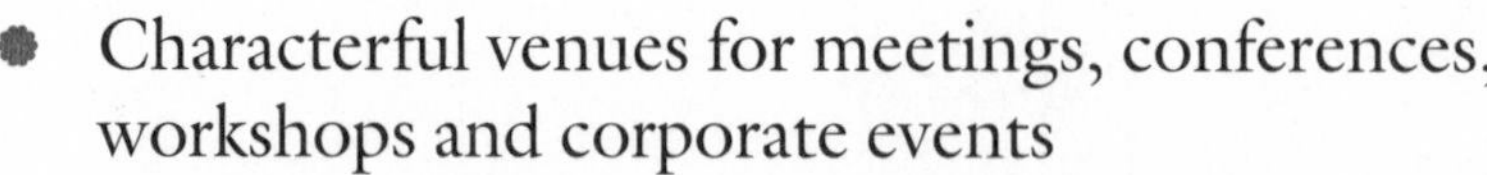

- Characterful venues for meetings, conferences, workshops and corporate events
- Reliable, comprehensive, quality content
- Intelligent, dedicated venue search capabilities
- Sophisticated location and map searches

Visit Bestlovedhotels.com and register your details on-line now to receive special offers, discounts and opportunities available to the Professional Corporate Planner only.

GUEST SURVEY

Please tell us about your stay, the more we know the more reliable our future editions will be.

Hotel name ______
Name of guest ______
Address ______

______ Postcode ______
Tel: ______ Fax: ______
E-mail: ______

Reason for stay

Business ☐ Conference ☐ Pleasure ☐ Dining ☐

How did you find your visit?

	Excellent	Good	Not Good	Poor
Public Rooms				
Bedrooms				
Restaurant/Food				
Comfort				
Facilities				
Service				
Courtesy/friendliness				
Value for money				

Please tick only one box for each aspect of your stay.

Additional comments:

______

Do you have a best loved hotel?

Name of hotel ______
Location ______

Hire car information:

Did you rent a car to get to the hotel? ☐ Yes ☐ No
From where: **Herts Avis Europcar** Other ______
(please circle)

Airline information:

What airline did you use to arrive in the British Isles?

______

BLD01/SF

ORDER CARD

Best Loved Hotels of the World 2001 - PRICE LIST

	UK£	US$	EIRE£
UK & Ireland Directory	14.99	19.95	15.99
Amex cardholders price	**13.99**	**17.95**	**14.99**
Add for post and packing	*4.50*	*3.00*	*4.50*

Postage to Europe - £6; to any other country - £10

Orderlines

UK: 0870 586 2010 Fax: 01548 831074
US: 800-808-7682 Toll free fax: 800-572-8131
E-mail: bookorder@bestlovedhotels.com
or order on line at www.bestlovedhotels.com

Order by post

Fill in your details and send this slip to the **FREEPOST** address below:
Best Loved Hotels of the World
Clientbase Fulfilment Ltd
FREEPOST (SWB40527), IVYBRIDGE PL21 0ZZ (UK only)

Please send me Best Loved Hotels of the World 2001
Copies required ☐ @ ☐ each **£/$***
Add for post and packing per copy **£/$*** ....
TOTAL **£/$*** ....
* Please circle the currency you are using

Payment method

Charge/Credit Card ☐ Personal Cheque ☐*
*Cheques to be made out to "World Media Publishing Ltd"

Please charge my account

American Express ☐ Diners ☐ Mastercard ☐ Visa ☐

Expires end

☐ I enclose my order on company letterhead. Please invoice my company (UK only).

Name (Mr/Mrs/Ms) ______
Company ______
Address ______

Zip/Postcode ______ Country ______
Tel ______ Fax ______
E-mail ______

Signature ______

Please allow at least two weeks for delivery. BLD01/OF

ORDER CARD

Best Loved Hotels of the World 2001 - PRICE LIST

	UK£	US$	EIRE£
UK & Ireland Directory	14.99	19.95	15.99
Amex cardholders price	**13.99**	**17.95**	**14.99**
Add for post and packing	*4.50*	*3.00*	*4.50*

Postage to Europe - £6; to any other country - £10

Orderlines

UK: 0870 586 2010 Fax: 01548 831074
US: 800-808-7682 Toll free fax: 800-572-8131
E-mail: bookorder@bestlovedhotels.com
or order on line at www.bestlovedhotels.com

Order by post

Fill in your details and send this slip to the **FREEPOST** address below:
Best Loved Hotels of the World
Clientbase Fulfilment Ltd
FREEPOST (SWB40527), IVYBRIDGE PL21 0ZZ (UK only)

Please send me Best Loved Hotels of the World 2001
Copies required ☐ @ ☐ each **£/$***
Add for post and packing per copy **£/$*** ....
TOTAL **£/$*** ....
* Please circle the currency you are using

Payment method

Charge/Credit Card ☐ Personal Cheque ☐*
*Cheques to be made out to "World Media Publishing Ltd"

Please charge my account

American Express ☐ Diners ☐ Mastercard ☐ Visa ☐

Expires end

☐ I enclose my order on company letterhead. Please invoice my company (UK only).

Name (Mr/Mrs/Ms) ______
Company ______
Address ______

Zip/Postcode ______ Country ______
Tel ______ Fax ______
E-mail ______

Signature ______

Please allow at least two weeks for delivery. BLD01/OF

BEST LOVED HOTELS 2001

Ordering copies of the Best Loved Hotels of the World is easy; you can telephone, fax, e-mail, order on line or send us this slip by **FREEPOST** (UK only; no stamp required) to the address below:

Best Loved Hotels of the World
Clientbase Fulfilment Ltd
FREEPOST (SWB40527),
Ivybridge, PL21 0ZZ

For telephone or fax orders, call:

IN THE UK

Phone: **0870 586 2010**
Fax: **01548 831074**

IN THE US

Phone: **800-808-7682**
Toll free fax: **800-572-8131**

E-mail: **bookorder@bestlovedhotels.com**
or order on line at www.bestlovedhotels.com

When ordering, quote your charge/credit card number and expiry date. Remember to allow for the cost of post and packing. Full details are on the previous page.

Use your American Express chargecard and save - see over

BEST LOVED HOTELS 2001

Ordering copies of the Best Loved Hotels of the World is easy; you can telephone, fax, e-mail, order on line or send us this slip by **FREEPOST** (UK only; no stamp required) to the address below:

Best Loved Hotels of the World
Clientbase Fulfilment Ltd
FREEPOST (SWB40527),
Ivybridge, PL21 0ZZ

For telephone or fax orders, call:

IN THE UK

Phone: **0870 586 2010**
Fax: **01548 831074**

IN THE US

Phone: **800-808-7682**
Toll free fax: **800-572-8131**

E-mail: **bookorder@bestlovedhotels.com**
or order on line at www.bestlovedhotels.com

When ordering, quote your charge/credit card number and expiry date. Remember to allow for the cost of post and packing. Full details are on the previous page.

Use your American Express chargecard and save - see over

Do you have a Best Loved Hotel?

Here is your chance to nominate one or two of your Best Loved Hotels and to let us know why you have chosen them. Is it associated with a special event? Or a special memory? Please let us know.

Your choice and comments will help us determine the Best Loved Hotels of the Year for 2001 and may become the Best Loved Quotation for that hotel. If we use your quotation, ***we will send you the next year's edition FREE OF CHARGE.***

Best Loved Hotel ______
Date Stayed ______
It is my Best Loved Hotel because:
" ______ "

Best Loved Hotel ______
Date Stayed ______
It is my Best Loved Hotel because:
" ______ "

Your name ______
Address ______

Zip/Postcode ______
Country ______
Telephone: ______
Fax: ______
E-mail: ______

Signature ______

FREE BROCHURE SERVICE

If you see an hotel in this book and want to know more about it, simply circle its page number below, fill in your name and address details, and post the card to us.

As soon as we receive your request, we shall arrange for the brochures to be delivered to you as soon as the postal services allow.

There will be no delivery or postage charge for this service.

BEST LOVED HOTELS 2001

Suite 11, The Linen House, 253 Kilburn Lane,
London W10 4BQ, United Kingdom

Tel: +44 (0)20 8962 9555 ◆ Fax: +44 (0)20 8962 9550
E-mail: freebrochure@bestlovedhotels.com
Website: www.bestlovedhotels.com

BEST LOVED HOTELS 2001

Free Brochure Service

Please send me full details on the hotel(s) whose page number is circled on the right.

Name ______________________

Address ______________________

____

____

City ______________________

Zip/Postcode ______________________

Country ______________________

Tel: ______________________

Fax: ______________________

E-mail: ______________________

From time to time we publish special offers, news and hotel updates as well as share your data with other reputable third parties. If you do not wish to receive anything from third parties simply tick here ☐.

BLD01/BR

20	49	79	114	148	184	214	244	279	313	343	378	414	443
21	50	80	115	149	185	215	245	281	314	344	379	415	444
22	51	81	116	150	186	216	246	282	315	345	380	416	445
23	52	82	117	151	187	217	247	283	316	346	381	417	446
24	53	83	118	152	188	218	248	284	317	347	382	418	447
25	54	84	119	153	189	219	254	285	318	348	384	419	448
26	55	85	120	155	190	220	255	286	319	349	385	420	449
27	56	86	121	156	191	221	256	287	320	350	386	421	450
28	57	87	122	157	192	222	257	288	321	351	387	422	451
29	58	88	123	158	193	223	258	289	322	352	388	423	453
30	59	94	124	159	194	224	259	290	323	353	390	424	454
31	60	95	125	160	195	225	260	291	324	354	391	425	455
32	61	96	126	161	196	226	261	292	325	355	392	426	456
33	63	97	127	162	197	227	262	293	326	356	393	427	457
34	64	98	128	163	198	228	263	294	327	357	394	428	458
35	65	99	129	165	199	229	264	295	328	358	395	429	459
36	66	100	130	166	200	230	265	296	329	359	396	430	460
37	67	101	131	167	201	231	266	297	330	360	397	431	461
38	68	102	132	168	202	232	267	298	331	361	398	432	462
39	69	103	133	169	203	233	268	299	333	362	399	433	463
40	70	104	134	170	204	235	269	300	334	363	400	434	464
41	71	105	135	176	205	236	270	301	335	364	401	435	465
42	72	106	136	177	206	237	271	302	336	365	402	436	466
43	73	107	137	178	207	238	272	303	337	366	408	437	467
44	74	108	138	179	208	239	273	304	338	373	409	438	468
45	75	109	139	180	209	240	275	305	339	374	410	439	469
46	76	110	140	181	210	241	276	306	340	375	411	440	
47	77	111	141	182	211	242	277	307	341	376	412	441	
48	78	113	142	183	213	243	278	312	342	377	413	442	

GUEST SURVEY

Please tell us about your stay, the more we know the more reliable our future editions will be.

Hotel name ______________________

Name of guest ______________________

Address ______________________

____

Postcode ______________________

Tel: ______________ Fax: ______

E-mail: ______________________

Reason for stay

Business ☐ Conference ☐

Pleasure ☐ Dining ☐

How did you find your visit?

	Excellent	Good	Not Good	Poor
Public Rooms				
Bedrooms				
Restaurant/Food				
Comfort				
Facilities				
Service				
Courtesy/friendliness				
Value for money				

Please tick only one box for each aspect of your stay

Additional comments:

____

____

____

____

____

Do you have a best loved hotel?

Name of hotel ______________________

Location ______________________

____

____

Hire car information:

Did you rent a car to get to the hotel?

☐ Yes ☐ No

From where:

Hertz **Avis** **Europcar** Other

(please circle)

Airline information:

What airline did you use to arrive in the British Isles?

____

BLD01/SF

Use this £5 voucher at selected Best Loved hotels

YOUR PURCHASE of this 2001 Directory of the Best Loved Hotels of the World entitles you to the four £5 tear-off vouchers opposite.

To redeem them, just make a reservation to stay at any of the participating hotels (see other side of opposite page) or book a table for two for a meal at one of them. When making your reservation, you must tell the hotel of your intention to use the voucher.

£5 off your stay or..

If you use your voucher in association with booking accommodation, you will have £5 deducted from the standard charge (rack rate) for the room.

... two free glasses of wine

If you choose to take a meal, there must be two of you, your voucher will entitle you to a glass of house wine each. It is as simple as that.

It's a gift!

If you wish to give the voucher to someone else, there is no problem, it is entirely transferable. The rules, however, are the same.

Please refer to full terms and conditions on the voucher.

Hotel bedroom copies do not contain any vouchers.
If you would like to purchase your own copy please see order card or go to www.bestlovedhotels.com

---

Airmail

No stamp needed UK only

Clientbase Fulfilment Ltd
FREEPOST (SWB40527)
IVYBRIDGE PL21 0ZZ

No stamp needed UK only

Clientbase Fulfilment Ltd
FREEPOST (SWB40527)
IVYBRIDGE PL21 0ZZ

Or two glasses of house wine

BEST LOVED HOTELS OF THE WORLD 2001

Voucher

This voucher may be redeemed at any participating 2001 Best Loved Hotel (see overleaf and refer to their page in the directory or go to www.bestlovedhotels.com) for its face value against the room rack rate OR two glasses of house wine subject to the conditions shown overleaf.

2284756347

VALID until 31 December 2001

Jeffrey Epstein
Publisher, Best Loved Hotels of the World

Or two glasses of house wine

BEST LOVED HOTELS OF THE WORLD 2001

Voucher

This voucher may be redeemed at any participating 2001 Best Loved Hotel (see overleaf and refer to their page in the directory or go to www.bestlovedhotels.com) for its face value against the room rack rate OR two glasses of house wine subject to the conditions shown overleaf.

4500883108

VALID until 31 December 2001

Jeffrey Epstein
Publisher, Best Loved Hotels of the World

Or two glasses of house wine

BEST LOVED HOTELS OF THE WORLD 2001

Voucher

This voucher may be redeemed at any participating 2001 Best Loved Hotel (see overleaf and refer to their page in the directory or go to www.bestlovedhotels.com) for its face value against the room rack rate OR two glasses of house wine subject to the conditions shown overleaf.

2800246302

VALID until 31 December 2001

Jeffrey Epstein
Publisher, Best Loved Hotels of the World

Or two glasses of house wine

BEST LOVED HOTELS OF THE WORLD 2001

Voucher

This voucher may be redeemed at any participating 2001 Best Loved Hotel (see overleaf and refer to their page in the directory or go to www.bestlovedhotels.com) for its face value against the room rack rate OR two glasses of house wine subject to the conditions shown overleaf.

3184947849

VALID until 31 December 2001

Jeffrey Epstein
Publisher, Best Loved Hotels of the World

Stay at any of these Best Loved Hotels (or enjoy a meal at one of them) and save using the voucher overleaf

Aberdeen Lodge
Ahernes
Alexander House Hotel
Angel Hotel
Bailiffscourt Hotel
Ballynahinch Castle Hotel
Bath Lodge Hotel
Beechleas Hotel & Restaurant
Bignell Park Hotel
Bindon Country House Hotel
Blakes Townhouse
Bonham
Borrowdale Gates
Brockencote Hall
Brookhouse
Buckland-Tout-Saints
Budock Vean
Bunchrew House Hotel
Burford House
Bushmills
Butlers Town House
Cameron House
Castle House
CastleHyde Hotel
Channings

Charlton House
Chesterfield Mayfair
Christopher Hotel
Cliffe Hotel
Colwall Park Hotel
Combe Grove Manor
Combe House at Gittisham
Corse Lawn House Hotel
Cotswold House Hotel
Coul House Hotel
Court Barn
Court Hotel
Craigellachie Hotel
Cranley
Crewe Hall
Cringletie House Hotel
Cromlix House
Crosby Lodge
Crown at Whitebrook
Crown Inn & Hotel
Culdearn House
Dale Head Hall
Devonshire Hotel
Dundrum House Hotel
Eastwell Manor

Empire
Enmore Hotel
Esseborne Manor
Fairyhill
Fawsley Hall
Fayrer Garden House Hotel
Feathers, The
Flackley Ash Hotel
Flemings Mayfair
Flodigarry Country House Hotel
Four Seasons Hotel
Gilpin Lodge Hotel
Glenapp Castle
Glenmorangie House
Glenmoriston Arms Hotel
Glin Castle
Grants Hotel
Gregans Castle
Haley's Hotel & Restaurant
Halpin's Hotel
Hatton Court
Hibernian Hotel
Holbeck Ghyll Hotel & Spa
Holly Lodge
Holne Chase Hotel

Hotel Eilean Iarmain
Hotel Maes-y-Neuadd
Howard
Hunstrete House
Inn at Ardgour
Inn At Lathones
Inn on the Green
Judges at Kirklevington Hall
Kensington House Hotel
Killarney Royal Hotel
Knockinaam Lodge
Knockomie Hotel
Knockranny House Hotel
Lake Country House
Langar Hall
Linthwaite House
Little Admiral
Lovelady Shield
Maison Talbooth
Manor House
Mansion House Hotel
Matfen Hall
McCausland Hotel
Melvin House Hotel
Mere Court Hotel

Merrion Hall
Michaels Nook
Milestone
Mill End Hotel
Miller Howe Hotel
Millstream Hotel
Montague On The Gardens
Montcalm Hotel Nikko London
Moore's Hotel
North West Castle Hotel
Number 41
Nuthurst Grange
Old Bank Hotel
Old Manor Hotel
Old Priory Hotel
Orestone Manor
Owlpen Manor
Pale Hall Country House
Pen-Y-Dyffryn
Penmaenuchaf Hall
Pheasant
Pier at Harwich
Plough At Clanfield
Powder Mills Hotel
Prince Hall Hotel

Risley Hall
Rosleague Manor
Royal Marine Hotel
Rubens At The Palace
St Martin's On The Isle
St Michael's Manor
St Olaves Hotel
Stonor Arms
Swinton Park
Swynford Paddocks Hotel
Taychreggan
Thornbury Castle
Three Lions
Tides Reach Hotel
Tillmouth Park Hotel
Tyddyn Llan Country House
Waren House Hotel
Waterford Castle
Waterman's Lodge
Westmorland Hotel
Willington Hall
Windsor Hotel
Woodside Hotel
Woodstock Hotel

Terms & Conditions

1. Each purchase of the Best Loved Hotels of the World Directory entitles the buyer to £20 worth of vouchers.
2. All reservations (accomodation or meals) must be made in advance and are subject to availability.
3. The voucher may not be used in connection with any other promotion.
4. Each voucher cannot be used in combination with other Best Loved Hotels vouchers.
5. Offer valid until 31st December 2001.
6. A voucher may be exchanged for £5 off the prevailing rack rate at time of reservation OR two glasses of house wine per couple dining in the hotel restaurant.
7. The voucher is transferable but the above conditions apply in full.

Stay at any of these Best Loved Hotels (or enjoy a meal at one of them) and save using the voucher overleaf

Aberdeen Lodge
Ahernes
Alexander House Hotel
Angel Hotel
Bailiffscourt Hotel
Ballynahinch Castle Hotel
Bath Lodge Hotel
Beechleas Hotel & Restaurant
Bignell Park Hotel
Bindon Country House Hotel
Blakes Townhouse
Bonham
Borrowdale Gates
Brockencote Hall
Brookhouse
Buckland-Tout-Saints
Budock Vean
Bunchrew House Hotel
Burford House
Bushmills
Butlers Town House
Cameron House
Castle House
CastleHyde Hotel
Channings

Charlton House
Chesterfield Mayfair
Christopher Hotel
Cliffe Hotel
Colwall Park Hotel
Combe Grove Manor
Combe House at Gittisham
Corse Lawn House Hotel
Cotswold House Hotel
Coul House Hotel
Court Barn
Court Hotel
Craigellachie Hotel
Cranley
Crewe Hall
Cringletie House Hotel
Cromlix House
Crosby Lodge
Crown at Whitebrook
Crown Inn & Hotel
Culdearn House
Dale Head Hall
Devonshire Hotel
Dundrum House Hotel
Eastwell Manor

Empire
Enmore Hotel
Esseborne Manor
Fairyhill
Fawsley Hall
Fayrer Garden House Hotel
Feathers, The
Flackley Ash Hotel
Flemings Mayfair
Flodigarry Country House Hotel
Four Seasons Hotel
Gilpin Lodge Hotel
Glenapp Castle
Glenmorangie House
Glenmoriston Arms Hotel
Glin Castle
Grants Hotel
Gregans Castle
Haley's Hotel & Restaurant
Halpin's Hotel
Hatton Court
Hibernian Hotel
Holbeck Ghyll Hotel & Spa
Holly Lodge
Holne Chase Hotel

Hotel Eilean Iarmain
Hotel Maes-y-Neuadd
Howard
Hunstrete House
Inn at Ardgour
Inn At Lathones
Inn on the Green
Judges at Kirklevington Hall
Kensington House Hotel
Killarney Royal Hotel
Knockinaam Lodge
Knockomie Hotel
Knockranny House Hotel
Lake Country House
Langar Hall
Linthwaite House
Little Admiral
Lovelady Shield
Maison Talbooth
Manor House
Mansion House Hotel
Matfen Hall
McCausland Hotel
Melvin House Hotel
Mere Court Hotel

Merrion Hall
Michaels Nook
Milestone
Mill End Hotel
Miller Howe Hotel
Millstream Hotel
Montague On The Gardens
Montcalm Hotel Nikko London
Moore's Hotel
North West Castle Hotel
Number 41
Nuthurst Grange
Old Bank Hotel
Old Manor Hotel
Old Priory Hotel
Orestone Manor
Owlpen Manor
Pale Hall Country House
Pen-Y-Dyffryn
Penmaenuchaf Hall
Pheasant
Pier at Harwich
Plough At Clanfield
Powder Mills Hotel
Prince Hall Hotel

Risley Hall
Rosleague Manor
Royal Marine Hotel
Rubens At The Palace
St Martin's On The Isle
St Michael's Manor
St Olaves Hotel
Stonor Arms
Swinton Park
Swynford Paddocks Hotel
Taychreggan
Thornbury Castle
Three Lions
Tides Reach Hotel
Tillmouth Park Hotel
Tyddyn Llan Country House
Waren House Hotel
Waterford Castle
Waterman's Lodge
Westmorland Hotel
Willington Hall
Windsor Hotel
Woodside Hotel
Woodstock Hotel

Terms & Conditions

1. Each purchase of the Best Loved Hotels of the World Directory entitles the buyer to £20 worth of vouchers.
2. All reservations (accomodation or meals) must be made in advance and are subject to availability.
3. The voucher may not be used in connection with any other promotion.
4. Each voucher cannot be used in combination with other Best Loved Hotels vouchers.
5. Offer valid until 31st December 2001.
6. A voucher may be exchanged for £5 off the prevailing rack rate at time of reservation OR two glasses of house wine per couple dining in the hotel restaurant.
7. The voucher is transferable but the above conditions apply in full.

Stay at any of these Best Loved Hotels (or enjoy a meal at one of them) and save using the voucher overleaf

Aberdeen Lodge
Ahernes
Alexander House Hotel
Angel Hotel
Bailiffscourt Hotel
Ballynahinch Castle Hotel
Bath Lodge Hotel
Beechleas Hotel & Restaurant
Bignell Park Hotel
Bindon Country House Hotel
Blakes Townhouse
Bonham
Borrowdale Gates
Brockencote Hall
Brookhouse
Buckland-Tout-Saints
Budock Vean
Bunchrew House Hotel
Burford House
Bushmills
Butlers Town House
Cameron House
Castle House
CastleHyde Hotel
Channings

Charlton House
Chesterfield Mayfair
Christopher Hotel
Cliffe Hotel
Colwall Park Hotel
Combe Grove Manor
Combe House at Gittisham
Corse Lawn House Hotel
Cotswold House Hotel
Coul House Hotel
Court Barn
Court Hotel
Craigellachie Hotel
Cranley
Crewe Hall
Cringletie House Hotel
Cromlix House
Crosby Lodge
Crown at Whitebrook
Crown Inn & Hotel
Culdearn House
Dale Head Hall
Devonshire Hotel
Dundrum House Hotel
Eastwell Manor

Empire
Enmore Hotel
Esseborne Manor
Fairyhill
Fawsley Hall
Fayrer Garden House Hotel
Feathers, The
Flackley Ash Hotel
Flemings Mayfair
Flodigarry Country House Hotel
Four Seasons Hotel
Gilpin Lodge Hotel
Glenapp Castle
Glenmorangie House
Glenmoriston Arms Hotel
Glin Castle
Grants Hotel
Gregans Castle
Haley's Hotel & Restaurant
Halpin's Hotel
Hatton Court
Hibernian Hotel
Holbeck Ghyll Hotel & Spa
Holly Lodge
Holne Chase Hotel

Hotel Eilean Iarmain
Hotel Maes-y-Neuadd
Howard
Hunstrete House
Inn at Ardgour
Inn At Lathones
Inn on the Green
Judges at Kirklevington Hall
Kensington House Hotel
Killarney Royal Hotel
Knockinaam Lodge
Knockomie Hotel
Knockranny House Hotel
Lake Country House
Langar Hall
Linthwaite House
Little Admiral
Lovelady Shield
Maison Talbooth
Manor House
Mansion House Hotel
Matfen Hall
McCausland Hotel
Melvin House Hotel
Mere Court Hotel

Merrion Hall
Michaels Nook
Milestone
Mill End Hotel
Miller Howe Hotel
Millstream Hotel
Montague On The Gardens
Montcalm Hotel Nikko London
Moore's Hotel
North West Castle Hotel
Number 41
Nuthurst Grange
Old Bank Hotel
Old Manor Hotel
Old Priory Hotel
Orestone Manor
Owlpen Manor
Pale Hall Country House
Pen-Y-Dyffryn
Penmaenuchaf Hall
Pheasant
Pier at Harwich
Plough At Clanfield
Powder Mills Hotel
Prince Hall Hotel

Risley Hall
Rosleague Manor
Royal Marine Hotel
Rubens At The Palace
St Martin's On The Isle
St Michael's Manor
St Olaves Hotel
Stonor Arms
Swinton Park
Swynford Paddocks Hotel
Taychreggan
Thornbury Castle
Three Lions
Tides Reach Hotel
Tillmouth Park Hotel
Tyddyn Llan Country House
Waren House Hotel
Waterford Castle
Waterman's Lodge
Westmorland Hotel
Willington Hall
Windsor Hotel
Woodside Hotel
Woodstock Hotel

Terms & Conditions

1. Each purchase of the Best Loved Hotels of the World Directory entitles the buyer to £20 worth of vouchers.
2. All reservations (accomodation or meals) must be made in advance and are subject to availability.
3. The voucher may not be used in connection with any other promotion.
4. Each voucher cannot be used in combination with other Best Loved Hotels vouchers.
5. Offer valid until 31st December 2001.
6. A voucher may be exchanged for £5 off the prevailing rack rate at time of reservation OR two glasses of house wine per couple dining in the hotel restaurant.
7. The voucher is transferable but the above conditions apply in full.

Stay at any of these Best Loved Hotels (or enjoy a meal at one of them) and save using the voucher overleaf

Aberdeen Lodge
Ahernes
Alexander House Hotel
Angel Hotel
Bailiffscourt Hotel
Ballynahinch Castle Hotel
Bath Lodge Hotel
Beechleas Hotel & Restaurant
Bignell Park Hotel
Bindon Country House Hotel
Blakes Townhouse
Bonham
Borrowdale Gates
Brockencote Hall
Brookhouse
Buckland-Tout-Saints
Budock Vean
Bunchrew House Hotel
Burford House
Bushmills
Butlers Town House
Cameron House
Castle House
CastleHyde Hotel
Channings

Charlton House
Chesterfield Mayfair
Christopher Hotel
Cliffe Hotel
Colwall Park Hotel
Combe Grove Manor
Combe House at Gittisham
Corse Lawn House Hotel
Cotswold House Hotel
Coul House Hotel
Court Barn
Court Hotel
Craigellachie Hotel
Cranley
Crewe Hall
Cringletie House Hotel
Cromlix House
Crosby Lodge
Crown at Whitebrook
Crown Inn & Hotel
Culdearn House
Dale Head Hall
Devonshire Hotel
Dundrum House Hotel
Eastwell Manor

Empire
Enmore Hotel
Esseborne Manor
Fairyhill
Fawsley Hall
Fayrer Garden House Hotel
Feathers, The
Flackley Ash Hotel
Flemings Mayfair
Flodigarry Country House Hotel
Four Seasons Hotel
Gilpin Lodge Hotel
Glenapp Castle
Glenmorangie House
Glenmoriston Arms Hotel
Glin Castle
Grants Hotel
Gregans Castle
Haley's Hotel & Restaurant
Halpin's Hotel
Hatton Court
Hibernian Hotel
Holbeck Ghyll Hotel & Spa
Holly Lodge
Holne Chase Hotel

Hotel Eilean Iarmain
Hotel Maes-y-Neuadd
Howard
Hunstrete House
Inn at Ardgour
Inn At Lathones
Inn on the Green
Judges at Kirklevington Hall
Kensington House Hotel
Killarney Royal Hotel
Knockinaam Lodge
Knockomie Hotel
Knockranny House Hotel
Lake Country House
Langar Hall
Linthwaite House
Little Admiral
Lovelady Shield
Maison Talbooth
Manor House
Mansion House Hotel
Matfen Hall
McCausland Hotel
Melvin House Hotel
Mere Court Hotel

Merrion Hall
Michaels Nook
Milestone
Mill End Hotel
Miller Howe Hotel
Millstream Hotel
Montague On The Gardens
Montcalm Hotel Nikko London
Moore's Hotel
North West Castle Hotel
Number 41
Nuthurst Grange
Old Bank Hotel
Old Manor Hotel
Old Priory Hotel
Orestone Manor
Owlpen Manor
Pale Hall Country House
Pen-Y-Dyffryn
Penmaenuchaf Hall
Pheasant
Pier at Harwich
Plough At Clanfield
Powder Mills Hotel
Prince Hall Hotel

Risley Hall
Rosleague Manor
Royal Marine Hotel
Rubens At The Palace
St Martin's On The Isle
St Michael's Manor
St Olaves Hotel
Stonor Arms
Swinton Park
Swynford Paddocks Hotel
Taychreggan
Thornbury Castle
Three Lions
Tides Reach Hotel
Tillmouth Park Hotel
Tyddyn Llan Country House
Waren House Hotel
Waterford Castle
Waterman's Lodge
Westmorland Hotel
Willington Hall
Windsor Hotel
Woodside Hotel
Woodstock Hotel

Terms & Conditions

1. Each purchase of the Best Loved Hotels of the World Directory entitles the buyer to £20 worth of vouchers.
2. All reservations (accomodation or meals) must be made in advance and are subject to availability.
3. The voucher may not be used in connection with any other promotion.
4. Each voucher cannot be used in combination with other Best Loved Hotels vouchers.
5. Offer valid until 31st December 2001.
6. A voucher may be exchanged for £5 off the prevailing rack rate at time of reservation OR two glasses of house wine per couple dining in the hotel restaurant.
7. The voucher is transferable but the above conditions apply in full.